Gun Digest

1995/49th Annual Edition

EDITED BY KEN WARNER

DBI BOOKS, INC.

CONTENTS

FEATURES

DEPARTMENTS

CATALOG

ABOUT OUR COVERS

When gun talk turns to small, concealable handguns, one type is invariably brought to the fore—the double derringer. Basing their guns on the classic two-barrel derringer design made famous by Remington nearly 130 years ago, American Derringer Corp. has been turning out excellent, modern, stainless steel examples of the kind with mechanical improvements to serve a number of needs.

Our front cover shows to good advantage the pleasing lines of the Model M-4 Alaskan Survival Model with 4.1-inch barrels chambered for the 45-70 (top barrel) and 45 Colt/410 3-inch shotshell (lower barrel). Used as a survival gun, it's capable of taking small game at short range and can be used for self-protection against snakes and the like, or for larger game should the need arise. At top right is the standard M-4 chambered for 45 Colt that will also shoot the 410 3-inch shotshell.

The lower guns are two American Derringer Model M-1s, chambered for 38 Special and 44 Magnum. Available in over fifty different rifle and handgun calibers, the M-1 is made of high tensile strength stainless steel to handle real powerhouse cartridges. They're designed to be the ultimate short-range backup guns for sheer power, ruggedness and reliability.

On the back cover, at top left, is the American Derringer Model 7, intended as a backup or hideout gun for law enforcement officers. At 7½ ounces, it is the lightest pistol available chambered for 38 Special, 44 Special, 32 H&R Magnum or 380 ACP and, as shown, it's also chambered for 22 Long Rifle. It's finished in matte gray to eliminate reflections and has thin rosewood grips. In the middle is the American Derringer Model 6 over/under chambered for 45 ACP, but also available in 45 Colt/410 and 357 Magnum. It was designed to provide ranchers, campers, fishermen, farmers, hikers and hunters with a small, lightweight gun for shooting snakes and small game at short range. It has 6-inch barrels and weighs just 21 ounces.

The American Derringer DA 38 at right is a double-action-only stack-barrel that's also made of stainless steel with an aluminum frame. It has 3-inch barrels, weighs 14.5 ounces and has an overall length of 4.85 inches. Used as a backup gun for law enforcement, the DA 38 can be had chambered for 38 Special (shown), 9mm Parabellum or 357 Magnum for ammunition compatibility with service guns. In 357 Magnum, it's billed as the world's lightest gun in that caliber. This is a slim, easy-to-carry gun of high quality and workmanship.

Photos by John Hanusin.

GUN DIGEST STAFF

EDITOR-IN-CHIEF
Ken Warner

SENIOR STAFF EDITOR
Harold A. Murtz

ASSOCIATE EDITOR
Robert S.L. Anderson

PRODUCTION MANAGER
John L. Duoba

EDITORIAL/PRODUCTION ASSOCIATE
Jamie L. Puffpaff

EDITORIAL/PRODUCTION ASSISTANT
Holly J. Porter

ASSISTANT TO THE EDITOR
Lilo Anderson

CONTRIBUTING EDITORS
Bob Bell
Doc Carlson
Edward A. Matunas
Layne Simpson
Larry S. Sterett
Hal Swiggett
J.B. Wood
Don Zutz

ELECTRONIC PUBLISHING MANAGER
Nancy J. Mellem

ELECTRONIC PUBLISHING ASSOCIATE
Robert M. Fuentes

GRAPHIC DESIGN
Jim Billy
John L. Duoba

VICE PRESIDENT/MANAGING EDITOR
Pamela J. Johnson

PUBLISHER
Sheldon L. Factor

DBI BOOKS, INC.

PRESIDENT
Charles T. Hartigan

VICE PRESIDENT & PUBLISHER
Sheldon L. Factor

VICE PRESIDENT—SALES
John G. Strauss

VICE PRESIDENT/MANAGING EDITOR
Pamela J. Johnson

TREASURER
Frank R. Serpone

S&W's MASSIVE M&P...

...Meant To Be A 41 For Cops

by GARY M. BROWN

The Smith & Wesson M58 Military & Police Revolver was designed for the lead bullet "police" 41 Magnum cartridge.

IN 1964, AT the urging of such notable firearms writers as Elmer Keith and Charles "Skeeter" Skelton, Smith & Wesson and the Remington Arms Company combined to introduce the 41 Magnum revolver cartridge. The same team had, of course, brought the 44 Remington Magnum to the shooting world in 1956.

While some championed the need for a handgun round to bridge the gap between the mighty 44 Magnum and 1935's phenomenon, the 357 Magnum, others disputed the entire theory. The latter group maintained that the proposed 41-caliber round could do nothing a down-loaded 44 Magnum or an up-loaded 44 Special couldn't do as well, if not better. Still, the proponents of the 41 promoted the cartridge, which they said would combine the higher velocity of the 357 with increased diameter and frontal area, yielding a round that would provide better penetration, somewhat lessened recoil, and excellent killing power. The 41 was to be all things to all people, especially law enforcement people.

Therefore, in 1964, Smith & Wesson introduced their Model 57 Target Revolver in 41 Magnum. The Model 57 was virtually identical

The M58, pictured with 1970's accoutrements, represents the ultimate big-bore police service revolver rig according to Brown.

(except for caliber) to the firm's Model 29 44 Magnum. After a rather indifferent beginning, the Model 57 continues today in S&W's current line (as does the stainless steel version of the piece, the Model 657, which was introduced much later). The only thing really unique about the Model 57 back then was its offering of a 6-inch barrel (along with 4- and 8³/₈-inch versions) as opposed to the 6¹/₂-inch standard mid-length barrel of the Model 29 44.

It is the other 41-caliber revolver introduced by S&W we're discussing here. The $140 price tag of the Deluxe Model 57 and its "fragile" adjustable target sights made it an unlikely candidate for law enforcement usage. So Smith & Wesson provided an enlarged version of their famed Model 10 38 Special Military & Police Revolver, the heavy-barreled model of 1957. The big M&P was chambered for the 41-caliber round.

The Model 10 was built on the mid-sized K frame, but the new gun was based on the massive N frame. The bigger frame was necessary to provide a cylinder large enough for six 41-caliber rounds and to add heft to keep recoil manageable. The new gun was officially designated the Smith & Wesson Model 58 41 Military & Police Revolver.

The 41 Magnum factory round offered by Remington (and subsequently Winchester) took two forms. The first was a 210-grain jacketed softpoint that possessed full magnum ballistics. The second offering featured a 210-grain Keith-style *lead* bullet that was down-loaded to a bit over 900 fps velocity, having in excess of 400 foot-pounds of energy at the muzzle when exiting a 4-inch tube. This so-called light load was touted both as a practice round for the magnum as well as being ideal for police usage.

Nowhere in the formal description of the gun did the term "Magnum" appear, although the right side of the barrel, at least on late versions, was roll-marked 41 Magnum. The magnum designation was officially eschewed because, even though the full-power version of the 41 round would fit and was safe to fire in the Model 58, Smith never intended the gun to be used with the hot round. The M&P design made the use of the magnum loading hard to justify. All non-target M&Ps featured "fixed" sights only, regardless of caliber. The Model 58's sights were a simple ¹/₈-inch serrated ramp front and a corresponding square notch milled in the gun's topstrap. The hammer and trigger of the Model 58 were the narrow "service" variety, not the very

wide versions of the Model 57. The Model 58's grips were the Magna variety, most of them in the P.C. (Police Combat) configuration, which meant they were noticeably rounded at their bottoms.

The grips on the Model 58 were absolutely horrible when it came to controlling the hard-kicking 41 Magnum version. These service-type stocks could have easily been replaced with better designs, but few individual officers, let alone departments, would spend the additional money. So, it was always *intended* that the Model 58 would be limited to firing the lead light load (or its handloaded equivalent). The gun was offered initially at a very reasonable retail list price of $80 for the blued version and $85 for the nickel-finished model.

In an ideal world, the Model 58 *should* have gone on to fame and fortune as the all-time "ultimate" police duty revolver, but it was not to be. Almost from the beginning there was resistance. "Regulations" of many (if not most) police organizations stipulated 38 Special fixed-sight duty revolvers—period! Money, it appears, has always been a consideration in the purchase of police service weapons, and the mid-1960s were no exception. While the new gun and cartridge may have been superior to the standard-issue 38, the cost of such replacement would have been high. There was also considerable controversy about issuing a magnum revolver to cops (even if they were supposed to use the *non*-magnum load) from a public relations point of view. Many departments didn't want to incur the wrath of the public by blowing to pieces "poor misunderstood victims of society" with mean, nasty magnums.

However, none of the above reasons really led to the downfall of the Model 58. Several police organizations did adopt the gun. By choice or by chance, the 210-grain jacketed softpoint full-magnum load found its way into those Model 58s used for police service. The full-power round, in a gun designed for it, was spectacular not only in performance but in recoil and muzzle blast as well. When touched off in the Model 58, which was offered only with a 4-inch barrel, the round must have been a

log. At the time it was dropped, in 1978, the suggested retail price had increased to $175 for the blued model. That seems still somewhat of a bargain, but virtually *no* Smith & Wesson handguns were actually available at anywhere near their published list prices during that time period. They were *much* higher!

Pictured is the author's current Model 58 41 Military & Police Revolver, in new and unfired condition, in its original box with all packaging materials and accessories. The gun, in the N271XXX serial number range, makes it one of the final pieces of its type to be produced. Your reporter had a long and pleasant association with a nearly identical Model 58 bought in the mid-1970s. Since the gun was generally available back then, it was carried on a daily basis for personal protection and was excellent in that role. There were no sharp adjustable sights poking into one's side when

ing problem after several boxes of ammo had been put through it. I fitted the piece with a set of factory Goncalo Alves checkered target grips, which happened to perfectly fit my very large hands.

Today, the availability of myriad high-capacity semi-automatic pistols shooting ammunition with comparable ballistic performance would probably preclude my carrying the Model 58. Add to that its current NIB (New In Box) collector value of approximately $400, which provides yet another reason to keep hands off.

I traded the first Model 58 for an even more valuable "collector" Smith, shortly after the gun was discontinued in 1978. It was still in "as-new" condition, and I missed it immediately. Perhaps figuring that I'd one day own another, I saved the Bianchi 5BHL lined holster, the HKS Speedloader, the eighteen-round Case-Gard ammo wallet and an older box of Remington lead SWC

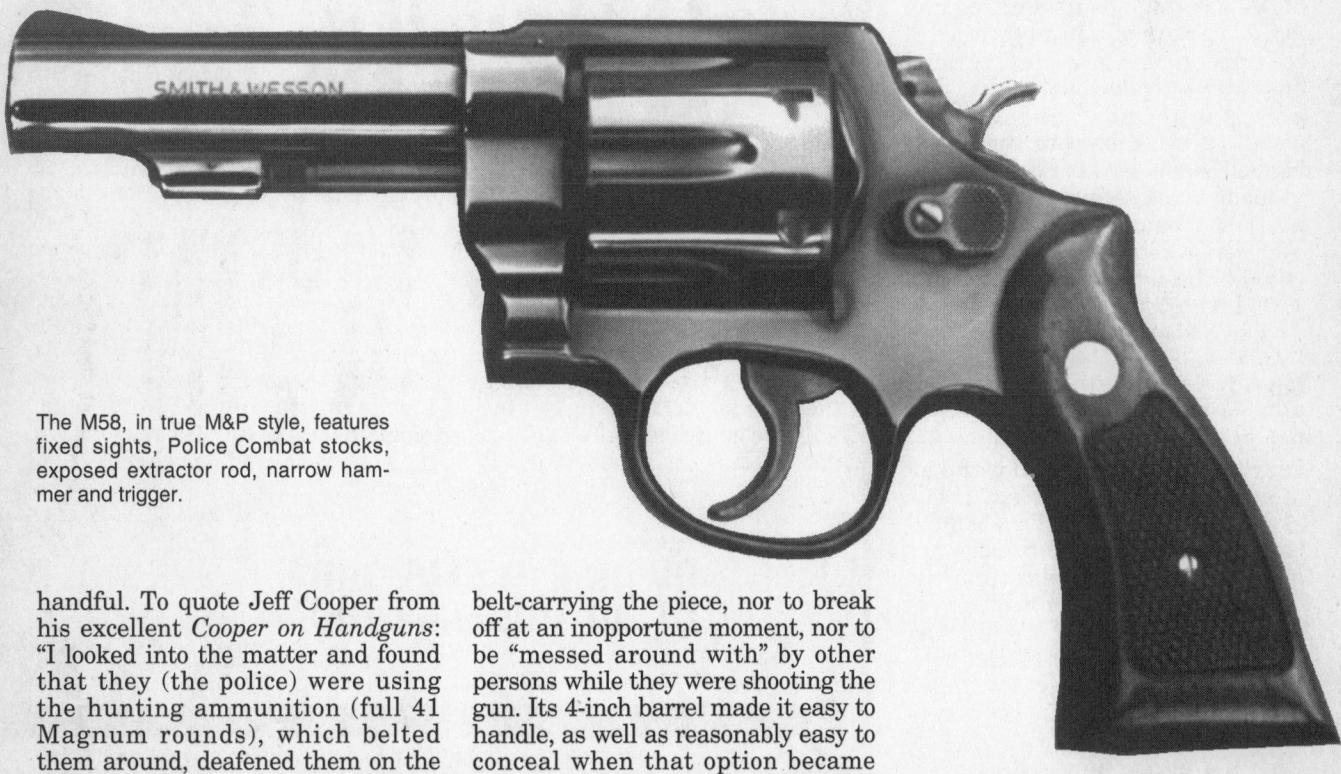

The M58, in true M&P style, features fixed sights, Police Combat stocks, exposed extractor rod, narrow hammer and trigger.

handful. To quote Jeff Cooper from his excellent *Cooper on Handguns*: "I looked into the matter and found that they (the police) were using the hunting ammunition (full 41 Magnum rounds), which belted them around, deafened them on the indoor range, and terrified their lady cops." This, more than any other single factor, seems to be the reason that the Model 58 failed to live up to the high expectations set for it by Smith & Wesson and the writers who had hyped its development and manufacture.

The Model 58 held on from its 1964 introduction through S&W's 1977 product catalog. There is no mention of the gun in the 1978 cata-

belt-carrying the piece, nor to break off at an inopportune moment, nor to be "messed around with" by other persons while they were shooting the gun. Its 4-inch barrel made it easy to handle, as well as reasonably easy to conceal when that option became necessary. I never fired a magnum round from the piece. From this particular gun, the lead police load was extremely accurate, as well as very easy to control. Initially, there were some leading problems; this later seemed to correct itself. Whether the barrel "smoothed out" after being shot a bit, or whether (as later reported) I had gotten some early "soft" lead projectiles, I'll never know for sure. The gun no longer had a lead-

rounds that I'd had with my initial gun. I recently purchased the replacement Model 58 pictured in this piece and, with the addition of the original accoutrements from the late 1970s, still have the option of carrying the ultimate N-frame, big-bore police service rig, featuring the Smith & Wesson 41 Military & Police Revolver, the largest ever of its type. •

ONE OF THE REASONS I like a good, long walk in the woods, with an eye out for small game and some favorite firearm packed along, is that it gives me the opportunity for a flavorsome meal cooked on an open fire, and very little weight gain. By the time I've hunted a fine squirrel, say, made the kill, skinned it out, and cooked it up, I've used up most of the calories it provides. But I've had a wonderful time. And I couldn't find that flavor in a five-star restaurant if there was one within 200 miles.

Last fall, after hearing all those stories about ugly assault weapons with no sporting purposes from experts in the media, I thought I might try my new Intratec DC-9 in the woods. The Intratec is a simple, friendly pup of a pistol, with a firearm's equivalent of big feet and floppy ears. You have hopes it will grow into something worthwhile, but while it's a pup you enjoy it. Straight blow-back, big open sights, a comfortable grip, and a handy magazine to hold on to, it looks ferocious enough to scare a politician. It's great fun to shoot, and accurate enough if you take your time. That big bolt slams forward hard enough to make quick second shots chancy, but what kind of squirrel hunter ever gets a second shot? My experience has been that if I miss the first shot, I will just have to wait around for a second squirrel.

The ventilated shroud around the barrel, which has so alarmed Senator Feinstein she has prepared federal legislation against such a "witch mark," I have found useful for attaching a sling. Maybe not a sling exactly, but a strap off a shoulder bag. I just clip one end through one of the ventilating holes, and the other end clips on the doohicky at the end of the receiver. Works great. Lean against a tree, prop the magazine on a fallen log, push out against the strap, and you can get a very steady hold. You need a steady hold even if you are hunting squirrels with a Kimber or a Walther target rifle.

My Intratec is not going to win any benchrest contests, but it is reasonably accurate for an inexpensive 9mm with a 4-inch barrel. I have a feeling a lot of old flintlock and percussion cap squirrel hunters would have been delighted to trade "old Betsy" for an Intratec, and brought home more squirrels than I could. I've read a lot about the inadequate stopping power of 9mm hardball, but not on squirrels. It does *fine* on squirrels; bigger hole than a 22, but not much more meat loss.

The morning I went out for hunting, I decided I would have curried squirrel for lunch, or maybe supper, or curried something. A good dish takes only a little care and some thinking beforehand. I walk with a daypack on my back that weighs barely 10 pounds, but can provide me with a gourmet meal if I do my stuff. In plastic bags, I put one cup of rice, a small to medium onion, and two tablespoons of curry powder. I also bring some cooking oil in a 4-ounce bottle. All it takes beyond that is some water and, of course, a squirrel.

I have a quart pot for the rice, a medium skillet, pie pan for a plate and a small folding grill. I found a heavy knife-fork-spoon combination from some European army in a surplus store. The fork is all I need, or the spoon, since I carry a small knife anyway. But it is a nice set and I like to see them click together. They are indestructible, and I have had them since the defeat of whichever European army—German, maybe. Water I can get from a little stream, and since I boil it, I don't worry about *giardia*.

All hunting involves getting yourself to where the game is, approaching the game near enough to take it, and doing just that. You'd think anybody could do it. And the truth is, I've seen some pretty non-literary types do just fine at it. Let's say it takes practice, and patience is the hunter's virtue. I've often thought some of those mystics who sit and meditate silently for hours would make great still-hunters, and I guess if they could break away from their meditations, they would. But that's what I pretend to be. Nature-mystic,

WALKIN' AND HUNTIN' AND EATIN'

BY HOWARD MCCORD

great hunter demon silent as a rock, a brooding Nemesis plotting the death of squirrels, and the eating of them afterward.

The secret is to go into the woods to a place where there are squirrels, sit down, get in position, and disappear from their awareness by your solidity and quiet. Even though they may know better, in half an hour they will think you are a rock, or a sleeping bear, or a tree stump. They will begin to move about. Don't turn

Writer's Intratec DC-9 put him one up on the food chain over this plump squirrel.

and look when you hear one. It can run away and hide before you get turned. Just sit and wait. If you are a perfect hunter, a squirrel will come to rest exactly where you have aimed your TEC-DC9. If you are not perfect, you may have to move the pistol slightly. It is all very simple—if you are perfect. While you wait, think about cooking.

Busy in the leaves, then on the branches, then suddenly quiet and attentive, he was right there, even if I had to move the pistol a little. Too-wide rear sight let a little squirrel red highlight the front sight as I squeezed. Suddenly a very loud forest and all the other squirrels still and silent, shocked. Squirrel was a heavy-bodied male, ripe on the good food of the forest, which he was to become himself to the predator next highest on the food chain.

I made the necessary incisions and cuts, and peeled off his coat. Down by the creek, I had a little spot where I built a fire under the grill, washed the squirrel off and cut him into quarters. Another of McCord's Famous Discoveries: cut a piece of plywood about 12x15 inches—the same size as that plastic foam seat I believe in carrying. Makes a dandy cutting board and dining table, and slips in your pack just in front of the plastic foam seat, which pads your back when in the pack, and keeps your bony butt warm when out.

Get the fire going. Put the oil in the skillet, chop up the onion on the board and fry the onion slices til brown. In the meantime, in half a Sierra cup of water, add the curry powder and mix. When the onions are brown, add the curry paste, and drop in the squirrel pieces. Fry and brown for two or three minutes. Then add two cups of water and let simmer. This may take forty minutes or so, depending on how tough the meat is.

At this time, I always reach in the pack and pull out that bottle of red wine that just seems to be there. Sip two glasses (or half Sierra cups) slowly over the next half-hour. Contemplate the hunt, the forest, the little stream, the cloudless sky overhead. Take some quality time out for yourself.

Then put on the rice. One cup of rice to two cups of water. Bring to a boil, cover, and you have fifteen minutes to wait. By then the squirrel should be done, you will be on your third cup of wine, the rice will be fluffy and pure, and all you have to do is put the rice in the pie pan, and spoon the rich curried squirrel over it. If you are smart, which I never am, you remembered to bring a small jar of chutney as a garnish. A small loaf of French bread hardly adds to the pack's weight, and a real frontiersman will remember that. I don't know where you'll eat better than right where you are.

Why, I bet even Senator Feinstein would enjoy such a civilized repast.

* * * *

Early last summer, I was down in my basement study reading *The History of Herodian*. This is something I do when the "Washington Scene" gets too painful. There is nothing like brooding over the follies of the late Roman emperors to make our own politicians' foibles pleasantly ridiculous. Sunk into the tumultuous times of Commodius, I was aroused by the cries of my youngest daughter, Eva. "Dad, there's a woodchuck eating your tomatos!"

So much for Commodius. His outrages had just been exceeded, and even the crew in D.C. slipped from my consciousness. I had raised those tomatoes from seedlings. They were beautiful, they were red, plump, tasty, and they were mine! Not Mr. Woodchuck's.

Small, even cute, this PX-22 still filled the pot after a hunt from garden to garage.

Braised Groundhog in Spiced Red Wine Sauce

$^1/_2$ lb. lean bacon; finely chopped
1 5-lb. groundhog, cut into
   serving pieces; or use 2-3 3-lb.
   groundhogs, cut into serving pieces
$^1/_2$ t. salt
$^1/_2$ t. black pepper
$^1/_2$ cup flour
$^1/_2$ cup wild onion, finely chopped

$^1/_2$ t. garlic, finely chopped
1 cup dry red wine
1 cup chicken stock
2 T. brandy
1 t. red currant jelly
1 bay leaf
$^1/_4$ t. dried rosemary
$^1/_4$ t. dried thyme

In a heavy flame-proof 5-quart casserole, cook the bacon over moderate heat until crisp. Drain the bacon and set the casserole aside.

Wash the groudhog quickly under cold running water and pat dry with paper towels. Sprinkle the pieces with salt and pepper and then dip them in flour, shaking off any excess flour. Heat the casserole until the fat sputters.

Add the floured groundhog pieces a few at a time and brown them evenly on all sides. As they are done, transfer the groundhog pieces to a plate. Pour off all but two tablespoons of fat from the casserole and in it cook the onions and garlic, stirring frequently, for 6 to 7 minutes. Pour in wine and chicken stock and bring to a boil over high heat, scraping off any brown bits stuck to the bottom of the casserole. Stir in brandy, currant jelly, bay leaf, rosemary and thyme. Return the pieces of groundhog to the casserole; add the drained bacon, cover the casserole tightly and simmer over low heat for 2 hours or until the meat is tender but not falling apart. Pick out the bay leaf and taste for seasoning. The dish should be quite peppery.

Serve the groundhog directly from the casserole.

Credit: *Wilderness Cooking* by Berndt Berglund and Clare Bolsby (1973).

You'd think in a house of forty or fifty firearms, I'd have a woodchuck powderstick ready to go. But the quickest thing I could grab was a little American Arms PX-22, a Walther TPF clone I had purchased a few months back. Something for James Bond on a light-duty afternoon. I had it stoked with some hollowpoints and played with it at the range a week before. It did everything I asked it to do, and gave me no trouble.

I grow my tomatoes in the front yard, over by a retaining wall that keeps the yard out of the driveway. When I came out the door, the woodchuck was sitting on the retaining wall helping himself to patio tomatoes. When he saw me coming, he ran back on the wall a ways, then dove off onto the driveway. I couldn't shoot from there anyway, as a neighbor's house might have taken a ricochet. I went over the wall after him and saw him disappearing into the open door of my garage. There were plenty of hiding places in there for a woodchuck, but this one wasn't smart. He didn't hide, but kept moving around. Two shots at about 15 feet got me a woodchuck.

A few years ago, my sister, knowing my predilection for cooking up whatever I shoot, sent me *Wilderness Cooking* by Berndt Berglund and Clare Bolsby (1973). This is a text to preserve next to Horace Kephart's *Camping and Woodcraft* (1917). No gentleman traveler in the wilderness should be ignorant of either of these books, for they will ensure a warm, safe camp and mighty fine eating,

given just a bit of skill and luck on the traveler's part. By mid- to late summer, woodchucks, or groundhogs as some call them, are fat and sassy on your and your neighbor's garden produce, young corn and soybeans from the local fields, and other tasty ditchbank and hedgerow provender. They are the largest members of the squirrel family, and quite delicious.

Since I was home and had a full kitchen to use, I thought I'd do something a little fancier than I would on the trail, where I would probably just brown and simmer him with some salt and pepper and a chopped onion or two. "Braised Groundhog in Spiced Red Wine Sauce" stared at me from page 129 in *Wilderness Cooking*.

I baked a few potatos, put some frozen peas in the microwave, put the butter out on the table with some warm dinner rolls, and just on schedule hunting buddy Charlie Mangus drove up and supper was on. Again, I recommend a nice red wine from a screwtop bottle. You don't want to get too fancy eating woodchuck. Though with this recipe, you'd be excused if you cracked the Chateauneuf du Pape '89 you've kept in the gun safe all this time. It is first-rate eating.

* * * *

I learned to shoot in the summer of 1938, when I was five years old. My mom and dad took me out to the desert with the little rifle my dad had learned to shoot with in 1913,

Hank, the rifle, put three shots in half an inch at 20 yards. The writer helped.

"HANK"
3 shots
20 paces
½ inch

WINCHESTER '02
Boy's Rifle

Standing tall here with the 3-pound 22 of his boyhood, McCord uses it seated, preferably in comfort and with a rest.

when he was five. It was a Winchester Model 1902 single shot 22 chambered for Short, Long and Extra Long, and weighed 3 pounds. My dad set up a short piece of red sewer pipe against a sand dune, got down with me and showed me how to sight, and when I pulled the trigger, the pipe split right in two, hit dead center. I don't know who was proudest, me or Dad. We've owned the rifle eighty years now, and I've taught my own children to shoot with it. I moved on to other rifles when I began to shoot on the Junior NRA target rifle team, and the Junior ROTC team from eighth grade on. But I didn't own another rifle until I was sixteen, and I accounted for more jackrabbits, cottontails and assorted other small game with that '02 than with all my other firearms put together.

I spent ten summers at my uncles' ranches on the Rio Feliz in southern New Mexico and hunted every afternoon with my cousin Tom. Those were years of drought and over-grazing for the war effort. We ran cattle, Merino sheep, and Angora goats for mohair, and the figuring was five jackrabbits ate as much as one sheep. We certainly had no shortage of jackrabbits, try as we might to keep the numbers down. We considered the mature jacks too tough to eat, but young jacks were tasty, and every cottontail we took ended up in the pot.

In later years, I hunted less and less with the '02. While it was a joy to carry, it was sized for a boy, and my years on the rifle team had made me used to peep sights, so I gradually switched my allegiance to a Marlin 39A with a Williams receiver sight. But I never forgot my '02, and this fall I took that old favorite along when I slipped my day-pack on my shoulders and headed out for the woods.

I estimate I put 50,000 22 Long Rifles through it during the years I used it, but the rifling is still sharp—testimony to the gentle ways of regular Long Rifles on barrels. I shoot PMC Target 22, or Remington 22 Target, in it now to keep the pressures low and to have the least deviation, shot to shot. Remington provides a 40-grain solidpoint at 1150 fps (probably less from the '02's 18-inch barrel), which gives 117 foot-pounds muzzle energy. You can increase the killing impact a bit by filing off the solid point to a flat-nose, using one of those handy gizmos you slip over the bullet to keep your filing true. I do that for woodchuck, but not for anything smaller. I can keep my shots within an inch or two at twenty paces, and given the tiny notch in the rear sight, and my old eyes, I am satisfied with this result.

When I walk out to the woods, I'm never sure what I'll have for dinner. Over the years I've dined on many different "small deer" as Kephart calls them. "All's meat that comes to a hungry man's pot," he says, and I'm a believer. He claims prairie dog is as good as squirrel, porcupine is good, "and that of a skunk is equal to roast pig." All the cats are good, but dog is by far the best, though the early traveller, Hart Merriam, ranked it second to panther. If I ever do shoot a mountain lion, I am bound and determined to cook him up and try. But for a contemporary witness I have to call on my son Robert, who has spent the last two years in China and feasted on more species of animals than I by far. He's had leopard, which he found OK, but it was second to the three different dog dishes he has been served: chopped dog, spicy dog and dog soup.

I figure household pets are off limits, but if I run across a feral dog that tries to eat me—and such are not unknown in these parts—I will try some spicy dog of my own. But today I thought of gentle birds, and put a couple of apples in my pack and a little baggie with two tablespoons of brown sugar. What I had in mind was a fat grouse.

A few years ago, I spent a summer teaching in Alaska, and since my classes were in the evenings, I spent the days wandering the woods and mountains around Juneau. Grouse were plentiful and divinely stupid and fearless, and there were many times I could have taken one with a rock or a stick. Down in the lower 48, they are considerably more alert, and the sharptail grouse of the Dakotas can be a real challenge, the Western sage hen a little less so. I suppose proper hunters go after grouse with shotguns, and shoot at flushed birds. I had learned a little different approach on the ranch, hunting quail and dove with a 22. I am no Ad Topperwein and would never think of trying to down a fly-ing bird with a 22. But head shots at sitting birds 15 or 20 yards off are just the thing for old small-bore target shooters.

Some days, instead of going after jacks, Tom and I would go back to the corrals where a wise bird might pick up some spilled grain easily enough. We would hide by the fences, rest our rifles on top, and wait. We specified head shots only. We either got a clean kill or a miss, but we usually got two quail or dove in an hour, and a fine supper soon after.

I now had in mind a forestfire burn some ten years old south of my land in the state forest. I had seen grouse along the edge of it before, as they seemed to like the more open burn for foraging and the woods for quick retreat. It was an hour's pleasant walk away, as long as you knew the local greenbriar. An excursion into a thick patch of that might delay you a bit and ruin your temper for a while.

Greenbriar likes the ridges, so I kept just below, cut over a saddle, and swung southwest around the high point on my place, then edged south below the ridgeline. When I saw the open area of the burn through the trees, I began to move cautiously, alert for movement up ahead. As quietly as a bumbling human can, I approached the edge of the burn and spotted a place where I could sit back under a tree and have a good view.

Quiet attentiveness to all things, inner and outer, is the secret to good hunting and good meditation. All the hunters in your ancestry wait with you. The long double helix of your DNA remembers all life, and the hunters are there. If they seem too distant to be of much help, at least try to be as patient as they were, as still and as silent. More things are achieved by quiet in the woods than by great activity.

Some stirring down the slope, some flutterings, and then a bevy of busy feathered folk came closer. The sun was pleasant, I was in shadow, my knees drawn up to make a fine rest for the '02, and I waited for a plump grouse to settle on the ground for a moment or longer, attentive to a delicacy, and then: Pow! The 22 made just enough noise to send the other birds into the air, but my dinner lay quietly, the bullet passing just beneath the skull through the neck. A certain amount of luck, no doubt, played a role in the shot placement, but not according to me, at that moment. After all, couldn't I still shoot a possible at 50 feet with my target rifle? Well, sometimes. The bullseye on a 50-foot target is smaller than the 22 bullet. Why not, I told myself, say you aimed to break its neck. And did. And so I do.

I opened the grouse with my Marble 33, the exact tool for the deed, cleaned him out, then put him in my pocket and headed back to my hollow and the little creek that flowed there some months of the year.

I had a favorite spot on that creek where I had a fire ring I often used. When I arrived, I started a bigger fire than usual and heaped it up. Then I went to the stream and washed out the grouse. I salted the cavity, and cut my two apples into small pieces and stuffed them in, then I put in the maple sugar. I put the bird down on the cooking board and walked down to the stream to a small clay deposit I had used before. It was mud-pack time. I dug a big double handful of clay, brought it back to the board and kneaded the clay out flat and smoothed out a sheet about $3/4$-inch thick and 10x12 inches. I put the bird in the middle of the sheet and went back to the creek and dug two more handfuls. I made another big mud pancake and put it over the bird, sealing all around. There should be no hole or crack through which steam or juices might escape. I left the feathers on the grouse. Then I scraped a place in the coals, put down the mud-wrapped grouse, and heaped the coals back over it. I added more wood and eased back into fire-tending, meditating and red-wine-sipping modes. I even found time to take a ramble down the creek to see how the property was faring.

Mud baking is probably about as old as hunting and not eating it raw, but it requires a good clay that won't crumble as it dries and will keep the seal. Two hours is about right for most meals. Better a little longer than rawer, so be patient. When you think it's ready, take it out and crack it open. All the juices will be there, and the feathers and skin will come off with the clay. You are left with a delicious grouse, apple-stuffed, and you can eat it right from the clay plate you just made.

If your luck holds, you'll get to walk home in moonlight. ●

ALL THOSE OTHER 30-30s

by JOHN MALLOY

Robert Malloy thinks his receiver sight makes his Stevens 325 shoot better than the writer's.

THE LEVER-ACTION rifle and the 30-30 Winchester cartridge have a relationship nearly unique in firearms history. Most people automatically class a lever-action rifle as a "thirty-thirty," and conversely think of rifles using the 30-30 cartridge as lever-action rifles.

In his 1965 book, *Cartridges of the World*, Frank Barnes obviously had the traditional lever action in mind as he described the 30-30 Winchester cartridge:

"Its popularity is due in a large measure to the fact that the cartridge has always been available in short, light rifles and carbines."

There is a lot of truth to this, but there is another side to the coin.

Members of the firearms fraternity are well aware that lever-action rifles have been made, and are still being made, in many calibers other than 30-30. Most are also at least passingly aware that 30-30 rifles other than lever actions have been made.

What is surprising is how many of those "other" 30-30s there actually are. Lots of 30-30 rifles were made—and continue to be made—in a variety of makes and action types. It is just possible that those other 30-30s may have had some influence in making the 30-30 the popular cartridge it is today.

The well-known story of the 30-30 began in 1894, when Winchester offered John M. Browning's latest lever-action design as its Model 1894. It was the first American rifle chambered for a smokeless powder hunting round, the 30 Winchester Center Fire (30 WCF) more commonly known now as the 30-30 Winchester.

Authorities generally agree that the 30-30 cartridge itself was introduced in 1895, in the summer of the year after the rifle's introduction. Obviously, Winchester had developed the cartridge some time before, and there is some claim that the company actually introduced the cartridge in 1894, loaded for a short time with blackpowder.

It doesn't really matter. We know the smokeless hunting round appeared in 1895, and it took the hunting world of a century ago by storm. Thus, 1995 is the true centennial of the 30-30.

Everyone who tried it praised its flat trajectory and amazing stopping power. To us, in these days of belted magnums, this may seem strange. But, remember, when the new round was introduced, the principal deer cartridge used in America was the 44-40! With the 30-30, shooters gained extra effectiveness and still kept the familiar, trim lever action.

Such an excellent cartridge as the 30-30 in Winchester's new lever-action rifle meant that other lever actions would soon be made to handle it. Marlin, and then Savage, quickly included the chambering. As time went on, tradition in some areas made "lever action" and "30-

for both the '94 and the Single Shot took place in the summer of 1895. Strangely, though, the December, 1896, Winchester catalog does not list this chambering for the Single Shot.

It may simply have been an error of omission. If, however, it was not available then, it is interesting to speculate on the reason.

The action of the 1894 lever-action rifle was plenty strong enough for the new smokeless 30-30 round. The common low carbon or "mild" steel had made satisfactory barrels for blackpowder loadings. However, the combination did not work for the 30-30; the mild steel barrels would not stand up to extensive firing of the smokeless loads.

steel barrels, sold at a slightly higher price.

Sales of the Single Shot in 30-30 caliber were never large. When old-timers referred to the "Winchester 30-30," they always meant the '94.

Still, the chambering of the 30-30 in the Single Shot, one of the most accurate and highly regarded rifles of its day, was significant. The inclusion of the 30-30 in the gun's extensive lineup of cartridges, which included all the effective centerfire cartridges of the time—22 Winchester Center Fire to 50-110 caliber—gave the new round a prestige it might not have had if its chambering had been restricted to the lever action alone.

Remington had been Winchester's

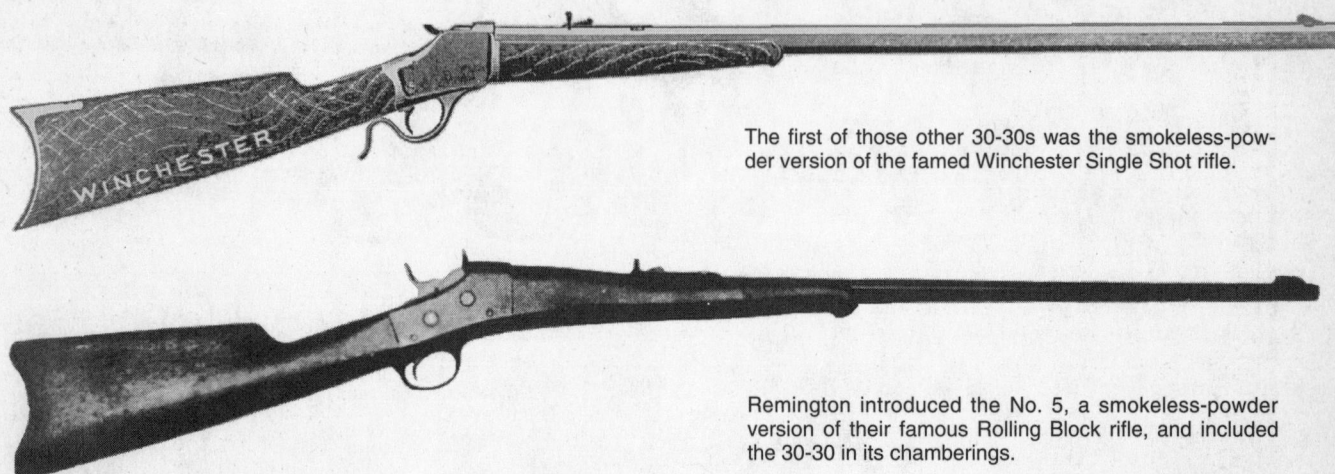

The first of those other 30-30s was the smokeless-powder version of the famed Winchester Single Shot rifle.

Remington introduced the No. 5, a smokeless-powder version of their famous Rolling Block rifle, and included the 30-30 in its chamberings.

30" almost interchangeable terms.

Not without reason. Numerically, the vast majority of all the rifles chambered for this round have been lever actions.

But not all.

The first of the other 30-30s were single shot rifles. Winchester had brought out its Single Shot rifle after purchasing the design from John M. Browning. It was the first firearm design Browning ever sold, and the first Winchester rifle that could handle long, powerful cartridges. It began a relationship between Browning and the Winchester company that led to the development of many Winchester offerings, including the 1894.

Winchester advertised its Browning-designed Single Shot rifle as made "for all desirable cartridges from 22 to 50 caliber." As a matter of course, the company chambered the Winchester Single Shot for the new 30-30 cartridge.

But, perhaps not right away.

It is generally recorded that the introduction of the 30-30 cartridge

By 1895, Winchester had developed new barrel-making equipment that could machine its new and much stronger nickel steel. This allowed the introduction of the 30-30 smokeless cartridge and rifles in August of that year.

The light, handy Model 1894 in its powerful (for the time) 30-30 loading was an immediate success. The demand may have been so great that the Winchester plant was simply unable to spare any great amount of the scarcer nickel steel to adapt into barrels for the Single Shot. That earlier rifle was already selling well in other calibers.

The Single Shot was soon available in 30-30, of course. Winchester advertising stated the Single Shot was available "in all desirable calibers," and the new smokeless round had certainly become one fast!

Until it was discontinued in 1920, the Single Shot was offered in 30-30 and other smokeless calibers. Mild steel was still used for some blackpowder chamberings, and the smokeless models, with their nickel

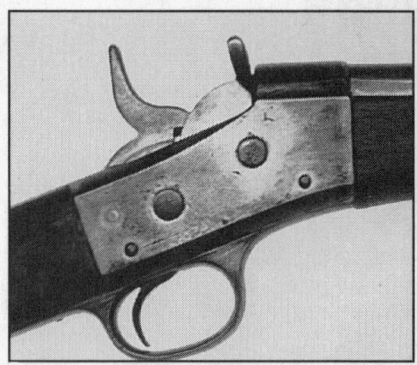

The rolling block action was a strong one, and changes were made to adapt it to smokeless powder cartridges, which included the 30-30.

big rival since the days following the Civil War. The company's rolling block single shot rifle had been used for decades with blackpowder cartridges for military and sporting use around the world.

About 1897, the company introduced a smokeless-powder version capable of handling the higher-pressure rounds becoming popular. With an eye to military sales, the new special No. 5 rolling block was offered in 30-40 Krag and 7mm Mauser military loads. Remington could not ignore the popularity of the new hunting round and brought out a sporting version of the No. 5 and included the 30-30. The rifle was eventually offered also in 303 British, 32 Special and the smokeless versions of the 32-40 and the 38-55 cartridges.

In the line until about 1905, the 30-30 rolling block showed that the cartridge was of interest to a company that did not market a lever-action repeater.

The interesting Remington-Hepburn No. 3 rifle was also made in 30-30 caliber. This falling block, side-lever single shot had been old-timers and the newest and best of the time.

At any rate, Remington's Lee was the first bolt-action 30-30. The idea would appear several more times, we shall see, as time went by.

Lever-action and single shot rifles had dominated the hunting scene in America since the Civil War, with bolt actions running only a distant third.

After the turn of the century, other action types appeared. In 1906, Remington introduced a semi-automatic centerfire, the Browning-designed Model 8, followed in 1912 by its slide-action high power, the Model 14.

Perhaps because they really disliked chambering their rifles for the Savage-Stevens line, as we shall see, wound up with more types of non-lever-action rifles chambered for the 30-30 than that of any other company.

The Remington rimless cartridges come into the story in another way. By the second decade of this century, single shot, lever-action, bolt-action, slide-action and semi-automatic hunting rifles were in regular use. Perhaps this is the logical place to answer a question that is bound to come up.

Was there ever a semi-automatic 30-30 manufactured?

The answer is clear: probably not.

A number of books concerned with firearms values have listed the Standard gas-operated semi-auto as

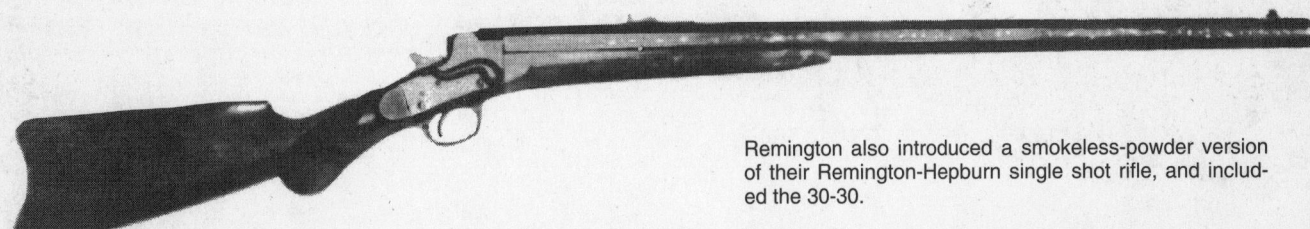

Remington also introduced a smokeless-powder version of their Remington-Hepburn single shot rifle, and included the 30-30.

made since 1880 in blackpowder calibers. About the same time as the introduction of the No. 5 Special, the Remington-Hepburn was introduced in a "High Power" smokeless version. Besides the 30-30, calibers offered were 30-40, 32 Special, 32-40, 38-55 and 38-72. The Remington-Hepburn was made until about 1907.

During the last decade of the 1800s, the bolt-action rifle saw widespread use as a military arm, but Americans did not favor that type for hunting.

Remington had introduced a bolt action, the Remington-Lee, for military trials prior to 1890. When the 30-30 became popular, a sporting version was introduced in 1899 and stayed in the Remington line until about 1907. Besides the 30-30, the smokeless-powder version of the Lee offered other common hunting and military rounds of the time. Other reported chamberings included the 6mm U.S. Navy, 30-40, 7mm, 303, 7.65mm Mauser, 32 Remington, 32-40, 35 Remington, 38-55, 38-72, 405 Winchester, 45-70 and 45-90.

The Remington-Lee was ahead of its time and was not particularly popular. Only a few thousand in all calibers were made. But the optimistic offering of calibers included both old and new rounds of the time. The 30-30 may have benefited by being associated with both proven competition's popular cartridges, or perhaps because the rimless cartridge case was used in most military magazine rifles of the time, Remington designers introduced their own line of rimless cartridges.

The 25, 30 and 32 Remington were the ballistic equivalents of the 25-35, 30-30 and 32 Special rounds developed by Winchester. A new round, the 35 Remington, was also introduced.

In 1911, the Stevens firm (which was not to be affiliated with Savage until 1920) introduced its first lever-action repeater, the Model 425. The company had never cataloged a 30-30 rifle, although their falling block Stevens-Ideal Model 44½ was available in that caliber on special order. Recall that the 30-30 cartridge was then but a decade-and-a-half old. It had become the most popular round for lever-action rifles, but was there any guarantee that its popularity would last?

Just five years before, Remington had introduced its line of more modern-looking rimless cartridges. Stevens made a decision to go with progress and chambered their new rifle for the 25-30-32-35 Remington cartridges. Within five years, the new rifle, actually a good design, was dropped from the line.

Of course, there is no real connection, but, seemingly to atone for poor judgment in rejecting the 30-30, the

The Remington-Hepburn's side-lever dropped the breechblock, here in the open position, and the firing pin had to travel uphill.

a 30-30. This rifle was the first American gas-operated hunting rifle made in the U.S. and was produced for only a short time around 1910. The action was operated by a sliding forearm, and the gas port could be plugged and the rifle used as a slide action. Was it really a 30-30?

Trying to trace the origin of this idea, we find that firearms authority Phillip B. Sharpe mentioned in his 1947 revision of *The Rifle in America* that the Standard catalog stated the rifle was "supplied in .25-35, .30-30 and .35 calibers."

One must realize, however, that the 30 Remington cartridge was first referred to as the 30-30 Remington. The writers of the catalog apparently just used the Winchester terminology to describe the 25 and 30 Remington cartridges. The Standard rifles are known in calibers 25, 30 and 35 Remington. These rimless cartridges feed well from the box magazine used. It seems only logical, that having designed the box magazine for a rimless case, the company would stick with the Remington line of rimless cartridges.

To further clarify the situation, Sharpe himself, writing for the *American Rifleman* in September, 1951, specifically stated that the calibers in which the Standard rifles were made were 25, 30 and 35.

and the switch to sporting style was relatively easy. The original 30-06 caliber was offered, as was the 7mm Mauser. Spurning the 30-30, Remington also offered its 25-30-32- 35 rimless line.

Winchester introduced a new bolt action, the Model 54, in 1925. It was based in large part on the Mauser and 1903 Springfield designs.

What chamberings would sell in the new rifle? The standby 30-06 was becoming very popular as a hunting round, and that seemed a sure thing. They also felt confident about the acceptance of their spectacular new 270 round. To broaden the appeal to hunters, that popular deer cartridge, the 30-30, was added about 1927 or 1928.

Model 54's range of chamberings: Other than the 30-30, there was the 22 Hornet, 220 Swift, 250 Savage, 257 Roberts, 270, 7mm Mauser, 30-06, 7.65x53mm Mauser and 9x-57mm Mauser.

Viewed in this light, the 30-30 seemed a reasonable choice to include. However, firearms experts of the time ridiculed the 30-30's inclusion in the Model 54 lineup, calling it the worst possible choice for a bolt-action rifle cartridge. Still, when the rifle was tested, they marveled at how accurate the old round could be.

After World War I, Savage Arms Company wanted to expand its production capabilities and purchased the J. Stevens Arms and Tool

The Remington-Lee sporting rifle was the first bolt-action rifle to use the 30-30 cartridge.

Winchester's 1925 bolt-action sporting rifle, the Model 54, was originally introduced in calibers 30-06 and 270 Winchester, but soon included the 30-30.

That should put the matter to rest.

But, still, one wonders. Why was the 30-30, the most popular sporting cartridge of all time that was actually introduced as a sporting cartridge, never used in a semi-automatic rifle?

Winchester's attempt at a bolt-action sporting and military rifle, the 45-70 Hotchkiss, had not been very well received, and therefore relatively few of them were made. Remington's Lee bolt action, with its large selection of calibers, also had not been popular.

World War I changed America's thinking about the bolt-action rifle.

Returning doughboys had been introduced to powerful bolt rifles during the war, were comfortable using them, and wanted something similar for hunting.

During the 1920s, a number of bolt-action hunting rifles were introduced.

Remington's 1921 offering, their Model 30, was based on the 1917 Enfield action. Remington had manufactured the 1917 during the war,

Shortly after Winchester's initial introduction of the Model 54 in 1925, Captain Edward C. Crossman, a noted firearms authority, tried out one in the 270 chambering. His description is of interest. Crossman praised it as a "modern rifle, firing modern cartridges and designed for the up-to-date man who has kept the moss off his back, and who realizes that there is not enough game left for us to go fooling around with 30-30s and rifles of that obsolete class."

The Model 54 design was improved in 1930, and the 30-30 chambering was dropped within a few years. The forerunner of the famous Model 70, the Model 54 was made from 1925 to 1936. To show the degree of Winchester's uncertainty as to what would sell, look at the

Company in 1920. Stevens, as we know, had never cataloged a 30-30 rifle. Savage had chambered the 30-30 only in the Model 99 lever-action rifle.

In 1920, the year of the Stevens acquisition, the company introduced a new short-action, high-power, bolt-action sporting rifle to the American market. It was chambered for the 250 and 300 Savage smokeless powder cartridges they had developed for their Model 99.

The Model 1920 was the first really compact, short-action bolt rifle offered. However, with the growing popularity of the 30-06, it was phased out in favor of the longer-action Models 40 and 45. These were introduced in 1928 and remained in the line until 1940. Mechanically the same, the Model 40 was the stan-

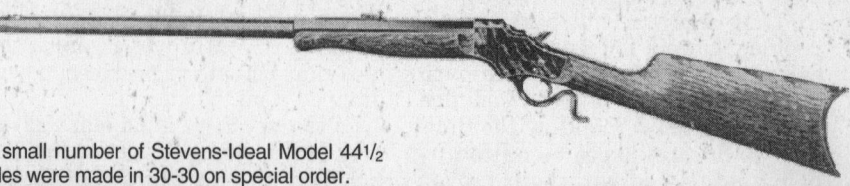

A small number of Stevens-Ideal Model 44½ rifles were made in 30-30 on special order.

dard version. The Model 45 "Super Sporter" had better wood, checkering, and an optional Lyman receiver sight.

The new rifles had an action featuring a thick receiver with an ejection port, instead of the open receiver style of the Mauser. The stiff receiver allowed the bolt to lock behind the ejection port, giving a fairly short, smooth bolt throw.

The longer action had been specifically designed to handle the 30-06, which was on its way to becoming one of America's most popular hunting rounds. Savage kept its compact 250 and 300 Savage rounds in the lineup, and also added one more that they felt would be a sure seller—the 30-30.

Because it was based on a shotgun action, it was logical to offer the 219 as a utility gun with interchangeable rifle and shotgun barrels. The Model 221 was a 30-30 caliber with an extra 12-gauge shotgun barrel. The Model 222 had a spare 16-gauge barrel, and the Model 223 was a 20-gauge.

The 30-30 was the powerhouse cartridge of the Savage 219 and was its most popular chambering. However, the rifle was also offered in 22 Hornet, 25-20 and 32-20. These were perhaps the most widely used small game centerfire cartridges of the time.

Savage production during World War II had been devoted to military arms, primarily the Thompson sub-

the rear of the receiver for added strength.

Of note was the barrel attachment. The barrel threaded into the receiver from the front, and headspace was controlled by a large barrel nut in front of the receiver. The nut also clamped the recoil plate in place. This system worked very well and cut production costs. It is still used on Savage bolt-action rifles today.

I bought a secondhand 325 back in the mid-'60s. A rifle that appeared hardly larger than a full-size 22, it carried easily and was an accurate shooter.

My brother has one equipped with a peep sight. Horribly abused before it joined the family, it has little fin-

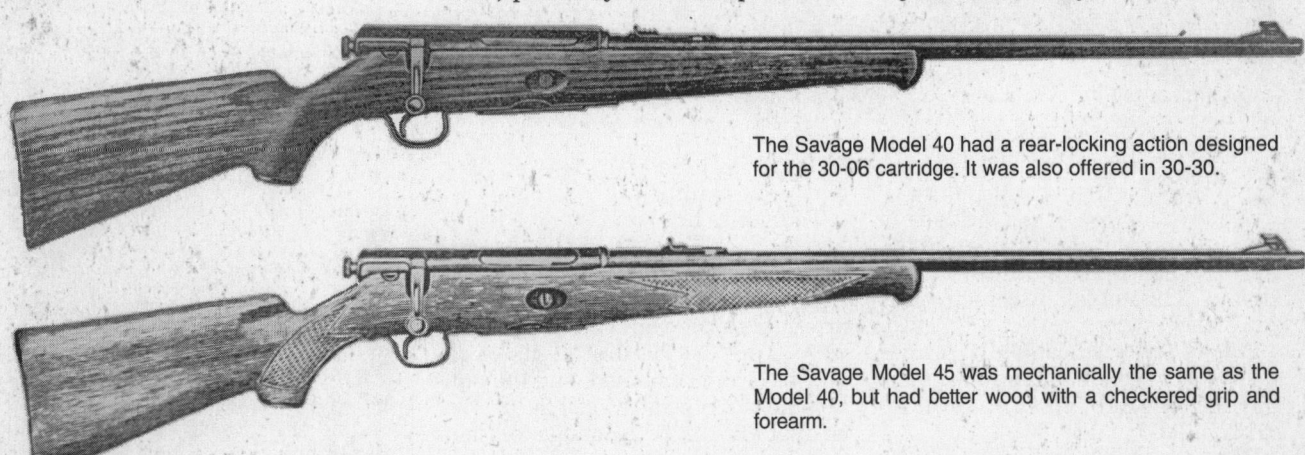

The Savage Model 40 had a rear-locking action designed for the 30-06 cartridge. It was also offered in 30-30.

The Savage Model 45 was mechanically the same as the Model 40, but had better wood with a checkered grip and forearm.

Savage also reintroduced the single shot 30-30. The Winchester and Remington single-loaders had faded out of the hunting rifle picture in the years following World War I. But in the 1930s, the Great Depression created a demand for less-expensive firearms that would still be serviceable hunting guns.

In 1938, a decade after the introduction of its new bolt-action rifles, Savage introduced a single shot 30-30 rifle based on its hammerless break-open shotgun action.

Weighing only about 6 pounds, the handy Model 219 rifle sported a 26-inch barrel, yet the overall length was only 42 inches. The longer barrel gave it the full velocity and sight radius of a traditional 26-inch, 30-30 lever-action rifle in a shorter, lighter package. It was well-liked.

With the coming of World War II, the Model 219 drifted out of the line. It returned about 1959 and remained until 1965. Then, it was replaced for two years—1967 and 1968—by the 219L, which used Savage's less-expensive side-lever break-open action.

machine gun and the British No. 4 rifle. Production of the Model 219, along with most other sporting arms, was suspended during that time.

Production of the Models 40 and 45 did not resume after the war. Instead, in 1947, Savage introduced a new, low-priced, bolt-action centerfire rifle, the Stevens Model 325, in 30-30 caliber. This gun had a 21-inch barrel and weighed only about 6 pounds. A slightly fancier version, the 325S, had a receiver sight and sling swivels. A companion rifle, the Stevens 322, was chambered for the 22 Hornet.

The little Stevens was a real innovation. A simple, sturdy bolt action, it could be made at a portion of the price of the traditional Mauser-based design. Its single front locking lug was at the upper position of the bolt when the action was open and locked into a recess on the right side. Thus, even with a front locking lug, the cartridge did not have to jump over a locking-lug recess while going from the magazine to the chamber. The root of the bolt handle turned into

ish on the stock, and the "engraving" on the metal is really rust pockmarks. In spite of its hard life, it will still regularly keep five shots in about an inch at 50 yards.

The Stevens 325 was well received by post-war hunters. Within a few years, in 1950, it was reintroduced with minor changes as the Savage 340. The first 340 had a slightly shorter 20-inch barrel and was advertised as a "carbine-style rifle." A wheel-adjustment Dockendorff-type open rear sight was standard, and a round bolt knob replaced the butterknife handle of the 325.

The 340 was a popular rifle and remained in the Savage line for over thirty-five years.

During this time, a number of options and variations were offered. The 340S had a receiver sight. The 340C was a carbine with an 18-inch barrel. Barrel lengths of 20, 22 and 24 inches have been standard at different times on different variations. As time went on, a gas shield knob was added at the rear of the bolt. Toward the end of production, pressed checkering and a reshaped

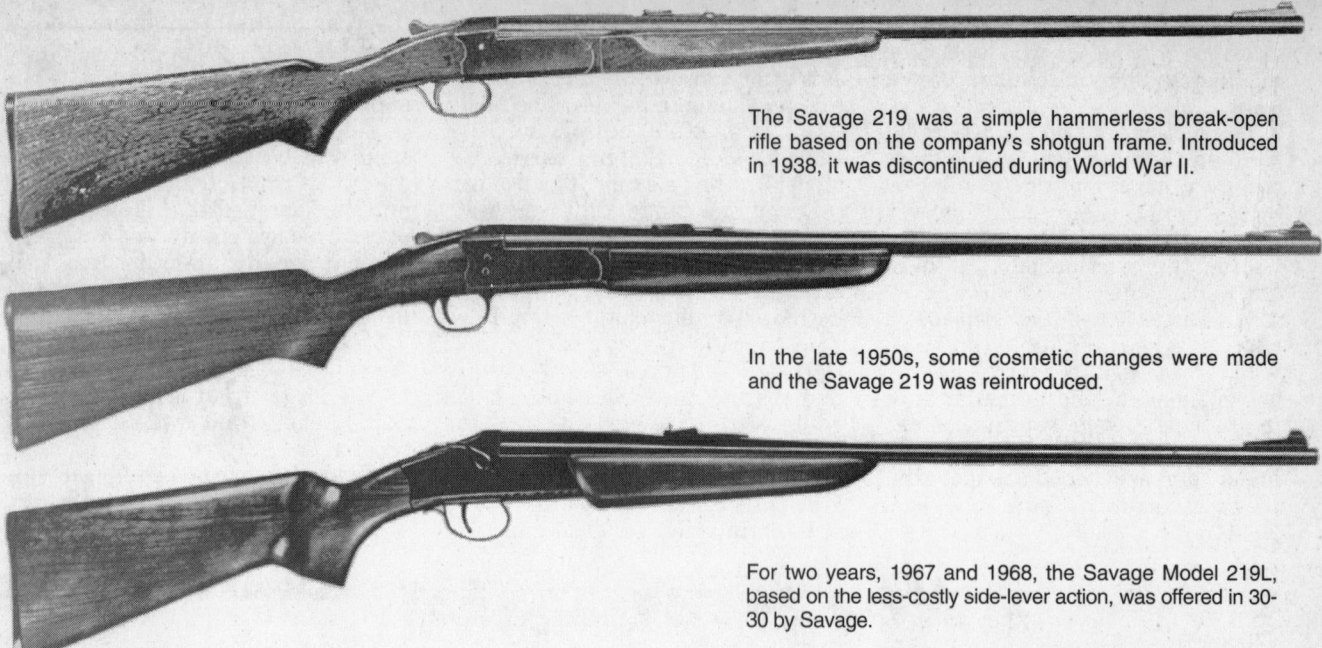

The Savage 219 was a simple hammerless break-open rifle based on the company's shotgun frame. Introduced in 1938, it was discontinued during World War II.

In the late 1950s, some cosmetic changes were made and the Savage 219 was reintroduced.

For two years, 1967 and 1968, the Savage Model 219L, based on the less-costly side-lever action, was offered in 30-30 by Savage.

stock and trigger guard appeared. The 30-30 was the most popular caliber, but others were added as seemed appropriate. Besides 30-30, the 340 has been available in 22 Hornet, 222 and 223 Remington and 225 Winchester.

A lower-cost version with cheaper wood was marketed for a time as the Springfield 840, in caliber 30-30 only.

Through all these variations, the Savage 340 variants remained sturdy, no-frills rifles. They received little attention from the firearms press, but the hunters who used them thought well of them. The Model 340 remained in the Savage line through 1985. Following financial difficulties, the company simplified its line in 1986 and discontinued the gun.

However, long before that time, Savage introduced two new styles of 30-30 rifles to hunters. In the early 1970s, they brought out the Model 24V combination rifle/shotgun and the Model 170 slide-action rifle.

The 24V was a new gun, but in basic concept it dated back to the Stevens 22-410. That break-open gun, a 22 rifle barrel over a 410 shotgun barrel, was introduced in 1938, the same year as the Savage 219 single shot break-open 30-30.

The idea of a rifle and a shotgun on the same frame was nothing new. European guns with rifle and shotgun combinations of two, three and even four barrels had been made. Some even had rifle barrels for the 7.62x51R caliber—the metric designation for the 30-30! Savage,

though, defined the idea for American standards.

The useful little gun became popular. During World War II, substantial numbers were purchased by the Army Air Forces for use as survival arms. After the war, the designation was changed—the first digits of 22 and 410 were combined, and the gun became the Savage Model 24. In the early 1960s, a 22/20-gauge version was added.

Although it was offered as a small game combination, many who hunted both deer and small game during the same season (your writer included) welcomed the new gun. It was a compromise, but a 22 Long Rifle in the top barrel and a rifled slug in the 20-gauge tube would allow careful shots at either squirrels or deer. The stage was set for a larger version.

In the mid-1960s, the introduction of the Model 24V in 222 Remington and 20-gauge proved the new gun workable as a centerfire rifle. When it became available as a 30-30, in the mid-1970s, sales increased. At last the mixed-bag hunter could go afield with one gun in his hands that—for the first shot—would do the job as well as his pump shotgun or his lever-action rifle.

And, as a rifle, it shot well. A "Testfire" writeup in the 1975 GUN DIGEST reported average groups at 100 yards between 2 and 3 inches. Perhaps not benchrest accuracy, but nobody bought the 24V as a target rifle. As a hunting gun, it certainly could hold its own.

The 24V became a mainstay of the

The 30-30 was the only big game round offered for the Savage Model 219 rifle. For varmints and small game, there were 22 Hornet, 25-20, and 32-20 chamberings.

American hunting scene. Besides the most popular 30-30 chambering, the rifle barrel was also offered for 22 Hornet, 222, 223, 357 Magnum and 357 Maximum.

Over the years, changes were made in barrel attachment, sights, stocks, and a number of small parts. Changes were represented by a series designation, beginning with Series A.

In 1989, the Savage 24F was introduced. Its modified frame added a cross-bolt safety and made the combination gun even more versatile by allowing a 30-30/12-gauge option. At the time of this writing, the 24F in 30-30 is available as the standard

24F, with a 20-gauge barrel, and as the 24F-12, a 30-30 over a 12-gauge. Both have black polymer stocks. The 12-gauge version has screw-in choke tubes.

The slide-action Model 170 was a 30-30 rifle based on the Savage-Stevens pump shotgun action. Introduced in the early 1970s, it was also cataloged in 35 Remington caliber. Such rifles must be rare; every 170 I have seen is a 30-30. Later variants such as the 170C, a carbine version offered in 1974 with an 18 1/2-inch barrel, were cataloged as 30-30 only.

The 170 is not a particularly light rifle for a 30-30, tipping the scales at 7 pounds or more with its standard 22-inch barrel. Perhaps the extra weight of the barrel helped give it its reputation for accuracy—all 170s seem to be good shooters. The tang-mounted slide safety is convenient and finds favor with those who don't care for the traditional lever-action hammer. I have owned two of these Model 170s. Although the tubular magazine requires flat or blunt pointed bullets, I have fired a number of different loads through them and they shoot well.

Remington had brought out the first bolt-action 30-30, the Remington-Lee Sporter, which had been produced shortly after the introduction of the cartridge. By the mid-1960s, the company's Model 700 was selling well, but it had nothing to offer in the lower-price field. Anyone wanting an inexpensive new bolt-action hunting rifle bought a Savage 340.

In 1967, Remington entered the lower-priced bolt-action market with its Model 788. The interesting action was somewhat reminiscent of the old Savage Models 40 and 45. It had a solid receiver with an ejection port, rather than separate front and rear receiver rings. The nine locking lugs were rearward of the ejection port. Some shooters still do not favor a rear-locking action because, in theory, it can stretch during firing. In practice, it did very well, indeed, and the 788 developed a reputation for fine accuracy.

The initial offering in the 1967 Remington catalog was in four calibers: 222, 22-250, 44 Magnum and 30-30. The slow-selling 44 was dropped after a few years. By that time, the 6mm Remington, 243 Winchester and 308 Winchester had been added. Few people chose the 30-30 in the face of such options. The 1972 Remington catalog was the last to list the 30-30, and it was dropped during that year. By 1984, the Model 788 had been discontinued. By then, its offerings included, as well as the 30-30, the 222, 223, 22-250, 6mm, 243, 7mm-08, 308 and 44 Magnum.

Almost unnoticed, the 788 in caliber 30-30 had a small but dedicated following. Rifle shooting with cast bullets had never faded completely away after the common use of smokeless powder and jacketed bullets, but relatively few center-fire rifle shooters were interested in lead bullets. Then, in the late 1950s and early 1960s, a series of *American Rifleman* articles by Col. E.H. Harrison, and the appearance of the Lyman *Handbook of Cast Bullets*, revived interest in that

The writer has acquired other hunting rifles since purchasing his Stevens 325 second-hand in the early 1960s, but the little rifle still makes it into the woods.

The Stevens 325, introduced after the end of WWII, was a light, simple 30-30. About the size and weight of a full-size 22, it sold at a low price.

The Stevens 325 contained some real innovations. Its single forward locking lug locked sideways, so the cartridges did not have to feed over a recess. The "butterknife" bolt handle turned into a receiver recess for extra safety. The barrel nut forward of the receiver controlled headspace adjustment.

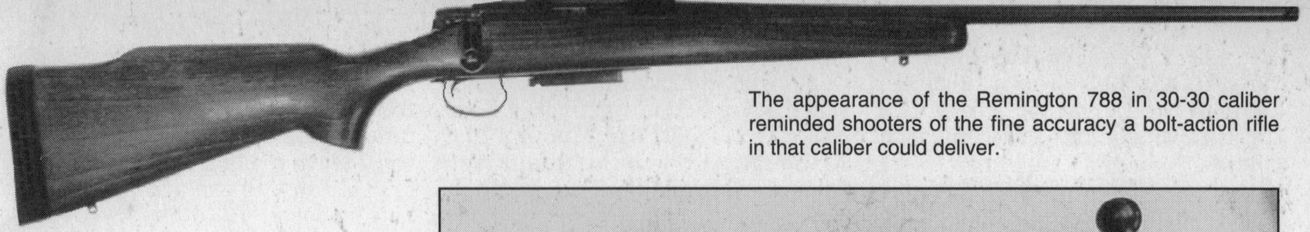

The appearance of the Remington 788 in 30-30 caliber reminded shooters of the fine accuracy a bolt-action rifle in that caliber could deliver.

The nine locking lugs of the Remington 788 are at the rear of the bolt, but the massive receiver makes a very solid action. The rifle had a reputation for good accuracy.

phase of the shooting sports. The 788 arrived on the scene as this interest was growing.

Most modern rifle cartridges had too much case capacity for the lighter charges used with cast bullet loads. The best cartridge case for cast bullets would have moderate capacity and a long neck to cover the lubrication. The 30-30 met those requirements and was seen in a new light. With a solid, accurate bolt-action rifle in that chambering available, cast bullet enthusiasts discovered what Winchester 54 shooters had discovered four decades before: the 30-30 can be an exceptionally accurate cartridge.

The Savage 219 single shot rifle had drifted out of the company's line for some time, then drifted back in about 1959. The reappearance was important enough to spark a mention in the 1960 GUN DIGEST. Apparently there was still a market for single shot 30-30s.

About 1963, Harrington & Richardson brought out a single shot 30-30. Like the Savage offering, it was based on a break-open shotgun design. Built on the latest version of the H&R Topper shotgun frame, the new rifle was an outside-hammer single. H&R had made 30-caliber military rifles under contract and, indeed, had been the largest single manufacturer of the M-14. The company had the equipment for rifling barrels, but had not had a centerfire rifle in their product line.

The Topper Model 158 was brought out originally in 30-30 and 22 Hornet, and for a few years in 22 Jet.

Combinations with extra 20-gauge or 410 shotgun barrels were also offered. Specialty models with full-length forearms, straight stocks, pistol grip stocks, gold-plated triggers and nickel-plating were offered.

To keep these variations organized, H&R used a remarkably simple method. The receivers had the company name and the barrels had the model number and caliber. Thus, a number of barrels could be used with the same basic receiver to produce a large number of variants to entice the shooting public.

At only a shade over 5 pounds, and with a 22-inch barrel, the little H&R 30-30 was a reasonably potent rifle in a very compact form. Taken down, it fit easily in most suitcases. I have taken mine along when I didn't

In 1950, the Stevens 325 was modified and introduced as the Savage Model 340 in this catalog illustration.

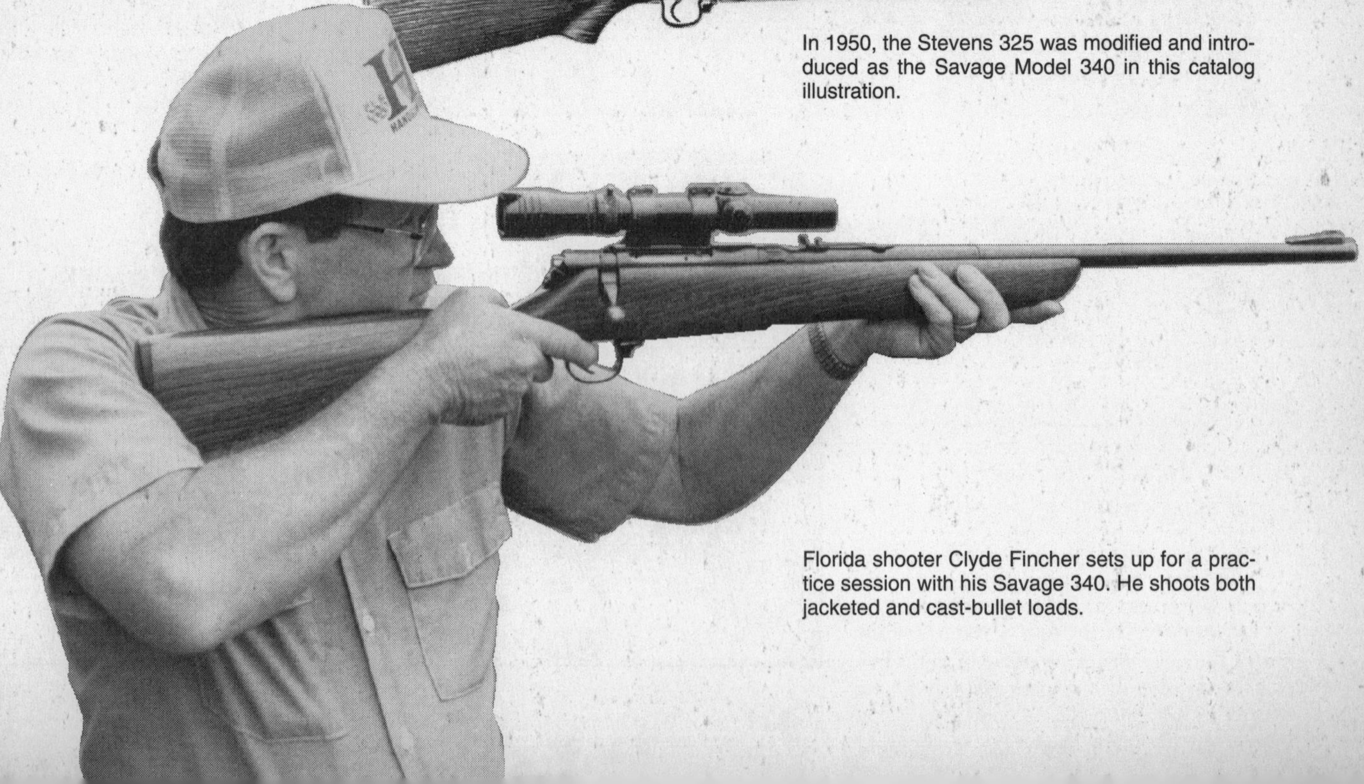

Florida shooter Clyde Fincher sets up for a practice session with his Savage 340. He shoots both jacketed and cast-bullet loads.

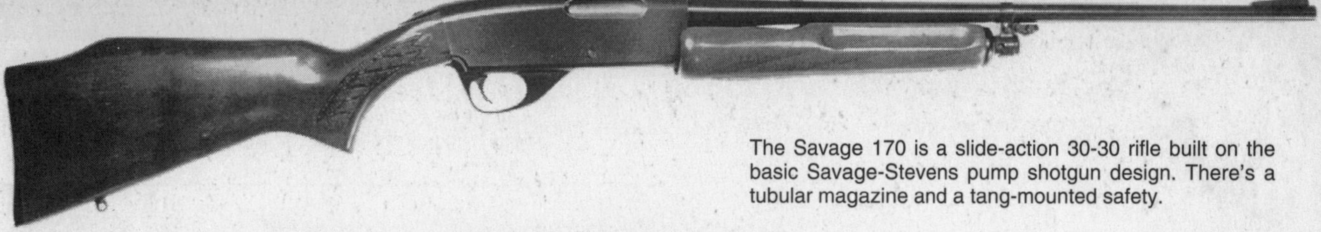

The Savage 170 is a slide-action 30-30 rifle built on the basic Savage-Stevens pump shotgun design. There's a tubular magazine and a tang-mounted safety.

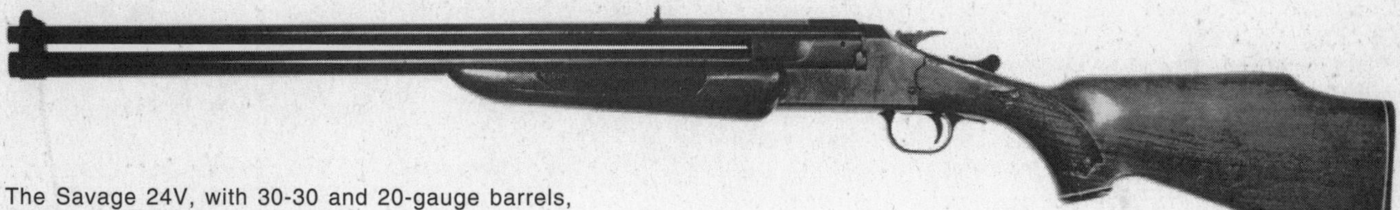

The Savage 24V, with 30-30 and 20-gauge barrels, became the choice of hunters who hunted deer and small game at the same time. This is an early 24V, a series A.

The latest Savage under/over combination gun is the Model 24F, which offers the 30-30 with either a 20- or 12-gauge shotgun barrel. It sports a black polymer stock and some mechanical changes.

really expect to get in any hunting, but wanted to have a centerfire rifle, just in case.

Some people liked the little rifle, but wanted a bit more power. In Louisiana, where I lived at the time, local gunsmiths offered a simple way of getting it. They would transform the H&R rifle into a 30-40 Krag by simply running a chambering reamer into the barrel.

At the time, I wondered about the safety of doing this with an action originally designed for low-pressure shotgun loads. No one ever had any problems, and in 1972, H&R added 44 Magnum and 45-70 to the caliber offerings of this design.

The growth of ammunition reloading as a hobby in the 1960s tied in well with the availability of the single shot H&R 30-30s.

The cartridge had always been factory-loaded with flat- or round-nose bullets to avoid the danger of the bullet of one cartridge firing the primer of the cartridge ahead in a tubular magazine.

The box magazine of the Savage 340, of course, did not have this problem, but few people reloaded the 30-30 when it was introduced. The H&R came along at a time to catch the fancy of reloaders who wondered how this round would do with pointed bullets. Apparently, it did very well indeed. One member of the shooting club to which I

belong uses his scoped H&R 30-30 with spitzer handloads for deer every season.

In 1985, the Harrington & Richardson firm, after being in business for 114 years, had financial problems and went out of existence. The assets were acquired by a group of investors in 1987, and production of a small line of selected firearms was resumed. The guns were marketed under the New England Firearms name.

Included in the offering for 1988 were several NEF Handi-Gun rifle/shotgun combinations based on the previous H&R Topper design. Available with 12- or 20-gauge shotgun barrels, the rifles were offered in 22 Hornet, 223, 45-70 and, of course, in 30-30!

The next year's NEF catalog offered the rifles alone, without the extra shotgun barrel, cataloged as the Handi-Rifle. Calibers for 1989 were the same as before.

I am reminded of my concern that the original H&R break-open action might not be strong enough for the higher pressure of the 30-40 Krag cartridge. Along with the 30-30, the NEF catalog current at the time of this writing lists the Handi-Rifle in these calibers: 22 Hornet, 223, 243, 270, 30-06 and 45-70.

Since 1991, the H&R brand name has returned to the market. The same company now makes rifles sim-

The new Savage 24F has a crossbolt safety in the frame, in addition to the rebounding hammer with barrel selector.

ilar to those they produce as NEF guns, but with the H&R 1871 trademark. However, they are essentially varmint rifles and do not include the 30-30 chambering.

In 1986, just after the original H&R rifles went off the market, another single shot 30-30 rifle, the Thompson/Center Contender carbine, entered the scene.

The Contender pistol had been introduced in 1967. Silhouette shooting as a sport was sweeping across the country, and the new pistol became popular for such matches. For 200-meter rams, one of the popular chamberings had been 30-30

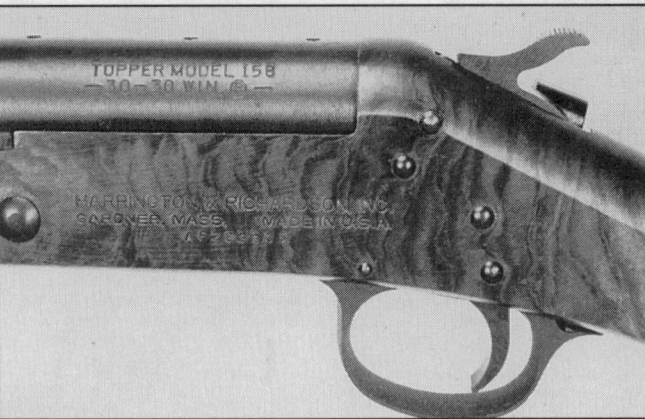

Based on the Topper shotgun, H&R's Model 158 30-30 was a light and compact 30-30 that shot well.

H&R kept its numerous variations straight by making frames alike and putting model numbers on the barrels.

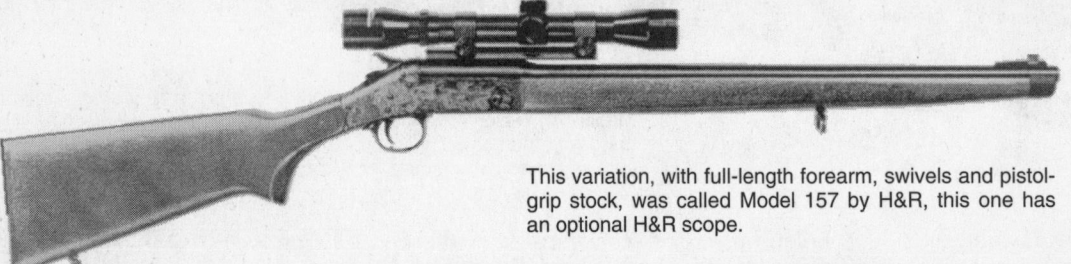

This variation, with full-length forearm, swivels and pistol-grip stock, was called Model 157 by H&R, this one has an optional H&R scope.

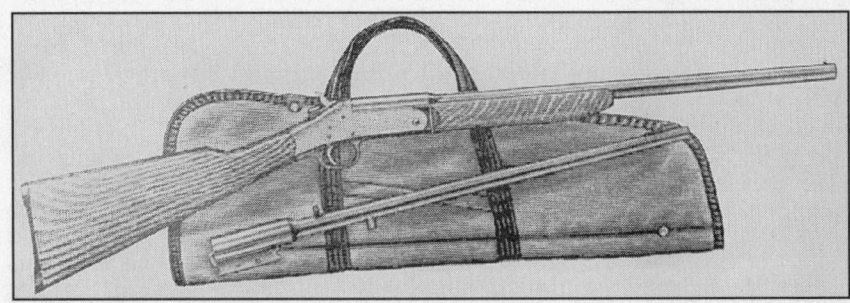

Early on, H&R offered combinations which included a rifle barrel and a shotgun barrel to fit the same frame and forearm.

Winchester, added to the line in 1969.

After almost two decades of production as a pistol, the new rifle option appeared in 1986. The Contender was offered with a longer barrel and shoulder stock as the Contender carbine, and 30-30 was one of the initial chamberings. A kit of the carbine barrel and stock became available for those who already had a Contender pistol.

The Contender carbine weighs only about 5 pounds and has a 21-inch barrel. It has found a following among those who can use such a light, compact rifle. It fits women and young people well, and for the youngest of young people, a special youth version is available with a 16½-inch barrel and a stock 2 inches shorter than standard. The 30-30 is a good balance of power and recoil for this light rifle and, of course,

spitzer-bullet handloads can be used that are not available in factory offerings.

It seems almost assumed that Contender carbine owners will be handloaders. The calibers in which this rifle has been offered provide plenty of opportunity for experimentation with various loads. Besides the 30-30, the little rifle has been offered in these chamberings: 17 Remington, 22 Hornet, 222, 223, 7mm TCU, 7-30 Waters, 357 Maximum, 35 Remington, 375 Winchester, 44 Magnum, 45 Colt and 45-70.

Although the 30-30 was designed for a lever-action rifle, non-lever-action 30-30 rifles have been around for about as long as the cartridge itself. Those other 30-30s have been made in regular production as falling block, rolling block and break-open single shots, and as bolt-

action, slide-action and combination gun types. They are still available as the Savage 24F, the New England Firearms Handi-Rifle, and the Thompson/Center Contender carbine.

Have we covered them all?

The more we look, other interesting tidbits turn up.

Back in the 1890s, Andrew Burgess, inventor of the Burgess sliding-grip shotgun, reportedly made some of the unusual guns as rifles in 30-30 caliber.

More recently, about 1970-75, the Clerke firm of Santa Monica, California, made rifles that were essentially copies of the Winchester Single Shot. Made for modern calibers from the 223 to the 458, they also included the 30-30 in their line.

About the same time, a Spanish firm in Eibar, Spain, made a copy of the Remington rolling block as the

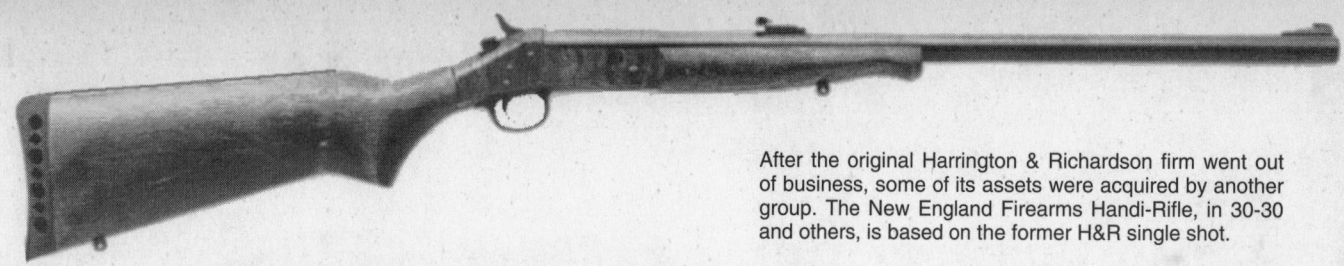

After the original Harrington & Richardson firm went out of business, some of its assets were acquired by another group. The New England Firearms Handi-Rifle, in 30-30 and others, is based on the former H&R single shot.

Star Carbine during 1973-75. Never imported into the U.S., it is rarely seen here. The 30-30, of course, was one of the chamberings.

Even more recently, the Sile company of New York, in 1992-93, offered conversions of surplus SMLE bolt-action rifles as sporters in 30-30 caliber.

The 30-30 cartridge has endured for a century. It might well have retained its popularity even if it had only been available in lever-action rifles. As we have seen, however, it was also chambered in a variety of other rifles that offered the best cartridge choices available throughout the past century.

Its inclusion in the lineup of the best of the time confirmed its place as a round to be considered seriously. Its use in different rifle types broadened its usefulness and versatility. While thinking of the 30-30s century of popularity, perhaps it is appropriate to give some credit, at least a little, to those "other" 30-30s. ●

The Contender carbine is easy to handle, especially suitable for women and children. Mrs. Eric Brooker shoots a Contender.

Starting life as a single shot pistol, the Thompson/Center Contender was offered as a carbine in 1986, and 30-30 was one of the initial chamberings.

Selected Bibliography

Barnes, Frank C. *Cartridges of the World*. Chicago: The Gun Digest Co. 1965.

Blackwell, Wayne. "Cast Bullet Accuracy with a Bolt-Action 30-30." *Handloader* 63, Vol. 11, No. 5 (Sept-Oct., 1976) p. 38-41.

Carmichael, Jim. "Cast Bullets for the 30-30." *Handloader* 20, Vol. 4, No. 4 (July-Aug., 1969) p. 22-24.

Crossman, Capt. Edward C. "The Winchester-Springfield." reprinted in *The Winchester Collector*, Vol. 16, No. 4 (Fall 1993) p. 15-16.

de Haas, Frank. *Single Shot Rifles and Actions*. Chicago: The Gun Digest Co. 1969.

de Haas, Frank. *Bolt Action Rifles* Northfield, IL: The Gun Digest Co. 1971.

Flayderman, Norm. *Flayderman's Guide to Antique American Firearms*, 4th Edition. Northbrook, IL: DBI Books, Inc. 1988.

Hatcher, Julian S. "New Savage Hi-Power Rifles." *American Rifleman*, Vol. 98, No. 7 (July, 1950) p. 38.

Madis, George. *The Winchester Book*. Brownsboro, Texas: Art and Reference House. 1979.

NRA Technical Staff. "Savage Model 219." *American Rifleman*, Vol. 107, No. 8 (August, 1959) p. 55-58.

Sharpe, Philip B. *The Rifle in America*. New York: Funk & Wagnalls. 1947.

Sharpe, Phil. "Standard Automatic Rifle." *American Rifleman*, Vol. 99, No. 9 (Sept, 1951) p. 56.

Smith, W. H. B., and Joseph E. Smith. *The Book of Rifles*, 3rd Edition. Harrisburg, PA: Stackpole. 1963.

Stebbins, Henry M. *Rifles, A Modern Encyclopedia*. Harrisburg, PA: Stackpole. 1958.

Sterett, Larry S. "Testfire Report, Savage 24V-A." GUN DIGEST, 29th Edition. Northfield, IL: The Gun Digest Co. 1974.

Trzoniec, Stan. "Harrington & Richardson Enters a New Phase of Firearms History." *Gun World*, Vol. 33, No. 6 (January, 1993) p. 38-42.

West, Gene. "30-30 Bolt Action Handloads." *Handloader* 19, Vol. 4, No. 3 (May-June, 1969) p. 40-41, 56.

Williamson, Harold F. *Winchester, The Gun That Won The West*. New York: A.S. Barnes. 1952.

by ROBERT J. ROBEL

The author's short-barreled Winchester Model 70, laced-on cheekpiece and all, carries countless pleasant memories of the hunt.

The Joys of the NOSTALGIC HUNT

The old 30-06 Springfield is now a 308 Norma Magnum with a 6x Firearms International scope for long-range shooting.

A forty-year-old pair of binoculars that brought back memories and set the stage for the author's nostalgic hunt—and went along for the trip, too.

This Leica IIIf camera with its spectacular Elmar 50mm f/3.5 lens, and adaptable Elmar 90mm f/4 lens, and Weston exposure meter recorded many years of cherished hunting experiences—and this last one, too.

Downed in classic fashion, this big five-pointer was killed on the
Vermejo Park Ranch.

BUG-EYED and filled with excitement, and very young, I pried open the long wooden shipping carton. With mounting disappointment, and for three long months, I had watched the Railway Express truck pass my house many times. Today, the truck stopped and left the box. A year earlier, I had joined the National Rifle Association for the sole purpose of being able to order a surplus Springfield rifle from the Director of Civilian Marksmanship. It had finally arrived.

Youthful impatience was evident as I hammered on the old screwdriver to pry up the lid of the box. Inside was an ugly mess—a Springfield 1903-A1 covered with cosmoline and wrapped in brown paper. I reverently removed the brown wrapping and painstakingly cleaned the rifle. It was classed as unserviceable, but it looked as if it had never been shot before. The headspace was okay and the inside of the barrel was mirror smooth.

I discarded the military stock and used a mongrel set of wood chisels to fit the barreled action into an "irregular" Bishop stock blank. After a neighbor helped me drill and tap the action for a receiver sight, my first big game rifle was ready to be shot. Factory ammunition was too expensive, so I acquired some military surplus rounds. The groups were big and the stock was clumsy, but it was my rifle.

Looking back forty-five years to that series of events is nostalgic... an early experience I never want to for-

get. I still have that rifle and cherish it dearly.

Wisconsin researchers report that hunters evolve through five distinct behavioral phases. Starting out with the "shooter phase," novice hunters are interested in getting lots of shooting. This phase is replaced by the "limiting out phase," in which the hunter becomes obsessed with filling the bag. Selective hunting follows the limiting out phase and is termed the "trophy phase." Experience gained during the first three phases sets the foundation for the fourth one, the "methods phase." In this phase, the hunter concentrates on the quality of decoys, tone of turkey calls, precision of rangefinder telescopes, and other such methodologies. The Wisconsin researchers conclude that the last phase is the "sportsmanship phase," or mellowing out.

Those researchers were correct as far as they went. Most of us have passed through or are passing through those phases of hunting. Looking back, I can recall each of mine, and so will most hunters if they are honest with themselves. This study is interesting, but those researchers were not old enough to recognize the ultimate phase enjoyed by the ardent hunter, the one reserved for hunters over fifty. The five early phases of hunter evolution are necessary ingredients of the ultimate stage, the "nostalgia phase."

The nostalgia phase was evident as I glassed for elk in this aspen

park of northeastern New Mexico. My 7x35 binoculars swept across the meadows and mountain hillsides just as they had done on the sagebrush plains of Wyoming many years before. The seeds of this nostalgic hunt were sown last year when I came across my old binoculars on the top shelf of a storage closet. Purchased almost forty years ago for my first antelope hunt, and subsequently used on big game hunts in Colorado, Idaho, Alaska and Canada, they hadn't been hunting for over two decades. I own an expensive pair of modern roof-prism binoculars, but for some niggling reason, I chose to have this old pair cleaned and aligned.

When they returned from the New York optical firm, I was taken by their resolution, their balance and their comfortable feel. I put the dent in the barrel thirty years ago while stalking a mountain goat in southern British Columbia; the chipped objective lens was a souvenir of a bad fall on a talus slope while hunting sheep in the Yukon Territory; and the discolored leather case brought back memories of thirteen days of relentless rain on a twenty-one-day pack trip into the Wrangell Mountains of Alaska. If this one piece of hunting gear could rekindle so many memories, how much more enjoyable would it be to saturate a hunt with memorabilia from the past forty years of hunting? With that goal, I set out.

Rummaging through my hunting paraphernalia, I assembled a collection of hunting equipment reminiscent of the early days of Elmer Keith and Jack O'Connor—two hunter/writers who had an enormous influence on me during my early formative period. The old Springfield plus a Winchester Model 70 of similar vintage would be my arsenal, the Anchor 7x35mm binoculars would be my eyes, an old Leica III would record the trip on film, and my threadbare Comfy down jacket would protect me from the cold. Other items included a worn skinning knife, a solid leather cartridge case, an old leather Stetson hat, leather boots (non-insulated with honest-to-goodness leather laces), and an elk-leather shirt. My wife thought I was a case for the fellows in the white jackets as I spent over six months repairing, cleaning and reconditioning hunting gear for my nostalgic hunt.

My first big game rifle had evolved with me during my hunting years. The receiver sight gave way to a telescopic sight, the heavy stock was replaced with one weighing much less, the original barrel was turned down and shortened, and the rifle had been rechambered to 308 Norma Magnum in the early 1960s. What was a clumsy 9½-pound rifle forty-five years ago was now a sleek beauty weighing only 8 pounds. The other rifle with me was a prewar 30-06 Winchester Model 70 rebored by P.O. Ackley to the 35 Improved Whelen. Its 4x Zeiss scope rested low in a Conetrol mount.

The vast Vermejo Park Ranch was the chosen location for this hunt. The ranch encompasses over 500,000 acres of the Sangre de Cristo mountains of New Mexico and is noted for its quality elk hunting. Boone & Crockett record-class elk are not too common on the ranch, but hunters kill a goodly number of nice 6x6 bulls each year. Lodging is superb. I used to enjoy drafty tents, leaky air mattresses, greasy camp cooking, and a splash of cold water on my face in the morning, but not anymore. Let the young nimrods put up with these conditions. My aging carcass now requires a comfortable bed, palatable food and a warm shower to remove the chill from my cold bones and relax sore old muscles. The Vermejo provides these amenities for us over-the-hillers.

I arrived a day early to check the zero of my two rifles. My Whelen was zeroed to be 3 inches high at 100 yards, on at 225 yards and about 8 inches low at 300 yards. While shooting it, I recalled checking that rifle's zero along the bank of the Nisutlin River in the Yukon Territory thirty years ago. My Indian guide was watching as I touched off the first shot. The bullet struck exactly where it was supposed to. My guide was speechless when I turned around. Blood was flowing down from a nasty gash above my eye where the scope had cut through to the bone. That was not the way to favorably impress a guide just before venturing forth on a thirty-day pack horse quest for grizzly bear and Dall's sheep. We used a darning needle and dental floss to stitch me up that afternoon. A deep crescent-shaped scar above my right eye reminds me of that mishap each morning when I shave.

As hunters became better acquainted after dinner the first night at the Vermejo, we discussed rifles, of course. Four of the six fellows at my table would be using 7mm Remington Magnums, new and shiny, but without memories. How sad for those hunters. My rifles had been with me on hunts before. They had accounted for grizzly and black bears, mountain goats, caribou, moose and elk, plus bighorn, Dall's and Stone's sheep. Confidence in rifles comes only from successful experiences with them. These two rifles were filled with pleasant memories. Nostalgia through and through!

I was fortunate that Bob Daugherty would be my guide on this hunt. Bob had guided me several years previously on a successful mountain lion hunt when the mercury hovered around zero for five days. He also accompanied my wife and I in quest of a black bear on the Vermejo Ranch just two years previous. Both of those hunts were filled with colorful recollections.

Bob described the type of terrain and cover in which we would hunt: thick timber interspersed with small grassy parks. Elk were not too plentiful in the area, but some nice bulls had been seen there by cowhands earlier in the fall. The likelihood of a long shot was minimal. My 308 Norma had a 6x scope and a 24-inch barrel for long-range shooting, so I chose to use the trusty 35 Whelen with its 4x scope and 20-inch barrel.

The late Vernon Speer had personally sold me some 250-grain soft-point bullets in 1951, and they had

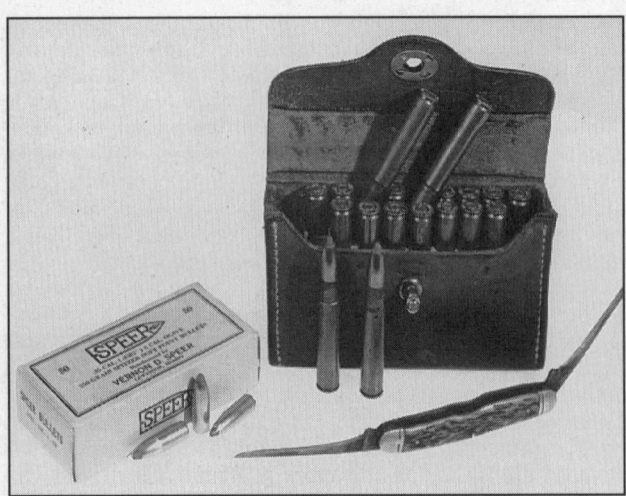

The original Speer bullets, the old leather belt-pouch, the worn but very useful muskrat pattern folding knife—all in the nostalgia package.

A leather Stetson hat that protected the writer from sun, rain and sleet for years—and acted as a rest for the forearm of a rifle—came out of retirement for this one.

always performed outstandingly on big game. I had those bullets loaded in resized 30-06 cases to travel at 2600 fps. The Zeiss scope on the rifle had the European four-post and crosshair reticle. The rifle-scope-bullet-load was a combination in which I had great familiarity and confidence.

Killing power of cartridges is discussed at length in gun rooms and over campfires. I have used the high-velocity 25- and 27-caliber magnums with good success on light big game like antelope, deer, mountain goats, mountain sheep and caribou. But give me a heavy bullet at moderate speed for heavy big game such as elk, moose and grizzlies. The standard kinetic formula measures the energy of a bullet for heavy animals. My past experiences hunting big game prompted me long ago to rely on the Momentum Value (MV) as a measure of killing power for large big game animals. MV is the bullet weight in hundreds of grains times the velocity in hundreds of feet per second. My 35 Whelen with its 250-grain bullet at 2600 fps has a 65 MV at the muzzle compared to the 41 MV for a 130-grain bullet from a 270 Winchester at 3140 fps, or the 50 MV of a 175-grain bullet from a 7mm Remington Magnum at 2860 fps. At 300 yards, the 250-grain bullet from my 35 Whelen has a 52 MV compared to the 130-grain bullet's 20 MV, or the 37 MV of the 175-grain bullet. The momentum of a heavy bullet allows it to smash through tough bone as it penetrates deeply to the vital organs of big animals. Past one-shot kills of grizzlies, moose and elk all reinforce my confidence in the Momentum Value as a reliable measure of killing power for those big animals.

It was below freezing as we left the ranch headquarters that first morning. I donned my leather shirt and hat, and snuggled into the down jacket I wore on my first real big game excursion. Later, in Alaska, that down jacket and I encountered thirteen days of rain. I can recall standing so close to a roaring fire to dry out that hot embers and sparks burned holes through the outer twill covering the jacket. Those small holes were still there rekindling memories, including a wet sleeping bag that reeks of smoke decades later. Those memories are not of an experience I would care to repeat. Time has mellowed some sour ones for me, but not wet cold clothes and soggy sleeping bags. My hunting memories are sweet and sour, but more sweet than sour.

The next morning, a four-wheel-drive pickup truck transported us fifteen miles to the southern part of the ranch in a short forty minutes. The road was little more than a cattle trail, but the ride was luxurious compared to the pounding I've experienced on saddle horses. I recall averaging less than fifteen miles per day in Alaska, riding into sheep country.

The eastern skyline was barely visible as we left the vehicle and began hiking up the gently sloping mountain to a plateau 2 miles away. Bob wanted to get us there at dawn in hopes that elk would still be feeding in one of the small grassy parks that dotted the length of the plateau. As we approached the plateau, a magpie scolded us severely and a raven winged its way far overhead. We glassed the first small park in vain. Onward to the second park where we spotted thirty-six cow elk. Backing off, we circled downwind of the grazing cows and edged onward to the third park in the series. Points of aspens jutted out into the middle of this long narrow park. No elk in sight. Onward to the next park, and the next, and the next.

The sun was now well above the horizon and the peak of morning wildlife activity was over. We had traversed the full length of the plateau and spotted only cow elk. Elk sign was still abundant as we meandered the timber during the late morning and early afternoon, but we saw no elk.

Back to the parks in the evening: The first two were empty, but a couple dozen elk were in the third. A spike and a 4x4 bull graze among the cows. The larger bull was tempting, but Bob discouraged me from taking him on the first day of our hunt. We saw no more elk that evening and arrived back at the truck well after dark.

The next two days were windy and cold. Deep snow accumulated in the higher elevations of the Vermejo and restricted our hunting to lower areas. Although we saw cows and calves each day, not a single bull showed himself. That 4x4 bull I passed up the first day was beginning to haunt me. The lack of a shootable bull elk was a rerun of a hunt in Idaho. On that hunt, my guide and I were in the Selway-Bitterrot Wilderness Area for ten days before we sighted a bull. Deep

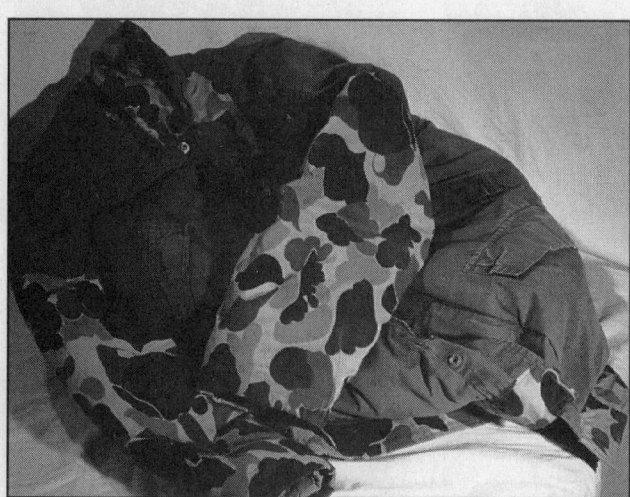

The worn sleeves and collar of this Comfy down jacket were covered with camouflage fabric to prepare it for another memorable hunt.

These quality leather boots with real leather laces have provided solid footing for many big game hunts across North America—and did it this time, too.

From up above, the Vermejo's long-running ridges are an open book if you know the country and own good glasses.

(Right) From down in the flat, the Vermejo's ridge pattern doesn't seem so easy to solve, but the flat travels easy.

(Below) The author checks his rifle's zero before heading out on any hunt, and this was no exception.

(Above) With the venerable 35 Whelen over his shoulder, the author uses his memory-ladened 7x35 binoculars to locate elk on the Vermejo.

(Left) Meat in the panniers—a really classic way to finish off a Western elk hunt.

snows and strong northern winds produced a chill of minus 40 degrees. I finally scored on the eleventh day. We had crossed the fresh tracks of a small herd of elk in mid-afternoon and followed it less than twenty minutes before we came upon them feeding on a hillside 200 yards away. Seven cows and a pair of 5x5 bulls. Leaning against the trunk of a massive ponderosa pine, I lowered the safety on my Springfield and dropped one of the bulls with a 200-grain Partition bullet from the 308 Norma Magnum. That scene is still vivid in my memory.

We left the Vermejo lodge an hour before sunrise the fourth morning and drove twelve miles through a howling blizzard. The 40-mile-per-hour wind and temperatures in the low teens produced a wind chill of minus 30 degrees. My down jacket protected me from the ravages of Mother Nature as we trudged through ankle-deep snow. From a ridgetop, we watched a herd of at least 300 elk feeding in a sheltered valley far below. Mostly cows and calves, and a few spike bulls as well. Two hours of hard hunting resulted in a growling stomach, cold feet and tingling ears, but no bull elk.

Continuing along the old logging road, we crossed the fresh tracks of a large elk, and we set off in hot pursuit. Through dense spruce thickets and open aspen stands, the tracks meandered toward some second-growth pine. I followed close behind my guide, stepping in his footprints to reduce noise. Then, the guide stopped and pointed to the hind quarters and yellow rump of an elk, 40 yards in front of us. Bob thought he saw antlers, but the pine trees were too dense to determine size. Kneeling down, I braced my rifle against the trunk of an aspen and peered through the scope at the rear third of the elk. The animal shook the snow from his back and lay down, fallen timber and small trees hiding him. Now what?

Bob signaled me to follow and we silently circled upwind of the bedded elk. The elk got a whiff of us and stood up—a small 5x5 bull, only 40 yards away. I winced as Bob told me not to shoot. "Wait for a larger one," he said.

Just as I was about to object, the little bull stepped into the undergrowth and disappeared. I was dumbfounded—the second to the last day of the hunt, and I pass up a 5x5

bull elk. Is this a nostalgic hunt, or is senility setting in?

I was wool-gathering as we trudged along a sparsely wooded hillside through at least 3 inches of new snow. Then, Bob stopped to examine another fresh set of elk tracks. He smiled, "If we catch up with this one, he'll be worth shooting."

This elk was feeding as it crossed through open meadows. For half a mile, there was no elk. The tracks were almost smoking fresh and droppings wet and warm. Another half-mile of trailing becomes physically exhausting, passing through a large aspen stand with numerous windfalls. Bob stopped short as we topped a small rise. The bull stood at the edge of a spruce thicket 70 yards ahead. Slowly settling into a sitting position, I put my leather Stetson on the fallen log in front of me. The forearm of the Whelen was solid on the crown of the hat as I eased off the safety.

Like a television flashback, I clearly saw myself positioning that same rifle across that same leather hat in southern British Columbia. On that occasion, the quarry was a large sow grizzly bear feeding on blueberries at dusk. It had been a long afternoon stalk across talus slopes and steep grassy hillsides. The crosshairs settled motionlessly on the shoulder of the grizzly as I squeezed the trigger. Fire belched from the muzzle of the short barrel when the firing pin struck the primer. The 250-grain bullet sped into the bear's boiler room. Another one-shot kill was recorded for me in that rifle's series of nostalgic events.

Reality was restored as Bob whispered, "It's a big 5x5, take him now before he catches our wind, hit him in the shoulder. Shoot now," Bob said, "before he gets into the timber." The crosshairs were motionless as the rifle barked.

The elk disappeared before I recovered from the recoil. Bob was all smiles. The elk went down and hardly kicked. Again, the old Winchester, rebored by the late P.O. Ackley, and the 250-grain bullet designed and produced by the late Vernon Speer did their jobs well. The heavy antlered bull added flavor to this pleasant experience and helped etch the memory into the deep reaches of my aging mind.

Reverently, I removed the spent cartridge case from the chamber of the rifle and the loaded cartridges

from the magazine. Placing them methodically back into the leather cartridge case on my belt, I recalled doing the same thing several years ago after killing an antelope in northeastern Wyoming.

Bob did not permit me to relive that experience as he extended his warm congratulations. We both were elated.

After admiring the animal briefly and recording the event with my camera, I unfolded my old Case knife and began to open up the body cavity. My knife was used to this, having gutted and skinned dozens of big game trophies in the past. The blade was worn thin from use, but it still held an edge like no other knife I have owned. While resharpening the two blades, I traveled back in time to 1958 when this knife was the only instrument available to skin and to flesh the hide of a huge boar grizzly deep in an alder thicket in the Pelly Mountains of the Yukon. That bear challenged the ability of the knife. It had to be sharpened every 10 minutes or so as the tough hide dulled the thin blades. Gutting the bull elk hardly took the edge off the blades, but I resharpened them anyway out of habit. This knife will continue to be my companion on future hunts and will always rekindle fond memories as I use it.

My hands were stiff from the cold when we finished gutting the bull. A 3-mile hike through the blowing snow got us back to the pickup by noon. At the ranch headquarters, we gulped down a hurried lunch then rounded up a couple pack horses.

Mid-afternoon found us quartering the bull and loading the pieces in pannier sacks on the two horses. Snow continued to fall as the horses were led back to the road at dusk. We unloaded the horses in the light of the headlights of the truck, then settled our tired bones in the cab and headed back to the lodge. Mesmerized by the experiences of the last four days, my encyclopedia of nostalgia was again enriched.

We all look forward to experiencing more hunts in our lifetimes. Each will be of higher quality because each will benefit from previous hunts. Hunts should become richer experiences as a hunter ages. The earlier a hunter enters the nostalgia phase, the more rewarding a lifetime of hunting experiences will become. Be sure to include some nostalgia in your next outing; it will be an experience you won't forget. ●

Darra Is Still There...

And Still Makes Guns

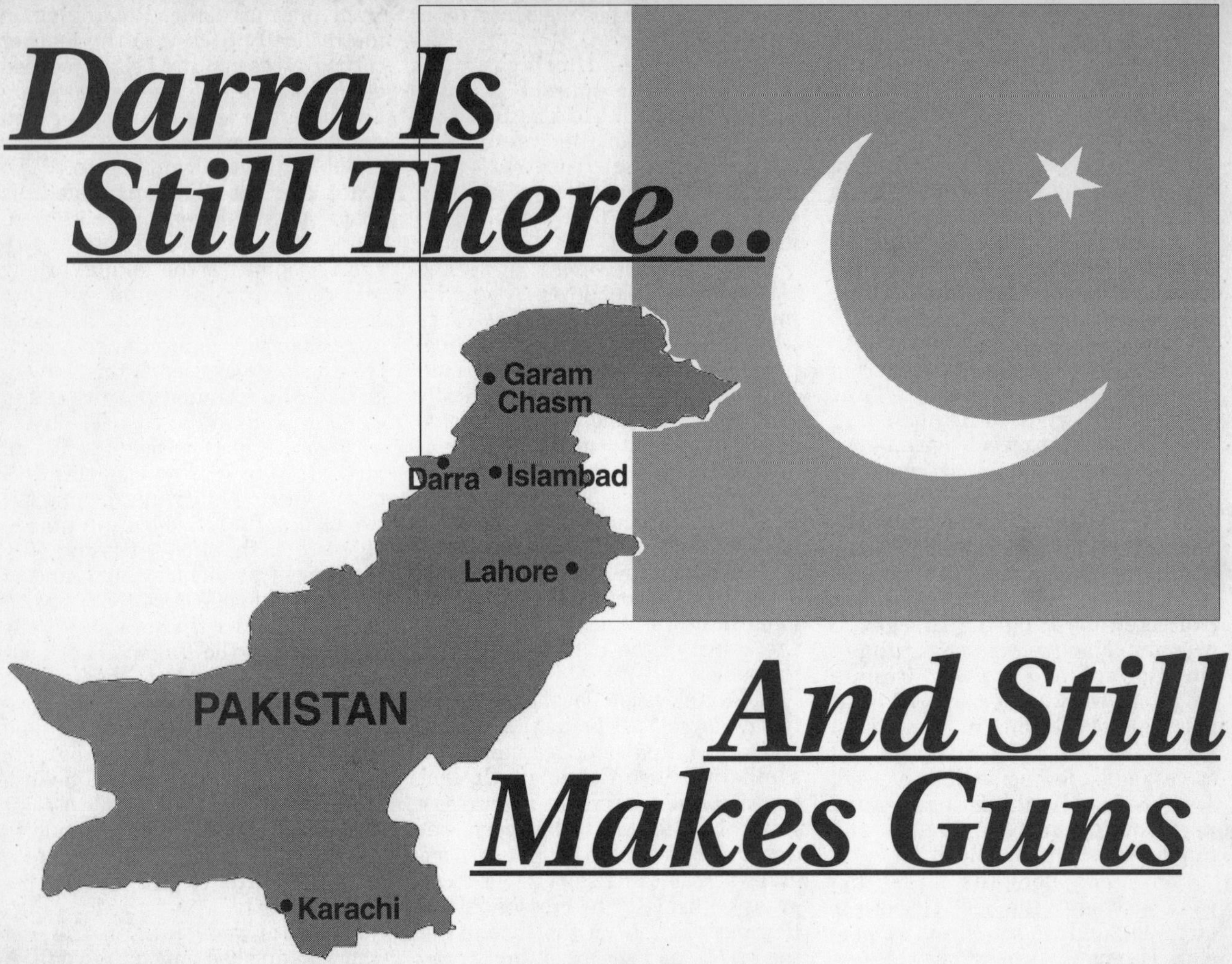

Garam Chasm

Darra · Islambad

Lahore

PAKISTAN

· Karachi

by RAY ROSE

A MAN WEARING a turban asks you, "You want to fire rocket? How 'bout buying a Dragunov? Some hashish?"

No, it's not East LA; it's Darra, Pakistan.

Darra, Pakistan (42 km south of Peshawar) is a Mujahadeen tribal area, tribal in the sense that the area is anarchical. There is no written law and no police force. It is a place where one can browse through a hundred shops containing AK-47s, 5.56mm AR 70 Berettas, M-16s, Stealth pen guns and brass knuckles, the special kind with attached kidney knives handy for breaking noses and slicing open cheeks in one blow. And I went there once.

Before gaining passage to this tribal area, I had to present travel permits at a police checkpoint. Conveniently, my Pakistani friend Mukhtar had connections with these particular police at this particular

Inside a Darra gun shop—take your pick. The writer tried a little bit of a lot of things.

checkpoint, so after a few hugs and cheek-kisses, we were allowed entry with forged permits.

Entering Darra, Mukhtar's Japanese-car tires crunched on the dirt road. To my right, out my window, I spotted a row of Muslims kneeling and kissing the baked ground. They were facing East, praying.

"La ilaha illa ilah," said Mukhtar, pointing to the pious Muslims. "This means," Mukhtar continued, "that there is no god but God." And he further explained that the word "Islam" comes from the word "Salam," which in Urdu means peace.

So in this country where Islam commands one to surrender to peace, there are gun shops and hashish dens. History forgets when Darra began its gunsmith copy-catting, but in 1809 Mountstuart Elphinstine traveled through Pakistan and noted seeing long-barreled muskets. In 1897 emerged the business of reproducing the British Lee Enfield rifle—the sniper's favorite—in Darra (source: Insight Guides, Pakistan, 1990).

We stopped in a gun shop owned and operated by one of Mukhtar's many friends and sipped tea. I noticed surface-to-air rockets and launchers. These were Pak-built RPGs, a model improved on from the RPG-7s captured from Soviet forces in Afghanistan. In fact, most rifles were of the Russian AK-47 variety, obviously from the Soviets next door. There were guns of the American M-16 genre, including the A1 and the heavier, more reliable A2 variety; there were Italian models, among them the Franchi and the Beretta; German models, 9mm Heckler & Koch; French makes like the MAT 49; and, ironically enough, precise renditions of the Israeli 7.62mm Galil assault rifle. In the rear, behind a glass case, were hand grenades, renditions of the British L2A2 grenade packed with the standard 6 ounces of RDT/TNT, and midst the grenades, an odd number of 12-bore Ithaca 37s.

In a field out behind the shop, I test-winged a few grenades, their handling just as efficient as any American-made grenade. I also used a M203 launcher and found I could hit point targets at 160 yards.

Later on in the day, a smiling, Japanese fellow entered the shop, interrupting our tea break. He was wearing Madonna cut-offs and Converse low tops.

"Hello," he said loudly, "I want to shoot missile."

Midst gunfire and the din of Darra's factories, gunmaking Muslims take time to worship.

The wild west of Garam Chasma, an important staging point for the Mujahadeen anti-Russian war effort.

"Yes, please," said the shopkeeper, using standard British English. He de-shelved a rocket and a launcher, and holding the weapon said, "One go is 100 U.S. dollar, cash." And he handed the launcher to the Japanese fellow.

"Oh, very expensive," he replied. And from his Tokyo fanny-pack he slipped out a crisp U.S. $100 note, as if he were prepared to pay this sum, and handed it to the shopkeeper.

"OK," said the shopkeeper and led the Japanese lad out to the back field. Eighty yards away stood a lone tree. The Japanese lad would fire the missile at the tree and blow it from its roots. The anticipation of this gradually drew a crowd of twenty. The lad took the missile into the launcher, lost his balance from its weight, regained his balance, steadied himself, and with squinted eye took aim. He triggered the missile, spraying white rocket smoke in his face, and the warhead went side-winding off target, whistling faster and faster to the ground, while the onlookers wrapped their heads in their arms and ducked.

Thud. The missile plowed into the mud and did nothing. The Japanese lad opened his eyes and, like a golfer who muffed a ball, threw down the launcher. Bored, the shopkeeper calmly walked over to the missile, picked it up and cleaned the mud-clumps from it. "Easy coming, easy going," he said and laughed crazily.

The Japanese guy, realizing that he was outnumbered by 700 to one, laughed along.

After the excitement settled, I visited a dirt-floored warehouse where weaponry was manufactured on old machine tools. I didn't know whether these family-run workshops could be efficient in the thousands of operations necessary to produce one machinegun, or safe. Shells were loaded with a Lee Turret press, self-

Browsing and fooling around in Darra. Gun shops there offer the full small arms gamut.

indexing and progressive. And for used firearms, a rebluing process was performed with *no* safety precautions. One Pakistani boy, nine years old, had his face splattered with lack-of-safety-precaution scars and was still dutifully performing this task. He wore no safety mask and his gloves were made of cotton, not rubber. Most astounding was the steel casting performed in dug-out sand holes and how the shop workers would handle the near-molten metal pieces with their hands.

With these archaic production methods in mind, I quizzed shopkeepers on what problems their guns most usually encountered. Broken extractors, jammed safety buttons,

faulty ejectors and notorious bridge screw mishaps were most on the list. Nothing extraordinary.

I now wanted to shoot some guns. All safety precautions were dismissed as, for example, in a 7mm Mauser we fired 300 Savage rounds. And we fired the guns straight into the sky while standing in the middle of the main road. In the submachine gun line-up, I zipped away bursts from 9mm Micro-Uzis, mirror images of the bonafide Uzi, as were mirrored exactly the MAT 49s (French submachine). Despite the lack of safety precautions, the utter lawlessness of it all provided me with a pure madcap rush. There was nothing I could do in Darra to get

arrested or even accosted by the police or government officials. There were none.

By the end of my visit to Darra, I had concluded all their weapons, save for the Japanese guy's dud RPG-7, to be surprisingly reliable. They all dealt out high energy dumps as they were designed to do. And to those interested in smuggling, their costs (AK-47s for under $1300) were very competitive.

I then left Mukhtar and traveled by overnight bus, north to Garam Chasma (Hot Springs). G.C. was a popular Mujahadeen staging point for entering the war fields of Afghanistan. When I arrived, it was dark, so I settled into an im-

pressive hotel owned and operated by a Mr. Abbis who looked like an Aladdin genie. He maintained a swimming pool filled with hot spring water. This served as a gorgeous break for the traveling gun connoisseur.

The following morning, I wandered through the one-lane bazaar and dabbled in tea shops, talking with those Mujahadeen who could speak English. I met one, a sixteen-year-old, who after a few months in a French war-hospital was certified to perform surgery and gynecological duties, or so said his license. His body was sixteen, but his eyes were thirty-five. He expounded on the terrors of the war in Afghanistan: the Russian planes that showered bullets on villages, the days without food or water in the desert, the carnage, the carnage and the carnage.

He also pointed out that Garam Chasma, thanks to the U.S. government, was a well-equipped ammo dump for the Mujahadeen effort, (This recently changed as the U.S. stopped aid to Pakistan after discovering nuclear arms manufacturing.) Because of this U.S. military aid, my being an American brought honor and respect as opposed to the disrespect I received in the tea-houses of Iran and China and parts of India.

In Garam Chasma, no one offered me a hand grenade or hashish, but they did offer me guided horseback tours, at the tune of $100 a day, over the Dorah Pass into war-riddled Afghanistan. Due to my case of dysentery and fear of dive-bombing MIGs, I declined. Instead, I ambled down the bazaar and priced U.S. military supplies that were being sidetracked from the war effort and sold at a profit. U.S. Army-issue sleeping bags, unused, were $10 each. Other U.S. military items such as boots and camo-fatigues were similarly priced: dirt cheap for myself and unattainable for the penniless Mujahadeen. Rather than wear the U.S.-donated Army gear, the troops wore sandals or hard rubber rain boots a few sizes shy of a good fit.

All told, the Afghan Mujahadeens and the people of Pakistan, despite their love affair with guns, are surprisingly friendly and hospitable. They are not full-tilt, war-crazed terrorists, but guns and gunsmithing, with or without Western military aid, will continue to exist there and in developing nations the world over. •

Read what the experts say
about the new BOSS.

BALLISTIC OPTIMIZING SHOOTING SYSTEM The new patented BOSS allows you to fine-tune the accuracy of a Browning rifle. The BOSS allows you to shoot with unbelievable precision — with any factory load. But, don't just take our word for it, read what the experts say.

"The biggest improvement in rifle accuracy to come along in the last 100 years."
BOB MILEK
Field Editor — Guns & Ammo, Petersen's Hunting

"With the BOSS it is now possible for any shooter to fine-tune a rifle better and with far more versatility than has been possible by even the world's finest custom gunsmiths."
STEVE COMUS
Managing Editor — Gun World Magazine

"Simple to adjust, nothing to wear out or break, relatively inexpensive, the BOSS is a giant step forward in the long search for that evasive one-hole group."
AL MILLER
Associate Editor — Rifle Magazine

"Browning has made accuracy as easy as twisting a knob."
ROBERT HUNNICUTT
Senior Associate Technical Editor — American Rifleman

"Could well be the most significant improvement in accuracy to come along in a long, long time."
JON SUNDRA
Shooting Editor — Guns, Shooting Industry, Guns & Hunting
Author of the book, "Complete Rifleman"

"I shot my tightest group ever with a Browning BOSS rifle."
BILL MILLER
Hunting Gun Columnist,
Editor — North American Hunter Magazine

"The BOSS is a major achievement regarding the basic approach to rifle accuracy."
RICK JAMISON
Shooting Editor — Shooting Times
Author of the book, "The Rifleman's Handbook"

"Browning has taken a path toward solving the riddle of accuracy, opening the door to the 21st century of rifle performance."
JIM CARMICHEL
Shooting Editor — Outdoor Life
Author of "The Book of the Rifle"

"For an out-of-the-box factory rifle with factory ammunition, it just doesn't get any better. It's a fabulous system!"
CRAIG BODDINGTON
Senior Field Editor — Petersen's Hunting Magazine

"A major breakthrough for Browning and a real boon for shooters."
GRITS GRESHAM
Shooting Editor — Sports Afield
Host — ESPN's TV Series, "Shooting Sports America"

Patent # 5,279,200

NEW A-Bolt II with BOSS
New A-Bolt II's are available with optional BOSS except Micro Medallions and 375 H&H.

BAR Mark II with BOSS
The BOSS is optional on all BAR Mark II rifles.

WE'RE LEADING THE WAY INTO THE FUTURE!

WITNESS

Multi-caliber versatility for the twenty-first century.

Even more than today, the citizens of the future will look for economy and value. The versatile *WITNESS* will still fill the bill. With models for competition, duty, home defense and casual plinking...sizes from standard to subcompact...ported and nonported...standard length and extra-long compensated models...seven calibers (22LR, 9mm, 9x21, 40S&W, 38 Super, 45ACP, 10mm)...all steel frame and slide construction...there's a *WITNESS* for everybody and every purpose. Best of all, the *WITNESS SERIES* has a host of accessories, so the value minded citizen may upgrade or convert the *WITNESS* to meet the challenges of the future.

See the complete line of EAA products at your local firearms dealer, or send $2 for our current color catalog. Dealers, send your current FFL, retail tax certificate *and your phone number* for a catalog.

ASTRA

The dawn of a new era of high performance *super pistols*.

No pistols in the world are as ahead of their time as the *A-75* and *A-100*. The mighty little *A-75* (9mm or 40S&W; 45ACP available October 1994) is ASTRA's *selective double/single action super-compact*. With all-steel construction, adjustable three-dot sights, and triple safety system *including a de-cocking lever,* the sleek *A-75* is ASTRA's hottest model. The *A-75* was voted **The 1994 Pistol of the Year** by the National Association of Federally Licensed Firearms Dealers. The *A-75* is also available with an aluminum frame, making it one of the lightest 9mm's in the world...24 oz. The double-action *A-100* (9mm, 40S&W, 45ACP) is an equal in both quality and function to some other popular pistols costing twice as much. It comes with a law enforcement-approved de-cocking lever and a new higher capacity magazine. (A new lightweight *A-100* will be introduced with an aluminum frame in late 1994.)

The *A-75* and *A-100* will be available mid-1994 with optional night sights.

EUROPEAN AMERICAN ARMORY CORP.

P.O. Box 1299 ■ Sharpes, FL 32959 ■ 407/639-4842

© EAA 1994

KEEP YOUR GUNS FROM BECOMING HOT.

Don't let your guns end up fenced or fried. Get the better, *total* protection of a Browning/ Pro-Steel gun safe. The entire Browning lineup is new this year and every safe is better than ever. Like all new Platinum and Gold Series models with Uni-Force™ cam design. Multiple, independent assemblies actuate massive 1-inch diameter bolts. A special shock dissipating design further frustrates the most determined attacks to the bolt ends.

New this year, all series have versions available with the *Certified Browning Fire Safe* option. Browning safes are *independently tested* and *certified* by Omega Point Laboratories to standards you should demand. In a 1,200° F test fire the inside of a Browning fire safe stayed below 300° F for thirty minutes. The test simulated the duration and extreme heat of an average house fire. Safe exterior temperatures were so hot, in fact, that the handle and dial literally melted off the test safe's door. Yet contents — loose paper and a Browning shotgun — remained safe inside due to our advanced inner liner and dual layer insulation design.

Browning Platinum Plus with Uni-Force Cam system. Fire resistant door panel removed to show locking mechanism.

See the Browning/Pro-Steel fire certification test for yourself. Send $5.00 for a VHS video and a comprehensive 132 page catalog of Browning Hunting & Shooting products (itself a $2.00 value). Browning, Dept. D8, One Browning Place, Morgan, Utah 84050-9326, or phone toll-free 1-800-333-3288.

THE BEST THERE IS.

Leather goods courtesy of Don Hume, Inc.

THE SIG SAUER P 226...
Full-Time Safety, Impressive Firepower

Firepower? When your situation demands maximum firepower, the Sig Sauer P 226 will always deliver. Developed specifically for today's law enforcement officer, the Sig Sauer P 226 can deliver 16, 9mm rounds (21 optional) rapid-fire at outstanding accuracy. Adjustable high-contrast sights provide easy target acquisition even when visibility is diminished.

Safe...Always! The unique multiple internal safety and decocking feature make the P 226 the safest gun you can carry under *any* conditions. The loaded and decocked weapon puts the hammer in register with the safety intercept notch, so firing is possible only when the trigger is pulled.

It is the perfect transitional weapon from revolver to semi-automatic. Now being carried by many elite law enforcement agencies in the U.S. and Europe, it has proven itself to be the most efficient, safe and reliable handgun in the world.

Contact us today for the name of your nearest Sigarms dealer. He's anxious to show you the safest ...and most effective gun you can carry.

SIGARMS

SIGARMS, Inc.,
Industrial Drive,
Exeter, NH 03833

THE SIG SAUER P 226...YOUR TACTICAL EDGE!

THE FIRST PRACTICAL

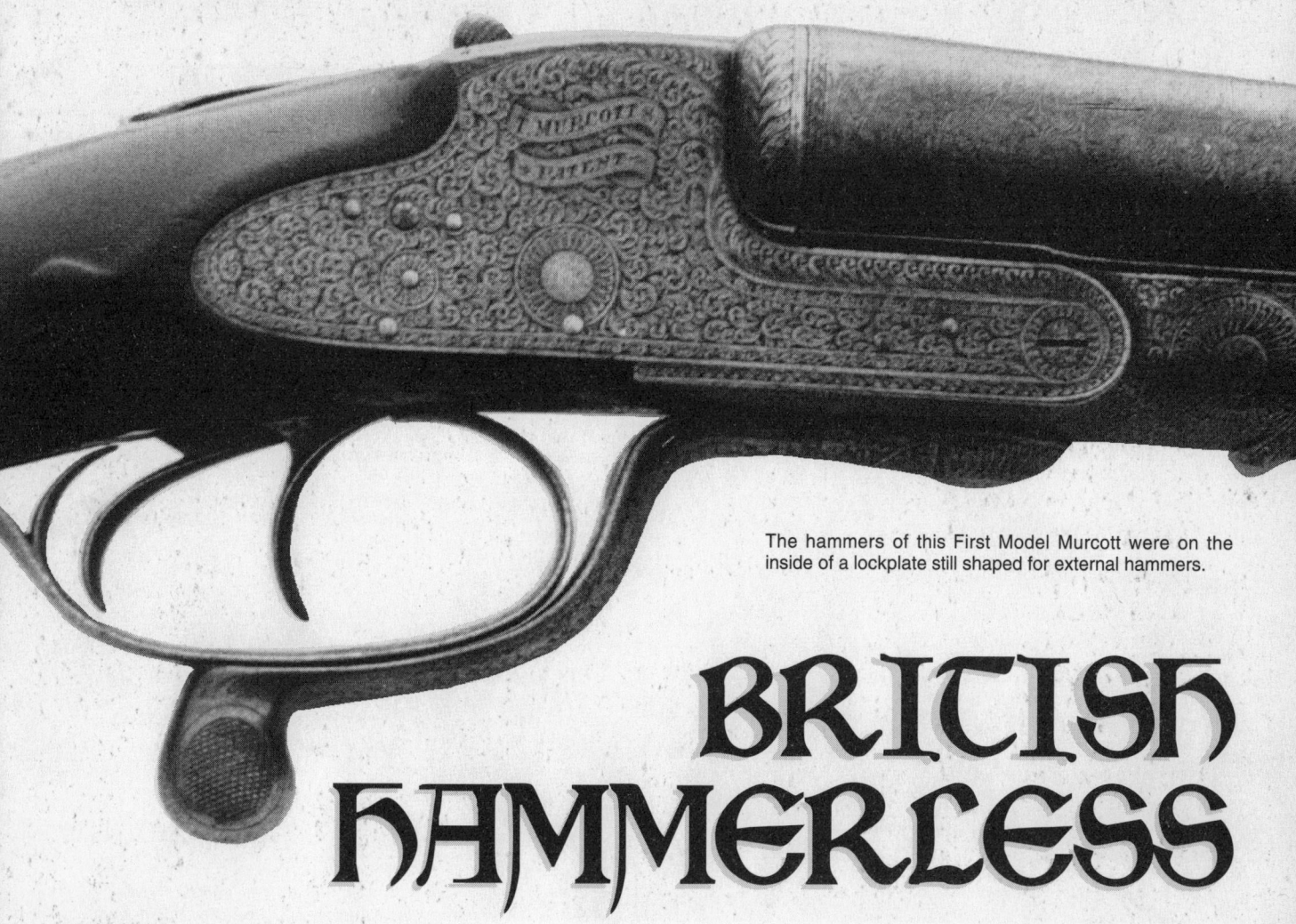

The hammers of this First Model Murcott were on the inside of a lockplate still shaped for external hammers.

BRITISH HAMMERLESS

by JACK BARTLETT

LONDON, ENGLAND, in the 1860s—a city of long-skirted gals, gas and oil lamps, hansom cabs and top-hatted, frock-coated men, all sporting muttonchop whiskers and massive moustaches. One such Britisher was Theophilus Murcott, gunmaker and businessman, who started his business in 1854, building muzzle-loading shotguns and rifles. In the '60s, Brits were still into front-loading despite the fact that a Frenchman, one Lefaucheux, had just sent over his pinfire hammer gun that loaded at the wrong end with a cartridge.

Our Theophilus was no stick in the mud. Many British gunmakers (including the first Greener) and many old-time sportsmen roundly condemned the first breechloaders,

but Murcott was all for change and improvement. Soon the pinfire was supplanted by the centerfire cartridge, and on the drawing boards the designers were producing their most exciting development yet—the hammerless shotgun.

Several British gunmakers had been experimenting with the idea of building guns without external hammers. Daw's gun was introduced in 1862 and Green's in 1866, but neither was completely successful. Our Theophilus, in 1871, designed and built his very, very short-lived, but immortal, double-barrel, non-ejector, hammerless shotgun, a sidelock with

Damascus barrels, of course, well-balanced and having all the attributes of a "best" British shotgun. To this gun can be awarded the accolade for being the first successful British gun without hammers.

As you can see in the drawings, the sidelocks might have come from any quality hammer gun, though now the strikers rest in the "innards" of the lock. Theophilus did, in his first gun, employ the ordinary "double grip" underlever system, the strongest method ever designed for locking barrels to action, and also the slowest. In later models, he used a snap action, the underlever being

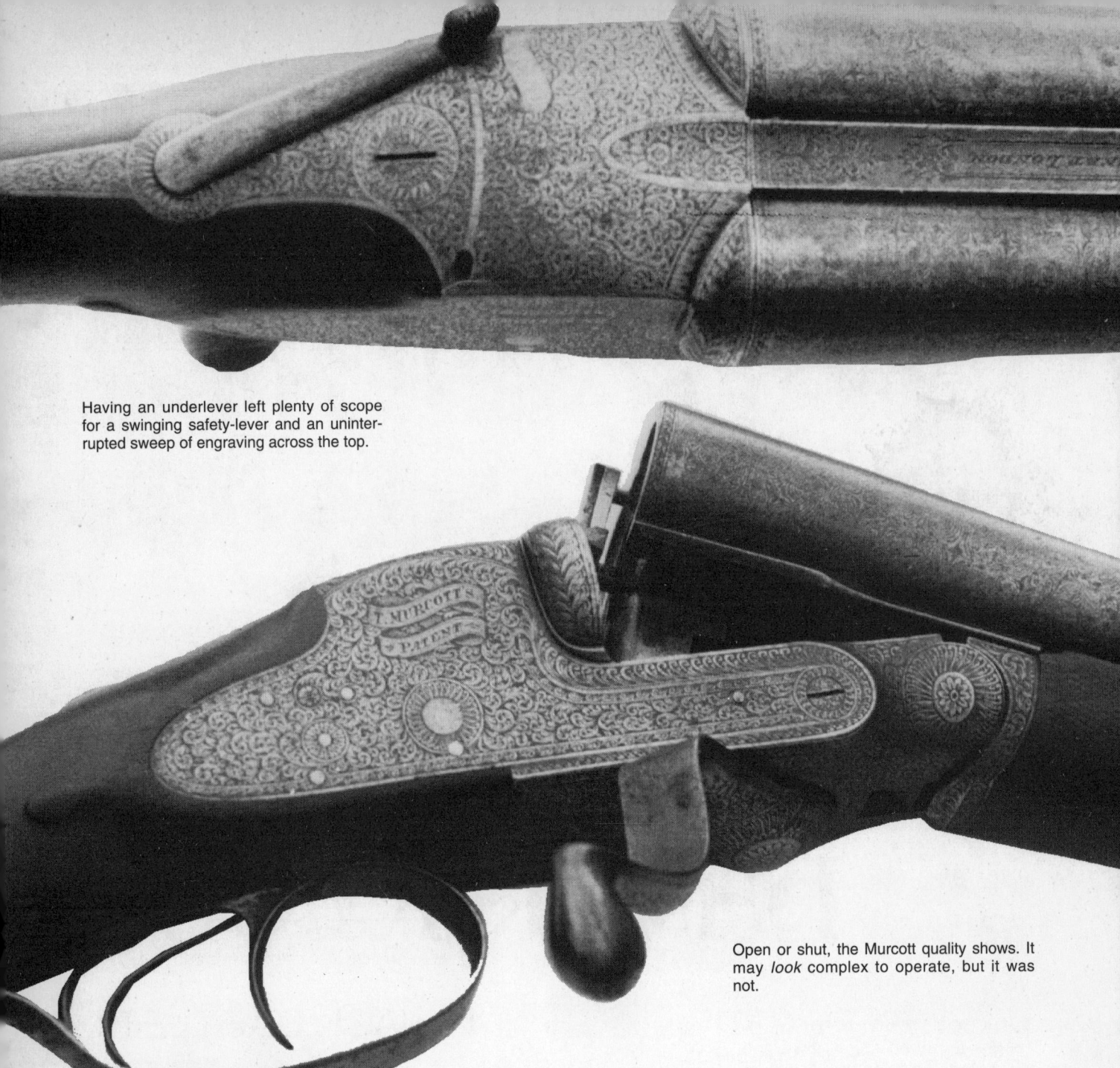

Having an underlever left plenty of scope for a swinging safety-lever and an uninterrupted sweep of engraving across the top.

Open or shut, the Murcott quality shows. It may *look* complex to operate, but it was not.

forced forward to withdraw the bolt from the bites in the lump, and also to extract the bolt from its hole between the barrels above the extractors.

Theo also employed a rather peculiar very, very long safety bolt lever, which swung from Fire to Safe by being rotated across the top of the action. This safety only bolted the triggers and did not have the advantage of a modern intercepting sear.

But to continue with the career of Theophilus. In 1861, he moved from his original premises to a more prestigious address at 68, The Haymarket, London, a retail shop where the London "swells" of the day could foregather to discuss their shooting and the new guns they were going to purchase. At the rear of the gunshop was a fully equipped workshop staffed by many of the foremost bench gunmakers of his day. And there he was to build and sell both models of his hammerless gun until 1878 when his business closed. Did he cease trading because of advancing years and illness? History, unfortunately, does not record. But we do know that in 1879 the famous W.W. Greener took over these premises, using them as his London agency for the sale of shotguns and rifles built in his Birmingham factory.

This was not the end for the Murcott hammerless gun. No more were built, but the existing guns continued to give their owners yeoman service. Old Jack—your reporter—has been shooting in Britain since 1927 and during those chequered years has encountered many, many sportsmen still shooting the old Murcott.

Now, I'm sure people from the U.S. of A. all know that our large midland manufacturing city of Birmingham is the place where many, many guns were built. Did not we supply 577-caliber muzzle-loading Enfield rifles when you had that shindig 'twixt North and South? And did not a "Greener" sit atop the Wells Fargo coaches? In the gun quarter of "Brum" (as we call that city) were dozens of self-employed outworkers, who each (in their own small workshops) did one particular job on the building of a shotgun. One filed the action, another set up tubes into pairs of barrels, another crafted superb slabs of walnut into gunstocks.

One such family, originally in business as barrel filers for three generations in Birmingham, when bulldozers bit deeply into their old red brick workshops, moved to rural Herefordshire to continue their trade as gunmakers and barrel filers. These are the Pierces, a father and two gunmaker sons together with a daughter who does the accounts and shopwork. Hereford is the border county marching alongside Wales, where white-faced Hereford cattle were early bred.

Well, on a recent visit to the house of the Pierces, The Gun Room in Etnam

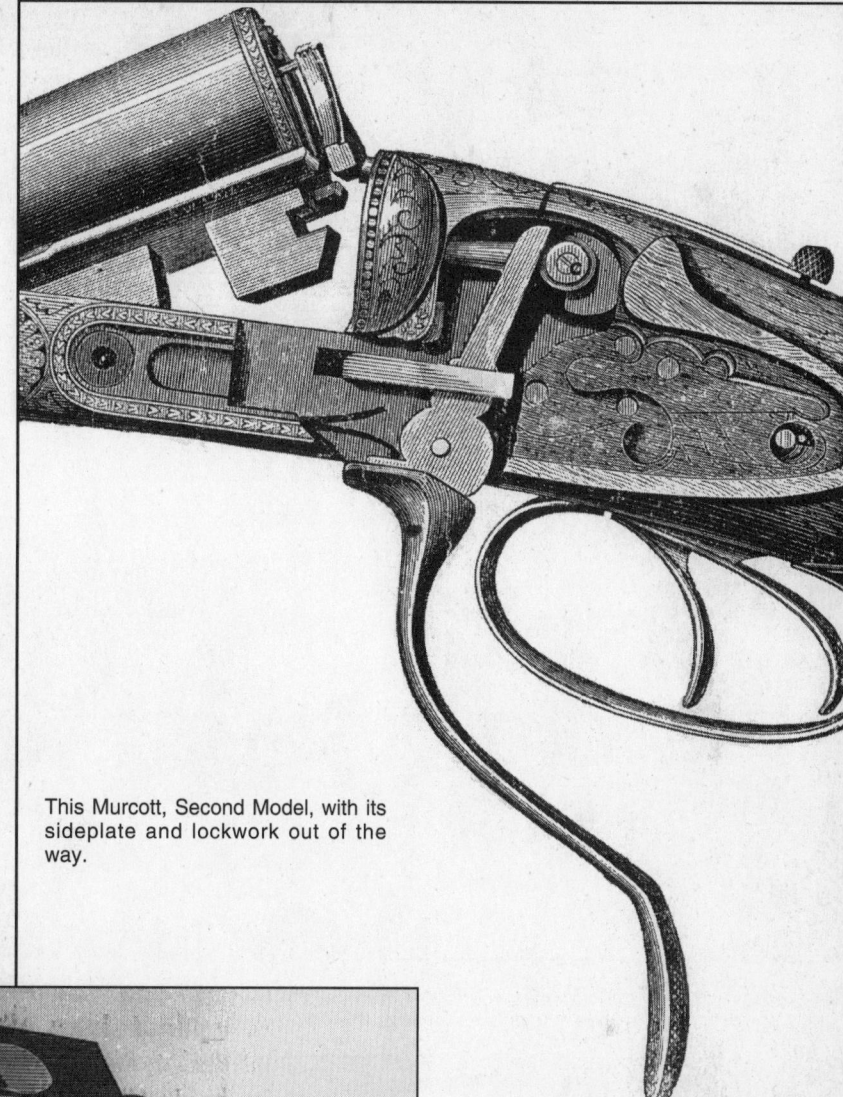

This Murcott, Second Model, with its sideplate and lockwork out of the way.

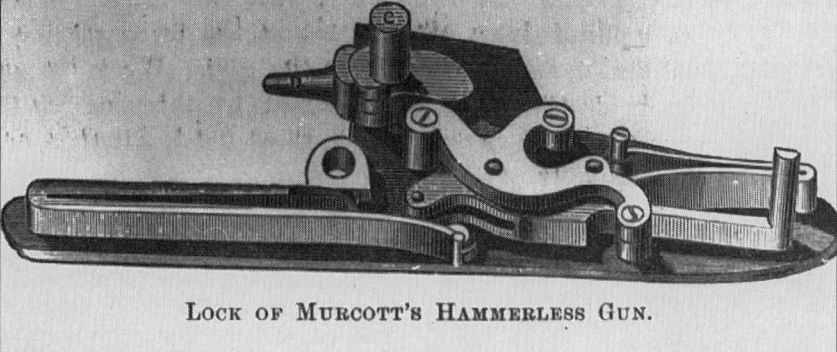

LOCK OF MURCOTT'S HAMMERLESS GUN.

Ah, but they were springmakers in those days, were they not?

Street, Leominster, Herefordshire, Stan Pierce, head of the firm, thrust into my hands one of the very first, double-grip underlever hammerless Murcotts. Considering its age—about 114 years—it was in excellent condition, the Damascus barrels free from pits, and the original British blackpowder proof marks supplemented (at some later date) by proof for nitro powders. Instructions from the lucky owner were to refurbish the Murcott as new.

The Pierces did just that. When

old Jack returned a few weeks later, there she was, Damascus tubes a beautiful shade of copper brown, the stock gleaming with a London oil finish, the engraving crisp and clear, furniture, trigger guard and underlever a deep dense blue.

She now appeared as the sleeping beauty after a century's repose—crisp, lovely and pristine. For the Pierce family has reconditioned many such British classical guns for customers in the U.S.A., Britain, the Middle East and Europe.

In particular, they are past mas-

ters at the art of building new barrels for shot-out classical best guns. Complete new barrels are, of course, extremely pricey although many a best British gun is well worth the expense. Five and twenty odd years ago, British gunmakers introduced the system of re-sleeving shotgun tubes. The old barrels are sawn through just ahead of the breech, leaving the lumps and ejectors still working exactly as they should to the action of the gun. The old tubes are discarded and completely new tubes are then slotted into the old breeches. New ribs (or the old ones if the customer wishes to retain the original builders name thereon) are then re-laid on the pair of tubes, wedges are soldered between the barrels and, finally, David Pierce processes the barrels through his tanks and they emerge carrying a deep, dense hard blue.

Old Jack was delighted when Stan

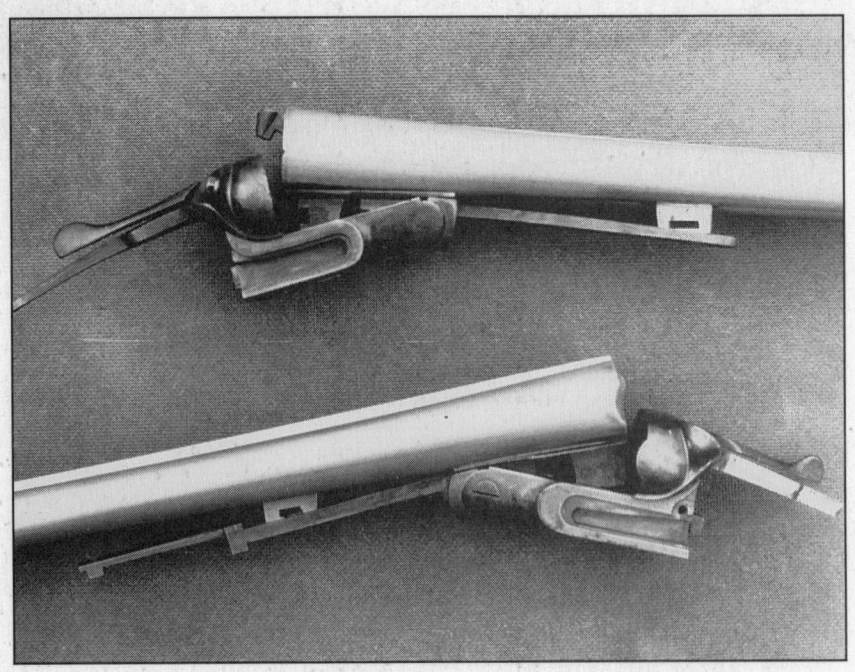

Mark and David Pierce, Birmingham apprentice-trained gunsmiths in their workshop. Note the chopper lump tubes ready to be joined into pairs.

Top: 10-bore hammer gun, built by Holland & Holland in the 1880s. Bottom: 10-bore hammer gun, built in the 1880s by Purdey, both for customers in the USA. Both now have the tubes re-sleeved by Pierce & Son, Gunmakers, Leominster, England.

Pierce thrust into his hands the two guns shown in the photograph. Both were in 10-bore and hammer guns, obviously built about the 1880s. One came from the famous house of Purdey and t'other from Holland & Holland, both London gunmakers producing work of the highest standard. These guns were sent from the U.S. to have their shot-out tubes resleeved, and my photograph shows the superb craftsmanship of the Pierces. Both barrels are, of course, in the white and show the work before reblueing has been carried out.

As most American shotgunners are no doubt aware, although there is no legal requirement for guns built in your country to undergo a statutory proof, all guns built in Britain, or imported into the country from a manufacturer whose state does not have a reciprocal proof house agreement with us, *must* be sent to either the Proof House in London or Birmingham where the weapon is fired with an excessive charge to prove its safety with standard cartridges. And sleeved barrels are reproved.

When the system of re-sleeving was introduced, the Proof Masters in charge of the Proof Houses had grave doubts about the safety of the system. Today it has been clearly demonstrated that a shotgun, even one built seventy to eighty years ago, is far safer to use with re-sleeved barrels than with the original old tubes.

Incidentally, though we have no knowledge of the history of these two 10-bores, might old Jack hazard a guess they were originally built for American gunners who shot live pigeon from traps. If this was indeed so, I trust they won a sackful of dollars, and I'm sure that refurbished and sleeved, they could serve their new owner for another hundred years. Murcotts are like that. ●

The First Model Murcott, after restoration by the Pierces, snuggles down beside some of its contemporary shooting literature—its best gun lineage is clear.

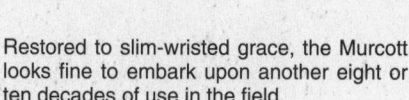

Restored to slim-wristed grace, the Murcott looks fine to embark upon another eight or ten decades of use in the field.

Whiteface Has Left Us

Jack Bartlett died in 1993, full of seventy-seven years and what looks to have been a most satisfactory life. He was at Dunkirk in the Hitler War, and then did a spell at Bomb Disposal.

When all that was over, he set about being a carpenter and a civil engineer and a father and husband and, from 1977, a gun writer on all shooting subjects.

In England, he called himself "Whiteface" in print, as his sort of chap from Hereford—where the cattle come from—is wont to do. As you can tell from his writing, he had a lot of that sort of fun.

He left his wife, Joan, and three children, Pat, Alan and Eileen—and a great many readers.

Ken Warner

"WHILE SPORTSMEN are not usually of a grieving or worrying nature, that they are not altogether satisfied is evinced, from time to time, by their demands on the manufacturers for improvements in the appliances which they use in their various sports. In no instance is this trait more noticeable than it is among those who use firearms."

So began Robert A. Kane's mid-1908 spirited commentary describing the attitudes of a generation of American outdoorsmen toward the providers of sporting arms. With the turning of the century, advancements in all areas of science influenced the entire arms-producing industry, effecting obsolescence at a frightening pace. The Sharps, the Ballard, and the percussion ignition system had outlived their usefulness. Arms companies that could not adapt were weeded out unmercifully. For survivors, with the toppling of various competitors fresh in memory, there was a satisfying security in having produced the top-of-the-line goods for over a half-century. At the same time, widespread publicity of the remarkable progress in military science, and what was happening in the world of ordnance, was broadcast through the medium of the sporting press.

A new breed of gun enthusiast was being cultivated. Educated by experts through a variety of publications that catered to him, the pre-WWI gun crank was decidedly more sophisticated than the generation that had preceded him. He had an understanding that his guns were something more than mere tools.

This performance and value conscious shooter tended to specialize, and to own several guns. Now, with leisure time on his hands, and surplus dollars in his pocket, he became increasingly aware of the deficiencies of the implements of his sport. With increasing regularity, suggestions for a new model gun, or an

Ashley Haines as a young man, about 1899.

improvement in an existing model, were advanced by experimenters and visionaries in the forum that the gun columns of the outdoor magazines provided. There existed a continual, but woefully unorganized, cry for up-to-date models. This public felt armorers had not learned to anticipate the shooter's needs and

Ashley Haines

desires, or even to be mildly receptive to suggestions.

Taken as a whole, arms makers were successful in thwarting this new order of malcontents. New England gun manufacturers were protected somewhat by stiff duties and tariffs from the danger of foreign producers grabbing a disproportionate share of the U.S. market. American patent laws were liberal and well-administered. It was generally considered that domestic manufacturers resisted the crank's petty activity, and rationalized their own position. To bring out new guns was expensive and troublesome, they maintained. The costly retooling and training of employees was to be considered as well. Besides, the scattered opinions of a few cranks did not necessarily constitute a demand. Product lines were not broken, and didn't need fixing.

The independent and dictatorial gunmakers steadfastly ignored the politely worded suggestions of well-intentioned individuals claiming to represent the desires of the mainstream of the shooting fraternity. If the steadily growing group of critics would ever hope to modify the gunmaker's outlook, they would need a gritty, not easily silenced spokesman to champion their cause.

Among those who dreamed the dreams and saw the visions was a young Canadian with some ideas and notions of his own. By 1904, he busied himself sharing his convictions and observations, and displaying his competence to the readers of American outdoor magazines in letters written to the editors. In the pages of the gun columns of *Outdoor Life* and *Field and Stream*, communications over the signature of Ashley A. Haines attracted a wide attention.

Haines himself felt the commonly acknowledged dissatisfaction with the way gunners preferences were ignored. He was a member of the very vocal minority. "I am probably about as much a crank and hard to suit concerning firearms as can usually be found," he admitted.

In the first few years of this century, these columns in sporting magazines were a forum for the expression and sharing of ideas, opinions and preferences of the readers. Reader input was encouraged and comprised the bulk of the columns' contents.

Haines' brief commentaries were solidly drawn from experience. His uncommon expertise and assertiveness earned him a considerable amount of magazine space, an ever-increasing exposure, and a minor following. In short order, Ashley Haines blossomed into a regular and welcomed contributor, his byline as recognizable as his contemporaries Lt. Townsend Whelen and E.C. Crossman, themselves budding gunwriters. He quickly achieved notoriety.

These obvious talents did not go unnoticed by *Outdoor Life* managing editor J.A. McGuire, who recruited Haines for a vacancy on his magazine's masthead. In 1905, Haines took command of the Arms and Ammunition column of the magazine as its first editor. He maintained this position in what appears to have been an on-again, off-again arrangement for the next eight years.

McGuire soon tired of suffering through page after page of Ashley's longhand manuscripts. Haines' penmanship was "unbeautiful." One of the first orders of business was to ship northward a rickety office surplus American typewriter. Haines never quite got used to the contraption, but continued to use it to peck out his monthly material, one-fingered, for many years.

By 1908, McGuire recognized Haines' intensifying popularity and invited him to supply an auxiliary Question and Answer column to respond to subscriber's questions within his field of experience. McGuire believed that Ashley had given the "subject of arms and ammunition for the hunter as much thought as any man in America."

Ashley Amos Haines was born in Michigan on the 13th of January, 1871. In 1885, Ashley's family traveled by covered wagon to eastern Kansas. They soon uprooted and settled in southwestern Kansas, near the town of Garden City, where young Haines spent his teenage years.

After a try at placer mining in Idaho, Ashley relocated to Montana. In 1901, he homesteaded 160 acres of Canadian topsoil, known to *Outdoor Life* readers as the "Last Gasp" ranch, in a narrow valley he often referred to as "Obscurity Holler," 11 miles out of the sparsely populated town of Salmon Arm, British Columbia. Here he established a local reputation as a natural-born farmer, putting up crops of wheat,

by JIM FORAL

AN APPRECIATION

ARMS AND AMMUNITION

A New Cayuse on the Range—The .22 Colt Auto

By Ashley A. Haines.

It's the finest little cayuse that has ever trotted out of Hartford; take my word for this. It's a strange appearing little critter, at least so one will pronounce it when first having a look at it. When one gets his front feet on it, however, and has a chance to put it thru its paces, he calls it the thorobred of the cayuse family.

Now, what's this all about? Listen.

I am not one of the many who advocated such an arm—in fact, when the Colt people asked me for an opinion as to which of two types of one-hand .22 arms would likely prove the most popular, I unhesitatingly voted for the revolver. We got the gun—first for the .22 W. R. F. cartridge, then for the .22 short and long cartridges, and later for the .22 long rifle. And good guns many have found them, too, tho in some respects some of us have thought slight changes, if made, would improve them in design. While the .22 Colt revolvers, that have been men-

tioned, have many desirable features to recommend them to many shooters, at the same time I am of the opinion that this new

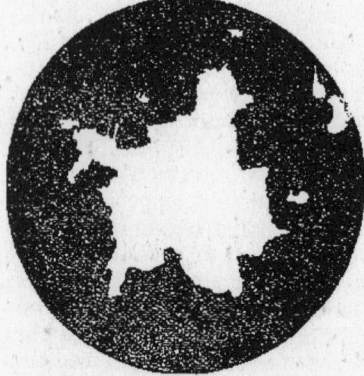

Target No. 2.—Same number of shots and same conditions as for No. 1. By author.

Colt will be found the one that will be sought for more by the pistol cranks. My acquaintance with the little animal has been rather brief, but for all that I am strong for this new Colt. Ten shots at one feeding will look good to the rapid-fire specialist and as this new Colt feeds only on the cheapest, tho best of fodder, this rapid fire man will be sure to feed this little beast an awful lot of the long rifle Lesmok and semi-smokeless stuff. And it has a most voracious appetite. After getting a full feed, the pulling of the trigger a few times spells m-o-r-e, more, just as plain as can be. And it's the greatest pleasure imaginable to gratify its appetite.

Now let's see if we can write something real serious like. No doubt most of the readers who are at all interested in shoot-

287

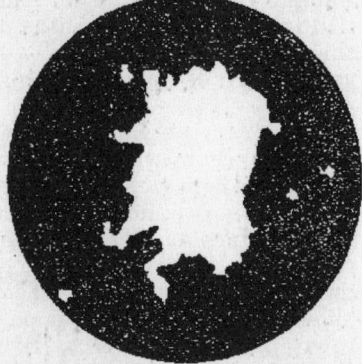

(Target No. 1.)—50 shots off-hand at 30 feet at 2¾ inch bull with Colt .22 auto pistol. Magazine full—10 shot—fired at one hold—that is without lowering hand until magazine was empty. Neither rapid nor slow fire—merely medium time. By author.

Across the pages of the shooting press, llike this column from the March, 1916, *Outdoor Life*, Ashley Haines and his correspondents wrote new chapters in firearms history.

hay and timothy. He also kept a few cows and chickens.

Despite the lack of formal training, Haines was a talented and highly competent communicator. What he wrote was presented in a sensible, direct manner, and always with clarity. The reader never finished a Haines article confused or uncertain. There was also a knack for authoritatively demonstrating his sophistication without patronizing. His gentle manner left the readers with the impression they were not being instructed or sermonized, but were reading letters from a friend.

Today's followers of Haines' material would, on occasion, be sent scurrying for a dictionary to look up such archaic terms as *anent, cavil* and *propounded*. These were, however, much-used terms then.

As did so many of his contemporaries, Ashley Haines had a penchant for the use of many words when a few would do. This is not to be considered a fault. It was a writing style of the day, a holdover from the superfluity that characterized the literature of the late 19th century. Brevity and concision would not fall into fashion until some years

later. Publishers saddled with space limitations would see to that.

Haines commonly used repetition as a device to emphasize or illuminate his point, or to reinforce a conclusion. When one considers that his readership was comprised of individuals from all levels of education, background or knowledge, from the rankest beginner to the critically expert with opposing viewpoints or experiences, it seems that this tactic would have tended to benefit the entire lot.

He also had a flair for digression. For instance, a segment of his text might begin with the words, "Before proceeding further, I want to state..." or "Just one more word regarding..." From the original thought he would stray to temporarily pursue a distant detail. Despite the detours, the destination was arrived at ultimately. Doubling back from the tangent to his source three paragraphs later, he would write, "But to return to..."

Haines himself had no gimmicks, no distinguishing personal peculiarities. He wore no big hats, had no bushy sideburns, and didn't wear sunglasses indoors. His trademarks, and his appeal, were his skills, experience and expertise. Among his readers, Haines was respected for his practicality. Since he daily used guns, his opinions and evaluations were based on experience and carried a special merit.

Among the members of the A.A.H. fan club was Arizonan R.L. Stevensen, whose letter to the editor of *National Sportsman* in April, 1909, effectively summarized the opinion of a continent of sportsmen. He wrote: "When it comes to guns from a practical standpoint, Mr. Ashley A. Haines is hard to beat." "Haines has few equals," declared another supporter, "...his practical knowledge of rifles and ammunition covers about everything." Mr. F.M. Bivin, whose byline appeared in the press from time to time, had this to say: "I unquestionably place Mr. Haines at the head of the present generation of writers on rifles."

Haines' humility was as apparent as his expertise. When his spirited readership had flung the label "expert" around a little too freely regarding him, Haines confronted the praise and was compelled to respond. He feared that his fans had "over estimated my abilities in several directions." He must have been blushing when he wrote, "I am not posing as an expert nor a 'would-be know-all'; such a man as the latter is detestable."

In 1906, Haines found fault with emerging rifle stock design trends and with the impractical direction they were heading. He was especially critical of the shaping and placement of poorly designed pistol grips. Haines disapproved of the grips adorning the Winchester Model '73 and the Remington-Lee, but of all the guns that needed a decent pistol grip, the straight-stocked Savage Model 1899 was at the top of the list. At the time, the Savage people would supply a stock with a pistol grip ("so-called") for an additional $2.50, but its design didn't satisfy Haines and a handful of his believers, who regarded the Savage grip as a non-functional ornament. Even at that, its ornamental value "...seemed rather doubtful."

Haines' complaint was that the Savage lever gun's grip was positioned too far to the rear of the trigger to be grasped during firing and furnished no substantial support for the hand. A 1906 *Outdoor Life* article dealing with rifle stocks, which covered several pages, expressed his annoyance. An illustration in the October issue pinpointed the location of the pistol grip as he imagined it should be. Haines' handful of properly shaped pistol grip was near enough to the trigger that a slight curve in the Savage lever was required. In 1910, Savage decision-makers concluded that Ashley's suggestion contained enough merit that they bent to the ample leverage applied by Haines, and others. For a few years, a Savage Model 1899 pistol grip stock, Model Haines, was offered as an extra-cost option. A lavish Circassian walnut-stocked, engraved specimen in 303 Savage caliber was shipped to Salmon Arm for the approval of its instigator.

Earlier in 1906, Haines suggested an intermediate-sized cartridge to fill the rather noticeable gap in the line-up of chamberings for the 1892 Winchester lever action. He proposed a 35 Hi-Power—a 44-40 shell necked to 35-caliber—that would fill the slot between the 32-20 WCF and the 38-40 WCF. In a nickel-steel barrel, a load of 24.5 grains of Lightning should give a 180-grain bullet a velocity of 1900 fps, he estimated. The 35 Hi-Power received a very respectable degree of support. Pasqual de Angeles, a familiar name in the era's sporting press, ventured a prediction: "It is quite probable that this rifle and cartridge would supplant even the ubiquitous 30-30 in the affection of the shooting public."

A rally was recommended. Californian L.E. DeRieux initiated it. In the *Outdoor Life* columns of November, 1906, DeRieux had this to say: "Should the subscribers of *Outdoor Life* think enough of such an arm to petition the Winchester Arms Company to put it out, you may put my name down for one of the first on the market."

Winchester never brought out Haines' 35 Hi-Power, of course. If they had, it might have interfered with sales of their 1907 model, unleashed upon the American public in January, 1907, and presumably well past the drawing-board stage when Haines burst into print with his 35-caliber suggestion. The origins of its proprietary chambering, the 351 WSL (Winchester Self-Loader) have been historically chalked up as the good idea of New Haven ballisticians. The fact that it launched a 180-grain bullet at 1861 fps is probably just a bizarre coincidence.

Haines had a special fondness for the 1892 Winchester. The folks at Winchester built a fancy 38-40 rifle to special order for him with the forend 2 inches shorter than standard length. This was Haines' conception of the ideal '92. "ASHLEY A. HAINES" is engraved on one side of the receiver, and his brand, the Diamond A, appears on the opposite side. This old '92 is still closely held by the Haines family.

Although he was a lever-action fancier, Ashley admired the trombone action and felt that it had a place in America's game fields. He didn't, however, approve of the way the slide was operated. To him, the movement should be reversed, in the shorter rifle calibers, at least. A rifle had an awkward, unsightly appearance with a vacant space between the forearm and the front of the receiver. Haines admitted that there was no particular advantage to his method, aside from a possible improvement in the arm's balance, and the freedom from the forearm wobble generally associated with pump-action rifles, but it would be neater appearing.

In his younger days, about 1900, Haines had gone to the trouble of fashioning a wooden prototype of his reversed forearm slide action. His machine worked perfectly and was shown to several gun manufacturers, none of whom criticized it adversely.

Haines indicated it was thoroughly examined by "one of the most noted firearms inventors of today," presumably John Browning. Nothing ever came of this Haines idea.

Haines also had some thoughts about what the ideal sportsman's knife should look like, and illustrated his opinions in issues of *Outdoor Life* and *Field and Stream* in early 1908. His six-inch miniature Bowie-type knife featured a thin, wide and curved blade 3½ inches long. The Marble Safety Axe Company of Gladstone, Michigan, made the prototype according to his pattern and indicated they would be pleased to add it to their product line, if enough interest was generated to make it a paying proposition. Evidently, enough orders were received. By the spring of 1910, the popular Haines Model hunting knife hung from the belts of America's outdoorsman from coast to coast.

When large-scale distribution of the Smith & Wesson Bekeart Model, known officially as the 22/32 Heavy Frame Target Revolver, began in 1911, a borrowed specimen fell into the awaiting hands of A.A.H. On the whole, Ashley was "so favorably impressed" with the little gun that he ordered one for himself. Twenty dollars bought an awful lot of revolver in 1913. North-of-the-border types, including our Mr. Haines, were obliged to be separated from another six bucks for duty. Even at that, Haines felt that he got his money's worth. The gun had one distracting flaw, however: The grips were too small.

"I very much doubt if the designer of that grip is satisfied with it," was Haines' remark.

The small stocks, holdovers from the petite pocket revolver grips issued with the older 32 Hand Ejector, weren't even close to Haines' idea of the hand-filling grip a target revolver required. Haines urged S&W officials to provide properly shaped grips. Enough target shooters of the era echoed those senti-

Photo Credit

The author wishes to thank Lyle Haines for the use of family pictures of his uncle, and Col. Rex Applegate for the use of photos of his Haines Model revolver and others.

ments that S&W developed and shortly offered optional stocks.

The same problem, as Haines saw it, existed with the 22 single shot Perfected Target Pistol which was very popular with serious pistol shooters back then. This model was a cylinderless pistol adapted from the 1891 Model Smith & Wesson. The grips on the Perfected Model were determined also to be badly engineered. A longer set of stocks, which Ashley considered to be "saw handles," made better grips than the ones they replaced, but they were still a "poor substitute for a target stock" he wrote in February of 1914. Haines might have approved of Smith & Wesson's Magna stocks that appeared in 1938.

In 1908, when Colt was contemplating a 22 target revolver, they contacted Haines. Colt executives intended to base their 22 on the 32-caliber New Police frame, which Ashley viewed as entirely practical. He re-expressed his opposition to guns of small caliber being built on frames developed for 44- or 45-caliber cartridges. Haines proposed a quarter-inch more space between the grip and the rear of the trigger guard, and a grip that slanted back somewhat. These suggestions required the fabrication of a new frame, so Colt ignored Haines' recommendations. Not surprisingly, the bulk of complaints from the buyers of the new Colt 22 target revolver centered on Haines' points.

When the century was young, the successful semi-automatic rifle originated. The era's riflemen were divided between those that viewed the autoloader suspiciously and considered it a fad that would surely pass, and those who envisioned the self-loader dominating the arsenals of the future. The times were so progressive that one forward-looking 1910 *Outdoor Life* correspondent prophesied a U.S.-made autoloader producing a velocity of 3500 fps would be available by 1915. We're still waiting for that one.

Before examining the Remington Model 8, new to the market in 1906, Haines belonged to the former group. In 1907, he put a 35-caliber sample to the test and was impressed with its strong and simple mechanism and marveled at its absolute reliability. Its takedown feature, he felt, was a practical touch. In his evaluation, which can be found in the February, 1908, number of *Outdoor Life*, Haines reported no difficulties and no weak points. He did, however, pinpoint some minor need for

Haines never fully left the lever actions, Winchesters or Marlins—like this one—or Savage behind. He was practical about such things.

improvement. He wrote: "The shotgun butt doesn't appeal to me, and a rifle with rifle buttstock and properly shaped pistol grip would suit me much better."

Haines' stock preferences were apparently shared by enough sportsmen that Remington was obliged to listen. After sufficient numbers of Haines-prompted letters crossed the proper Ilion desks, Remington officials consented to supply the A.A.H.-suggested features as options. Increasing the capacity of the Model

8's magazine by one round, as Haines had wanted, was not as easily remedied. The capacity remained the standard five rounds.

Since Haines appeared to be fond of Remington products, we can assume sentiments were mutual. In 1912, Remington unveiled its hammerless slide-action Model 14 which had been "repeatedly called for by American shooters for years." Ashley Haines tested one of the first guns off the assembly lines and then published his appraisal in the March,

1913, issue of *Outdoor Life* magazine.

In his write-up, Haines heartily approved of the location of the pistol grip, close to the trigger guard, "where a pistol grip should be." He discovered, however, two features on the new model pump gun that he disliked: "The sights are rather too close to the barrel," he wrote. The suggestion to provide higher sights is one Remington engineers took to heart, we are told. In addition, A.A.H. predicted that a lot of unwanted brush and twigs would find their way into the space between the front end of the barrel and the magazine tube, resulting in some annoyed Model 14 owners. This defect, Haines felt, was important enough that the manufacturers should consider a remedy. By 1918, a thin steel deflector joined the barrel and tube.

Late in 1904, through the *Outdoor Life* arms and ammunition columns, Ashley Haines published a short article dealing with his perception of the ideal revolver. He admired the rugged functional styling of the Colt Single Action Army. Its principal shortcoming, he opined, was its clumsiness and slowness to load and unload. If the Colt could be cross-bred with a Smith and Wesson double-action revolver, combining the best features of the two systems, the single-action mechanism of the Colt and the swing-out cylinder of the S&W, the perfected six-gun would result.

With a swing-out cylinder, loading would be simplified considerably. In addition, all six spent cases could be ejected with one push on the ejector rod, an all-important consideration. The revolver of Haines' daydreams would be a 38 S&W Special, with a 6- to 6½-inch barrel, weighing about 32 ounces. He submitted a simple drawing illustrating what he had in mind, and delivered his opinion that such a gun would be well received if a gunmaker could be coaxed into producing it.

Haines' brief outline caught the attention of an astonishing number of readers, and generated a wholly unexpected volume of input from the 1905 revolver enthusiasts.

In the months that followed, the Haines-proposed pistol was the topic of lively discussion in the gun columns of *Outdoor Life*. Its popularity was contagious, extending into the gun departments of at least six other magazines. Haines suggested to a continent of revolver cranks that they had better get busy and make

their feelings known to gunmakers if they ever expected the idea to advance past the fanciful notion stage. If Colt and Smith & Wesson representatives kept posted on developments in the sporting press, they were prepared for the deluge of letters and penny postcards from every corner of the nation.

The question of what to call the revolver arose. A friend of Mr. Haines' suggested a name. Pascal De Angelis, of Utica, New York, writing in the December, 1905, number of *Recreation*, spread the word. He urged readers to refer to the gun they wanted as the "Haines Model" when they petitioned manufacturers. By early 1906, readers realized that Ashley Haines and the nameless revolver were too closely identified by association for any other designation to be appropriate.

Haines, a self-professed "common man" not seeking notoriety, modestly objected to the honor. He made a futile attempt to share the responsibility with experimenter A.W. Lowdermilk who had contributed some minor suggestions in the revolver's design. Lowdermilk, in the meantime, had published a similar insistence in *Outdoor Life*. Haines' objections notwithstanding, the name stuck. The "Haines Model" it was.

Colt leaders sifted through the mailbags and issued the response that the matter of a demand for the Haines Model would be examined. Oregonian Frank R. Morrissey offered that a count be taken of all who would buy such a gun, thereby proving the demand and demonstrating a ready market. Haines, the originator of the movement, was convinced that a manufacturer could yet be induced to build the guns and led the clamoring. An indication of the proposed 38 Special's following was the extent of the petition in the November, 1905, *Outdoor Life*, intended for the benefit of the skeptics at Colt. Nearly a hundred shooters subscribed for a Haines Model if it should be made. Several agreed to buy two or more. A second census, printed a few months later, listed dozens of additional pledges. Meanwhile, Bob Kane and Capt. A.H. Hardy, influential men during this period, kept the heat on by writing thousands of words in complete support of Haines' revolver as did a host of lesser-knowns.

Although the cause of the Haines Model was met with favor by the

overwhelming majority of readers, there appeared a lone critic. The ever-abrasive E.C. Crossman couldn't understand why anyone, including A.A.H., could not be contented with either a single-action *or* a double-action revolver. There appeared to be no apparent benefit in blending the two. Many of the advantages of the proposed revolver, Crossman felt, were "mostly in the head" of Ashley Haines. Crossman snidely summarized his position in February of 1908: "The poor carpenter invariably blames his tools."

In 1907, Colt momentarily pacified the mob by promising to take up the matter of a demand with those who couldn't be expected to know, their distributors and jobbers. Reports allegedly filed by agents at the distribution level indicated that they were unaware of any terrific call for a new model revolver. The results of this brand of marketing research provided the excuse for the people at Colt to declare the demand was insufficient to be profitable.

Oddly, Smith & Wesson, judging from the evidence that has survived, showed no interest in the project whatsoever. Presumably, there were some well-founded fears at S&W that production of Haines' Single Action may have had an effect on the sales of their recently introduced double-action 38 Special.

Finally, after all the discussion, appeals, national attention and the untiring efforts of Mr. Haines and his supporters, Colt positively refused to manufacture the gun "for various reasons." Colt executives could not be swayed on the decision.

When Haines considered that the use of magazine space could be better devoted to other topics, he quietly accepted the finality and abandoned the project. With some Haines Model fans, however, the matter wasn't killed so cleanly. Early in 1913, Ashley admitted he still received letters from die-hards, almost on a weekly basis, interested in rekindling the campaign.

In the wake of this failure, there was a rash of six-shooter modifications by clear-thinking mechanics. One involved a short-cylindered double-action Colt. With its barrel set back, this pistol delivered accuracy unobtainable from the factory's offerings. One ingenious citizen took a perfectly good SAA Colt 45 and successfully converted it into a hinged, top-break affair. The cartridges were ejected simultaneously and automatically. All of this

delighted Ashley Haines, of course.

A year after Colt delivered the fatal gut shot to the Haines Model, the issue was revitalized by Gus Peret of Yoncalla, Oregon. In the June, 1910, issue of *Outers*, Peret stunned subscribers with the startling announcement that "at least one Haines Model Revolver will be made." Peret knew something about revolvers. As the traveling exhibition shooter for the Peters Cartridge Company, he was as proficient a pistol shot as any man in the United States.

Peret enlisted the services of J.W. Cowan, also of Yoncalla, to build the revolver. "A very fine gunsmith" are the words Peret selected to describe Cowan. Working strictly with hand tools and primitive machinery, Cowan whittled out the frame and lock parts from a block of steel. Other revolver components were gathered. A 38 Special 1905 Target barrel, and a cylinder and yoke were ordered from Smith & Wesson. The parts department at Colt provided a Single Action Army trigger guard, backstrap and a set of grips.

Initial plans called for the use of the Colt SAA hammer. Due to differences in S&W and Colt cylinder dimensions, the Colt hammer couldn't be made to work. This turned out to be a blessing in disguise. Cowan designed and fabricated a new hammer. A modification was its lower spur, which allowed the pistol to be cocked with the ball of the thumb during rapid-fire. A button through the center of the hammer is the cylinder latch release. Pressing the button unlocks the cylinder, allowing it to swing to the left for loading and simultaneous ejection. A scalloped section of the frame was necessary for proper clearance when ejecting shells. The handmade trigger was patterned after the Colt SAA trigger. Its increase in width was inspired by the trigger on the S&W Russian Model Target revolver. The front sight was a Sheard gold bead, the rear modeled after the S&W 1905 target sight.

By the summer of 1910, Cowan completed the revolver and Peret took delivery. Peret recorded an impression: "The revolver has lived up to all the good things that has (sic) been said about it in the past, and it certainly has the finest balance and hang of any revolver I ever owned or saw anyone else own." Peret used the Haines Model 38 Special in his trickshooting demonstrations until 1935.

In 1914 he wrote: "I have some 26 revolvers, but this is the best one I own. For the past four seasons I have used it in all my work and it is perfection in the revolver class."

Cowan built a second Haines Model for another client. It was stolen in the mail, en route to a Chicago lawyer. The existence of a third specimen is rumored. Cowan's gunsmithing charges for the Haines Model was reportedly $50. The additional cost of factory-provided components needed to be factored into the total as well.

Peret's announcement revived a short-lived interest in the Haines Model. Perhaps the cost of a handmade conversion, too steep for most folks, kept its staunchest advocates from placing an order with J.W. Cowan. In 1932, Colt's advertising manager, who evidently had not been around in 1910, happened to become aware of Peret's Haines Model. In a personal letter, he asked Peret for the privilege of examining the gun. Colt, at the time, was considering introducing a new model of revolver to commemorate their 100th Anniversary in 1936.

By analyzing Peret's gun, he supposed: "...we might get from this arm of yours a suggestion which would really be worthwhile." Evidently, Mr. Haines was contacted for his input into the matter. Over the years, Ashley had enjoyed a continuing good relationship with both Colt and Smith & Wesson. Both companies respected him and held him in the highest regard.

However seriously it may have been considered, Colt officials concluded that "...our 100th Anniversary would have to pass without such an arm seeing the light of day."

At the Philadelphia Sportsman's Show in 1935, Peret happened to bump into R.F. Sedgley, the custom gun builder famous for his semi-mass-produced Springfield sporters. The two had a long visit, and Sedgley quizzed Peret at considerable length about his Haines Model. Sedgley confided he was thinking about producing some of the guns for "wealthy customers who wanted such an arm." Apparently, the idea never progressed past the discussion stage.

By 1912, Ashley Haines had convincingly demonstrated the might of his pen and the effect of a single individual's influence on the arms industry. Inspired by his example and encouraged by his success, the staff and readership of *Outers* magazine rummaged through an assortment of worthwhile causes to champion. The day of the automatic pistol was at hand. The 1911 Colt 45 ACP, newly on the market, had a wide appeal, but sales to civilians were slow. The high cost of ammunition kept many owners from practicing and potential owners from buying.

What was needed, they were convinced, was a rimfire understudy to the 45 auto, using cheap ammunition. A crusade was initiated to bring it about. Over the course of the next two years, numerous *Outers* articles suggested designs and desirable features. As a result of increasing publicity, support for a 22 autoloading pistol grew with a vigor. As a part of the scheme, the advocates employed petitioning tactics, *a la* Haines, to badger Colt and Smith & Wesson into submission. The unrelenting pressure confirmed that a demand was genuine, and a market existed, and convinced Colt officials of the profitability factor. Irrepressible rumors evolved into reality, and the 22 Colt Automatic, later known as the Colt Woodsman, was announced in 1915.

The victorious advocates, in a self-congratulating frenzy, busied themselves distributing the credit. Our man Haines, however, was not among them. None of the dreaded letters postmarked Salmon Arm, British Columbia, ever arrived in Hartford. Rather, Colt executives had valued Ashley's opinion to such a degree that they solicited his input concerning the proposed gun's popularity. A new model of 22 revolver would have been his preference. He made his thoughts clear when he evaluated the new Colt 22 in March of 1916. He wrote, "I am not one of the many who advocated such an arm."

Despite this, Haines was instantly impressed with the little gun and put together a glowing review. Ashley used his Colt for shooting grouse, snowshoe rabbits and "pine squirrels galore" during the winter of 1915, often at temperatures to 26 degrees below zero.

Primarily, Haines sought to educate his readership and provide them with information on current developments on the national shoot-

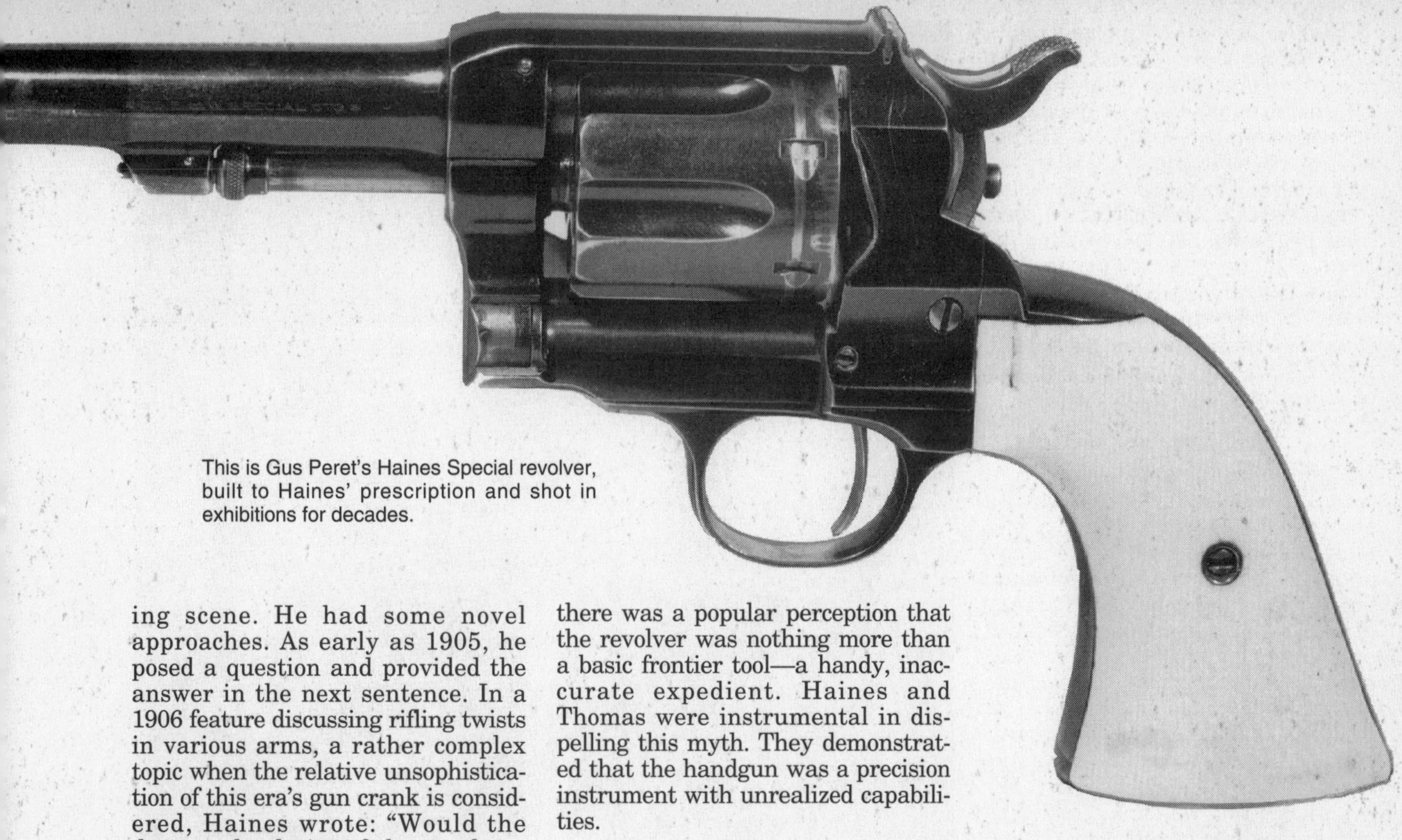

This is Gus Peret's Haines Special revolver, built to Haines' prescription and shot in exhibitions for decades.

ing scene. He had some novel approaches. As early as 1905, he posed a question and provided the answer in the next sentence. In a 1906 feature discussing rifling twists in various arms, a rather complex topic when the relative unsophistication of this era's gun crank is considered, Haines wrote: "Would the decreased velocity of the revolvers explain the quicker twist used? It seems to me that it would."

This interesting technique provoked momentary thought on the part of the reader. It had the added effect of maintaining their attention and preparing them for the balance of the article.

In a brilliant editorial move, *Outdoor Life* editor McGuire teamed Ashley Haines with Chauncey Thomas, the two most respected personalities of the period's sporting press, for a 1917-18 educational series of articles. Their pairing seemed to be tailor-made. A deep mutual respect was very much in evidence, C.T. and A.A.H. had been saying nice things about one another since 1910. The two hard-core SAA buffs engaged in a casual pen pal-type exchange of letters, which were subsequently published for the benefit of the subscribers. Presented under the guise of engrossing entertainment, the readers of the letter swaps became better informed gun cranks without even realizing it.

Almost exclusively, the subject of the monthly conversation was the revolver and revolver shooting. In an era when precision military rifle shooting and trapshooting had gotten tremendous exposure, handguns were badly neglected topics. Among a good percentage of the population,

there was a popular perception that the revolver was nothing more than a basic frontier tool—a handy, inaccurate expedient. Haines and Thomas were instrumental in dispelling this myth. They demonstrated that the handgun was a precision instrument with unrealized capabilities.

Peret's Haines revolver was a six-shot 38 Special, basically a Colt SAA with a swing-out cylinder.

The two proved conclusively that a properly tuned 44-40 Colt SAA was accurate enough to produce 2-inch 50-yard groups. To coax maximum accuracy from a six-shooter, Haines advocated shooting from a seated rest. So did Thomas, who often shot from the prone position. Ashley drew up a diagram of his rest, walking the reader through gun positioning, elbow placement and other fine points of rest shooting. All of this came as a shock to some. Real men, after all, had always shot standing on their hind legs, and used a one-hand hold.

The Haines-Thomas dialogue included lengthy discussions concerning handloading techniques with smokeless powders, casting lead alloy bullets that were fit to shoot, and causes and cures for offshots, poor grouping and key-holing. They pointed out the relationship between cylinder and barrel diameters and their crucial alignment, the absolute necessity of proper bullet to barrel fit. They explained how these inter-related factors contributed to successful results with the revolver. For most folks, this was their first exposure to any sort of technical six-gun material.

The 45 Colt was favored by both men. And revival of the 44-40, loaded with smokeless powder and good,

Gus Peret looks like the sort of fellow who would listen to all the stories, then say, "There will be at least one Haines Special," and have it built.

This is Walt Cowan, maker of the Haines Models, who reportedly got $50 for his time on the first one.

properly fitting bullets, is attributable to their discussions.

When the two disagreed on an issue, the reader would have benefited from the presentation of both sides, and may have been stirred to devote additional thought to these matters. The average reader, exposed and awakened to the niceties of pistol shooting, doubtlessly for the first time, profited greatly from McGuire's staged letter swapping. As a consequence, the American handgunner emerged with a better understanding of the technical aspects of his sport. The duet of Haines and Thomas, done as only they could do it, promoted hand-gunning as an art and advanced it as a science.

When the subject of 22 rimfire ammunition was brought up, Haines continuously stressed his dislike for the 22 Long Rifle cartridge. His chief complaint was that it was outside lubricated and, therefore, had the bad habit of attracting dirt, lint and filth to its wax-lubricated bullet, creating chambering difficulties. The waxy coating would often flake off, particularly in very cold weather,

and lodge in the gun's mechanism and magazine tube. Jamming, feeding and leading troubles resulted. In general, Haines found the outside lubricated 22 Long Rifle round to be something of a nuisance. Ashley admired the Winchester 1903 autoloader and its special inside-lubricated ammunition, the 22 Winchester Automatic cartridge. He was once asked to select a favorite, if allowed to keep but one rimfire rifle. Haines responded that it would surely be the 1890 Winchester pump gun, chambered for the powerful 22 WRF. The inside-lubricated, flat-nosed bullet was the reason for his preference, he wrote. When the Remington Arms Company considered bringing out a rimfire semi-automatic rifle in 1913, they wisely sought Haines' thoughts before the decision was made. Remington paid attention, and the inside-lubricated 22 Remington Automatic round was the result.

Haines admired the simplicity and strength of single shot rifles, an action type that, by 1914, had generously fallen into a state of disuse. In his earlier years, he had owned and used several Sharps rifles. He was very much attached to a special-order 30-40 Krag Hi-Wall Winchester with a Swiss buttplate. Haines wrote about other favorite Winchester single shots in calibers 38-55 and 40-90 Sharps Straight.

Although he never had the pleasure of owning one, the old Ballard Pacific rifle appealed strongly to him. He considered this model to be "the best rifle the Marlin people ever turned out." In the early 1920s, Ashley dropped a very strong hint that Marlin would be wise to resurrect the Ballard Pacific in an 8-pound hunting rifle—"a real hunter's real rifle."

Haines expended considerable thought to the construction of the ideal single shot action. It would eliminate what he considered to be weaknesses in the Sharps, Ballard and Winchester mechanisms, and combine the strengths and good points of each. He carved out several wooden working models, but evidently never tried to interest a manufacturer an producing the Haines Model Single Shot rifle. Nothing ever came of this either.

In the fall of 1914, Ashley relinquished his position on the staff of *Outdoor Life* for reasons not disclosed. In a private correspondence, an associate expressed the sentiment that a replacement with Haines' practical experience would be hard to find. He added: "A man who attempts to handle a deal like that from a factory catalog is apt to hit the ground hard."

Although absolved of his editorial responsibility, Mr. Haines continued to be a valued and regular contributor to the magazine. He also expanded his writing into the gun columns of other sporting magazines.

Even though he had experienced the progression from blackpowder to smokeless, had witnessed the spectacle of the evolution from muzzleloader to bolt action, cap and ball revolver to automatic, Haines himself was resistant to the changes. Of all the sporting arms he had handled in his career, his personal choices leaned toward basic working guns. By his own admission, his long-lasting first impressions of beauty and reliability in guns were formed in the 1880s. His firearms preferences were, for a gunwriter, decidedly out of date. He once wrote: "I'm ancient in my likes, I know, but I still prefer most of my firearms with the outside swing hammer."

If he were limited to one six-gun, for instance, it would be "the Single Action Colt, with 7½-inch barrel, sighted my way, and chambered for the 44-40, rubber stocks and blued finish—just plain Colt all thru but best for A.A.H."

It was the fate of young Ashley Haines to begin his shooting career with a double-barrel muzzleloader whose barrels and stock were kept together with many wrappings of wire. After his duck and prairie chicken shooting experiences on the Kansas range, he used the "scattergun but little and cared for it hardly at all." Haines preferred to do his small game shooting with a 22 rifle or revolver. If he were pinned down on shotgun selection, he admitted as late as 1920, it would be a 12-bore Ithaca 8-pound hammer gun of "inexpensive grade." His choice of a favorite rifle was just as curious. After the War, he considered it and concluded: "We could have managed very well if the 44 Winchester of the days of 1873 had marked the last development in rifles for sporting purposes. Exile me in good big game country—and give me a '73 Model, and I could get along quite contentedly."

Although a lever-action fan, Haines was certain that many hunters would shelve the guns of Winchester and Marlin as the trombone action shook the stigma of the Colt Lightning and increased in popularity. By early 1914, Ashley was editorializing his desire and inciting reader interest in another pump gun. "When will the Remington-UMC people offer us a trombone action designed to handle the 32-20 and 25-20 cartridges?"

What he wouldn't tolerate was made abundantly clear. He insisted that the entire rifle for these small cartridges should be proportioned accordingly, with a mid-sized receiver and streamlined stock. The complete gun should weigh no more than 5½ pounds. He cautioned Remington not to try to slip in a 32-20-adapted Model 14½, the carbine version of the Model 14 chambered for the 44-40. A new scaled-down frame, proportional to the cartridge, was necessary. Remington responded after postwar production was resumed.

In 1923, another Haines-provoked invention hit the shooter's marketplace. The lightweight centerfire Model 25 pump embodied each of the features Haines and his gang of letter writers had said they wanted.

Although discontinued for many years, some people still consider the Model 25 to be the ideal small game rifle.

A.A.H. had devoted much thought to areas other riflemen would have considered trifling, or wouldn't have considered at all. Take rifle sights for example. The factory-provided barrel sights didn't appeal to him. Moreover, he felt their methods of attachment had serious flaws and should give way to better ones. Most rear sights on American-made rifles in those days were fastened to the barrel by means of a dovetail slot cut in the barrel. In many cases, the front sight was attached in the same way.

Lever-action guns were particularly offensive in this regard. Their magazine tubes were connected to the barrel with a band, which was also dovetailed to the barrel. On some rifles, the forearm was held in place in similar fashion. Haines felt, as did a number of others, that sight slots cut into a barrel weakened it, and caused an irregular vibration throughout its length, theoretically affecting accuracy. The solution, as Haines saw it, was to have the sight bases, front and rear, forged integral with the barrel. Proper sights could them be installed on the rear base with the use of screws. Front sight blades needed to be pinned securely in place, he insisted.

Haines was a fan of the tang-mounted aperture sight made by Lyman and Marbles. He also spoke highly of the Lyman receiver sights that were, at the time, just catching on. In 1909, he suggested that gunmakers drill and tap holes on rifles meant to receive these sights. A lot of rifle toters lived a long way from a gunsmith, he pointed out.

Incidentally, or coincidentally, one of the first Model 54 Winchesters off the production line, a deluxe grade 270 WCF with a two-digit serial number, was presented to Ashley Haines by Winchester Repeating Arms in 1925. Its sights were held to the barrel precisely in the manner Haines had recommended for so many years.

Early in his career, Haines had urged gunmakers to fabricate open rear sights from unpolished steel, which would decrease reflection and allow for better sight definition. When Savage released a new model of 22 semi-automatic rifle in the spring of 1913, a specimen was forwarded to Haines for a critique.

This is what A.A.H's leather stamp looked like. It is, of course, a small version of his cattle brand.

even suggested a cartridge, "properly proportioned," of course, for the rifle. Its shell would be rimless, its caliber 25. It should hold enough powder to drive a 100-grain bullet to 2500 fps.

"The ideal featherweight high-power should weigh no more than 5½ pounds."

Although he preferred a lever action, by 1919 he was willing to make some concessions. He wrote: "Well, if we simply can not get a lever action properly proportioned for some suitable cartridge, then let it be a bolt action, and possibly, even A.A.H. might take kindly to it."

There were many good things to say about the rifle. Regarding its sights, however, he pulled no punches. He had this to say: "Just why they should send out such an excellent rifle with such inferior sights is past me. Possibly the day may come when makers can be persuaded that an open rear sight of the non-glaring sort would be appreciated by the shooting public, but evidently that day has not quite arrived."

In 1919, Stevens proudly unveiled their Model 10, a queer-looking single shot pistol with a cocking knob rather conspicuously attached to the rear of the gun. Company officials expressed a sample up to Salmon Arm, no doubt hoping for a flattering appraisal. Initially, Ashley was unable to produce small groups with the pistol "...nor should I expect to with any of the sights I have so far had on this gun," he added. Haines appreciated Stevens products, but his description of the rear sight bordered on the unkind: "A great big square notch appearing large enough when aiming to drop a 2x4 scantling in edgeways."

A smaller rear sight insert, frantically mailed from the factory, was still too big to suit the tastes of A.A.H. Ashley wholeheartedly approved of the pistol's grip, which fitted him perfectly. "But those sights!"

Stevens redesigned the pistol's sighting system. Haines left them with little choice.

"Overweight, unnecessary weight, has long been a conspicuous cause of complaint against American rifles." Those were not the words of Ashley Haines, but those of A.C. Gould, written during the blackpowder days of the late 1880s. The desire for lightweight rifles was not a new thing. Since Haines began to write, he had campaigned for lighter rifles, especially his favored lever action.

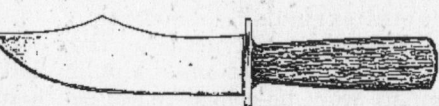
In April, 1910, *Outers* magazine was offering the $2.50 (a big price then) Marble's Haines knife as a contest prize.

About 1913, a renewed zeal for the project became evident in his columns.

Winchester and Savage responded halfheartedly with featherweight versions of the existing models in their line. This basically involved paring the excess steel from barrels and, in Winchester's case, shortening magazine tubes. What the makers offered, or "handed the shooters," essentially was a shorter and very much lighter barrel screwed into a standard lever-action frame. This approach didn't pacify Haines, who felt entitled to the "real thing," a compact new model gun with the receiver proportioned to the barrel and to the cartridge.

Shotgun manufacturers, after all, didn't put out their double shotguns on a single receiver. Each gauge was built on a separate frame size. Haines felt that the rifleman was entitled to the same consideration.

In a 1919 *Outdoor Life* article, a persistent Ashley Haines again pestered Winchester and Savage for an improved "properly proportioned" rifle: "What is wanted is an arm built with its receiver as small as can accommodate properly the cartridge it is to handle."

Almost as an afterthought, he

As was frequently the case, Haines' continual harping triggered a result. By the summer of the next year, Savage proudly promoted their entry into the bolt-action field, the Model 1920. At just under 6 pounds, this short-actioned 250-3000 remains one of the slickest little guns ever to come out of a New England arms plant.

Even the reloading tools supplied by the era's makers were not immune to Haines' censure. The #3 Ideal tool, later to be known as the Lyman/Ideal 310, was the subject of a specific fault-finding: He found bullet-sizing to be "altogether too slow." The tool's punch had to be completely withdrawn for every bullet sized. Haines' simple remedy was to cut a slot, or hole ("a very simple thing to add a hole, surely") in the mid-section of the sizer to permit cast bullet insertion without removing the punch each time. Haines devised a simple lever to retract the plunger past this opening.

Despite Haines' relentless pressure, Ideal refused to yield. He may have obtained patent protection for his modification at some point, but in 1923, Haines contributed his idea to the handloading fraternity, free for anyone to use.

In 1914, Haines' attention turned to certain Ideal moulds lacking crimping grooves. Together with a relentless band of adherents, A.A.H. conducted the letter-writing ritual, but was unsuccessful in penetrating to the seat of reason. "I have wasted a lot of good paper writing Ideal," he proclaimed. The matter was rehashed publicly from time to time during the next few years without the hard-headed policy makers at Ideal softening.

By 1919, Haines, obviously irritated, displayed an uncharacteristic peevishness in that year's August number of *Outdoor Life*:

"And here's to the Ideal people: Why not give us new moulds for revolvers and tubular magazine rifles casting bullets with crimping grooves? We realize that you have supplied such moulds in a few calibers; why not in all?"

He brazenly suggested the grooves be sloping, and should be square-shouldered. And he continued with his usual directness "...just another matter before I ring off: Why not make your tools of a better material, finish them equal to the old Winchester tools and blue them, of course? What's wrong with the Ideal people, anyway?"

In 1924, still harping on Ideal for their steadfast refusal to consider his demands, he applauded the example of Modern-Bond, new on the reloading scene, for adding crimping grooves to its recently introduced line of bullet moulds.

Before the Great War, the most undesirable feature of the 1899 Savage, at least the ones chambered for the speedy 22 Hi-Power and the 250-3000, was that it was offered only in a takedown version. Continual shooting of these so-chambered Savage lever guns off the shoulder of A.A.H. resulted in a steadily deteriorating accuracy and a gradual but inevitable sloppiness at the barrel/receiver junction. A nation of riflemen, who had scratched their high-velocity itch by purchasing the trendy Savage takedown, shared Haines' sad experience of unaccountable lost grouping and barrels that rattled in their frames.

In a mid-1919 number of *Outdoor Life*, Haines offered his solution: "...a solid frame might do the trick." Repetition for emphasis is found elsewhere: "If the solid frame will prove the remedy, I'll have one, provided the Savage people ever bring one out, which I believe they will do well to seriously consider...By all means, give us the present model in solid frame or offer some remedy for the disease that afflicts their present takedown when found in their 22 Hi-Power and 250-3000 calibers."

After the 1918 Armistice, the focus at the Utica plant was once again sporting arms. Newly attuned to market demands, influenced to some degree by Ashley Haines, the entire line of Model 1899s was revamped in 1920-23. Needless to say, the solid-framed 22 Hi-Power and 250-3000 were manufactured and cataloged as regular items.

In the fall of 1920, Mr. Haines published a simple suggestion that certain Colt and Smith & Wesson double-action models could be easily modified into highly desirable revolvers that were particularly well adapted to rapid-fire. Steps in improving Haines' exclusively double-action six-gun included eliminating the hammer spur, and smoothing and reducing the self-cocking pull of the trigger for better control. It also involved completely concealing the hammer under a shield, attached with screws, which would-effectively weatherproof the revolver. Colt and S&W, with a wide variety on the market, didn't share Haines' enthusiasm for this proposed improvement. Haines pictured this sort of a gun as the optimum pistol for aerial target shooting, but would make a good all-round gun for someone willing to practice with it.

In the 1940s, however, Colt came out with an optional hammer shroud, a detachable metal hood that could be installed on the Detective Special and certain other Colt double actions. Its purpose was purely offensive. It provided a means to cover the action of the hammer, making it possible to fire from the pocket, or to draw the gun quickly without getting needless projections, such as hammers, caught on clothing. Everyone marveled at the originality of Colt's idea.

Not every Haines-provided suggestion was rushed to a drawing board, of course. A odd-looking buttplate, for example, long on practicality, but short on appearance, died soon after its description in the September, 1909, issue of *Outdoor Life*. The smooth steel buttplates, supplied as standard on rifles of that era, had the habit of slipping from the shoulder of the firer. Mr. Haines suggested that a sharply checkered skeleton buttplate of steel, with a pad of soft rubber studs projecting from its center, would do wonders in keeping a buttplate on a man's shoulder. He went so far as to invite the enterprising concern of the Marble Safety Axe Company to turn them out as an aftermarket accessory. Marble's reaction is unrecorded, and the Haines model buttplate never saw production.

Ashley was a believer in the 1886 Winchester lever-action rifle. He

A.A.H. (left) poses with a moose head. The other man is Brock Price, who has a Model '86 45-70, while Haines holds a presentation Model 54 270-caliber. The picture was taken about 1926.

prodded New Haven non-stop to chamber the gun for the Model 1894 series of cartridges: the 25-35, 30-30, 32-40, 32 Special and 38-55. For reasons that are obvious, Winchester never listened too intently.

After a long hard day with the axe or the shovel, A.A.H. was obliged to stay up into the night answering letters from readers and producing manuscripts by lantern light. It

Haines at about eighty. His rifle is a Winchester Hi-Wall in 40-90 Sharps Straight. Note the Haines-made cartridge holders on the butt of the rifle, and on his belt.

seems obvious that Mr. Haines sometimes felt that editor McGuire pressured him with deadlines, and didn't quite realize what he was up against. Ashley was often forced to apologize for delays in getting his material to the editor's desk on time. If Haines' alibis were perceived as excuses by the editor, they were offered as explanations to the readership. He was a master at the technique.

For example, ammunition was occasionally held up in Customs. A promised delivery of powder or primers could have been frustratingly late, or an expected test rifle may not have shown up on time. Ashley may have been overcome with the "grippe" or convalescing from the flu. The weather and conditions of the Rocky Mountains played a role. It could be rainy or wet, or the snow lay too deeply on the ground. Salmon Arm, British Columbia, was not exactly located in the Banana

Belt. Winter temperatures of 40 below were not unheard of. Once, during a snowstorm, Ashley conscripted a son to hold an umbrella over his revolver rest so that the sights would not be obscured. Accuracy testing was completed on schedule.

Haines' excuses were, I suspect, intended to entertain and amuse as much as account for missing data that would wait comfortably until next month's issue. Consequently, readers came to know Ashley Haines as a man not much different than they were, subject to the same obstacles, trials and setbacks that haunted them all.

A.A.H. established a widespread reputation for turning out first-rate leather work. For personal use, and on an uncommon custom-made basis, he produced holsters, cartridge and money belts, knife and axe sheaths, and other leather outdoor gear. He was especially proud of his "seamless cartridge belts, made from California calfskin. Finished items were decorated with the trademark Diamond A stamp. Photos of examples of Haines' workmanship graced the pages of *Outdoor Life* from time to time. He is known to have devoted at least one magazine article to the subject of leather working. Haines-made leathergoods continue to crop

up occasionally across Canada and the United States.

One of Haines' lesser known talents was writing poetry. He displayed a knack for composing rhyme that would appeal to a gun crank. Some examples were quite lengthy. One ode, which appeared in the December, 1920, issue of *Rod and Gun in Canada*, a passer-by's thoughts upon looking into the front window of a used gun store, and wondering what tales could be told if old guns could speak. Two selected verses:

> They speak of beleaguered wagon train,
> Of arrowy showers and leaden rain,
> And of Red Man circling near,
> They tell of the fight and the battle won—
> By nervy men the deed was done
> And by women unknown to fear—
>
> Rusty and dusty and battered and marred
> These Old Reliables speak of a hunt of Long Ago,
> Frontier privations and border strife,
> The fiery stake and the Scalping Knife
> Days that no man again may know,
> "Ancient," and "Obsolete" and "Out-of-date"
> Yes, but they merit a better fate
> Than accorded them in the window here.

When it came to getting what he felt was wanted by the shooting public, Haines employed some tactics that became standard. First, he made a suggestion. Then he urged, repeatedly, if need be. Often he would write in a mildly belittling tone to emphasize his intentions. If this failed, he shook a calloused fist under the noses of gun company executives, reissuing his demand. One has to wonder if Haines, self-described as a "peaceable sort of critter," looked forward to that final attention-producing step.

Early in his career, Mr. Haines naturally cultivated a considerable following. With continued exposure in the various gun columns, he quickly developed into something of a personality, capable of significant influence. His position in the public eye, however, carried with it a tremendous burden. The man from Salmon Arm was suddenly elevated to what must have been the unanticipated status of a role model for his young readers.

There can be no doubt that uncountable gunstruck skinny kids, adolescents and other assorted beginners were affected by A.A.H. as much as any adult in their lives. Elmer Keith, as an example, was among the notables who spent their formative years heeding the gospel according to Ashley Haines. Keith would later remark on Haines' considerable impact on his boyhood, and acknowledged a debt to his mentor.

Haines was aware of the powerful influence he exerted upon the youngsters who admired him and turned to his columns for guidance. He recognized an obligation to the impressionable youth of North America. This is one of the reasons Haines stressed the use of firearms solely for sporting and recreational purposes, and avoided their offensive and defensive applications as weapons almost altogether. For instance, when A.A.H. finally responded to the many reader inquiries concerning the Model 1911 Colt 45 ACP in January of 1913, he began: "No, I am not interested in the slightest in this arm for the purpose for which it was originally intended, but as it can be used for hunting and target shooting as well as 'shooting it out'...I avail myself to give my impressions of the arm and cartridge."

Mr. Haines advocated hunting in every form and supported sport shooting as wholesome recreation. Further, he promoted the involvement of youth in these activities and encouraged fathers to train their sons in the use of guns, and instill an appreciation for the rifle. For his own boy, Ashley bought a new $5 Winchester Model 1904 22 single shot. It was an inexpensive gun, but one he considered to be an "excellent selection."

In 1919, Haines sold Last Gasp. He uprooted four children and made a move to Washington state to be closer to proper medical care for his ailing wife. He intended to buy a ranch and settle there, but land proved to be too costly. He moved back to Salmon Arm and bought an undeveloped 80 acres, 14 miles from town.

During the early 1920s, Ashley busied himself clearing his small farm, building a dwelling house, barn and chicken coop. He supported the family as a woodsman, pulling a crosscut saw and swinging an axe. He hewed bridge timbers and telephone poles and cut firewood. In addition, he trapped lynx, as well as sharpened saws, axes and other implements of the woodsman. He

made fancy holsters and money belts, and continued to write for the magazines.

By 1924, Haines offered another excuse for the poorer grouping of the rifles he continually tested. His eyesight was failing steadily—cataracts. A special aperture sight that attached to the lens of a pair of spectacles proved to be somewhat of a temporary remedy and allowed him

Haines spent most of his working life cleaning timber like this with hand tools. The work didn't break him, but he bent some.

to continue his beloved pistol shooting for a short time.

More health problems plagued Mr. Haines. He was afflicted with crippling arthritis, which had a tremendous effect on his vigorous and active lifestyle. This condition was said to have been brought on by a lifetime of overwork. Deafness in one ear, the result of quinine treatment for the malaria he had contracted in 1906, further complicated his overall health. As a consequence, he became less active as a shooter and writer. A.A.H. contributed to *Rod and Gun in Canada* on an infrequent basis in the mid-1920s. From time to time, a Haines-written article appeared in *Field and Stream*. He quit writing altogether in 1932. Ashley A. Haines was blessed with a long and productive life. He died in May of 1957, aged eighty-six years.

If Haines were around these days, he would find that in the mod-

ern gun marketplace, there are very few unfilled niches. With the arms industry's fingers on the pulse of the gun-buying citizenry, there is little chance a potentially profitable market is overlooked. Gunmakers now stand ready to provide us with specialized firearms for every conceivable application and are eager to meet a reasonable demand before a competitor beats them to it. Gun

company executives still get plenty of mail with an insistent tone, I am told. It behooves them to remain attentive.

There was a period in our history when we needed a man who was not intimidated by arms makers willing to provide only what they pleased. The cause required a strong, respectable leader to stir up consumers and band them into a loud unified voice. Haines showed his generation the colossal influence of an individual, the power of persistence, and the futility of asking nicely. The right man happened upon the scene at about the right time. I suspect that his destiny was not to be thrust into obscurity by the passage of the decades and our tendency to neglect the past, but Ashley A. Haines has become an unrecognized, forgotten figure. He's worthy of a more prominent position in the history of arms and ammunition, but it's hard to see how he'll get it. ●

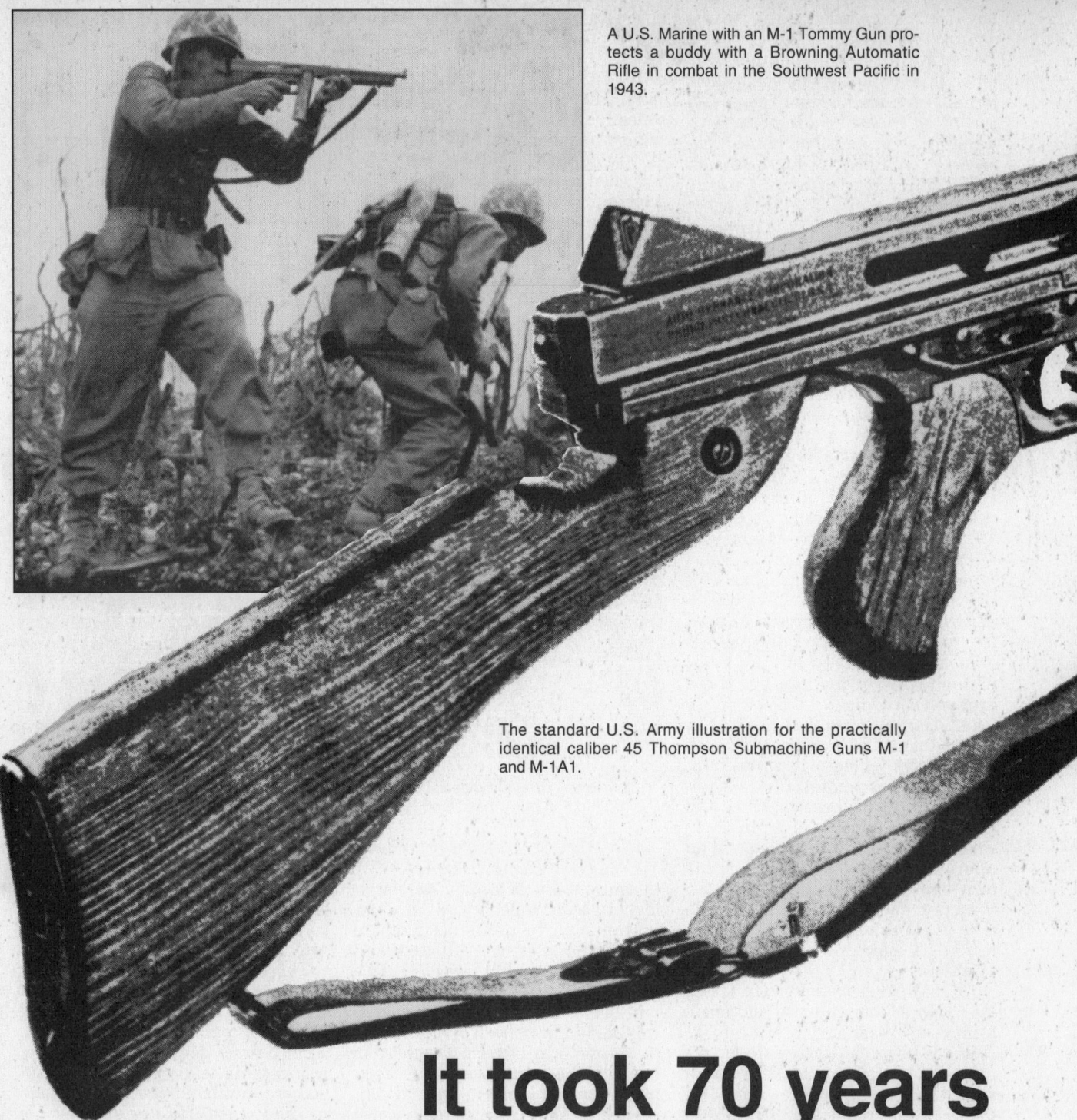

A U.S. Marine with an M-1 Tommy Gun protects a buddy with a Browning Automatic Rifle in combat in the Southwest Pacific in 1943.

The standard U.S. Army illustration for the practically identical caliber 45 Thompson Submachine Guns M-1 and M-1A1.

It took 70 years to run the full course...

FROM TOMMY GUN

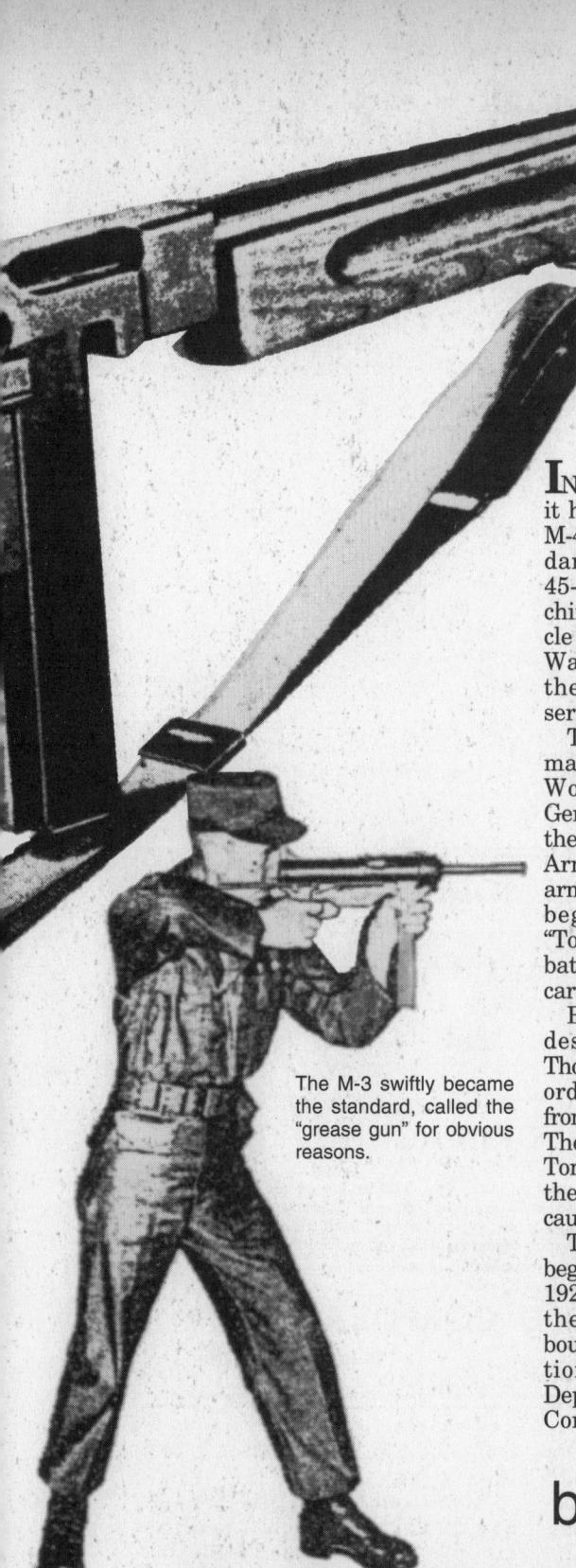

The M-3 swiftly became the standard, called the "grease gun" for obvious reasons.

IN 1993, THE U.S. Army announced it had adopted the 5.56mm Carbine M-4, a shortened version of the standard M-16A2 rifle, to replace the 45-caliber M-3 and M-3A1 submachine guns issued to armored vehicle crews. These date back to World War II, and they were the last of their kind in U.S. Armed Forces service.

The American development of submachine guns began at the end of World War I, in 1918, after the Germans and Italians had first used them in combat. At that time, U.S. Army Ordnance Department small arms expert Col. John T. Thompson began work on his legendary "Tommy Gun" built to fire the combat-proven 45 Colt automatic pistol cartridge.

By 1921, the basic Tommy Gun design was perfected, and Col. Thompson's Auto-Ordnance Company ordered 18,000 of its basic actions from Colt Patent Firearms Company. These were enough to build all the Tommy Guns sold until 1939, when the first huge World War II orders caused it to be put back in production.

The Army and Marine Corps began testing the Tommy Gun about 1920, but it was seven years before they bought any. The first were bought to replace 182 guns requisitioned from the U.S. Post Office Department in 1927 to arm a Marine Corps Expeditionary Force sent to China. The Post Office Department had bought them to protect the mails from robbers ravaging them at the time.

Deployment of Marine Corps Expeditionary Forces in Nicaruga and other places in the late 1920s caused them to buy more Tommy Guns. By 1930, the Marine Corps had some 340 in service, and the Army had a small number for testing as an auxiliary weapon on armored vehicles. These were all the original Model 1921 Thompsons with a vertical grip under the barrel. The government designated them "Cal. .45 Thompson Submachine Gun M-1928."

Since the gun was proving an effective, rugged and reliable weapon, the Army Ordnance Department was instructed to standardize its design. This was done by making only one change of any importance: The military had found the vertical front grip clumsy, and it was replaced with simple forend stock. This improved model was adopted for limited procurement in 1932 as the "Cal. .45 Thompson Submachine Gun M-1928A1," and in 1936 it was redesignated as a standard Armed Forces weapon. By 1939, several thousand Tommy Guns had been procured and issued to the Army, Navy and Marine Corps.

In the 1930s, the Armed Forces did a great deal of testing to determine how and by whom the Tommy Gun should be used. The Army adopted it for use as "additional armament" for its tanks and other armored fighting vehicles, with one gun to be issued to each.

Both the Army and Marine Corps tried to figure a way to insert the gun into regular infantry units. Both services had the basic twelve-man infantry squad: a squad leader armed with a rifle or 45 pistol, nine riflemen carrying the new M-1 Garand rifle, a BAR rifleman, and an assistant squad leader with a

by KONRAD F. SCHREIER, JR.

TO GREASE GUN

Men of a U.S. Cavalry 1939 motorcycle scouting-patrolling detachment with their caliber 45 Thompson Submachine Guns M-1928A1.

This ad for the Auto-Ordnance Tommy Gun appeared in military magazines in 1942.

Model 1903 Springfield rifle fitted with a grenade launcher. There was no place in this organization for a man armed with a Tommy Gun.

When World War II began in 1939, the Army began to rearm, and one of its first orders was for 900 Model 1928A1 Thompsons. At the same time, the British government began placing substantial orders for them. By 1940, U.S. orders for Tommy Guns had increased to over 20,000, and the original stock of actions Colt had made back in 1921 began to run out very quickly.

The Tommy Gun had to be put back into production, but Colt had large orders for its pistols, machine-guns and automatic cannon, and could not handle the job. A new maker had to be found.

Auto-Ordnance Corporation, owners of the Tommy Gun design, contracted with Savage Arms to build the guns. The original tooling was owned by Auto-Ordnance, and they had it transferred to Savage which helped them get the gun into production by the end of 1940.

As the Thompson was getting into mass production, the Army Ordnance Department began testing all submachine guns offered to them. They tested twelve in 45-caliber and another eight in 9mm Parabellum, but none of these were as good as the Tommy Gun. So, none were adopted.

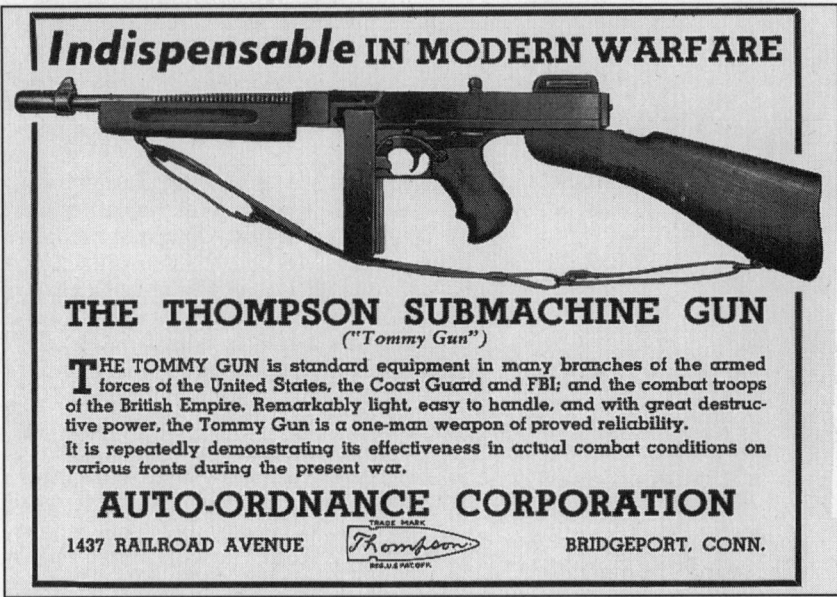

By 1940, our Armed Forces were getting enough Tommy Guns to make it necessary to issue instructions on how to use them. These appear to have originated in the Marine Corps, and they never did change much. They not only apply to the Tommy Gun, but to any submachine gun.

Basically, they said that a submachine gun could, like a rifle, be fired from either the regular prone, sitting, kneeling or standing positions. Like the Browning Automatic Rifle, they could also be effectively fired from the hip in the "assault position."

Submachine gunners had to exercise careful fire discipline to deliver effective fire and conserve ammunition. The most effective fire was delivered by triggering short bursts of two to four rounds at a time. This proved the best way to achieve hits at ranges from 50 to 100 yards where the gun was most effective. Longer bursts tended to be wild and waste a lot of ammunition, since the guns all fired from an open bolt which disturbed the gun's aim.

Combat experience quickly proved these directions on how to use submachine guns were correct. First, their maximum effective range was about 200 yards. They were particularly effective in close combat conditions encountered in jungle warfare, street fighting and the like. Their high rate of fire, 650 to 750 rounds per minute, was quite manageable as long as they were fired in short bursts, and troops found this technique easy to learn.

The Tommy Gun's most serious disadvantage was its weight of about 13 pounds with a sling and loaded twenty-round magazine. The gun, along with the four to eight loaded magazines its user carried, made quite a load. Another problem was its cost. In 1941, a Tommy Gun cost $200, almost twice as much as an M-1 Garand rifle! Part of this was because the Thompson was rather difficult to manufacture.

The Army completed a reorganization in early 1942, under which more submachine guns were required. They were authorized for every armored fighting vehicle, including half-tracks and self-propelled artillery. Special units like airborne battalions and cavalry reconnaissance companies had as many as 10 percent of their men armed with them. Although they were not authorized for regular infantry units, more and more were being issued to the infantry as "special weapons."

By mid-1942, it had become obvious things would have to be done to ensure that the supply of these guns would keep up with the steadily increasing requirements. Since the Tommy Gun was the only one in production, work began on making it simpler and less costly.

The first change produced the Model 1928M-1 with a much simpler, less expensive rear sight and loosened finish requirements.

In April, 1942, the Thompson M-1

was adopted, and it was much changed. Gone was the bolt's complicated Blish "hesitation lock," the Cutts muzzle climb compensator and the detachable buttstock feature, all of which had been found unnecessary to the effective operation or use of the gun. In addition, the operating handle was moved from the top to the right side of the gun's receiver. With these changes, the cost of the M-1 Tommy Gun fell to $70.

In October, 1942, another cost-cutting simplification was made, resulting in the M-1A1. The complicated cam-operated firing pin was replaced with a simple fixed firing pin in the face of the bolt. This eliminated a lot of critical machining and worked as well or better than the original system. This change and additional production engineering brought the price of the M-1A1 Tommy Gun down to about $45.

When all Tommy Gun production was stopped in 1944, some three million of them had been made. About half of these were issued to the U.S. Armed Forces, the rest going to Great Britain, Russia, China, the Free French and other Allies as Lend-Lease military assistance.

By the time the Tommy Gun went out of production, our Armed Forces had realized how useful they could be. Many Army and Marine Corps infantry units, particularly in the Pacific Theater of Operations with its jungle warfare, had replaced one of their infantry rifle squad's Garand rifles with a Tommy Gun. The 10,600-man Army armored divisions could require some 2800 of them. All special airborne, mountain and similar special purpose regiments had large numbers of them.

The Army anticipated the eventual huge requirements for submachine guns as early as 1939, when it had looked at other designs. This led to a number of other submachine guns being procured and issued.

One of the first was the 45-caliber Reising, a commercial venture of the Harrington & Richardson Arms Company. This gun was designed by Eugene M. Reising in 1941 to be easier to manufacture and several pounds lighter than the Tommy Gun. After some development problems were overcome, the Marine Corps ordered a quantity of them early in the war when Tommy Guns were in short supply.

There were two models of the Reising: The Model 50, with a conventional full wood stock, and the Model 55 with a half wood forestock and folding wire butt. Neither model was ever officially adopted by the U.S.

Unfortunately, the Reising had some serious deficiencies as a military weapon. It was very prone to fail when exposed to mud, sand and similar dirty conditions encountered in combat. It was also somewhat fragile for military use. After very lit-

This is the unsuccessful Auto-Ordnance caliber 45 Thompson Submachine Gun T-2 replacement for their Tommy Gun.

tle actual combat use, the Marine Corps discarded them. They had become so disliked it is said Marine Corps Gen. Merrit A. Edson ordered some 4000 on hand in a forward area depot in the Pacific condemned and dumped in the ocean before they could be issued to "his Marines." Gen. Edson was a noted rifleman.

The majority of the 100,000 Reisings manufactured during World War II proved completely adequate for uses not involving ground combat. A large number were issued as part of the small arms complement on Army and Navy ships, and for rear area guard use. Civilian law enforcement agencies and war production plant security departments were allowed to procure them since they could not get Tommy Guns. If nothing else, the Reisings helped relieve the early war submachine gun shortages.

Another submachine gun the Army procured which served in a special role was the Marlin United

This ad for the H&R caliber 45 Reising Submachine Gun Model 50 appeared in military magazines in 1941.

This photo of the High Standard-Marlin 9mm Submachine Gun UD M42 was taken when the gun was first tested. This gun was only used by the OSS for European clandestine operations in World War II.

This is the Inland-Hyde caliber 45 Submachine Gun M-2 replacement for the Tommy Gun which never went into production.

This ad for the H&R caliber 45 Reising Submachine Gun Model 55 appeared in military magazines in 1942.

Defense UD M42, the only American World War II 9mm submachine gun. This gun was designed by Carl Swebilius of High Standard in 1941, and about 30,000 were procured specifically to fill the Office of Strategic Services—OSS—requirement for a 9mm submachine gun for use in their clandestine operations against the Germans. The UD M42 was rated a "satisfactory" weapon, but all that is known about its issue and use is that the Free French Resistance Forces received about 2405 of them before the 1944 D-Day landings in France.

In the ongoing effort to replace the Tommy Gun with a simpler and less costly submachine gun, Auto-Ordnance submitted their redesigned T-2 Tommy Gun in 1942. The gun was unsatisfactory in a number of respects, and this project was dropped.

The Tommy Gun replacement developed by George J. Hyde was more successful. Hyde began developing his submachine gun as a private citizen in the 1930s; an early model had been tested by Army Ordnance in 1939, and selected for further development in 1941.

Hyde went to work for General Motors' Inland division in connection with their production of the M-1 Carbine in 1941, and Hyde and Inland produced a prototype submachine gun that passed a superior test in late 1941. After some very minor changes, the Inland-Hyde was adopted in April, 1942, as the "Cal. .45 Submachine Gun M-2" as a substitute standard for the Tommy Gun.

Unfortunately, the Inland-Hyde M-2 was hit by serious problems which were no fault of its own. There were no available production facilities to make it or materials priorities for it due to other more urgent projects. In addition, the modifications being made to the Tommy Gun were beginning to allow delivery in required quantities. Then, the Army began issuing a bewildering series of submachine gun design requirements, and the Inland-Hyde M-2 didn't seem to meet any of them. After a small number of pre-production prototypes, the M-2 was declared "obsolete" in June,

1942, and the handy little gun became a museum curiosity.

However, by the time the M-2 project was terminated, Col. Rene R. Studler, one of the Army Ordnance Department's best engineers, E.C. Sampson, a GM production engineer, and George J. Hyde had teamed up to produce a set of requirements for another Tommy Gun replacement:

1. It had to be as cheap and easy to manufacture as the British Sten submachine gun.
2. It had to fire the U.S. 45-caliber pistol cartridge and be easily convertible to fire the 9mm Parabellum round.
3. Its action had to be highly resistant to the entry of sand, dust and other dirt.
4. The gun would fire with a full-automatic rate of only about 500 rounds per minute to make short-burst fire easy.
5. The gun was to weigh about 10 pounds loaded.

Inland Division of GM quickly built five prototypes of the design, shipping them to Aberdeen Proving Grounds for testing.

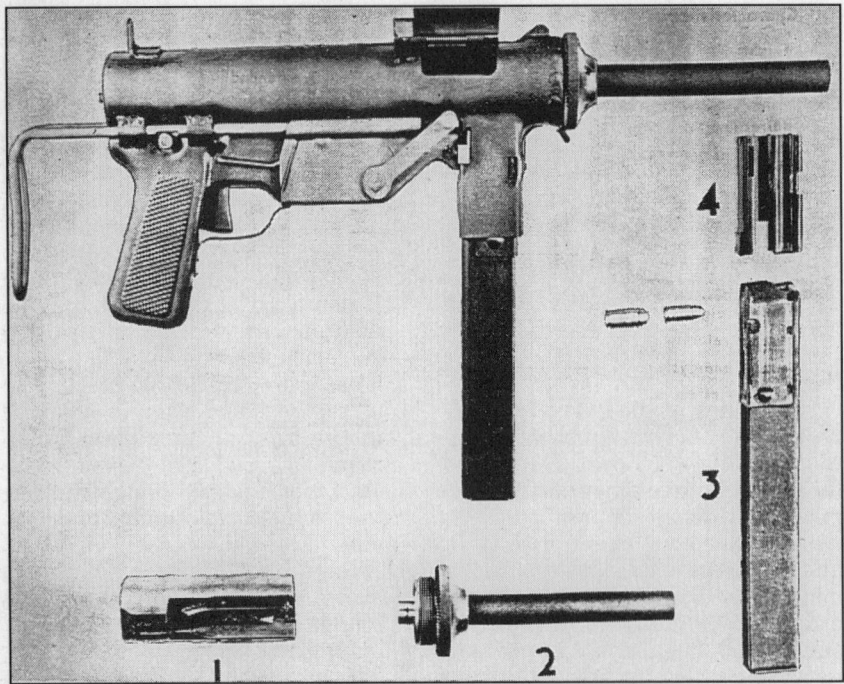

These GIs in northern Europe in early 1945 are armed with a caliber 45 Grease Gun, two M-1 Garand Rifles and a Browning Automatic Rifle, all ready to go into action.

The caliber 45 Submachine Gun M-3 which replaced the Tommy Gun with its 9mm conversion kit: 1) 9mm bolt, 2) 9mm barrel assembly, 3) 9mm magazine and 4) 9mm magazine well adapter.

The prototypes met all the requirements, and they also passed the best test of any submachine gun the Army has tested before or since. By December, 1942, the people throughout the Army whose troops would use it had seen it, and universally they recommended its adoption.

Of course, there were all manner of suggestions on how to improve the new design, but Col. Studler and the other small arms people succeeded in thwarting them. All they would have done was delay getting the new gun into production or make it harder to mass produce.

On December 24, 1942, the new design was adopted by the Army as the "Cal. .45 Submachine Gun M-3" and immediately ordered into production. While GM's Inland Division was too involved in M-1 Carbine production to take the job, GM's Guide Headlamp Division took it on.

Guide Headlamp built 591,000 M-3s during the war. They also built some 25,000 9mm Parabellum conversion kits which included a bolt, barrel assembly, magazine well adapter and magazines.

This is a 1950s U.S. Army composite photo of the standard submachine gun firing positions. The gun in them is the caliber 45 M-3A1 Grease Gun.

The principal use of 9mm M-3s was far in the future. As a stopgap when NATO "standardized," 9mm M-3s were placed in U.S. tanks in Europe in the '70s, even though more sophisticated 9mm small arms were in other NATO tanks.

By mid-1943, the first M-3s were in the hands of troops, and they proved effective, reliable weapons. They were superior to the Tommy Gun in practically all respects, but they were very untraditional looking and ugly guns. The GIs immediately named the M-3 the "Grease Gun" for its similarity to one of these automotive tools.

By 1944, the Grease Gun had proved itself an excellent combat weapon. It saw extensive service in the European Theater in 1944-1945, and with troops in the Pacific at the same time. Most of the M-3s went into action with units sent into the field directly from the United States; however, by the end of the war they were being issued to replace some combat units' Tommy Guns.

In April, 1944, when its production was well under way, a project to improve and further simplify the M-3 was begun. The improvements were based on both manufacturing and combat experience. In December, 1944, the improved M-3A1 was adopted to be co-standard with the M-3, and to replace it in production.

The changes included replacing the M-3s crank cocking handle with a simple cocking hole in its bolt. A simple magazine loader was incorporated in the M-3A1s wire stock. The M-3A1 went into production in early 1945; however, diminishing requirements held its World War II manufacture to some 30,000.

Not only did the M-3/M-3A1 project produce a very successful submachine gun, it also met the low cost requirement. The average cost to the government in World War II was $18, less than half the lowest amount ever paid for a Tommy Gun.

Although the M-3 and M-3A1 were co-standard in the U.S. inventory after World War II, there were still large stocks of Tommy Guns in depot reserve storage when the Korean War broke out in 1950. These were issued to both U.S. troops and the United Nations allies, including the South Koreans. However, the U.S. Army wanted to have the M-3A1 as general issue to its troops, and so it was put back into production.

The Korean War M-3A1 Grease Gun production contract went to the Ithaca Gun Company. They used World War II production machinery, tooling, jigs and fixtures that had been carefully put in storage at the end of the war. During the Korean War, Ithaca produced some 700,000 M-3A1 Grease Guns.

Although the use of the submachine gun declined after the Korean War, the M-3 and M-3A1 remained co-standard models, and there were still large numbers of "limited standard" Tommy Guns in "war reserve storage." The Viet Nam War brought all of them into action another time, and before it was over, the available stocks of Tommy Guns began to become exhausted.

As a direct result of the introduction of the submachine gun-sized M-16 in the Viet Nam War, the use of submachine guns by regular U.S. Armed Forces ground troops further declined; their use as auxiliary armament for armored fighting vehicles, and for arming troops who could not easily carry a rifle, did not.

The U.S. Army actually tested and procured limited quantities of the compact carbine or submachine gun versions of the M-16 rifle as far back as the Viet Nam War, but these were always limited procurement special use weapons. This situation changed in 1993, when the 5.56mm Carbine M-4 version of the M-16A2 was selected to replace the M-3A1, which was still in use as an auxiliary weapon for armored fighting vehicles and other uses. Of course, there are still both M-3 and M-3A1 submachine guns in war reserve storage. That's the way we do it. ●

A FEW YEARS AFTER the 284 Winchester came along in 1963, I used it as the basis for a custom wildcat rifle that combined the great old FN Supreme action with a Douglas Premium barrel of 24 inches. Chambered for the efficient little 25-284 round, and carrying a variable scope, the outfit proceeded to take a chunky six-pointer in the scrub of central Wisconsin's sand country before heading south for two more whitetails in the low-hanging live oaks of Texas' hill country.

But my Uncle John and his coterie of carbine carriers could only shake their heads sadly and scoff. Three deer down, quickly, meant nothing. What was this world coming to? As a brush gun, my latest project was all wrong, every bit of it! Brush guns didn't have long barrels; they'd get hung up in the tangles. Nor were they supposed to be turnbolts, which are far too slow for repeat shots when white flags go flying in the thicket. Variable scopes with high magnifying powers were clearly out of place in those cramped quarters. And everyone knew that fast, pointy, lightweight rifle bullets deflected off spider webs. I expected them to ask me to open up my freezer's lid and let the packaged venison run back to the wild, because it simply shouldn't have been bagged by that kind of rifle in that kind of cover!

Thus has the power of tradition built upon erstwhile logic stereotyped the so-called American "brush gun." For big game, the rifle (carbine, really) should be short of barrel for handiness, relatively broad of bore, and teamed with heavy, blunt-nosed bullets that travel at pedestrian velocities. Put these features together in a pump, lever, or autoloading action, and it fits the established public image of a brush rig.

Americans have also conjured up a vision of the ideal shotgun combo for small game hunting in covert and bramble patch. It, too, has come to

A NEW LOOK AT

A high-intensity modern cartridge can anchor a deer quickly with an accurate placement near the central nervous system. And a scoped rifle of that sort, such as this Weatherby, can thread high-speed bullets through the thicket.

Carbines have long been celebrated as optimum brush guns, because they are handy, short-barreled, light, and have a fast repeating action. All that's just fine. But does it mean the more modern cartridges and turnbolts don't fit the category?

have stumpy proportions. Its barrels range from those of sawn-off riot guns, such as the Model 97 Winchester, to those modern repeaters with 21- to 24-inch tubes and doubles with 24- to 25-inchers. According to prevailing concepts, said scatterguns should have open chokes that spray fine shot all over the sky, and straight (English-style) grips have also slipped into the equation. And scaled-down smallbores are emphasized.

But just how valid is the established brush gun concept? Do we really *need* guns and loads that fit those moulds, those images? Might the basic concept, in fact, not be based on some erroneous judgements that have been set by logic rather than science? And could there just be other ways of approaching brush-country hunting with even greater effectiveness than with the traditional guns and loads?

A dictionary I have defines the word "mystique" as, "a framework of doctrines, ideas, or beliefs constructed around a person or an object endowing it with enhanced values." Given that definition, my experiences during the last half-century cause me to wonder if the American brush gun concept isn't more of a mystique than a necessity. For although I hunted ruffed grouse and woodcock quite hard, and although I spent many delightful seasons listening to beagles in the cottontail brambles, I never did follow the conventional wisdom into stumpy, open-bored shotguns. Moreover, despite an admitted prejudice toward wing-shooting and shotguns, I have dragged about forty big game animals from the deer forests; here my penchant wasn't the heavy-caliber carbine, either, but rather the modern, high-speed stuff generally done up in turnbolt style. Methinks, therefore, that we have more than adequate room for a thinking man to do a 180-degree flip-flop and successfully, if not *more* successfully,

THE BRUSH GUN MYSTIQUE

by DON ZUTZ

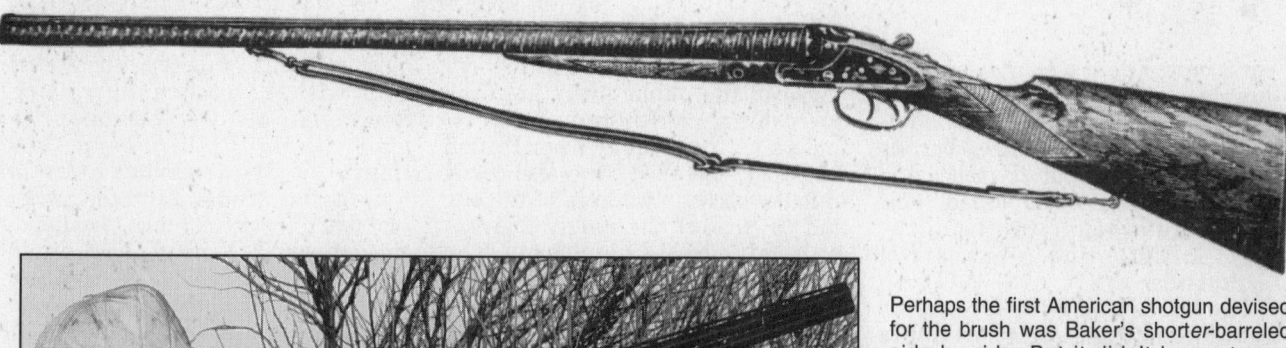

Perhaps the first American shotgun devised for the brush was Baker's short*er*-barreled side-by-side. But it didn't have stumpy tubes, and its left barrel was bored Modified for a huskier pattern on follow-ups.

What's all this talk about needing a stumpy shotgun in the thicket? A longer barrel swings smoother and carries into a more positive follow-through. And it'll get on target quickly, too, if the hunter bothers to develop a mounting technique.

employ equipment that is diametrically opposed to those of the evolved, traditionally accepted, brush gun and load.

Take the shotgun side of this issue, for example. That the eastern upland environs of our New Nation held much of its game in heavy cover can't be argued. Ruffed grouse, woodcock, turkey and cottontails were generally different than the open-field birds of England. That could be why, around the turn of the century, Baker of Batavia, New

less powders helped it over the hump. Today, many of the Spanish gunmakers offer their copies of the XXV, the one by AyA having gained some followers. Others, like Grulla and Arrieta, will build XXVs on order.

The interesting thing is that Churchill didn't conjure up the XXV as a true brush gun. Churchill's main argument was that the gun got on targets yards sooner. Frankly, I believe he was mainly displaying his salesmanship, and that the XXV was

foibles. It becomes a poke-and-hope piece, since there's not enough barrel length to provide inertia, which converts into momentum, for a smooth swing and positive follow-through. Poke-and-hope, of course, is another way of saying "snap shooting," which is the least efficient of all wingshooting methods.

At one time, I hunted ruffed grouse with a passion. Most of this hunting was done without a dog, and toward the end of the episode I could count about 400 birds bagged. My

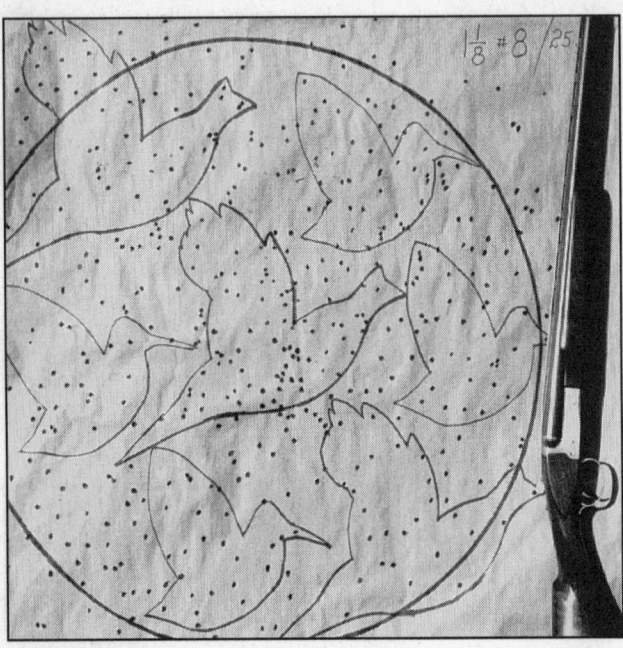

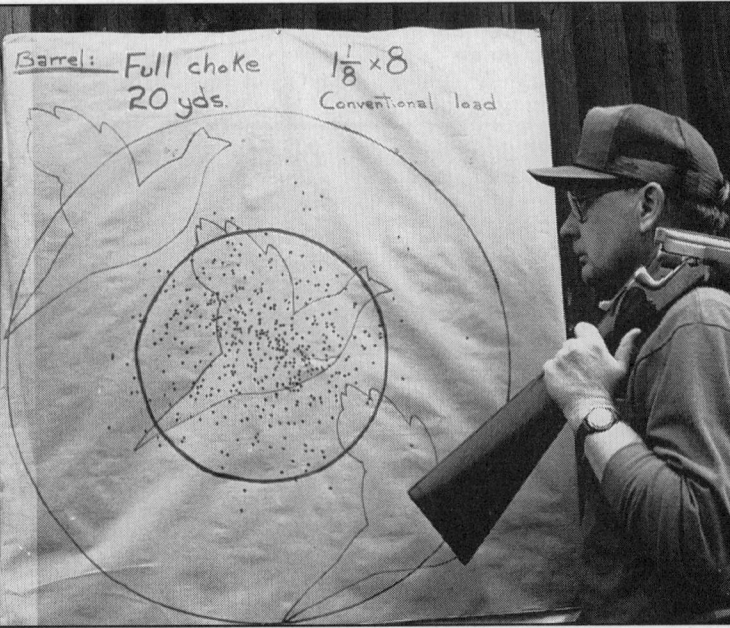

The writer agrees with the old idea that the first pattern for brush-type bird hunting should be open, sorta like this, but...

...for the second shot, he prefers a tightly packed pattern to hammer its way through the foliage and still put multiple hits on the bird. Brush picks off pellets all too well.

York, brought out a shorter-barreled double advertised simply as the "Baker Brush Gun." A trim, hammerless piece, its Damascus barrels were bobbed to about 26 inches and bored Cylinder and Modified. This was quite a departure from the norm in those lingering years of blackpowder.

The current mania for stubby upland shotguns didn't emanate from the Baker Brush Gun, of course. That gun faded gently into the past, hunters continuing to opt for 30-inch, Full-choked barrels on their doubles and newfangled repeaters.

If any short-barreled innovation had a carryover effect on American shotgunners, it was the XXV gun introduced by London gunmaker Robert Churchill between the world wars. The XXV got its name from its barrel length, which was 25 inches. The XXV was controversial for years, but more efficient smoke-

introduced to generate controversy and lead the public away from the on-rushing over/unders; for over/unders not only broke from British traditions, but they were also costly to make because workers of the day had to cut out the deep receivers with only simple hand tools. The main point is, however, that Churchill didn't buckle under criticism, and the XXV did much to solidify the short-barreled shotgun's acceptance.

The question is: Do we really need ultra-short barrels and fanned-out patterns in the uplands? I doubt it. No amount of barrel shortening can compensate for poor shooting technique, and few hunters take this phase of their sport seriously. If they did, the Skeet fields would be jammed.

In many respects, the short-barreled, open-patterning upland gun merely exacerbates a hunter's

most efficient guns were a Merkel O/U with 28⅝-inch barrels; a Remington M1100 12-gauge with plain (no rib), 26-inch barrel and Improved Cylinder choke; and a Remington Model 1100 20-gauge Lightweight with 28-inch, Modified-choked barrel. None of those would be the shining apple in the eye of a current upland enthusiast who gets his experience from colorful magazines, but time and again I scored fabulously with those guns. One instance stands out...

A young neighbor bought land in central Wisconsin and invited me along to cruise it during the late grouse season. The bird population was high, and he burned over a half-box of Federal ⅞-ounce 28-gauge ammo through an AyA double for just a brace. Meanwhile, my Merkel's lower barrel dropped five birds with five shots, and I was never invited back. Even on fast flushes, the Merkel's barrels were manageable and smooth.

When Remington's Model 1100 20-gauge Lightweight came out, I traded for one with a 26-inch, Improved Cylinder barrel. Then I proceeded to miss more than I cared to. After analyzing the problem, I traded that barrel for a longer 28-incher with Modified choke, and my fortunes returned. The longer barrel aided in a smooth stroke that flowed into a positive follow-through. And insofar as getting hung up in the

former has over-emphasized the explosive start.

Now about patterns in the brush: Theory has long recommended the Cylinder bore. Baker put that into the first barrel of the Brush Gun, and some writers who operated in the first half of this 20th century praised the Winchester Model 97 riot gun for gathering upland harvests. The reason is obvious: A wide pattern leaves more room for human pointing error. And there is probably little wrong with Cylinder bore,

My Merkel's top barrel threw snug, Full-choke shot strings, and I let it do just that. In the lower chamber I placed a handloaded "scatter load" for an Improved Cylinder performance, but in the top I frequently used a 3$\frac{1}{4}$ drams equivalent, 1$\frac{1}{8}$-ounce, field loading with hard or copper-plated #6s. That was too gross for a lot of grouse and woodcock hunters who thought anything heavier than #7$\frac{1}{2}$s spoiled the aesthetics of a hunt, but I beg to differ. Lost cripples spoil the scene more than

Yup, old-timers could lay 'em in there with the 38-55, but when tested, this Winchester couldn't punch 'em home the way the 270 and 280 did.

Outshooting all the older brush guns in actual firings through cover was a Mark X Mannlicher 270 using max-pressure handloads and the 150-grain Hornady and Power Point projectiles.

thicket is concerned, forget it! The only time I can remember being tied up in brush was with a 26-inch-barreled gun!

America's upland hunters can learn something from Sporting Clays, a game that is set up in woodlots to simulate field-type shooting. The top-scoring folks here aren't using stumpy hunting guns; they're swinging long-barreled stuff, many opting for 30- or 32-inch tubes on O/Us, with those of 28 or 30 inches on autoloaders. Such lengthy barrels are smoother and more likely to supply follow-through momentum. And, since Sporting Clays targets spring faster than any game bird ever flushed, the longer guns prove themselves less of a hindrance than mere logic suggests. Indeed, the difference between a poke-and-hope hunter and an advanced Sporting Clays shooter is that the latter has developed a total technique, whereas the

Skeet or Improved Cylinder chokes for the first shot in a covert or bramble patch.

But I beg to differ when it comes to second and third shots. A generously spread pattern cannot hammer its way through cover. Hang a patterning sheet 30 yards out in grouse cover some day and let go with 7$\frac{1}{2}$s, 8s, or 9s. Then see how much shot got through in sufficient density to ensure multiple hits. You'll be amazed at the weak spots caused by pellet deflections.

Despite popular notions about open chokes, tight patterns are the best for follow-up shots in the brush. They'll slug their way through. By concentrating a high density in a smaller area, one is guaranteed a better chance of multiple hits. And in thick cover, multiple hits are needed for positive retrieves. One-pellet hits may drop a bird, but it'll run off, a lost cripple.

just another 0.010-inch of pellet diameter! And I might observe that a centered hit with a Skeet pattern is also a centered hit with a Modified, Improved Modified, or Full choke pattern!

If one has read the foregoing commentary carefully, then he has already reached my conclusion that the best brush-country shotgunning equipment isn't an amputated barrel with a wildly patterning gun/load duo. The answer is improved technique, grooved in low-gun Skeet or Sporting Clays. No gun can compensate for the physical faults of a dilettante.

Now, what about big game rifles, carbines, and loads? Do we need lever-actioned carbines, pumps, autoloaders or double rifles in the timber? Must our cartridges host robust, round-nosed bullets that roll along with the speed of a bowling ball?

Straight-gripped doubles with between-the-hands balance, like this sidelocked Merkel, have always been great in the thicket. The writer likes them, with 27- to 28-inch barrels, thank you.

If your answer to the above is "yes," pause for a moment and remember how 16-pound bowling balls deflect off much lighter pins! An older friend and I gave that some thought years ago, and we set up actual deflection tests in a wooded area. He supplied the older bell bores—the 38-55, 35 Remington, 45-70, 32 Winchester Special, and 348 Winchester—while I brought the more modern "hot stuff." And after intermittent shooting during two winters, we came to one conclusion: *all* bullets deflect! The 35 Remington's 200-grainer wasn't any more positive than a 270's 130-grainer. That result should have knocked the ol' brush gun myth right into a cocked fedora, but there are some added observations that argue in favor of a new approach to brush rifles.

Our testing indicated that the bullets most likely to tip and carom were those with the slowest spin. Bullet weight alone wasn't impressive. One of the worst performers was the 32 Winchester Special, which gave a 170-grain bullet a 1:16-inch spiral. Its blunt-nosed bullet upset on minor contact, as did some 255-grain slugs from the 38-55's slow rifling. And although many casual hunters believe that the 44 Remington Magnum and 444 Marlin are the *ne plus ultras* because of their heavy, blunt bullets, they were also readily bumped off line by light foliage, thanks to their lazy 1:38-inch spin.

If our brush shooting uncovered anything, it was that a high-velocity loading with a fast rifling twist and a projectile bearing a high ballistic coefficient rating could actually out-shoot the vaunted and traditional brush cutters at their own game! Some of the best point-of-aim hits came from a Mark X Mannlicher-stocked 270 Winchester. When loaded to maximum pressures with H-4831, it laid Power Points and Hornady 150-grainers into the bullseyes even though we saw definite twig-wiggle during bullet passage. Ditto for my Remington Model 725 in 280 Remington using reloads stuffed to maximum with 154-grain Hornady Javelins, a recipe that took three straight whitetails for me in Wisconsin scrub with just a trio of shots. The 270 had 1:10-inch rifling; the 280 had 1:9½.

What's behind this performance of high-velocity outfits and their slender, pointy, quick-spinning bullets? Gyroscopic stability. Watch a kid play with a toy gyroscope. When it's spinning smartly, it'll bump into something, totter a mite, but rapidly regain its upright posture. When it slows down, however, it'll wobble radically on contact and, quite often, topple. So, too, with bullets in flight. Those with a fast rotational velocity tend to settle back into a stable flight better than those with a slow spin, which wobble and/or flip after nipping brush to slant away from the line of sight and frequently keyhole.

While it does clash with cherished traditions, then, the modern high-velocity cartridge isn't a bust in the brush. But in reality the whole subject is rife with variables. And at the risk of being repetitious—all bullets deflect, including those of the ol' 38-55, 45-70, and 44 Magnum!

In fact, the practice of blasting away at deer shielded by brush is passé. So are open sights and the idea that 4- to 5-inch groups are "good enough to hit a deer." That sloppy attitude only cripples and loses deer by placing the bullets in non-vital spots. To level a brush-country trophy, scoped rifles with MOA accuracy loads are ideal; they can help a hunter locate open tunnels through cover and, at the proper moment, thread a high-impact projectile through it for a perfect hit in a vital spot. There is no need for coarse, by-guess and by-golly holding and shooting. Scopes and accuracy loads can transform timber and thicket deer hunting into something as precision-oriented as sniping at antelope and prairie dogs on the high plains.

The modern, high-intensity cartridge is also a prime candidate for current woods hunting, because its shocking power has the potential for a quick knockdown. There's nothing automatic about a lightning-like kill, of course, but the old-timers don't deliver that with certainty, either. Remember the old advice to sit down and smoke a pipe before trailing a hit deer? It came from the past, because a high percentage of the deer struck ran off and had to be trailed. The idea was to let them run off, lie down, and stiffen before the hunter took the trail. But try that

If Sporting Clays shooters can win championships with long-barreled guns on simulated field-type stands, why do hunters need such ultra-short barrels? Bobbed barrels won't compensate for lack of technique.

"smoke a pipe" routine in these days of overcrowded woodlots and forests, and somebody else will have sent the final shot home, tagged, and dragged out your deer before you get close! Today, you can't afford to let a deer run far, and a shocking hit is far better than a milder one.

Shot placement is also a factor in brush hunting. The best impact areas for quick knockdowns are the head, neck and high lung near the spine. Low shots to the brisket merely hit the heart or low lungs, which aren't positive knockdown areas; they're too far from the central nervous system. Deer hit in the heart can run unbelievable distances. The key is holding high. My quickest knockdowns in the brush have come from high lung and spine placements.

Whether it's the smoothbore or a rifle, then, the aged "brush gun" concepts can be questioned and, in many instances, proved wrong or outdated. Changes in technology and hunting conditions have given us opportunities to flex some ingenuity and apply new approaches for improved results. The former brush-gun mystique left a lot to be desired!　●

From .416 to .22 LR
WE'VE GOT IT ALL!

26 Models
290 Variations
42 Calibers
3 Gauges
25 Barrel Lengths
19 Stock Variations
16 Grip Variations

Pictured at right is a modest sampling of the extensive firearms line manufactured by Sturm, Ruger & Company, Inc.

PLAY IT SAFE!

BENELLI 20 GAUGE SHOTGUN
LIGHTWEIGHT, FAST HANDLING, RELIABLE

The Benelli 20 gauge is quick and easy to handle, making it an ideal choice for smaller-framed shooters.

At 5¾ pounds, the Benelli Montefeltro 20 gauge is the perfect lightweight companion for a long day in the field. The low recoil of this 20 gauge semiautomatic shotgun makes it a natural choice for many upland game shooters.

The heart of the Benelli 20 gauge remains the famous Montefeltro rotating bolt, the same operating system found on *all* HK Benelli shotguns. A rugged and simple inertia recoil design, this bolt system functions reliably with all standard 20 gauge shells without adjustment.

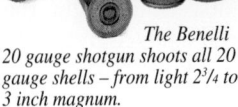

The Benelli 20 gauge shotgun shoots all 20 gauge shells – from light 2³/₄ to 3 inch magnum.

Benelli 20 gauge Montefeltro Super 90 shotgun

Unlike most semiautomatics, there is no complicated gas system that collects grime and powder residues. No complex cylinders and pistons to maintain. And the entire shotgun can be disassembled in seconds without tools for easy cleaning.

The dependable Benelli inertia recoil action is coupled with a 26-inch vent rib barrel for optimal balance and quick handling. Screw-in choke tubes are steel-shot safe and the buttstock drop is easily adjustable for a custom fit.

Lightweight, but built to stand up to the toughest shotgunning, the Benelli Montefeltro 20 gauge represents a unique combination of technologically advanced engineering and classic European styling.

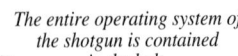

The entire operating system of the shotgun is contained in the bolt.

For more information and the location of your nearest Authorized Dealer, contact:
Heckler & Koch, Inc.
21480 Pacific Boulevard
Sterling, Virginia 20166 USA
Telephone (703) 450-1900

Call 1-800-262-2079 for your 40-minute Benelli/HK video tape. $6.95 shipping & handling, please have VISA or Mastercard ready.

IT ALL STARTED somewhere back there in the dim recesses of history when a real shootist carefully carved his initials in his supply of lead musket balls. In more recent memory, it was the heroic Lone Ranger who kept the tradition alive with those distinctive solid silver bullets of his. Now in an era of mass culture and production, other statements are being made by shooters—this time on the heads of their cartridge cases and the sidewalls of their shotshells.

The day of the boutique cartridge has arrived. And the options are endless.

Suppose you would like to see your name as a headstamp. Midway Arms—that purveyor of bulk brass and bullets—just may already have it cataloged. If your name is Bill, Bob, Jim or John and you shoot a 357 Magnum, you're really lucky.

Your proper name is right there on the headstamp of Midway's cataloged handgun brass. Midway calls it their personal series.

If you're not luckily named, you could settle for Midway brass commemorating one of the enduring celebrities of handgun fame stamped on the head of the very cartridge he championed: Keith on the 44 Magnum, Cooper on the 45 ACP, and Jordan on the 357 Magnum. Midway naturally

BOUTIQUE CARTRIDGES ARE HERE...

Any Bill, Bob, Jim or John will do. If he has or can get a 357 Magnum, he can have personal Midway brass.

by HOLT BODINSON

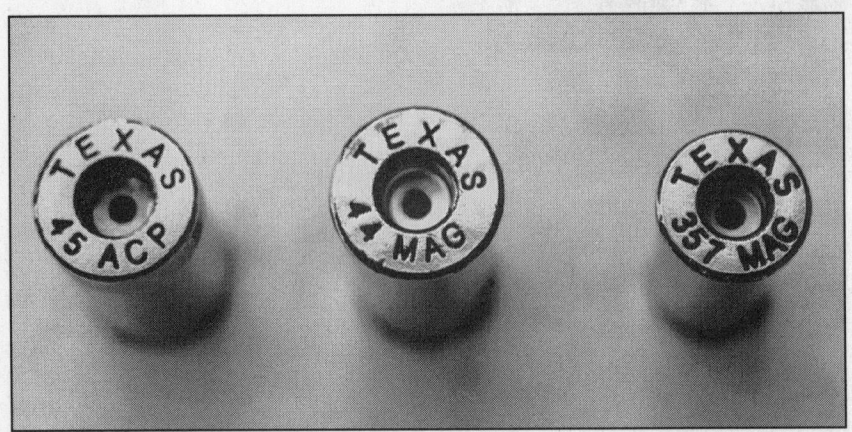

In these cases, you can stuff the loads of Jeff's, Elmer's or Bill's fancy—Midway makes 'em this way.

Any Texicans who favor wimpy stuff like 9mm or 38 Special are out of luck—Midway's Texas series is for serious cowboys.

calls this line of boutique brass the celebrity series.

And, if you hail from the great state of Texas, well, "Howdy, pardner!" Midway has created the Texas line of nickel-plated 357 Magnum, 44 Magnum and 45 ACP brass that has "TEXAS" stamped on the head of each case in a big and brassy Texas way. Even if you're not a Texan, these cases represent an interesting and beautiful example of boutique cartridge case making.

In terms of cost, there is a quantum leap from Midway's cataloged named brass to truly personalized cartridges. Still, the technology and willingness of smaller custom ammunition makers to accommodate special requests and produce boutique products has never been greater.

Two prominent brass artists working to fill special orders are Art Alphin of A-Square/A-Cube and Jim Bell, Jr. of MAST Technology. Through a computerized process, these ammunition makers can create a custom headstamp in any language and can, English apart, imprint the brass using Latin, Greek, Cyrillic, Hebrew or Arabic alphabets. Since both companies draw their own brass, such small runs of special cases are piggybacked on commercial runs of the same caliber. Delivery times thus vary, depending upon caliber demand.

Classic examples of such artistry were the special 100-case runs they produced for Safari Club International's "World's Most Dangerous Game" series of commemorative rifles. Pictured nearby are Art Alphin's 404 case marked "SCI 93—Tiger 404" which accompanied Al and Roger Biesen's Bengal tiger rifle in 1993; and Jim Bell's 416 Rigby case carrying the complex headstamp reading "Simba—M'Bogo. SCI. .416. 94." One hundred of Bell's special cases accompanied Frank Wells' stunning 1994 rifle, paying tribute to the African lion and Cape buffalo—Simba and M'Bogo—scripted in Swahili.

Proprietary cartridges are almost a separate group unto themselves in any discussion of customized headstamps. From a collector's viewpoint, they are among the most interesting of all. Art Alphin's "A-Square .416 Chapuis," developed to achieve 416 Rigby velocities at lower pressures for the Chapuis brand of double rifles, and the "A-Square .450 Walker," which is essentially the

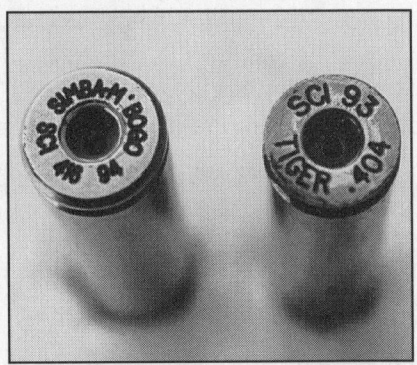

When price is hardly any object, as when Safari Club attempts a splash, you can afford just 100 cases done up thus.

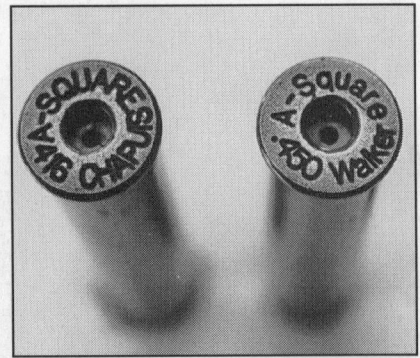

This is a little different. These are real cases for real guns in uncommon calibers.

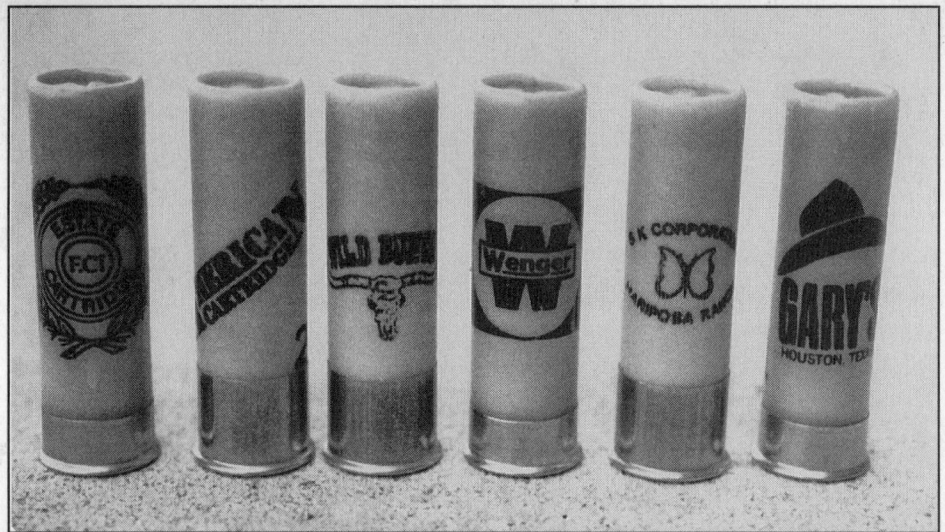

If you buy 10,000 shells at a time, your own load and your own case design is no problem and costs hardly any extra. You want fewer—well, they cost a little more each.

(Below) Here are some more moderately odd ones, but the headstamps simply tell what they are.

For a company like Dakota, dealing in big tickets, its own brass is a nice way to go.

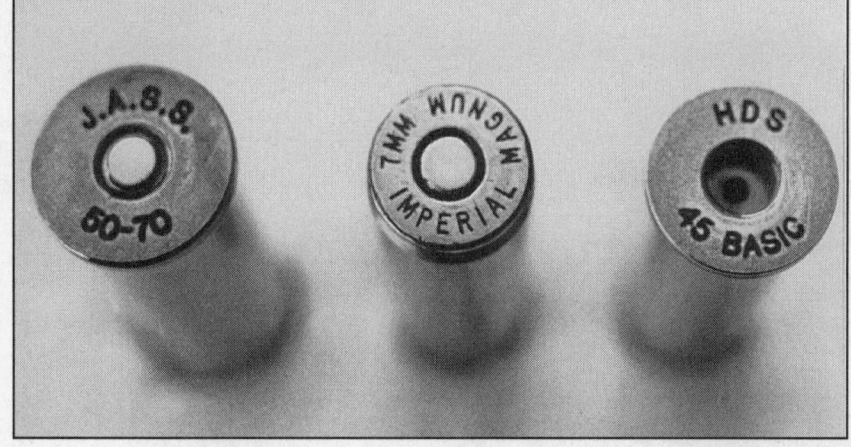

same case necked out to 45-caliber, are shown here. Also pictured are headstamps from the A-Cube-produced brass for the Dakota series of big game cartridges based on the 404 modified case, and the "Imperial 7mm Magnum"-marked case—another improved 404 design—that was made in Venezuela for the Imperial Cartridge Company of Canada.

What specialized headstamps do non-commercial clients order on standard cases? Everything imaginable from proper names to birthday and Christmas designations. Unfortunately, these special headstamps are so private and personal no photographs were available. And that is, after all, as it should be.

Typically, there is an initial set-up charge to make the custom headstamp die. Title to the special die remains with the customer, but possession remains with the case maker. The charge per custom case is based upon variables such as the number ordered, caliber, whether or not

unstamped brass of the caliber requested is on hand or in the production schedule, and whether the customer wants brass only or loaded ammunition. For example, Jim Bell of MAST Technology currently quotes a price of $500 to produce a customized headstamp die with no additional charge for stamping the customer's brass, if and when a run of that caliber is being manufactured.

Not to leave shotgunners out in the cold, Estate Cartridge, Inc., of Willis, Texas, will provide personalized shotshells, private brand shotshells, and shells loaded to the customer's specifications and packaging requirements. Estate reports it can't keep up with the demand for its boutique products. Pictured are just a few of their recent private and "estate" brands that incorporate names, special messages, corporate logos and addresses like "Gary's of Houston," "Mariposa Ranch," "The Wild Bunch," "American Cartridge," and "Wenger."

And if you were thinking the price

of "named" shotshells might be outrageous, you will be pleased to learn that Estate's prices are almost in line with run-of-the-mill commercial ammunition. For example, a case of shotshells contains 500 rounds. To imprint your logo or name on a standard load, the price currently quoted is no charge for 200 or more cases, $5 per case for 100 cases, $10 per case for 50 cases, and for only one to two cases $100 above the base price of a case of shells (approximately $100). In short, about $200 per case in small lots—which comes out to $10 per box of 25 personalized shells. And that's a bargain.

Today's boutique cartridge services are unique, intriguing and give way to all sorts of flights of fancy, depending, of course, on the depth of one's pocketbook. They're a new twist in the ever-evolving sporting ammunition field and a great way to memorialize a special person, company, firearm or event, depending, again, on the depth of your pocketbook. ●

by DON ZUTZ

SHOTGUN REVIEW

although also cycling all 20-gauge loads interchangeably, is recoil-urged.

The Browning Golds have additional interesting features. Given a tilting-type bolt, the gun's receiver is somewhat more compact than is usual. Moreover, the receiver is made of a lightweight material that keeps the 20-gauge just below 7 pounds with a 28-inch barrel, while the 12 runs about 7½ pounds with the 28-inch barrel. Both gauges are equipped with Invector choking, but it must be pointed out that the 12-bore has overbored barrels and uses the Invector Plus tubes.

The Golds further utilize a short-thrust piston rod rather than lengthy action bars. This tends to reduce the amount of powder gas residue that seeps back into the action area, meaning the gun will general-

available, as are straight or pistol grips. With engraving patterns from the old Foxes, these repros are thoroughly delightful compared to the dull, drab repeaters that are now in vogue.

One final observation is that gunmakers have smiled on the 28-gauge this year. Harrington & Richardson 1871 is making a 28-gauge, break-action single under the New England Firearms banner, and it's a better selection than the 410 for beginners and milady. Remington has made the 28 a permanent part of the Model 870 Express line, while American Arms has a neat, trim 28 in its Silver Series of stackbarrels.

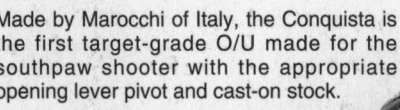

Made by Marocchi of Italy, the Conquista is the first target-grade O/U made for the southpaw shooter with the appropriate opening lever pivot and cast-on stock.

petitive niche area, especially in the turkey and deer slug categories. The traditional wood and glossy blue are also fading; more and more stock/forearm finishes are becoming an ugly (in my opinion) black. The utility of synthetics and matte finishes can't be questioned, of course, and the all-weather, no-glint concepts do attract new sales. But wouldn't it be awful if the current and future generations began to believe that these are the classics?! It's like showing up for a fine southern quail hunt with an assault rifle!

Few entirely new designs have come forth for '94. The main thrust is Browning's entirely new autoloader, the Gold. Dropped are the Browning A-500s which failed to excite scattergunnners. The Gold semi-auto is made in 12- and 20-gauge, and both sizes are fitted with self-metering pressure valves to handle all 2¾- and 3-inch loads interchangeably. This is the first gas-operated 20 to be so offered; the Benelli 20,

ly remain cleaner. In the hands, the Golds point very nicely. They sit down well and provide comfortably rounded gripping spots. We look forward to bird hunting with the Gold. And if aspects of it have something in common with the now-obsolete Winchester Super-X Model 1, it's because both were designed by the same man, Joe Badali.

Although I bemoaned the lack of beauty in many of the current shotguns, the people at Connecticut Shotgun Manufacturing Co. have bucked the trend with reproductions of the Ansley H. Fox shotguns. These are hardly what the frugal-minded duck hunter will focus on, as they have starting prices of $5,650, but the display models shown at the 1994 SHOT Show in Dallas were impressive. Currently made in 20-gauge only, they have Circassian walnut, hand checkering and finish, and case-colored frames which, somewhat unlike the original Foxes, have scalloped lines to greet the stock's jaws. Otherwise, the guns essentially follow the Fox format with a rotary bolt and either the basic twin triggers or Fox Kautsky single trigger. A Fox-style beavertail is also

Ruger, too, is beginning to chamber the Red Label O/U for the 28-gauge, and Browning will have 28-gauge BPS slide-actions.

And with that, we move into the exploits of individual gunmakers.

American Arms, Inc.

This company focuses on introductory-level shotguns at modest prices, and it is one of the few around with an assortment of side-by-sides priced below a king's ransom. These doubles, plus the firm's Silver Series of over/unders, have excellent handling qualities.

New for '94 is a Silver Series O/U with 24-inch barrels for turkey hunting or fast-action uplanding in the grouse woods. The gun has a traditional finish rather than camo. There is also a very dynamic Sporting

THE TWO LEADING shotgun stories for 1994 may very well be the availability of models promised in 1992 and 1993, along with the diminishing beauty of bird guns. Despite technological advances in manufacturing, the production lines have not kept pace with the marketing end. All of this has kept shooters in limbo, wanting a certain shotgun but not being able to buy one or, in many instances, not even being able to see and handle one. Thus, 1994 will be a year of catching up.

And then there is the trend to (ugh!) black. The pretty parts are suddenly missing on many current shotguns in this com-

Clays over/under made on a Franchi design to sell well below a cool thou. If a gun writer ever could justify saying, "It's a lot of gun for the money," this is where the expression fits!

Baikal

American shotgunners first became interested in Russian-made Baikal shotguns when Soviet shooters blew the socks off Yankee Skeetmen in Olympic competition. Unfortunately, the first such guns to be shipped to the USA in the 1970s were hardly of the same quality as those swung by Soviet interna-tional marksmen, and we lost interest. But now, with most-favored-nation trading status, the state of Russia is trying again. Handling these guns will be KBI, Inc.

The main thrust is the Baikal IJ-27E-1C O/U. It has a mechanical single trigger that is actually quite crisp, and a novel feature permits the shooter to select between load extraction or ejection via a slot-head screw adjustment. An initial impression is that the makers could do a somewhat better job of finishing. However, the retail price at this writing is just $479, so it is an introductory-level piece, albeit with promise should the maker ever slick it up.

Beretta USA Corp.

A pair of over/unders are new at Beretta this season. One is an economy version of the Onyx called the Model 686 Essential. The "Essential" moniker derives from the fact that, to reduce cost, practically everything has been removed except the very essential components. Done in a dull finish like the Onyx, the Essential has no side ribs joining the barrels, and certain other shortcuts have been made.

Bernardelli

This franchise has bounced around the U.S. like a tennis ball hammered by Martina Navratilova. It's now at Miami-based Armsport, Inc. While nothing new appears, the Bernardelli line is always an excellent offering with well-made side-by-side and over/under pieces.

Browning

Along with the semi-auto Gold guns mentioned above, Browning has come up with a bolt-action shotgun that wasn't put into the 1994 catalog. The

Beretta has a new set of Sporting Clays O/Us which sport the broad "Strada" rib that spans 12.5mm, meaning close to a half inch.

The Bernardelli line, such as this 28-gauge Roma 6, is now being handled by Miami-based Armsport.

Another new O/U is pointed toward Sporting Clays. Called the 686 Silver Perdiz Sporting, it hosts the wide *Strada* rib (12.5mm, or nearly a half-inch) and is chambered for the 3-inch 12-gauge cartridge. Thus, the gun is suited for Sporting Clays or the field.

Since Beretta owns a chunk of Benelli, it is using the brilliantly conceived Benelli Monte-feltro (recoil operated) action on a new semi-auto, the Pintail. Its frame pivots on beefed-up components for strength and longevity. The gun shoots all standard and 3-inch 12-gauge loads interchangeably without any need for mechanical adjustment. It's a beautifully simple design available with 24-, 26-, or 28-inch barrels, including a rifle-sighted number.

One final point is that Beretta is now offering special choke tubes for steel shot compatibility under the "SP" designation. Extra-length choke tubes are also being cataloged.

gun seems to follow the concept used by Tar-Hunt to improve slug accuracy. However, Browning's 12-gauge bolt gun differs in that it has a smooth bore and can double for turkey hunting as well as slug shooting. The gun comes with a pair of extra-length screw-in tubes, one Extra Full for heavy turkey loads, the other an elongated rifled tube for sabot shooting. The receiver will be drilled and tapped for scopes, and this metallic nucleus will be placed into a (guess what?) black synthetic stock.

Relatively new in the Citori line is an assortment of higher-grade target guns. Browning extends the gold theme here, tagging one the Golden Clays GTI and another the Golden Clays Citori Skeet. The new Pigeon Grade Special Sporting O/U also carries a gold-bordered frame, as does the BT-99 Golden Clays trap gun.

In one of those catch-up situations, the Browning Recoilless trap gun, cataloged at least two seasons ago, is finally showing up on dealers' shelves with 27- or 30-inch trap barrels.

A last note is that the 28-gauge and 410-bore Citoris now have Invector choke versatility.

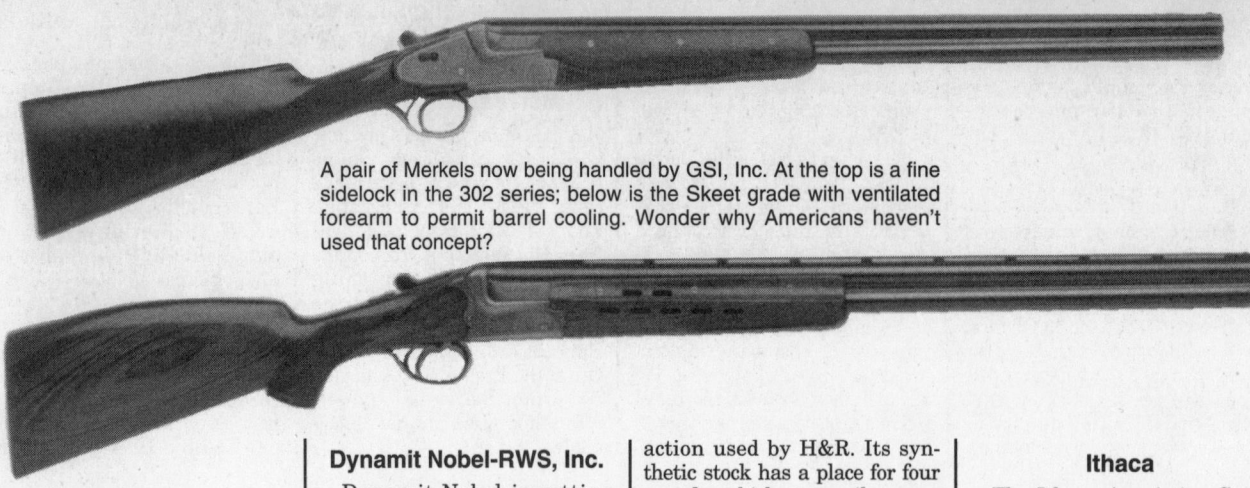

A pair of Merkels now being handled by GSI, Inc. At the top is a fine sidelock in the 302 series; below is the Skeet grade with ventilated forearm to permit barrel cooling. Wonder why Americans haven't used that concept?

Connecticut Valley Classics

The CVC stackbarrels are based on the designs introduced by Classic Doubles International, which had a short run before finances and its Asian manufacturer fell apart. Production has dragged at CVC, but barrel assemblies are now in production, and they should begin to appear. If they're equal to the original Classic Doubles, they're worth the wait.

Dynamit Nobel-RWS, Inc.

Dynamit Nobel is getting serious about its new Rottweil over/under competition gun. Once made in Italy by Gamba, this gun is now being produced in Germany under the direct supervision of D-N people.

Harrington & Richardson 1871

Remember the Snake Charmer, a handy little 410 that served for everything from potting small game to self-defense and snake whacking? H&R 1871 is back with a similar concept that's entirely legal. The gun is based on the 410 break action used by H&R. Its synthetic stock has a place for four rounds, which are easily accessible. The barrel is a 19½-incher. It won't win the Grand American trapshoot, but it'll serve on a lot of hikes, fishing trips, and pick-up hauls into the boonies.

HHF Shotguns

A totally new name in U.S. sport shooting, HHF distributes a line of Turkish-made shotguns, both side-by-sides and over/unders. These are turned out in the little village of Huglu, Turkey, in a cottage industry setting. Each craftsman applies his skills, often at home, and the guns come together in a modern facility and indoor test range.

The O/Us have fine modern lines and stock dimensions. Target-grade guns used by European shooters are said to have excellent staying power, thanks to properly fitted hardened parts. Much of this line will pivot on custom work with a lag of about 3-4 months. About the only thing different from other doubles is that the engraving tends to be a bit Eastern (Arabesque). Otherwise, the guns I've handled and seen taken apart looked just fine. The people at HHF may just be uncorking the surprise of the year.

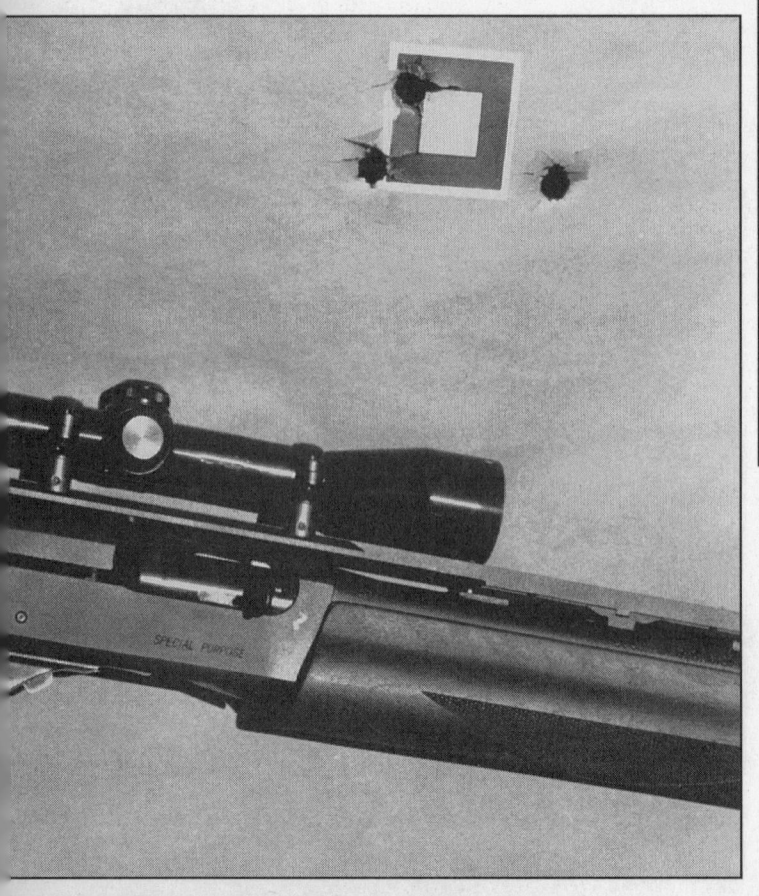

A new, stronger and stiffer cantilever now sits astride the Remington SPS 11-87 and 870 Deer Guns to provide repeatable accuracy such as this 3-shot group shot at 100 yards from benchrest.

Ithaca

The Ithaca Acquistion Corp. continues to struggle with its line of Model 87 pump guns, but recently it has taken on the Italian-made line of Fabarm doubles. These have been around the stateside block a few times, too, like the Bernardellis, but they're also pretty good side-by-side and O/U pieces in the moderately priced field.

Marlin

Once heavily into bolt-action shotguns, Marlin returns with the Model 512 S, meaning a rifled-barrel turnbolt that's aimed specifically for saboted slugs. It's 1:27-inch rifling twist is fast and won't do all that well with round-nosed, Foster-type slugs. But with plastic-encased sabots, it's right on. The rig has attractive sporter lines and open sights plus a drilled and tapped receiver top. The price isn't astronomical.

Marocchi

Perhaps known better as the Conquista, Marocchi's O/U tournament gun that first appeared here as a Sporting Clays piece has been carried to trap and Skeet configurations for 1995. An innovation is a left-hand version that has the opening lever pivoted for southpaws, along with the correct cast-on angle for lefties. To identify these, the trigger guards are engraved with "Sporting Left." The guns have very good swing dynamics and are imported by Precision Sales International, Inc.

Mossberg

Mossberg's Model 9200 autoloader is finally at hand. The 24-inch-barreled form is the 1994 National Wild Turkey Federation gun. Other variants are available, including a camo-covered gun.

Krieghoff

The K-80 remains solidly entrenched here as the main action nucleus. However, the increasing interest in small-bore Sporting Clays has prompted the development of a medium-weight barrel to accept slip-in small-bore inserts, thus converting a 12-gauge to a lesser bore.

Merkel

Things got shaky at Merkel for a time, but an infusion of new cash has the place running again. The American importer is GSI, Inc. Get 'em while they're hot, because the wages of German workers are scheduled to rise each year as the once-split nation regroups. Clay target grades and beautiful sidelocks are here, and the sidelocked SxSs have excellent weight distributions for American uplanding.

Remington

Remington's main move for 1994 is a pair of Model 11-87 and 870 Special Purpose Deer Guns with synthetic stock/forearm assemblies and, more importantly, a new cantilever scope mount that is stronger, stiffer, and permanently brazed to the barrel. A matte finish

covers the metallic parts. Also in the slug gun category are two 20-gauge Deer Guns with rifled barrels and the newly strengthened cantilever mount. Built on the M1100 and 870 Lightweight frames, these 20s have Monte Carlo stocks of walnut. Remington's M1100 Special Field will now wear a 23-inch barrel rather than the original 21-incher, and the long-awaited Peerless O/U is finally beginning to appear in gun shops.

Rizzini

Always an excellent Italian-made shotgun line, but not widely distributed, the Rizzini guns are now being handled stateside by Lou Alessandri and Son, Ltd., of Rehoboth, Massachusetts. The O/Us are spirited and handsome. Rizzinis should interest the advanced gun collector or shooter.

Ruger

Surprise, surprise! I had barely seen the Ruger catalog listing the 20-gauge, 30-inch-barreled, Sporting Clays version of the Red Label when a shooter showed me one. Normally it takes Ruger a lot of time to get a fresh product on the market. Is Clinton like

Mussolini, getting the trains to run on time?! Not only is the Ruger 20-gauge Sporter available, but it is overbored a normal 0.615-inch bore to 0.633-inch. That might make it the first overbored 20 ever mass produced. And it doesn't stop there! All Ruger 12-gauge barrels will also be overbore, be they Skeet, Sporting, or field; the bore diameters will be about 0.743-inch compared to the normal 0.729-inch for 12s. Thus, the screw-in choke tubes will be specially sized to match the bores.

As already mentioned, the Red Label will also be made in 28-gauge in 26- and 28-inch barrel lengths. They're quite trim at about 6 and 6¼ pounds, respectively, with their pistol-gripped stocks.

Stoeger

The Brazilian-made IGA SxS and O/U models have had some improvements in line. They show less bulk these days, and a straight-gripped design has come along. The IGAs don't have the world's best trigger pulls, but they are husky and rugged for day-in, day-out hunting at a very modest price.

At hand is a new Tikka O/U, the Model 512S. This is the old

Valmet Lion design beefed up with a sliding top bolt (a la the current Krieghoff 32 and K-80). It's a good looking gun and seems quite serviceable.

Tar-Hunt

I'm still not sure whether this is a shotgun or not. But it is a superbly accurate, bolt-action, 12-gauge slug gun with variously rifled barrels for sabots, Foster slugs, or a compromise. For 1994, a variety of stocks is being offered in synthetic or custom wood. The trigger on this one is rifle-like. Also, look for the company to bring out a new, mushrooming, 1¼-ounce slug of pure lead, which retains its accuracy despite firing setback forces, and has been known to deliver instant knockdowns via hydrostatic shock when used with fast-twist rifling (around 1:27). The slug will be sold under the "Lightfield" company name.

Weatherby

Weatherby is getting deeper into shotguns. The same custom shop work that was once centered on Mark V magnum rifles will be offered for the firm's list of O/Us. The guns can now be had with straight, semi-pistol, and full pistol grips plus the customer's choice of wood and dimensions, all upon special order, of course. The Grade II and III Orion Classic Fields are lookers!

For 1994, the main additions are in the Orion category, where some innovations have been employed for a greater selection in styling.

Winchester/USRAC

The company continues to play games with its 22-inch-barreled Model 1300 pump gun. A new pattern is the Real-tree Turkey camo, but (ugh!) wouldn't you know it? The remaining two are colored like the ace of spades! These are tagged the Black Shadow Turkey and Black Shadow Deer. Obviously, both have black composite stock and forearm plus matte-finished metals, and they're rightly drilled and tapped for scope mounts. And the Model 1001 O/U listed last year? Sorry, I haven't seen any, either.

In general, then, we do have a bunch of working shotguns at hand, but I do wish more people would begin to make pretty pieces again! Enough already with this black stuff! ●

I still haven't figured out if the Tar-Hunt rifled turnbolt is indeed a shotgun, but it handles sabot slugs with amazing accuracy.

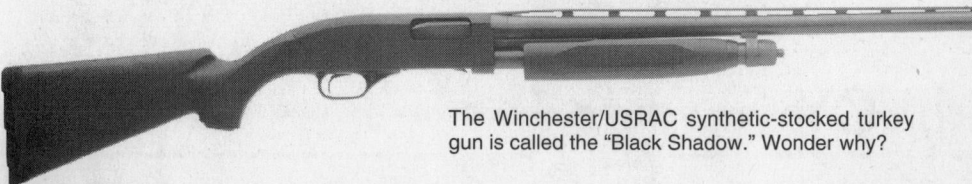

The Winchester/USRAC synthetic-stocked turkey gun is called the "Black Shadow." Wonder why?

THE RECENT popularity of new 10mm/40-caliber automatic pistol cartridges has emphasized a point easily overlooked: All the other automatic pistol cartridges in common use today were also the ones in common use during the first decade of the century.

It is difficult to think of them as old-timers. Even those who truly appreciate the revolver admit that the semi-automatic pistol is "more modern."

Yet, the development of cartridges that allowed the automatics to be-come popular began over a century ago. Almost every conceivable cartridge had been tried before World War I. Most failed. The ones that survived were all firmly established before 1910. They proved so useful they remain in common use today.

To understand how this came about, consider the rapid changes that occurred in the late 1800s. Within just a few decades, muzzle-loaders had been supplanted by breechloaders, and single shots were overshadowed by repeaters.

By 1886, France had introduced a small-bore smokeless-powder rifle cartridge. By 1891, most of the world powers had adopted smokeless-powder repeating rifles of small bore size.

Into this picture of rapid change, with the acceptance of rapid-fire arms and the availability of smokeless powder, came the automatic pistol.

The first of the new pistols to reach production was the Austrian Schonberger. The unusual friction-delay design of 1892 was short-lived, but it showed that a hand-

EARLY AUTO PISTOL CARTRIDGES

Good Ideas That Did Not Die

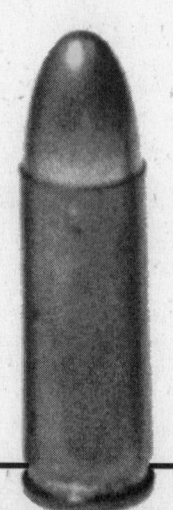

by JOHN MALLOY

gun of semi-automatic type was indeed feasible. Little is known about the Schonberger cartridge, except that it used a bullet of about 8mm diameter. It probably was rimmed and may have been straight-sided, similar to revolver rounds of the time.

The Schonberger reached the market first, but had not been a success. The first successful semi-automatic pistol was the 30-caliber Borchardt. Developed by naturalized American inventor Hugo Borchardt, it was produced in Germany in 1893, a year after the Schonberger.

We can imagine Borchardt's frustration during the development of his pistol. He was working on an innovative pistol design in which no existing cartridge would work. With little to guide him, he was forced to design his own.

We cannot know Borchardt's thinking in designing his new cartridge, but it is clear that he had four decisions to make.

First, the shape of the case would have to allow both feeding from the magazine and positioning in the chamber. In revolvers, the cartridges were positioned by the rims. Rims, however, would not allow proper feeding from the innovative new grip-mounted detachable magazine system he was developing. In 1888, the Germans had adopted a rimless, bottleneck rifle cartridge. Borchardt decided on a scaled-down version of such a cartridge.

The second decision involved the caliber or bullet diameter. It is not known why he chose a 30-caliber

The survivors: The most common automatic pistol cartridges in use throughout the world today—all introduced before the end of the first decade of this century: 1) 25 ACP (1906); 2) 30 Luger (1900); 3) 30 Mauser/7.62mm Tokarev (1893, as 30 Borchardt); 4) 32 ACP (1899); 5) 380 ACP (1908); 6) 38 Super (1900, as 38 ACP); 7) 9mm Bergmann-Bayard/9mm Largo (1901, as 9mm Mars); 8) 9mm Luger (1902); 9) 45 ACP (1905).

The 30-caliber Borchardt pistol was the first successful automatic pistol, introduced in 1893. Its cartridge outlived the pistol; known as the 30 Mauser or 7.62mm Tokarev, it is still in common use. This Borchardt is in the Metzger collection at College Station, Texas.

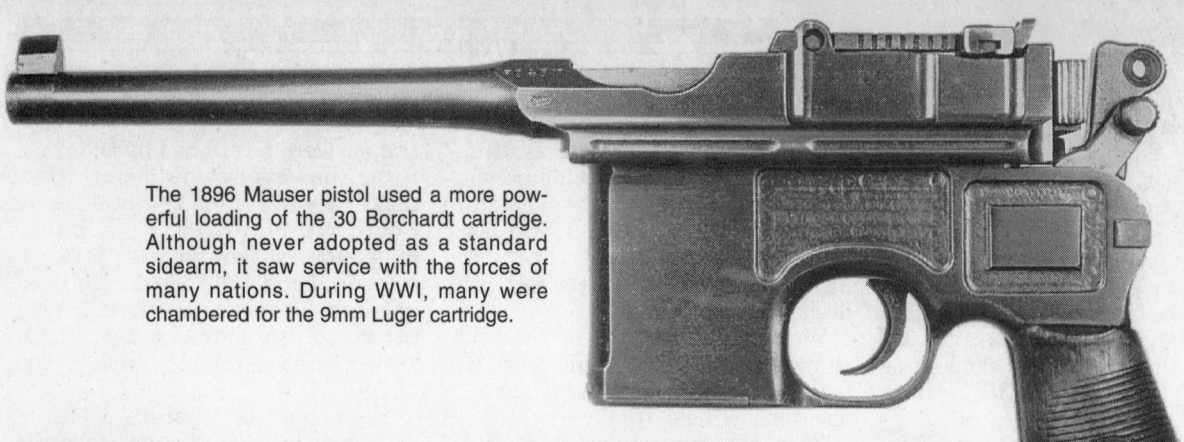

The 1896 Mauser pistol used a more powerful loading of the 30 Borchardt cartridge. Although never adopted as a standard sidearm, it saw service with the forces of many nations. During WWI, many were chambered for the 9mm Luger cartridge.

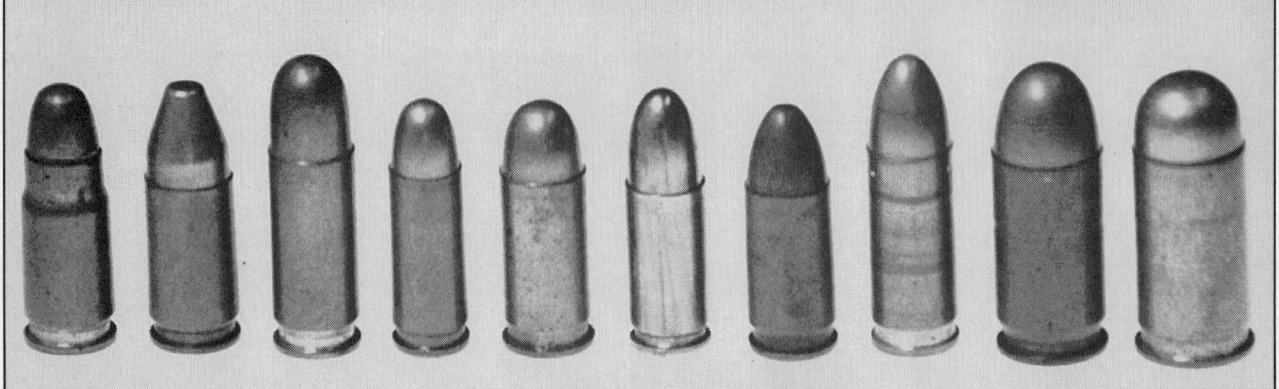

Military automatic pistol cartridges adopted by some of the world's governments prior to World War I: 1) 30 Luger (Switzerland, 1900); 2) 9mm Luger (Germany, 1904); 3) 9mm Bergman-Bayard (Spain, 1905; Denmark, 1910); 4) 7.65mm Mannlicher (Argentina, 1905); 5) 9mm Browning Long (Belgium, 1903; Sweden, 1907); 6) 8mm Roth-Steyr (Austria, 1907); 7) 9mm Glisenti (Italy, 1910—original had truncated-cone bullet); 8) 9mm Steyr (Austria, 1912); 9) 45 ACP (U.S., 1911); and 10) 455 Webley Self-Loading (Great Britain, 1912).

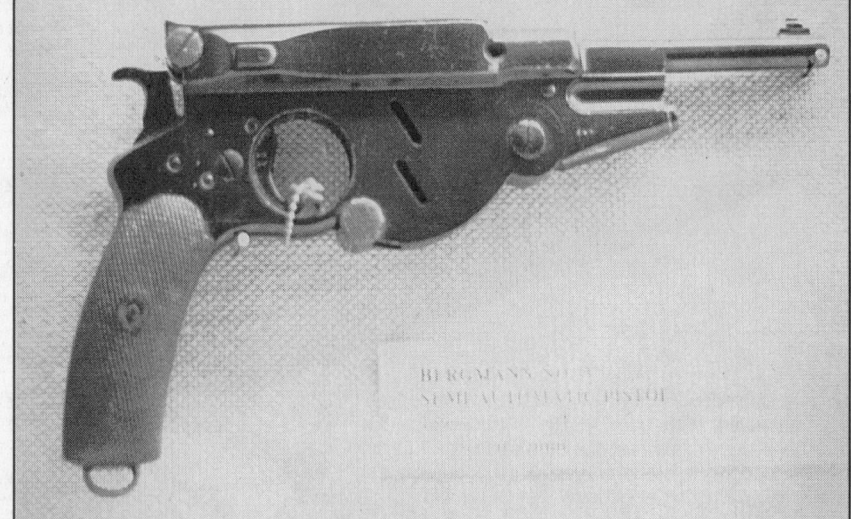

Bergmann pistols of the 1894-1896 period were the world's first successful blowback pistols, although their unusual tapered cartridges soon became obsolete. This specimen is in the Winchester Museum at the Buffalo Bill Historical Center in Cody, Wyoming.

bore for his pistol. Perhaps he kept up with firearms developments in America and was aware of the U.S. Army's preference for a rifle of that bore size. Mauser had made a 31-caliber (7.65mm) rifle for Belgium in 1889, so the tradition of bore designations in even millimeters had already been broken. Still, the 30-caliber—not a logical choice within the metric system—was selected by Borchardt.

For his third decision—length—it is obvious the overall length of the cartridge could be no longer than the grip of his pistol could accommodate—about 30mm. The critical decision was thus the length of the cartridge case. It is difficult to speculate as to whether European or American influence guided him here. The final case length was about 25mm (almost exactly 1 inch) long.

Once the shape, caliber and length had been decided, however, the fourth decision—the diameter of the base of the round—was relatively simple. Here, European measurements provided the nearest even number that was satisfactory. The obvious choice for a maximum base size was an even 10mm (.3937-inch). This was a fateful and fortunate selection, as it allowed cases of that size to be later opened up to use 9mm bullets.

The Borchardt pistol was a real pioneer. Large and clumsy by today's standards, its locked-breech mechanism worked well, and it influenced design for some time to come. About 3000 were made.

The Borchardt cartridge, however, was in some ways the real breakthrough. Its rimless body fed smoothly through the magazine and its bottleneck shoulder positioned it properly in the chamber. It was the first successful automatic pistol cartridge, showing the real promise of this handgun type for the first time. It was also (and this caught the attention of the time) the world's first *high-velocity* handgun cartridge. Later known by other names such as 30 Mauser and 7.62mm Tokarev, it was destined to be one of the world's most successful pistol cartridges.

During the 1890s, the Mauser firm had grown tremendously through the sales of military repeat-

(Above) The Mannlicher Model 1901 pistol used a low-powered 7.65mm straight-case cartridge. Although it saw limited military use, it was surpassed by pistols chambering more powerful rounds. This specimen is in the Winchester Museum at Cody, Wyoming.

(Left) The automatic pistol cartridges of John M. Browning, from left: 1) 32 ACP (1899); 2) 38 ACP (1900); 3) 9mm Browning Long (1903); and 4) 25 ACP (1906) are all semi-rimmed. The 45 ACP (1905) and 380 ACP (1908) are true rimless designs.

Line drawing by John Malloy: Cartridges introduced by Bergmann during the period 1894-1901: 1) 5mm grooved; 2) 5mm grooveless; 3) 6.5mm grooved; 4) 6.5 grooveless; 5) 8mm; 6) 8mm Simplex; 7) 7.63mm (7.8mm); 8) 9mm Mars. Moderately popular during this period, most had been discontinued by the end of WWI. The 9mm Mars alone (as the 9mm Largo/Bergmann-Bayard) is still in use.

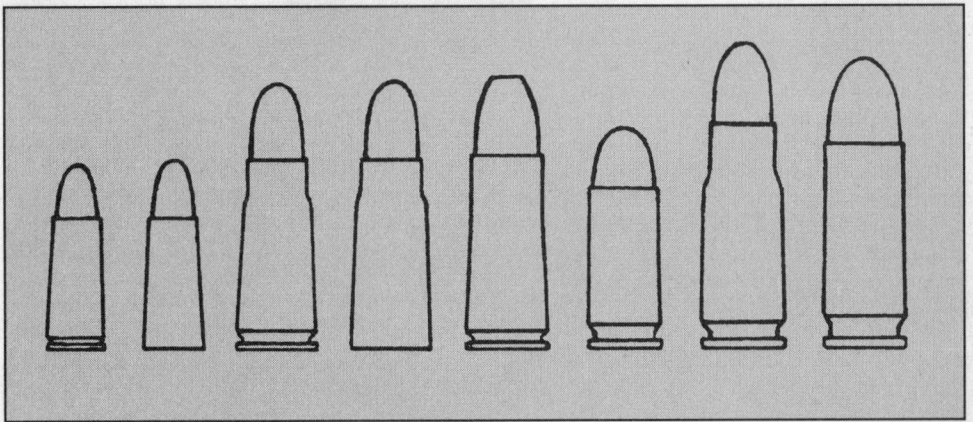

ing rifles. Paul Mauser realized that good military sales of semi-automatic pistols were a possibility. In 1896, Mauser introduced the famous locked-breech pistol, later affectionately called the "broomhandle."

The cartridge was dimensionally identical to the 30-caliber (7.65mm) Borchardt, using the same case and bullet as the round introduced three years before. The Mauser loading, however, was substantially

more powerful, stepping up the velocity. Known as the 30 Mauser (7.63mm), it became world famous for its power and flat-shooting characteristics.

The Mauser pistol, although never adopted as the official pistol of any nation, overshadowed the Borchardt and other early semi-automatics. Its manageable size and greater power made it immediately popular.

Before the end of 1898, German-

born Andreas Schwarzlose of Austria had introduced a nicely balanced locked-breech pistol. This "Standart" pistol used a rotating bolt. The Mauser's popularity made its cartridge the standard of the time, so the Schwarzlose was chambered for the 30 Mauser round. These Schwarzlose Standart pistols are very rare today, most apparently going to Russia in 1905, and they were never returned.

In 1900, the Austrian firm of Mannlicher introduced a weak locked-breech pistol chambered for a lower-powered cartridge of the same 7.65mm bore diameter. However, it used a shorter, straight-cased cartridge.

A stronger model was not introduced until 1903. It, too, never achieved any real popularity, even though it used a new, more powerful 30-caliber (7.65mm) Mannlicher bottleneck cartridge. Perhaps not surprisingly, the new bottleneck round had exactly the same dimensions as the Borchardt and Mauser rounds.

Within a year of the Borchardt's introduction, the German firm of Bergmann introduced a low-powered semi-automatic pistol. A number of different models and calibers were produced between 1894-1896 and were the first blowback pistols ever produced. The design of the guns was apparently the work of Louis Schmeisser, a Bergmann employee, but there is speculation that Theodor Bergmann himself had a hand in designing the cartridges.

Keeping in mind that he had little to guide him, Bergmann's unique cartridges still seem unusual to us. The first was a 5mm round that positioned itself in the chamber on the walls of its sharply tapered case. Because it was literally blown back out of the chamber as a means of extraction, the case was made with no extractor groove. Next came a 6.5mm number which had both a bottleneck and a pronounced taper. It, too, started without a groove. For convenience of unloading, extractor grooves were later added to both the 5mm and 6.5mm cartridges.

Another innovative design, an 8mm round, had a straight case neck, but a tapered rear portion for positioning.

In 1897, Bergmann introduced a locked-breech pistol. The cartridge was almost identical to the 30-caliber Borchardt and Mauser rounds, but the shoulder was formed farther back from the case mouth. This gave a longer neck for the same overall length. Perhaps to avoid confusion with the earlier rounds, the cartridge was sometimes called the 7.8mm Bergmann.

The first Bergmann 8mm round had a straight case neck, but a tapered rear portion for positioning in the chamber. As the turn of the century approached, a shorter, straight 8mm cartridge, known now as the 8mm Simplex, may have been the first automatic pistol cartridge to position itself on the case mouth. The exact date of introduction of this round, however, is in some question. By the end of World War I, most of the Bergmann cartridges had gone out of production.

In about 1901, however, Bergmann's biggest success was introduced. The 9mm Bergmann Mars cartridge was straight, rimless, and headspaced on the case mouth. Probably by coincidence, because 10mm was a logical case base diameter for a 9mm bullet, the base and body dimensions of the case are close to those of the Borchardt/Mauser rounds.

The Mars cartridge was a powerful one for the time. It was adopted by Spain in 1905 and Denmark in 1910. The pistol contracts were handled by the Pieper firm of Belgium, who added their tradename "Bayard." Although known as the 9mm Largo in Spain, the round is generally known as the 9mm Bergmann-Bayard.

Limited numbers of Bergmann pistols in 7.5mm, 10mm, 11mm and 11.35mm were reportedly made. These seem to have been largely experimental. Both the pistols and the ammunition are extremely rare. In some cases, not even a single specimen is known to exist today.

Hugo Borchardt, while develop-

ing his pistol, had worked with a German engineer named Georg Luger. The two men were both in their forties and apparently worked well together. Toward the end of the 1890s, Luger began a redesign of the awkward Borchardt mechanism into a more compact package. Borchardt apparently worked with Luger on this project at Deutsche Waffen- und Munitionsfabriken (DWM), but the exact relationship between the two at that time is not known.

The result, however, is well known:

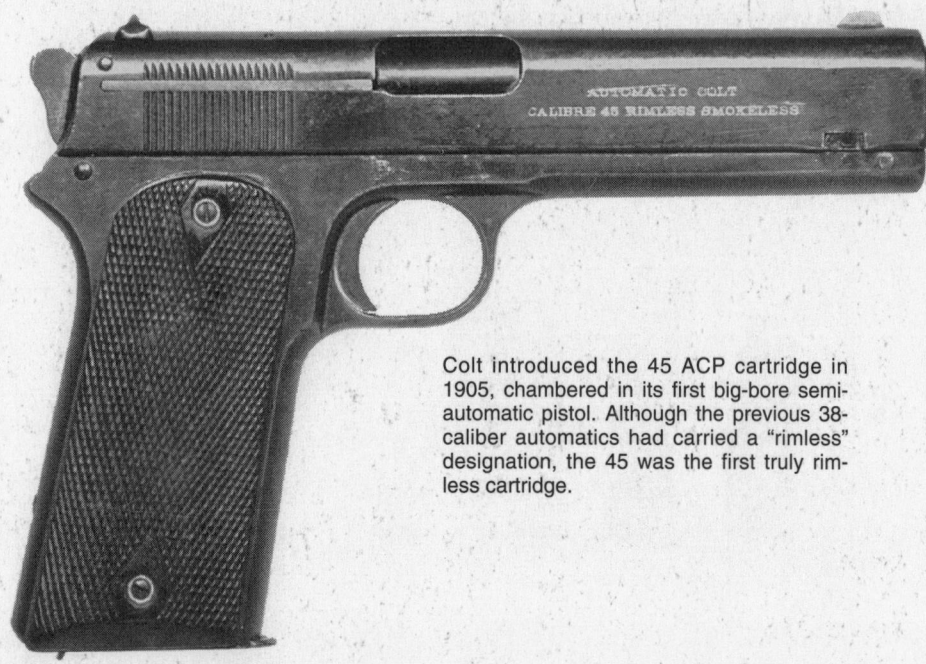

Colt introduced the 45 ACP cartridge in 1905, chambered in its first big-bore semi-automatic pistol. Although the previous 38-caliber automatics had carried a "rimless" designation, the 45 was the first truly rimless cartridge.

the famous Parabellum, or Luger, pistol.

Because the Luger had its recoil spring inside the grip frame, less space was left for the cartridge magazine. The Borchardt round was therefore shortened, and the resulting cartridge became the 30-caliber (7.65mm) Parabellum or Luger.

It used the same bullet and base diameters, and kept the bottleneck shape. The power level, although less than that of the 30 Mauser loading, was close to that of the original 30 Borchardt.

By 1900, the 30 Luger had already been adopted as the military sidearm of Switzerland. The German military, however, declined the chance to adopt it.

In 1902, a Luger pistol for a new 9mm cartridge was introduced. DWM made the new round simply by shortening and straightening the

30 Luger case to hold a 9mm bullet. The overall length of the new cartridge was the same as that of the original 30-caliber one. Thus, no change in any part of the pistol, other than the barrel, was required.

The new round was adopted by the German navy in 1904 and by the army in 1908. As the cartridge of the famous P08 Luger pistol, it became known worldwide as the 9mm Parabellum or 9mm Luger.

Also in 1908, another "enlarged" cartridge was introduced. Mauser, using the same technique that had

In 1908, when the German army adopted the 9mm Luger round in the P08 pistol, the cartridge started on its way to becoming the most widely used military pistol round of all time. (Courtesy of Robert Malloy.)

produced the Luger round, opened its 30-caliber case to 9mm, creating the powerful 9mm Mauser Export cartridge. It was developed for the "Export Model" Broomhandle, but had a relatively short life, being discontinued in 1914. When World War I commenced, 1896 Mauser pistols were chambered for the 9mm Luger round to avoid supply problems.

In 1910, two years after the P08's adoption, the Italian government adopted a cartridge of the exact dimensions of the 9mm Luger, but loaded to a much lower power level. Although it is visually identical, the Luger round had pressures too high for the weak Italian Glisenti pistol. The Italian round is known as the 9mm Glisenti.

While all this had been going on, American firearms genius John M. Browning had been working with semi-automatic pistol designs of his

own since the middle 1890s. He had already developed several working machineguns, and one had been accepted for U.S. service in 1895. However, he had always worked with existing cartridges, and they were always rimmed. His machineguns, for example, were chambered for the popular rimmed rifle cartridges of the time, including 44-40, 45-70 and 30-40 Krag.

Now, for the first time, he was designing mechanisms through which no current cartridge would work properly. The obvious solution

was to design his own. His experience with the positive positioning of a rimmed cartridge influenced his development of cartridges for his semi-automatic pistol designs. These rounds have come to be called "semi-rimmed."

They have extractor grooves and, at a casual glance, do not appear to have a rim. However, they are not truly rimless. A small flange at the base is of slightly greater diameter than the body of the case.

The first round introduced—the 32 Automatic or 7.65mm Browning—was destined to become one of the most widely used cartridges of all time. It was marketed by Fabrique Nationale (FN) of Belgium in 1899, chambered in Browning's compact blowback pocket pistol. The light, flat 32 was soon made available in several improved models by Fabrique Nationale, and almost as quickly it

was copied by armsmakers all over the world.

R.K. Wilson, writing in the 1930s, estimated that over 80 percent of all makes of automatic pistols made up to that time were chambered for the 32 Automatic cartridge!

At this point, we should consider some other possibilities for the origin of this cartridge. It has been mentioned by some that Browning could have used the Bergmann 8mm Simplex as a pattern for the 32-caliber round. It has also been mentioned that perhaps Winchester engineers developed the cartridge for Browning. When the record fails to clear up such points, we must rely on our knowledge of the man himself.

Browning, prior to his relationship with Winchester, had never been more than 100 miles from Ogden, Utah. By the time he began work on his automatic pistols, he had made the long train trip to Connecticut a number of times, but a trip to Europe was still many years into his future. He would have been interested in any European developments, of course, but the chance that he actually had an opportunity to try out the early European pistols or cartridges before he began his work seems remote.

In addition, the date of introduction of the 8mm Simplex is in some question. It seems unlikely that the round could have been in widespread use prior to Browning's pistol development. More likely, the 8mm and 32 Auto rounds were actually contemporaries.

If we accept the 32 Automatic as an original design, can we then credit Winchester engineers with it? We must remember Browning's reputation as an impatient genius. Having begun development of automatic pistol designs, he would have tried the available cartridges first. Indeed, his early patents show rimmed revolver-type cartridges in the drawings. Having found existing ammunition designs unsuitable, would he then have mailed a letter to Winchester, suspended work, and waited for the Winchester experts to design a suitable cartridge, produce a trial lot, then ship the new ammunition back to Utah? Such patience does not tie in with what we know of the man.

Consider this: The Browning Brothers store was a jobber for Winchester ammunition and had access to all types of cartridges to use for experimental work. By the

With the adoption of the Model 1911 Colt 45-caliber pistol, the United States became the first nation to have a standard-issue automatic pistol of a caliber larger than 9mm.

The first successful automatic pistol cartridge in some of its several forms: from left, a rare original 30 Borchardt cartridge, a 30 Mauser and a 7.62mm Tokarev. A century later, pistols are still being made for this 1893 design.

mid-1890s, 32- and 38-caliber revolvers were very popular. There were a number of 32-caliber rounds—the 32 Merwin & Hulbert Long, 32 Harrington & Richardson, 32-44 target load and the new 32 Smith & Wesson Long—that were the same bullet diameter as Browning's later 32 Automatic cartridges.

It seems plausible that Browning shortened some of these to a case length he felt to be suitable for a magazine inside the grip. He would then have reduced the rim until the cartridges fed smoothly over each other, leaving a slight flange to position the round in the chamber. The semi-rimmed pistol cartridge was probably born in this manner.

Once the round satisfied Browning, Winchester would probably have produced quantities for his experimentation, glad to be on the ground floor of something that might be a big seller. The company actually was the first American firm to produce the cartridge as the 32 Automatic Colt Pistol (32 ACP) when Colt chambered a Browning-designed pistol for it in 1903. Even considering Winchester's involvement, it seems likely that the semi-rimmed 32 ACP was a true Browning design.

Concurrent with his work with the blowback 32, Browning developed a locked-breech 38 pistol for Colt, which was introduced in 1900. The cartridge—the 38 ACP—is similar in general shape to the smaller 32. It is easy to imagine its origin by shortening the 38 Long Colt revolver cartridge case and making it semi-rimmed.

The popularity of FN's 32-caliber pistol sparked ideas of a larger-caliber FN pistol suitable for military use. Apparently, it was felt desirable to retain the simplicity of the blowback design, so shortening the 38 ACP case and using a lighter bullet and reduced powder charge allowed this. The resulting cartridge, introduced in 1903 and known as the 9mm Browning, came to be known later as the 9mm Browning Long.

When the idea of a small hideaway pistol came up, no suitable cartridge existed. Browning designed a small automatic for a new cartridge, the 25 ACP. True to his original design, it used a short semi-rimmed case. Introduced by Colt in 1906, it was the last of the semi-rimmed cartridges.

By that time, Browning's work had reached completion on a new 45-caliber pistol for Colt. Introduced late in 1905, the new gun used a true rimless cartridge that positioned itself at the front of the chamber on the mouth of the cartridge case. The cartridge, the 45 ACP, became the U.S. Army's official pistol cartridge in 1911, with the adoption of the famous Colt Model 1911.

Browning's last automatic pistol cartridge, the 380, was also rimless. Introduced in 1908, it was immedi-

pistol. The attempt failed because the felt recoil was so punishing to the shooter. The words from a British army test trial sum it up: "No one who fired once with this pistol wished to shoot it again." Both Mars pistols and the ammunition are very rare today.

Yet, the 450-caliber cartridges are of particular interest. Although they failed, they gave Webley & Scott, England's largest manufacturer of military sidearms, the notion that a semi-automatic pistol of that bore size might be a worthwhile project.

Browning and Colt had shortened

least in experimental form. In appearance, it was very similar to the later 45 ACP, but used a case of slightly different dimensions and a flatpoint bullet. I can't help but speculate that the pistol Bergmann submitted for the 1907 U.S. Test Trials actually was chambered for the 11.35mm cartridge, for it would not fire the 45 ammunition furnished for the trials.

About 1904, Danish engineer Jens Schouboe, having introduced an earlier 32-caliber blowback pistol, brought out a 45-caliber version. The cartridge, known as the 11.35mm Schouboe, was unique. To keep pres-

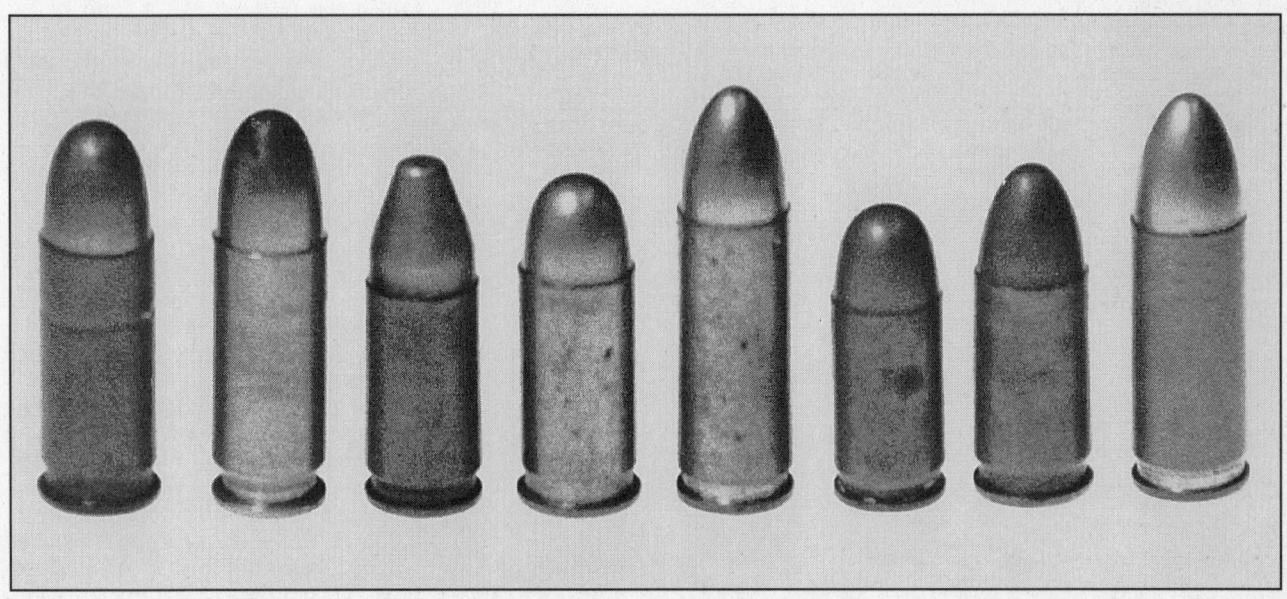

Cartridges of about 9mm bore size turned out to be the most widely used for full-size or military-style holster pistols, and a number of pocket pistols: 1) 38 ACP (1900); 2) 9mm Bergmann-Bayard (1901); 3) 9mm Luger (1902); 4) 9mm Browning Long (1903); 5) 9mm Mauser (1908); 6) 380 ACP/9mm Browning Short (1908); 7) 9mm Glisenti (1910—original had truncated-cone bullet); 8) 9mm Steyr (1911).

ately popular. The same length as the 32 Auto, it could be adapted to many of the same pistols, and its greater frontal area and heavier bullet made it more effective. In the United States, it was called the 380 ACP or 380 CAPH (Colt Automatic Pistol, Hammerless). In Europe, it became the 9mm Browning Short, Corto or Kurz.

The Browning-designed Colt 45 wasn't the first semi-automatic pistol of that caliber. Around 1898, Hugh Gabbett-Fairfax introduced his ill-fated Mars pistols in England. The original caliber was 360, followed by pistols of 8.5mm, 9mm, 10mm, 450 Long, 450 Short and 472 calibers. Few pistols were made, but the Mars guns were a pioneering attempt at a high-velocity, big-bore

the old blackpowder 45 Colt cartridge and made it rimless (with a case head almost identical to that of the military 30-06 rifle cartridge) to form the 45 ACP. Webley used the lengthened 455 revolver cartridge designed for the Webley-Fosbery revolver, made it semi-rimmed, and it became the 455 Webley Self-Loading round. A 455 Webley semi-automatic pistol was offered for commercial sale in 1904, actually a year before the big-bore Colt was announced. However, the much-redesigned British pistol was not adopted until 1912, a year after the improved Colt 45 had been accepted for U.S. Service.

By about 1903, Theodor Bergmann added a new 11.35mm cartridge to the Bergmann line, at

sures within the limits of his blowback design, Schouboe used a very light bullet consisting of a copper-jacketed wood plug with a disc of aluminum at the base. Total weight was slightly over 60 grains. The light bullet achieved very high velocity (about 1600 fps) with surprisingly good penetration. Accuracy was poor, though, and the gun went out of its limited production after about 500 had been made.

About 1897, a 5mm bottleneck cartridge was introduced for the Spanish Charola y Anitua pistol. Later adopted for the Belgian Clement pistol, it is commonly known to collectors as the 5mm Clement.

About 1902, in Austria, the small 7.65mm Roth-Sauer cartridge was introduced. Of about the same power

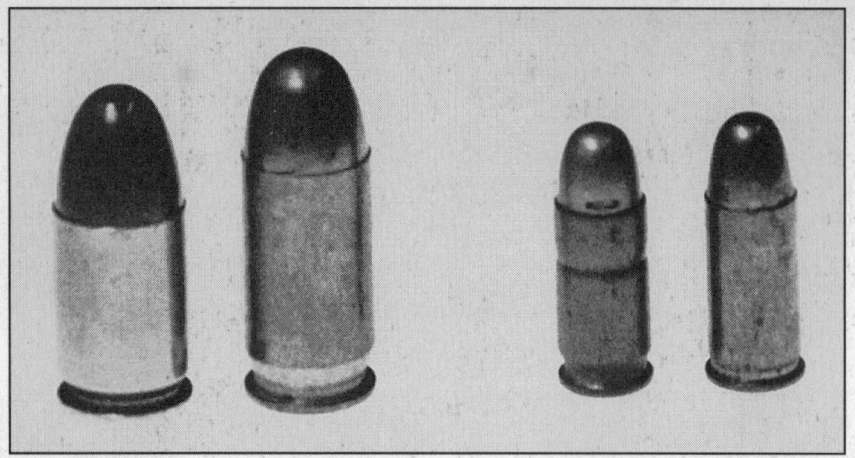

Interesting designs that did not achieve widespread use: from left, the 11.35mm Schouboe used an extremely light copper-covered wood bullet to attain high velocity. A 45 ACP is shown for comparison. The 35 S&W had a jacketed nose and a lead body, locked together by slots in the nose cap. A 32 ACP is shown for comparison.

Original 30-caliber cartridges and the 9mm rounds developed from them by straightening the case: from left, a 30 Mauser and a 9mm Mauser, a 30 Luger and a 9mm Luger. The 30 Mauser round remained in widespread use, while the 30 Luger was overshadowed by the 9mm.

on the Belgian Clement design. The 32 ACP would have been a logical choice of calibers, but the firm apparently did not like the idea of chambering their pistol for a cartridge associated with their rival, Colt.

Instead, a new round, the 35 Smith & Wesson, was designed, but it was not really of 35-caliber—it's a 32! Except for having a true rimless case, it was only slightly different from the 32, with no increase in power.

The greatest difference was in the bullet. Smith & Wesson believed that jacketed bullets were necessary for functioning, but would wear the bore excessively. They designed a two-piece bullet with a lead body and a jacketed nose. The lead was swaged into the nose cap, with slots in the nose cap serving to lock the two parts together into a single unit.

The late arrival, higher cost and limited availability of the 35 S&W cartridges contrasted poorly with the worldwide popularity of the 32. S&W later dropped the 35 in favor of the 32, but by then they had passed the prime period of pocket-pistol popularity. Both 35 S&W pistols and cartridges are scarce today.

Just prior to World War I, in the 1913-14 period, several tiny automatic pistols were introduced in Europe. Their cartridges—the 2.7mm Kolibri, 3mm Kolibri and 4.25mm Erika (later known as the Liliput)—made the 25 ACP look huge by comparison. Equivalents for the diminutive rounds are about 11-,

as the 32 ACP, the case is shorter and the two will not interchange. The Roth offering could not compete with the already established Browning-designed 32.

In 1907, Austria adopted the 8mm Roth-Steyr as its military cartridge. The straight-cased cartridge was of reasonable power for its bore size, but was soon discarded when Austria adopted the 9mm Steyr-Hahn pistol in 1912. The larger straight-cased 9mm Steyr cartridge, introduced in 1911, was dimensionally very similar to the 9mm Bergmann-Bayard round introduced a decade before.

In 1913, Smith & Wesson entered the pocket-pistol market, introducing its first automatic pistol. It was based

This 1912 Steyr-Hahn is ready to be loaded with a clip of 9mm Steyr cartridges. The pistol was the last military sidearm to be loaded with a stripper clip.

12- and 17-caliber, respectively. Except for the easy concealability of the miniature pistols, it is difficult to imagine any effective purpose for them. The pistols and their cartridges are very rare today, and after World War I, little that was new appeared in the world of automatic pistol cartridges.

The 9mm Luger became widely accepted and a number of new pistols were designed for it. It effectively replaced a number of other cartridges as military rounds.

In 1925, Japan adopted the Type 14 pistol chambered for the 8mm Nambu cartridge. This bottleneck design, essentially an enlarged copy of the 30 Luger round, may have been used in Japanese pistols since about 1902. The Japanese apparently did not trust ordinary soldiers with pistols; production was low, relative to that of other countries. Use of the cartridge essentially ended with the defeat of Japan in World War II.

In 1929, Colt increased the velocity of its 38 ACP cartridge, calling the new loading the 38 Super. The bullet and case remained exactly the same, but because of increased pressures, the Super should never be fired in the older 38 ACP guns.

About 1930, the Soviet Union adopted the 30 Mauser cartridge, which had been used in their Mauser and Schwarzlose pistols since before the 1917 Revolution. Chambered in the new Soviet-designed Tokarev pistol, it became known as the 7.62mm Tokarev.

If anything could be called a new development, it would probably be the 7.65mm French Long cartridge for the French 1935 pistols. Actually, the cartridge was our top-secret round for the U.S. Army's World War I Pedersen device of 1918. The French apparently thought it would make an ideal military pistol cartridge. Five years later, when the Nazis occupied France, they chose not to continue production of the French pistols.

So, the early cartridges were the ones that continued, and their use spread throughout the world.

In the past decade or so, some high-powered automatic pistol cartridges have been made in limited quantities for specialized long-range silhouette or hunting uses. They include the 44 AutoMag, the 45 Winchester Magnum, and the more recent 475 and 500 rounds for the Wildey and Desert Eagle pistols. These big boomers fill a small niche that did not exist for the unsuccess-

ful Mars pistol back at the turn of the century.

But, for general use—be it for recreation, personal defense, military or police—the same pre-World War I auto pistol cartridges have remained the rounds of choice for the vast majority of shooters and manufacturers.

Until really recently.

In the past few years, we have seen a tremendous flood of 10mm and 40-caliber pistols, at least here in the United States. Certainly, the trend to these new cartridges shows that something new and better has finally arrived, doesn't it?

Well, perhaps.

A 10mm cartridge of the early 1900s that looks almost identical to the 40 Smith & Wesson was described by R.K. Wilson in his 1943 book on automatic pistols. He speculated that it may have been adapted to an early Roth pistol.

It is reported by some that a 10mm Bergmann pistol was tested

and rejected by the British in 1902. Two different cartridges were provided. One was a high-velocity (10mm Lite?) round.

In 1903, Colt experimented with a 41-caliber pistol for U.S. government tests. About 1911, Colt also developed a 9.8mm cartridge for European military trials. In 1919, Birmingham Small Arms (BSA) in England produced a small number of experimental 40-caliber pistols. Interestingly, none of these efforts to introduce a pistol cartridge of about 40-caliber met with any success.

It will be interesting for our offspring to look at the automatic pistol scene after the first decade of the next century. Perhaps the new 10mm/40-caliber cartridges will truly dominate the pistol world. Perhaps they will be just a postscript. In either case, there is a strong chance that some of the cartridges developed by the end of the first decade of *our* century will still be around.   ●

Bibliography

Bady, Donald B. "The .45 ACP Cartridge" *American Rifleman*, Vol. 105, No. 3 (March 1957), p. 22-24, 68-69.

Bady, Donald B. "The Automatic Pistol in Denmark" *American Rifleman*, Vol. 107, No. 1 (January 1959), p. 19-21.

Bady, Donald B. *Colt Automatic Pistols*. Borden, Alhambra, CA: Borden, 1973.

Barnes, Frank C. *Cartridges of the World*, 4th Ed. Northfield, IL: DBI Books, 1980.

Betz, Col. W.R. "John M. Browning's FN Pocket Pistols, Part One" *American Rifleman*, Vol. 136, No. 3 (March 1988), p. 40-43, 80.

Browning, John, and Curt Gentry. *John M. Browning, American Gunmaker*. Doubleday & Co., 1964.

Dickey, Pete. "Steyr's Oldest and Newest Pistols" *American Rifleman*, Vol. 131, No. 3 (March 1983), p. 22-25, 71.

Ezell, Edward C. *Handguns of the World*. Harrisburg, PA: Stackpole Books, 1981.

Goodman, Roy G. "The .455 Webley & Scott Pistol" *American Rifleman*, Vol. 110, No. 5 (May 1962), p. 40-43.

Hatcher, Julian S. *Textbook of Pistols and Revolvers*. Plantersville, SC: Small Arms Technical Publishing Co., 1935.

Hogg, Ian V. *The Complete Illustrated Encyclopedia of the World's Firearms*. New York: A&W Publishing, 1978.

Hogg, Ian V., and John Weeks. *Pistols of the World*. San Rafael, CA: Presidio Press, 1978.

Minor, Elliott L. "Origin of .32 ACP Cartridge" *American Rifleman*, Vol. 118, No. 4 (April 1970), p. 60-61.

Nielsen, Finn I. "The Belgian Pistol Used by Denmark" *American Rifleman*, Vol. 118, No. 9 (September 1970), p. 64-65.

Olson, Ludwig. "The Controversial .45 Auto" *Rifle 105* (May-June 1986), p. 22-25, 61-67.

Rogers, Patrick F. "Colt's Early Automatic Pistols" *American Rifleman*, Vol. 132, No. 12 (December 1984), p. 28-31, 67-69.

Schroeder, Joseph J., Jr. "Bergmann Automatic Pistols" *American Rifleman*, Vol. 114, No. 10 (October 1966), p. 38-42.

Shimek, Robert T. "The .45s That Failed" *Guns & Ammo 1984 Handgun Annual* Vol. 1, No. 1, p. 102-105, 190.

Simmons, Donald M., Jr. "Smith & Wesson 35 Auto Pistols, A History for Collectors" *Gun Digest*, 30th ed. (1976), p. 144-153.

Smith, W.H.B., and Joseph E. Smith. *Books of Pistols and Revolvers*. Harrisburg, PA: Stackpole Books, 1968.

Sterett, Larry S. "Mars Automatic Pistols" *Gun Digest* 15th ed. (1961), p. 121-129.

Stewart, James B. "Bergmann System Military Pistols" *Gun Digest* 27th ed. (1973), p. 124-132.

by HAL SWIGGETT

HANDGUNS TODAY:

SIXGUNS AND OTHERS

A FEW CHANGES here and there—*modifications* may be a better way to say it—nothing really new except it's rejuvenated and beautifully done:

Navy Arms

SHOT Show booth #3361 (Dallas Convention Center, 1994) was a hotspot for wheel-gun enthusiasts. Val Forgett had on display his reproduction of the 1875 Schofield revolver. According to Roy Jinks' great book, *History of Smith & Wesson*, Major George W. Schofield put the ball in play in the spring of 1870. September 9th of that year, S&W sent him a Model 3 and 500 cartridges. At no charge.

The Major was impressed with Model 3, but felt it could stand improvement for cavalry use. A patent was issued to Schofield June 20, 1871. His first change? Move the barrel latch to the frame rather than on the barrel.

Schofield continued his work with the Model 3, but in the meantime the Ordnance Department adopted Colt's 1873. Schofield, a Colonel by then, made an appearance at the War Department informing them of his improvements in the Model 3. On September 8, 1874, S&W signed a contract to deliver 3000 Schofield revolvers to the U.S. Army at a cost of $13.50 each. On April 26, 1875, they received three of those 3000. Plus, by then the Army had placed an order for an additional 3000. There were a few modi-

fications later, but now you know how the Model 3 Schofield made it to 1875.

When this single action was dropped by the military, two dealers bought most of them. Many barrels were cut to 5 inches. Wells Fargo took a liking to those 5-inchers, as did General George Armstrong Custer and Jesse James.

Now, you can get a replica of the Cavalry 7-inch with military markings or 5-inch with Wells Fargo markings. Chamberings for both are 44-40 or 45 Colt. Plus all this background, thanks to *History of Smith & Wesson* by Roy Jinks.

Navy Arms' replica 1875 Schofield revolver is beautifully done in 44-40 or 45 Colt.

Swiggett and his new Signature Series shoulder holster, custom-built by American Sales. Each holster has Hal's signature.

Freedom Arms

Now it's the Model 555 in 50 Action Express (50 AE). Featuring a 325-grain bullet at 1400 fps, it is billed as an excellent cartridge for deer-sized game or as a backup when hunting dangerous game. Bullet diameter is .510-inch. Handgunners who thought they had everything now have another step to take. Barrel lengths are 4$\frac{1}{2}$, 6, 7$\frac{1}{2}$ and 10 inches, and it is offered in both Field and Premier Grade.

FA's lineup now includes Models 252 (22 rimfire), 353 (357 Magnum), 454 (454 Casull, 45 Colt or 44 Magnum) and 555 (50 AE). Is it complete? Only time will tell.

Another option from Freedom Arms that isn't often mentioned: my personal 4$\frac{1}{2}$ Premier Grade can be dressed any of three ways—454 (as it started out), 45 Colt or 45 ACP. A cylinder for each cartridge. I do not believe in shooting cartridges of less than chamber length. Sooner or later, those who do will find cases harder—or impossible—to extract. Trust me.

Always something new from FA. Now they offer their own 357 Magnum 180-grain bullet with two cannelures so it can be loaded for their M353 or conventional cylinders.

Colt

Hard times: Keeping their doors open and turning out fine products is a situation Colt has lived with for years. Their Python 357 Magnum will live forever with those of us who truly appreciate fine workmanship. This company's stainless steel Anaconda is hard on the Python's heels. First in 44 Magnum, with barrel lengths of 4, 6 and 8 inches, and now in a 6-inch 45 Colt. Fans of either cartridge haven't tried them all until a day with an Anaconda has been added to their education.

Thompson/Center

The 300 Whisper in T/C guns is leaving many of us awestruck. J.D. Jones, its inventor, feels the same way. Just yesterday, as this is written, he told me he had fired at least 15,000 rounds and still can't believe what happens.

The 300 Whisper is based on a 221 Fireball case expanded to accept 30-caliber bullets. It handles, graciously, anything from 125- to 220-grain bullets. J.D. named it "Whisper" because Sierra's 220-grain MatchKing leaves the muzzle at only 1020 fps. This makes it a highly efficient subsonic match round losing only 70 fps in its first 200 yards of flight.

Cor-Bon, distributor of 300 Whisper ammunition, says the 125-grain Nosler Ballistic Tips

Ruger

High-gloss stainless steel finishes, recreating the appearance of nickel-plated Old West revolvers of many peace officers, is "it" from Ruger this time around. They're far more durable, to be sure, than early-day plating. Blemishes and scratches can be restored to like-new by simple polishing and buffing. No more peeling.

Still preserving the "frontier" image, the Single-Six is also offered with fixed sights. This 22 rimfire comes with interchangeable LR and WMR cylinders and rosewood grips.

Blackpowder fans haven't been left out. Old Army, Ruger's cap-and-ball sixgun, is available with fixed sights, too. Their words, "The new fixed sight models, in both blued and stainless steel finishes, closely represent the appearance and function of those early revolvers, but with modern materials, technology and design features, such as steel music-wire coil springs."

Smith & Wesson

I have been working with two S&W 44 Magnums, both Model 629s—meaning stainless steel. Both with 8 3/8-inch barrels. One, the least used, is just that, a straight M629. The other has seen more than a little duty. The reason? It is their M629 Classic DX. A "huntin' handgun." My kind.

Topped with Redfield's three-ring mount and Bausch & Lomb's excellent 4x scope, it not only does a great job on the range, but in the field as well. To

prove it, I set up a hunt with Doug Luger, a fine professional hunter.

One of my "victims" was 15-year old Chris King who had never shot any handgun bigger than 22. The other, a Bandera, Texas, banker well-versed in handgunning. Chris, with a single shot, put his name on a right-handsome blackbuck antelope. After proving his ability on several small rocks, Banker Finley tagged two trophy axis bucks with as many shots. Neither did a lot for Winchester that day, so far as expending ammunition.

Rossi

A pair of right-handy 44 Special stainless steel revolvers are imported from Brazil by Interarms. They have 3-inch barrels, 8 inches overall, and weigh in at 27.5 ounces.

The Model 720 wears an adjustable, white-outlined rear sight with a red-insert ramp up front. The Model 720C—they call it "Covert Special"—is the same revolver, but with fixed sights and a shrouded hammer. This one is double-action-only.

Both are five-shot, feature a full-length ejector rod shroud and custom combat-style grips for positive, non-slip control.

Freedom Arms big 50 AE alongside their 22 rimfire shows the whole spectrum.

start at 2050 fps and 150-grain NBTs at 1850 fps. I can testify to their effectiveness. During SCI's Handgun Meat Hunt for the Needy on the fabulous Y.O. Ranch (deep in the heart of Texas), I had the privilege of guiding Ken French, a T/C honcho. He took three whitetails, two bucks and a doe, with three shots.

This is a proprietary cartridge invented by J.D. Jones. Factory Cor-Bon ammunition, loading dies and ammunition components are available through SSK Industries.

Effectiveness? Cor-Bon's 300 Whisper factory ammunition, out of 10-inch T/C pistol barrels, will usually exceed factory 30-30 ballistics in the same barrel lengths. With a lot less noise and recoil.

Short revolver fans haven't been left out by Colt. Here is their 4-inch Anaconda.

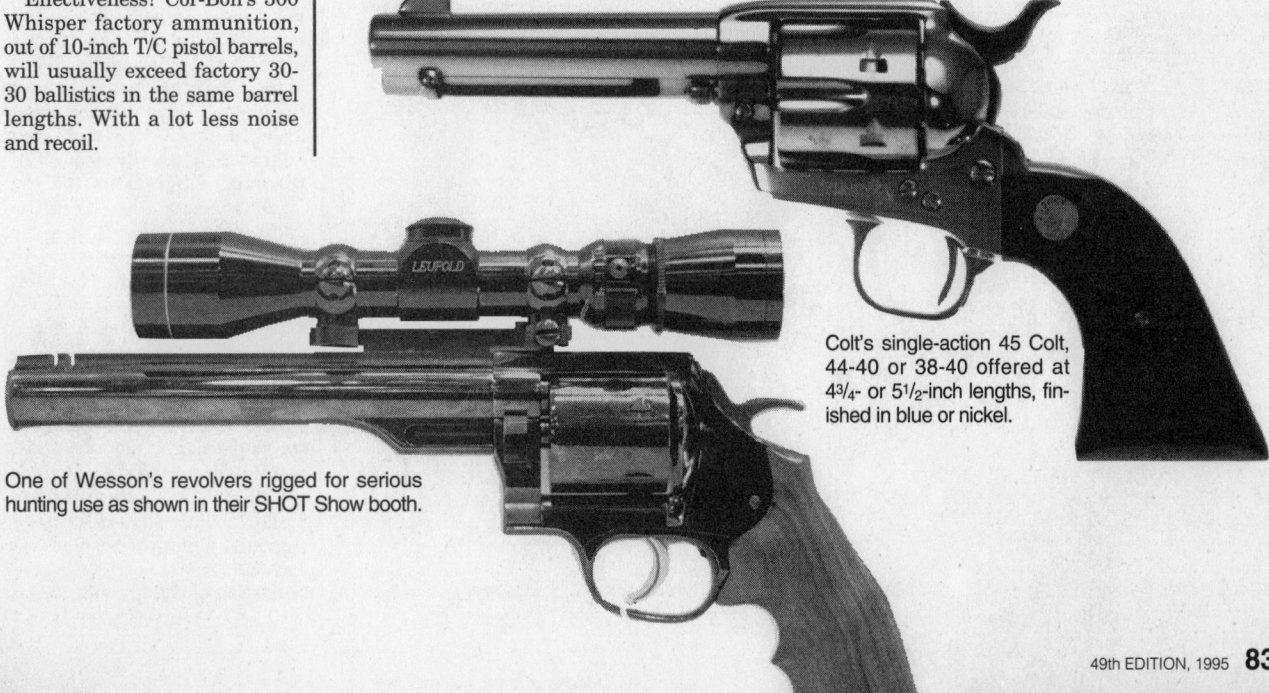

One of Wesson's revolvers rigged for serious hunting use as shown in their SHOT Show booth.

Colt's single-action 45 Colt, 44-40 or 38-40 offered at 4 3/4- or 5 1/2-inch lengths, finished in blue or nickel.

Mitchell Arms

Might as well get it in here: Mitchell Arms has dropped 44 Magnum from their line of single-action chamberings. The Bat Masterson Model has 4³/₄ inches of barrel and a nickel finish; the U.S. Army model has 5¹/₂ inches of barrel. Both offered in 357 Magnum or 45 Colt. Also dropped from this single-action line are adjustable sights. A pity.

North American Arms

This Utah-based company offers four mini single-action rimfire revolvers. Mini-Master has a 4-inch vent-rib-appearing barrel, adjustable rear sight and red insert ramp up front. Black Widow, same song and verses except with 2-inch barrel. Both are offered in 22 Long Rifle or WMR, or as a combo utilizing both cylinders.

Harrington & Richardson

So new it didn't make their catalog is H&R's Model 949 Classic Western Revolver. It is a nine-shot and features a "Western" look in spite of its double-action capability. There is a loading gate, shrouded ejector rod and authentic case-colored backstrap and frame.

Those of us admitting to remembering the 1950s, '60s and '70s notice the only difference is a transfer bar safety system. The original 949 was made from 1960 through 1985 and was called "Forty Niner."

New England Firearms

This company picks up a couple of the earlier Harrington & Richardson revolvers in 22 Long Rifle, 22 WMR and 32 H&R Magnum. Barrel lengths are 2¹/₂ and 4 inches. Their target-grade, heavy-barreled, adjustable-sight revolver is offered three ways: nine-shot 22 Short, Long or Long Rifle; six-shot 22 WMR; or five-shot 32 H&R Magnum. Models: Lady Ultra is 3-inch and 32 H&R Magnum; Ultra Mag is 6-inch and 22 WMR. Ultra is also a 6-incher but in 22 Short, Long or Long Rifle.

Taurus

Bigger and bigger. Both the company and its guns. This time they offer an all-new, big, heavy Model 44 44 Magnum, not an adaptation of anything

Whitetail dropped at 80-90 yards with a single shot from Ken French's 300 Whisper and the 125-grain Nosler Ballistic Tip.

(Right) The 300 Whisper, T/C's newest chambering, handles bullets from 125-grain to 220-grain. The case, designed by J.D. Jones, is a blown-out 221 Remington.

(Below) Ruger's New Model Blackhawk 45 Colt now in high gloss stainless finish, 4⁵/₈- or 7¹/₂-inch barrels.

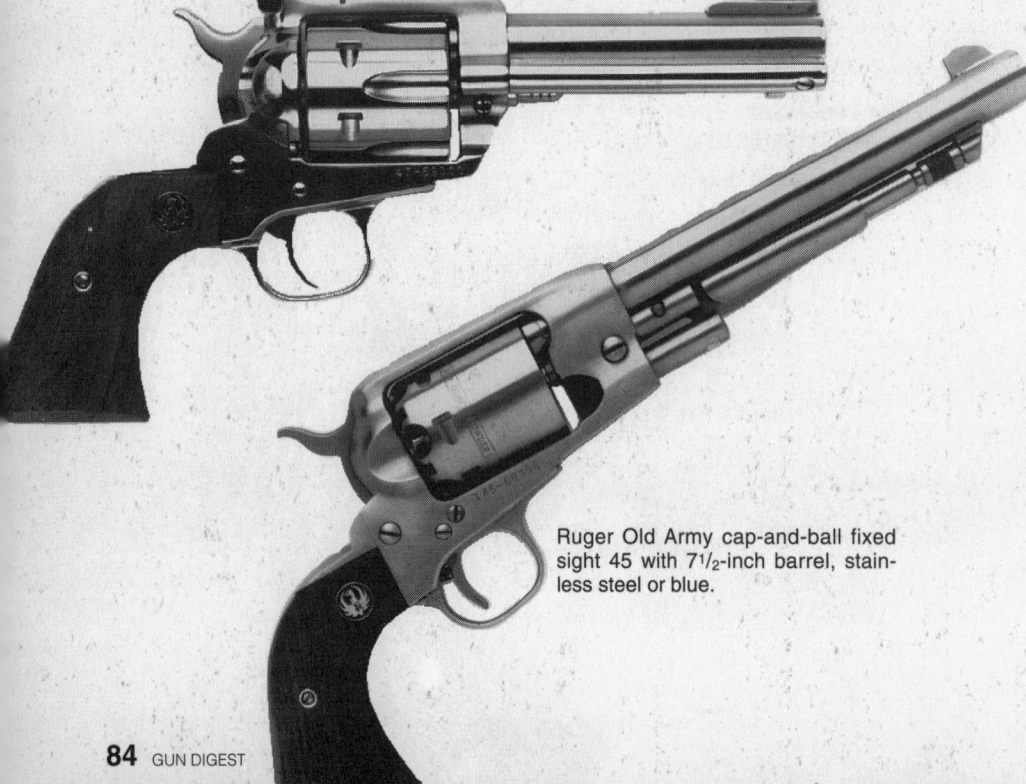

Ruger Old Army cap-and-ball fixed sight 45 with 7¹/₂-inch barrel, stainless steel or blue.

in their line. Three versions: 4-inch with a solid rib at 44³/₄ ounces and 6¹/₂- or 8-inch with vent ribs at 52¹/₂ or 57¹/₂ ounces. Double action and six-shot. Blue or stainless steel.

All three barrel lengths feature Taurus' integral compensating system which consists of two rows of four cylindrical ports cut into each side of the barrel's top surface to the immediate sides of the front sight. Their craftsmen relieve the barrel's rifled interior diameter to form an expansion chamber. This allows part of the expanding gas behind the bullet to escape. The result is that escaping gas pushes the muzzle down, resulting in reduced muzzle jump and felt recoil. Their catalog copy writer calls it "taking the 'ouch' out of firing these big bruisers."

Competitor

Al Straitiff and his Competitor single shot, cannon-breeched pistol have survived their growing pains. His centerfire 5mm cartridge and adapters for Remington's 5mm rifles are ready for marketing.

His list of chamberings totals 240 types. Barrels are inter-

Smith & Wesson's 8³/₈-inch stainless 44 Magnum took three trophy animals in a single day—a fine hunting handgun.

changeable, meaning one receiver takes any and all, and changing takes no more than three minutes. Two ambidextrous grips are offered—synthetic or laminated wood.

Charter Arms

Nick Ecker's newest is a slick little 38 Special Off Duty with no visible hammer. It is double-action-only, nickel, and with a Neoprene combat grip. One of CA's Bulldog Pug 44 Specials is a frequent companion of mine.

European American Armory

EAA's Big Bore Bounty Hunter single-action revolvers are offered in 4¹/₂ or 7¹/₂ barrel lengths and in 357 Magnum, 44 Magnum and 45 Colt. Finishes are blue, color case-hardened, chrome or blue/gold two-tone.

The Small Bore Bounty Hunter is offered with 4³/₄-, 6- or 9-inch barrel length, with two cylinders in 22 Long Rifle and 22 WMR. Finishes are blue or blue/gold two-tone. Grip options are rosewood micarta or ivory polymer. And, best of all, with a fully adjustable rear sight.

Texas Longhorn Arms

Bill Grover and his right-hand single action are truly off and running. A 40x100-foot, concrete-floored new plant, new equipment to keep a half-dozen full-time employees busy, corporate offices near Houston and a Texas flag flying over that new installation.

About his right-hand single action: it really is. It loads from the left side and its trigger edge is even with the right side of the trigger guard. Truly a right-hand sixgun. This, in itself, should prove Samuel

Colt was indeed left-handed. On Colt single-action revolvers, the trigger is flush with the left side of their trigger guard.

Ithaca

Here we go again. This time they tell me it's a "for sure."

This Model 20 single shot, change-barrel pistol has been kicking around for a long time. In fact, my collection includes one of the originals with an extra barrel.

Delivery will be with two barrels. Choice of length is 10 or 12 inches. One barrel will be 44 Magnum, the other 22 Long Rifle. Frames and barrels will

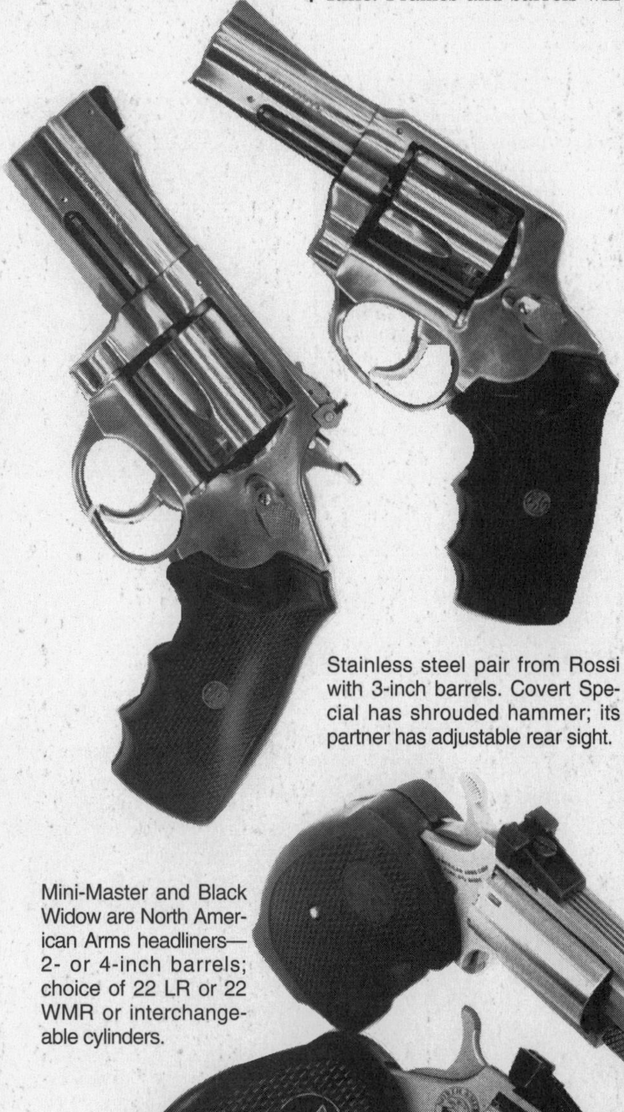

Stainless steel pair from Rossi with 3-inch barrels. Covert Special has shrouded hammer; its partner has adjustable rear sight.

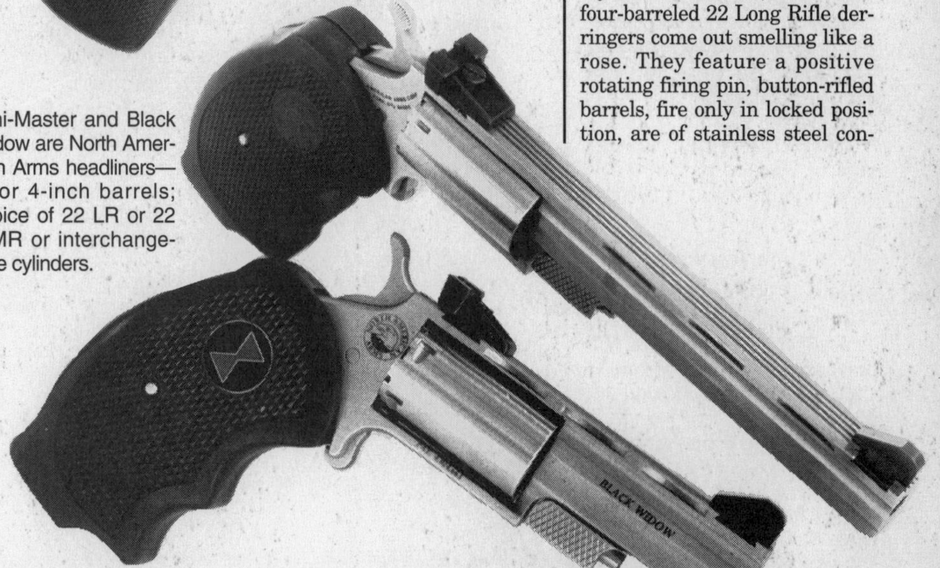

Mini-Master and Black Widow are North American Arms headliners— 2- or 4-inch barrels; choice of 22 LR or 22 WMR or interchangeable cylinders.

have a sandblasted, matte-blue finish. The ambidextrous grip and forend are of high-grade American walnut with satin finish.

Their literature, and their word to me eyeball-to-eyeball, agreed these would be available in June of 1994.

Sidewinder

Here we're talking b-i-g. Weighing in at 63 ounces, with its unfluted cylinder and 7¹/₂-inch barrel, this stainless steel 45 Colt/410 3-inch shotgun/45-70 digests a half-dozen of either with ease.

Its choke tube must be installed to effectively fire those 410 shotshells. The pattern, by the way, will surprise you. At 10 yards, using a 20-inch circle, patterns ran right at 90 percent. Amazing, to say the least. The tube must be removed before firing bullets.

Metallic cartridges, both 45 Colt and 45-70, provided acceptable accuracy. However, to get the most out of those, one must resort to handloads. It takes 300-grain bullets to obtain optimum results with the Sidewinder.

Recoil? Nil according to a trusted friend. This big revolver is so new I hadn't heard about it until talking, via AT&T, to that long-time friend. The above information came from him because time ruled out trying to get my hands on a Sidewinder, and I did want you to know about it. To find out more, contact Darvin Carda at D-Max, Inc.

HJS Derringer

Manufactured right here in my Lone Star state, these little four-barreled 22 Long Rifle derringers come out smelling like a rose. They feature a positive rotating firing pin, button-rifled barrels, fire only in locked position, are of stainless steel construction and would cost $1.44 to mail. Four and a half ounces at 23 Cents plus 29 cents for the first. Except that our post office department would frown on such action.

Length of this "little one" is 3^{15}/$_{16}$ inches, height 2^3/$_4$ inches and width ^{5}/$_8$-inch. HJS also catalogs a single shot 38 S&W or 380 Auto chambered single shot with those same dimensions.

Thunder Five

Big as this one is, there is very little to say about it. Other than the fact it weighs 49 ounces, has a 2^1/$_8$-inch barrel and a five-shot cylinder length of 3^3/$_{16}$ inches.

There are two models: one accepts 45 Colt or 3-inch 410 shotshells. The other shoots 45-70 cartridges. The frame, barrel and sight is one casting, including rifling. Single action trigger pull is the best feature at 40 ounces. Two and a half pounds.

About its cast-on-the-frame sights. My Oehler 35P front screen, at 8 feet, gave its all to a single 45 Colt shot. As for accuracy, I found 410 ^{1}/$_5$-ounce slugs best of all.

The 45-70 is built to accept only those factory cartridges loaded for older rifles such as trapdoor Springfields and not current 300-grainers loaded for modern firearms.

XL Single Shot Pistols

Manufactured by RPM barely outside Tucson, Arizona, these guns have had great success in silhouette shooting. They are off-shoots of the Merrill of a good many years back. One particular feature making them different than any other is a thumb-activated lever atop the left grip. This must be depressed before the pistol will fire.

Those interested in tiny groups "way out yonder" would do well to check out this single shot.

Cimarron Arms

Newest in this stable is the "Thunderer." Two versions: 3^1/$_2$- or 4^3/$_4$-inch, either modern blue or charcoal blue. Calibers are 45 Colt, 44-40, 44 Special and 357 Magnum.

Thunderer's frame and hammer are case-colored. Grips are smooth walnut with hand checkering available at a slight extra cost. These are Old Model (blackpowder) reproductions. Should you have access to an early issue, put them side by each other. It's great.

The owners discovered Houston's fast life wasn't all that great, so they moved to the heart of our Hill Country.

M.O.A.

Richard Mertz has added stainless steel to this "falling block" pistol line—both receivers and barrels. He has also gone dealer direct, pointing out at the same time, delivery averages about six months.

Another innovation is that extra barrels can be fitted to your receiver at the factory. Once fitted, they can be changed by the customer with a spanner wrench.

Lone Eagle

This single shot pistol comes from Magnum Research. Barrel length is 14 inches. Weight varies from 69 to 71. Caliber (chambering) makes the difference here. Barrels are Mil Spec chrome moly steel hardened to 26-32 Rockwell C. Breech and other components are heat-treated gun quality 4140 steel.

Davis Derringers

Derringers, little over/under pistols, are mighty handy "comforters." Davis Industries lists a 2.4-inch O/U in 22 LR, 22 WMR, 25 ACP and 32 ACP. Then there is a 2^3/$_4$-inch in 38 Special. And a lot more. All come in either chrome or black Teflon.

Harrington & Richardson's Model 949 is back. Through 1985, this one was cataloged as Forty Niner; for H&R 1871, it's a classic.

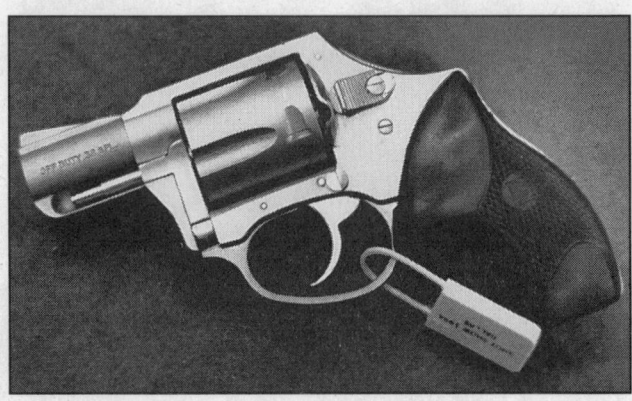

Charter Arms 38 Special 2-inch Off Duty is now offered with no visible hammer and nickel finish.

Cimarron Arms has added Thunderer to their authentic reproductions in 3^1/$_2$- or 4^3/$_4$-inch; choice of two finishes: modern blue or charcoal blue; chambered for 45 Colt, 44-40, 44 Special or 357 Magnum.

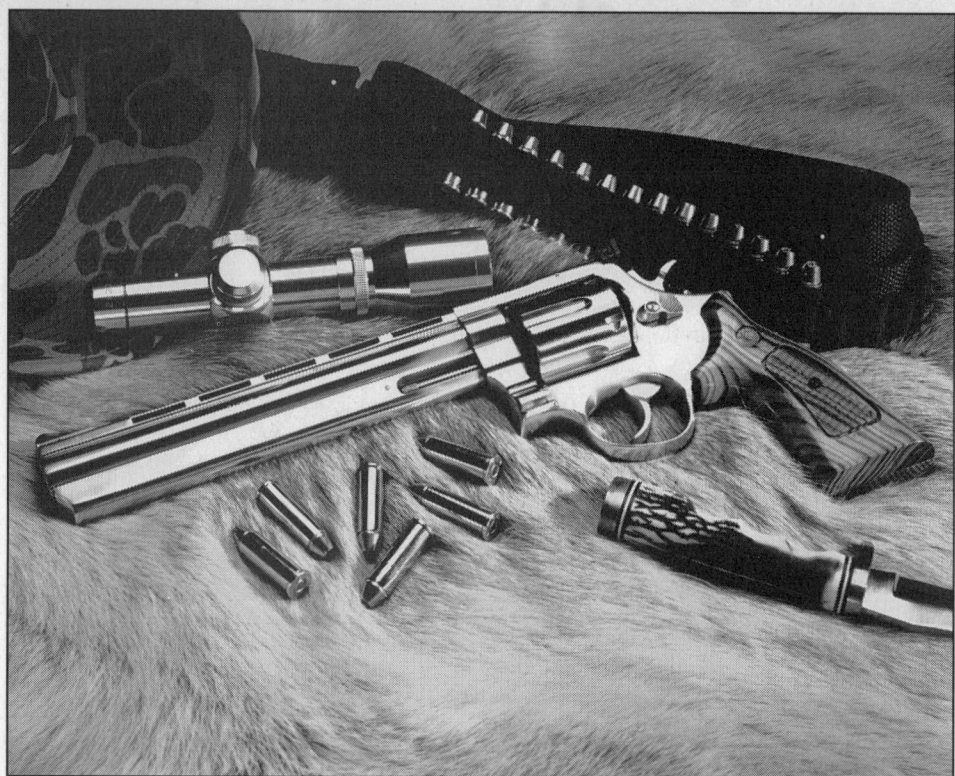

(Above) European American Armory's Small Bore Bounty Hunter provides an adjustable rear sight.

(Left) Bigger and better Taurus stainless steel 44 Magnums in 4-, 6½- or 8-inch barrel lengths. Taurus' integral compensating system is there, too.

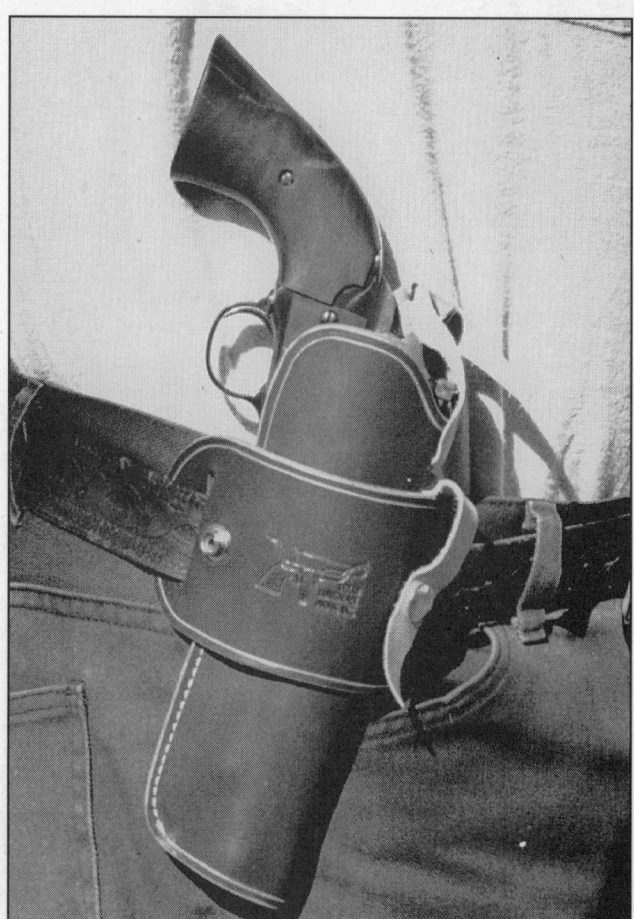

Bill Grover's (Texas Longhorn Arms) four-way holster can be worn right- or left-hand, and right- or left-hand crossdraw.

American Arms

Maybe best noted for fine shotguns, this company also imports five single-action revolvers (centerfire) plus four blackpowder cap and ballers.

There is a 4¾-, 5½- or 7½-inch 357 Magnum, 44-40 and 45 Colt. Then there is a 4¾-, 6- or 7½-inch Buckhorn, with or without adjustable sights. This last one is in 44 Remington Magnum/44 Special. One of the Regulator models offer a bird's-head grip.

Finishes are blue or bright nickel.

Cap and ballers include an 1847 Walker, 1851 Colt Navy, 1860 Colt Army and 1858 Remington Army. This last one is offered in both stainless steel or blue with brass frame. You really do need their catalog for details.

Bear Arms

How many times have you put three bullets into a 100-yard group measuring .192-inch center to center? It was a first for me. The cartridge? A 250 Savage Improved (Ackley). Steve Branham's highly customized XP-100 Remington (all that's still Remington is the action) wears a 16-inch heavy (.768-inch at the muzzle) barrel and a synthetic stock. Its scope is a Burris 2.5-7x in that company's mount.

My load? Nosler 100-grain Ballistic Tip over a hefty charge of H-414 and set off with a Winchester large rifle primer. Velocity? According to Ken Oehler's 35P, 2888 fps. A factory load, clocked at the same time, did 2329 fps. Actually my load does better than factory figures out of rifle barrels. My widest group out of Steve's pistol was .555-inch. Most were give or take halfway between. Yes, Steve's pistol is a shooter.

Hip-Grip

A right-handy little device is Barami's Hip-Grip. It replaces a short-barreled carry revolvers' regulation grips and is so designed to take advantage of the trouser belt. Recommended, according to their literature, for plain clothesmen, detectives, off-duty policemen, bank tellers, retail businessmen, truck drivers...any authorized citizen.

I first met these folks, the Barishes, at a NSGA show long years ago. Was among the first to put them in print and felt it time to do so again. It really is a handy item.

Signature Series Shoulder Holster

A new Signature Series shoulder holster designed by this writer is being marketed by American Sales & Mfg. Co. Weight of the hunting handgun is distributed between one shoulder and the belt. Plus, it is individually made for each order from top-grain leather and fully lined, to fit your specific model, barrel length, scope and mount. An outline drawing of your gun is requested along with your height, weight and shirt size. Truly custom made for each individual and with or without cartridge loops.

Semmerling LM-4

This one could have been up front because it comes from American Derringer, but there really is a reason for making it the finale.

Semmerling is a unique, pocket-size, 5.2x3.7x1-inch, pistol. It is chambered for 45 ACP, and though it looks like an autoloader, it really is a double-action manual repeater with five-round capacity fed from a magazine. The first round, carried in the chamber, is ready for instant use; the remaining four can be fired almost as fast as an autoloader by operating the slide with the opposite hand. This maybe sounds weird, but I've done it and it works. Fast.

I first met Bob Saunders, founder of American Derringer, around 1970. He walked through my door one morning, package in hand, and asked if I would consider making photographs for him to put together his first brochure.

The package contained a tiny 25 ACP autoloader. Admitting up front he had no financial backing, he hoped I would accept a pistol for payment. I assured him that wasn't neces-

sary. I would gladly help him get started with a few pictures.

When he came back to get the prints, he asked if I had a special serial number. Without thinking, I said, "13 sounds like a good number."

A few weeks later he walked in and handed me gun number 13. Then he disappeared for several years, surfacing, finally, in Waco, Texas. Sometime later, I noticed he had 45 Colt listed under his derringers. I asked him, "Have you ever made one in 45 Colt?"

"No, but I will if anyone ever orders one." With that I told him I would like to have one.

Maybe a dozen years had passed.

Sometime later, a package arrived and in it was my 45 Colt derringer—serial number

HJS four-barreled stainless steel derringer, Texas-made for 22 Long Rifle.

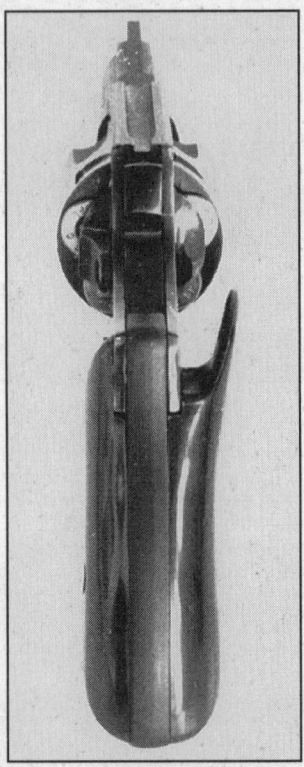

13. With it was a penned note on his letterhead and signed "Bob." It read, "Thanks Hal."

That was the Bob Saunders I knew.

He died in October of 1993. Elizabeth (Mrs.) Saunders heads the company and continues to offer all guns listed in his brochure. Including this Semmerling. ●

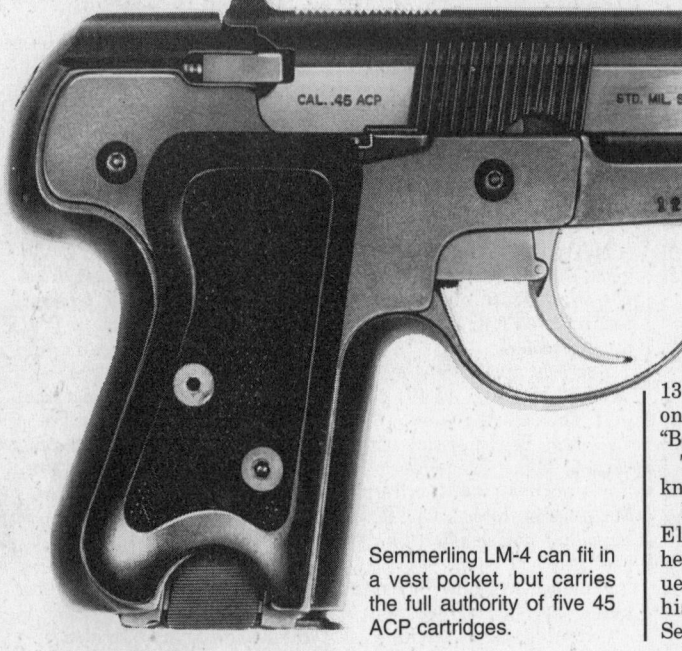

Semmerling LM-4 can fit in a vest pocket, but carries the full authority of five 45 ACP cartridges.

Hip-Grip, from Barami, is actually a handle holster for those who need a small handgun close by, but don't want holsters.

Davis Derringers added 32 H&R Magnum in two barrel lengths, 2³/₄ or 3³/₄ inches, and a choice of chrome or black teflon.

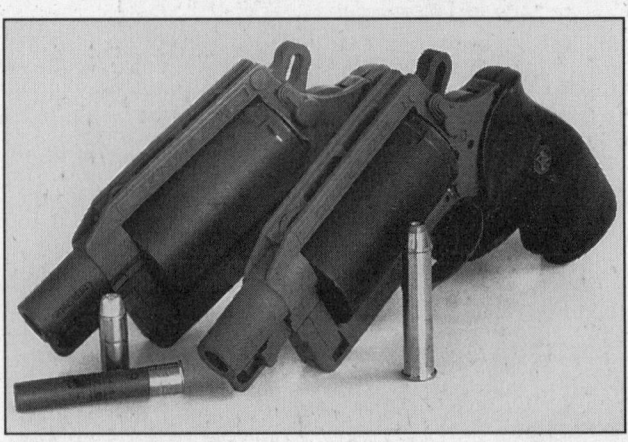

Thunder Five weighs in at 49 ounces with its 2¹/₈-inch barrel and five-shot cylinder. One model is chambered 45 Colt/410 3-inch. The other is 45-70.

by J. B. WOOD

HANDGUNS TODAY:

AUTOLOADERS

LET'S BEGIN WITH the biggest, the pistols in 50 Action Express. The first one, of course, was the Desert Eagle from **Magnum Research.** Now there are two more. **AMT** has the Mark V Automag, in stainless steel. **L.A.R.** has the blue steel Grizzly Mark V. I have fired both of these, and the recoil is substantial, but not as fierce as you might think.

Also new from **AMT** is a slightly enlarged DA-only Back Up in 45 ACP. As this was written, I have handled only a prototype, so I can't report on its shooting characteristics, but the increase in size is just enough to accommodate the larger round, and no more. The magazine will hold five rounds. As with all AMT pistols, the material is stainless steel.

In the same category—small pistols in large calibers—is the new 9mm **Kahr.** It is very small and flat, no larger than the average medium-frame 380 pistol. It's DA-only, all-steel, and is a true hammerless. The only external controls are a slide latch and the magazine release button. The single-line magazine holds seven rounds. They call it the K9, and it's a very neat little gun.

The news from **Colt** includes an item on their 9mm Model 2000—it has been dropped from the line and will be replaced by another pistol now in the design process. Meanwhile, they have produced a new pistol in 22 Long Rifle, the Cadet. It has the fine grip angle of the old Woodsman, stainless steel construction, and a heavy barrel with a ventilated rib. The price will be competitive. A remake of the Woodsman would have been *very* expensive.

Smith & Wesson has the Performance Center Compacts, in 9mm, 40 S&W and 356 TSW. Magazines hold ten rounds in the 40, and thirteen rounds in the other two. All will feature hand-fitted titani-um-coated spherical barrel bushings and oversize hand-lapped frame rails. Back by popular demand is the compact Model 4516 in 45 ACP. In the 22 department, the Model 41 has re-contoured walnut grips and a Millett rear sight. The Model 2206 also has a Millett sight and Herrett walnut grips.

There is also the S&W Sigma Series, real high-tech. They have twelve patent applications on these. The first will be a 15+1 40 S&W and a 17+1 9mm. Grip angle, frame design, and backstrap are all set up for quick target acquisition. The steel slide and polymer frame are both environment resistant.

The new P94 from **Ruger** is trimmer and lighter than the original pistols and is sized midway between the full-sized gun and the compact P93. In 9mm, the P94 magazine holds fifteen rounds, and the count is eleven in 40 S&W. The weight is 33 ounces. There is also a P94L, with an integral laser in a built-in housing that is part of the frame. The P94L is available only in 9mm. The usual options are offered—manual safety, DA-only, or decocker.

The big news from **Beretta** is the Model 8000, a compact DA in 9mm and 40 S&W that has a rotating-barrel locking system. It will be available in several variations—stainless steel, DA-only, and a conversion unit for the 41 AE cartridge. The Model 8000 in 9mm has a fifteen-round magazine, and ten rounds will fit in the 40 S&W. It is unlike any Beretta previously made, and the prototype I examined had a perfect feel in the hand. Also new from Beretta is the

The new Compact Baby Eagle from Magnum Research, here in matte chrome, with a frame-mounted safety-lever.

The Kahr K9—a very flat, compact seven-shot 9mm.

Model 98 with the resurrected name "Brigadier." In 9x21mm chambering for competition, it has a new slide configuration, with a pronounced swell at the locking point.

The **Heckler & Koch** USP, in 9mm and 40 S&W, is now available with nine different control arrangements—DA-only, decocker, left or right side, and six others. The built-in "rails" at the front of the frame allow easy mounting of

S&W's 356 TSW Compact; there are others in 9mm and 40 S&W.

The Olympic Arms re-make of the Whitney Wolverine is well under way. Here are two of the new frames.

A size comparison: The AMT 380 DAO Back Up and the new one in 45 Auto.

model of the precision-made and elegant **Coonan** 357 pistol. This year, there is the Classic from Coonan, with an integral compensated barrel and a fully adjustable rear sight.

The **Bersa** Thunder 9 has finally arrived from Argentina, and it was worth the wait. In 9mm with a fifteen-round drop-free magazine, it has ambidextrous controls and beautiful engineering. Don't be fooled by the moderate price—this is a high-quality piece. This remark also applies to the medium-frame Bersa pistols in 22 LR and 380 ACP. **Eagle Imports** is the U.S. agency.

Nationwide Sports Distributors now has the excellent 9mm **Daewoo** DP-51, the pistol with the unique triple-action firing system. New this year is a version in 40 S&W, the DH-40, with a 12+1 capacity. I have fired the 9mm version extensively, and its performance has been flawless. **ChinaSports** has the interesting 9mm Model 77B, with one-hand slide retraction via the movable front of the guard. I have also fired this one, and it works well.

From **Ram-Line**, there is a neat compact treatment of their 22 LR pistol. Called the Ram-Tech, it is offered with fifteen- or twenty-round magazines. The resurrection of the Whitney Wolverine by **Olympic Arms** is coming along, and they have tentatively re-named it the Partner. However, there is a chance they can call it the Wolverine, they say.

Phoenix Arms, maker of the old reliable Raven 25 ACP, has a new pair of pistols in 22 LR and 25, the HP-22 and HP-25. I have tried the HP-22, and I am

accessories, such as their new UTL (Universal Tactical Light). This is no ordinary flash light. It exceeds SOCOM requirements for full facial recognition at 25 meters.

Glock has the new Model 24, in 40 S&W, a long-slide competition pistol similar in design to the Glock 17L. It will be offered in compensated and non-compensated versions. Both will have factory-installed competi-

tion triggers and drop-free magazines. The drop-free magazine feature is also now available on all models.

Browning is now offering the venerable Hi-Power in 40 S&W chambering. I would imagine there are plans to have the BDM in this caliber sometime in the future. The compact PT-908 from **Taurus** now has a big brother, the PT-945 in 45 ACP chambering, and it is only slight-

ly larger than the 9mm version. At **Magnum Research**, the Baby Eagle (earlier known, elsewhere, as the Jericho) is now available in a nice little compact version.

European American Armory has the **Astra** A-75 in an aluminum-frame version that weighs only 23 ounces. It's in 9mm or 40 S&W, and measures 6$\frac{1}{2}$x4$\frac{1}{2}$ inches. Last year in this space I noted that there is a compact

Springfield's XM4 high-capacity 1911A1 comes now in 9mm or 45.

The Laseraim Series I, this one in 45 ACP chambering, offers real high-tech machining.

Here's HK's USP with their Universal Tactical Light mounted, one of nine combinations.

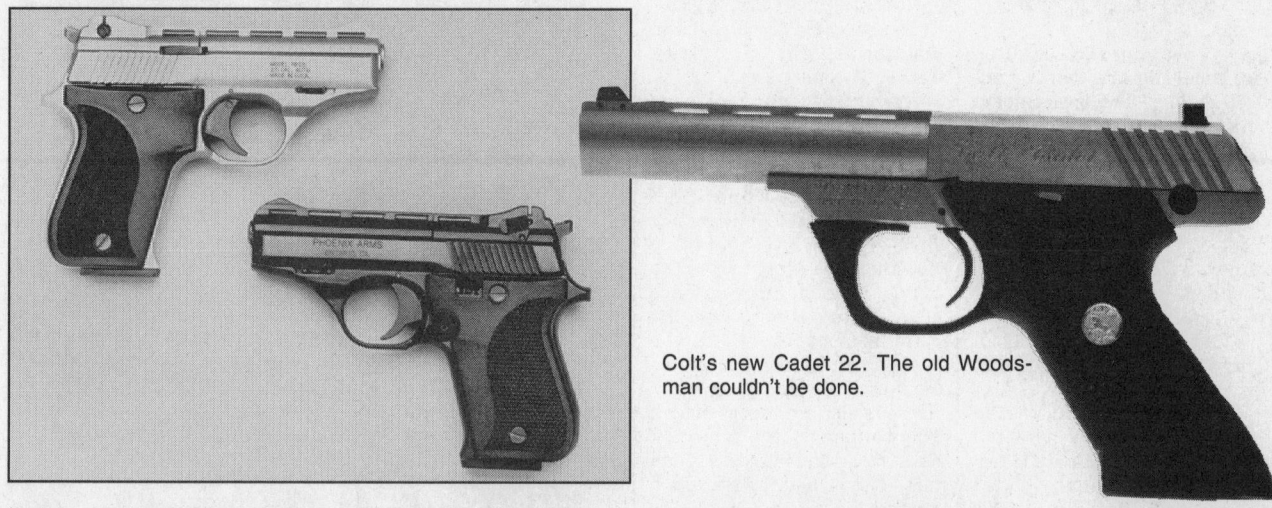

In satin nickel and blue, the HP-25 and HP-22 pistols from Phoenix Arms.

Colt's new Cadet 22. The old Woodsman couldn't be done.

Beretta's Model 8000, for cops first, in 9mm and 40 S&W, has a rotating-barrel lock.

S&W's new ergonomic Sigma will come in 9mm and 40 S&W.

This is S&W's Model 2206 target pistol—Millet sights, Herrett grips.

MKS Supply's JS series includes this eight-shot 9mm called, at 32 ounces, the Compact Polymer.

Ruger's KP94 is mid-sized and comes in six versions in 9mm and 40 S&W.

Ruger's KP94 Laser Pistol in 9mm (only) has the laser built into the frame.

amazed that this excellent little gun retails for less than a hundred dollars. The satin-nickel version looks exactly like stainless steel.

Springfield, Incorporated, has announced a new GM-pattern pistol, the XM4. Its frame is made of a tough polymer called Xanex, and the slide and the moulded-in rails are stainless steel. In 9mm, the capacity is 18+1, and in 45 ACP, it's 13+1. There are numerous "custom" features in the design.

I am glad to report the return of one of my personal favorites, the **Bernardelli** pistol that was originally called the P018. It's now the P. One. Though its external look is a little different, it still has all of the good original features. Among these are the forged steel frame, slide and barrel. The frame rails are full-length, and the ergonomics are outstanding. It is also now available in 40 S&W. The U.S. agency is **Armsport**.

J.O. Arms of Houston, Texas, is now offering the Kareen and Barak pistols made by **KSN Industries** in Israel. These are in 9mm and are essentially the good old Hi-Power with a few custom features. The Barak is a compact version. A 40 S&W chambering will soon be available.

KBI, Incorporated, still has the good 9mm pistols from Hungary, based on the Hi-Power, in SA and DA versions. A

45 ACP chambering is now offered, the GKK-45. The tiny and beautifully made PSP-25 is still available. The newest addition is a commercial-grade Makarov from Russia, in 9x18mm or 380 ACP chamberings.

A while back, **Emerging Technologies**, the Laseraim people, bought **Wyoming Arms**. The pistol was extensively re-designed (I was involved in this), and it emerged as the Laseraim, in three versions. The Series I has an extended dual-port compensator and a distinctive slide top with five lightening cuts that also serve to cool the barrel. The chamberings are 45 ACP and 10mm, and the material is stainless steel. The lower front of the frame has built-in laser-mounting rails. There is also a compact model. The workmanship is superb. I have put a lot of rounds through these pistols, and their function is perfect.

Nehemiah Sirkis has re-designed his small 9mm DA-only pistol for **Intratec**, and their name for it is the Category 9. It has an 8+1 capacity, and weighs only 18 ounces. A true hammerless, it is striker-fired and has a sliding trigger. I have not had an opportunity to try it, but it seems to be a neat little package.

From **Century Arms**, the Czech Model 52 is now also available rechambered to 9mm. An armorer's kit is offered for the Model 52, containing every part for the pistol (in various quantities) except the frame and slide. They also have the East German Makarov in 9x18mm, and the Argentine-licensed copy of the Hi-Power. On all of these, the prices are very reasonable.

MKS Supply has a new compact 9mm lightweight in their line of moderately priced guns. The JS-9mm Compact Polymer weighs just 32 ounces. It is single action, hammerless, and the capacity is 8+1. The new grip has a nice contour, and the gun has low-profile three-dot sights.

For those who liked the sturdy little 25-caliber external-hammer pistols from **F.I.E.** and **Excam**, a slightly re-designed (and slightly smaller) version is now available from **Heritage Manufacturing**. It is offered in a standard model (H25B), all blue with smooth wood grips, or a fancier one (the H25G), with gold-plated small parts and checkered wood grips. ●

JOSEPH SZECSEI'S

Fabulous Repeating Double Rifles

by HOLT BODINSON

From the top: No. 1, an over/under four-shooter in 375 H&H Magnum; No. 4, an over-under four-shooter in 9.3x64mm with one-piece bolt; No. 3, another four-shot 9.3x64mm over/under; No. 2, a side-by-side 375 H&H Magnum, one-piece barrels rifled by EDM, set up with dual-magazines to make it an eight-shooter.

THEY WERE NEW. They were radical. And gunmakers at the 1993 Reno-based Safari Club International and American Custom Gunmaker's Guild shows flocked to see Joseph Szecsei's SCI exhibit of his remarkable repeating double rifles.

Joseph Szecsei (pronounced Seh-chay) is not your typical gunmaker. Born in Hungary and displaced by World War II, he wandered the world taking odd jobs before finally emigrating to Canada in 1951, where he found work as a tool and die maker with the Ford Motor Company. Gunmaking had always been his passion, but not his profession, and Szecsei can spin yarns for hours about his youthful confrontations with the Hungarian security police who did not care one whit for his homemade bolt-action and break-open 22s. There were also conversions of military rifles into shotguns—all, by the way, machined on a self-built metal lathe, the loss of which Szecsei regrets to this day.

After five years with Ford, young Szecsei opened his own tool and die shop in Windsor, Ontario, to carry out contract work for the automotive industry. The business proved highly successful and expanded into a major stamping operation, where today Szecsei fabricates as many as eighteen major components for Ford's mini-vans series.

Economic success brought with it the leisure time to enjoy big game hunting. It was an incident in 1989, during a hunt in the Zambezi Valley of Zimbabwe, that challenged Joseph Szecsei to make a creative jump in double rifle design. The actual circumstances were not all that unusual for an elephant hunt. He was shooting a Heym over/under double rifle in 458 at the time. Having fired both barrels at a trophy bull, which dropped to the shots in dense brush, Szecsei broke open his gun and looked down at the deep breech to load two more cartridges. During those critical seconds when his eyes were off the potentially explosive scene in front of him, and with an unloaded rifle in his hands, he was charged by a yet-unseen bull and then another. Had it not been for the fast footwork and warning shots of his professional hunter, Szecsei is convinced he would have returned to Canada in a casket.

But "what if," he thought, a way could be found to combine the best features of a double rifle with those of a bolt-action repeater. It was an intriguing thought, and upon returning to Canada, this craftsman and inventor began to transform a radical concept into reality in the environment of a highly sophisticated tool and die shop. At his command were state-of-the-art computer-operated machine tools and the programmers necessary to turn rough requests into metal parts. Szecsei observed that if he needed a barrel band, bolt, rear sight, sear or firing pin, he need only describe it to his young computer whizzes and it would be made. By dramatically reducing the time it took to turn ideas into finished parts, the creative side of Joseph Szecsei had free reign, and

by 1994 he had produced seven of his repeating double rifles—each one distinctly different—and is now working on designs number eight and nine.

The heart of Szecsei's designs is a compact, two cartridge-holding bolt that locks up in the rear through a rotating interrupted thread "cannon breech" (although in the latest design, No. 7, the interrupted thread-type lugs have been replaced by three conventional solid lugs). The double bolts have two firing pins, two independent sears activated by two separate triggers. The latest trigger design in rifle No. 7 adds an interlink that actually pulls the sear down and out of engagement in a foolproof and positive manner. A Greener-type half-round through-bolt safety locks both sears and triggers.

The over/under and side-by-side

designs have integral magazines, although Szecsei used detachable magazines in side-by-sides Nos. 2 and 7. As built with integral magazines, the over/unders take one round in the chamber and one in each well of the side-loading, hinged magazine, providing four shots with one stroke of the bolt. The side-by-sides accept one round in chamber and two in each well of the bottom-loading magazine, providing the hunter with six shots with two strokes of the bolt. The No. 7 detachable magazine-fed side-by-side in 416 Remington, pictured and currently under construction, holds three cartridges in each magazine, giving eight shots with three movements of the bolt.

The extractors on the bolts are similar to Sako design, and both fixed and spring-activated pin ejectors have been used in the various

This is the No. 4 and its locking lugs, one-piece bolt, double triggers and in-the-stock safety.

Massive double bolt of the No. 6 rifle is seen here picking up and chambering two 458 Winchester Magnums at once.

rifles. Szecsei favors pin ejectors because of the positive spring-loaded force they provide to the ejection cycle. As might be expected, the extraction/ejection process is non-selective. If you fire only one barrel and retract the bolt to reload, both a fired and an unfired round are ejected simultaneously. In practical hunting terms, it's not even a consideration given the firepower inherent in the design.

An intriguing design feature Szecsei has incorporated into the extraction cycle is a threaded gas port plug. If for any reason extreme pressures were experienced and extraction became difficult, the threaded gas port plug can be removed, providing sufficient access to the extractor so it can be held solidly against the case rim. This ensures it does not ride over the rim or rip through the outer edge of the rim when the bolt is forcefully withdrawn.

The receivers and bolts have been machined from pre-hardened steel, bringing the completed weights of the seven rifles built to date to between ten and twelve pounds. Szecsei indicates he would like to lower those weights and is currently building rifle No. 9—a 7mm Remington Magnum/458 Winchester Magnum over/under—using titanium. Converting the receiver and bolts to titanium, Szecsei calculates he will be able to reduce the weight of those components by 40 percent, double their strength over steel, and still achieve a Rockwell hardness of about 32 to 36. Again, he has the machine tools to do it.

Double rifle barrels and their regulation has always been the "black art" of double gun manufacture—not so, though, in the more modern designs that dispense with solid ribs and have two independent barrels adjusted by various methods. As clearly illustrated here in rifle No. 7, Szecsei typically incorporates an adjusting ring/clamp around the barrels that can be tightened or loosened using three screws to converge the points of impact of both barrels. The dovetailed sleeves at the muzzles are also part of the adjusting system. Accuracy? Three to four inches at 100 meters is the norm. And as big game hunter Szecsei likes to point out, such performance is very sufficient for dangerous game at close ranges. Nevertheless, he is intrigued with the prospect of chambering the

A home shop for a fellow like Joseph Szecsei includes lathe, mill, surface grinder and perhaps anything else he wants.

No. 7 is an eight-shooter side-by-side in 416 Remington Magnum, and Szecsei works on it himself at home when he can.

The classic view of the big-bored double rifle is backed up here by six more quick shots, available with three strokes of the bolt in Szecsei's No. 7 rifle.

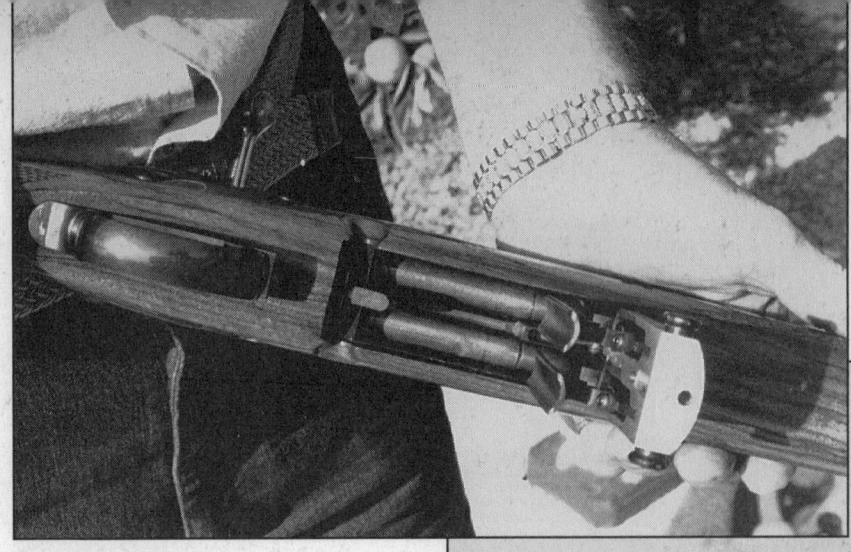

The No. 5 design loads from the bottom—just pop the cover and drop 'em in.

Two 458s in the side magazine of the No. 6 design, an over/under.

Joseph Szecsei and a Hungarian boar which fell to his No. 2 rifle—a 375 H&H Magnum.

Bodinson (left) found the Szecsei rifles soundly built and balanced.

rifles for lighter hunting calibers and tightening their accuracy requirements.

An interesting sidelight to Szecsei's barrel experiments is that the most accurate barrel he ever produced was the No. 2 375 H&H which was machined from one piece of steel and rifled using the EDM process. And though Joseph is normally very open about discussing his designs, rifle No. 8 remains somewhat of a secret. The most we can say is that it will be a repeating drilling in calibers 500 Jeffery and

223 Remington. Just think about that for a moment.

Although slightly unconventional in appearance, every one of Szecsei's rifles balances nicely and handles well. The bolt throws are extremely short and fast. As impressive as the unique designs of these double rifles is their execution. The quality of the intricate machining is simply remarkable.

And he doesn't want to manufacture them!

While Szecsei holds worldwide patents on his designs, he is not the

least bit interested in blending gunmaking with automotive parts production. Gun design has been a challenging and relaxing hobby, and he wants to keep it that way. So he is actively interviewing the established gunmaking firms (largely European) that are beating a path to his door to secure licensing and manufacturing rights.

He's an interesting man with a remarkable series of thoroughly original designs. Will we one day be able to buy a Szecsei repeating double rifle? One can only hope. •

THEN.

• **Strength of the same, proven Mauser-type action.** This design is considered by many the most reliable of all bolt actions ever made.

(Cutaway view)

• **Positive ejection with the original blade-type ejector.** No other system gives you more control. Pull slowly to simply pluck the round from the action. Open the bolt quickly for clear ejection. The blade ejector relies on no springs or mechanical parts so it's extremely reliable.

MODEL 70 · PRE-'64

The Return of the Pre-'64 Type Model 70.

Top: Original Pre-'64 Model 70 serial number 487982.
Bottom: Today's Model 70 Classic Featherweight.

After 30 years the classic rifle of all time is back... because it's better.

The original Pre-'64 Model 70 earned a following unmatched by any other rifle design ever. No rifle has ever earned the affection of more gun experts, target shooters and serious hunters than the Winchester Model 70.

"The Rifleman's Rifle."

When you compare the features found on the original with the new "Classic" Model 70 you'll see all the features that inspired gun writers to call it "The Rifleman's Rifle." Claw extractor, controlled round feed, blade-type ejector and cone-to-breech design. Plus you'll notice a level of quality manufacturing and tight tolerances that, in many cases, exceeds that found on the originals. Today's new "Classic" Model 70s with Pre-'64 type actions are better than ever before.

It's been nearly 30 years since the last of the original Model 70s left the Winchester firearms factory. And there's never been a Winchester that more people asked to have back. Well, now they're back, and better than ever. So don't hesitate to get your own piece of the Model 70 legend.

• **Same controlled cartridge feed that made the original standard equipment for Africa-bound hunters.** The moment the cartridge leaves the lips of the magazine it engages between the claw of the bolt. Gravity plays no part. The claw is always guiding the cartridge with your rifle in any position—a confidence advantage, especially when hunting dangerous game.

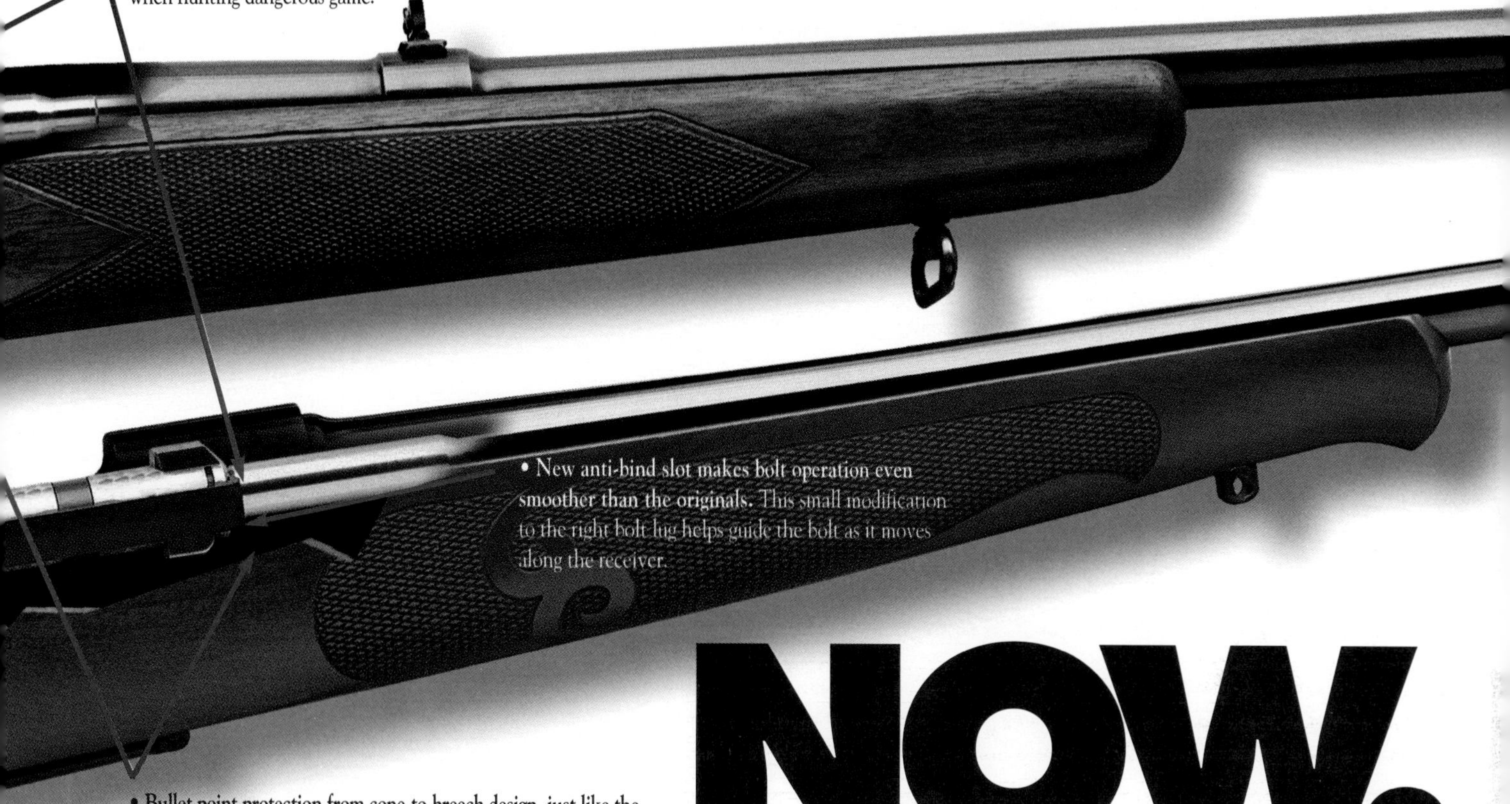

• New anti-bind slot makes bolt operation even smoother than the originals. This small modification to the right bolt lug helps guide the bolt as it moves along the receiver.

NOW.

• **Bullet point protection from cone-to-breech design, just like the originals.** As a bullet enters the chamber it is guided into the chamber without risking damage to the exposed lead point. Flawless points assure a higher level of accuracy with all bullet shapes.

Pre-'64 type action or push feed design. Your choice.

One big advantage you couldn't get with the originals is a choice between the new Pre-'64 type action on all new "Classic" models and our proven push feed action design. Both have superb performance records and possess accuracy coveted by shooters world-wide. The push feed — with its base-surrounding bolt face design — lends itself better to certain calibers. Both are available in more stock styles, calibers and configurations to match many more needs than ever before. In fact, you can choose from over 140 different Model 70 specifications — because when it comes to serious hunting and shooting, not just any rifle will do.

Model 70 Classic Stainless (also available in push feed design)

Model 70 Classic Featherweight (also available in push feed design)

NEW CALIBER 284 Win.

Model 70 Classic DBM (also available in push feed design)

Model 70 Ranger

Model 70 Lightweight

WINCHESTER ®

For a free catalog write: U.S. Repeating Arms Company, Dept. V027, 275 Winchester Ave., New Haven, Connecticut 06511-1970. Winchester is a registered trademark licensed from Olin Corporation.

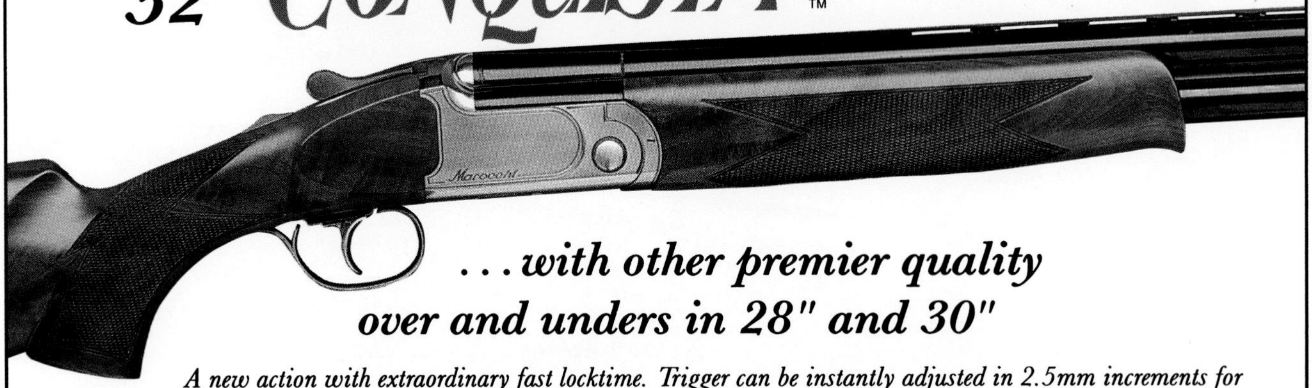

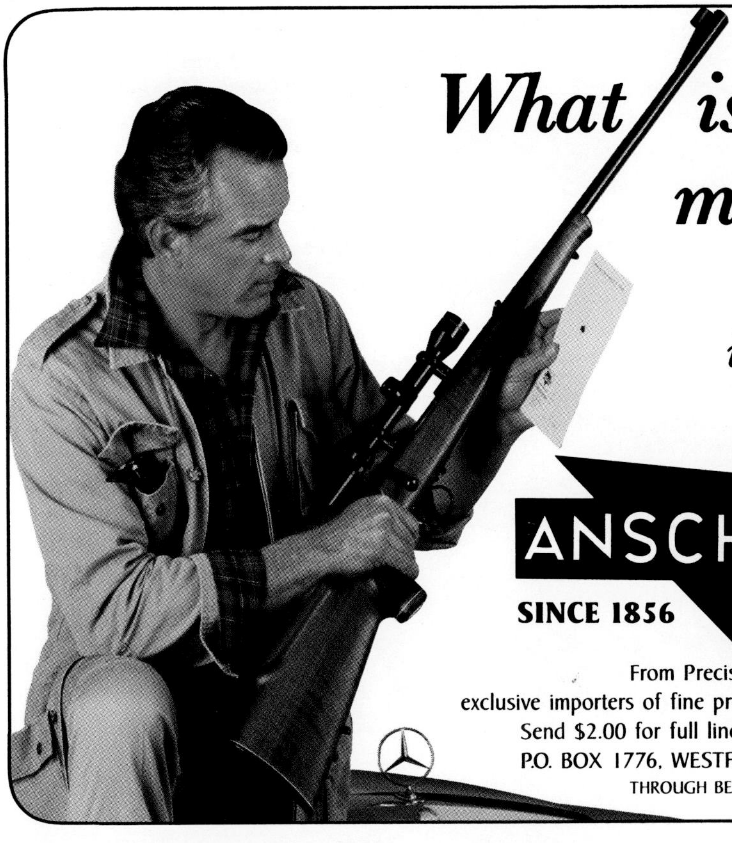

A Modern TRAIL GUN

by C.E. Harris

An old pattern and a new cartridge make a great Ruger

SMITH & WESSON coined the term "Outdoorsman's Revolver" to describe shorter, lighter versions of adjustable-sighted target guns. They were built to use high-velocity cartridges for flatter trajectory and greater killing power than standard target loads. The K-22 had recessed chambers for use with 22 Long Rifle high-velocity ammunition. The N-frame 38/44 was similarly designed for high-velocity 38 Special (now +P). Both were marketed under the S&W "Outdoorsman" trademark in the 1930s. Neither were lightweights. The K-22 was the heaviest 22 rimfire revolver of its era, at 36 ounces. The 38/44 Outdoorsman weighed as much as a Colt 45 Single-Action Army with 7½-inch barrel—42 ounces.

Since World War II, the trend has been to produce smaller and lighter trail guns. The logic behind this was that greater portability was worth a minor sacrifice in ballistics and hitting ability. Actually, I don't care to give up either. Why can't a compact revolver be accurate, rugged, reliable, flat-shooting and hard-hitting? There is no technical reason why not. People have spent their entire lives in search of the perfect trail gun. For me, the search is over. It's a Ruger 4⅝-inch 32 Magnum Single-Six. Let me tell you why.

The J-frame Smith & Wesson 22 Kit Gun, Ruger Bearcat and Single-Six first appeared in the late 1950s, and typify today's popular image of a rimfire trail gun. I've tried them all. While they are handy and accurate, a 22 simply lacks authority for animals as large as a woodchuck, my performance standard. The Smith & Wesson 38 Chief's Special has served me well for such use for over twenty

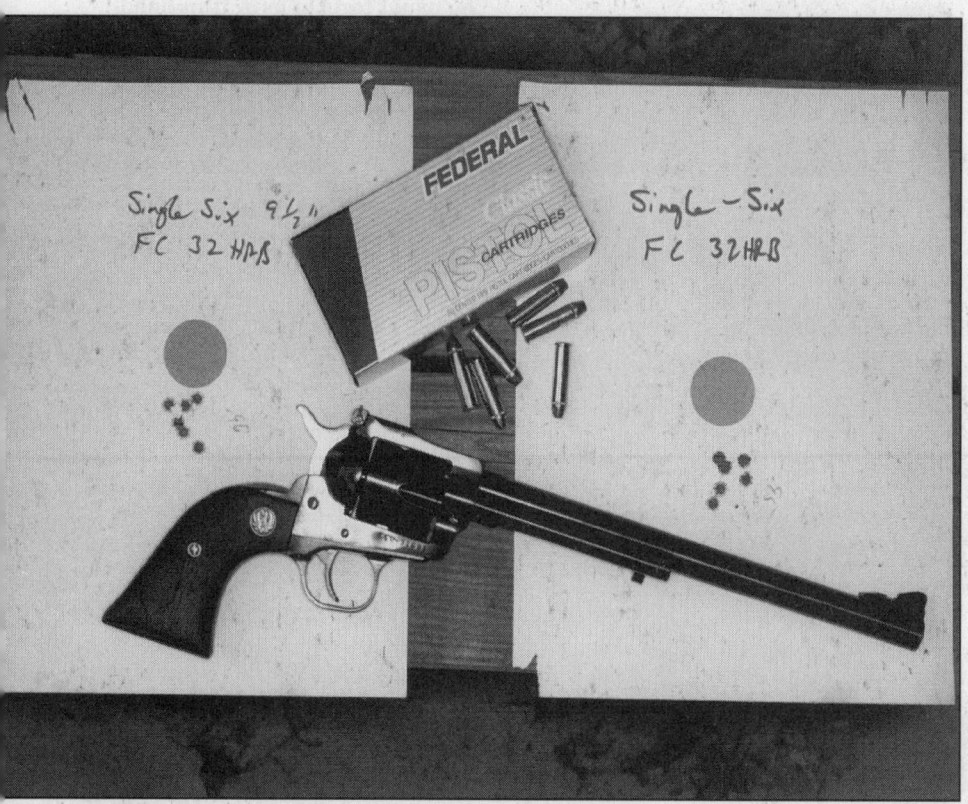

Harris started with Ruger's longest barreled 32 H&R Magnum, which shot groups like these with Federal ammo at 25 yards.

years. I've worn out two of them and am now on my third. I do like the gun, but it lacks ruggedness. My current Chief's is a 3-inch heavy, full-lugged barrel with adjustable Kit Gun sights, and is the most accurate example of the model I've ever owned. If the Chief's were more sturdy and flatter shooting, it would be perfect.

The Ruger SP101 appears suitable, certainly sturdy enough, but is about a quarter-pound too heavy. It is certainly accurate enough for defense, but neither the 38 nor the 32 Magnum versions I fired were accurate enough for small game. A friend's SP101 in 9mm is quite accurate. His happens to shoot dead on with his favorite load and has potential. But too much is left to luck here for me to plan on it if I buy one. Adjustable sights are available on the 22- and 32-caliber SP101 models, which are a help. But in my experience, the gun is less accurate than the Single-Six in the same caliber. The Single-Six also has the advantage of being substantially less expensive.

I have not found a centerfire semi-auto pistol which I consider really suitable for trail use. I have no use for a handgun for field use unless it is accurate enough for hunting small game. To me, this means being able to average 2-inch or better, five-shot groups at 25 yards, hand-held, with factory iron sights, from a supported field position. It's easy to find a handy, accurate revolver. Almost any decent 38 Special will shoot 2-inch groups with factory wadcutters. Find me a semi-auto that does this, with a handload I can make, which weighs two pounds or less, costs less than $300, and you may change my mind, but I don't expect a line to form soon.

It's true that quality 22 semi-autos, such as the Ruger, easily meet this accuracy standard, and the new composite-framed KP-4 is certainly light enough. But the power of a 22 rimfire is still marginal. Accurized 38 and 45 target guns have enough power and accuracy, but are about 10 ounces too heavy for a field gun. An alloy-framed accurized Colt Commander is as close as I ever got, but I gave the gun away to a friend going overseas, and never saw it again.

Accurate and light revolvers are common, digest a variety of ammunition without fuss, and don't scatter brass all over. This makes them

One 2-pound solution Harris knows well is a 3-inch Chief's Special in 38, a speedloader and a few rounds.

highly attractive for trail use. I'd like to explain some background here.

In 1977, I wrote in *American Rifleman* that a "basic load" of trail handgun and ammunition should not exceed 40 ounces. Those parameters made sense to Ken Warner when he edited my original manuscript then, and I think they still do. Today, my preference leans toward limiting the weight of the handgun/ammunition package, minus holster, to 2 pounds, for short trips. Of course, you can easily carry a heavier gun and ammunition when on horseback or while driving a vehicle than when on foot. The duration of an outing is probably the determining factor, because while a revolver and a dozen rounds are usually adequate for a day or weekend trip, a box of fifty is more reassuring on a longer trek, or if you intend to do some practicing.

As I enter my mid-40s, a heavy sidearm is an obvious nuisance. I would rather have the firearm readily available without being constantly reminded by gravity that it is there. This feeling severely reduces the utility to me of cartridges more powerful than the 38 Special. If you opt for a 22, you get reduced weight and

bulk, but also give up a lot in performance, so a compromise is needed.

The usual targets for a trail handgun are small game, but I prefer the chosen round also be adequate for the occasional marauding larger varmint, such as a feral dog, rabid fox or raccoon, and also have reasonable potential for defense use. I don't live in bear country, so energy comparable to the 38 Special is entirely adequate, about 200 to 250 foot pounds.

Some people, Ken Warner among them, feel the 22 WMR makes sense as a trail gun. Personally, I dislike its sharp report and the cost of its ammunition, which exceeds that to assemble a more effective cast-bullet handload in a larger centerfire. The accuracy of the 22 WMR from a handgun is generally inferior to the 22 Long Rifle.

The 38 Special is close to ideal for the trail handgun. It has ample power and accuracy, and there are a variety of excellent factory loads. The cartridge is easy to reload and is available everywhere. Wadcutters, +P lead hollowpoints and shotshells provide a good basic ammunition mix. My current Model 36 heavy barrel weighs 24½ ounces. When carried with two Speer shotshells and three wadcutters in the

Another 2-pounder is an old Colt Woodsman and a box of cartridges—handy, shoots good, but it's a 22 rimfire.

cylinder, plus two spare speedloaders (one each of 148-grain wadcutters and 158-grain lead hollowpoint +P), the package weighs only 2 pounds, without holster. That's the same as a pre-war 4½-inch Sport Model Colt Woodsman with one magazine and a paper box of Long Rifles!

However, the S&W Chief's Special is at its design limits when used with +P loads. Having worn out two guns in twenty years, I now shoot *very* few +P loads, about a cylinderfull per year for refamiliarization. My favorite 38 Special field loads are either factory or handloaded target wadcutters and Speer shotshells. The cast H&G No. 50 wadcutter approximates standard 158-grain service velocities with 3.5 grains of Bullseye, or 4.2 grains of SR-7625 or W-231. This gives a little more "zip" than mid-range target loads, with good killing power.

Beyond 25 yards, the trajectory of the 38 Special is not as flat as I like. While handloaded wadcutters pass the "woodchuck test," getting solid hits beyond 40 yards is problematic. I have always wanted something a little faster and flatter, but not exceeding the light recoil of the 38 Special.

In the early 1980s, Ellis Lea introduced me to the 32 S&W Long. Until

then I never thought much of this wimpy looking round, in which the usual factory loading fires a 98-grain lead round-nosed or full-wadcutter bullet at about 720 fps. Handloaded, the 32 S&W Long is a different story. When used in a strong, solid-frame revolver like the post-war Colt Police Positive Special or the 41-framed Officer's Model Target, the post-war Smith & Wesson Regulation Police (Model 31) or K-32 Target, the 32 S&W Long is easily coaxed to 32-20 levels.

The 32-20 Winchester was the best small game handgun load ever invented, producing about 1000 fps in a six-inch barrel. Factory loads offered either 100-grain softpoints or a flat-nosed lead bullet of the same weight. The 32-20 defines the performance envelope for the ideal trail gun, if you could get those ballistics in something as accurate as a 38 wadcutter.

When the 32 S&W Long is handloaded to 32-20 levels, in a strong revolver, its accuracy rivals the best 38 Special match wadcutter target ammunition. The trajectory is flat enough that hitting a woodchuck-sized target is easy beyond 50 yards. A fine shot can shoot competitive scores on the NRA Hunter's Pistol Silhouette course out to 100 meters.

So I fell in love with the 32 S&W Long. My Colt Officer's Model Target was made in 1940. Ordinarily, it would be more of a collector's item than a shooter because this model is scarce in this caliber. To my extreme good fortune, my example had a few external dings, which took it out of the prime collector category, so I have used it heavily with no regrets. It has endured nearly 10,000 rounds of 100-grain SWC cast bullet handloads at about 1000 fps, mostly with 3.5 grains of W-231 or SR-7625 powder. This load is maximum even for the 41-frame Colt and is excessive for small-frame 32 S&W Long revolvers, but my Officer's Model 32 remains tight and wonderfully accurate. Its one drawback is that it weighs 37 ounces and isn't even close to pocket-sized.

The only disadvantage I saw to the 32 was that no strong, accurate, handy revolvers with adjustable sights were available. The Officer's Model was wonderful, but carrying it and the S&W Chief's Special on different occasions made me want a strong, compact 32 revolver that approximated the Officer's Model's ballistics and accuracy. While cast semi-wadcutters were effective enough, a fast-expanding JHP varmint bullet would make the round more flexible. Getting handloaded 32-20 softpoint bullets to expand reliably in the 32 S&W Long requires hotter loads than I want to shoot in the old Colt.

That has all changed now.

In 1984, the 32 H&R Magnum was introduced by Federal Cartridge Corporation. Nobody was sure whether this modest round would survive in an era where bigger is widely believed to be better, but I feel it is the best trail gun and Hunter's Pistol Silhouette cartridge ever. The ballistics of the 32 Magnum closely approximate the 32-20 Winchester, but are achieved in a smaller, more efficient case which is a lot easier to reload. Smith & Wesson and Ruger both offer handy trail guns for this caliber.

Factory 32 Magnum loads feature either a 95-grain flat-nosed lead bullet or an 85-grain Hornady XTP hollowpoint at 1050 fps, from a 4⅝-inch revolver barrel. Operating pressures of the 32 H&R are about 10 percent above the 38 Special +P, but substantially less than the 357 Magnum. Some handloaders feed the Ruger 32 handguns hotter handloads that substantially exceed factory ballistics, pushing 1300 fps, but neither Ruger nor I recommend it. A modest velocity of 1000-1100 fps will give all the terminal effect that a cast semi-wadcutter has to offer.

If you want rapid expansion, you don't need to load hot to get excellent performance with the Hornady XTP bullets. They expand reliably in 32 S&W Long handloads suitable for the smaller frame guns, like the S&W Model 31, down to 800 fps. The XTP bullets perform best at around 1000-1100 fps. At these velocities, they produce exit holes in wax blocks that are indistinguishable from those of 38 wadcutter loads, or about the size of your thumb. The big difference

is that they are more accurate and shoot flatter, permitting 100-yard kills on chucks without holdover.

My Colt's 6-inch barrel permits attaining 1000 fps or so with modest pressures, but I never felt its longer sight radius was much of an advantage, when compared to its weight and bulk. I hit most field targets within 40 yards about as well with the Chief's Special. The trajectory of the 38 was the problem, not its accuracy.

I decided it would be interesting to explore the effects of sight radius and barrel length upon hand-held accuracy with a reasonably priced, readily available, modern 32 trail revolver. The Ruger Single-Six fills the bill per-

fectly. The questions I wanted to answer were: Just how important is a longer sight radius to make a revolver easy to hit with and will a handy barrel length still permit me to approach the energy of 38 Special +P loads in a revolver of the same size?

I obtained a 9½-inch Single-Six chambered for 32 H&R Magnum because it provided the opportunity to explore the effect of reduced sight radius separately from barrel length. I first established a baseline accuracy level of the Single-Six with the longest factory barrel and sight radius.

Firing factory Federal 32 H&R Magnum 85-grain JHPs, the aver-

Harris's choice of a test gun let him move the sight first, *then* start experimenting with barrel lengths.

The end result was a trail-handy 4⅝-inch barrel and factory-load groups not much worse.

ACCURACY DATA FOR RUGER SINGLE-SIX 32 H&R MAGNUM*

Barrel (ins.)	Bullet (Wgt. Grs.)	Bullet (Type)	Load (Grs./Powder)	Vel. @10ft (fps)	SD	Group (ins.) Small	Large	Avg.
Handloads—Baseline data for 32 S&W Long in Factory Barrel								
19½	100	Saeco cast SWC	3.5/SR-7625	1121	19	1.56	2.28	1.97
19½	85	Hornady XTP	3.5/SR-7625	1124	28	1.55	2.37	2.03
Factory Loads—Baseline Data for 32 H&R Magnum								
9½	85	Federal JHP	Factory	1193	63	0.73	1.85	1.19
29½	85	Federal JHP	Factory			0.86	1.75	1.30
7½	85	Federal JHP	Factory	1131	33	1.22	1.85	1.51
5½	85	Federal JHP	Factory	1098	13	1.21	2.04	1.60
45/8	85	Federal JHP	Factory	1077	15	0.95	1.67	1.24
Handload—Velocity vs. Barrel Length 32 S&W Long								
9½	100	Saeco SWC	3.5/SR-7625	1109	24			
7½	100	Saeco SWC	3.5/SR-7625	1101	18			
5½	100	Saeco SWC	3.5/SR-7625	1063	29			
45/8	100	Saeco SWC	3.5/SR-7625	1035	31			
Handloads—32 S&W Long in Shortened Barrel								
345/8	85	Hornady XTP	3.5/SR-7625	1004	28	1.52	2.12	1.91
445/8	85	Hornady XTP	4.0/SR-7625	1161	10	1.29	2.23	1.80
345/8	100	Saeco SWC	3.5/SR-7625	1035	31	1.38	2.10	1.77

Loads for other Trail Guns

Barrel (ins.)	Bullet (Wgt. Grs.)	Bullet (Type)	Load (Grs./Powder)	Vel. @10ft (fps)	SD	Group (ins.) Small	Large	Avg.
Colt Officer's Model Target 32 S&W								
36	85	Hornady XTP	3.5/SR-7625	1064	28	1.45	2.28	1.83
46	85	Hornady XTP	3.7/SR-7625	1104	19	1.08	1.94	1.47
36	100	Saeco SWC	3.5/SR-7625	1087	13	1.20	1.66	1.46
Smith & Wesson Model 36 Heavy Barrel								
3	148	Federal WC	Factory	721	11	1.53	2.27	1.96

*Average of six consecutive 6-shot groups at 25 yards fired hand-held from sandbags with no iron sights.
1These 32 S&W handloads OK for S&W K-22, Colt Officer's Model and similar solid-frame guns only. For smaller frames consult published data. Bullet sized .313; Lee Alox-beeswax.
2Test effect of reduced sight radius after setting front sight back to position used for 45/8-inch Ruger barrel.
3These 32 S&W handloads OK for S&W K-22, Colt Officer's Model and similar solid-frame guns only. For smaller frames consult published data.
4These 32 S&W handloads for Ruger and Colt Officer's Model only!

age extreme spread of five consecutive six-shot groups at 25 yards was 1.2 inches. The best groups were around ¾-inch. These results accurately define my ability to hold and see the sights. I then moved the front sight rearward to the same position as on the 45/8-inch barrelled version. Using the same ammunition, the average group size opened only slightly, to 1.3 inches for the same number of targets. No individual group exceeded 2 inches, and the difference in average group size is statistically insignificant. The velocity of factory 85-grain JHP loads in the 9½-inch barrel was an impressive 1196 fps.

The next step was to chop the Single-Six barrel off in increments, chronograph the factory loads at each step, and repeat the group series. The tests would stop with the 45/8-inch barrel which establishes the SAAMI ballistic parameters for the cartridge. This was accomplished by taking to the range a portable vise, hacksaw and extra blades, mill file, carpenter's square and case chamfering tool. I had found in my previous tests of 22 rifles (Gun Digest, 46th Edition, p. 157) that hand cutting, squaring, chamfering, careful visual inspection and patience shoots as accurately as a lathe job. This permitted all the firing comparisons to be completed side-by-side on the same day. The results are quite revealing and are detailed in the accompanying table.

Cutting straight to the bottom line: By the time you cut the 9½-inch barrel back to 45/8 inches, the velocity of factory 32 Magnum loads drops about 24 fps per inch, from 1193 fps to 1077 fps. Despite this 19 percent drop in striking energy, from 268 to 219 foot pounds, the short barrel is still quite respectable, its energy being equal to a 158-grain 38 Special slug at 789 fps, the same as my full-power wadcutter handloads.

The accuracy attainable when firing over sandbags was every bit as good with the shortened barrel as with the original long one. My test series with the hacksawn, filed and deburred barrel averaged 1¼ inches! The smallest group in that series was just under an inch, the largest less than 1¾ inches. This could be readily repeated with handloads with the XTP bullets using either W-231 or SR-7625 powders.

When using 32 S&W Long cast bullet handloads with a faster powder (SR-7625), the velocity dropped about 15 fps per inch, from 1109 fps in the original 9½-inch barrel to 1035 fps after cutting it. This resulted in a 13 percent loss in energy, from 273 to 237 foot pounds. That is comparable to the energy of a 158-grain 38 Special slug moving 823 fps, approximately the results obtained with factory +P in the 3-inch Chief's. Accuracy was not affected, remaining just under the 2-inch mark. This is entirely acceptable, considering the jump of the lead bullet when firing 32 S&W Long ammunition in the .15-inch longer 32 Magnum chamber.

I felt somewhat lucky that the 32 S&W Long handloads developed for my Officer's Model Colt also shoot well in the Ruger. I had hoped this would be true so I wouldn't have to load two types of ammunition. However, such may not be the case with other guns. An exception occurred in testing the Speer 100-grain JHP bullet, which didn't tolerate the jump well from the 32 S&W Long case in the Magnum cylinder. Groups with the this bullet, using the same charge which shot well with the Saeco 100-grain cast bullet of the same weight, enlarged from neat 1¾-inch clusters in the Colt to over 5 inches in the Ruger. The Hornady XTP bullets showed no such finicky tendency.

So, the moral for all you "Outdoorsmen" out there is that this little experiment tells me the Ruger Single-Six 32 H&R Magnum with 45/8-inch barrel offers all one could ever want in a trail gun. It is as accurate as a rare, collectible Colt, far less expensive, easier to find, and a lot handier. It provides striking energy that compares to the 38 Special +P, with lighter recoil and flatter trajectory.

My trusty old Colt can now be lovingly cared for and put out to pasture, as an old friend to be enjoyed with nostalgia, but no longer abused by heavy use. The trim Ruger is going to be my steady companion, having earned it spurs and demonstrated it can cut the mustard. •

by SIDNEY DU BROFF

These are proofmarks, stamped on barrels when they pass proof.

What do they do
in Proof Houses?
Well, it isn't all...

Sitting In Charlie's Chair

Device for testing single shotgun barrels, which are submitted here for testing from all over the world.

THE PROOF MASTER handed me a gun barrel. "Hold it up to the light," he commanded. "What do you see?"

"Circles."

"What kind of circles?"

"Not very good ones. More like eggs."

"Not concentric?"

"Definitely."

He nodded in approval. "You're on your way to becoming a Proof Master."

It was a good start. But the process might take twenty years.

I was at the London Proof House, the oldest proof house in the world, where they have been checking out guns since 1637. The need for such an institution arose from the fact that people—definitely not gunmakers, but armorers, blacksmiths and the like—wanted in on what was some very brisk action.

The gunmakers, not very happy about the competition, which was also an affront to their professional pride and skills, went marching off to see King Charles I, petition in hand, and asked for a charter.

"Now diverse Blacksmiths and others," they contended, "inexpert in

Gun-tester Pat with a Damascus-barreled, round-action, Scottish-made hammer gun, well over a hundred years old, which had just passed proof—nitro proof.

The Board Room in Birmingham.

Gun-tester Pat with revolver—they shoot all the chambers in each gun they test.

the art had taken it upon themselves to make, try and prove guns after their unskilful way, damnifying the Gun-makers in their particular trade and causing much harm and danger through much unskilfulness to the King's loyal subjects..."

The King was sympathetic and gave them their charter. They now had the rights of "search, view, gauge, proof, trial and marking of all hand-guns, great and small, dags (a heavy pistol) and pistols in London or the suburbs or within ten miles radius."

There were sixty-two gunmakers. They became The Worshipful Company of Gunmakers. One would be a master, who would serve for a year. But definitely no "Armourers and Blacksmiths." They were blackballed for life.

Gunmaking was more than just making guns. It was a way of life. Members were supposed to feel "brotherly love and amity" toward each other. To encourage these feelings, an annual dinner was held on the first Thursday after the Feast of St. Bartholomew the Apostle. Attendance was mandatory. Wives, however, didn't have to come, if not inclined, or if husbands felt disinclined to bring them. The cost was half a crown each—two shillings sixpence. Those who couldn't be both-

ered to show up at all paid a one pound fine.

If a member stopped feeling brotherly love and amity toward a fellow member, and punched him in the face, that cost him forty shillings—two pounds. The same amount was imposed if a member said some really unpleasant things to a fellow member. It was a lot of money back then, considering that it represented a month's wages for many a worker.

Members were also expected to be present at the funerals of fellow members and their wives. Failure to attend, without a good excuse, resulted in a ten shilling fine.

For a boy who wanted to learn the gun trade—and getting the chance was considered a privilege—it was necessary to serve a seven-year apprenticeship. He was required to make a gun, which he presented when his seven years were completed. It was the "Proof Piece." The Master, and his Wardens, inspected it carefully. If work and worker were deemed satisfactory, the fellow could use the gunmakers' symbol on his work: G.P. and a crown. That mark is still in use today.

As I set aside the obviously defective gun barrel, the bell rang here at No. 48 Commercial Road, in the scruffy East End, where the Proof House is inconspicuously located. In

Pat examines a gun barrel by holding it up to the light to determine if the circles are concentric.

a little while a girl appeared, a pleasant-looking young woman who seemed somewhat out of place here. The Proof Master presented her with a gun. Well, not exactly a gun. It had once been a gun, an autoloading pistol which she had brought in earlier as part of a consignment for her gun-importing employer. Now, more accurately, she was collecting the bits and pieces that used to be an autoloading pistol. This one hadn't made it through proof.

The girl, putting a brave face on, thanked the Proof Master politely and went off with her little package. Proof Master, Mr. A.C. Bedford, showed little remorse, delighting, he told me, in the title he had earned through diligence and perseverance: "The Butcher."

"No matter what the origin of the gun," he said, "it is subject to the very same exacting proving. And it will be the same while I am here." He quoted the saying on his wall. "If In Doubt Throw It Out!"

A British firm, importing guns in the white from Spain (not yet proved), doing them up a bit and selling them under their own name, was once having some difficulty. "I was failing gun after gun," Proof Master Bedford said, "because they weren't good enough."

The firm brought the Spanish Proof Master to London to see how English Provisional Proving was carried out: 9½ drams of blackpowder went into a 12-gauge proving shell loaded with 1¾ ounces of #6 shot and two felt wads.

"He was horrified," A.C. Bedford said, pleased. "He said it was absolute butchery."

"I said this is what English guns must stand up to."

This is a private company. It is owned and run by the English gunmakers. It is not supposed to make any money or lose any, either. The idea is to break even.

An individual who brings his gun in for proving, whether single or double barrel, pays about $16. If he, an importer or manufacturer, brought in guns in multiples, the cost is roughly $15 each for a double, $7.50 each for a single.

Representatives of Holland & Holland and Purdey sit on the board. When they meet, here in this damp basement known as "The Court," they wear robes and badges. They put them back on again for their annual dinner, with all guests expected to be in formal attire. This is the occasion when the new Master is sworn in, with the outgoing one giving up the keys to the Proof House, all part of the ceremony.

Firing is done from the outside, by pulling the cord—a sensible idea if you're firing really heavy loads.

Now, in the "Court," seated in the regal armchair normally reserved for the Master, at the head of the long wooden table, and around which at other times sit the luminaries of British gun making, I was graciously initiated into the domain that not only tests guns to ensure they are safe to use, but provides a "mystique" to go along with it. That included a prohibition on photographing even the Master's Chair—as well as anything else in the place.

"The mystique must remain," Proof Master Bedford intoned.

"What mystique?" I asked.

"The mystique of proving."

I wouldn't have thought that testing a gun to ensure its safe construction required either ritual or mystique. But then how many proving facilities have a resident ghost to engender such an aura?

I waited to see if Charlie would appear. Once an employee who had blown himself up at some point during the past 350-plus years, Charlie was now a ghost and has a predilection for sitting in the chair I now occupied. I don't really believe in ghosts; I've never encountered any. But neither do I disbelieve, particularly since everybody in Britain takes their presence for granted. Not necessarily malicious, ghosts are just part of the heritage, part of the aura and the mystique. Proof Master Bedford, who doesn't believe in ghosts either, frequently encounters Charlie down here. Maybe he was sulking because I was sitting in his chair.

Mystique aside, just exactly what do proofmasters do? And why?

All guns made in the United Kingdom have to be proved. Makers can take their chances and have it done in London, or at the Proof House in Birmingham, which was established in 1813 (the year it became an offense to sell a gun in the UK that had not undergone proving), where they function with less mystique and where, it is said, the chances of getting a borderline gun through are somewhat greater.

Military arms are not tested here. They are inspected by military ordnance. Should they be released for sale to the public, however, they would then be proved in exactly the same way as sporting guns.

First, the proof people look at the gun carefully. Minor faults won't necessarily prevent passage, as long as safe use isn't going to be a problem. Next comes "shadow viewing."

Here, the barrel, or barrels, are held up to the light. The inner and outer surfaces are inspected both from the breech and the muzzle. They look for broken or distorted shadows. If the shadow isn't concentric, it means there are bulges or dents in the barrel. These faults are easy to miss with distortions that go no more than .002-inch. This is where knowledge, skill and experience make the difference.

They then gauge the barrels for bore sizes, which are stamped on them before they are proved. Chamber length, diameter and rim depth are checked, and also the action, to see that it functions safely and closes properly. They then lock the barrels into a recoil carriage or vise, and a proof cartridge, which develops between 60 and 80 percent more pressure than normal, is fired. A 12-gauge shotgun, with a 2½-inch chamber that normally creates 3 tons of pressure, is thus expected to take between 4.8 and 5.4 tons. For rifles and handguns, 30 to 45 percent more than normal is the usual proof test.

Part of the carriage pulls the trigger or triggers. If barrels only have been submitted, a cylindrical device is fitted into the breeches. Ever mindful of how Charlie met his end here, the testers watch the firing

(Above) Cartridges are left in the barrel after firing for further examination. Stripes on the cartridges indicate velocity.

Automatic arms waiting to be deactivated, then sold to the public.

process from behind safety glass. They then clean the barrels to get rid of the fouling, and shadow view once again. They check the action to see if it's still tight against the face of the barrels, and inspect for cracks or distortions. If all is well, proofmarks are stamped on the flat side of the barrels and action. Even if a gun doesn't make it first time around, often it can be repaired, or otherwise restored, and will make it on the second go.

Double barrel shotguns, English and others, go through two proofs. "Provisional" comes first, and happens in the early stage of manufacture in the country of origin. The idea is to keep the maker from continuing to work on defective tubes. Single barrel guns are not subject to Provisional Proof. Definitive Proof happens when the gun is finished, or almost finished. They use nitro-based powder, because it's faster burning and applies the pressure at the breech end of the barrel.

British guns—that means shotguns, almost the only sporting arms that ever come here—always make it through proof. Any defects would be discovered at the time of Provisional Proving; the defects would then be corrected before re-submission.

All guns coming into Britain have to be proved in one place or another.

The coat of arms at the Birmingham Proof House gate—dates and such are important in England.

A familiar publication on the loading desk at the Proof House: *Cartridges Of The World.*

Proof Master Scott standing in front of photographs of illustrious predecessors—a long line, they make.

There are reciprocal arrangements with a number of countries—Germany, Austria, Czechoslovakia, Ireland, France, Italy, Belgium and Spain—whereby their guns are proved in country of origin by an acceptable proof house. What's acceptable? A proof house that is available to individuals, manufacturers and importers and will allow themselves to be inspected by representatives of the English Proof House.

Private testing, in one's own manufacturing facilities, doesn't count, such as in the U.S. However, American-made guns are not having a problem, considering the strict consumer protection laws in the United States. One importer of U.S. guns with whom I spoke told me he had never had a failure. If anything, the Proof Master said, American guns are over-engineered.

The guns that don't make it through—and these are less than 1 percent—can come from anywhere. They are usually older guns that are submitted, or re-submitted for up-to-date proving, without which they could not be legally sold. Or they may be guns that are unsafe and present a danger to the current user, who might want the reassurance of an up-to-date proving.

The ultimate owner now knows that his gun is safe. Allen C. Bedford, Proof Master, recently retired, wouldn't have it any other way. While there are those in the gun trade who will probably disagree, Bedford has no doubt that he was always the right man in the right job. There can be little doubt that he loved the work and brought devotion and dedication to it.

He started work at the Proof House in 1960, and became Proof Master eleven years later. He began his working life as an apprentice in an aircraft factory in Bristol, in the West of England. During World War II, he served in the Royal Engineers. To work here, one needs to know about guns—and like them—the way Bedford does, have a good mathematical background, and a good general education. The other six men who work at the Proof House qualify on all counts.

For all of them this is no mere job, but a large and important part of their life. It's obvious for anyone to see that Allen C. Bedford, Proof Master these many years, has always liked it that way. •

by LAYNE SIMPSON

RIFLE REVIEW

A-Square

A-SQUARE'S NEW Hamilcar is basically a trimmer and lighter version of the Hannibal. Built around a highly refined P-14 Enfield action, nominal weight is 8 pounds with a wood stock and a half-pound less with a synthetic stock. The first Hamilcar built weighed 8³/₄ pounds with what has become one of my favorite scopes for open country hunting, the Bausch & Lomb 2.5-10x Elite 4000. The new rifle is available in 25-06, 257 Weatherby Magnum, 6.5x55mm Swedish, 264 Winchester Magnum, 270 Winchester, 270 Weatherby Magnum, 7mm Remington Magnum, 7mm Weatherby Magnum, 7mm Shooting Times

Simpson found Tom Volquartsen's Firefly 22 Short conversion of Ruger's 10/22 accurate and great fun to shoot.

In calibers from 7mm STW to 338-06, the Hamilcar is a trimmer, lighter version of A-Square's Hannibal.

Westerner (STW), 300 Winchester Magnum, 300 Weatherby Magnum, 338-06, and 9.3x62mm Mauser. Optional barrel lengths are 20 to 26 inches. Of special interest to those who buy a Hamilcar in 338-06, that cartridge has been added to A-Square's ammunition line in four loadings, with the 250-grain Sierra as well as the A-Square Dead Tough, Lion Load and Monolithic Solid bullets of the same weight, all at a nominal 2520 fps.

I tried three of A-Square's four 7mm STW factory loads in the Hamilcar. My Oehler 35P said average velocity in the 25-inch barrel was 3437 fps for the 140-grain Nosler Ballistic Tip load, 3271 fps for the 160-grain Nosler Partition load, and 3256 fps for the 160-grain Sierra load. Average 100-yard accuracy was 0.88-inch, 1.34 inches, and 1.12 inches, respectively. In the 26½-inch barrel of my custom Model 700, the loads averaged 3512, 3303, and 3318 fps. When I zero the Ballistic Tip load 3 inches high at 100 yards, it's down less than 5 inches at 400.

As I predicted last year, A-Square rifles are now chambered for a new Super 30 cartridge. Called the 300 Petersen, the rim of its totally new beltless case is a bit smaller in diameter than that of the 378 Weatherby

Magnum case. That makes it better suited for Remington 700 and Winchester 70 actions. Muzzle velocity with the 180-grain bullet in a 26-inch barrel is said to be the same as that of the 30-378 Weatherby Magnum, or 3400 to 3500 fps. A-Square will offer unprimed cases as well as several factory loadings. Rifle options are A-Square's Hannibal and the Model 70 Super Grade from USRAC's custom shop.

Browning

The A-Bolt and BAR Mark II rifles are available with what Browning calls the Ballistic Optimizing Shooting System (BOSS, for short). The device attaches to the muzzle and is basically a combination recoil brake and barrel vibration tuner. I've not shot one, but others who have say it works. Both rifles are available in various standard and belted magnum chamberings, and since the BOSS is 2 inches long, actual barrel length with all calibers is around 22 inches.

Cooper Arms

Cooper Arms' line of extremely handsome high-quality rifles continues to grow in number and now includes right- and left-hand actions. The Model 36 family is available in 22 rimfire, 22 Hornet and 17 CCM, the latter a centerfire cartridge that pushes a 20-grain bullet along at about 2700 fps. As its name implies, the Model 36 BR-50 was created for the relatively new (but growing) sport of benchrest competition with 22 rimfires. Moving on up in power, we have the Model 21 Varmint Mach IV, 221 Fireball, 222, 223, 6x45mm and 6x47mm. Those chamberings also are available in a standard-weight rifle called Custom Classic. The Model 36 Featherweight and BR-50 rifles have synthetic stocks, but all others wear walnut ranging from standard grade to extra fancy.

D&J Custom

Transforming the Ruger 10/22 autoloader into a precision tackdriver is not exactly a new idea, but Kentuckian Don Fraley, who owns D&J Cus-

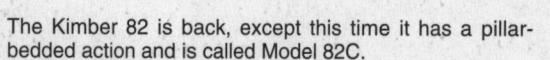

The Kimber 82 is back, except this time it has a pillar-bedded action and is called Model 82C.

tom Gunshop (and D&J Custom Bullets) is the only gunsmith I know who eliminates the clamp-in style of barrel installation when doing so. Don accomplishes this by line-boring and threading the receiver, and then screwing in a match-grade barrel. The barrel is bedded full length in its new walnut or fiberglass stock with the action left free-floating. This is done because Fraley believes the aluminum alloy receiver lacks the rigidity to support a heavy target-weight barrel without warping slightly, and therefore affecting accuracy. He sells complete rifles and barreled actions or will fit a new barrel to a customer's 10/22. If you have your rifle rebarreled, don't forget to include the trigger job with its new light-weight speed hammer and spring kit. Fraley also sprinkles magic accuracy dust on Ruger's 77/22 bolt gun in 22 LR and 22 WMR, and is already taking orders for what he says will be the sweetest and most accurate little 22 Hornet you'll ever shoot.

Eagle Arms

Eagle Arms builds some of the world's most accurate AR-15 rifles. I know this to be true because an EA-15E2 H-BAR Golden Eagle with its heavy Hart barrel averaged 1/2-MOA in my hands while digesting its favorite loads. Called the EA-15E2 Eagle Eye, a new Eagle Arms hatchling, it weighs a nominal 14 pounds, or a couple pounds more than the Golden Eagle. It has a flat-top receiver

with an integral Weaver-style sight mounting base, a weighted buttstock to counterbalance the extremely heavy 1-inch diameter 24-inch barrel, adjustable handrest, tubular aluminum handguard, and national match trigger and sights. The seventh member of the Golden Eagle flock, the Eagle Eye is sure to be seen in many winner's circles.

If you don't see exactly what you want in the standard-production lineup, the custom shop will build one your way. Those boys will also upgrade AR-15 rifles made by Colt and others. In addition to complete rifles, Eagle Arms sells forged receivers, barrel assemblies, and various component parts, all match grade.

Harrison Gunworks, Inc.

Co-owned by Randy Brooks (who also owns Barnes Bullets) and his daughter, Jessica, Harrison Gunworks is building some of the nicest big game rifles I have examined lately. One model aptly called the Lightweight weighs only 5 1/2 pounds due mainly to its synthetic stock and Swiss-cheesed Remington 700 action. Another, called the Safari, is built around a '98 Mauser or Model 70 action and is available with a walnut or synthetic stock. Caliber options range from the 223 Remington for varmints to 7mm STW for elk to 358 STA for brown bear to the various 416s and 458s for even bigger stuff.

H-S Precision

The new Pro-Series by H-S Precision is basically a super-accurate tackdriver built around the Remington 700 action that can be taken down so nobody would ever guess there's an elk rifle in your duffel bag. The patented takedown system compensates for normal wear of the interrupted barrel shank threads. Two synthetic-stocked versions are available, the 12-pound Tactical for law enforcement and the 8-pound Sporter

Built around '98 Mausers, Peters & Hosea rifles have English-style stocks and other niceties such as Warne quick-detach scope mounts and Express-style open sights.

(Above and right) Browning calls the combination muzzlebrake/vibration tuner attached to the muzzle of this BAR a Ballistic Optimizing Shooting System (BOSS for short).

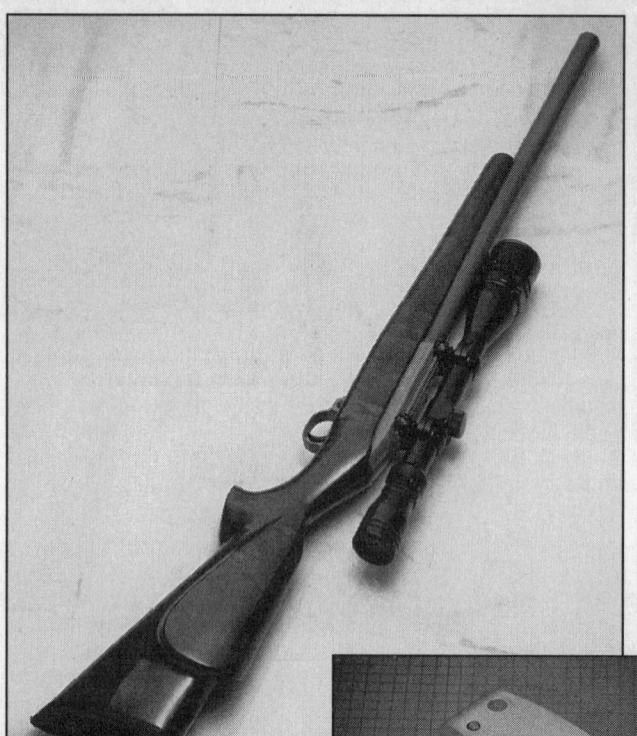

(Above and right) Don Fraley at D&J Custom eliminates the clamp-in style of barrel installations when building a super accurate rifle around Ruger's 10/22 action—he bores and threads for the barrel.

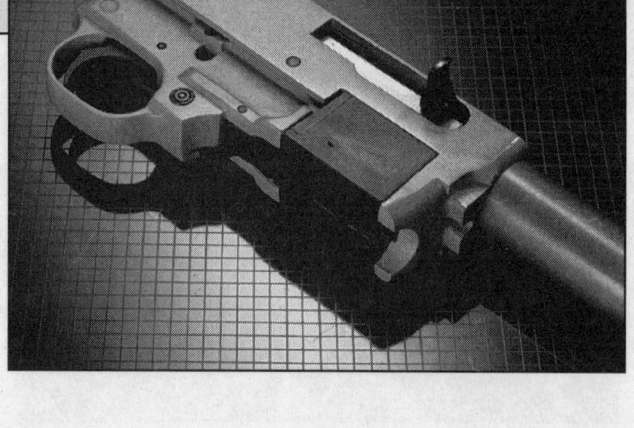

buttpad, and steel grip cap) and Super America (AAA-grade Claro, ebony forend tip, classic stock with beaded cheekpiece, 22-lpi wrap-around checkering, black rubber buttpad, and steel grip cap). The Custom Shop Super America can be all that plus have extra-cost options such as skeleton-style steel grip cap and buttplate, quarter-rib with express-style sights, jewelled bolt body, checkered bolt knob, and rust blue finish. There's also a limited-production Custom Match.

Each rifle is accuracy tested in a 50-yard tunnel with RWS R50 ammo and then shipped with its test target. Before escaping the factory, a Classic has to squeeze five bullets into .400-inch or less, and a Super America has to do the same for ten shots. It's great to see one of

day at the range with a pre-production model and was impressed with what I saw, to say the least. Five-shot groups at 100 yards with seven saboted slug loads averaged as follows:

Win. 3″ Hi-Imp.	2.3 ins.
Win. 2³/₄″ BRI	2.4 ins.
Rem. 3″ Copper Solid	2.8 ins.
Win. 2³/₄″ Hi-Imp.	2.8 ins.
Rem. 2³/₄″ Copper Solid	2.9 ins.
Fed. Prem. 2³/₄″	3.1 ins.
Win. 3″ BRI	3.4 ins.

I've seen deer rifles (and deer hunters) have to work mighty hard to reach such a level of accuracy.

The new Marlin slug gun came with a quick-detach Weaver mount, making it easy for me to attach a springwater clear Leupold 1.75-6x Vari-X III. Remington's new 3-inch Copper Solid was my pick of the saboted slug load litter for serious whitetail work. The 57-caliber, 500-grain hollow-nose slug exited the Slugmaster's 21-inch barrel at an average of 1464 fps for almost 2400 foot pounds of punch. With its 100-yard energy delivery of just over 1700 foot pounds, gun and load equals 444 Marlin factory load performance at that range. That's a lot more authority than delivered by any other 12-gauge slug load. The Model 512 is built specifically for shooting saboted slug loads, but at an average of 4.3 inches with Winchester's Foster-type load, the one I shot wasn't exactly a slouch in the accuracy depart-

for you and me. You can buy a rifle with one barrel only, or you can buy it with as many barrels in various calibers as your heart desires and your bankroll stands. The two models are also available with a right- or left-hand action.

Kimber

The Kimber Model 82 in 22 Long Rifle is back as Model 82C. The company is Kimber of America, Inc., of Clackamas, Oregon, and Greg Warne who was a co-owner of the original outfit is why it has arisen from its ashes. I've held several of the new rifles in my hands, and they were absolutely gorgeous. The only design differences I noticed on the new Model 82C are pillar bedding, a slightly trimmer forend and a four-round detachable magazine that fits flush with the bottom metal. Five- and ten-round magazines are also available. The 82C weighs a

Ruger's 10/22 International is available with blued or stainless steel barrels, and has a certain look about it.

nominal 6¹/₂ pounds, has a 22-inch barrel and measures 40¹/₂ inches overall. Unlike the grooved receiver of the Model 82, the 82C is drilled and tapped for Warne scope mounts. As has always been the case, everything on a Kimber that looks like wood and steel is wood and steel. Also as expected, fit and finish are flawless.

The two standard models are Classic (standard-grade Claro walnut, classic-style stock with no cheekpiece, modest 20-lpi checkering coverage, red rubber

the most handsome rifles ever built back in production, and it's just as great to see it's still made in America.

Marlin

Marlin's new 12-gauge Model 512 Slugmaster with its turn-bolt action, fully rifled barrel, adjustable sights and quick-detach scope mount looks like a rifle, shoots like a rifle, and hammers game like a rifle. That's why you're reading about it in a rifle report. Just before Thanksgiving of '93, I spent a

ment with anything I fed it. Marlin should sell lots of this one.

In the 22 rimfire department, Marlin's new Model 880SS bolt action has a stainless steel barreled action and a synthetic stock. Also new is a slightly modified version of the Model 2000 target rifle. Called the 2000A, its stock has an adjustable cheek rest and a wrist shaped for right- and left-hand shooters.

The Model 922M autoloader in 22 WMR that was new last

year never made it to the production line, but Marlin officials say you should be able to buy one during 1994. In case you've forgotten, it has a walnut stock, a 20½-inch barrel, seven-round detachable magazine, and weighs 6½ pounds.

To commemorate the 100th birthday of its Model 1894 rifle, Marlin is offering a deluxe limited-production version called the Century Limited during 1994 only. Chambered for 44-40, it has a 24-inch tapered octagon barrel with eight-groove rifling and a twelve-round tubular magazine. The receiver, breech bolt and lever are case-colored and engraved by Giovanelli of Italy. The semi-fancy walnut butt-

in importance, the following walnut-stocked Marlin rifles now come standard with cut checkering on their buttstock and forend: 336CS, 444SS, 1895SS, 1894S, 1894CS, 39AS, 39TDS and 922 Magnum.

Peters & Hosea Gunmakers

Owned and operated by two former Kimber employees, Peters & Hosea is a new firm dedicated to building top quality English-style magazine rifles. All are built around the '98 Mauser action at the Beaver Creek, Oregon, facility. The Dominion Grade features a semi-pistol grip stock of Moroccan walnut with hand-cut checkering, rubbed oil finish,

Remington

During '93, I managed to wring out several Remington prototypes that were scheduled for introduction in '94. One was the Custom Shop's new 6¾-pound Model 700 AWR (Alaskan Wilderness Rifle). Available in 7mm Remington, 300 Winchester, 300 Weatherby, 338 Winchester, and 375 H&H belted magnum chamberings, it has a 24-inch barrel and a Kevlar-reinforced fiberglass stock. With its stainless steel barreled action hidden by a satin black finish, this one is for those who like the idea of a totally weatherproof rifle but don't like the "unfinished" look of naked steel. The 7mm Mag-

a chuck's whisker above dead on at 300 where it delivers close to 900 foot pounds. That, my friend, is flat-shooting, tack-driving, chuck-busting performance in any varmint shooter's book.

Install a lightweight 24-inch match-grade barrel in 22 Long Rifle and trimmer synthetic stock on the 40-XRBR action and you've got the 40-XRKS. Its match-dimension chamber and benchrest-grade barrel will surely enable its owner to enjoy quite a dead-eye reputation among any group of serious squirrel snipers.

In the standard-production department, we have the 9-pound Model 700 Sendero with its synthetic stock and heavy

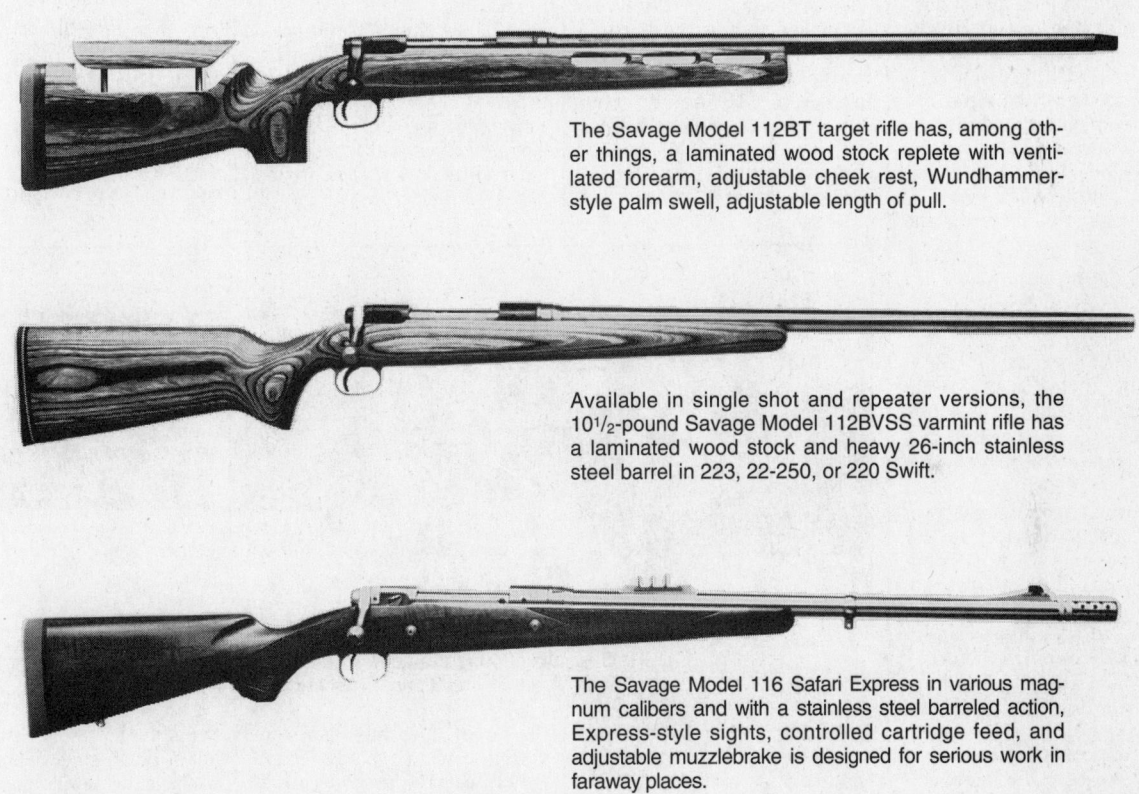

The Savage Model 112BT target rifle has, among other things, a laminated wood stock replete with ventilated forearm, adjustable cheek rest, Wundhammer-style palm swell, adjustable length of pull.

Available in single shot and repeater versions, the 10½-pound Savage Model 112BVSS varmint rifle has a laminated wood stock and heavy 26-inch stainless steel barrel in 223, 22-250, or 220 Swift.

The Savage Model 116 Safari Express in various magnum calibers and with a stainless steel barreled action, Express-style sights, controlled cartridge feed, and adjustable muzzlebrake is designed for serious work in faraway places.

stock has a straight wrist, curved brass buttplate and cut checkering. The forend is checkered and held in place by a steel nosecap.

In the things discontinued department, Marlin no longer offers the 218 Bee, 25-20, and 32-20 chamberings in its standard 1894, but the handy little woods gun is still available with a 20-inch barrel in 44 Magnum/44 Special and an 18½-inch barrel in 38 Special/357 Magnum.

Last, but certainly not least

reinforcing crossbolt and buffalo horn forend tip. Also included are rust blue finish, hinged floorplate, Kimber double-lever scope mounting rings, Express-type rear and barrel band-type front sight, and just a touch of English scroll engraving. The more expensive Empire Grade has all that plus fancy walnut, trapdoor grip cap, monogramed silver oval in the stock, and more extensive engraving coverage. Other custom options are also available. Darned handsome rifles.

num I toted on the Alaska Peninsula shot good, looked good, worked good on caribou. There's also a 7¾-pound Model 700 APR (African Plains Rifle), with laminated wood stock, satin blued steel finish, and a 26-inch barrel.

One new 40-X is the 40-XBS with a stainless steel barrel and action. A 220 Swift, the 40-XBKS (synthetic stock) I shot averaged .41-inch for five five-shot groups at 100 yards. When zeroed 2 inches high at 100 yards, the Ballistic Tip was

24-inch barrel in 25-06, 270, 7mm Remington Magnum and 300 Winchester Magnum. This one was designed for the deer hunter who sits and glasses a lot and walks very little. There's a Model 700 Varmint Synthetic Stainless Fluted, a heavy-barrel varmint rifle with a synthetic stock, stainless steel action, and a 26-inch stainless barrel.

Remington's new variation of its Model Seven carbine has a slightly longer 20-inch barrel, synthetic stock, and stainless

The new Mark V Sporter is the least expensive Mark V rifle Weatherby has ever built—available in almost all chamberings.

steel barreled action. Nominal weight is 6¼ pounds, and you can get one in 243, 7mm-08, and 308.

Remington kicked off its series of limited-production Model 700 Classic rifles chambered for classic cartridges in 1981 with the 7x57mm Mauser. For 1994, it's the 6.5x55mm Swedish. The prototype I used to bag a handsome fallow buck at the 777 Ranch near Hondo, Texas, has a 24-inch barrel with a 1:8-inch rifling pitch. The twist rate stayed the same, but the rifle you'll buy will have a 22-inch barrel. That deer, by the way, was taken with a single round of Remington's equally new 140-grain loading of the 6.5 Swede cartridge.

Ruger

The most exciting news from Sturm, Ruger & Co. for '94 is the marvelous little Model 77/22 in 22 Hornet. Available with scope mounting rings only (77/22RH) or with rings and open sights (77/22RSH), Ruger's handy varmint rifle has a 20-inch chrome-moly barrel, walnut stock, six-round rotary magazine, and weighs a nominal 6 pounds. Rifling twist rate is 1:14 inches, which means that bullets as heavy as 55 grains will stabilize in turkey loads (older Hornet rifles have a rifling twist rate of 1:16 inches).

International Carbine is what Ruger is calling the latest edition of the 10/22 autoloader. It has an 18½-inch barrel and a Mannlicher-style stock that terminates at the muzzle with a metal nosecap. Sling swivels are there, but they're the non-detach type. This little bunny rifle is available with a stainless steel barrel and the aluminum alloy receiver finished to match (K10/22RBI), and black coated receiver with blued steel barrel (10/22RBI).

Sako

Sako is planning to build a limited number of rifles in 7mm Shooting Times Western-er (7mm STW) during 1994.

That's all I know about it for now.

Savage

Why did Savage officials decide to start calling rifles built around the Model 110 action Model 111s, 112s, 114s and 116s? Beats me. In fact, I've yet to ask a Savage official that question and get the answer. At any rate, I won't be surprised to see the various model designations eventually replaced by the old (more familiar) 110 designation sometime in the near future. For now, Savage's '94 catalog shows twenty-four different variations built around the Model 110 action, of which half are new for '94. Standard chamberings include 223, 22-250, 220 Swift, 243, 250-3000, 25-06, 270, 7mm-08, 300 Savage, 308 and 30-06. The belted magnums are Remington's 7mm, and Winchester's 300, 338 and 458.

The Model 112BT target rifle in 223 and 308 has a laminated wood stock with an adjustable cheek rest and a heavy 26-inch stainless steel barrel. The barrel has a black finish and is threaded for a sight base which is included in the package.

The Model 116SE (Safari Express) has a stainless steel barreled action and possibly the most handsome stock ever carved from a walnut tree by

Savage. Introduced in Winchester's 300, 338, and 458 Magnum chamberings, the 24-inch barrel wears a three-leaf express-style rear sight, ramped blade up front, barrel band-style quick-detach sling swivel post, and Savage's new muzzlebrake. An exterior sleeve on the "AMB" (adjustable muzzlebrake) provides a reduction in recoil and muzzle jump when in its open position, or shuts off the brake when in its closed position. In other words, you can use the brake at the range, where it's convenient to double up on the ear protection, and then with a twist of the wrist, close its gas ports for field use. The bolt of

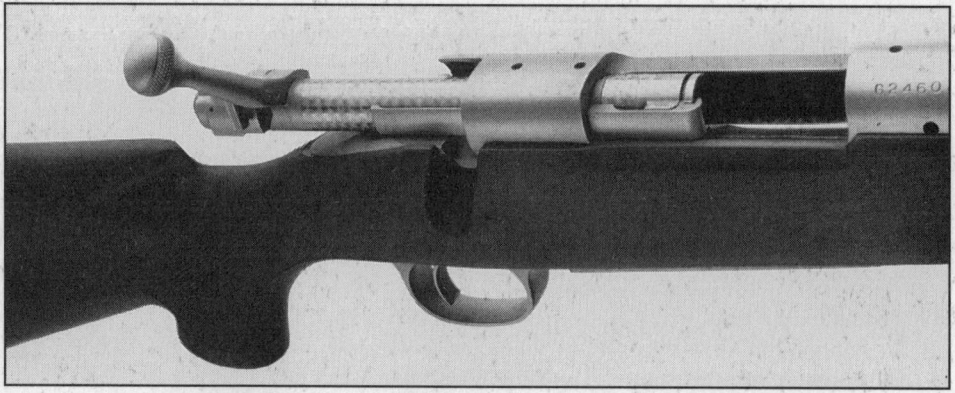

USRAC is now offering the controlled-feed option with pre-'64 style extractor on more of its Model 70 variations. Progress is everything.

the 116SE also has been converted to what Savage technicians describe as controlled-round feed design. This was accomplished by removing part of the counterbore wall of the bolt face so the rim of a cartridge can slip behind the extractor as it is being chambered.

Another extremely handsome new rifle in the Savage lineup is called Model 114CU. Available with a 22-inch barrel in 270 or 30-06, or a 24-inch barrel in 7mm Remington Magnum or 300 Winchester Magnum, the Classic Ultra weighs a nominal 7¼ pounds and has a classic-style, oil-finished walnut stock with cut checkering. It also has a detachable box magazine, and

all metal is given a high-gloss polish job prior to being blued.

There are three new synthetic-stocked variations with stainless steel barreled actions, the Model 116FCSAK (detachable magazine, fluted barrel and ABM muzzlebrake), Model 116FSK (no flutes and standard muzzlebrake), and Model 116FSS (no flutes or muzzlebrake). The Model 112BVSS is a heavy-barrel varmint rifle. Replace its stock with a synthetic and you have the Model 112FVSS. Replace the repeating actions of those two with single shot actions and you've got Models 112BVSS-S and 112FVSS-S. The Model 112FV is the same as

the Model 112FVSS except it has a blued steel barrel. Then we have the new economy-grade rifles: Model 111G with a classic-style, walnut-colored hard-wood stock and Model 111FC with quick-detach magazine and synthetic stock.

Holy confusion Batman, that's a lotta new models.

Steyr/Mannlicher

Steyr/Mannlicher rifles rank among the finest in the world, but a number of factors have caused their prices to zoom far beyond the working man's budget. Last time I looked, the Model M Sporter costs today almost exactly what I paid for my wife's brand-new Volkswagen Beetle some years back.

The new Model III Professional ain't cheap either, but you will get five bucks change from one of today's thousand dollar bills—if you don't pay state sales tax. It has a 23.6-inch barrel and synthetic stock, weighs 7½ pounds, is available in 270, 30-06 or 7x64mm, and can be had with single or double-set trigger. Other models are available in the more popular American chamberings, as well as those most Americans seldom see: 5.6x50mm Magnum, 5.6x57 Magnum, 6.5x57mm Mauser, 9.3x62mm Mauser, 6.5x68mm, 6.5 Swede and 9.3x64mm.

Ultra Light Arms

Last year, it was the new Model 20RF, a 5¼-pound 22 rimfire version of Ultra Light Arms' fantastic little Model 20 centerfire. This year, it's a heavy-barrel version of the 20RF designed for the rapidly growing sport of BR-50 benchrest shooting. All 22 rimfires built by ULA to date have been single shots, but company officials hope to eventually offer a Model

Custom Limited Edition Centennial with its 26-inch half-octagon barrel, curved steel buttplate, highly engraved receiver, extra-fancy checkered walnut, and Lyman tang sight. Only 94 will be built, so the price puts this one out of the using category for most of us. Next is the Limited Edition High Grade with less of everything, but still a very nice rifle at about the cost of two and a half standard-grade Model 94s. Take away the tang sight, reduce the checkering coverage, pick out a plainer piece of wood, really get conservative on the receiver engraving, and you've got the Limited Edition Grade I. Its tang is drilled for the Lyman sight, so you can order one through your USRAC dealer and install it yourself. Regardless of which of the three variations you decide to buy, don't forget to stock up on Winchester's special run of 30-30 cartridges. The ammo box matches the rifle box in design.

As other things different

ably. The fiberglass stock is fire-engine red, but other color options are available for the more conservative in nature among us.

While shooting a Firefly rather extensively, I recorded the following five-shot group averages from the 25-yard benchrest: Fiocchi Golden Match (0.28), RWS R-25 (0.31), CCI HVHP (0.44), CCI HV (0.47), Winchester HVHP (0.49), CCI CB (0.51), and CCI Target (0.83). Overall aggregate accuracy with all ammo was well under ½-inch. If you have ever shot 22 Short ammunition in rifles chambered for the 22 Long Rifle cartridge, you can appreciate that level of accuracy. The Firefly fed and functioned 100 percent smooth and bobble-free with all types of ammo.

I grew up on a farm and seldom used anything but 22 Shorts for all my small game hunting. Some of today's experts say the little cartridge is for plinking only, but back then it killed rabbits and squir-

220 Weatherby Rocket, a sharp-shouldered, blown-out version of the 220 Swift. It lasted into the 1950s, and I still own a Weatherby rifle on the FN Mauser action in that caliber. The 375 Weatherby Magnum, an improved version of the 375 H&H Magnum, and a favorite of firearms writer Warren Page, was discontinued soon after Roy introduced his 378 Magnum. Latest to feel the axe's cruel bite is the 224 Weatherby Magnum, our first (and probably last) belted 22. On a more cheerful note, the Varmintmaster in which the 224 used to be available is still offered in 22-250. Before leaving the subject of things discontinued, we have to say Weatherby's Vanguard series of rifles is also history.

The famous Mark V rifle is still with us. You can buy one in plain-vanilla chamberings such as 270 Winchester and 30-06, or go for more speed with a Weatherby Magnum in 240, 257, 270, 7mm, 300, 340, 378, 416 or 460 calibers. Wood-stocked Mark V

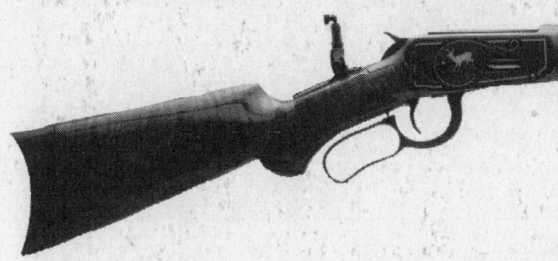

The limited-edition Centennial High Grade with its half-octagon barrel, tang sight, engraved receiver and fancy checkered wood is one of several ways USRAC is celebrating the Model 94's 100th birthday—and it is *very* handsome.

20RF repeater with a detachable magazine as well.

USRAC

Several Model 70 variations are now available with either the push feed or controlled feed type bolt. The former has the post-'64 style extractor and ejector. The latter has the pre-'64 style extractor and ejector and is now available in Super Grade, Custom Sharpshooter, Sporting Sharpshooter, Super Express, Classic, Stainless, Classic SM, DBM, DBM-S, Sporter and Featherweight configurations.

USRAC is celebrating the Model 94's 100th anniversary in a couple of ways. For one, the receivers of all variations, including the Big Bore, Trapper, Wrangler and Ranger, built during 1994 will wear the inscription "1894-1994." For two, USRAC is building a limited number of high-grade 94s in three variations, and they are the most handsome I've seen in several decades. Starting at the top, we have the

from last year go, the 32 Special has been dropped from the Model 94, the 220 Swift has been added to the Model 70 Heavy Varmint and Custom Sharpshooter, the 284 Winchester is now available in the Model 70 DBM, and you can now buy a Model 70 Super Express in 416 Remington Magnum.

Volquartsen Custom, Ltd.

Called the Firefly, Tom Volquartsen's latest transformation of the Ruger 10/22 autoloader into a precision shooting machine is chambered for the 22 Short. Tom covered every detail, right down to modifying the rotary magazine so it will handle the shorter cartridge. The Firefly has a heavy 16½-inch stainless steel barrel with a muzzle diameter of .920-inch. Overall length is 35 inches and weight with a Bausch & Lomb 2-8x Compact scope is 7¼ pounds. Its trigger breaks crisply at 33 ounces. A new lightweight speed hammer decreases locktime consider-

rels as dead as I figured they ought to be killed. And it still does, for that matter. Besides, a box of Shorts was about 20 cents less than Long Rifles in those days, and you wouldn't believe how far two dimes would go in other places back then. At any rate, playing with the Firefly reminded me of how pleasant the mild-mannered little 22 Short is to shoot. It's extremely quiet, cartridge recoil is virtually nonexistent, and when shot in Tom Volquartsen's Firefly, it's more than accurate enough for the country boy in all of us.

Weatherby

Four Weatherby chamberings have been introduced and eventually discontinued since the company began building rifles during the 1940s. The first was the 228 Magnum on a shortened Holland & Holland belted case. Loaded with a 70-grain .228-inch bullet, it appeared in the first Weatherby catalog, but was soon dropped. Then there was the

variations presently available are Deluxe, Lazermark, Safari Grade, Custom, Crown Custom and, probably the best buy of the bunch for the money, the economy-grade Sporter. Available in Weatherby calibers from 257 through 340, the new sporter is available in 270 Winchester, 30-06, and four other belted magnums, 7mm Remington, 300 Winchester, 338 Winchester and 375 H&H.

Mark V rifles with synthetic stocks are called Alaskan (electroless nickel metal finish) and Weathermark (blued steel). All models are available with Weatherby's optional Accubrake muzzlebrake.

Weatherby's '93 catalog introduced an extremely handsome variation of the Varmintmaster called Whitetail Deluxe. Chambered for the fine little 250-3000 Savage cartridge, it has a 22-inch barrel and was rated at 6 pounds. According to Ed Weatherby, that one still sits on the back burner along with Varmintmaster actions in 270, 30-06, and other interesting calibers. ●

by EDWARD R. CREWS

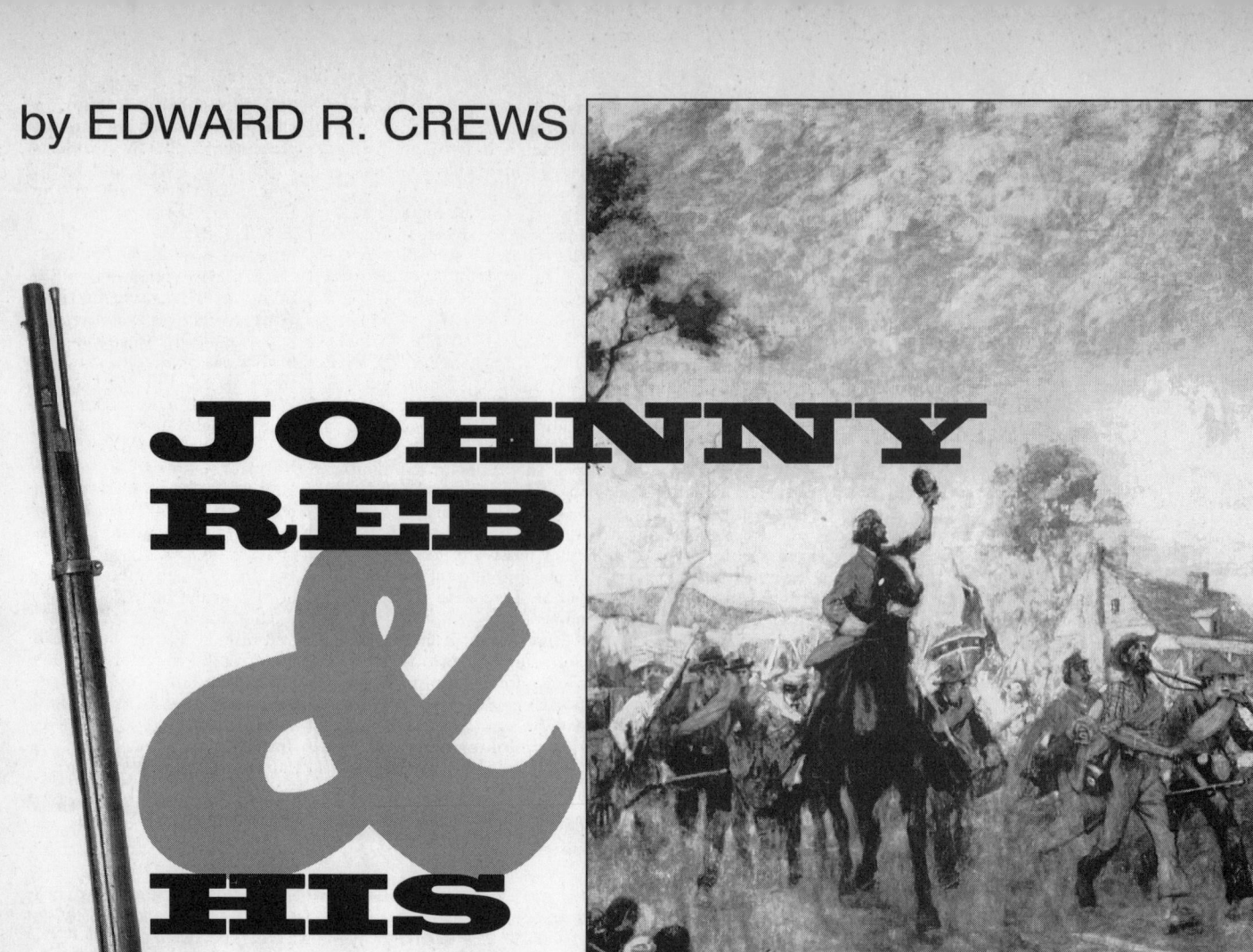

JOHNNY REB & HIS GUNS

This unmarked Confederate rifle in the Springfield pattern is proof the South had an ordnance system. (Virginia Historical Society photo.)

No JOHNNY REB manning the Confederate line at Mayre's Heights could be unimpressed at the spectacle before him. On an open plain between this high ground and the nearby town of Fredericksburg, Virginia, thousands of Federal troops were massing for an attack.

William M. Owen, a Confederate artillery officer, watched on December 13, 1862, as the enemy soldiers ran toward him behind unfurled battle-flags, chanting a deep-throated refrain—Hi! Hi! Hi! "How beautifully they came on," he wrote years later. "Their bright bayonets glistening in the sunlight made the line look like a huge serpent of blue and steel."

Union Major General Ambrose E. Burnside was hurling his Army of the Potomac against the Southern

defenses. He wanted to rout General Robert E. Lee and his Army of Northern Virginia, and then march into Richmond about 50 miles south and end the war. Burnside had massed 27,000 men for the attack on Mayre's Heights; Lee had only 6000 defending it. Although Federal assaults earlier that day had failed elsewhere along Lee's line, Burnside hoped this attack would work.

The Union attack, however, was doomed to fail. Lee held a superb defensive position. Mayre's Heights commanded nearby terrain and was studded with artillery. At its base, a breast-high stone wall provided shelter for the Georgia infantrymen of Cobb's Brigade. Also, many of Lee's men had rifled muskets, the war's most common infantry weapon. A properly trained soldier could hit tar-

Stonewall Jackson reviews his troops during his famous Valley Campaign of 1862. So much enemy equipment was captured that the Confederates found themselves well-armed when the fighting ended. This mural is in the gallery with the Southern gun collection. (Richard Cheek photo.)

gets at 300 yards, firing three rounds a minute.

That so many of these weapons would be in Southern hands was a miracle. When the various states that comprised the Confederacy left the Union in 1860 and 1861, they had few modern military rifles. U.S. arsenals seized by the South held older, less-desirable guns. Plus, the South had virtually no rifle-making facilities. Perceptive Southern leaders knew that a Union naval blockade eventually could slow, and probably halt, imports. All these factors produced an ill-armed military.

"At the commencement of the war, the Southern army was as poorly armed as any body of men ever had been," wrote John H. Worsham of the 21st Virginia Infantry Regiment. "Using my own regiment as an exam-ple, one company of infantry had Springfield muskets, one had Enfields, one had Mississippi rifles, and the remainder had the old smoothbore flintlock musket that had been altered to a percussion gun. The cavalry was so badly equipped that hardly a company was uniform. Some men had sabers and nothing more, some had double-barreled guns. Some had nothing but lances, and others had something of all. One man would have a saber, another a pistol, another a musket, and another a shotgun. Not half a dozen men in the company were armed alike."

That situation had changed dramatically by late 1862, as Burnside and his men learned at Fredericksburg.

Federal commanders initiated the attack around noon. Their men had to cross about 600 yards of open ground to reach the Confederate position. Union troops began taking casualties as soon as the advance started. When they were within 125 yards of the stone wall, Cobb's infantrymen shouldered their muskets.

"A few more paces onward and the Georgians in the road below us rose up, and, glancing an instant along their rifle barrels, let loose a storm of lead into the faces of the advanced brigade," Owen wrote. "This was too much; the column hesitated, and then, turning, took refuge behind the (nearby earthen) bank."

Burnside repeatedly sent assault waves against the enemy lines all day. Only the arrival of night ended the fighting. No Billy Yank came closer than fifty yards to the stone wall. Federal losses were 8000 compared to 1600 for the South.

Fredericksburg was a testament to the Army of the Potomac's courage. It also showed that the rifled musket was ending the sweeping, grand Napoleonic charge. This weapon represented a significant technological gain in warfare. It was powerful enough, accurate enough and had enough range to pound apart the most determined attack a foe could mount. The industrialized North could supply hundreds of thousands of these arms to its soldiers with comparative ease.

The agrarian South, however, faced staggering supply problems. Against all odds, the Confederacy did get sufficient modern arms to its troops. That required hard work, organization, improvisation and the talents of a remarkable man—Josiah Gorgas. Nobody in the Confederacy would do more to get rifles for Johnny Reb.

A Pennsylvanian, West Pointer and pre-war professional soldier, Gorgas became chief of Confederate ordnance early in the war. Before it ended, he would run thousands of guns through the Yankee blockade and build a Southern weapons industry from scratch. Southerners in 1861 might have gone to war with fowling pieces and old smoothbores, but by mid-1863, thanks to Gorgas, they generally had equipment that matched their Federal foes'. One Southern leader succinctly and accurately described his wartime achievements: "He created the ordnance department out of nothing."

Gorgas knew early on that the rifled musket would play a key role in the conflict, and the Confederacy would need large quantities of them. He also understood its capabilities. Compared to today's military rifles, the typical Civil War musket was heavy, big, cumbersome and fired a huge bullet, often more than half-an-inch in diameter. Such muskets required twenty steps to load. A soldier typically did this standing upright and holding his weapon in front of him with its butt on the ground. Ammunition came in paper cartridges that contained a bullet and a standard charge of blackpowder. Johnny Reb would bite off a cartridge end, pour the powder down the barrel, discard the paper, place the bullet in the muzzle and ram it to the breech using a ramrod carried in a channel beneath the barrel. The Civil War musket's ignition system relied on the percussion cap, a metal cap filled with fulminate of mercury. The system was reliable and could function in all weather conditions.

The same could not be said of the previous generation of military shoulder arms. The flintlock muzzle-loader depended on a piece of flint striking a piece of metal to create a spark. Much could go wrong with this process, and damp powder doomed it. Knowing the flintlock's limitations, both Civil War armies eagerly embraced the percussion system.

Average Johnny Rebs and Billy Yanks in the infantry used the same weapons and used them the same way, both as individuals and as members of military units.

For much of the conflict, officers in blue and gray deployed troops in large, concentrated units that shot in volleys. This allowed commanders to mass fire and to control fire rates. The only way to move men into these combat formations was through standardized maneuvers, which explains why the 19th century American soldier spent much time drilling.

Although presented with a powerful, comparatively long-range weapon in the rifled musket, generals stuck with those formations and tactics appropriate to the short ranges and inaccuracy of the smoothbore era. Surprisingly enough, leading commanders on both sides failed to immediately grasp the rifle's destructive power. Not only did Burnside embrace the frontal assault at Fredericksburg, but so did Lee at Gettysburg, Ulysses S. Grant at Cold Harbor, and Confederate Lt. Gen. John B. Hood at Franklin, Tennessee. At all these places, the results were disastrous.

As the war progressed, however, the average soldier realized the value of entrenching. Southern infantrymen became adept at creating trenches and rifle pits whenever they stopped, using tin cups and plates as well as shovels to put a few inches of dirt between them and the enemy. The 1864-65 Petersburg campaign, in fact, was largely a fight between entrenched armies that knew a direct attack against such works was tantamount to suicide.

For the average Confederate soldier, combat was a terrifying experience. It also was hard work. To begin, loading the rifle was difficult. Even veteran soldiers could easily forget what they were doing in the heat of battle. Sometimes they loaded a bullet first, powder second, or jammed load after load down the barrel without capping the nipple. Blackpowder also quickly clogged musket barrels and wrapped the battlefield in clouds of dense smoke that made seeing targets difficult, if not impossible.

Johnny Reb also endured his rifle's hefty recoil. Sam Watkins, a Southern soldier, reported firing 120 rounds during the Battle of Kenesaw Mountain. Afterwards, his arm was battered and bruised. "My gun became so hot that frequently the powder would flash before I could ram home the ball," he wrote, "and I had frequently to exchange my gun for that of a dead colleague."

How good a shot was Johnny Reb? We'll probably never know. While the rifled musket could perform outstandingly, and many

Southerners lived in a society that prized good guns and marksmanship, battle imposed great demands on the best of shots. The danger, excitement, loading process and smoke-covered battlefields made accurate shooting extraordinarily difficult. One historian has estimated that for every casualty produced, 200 rounds were fired. Others believe the figure to be much higher.

If the tactical implications of the rifled musket were sometimes imperfectly understood, its value as an improved shoulder arm was easily grasped. So Confederate officials knew that getting these weapons into Johnny Reb's hands was vital,

and Confederate ordnance chief Gorgas energetically set to work on the problem from the war's start. He knew only three sources of supply existed: capture, import and Southern manufacture.

The Confederacy turned to capture first. As each Southern state left the Union, it seized any Federal arms held at arsenals or armories within its borders. The pickings were lean. These establishments did not have many modern arms. They mainly held older government models of little value. Among these was the U.S. Model 1822 musket, a 69-caliber smoothbore. Many were converted from flintlock to percussion, but the improved ignition system did

Anthony Sydnor Barksdale (1841-1923) of Charlotte County posed with his rifle for this ambrotype (ambrotypes are reversed photos), taken in 1861 when Barksdale was twenty. He served as a private in the 14th Virginia Infantry Regiment and later transferred to Edward R. Young's battery in Mosely's Battalion. Captured in Petersburg in 1865, he was a prisoner of war at Point Lookout for several months. (Virginia Historical Society photo.)

not compensate for their unrifled barrels. Their range and accuracy was limited. Hitting a specific target more than 100 yards away relied on luck as much as skill.

Once the fighting began in earnest, the Confederacy wasted little time in seizing modern Union weapons whenever they became available. Federal prisoners, battlefield gleanings and captured warehouses yielded first-class arms for the Cause.

As veteran Southern infantryman Worsham noted: "When Jackson's troops marched from the Valley (of Virginia) for Richmond (in 1862) to join Lee in his attack on McClellan, they had captured enough arms from the enemy to replace all that was inferior; and after the battles around Richmond, all departments of Lee's army were as well armed."

Probably the most preferred capture from the Yankees was the 58-caliber Springfield, which came in several models. This rifled musket was superior and typical of its type. The weapon weighed roughly 9 pounds, was 58 inches long, and saw more service with the U.S. Army than any other rifle. Government and private armories produced hundreds of thousands during the war.

Also especially desired by Johnny Reb was the U.S. Model 1841. It was first issued in 54-caliber, but many were altered to 58-caliber, and a fair number came into Confederate hands through Federal arsenals in Southern states. This weapon was commonly known as the "Mississippi rifle," from its Mexican War service with Mississippi volunteers commanded by Jefferson Davis.

Confederates also were delighted to get their hands on Federal breechloaders like the Sharps and Spencer. Both represented significant gains in rates of fire and ease of loading.

To load the Sharps, a 52-caliber breechloader, the soldier pulled down the trigger guard. This caused the breechblock to drop and opened the chamber into which was inserted a linen or paper cartridge filled with powder and a bullet. The Sharp's rate of fire was three times that of a musket.

The Spencer fired metallic cartridges. Its tubular magazine in the buttstock held seven rounds. A skilled operator could fire twenty-one rounds per minute. Unfortunately for the South, captured Spencers suffered from an ammunition shortage as the Confederate industry frequently was incapable of meeting cartridge needs created by the weapon's firepower abilities.

Though infantrymen seldom carried revolvers, the Confederate cavalry loved them, especially captured Colts. These were Northern-made, but saw widespread use in both armies. Six-shooters in 36- and 44-calibers, their cylinders could be loaded with paper, foil or sheepskin cartridges, or loose powder and ball. Ignition required a percussion cap on each nipple at each chamber.

Imports were another vital source of armaments. Europe eagerly provided guns to both sides. Southern weapons had to come through the Federal blockade, and a surprisingly large volume made the trip.

Europe offered some superlative weapons and some junk. Particularly despised by Johnny Reb were rifles made in Austria and Belgium. Unwieldy, inaccurate and unreliable, they were dead last on his wish list.

The most desired import was the 577-caliber Enfield. A British-made musket, the Enfield was rugged and accurate. The Enfields came in several styles, including a carbine. Southern cavalry was particularly attached to the latter, even though as a muzzleloader it lacked the rapid-fire quality of Union repeaters. Another popular and well-crafted British import was the 44-caliber Kerr revolver.

Great Britain also supplied some of the war's best sharpshooter rifles: the 44-caliber Kerr and 45-caliber Whitworth. Southern marksmen treasured these guns, which enabled them to hit targets at 1000 yards. The most famous long-range shooting incident of the war occurred on May 9, 1864, during the Battle of Spotsylvania.

Several Southern marksmen are given credit for what happened, but it is impossible to know who did the shooting. One version of the incident comes from Captain William C. Dunlop who commanded the sharpshooters of McGowan's Brigade. This Confederate unit was ordered to move ahead of the main body of Southern troops to scout for Federals that day. Dunlop concealed his men in position along a ridge where they could see the Union VI Corps deploying on a distant hill. Immediately, Dunlop's men began firing with telling effect.

Among Dunlop's troops was a Private Benjamin Powell of South Carolina, who carried a Whitworth that day and was looking for impor-

Confederate "Sharps" carbine by S.C. Robinson, a direct copy of the U.S. Sharps model. Lockplate and top of barrel read "S.C. Robinson, Arms Manufactory, Richmond, VA 1862." (Virginia Historical Society photo.)

Whitney "Mississippi" rifle made by Eli Whitney in 1851, U.S. Model 1841, U.S. percussion rifle in unaltered, original configuration. (Virginia Historical Society photo.)

tant targets. One soon presented itself. Powell could see a Yank officer moving along the enemy firing line, giving commands and viewing the field through binoculars. His behavior and the staff trailing behind him suggested this was an important man.

Powell decided to shoot him. The round traveled 800 yards and struck General John Sedgwick, the corp commander, in the left cheek, killing him. Only moments earlier, the general had tried to calm his troops who were agitated by the sniper fire. They "couldn't hit an elephant at this distance," he said seconds before he died.

One of the most intriguing weapons that made it through the Union's naval blockade was the Le Mat revolver, which could fire nine 41-caliber rounds from its main barrel plus buckshot from a shorter one. (Oddly enough, its main barrel's caliber is variously reported as ranging from 40- to 42-caliber.) The idea for this monster came from Jean Alexander Francois Le Mat, a New Orleans doctor. Once the Confederacy accepted his pistol, the doctor headed for France where it was produced. A carbine model also was developed.

The last source of weapons was from within the Confederacy. Given the virtually non-existent manufacturing base there, Gorgas achieved astonishing results, creating government armories as well as inspiring various private firms to enter the armaments field.

The best Southern-made weapons came from government operations in Richmond and Fayetteville, North Carolina. Early in the war, the Confederacy captured Federal gunmaking equipment at Harper's Ferry. This was used at both Confederate plants to produce 58-caliber muskets, known as Richmond and Fayetteville rifles.

These two factories were not the only source of "home-grown" weapons. Other production facilities sprang up in Georgia, Louisiana, South Carolina, Mississippi, Texas and Alabama. Quality and volume varied greatly from factory to factory, as the case of the Confederate "Sharps" proved. These were versions of the Sharps carbine Model 1855, made by the Richmond firm of S.C. Robinson Arms Manufacturing Company. Forty were sent for field-testing to the 4th Virginia Cavalry Regiment in the spring of 1863. The gun was not a success. Reportedly

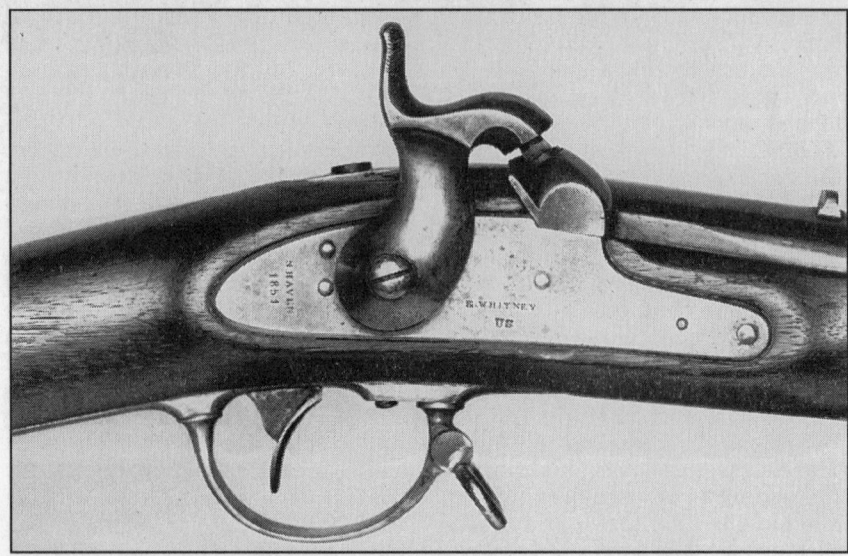

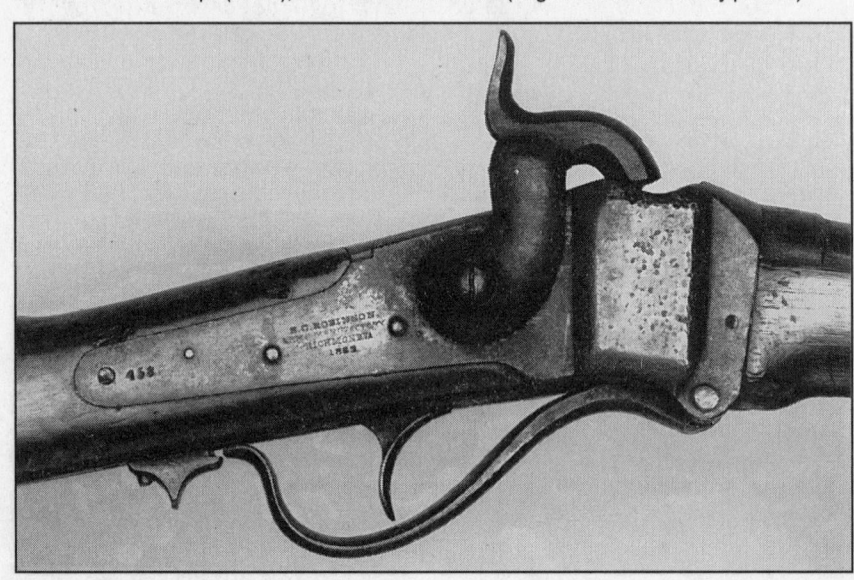

Whether marked "U.S.," like this Whitney Mississippi Rifle (above), or "RICHMOND VA," as it says on the Robinson Sharps (below), the Rebs used them all. (Virginia Historical Society photos.)

seven of nine burst during firing. Furious, an officer of the regiment, Lieutenant N.D. Morris, fired off a letter to a newspaper, *The Richmond Whig*, which ran a story on the weapons under the headline "An Outrage."

"The lieutenant suggests," ran the article, "that the manufacturers of these arms be sent to the field where they can be furnished with Yankee sabres, while the iron they are wasting can be used for farming implements!"

Ordnance officials rushed to defend the producers and the carbines, suggesting the soldiers using the weapons had not been trained properly, but the bad reputation stuck. Captain W.S. Downer, superintendent of the Richmond armory, also reported to Gorgas that somebody should remind the

letter-writing lieutenant about army procedures. "I would also suggest that Lieut. N.D. Morris, of Capt. McKinney's Co., 4th Va. Cavalry, be notified to communicate with the Department through his proper officers, rather than through the columns of a newspaper."

Besides government plants, private firms got involved in weapons production. For example, Davis and Bozeman of Coosa County, Alabama, made 58-caliber rifles. J.&F. Garrett Co. of Greensboro, North Carolina, produced the 52-caliber Tarpley carbine, the only breech-loading gun patented, manufactured and offered for general sale in the Confederacy.

Private industry made its biggest contribution to weapons production by making pistols. When the war

English Whitworth Sharpshooter's rifle with telescope mounted along the left side of the barrel. This gun was one of twelve purchased in England in early 1863. (Virginia Historical Society photo.)

T.W. Cofer revolver, Second Model, 36-caliber, invented and patented by a Portsmouth, Virginia, gunsmith who made about fifty of them before the fall of Norfolk and Portsmouth in May, 1860. (Virginia Historical Society photo.)

began, the Confederacy had no revolver manufacturers within its borders. But wartime entrepreneurs appeared like Spiller and Burr, Griswold and Gunnison, and Leech & Rigdon.

Many entrepreneurs found that making weapons for the South was a difficult business indeed. Consider the story of Charles Rigdon, for example, a Southern sympathizer who lived in St. Louis. He moved to Memphis when the war started and formed a partnership with Thomas Leech to make swords. Advancing Union armies forced the pair to move to Columbus, Mississippi, and then to Greensboro, Georgia, where they made 36-caliber revolvers, which were copies of Colt's pistols. The partnership eventually collapsed. Leech kept making revolvers in Greensboro. Rigdon opened a new pistol firm in Augusta, Georgia—Rigdon, Ansley & Co.—that operated until the war's end. Interestingly enough, Samuel Colt sued the company for illegal use of his revolver patents.

One non-issue weapon that came from private manufacturers was the shotgun. Often brought from home, shotguns were popular among certain Confederate cavalry units, particularly in the Western Theater. Shotguns had limited range, limited tactical value and took a long time to load. But at close quarters they were devastating. The 8th Texas Cavalry, better known as Terry's Texas Rangers, were particularly fond of scatterguns. During the Southern retreat from the Battle of Shiloh,

this unit used these weapons effectively. Ordered to charge Union infantry pursuing the Southern army, the Texans swept forward, halted about twenty steps from the Federal line and fired their shotguns. Each barrel was loaded with fifteen to twenty buckshot. The Federal pursuit fell apart and a retreat ensued. The Texans then put their shotguns aside and pursued the enemy on horseback, firing their revolvers.

Much of the success of Southern weapon production came from the use of slave labor. African-Americans worked in armories and played a key role in the armament industry's labor force. For instance, the Georgia pistol firm of Columbus Fire Arms Manufacturing Co. hired forty-three blacks in 1862 and aggressively tried to find more during the rest of the war.

For blacks, working in weapons production was a mixed bag. It often meant separation from loved ones, hard work, long hours and daily rations of bacon and cornmeal. However, the work gave them valuable skills and provided an unprecedented degree of freedom.

Although the Confederacy ultimately lost the war, it did not do so due to a lack of weapons and ammunition. Granted, the Southern ordnance system had flaws. Armies in the East tended to be better supplied than those in the West. Units in either theater, even late in the war, might carry a hodgepodge of weapons, mostly rifled muskets but sometimes smoothbores, and this variety made ammunition re-supply a headache. Some of the Southern-made rifles and pistols did not meet

the standards of Northern or British factories, but on balance Gorgas did a remarkable job.

One anecdote makes the point. When Lee surrendered at Appomattox in 1865, his army was small, sick, ill-clad and poorly fed. However, most men were armed and, on average, each carried seventy-five rounds of ammunition.

Today, Confederate guns are scarce and costly. But the interested student of Civil War firearms can see one of the world's best collections of Southern weapons at the Virginia Historical Society in Richmond. The society owns an extraordinary collection of rifles, pistols, swords, belt-plates and buttons given to it in 1948 by Richard D. Steuart, a Baltimore newspaperman who had two grandfathers and nine uncles who served the Confederate cause. For many years, the collection was displayed to feature the weapons themselves as artifacts and objects of interest.

In 1993, the Virginia Historical Society decided to display its collection in an innovative way. The weapons were moved into a gallery decorated with life-sized murals of Civil War battle scenes. The new display uses the guns to tell the story of how the South armed itself. For the neophyte or life-long scholar of the conflict, the new display is entertaining and informative—you can *see* Johnny Reb and his guns. ●

For more information on the society and its collections, write: Virginia Historical Society, P.O. Box 7311, Richmond, VA 23221-0311 or call 804-358-4901.

by DOC CARLSON

BLACKPOWDER REVIEW

THE INCREASING interest in hunting with old-style firearms—an easy-to-see trend—is probably, as much as anything, the desire to put the "hunt" back in hunting. Whatever the reason for the continuing growth of this part of the hunting sport, both new companies and familiar names are providing new products for this ever-growing specialized sport. Let's take a look at a few:

One new product stirring great interest in shooters with a nostalgic bent is the Schofield revolver being reproduced by **Navy Arms Co.** It's very well done, an exact copy of the revolver designed by Schofield for use by the U.S. Army. Some 8900 of the guns were made between 1875 and 1877. The

pistol fired a 45-caliber cartridge slightly shorter than the Colt, hence the old designation of the cartridge for the 1873 Colt Single Action Army as 45 Long Colt. The guns were phased out after a few years of use in favor of the Colt Single Action and were sold on the surplus market. Many found their way into the hands of the people moving West, and the Schofield was a favored arm of the cowboy. Some of the surplus guns were cut down from their original 7-inch barrel length to 5 inches. Wells Fargo used many of these guns for some years.

The reproduction gun is made in both 44-40 and 45 Colt calibers, and is available in a 5-inch barrel, called the Wells Fargo,

and the original 7-inch version, called the Army. The price will be $795 and deliveries are scheduled to begin in March of '94.

Another rather interesting new gun on the market is produced by **U.F.A. Inc.** The gun resembles a Winchester High Wall single shot from a distance. It has an enclosed action with a center-hung hammer and single trigger. It is available in 40, 45 and 50 calibers as well as 12-gauge smoothbore. Barrels are interchangeable and, as the sights are on the barrels, they need no rezero when taken off and replaced. The possibility of having one gun with multiple barrels for various types of hunting is an interesting one.

All internal parts are stain-

less steel, and the gun is available with either a brushed matte or high-polish blued finish or stainless steel with a brushed matte finish. The standard stock is of laminated wood with premium walnut available as an option.

Called the Legend, the rifle offers Marble's open sights installed on the barrel or a scope mount is available, if you wish. Prices start at $834, with extra barrels and other options available.

Modern Muzzleloading continues to expand their line of in-line hunting firearms and accessories. They have added a new rifle called the Wolverine, which they describe as "a no-frills, lean, mean, hunting machine." This is their well-

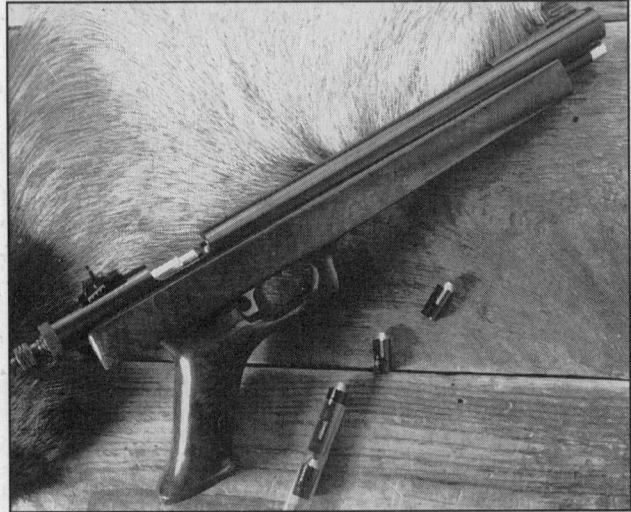

Modern Muzzleloading's Hawkeye target pistol promises a lot of competitive accuracy, tradition-be-durned.

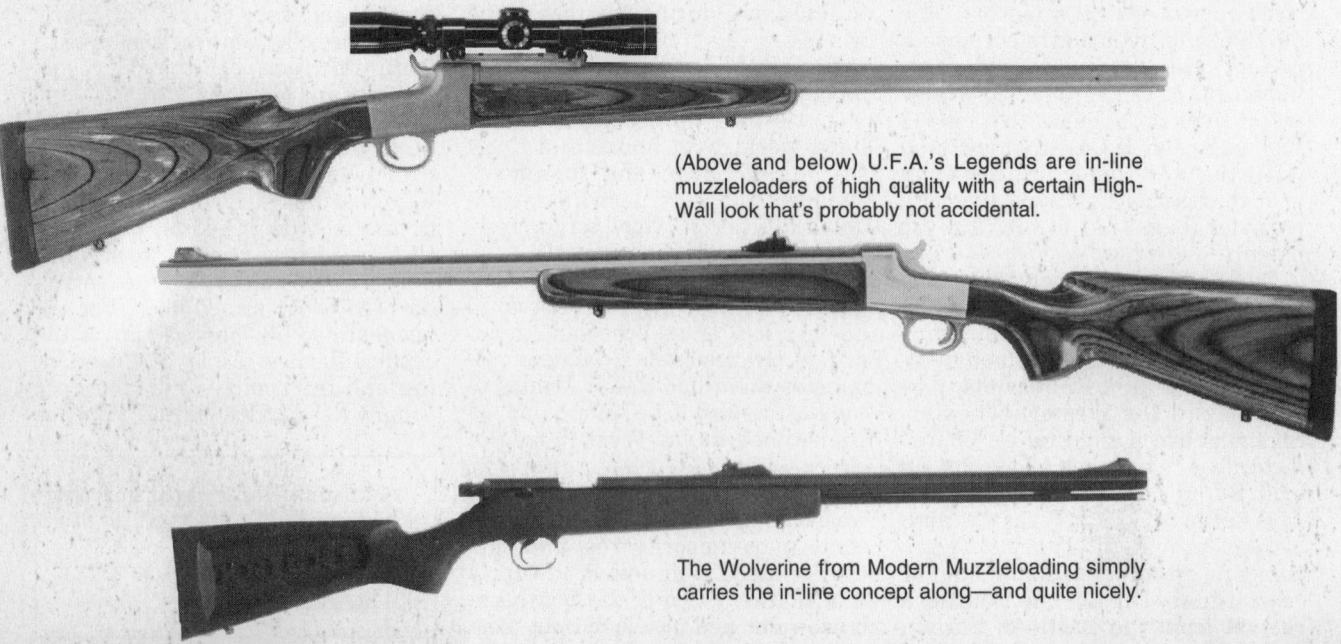

(Above and below) U.F.A.'s Legends are in-line muzzleloaders of high quality with a certain High-Wall look that's probably not accidental.

The Wolverine from Modern Muzzleloading simply carries the in-line concept along—and quite nicely.

tried, basic in-line action with a 22-inch barrel, 1:28-inch twist, fully adjustable trigger, removable breech plug, adjustable rear sight and patented double safety system, all mated in a lightweight moulded Fiber-Lite stock. It is priced at a very reasonable $249.95, which sure should find favor among those looking for a high-quality rifle at a good price. It's available in 50-caliber only, intended for use with slugs, not balls.

Modern Muzzleloading also has an in-line heavy caliber pistol. The Hawkeye has a tapered 12-inch barrel with a fast 1:20-inch twist in either blued or stainless steel. There's an aluminum ramrod, and the target-styled composite stock comes in either black or in simulated burl walnut that looks more like wood than wood.

There are the usual features—removable breech plug and adjustable, target-quality trigger. A fully adjustable rear and bead front comprise the sighting equipment. The gun should shoot either round ball or slug-type projectiles with equal accuracy, I would think. Priced at $349.95, this big pistol should interest both plinkers and small game hunters.

These same Centerville, Iowa, folks have brought a couple of new wrinkles to the ignition process also. The first of these is simply a redesign of the standard nipple. They have double-tapered the neck of the nipple so that while there is

large rifle magnum primer—the sort found in centerfire cartridges. The entire capsule, which resembles a centerfire pistol cartridge, is inserted into the breech of the in-line rifle and gives very hot, sure ignition. This should find favor with those who hunt dangerous game or spend a large chunk of their hard-earned income on a once-in-a-lifetime hunt and don't want to take the chance of a misfire.

Thompson/Center Arms pioneered the mass-produced muzzle-loading rifle with their T/C Hawken many years ago. When it first came out, the Hawken was decried as a non-traditional gun that would ruin the sport of hunting with muzzleloaders and flood the woods with hunters that were somehow "impure" due to their use of this new mass-produced rifle. The comments then were much the same as the in-line type of front stuffer is viewed by some today. The Hawken, rather than hindering the sport, fostered impressive growth of interest in muzzle-loading and is greatly responsible for the many special muzzle-loading hunting seasons in place today.

year, now comes in stainless steel. There are those who like the relative ease of taking care of this corrosion-resistant material. The gun has a Rynite stock to boot, as well as a 21-inch barrel with a 1:38-inch twist for slug projectiles. There's an adjustable Timney trigger, open sights and the rifle is drilled and tapped for T/C's Thunderhawk scope rings or the quick-release mounting system.

In the accessory line, T/C has added a Hunters' Starter Pack that includes a bullet starter, plastic capper, patch puller, powder measure and two quick loaders. It contains everything to get the hunter started except powder, caps and balls. It is available in 50- or 54-caliber.

T/C also offers their Break-O-Way sabots in 50- and 54-caliber preassembled with pure lead, hollowpoint bullets. These sabots consist of two plastic halves held together by a greased base wad, which helps

with fouling. They separate immediately upon leaving the muzzle and have given good accuracy in the shooting that I have done with them.

White Muzzleloading Systems is showing a new rifle that attracted my interest. The White folks have a complete line of in-line action guns that they combine with bullets of their own design to make up their shooting system. They have added, this year, the Green River line of guns. These rifles have the same accurate barrels as their other guns and are intended to be paired with the Super Slug projectiles. However, the Green River rifles are of traditional sidelock design with lines that will appeal to the more traditional-minded shooter.

There's a Manton-type hooked breech with all the "doglegs" in the flash channel straightened for much better ignition. The gun also uses the new Super

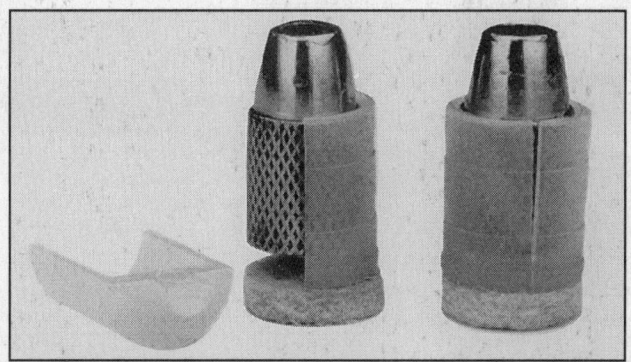

They're not messing around. The Break-O-Way T/C sabot is meant to kill deer.

Thompson/Center went all the way with the SST Thunderhawk—it's Rynite and stainless steel.

enough taper at the base to hold the cap securely, the upper part allows the cap to fully seat with very little pressure. This eliminates a very common cause of misfires using the percussion cap. Of course, those of us who are pure of heart and use the more reliable flintlock ignition do not have to deal with this problem. Unfortunately, in-line actions are not available in flintlock, yet!

The other ignition upgrade is a complete system that uses a plastic "capsule" containing a

T/C has now introduced a deluxe version of this famous rifle. Available in 50-caliber, the gun follows the form of the standard rifle with the addition of high-luster blue and a select-grade walnut stock. The patch/cap box is left off, and the hardware is all steel with the same high-gloss blue as the 28-inch barrel. The rifling twist is the standard 1:48 inches T/C has used for years. This is a *very* nice looking rifle.

The Thunderhawk, T/C's in-line action rifle brought out last

This T/C Hunter Starter Pack leaves only powder, balls, caps and a bag to buy.

Nipple the White folks brought out this year. The internal design of this nipple is supposed to give a hotter, faster flash to the powder for quicker, more positive ignition of both Pyrodex and blackpowder. The new nipple has a shoulder area that is shaped as a 5/16-inch hex nut so standard wrenches will fit it. I like that idea.

The Green Rivers are stocked in a fiber-composite base covered by a highly figured walnut crotchwood finish that is so wood-like as to trigger arguments that it is indeed wood. The styling is pretty typical 19th-century English sidelock sporting rifle. This type of stock design handles recoil well and points naturally. This line of Green River rifles, based on the traditional English hunting rifle, will be very popular with modern-day hunters. The quality is top notch, and the form and line are appealing.

Traditions, Inc., is another outfit with a very complete line of rifles. Beyond their hunters' guns, there's a nice Kentucky flintlock rifle, a good-looking copy of an English half-stock percussion fowler and two choice target rifles. The target rifles are special.

Both are styled after the half-stock, percussion target rifles of the mid-1800s. The Creedmore model is patterned after both American and English guns of the period. It sports a 32-inch barrel and is intended to shoot a 451-caliber slug. The lock is case-hardened, and the rest of the steel metalwork is blued. The walnut stock is of pistol grip half-stock design finished off with a black forend tip that passes for horn.

The other gun copies a mid-19th-century Alexander Henry target/hunting rifle. The caliber is the same as the Creedmore rifle. Sights on both guns are tang-mounted, Vernier-type aperture rears coupled with adjustable tunnel front sights. Either would be at home in the hunting field as well as on the target range. The Henry carries its own ramrod; the Creedmore ramrod must be carried separately as there is no provision for it on the rifle. This was, however, not uncommon in the hunting field of yore. If you are into English-style guns or target rifles, these are worth a look.

Connecticut Valley Arms has new guns for the hunter this year in the Wolf series. Stocks are a patented polymer, available in black, gray or Realtree camo pattern and are called Lone Wolf, Grey Wolf and (what else?) Timber Wolf. Actions and barrels are dull matte blued; barrel is rifled for slug shooting. The hammers are offset—bent to the right—which makes them very easy to cock, especially when a scope is mounted. The oversize trigger guard is plenty roomy for use with gloves.

CVA offers a very similar rifle with a laminated stock, 26-inch barrel with 1:48-inch twist and many of the same features as the Wolf series, but priced under $170. This plain-vanilla working rifle is solidly made and will serve the hunter on a budget very well.

Lyman Products, the reloading and sight people, are remaking the old-time tang sights for the '94 Winchester, so popular in days gone by. These will work on many new muzzle-loading arms, too. If you are looking for a traditional-looking aperture sight for your muzzle-loading gun, this might be worth a glance. The only thing to check is to be sure that your rifle's tang-to-barrel angle is about the same as the '94 Winchester's. Lyman is also making their popular receiver sight with a base to fit many of the more popular in-line action muzzle-loading rifles.

Hornady Manufacturing Co. is offering their sabot in 45-, 50-, 54- and 58-calibers. This is the same sabot they have been selling mated to their XTP pistol bullets. By being able to buy

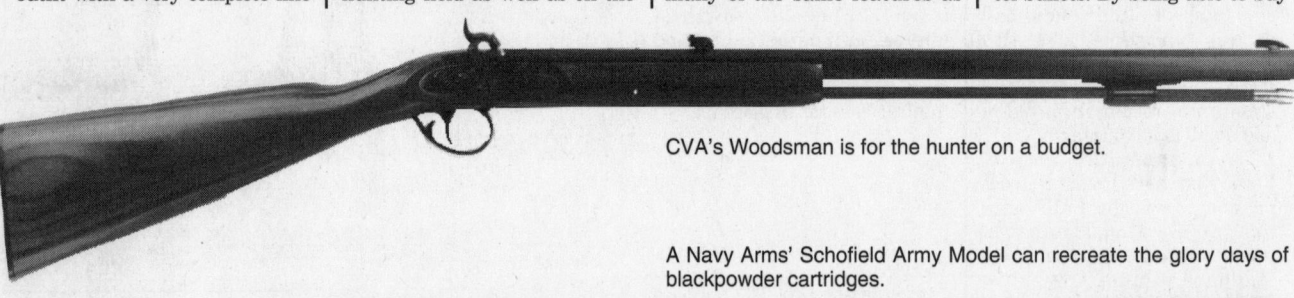

CVA's Woodsman is for the hunter on a budget.

A Navy Arms' Schofield Army Model can recreate the glory days of blackpowder cartridges.

the sabots in packs of 50, the shooter can mate them to whatever pistol bullet he likes.

This Nebraska company also has a new lube for either patched round ball or conical bullets. It is all natural, made from animal fats, they tell me. This should duplicate the old-time tallow that works so very well for breaking in a barrel and shooting.

The other thing Hornady has new this year that might have some interest to muzzleloader shooters is a new chronograph. This is a very simple-to-operate outfit that comes with a tube that stores the screens and legs, which then convert the tube to a stand for the screens, preset at 24 inches. Nothing else to buy or build. It will store up to five shots and is priced at less than $150. Now darn near anyone can afford to own and use a chronograph. There is nothing that will separate fact from fiction, when working up loads, better than a chronograph.

Another outfit that anyone who is shooting, or thinking about shooting, muzzle-loading firearms should know about is **Mountain States Muzzleloading.** This West Virginia-based company is a supplier for darn near everything that one could possibly want in the muzzle-loading line. Their 250-page catalog is chock full of goodies to delight the heart of the muzzleloader shooter. Their catalog, which sells for $5, is arranged so that everything is in alphabetical order, making it easy to find things. You don't need an index. A rather novel idea, I thought.

A relatively new product they have put together is a Premium Muzzle Loading Hunter/Shooters Kit. This contains everything one would need to shoot and clean a muzzle-loading arm, except the ammunition. The whole thing is contained in a shooting and storage box with a lift-out tray. Priced at $65, it really is a good idea for the beginning shooter who wants to go a bit beyond what the average shooting kit contains.

If you are into muzzle-loading pistols, especially revolvers, and need a holster to carry said hogleg, **Oklahoma Leather Products Co.** has two new ones to satisfy the needs of the Civil War buff. Embossed either "US" or "CSA," these cavalry-style holsters are sized to fit Colt or Remington revolvers of the Civil War era. The "US" holster is finished black, the "CSA" version is in brown, as is right for the originals. If your local dealer doesn't carry these reasonably priced holsters and the other leather products for muzzleloading made by the Oklahoma Leather folks, have him drop them a line. It's pretty good looking stuff. •

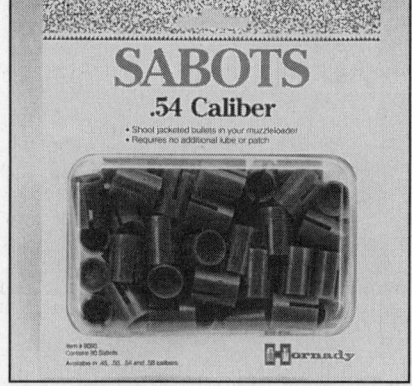

Add-your-own bullet sabots from Hornady in 45, 50, 54 and 58 calibers are new.

Here's T/C's new deluxe version—the Hawken Custom—of the rifles that were once controversial.

This little chronograph is—or can be—an eye-opener in more ways than one.

The stuff of Civil War dreams in leather from Oklahoma Leather Products.

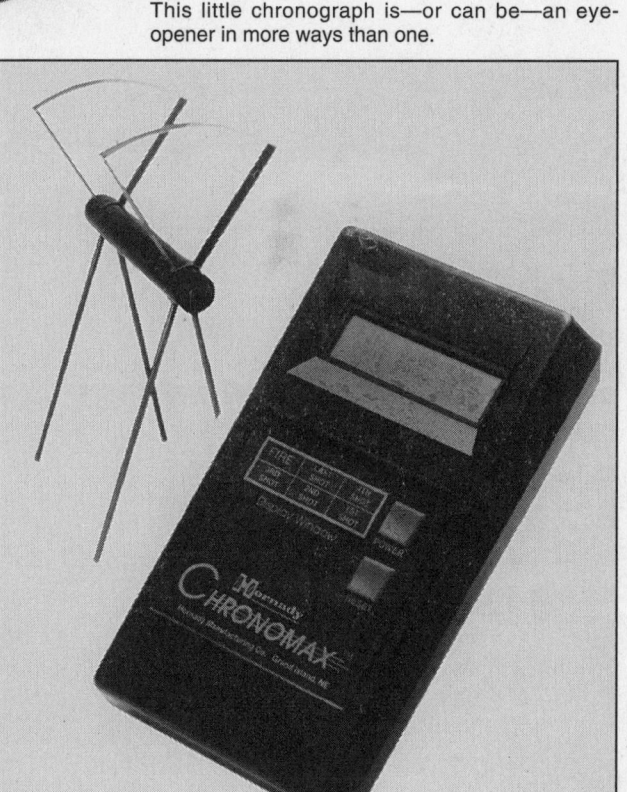

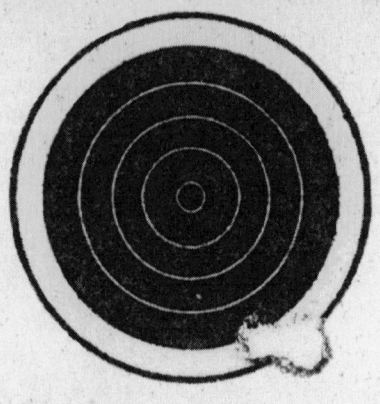

Writer Konrad Schreier shot this group (five shots, prone, rifle unzeroed) in 1942 with an M-2 Springfield. He knows about...

THE 22 RIFLES

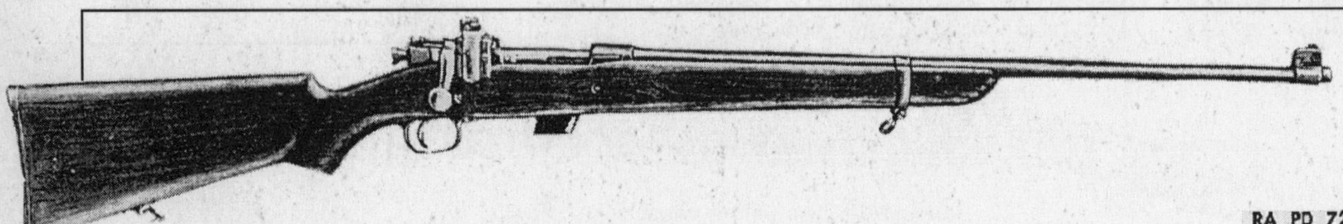

RA PD 72602

Figure 44—Rifle, U.S., Cal..22, M1922

The Springfield 22 rifles—M1922, M-1 and M-2—as shown in a U.S. Army World War II Ordnance Supply Catalog ORD 3 SNL B-1.

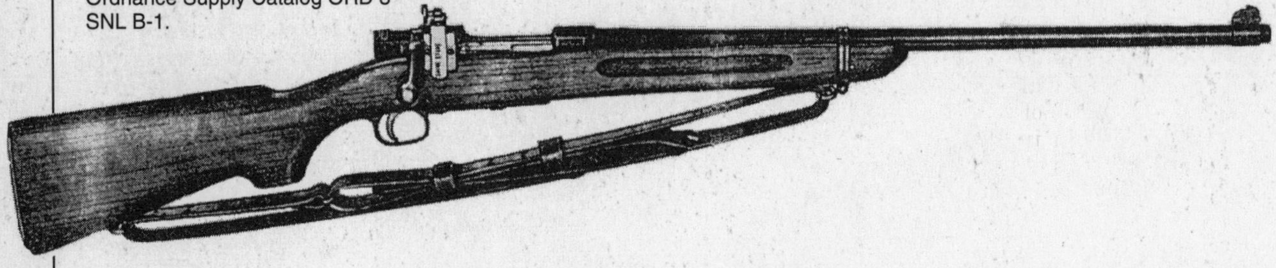

RA PD 81893

Figure 45—Rifle, U.S., Cal..22, M1

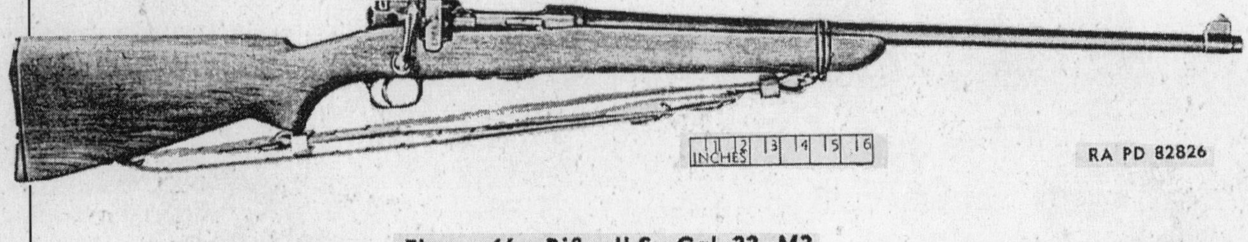

INCHES 1 2 3 4 5 6

RA PD 82826

Figure 46—Rifle, U.S., Cal..22, M2

MANY OF US who served in the U.S. Armed Forces in World War II got our first military live-fire training with 22 rimfire rifles. Only 10 or 20 percent of us had any previous formal rifle training, so the 22 was as good a way to begin our training as there was.

Those 22 rimfires were nothing new to the U.S. Army. They had been in use since before 1910. The 22 was used to begin the training of many novice soldiers in World War I.

the regular 30-06 Springfield or modifications.

Production of the 22 M1922 began at once, and in all, 1500 of them were produced. As soon as they were in service as training rifles, problems involving their bolt and magazine caused work on an improved model to begin.

The improved design was designated the U.S. Rifle M1922M-1. It overcame the basic problems of the original model, and with the help of improved 22 rimfire ammunition, it

20,000 Springfield 22 M-2s were built between 1932 and 1942 when its production was stopped in favor of urgent World War II combat weapons production. At the same time, Springfield Armory rebuilt many 22 M1922s and M1922M-1s to the 22 M-2's standards.

All models of the Springfield 22s were built with the same front sight as the issue Springfield, and they all had the Lyman 48 receiver rear. For serious target shooting, it was easy to replace the military front sight

WORLD WAR II
OF

by KONRAD F. SCHREIER, JR.

The reasons the U.S. Army considered 22 rifle training useful were many. A major one was that the 22 required only very simple, inexpensive ranges which could be constructed almost anyplace. The ammunition was much cheaper than regular 30-06, and the minimum recoil let soldiers learn without getting the bad habit of "flinching." The only problem in World War I was that there was no repeating bolt-action 22 rimfire rifle suitable for the kind of training the U.S. Army required.

While World War I was still in progress, the Army ordered its Springfield Armory to develop a 22 rimfire training rifle based on the standard cal. 30 Rifle M1903, the 30-06 Springfield. The first version of this rimfire rifle was the U.S. Rifle, cal. 22 M1922.

The 22 M1922 was tested with the full military stock and with a new stock configured like that of civilian 22 target rifles coming on the market at the time; the latter pattern was the one adopted. The rifle also used the then-new Lyman 48 receiver sight, and it had a five-round detachable box magazine. However, many of its parts were either those of

also was a more accurate rifle. Some 19,500 of the M1922M-1s were built in the late 1920s and early 1930s, and many of the original 22 M1922s were returned to Springfield Armory and rebuilt into M1922M-1s.

By 1930, the 22 M1922M-1 was not only widely used throughout the U.S. Armed Forces, but large numbers were issued to the Reserve Officers Training Corps (ROTC) at many military academies and secondary schools, since 22 rifle competition had become very popular not only in the Armed Forces, but among the ROTC academies and schools. In open competitions in which any rifle could be used, qualified commercial 22 target rifles, particularly the legendary Winchester Model 52, were shooting far better scores that the 22 M1922M-1. Springfield Armory was ordered to redesign its 22 rifle again, and the project was given to a development team including their legendary designer John C. Garand.

In 1932, the improved Springfield-designed U.S. Rifle, cal. 22 M-2 was introduced. Although there were several modifications made in its bolt during its manufacture, it was always a superior 22 target rifle, and

with a commercial globe target sight, but the use of a globe sight was not allowed for military match or training shooting. With good target ammunition and a globe front sight, the Springfield 22 M-2 could, and often did, outshoot the best pre-World War II 22 target rifles, including the great Winchester Model 52.

Today's Springfield rifle collectors find markings on these 22s very confusing. Military M1922s are very rare since most of them were upgraded, and so are M1922M-1s. To make things even more confusing, some M1922M-1s were originally marked M-1s without the 1922 marking. When the earlier models were upgraded to the M-2 standards, they were marked M1922M-2, M1922M-11 and M-11.

To further confuse the problem, post-World War II Ordnance Department manuals show all types from the original M1922 to the last M-2s of early World War II still in the U.S. Army inventory.

By the end of the 1930s, the U.S. Army used 22 rimfire rifle training very widely. Every post, camp and station had a 22 rifle gallery range, and *American Rifleman* magazines of the day show match scores reflecting fierce competition. These not only involved the Regulars, but also the National Guard and many ROTC units. Even the Military Academy at West Point participated. The Army had published "Range Practice, Caliber 22 (Small Bore Practice)" which describes in detail how the Army did it. Most of the shooting was at standard National Rifle Association smallbore targets, but there were also "landscape target" regulations, and a set for anti-aircraft rifle firing.

While much of the Army's 22 rifle practice was done on 50-foot indoor smallbore gallery ranges, it was also shot outdoors at 50-, 100- and 200-yard ranges. The Army's "Table of Fire" ballistic data for the standard-velocity 22 Long Rifle cartridge gave firing data for ranges up to 300 yards.

The landscape target was a large lithographed paper picture represent-

Range (yards)	Velocity	Bullet energy	Time of flight	Drop at target	Ordinate of trajectory half range	Mean accuracy	Angle of departure
	Feet per second	Foot-pounds	Seconds	Inches	Inches	Inches	Minutes
0	1,100	102	-----	-----	-----	-----	----
25	1,070	95	0.068	0.89	0.24	0.14	3.5
50	1,020	89	.140	3.17	.98	.33	7.6
75	980	84	.214	8.06	2.28	.45	11.7
100	950	79	.292	14.82	4.08	.57	15.8
125	920	75	.372	24.73	6.78	.80	20.5
150	890	71	.455	36.64	10.02	.98	24.9
175	860	67	.541	50.80	14.20	1.13	29.6
200	840	64	.630	72.93	19.10	1.25	34.3
225	810	61	.720	93.04	28.30	1.45	39.7
250	790	58	.812	118.21	31.87	1.65	44.7
275	770	55	.911	147.20	39.87	1.88	50.8
300	750	52	1.005	177.12	48.69	2.12	55.7

This table of fire for the standard-velocity 22 Long Rifle rimfire cartridge used in 22 training rifles in World War II is from the Army's TM 9-1990 and still works for standard-velocity 22s.

The Remington, Stevens and Winchester commercial 22 rifles as procured by the U.S. Army in World War II as shown in U.S. Army World War II Ordnance Supply Catalog ORD 3 SNL-B1.

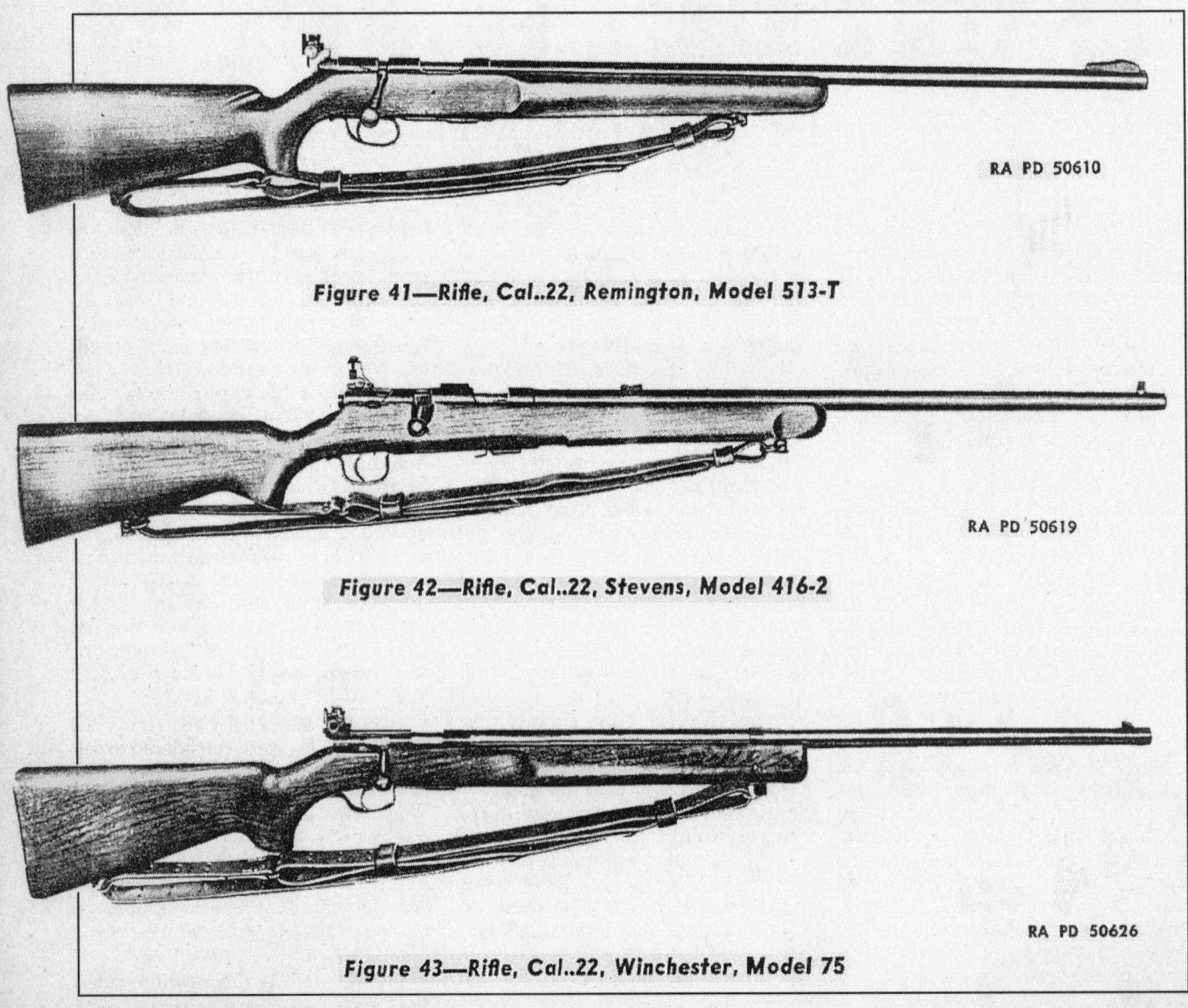

RA PD 50610

Figure 41—Rifle, Cal..22, Remington, Model 513-T

RA PD 50619

Figure 42—Rifle, Cal..22, Stevens, Model 416-2

RA PD 50626

Figure 43—Rifle, Cal..22, Winchester, Model 75

(Above) The U.S. Army caption for this 1942 photo reads "With a miniature moving target, and using small bore ammunition, a range officer shows these men how to blast a plane out of the sky with a rifle."

This early World War II photo shows a 22 Springfield rifle mounted as a subcaliber rifle on a M1905 Field Gun, probably fired on paper landscape targets.

ing the kinds of targets a military rifleman would encounter in the field. It was fired at a range of 1000 inches—83 feet, 4 inches—to simulate a range of 1000 yards, and the instructor carefully designated targets. Scoring counted the hits on those designated targets. Then the shooters had the boring chore of pasting transparent tissue patches over their hits.

The landscape target was also used to teach machinegunners. They fired at it with 22-caliber modifications of the standard Browning Machine Gun. The 22 cartridge also trained antitank gunners with spe-

cial adapters for 37mm and 57mm antitank guns. These mounted the stockless, sightless U.S. rifle, Subcaliber, cal. 22 M-2A1, a variation of the standard M-2 Springfield. Cal. 22 M-2A1s are very rare rifles since most of them were later converted into standard M-2s.

The landscape target system worked quite well, and it was widely used in the World War II era. The trainees also enjoyed it much more than they did punching holes in standard bullseye targets.

In the 1940-41 rearmament period, the Army made vast use of 22 rimfire rifle training. Shooting were 200,000 ROTC cadets in some 300 colleges, high schools and military academies. Nearly 5000 U.S. Army Officers and enlisted men detailed as ROTC instructors prepared their cadets for service with 22s.

At the same time, the National Rifle Association and other organizations offered 22 rimfire rifle training to familiarize people who would serve in the Armed Forces with firearms. Their programs, and those of the ROTC, worked from Col. Townsend Whelen's *Small Bore Rifle Handbook*, first published in 1936 by the Sporting Arms and Ammunition Manufacturers Institute, an excellent basic 76-page manual.

Getting into World War II on December 7, 1941, gave new priority to the 22 rifle basic training program. At the same time, Springfield Armory stopped producing the M-2 22 rifle to concentrate on combat weapons. Manufacture and supply of spare parts for their 22s held up for the rest of World War II, and a very limited number of M-2s were made up from parts on hand.

In February, 1942, the War Production Board froze the sale of all 22 rimfire rifles costing less than $50 so they could be rationed for sale for "essential purposes." At the same time, they froze the sale of 22 rimfire ammunition since the Armed Forces were taking the entire supply. The Army was expanding at an incredible rate, and so was the need for 22 rimfire rifles for indoctrination training.

This led the Army to procure commercial 22 target rifles for training use. These were to have full-size stocks and to cost less than $50 each. Thus, the Army procured the Winchester Model 75 Target, the Remington Model 513T Matchmaster, and the Stevens Model 416-2 Target. All three were accurate, magazine-loading, bolt-action rifles, though they were not as good as the Springfield 22 M-2. Large numbers of these were delivered to the U.S. Army in 1942 and until the requirement for them was filled in 1943.

These commercial target rifles were all somewhat modified to suit the U.S. Army's requirements. The most noticeable changes were flat Parkerized metal finish and military oil finish stocks. They all used commercial receiver rear target sights, and they all had blade-type front sights, not globe sights.

These military procurement 22s were all stamped with the U.S. property and acceptance marks. However, they were not stamped with inspection marks since they were commercial products procured for non-combat use and did not require them.

The commercial U.S. Army 22 training rifles were considered excellent. However, most of the competition shooting by Army rifle teams in World War II was done with the superior Springfield 22 M-2 rifles.

When the U.S. Navy went to war, it found that it had neglected small arms firing training. This was immediately corrected by adopting the Army's programs including basic training with 22-caliber rimfire rifles.

Mossberg 22 Model 44-US rifle used in World War II, shown here in a 1944 U.S. Navy training manual.

However, when the Navy requested a large number of 22s, the U.S. Army—which supplied their small arms—could not supply them from regular stocks. Fortunately, the Ordnance Department quickly found a commercial source for the rifles the Navy needed.

And so the Navy got enough Mossberg Model 44-US target rifles to fill their needs. This rifle was in the same class as the commercial Winchester, Remington and Stevens 22s. The Mossberg had a target-type rear sight and a special military-type post front sight. It had the Parkerized metal finish and oil-finished wood stock. The Navy found it completely suitable for their 22 rifle training programs.

The Marine Corps had been using the Army's 22 rifles and 22 rifle training program all along, but they wanted something more: a semi-automatic 22 training rifle which more closely simulated the now-issued M-1 Garand rifle. When they originated this requirement for a semi-automatic 22 training rifle in 1942, there was no commercial or military 22 which met it.

The Marines had already adopted the Reising submachine gun made by Harrington & Richardson Arms Company, and their requirement for a semi-automatic 22 training rifle came to the attention of its inventor, Eugene Reising. He designed a new semi-automatic 22 rifle to fill it.

In late 1943, the Marine Corps adopted Reising's new semi-automatic training rifle, the Harrington & Richardson Model 65. It was built to meet military requirements with Parkerized metal, oil-finished wood, and a target rear sight with a military front sight resembling that of the 30-06 Springfield rifle.

It was a simple blowback 22 semi-automatic, but its operating handle in a slot in the bottom of its forestock

This ad appeared in November, 1944. Called "The General" here, later they renamed it "The Leatherneck."

was a unique feature adopted from Reising's 45 submachine gun.

The H&R Model 65 proved perfect for the Marine Corps' requirement for a semi-auto 22 training rifle. It remained in service decades after World War II. It didn't take H&R long to manufacture all the Model 65s the Marines required, and in late 1944 the company received permission to offer the rifle for commercial sale as an early "reconversion" peace-time product. For some unknown reason, H&R called the commercial version of the rifle, which came with full Parkerized metal and oiled wood finish, "The General" Models 150 and 151. Soon after the end of the war they renamed it "The Leatherneck" as a tribute to the U.S. Marine Corps. Commercial "Leathernecks" do not, of course, carry U.S. property and acceptance marks.

All these World War II commercial military training 22 rifles have always been hard to find outside the U.S. Armed Forces. There are a number of reasons for this. One is that a modern 22 fired with modern ammunition and taken care of will last almost indefinitely, even in constant use. Another is that when a 22 was sent to a military facility for overhaul or repair, it would be scrapped if the cost to fix it was more than the price of a new rifle. A new one would be issued instead.

The stocks of 22 training rifles used in World War II lasted long afterward. The 22 Springfield M-2 was shooting into the 1970s. In the late 1970s, the U.S. Army Supply Bulletin "Army Adopted Items Selected for Authorization, List of Reportable Items" listed as "Rifle, Caliber .22, Training Grade, M13" the Winchester 75, the Remington 513T and the Mossberg Model 44-US! By that time, all of these rifles had been out of production for some twenty-five years! ●

Note: As an ROTC cadet, the author went through the U.S. Army World War II 22 rifle training program, and then as a member of the Ordnance Department, he occasionally had to deal with the 22 rifles used in these programs. All the information here was drawn from, or checked with, official U.S. Armed Forces publications.

The Harrington & Richardson 22 Reising semi-automatic rifle procured by the U.S. Marine Corps during World War II as shown in a U.S. Marine Corps manual.

Natural Pointers.

Bred over generations.

Sculpted in form, flawless in function.

Like a polished gun dog, our Model 11-87™ Premier™ autoloader has a natural instinct for upland hunting. You could say it was bred for the task, coming as it does from a long line of field-proven autoloaders. But this one is fitted with our exclusive light contour barrel, which makes it a half-pound lighter in weight – and a whole lot faster on point. It's superbly balanced, so it goes to your shoulder like it belongs there, then swings with remarkable ease. And late in the day, you'll feel the difference that half-pound makes, because this classic shotgun won't wear you out carrying what you don't need. It's available with 26", 28" or 30" barrel, each with Rem™ Chokes. And a custom-fitted hard case is standard. The Remington® 11-87 Premier. It's pure pointer.

Remington.

IT'S WHAT YOU'RE SHOOTING FOR.

MAKE NOISE)))))))))
((((((((((TO KILL DEER

The right sounds don't spook 'em

by FRANCIS E. SELL

"**M**AKE THE RIGHT noise in the right time and place, and you'll see plenty of deer—easy shooting, too."

That was Sam Whitstone, Siawash Indian, trapper and woodsman, giving me expert advice on deer hunting when I was a lad with my first deer rifle.

He added another bit of woods wisdom that has excellent application: "Walk a little; look a lot."

My Siawash friend has long since gone to the Happy Hunting Grounds, but all my life I have used his woods wisdom to give me easy deer shooting. The last fourteen deer to fall before my rifle were taken with exactly fourteen shots. All easy shooting because I made the right noise, in the right place. And that takes plenty of deer hunting know-how.

In addition to making the right noise in the right place, there is a time to remain silent beyond the telling. All this takes in a lot of deer hunting territory. No one, not even the silent Indian, ever moved through the woods without making some noise. The pattern of the Indian's noise, and that of all truly skilled woodsmen, is something else again. The noise is "in place" as to time of day and weather conditions, and more importantly, it is in place relative to game activity. Deer expect noise in the cover at certain times and places.

In heavy cover we see deer obscured by the trees, like this one moving out of his day bedding in the security cover. Note how a deer blends in with the natural landscape. This buck has just left heavy cover to move out to feed.

There is a woodland pattern of deer activity tied in with the weather. Let's consider normal weather in typical deer cover. When the weather is stable and there are no storms in the offing, the thermal wind drift is upslope on hills and in draws from late morning until late evening. Then, as the cover cools after sunset, the thermal wind drift changes to downslope and downdraw or creek, holding to this drift all night, until well after sunrise. Then the change is again to upslope, up-valley, creek and draw, always from the lower to the higher ground.

Deer use these thermal wind drifts in their feeding and bedding.

They expect a pattern of noise on the trails between feeding and day bedding grounds. They usually bed during the day on higher ground than where they feed. Then in moving out to feed, they have a wind—a thermal updrift—from the feeding ground to be tested by those sensitive black noses. Quiet as they are, deer do make noise on the trails leading into the feeding area. This pattern of noise is part of their security setup.

After feeding, they bed directly in the feeding grounds. When morning comes, they feed again, and move slowly toward their day bedding area. The thermal wind drift is still downslope, from the night reversal, so they have a nose on the wind coming from the bedding thickets. They move slowly. They browse along the way. They stop to test the wind and listen to the sound pattern of other deer upslope. All of this must be taken into consideration by a hunter if he is to see more than fresh tracks in heavy cover.

If a storm is growling across the deer cover, then the wind drift pattern is changed. A north storm moves the air from north to south, but in the heavy deer cover, there are ridges and draws that change this overall wind direction. Over some terrain with some storms, there is actually wind drift from east, west and south on the ground. Unless the storm is severe enough to drive the game into the best sheltered section, they will take full advantage of the ground wind drift in their feeding and bedding cycles.

In a severe storm, deer will stop their feeding, regardless of the time of day, and seek out the most sheltered areas for their bedding, where they wait out the storm. These security spots are much different than the average once-a-year deer hunter might suppose. If a storm is coming out of the north, one might suspect that the most sheltered spot would be at the foot of a south slope. Actually, this isn't so.

I recall cruising timber in some excellent deer cover after a severe storm. I counted the number of windfalls, those broken trees that must be removed by salvage logging. A few trees were blown over on the storm-facing ridge. Then in the lee of the ridge for two or three hundred feet from its top, I found no down timber. Instead there was a profusion of deer beds, all facing downslope, where the deer had sheltered during the severe storm.

This, incidentally, is the pattern of all deer bedding. An experienced hunter can look at a deer bed and know when it was made if he knows the weather pattern for the past twenty-four hours. They always bed back to the wind, depending on their noses to give them warning of any danger approaching from that direction. They depend on their ears and eyes to give them fair view of the cover downslope. Each was different, but collectively they covered all the downslope area in the immediate vicinity.

At the bottom of the ridges, I found the greatest storm damage. Trees were blown over, broken off and stacked. The storm, striking the facing ridge at sixty miles an hour, came over the ridge, which deflected it upward and created a sort of vacuum, then turned downward in consequence, at a velocity about twice that on the facing ridge.

Look as I might, there were no fresh deer tracks here, nor did I really expect to find any. This was the famous Columbus Day storm that hit southwestern Oregon in the middle '60s. While my timber cruise had nothing to do with deer hunting, it did tell me a lot about game response to a severe storm.

But to get back to actual deer hunting, I want to report an episode that occurred in Maine. This report came from a dedicated deer hunter of that state. The hunter writing me said that he had a heart problem, and his doctor told him that he couldn't hunt deer that season. In short, he wasn't to join in those tub-thumping drives, hike all day fighting brush, covering miles of forest.

He eventually wrangled permission to go along with his deer hunting friends and do a bit of trail watching, provided he didn't overexert—walk a little; then rest. Don't try to cover more than 1/4-mile in any one day, going and coming. So he became a "lazy Indian" hunter—not the silent Indian who reportedly glides through the forest without a sound—a type of movement only the deer predators came close to achieving, which is very alarming to the deer.

This handicapped hunter got on a deer trail just after good shooting light. He followed it slowly, walking a little, looking a little, toward a

Sell learned about noise in the woods by making lots of it, very quietly, for a long time.

ridge north of camp. He downed a beautiful six-point buck, one of the largest he ever took. He walked in on him around a turn in the trail he followed, getting the shot at about 40 yards. The buck was looking back over his shoulder, trying to see what was making the slight noise on his backtrail. What kept that buck from being alarmed was the fact that the noise pattern was in place. The deer using that particular trail between their bedding and feeding expected some noise on that trail at that time. And the weather being stable, the thermal wind drift was still downslope, giving the buck a wind from the security cover toward which he was casually moving.

During the ten days this hunter was in camp, he did his hunting with a camera, getting the pictures of three other bucks. His hunting partners "hunted high and low," covering miles of territory without seeing more than a lot of fresh tracks. All that activity is why they failed.

Deer have a distinct pattern of activity in heavy cover—east or west, north or south. If a hunter confines his activities to that pattern, he is going to see a lot of game. When a hunter confines his activities to their pattern of noise, he is not going to put up a deer well beyond his line of vision in heavy cover.

Deer move slowly. They stop to evaluate the sounds; they browse along the woodland trails. This

The click of the camera alerted this doe at a full forty yards in mid-morning with plenty of normal woods noise about.

adds up to a pattern of sound and movement which I have used for years to give me easy shooting. If it is toward late evening, I usually move around the section in which I expect the deer are using for day bedding, and do a bit of trail watching on the escape trails leading out of the bedding area. These trails usually are distinctly marked and are laid out so they get the thermal wind drift across them from the feeding area after the morning wind reversal. On several occasions they have paid off for me during the midday and early afternoon, when there is less deer movement than at any other time.

After this trail-watching period, when the deer begin to move out toward their evening feeding, I have had very good luck just working slowly along the winding trails leading toward the feeding area.

Sometimes I have taken my buck directly on the trail I followed, sometimes I have taken him on another trail adjacent to the one I was on. Sure, I made noise, but it was timed to the noise the deer made, and in a position where they expected noise at this particular time of day.

After feeding and night bedding in the more open area, the thermal reversal gives them good coverage for their return trip up ridges and draws to their day bedding thickets. I have often still-hunted—slowly stalked—these trails, seeing any number of deer as I moved upslope toward the day bedding. Indeed, I have actually taken deer after they have bedded for the day, moving slowly in toward their bedding ground while the thermal wind was still downslope.

But if a hunter were on those same trails after the thermal reversal sends the scent pattern uphill and updraw, he could touch off all the deer in the vicinity without seeing any. Last season I spent an hour going around a section where I knew the deer bedded, moving well around the entire area. What I wanted and finally obtained was a trail watching position where I could see the escape trails leading out of those thickets.

I watched those trails downslope from me, angling along the ridge, for two solid hours before a stumble-bum hunter came into the bedding thickets, totally disregarding the slight wind drift ahead of him. My trail watching paid off with a nice three-point buck (Western count). The range was about forty yards, the buck moving slowly. No problem in clipping him behind the ear.

Once, during a hunt with an old Chinook Indian trapper and woodsman, he told me that the hardest problems for most hunters was to sit down and remain still. They stand up, sit down, cough. They put their gun where they have to do a lot of moving to get it when a deer comes along, though usually they don't see any unless they are looking across a canyon, a long way off.

He told me all this while sitting under a sheltering spruce, in the dry, watching a maze of trails leading into about three acres of heavy sheltering cover, mostly dense black huckleberry. Before settling down for his trail watching, he had cut two forked sticks. He pushed those two sticks into the ground and placed his rifle in the formed cradle, muzzle pointing toward those trails coming out of the thickets. Later in the evening, when I had grown quite restless, three does came cautiously

out of the thickets, stepping lightly, noses to the thermal updraft, moving cautiously toward their feeding ground. Then a forked horn came out and my Chinook Indian friend dropped one with a neck shot, range about sixty yards.

Sometimes there is a rain in the heavy cover. This is a pattern of noise beyond that made by the deer in their travels, and it is an excellent advantage in hunting. During the rainy period, the wind drift is always from the higher to the lower ground. Deer using the more open feeding areas during such a storm period often change trails, coming into the feeding area from the lower ground, giving them good nose coverage.

During the rut, when the deer are about their annual mating, the trails between security cover may be used at any time of day, the bucks seeking out the does in heat. At this time, the bucks travel the trail without a great deal of regard for wind coverage, following the scent patterns laid down by the does. This is an excellent time for trail watching on the trails between patches of security cover. But it must be remembered that even during the rut, there is no premium placed on unusual noise or movement. To make this trail watching pay off, a hunter must remain quiet at all times.

I, like all experienced woodsmen, am very critical of loud drives. The still-hunting drive is much more productive. Both the standers and the drivers will see more deer. But it takes plenty of woods savvy to make the silent woodsman's drive—and I use the word silent advisedly. The drivers work the trails leading into the day bedding area. Moving with the wind, usually. Working through the heavy security cover slowly, cautiously.

The hunters on stand are covering the escape trail leading out of these security thickets. The entire drive is silent, compared to the orthodox drive. The only noise made is that of unalarmed deer, produced by the drivers on the deer trails. The shooting will be at deer not greatly alarmed, generally moving at a cautious walk.

Such driving is based on a careful reading of the entire cover, the ability of hunters to take trail-watching stands and remain quiet for several hours. Fields of fire must be carefully selecteds so there is no shooting back into the cover the drivers are working. •

A $600 SCOPE ON A $200 RIFLE?

—it works just fine!

by ROB LUCAS

The author votes the top-dollar scope ticket, regardless of the rifle—this is, clearly, a Zeiss scope.

IT WAS A SHOTGUN wedding for this unlikely couple, a $200 Marlin lever action and a $600 Zeiss scope. With barely a week left before the 1991 Michigan gun deer season, I had two choices—clamp my favorite 1.5-4.5x Zeiss Diavari C on the Marlin or hunt with iron sights. Reluctantly, I bought a set of Weaver QD rings and a one-piece base, and while the Loctite cured, I glared at the Zeiss-scoped Marlin thinking that the Q in QD stood for "Quick," and the D was for "Divorce"—right after the season.

How I got in this predicament goes back to that summer when my brother-in-law, Tim Bellefluer, called to say he was coming to our family deer camp in Upper Michigan. At age forty-eight, Tim was taking up deer hunting. I didn't ask why, but there were two small details: He had no deer rifle—in fact, no gear at all—and his travel year was booked until October. There was no way we could get together in Illinois before deer season.

Tim said he wanted his own rifle and not just a family loaner, and I liked the sound of that. I asked what kind of a rifle he thought he might like.

"I always wanted a lever action," Tim answered, with passion.

Wouldn't you know it would be a levergun? I was just recovering

from my third case of the Levergun Fever.

This time a 44 Magnum Browning copy of the Winchester Model 1892 carbine got sold for cash. Like Tim and so many other deer hunters, I always wanted a light lever-action deer rifle, too, but the balance between portability and performance was tricky, and compromises had to be made. In 1990, I convinced myself I needed an iron-sighted, 20-inch-barreled deer gun to carry into those dark, swampy places that big bucks like and I usually walked around, and where shots would be close. Evenings out there, as darkness and prime hunting time approached, I kept checking the Browning's century-old buckhorn sight picture against a patch of snow near my blind. Yup, the thin front blade and rear notch were still visible—no problem. But when a decent six-point buck crossed in front of me after sundown, I saw nothing but blurry black metal against a black evergreen background and the deer walked away. Not the rifle's fault—my fault.

I knew better. That cat's been out of the bag for years. Scopes work as well at short range as they do long range, for all kinds of short-range deer hunters—muzzleloaders, shotgunners, big-bore handgun hunters,

even bowhunters. Scopes do the job for the African dangerous game hunter and for the target shooter, like the fourteen-year-old kid who regularly beats me at the bowling pin game with his Aimpointed Ruger against my iron-sighted 22 Beretta 87. Holster guns need iron sights; deer rifles, including lever-action brushguns, need scopes.

I told Tim a scoped lever action was not a bad choice for the paper-mill forests and pine plantations around our deer camp, and the longest shot he'd see might be 150 yards. So we agreed that a really great brother-in-law would take care of everything for him.

Would a check for $300 cover it? Better make it $350, and I hung up the phone thinking it would be a leadpipe cinch. There was no rush and every store that sold hunting rifles or equipment sold inexpensive 94s or 336s.

At the time, I had a serious scope project in progress. I had decided to replace the Zeiss 1.5-4.5x Diavari C on my 35 Whelen Improved elk and mule deer rifle with my new Zeiss, a 4x32 Diatal C, that my wife had given me for Christmas.

The Whelen was built in 1986, starting from an Oberndorf military action, McGowan #3 barrel, and Brown Precision fiberglass stock. I like small, high-perfor-

mance scopes, and this 1.5-4.5x was the smallest variable wearing the Zeiss brand. That Zeiss-Whelen outfit went into some remote, rough places, including Montana's Bob Marshall Wilderness and Wyoming's Jim Bridger, and it became the most successful rifle I've ever owned. When Nosler brought out a 225-grain, 35-caliber Partition bullet, I settled on it and 57.5 grains of IMR-4064 for 2670 fps as a flat-shooting, powerful all-purpose load. In Montana, we chased whitetail deer in the same brush-choked coulees where grizzlies liked to lay up, and it was comforting to know I had 35 Whelen horsepower in case I did stumble into a big bear.

The longest shot I made with the Zeiss/Whelen was 330 yards, oddly enough on a whitetail buck; the shortest was a mule deer at 40 yards, both shots taken with the variable turned up to 4.5x. In fact, 90 percent of the time it stayed on 4x or 4.5x, so I made the scope swap to the 4x32 Diatal C, which was Zeiss' smallest fixed-power glass.

All of which left my all-time favorite Zeiss 1.5-4.5x temporarily unattached.

A binocular salesman once explained to me how all Zeiss lenses are ground and polished so perfectly they're "actually rated 3 percent cleaner than air" and that's why a pair of 7x42s cost $1000. Whether "cleaner than air" is a concept or a sales pitch I don't know, but only a guy like Bob Bell should attempt a technical discussion comparing the lens quality of premium European brands like Kahles, Steiner, Swarovski, Schmidt & Bender or Zeiss versus the best American scopes named Leupold, Burris, Redfield, etc. Bob Bell I ain't, but I'll try to explain in a nutshell why I'd rather lay out $700 for a new Zeiss or Schmidt & Bender scope than for another new rifle.

Looking through the most expensive glass money can buy, I see a flat, "hard-edged" brightness, images that have no fuzz and wide open backgrounds without cloudiness, from one edge of the field to the

stocks for under $250. Used 30-30 94s were everywhere for around $200, a few nice pre-'64 30-30s and 32 Specials were $400-plus. The trouble with the Winchester 94 was there were so many to look at I couldn't pull the trigger. I kept thinking I'd find a better one tomorrow.

I could hardly pass up, on Tim's behalf, of course, the Expo-sized summer gunshows at the fairgrounds, where I found more good Winchester guns to look at. One rifle I will always regret having to pass on (Tim would have loved it) was a new-in-the-box Winchester Model 64 32 Special Deer Rifle. This was a 1950s-vintage rifle with a 24-inch barrel, 2/3-length magazine, pistol grip stock, factory checkering on the

the hammer, red-painted on the left side and "Safe" on the right.

I kept coming back to the Marlin 336, and I think a picture in the 1960 Gun Digest is the reason why. In that issue's catalog under "U.S. Rifles" is a Marlin 336 wearing a scope. On the same page is another Marlin marketed as the "J.C. Higgins Model 45," with a Weaver one-piece base, Weaver rings and a straight-tubed J.C. Higgins 2½x scope that looks like it belongs there. So thirty years ago, Marlins wore scopes. Gradually, I discovered the two most popular lever-action rifles of all time, the Winchester 94 and Marlin 336, were not interchangeable in other ways, too.

I definitely thought the Marlin's lever felt smoother, easier going and

Benching a lever gun requires more handholding and a lot less sandbagging.

other. Close-range targets in low-light hunting, like a gray whitetail deer standing against jackpines, are resolved with sharpness that is sometimes startling. That's why I use them.

Off and on from June to September, I toured the neighborhood gunshops, the big discount chainstores, and the all-sports superstores. The Winchester Big Bore Side Eject 94 was my first choice for Tim, particularly in 307 Winchester caliber since the 375 Winchester was already gone from the catalog. Pretty ones with nice walnut and deep bluing and a Bushnell 1.5-4.5x on top were available below Tim's $350 ceiling, as were iron-sighted Side Eject 30-30 Ranger models with hardwood

grip and forend, and the guy wanted only $600 for it.

Luckily, I reminded myself that Tim did not need an expensive, iron-sighted relic, no matter how cool. And neither did I, as it was becoming obvious I was fighting off my fourth bite of the Levergun Bug.

I had never owned or even fired a Marlin rifle. New Marlin Model 336s with wood stocks sat on discount store shelves priced at a measly $189. I found new 30-30s with real walnut stocks in local gunshops for between $249 and $329. Unlike the newly engineered Side Eject 94 Winchester which had an unobtrusive transfer bar safety, all new Marlins were the same old gun with a new through-bolt safety just below

coming, and it had zero side-to-side wobble. The lever also locked up snug against the grip frame with a firm, tactile click, and it stayed locked. This was important for a newcomer to rifles. The more 336s I held, handled and shouldered, the more I liked the long, swept-back pistol grip, and the way the rounded receiver felt dangling in one hand, which is the way I like to carry a brush gun. At the top of the list of Marlin's qualities was its solid-top, side-ejecting receiver, a receiver made to carry a scope just like the guns in the 1960 Gun Digest.

In September, I visited a gunshop off the beaten path and found a brand-new 1991 336CS with a red rubber recoil pad, new cross-bolt

The results—a 1½-inch group fired at four different scope powers—can lead to grins.

LEUPOLD 100 YARD TARGET

safety, and Marlin's new, darker walnut wood. That stock caught my eye, but the reason I took a closer look was the tag tied to the finger-loop. This six-shooter was a 35 Remington and not another 30-30. The price had been knocked down a couple times from $329 to $275, and when I asked why, the shop owner said I was the first customer to look at it in months. I checked it over every way I could think of and told him to wrap it up, adding I wished he had one more Marlin just like it. He walked to the discount rifle rack and pulled down a dusty old gun I thought, at first, was a plastic-stocked BB gun replica of a 336CS. But it, too, was stamped "35 Remington" on the barrel.

This ugly duckling was a two-year-old, unfired display model with shopworn wood and flecks of rust along its thinly blued barrel. There was a dent or two in the forend and some scratches in the buttstock that went all the way through the high-sheen finish. This walnut was the older, yellowish Marlin wood, much lighter than the 1991 gun I'd just bought. But the grain ran in the right direction, close and straight all

the way to the action, and the inlet-ting looked as good or better than any Marlin I'd seen in the last four months. The lever felt stiff and tight like the new gun; the trigger pull was a 10-pounder, but broke clean. Yes, indeed, under the surface neglect was a brand-new rifle, com-plete with a dusty box and paper-work. The price was $229, and the shop owner said he was tired of singing happy birthday to it. I said $200.

For $475, the family had two new deer guns. The shiny new one would, of course, be Tim's, and I'd keep the ugly duckling for a rainy day. Somewhere in my basement assort-ment of spare gear was my first good scope, a straight-tubed Weaver V4.5W. This all-steel scope was heavy by today's standards, its plain crosswire reticle hard to see com-pared to a duplex, and the glass was-n't the clearest. But it would do for any target I needed to hit with a 35 Remington.

I set up Tim's Marlin with a new, modern 1.5-5x straight-tube variable scope that brought it to under 7½ pounds carrying weight. This scope had a bottom-power field of view 70

feet wide at 100 yards and plenty of magnification for longer chances.

I chronographed Tim's rifle with every 35 Remington factory load I could find, and the results were enlightening.

Silvertips were the most accu-rate—five-shot group averaged 3 to 3½ inches. No factory 35 Remington load came close to the 2080 fps facto-ry standard. I had to wonder if both Marlins would have to be loaded down to get good brush gun accura-cy, say, 2- to 3-inch five-shot groups at 100 yards. Figuring Tim needed close-range accuracy, I saved him a box of Silvertips.

Ten days before the November 15 opening day, I hauled my amber-stocked ugly-duckling Marlin to the basement and went looking for the old Weaver. Looked everywhere; could not find the Weaver. My know-it-all wife reminded me that Mr. Generosity gave away the Weaver years ago, a present to our son-in-law. Great news. Went back upstairs to look through the gun cabinet. Then I saw the 1.5-4.5x variable Zeiss Diavari, worth three times the price of the Marlin, sitting on the shelf look-ing lonesome. And you know the rest. The Immutable Law of Rifle Economics, big bucks for the rifle and small change for the scope, lay rent and ruined on my basement floor.

I wish I had a great Marlin story from 1991, but Tim didn't see a deer his first season and the one I got was routine, 30 yards in bright daylight using my 257. I did carry the Zeiss-scoped Marlin back into the thick stuff, and there was something just right about it, so I held off the divorce. In 1992, I again took the Marlin to Michigan as a backup gun, and the spike buck we got together is a brush gun story.

In the '92 season, I first carried my flat-shooting 257 Roberts and walked the high ground. Evenings, the family sat in our cozy hunting cabin talking about deer, deer guns and scopes, and naturally I took a verbal pounding for showing up two years in a row with a "yuppie scope on a workingman's rifle."

Late in the evening of the fourth day, I returned to my truck, stowed the 257 and rucksack, and glassed the mile-long treeline behind me with 7x20 mini-binoculars. It was well past 5:30 p.m., the red haze on the horizon was about gone, and there on the hardwoods' edge, wait-ing patiently for me to clear out, were four gray shapes that hadn't been there when I walked through at 5:20.

I got back there next afternoon and looked over my problem: a wide-open new rye field and not a stick of clover for 400 yards. I had to find a hidey-hole back in the hardwoods where vision would be cut down to a 50-yard radius, and my chances of being in the right spot at the right time were slim at best. But this was the kind of close-range potential for which I had brought a back-up rifle, the Zeiss-scoped Marlin. I piled up some deadwood, stretched out on the ground with the Marlin beside me, and waited for it to be 5:30 again.

Two deer showed up at dusk, both does. The gray of their hides was a perfect blend with the hardwoods around them. Moments later, three more deer grew out of the ground, the five of them strung out between 30 and 50 yards from my blind. It was so late in the evening, the light in the trees so thin, that I could only see deer when they stood broadside to me—facing me, they evaporated. And there was one other tactical detail—they were behind me. Even if I could see to shoot, I had to roll on my left side while bringing the Marlin over my right hip.

No way could I see horns with my eyes, but one gray shape was bulkier than the others, so I concentrated on him, slowly wriggling into a prone position one millimeter at a time. And it grew darker and darker. By the time I was in position for a broadside poke at that deer, he was 30 yards out in the field nipping at rye tips, with about a jillion skinny hardwood trees between us. I got the scope up where I could look at him through the trees—the Zeiss was set on 2x—and it was magic. On the other side of the fat Plex reticle was a black-and-white photograph of a spike buck. Blam.

My brother Ken was in the area, heard the shot and came on the run. By the time he found me in the gathering darkness, I was busy trying to manipulate a knife in one hand and a flashlight in the other. Ken spied the 35 Remington leaning against a nearby tree, Zeiss scope covers back in place protecting my valuable glass.

"Don't tell me that upside-down thing..." he said, laughing.

I told him if he was going to insult my deer rifle, he could either grab the light or start cuttin'. We set up his camera for some pictures, but without

(Left) Writer's 35 Remington has an excellent conversion rate—it turns at least one deer into venison every season.

(Above) Potent on deer, there's enough factory load variety in the 35 Remington to suit most rifles.

a flash all his prints picked up was my grinning mug.

Through two seasons in a two-deer county, the Zeiss/Marlin has put three whitetails in various freezers, taking one Silvertip and two Core-Lokts for the jobs. Nothing big yet, but I sure like the trend. From the perspective of a hunter, as opposed to a banker, the $600 Zeiss scope perfectly compliments the $200 Marlin, and that quick divorce I had scheduled a few years back isn't going to happen. Here in 1994, the Marlin's having its third deer season and it's no longer a backup rifle—I've got something else in mind for that job.

There are a few things I can tell you about owning, shooting and hunting whitetails with a Zeiss-scoped Marlin rifle:

First, a Zeiss/Marlin is a short-range deer gun—about 150 yards is the limit for its 20-inch barrel and the ninety-year-old 35 Remington cartridge. That 150 is about a football field further than I can usually see in jackpine plantations and tag alder thickets where I'm likely to be carrying the Marlin. For stalking or sitting quietly in the trees, I leave the Zeiss on 1.5x to get that huge crystal-clear field of view. Actually, I'm guessing about 150 yards because that's what I read and because that was the yardage between the Marlin and the biggest deer taken so far with it, a very large doe. I held for a center lung hit, the

Core-lokt landed two inches low, and she ran all of about 30 yards. I carry the Marlin thinking I'll shoot close, close as in "How much time is there between a buck's snort and his first jump?"

That idiot-proof safety I disliked three years ago I now appreciate. The Winchester and Marlin tubular magazines are unloaded by jacking the rounds through the action. With that beefy block of metal between the hammer and firing pin, I point the rifle in a safe direction and crank away. It's a good safety. For jump-shooting or blind-sitting, I prefer the half-cock notch, from where an educated thumb can either haul back the hammer extension in a hurry or, with a fingertip touching the trigger, ease it back without a sound.

A Marlin 336 will shoot, and so will most lever guns once you learn the trick. Benchresting a brush gun calls for a good handload, a strong supporting left hand and arm, and a conscious thought of "follow through" with the reticle after the trigger breaks. My rifle likes a Frank Barnes load—36.5 grains of IMR-3031 with the 200-grain Core-Lokt round-nose and WLR primer—for 2050 fps, which exceeds all the factory loads I've clocked. Despite a crisp 10-pound trigger pull, a hammer that hits with a crash and a short barrel that jumps quick, five-shot groups over sandbags go into 2½ inches, and less on good days.

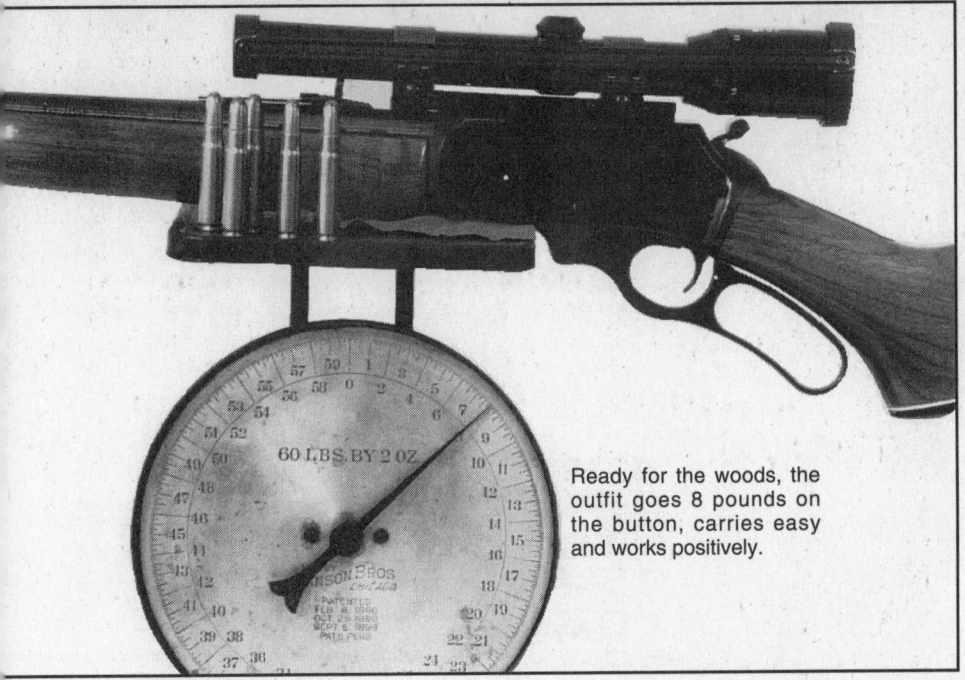

Ready for the woods, the outfit goes 8 pounds on the button, carries easy and works positively.

My theory on the short-range effectiveness of blunt, slow 35-caliber bullets, why they outperform their paper ballistics, is that they slow down so much more inside the target. What relatively low remaining energy carried is transmitted. The 35 Remington is a gentle killer, if that can be said, meaning very little meat is bloodshot compared to the faster, smaller deer calibers.

I can also tell you that a Zeiss-scoped Marlin is not nearly as conspicuous as you might think. On looks alone, this straight-tubed, flat-black variable scope is merely business-like, riding low above the Marlin's receiver, the same timeless hunting rig shown in the 1960 GUN DIGEST. At the target range, the Marlin and I usually sneak by without a scratch, and it's only when somebody takes a second look and recognizes those white Zs on the turret caps that the fun begins.

There have been a few strange encounters. One guy figured I just got off the turnip truck, bought a used Marlin with a Zeiss on top and didn't know what it was. Another gentleman offered me $300 for the Marlin, saying its serial number was exactly 100 digits older than his 30-30 Marlin. He only wanted it, naturally, if the scope went with. A few lever-gun bashers have accused me of misconduct, aesthetic uncorrectness, one-upsmanship, or just flat throwing good money away. I guess there is no accounting for taste.

Best of all, it's a fun rifle to shoot. No matter what other rifles I'm testing, final zeroing, chronographing or whatever, I always take the Marlin along and crank a few magazine-loads through the action. It is a hunting rifle I'll never get tired of owning or, at under 8 pounds loaded with five Core-Lokts, of carrying. Sometimes I shoot over sandbags, but mostly I blast away either sitting or standing as I would be in a hardwood stand. The Marlin doesn't make much noise, doesn't kick hard or punish my cheek.

My wife says I grin when I'm shooting the Marlin. That's because I'm smug. Why not? There's nothing to improve—I've got 200 nickel-plated Remington cases stuffed with an accurate Core-Lokt hunting load and a scope that's as clear as it gets at close range. Think about it.

I like the Zeiss/Marlin so much that I've been messing around with another upside-down rifle, a Schmidt & Bender/Savage 99E in 250-3000. I bought this pre-WWII gun from a friend who inherited it and then chopped it off at both ends for his diminutive wife, leaving only 18 inches of barrel length and 12¼ inches of buttstock between the trigger and the oversized 1-inch recoil pad. But the Model 99 action was absolutely clean and tight, and I offered almost the same money for it as for the ugly-duckling Marlin which I now prize. Did I get lucky twice in a row, accuracy-wise? Yes

and no, but maybe that's another story. It *is* a keeper.

I heard the all-time insightful put-down of a Zeiss-scoped Marlin as I was tuning up for the 1993 season. My nearest neighbor on the 100-yard range was a dedicated varmint shooter with a pair of big-scoped 22-250 Remingtons. We talked about the spring prairie-dog plague that hit southern Colorado and ended his season early, leaving him with a batch of so-so reloads to burn up. He was curious as to why I had mounted "that fine instrument" on a Marlin.

I told him I liked the view.

He told me the Marlin can't convert.

"It can't what?"

Turned out he was a math teacher in the local high school. He said the advantages that I paid for in the expensive Zeiss were subtle degrees of image resolution, measurable just like rifle accuracy in minutes of angle. Therefore...with a light 20-inch barrel, a cartridge like the 35 Remington with a maximum reach of 150 yards, and best groups of three minutes of angle...the Marlin had neither the accuracy nor the range to convert those subtle advantages into hits. A Marlin can't convert.

It was interesting, a sort of Law of Diminishing Returns for lens quality based on inherent accuracy. With the Zeiss I could see the eye of a gnat, but with the Marlin I couldn't shoot it out. Sounded plausible, but I plan to ask Mr. Bell if any such law exists.

Just ask my brother-in-law, Tim Bellefleur, if he thinks a Marlin is worthy of a great scope. Tim is a salesman, and he'll say a Marlin 336 is "user friendly," better than the competition, and the best deer gun for the money ever made. Tim likes my Zeiss, but will invest his hard-earned cash in the more compact $500 Swarovski 1.5-4.5x, a scope with the same Plex reticle as the Zeiss C, explaining his choice to Marlin-bashers with a rhetorical question: When was the last time anybody saw a pair of used Leica binoculars for sale?

I think the $200 Marlin rifle and $600 Zeiss scope is a marriage that will hold together because there's a consideration far more important than money. You see, a Marlin can convert. Mine converts whitetail deer into venison steaks, chops and sausage annually. ●

ELMER

by
GENE
BROWN

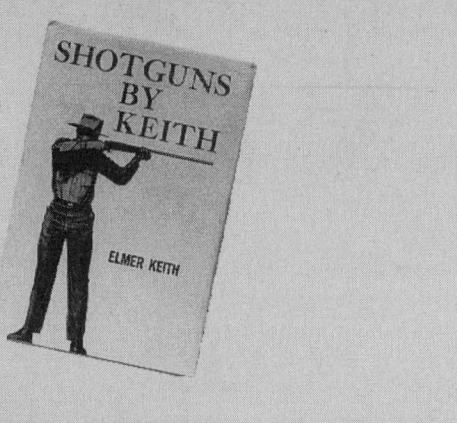

KEITH—
THE MAN AND
HIS BOOKS

SINCE THE LATE 18th century, there has been an ongoing interest both here and abroad in the collecting of books on guns and hunting. The past ten years have shown a dramatic surge in this interest.

The availability of many sought-after publications has decreased immensely while their value and price has increased proportionately. Collectors have discovered that certain books by Jack O'Connor, Robert C. Ruark, Charles Sheldon, Karamojo Bell, Theodore Roosevelt, Townsend Whelen—to name a few of the more popular sporting writers—have oftentimes risen tenfold from their original bookstore prices of a few years back.

According to numerous specialist book dealers in the United States, and even a few I have talked with in London and Edinburgh, it appears that the all-time winner in sporting-book price appreciation and appeal could be the late dean of American firearms writers, Elmer Keith, who over a period spanning almost fifty years wrote ten books on guns, hunting and the outdoors.

In 1979, as a curious collector of guns and hunting books, I approached Mr. Keith at his home in Salmon, Idaho, to try and determine just how many of his books were published and what their publications figures might be. Keith, in typical fashion, tipped back his oversized hat, chomped down on a cigar and said that he'd never given it much thought, but if I was interested, he would allow me to go through his files. Maybe together, he said, we could come up with the facts.

My search into the facts and figures of Keith's literary background eventually evolved into a two-year off-and-on program with his help that resulted in the following bibliography. This list is confined only to his books and does not include the hundreds and possibly thousands of articles he wrote for periodicals of which the first was written and published in 1925.

Eleven years after his first article about competition shooting was published in the *American Rifleman,* and Keith's fame as a guide, hunter and developer of different calibers and types of bullets had risen, he was commissioned in 1936 by the Samworth Publishing Company, also known as the Small Arms Technical Publishing Company of Onslow County, North Carolina, to write three books. The first book, a manual covering the selection, use and loading of the most suitable and popular revolver cartridges, is called *Sixgun Cartridges and Loads.*

In the late 1920s, S. Harold Croft, a Philadelphia sportsman, had visited at Elmer's first ranch outside of Durkee, Oregon. Their love of pistols and marathon shooting sessions in the Oregon desert developed into a mutual respect and lifelong friendship. It was Croft to whom Keith dedicated this first book.

The book, orange in color, is a hardbound work measuring 4³/₄x7³/₄ inches and contains 151 pages. An estimated 5000 of them were published between December of 1936 and into the late 1940s.

To be a first edition, a copy of this book, of which Elmer estimated about a thousand were published and sold, must state "Published December 1936" on the title page. Other editions had a simple 1936 copyright date, while others stated publication dates of 1941, 1945 or 1946.

The first edition copy, in good original condition with a dust jacket, currently sells for between $75 and $125. Signed copies are even more. There is also a modern reprint of this book which sells for about $20.

The second book in this series for Samworth is also rather small in size and is titled *Big Game Rifles and Cartridges,* featuring drawings by Philip Plaistridge. It, too, was published in 1936 by Thomas G. Samworth, Small Arms Technical Publishing Company, now listed as being in Plantersville, South Carolina.

It is hardbound, green in color, and like the first book by Keith, measures 4³/₄x7³/₄ and has 161 pages. Records are sketchy on this one. Keith believed that about 5000 of them were published by Samworth, and perhaps the same amount when it was eventually republished by Stackpole in the late 1940s. He said that he couldn't be precise about the quantity, but figured that in all a little over 10,000 of them had been published.

A modern reprint of this book is also available for about $20. First editions vary from about $75 to $125 with signed copies fetching more.

The third part of this Depression-era deal was to include a book about varmint hunting. Elmer, now ranching on the North Fork of the Salmon River in Idaho without benefit of running water or electricity, com-

pleted the manuscript for this book, sent it off, but somehow the book was never published and, to his knowledge, was lost or destroyed and never seen again. Recalling those days of living mainly on venison, potatoes and whatever he could make writing and guiding, he said with chagrin that he never received any money for his work on this last book for Samworth.

His next book, published shortly after World War II, is the rarest and most sought after by collectors today. Elmer said that it, next to *Sixguns, the Standard Reference Work* which

came out years later, is his favorite book of all that he did.

Published by Standard Publications, Inc., Huntington, West Virginia, in 1946, *Keith's Rifles for Large Game* is indeed a beauty. This work, dedicated to his wife Lorraine, is a black hardbound book with silver lettering on its cover. Including the index, this book contains 405 pages and has hand-drawn illustrations and photographs throughout. It was edited by Christian Lenz, an accomplished author in his own right, whose most well-known book is *Muzzle Flashes.*

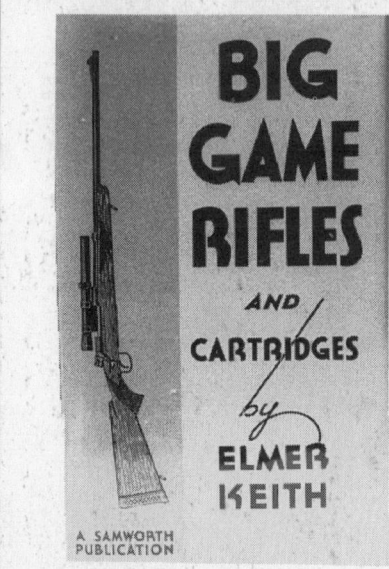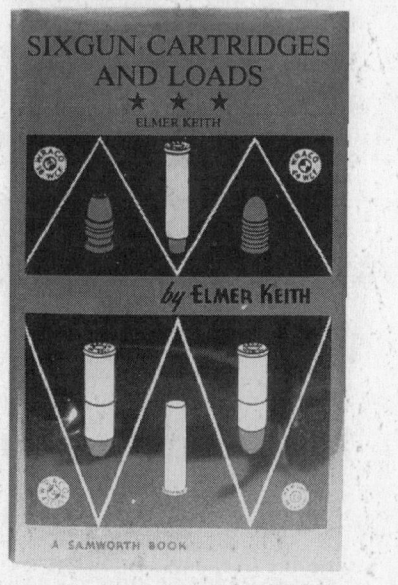

Big Game Rifles and *Sixgun Cartridges and Loads* by Elmer Keith. Published in 1936 by Samworth Publications. These are the first two books written by Keith.

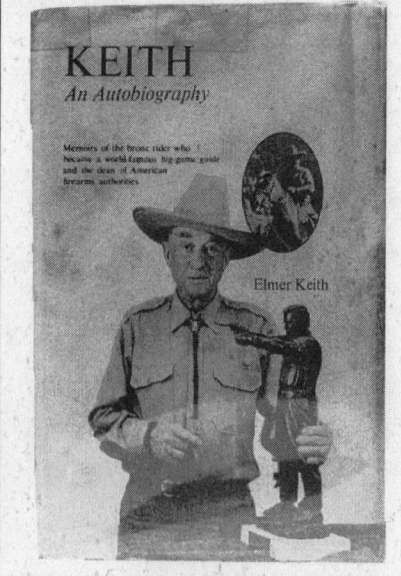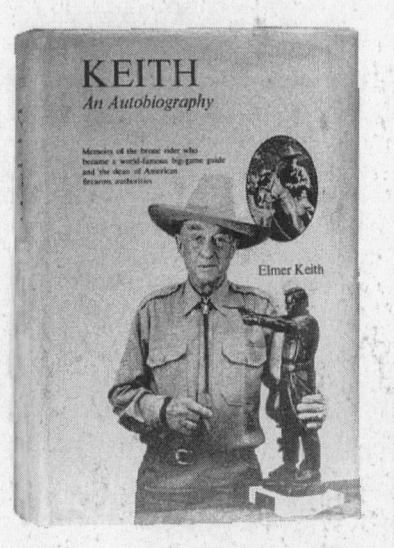

Two different editions of *Keith, An Autobiography.* At left is the first; the later book-club edition is smaller in size, but contains the same text.

Approximately 2000 copies of *Rifles for Large Game* were published, of which about 1000 sold for $10 each. Not a cheap price for a book in those days when it was not uncommon for a working man with a family to receive a weekly paycheck of less than $50.

Elmer said that he had reason to believe that about 1000 copies of this book were destroyed by water damage while being stored in a warehouse. He said that, all things considered, there could easily be far fewer than 1000 first edition copies of this book remaining, which accounts for their extreme scarcity and growing price.

There is now a reprint of this book, in a hardbound edition, available for about $40. The original is a far cry from that owing to its extreme rarity, presently selling for between $600 and $1000. The last unsigned copy I saw change hands was in October of 1983 at the autumn Spokane, Washington, gun show. I have since seen a very nice signed copy sell for over $1300.

An advanced collector of books on guns and hunting traded a specialist book dealer from Montana a Weatherby rifle valued at $850 for a copy of this book. Since then, I have only seen a few of these books available and only through mail-order catalogs. Each time I called to inquire about them, they had already been sold.

About a year after this highly sought-after and scarce book made its debut, Elmer was contracted by Little, Brown and Company of Boston to do a comprehensive work on hunting. It eventually came out as *Elmer Keith's Big Game Hunting* with the first edition appearing in 1948. It was published simultaneously in Canada by McClelland and Stewart, Limited. A second edition by Little, Brown and Company was published in 1953.

This indeed comprehensive work centered on Keith's vast hunting experience in North America. It is a 420-page book measuring 6½x9 inches with illustrations by Bob Kuhn and the author. Elmer, incidentally, told me that he drew most of the illustrations for his books while visiting doctor's or dentist's offices. He didn't elaborate, just mentioned it one day as we were driving from his home in Salmon, Idaho, to a gun show in Los Angeles.

There were 5000 copies of this book published, and when found today on the shelves of used and rare book dealers, it's usually priced between $50 and $100, with the 1953 edition selling for a bit less. Signed copies usually go for about $100 in today's market.

Elmer was not overly enthusiastic about his next book, *Shotguns by Keith*, which was published by Stackpole in 1950 and had several reprint editions, some by Bonanza Publishing. On numerous occasions, Elmer spoke highly of Major Charles Askins, Sr. to whom this book was dedicated.

Six-guns and large caliber rifles were Keith's main forte, and he admittedly found it difficult to put his whole heart, even though he produced what some scattergunners claim to be a more than competent work, into something about shotguns. The first edition of this book is red in color with ensuing ones being brown. It also measures 6x9 inches and contains 334 pages.

Elmer estimated the press run on this book to be about 10,000, including editions both by Stackpole and Bonanza. Depending upon condition, this book is around $25 to $75. I have seen signed editions with mint

Elmer Keith's *Big Game Hunting* on the right was first published by Little, Brown and Company in 1948 with a subsequent 1953 edition. Portions of this book appear in *Guns and Ammo For Big Game Hunting* published by Petersen Publications, Los Angeles in 1965.

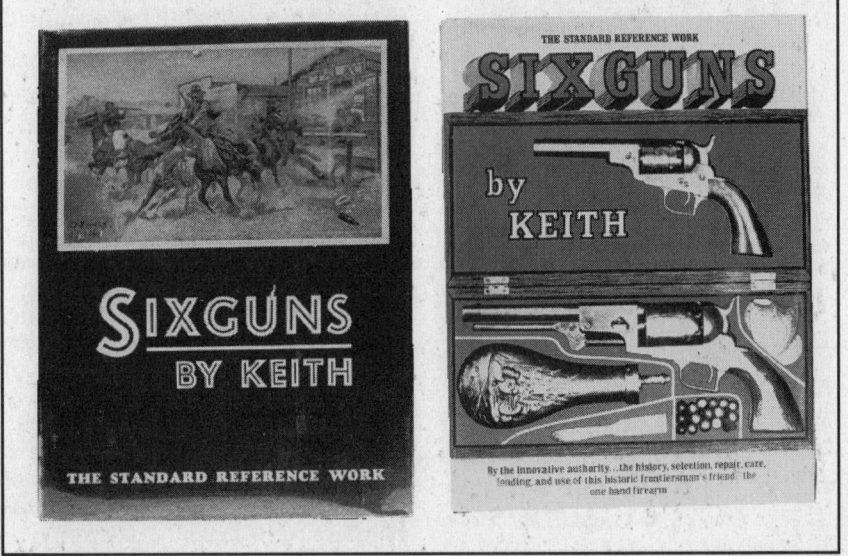

The first edition of *Sixguns by Keith, the Standard Reference Work* is at left. It was published in 1955, and followed by a later edition that has gone through several printings.

dust jackets carrying an asking price of $100.

By now, Keith had moved with his family from the ranch in the North Fork area, sometimes referred to as Gibbonsville, to a home on the west edge of Salmon, Idaho. From this location, he made his first trip to Africa, joined the editorial staff of the *American Rifleman* and began to put the finishing touches on his real labor of love, *Sixguns, the Standard Reference Work* which came out in 1955.

This wheelgun classic was first published by Stackpole and is dedicated to his wife Lorraine..."the lady who has shared the vicissitudes of life with me for the last 30 years and helped to make this book possible."

The first edition of this book is a green, hardbound version with 308 pages. On its dust jacket is an illustration by Western artist Charles Russell featuring horses, cowboys and smoking six-guns on the dirt street in front of a saloon. A later edition by Bonanza has a plain, lettered red and white dust jacket. The preface for it was written by Judge Don Martin of Salmon, Idaho, a longtime friend of Keith.

A little over 10,000 of these, according to Elmer, were initially published by Stackpole. He was not exactly sure as to how many were later done by Bonanza Books, but knew that it was in its 10th printing by 1981. He estimated, of both editions, that more than 20,000 were published.

Prices on this book vary with a ragged copy at a gun show or in a used book store with an asking price of $40 or so on up to mint condition, signed copies in the $200 range. The Bonanza editions are usually priced about 30 to 50 percent less.

The next Keith book was part of a two-volume set, of which the other half was *Mister Rifleman* by Townsend Whelen. Elmer's half of this effort, published in 1965 by Petersen Publishing, Los Angeles, was *Guns and Ammo For Big Game Hunting*. It featured illustrations by Bob Kuhn, contains 384 pages and measures 9x11 inches.

Portions of this book are reprinted from the 1948 Little, Brown and Company edition of *Elmer Keith's Big Game Hunting*. Initially, Elmer estimated that about 5000 of these had been published, but after going through some long buried files, he determined that the number was closer to 10,000 for *Guns and Ammo For Big Game Hunting*. Occasionally, sporting book collectors find this book as part of the original, complete boxed set, but it is generally found singly. The price for the Keith side of the set is currently ranging from between $75 for a good copy in dust jacket all the way up to $200 for a signed copy.

During the late autumn of 1957, Elmer received an invitation from a group of professional African guides to come over and hunt game on the Dark Continent. This eventually led to another book centered on hunting which outlined that first trip and ensuing adventures Keith had in Africa. This book, *Safari*, published in 1968 by Safari Publications, La Jolla, California, was produced under the direction of Truman Fowler. It is dedicated to Captain M. St. John Lawrence and to All Members of White Hunters (Africa) Ltd. and the members of the East African Professional Hunters Association.

Aside from having the book partially dedicated to him, John Lawrence also did the introduction. The publica-

Two different versions of *Shotguns By Keith*. It was originally published by Stackpole in 1950 and has gone through several reprint editions.

Keith's Rifles for Large Game, 1946, Standard Publications, Huntington, West Virginia—his most scarce and sought-after book which has gone up in price considerably over the past ten years.

Cover of Elmer's last book, *Hell, I Was There*, published by Petersen Publications, Los Angeles, expressed a lot of his attitudes toward life.

tion figures on this green, hardbound, 167-page book were 10,000 copies. It measures 8¹/₂x11¹/₄ inches. And this particular collector's book could be the guns and hunting sleeper of all time in light of what several dealers in used and rare books have said.

They say it has several things going for it—Keith's name and reputation, guns, adventure and African hunting, and the relatively limited number of them available—which could prove in the future to make it a book of some substance in potential worth.

In four years I saw, only at gun shows and at no used bookstores, only four copies, and they were priced from $100 to $150, which is considerably higher than its original price of $15.

More years would pass before the inevitable...a book about the life of Elmer Keith ranging from his turn-of-the-century boyhood days on the American frontier, which was being laid to rest, on up to the time when he was awarded the first Handgunner of the Year trophy in 1973. The Winchester Press, in 1974, published *Keith an Autobiography* which was advertised as "Memoirs of the bronc rider who became a world famous big game guide and the dean of American firearms authorities."

Designed by Nina Wintringham and dedicated to Keith's parents, his wife, and son Ted's family, this is a brown hardbound book with 381 pages and numerous illustrations. It, in first edition, measures 6¹/₄x9¹/₄ inches. The foreword was written by Judge Don Martin. Winchester Press produced an estimated 5000 copies, but figures on a later, smaller-in-size, book-club edition are unavailable.

From my research, this book-club edition appears to be somewhat scarcer than that published by Winchester Press. I have yet to see one offered at a gun or Western Americana show, and used and rare book dealers say they seldom see it. As to the value of the book-club edition, I cannot say. However, the Winchester edition has been going up. I have seen a signed edition at the bi-annual 4600-table Great Western Gun Show in Los Angeles, with dust jacket, for $100, which sold the same day it was offered.

There would be more of the Keith story published in yet another book. An expanded and somewhat revised

Gene Brown and Elmer Keith, May 2, 1979, in front of the Keith home at Salmon, Idaho.

version of Keith's autobiography entitled *Hell, I Was There* was released by Petersen Publishing, Los Angeles, California, in 1979.

This 308-page work has proven to be the biggest selling Keith book of them all. As of 1981, more than 20,000 had been published, according to Elmer.

In 1979, Elmer signed about 1000 labels which were attached to the inside of *Hell, I Was There* and sent out to the first buyers. An unsigned copy of this book is currently available through some mail-order houses for about $20. I have seen signed copies for sale, which include their original shipping boxes, with an asking price of $175.

In addition to the foregoing books by Elmer Keith, there were special editions which seem to have vanished into the air. Among these extremely hard-to-find Keith books are simulated leatherbound editions of *Sixguns, the Standard Reference Work* and another of *Guns and Ammo For Big Game*. Elmer said that approximately 2000 of the simulated leatherbound *Sixguns* were published by Stackpole Publishing and the same number of *Guns and Ammo For Big Game* were published by Petersen. The only copies of these I have ever actually seen were in Keith's own library.

Over the past years I have not—at gun shows, in used and rare book stores or through catalogs—seen one of these books offered for sale. The last copy of the simulated leatherbound *Sixguns* I was aware of went to a collector in Pasadena,

California, in the spring of 1981 for a reported $250.

Other, even more scarce, examples of Keith's writings are the original hand-corrected manuscripts. To Elmer's knowledge, in 1980, a collector in eastern Montana had the original manuscript for *Sixguns, the Standard Reference Work*. The one for his 1974 biography was somewhere in Los Angeles, and the *Hell, I Was There* manuscript was with a collector in northern Idaho. The rest, he thought, were either lost or inadvertently destroyed by publishers.

Letters written by Elmer Keith turn up occasionally at gun shows, but usually only as display pieces and are not for sale. Keith was a prolific writer whose stated daily goal was 5000 words. How scarce and/or valuable his letters will become only time will tell.

Numerous articles by Keith can be found in the *American Rifleman* magazine dating back to 1925. The majority of his writing for this magazine was during the years from 1950 to 1955. He was featured on the cover of this magazine in 1928, 1931 and 1936. He also wrote for *Outdoorsman, Western Sportsman* and *Guns* magazine. His monthly column was a regular feature in *Guns and Ammo* magazine for more than twenty years.

The publication figures and descriptions of the foregoing books were checked and verified by Elmer Keith at his home in Salmon, Idaho, in June of 1981.

Elmer Keith died February 14, 1984, in Boise, Idaho. ●

by LEN McDOUGALL

POOR MAN'S DEER RIFLE

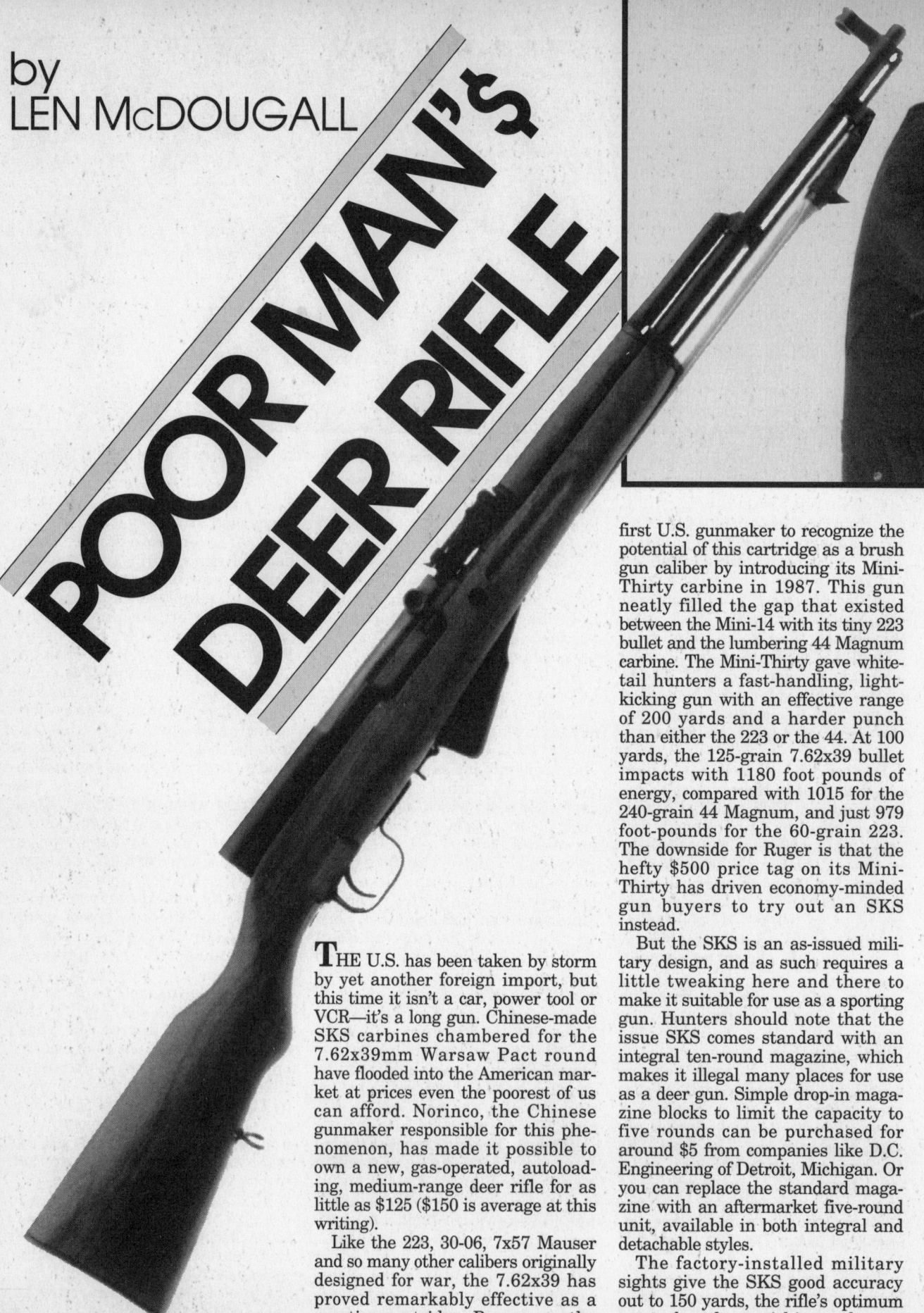

THE U.S. has been taken by storm by yet another foreign import, but this time it isn't a car, power tool or VCR—it's a long gun. Chinese-made SKS carbines chambered for the 7.62x39mm Warsaw Pact round have flooded into the American market at prices even the poorest of us can afford. Norinco, the Chinese gunmaker responsible for this phenomenon, has made it possible to own a new, gas-operated, autoloading, medium-range deer rifle for as little as $125 ($150 is average at this writing).

Like the 223, 30-06, 7x57 Mauser and so many other calibers originally designed for war, the 7.62x39 has proved remarkably effective as a sporting cartridge. Ruger was the

first U.S. gunmaker to recognize the potential of this cartridge as a brush gun caliber by introducing its Mini-Thirty carbine in 1987. This gun neatly filled the gap that existed between the Mini-14 with its tiny 223 bullet and the lumbering 44 Magnum carbine. The Mini-Thirty gave whitetail hunters a fast-handling, light-kicking gun with an effective range of 200 yards and a harder punch than either the 223 or the 44. At 100 yards, the 125-grain 7.62x39 bullet impacts with 1180 foot pounds of energy, compared with 1015 for the 240-grain 44 Magnum, and just 979 foot-pounds for the 60-grain 223. The downside for Ruger is that the hefty $500 price tag on its Mini-Thirty has driven economy-minded gun buyers to try out an SKS instead.

But the SKS is an as-issued military design, and as such requires a little tweaking here and there to make it suitable for use as a sporting gun. Hunters should note that the issue SKS comes standard with an integral ten-round magazine, which makes it illegal many places for use as a deer gun. Simple drop-in magazine blocks to limit the capacity to five rounds can be purchased for around $5 from companies like D.C. Engineering of Detroit, Michigan. Or you can replace the standard magazine with an aftermarket five-round unit, available in both integral and detachable styles.

The factory-installed military sights give the SKS good accuracy out to 150 yards, the rifle's optimum range, but those wishing to have a

The author's four-season field test of the Norinco SKS bordered on the unreasonable, at times. The test gun was routinely exposed to hardships no sensible hunter would experience.

scope mounted may have difficulty finding a qualified gunsmith who will do the job (an awful lot of gunsmiths regard the SKS with the same disdain once expressed by American car dealers when they looked at a Toyota). Probably the simplest way to mount a scope on your SKS is to buy a replacement receiver cover with the mount already installed. These assemblies start at about $30 and are available from Tapco, Inc., of Smyrna, Georgia. The one complaint I've encountered with these units is that they don't allow sufficient eye relief with the factory stock.

My own scope mount is a custom job from The Lock, Stock & Barrel Shop of Traverse City, Michigan. It consists of a 9-inch aluminum alloy mount rail held in place by four tapped machine screws with a layer of epoxy sandwiched between the mount and receiver cover for added stability. The extra-long mount allows more latitude when adjusting for proper eye relief.

One thing to be aware of when mounting a scope on the receiver cover is that few of the covers are completely immobilized when the connecting pin is cammed and locked in place. Since even a minute amount of movement at the scope will translate into an appalling variation in the bullet's point of impact at 100 yards, stabilizing the receiver cover is an absolute necessity. Fortunately, this is an easy fix that can be accomplished by inserting a thin rubber shim (bicycle tire inner tube works fine) between the receiver and the

squared lug at the rear of the receiver cover. With this shim in place, the connecting pin will lock down tightly and the receiver cover will stay in the same position shot after shot.

The SKS trigger pull is about what one would expect from a military rifle: heavy, creepy and sloppy, but manageable enough to get the job done. The easy disassembly of the SKS and the interchangablity of its components make having a spare trigger assembly—as well as other spare parts—a good idea. Spare, snap-in trigger assemblies can be purchased from Tapco, starting at $33 for the type with a stamped trigger guard, and $39 for those with milled trigger guards. For safety's sake, never attempt any adjustments or modifications to the trigger assembly.

Another problem common to at least some of the SKS rifles is their maddening tendency to lock up with the bolt in the closed position and an empty cartridge still in the chamber. The problem is usually caused by a burr around the inside circumference of the chamber mouth. The problem can be solved by chamfering the chamber mouth to remove the burr and polishing the chamber wall, a simple operation that costs about $15.

Jamming can also occur as the result of excessive spring force on the recoil spring rod assembly and the ejector rod located inside the rear sight block. With the recoil spring rod assembly fully extended, the spring is still under considerable tension and is so long that it bulges out

in a wavy fashion from the sides. On my test rifle, these bulges were hanging up on the bolt carrier during recoil, impeding its travel and preventing the gun from cycling smoothly, particularly in cold weather. With considerable trepidation, I began shortening the recoil spring, two coils per cut, until the SKS functioned flawlessly with all types of ammunition. At that point, I had cut fourteen coils from its original length.

Next came the ejector rod spring. I reasoned that removing two coils from the twisted music-wire spring would increase ejection force and travel while still maintaining sufficient tension on the ejector rod to hold it firmly in place with the rifle assembled. I'm happy to report that the spring-cutting operation was a success and is now being used by at least one gun dealer to help cure jamming problems with the SKS rifles he sells.

The issue SKS carries its own cleaning kit under a trapdoor in the butt and a cleaning rod locked in place under the barrel by the folding bayonet. All of these, including the bayonet, can be valuable tools for the serious trophy hunter who routinely ventures deep into the boonies where the big bucks hide during daylight hours. The utility of the cleaning rod and kit is obvious, and the seemingly useless bayonet can be folded down at a 90-degree angle to the barrel and shoved into the ground to provide a pretty fair rest for long-range shooting from the prone position. Strangely, using the bayonet as a rest doesn't seem to affect the bullet's point of impact at all, which defies logic for those of us who subscribe to the floated-barrel theory.

A common complaint about the SKS carbine is that its stock is too short. Most men will find themselves all scrunched up while shooting. Those who find the short stock hard to get used to can purchase full-size synthetic replacement stocks for as little as $50. Slip-on rubber recoil pads can also be used to stretch the stock an extra inch or so.

Out of the box, every new SKS I've fired has been capable of placing three shots into 3 inches at 100 yards, more than adequate for use as a brush gun. Those rifles that fail to do so consistently are most likely victims of their own ammunition. The Chinese-made ammunition is apparently not manufactured to the same tight tolerances as American ammunition, and it isn't unusual for a "flyer" to open up an otherwise snug group to 7 inches or more. The cure for this problem is usually as simple as buying a box of American-made hunting cartridges.

SKS owners who wish to maximize the performance of their carbines will find a wide variety of aftermarket accessories to choose from. Whitetail hunters who frequent thick, brushy areas where a lightning-fast second shot might mean the difference between elation and frustration can install a muzzle-brake that will reduce muzzle climb to almost nothing. I've tested the rather massive model from D.C. Engineering and was impressed enough to make it a permanent feature on my own SKS. At $19.50 it costs a couple of dollars more than some others, but the increase in rapid-fire control it provides makes it a bargain at twice the price. The only problem caused by installing some muzzlebrakes is that their diameter will not permit the cleaning rod to be withdrawn. This dilemma is easily fixed by simply filing a flat spot onto the knob at the muzzle end of the cleaning rod, allowing it to clear the muzzlebrake with the bayonet folded out at a 90-degree angle.

Aftermarket detachable box magazines have also become popular with SKS owners who find the standard trapdoor cup magazine too restrictive. The companies submitting magazines for my four-season field tests were USA Magazines of Downey, California; D.C. Engineering; and Tapco, Inc. The five- and thirty-round models from USA Magazines are made from stamped and spot-welded steel with Zytel followers; the five- and thirty-seven-round models from D.C. Engineering are made from heavy-gauge wire-welded steel with stamped steel followers; and the thirty-round mag from Tapco is composed entirely of Zytel. (Tapco does not offer five-round hunting magazines).

The magazine tests were enlightening to say the least. Three different guns were used to ensure a fair sampling, but the one variable that couldn't be controlled during initial tests was the outside temperature, which was minus 12 degrees Fahrenheit. The Zytel mag from Tapco suffered a cracked lip and jammed the gun on the second round. A quick visit to my favorite gunsmith netted seven more of the Tapco mags, but the initial failure was more than just a fluke. Four of the seven new mags

also suffered cracked lips on the first loading and two of them suffered cartridge nose-dives that actually broke out the front of the magazines. Only one of the Zytel magazines emerged from the first firing unscathed. These failures were apparently caused by the extreme cold and didn't occur in warmer temperatures.

The samples from USA Magazines appeared to work very well on the first loading, but subsequent tests in warm temperatures revealed some disturbing problems. Despite repeated cleaning and lubrication with silicone, the Zytel follower in one thirty-round mag consistently stuck fast after about ten rounds, and the magazine had to be disassembled each time to free it. Of the five thirty-round mags we tested from this company, all but one experienced problems with sticky followers, but three of them were cured after a couple shots of silicone.

The five-round mag from USA Magazines also had a few problems, although jamming wasn't one of them. The most noticeable glitch was the way the magazine fit into the gun, so tightly that considerable wiggling and shoving was needed to lock it in position and only a hearty pull could remove it. Since all detachable mags require that the rifle's bolt be locked to the rear before they can be inserted or withdrawn, using the five-round mag was made even more difficult by its failure to engage the locking mechanism after the last round was fired. That meant the bolt had to be held to the rear manually and the lock slid into place with a finger of the opposite hand before the magazine could be removed. One of the thirty-round mags also had this same problem.

The winner in our magazine tests was D.C. Engineering. Their strongly built wire-welded five- and thirty-seven-round (yes, thirty-seven rounds) magazines are ugly as a mud fence compared to those of their competitors. But after running twenty-five rounds through the five-round mag and 117 rounds through the thirty-seven-round unit without so much as a hiccup, there seemed to be little point in continuing. They might be ugly, but they sure can cook.

Wood-to-metal fit of the SKS I used in my four-season field tests was satisfactory, and even good considering the rifle's price tag. The finish of the Tung-wood stock was mediocre, but then the gun was never

meant to be aesthetically pleasing, only functional. My biggest complaint was with the less than precise way the action was mounted into the stock, and I think having it glass-bedded would probably bring about a noticeable improvement in accuracy.

However, the SKS will never be a sharpshooter's rifle, and, again, it was never intended to be. Although the 7.62x39 bullet is considered a 308, the SKS barrel has a land diameter of .311-inch and a groove diameter of .313-inch. It shoots .308-inch bullets just fine, maintaining enough accuracy to get the job done at 200 yards.

For the handloaders among us, I want to point out that *only* .308-inch bullets are recommended for reloading the 7.62x39 cartridge, and propellant charges reflect that. Attempting to shoot a .311-inch bullet with the same powder charge recommended for a .308-inch could result in very high breech pressures. As with any caliber, be safe when reloading the 7.62x39 and always adhere to the recommended loadings.

After thoroughly abusing it for a solid year in all types of weather, my final impression of the SKS is that it's a solid, well-made rifle, in spite of being a bit rough around the edges. The massive two-piece bolt is built much stronger than it needs to be, and both components appear to have been milled from solid steel. Toolmarks are evident throughout the gun, but critical bearing surfaces are smooth and polished. External metal surfaces are nicely blued and appear to have been coated with a rust inhibitor (my test gun was weatherproofed because it was exposed to weather and abuse that a sporting rifle would never see). It's apparent that the SKS and the AK-47 share the same bloodline, but whereas the AK has stamped and riveted metal parts that, in my opinion, give it a "tin can" look, the SKS has the feel and appearance of a firearm that was designed to last a lifetime.

The 7.62x39mm SKS rifle won't appeal to everyone, and I certainly wouldn't recommend that anyone trade in their existing deer rifle for one of them. But if you've been looking for a solid, utilitarian, budget-priced brush gun that doesn't mind a little abuse, or if you have a young hunter in the family who needs a first deer gun, this is one sturdy little autoloader. •

A Workhorse Trapline 22

The Remington 510-X on bags at the range. It's stocked in maple, fitted to the writer.

DURING THE '70s and '80s fur boom, when fox pelts were worth well above $50 and raccoon not far behind, I ran a trapline full-time for the month of November each year. In those days, the most popular fox trap was the #1½ coil spring foothold. Its small jaw spread and modest spring strength were more than adequate for the lightly built fox.

During the middle '70s, however, the coyote expanded his range into Maine's evergreen forests. Being a canine, he was, of course, fascinated with the urine and gland odors used for fox trapping, and soon started showing up in our fox traps.

Eastern coyotes are big animals, weighing from 20 to sometimes 50 pounds or more, and they fight a trap hard and relentlessly. I held the first coyote I caught, but the next two pulled out right in front of me. When I tried to approach close enough to shoot them with my Ruger Single-Six 22 rimfire revolver, they redoubled their struggles and the little #1½ fox traps couldn't take it.

I decided I needed a 22 rifle to shoot trapped coyotes at a distance while they were still fairly calm. I wanted something inexpensive but reliable, rugged enough to take the abuse of trapline work, a gun I could toss in the front seat of the truck and not pamper much.

At a gun show, I found a used single shot bolt-action Remington 510-X Targetmaster with a ¾-inch tube Weaver B6 scope on it. I had the barrel cut down to 18 inches to make handling easier and sighted it in at 30 yards with 22 Shorts.

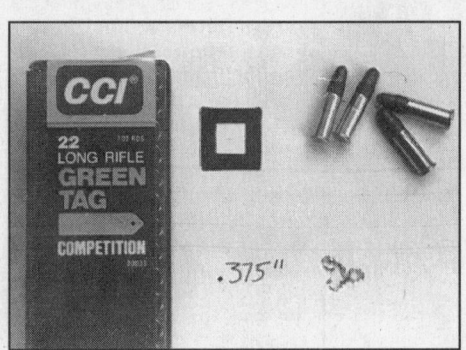

CCI's Green Tag grouped five shots into .375-inch at 50 yards—excellent accuracy.

Eley Match Xtra puts five shots into .50-inch at 50 yards when Noonan does his part.

Shorts are best for shooting trapped animals as they will kill cleanly when placed in the brain, but aren't powerful enough to exit. Faster loads penetrate the head completely and often exit out the back of the neck or back, lowering pelt value.

Bullet placement is critical with this type of work, so I needed at least some accuracy. I remember being mildly surprised at how small those 30-yard groups were, although I didn't measure them. I hadn't expected more than just ade-quate accuracy from the inexpensive single shot.

At the time, I was trapping a lot of old farm country with abandoned farms, overgrown back fields, and old apple trees. It was ideal ruffed grouse habitat, and I saw birds daily. One day, I spotted a bird pecking gravel in the old farm lane ahead of me and, as I drove closer, it occurred to me that the bird's head looked bigger than the groups the 22 had shot at that distance. I stopped the truck slowly, eased the door open, slid a Short into the chamber of the Remington, and slunk a few steps to a tree. I braced the gun against it, crosshaired the grouse's head and pulled the trigger.

At the pop of the Short, the bird flopped over and flapped crazily in circles on the ground. When it quieted down, I picked it up; there was a hole right through the head, dead center. There's a lot of satisfaction to a shot like that, and both the bird and the gun felt good in my hands as I walked back to the truck.

A little while later I spotted

another grouse, and the Remington hit that one right in the head, too. When a third bird joined the others, I realized that I'd stumbled onto a real prize. I found myself moving lesser objects out of the way on the seat beside me and laying the gun there respectfully, instead of just tossing it in like I had before.

Eventually, I saw a coyote bouncing around ahead in one of my fox traps. I stopped the truck a distance back to avoid exciting the animal and approached on foot. The big canine was getting agitated, so about 40 yards away I leaned against a tree. When he stopped to look at me, I put the crosshairs in the center of his high forehead. Coyotes are relatively

Right side view of action and pistol grip, a grip fitted to its maker. Note the trigger shoe and original trigger guard.

easy to kill with a hit anywhere in that area. At the shot he flopped over, stone dead. Bingo! I had my trapline coyote gun.

I forget exactly how many grouse I head-shot that fall, but it was well over twenty. I killed several more coyotes, and never lost one. By the end of the trapping season I was right in love with the little Remington. I still am.

I trapped full-time each fall until the late '80s, and the 22 always went with me. You always see game when running traps, and the gun picked off a lot of bonus grouse, squirrels and rabbits. It accounted for a lot of fur, some of which I would have lost without it. Better fox/coyote traps became available, but I still routinely shot all coyotes with the rifle, usually from 20 to 30 yards. When I trapped raccoon in heavily set-

tled areas, I used very small traps to avoid hurting pets, and occasionally a coyote would get a toe or two stuck in one. The Remington saved some of them for me.

One time, I was nuisance-trapping raccoon at a local town dump, carrying just my pistol. I rounded the corner of a wall of trash and there was a coyote in a coon trap. He was in the red color phase, as red as a fox in the early morning sunlight, and I decided to take a picture. I trotted back to the truck for the camera, and almost as an afterthought I slung the rifle over my shoulder.

When I returned both coyote and trap were gone! I heard brush rattle to my left, and there was the coyote, the trap still on his foot, hung up in a bunch of alders.

I literally dropped the camera, dug frantically in my pocket for a shell, and fumbled it into the chamber. The coyote never moved, and I shot him in the face at about 20 yards. He had pounded the trap so hard that a rivet had opened, coming free of the chain. Coyotes are hard on equipment.

Whenever any furbearer acted like it might pull out, I shot it from a distance. You develop a sense for animals that are poorly held; I'm sure they can feel some give to the trap, and when you approach, they get a little more frantic than solidly held animals do. They know they've got one last chance. You get a gut feeling: better shoot this one from back here, right now.

Once, I was checking a pair

of fox traps about 100 yards apart, in a farm pasture right near a small town. The first set was behind a brushy fencerow. When I got about 50 yards from it, a big bobcat jumped up and stared at me over the brush.

I was astonished; bobcat catches were infrequent, and definitely the last thing I expected this close to town. The cat went crazy, snapping back and forth at the end of the chain. Something told me not to get much closer, but I ran ahead to a fencepost, rested the gun on top and whistled. The cat stopped momentarily and stared at me over the brush, and I shot him in the forehead.

When I lifted him up, the trap stake pulled free of the ground. We'd had some rain, and the wooden stake had loosened in the wet clay soil enough for the long-legged cat to jerk and pump it loose. The big male later weighed in at 32 pounds, large for Maine. I would have lost him without the Remington.

After I calmed down a bit, I walked to the second set, and there was a cat in that one, too! It sat still, crouched in a ball, staring at me, but after the first cat I didn't take any chances—I shot it at about 20 yards. It was a smaller 15-pound female, solidly held. Possibly they were traveling together.

The Remington became an essential trapline tool for me. I shot all trapped bobcat with it. I took to shooting fox, too, as it was very quick and stressed the animal less than approaching closely to stun them. I'd place the bullet on the side of the head at the base of the ear, making sure there was no exit hole in the neck, which was always a problem with face-on shots on these light animals.

Every year, I would catch a fisher or two and the occasional otter in my fox or coon sets, and I always shot these valuable furbearers with the Remington, again through the side of the head to avoid holes in the neck. Both these animals fight a trap violently when approached, and it was much easier to shoot them from a distance while they were relatively quiet. It also prevented possible pullouts.

Skunks were common catches on the fox line, and the rifle was the perfect tool for dispatching them safely with head shots from a distance.

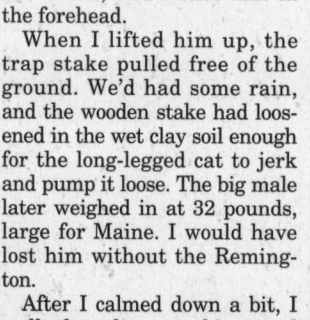

I usually used the revolver on raccoon, but several times I had raccoon take a trap on a pronged fox drag up into a tree. I shot them from the ground with the rifle. I'd much rather climb a tree after a dead raccoon than a live one.

My confidence in the Remington increased to the point where I just assumed that if I got the crosshairs on something, it was dead. The gun hit things with monotonous regularity. Of course, if you have confidence in a rifle, you shoot better anyway. Bear in mind that most of this shooting was at stationary objects at reasonable ranges, and from a rest. I could take very deliberate shots. I missed occasionally, but it was always my fault, not the gun's. If I did my part, the Remington would place bullets with surgical precision.

One day a fox crossed the road ahead of me. I pulled the truck over, grabbed the Remington and hopped out. The fox ran out in the middle of a mowed field and stopped to sit on his haunches and stare back at me. I chambered a Short and laid down with the rifle over a hay bale.

It was a good distance, and there was a steady breeze coming from the left. I held a bit more than an inch above the very tip of his left ear and squeezed off a shot, and a second later the fox slumped in a heap. It was 75 paces to him, and there was a bullet hole almost exactly between his eyes. Carrying the $70 fox back to the truck, I felt like I owned Supergun.

Curious about how well the gun really would shoot, I finally sat down at a bench. Through the Weaver B6, I could group Winchester high-velocity Shorts into 3/4-inch at 30 yards. At 50 yards, groups opened to over an inch and were a full inch below point of aim. I was lucky I had even hit that fox.

I knew I needed more reach and accuracy for longer shots, so I tried some 22 Long Rifle ammo. Winchester's Super-X high-velocity hollowpoints grouped into just a hair under an inch at 50 yards. In addition, the gun put both the Winchester Long Rifles and Shorts into exactly the same point of aim at 30 yards, a real asset. From then on I used the Shorts only on trapped animals out to about 30 yards, and the Long Rifle hollowpoints on everything else.

The restocked Remington fits the author perfectly. It works in a variety of hunting positions.

When working a trapline, you'll sometimes see raccoon during the day, often sleeping in trees. The Remington has knocked down a number of them over the years. I use Long Rifle hollowpoints on these tough animals, and always try for a head shot. Sometimes you'll surprise a raccoon on the ground. If you charge right at them, yelling and barking like a dog, they'll go right up a tree, where they're easily shot. I remember a pair of them crossing the road ahead of me into a stand of pines. I slammed on the brakes, grabbed the Remington and gave chase. It took me a while to find them up in the thick evergreen branches, but eventually I carried two $30 raccoons back to the truck.

Under the right circumstances, the 22 Long Rifle will kill fairly sizable game. For several years, I trapped dairy farm country, where coon and black bear populations were high because of all the cornfields. Each year, bears would spring half a dozen or so of my coon and fox sets. Their big feet spanned the jaws of the traps and set them off without getting caught.

One day, I pulled up on a logging road and stuck my head out the truck window to check a trap back in the spruces, only to see a small black bear staring back at me. He had just got caught, because the area wasn't torn up at all. I debated leaving him alone and letting him pull out, but the farmer whose land I was on had a lot of bear damage in his corn. Besides, I like bear meat.

I shot him in the ear with the rifle, using a 22 Long Rifle hollowpoint, and he dropped in his tracks. He was only held by one toenail, and it popped off while he was thrashing around. He weighed about 60 pounds, was corn-fed and delicious, and the farmer was delighted.

Some people claim the 22 Long Rifle will regularly kill deer, but I've never attempted it. I'm sure it can be done if conditions are perfect, but bullet placement is just too critical. I don't think power and penetration are adequate to kill consistently, or compensate for a poor shot. I've killed several deer with head shots with the more powerful 22 WMR, which will usually penetrate the head completely even with hollowpoints, but I also lost one after a very solid hit, and consider that cartridge marginal at best. I've butchered a few pigs with the 22 Long Rifle, and in my opinion, the 22 WMR is far better for this job, too. Maine bear trappers routinely shoot trapped bear with the 22 WMR; most consider the Long Rifle inadequate.

The 22 rimfire is a very versatile small game cartridge. In addition to trapline duty, I did a lot of hunting with the Remington, and long ago lost track of the head-shot squirrels, rabbits and woodchucks it has accounted for. It's done pest control duty, too; it has knocked plenty of pigeons and starlings out of trees and has done-in an occasional crow, barn rat, porcupine and feral cat, and a few swimming muskrats and turtles. A good 22 rimfire rifle is a valuable tool in rural areas.

Through the years, I steadily upgraded the gun. The original stock was a bit cumbersome, so I took some wood out of the pistol grip and shortened and narrowed the forend. The trigger was awful, with a lot of creep and a heavy pull, so I had a gunsmith work on it. There's still a bit of travel, but it now fires crisply at about 2 pounds once you take up the slack. I added a trigger shoe, which made a big difference in the feel.

The little Weaver B6 was fine for controlled shots on trapped animals, but it was too cramped for the quick handling needed for hunting. When my long traplines ended in the late '80s and I began using the gun mostly for hunting, I put a full 1-inch centerfire scope on it, a Bushnell 6x Sportview. This is a very clear, sharp scope, with a big light-gathering 40mm objective lens. Field of view is a full 20 feet at 100 yards, one reason I like fixed-power scopes. The duplex reticle is thick enough on the edges to make centering quick, important in a hunting scope, yet the center crosshairs are fine enough to let me see a half-inch bull at 50 yards. The added heft of the 10-ounce scope, positioned right over the action, helps balance the light rifle and makes handling steadier. This scope is an excellent match for 22 rimfires intended for serious small game hunting.

A couple of times the point of impact changed when the scope was bumped and the inexpensive grooved receiver mounts slipped. I had a gunsmith drill and tap the receiver for Weaver's #21 bases, mounted the scope with Weaver rings, and have had no trouble since.

With the new scope and higher bases, the stock's comb was too low. In a moment of irrational affection for the Remington, I decided to restock it. The nicely grained maple blank only cost $10, and who counts the hours spent on a labor of love, anyway?

The Remington now wears a thumbhole stock that fits me perfectly. I can shoulder the gun with closed eyes and when I open them I'm looking at the crosshairs. The pistol grip is positioned so just the tip of my trigger finger rests on the trigger shoe, and the flat-bottomed forend is very stable on a rest. It's a nice handling gun, too, quick to shoulder and point. The light wood has mellowed yellow with age and is pleasant to contemplate while sitting in the sunny October squirrel woods.

I glass-bedded the action and free-floated the barrel, then tested it with a variety of match ammo. CCI's Green Tag grouped five shots into .375-inch at 50 yards, Eley's Match Xtra into .50-inch at the same distance. Not too shabby.

I prefer high-velocity hollowpoints for squirrel hunting because of better bullet expansion and a bit longer reach, so I tested some different brands. CCI's Mini-Mag did best in my Remington, shooting consistently into .750-inch at 50 yards—pretty good for commercial hunting ammo. With this load, I can hit and kill squirrels consistently out to 60 yards. This load has done well for me in a number of different guns.

I realize the Remington is no match rifle, and other more expensive and finely tuned guns will shoot better. But for an inexpensive mass-produced gun it does quite well, thank you. And it's utterly reliable. Besides all the hunting, trapping and plinking, there have been many target sessions of hundreds of shots, and some of over a thousand at a sitting. During the twenty years I've owned the gun, I'll bet I've put close to 10,000 rounds through it. The simple bolt always feeds smoothly, never jams and extracts easily.

Jack Heath, Remington's historian, tells me that about 20,000 of the Model 510-Xs were manufactured between the years 1964 and 1967. It didn't have a special match chamber or barrel, although the rigidly made action helps accuracy. It's just a particularly well-made gun—one good gun, you might say. •

by **DICK EADES**

A Real 28-Gauge

THE YEAR WAS 1961. I was shooting Skeet with the Ft. Hood, Texas, team and hoped to enter the 28-gauge events. I shot a borrowed gun several times with indifferent results. I wanted to buy one of my own, but money wasn't too plentiful and a new Browning Superposed cost a bit more than $500.

The NSGA Show (National Sporting Goods Association) in Chicago offered me a look at the Charles Daly shotgun line. At that time, Daly guns were being made in Japan by B.C. Miroku Co., now producers of the Browning Citori line. At that show, I met the sales manager of the Daly Company, Joe Salisbury, and had a short conversation with him. I looked at the guns displayed and realized they were of very good quality and priced far below the Browning products.

After returning home from that show, I telephoned Salisbury and asked him if he would sell me a 28-gauge gun, choked Skeet and Skeet. I was thrilled when he agreed to ship the gun upon receipt of a check for $225. I mailed the check and haunted the Express office until the gun arrived.

The new gun was a dream. It weighed less than 6 pounds and had a slender forearm and delicately shaped buttstock, fitted precisely to the engraved metal of its diminutive receiver. It performed on the range as nicely as it looked and felt. Patterns from both barrels were large and perfectly centered to point of aim. I was thrilled as my 28-gauge scores soared. The first registered shoot in which I used the little gun was a big one with lots of competition. I ran fifty straight with the Daly and won the 28-gauge event, getting myself "4

punched" into AA class in the process.

No matter, the gun was a delight to swing and shoot. In design, the gun was much like a Browning with single trigger, selective ejectors and non-automatic safety.

Several of my fellow team members asked to shoot the gun and I proudly allowed them to try it out. One was so taken with it, he asked if I could get one for him. I thought so and called the Daly company again, asking if we could repeat the sale at the same price. They agreed and another $225 check was posted.

Several days later, a box arrived by UPS and I opened it, expecting to see another gun like the one I was shooting. Instead, this one was much bulkier than mine. It weighed almost 2 pounds more and lacked the petite dimensions mine displayed. Obviously, this second gun was a 20-gauge that someone had fitted with 28-gauge tubes. I called the company to inform them that an error had been made.

Mr. Salisbury assured me that there was no error. According to him, the only 28-gauge guns they imported were, indeed, 20-gauge receivers fitted with 28-gauge barrels. I kept insisting that my gun was far smaller than the second one he had sent, and I wanted another one like my original. Finally, he asked me for the serial number of my gun, which I read to him on the telephone. As soon as he heard the number, he told me that my gun had been shipped in error and that I must return it at once. I replied that there was no way I would return the gun; he had cashed my check and I

already had it back from my bank. According to my thinking, the gun was mine and would so remain.

Salisbury told me all sorts of horror stories about the gun. It wasn't a production model. There was no warranty on the gun. There were no repair parts available for it. If anything broke, I couldn't get it repaired.

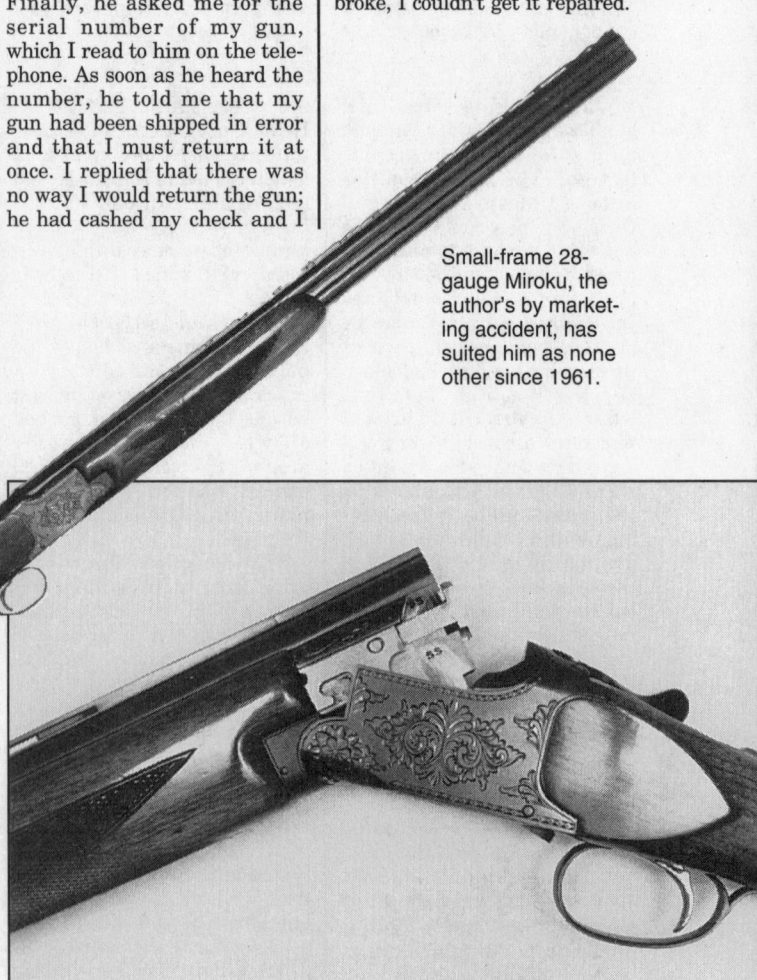

Small-frame 28-gauge Miroku, the author's by marketing accident, has suited him as none other since 1961.

Scaled right down to the 28-gauge shell, there aren't many like this in the U.S.

I quickly informed him that the darn thing wasn't born, it was built, and if it broke, I could get it fixed. If there were no parts, replacements could be made. In short, there was no way I would give up my positively favorite 28-gauge shotgun.

Over the next few months, I had several telephone calls from Salisbury, offering trades, cash and other inducements to return the gun. His final offer was a new Diamond Grade Daly in any gauge I wanted, even trade for my little 28. Again, I refused and told him to forget the gun existed since he would *never* get it back.

About a year later, I happened to see Joe at another show. I repeated that the gun was going to stay with me, but asked him why he was so desperate to get it away from me. He grinned, then told me the story.

According to Joe, the gun was one of thirty-seven they had imported while considering adding it to their line. They decided not to add the gun since it would sell for more than their other standard grades, and they did not think it was a practical marketing approach. He went on to say he wanted to get it back since he knew where he could sell it for several times the price I had paid for it. We adjourned to the local bar and I offered him a drink as consolation for his failed attempts.

Since then, I've heard several other stories of the gun's origin. Probably the most believable is that this small-framed Daly is still being made by Miroku, but it is their domestic model and has never been exported for sale. There is a chance that it is also made in 410, but I know of no one who has seen one. Several shotgunners I know report having seen another of these little 28s in this country, but I have found only one other in the thirty-plus years I have owned this one. The owner of the other one feels about his the way I do about mine. It's his and will remain his as long as he is on this earth.

If you happen to run across one of these tiny 28 gauges, please let me know. Y'know, they can't be repaired and it would be a shame to be stuck with one. Out of the goodness of my heart, I'll pay $225 for any one I may be offered. I might even pay $250 for one in 410-bore. ●

by LARRY S. STERETT

A Very Good Mossberg

IT WASN'T THE first rifle I ever purchased, nor even the first gun. I never took it to Africa, or to Canada, or even to Mexico. Nor was it used to bag my first whitetail. It *was* my first bolt action, and for many years it thinned out the local ground squirrel and groundhog population. It was, and still is, one good gun.

My introduction to small-bore shooting took place on the high banks of a small stream flowing through the pasture of my uncle's farm. Dick had been a Navy pilot in the Pacific in World War II, and when he returned home, he went into farming with his brother. One Sunday afternoon, he and my Aunt Pink decided it was time I learned to shoot. Dick unpacked his trunks and out came his rifle, a Savage Model 19 NRA Match rifle. It had a 28-inch barrel topped with a blade front sight, an adjustable aperture rear sight, and scope mount bases to which had been fitted a Winchester 4x scope. To me it looked like a million dollars, or at least 100 shiny silver ones.

Uncle Dick stuck a couple of boxes of 22 Long Rifles in his pocket, told me to pick up and carry the rifle, and it was off to the creek. There I learned to concentrate on breath control, trigger squeeze and sight picture, while shooting at small pieces of wood tossed down onto the opposite bank, or drifting slowly downstream. The time went by too rapidly; two boxes of cartridges just don't last long when you're having fun plinking. I was hooked on shooting. The Savage was nice, but it was a bit heavy, and the five-shot magazine had to be removed and loaded too frequently. I wanted a rifle of my own.

Mowing lawns at 25¢ each, or 50¢ if it was a really large one, doesn't mount up very fast. Nor does delivering papers at $3 per week, or odd jobs at 25¢ per hour. The process does allow plenty of time to peruse the "wish books" and *Sports Afield, Field & Stream, Hunting & Fishing,* and *Outdoor Life* to determine which was the best rifle. I couldn't afford to subscribe to the magazines, except *Hunting & Fishing,* which was $1 per year, but another uncle kept me supplied with some of the others.

Eventually, I purchased a rifle from Montgomery Ward & Company in those dream days of yesteryear when you could buy sporting arms from mail-order houses and walk through town carrying your new rifle on your shoulder. It was a good rifle, but it couldn't easily be fitted with a scope, and I wanted a rifle with a scope. The local hardware store carried mainly Winchester rifles, and every so often a Remington, and could order the others, but none of them seemed to be what I wanted. Sears, Roebuck & Company, Montgomery Ward, and even Spiegel's carried good selections of most of the popular brands of rimfire rifles, and whenever a new catalog arrived, I turned to the sporting goods section first.

I'd been saving money, and finally I decided. The rifle had everything I wanted: a bolt handle with round knob positioned close to the trigger, just like the gun writers said was necessary for rapid bolt operation; a genuine walnut stock with cheekpiece (something most other rimfire rifles did not have); a streamlined trigger guard with moulded finger grooves (which most other rimfire rifles did not have); and a "safety cover plate" attached to the bolt to cover the ejection port during firing and whenever the bolt was closed (another feature other rimfire rifles did not have).

Those were all good features, but there were more. It had a barrel band, quick-detachable sling swivels, and not two, but three sights—an open sight adjustable for windage and elevation, and with choice of aperture or V or U notches; a hooded ramp front sight with four fixed, interchangeable inserts; and an S130 peep rear sight adjustable for windage and elevation. The rear aperture sight could also be adjusted to increase the sight radius, and the cross arm swung out of the way when using the open field sight or a scope. And the rifle was factory drilled and tapped to accept scope mounts.

There was still more: The trigger was well shaped, plus grooved to reduce finger slippage, and it was adjustable for let-off. The safety was located at the rear of the receiver, literally under the thumb—a green plastic indicator with an S on it and a red one with an F, both inset in the stock, indicated the respective positions.

Finally, there was even more—it would shoot any 22 Short, Long or Long Rifle cartridge; it had a tubular magazine with side ribs between the magazine and barrel to give it a

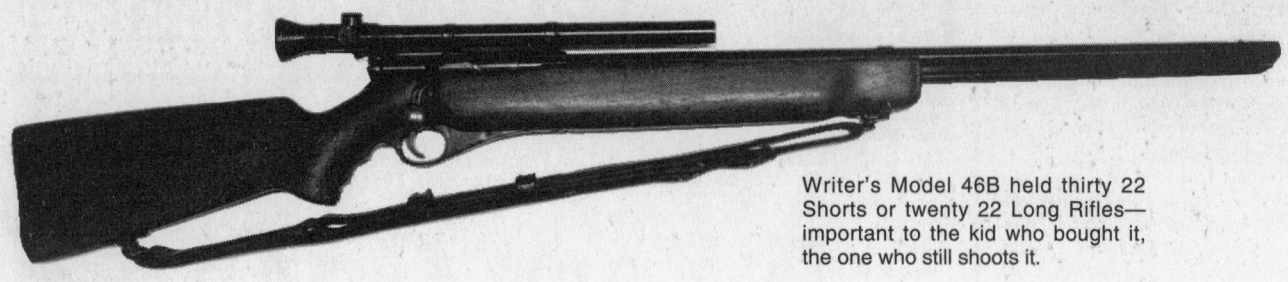

Writer's Model 46B held thirty 22
Shorts or twenty 22 Long Rifles—
important to the kid who bought it,
the one who still shoots it.

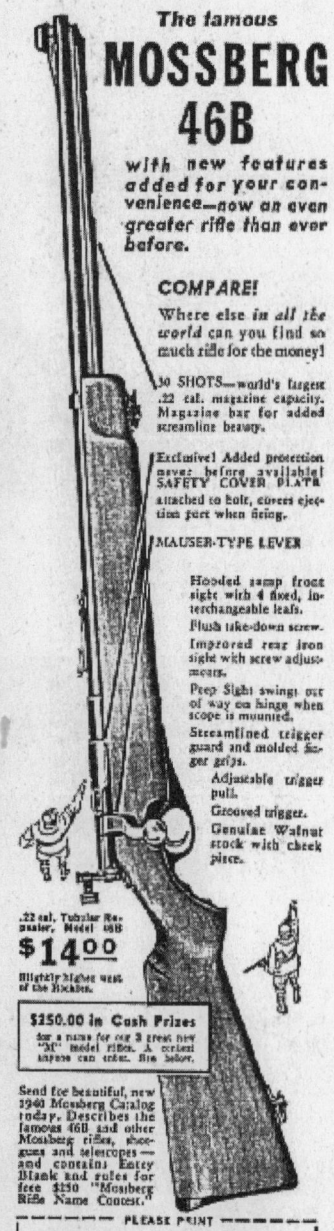
In April, 1940, this is what Moss-
berg had to say about the 46B,
and the story worked on Sterett.

real streamlined appearance;
and, the clincher, it held more
cartridges than any other rimfire rifle in the world then on
the market. The Mossberg Model 46B had a magazine that
extended almost to the end of
the barrel; it held thirty 22
Shorts, twenty-three Long or
twenty Long Rifle cartridges.
That did it! I ordered a Mossberg Model 46B rifle.

The Model 46 was introduced
in 1935, and changed to the 46A
in 1937; the original 46B, having a twenty-round 22 Short
capacity, made its appearance
in 1938. With an extended magazine tube, side ribs and a couple of other changes, the streamlined Model 46B was introduced in 1940. It was discontinued after World War II
started, when Mossberg's production of rimfire rifles was
mainly limited to box magazine bolt actions used as military trainers. In the U.S., it
was the 44-US, and in Great
Britain it was apparently the
42M. Following the war, the
Model 46B was returned to
production, but at a price a bit
higher than the $14 it had
been in 1940.

Having finally accumulated
enough money, I filled out the
order form, enclosed a postal
money order for $24.53, and
rushed off my order to Montgomery Ward for a Mossberg
Model 46B Bolt Action 22
Rifle. The wait for the long

box to arrive at the post office
seemed to last forever, but
eventually there was a package for me.

Rushing home, I carefully
unwrapped and opened the box
to reveal a streamlined beauty
of polished blued steel, with a
shiny bolt knob, and genuine
walnut stock with cheekpiece.
After opening and closing the
bolt several hundred times, at
least, checking to make sure
the sling swivels really were
quick-detachable, and removing the hood on the front sight
to see if the four interchangeable inserts really did, I was
ready. With a peanut butter
sandwich, homemade cupcake,
apple, water-filled canteen and
four boxes of 22 Long Rifles in
my knapsack, I picked up the
new rifle and headed for the
abandoned quarry west of
town.

Using my knapsack for a
pad, and the four free targets
the hardware dealer had given
me when I bought the ammo, I
tried the aperture sight, the
open field sight with the U-
notch, V-notch, and the aperture (too far from the eye to be
useful) and the four front sight
inserts—post, bead, aperture
and inverted V. Everything
worked. I liked the aperture
front, but it obscured too much
of the target, except for the
bullseye, so I settled on the
rear aperture and bead front
with the U-notch on the open
sight, if needed for some reason. It was sighted in at 50
paces, or about 50 yards.

Over the next few years, the
46B accounted for an untold
number of ground squirrels,
the thirteen-stripe variety, and
a much lesser number of
groundhogs. One favorite territory for the squirrels was a
gently sloping pasture with a
high bank on one edge. It was
only a couple of acres in size,
and milk cows were kept in it
overnight. During the day it
was empty, and the cows had

grazed it clean, making any
bump that wasn't a cow patty
very obvious. Sitting along the
fence opposite the bank, I could
watch the entire pasture.
When a ground squirrel stood
up to survey the terrain, it
soon became food for the crows
and hawks. For the groundhogs, it was a hayfield behind
an abandoned barn. There was
a hedge along one side, and a
small dip across the center of
the field that divided it into
two fairly even sections. The
groundhogs liked to den under
the hedge and come out into
the alfalfa and red clover to
feed. After buying a Mossberg
No. M4 (b) 4x scope, complete
with mount, for $10.06 from
Hudson Sporting Goods, and
mounting it on the 46B using
the factory drilled and tapped
holes, I was ready to do major
damage to the hay feeders.

Late spring, just after
Memorial Day, the Fourth of
July, and Labor Day, times
when the hay was mowed and
put up, were the best times of
the year. The stubble was
short, making the groundhogs
easier to spot, and early morning and late afternoon were the
best feeding times. Using
Super-X or Kleanbore hollowpoints, the 46B generally
accounted for two or three
beasties per week during the
summer months, in this and a
couple of nearby hayfields.
None of the shots was over 75
yards, and the Mossberg rifle
and scope did its job well.
Today, the 46B combo is just as
accurate as it was back then,
but the pastures are now cornfields, even the hilly ones, the
hedges are gone, as are the
fence rows, and there just
aren't as many ground squirrels and groundhogs around.
Thankfully, there are still
plenty of rabbits and squirrels
around in season, and a well-
placed hollowpoint from the
46B will still do the job. It's too
good to retire. ●

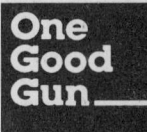
by TED STEPHENS

A Hard-Working Browning

A 4x4 blacktail in California's brush country—routine for the much-shot Browning.

THE RIFLE WAS made in 1966, even though I bought it new in February, 1971. I was fifteen years old and had been saving my paper route money from 1966 or thereabouts. This was the rifle I chose to launch me into serious hunting gear, and looking back over the last few decades, it is fair to say it lived up to the task.

I had already shot some game with the 30-30 and the 243, but this rifle that started it all is an FN/Browning Safari Grade in 270 Winchester. The checkering is all worn smooth, and I have refinished it four times. We're on our third barrel. The first one came off when it was still in pretty good shape, but the second—a Shilen 24-inch #5 contour 1:20-inch twist, select match-grade stainless—had approximately the first 4 inches of rifling worn smooth when I replaced it with a Shilen 24-inch, #4 contour 1:10-inch match-grade in 1989.

With this rifle, I shot my first 30-inch-plus mulie, my first six-point bull elk, my first bear, coyote, wild boar, kudu, gemsbok, impala, moose, caribou...It has always been lucky. In 1988, the year before I re-barreled it, in one fall it shot a 70-inch moose, a monster caribou, a 34-inch mulie, a bull elk, and another fine mulie, all with one shot each. No wonder when our raft turned over in Alaska the first thing I did was dive for my gun case! It has also been nice to have a rifle with the simple Mauser design that could be completely stripped with a screwdriver for the guard screws and one four-penny nail!

My journal shows I have shot approximately 170 head of big game with this 270. About 100 of these have been wild boars I was hunting or while backing up other hunters. No matter how heavy the rifle was or how tired I was, I have always enjoyed carrying this rifle with me. It has always had the feel that is hard to describe with words. The load has always been a straightforward formula in Winchester cases and Win-

(Left) It was a one-day pack and a two-day pack out, but the author's heavy barreled 270 felt light on this trip with a 7x8 mulie.

(Right) A 6x6 bull and the author's 270 brightened up this rainy Idaho day.

chester primers: 58 grains of H-4831 or 53 grains IMR-4350 for the 130-grain Sierra SBT; 52 grains of IMR-4350 for the Sierra 140-grain SBT or HPBT; and for bigger game, 51 grains of IMR-4350 or 54.5 grains of H-4831 for the 150-grain Nosler Partition.

For deer, black bear and wild hogs, you could never find a better cartridge than the 270. With a well-placed shot, you have your game. I have shot several elk with the 270, and I now believe for any shot at any angle, one needs more power.

With its heavy stainless barrel, Buehler mounts and rings, and a fixed 6x Leupold, my 270 weighs 9¼ pounds. Some may feel that weight is excessive, but it has "weighed in" again and again when the wind was blowing or I had a poor shooting rest. As a matter of fact, I have backpacked in several areas that were so rugged, other hunters stayed away. That old 9¼-pound rifle never bothered me a bit with a big load of meat and an oversized rack on my back.

The most consistent bedding method I have found for FN/Browning rifles is to pillar-bed both guard screws, glass-bed support the entire action, bed the barrel swell and free-float the rest of the barrel. For a pure rugged hunting rifle, I free-float the barrel with about .050-inch clearance so it is easy to clean the channel with a bandanna in the field. I have also found by undercoating the entire unfinished stock with a 10 percent Varathane liquid plastic with 90 percent mineral spirits carrier, the stock is very stable, quiet and feels good. A normal oil finish goes on top of the soaked-in Varathane base.

Many of us have a feeling that some rifles are just lucky. I know I do, especially after considering the luck this one has always had. One of the few big game animals I had not been successful on was mountain lion. I'd looked for a big tom with other rifles several times, with no luck. I had seen big-looking cats when hunting deer with my beloved 270, but never had a tag with me. This last January, when looking specifically for a big tom, I packed it. One shot did it, and I headed home with a big cat. Some rifles just work this way, and I imagine that is why Jack O'Connor talked of being buried with his favorite pair of Model 70s in 270.　●

by LEE ARTEN

Colt's Conversion Unit

I WAS LOOKING for a double-action 22 revolver in Pat's Sports Shop in 1979. When I walked out, instead of a Smith or a Charter 22, I was carrying a used Colt Conversion Unit (CCU) for my Colt 1911 45 ACP. In the years since, I have come to regard that $80 purchase as arguably my best gun deal to date. The 22 conversion is definitely the best half-gun I own.

The CCU allows 22 Long Rifle ammunition to be fired through full-size 1911 and 1911A1 pistols in 45 ACP, 38 Super, and 9mm Luger. It consists of a slide assembly, 22-caliber barrel, floating chamber, barrel bushing, ejector, recoil spring, slide stop and magazine. Because I'd been reading gun magazines for years, and never left a sporting goods store without an armload of catalogs, I knew about the conversion, but before Pat starting selling mine to me, I hadn't actually seen one.

I liked what I saw. The blued slide was a lot easier on the eyes than the military Parkerizing on my 45's frame. I liked the Colt Accro sights better than the aftermarket Micro set I'd put on the 45. That rear sight looked like it had just been stuck onto the 45 slide, no matter how many times I looked at it.

The literature that came along said, "The Colt 22 Cal. Conversion Unit makes target practice possible at approximately one-seventh the cost of 45 caliber shooting."

I liked the idea of more shooting for less cost and started out to do as much of it as I could. The conversion quickly found a place in the gravel pit as a plinker and on my hip as a small game gun. The 22/45 worked fine in the woods, but at first can-rolling and clod-busting wasn't its strong suit. After just one box of 22s, the floating chamber would pack with lead, the slide would start failing to close, or fired cases would catch in the ejection port. I expected this from a semi-auto if it was left uncleaned long enough. Having it happen at the fifty-round mark seemed too much of a bad thing.

For a time, I thought I'd made a mistake in not holding out for a revolver. Before I did anything rash, I discovered that the malfunctions were basically my fault because I like bargains. When buying 22 ammo, I could always find a promotional

With the original box and Colt information sheet, the unit may be worth a bit more than the author paid for it back in 1979.

brand with a plain lead bullet for less than any other kind. Most of the el-cheapo brands grouped quite well in the 22/45, but firing them seemed to leave more lead in the floating chamber than went out of the barrel.

It took me longer than it should have to try different loads. Almost the first stuff I fired after the bargain rounds was Remington high-velocity, solid bullet ammo. The only difference I saw, at first, was that the Remington 22s came in a plastic box holding 100 rounds, not a pasteboard one holding 50. The difference that mattered, that kept my CCU shooting, was that the Remington bullets were plated. The plating looks like it could be scraped off with a thumbnail, but it slows leading enough so I can now shoot close to 600 rounds before the 22/45 needs cleaning.

Winchester Super-X and other plated ammunition works, too. Even the extremely cheap Sovereign Tiger Cat brand, imported from Mexico, feeds well. The Remington high velocity works best for me. It seems more consistent from shot to shot than Tiger Cat, and when I buy it ten boxes at a time on sale at the local Coast to Coast, it is cheaper than the Super-X.

I didn't shoot in target matches when I bought the Conversion Unit, and I didn't train beginning shooters. I have done both since, and the 22/45 works well in both roles. I have read reports that conversions are not accurate enough to use in even semi-serious target competition. Shooting my 22/45, I have been soundly beaten by other shooters with Ruger, Smith and High Standard target pistols. Since I have also fired good, tight groups using a modified Weaver and from a target stance, I attribute my poor scores to insufficient practice, the GI trigger, and the use of optics by most other competitors.

The trigger has since been demobilized, smoothed and lightened by about a pound, but I haven't added an Aimpoint yet. Despite the references to target shooting in the Colt literature, I think the Conversion Unit is really best used as a low-cost trainer and understudy for the serious pistol, the 45.

I have hunted rabbits with my 22/45 and fired some matches, but it has been used most in

From a classic target stance, or two-handed, the Colt Conversion Unit fits right in. It allows cheaper shooting.

(Right) Any holster that fits a target-sighted 45 auto will also carry the Colt Conversion Unit. An Uncle Mike's magazine pouch made for the standard Colt 45 magazine will also accept conversion unit mags.

(Left) Since the magazine holds ten rounds, a Colt Conversion Unit (left) can do a fair job as an understudy for high-capacity 45 pistols like the fourteen-shot pin gun shown to the right here. The increased recoil from the floating chamber also helps simulate the recoil of full-power pin or IPSC loads.

"Ideal for training new shooters," Colt said. It's true for the author's son Isaac, ten.

"Wow! I hit the target!" You hear that a lot from Isaac.

The Colt Conversion Unit and some of the best ammo that it likes. Remington high-velocity "golden bullet" ammo works best. Winchester Super-X does well too. Imported Tiger-Cat shoots more erratically, but doesn't jam the gun.

Accuracy is not supposed to be the Conversion Unit's strong point, but the author fired six of the ten shots on this slowfire target into a group that beats many fired with target pistols.

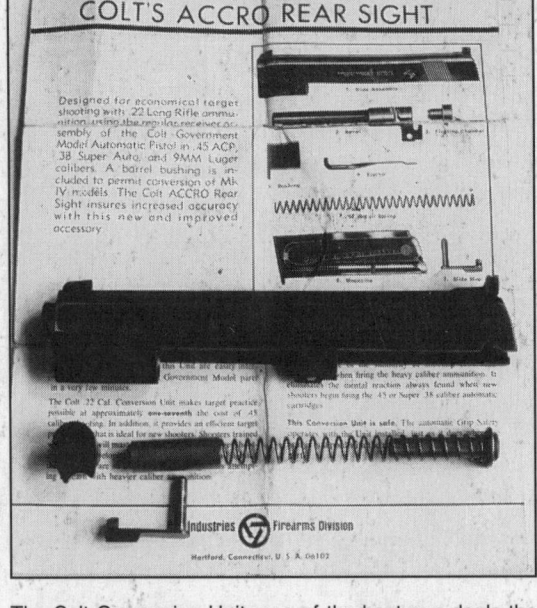

The Colt Conversion Unit, one of the best gun deals the author has ever made, despite being only half a gun. Colt hasn't made the Conversion Units since 1986.

practice for bowling pin competition. The range where I shoot during the winter was built to handle all police duty and target ammunition up to the 44 Magnum and 12-gauge slug loads. The pistol club there, however, allows only 22 shooting during club meetings. The 22/45 thus is the closest I can come in the cold months to practicing with the gun I use in matches.

My old 1911 frame with the CCU installed offers the same trigger and grip as the 45/45, plus similar sights. It also comes closer than the Rugers, Smiths and Brownings at the range at mimicking the recoil of full-power 45 ACP loads. The Colt literature, right after explaining that the unit is ideal for training new shooters because it is easier to shoot than a full 45, 38 Super or 9mm Luger, goes on to say, "It is well to note that the Floating Chamber, with which this unit is equipped, produces a recoil that is approximately four times the recoil of 22 Long Rifle ammunition when used in regular 22 caliber arms." Besides adding kick to simulate firing full-power ammunition, the floating chamber uses the minor recoil of the 22 Long Rifle round to operate a slide the same size as a regular centerfire slide. This makes it possible to have a 22 with the same weight as a standard 45, 38 Super or 9mm.

I can easily tell the difference between firing the CCU and the full 45. It is also easy to feel the difference between shooting the 22/45 and a stan-

dard 22 target pistol. I believe the increased recoil with the conversion helps when I am training for bowling pin matches. I think it would also be a help in practicing for any competition which stresses speed, power and accuracy. It is not as good as full-power practice, of course, but it is many times better than no practice at all.

The same kind of thing might be said for the CCU itself. Sometimes, it is not as good as either a full-power service pistol or a tricked-out, optically friendly 22 target gun, but the CCU, enframed, and in hand, is a lot better than no gun at all in most situations.

I'm glad I got my good half-gun when I did. The first time I checked the price of a new Conversion Unit, about five years after I bought mine, they were already going for $240. The last listing I saw for them, in the 1987 GUN DIGEST, was more than $300. According to the marketing department at Colt, the conversions have not been made since 1986. The parts department at Colt says they have no conversions and no magazines left.

Since they are no longer made, used conversions like mine, in good condition, in the original box, with the original literature, may be approaching the price of new ones in 1984. That makes my $80 deal look better and better, but I'm going to keep on letting my profits ride. Even though it is only half a gun, my Colt Conversion Unit is too good to let go. ●

by TRACY A. SANDERS

My Low-Cost Ruger 44

FELLOW SPORTSMEN talk, and the talk invariably turns to a favored gun. Failing logic, their choice is usually based on some irrelevant variable. The often-touted relationship between accuracy and the small fortune they paid for the particular gun in question does not seem to correlate.

Perhaps, for me, my lack of understanding stemmed from my father's heavy-handed influence. From the time I began hunting—merely as my father's afterthought, "Well, I guess you can come, ...set up decoys, carry coffee, retrieve birds, tote my stool, etc."—to present, my father stuck to the basics of hunting and their importance. Safety was pre-eminent, and I have knots on my head to prove it. Advanced instruction came, after my vision cleared, on the simple but important relationship of accuracy to hitting. Cost and aesthetics did not always enter into his equation.

Accuracy can be found, though not easily, in any firearm, by applying a certain degree of understanding of the involved variables, i.e. bullet weight, bore condition, type and amount of powder, just to name a few. On the other hand, hitting, which is the ability to connect the projectile with the intended target, is the responsibility of every hunter and is only found through countless hours of practice.

I suffer from two dreaded diseases. I am a frequent gun swapper, which has left me to often lament some of the deals that I have made over the years. I am also a pawn shopper, which my wife regrets because I just can't seem to pass up a good deal.

Thus it was on a cold, rainy Saturday, looking for some-thing to pass the time, I was struck by an original idea. I had heard a new pawn shop had opened down the road and decided I should welcome the new owner to the neighborhood. And there, I came across a much abused Ruger Super Blackhawk. The barrel had been bobbed off to the ejector rod housing, and much of the bluing near the muzzle was worn to a dull gray. The loading gate and some of the cylinder looked dinged. The factory grips had seen much abuse, and the grip frame had begun to develop a fine patina of rust. However, the barrel had been properly re-crowned, the bore was clean and pit-free, the cylinder lockup was tight, and the trigger, though heavy, had no creep. I decided this new find was to be my new woods gun. After much haggling, I walked out with my new $130 purchase and a good feeling for my newfound neighbor.

Over the next few days, I applied cold blue and eased the trigger return spring, thinned and sanded the grips, and gave them a goodly dose of varnish mixed with stain. I had intended then to shoot some reduced loads with soft, cast bullets imbedded with LBT bore lap compound to polish the barrel, but I got an invitation to help friends ready their deer lease for the upcoming season. They were intent on reducing the jackrabbit population—Texas jacks compete for the same vegetation and are considered varmints, so I graciously accepted. Two weeks later, I was somewhere north of San Antonio, surrounded by rabbits.

I had brought some handloads—a hard-cast RCBS semiwadcutter weighing 260 grains, over enough H-119. This load

It cleaned up nicely, and now serves up big slugs.

had always shot accurately for me. Sighting in, the groups seemed acceptable, not superbly accurate, but certainly practical.

As we drove around harassing the local rabbits, I saw a herd of what appeared to be large goats. Actually, they were Barbados sheep, whose numbers brought additional pressure on the resident deer population, and the truck lurched to a halt. After much running, stalking and gasping for air, I came upon my prey and took a young ram cleanly with a heartlung shot at 40 long paces. He slammed to the ground as though he had been introduced to Gorgeous George, the infamous wrestler. I sure was pleased with my cheap gun.

Later, when I finally benched the gun for accuracy, I used a new hard-cast bullet sent to me by my friend Dan, also a hand-gun enthusiast. The bullet is a 280-grain design by Lead Bullet Technologies having a large, flat frontal surface area (meplat). Remington cases filled with even more H-110 completed the combination. The first four shots grouped into an incredible .75-inch at 50 yards. The last two shots enlarged the group to 2¼ inches. I felt these should be called as fliers, but in a follow-up call to Dan, he assured me they were not. Still, within one week, a nice fat doe fell to this load, a spine shot at 70 yards. Gorgeous George had struck again.

I have swapped many fine arms over the years, but few have held my grateful attention like this one. It is inexpensive, unassuming, and does all I might have ever hoped. In my eyes, it is truly gorgeous. My Ruger 44 is one good gun. ●

by BRIAN PURDY

An Un-British Hunting Rifle

Everything in sight, except the detail of the checkering, was specified by the happy-owner-to-be.

MY ONE custom rifle was not built by a famous gunmaker, nor built for a wealthy man. It is not covered with adornment, and it's not intended to be a pampered collector's item, but it's mine, and it will be my son's, and it's a hell of a gun.

It all started on Bruton Street in London, at modest business premises with a sign "Holland and Holland, Gunmakers." The prices of the double rifles were so high that I have long since blanked them from my memory. I remember, though, that you had to pay the full price in advance, and then wait more than two years for delivery. I was more realistically interested in what Holland and Holland calls a magazine rifle—a bolt-action rifle. The basic, unadorned model of their magazine rifle sold then for the equivalent of $590. This was without any engraving, and with good, but not fancy, wood. Delivery was about six months on the pay-in-advance plan.

I had a chance, that first day, to take a close look at a standard magazine rifle. It could be ordered in calibers from a list provided by Holland and Holland. Stock dimensions were to your order, within specified limits, as were a few of the furnishings of the rifle. The style was basic European, with a narrow comb, rather more drop in the stock than I liked, and a short, narrow forend. The action was an unmodified Mauser, but with a hinged floorplate on the magazine. Fitting of the wood to metal was first grade, and the checkering was good, but not particularly fine. I would have

Purdy glories in the fit and finish, the jeweling, all the things that you can see—and the proven accuracy, too.

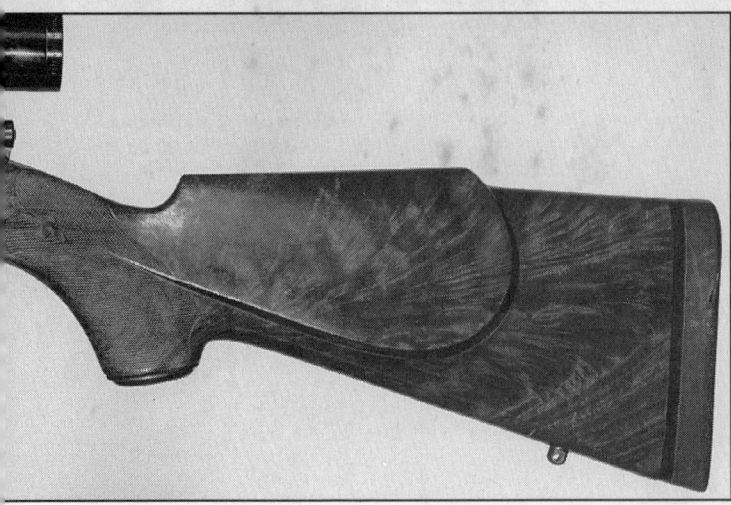

There are places where this favored Monte Carlo and cheekpiece shape would not be considered restrained, but that's how Purdy sees them.

Le tout ensemble put together by Bill Granger, now of Creston, B.C., has served nearly twenty happy years.

Proud owner Purdy anticipates generations of pleasure from the Granger rifle. The fun of this photo alone covers half the London price.

to rate it as a semi-custom rifle rather than custom, since all that the purchaser could specify were some personal accessories and his stock dimensions on the standard rifle.

Back home in Yellowknife, in the Northwest Territories, I considered the matter. I had been around guns since I took my first duck on the wing at age nine and had grown through a lot of guns and gun books. I thought I knew a bit about quality and design in sporting firearms, and I was sure that it was possible to have a better gun made in Canada, *completely* to custom specifications, for less than a Holland and Holland standard magazine rifle.

A few months later in Whitehorse, in the Yukon Territory, I saw some custom checkering and stocking work on a Winchester 97 shotgun. The work had been done by a local Whitehorse resident who lived just down the street. It didn't take long to knock on Ron Granger's door.

He soon proved to be the type of personable, expertly knowledgeable and competent sort of guy that you'd be happy to entrust with a tricky gunsmithing job. Ron showed us his tiny shop in a garage at the back of his home. Small though it was, it was fully equipped with everything necessary to work in wood or metal.

When I returned to Yellowknife, I decided that perhaps the time had come to see whether my dream rifle, custom built just for me, could be built by Ron Granger.

I wrote him, set out what I had concluded were the best components for my custom rifle, and asked for a price. I specified a Shilen barrel from Texas, a Sako Finnbear action from Finland, a Canjar single set trigger, and Fajen AAA, feather crotch, black or Claro walnut stock from California. I wanted extensive borderless 22 line per inch checkering in fleur-de-lis pattern, with ribbon, executed by Granger in the Yukon.

There followed a year's worth of the most satisfying exchange of correspondence I have ever had. Eventually, Granger said, "You must allow me the discretion of my own sense of design. I know enough of your personality now to be sure that you will be pleased with the outcome."

So much for my forend tip—this was no man to trifle with

such gewgaws. He also said he would need the full year to do the job, because he could only do the checkering I had asked for in short spells, due to the nervous strain involved.

Feeling that I had passed the Granger Test for Suitable Clients, I sent him a detailed and formal order for a rifle in 7mm Remington Magnum caliber, long throated to seat 175-grain bullets to the base of the cartridge case neck. I specified the action, trigger, barrel make and length, stock length and comb drop, type of checkering, sights, checkering and reshaping of the bolt handle, and fiberglass bedding. Stock wood and design, as well as the checkering pattern, were left to Granger's discretion, subject to my approval. I also told him to take all the time he needed to do his best work.

I was already feeling pretty good. Not only had I been able to specify very precisely what I wanted, down to the finest details of the checkering of the bolt handle, but the price I had been quoted beat Holland and Holland.

More than six months after it had been ordered, the stock blank arrived in Whitehorse. Granger got to work on it right away because of the delay, but sent me sketches of the line of the comb he proposed to build, stating "As so much time has fled by, I am working at the stock without first sending it to you—you will have clear right to send it back if not satisfied." He described the blank as an "eye popper," with deep red-brown feather pattern running the length of the butt, and the best blank he had his hands on.

When I first held the Granger rifle in my hands, I subjected it to the same searching examination I had given the Holland and Holland rifle several years before. The wood-to-metal fit was as if the stock, barrel and receiver had grown together. The bolt, and all interior parts of the receiver, glittered with evenly spaced jeweling whorls. The Canjar trigger let off at a clean 3 pounds unset, and at a touch when set. The safety catch was completely silent. The metal parts had been blued by Granger to a deep, highly polished black.

But the stock was the focal point of it all. The rich feather pattern in the butt immediately seized the eye and led it to the exquisite checkering work on the pistol grip and forend, with

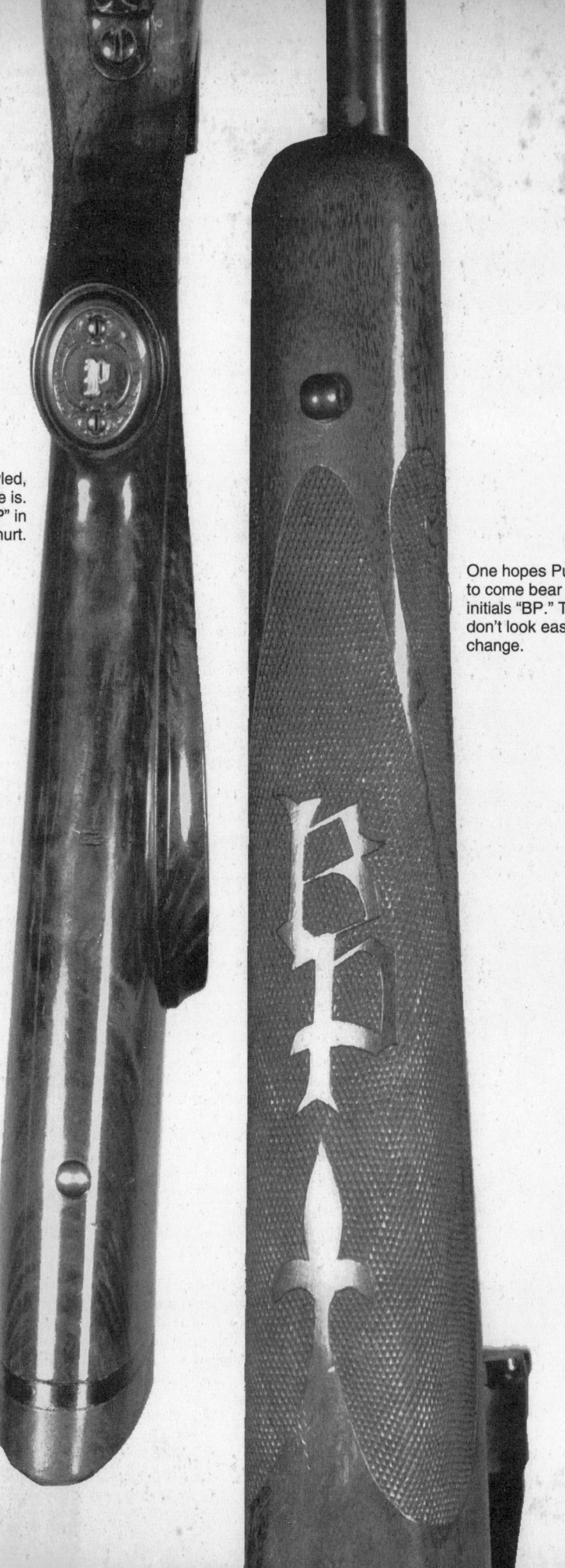

Very slimly styled, that cheekpiece is. Another little "P" in the buttcap can't hurt.

One hopes Purdys to come bear the initials "BP." These don't look easy to change.

the unique "BP" perfectly executed in the center panel. The sharp tipped diamonds of the checkering bit the hand enough to give the grip that checkering is meant for, but was fine enough to permit the glowing wood grain to show through. There were no runovers in the whole of the complex and extensive coverage.

Although the final coats of oil still had to be applied, I took the gun home to Yellowknife and fitted it myself with Conetrol scope mounts and a Leupold 2-7x scope. Nine days later, I used it to take the N.W.T. limit of five caribou, with six shots.

After this field test, Ron did a little final adjusting. He altered the angle of the bolt handle, and cut away some wood on the pistol grip to accommodate my rather large hand. This was a rifle truly fitted to its owner.

I then did my bit over the next month, by hand rubbing the stock with ten or twelve coats of linseed oil. This gave a deep, lustrous, easily repaired finish, which brought out the richness of the wood better than any other type of finish.

Finally it was done. I had my dream rifle, custom fitted to me, built to my specifications down to the finest details. The work had been superbly executed, and the components were the finest obtainable. The price? Well, I'm sure that both Holland and Holland's prices, and Granger's, are a lot higher now, but at the time, it beat the Holland and Holland price for their standard magazine rifle.

I've carried that gun a lot of miles now and looked at it hanging on the wall for a lot of hours. It's been a real field gun rather than a flashy showpiece. The Granger rifle has the kind of restrained elegance that doesn't grab the eye at 50 feet, but does bring knowledgeable shooters back for a second, and third, long warm look from up close. It will be with me until I get old, and then my son will have it.

I moved to Vancouver, British Columbia, a while back and for a couple of years didn't get a chance to go hunting. The third year, the rifle came down off the wall and went with me to the range for sighting. The first full-power load went into the center of the bull and the next four stayed within a half- inch of the first one. I looked in the general direction of London and smiled.

●

YOU COULD SPEND YEARS PUTTING TOGETHER A RELOADING BENCH LIKE THIS. OR, YOU COULD SPEND MINUTES.

A BENCH IN A BOX. ROCK CHUCKER PRESS, 5•0•5 RELOADING SCALE, SPEER RELOADING MANUAL, UNIFLOW POWDER MEASURE, ROTARY CASE TRIMMER-II KIT, HEX KEY SET, CASE LUBE KIT, CASE LOADING BLOCK, AUTOMATIC PRIMER FEED, POWDER FUNNEL, PRIMER TRAY II AND DEBURRING TOOL. DIES AND SHELLHOLDERS SOLD SEPARATELY.

At RCBS, we believe you should spend a lifetime using your reloading equipment, not accumulating it. That's why we created the Rock Chucker Master® Reloading Kit. It contains the world's most popular press, the Rock Chucker, plus all the accessories you need to reload like an expert. It costs considerably less than you'd pay for these items separately. It expands easily to progressive operation, with a Piggyback™ II conversion unit, which means you'll never outgrow it. Plus, it's guaranteed for life or forever, whichever happens to come first. So if you're ready to start reloading, spend your time wisely: visit your local RCBS dealer today.

RCBS®

TO DO IT RIGHT.

SPORTING EQUIPMENT DIVISION, BLOUNT, INC., RCBS OPERATIONS, 605 ORO DAM BLVD., OROVILLE, CA 95965.
FOR A COPY OF OUR FIVE BRAND SHOOTER'S CATALOG, CALL 1-800-533-5000 (CATALOGS ARE $2.00).
CCI • SPEER • RCBS • OUTERS • WEAVER

You won't find a better partner anywhere in the world.

The choice of the U.S. military and thousands of law enforcement agencies, the 92F has set a standard for reliability and performance that has yet to be beaten. This record has been consistently proven through exhaustive tests and, where it really counts, in the field with our military forces. Available in two operating systems, the Model 92 (9mm) and 96 (.40 cal.) pistols deliver the firepower, safety and ergonomics to meet your needs. Given the choice, why not go with a seasoned pro? See your authorized Beretta dealer or contact Beretta U.S.A. Corp., 17601 Beretta Dr., Accokeek, MD 20607. (301) 283-2191.

Model 92/96 Centurion and Model 92/96. *The high-capacity shortened and standard versions of the legendary pistol that protects America.*

Model 92/96D. *Double action only. Features slick slide system with no external safety lever and a bobbed hammer.*

Model 92/96 Centurion. *New shortened, high-capacity versions of the 92/96F models. 15+1 firepower (9mm) and 11+1 firepower (.40 cal.), with a compact sized slide and barrel.*

Model 92F Stainless. *All the features, reliability and firepower of the Standard 92F pistol. New matte stainless finish. Solid stainless slide and barrel. Black plastic grips.*

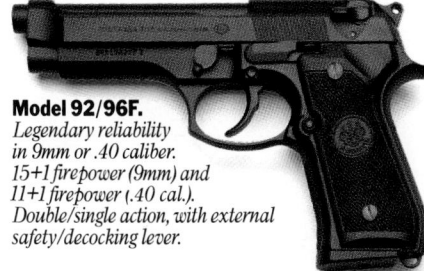

Model 92/96F. *Legendary reliability in 9mm or .40 caliber. 15+1 firepower (9mm) and 11+1 firepower (.40 cal.). Double/single action, with external safety/decocking lever.*

Model 92/96D Centurion. *Double action only version of the Centurion. Features slick slide system with no external safety lever and a bobbed hammer.*

Model 92EL. *The legendary reliability and features of the 92F...with bright blued finish, distinctive gold inlays and richly grained walnut grips.*

Beretta Operating Systems

F Models– *Double/single action, with external safety decocking lever.*

D Models– *Double action only without safety lever (slick slide).*

Beretta U.S.A.

3-dot and tritium night sights available.

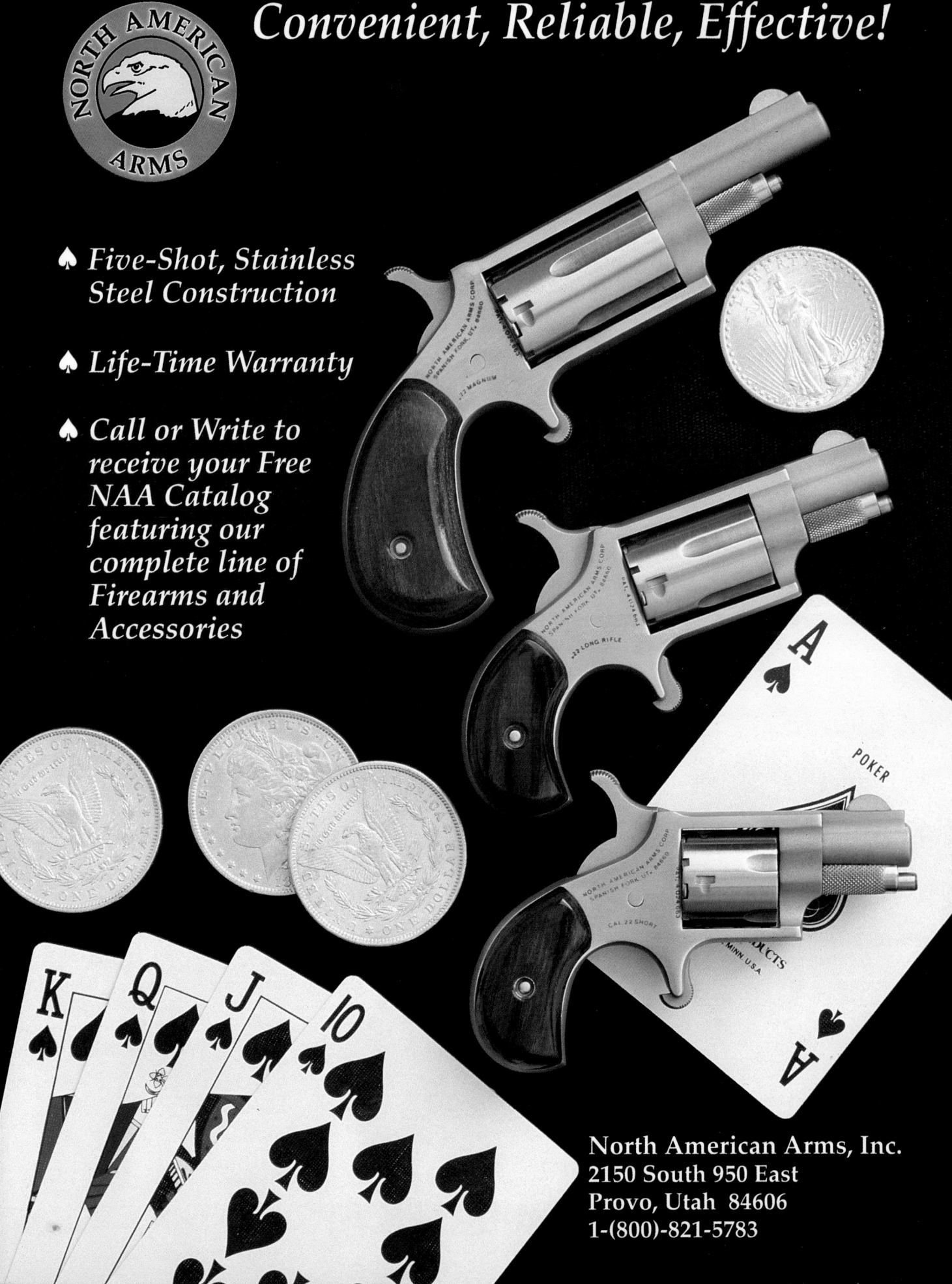

SHOOTING THE
ARISAKA RIFLE
MATCH

by JOHN MALLOY

Defeated but not humiliated, the writer manages a smile as he holds his Arisaka Match Rifle after his club's High Power competition.

I REALLY DIDN'T plan it.

When I went to that meeting of our local shooting club, I had no intention of shooting an old Japanese Arisaka rifle in the club's next High Power rifle match.

It happened this way:

One of the new members introduced himself as a collector of World War II Japanese military arms. He added that he enjoyed shooting them.

Now, our High Power match director is not a person who allows a centerfire rifle shooter to escape his attention. He immediately extended an invitation to the new member to participate in the coming match.

The new man explained that he couldn't. "I shoot only my Japanese rifles," he said. "I don't have a suitable match rifle."

I have always wanted our members to feel welcome and to be comfortable while participating in all the club's activities. Perhaps that is why I heard these surprising words issue from my mouth:

"Don't worry about that. You won't be the only one. I have a 7.7 Arisaka, and I'll shoot it in the next match."

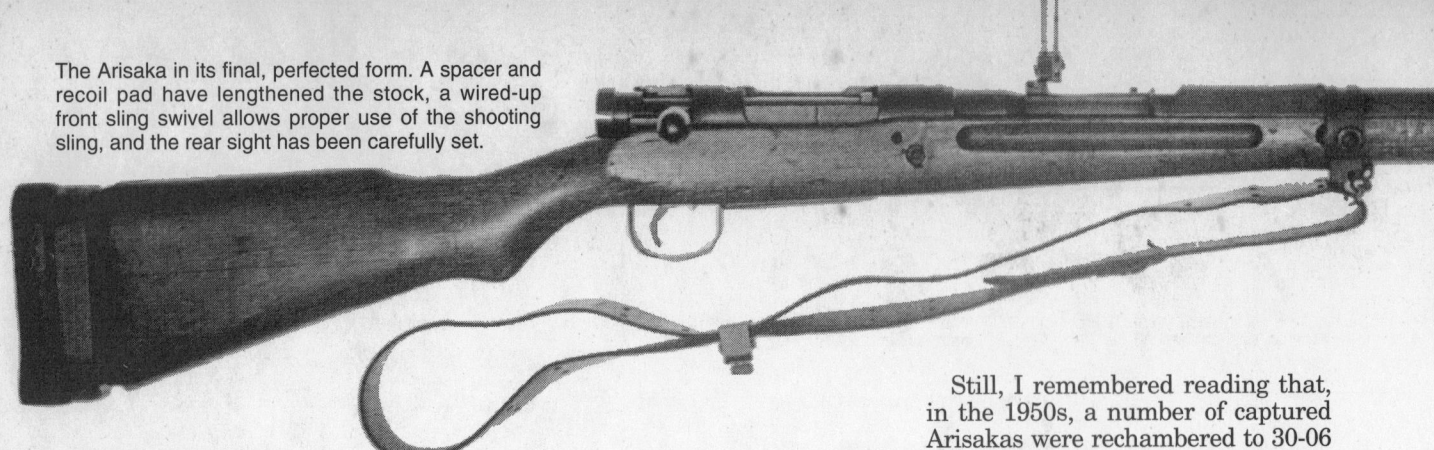

The Arisaka in its final, perfected form. A spacer and recoil pad have lengthened the stock, a wired-up front sling swivel allows proper use of the shooting sling, and the rear sight has been carefully set.

Once I had committed myself, I was faced with the reality of my rash decision. Nevertheless, I didn't want our new member to feel awkward, so I began preparations to use the ragged old Arisaka as my match rifle.

First thing I did was check my notes. I usually keep some sort of notes when I do some shooting, but that Arisaka must not have ranked very high in my esteem. No notes, but I did remember shooting it and hearing it go bang an undetermined number of years ago.

So, at least I know the clunker will fire. Better look it over.

The first Arisaka, in 6.5mm, was adopted by the Japanese in 1897. Use in the Russo-Japanese war showed a need for improvement, so a redesigned version, also in 6.5mm, came out in 1905. My rifle was the 1938 version, in which the caliber was changed to 7.7mm. If the 6.5 had been a junky-looking rifle with milled parts, the 7.7 was a junkier-looking rifle with stamped parts. The action was the archaic cock-on-closing type. The rifle originally had a wire monopod that pivoted at the lower band and a clattering dust cover over the bolt. Both were missing from mine. Apparently experienced Japanese soldiers lost theirs as soon as possible. The rifle had an aperture sight, but, with complete disregard for the theory of the aperture sight, it was in the same position as the old notch sight of the earlier 6.5 rifles. Attached to the sides of the sight's elevation slide were a pair of ridiculous folding "wings" for leading aircraft while trying to shoot them down.

At least it had a steel buttplate and a chrome bore. Specimens produced later in the war had wood buttplates nailed on, and the chrome bores were eliminated, as were the

adjustable sights. If anything good could be said about my rifle, it might be that it was the best of a bad lot.

Would the rifle shoot well enough? By now I had no thought of doing well in the match. My objective had become to escape humiliation. I was pleasantly surprised when a handful of Norma 7.7mm Japanese cartridges put holes on the paper and convinced me that the rifle shot well enough to meet this objective.

The problem then became one of ammunition.

I still had a handful of the Norma factory cartridges and another handful of empty brass. But I needed enough ammunition to sight-in, practice and fire the match.

Could 30-06 cases be safely reformed to 7.7mm Japanese? The practice has been discouraged due to the larger base diameter of the 7.7.

Still, I remembered reading that, in the 1950s, a number of captured Arisakas were rechambered to 30-06 (oversize chamber notwithstanding) to arm South Korean forces with a rifle that could use the standard U.S. rifle cartridge. Apparently, nothing very bad happened.

How much difference is there between the 7.7mm and 30-06 cartridge case bases?

A little time spent with a micrometer showed the difference to be somewhat less than I had anticipated.

The base diameter of six 7.7mm military rounds ranged from .470- to .472-inch. Miscellaneous Norma hunting loads of different vintages ranged .468- to .472-inch, with an average of .470-inch. These rounds were all full-power original cartridges designed to be fired in a 7.7mm chamber.

How did the 30-06 compare?

A double handful of original military and U.S. commercial loads ranged .465- to .468-inch. Military loads ran a tad fatter, averaging

Firing from the bench, the Arisaka met the accuracy requirements set by the writer. The short stock and lack of front sling swivel needed attention.

.467-inch, while the sporting loads averaged .466-inch.

Note that the ranges actually overlap, with the largest 30-06 equal to the smallest 7.7mm. The greatest difference still amounted to only .007-inch, while the average difference was only .003- to .004-inch. It seemed reasonable that moderate loads could be safely assembled in resized 30-06 cases.

Cases were easily formed with one pass in a 7.7mm sizer, then trimmed. For this particular rifle, neck reaming was not necessary.

To keep pressures low, I decided to try cast bullets and slow-burning powder. Lyman's #311291 and 44 grains of H-4831 had given good results in rifles of similar case capacity. Perhaps they would in the Arisaka, too. Trouble was, they wouldn't feed. Every shot jammed coming out of the magazine. Not too good for the rapid-fire stages.

My rifle apparently wanted only hard, pointed bullets. I unearthed a trove of pulled 303 British military bullets. Although dented and corroded, they were the right diameter, and plenty good enough for a clunker like the Arisaka. Sticking with slow-burning H-4831, I loaded them ahead of 49 grains for a moderate load. Back to the range.

The new load shot well enough,

Springfield stripper clips worked fine in the Arisaka and allowed its use in rapid-fire. The clips worked with both Norma reloadable cases and those of reformed 30-06 brass.

but the first shot showed me another problem. Wham! My thumb came back into my nose and I saw stars. All right, thumb to the right of the stock. I forget how many shots I fired before the bolt-release housing touched my nose.

Now, let me explain that some of my best friends have described me as "gangly" and my arms as "long and ape-like." Physical compliments aside, though, it was obvious that I could not comfortably shoot prone with that absurdly short stock.

I removed the buttplate and added a recoil pad. Better. I rounded off a piece of pine 1x2-inch and added that between the stock and the recoil pad. In business! Back to the range.

I made my final adjustments on the sight leaf from the bench. Shooting better than I expected. Actually, shooting pretty well. Everything is going into the black! That forward-mounted aperture sight is not too bad. It probably limited the field of view in battle, but on the target range it works all right. It actually seemed to sharpen up the front sight for my aging eyes. I made a note to use the bullets that were not corroded from now on.

Now to try the positions.

Uh oh! The sling swivels are on the left side. Okay for a carrying strap, but not good for effective use of the sling as a shooting aid. Ah, but here is the hole where the monopod used to be, in about the right place for a swivel. A piece of heavy insulated electrical wire—through the hole, formed into a loop and twisted at the side—solved the problem. I had a front sling swivel. Worked fine.

Shooting the Arisaka was getting to be a little bit of fun now. The rough inletting at the tangs and the other stock irregularities allowed a good grip. Almost as firm as good checkering. The rifle I had previously thought of as heavy and clumsy was steady and comfortable to shoot in standing, sitting and prone. It was grouping pretty well, and I was getting used to the unfamiliar but excellent sight picture. The cock-on-closing bolt actually made rapid-fire operation seem easier. Why would anyone use anything else for rapid?

Whoops! Rapid-fire! How was I going to reload during the rapid-fire stages?

The bases of the reformed 30-06 cases would obviously fit into Springfield stripper clips. Wonder of wonders! The Norma 7.7mm cases

also fit the clips, and the Springfield clips worked in the Arisaka as if they had been made for it.

My rifle was ready. I was ready.

The day of the match, my position "stood out" on the firing line. Ordinarily, we have a variety of rifles and calibers at each match. This one time, every other rifle was a 223 semi-automatic. Every one? Yes, the fellow with the other Arisaka didn't show up.

I felt a little awkward. I chose not to take sighter shots before the match began. Bad move. The aircraft lead wings on the rear sight slide must have snagged something, and my sight adjustment was gone. My first stage—standing—was way off. I didn't have much time during rapid-fire sitting for sight adjustments. Actually, much to the amusement of my fellow competitors, I used most of my first thirty record shots sighting in all over.

But by the last stage—twenty rounds, slow-fire prone—everything was clicking again. It was then that my Arisaka and I had our moment of triumph!

A light cross-wind had gradually increased, and no one seemed to have noticed. Recall that every other competitor was using a light 223. The groups were all shifted slightly to the left. Except ours. The big 31-caliber bullets seemed not to notice the change and plowed on through to form a centered group, and the highest score for that stage!

It was, of course, not enough. The Arisaka's aggregate was not good. We had been defeated, but neither the rifle nor I came away completely humiliated.

But that one experience was enough. To put that much work into getting a completely inappropriate rifle ready just can't be justified for such mediocre results. My Arisaka match rifle had its shot at glory and is now permanently retired.

Still...it was sort of fun.

Hmmm, just heard! To commemorate the fifty years since World War II, our Match Director is planning a special match. Competitors will be limited to rifles made during or before the war. He wants representative rifles of all the nations involved.

If I paid more attention to the Arisaka's sight adjustment... And if I worked up a load using more uniform bullets... And practiced more...

I can hardly wait. This should be an easy win for my Arisaka Match Rifle! ●

The East German Makarov

TESTFIRE TESTFIRE TESTFIRE

Left to right, 32 ACP, 380 ACP, 9mm Makarov, 9mm Parabellum. The Makarov is close in size to the 32 and 380, yet delivers more power.

As PEACE BREAKS out, East Bloc nations are now selling their military surplus and, since the factories are tooled up, producing these same models for export. The gun we tested was purchased at a gun show for $165 and was in virtually new condition. It came with a thumb-rest grip (right hand) plus the original Soviet-style grip, an extra magazine and a stoutly made russet-leather holster that wraps around the gun and holds it with a death grip.

There is, in fact, no gun designated "Makarov." This "Stasi" is a Walther PP clone, of all-steel construction. Hungarian-made guns by FEG have aluminum frames. The guns, with slight variations, are produced in Russia, China, and we hear, Poland and the Czech Republic.

The Makarov cartridge dates from the late 1930s. It is midway between the 380 ACP (9mm short) and the 9mm Parabellum cartridge in length. The round is believed to be a derivative of a German cartridge—the 9mm Ultra—developed in 1936, but the cartridges are not interchangeable. The Makarov case and bullet are slightly larger in diameter than standard 9mm Parabellum and with less taper. The groove diameter of the gun is .366-inch which is slightly over its .364-inch bullet diameter. Bullets for the 9mm Parabellum are .355-inch. Reloaders should use bullets of the proper diameter.

Essential to a police state is a good police/military pistol. This one would get my *ja wohl*! It fed and functioned flawlessly with Norinco steel-case ammunition and 200 rounds of CCI aluminum-cased Blazer ammunition. The CCI Blazer round delivers a TMJ (total metal jacket) bullet of 95 grains at an average 927 fps for five-round samples. These were clocked through an Oehler 35P chronograph on a brisk February day with the temperature near 40 degrees. The round is a bit under-powered by U.S. standards, but handloading can boost performance to a safe and effective velocity in the 1000-1100 fps range, according to loading data offered in the *American Rifleman* (December, 1993.) Starline offers brass, and Hornady and Sierra have bullets. If the Makarov catches on, which it looks to be doing, other companies will offer both brass and loaded ammunition.

Ken Alexander of CCI developed the Blazer loading and promises that a 92-grain Gold Dot hollowpoint will soon be

Women have no problem handling this gun. Report and recoil are slightly more than the 32 ACP, but not objectionably so.

The Stasi pistol offers a good grip and is just big enough for two-handed shooting.

The "Stasi" Makarov is about the same size as the old Colt pocket automatic—a favorite house pistol for many years.

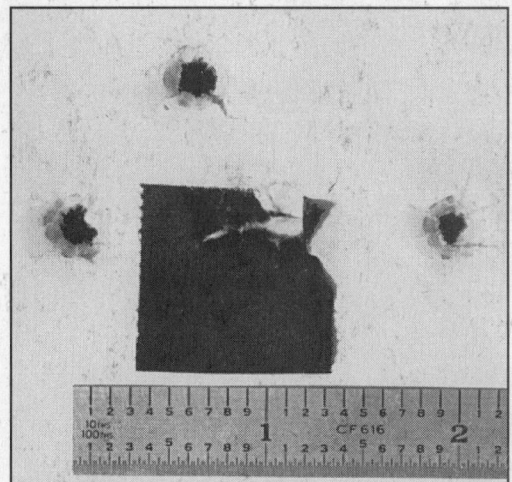

Five shots at 50 feet measured 2 inches. Rapid-fire at 7 yards was under 8 inches.

Field-stripping for cleaning is a simple operation.

available. Alexander reported that Walther-clone pistols from several countries were used in development of the CCI loading, and all functioned reliably with loadings ranging from 600 to 1300 fps. This is pretty impressive. Velocities above 1120 fps are getting into the proof range of pressures and 1300 fps loadings generate *dangerously high* pressures. While these guns are described as "hell for toughness," they are *not* indestructible!

The pistol was fired by both male and female shooters. Both rated the gun good as to the grip and handling aspects. The clean, square sights were considered very good. Report and recoil were judged not objectionable. Trigger pull was on the heavy side and somewhat creepy—expected in a military/police gun. For comparison, a venerable 32 Colt M1903 pocket pistol was also tested. The Colt grip was preferred by the male shooter who said the Colt had a crisper trigger, though terrible sights. Fit and finish were better than the Colt. With size and bulk equal to the pocket Colt, the Makarov pistol packs far more wallop than either the 32 or 380 rounds.

Accuracy tests were made from 50 feet to 35 yards. In spite of a cross-wind gusting to better than 20 mph, 2-inch five-shot groups were made at 50 feet without great difficulty. Rapid-fire eight-shot groups at 7 yards averaged just over 7 inches. At 35 yards, eight-shot slow-fire groups were about 8 inches, but drifted windward about 3.5 inches. For a military pistol with a 3½-inch barrel, this is *very* good.

Field stripping is simplicity itself. With an empty magazine in the gun, lock open the slide. Remove the magazine. Pull down the trigger guard and lock it by pressing it to one side. Pull back the slide to clear the frame, lift up on the rear and slip forward to clear the barrel. Remove the recoil spring. The spring has a flat end and a snug fit at the rear. It fits properly one way only. Reassemble in reverse order. The hammer area remained very clean through our shooting, but can be easily cleaned with a toothbrush.

In all, I rate this an excellent buy as a home defense gun.

C. Rodney James

NCP's Mach One Trap Gun

The monoblock of the Mach One has a deep hook on the face of the integral lump to pivot around the receiver hinge pin. Note the Mach One features an extractor, not an ejector; it raises all shells—loaded or fired—for manual removal.

ANY SHOOTER who has been very long in the game is familiar with Loctite for use on scope mount screws and grip screws. But how about assembling a shotgun using Loctite? The Loctite Corporation makes many different products, including super adhesives, and when NCP Products, Inc., of Canton, Ohio, decided to design a new single barrel shotgun for trapshooters, they investigated a special adhesive in place of silver solder. The result is not apparent, but NCP's trap gun barrel assembly is put together using a Loctite adhesive. It is literally impossible to get them apart without damaging the barrel.

The Mach One we tested tipped the scales at $10^3/_8$ pounds and was $50^1/_{16}$ inches overall with a 33-inch barrel. There is neither safety—trap guns do not require one—nor top lever. Pulling rearward on a release, located forward of the trigger, unlocks the barrel assembly and allows it to tip downward.

They mill the Mach One from a block of solid steel. The front is recessed to accept the mono bloc of the barrel assembly; the lower rear is milled to accept the trigger plate assembly. An underbolt, actually an integral part of the release mechanism, locks the gun when the bolt slides forward into the bite in the single monobloc lump.

The trigger plate can be removed by unscrewing a single screw on the rear tang of the block trigger guard. The trigger has a smooth, flat face and a let-off of $2^1/_4$ pounds.

The Mach One's monobloc offers a bit of difference. The lump on the bottom of the monobloc provides space for the bite and the hook for the hinge pin. Extending forward from the monobloc for nearly $6^1/_2$ inches is a sleeve, its forward 1 inch making a barrel band which serves as a hanger for the forearm.

The barrel is assembled into the monobloc sleeve using a Loctite adhesive. The resulting assembly has a yield strength of 110,000 psi and a tensile strength of 158,000 psi, according to the manufacturer. The shotgun would have to get to a temperature of 500 degrees Fahrenheit before any damage would be done to the Loctite bond.

The test gun was Pro-Ported—two rows of ports on each side of the ventilated rib—and had Briley screw-in choke tubes. It has been back-bored and, although chambered for standard $2^3/_4$-inch 12-gauge shells, the forcing cone had been changed to a long taper and our sample would accept $3^1/_2$-inch shells.

Topping the barrel was a one-piece ventilated rib machined from solid steel, .372-inch wide. Attached to the barrel at two locations—monobloc and muzzle—the rib is adjustable to change the impact point. This is accomplished by loosening two screws on the muzzle barrel band, moving the rib up or down, and then tightening the screws.

The surface of the rib was serrated to break up light reflec-

The NCP Mach One 12-gauge Custom Trap has an Etchen-style pistol grip on the Monte Carlo stock and a one-piece adjustable ventilated rib. Ahead of the trigger guard is the underbolt release, which withdraws the bolt from the bite in the rear of the lump to unlock the barrel assembly.

Note the clean but massive construction of the Mach One receiver and the forearm iron assembly. Gun is built to take trap competition pounding.

The muzzle band on the Mach One provides the support post for the front end of the adjustable ventilated rib. Loosening the two screws allows the rib to be moved up or down. Briley choke tubes are used in the Mach One; the choke tube wrench is shown on the left.

tions, and at the muzzle end there was a red bead. Halfway, the rib offered a silver center bead.

The beavertail forend and Monte Carlo buttstock on the Mach One is of American black walnut with a high-gloss finish, built by Brent Umberger. Ours had quality cut checkering at 20 lines per inch.

The buttstock had a length of pull of 14^3/$_8$ inches, with drops at the comb, heel of the Monte Carlo, and heel of ^{3}/$_8$, ^{5}/$_{16}$ and 1^5/$_8$ inches, respectively. The Etchen-style grip had a slight palm swell on the right side. There was a ^{15}/$_{16}$-inch thick Kick-Eze black recoil pad.

Wood-to-metal fit and metal finish on the Mach One were near perfect. All metal surfaces but the ventilated rib had a matte blue-black finish; the rib had a matte silver finish. Gold and black finished ribs are available as an option.

Since there are more 16-yard trapshooters than handicap shooters, the sample Mach One was patterned at 34 yards, or about the distance from the shooter at which the birds would be broken. Two choke tubes were used—.725- and .715-inch.

With Winchester AA Super-Lite and Fiocchi-Lite loads, each containing 1^1/$_8$ ounces of #8 shot, the Mach One produced five-shot pattern averages of 80.9 and 76.7 percent, respectively, using the .725-inch tube. Switching to the smaller tube, and using AA Super-Lite and Remington Premier Light loads, the latter with 1^1/$_8$ ounces of #8^1/$_2$ shot, the five-shot pattern averages were 88.4 and 86.3 percent, respectively.

Two other loads—the Victory Challenger with 1 ounce of #8, and Remington Premier containing 1^1/$_8$ ounces of #7^1/$_2$ shot—were patterned at 40 yards. The averages were 70.9 and 70.3 percent, respectively.

The adjustable ventilated rib was also checked to determine how much it altered the point of impact at 40 yards. Using the same load, setting the rib in its highest position lowered the pattern center about 3 inches at 40 yards. After patterning, the Mach One was taken to the practice range along with an assortment of factory loads and handloads. No mechanical problems were encountered, and fired shells were raised by the extractor for manual removal.

Currently, the Mach One sells for $3900, complete with a custom carrying case and a choice of stock wood—(American black walnut, English walnut or French walnut)—and ventilated rib finish. It also carries a five-year warranty. Considering the price of some production and semi-production trap guns, the custom Mach One gun is a bargain.

Larry S. Sterett

Ruger's Old Army

TESTFIRE TESTFIRE TESTFIRE

Results like this with a 250-grain bullet make the Old Army a serious handgun.

Ambidextrous Harris finds the Old Army good for lefties.

Traditional round ball best suits the Old Army's sights.

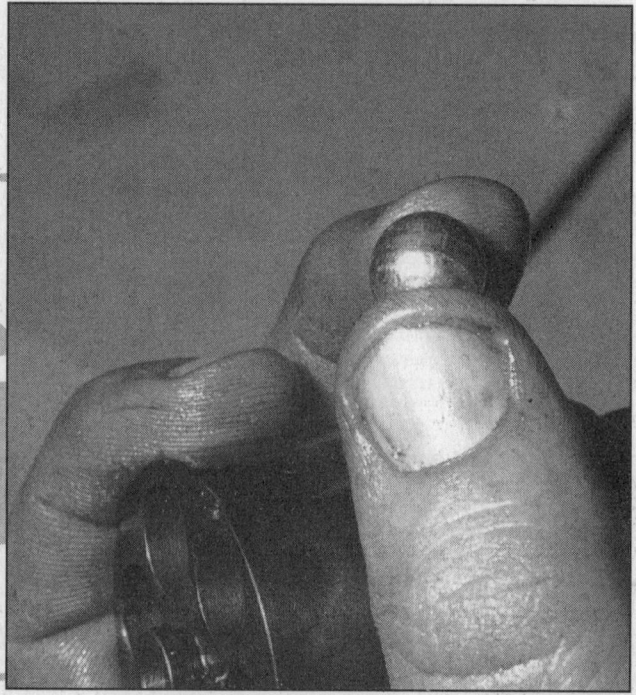

IN MY OPINION, every true handgun or blackpowder enthusiast should own a Ruger Old Army. "Why?" you ask? Because it is the best blackpowder revolver out there. It is the strongest and most accurate, has good adjustable sights and is of modern design and materials, being far superior to the old guns and replicas. Who would have thought that a modern blackpowder revolver would survive twenty years in today's market with no real competition?

History buffs say that Colt 1851 Navies or 1860 Armies are trimmer and faster handling. Well, they aren't that much trimmer or lighter; they surely don't take as powerful loads; their sights are poor; they're also less accurate. Wild Bill Hickock's 1851 Navy Colt 36 was 40 ounces and 13½ inches long, not exactly "handy." John Wesley Hardin's 1860 Army tipped the scales at 43 ounces, only three less than the Ruger.

The most compact revolver of "service caliber" during the pre-cartridge era was the Colt 1862 Police. Compared to a full-sized holster revolver, it is a "trim" piece with 5½-inch barrel, in 36-caliber with fluted cylinder—11 inches overall and weighing 39 ounces.

I don't consider an 80-grain, .375-inch round ball at 900 fps very inspiring from a gun as large as a Ruger GP-100. All the old guns had delicate, leaf-spring mechanisms which are less reliable in heavy use than the coil-spring Ruger. Sear springs were always the first thing to go in Colt single actions, and still are.

I can't dispute that the Ruger is hefty. It weighs 46 ounces and is 13½ inches long. It's not "pocketable." The Colt 1862 Police isn't very pocketable, either. The Old Army is powerful and accurate, developing energies exceeding 45 Colt factory loads. It is fully as accurate as

In the Harris tradition, it takes a lot of shooting to make a gun a keeper.

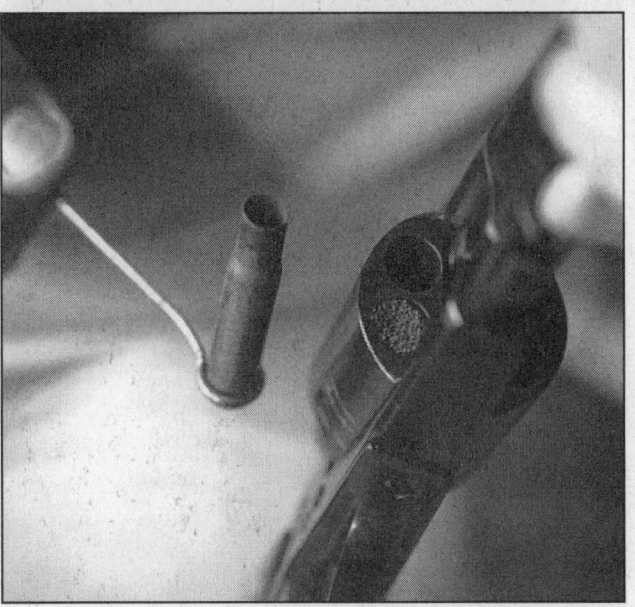

Dipped charges are the Harris way to go, once the load is established.

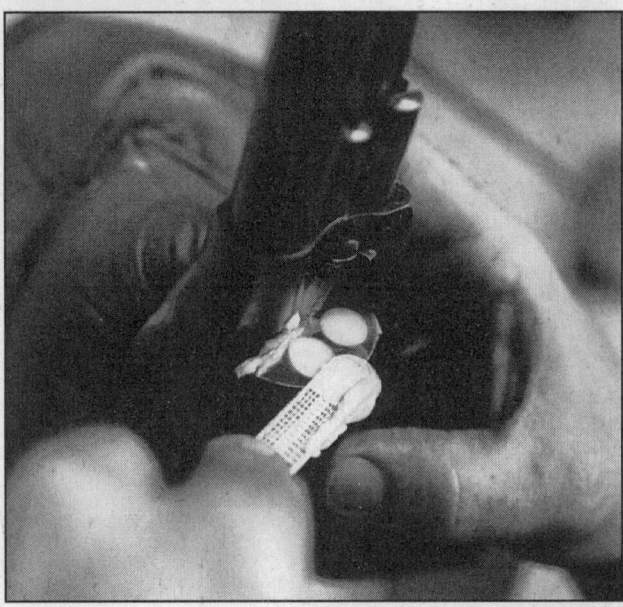

Topping the chamber off with Crisco (or your choice of lube) pays off.

Deep chamber recesses are part of the Old Army's charm.

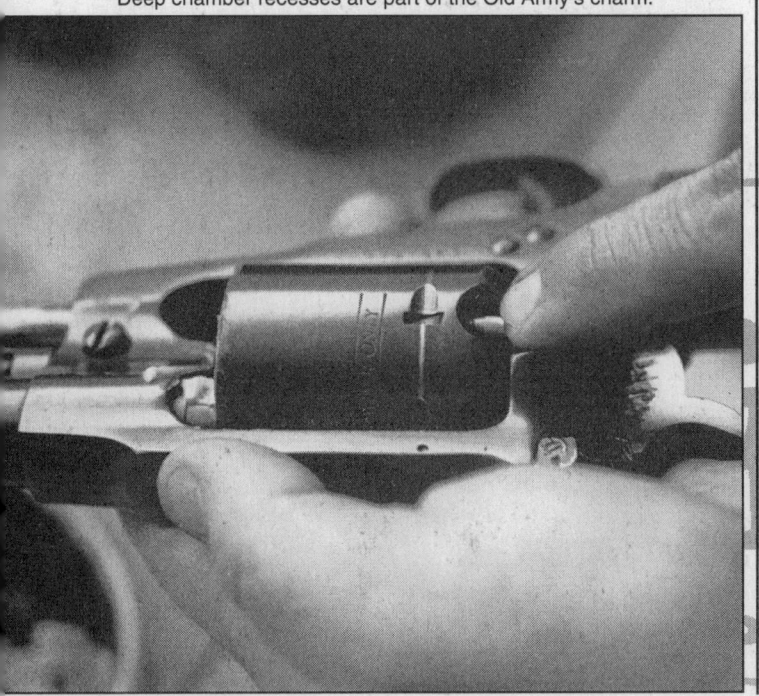

any centerfire revolver I have owned, except for tricked-out target guns. Mine is quite reliable. It is certainly more dependable than other percussion revolvers against which it may be compared.

The Ruger's deeply recessed nipples greatly reduce cap jams, compared to the old guns and replicas. With light target loads, occasional cap jams result from the cup lodging in the firing pin hole in the frame. With full charges of 30 grains or more, this isn't a problem because the cap effectively fragments. Another nice touch is that the Ruger's hammer nose clears the nipples when the hammer is fully down, so they aren't damaged by dry firing. Don't try *that* with a Navy Colt.

For deliberate aimed-fire, the Ruger is certainly easier to shoot well than the old guns or replicas. For point-shooting, the older guns have an edge, but I

was never into cowboy stuff. If a fellow wants one blackpowder revolver that is powerful enough to hunt with and accurate enough for serious target work, this one is it. The Ruger Old Army gives up only rapidity of reloading to its cartridge counterparts. If you can live within the six-round cylinder capacity, and two minutes to reload, a fellow could accomplish almost any sporting task a handgun is called to do with this gun. It is my favorite big-bore revolver.

Round balls are the traditional bullet for cap-and-ball revolvers, and fine for general use because they are easy to cast, accurate and frugal of powder and lead. Ruger recommends 20 grains of FFFg with a .457-inch round ball. This light load attains about 750-800 fps, approximating the energy of 38 Special wadcutter ammunition, and groups under 2 inches at 25 yards in my gun. The same

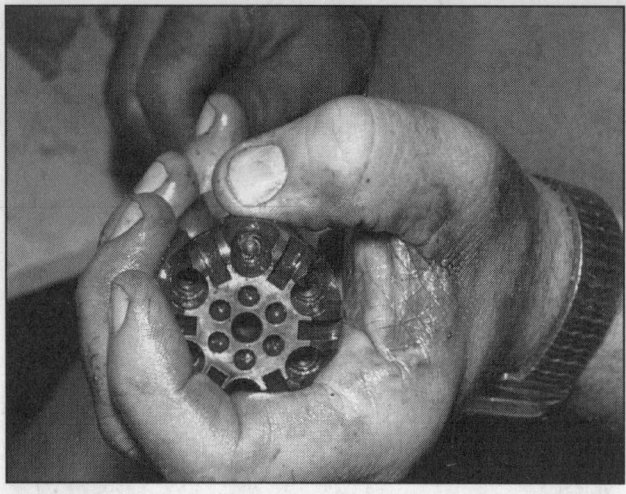

When it's cleaning time, one finds all sorts of nooks and crannies that need attention.

Tight ball fit, whether round ball or R.E.A.L. bullet, is important to *all* cap-and-ball revolvers.

round ball goes about 900 fps with 30 grains of FFFg, or the equivalent in Pyrodex, which approximates the energy of a 38 Special revolver with +P ammunition and is my choice for a field load.

The Old Army can safely handle as much sporting blackpowder or Hodgdon Pyrodex as the chambers will hold. Even with the heaviest loads, its recoil is moderate. Accuracy of round balls falls off over 1000 fps unless Ox-Yoke Wonder Wads are used over the powder. When these are used, you can fill the chambers with all the FFFg black, Pyrodex P or RS they will hold, producing velocities approaching 1200 fps and acceptable 2½ to 3-inch groups at 25 yards.

The sights on the Old Army are set up from the factory for round balls, as that seems to be what most people shoot. Using Ruger's recommended round ball load of 20 grains of FFFg, or the equivalent in Pyrodex, it strikes high in the ten-ring of the 25-yard timed and rapid-fire pistol target with the rear sight bottomed. The 155- to 185-grain cast semi-wadcutters intended for the 45 ACP shoot close to point of aim with the standard sights, if you can find a bevel-based mould that is easy to load and casts .453-inch in soft lead, which some do.

If you want to use heavier bullets, a front sight 0.10-inch higher is needed. This is a simple gunsmithing job. In a pinch, the Speer swaged lead 200- and 250-grain SWC bullets work acceptably, except that being undersize they creep forward in the cylinder with loads heavier than 25 grains of FFFg black-powder. The Lee 200-grain R.E.A.L. bullet is my choice for a heavier wadcutter bullet, because it is easy to load and shoots accurately with the same charges that work with round balls. For a heavier hunting load, 35 grains of FFFg, or the equivalent volume of Pyrodex RS, produces 2-inch groups at 25 yards, about 900 fps and 360 foot-pounds of energy. The 250-grain R.E.A.L., using 30 grains of FFFg, or the same volume of Pyrodex P, produces 2-inch groups or less at 25 yards and energies that exceed factory loads in the 45 Colt. The disadvantage of this heavy bullet is that you *must* change to a higher front sight to get a useful zero.

(EDITOR'S NOTE: The Ruger Old Army is now available in a fixed-sight version.)

In my experience, Hodgdon Pyrodex seems more consistent between batches than black-powder. It produces less fouling and permits more rounds to be fired while maintaining accuracy. Remember that Pyrodex is not non-corrosive and requires the same attention to cleaning that blackpowder does. Cleaning a blackpowder gun doesn't need to be the chore that it is in folklore. There are plenty of cleaners for those who shun water. The accompanying load table summarizes my best loads in the Old Army, so don't try to reinvent the wheel. I really like this gun, and if you try it too, you may appreciate why.

C.E. Harris

Ed Harris's Best Loads For the Ruger Old Army

Lee Measure	Bullet (Grs./Type)	Load[1] (Grs./Powder)	MV[2] (fps)	SD	—Extreme Spread (ins.)— Smallest	Largest	Avg.
1.3cc	143/.457" RB	20.0/FFFg	801	43	1.76	1.93	1.84
	wad, Farina fill	16.5/P	851	11	1.62	2.10	1.91
	200/Lee R.E.A.L.	20.0/FFFg	699	25	1.75	1.96	1.81
	wad, no fill	16.5/P	816	13	1.73	2.74	2.12
	250/Lee R.E.A.L.	20.0/FFFg	672	12	1.91	3.00	2.39
	wad, no fill	16.5/P	759	9	1.41	2.00	1.76
1.6cc	143/.457" RB	25.0/FFFg	931	32	1.42	2.40	1.88
	wad, no fill	21.0/P	942	19	1.59	2.30	2.00
	200/Lee R.E.A.L.	25.0/FFFg	864	7	1.06	2.55	2.01
	wad, no fill	21.0/P	940	31	1.45	2.51	2.02
	250/Lee R.E.A.L.	25.0/FFFg	781	31	2.04	2.56	2.22
	wad, no fill	21.0/P	876	12	1.68	2.08	1.83
1.9cc	143/.457" RB	30.0/FFFg	971	15	1.79	2.20	2.00
	wad, no fill	20.0/RS	883	30	1.21	2.52	1.80
	200/Lee R.E.A.L.	20.0/RS	836	29	1.28	2.42	1.91
	wad, no fill						
	250/Lee R.E.A.L.	30.0/FFFg	882	12	1.30	2.14	1.60
	no wad, no fill						
2.2cc	143/.457" RB	35.0/FFFg	1010	9	1.50	3.96	2.13
	wad, no fill						
	200/Lee R.E.A.L.	35.0/FFFg	1017	15	1.59	2.57	1.89
	wad, no fill	26.0/RS	914	41	1.08	2.43	1.82
	250/Lee R.E.A.L.	26.0/RS	913	32	1.81	2.17	2.03
	no wad, no fill	24.0/P	982	28	1.61	2.69	1.94

[1]Second load shown is for Pyrodex; P = Pistol, RS = Rifle/Shotgun

[2]Velocity at 10 feet.

Average of five, 6-shot groups at 25 yards from sandbag rests. CCI caps and Ox Yoke throughout, unless stated.

Bernardelli's P.One

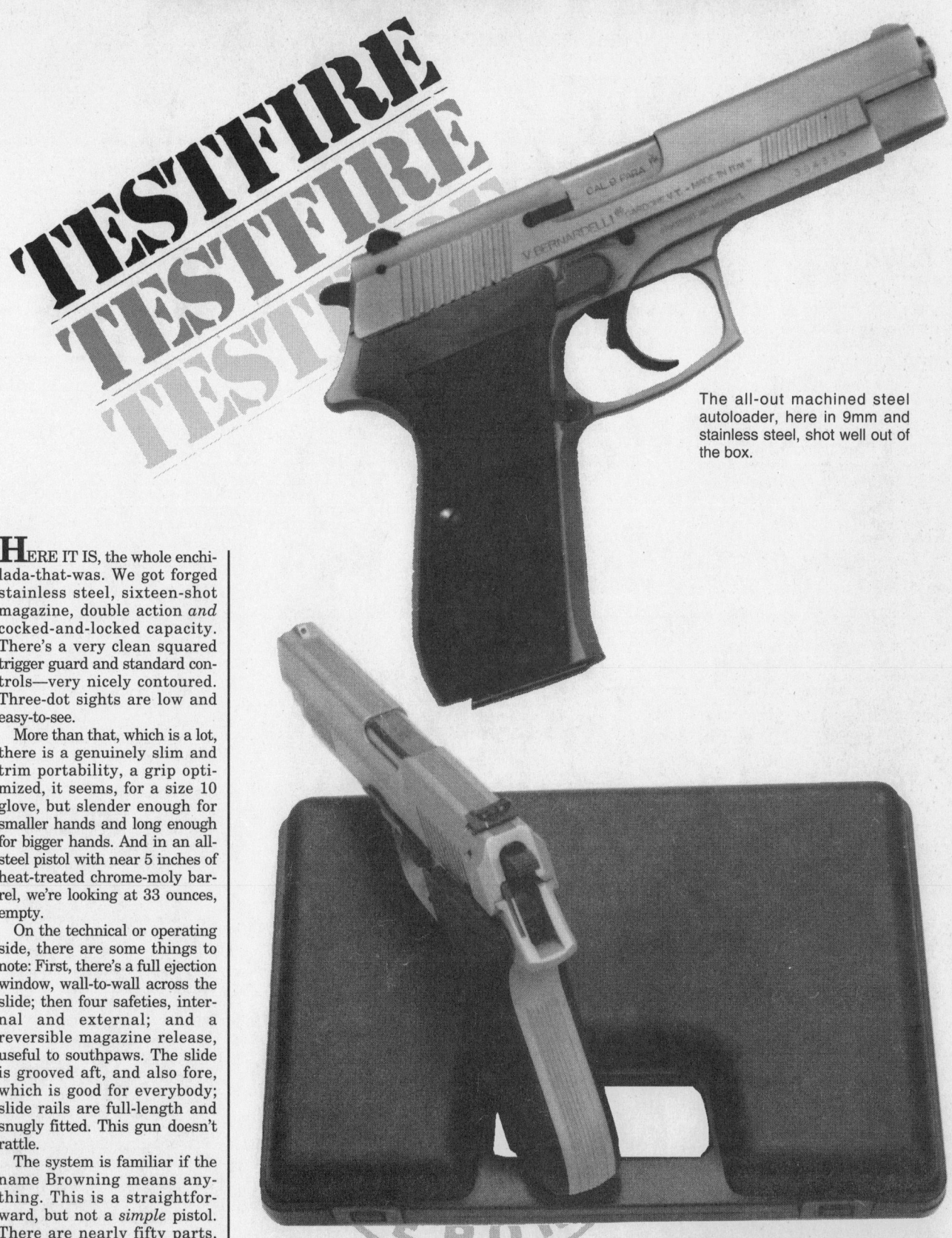

TESTFIRE TESTFIRE TESTFIRE

The all-out machined steel autoloader, here in 9mm and stainless steel, shot well out of the box.

HERE IT IS, the whole enchilada-that-was. We got forged stainless steel, sixteen-shot magazine, double action *and* cocked-and-locked capacity. There's a very clean squared trigger guard and standard controls—very nicely contoured. Three-dot sights are low and easy-to-see.

More than that, which is a lot, there is a genuinely slim and trim portability, a grip optimized, it seems, for a size 10 glove, but slender enough for smaller hands and long enough for bigger hands. And in an all-steel pistol with near 5 inches of heat-treated chrome-moly barrel, we're looking at 33 ounces, empty.

On the technical or operating side, there are some things to note: First, there's a full ejection window, wall-to-wall across the slide; then four safeties, internal and external; and a reversible magazine release, useful to southpaws. The slide is grooved aft, and also fore, which is good for everybody; slide rails are full-length and snugly fitted. This gun doesn't rattle.

The system is familiar if the name Browning means anything. This is a straightforward, but not a *simple* pistol. There are nearly fifty parts, not counting the magazine. And it is obvious Bernardelli's

In the slim-and-trim tradition, the Bernardelli offers the familiar controls in the familiar places.

Big hands feel good on the P.One. It answers the helm well—a nice piece overall.

No surprises here, either, except maybe those full-length frame rails.

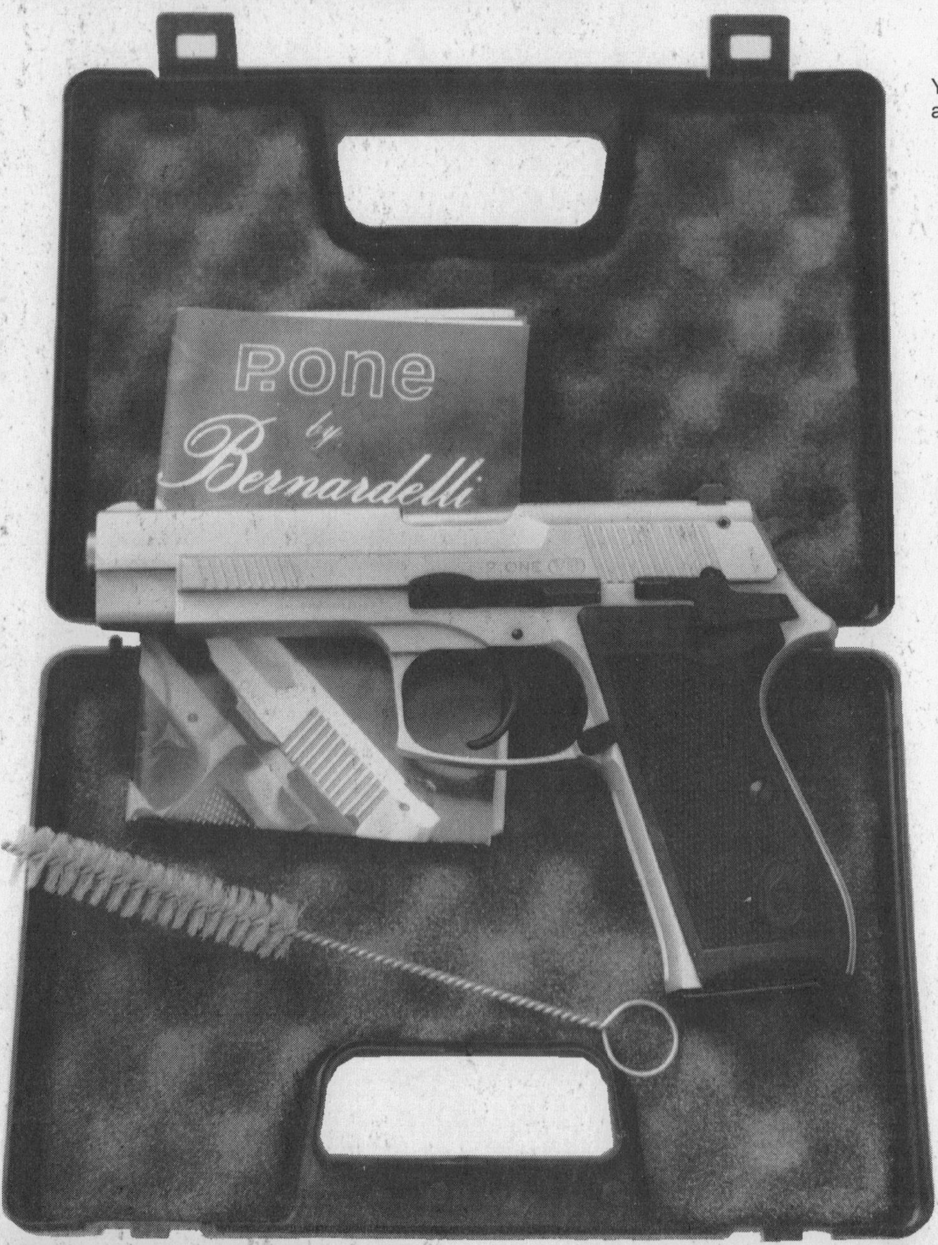

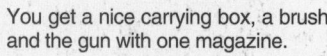

You get a nice carrying box, a brush, and the gun with one magazine.

machine tools work over every square millimeter.

It is also obvious that the work is very nicely accomplished. This is a personal firearm brought to a high degree of finish. It is no less than elegant.

The P.One shoots like it looks. You have to concede it the safety-conscious single-action trigger. It ain't crisp, even after considerable take-up. It is European in feel, but it is also consistent. (In "Sport" versions, this pistol is offered with a straight trigger and a different transfer bar to go with it.) The double action is very useful—it pulls clean and doesn't "stack" unduly. There is nothing (nor should there be anything) in the control system to eliminate the double-pull/single-pull feel; getting that under control takes practice.

Several shooters found that the gun, out of the box, shot to the sights, fired fast, grouped very acceptably. Time constraints forbade serious benching, but it is unlikely the P.One goes very far from the norm for a quality pistol.

High marks all around here are well-deserved. The Bernardelli P.One is an elegant conception in the Browning pattern. In either 9mm or 40 S&W, it's a classy sidearm in a fine tradition.

Ken Warner

S&W's Sigma

Yep, this combat gun has good internal clearances. You can see the sky through the gun here.

THERE HAVE BEEN a lot of new S&W model introductions the past few years. The firm has rung a full gamut of changes in handguns, revolvers and semi-autos alike.

And now comes a new gun—not a new model, not a rerun or a rework or an expansion or a contraction. The Sigma is, for S&W, as new as the Model 39 was in 1954. Then, the 39 told the world Smith was serious about self-loaders. An increasing profusion of S&W semi-autos since has affirmed that stand.

In the world of pistols as sidearms, handguns as arbiters of survival, the new Sigma is again serious S&W stuff. It is in the new mode, firepower without fuss, without bells, without whistles.

Yes, it's like a Glock. It had better be. That is, it has to compete in a market Glock substantially dominates. And it has to be every bit as much a new shot delivery system. On both counts, the Sigma gets off to a good start. The test gun was bobble-free, easy to shoot, performed exactly as cataloged.

It's a nice package. The Sigma weighs 26 ounces plus the magazine. It has a 4½-inch barrel. It holds sixteen 40 S&W rounds. And you can see through it. That is, the slide-frame clearances are engineered to provide a good deal of room, enough to see through, in fact. Although the inevitable comparative measurements are very close, the Sigma is a little less handful than is the Glock. And it's somewhat smoother on

The Importance of Being Glock

IT'S BEEN GOING on a good while and everybody talks about it without actually saying it: The handgun has changed again, fundamentally changed, and Gaston Glock did it.

No, it's not the better living through industrial chemistry, or the ready-moulded polymer parts, or the different fire control. It's not the completely different manufacturing process. It's the *package*. Gaston Glock made a new package to carry cartridges and deliver projectiles.

That doesn't happen often. In handguns, Sam Colt did it, and John Browning did it, and both of them created fundamental change. So has Gaston Glock.

And after he did it—in Austria in that reported 90 days or so of creative contract snaring, starting from scratch, that seems so improbable—mainstream pistolry flowed in a new direction. Sure, the old stuff works just fine, and a lot of it suits some purposes better than the new package, but it's still old stuff. All of it.

It's the different—the new—thinking that makes the colossal difference. Glock, dealing with Austrian military require-

ments more or less in his own vacuum, solved sidearm design functionally, with little use of traditional bells and whistles. There are bits and pieces hanging all over all the old stuff that simply are not there on a Glock.

It was *not* the new ways to make guns that did it, nor the new materials. A lot of people latched onto these and Glocked a lot of new models. No supremely successful design emerged from the patch jobs.

Now the message has arrived. Now a major someone has produced a Glock kind of package. This new entrant in the new mainstream is S&W's Sigma; there will be others.

A pistol is a package for carrying deadly force safely and delivering it expeditiously on demand. It turns out that meticulous fitting of parts, smooth metal surfaces, crisp triggers, mechanical safeties, multiple procedure options—all available in profusion on the old stuff—don't help. A handgun designed to be as easy to use as a ballpoint pen, a Bic lighter, or a desktop stapler is the better choice.

And that is the importance of being Glock.

Ken Warner

The Sigma gets simpler and simpler the more you look at it.

The Sigma comes with two magazines and a lot of ergonomics.

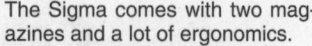

The 40 S&W version backs right up out of the other hand, but doesn't bounce and twist.

the surface and a little less blocky.

Beyond all that, the Sigma is the new ideal—you just pick it up and shoot it. No manual safeties; the same pull everytime; if it's loaded, it goes. Understand, if the round in the chamber doesn't go, you can't pull it again. Serious thinkers on this subject generally agree that given a misfire at a really bad time, the best way to survive is to get a new round up the spout and proceed, so the lack of a second primer hit is not crucial. The Sigma will fire without a magazine in place, another sound survival-related feature.

First out of the S&W Sigma box is the 40 S&W version. So we fired a 26-ounce machine

that delivers 180-grain bullets at right around 1000 fps. The natural question is, "What's that like?"

For whatever ingenious reason, involving ergonomics, internal ballistics, cycle time, grip angle and, probably, texture, it is not as tough as a Model 1911 shooting 45 ACP hardball. It sets up and back, and pretty quick, but the Sigma doesn't twist and buck like the much heavier 1911.

Trigger pull, in the Sigma system, is a straight pull-through-and-release of a striker. The Sigma trigger itself is articulated, and the joint serves as a safety device—only finger force which bends this joint will move the trigger; a fall, for

instance, won't. It is a most unobtrusive safety device.

The pull itself is definitely what we call "double action." It's quicker than a DA-revolver pull, a shorter and smoother (than an average revolver) trip. The weight of pull is under 10 pounds. One can "press" this one. So the shot becomes: present—sight—press—bang. It's very quick, very consistent.

Curiously, stuff that isn't there is bothersome at first. The apparent total lack of a "safety," which means no button or lever to manipulate, worries a little. Then there's no hammer, so the "Is it ready?" signals are more subtle. After a couple of magazines, that all disappears.

The Sigma is not a precision tool. It's better than that. From

the point of view of the Sigma, any concern with 2-inch targets is trivial. The design says, "If you want to plink, get some other gun, maybe a nice 22. This one is for business."

Despite the procedural, visual and structural similarity to the Glock family of fine autos, Sigma has given rise to more than a few patent applications, S&W says. They've been working at Sigma for two years as you read this.

In the time we spent with this new Smith, we learned that S&W knew what it was doing. Their gun is not imitative, but derivative. It impressed people who favor Browning P35s personally; the police are going to love it.

Ken Warner

HOOPER sc.

FRONTIER JUSTICE

Many gun laws made then are gun laws now.

by JOAN WENNER, J.D.

SOME OBJECTS were sacred to our society 100 years or so ago—the flag, apple pie and, particularly in the West, the trusty six-shooter once worn openly and slung loosely as one's sidearm. Firearms commanded respect, even if not totally accepted by all segments of the population.

From old lawbooks—circuit-riding judges often carried a few such volumes as mobile law libraries—numerous cases can be found still applicable today to firearms issues. The refinement and development of firearms-related legal principles and statutes provide an interesting roadmap back to the past. Some serious, some humorous, these real-life frontier cases provide a fascinating glimpse into erstwhile judicial efforts struggling to tame the untimid West by substituting courtroom justice for the personal kind.

Not surprisingly there were frequent cases to be decided around the

Territories involving guns—their possession, sale and, most notably, their use, both negligent use and the intentional doing-in of the other guy before he got you. These are the areas targeted here.

Some legal scholars contended the right to keep and bear arms was *not* a right conferred on the people by the Constitution and similarly phrased state constitutions, but rather a right thought "safeguarded from infringement" in those documents—an inherent and inalienable general right long antedating the adoption of the federal Constitution—and later said to exist independently.

The Second Amendment, according to interpretive court decisions, was designed to foster "a well regulated militia" necessary to the "security of a free-state." Constitutional provisions, they offered, referred only to a collective body, i.e., the

militia. A California court held the Second Amendment provided a limitation on encroachment by the federal government and not as a limit upon individual rights. Certainly, they reasoned, it was not a right that should be granted to desperadoes and other categories of irresponsible citizenry.

In an early Oklahoma case, the presiding judge wrote, "constitutional guaranties with respect to the bearing of arms, the word 'arms' means such weapons as are adapted to the efficiency of the citizen as a soldier, military equipment carried openly by militia," or, as mentioned by some later courts, impressed with historical background of earlier times, "that which were so employed when the constitutional provisions were adopted, such as rifles, shotguns, or muskets, and swords." In other words, "arms" meant those used solely as "weapons of war."

On the other hand, there were judges saying the term "arms" guaranteed to every person the right to bear arms for defending himself plus the state, and which could not be confined "within the limits fixed by the historical and military test but must be deemed to include arms customarily kept by law-abiding citizens for their protection." The right was not intentioned, it was said, for people to bear arms on all occasions and in all places, but "kept for ordinary purposes they're adapted to such as defense of person, property and the state."

Even at common law, the right to bear arms was not absolute—"the act of riding or going armed with dangerous weapons to the terror of the people" being an indictable offense.

Laws preventing the carrying of non-military-type weapons thus came into being and firearms laws continued to progress governing gun and rifle use (no firing within town limits) and ammunition sales.

A proliferation of accidental injury cases involving the sale of firearms and gunpowder, particularly to minors, also gained in frequency around the circuits. One Texas judge's laboriously prepared 1924 opinion detailed the reasoning behind holding sellers to a duty of prudence and care in the sale of these potentially dangerous objects and related supplies.

Powder was sold to a ten-year-old who was later injured when he placed it in a can and lit a match to it for the fun of fashioning a firecracker and seeing it explode. Evidence was presented that the store clerk didn't know the boy was inexperienced in using gunpowder and so didn't tell him to put a top on the can or bucket before adding a fuse to it and lighting the match. Under this particular fact situation, the clerk was not held responsible.

A like outcome had been reached in other earlier cases, such as an 1886 Iowa case involving the sale of a revolver to a minor thought to be experienced in firearms and "having nothing in his character or disposition rendering it dangerous to place a weapon of that kind in his hands."

Subsequently, the National Firearms Act of 1930 was eventually enacted regulating sales, and now, of course, laws place very strict duties on weapons sellers, including outlawing sales to minors.

Frequently, descriptions of criminal cases were also chronicled in considerable detail, particularly when the act alleged was not your routine witnessed self-defense shootout. Published rulings not only followed legal principles existing at the time, but also served to guide territorial legislatures in refining and adding to the growing body of criminal statutes, which are now the basis of many statutes today.

An example: A Nevada court in 1884 was called upon to decide whether an Esmeralda County defendant who shot another dead excusably did so in response to an attempted assault upon himself, or whether he committed murder in the second degree. Justice Leonard related the facts and testimony in the following court opinion:

The defendant Warren admitted killing the deceased John Darling but claimed the defense of justifiable homicide. He testified Darling had threatened his life on several occasions, especially on the evening previous to the shooting, and had corroborating witnesses.

Warren further testified that he met Darling the night before and Darling tapped him on the shoulder saying he wanted to see him. Defendant Warren stepped aside, and deceased shouted there were three _____'s that he was going to kill and that Warren was one of them; and he would fill defendant full of holes. He had a big pistol in his pocket which he started to pull and raised his hand to hit Warren and said, "I will see you again, you dirty _____." That later in the evening Warren was warned by different townspeople to look out for Darling.

Fearing an attack during the night, Warren put two chairs against the door, and threw himself down across the bed with his clothes on. Early the next morning, he went to the hotel by a back way. After stopping there for about an hour, Warren said he walked outside, saw the deceased down the street and to keep out of his way, went into the bar-room and walked up and down the floor for a while.

John Darling came along and when the defendant was within two feet of the saloon door he said, "I have got you now." Warren then pulled his pistol. "He made a dart at me, and just as he came at me I fired two or three shots before he got down." The defendant testified he thought the deceased had a pistol in his pocket where he had the previous evening.

A witness Green spoke on Warren's behalf that he saw Darling stop at the hotel door; that he made a move as if he was going in; that one hand was in his pocket; and he heard him say something but couldn't understand what; and then heard somebody else say, "You come to threaten my life again." Other witnesses, including one Miss Belle Harris of the bar-room offered testimony that the deceased was "quarrelsome especially when drinking, and was larger and stronger than defendant."

An assault is an unlawful attempt, coupled with a present ability, to commit a violent injury upon the person of another. It was of the first importance to defendant to show that Darling assaulted him at the time, or made demonstrations which, in view of all the facts, justified him, as a reasonable man, in believing that he was in danger of losing his life or receiving great bodily harm. Former threats alone did not excuse him.

A thoughtful Judge Leonard further commented an assault or attempted assault on Warren did not appear to be proven (but did order a new trial on other technical grounds). The defendant was convicted of homicide. Later cases throughout the West continued to require more than mere threats to life and limb to justify or excuse a homicide. And so it stands today.

The practice of carrying weapons and the widespread notion of the right of self-defense for all would certainly have led the majority of Westerners to agree with the famous William Blackstone's assertion that "self defense...is justly called the primary law of nature." But as seen above, that was a too-loose interpretation of the law by many courts.

Along with presiding judges, who were presidential appointees, having to travel long and arduous routes to each assigned territory county seat, constantly threatened by roving bands of outlaws, frontier trials organized upon arrival could also be hazardous. Sheriffs and deputies reportedly routinely collected guns from spectators. At one rather tense courtroom session over forty guns were confiscated. At other times, security was lax with guards often absent and found gambling at the local saloon.

To dispense justice in the Wild West was not then an easy task. It appears no less difficult now. ●

IN THIS PECULIAR age of semantic sensitivity and social correctness, the folks we once called "handicapped" or "disabled" are now called "physically challenged." So be it; I've never been one to go against society's grain. (Well, not that often, anyway.) Whatever the term, the thing to remember about physical impairment is that it could happen to any one of us at any time. And if,

in fact, it did, even if just temporarily, the person afflicted would suddenly find shooting a handgun, to say the least, something of a problem.

Pistols and revolvers are often thought of as one-handed guns, but even a simple, temporary injury to nothing more than a finger quickly teaches that shooting a handgun requires the use of *both* hands. And

for anyone whose disability is both permanent and more severe, it often requires a great deal more than that.

A few years ago, for example, I was briefly acquainted with a young woman who suffered from the rare adult form of muscular dystrophy. In spite of her disability, though, she was sufficiently fit to find a job as a civilian office clerk with her local

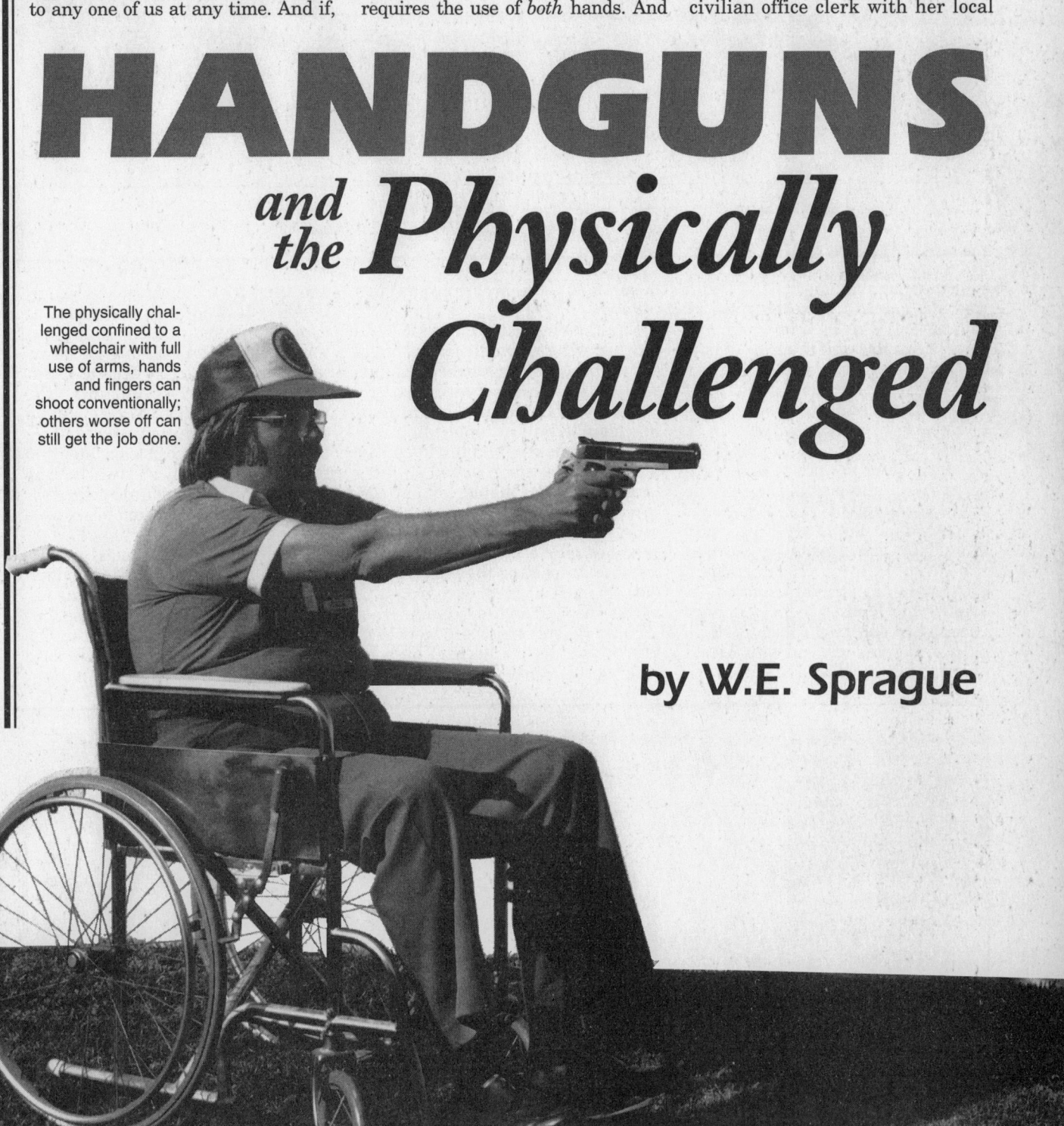

HANDGUNS

and the *Physically Challenged*

The physically challenged confined to a wheelchair with full use of arms, hands and fingers can shoot conventionally; others worse off can still get the job done.

by W.E. Sprague

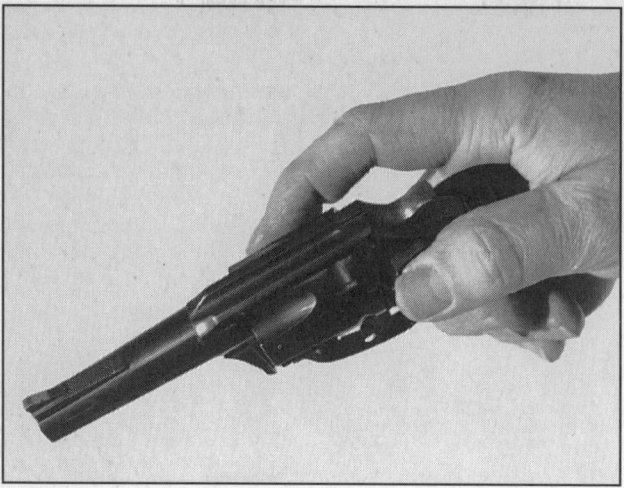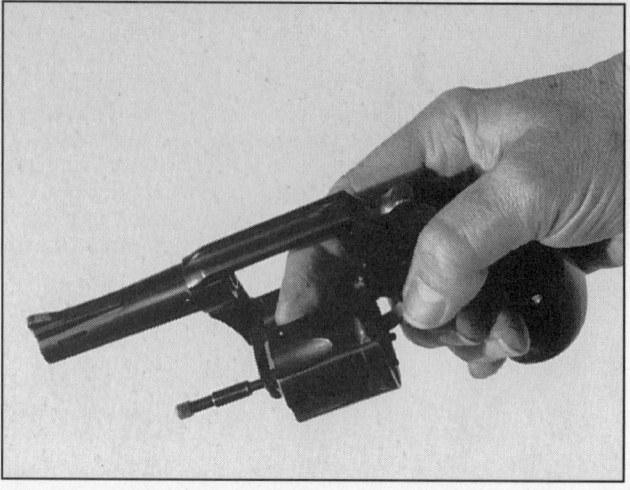

Shooting a revolver presents no special problem to the one-handed, reloading is a different matter. The cylinder can be opened, though, by working the latch with the thumb and pressing the cylinder outward with the trigger finger.

police department, with the result that she gained a disturbing insight into her city's rising crime rate, and soon began to think in terms of buying a handgun for personal protection The only trouble was that her debilitating condition cast serious doubt on her ability to use one.

Since she lacked the muscular strength either to work slides or load magazines, auto pistols proved to be out of the question. The same condition ruled out the heavy trigger pull of a double-action revolver. Further, the weight of the average handgun, either pistol or revolver, made it impossible for her to hold it high enough for deliberate, aimed fire. Still, she was determined, and with the aid of one of her new-found friends in the

department, the problem was soon resolved.

First, having determined that she *did* have the strength for a single-action pull, she purchased a lightweight, 2-inch revolver. Next, he taught her how to use both thumbs in a double-handed hold to quickly cock the hammer. And finally, under his guidance, she learned to hit a target at a reasonable combat distance by cocking the gun at her waist, swinging it up before her, and snapping off a shot just as it reached eye level, repeating the whole procedure for each succeeding round.

Her case, though extreme, is not unique. Where once there were very few physically challenged persons who were interested in guns and

shooting, their numbers are rapidly growing. It is not only the increasing threat of violent crime, but the current emphasis on enabling the physically challenged to participate in virtually any activity—including the use of handguns, for recreation if not defense—that brings this on. Chances are, in fact, that sooner or later you may find yourself approached by someone with a handicap, asking for your help in the matter of using a handgun.

Teaching the physically challenged person to manage a handgun can be a very rewarding experience, not only in the charitable sense, but in the challenge it presents to the instructor's ingenuity since, as the young woman's case amply demon-

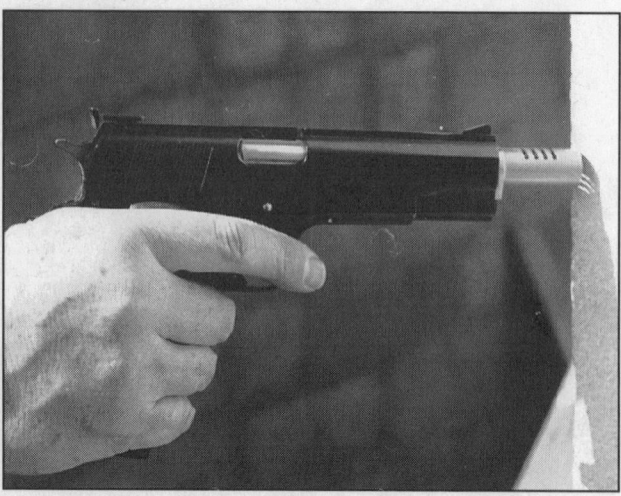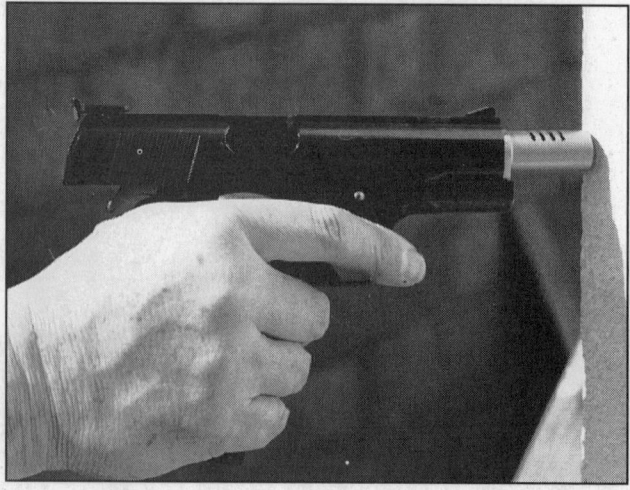

The one-handed shooter normally can't work an auto pistol's slide. Something like a King's Compensator Bushing, though, works it by simply jamming the muzzle end of the device against some solid surface and briskly shoving the gun forward.

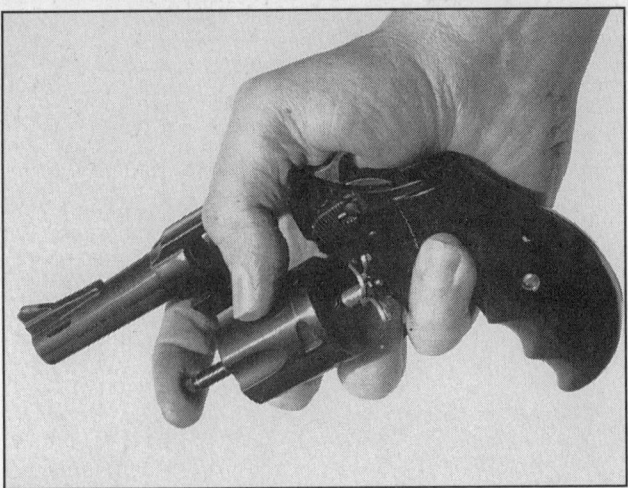

The single hand can "walk" around the frame to work the ejector rod and shake out the empties.

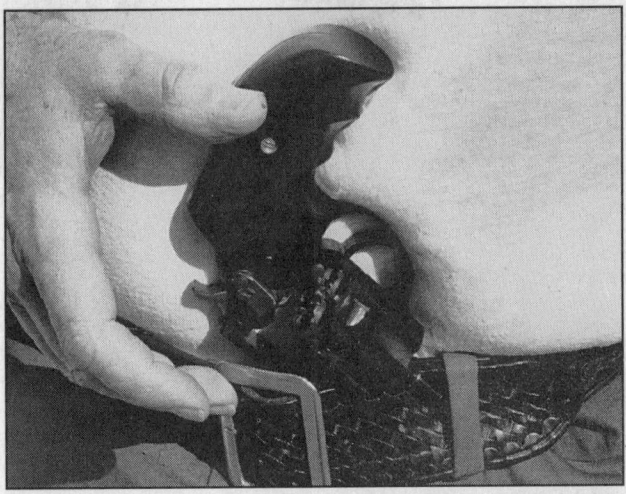

With the empties ejected, a revolver can be loaded with just one hand by shoving its muzzle into the belt or waistband.

strates, teaching involves technique perhaps more often than it does a particular gun or any special equipment. Moreover, the lessons learned in teaching a physically challenged person to use a handgun could one day prove invaluable to the person who undertakes the task, should he or she ever become disabled, even temporarily.

Speaking here of physically challenged persons means those with disabilities above the waist. A person confined to a wheelchair who still has the use of his or her hands and arms can shoot from a seated position, employing conventional methods, and nothing special is needed in the way of guns, techniques or equipment.

The disabilities that do indeed require something special range from missing or unusable upper extremities—arms, hands or fingers—to various vision problems. And in just about every case, there's a technique, a gun or device that can be used to compensate, allowing the physically challenged person to use a handgun successfully, even an autoloader.

For example, a simple shop-made lug, silver soldered to the side of the slide, can easily solve the problem. Gripping the gun in his "good" hand, the physically challenged shooter can work the slide by placing the lug against any handy surface, and shoving the gun forward—even the edge of his belt or the heel of his

shoe will do—allowing him to chamber the first round from the magazine, clear a jam or misfire, or lock the slide open at any time—or anything else that requires working the slide.

With either the Colt Commander or Government Model pistol, the same needs can be met by installing a King's Compensator Bushing. Made to reduce recoil, the King's device is essentially nothing more than a regular barrel bushing made with a liberal forward extension. Since the compensator extends well beyond the muzzle end of the barrel, the slide can be worked simply by bracing the muzzle device against a solid surface and shoving the pistol sharply forward.

A Colt-type magazine release should be no problem for someone restricted to one-hand. A butt release would require modification.

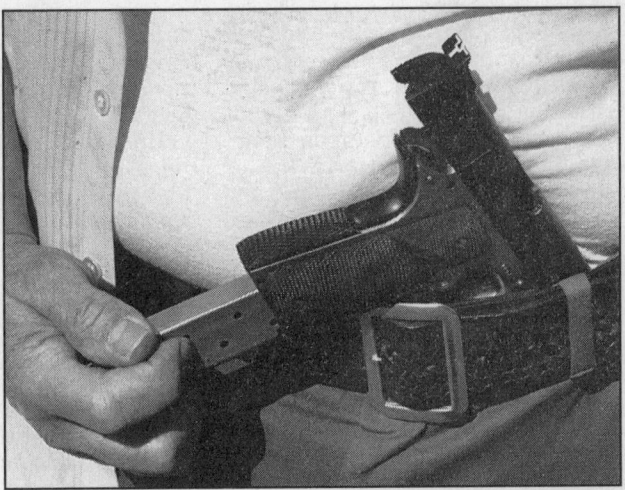

Jamming the gun into the belt or waistband permits a physically challenged shooter to insert a loaded magazine.

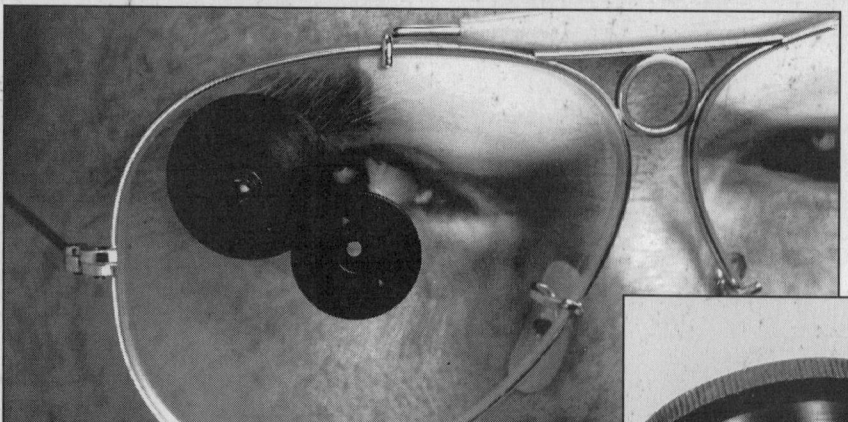

(Left) Faulty vision can sometimes be overcome for a shooter through the use of some non-prescription device such as the Merit Optical Attachment.

(Below) The Merit Attachment mounts with a small suction cup and has a pivoting arm.

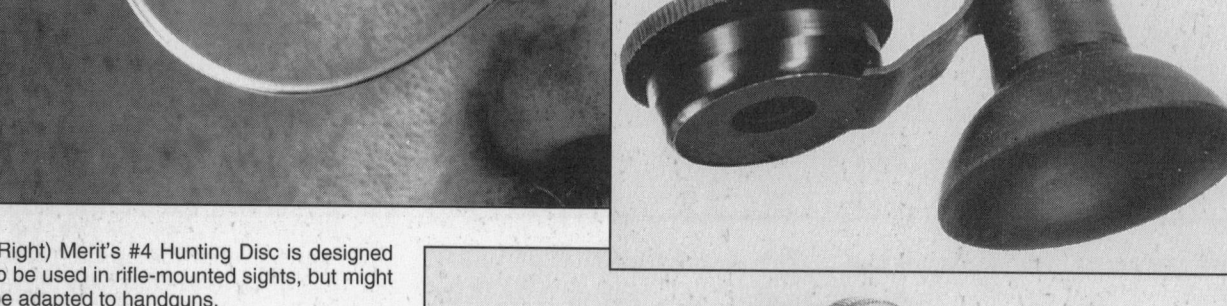

(Right) Merit's #4 Hunting Disc is designed to be used in rifle-mounted sights, but might be adapted to handguns.

Many unaltered pistols can be worked in much the same way, simply by butting the upper, forward "lip" of the slide against a convenient overhang, such as the edge of a bench or table, and shoving briskly forward. Years ago, there was a gun magazine account of an Army MP who devised a similar technique, using the edge of his GI holster. He carried his 45 with the chamber empty, but could match the shooting speed of most carried holstered pistols loaded, cocked and locked.

No matter the technique or modification, the one-handed shooter will find loading an auto pistol fairly simple. With the slide locked back, he has only to shove the gun in his belt or waistband, retrieve a loaded magazine from his pocket, pop it in place, withdraw the gun, and hit the slide release—all with one good hand. Having the magazine well funneled might further simplify loading, and installing an extended slide release might also help. As for loading the magazine itself, with a fair amount of practice, almost anyone can learn to thumb cartridges into place with one hand, while resting the magazine on a solid surface.

For ejecting an empty magazine, the one-handed shooter should have no difficulty with a Colt-type magazine release, since it's conveniently in reach of the thumb. Butt releases, though, are something else. One solution is to shove the gun into the belt or waistband, then work the catch with the one good hand. Another is to weld an extension to the catch, then shape it to permit its operation by pressure against some solid object. With either type of release, though, it might be a good idea to fit the base of the magazine with a so-called combat pad to keep it from being damaged when it's dropped. In shooting a revolver, the person who can only use one hand clearly has no problem since, disciples of the double-handed hold notwithstanding, in the firing phase, it's truly a one-handed gun. For loading and unloading, however, he or she will have to learn a few new tricks.

British troops, I've been told, were once taught to reload top-break Webley revolvers by first thumbing down the latch, then flipping the barrel downward, causing the empties to eject. Then, with the muzzle thrust in the belt, fresh cartridges could be loaded into the cylinder, the gun withdrawn and, with another flip of the wrist, re-closed.

A similar one-handed procedure can be used with modern revolvers with swing-out cylinders. The catch is released by the thumb, and the cylinder pressed outward with the trigger finger. If the direction of swing is incompatible with the hand in use, the cylinder can be opened with a gentle—repeat, *gentle*—flip of the wrist. This practice is normally frowned upon, but perhaps forgivable here.

With the cylinder open, the gun can either be put down and gripped again, or the fingers can be "walked" around the frame in such a way that, with the muzzle pointed skyward, the ejector rod can be used. With the muzzle then shoved in the belt, or held between the legs, the cylinder can be reloaded and swung or pressed closed. A variation of this technique can be used with single-action revolvers and others that use a pin to hold their cylinders in place. Rather than the muzzle, the butt of the gun is held between the legs, or in the shooter's waistband, to accommodate ejection.

Although considered minor as disabilities go, missing finger joints can nonetheless make shooting difficult. For example, cocking the hammer of either a revolver or a pistol is virtually impossible if the first joint of the thumb is gone. The two-handed shooter can, of course, use his other thumb. But if in addition to missing the thumb-joint of his dominant hand the shooter is also missing his other hand, he must rely on other methods.

One solution is to have an extension welded to the hammer spur, permitting the gun to be cocked against either the shooter's leg or some convenient object. As a matter of fact, even without an extension, many guns can be cocked this way, and the method, I'm told, was once taught to U.S. cavalrymen on the assumption that the horse-soldier's other hand would be busy controlling his mount.

Perhaps the most prevalent disability is that of faulty vision, which can range from simple nearsightedness or astigmatism, to partial or total blindness. I've been told a modicum of success has been had in teaching the totally blind to shoot by sound, but since there's no way to identify one's target, this procedure is clearly out of the question when it comes to defensive shooting and must be restricted to recreational shooting only. Even then, it requires special targets rigged to produce some sort of sound—along with a good deal of patient instruction by someone who's experienced in working with the blind.

However, in these days of affordable corrective lenses, high-tech laser surgery, and a surfeit of optical specialists, any lesser degree of faulty vision, even partial blindness, is by no means a barrier to shooting a handgun, defensively or otherwise. There are a good many people with extreme vision loss who might learn to use a handgun if only they realized they could.

One solution to this particular problem lies in having a special lens made for the master eye; specifically, one that will give the sharpest possible image of the sights when the gun is aligned for shooting, yet still provide a recognizable target. Even if nothing more than a blurred mass is visible over the sights, some very commendable shooting can still be done. This provision is, of course, far more suitable for recreational shooting than it is for self-defense, since the special lens cannot be worn all the time.

Making such a corrective lens is, of course, a matter for the skilled optical specialist, and in many cases he can do so, providing he knows exactly what is needed. And, often, the only way to demonstrate that need is with an actual handgun. So, *with his approval*, simply bring an unloaded gun to his office, show him what's required, and let him take it from there.

A good many people approaching so-called middle age can be technically classified as physically challenged, since they experience a minor loss of vision caused by the fact that the lenses of aging eyes begin to lose elasticity, resulting in one of two conditions—myopia or presbyopia. Myopia is the inability to see *distant* objects clearly, while presbyopia is the inability to see *close* objects clearly. Either is really no big deal—unless the distant object happens to be your target or the close object your handgun sights.

Most people who already wear glasses usually solve the problem by getting a pair of bifocals, glasses with the upper portions of the lenses corrected for distance vision and the lower portions corrected for close vision. But if the afflicted person doesn't already wear glasses, or doesn't feel like shelling out a $150 or so for a pair of bifocals, there are a couple of simpler, less expensive answers to the problem of aging eyes.

The first of these is to use a non-prescription device designed to sharpen visual acuity. One such is the Merit Optical Attachment, an ingenious little disc affair with an adjustable aperture and a short, pivoting arm that mounts on the shooter's regular or shooting glasses by way of a small suction cup. The arm, of course, allows the disc to be moved up out of the way when the device is not in use.

The "secret" of the Merit device lies in its adjustable aperture, much like the aperture of a quality camera. Like the camera, at its optimal adjustment, it not only increases the master eye's depth of field (the distance at which all objects seen are in sharp focus), but also compensates for changing light conditions. Together, these two benefits allow both the target and the handgun's sights to be seen clearly and cleanly.

Obviously designed for target shooting, be it "plinking" or formal competition, the Merit Optical Attachment is not well suited for spur-of-the-moment defensive shooting; going around all day with one mounted on your glasses would seem a bit impractical. Merit, however, makes several other shooting aids, one of which might conceivably be adapted to defensive handgun use.

Called the #4 Hunting Disc, it, too, has an adjustable aperture and is designed to fit any rifle-mounted receiver sight (a so-called peep sight) having a $7/32$-40 thread. A bit of imagination readily suggests that a good gunsmith might be able to mount a similar sight, complete with Merit's #4, on just about any revolver. Possibly even an auto pistol.

Still another aid to aging eyes, and one specifically designed to offset presbyopia, the Safety Bifocal Shooting Glasses are offered by Dillon Precision, the same folks who make those familiar blue, high-quality/low-cost reloading presses and accessories.

Priced at a mere fraction of regular bifocals, they're made with polycarbonate lenses (fitted in aviator-style frames and available in yellow, clear or smoke) that are 250 times as impact-resistant as glass. In fact, in a test conducted by the staff of the *American Rifleman*, the shot from two Federal field loads, fired at 25 yards, failed to penetrate them. And besides being tough, they're available in corrective powers of 1.5x, 2x, and 2.5x.

While space prohibits discussing them all, there are, of course, still other physical impairments which can make the use of a handgun seemingly impossible. But the operative word in almost every case is "seemingly." Ninety percent of the time, if the problem is approached objectively, some method can be found—be it a modified gun, a gadget of some sort, or a particular technique—that will allow the physically challenged person to use a handgun effectively. •

ROVING

WITH

KEPHART

by JOHN ROSS

DOWN THE RIDGE, beyond the valleys of Desolation and Defeat, the Smoky Mountains are quiet now. No clop of mule hoof on quartzite cobble, no laughter of shirttail boys skylarking home from Sunday service, no infectious front-porch fiddling dancing tunes up the hollow on the cool night air.

Vanished, too, are the coarse voices of tired men stripping timber from steepening slopes, the silent suffering of gaunt, old young mothers hunkered over smoky hearths cooking for hungry young'ns, the leaden tolling telling of one more passage from this toil to glory beyond.

No one's sproutin' corn or making mash or sneaking blockade whiskey out of a laurel hell knowing that before this night passes Old Smoky's spine's got to be crossed so the whiskey'll be in Tennessee come the morning sun. The high notes of Plott hounds bayin' a bear out around Blockhouse mountain are memories that drift up with the mists that give the mountains their name.

At last we were on a saddle of the divide, a mile above sea level, in a hut built years ago for temporary lodgement of cattle-men herding on the grassy "balds" of the Smokies. A sagging clapboard roof covered its two rooms and the open space between them that we called our "entry." The State line between North Carolina and Tennessee ran through this unenclosed hallway. The Carolina room had a puncheon floor and a clapboard table, also better bunks than its mate; but there had risen a stiff southerly gale that made the chimney smoke so abominably that we were forced to take quarters in the neighbor State...

Our dogs were curled together under the long bunk, having popped indoors as soon as the way was opened. Somebody trod on Coaly's tail. Coaly snapped Dred. Instantly there was action between the four. It is interesting to observe what two or three hundred pounds of dog can do to a ramshackle berth with a man on top of it. Poles and hay and ragged quilts flew in every direction. Sleepy Matt went down in the midst of the melee, swearing valiantly. I went out and hammered ice out of the washbasin while Granville and John quelled the riot. Presently our frying-pans sputtered and the huge coffee-pot began to get up steam.

"Wall, who dreamt him a good dream?"

"I did," affirmed the writer. "I dreamt that I had an old colored woman by the throat and was choking dollars out of her mouth——"

"Good la!" exclaimed the four men in chorus; "you hadn't orter a-told."

"Why? Wasn't that a lovely dream?"

"Hit means a she-bear, shore as a capshootin' gun; but you done spile it all by tellin'. Mebbe somebody'll git her to-day, but *you* won't—your chanct is ruined."

Classic Horace Kephart, this bear hunt in the Smokies from *Field and Stream.* All but forgotten today, Kephart was, for the first third of this century, the standard-bearer among outdoor writers. An outstanding shot with *schuetzen* rifles of the 1890s, he first wrote about guns and hunting and had strong opinions on gun control and ballistics. Some of his earliest thoughts he pulled together in "The Hunting Rifle," a series of chapters in *Guns, Ammunition & Tackle,* by A.W. Money and others, which was edited by Caspar Whitney and published in 1904 by the American Sportsman's Library.

Kephart's fame stems from his two major books, *Our Southern Highlanders* and *Camping and Woodcraft,* that have both been in print for about seventy years. *Our Southern Highlanders* was one of the primary factors that swayed public opinion to create the Great Smoky Mountains National Park.

With a linguist's ear and penchant for detail, Kephart's ascendancy in intellectual society had been meteoric. By age forty-one, he was chief of the St. Louis Mercantile Library, a frequent contributor to library journals, highly respected and, as he put it in a letter to a friend "...in a blessed rut."

In a secret notebook, "The Song of Barbarism," he inked his developing credo: "I love the wilderness because there are no shams in it." Kephart drank to excess and sought solace from city society on forays into the Ozarks. The library directors, alienated by his behavior, forced his resignation in 1903. His wife, equally estranged, left with their six children the following spring. Marriage and family firmly aground, career bashed in and on the rocks, Kephart was breaking up in a wild mid-life storm, his psychological counterpart to the St. Louis 1904 hurricane which he allegedly survived by clinging to a lamppost.

Of all this Kephart later wrote simply: "My health broke down..." From his father's home in Dayton, Ohio, he rapidly recovered and, on maps, went looking for a place where contour lines were close together and cities were not. He found it in the Big Smoky Mountains, 350 miles south.

Primeval, uncut, unmapped, unchanged for 10,000 years, the Smokies were a natural library where a student of the outdoor arts and philosophies could study unimpeded. Kephart took to it with the fervor of a sinner who'd found salvation.

Soon a regular contributor to outdoor monthlies, he turned his tramps into how-to-tales that taught the city-bound about the science of self-reliance in the woods. Outing published his *Book of Camping and Woodcraft* in 1906. Seven years later, Macmillan brought out *Our Southern Highlanders*, a collection of his yarns about the Smokies and his neighbors.

Camping and Woodcraft was the

precursor to the Boy Scout manual before the management took the outing out of scouting. It's the outdoors Old Testament, an American Britannica of practical advice on every conceivable aspect of camping, and then some.

How to pick a tent, pack a tent, pitch a tent; feather a camp bed out of balsam boughs; build fires that will warm you the night through; select proper clothing and food (com-

...good hearted, manly fellows who will take things as they come, do their share of camp chores, and agree to have no arguments before breakfast.

In the book, he doesn't cover firearms and fishing tackle...

I am saying nothing about guns, rods, reels and such-like because they are the things that every well conducted sportsman goes broke on, anyway, as a matter of course.

course, but do not worship it...it is only a gun and can kill nothing you miss with it."

Kephart was a fervent disciple of Nessmuk (George Washington Sears) whose philosophy was: "We do not go to the green woods and crystal waters to rough it, we go to smooth it. We get it rough enough at home..."

Kephart's credo was an extension:

ACROSS THE SMOKIES AND LIFE...

plete with nutrient tables and recipes for the likes of deviled cold fowl, fairly exotic provender up on old Smoky's backbone), even how to walk (toes pointed slightly inward), you'll find it all in *Camping and Woodcraft's* nearly 900 pages.

He's explicit about the hallmarks of good camp mates:

...but he does address "Marksmanship in the woods..." and he starts with a couple of comments about equipment. Get a 22 repeater, he advises, learn to drive tacks with it, and shoot it "at miscellaneous objects at unknown distances from 20 to 100 yards." His advice on hunting rifles: "Get the best you can, of

The best vacation an over-civilized man can have is to go where he can hunt, capture and cook his own meat, erect his own shelter, do his own chores, and so, in some measure, pick up again those lost arts of wildcraft that were our heritage in ages past...

The charm of nomadic life is its freedom from care, its unrestrained liberty of action, and the proud self-reliance of one who is absolutely his own master, free to follow his bent in his own way, and who cheerfully, in turn, suffers the penalties that Nature visits upon him for every slip of mind or bungling of his hand...

A crane or heron taken with the rifle was worth a picture in the hill country.

Kephart sought self-reliance at its most basic level. He revered America's pioneers. As librarian, he amassed a fine collection on the American West. But he longed not just to catalog the works of the Francis Parkmans or Teddy Roosevelts. He yearned to have been with Parkman riding with the Dakota along the Platte, to flesh the dry bones of history with sinew and gut.

Why not? Reared on the Iowa plains at Jefferson, he saw his home robbed by then still-wild Indians. His companion was Robinson Crusoe. And in the backyard were his hulk and fantasy island that were everywhere an imagination could roam.

Sublimating his bent for the outdoors, the young Kephart pursued the profession of scholar, as was the Kephart family tradition. Bright to the point of precocity, Kephart was seventeen when he graduated from Lebanon Valley College in his native Pennsylvania. He studied zoology at Boston University and discovered that city's public library, where he enjoyed "the blessed privilege of studying whatever I pleased..."

A year later, he was an assistant under librarian Willard Fiske at Cornell University. In 1885, Fiske, his mentor and benefactor, took Kephart to Italy to catalog possibly the world's finest collection of Dante and Petrarch.

To Yale in 1886 as assistant librarian, and marriage the next year to Laura Mack of Ithaca. He was writing for library journals, raising a family, and reaching for the pinnacle of his profession, a picture of propriety and prosperity.

While Kephart was at Yale, Sears published a slim volume, *Woodcraft*. Sears was "Nessmuk," and he gave us the art of going light. As philosophical as practical, *Woodcraft* added to one's knapsack but few ounces, yet for Kephart it was heavy stuff. Years later, he would dedicate *Camping and Woodcraft* to "The Shade of Nessmuk in the Happy Hunting Ground."

Offered jobs at Princeton and Cornell, Kephart turned them down in favor of the post in St. Louis. Here in the gateway to the frontier, he could proceed on his grand plan of continuing *"The Winning of the West* where Roosevelt had left it."

For a decade, his professional persona flourished, but increasingly his interests turned from the library. Ozark wilderness beckoned. His hunting and camping expeditions grew longer. His writings for the prestigious "Library Journal" ceased, supplanted by freelance pieces for outdoor magazines, many of them about firearms, such as "Scientific Sharpshooting" in *Cassier's Magazine.*

Increasingly, he spent his time in J.P. Gemmer's gun shop, the third generation of the establishment founded by Samuel and Jacob Hawken. Among Gemmer's clientele was Capt. Charles Askins "...a full-fledged gun crank even in those days, back in the nineties, driving gunsmiths crazy with his alterations..." Kephart by then had a reputation among St. Louis smiths as "dot verdammt rifle crank." He was experimenting, then, with bullet designs for the 30 U.S. Army (30-40 Krag). In 1899, he created a pattern that was numbered 308206 in the "Ideal Handbook." Moulds were made in two sizes, 125-grain and 170-grain, with the former reported to give the better accuracy out to 150 yards.

The mid-life storm that washed Kephart out of St. Louis left him at a little train station in Dillsboro in the foothills of North Carolina's Big Smoky Mountains. From his toe-hold in the foothills, a Baker tent pitched on a knoll above Dick's Creek, Kephart searched for an abode deep in the Smokies, up a cove, in the lee of a ridge where his neighbors would be honest-to-God pioneers.

Two months later, he bid adieu to Dick's Creek and took the train to Bushnell on the Little Tennessee River, now deep under Fontana Lake. Kephart was bound for a log cabin up on Little Fork of Sugar Fork, across from the abandoned Everett Mine of which he was to be caretaker.

Riding one mule with a second in tow, Granville Calhoun set out from Medlin, a tiny two-store hamlet ten miles up Hazel Creek, to collect Kephart and conduct him up the mountain to the cabin. He'd never met Kephart and was doing this as a favor to an official connected with the mine.

As Michael Frome writes in *Strangers in High Places*, Calhoun described Kephart as "medium all over," pale, weak and so sick he could hardly sit on the mule, let alone get it to go. Calhoun prodded the mule carrying Kephart, lolling and near lifeless, up the creek-side road. It was past dark when they reached Calhoun's house.

Calhoun thought he'd soon have a dead man on his hands, especially when Kephart refused supper and had to be undressed and put to bed. Thinking that his guest needed a stimulant, Calhoun offered a glass of wild strawberry wine, a potion that tastes of angels' song and kicks like the mounts that had just brought them up the mountain. At this, Kephart brightened and Calhoun knew he was dealing with a man deep in the tremens of an extended hangover. It took Calhoun three weeks, so Frome's story goes, to spoon-feed Kephart back to health.

Embellished to great degree, there's still a dram of truth in Frome's account. On a boarding-house wall across the mountains in Townsend, Tennessee, Kephart scrawled:

"Corks are in bottles and easy to pull,
    And that's why little Horace is always full."

Kephart's alcoholism would kill

To others it was bleak; to Kephart, living tough was its own reward.

him, but in the months between his bouts he wrapped his mind around the mountaineers; embraced their quaint, independent tradition. At last, Kephart was Crusoe, cast up on an island around which rushed the halcyon days of the new 20th-century sea. The tide flowed up into cleared coves where houses were made of sawed boards. But above was a vertical land where home was a two-room cabin of logs felled and hewn by hand. Kephart's mountains began above the strand.

Nearly every man in the settlement was a skilled axeman and a crack shot. Some of them still used home-made muzzle loading rifles with barrels over four feet long. Some of the women still worked at home-made spinning wheels and looms. Coonskins and ginseng passed as currency at little wayside stores. Our meager life had not substantially changed from that of the old colonial frontier.

Ever the librarian, he kept detailed notes, neatly written in scrapbooks, stored in a soap box under his bed. Meticulously, he filled the looseleaf binders with clippings and references on virtually every outdoor subject he encountered. He wrote up what he learned for outdoor magazines: *Field and Stream, Forest and Stream, All Outdoors, Outdoor Life, Outing, Sports Afield* and others. His portraits of a backwoods rifle maker and old-fashioned shooting match in the July and August, 1924, *American Rifleman* are classics.

Articles for outdoor magazines continued as his cash crop. Like all later gun writers, he reviewed new products, argued pro or con on the latest technology (he was an early advocate for boattailed bullets), and took issue with the insanity of ill-conceived gun control legislation:

...here is an article I read on the second page of the newspaper: 'Washington, May 17 (1921)—A bill by Senator Shields of Tennessee, designed to curtail the sale of firearms by penalizing the transportation of firearms of any other type than those approved by the Army and Navy, or State regulations, was approved today by the Senate Judiciary Committee.'

Fellow sportsmen! read that little item carefully, consider what it means, and then *do something!*

(From *All Outdoors*, May 1921.)

turies. The destruction took just twenty years.

Kephart became a staunch proponent for the creation of a national park in the Smoky Mountains. "I owe my life to these mountains and I want them preserved that others may profit by them as I have," he wrote. He labored for the establishment of the Appalachian Trail and laid out its route along the Smokies' main ridge.

In April, 1931, he and visiting writer Fiswoode Tarleton hired a Bryson City taxi for a run out to "the Big Chief's" who did a roaring moonshine trade. On the return trip, driver and passengers were inebriated alike. The car crashed on sadly, aptly named "Dead Man's Curve." At age sixty-eight, Horace Kephart was dead.

Kephart's possessions were turned over to the park service about the time the park was created in 1937. The plan had been to establish a "Kephart Room" focusing on life of Southern Mountaineers in a museum at Cherokee, North Carolina. But the museum was never built. In 1968, Michael Frome wrote the regional director of the National Park Service, raising the question of a Horace Kephart Memorial Center. The director referred the query to the acting superintendent of the park, Don Davis.

In his reply to his boss, Davis wrote: "As for establishing a Horace Kephart Memorial Center, I would not recommend it because we have memorialized Kephart by naming a mountain, creek and stream in the park after him...In talking to some of the old-timers around here, I understand that he led the life of a bum and was frequently 'on toots' lasting several days..."

Acknowledged as a founder of the Great Smoky Mountains National Park and the "Dean of American Campers" with a mountain, creek and stream in his name, and a pair of books still in print after three-quarters of a century; that's not a bad legacy for a bum. •

Ever the gun crank, Kephart here pretends to dispatch a rattler with a Luger pistol.

By 1910, Kephart was living in Bryson City, a sleepy county-seat community in the foothills of the Smokies. He boarded at Cooper House, and in a little office above Bennett's Drug Store, he wrote *Camp Cookery, Sporting Firearms,* and *Our Southern Highlanders.* Here he edited the *The Outing Library,* a series of reprints of famous adventure tales.

He tried his hand at fiction—"The Girl with the Turquoise Eyes" in *Field and Stream*; "The Trail of a Bullet" for *Flynn's*. "Back through the air to the muzzle of the gun and the finger of the foul fiend who pulled the trigger," the pulp's subhead pants. Fortunately, little more was published.

More and more, however, his interest turned toward expanding *Our Southern Highlanders* (Macmillan brought out the revised edition in 1922) and preserving what was left of the mountains and the heritage that had nurtured him.

His Hazel Creek sanctuary was no more. Loggers stripped bare the forest. Deer and bear were shot out. Clear trout streams silted brown with thin soil flushed from denuded mountainsides. Money from logging brightened, momentarily, the drabness of many a mountain family, but as a candle flame flares before failing, prosperity was short-lived, and when the timber was cut, the jobs were gone and so, too, was the forest which had sustained families for cen-

Cartridge Cases On The Trail

by Sam Fadala

EISENHOWER WAS president. A new Chevy cost two grand. And I was sixteen years old with a set of hunting wheels in the form of a 1929 Ford Model A that got about 25 miles for each 25-cent gallon of gas she drank. The Kofa Mountains were close by, and I enjoyed climbing around in them every chance I got.

One day as I perched on a high dirt ledge, I saw a spent cartridge case, a weathered 38-72 Winchester that luckily got itself half-buried. The headstamp was still sharply readable so that cartridge case was a storybook. I shuffled it back and forth in the corners of my imagination, conjuring pictures of the old-time hunter who possibly took aim at a sheep below the ledge that caught the ejected case.

For me, that first old empty brass cartridge case was a tiny metal history book of shooting. I had to find out what a 38-72 Winchester was, when the cartridge was born, when it died and what rifles chambered it. The lure was both nostalgia and shooting interest. Winchester's catalog of 1916 listed the 38-72 round. The cartridge appeared in 1895 along with the interesting box-magazine 1895 Winchester lever-action rifle, a model that was eventually chambered for the 30-06 Springfield cartridge, the only lever-action accorded that honor. Ammo for the 38-72 Winchester sold for $34 a thousand with lead bullet, a dollar more for jacketed softpoint or full-patch fodder. Primed cases were $24 a thousand in 1916; 275-grain lead bullets for reloading $10 a thousand, one dollar more for softpoint or full metal jacket.

Bullets weighed 275 grains and shuffled out of the muzzle a little faster than an echo bouncing off a canyon wall. Winchester dropped the 38-72 in the Model '95, and by 1936, the old cartridge was moribund, overtaken by smokeless "small bores" such as the 30-40 Krag, '06 and even the 303 British. The '95 was also known for its 35 WCF and 405 Winchester chamberings, both providing a lot of power in a lever gun.

I didn't and don't consciously look for cartridge cases on the trail. They sort of found me, each one a fragment from the world of firearms, ejected after a shot. That's why we find cartridge cases on the trail—somebody shoots there.

I'm hardly the only scavenger of such souvenirs. My compatriot Dale Storey, the gunmaker, has been picking brass up as long as I have, with equally absorbing results. His most fascinating are two 40-60 Marlin cases, both found on the Montana ranch of Dale's upbringing. These cases were interesting because Storey's great-grandfather owned a Marlin Model 1881 rifle chambered for the 40-60 Marlin cartridge. The connection between the cases and great-grandfather's rifle is obvious and valid. The gentleman hunted the ranch for years, starting back in what we fondly call "the good old days" before paved highways ribboned the West.

This old cartridge was found on a Wyoming ranch. It has the balloon head case. The bullet diameter is 45-caliber. Usually, the headstamp is readable, not so with this cartridge. It must be investigated in terms of cartridge dimensions.

The 40-60 Marlin brass pickup was personal for Dale. Most finds won't be, not directly at least, but each located case carries special intrigue: The shooter may have owned a rifle chambered for that round, or at the very least he has heard of it and wonders about its history. Only older case-finds are truly rewarding, however. Locating a 7mm Remington Magnum or 300 Winchester Magnum case doesn't wind my watch. I pick 'em up just because, but they generally end up in the round file, not the collection.

My most-found rounds are 30-30 Winchesters and 30-06s. These go back far enough that individual cases can be worth studying. The headstamp tells the story. I especially like 30-30 brass because I've owned several 30-30 carbines and one 30-30 rifle over the years. I can't turn down a 30-30 case. Nobody I know used the little 30 where I live—the most popular rounds in the West are the 30-06, 270, 7mm Remington Magnum and the 243 Winchester in that order. So when I find a 30-30 leftover, I bet it's going to be old, and it usually is.

Another oldie is the 25-35 Winchester, also a magnet for me because my first deer rifle was a Model 94 so-chambered. Remember that this 25-caliber cartridge was just as first as the 30-30 because it came out simultaneously with the latter round in 1895. The 25-35 and 30-30 were not the first smokeless rounds—both were preceded by the several military smokeless loads—but they were the first smokeless numbers to be used widely by sportsmen. The 30-30 was quite a rage in its day, and its day is not yet over.

The puny 25-35 case is also worth picking up. Only last season my son found a 25-35 empty. As recognizable as the old hourglass Coke bottle, I turned the little bottleneck case over and over in the palm of my hand. The headstamp read "REM-UMC 25-35." The silvery-colored primer protruded out from the head of the case, I noticed. REM-UMC stands for Remington-Union Metallic Cartridge Company, by the way.

Also this past season I found an interesting 30-30 cartridge—unfired and noteworthy in part because of where it was. I was deer hunting the badlands. Topping a rise, I found myself standing in a depression that was obviously a waterhole at one time. At the rim of the depression rested the 30-30 cartridge. It read "W.R.A. CO. .30 W.C.F.," Winchester Repeating Arms Company, 30-caliber Winchester Center Fire. The intact primer was of the old-fashioned type with a "W" stamped in its center. The bullet was full metal jacket, or as noted in old Winchester literature, full patch. Imagination is not taxed in drawing a picture of a hunter waiting by that waterhole for whatever may have come in and in the process losing one of his loaded rounds.

A cartridge similar in shape and style to the 30-30 has also crossed my path several times. It is the 303 Savage. Running across spent 303 Savage brass always surprises me because I don't believe many 303s found their way into my home territory in the good old days, and the cartridge hasn't been chambered in the Savage Model 1899 rifle since World War II, although Winchester still loads 303 Savage ammo with a 190-grain Silvertip bullet. The 303 came out in 1895, the same year as the 30-30, but it never has been billed as a first among sporting smokeless powder rounds. Of further interest is the fact that I've come across several loaded 303s, and bullets have varied not only in weight, but also in diameter. A REM-UMC load carried a .310-inch bullet of 180 grains weight. Another REM-UMC was loaded with a .311-inch 180-grain bullet. A 303 marked "303 SAV. S.A. CORP," for Savage Arms Corporation, had a .310-inch bullet that weighed exactly 178.5 grains. I've found several 30-40 Krag cases, which is not terribly unusual, and I've also run across an 8mm Lebel case—hardly an everyday occurrence.

I have a couple 303 British pick-

Here, a 45-60 Winchester cartridge on the right is compared with a 270 Winchester cartridge. This is a visual illustration of just how much cartridge design did change over the years and how unique individual cartridges truly are.

Three oldies that are still found in loaded form as well as spent brass are the 38-40 Winchester on the far left, the 25-35 Winchester in the center and the 45 Colt revolver cartridge on the right.

ups, too, but after all, our country had plenty of imported rifles in that caliber, so nothing odd there, and of course many 300 Savage cases and a few 35 Remingtons. There's a 33 Winchester and a 348 Winchester in the collection, too. A 7.65 Argentine loaded by Norma, vintage unknown. Plenty of 270s, but why not? The 270 is next to the '06 in popularity out West. One 405 Winchester, appropriately located in the black timber near Jackson, Wyoming. Now there was a fellow who knew how to bag an elk in the forest with one shot. A 32 Winchester Special marked "W.R.A. Co. 32 W.S." also fixed with the funny brass-colored copper-centered primer stamped with a "W."

And I've collected some wildcats. Not many, but a few, the most interesting, I think, a 35-caliber cartridge that began life as a 30-30 Winchester case. Also there's a 30-40 Krag treated to the same 35-caliber alteration. A 300 Weatherby Magnum, well-weathered, with a shoulder configuration not found on modern Weatherby rounds, became part of my holdings a few years ago. I have a lot of such pickups because I'm out there a lot. My most interesting trail-find? Probably a long case stamped "S U.M.C. H 40 3¼." It's a 40-caliber cartridge 3¼ inches in length. This brass case popped up near where I found a bison horn a couple years earlier. A cartridge case I ran across in the timber was of interest to me marked "9.3x74R," a foreigner that would be at home on elk or moose in the mountains. One 38-40 Winchester case and numerous 44-40 Winchesters are also among my treasures. Most of the time the found case is intact, but I've located plenty that were bent or flattened, probably beneath the hoof of a cow, or for that matter a deer, elk or other animal.

Discolored, of course, but with readable headstamps, the majority of trail cases are worth noting if not keeping. One doesn't go along with head down looking for spent brass, but hunters tend to go today where hunters went in the past, wherever the land remains intact, and that is why finding a cartridge case now and again is in the realm of reality. Most are centerfires. I've located a few rimfire cases, but very few of real interest.

Then there is the reverse of finding brass in the field. We leave it there. The little case does no harm. And even those of us who look for our empties won't find them all. This past season, I tagged a whitetail buck in the Laramie Range of Wyoming. The little Model 77 Ruger International 308 did its job with dispatch, a 150-grain Sierra boattail bullet closing the gap swiftly between the muzzle and the game. I flicked the slick bolt back unconsciously and the fired case flew out like a freed bird, burying itself in the knee-deep snow that carpeted those cold last-days-of-November hills. The case was lost. But probably not forever. Perhaps it will be found next season. Perhaps it won't be noticed for years or at all. But if it is located, it will be by another hunter who will pick it up, rolling it between his fingers to bring the headstamp into view. He will mutter under his breath, "A 308 Winchester. I wonder what it was shot at? I wonder if the hunter got his game?" The outdoorsman will look around him and he will see a rugged hill with two evergreen trees protruding like plastic make-believes in a crystal water ball, and though he won't know it, he'll be looking directly at the place where a man before him collected good food and a fine memory, leaving a fired cartridge case behind as an unintentional memento for another hunter. ●

by BOB BELL

SCOPES AND MOUNTS

I CAN HARDLY remember using iron sights to hunt, though I started with them, as everyone did a long time ago. I got my first scope in the late '30s, but it was on a 22, and I was still using irons on my Model 94 32 Special and Model 71 in 348—and had no trouble killing deer and elk with them at the ranges we usually encountered in Pennsylvania and Idaho.

But the little Weaver 29S I was using on my 22 showed me the advantages of a scope (though that model was nothing when compared with what you can get nowadays), so I had a 2.5x Texan installed on the Winchester 71. Stith in San Antonio did the mounting, a nice job. But I never liked the offset mounting necessitated by the wide 348 case and the top ejection of the Model 71, and soon went back to the iron sights—a nice bolt-mounted aperture sight—on the gun.

The Norman Ford Texan was a good scope. Jack O'Connor once called it a Lyman Alaskan with a Southern accent, but nevertheless I took it off and used the 348 when it was pouring rain. I later put the Texan on an '06, a restocked A3 Springfield, where it served me well. I will never forget that my first group was a five-shotter under an inch at 100 yards. By that time, Dick Thomas had installed a 5-MOA dot in it. Dick is still putting dots in scopes, but only in Leupolds now.

I got to thinking about all this when I was chuck shooting this summer. I was using a Model 700 Remington 22-250, a

caliber I've been using since the '40s, but it was fitted with a Bausch & Lomb Elite 6-24x. It was hard to imagine the difference between scopes, how far we've come optically in barely a half-century. A big variable that is state-of-the-art, compared to the little ³/₄-inch, low-power Weaver that was not even their top scope then. (That was the 330 model, and the slightly higher magnification 440 was supposed to be a good choice for long-range big game and even varmints. A lot of readers have probably never heard of those models.)

There are other differences. The 29S cost me (or, more likely, Dad) less than $10 in 1937, while the big B&L lists for more than $550 today. A 50+ times increase in cost, even allowing for inflation, oughta get the shooter something. And I can say it does. It gets us optics like we never dreamed of back then and mechanical perfection. Like

the cigarette ad used to say, we've come a long way.

Anyway, here's what has taken us farther this year.

Redfield has a bunch of new scopes this year, about half for handgunners, half for riflemen. Can't be fairer than that. For the first group, there are seven models, the 2¹/₂-7x Golden Five Stars in black, nickel and black matte finishes, and 2x and 4x Golden Five Stars with either black or nickel finish. For the rifleman, the 3-12x Ultimate Illuminator is now offered with target knob adjustments in either black or black matte finish. The Ultimate Illuminators are the only Redfields (except one Specialty 4x scope with .75-inch tube) that don't have 1-inch main tubes; the U.S. mod-

els measure 30mm, which is a bit bigger than the 25.4mm which equal an inch.

There is now a 6-18x with a choice of black or black matte finish and target knobs, for easier adjusting; the same scope is also available with hunting-style adjustments. There is also a new 4-12x with target knobs, finished in black only. Like the 6-18x models, it has an adjustable objective unit, so the shooter can eliminate parallax completely at a given range.

Parallax is usually unimportant, but can mean a miss instead of a hit when the target is small—like a crow, for instance. Of course, it should be eliminated for group shooting from the bench. Don't count on the scope's range markings, though. This is no criticism of Redfield. Any scope from any maker may have range markings that happen to coincide with actual distance, but after using literally hundreds of models, we've found few that do. Regard them as suggestions only, to get close, then make final adjustments by actually using the scope. When you're positive of your 200-yard setting, say, scratch a thin line with a pocketknife as a reference, so you won't have to go through the procedure again.

I guess the previous scopes could be used for big game if necessary—the UI models were designed for that with 3x as bottom magnification—but I've

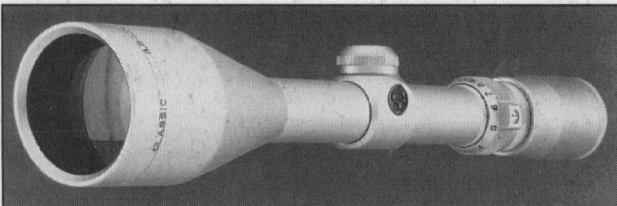

Simmons' 4x40 Whitetail Classic offers big field, plenty of eye relief.

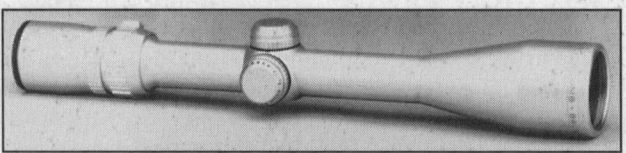

Bausch & Lomb Elite 4000 goes from 2.5x to 10x with 40mm objective and offers advantages of length in an optical system.

The Leupold Vari-X III is a 4.5-14x and has a 50mm objective which adjusts.

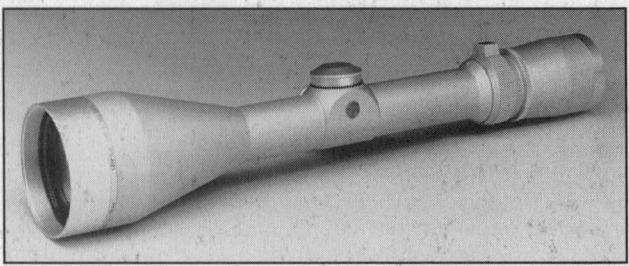

There is also a silver Vari-X III 3.5-10x in the Leupold line, also with 50mm objective.

never cared for big scopes on big game rifles. That's why I was glad Redfield has added two more small scopes to their line, a 1-4x Golden Star and a 1.75-5x low-profile Widefield. Neither has an enlarged objective, so both will sit low against the rifle as a hunting scope should.

This is my favorite size for a big game scope—if you can't aim at a critter with 4x or 5x, he's too far to shoot at. One of my favorite big game scopes for many years has been an older Redfield 1-4x. It's never let me down. So I'm glad to see these scopes. In the woods, I always carry the scope at 1x where it provides a big field (80 feet in the new 1-4x, 74 feet in the 1.75-5x); there's plenty of time to crank it up for a long shot if you wander out where you can see a long ways, but no time to turn it down for a fast woods shot when field is more important than power. Redfield also makes an intermediate eye relief shotgun scope of 1-4x that can be mounted ahead of an unaltered Springfield or Mauser bolt. It's a good solution to mounting a scope on such military rifles.

Currently, Redfield makes thirty-seven scopes in eight lines, if my count is correct. All but three have 1/4-MOA internal adjustments—more or less the standard in scopes nowadays. I've wondered about the necessity of this for years now. It allows precise zeroing for

Lyman and Unertl, for instance—but says he has trouble with Simmons and other makes which epoxy their reticles in place.

O'Donnell has long experience with dots. He used a 1-4x Redfield in the 101st Division in Vietnam when the shooting was more serious. He had two dots in the 1-4x, separated by 6 MOA, and used it on his M-16. Now he can put most any size dot you want in your scope, and if you want more than one, at any spacing.

I've been using Lee Dots since 1946 and like them. Just one suggestion: Don't get one too small. It should be at least 4 MOA at 2 1/2x and 6 MOA is usually better, unless you're hunting desert country. I have a Weaver 1.5-4.5x variable that has a 9-inch dot. It goes to 3 inches at top power, but the big dot is perfect in the woods.

Aimpoint, the Swedish maker of battery-operated red dot sights, lasers and other good stuff for shooters, offers new models, the Competition with 6-MOA dot and the Mag Competition with 10-MOA dot. These go with the older Aimpoint 5000 and 5000 Mag Dot, that have 3- and 10-MOA dots, respectively. Boosters in 2x and 3x are available for those who want more magnification. Aimpoints are seen more often on handguns and shotguns, but they're also suitable for rifles and are fast and easy to use, particularly at the shorter ranges.

one is more than 15 inches, not counting sunshade); in other words, they're getting into the sphere that barrel-mounted target scopes used to occupy. The curves of the lenses are shallower, thus don't need as much correction by following lenses, when the scope is longer. The action-mounted scopes favor the benchresters, of course, but don't make a noticeable difference to anyone else. It wouldn't surprise me if barrel-mounted scopes came back. In fact, I hear that a new maker is thinking of bringing back the excellent Lyman Super Targetspot. That should make lots of shooters happy.

For handgunners, B&L has two new Series 3000 Elites, a 2-6x and a straight 2x. The former has a 32mm objective, the latter 28mm. The 2-6x has constant 20-inch eye relief throughout its power range, whereas it's 16 inches on the other. Also a 3000 is the new 1.5-4.5x32mm with finger-adjustable 1/4-MOA

Buehler's President, Bob Ray, is retiring after forty years with the company. All production of the excellent bridge mount stopped in early 1994, though founder Maynard P. Buehler will continue making custom mounts only and will distribute any excess inventory.

Weaver (Blount, Inc.) has introduced a new 4-16x variable this year and a 2-10x, the former with an adjustable objective unit, the latter without. The 2-10x has a stainless finish, and a threaded sunshade is available for the 4-16x. These are additions to the smaller V3 and V9, and are built on similar one-piece tubes, as are the popular X models. The new models, obviously, will take care of all varmint shooting, and the lower magnifications will be suitable for big game. Both new scopes have Micro-Trac adjustments.

Conetrol, the sleekest mount around, is now available

Schmidt & Bender's Sniper is a 1.5-6x variable on a 30mm tube, shown here in an H&K mount.

Bushnell's 1.75-4x22mm Trophy is designed for turkey hunters and offers a heavy circle reticle with crosshairs.

varmint and target scopes, of course, but is a smaller adjustment than normally is required in a big game scope. A half-minute would be enough there, even a minute (like the old Lyman Alaskan) most of the time. This might be easier to build.

T.K. Lee Co. has been taken over by Mike O'Donnell after the retirement of Dan Glenn and the lackadaisical approach of another party. Mike can install dots in most scopes—Redfield, Leupold, Bushnell, Bausch & Lomb, Weaver,

Bausch & Lomb has expanded their Elite line with several scopes this year. Most notable is the 36x40mm; that should make the benchresters happy. This model has 1/8-inch finger-adjustable clicks for exact zeroing. The tube is one-piece, of course, and two sunshades, 3- and 5-inch, are included.

I've been using a lower power Elite on a heavy-barrel Model 700 in 22-250 for varmints and find it excellent. It's interesting, though, that these scopes are getting longer each year (this

clicks. It's obviously intended for short-medium use on big game. This scope has a 32mm objective; I'd be happier if it were a straight tube. At low power, I'm more than willing to trade some light for a smaller scope.

Bushnell has announced only one new scope this year, a 1.75-4x32mm Trophy for turkey hunters. It has a special reticle that features a thick plex with a heavy circle superimposed, and fine crosswires inside the circle. On 4x, the inner diameter of the circle subtends 6 inches at 40 yards, so it can be precisely zeroed. It has a 73-foot field at bottom power, 30 feet at 4x. That's plenty for turkeys and would be good for big game. Eye relief is long, 3.2 inches, so recoil should be no problem. Its internal adjustments are valued at 1/4-inch and are resettable.

in stainless steel, both rings and bases, in some configurations. These include (but aren't limited to) the two-piece Dap-Tar bases (WVRDT-2) that can be installed on the various Weaver-type top mounts made from aluminum extrusions. The Conetrol projectionless rings can then be utilized. The Dap-Tar bases bring windage adjustment to Weaver-style mounting, thereby permitting easy Conetrol mounting on dozens of military rifles, on airguns, on handguns. The tandem ring adjustment also allows the scope to remain centered over the gun after adjustment has been made. When attached, the WVRDT-2 base is 1/4-inch higher than the Weaver base it is affixed to. This can be important if using a large objective scope. DapTar bases can accept rings of 1-inch, 26mm, 26.5mm and 30mm, all made by Con-

Swarovski's Professional Hunter Series is largely machined from a solid bar of steel, tube included and has coil spring suspension system of the optical parts.

the Professional Hunter Series, they are being made on a one-piece aluminum alloy or steel 30mm tube with enlarged objective and ocular ends (except for the smallest, a 1.2-4x, which has a 24mm lens). Other sizes are 1.5-6x42, 2.5-10x42, 2.5-10x56 and 3-12x50. All have unusually long eye relief, 3.75 inches, except the smallest one, which has an even longer 4.5 inches and an 86-foot field at bottom power. This should be comforting on a dangerous game rifle.

Adjustments are unusual—most are 1 centimeter (about 1/3-inch) at a hundred yards, and again the smallest scope has a different value, 1.5cm per click. These scopes are on the heavy side, due to the 30mm tubes, ranging from 15.9 to 24.3

scope has an adjustable-focus eyepiece with built-in rubber ring to protect the eyebrow, though eye relief is more than adequate. All lenses are multicoated for high light transmission and contrast. Click values range from .20 on the 8x56 to .31 on the 1.5-6x. Weight varies from 14 ounces for the 4x36 and 6x36 to 21 ounces for the 2.5-10x56 in aluminum. Steel models are 1.1 ounces heavier. We've used the 8x56 for many years. It's an excellent scope and speaks well for the rest of the line.

Leupold is introducing a large-objective Vari-X III 4.5-14x this year. The scope has a 50mm lens, so can transmit a lot of light even at top magnification. This is another scope that can serve as a big game

etrol, so virtually any size scope tube can be handled. They're made in all three Conetrol standard grades. In another change, this one mostly for looks although a bit of weight is saved, George Miller has specified that the bases on some Conetrol mounts shall be fluted. Fine matte finish. No price increase, no waiting. High-gloss finish is available at extra cost, and stainless steel bases are now being made for some rifles.

Burris' big news right now is an 8-32x Signature scope that is available in several versions. Reticle can be a Fine plex, Peep plex or a Dot that subtends 2 inches at bottom power, 0.5-inch at top. There's a Posi-Lock version with the Fine plex reticle as well, and the Light Collector, which permits stopping down the objective unit to control light transmission, is available. Also made as the R/A for rimfires or airguns, this one is designed with a shallow depth of field and parallax settings for the distances usually found in competition.

The 8-32x Signature has a 44mm objective and eye relief of over 3 inches, is 17 inches long (less sunshade), and weighs 24 ounces. Field varies from 13 to 3.8 feet.

Posi-Lock is now an option on the 1.75-5x, 3-9x, and 3.5-10x50mm—all Fullfields. Handgunners also can get this option, which locks the reticle immovable after zeroing, on the Burris 2x, 4x, 1.5-4x, 2-7x and 3-9x LERs. Nobody needs the Posi-Lock more; the recoil from

The Pentax Lightseeker is a 6-24x—your choice of reticles, matte or polished finish, with oversize knobs and parallax adjustment.

Burris's Signature Series includes this 8-32x in five versions including an airgun model.

Redfield has target-style knobs on some Golden Five Star 6-18x and 4-12x scopes.

magnum handguns is tough on scopes.

The Peep plex reticle, a small open circle instead of intersecting wires at the center of a hex design, is offered in a new bunch of Burris scopes this year—the 3-9x, 3.5-10x50mm, 4-12x and 6-18x Fullfields; the 3-9x LER handgun model; and the Signature 2.5-10x, 3-12x, 6-24x and 8-32x.

Swarovski Optik has announced a new line of high-quality scopes this year. Called

ounces for the steel tube models. Aluminum models go 12.3 to 18.3 ounces.

From JENA (formerly aus Jena), from Europtik, features three variable and four fixed-power scopes: 1.5-6x, 2-8x42, 2.5-10x56, 4x36, 6x36, 6x42 and 8x56. Each is built on a thick-walled aluminum alloy tube (steel also available). Fixed-power tubes are 26mm, variables 30mm. All reticles (seven types available) are made of etched glass. Each

model at the lower powers and for varmints at the top end. It would be ideal on pronghorns, where its wide power range would come in handy. Like most scopes nowadays, this one also has multicoating, here called Multicoat 4—apparently to indicate the number of layers.

The 4.5-14x has an adjustable objective that focuses as close as 15 meters and either Standard or Heavy Duplex reticle. There's a simple range-esti-

Bausch & Lomb's Elite 3000 scopes include this 2x28 handgun model with 16-inch eye relief.

Simmons handgun scopes come in bright or dark in the Master Red Dot series.

mating function which uses the reticle and the power selector to estimate distance from 200 to 600 yards.

The Vari-X III 3.5-10x is now made with silver finish, for those who want to match a stainless steel gun. It's the tenth scope to be offered by Leupold with this finish.

An off-the-shelf 24x Leupold, incidentally, was used by Bob Frey of Airville, Pennsylvania, to break a record that had stood for six years. At the original Pennsylvania 1000-Yard Benchrest Club at Bodines, Frey put ten shots at 1000 yards in 4.076 inches. Nine of the 10 shots went in 2.90 inches. I wouldn't want Mr. Frey shooting at me at any distance.

Leupold has introduced a second line of optical goods, at a different price. Called the Wind River product line, it currently includes a series of binoculars in both porro and roof prism designs, individual and center focus.

McMillan Optical Gunsight Co. is the name of the newest scope company around and came into being because Gale McMillan wanted a glass sight that would hang together on the 50-caliber sniper rifles he builds out in Cave Creek, Arizona. He calls his creation the Visionmaster, and it comes in four versions: the VM I, II, III and IV. It's a 2.5-10x42mm with 1/4-MOA adjustments and

42mm non-adjusting front lens unit. It has thirteen layers of coating and a Mil Dot reticle etched on glass to prevent breakage. Duplex is also available. The one-piece tube is said to be waterproof and the eyepiece is rubber armored.

By the time you read this, an Ultimate Visionmaster should be available. It is intended for use where the light is bad. Also a 2.5-10x, it is planned to have a 56mm objective and a light-intensifying tube. Reticle is installed in the front focal plane, so there can be no impact shift with magnification change. I don't know the price of the latest model, but the 42mm Visionmasters are listed at $1250, so....

Pentax is introducing a 6-24x to its Lightseeker line, a move that will please many long-range shooters. This scope features a solid brass zoom tube, a reticle that is three times stronger than the industry standard, and high-resolution optics. Pentax scopes have seven-layer multicoating on all glass surfaces, both internally and externally, and the 6-24x has oversize internal optical construction. The new scope has either glossy or matte finish, and offers parallax adjustment, and oversize silhouette-type knobs for 1/8-inch adjustments. It is available with either fine crosswires or target dot plex reticle. Objective lens is 44mm; length is 16 inches;

weight 22.7 ounces. A sunshade and target-style knobs are available.

Pentax also is introducing an unusual magnification variable, a 3-11x, to their Lightseeker line. It has a 36mm objective and 1/4-minute adjustments. At just over 13 inches and an even 19 ounces, this scope can be used for either big game or varmints. It should be excellent for long-distance deer or antelope.

Premier Reticles are installed by Dick Thomas—exclusively in Leupold scopes—and have been around since 1945. Dick can do about anything you want in regard to reticles, even modifying the 6.5-20x to install the reticle in the first focal plane, if that's where you want it. He can also readjust focus parallax, boost fixed-power magnification, etc. Write for a more complete list.

Schmidt & Bender's latest is a 3-12x50mm variable. It is a sort of compromise between the 56mm-objective scopes, which a lot of hunters don't like the looks of, and the little ones. This is not to say the 3-12x won't serve in the twilight. It's excellent, with a twilight factor of 11.7 to 24.5, depending upon the magnification being used. Click value is 7mm at 100 meters, or about 1/3-inch, which is different than any American scope I can think of.

Other S&B scopes are available too, in 1.25-4x20mm, 1.5-

Conetrol's Weaver-adaptable bases are going to put Conetrol rings on a lot of guns.

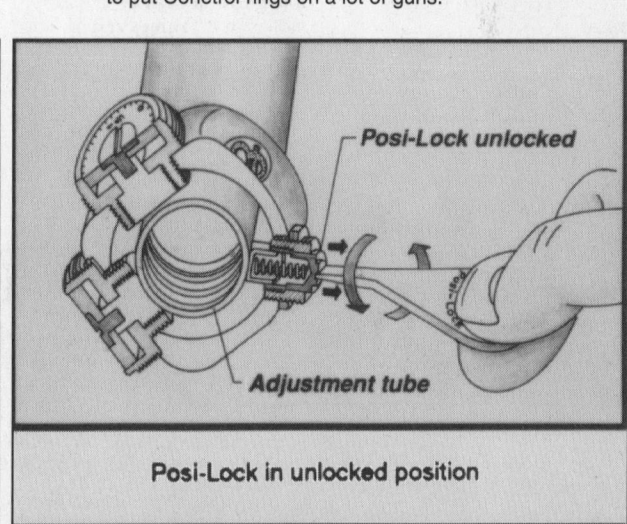

Posi-Lock in unlocked position

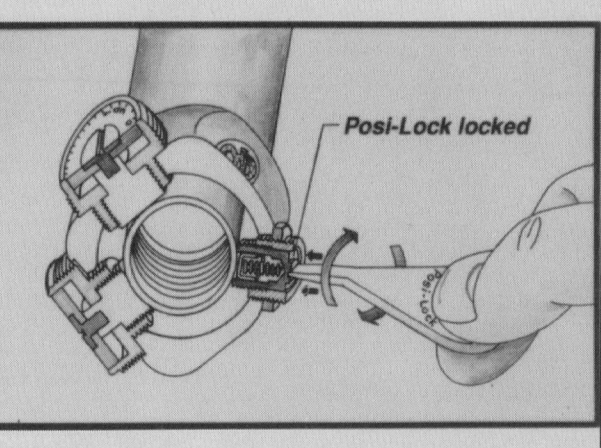

Posi-Lock in locked position

The Burris Posi-Lock system eliminates springs in favor of solidity, provided with the turn of a screw.

6x42mm, 2.5-10x56mm, 3-12x50mm and 4-12x42mm. All are built on 30mm tubes, though Dietrich Apel, who is now handling S&B scopes in the U.S., tells me we can get the fixed-power models with 1-inch tubes, if desired. Most of them can also be had with the reticle engraved on glass. I've had one of the small S&Bs on a 338 for years and can say first-hand it's excellent.

Swift has a bunch—five—of new model scopes this year, according to ad rep Bob Fichtel. These are the 2-7x40, 3.5-10x44, 4-12x40, 4-12x50 and, perhaps most interesting of all, a 1x30mm called the Fire Fly, that features a floating red dot as a reticle. Only 5.37 inches long, the Fire Fly has no parallax and unlimited eye relief, thus permitting shooting with both eyes open. This fast aligning electronic sight is suitable for rapid handgun shooting, paint ball guns and bows. A set of 30mm rings to fit Weaver-style bases comes with the scope.

Swift offers a dozen scopes for big game: a 2x20mm, 2.5x 32mm and a 4x32mm for handgunners, all built on 1-inch tubes, and a 4x15mm and 3-7x20mm for rimfires. Also rings for Weaver-style bases.

Simmons has now been offering scopes to hunters for ten years. It's not an easy field for a newcomer to break into, but we're glad to say Simmons has done it. Congratulations on their 10th Anniversary. My friend Dick Jackson used a Simmons 1-4x on his 270 to take a nice pronghorn in Wyoming during the past October, and a whitetail in Bradford county in December.

New this year are the 6x 40mm ProHunter, ideal for medium ranges, and a 4x40mm Whitetail Classic. This scope has a 34-foot field, which is greater than most 4x glasses offer, as is its 4-inch eye relief. The 44 Mag scope, a 3-10x44 model and Simmons' bestseller, is now available in buffed-silver finish to match a stainless rifle. This scope has all-brass working parts, a round wide-angle view and a Truplex reticle, with 1/4-MOA adjustments. Simmons also offers the Master Red Dot

collection—three 1x models, all built on 30mm tubes. One has a 4-inch dot and is intended for use on shotguns and rifles; the others have 12-MOA dots and are meant for handguns. They differ only in finish, one being black matte, the other silver. Master Red Dots are easy to use. There's an on-off switch that is turned to adjust illumination. These scopes come with 30mm rings, battery and other fittings. Like all red dot scopes, they are fast and easy to use in low-light situations. Turkey hunters especially like them—they're easily visible and the shotgun can actually be zeroed in.

Specifically for shotguns, Simmons is now offering two new scopes, a 2x32mm and a 4x32mm, the first in the ProHunter line, the other in the less expensive Deerfield. The ProHunter scopes have a special light-enhancing lens coating for target definition. Also new this year are silver finishes on the 3.5-10x40 wide angle and the 3.5-10x40 in the Whitetail classic line; the 3.5-10x44, the 4.5x32 and the 3-9x32 ProHunters; the 4x32, 3-9x32 and 3-9x40 Deerfields; and the 22 Mag for rimfires.

Warne continues to make his elegant adjustable double lever mount for an extensive line of rifles, both U.S.-made and foreign. The levers can be set at the angle desired. A recoil lug on the underside of the rings mates with a slot in the base to prevent forward or backward movement under recoil. Due to their dovetail fit and large areas of engagement, it is claimed

that the scope and rings can be removed and replaced without losing zero. Rings are available in several heights, so the scope can clear the barrel even if it's a heavy one and the scope has a large objective. Rings are also made in three diameters: 1-inch, 26mm and 30mm.

Zeiss is offering a new model that will be welcomed by woods and dangerous game hunters, a 1.2-4x Diavari Z. This scope is notable for its huge field and long eye relief—given as 32 meters (about 100 feet) at bottom power, 10 meters at 4x—and an eye relief of over 3 inches. Tube diameter is 30mm and weight is 17.3 ounces. Adjustment value is 1cm at 100 meters. There are 2.54cm in an inch, so clicks are worth about 1/3-inch. This scope is about 11.5 inches long, somewhat longer than many scopes of this power, so it gives plenty of latitude fore and aft to get the eye relief right.

Parsons Scope Service, under license from Lyman Products Corp., is recreating the world-famous Super Targetspot. Gil Parsons, who has been in the optical business for over thirty-five years, tells me he has been doing all Lyman's scope repairs in recent years. He hated to see the demise of the excellent Super Tragetspot (my buddy Bob Wise's favorite long-range scope; he has three originals) and decided to bring it back. He says the new version will be every bit as fine a precision optical instrument as the original. Many accessories will be offered, including a wooden box like the original. This offering is a joint venture between Parsons and master machinest Al Pauley, owner of Western Rifled Arms.   ●

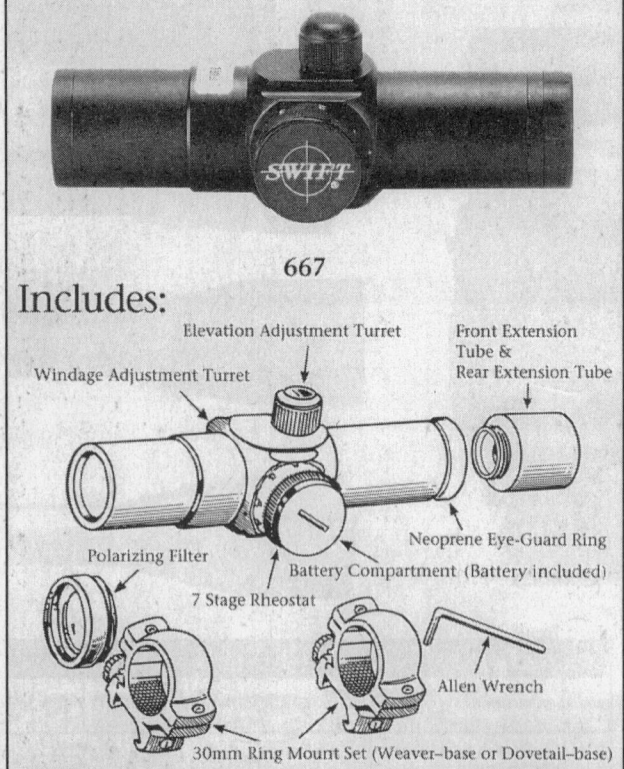

667

Includes:

Windage Adjustment Turret
Elevation Adjustment Turret
Front Extension Tube & Rear Extension Tube
Polarizing Filter
Neoprene Eye-Guard Ring
Battery Compartment (Battery included)
7 Stage Rheostat
Allen Wrench
30mm Ring Mount Set (Weaver–base or Dovetail–base)

Swift's Fire-Fly has a variable-intensity floating red dot, no parallax, and unlimited eye relief.

Warne QD scope mounts have adjustable (for locking position) double levers—a nice touch.

WHEN YOU BUY A
SMITH & WESSON
YOU GET MORE THAN
WHAT COMES IN THE BOX

When you purchase a Smith & Wesson it comes with the experience gained by 143 years of producing the World's most extensive line of handguns. It also comes with an unequaled commitment to each and every customer.

This commitment includes a Lifetime Service Repair Policy that says we will repair, without charge to any original customer, any handgun found to have a defect in material or workmanship for as long as you own the gun.

You also get a toll free customer service number, available coast to coast 8:00 am to 8:00 pm; special expedited priority repair service; two complimentary factory cleanings, and maintenance checks; and a network of factory approved warranty centers worldwide.

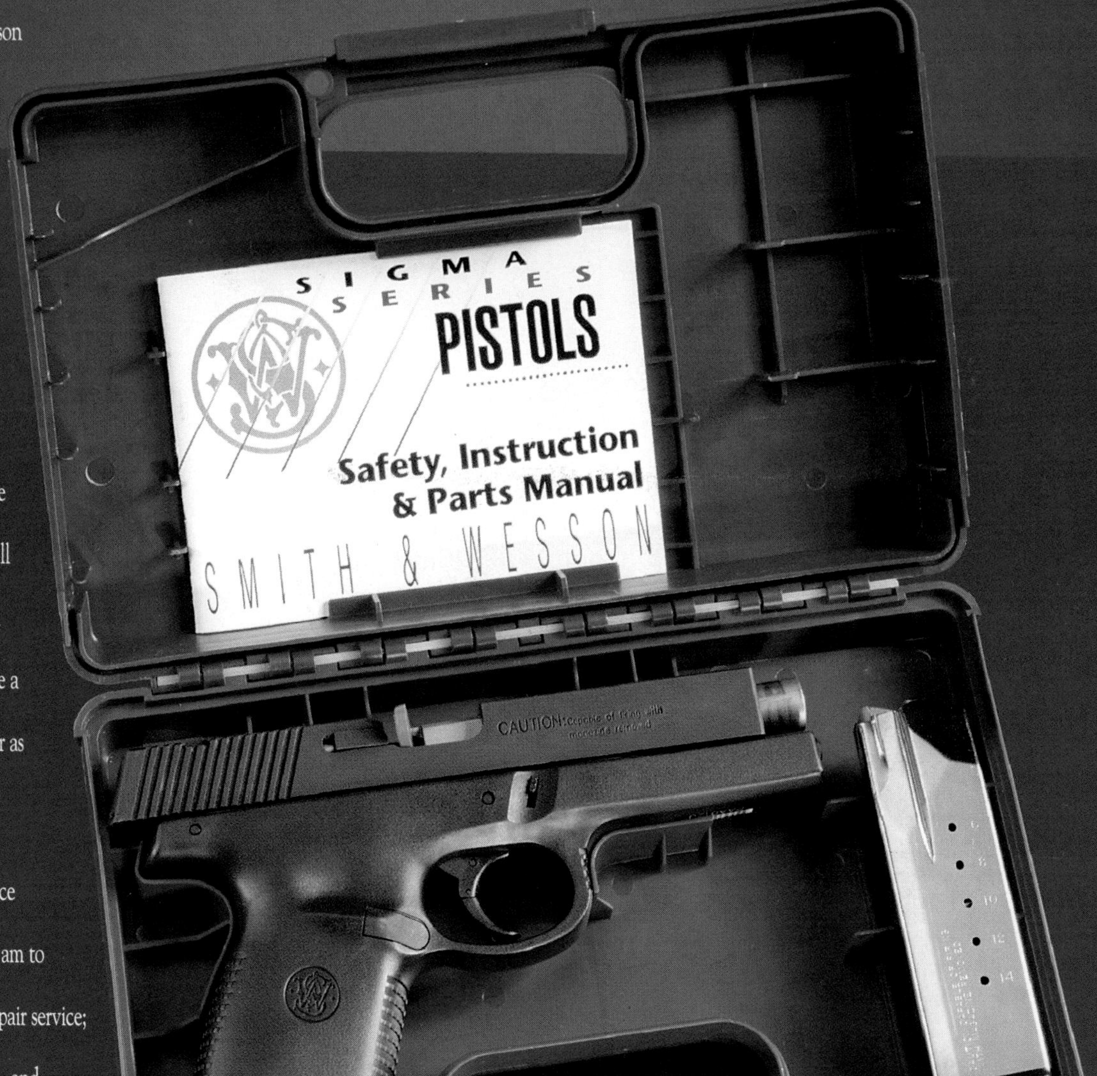

We call this the

SMITH & WESSON ADVANTAGE℠

For catalog with the complete line of Smith & Wesson revolvers and pistols and the location of a Stocking Dealer near you call 1-800-357-3844.

Smith & Wesson SW40F
Sigma Series™ Pistol Shown

CONTENDER®
Versatility...

All It Takes Is A Screwdriver.

For over 25 years, the Contender pistol has led the field of "hunting handguns." Its MOA accuracy has made it the top choice among serious handgun hunters as well as those who "bust steel." Many shooters will even tell you that the Contender will outshoot some of the rifles they own.

The Contender could stand alone with just these credentials, but there's more to a Contender than its accuracy. Contender barrels are interchangeable...in seconds. Remove the forend, punch out the pivot pin and you're now ready to install a new barrel.

We've got plenty of barrels to choose from: blued or stainless steel; 10", 14" and 16 1/4" and, they are all interchangeable. Calibers? We've chambered the Contender for 18 cartridges including the .410 bore shotshell; proven deer cartridges like .30/30 Win., .35 Rem., 7-30 Waters and the potent .375 Win. Even the awesome 45/70 Gov't. For varmints, you can't go wrong with a .17 Rem, .223 Rem or the venerable .22 Hornet.

T/C's Contender; the beauty of it is that you only need one gun, after that it's all a matter of barrels... and a screwdriver.

Check one out at your dealers. You'll see why it's America's #1 hunting handgun.

Dave Reilly with his 32" Dall sheep taken in the Wrangell Mountains of Alaska. Dave used a Super 16 Contender chambered for .45/70 Govt. Range was 200 yds.

THOMPSON/CENTER ARMS COMPANY, INC.

Write for our free catalog.

P.O. BOX 5002, DEPT. GD95
FARMINGTON ROAD
ROCHESTER, NEW HAMPSHIRE 03867

Shooters Tool™

A Blackie Collins DESIGN

The Shooters Tool™ by Case puts everything you need for scope mounting and adjustment in the palm of your hand.

When you're out in the field, you want to keep gear to a minimum. The new Shooters Tool™ gives you a #3 gunsmith slotted screwdriver, three hex bits (2.5mm, 7/64", and 3/32"), a coin slot screwdriver, and a Case 2" Tru-Sharp™ stainless steel blade. All components are rust-resistant and the durable Zytel® handle is conveniently sized to fit a vest or jacket pocket, shooter's bag, or gun case.

Closed Position diagram labels

2.5mm Hex

#3 Gunsmith Slotted

Coin Slot Screwdriver

Knife

3/32" Hex

7/64" Hex

Stainless Thumbscrews

Closed Position

ALSO AVAILABLE

the
NEW PROFESSIONAL
ultimate
HUNTER SERIES RIFLESCOPES
shooting
FROM SWAROVSKI OPTIK.
glasses

For the last twenty five years, almost all riflescopes were made the same way.

A manufacturer took one or more metal tubes, some optical elements, a reticle assembly, one or two leaf springs *(mounted horizontally)* and with some glue and gaskets, screwed everything together. If anything shifted or came lose, the scope would fail and so would you.

Swarovski is changing all of that with their new 30mm PH (Professional Hunter) series riflescopes*. The entire scope tube and central turret housing are machined from one solid bar of steel or aluminum alloy for incredible strength. The "zoom system" tube assembly and reticle are supported and cushioned by a unique "Four Point Coil Spring Suspension©" to handle the heaviest, recoil shock. And, Swarovski Optik is the only scope manufacturer in the world to do this.

Swarovski's premium optical performance is legendary. Now, with these revolutionary technical innovations, these new PH scopes are stronger, lighter and more dependable than any comparable scope.

They have the largest fields of view, the finest image quality, the highest light transmission and best reticles of any riflescope on the planet.

And, although these new scopes may cost a little more, they're worth it. There is a lifetime of value here and it's called Swarovski.

For more information on the new PH series of riflescopes, contact us.

For the moment of truth

SWAROVSKI
OPTIK

Swarovski Optik North America Ltd., One Wholesale Way, Cranston, RI 02920, (800) 426-3089

* Ten models available: 3-12x50, 2.5-10x56, 2.5-10x42, 1.5-6x42, 1.25-4x24, variable power in steel or alloy tubes.

USE A BIG RIFLE

by RAY ORDORICA

Business ends of four Ordorica rifles: 338 OKH, 416 Rigby, 458 Winchester Magnum and double 470 Nitro.

THE YOUNGSTER TOOK careful aim from a steady rest, squeezed the trigger and plastered his first deer with a well-placed shot. The deer jumped and was gone, and he never saw the deer again. No venison, no blood trail, no trace of tracks on the fall leaves. Stung by failure, the youngster quit hunting forever.

The fault lay not with the guy behind the rifle, but with the rifle itself. The youngster shot very well, but his rifle just wasn't up to the job.

His father, an acquaintance of mine, had provided a small-bore rifle, basically a varmint rifle, because the father was afraid of recoil. He passed along this fear and equipped the lad with a rifle that wouldn't do the job.

Another young man, another place and time, hunting his first deer, takes his shot with a 375 H&H Magnum, one he has shot hundreds of rounds through. He hit his deer in the neck, the deer fell, then jumped up and was gone. An enormous blood trail, however, led right up to the dead deer. The hunter in this case was me.

At the time, I had no hunting experience whatsoever, but I had read the experiences of many hunters. Some made sense and some sounded foolish. In every case where the writer's words made complete sense to me, the writer had recommended the use of big rifles for big game. I took that advice and have not regretted it.

Many folks who don't know any better, including lots of gun writers, think the 375 is a cannon, an enormous brute of a rifle. However, every experienced hunter I have met who has tried one considers the 375 not a cannon, but just a very fine general-purpose rifle.

It comes down to this: If you can shoot a big rifle well, and the big rifle weighs the same as a smaller rifle, why not use the big rifle? It's common sense: A big hole kills quicker and more reliably than a small hole.

Some folks try to tell me just the opposite: If a small rifle will kill a big game animal, why not use the small rifle for everything? The answer is that smallbores have an upper limit where they no longer kill well, but big rifles work well on anything. If they weigh the same, the only difference—repeat, the *only* difference—is the amount of recoil you feel when you shoot different rifles. You will feel exactly no recoil whatsoever when shooting any rifle at any game, so there is exactly no basis in fact for not using a big rifle.

I shot my caribou last fall with my double 470, a rifle that has consider-

Author's favorite rifle is his Churchill double 470, with which he shot his caribou one recent fall, using the rifle's iron sights. Caribou was 250 yards away.

Here's Ross Seyfried (in 1977) taking the recoil of his 8-bore double rifle. Shooting this rifle is great fun.

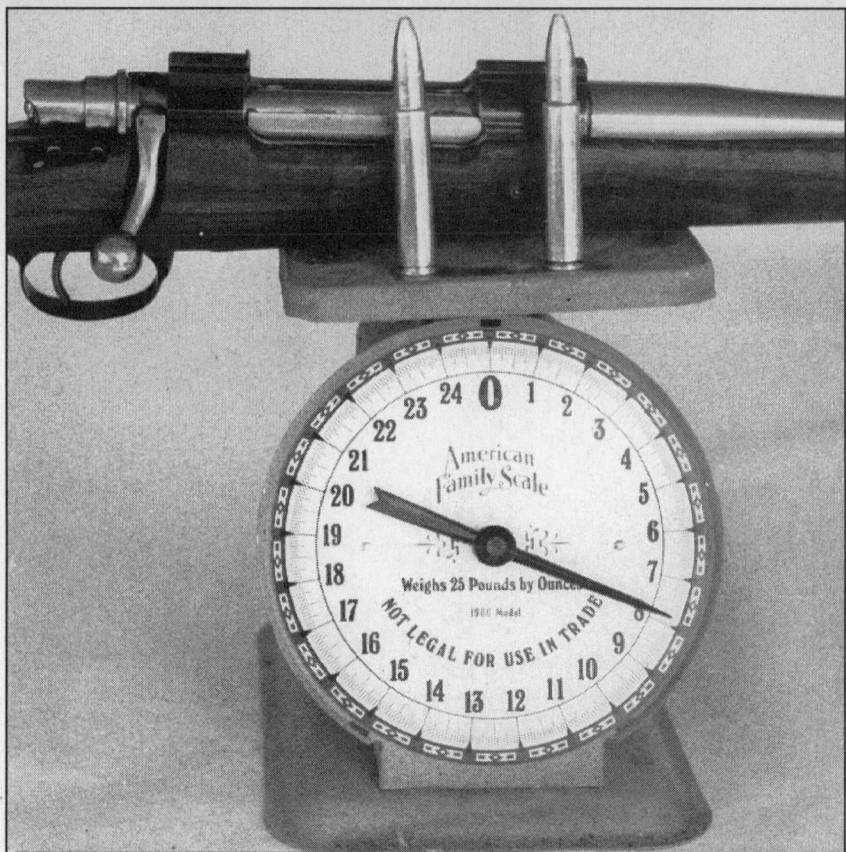

Writer's personal 416 Rigby on a modified Mauser 98 action goes just 8 pounds, unscoped but loaded.

Rear view of Ordorica's big four. The 10¼-pound double 470 handles much faster than any rifle here, but none of them is slow.

able recoil and a very loud report. I was unaware of any kick whatsoever at the shot, and the report was just a pleasant crackle down the valley. The bullet dropped the caribou where it stood, 250 yards away, and destroyed virtually no meat.

If you're afraid of any level of recoil at all, you're afraid of the recoil of your present gun to some extent, and you need to do your homework. I have written entire articles on coping with recoil and have made many tests with friends and acquaintances to see how well they can handle the recoil of big rifles. In *every case*, the shooter was able to shoot even my 8-pound 458 extremely well and, in most cases, asked to shoot it again.

There's a lot of baloney written about rifle choice. Most folks haven't ever shot a big rifle. Long ago and far away, one of the most popular rifles for all-around general African hunting (except for the big stuff) was a number called the 318 Westley Richards. It is so close to the wildcat 338-06 as makes no difference, there being a very slight difference in bullet diameter. This medium-bore cartridge tamed Africa as few other cartridges did. All those thousands of hunters didn't have their shoulders dislocated from recoil by a rifle that has ballistics not very far behind today's 338 magnum. They used the rifle easily and so could you.

Several things are necessary in order to kill an animal quickly. First, we must hit a vital spot. Second, we must hit that spot with a bullet that will hold together. Third, we must throw a big enough bullet. The bigger the wound channel, the quicker and more reliably the animal will die. If we fail in any one of these requirements, we are doing a great disservice to hunting as a pastime and to the grand game we hunt.

Any hunter worthy of the name needs to be a good shot. You owe that to the game. And there is no lack of best-quality bullets today, many available in factory loads.

Given good accuracy with premium bullets, how big is big enough? I have often heard a shooter say he can hit his animal with several shots, if needed, and therefore he doesn't need a rifle any bigger than the one he's using.

In my opinion, an adequate rifle ought to be able to anchor or definitely secure the game with one good hit—one hit, not several. The

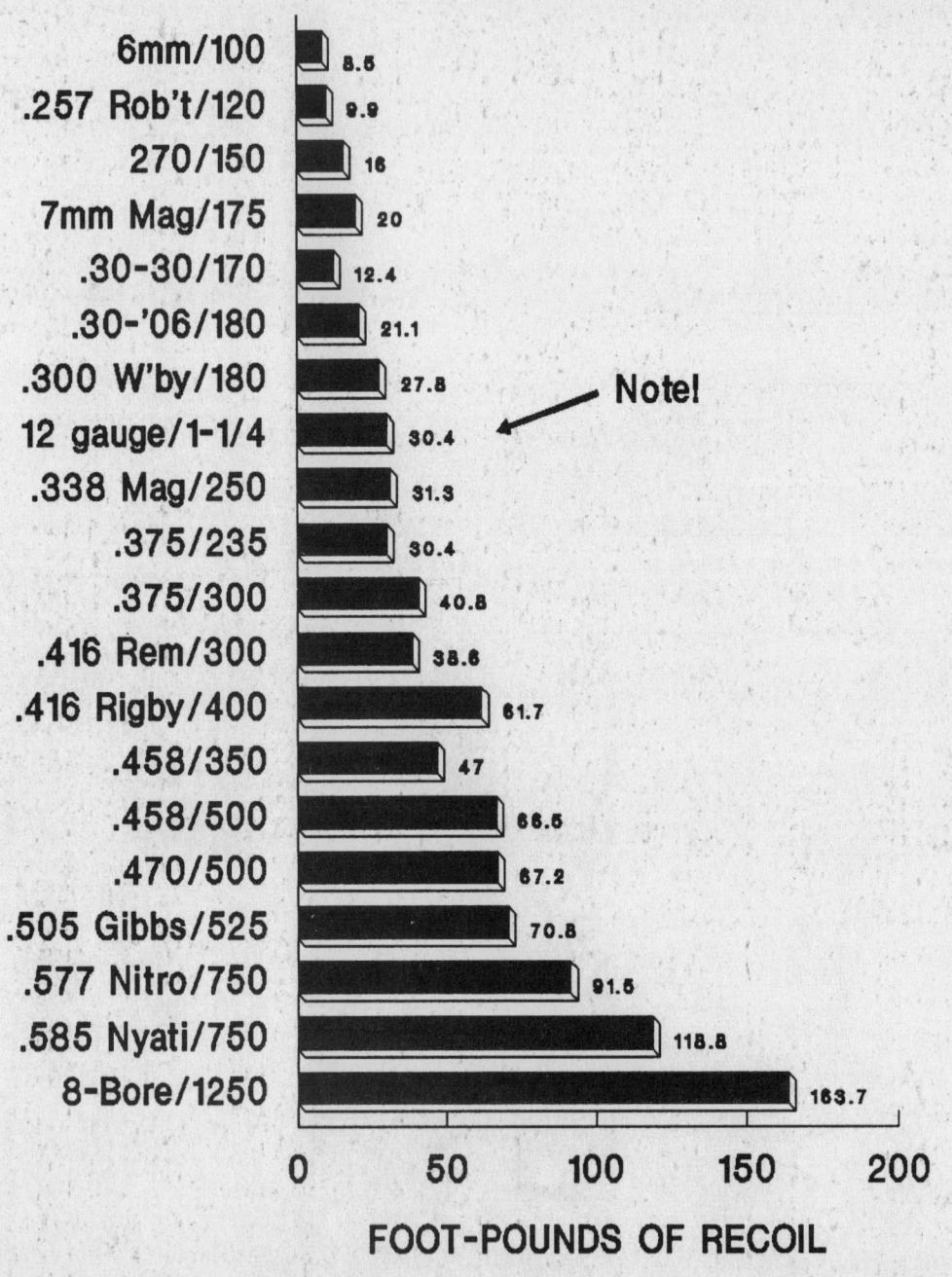

HOW MUCH KICK CAN YOU TAKE?
RECOIL COMPARISON

The bigger the bore, the shorter the rifle. Ordorica stocks his own bolt rifles, scopes them with QD mounts—clearly matches his Churchill double's buttstock.

Ordorica likes classic strengthening touches like an extended top tang. The Canjar single-set trigger, *fleur-de-lis* checkering and beaded cheekpiece are other favorites.

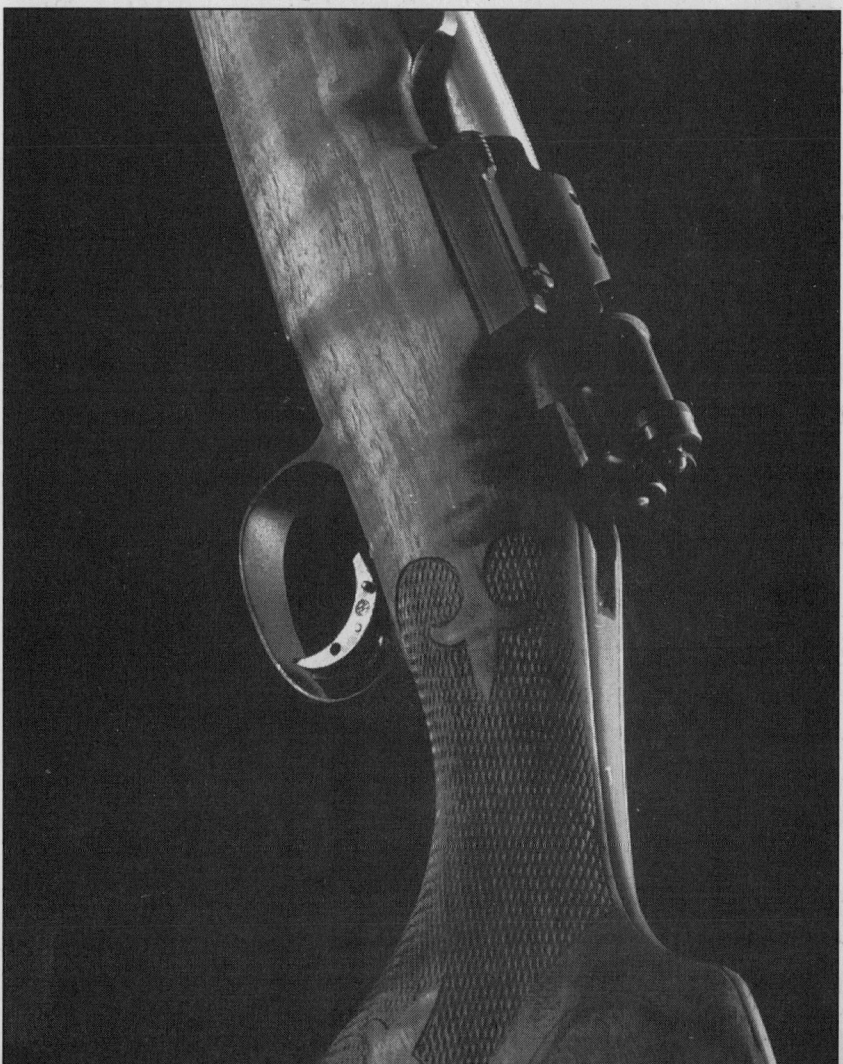

bullet ought to go completely through the game animal, though some argue this. Exit wounds usually bleed more than entrance wounds, and that tells me that the bullet should pass completely through the game animal, no matter how many bones it hits, if I want to see a good blood trail.

A friend of mine shot a moose last year with his 7mm Remington Magnum. He had a good rest and hit the moose well. However, the moose gave exactly no sign of having been shot. He shot again and got his moose, but he has sworn off that rifle for moose forever. He had been suckered into believing that a 7mm Magnum is a big rifle, which it's not.

The small-bore hunter might, probably will, have many one-shot kills to his credit. But press him and you'll find that often he has had to shoot several shots to anchor his game. Jack O'Connor had that attitude, and I suspect it made him some enemies. O'Connor knew his beloved 270 was not enough rifle for moose, yet he shot them and other large big game animals on many occasions with his little 270. He says in his *Rifle* book, writing of four moose shot with the 270, "One moose took two shots, one three, and one four."

"Differences of opinion make for good horse races!" said Elmer Keith,

Ordorica camped with his 470 in big bear country on Afognak Island, Alaska, in 1981. Rifle is bear insurance; the stogie kept mosquitoes at bay. (Sturdevant photo)

remarking on the fact that gun writers can produce controversy among their readers. Unfortunately, all gun writers don't have Keith's vast field experience, most particularly with the practical uses of big rifles.

Some gun writers are afraid of recoil and have said so in print. Some writers recommend small-bore rifles for nearly everything, as did O'Connor. He stated that he didn't like getting kicked by his rifle. I believe anyone in the business of recommending hunting rifles ought not to have his opinions biased by his problems with rifle recoil.

Almost anyone can handle a tremendous amount of recoil from any rifle that can be shot from the shoulder. You must know how or you can get hurt, but the ability can be learned. Trap shooters, millions of them, handle 30-06-class recoil, often for hundreds of rounds a day. Some hot duck loads fired from light shotguns produce recoil energy about the same as that of a 375. Don't tell me the average shooter can't handle a bit of recoil for a few shots per year!

Elmer Keith used big rifles, and he shot them for fun. Ross Seyfried shoots just about every type of big rifle on a regular basis and can handle the recoil of darned near anything. A bear guide I know shoots

his 416 from the bench for recreation. None of these guys are getting hurt.

Experienced Alaskan and African hunters always pick big rifles for big game. The conscientious man wants to see his game drop quickly to the shot. What good is a rifle that permits the game to disappear at the shot and perhaps run miles until it falls?

I'm not the first to say that we Americans have been spoiled by the absence of dangerous game in most of our hunting areas. If hunters got charged by wounded game, it wouldn't be long until bigger rifles were the norm. But that doesn't happen, and game animals are not given the consideration they ought to have.

Some time back, I was editor of two Alaskan hunting magazines. Hunters sent me stories of their hunting trips for use in my magazines, but I couldn't publish some of their tales in good conscience. One guy wrote of shooting two grizzlies on the same hunting trip with his 30-06 and losing both of them. He added that, "...this has happened to me on several other occasions." God only knows how many poor bears he shot and lost with his 30-06, trying to make his rifle do a job it was never intended to do.

In the opinion of many bear

guides, the 30-06 should never be used to shoot a grizzly. The 30-caliber rifles, magnums included, don't throw enough bullet metal to be any sort of *reliable* killer on Alaskan grizzlies. I have read and heard of too many failures with even the 375 on Alaskan grizzlies to ever rely on it if I had a bigger rifle. One guide recently bought himself a 458 to back up an archer because he felt his 375 was not enough rifle for a close-range encounter with a bear full of stickers.

I have shot three mule deer with the 375, using just three shots. One was neck-shot from about 75 yards, which left a good blood trail. Another, hit in the shoulder at about 30 yards, dropped on the spot. The third, a big dry Montana doe, was not only dead as a doornail when we found her, but was also gutted out by the shot, ready to pack.

The 375 didn't blow off legs or heads. It didn't spoil lots of meat. It performed as expected, nothing more. On my first hunt, I was also hunting elk, and I chose to use an elk rifle on my deer. I saw no reason to change and stuck with the 375 on later hunts.

There is no shortage of good big cartridges. We have the 338 Winchester Magnum and the 340 Weatherby. There's the big 375, and three 416s—the Remington, Rigby and Weatherby. There's a host of 40-caliber wildcats like the 416 Taylor, the 416 Howell and Van Horn, and the 425 Express.

There are also the really big ones, starting with the 458 Winchester Magnum, which greatly rewards the reloader. We also have the 460 Weatherby and some 45-caliber wildcats, the 450 and 460 G&A, and the 458 Lott, which is a useful extension of the 458 Winchester. In really, really big cartridges, we have the 505 Gibbs and the 585 Nyati.

While I would not be happy toting a 13-pound 585 Nyati up a sheep mountain, I would rather use it to shoot a sheep than I would a 6mm Remington. I read a horror story about a fellow shooting a sheep with his 6mm, "...until I was out of ammo." He got his sheep, but I wonder.

You can't count on luck in your hunting. Be prepared for the toughest game imaginable and arm yourself accordingly. In Alaska, when you hunt sheep you're also hunting grizzly (in many areas), and a big rifle is needed.

Weight is not a factor today. You

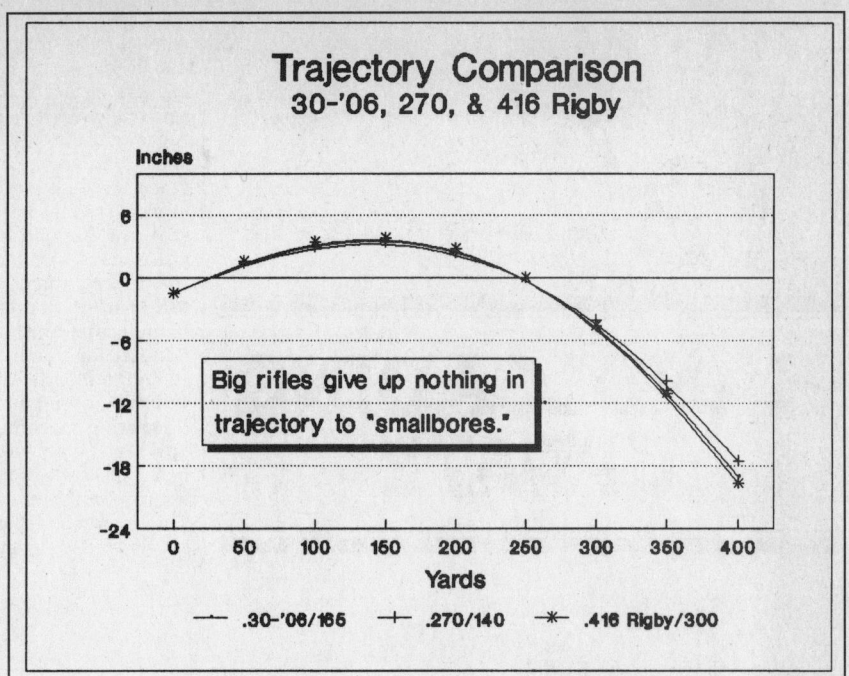

can have a 40-caliber rifle built to weigh, complete with scope and sling, well under 8 pounds. I have fired several light 40s, and they are quite pleasant when properly set up. With Mag-Na-Porting or the KDF muzzlebrake on the rifle, felt recoil is substantially reduced.

I would not hesitate to use a 416 Remington Magnum with suitable loads against all North American big game. I would use 350 to 400-grain bullets on moose or elk or bear in any terrain or cover, and go with 300-grain bullets at over 2800 fps for sheep or pronghorn or whitetails or mulies. While this is not to say there are not better cartridges for the smaller big game, this *is* to say 40s and larger will do it all, much better than anything smaller. They can always be loaded down to reduce power when desirable.

Next time you go hunting use a big rifle. Shoot it enough to get comfortable with it, give it an honest appraisal on the range and in the game fields, and I'll bet that you, too, will come to prefer big rifles for all your big game hunting. ●

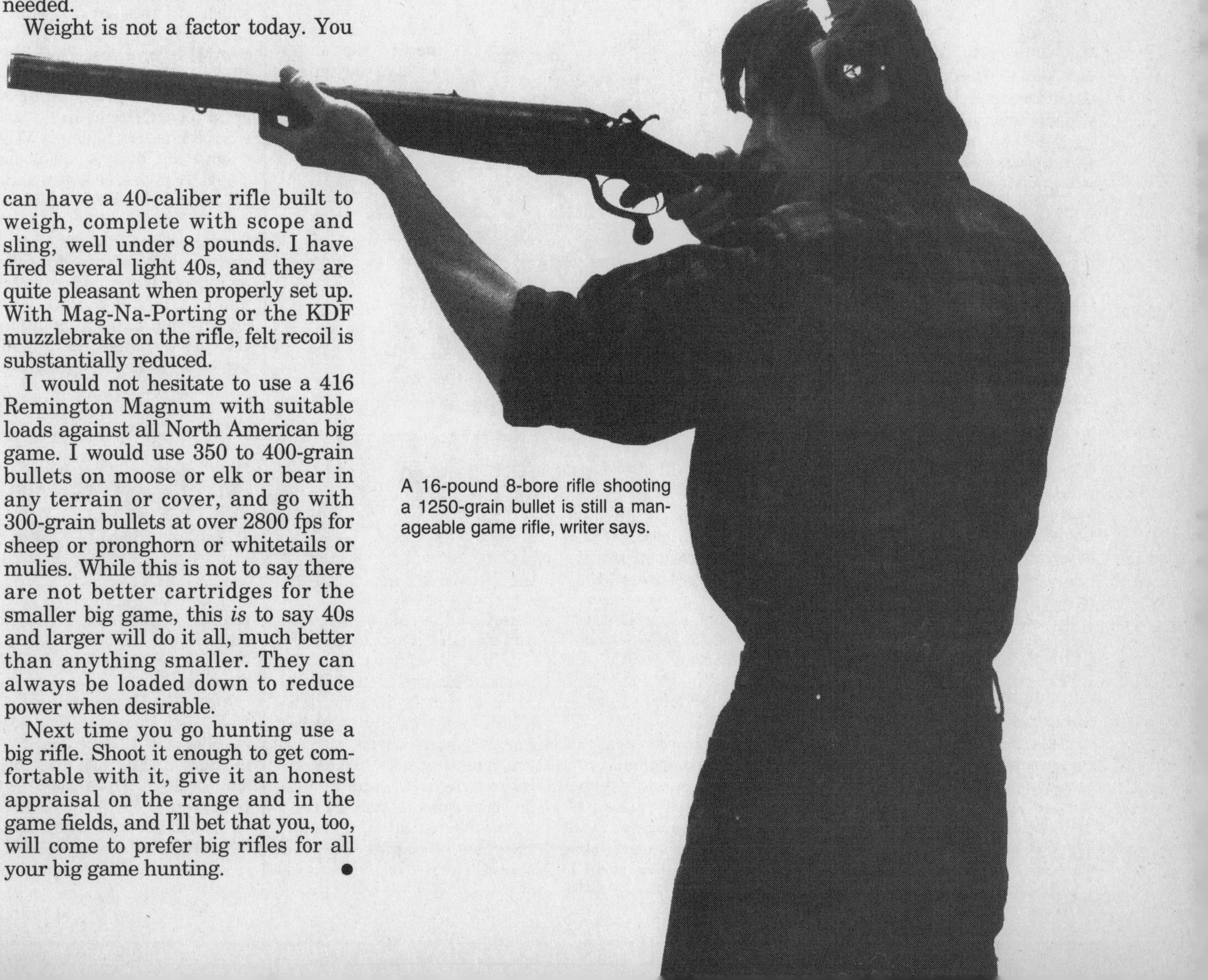

A 16-pound 8-bore rifle shooting a 1250-grain bullet is still a manageable game rifle, writer says.

by LARRY S. STERETT

HANDLOADING UPDATE

FEW HANDLOADERS today remember the Lyman Ideal 310 Tong Tool, but that's the device with which this shooter started his handloading career. With Norma 116-grain FMJ bullets, Remington primers, Du Pont No. 6 pistol powder, and cases obtained by firing a box of Winchester factory loads, many 9mm Luger reloads were assembled to feed a Mauser-manufactured World War II P-38 pistol. It was a slow process—decapping and sizing, changing dies, repriming, weighing all powder charges on a Herter's powder scale, changing dies, and seating the bullets—but it was a start. A powder measure soon speeded up the process, then a conventional press, using regular ⁷/₈x14 dies, replaced the 310 Tong Tool, and dies for additional calibers were added, plus a trimmer, and other miscellaneous equipment for loading metallics.

Equipment for loading shotshells started with a single-stage die used on a C-press, even slower than the 310, or so it seemed. Decap and size, recap, weigh and pour powder, seat and ram the over-powder and filler wads, dip and pour the shot, seat the over-shot wad and roll or fold with the new six-fold crimp. The paper cases would last for three or sometimes four reloads before they pin holed and were discarded. It was reasonably simple, and the reloads looked decent. As with the 310 and the metallics, the first shotshell reloader eventually was replaced, until the top was reached with a Hollywood

The manually operated Policlips MX93 bullet caster can turn out 800 to 1000 bullets per hour via a six-nozzle arrangement.

Some of the bullets possible when using the Policlips MX93 Policlips bullet caster. Extra six-cavity moulds cost under $100.

that could crank out 12-gauge reloads at about 1800 per hour, as long as someone kept all the hoppers and magazines filled with cases, primers, powder, shot and wads.

Today, the choice of available handloading components and equipment is much greater than in the days of the 310. Each year it keeps getting better. More powders are available, more loading information is

published, and literally there is more of everything to make the handloader's job easy. The loading gets easier as the reporting gets tougher.

Gun clubs, commercial handloaders, police departments and others needing large quantities of cast lead handgun bullets still find Magma Engineering equipment the best, but for smaller operations, the Policlips MX93 might be the answer. Manufactured in Italy, and distributed in North America by Policlips North America, the MX93 is a semi-automatic bullet casting machine. Manually operated, via two handles, it has a production rate of some 800 to 1000 bullets per hour. This is accomplished by a six-nozzle electric oven, automatic

cut-off of the casting crucible, and automatic ejection of the castings directly into a catch basket. Capacity of the MX93 is approximately 15 pounds of alloy, and a handy steel box functions as both base and storage. The six-cavity moulds are interchangeable, and moulds for most calibers, handgun and rifle, are available, although some might require longer to obtain. Currently the MX93 is

priced at $1000, with the extra six-cavity moulds costing under $100.

For large operators, **Magma Engineering Co.** has the needed equipment. The Mark VI Bullet Master casts 19,200 bullets per eight-hour shift and automatically separates the bullets and sprues. Temperatures are controlled ±7 degrees, and controllers are solid state with LED readouts. A divided pot assures optimum bullet quality and a float transfer device provides constant lead head pressure. Complementing the Bullet Master is the Lube Master, which can size and lube 34,400 bullets per eight-hour shift. It comes complete with Star dies for one caliber, and additional sizing dies are available in most calibers. Both machines work on 240 volts, although the Lube Master is available in a 120-volt version. For smaller casting operations, there's the Master Caster, which produces at a rate of 800 to 1000 bullets per hour, using Magma moulds.

For commercial reloaders, Magma also has a Case Master, which can swage/resize 41,000 cases per eight-hour day to SAAMI tolerances. They also offer the Pistol Load Master, a multimedia software data program for IBM-compatible personal computers having a VGA monitor and at least one floppy drive. It provides more than 1300 lead bullet loads for fifteen popular handgun cartridges from the 25 ACP to the 45 Colt and more than fifty digitally reproduced bullet and cartridge photographs, complete with dimensional data. In addition, the user can input up to 2 billion of his or her own loads and

records; loads can be displayed, edited and deleted. All for $39.95, plus $5.00 shipping and handling.

Mayville Engineering Co., Inc., has introduced a new reloader, the Model 8755 Steelmaster, for 3¹/₂-inch 12-gauge shotshells. A single-stage reloader, the 8755 will load either lead or steel shot. MEC has three Steel Conversion Kits to convert older loaders to handle the 3½-inch shells. There are also MEC 3½-inch pre-slit steel shot wads. Packaged 150 per bag, complete with loading data for both steel and lead 3½-inch shotshells, the new wads should be available at your local MEC dealer.

Lyman Products has some useful new products, starting with a power adapter to fit the Lyman Universal Trimmer. Consisting of a specially designed trimmer shaft with a standard ¼-inch Hex Adapter, it allows the trimmer to be used with a standard electric drill or power screwdriver. Complete with its own cutter and set of stop collars, the adapter can easily be removed for switching back to manual hand trimming without changing the caliber setting. There

bullet seating die; the other is a neck sizing die. Another new item is the carbide size bullet assembly, which includes the carbide size button, decapping rod, with spare decapping pin, and retainer. Now making loading dies for over 400 different handgun and rifle cartridges, Redding's range is from the 17 Remington to the 470 Capstick.

For blackpowder shooters, four new single- or double-cavity Saeco moulds are available, including two each in 40- and 45-caliber. Other new moulds in the Saeco line include one for a 180-grain FPGC 31-caliber; a 100-grain SWCBB and a 118-grain FP in 32-caliber; two 9mms, a 124-grain SWC-GC and a 140-grain SWC; a 9.2mm, 100-grain RNBB for the 9mm Makarov; a 148-grain

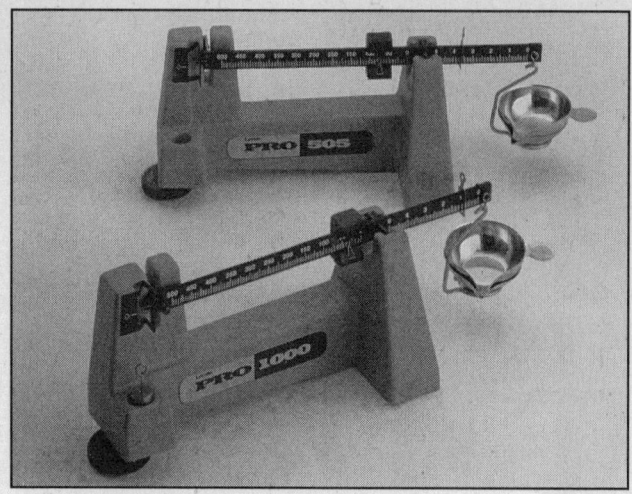

The Lyman Pro 1000 and Pro 505 reloading scales with high-impact styrene bases, leveling wheel, and easier to read beams.

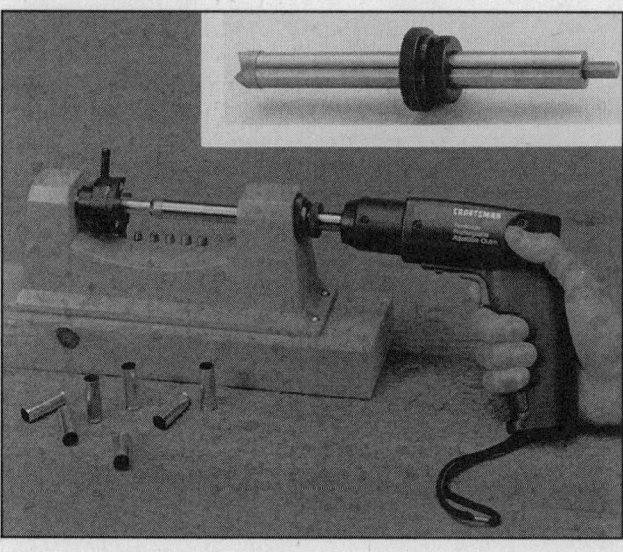

Lyman Products' new power adapter shaft makes case trimming much easier. It's available separately.

are two newly designed reloading scales, the Pro 1000 and Pro 505. They have improved platform systems, hi-tech bases of high-impact styrene with extra-large leveling wheels, easier to read beams and larger dampers for faster zeroing. Lyman also has two new 1-inch micrometers, as well as a steel Bench Wrench that will fit Lyman and RCBS hex lock nuts, Lyman die lock nuts, and the decapping rod and seating screw/expanding plug hex nuts as a start.

Redding-Hunter, Inc., has new three-die sets for bottleneck cases in addition to the regular two-die sets. There's the regular full-length sizer and the

WC for the 38/357 calibers; a 155-grain SWCBB in 40-caliber of 10mm size; a 365-grain RNGC for the 416 Rigby or others; a 200-grain SW in 44-caliber; and two 45-calibers, a 160-grain SPL for the 45 ACP and a 255-grain SWCGC for the 45 Colt.

Redding offers the Boss Pro-Pak reloading outfit—everything necessary to get started, except components. And there is now a new Competition Model BR-30 Powder Measure.

The **Bulletsmiths (Sierra)** introduced seven new bullets for handloaders in 1994. These include a 95-grain JHP and a 100-grain FPJ for the 9mm Makarov; a 150-grain FPJ for

the 38 Super, 9mm Parabellum, 9x21mm, or new 356 TS&W; a 300-grain JSP for the 45 Colt or 454 Casull; an 80-grain Blitz for the 7mm; a 135-grain HPBT for the 270 shooters; and a 215-grain SBT .338-inch for the 338 Winchester, 338 Lapua and 340 Weatherby Magnum cartridges.

Forster Products has their new Ultra bullet seater die with micrometer seating depth adjustments. Available in fifty-one calibers, ranging from the 22 Hornet to the 375 H&H, plus the Weatherby Magnum cartridges from 224 to the 340, the Ultra is graduated in 0.001-inch increments. There are also Ultra Upgrade kits for shooters already owning a Bench Rest Seater Die, a new "E-Z" expanding button on the Bench Rest Sizing Dies, and a new black oxide finish.

The "powder people," found at the **Hodgdon Powder Co.**, have a "New for '94" *Basic Reloaders Manual* listing a few loads for most of their powders and the more popular rifle and handgun cartridges and shotshells. Hodgdon currently has eight shotgun/handgun powders, including Clays, International Clays and Universal Clays, plus thirteen rifle powders, and four grades of Pyrodex–P, RS, Select and CTG. Loading data for the entire Hodgdon line of powders and most commercial cartridges, including a few wildcats, is available in The *Hodgdon Data Manual No. 26*, for $19.95, postpaid. It also includes data for Hercules, Winchester and IMR powders for rifle calibers, plus shotshells, and there are

sections on Silhouette cartridges and Pyrodex.

Starline has been manufacturing unprimed, unplated custom brass cartridge cases since 1976, cases available in handgun calibers only. Previously working for some of the world's leading ammunition manufacturers, Starline now sells brass direct to the consumer, in lots of 500 or 1000 ounces per caliber. The eighteen available cases range from the 32 H&R Magnum to the 445 Super Magnum, and include some hard to find cases, such as the 9x21mm, 9mm Makarov, 10mm Magnum,

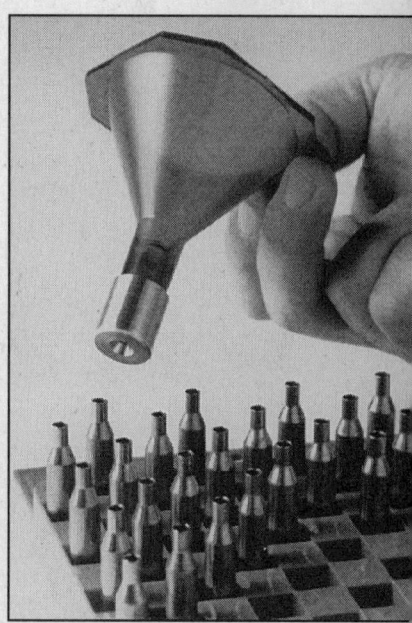

This adapter from Hornady makes powder charging of 17-caliber cases much easier.

The new RCBS Trim Pro Power Case Trimmer has a low RPM motor with spring-fed cutter—almost a small lathe.

Levers on the new RCBS Trim Pro Case Trimmer are easier to use and more accurate than draw collet systems.

The RCBS Cartridge Counter registers each time the Uniflow Power Measure dispenses a powder charge.

RCBS Pow'r Pull Bullet Puller for centerfire cartridges from 22 to 45.

plus, of course, the golden ones, 9mm Parabellum, 380 ACP, 45 ACP, 44 Magnum, 44 Special, 10mm and 45 Winchester Magnum. The quality of these cases is excellent.

Berry's Mfg., Inc., manufactures a line of plastic, hinged-lid ammunition boxes in sizes that will fit most handgun and rifle cartridges. The boxes examined were semi-transparent orange in color and had a fifty-round capacity. Berry's also manufactures plastic handgun cases of the type many handgun manufacturers now ship in. The model examined was black, foam-lined, with sliding locks and double handles, and large enough to hold an AMT Mark V 50 AE autoloader.

The most new items for handloaders are in the **RCBS** line. This includes a new Primer Guard hand-priming tool that seats primers rapidly, but safely, fits comfortably in the palm of most hands, and operates with a simple squeeze. It uses standard RCBS shellholders, comes with feed set-ups for both small and large primers, and the primer trap is easy to remove, install and fill. There is a new Pow'r Pull bullet puller for the rare mistakes we tend to make during handloading. A

three-jaw chuck grips the case rim (it is not for rimfire cartridges) and a rap on a solid surface, as with a hammer, drops the bullet and powder into the main chamber for reuse.

For the Uniflow Powder Measures, there's a new Cartridge Counter that registers each time the drum dispenses a charge. It can be attached to an AmmoMaster Auto, Piggyback, or mounted alone, to provide the number of charges thrown; A convenient reset knob returns the counter to zero.

To trim cases quickly and easily, RCBS has a new Trim Pro manual case trimmer with a lever-type handle, and a new lever attachment is available to upgrade existing RCBS trimmers to the Trim Pro level. There's a Trim Pro Power model to speed the trimming even more. The Trim Pro works with standard pilots and features flat plate shellholders, numbered the same as regular press shellholders.

Most handloaders do not think of the **Gun Parts Corporation** as being a source of items for reloading. However, if anyone is looking for universal shellholders to fit the Bonanza presses, plus RCBS and most other presses, Gun Parts might have them, and four for $5, plus shipping, is a bargain. Also available are loads of Lee Loader items, including priming tools, priming punch, star crimp dies, primer pocket cleaners, and even old-style threaded shellholders. There are also

shellholders and some parts available for the single-stage Five Star Loader, once manufactured by Numrich Arms.

Huntington still manufactures the firm's Compac Press. This press could be described as the 20th-century version of the 310 Tong Tool, but unlike the 310, which was designed for one-hand use, the Compac requires the use of both hands. It uses regular $7/8x14$ threaded loading dies and universal shellholders, and can be used to full-length resize most handgun and rifle cases.

Accurate Arms has acquired the Scot Powder Co., marking the first acquisition of one U.S. powder company by another in decades. The Scot powders, which are predominantly shotshell types, will continue to be marketed separately, and addi-

tions include a new Red Diamond powder of a type popular in Europe for many years. This double-base, diamond-shaped, sheet-cut, flake powder ignites easily, burns clean and offers low recoil in 12-gauge loads containing from $7/8$ to $1 1/8$ ounces of shot. (Accurate's Nitro 100 powder will now be sold under the Scot label.)

Another new biggie from Accurate Arms is the 345-page *Accurate Smokeless Powder Loading Guide Number One*.

This softbound volume provides loads for ninety-six rifle and fifty-six handgun cartridges, including not only popular commercial calibers, but many wildcat and obsolete ones as well. There are also more than a dozen specialized listings, including Desert Eagle loads, Schuetzen cartridge data, and NRA high power data, plus chapters on the history of reloading, record keeping and basic gun cleaning.

Handloaders wanting large quantities of unfired military caliber brass cases—50 BMG, 30-06, 308, and 223 Remington—and bullets should contact **Talon Mfg. Co., Inc.** All the components are unfired, having been recovered from disassembly of surplus ammunition, but there is a catch—the components are only available in lots of 10,000 or more. Talon also distributes the excellent Austrian Hirtenberger pistol and rifle cartridges, including some new 9mm frangible non-toxic and short-range non-toxic 223 and 308 training ammunition.

Finnish-made **Lapua** cartridges have been winning medals for decades, and some of our own military and Olympic shooters have used handloads featuring the .308-inch D-46 FMJ target bullet with the rebated heel. The D-46 and many other rifle and handgun bullets, plus unprimed cases from the 222 Remington to the 44 Magnum, are currently

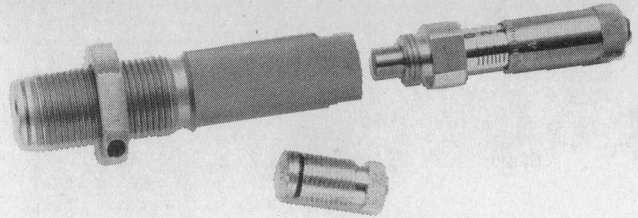

The Microjust Seater Stem by Hornady allows benchrest precision bullet seating. It replaces the threaded knob on the New Dimension seater die; one Microjust fits all such dies.

available to U.S. shooters through **Champion's Choice, Inc.** Bullet designs include the Mega, a mushrooming softpoint; the Scenar, a boattailed hollowpoint for target work; the Tera, a full copper bullet in .357-inch only for silhouette shooting; the MirR, spirepoint boattail softpoint; and the Lock Base, an FMJ design constructed to retain its velocity over extra long distances. The 250-grain Lock Base is one of the bullet designs loaded in the 338 Lapua Magnum sniper cartridge.

The **Hornady Mfg. Co.** now offers the Chronomax, a pocket-size chronograph powered by four AA batteries. Designed to measure velocities from 100 to 4999 fps, with an accuracy of 1 fps, the Chronomax uses separate skyscreens connected with a single cable and spaced 2 feet apart. The screens and legs install easily and store inside the tube for carrying when not in use.

Makarov handloaders will appreciate the new 9x18 Makarov Series III New Dimension die set and the 95-grain .365-

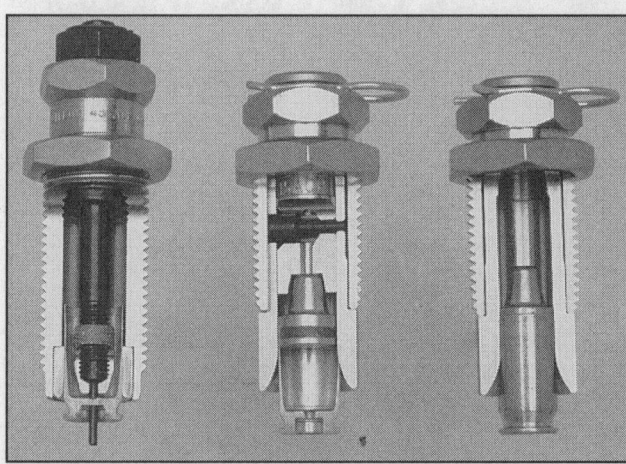

These sectioned views of Dillon's Dynamic Dies show the floating decap assembly, heavy decap pin, radiused mouths on bullet seater and crimp dies with the quick-release die inserts, and the hex lock rings and heads.

Dillon Precision Products, Inc., introduced their XL 650 a couple of years ago. For just under $400, it's one of the best deals around, and now they have a Universal Mounting Hardware Kit that will fit it, the Square Deal B, RL 1050, and RL 550B presses. Another new item is the 9x25 Dillon cartridge, and naturally the firm has the dies—full length carbide sizer, snap-together seater, and taper crimp—to handload it. The 9x25 Dillon cartridge is the regular 10mm case necked down to handle 9mm bullets, and **Briley** is currently chambering barrels for it.

inch Makarov bullets. Custom die sets are also available for the 50 Action Express cartridge, and Hornady New Dimension die set owners can turn their seating dies into benchrest-precision seaters by replacing the threaded knob with the new Microjust Seater Stem that is on the market.

Another accessory that every handloader of metallic cartridges needs is a case tumbler. The latest from Hornady is the M-3, which will hold up to 1000 38 Special cases. There's also a new Media Sifter to conveniently separate tumbler media from the cleaned cases.

Shotshell handloaders will appreciate the new Riser Legs for their 366 loaders, and a dust cover for the Apex, plus a Multipax Steel Shot Counter if they load steel shot. The Multipax features a cylindrical hopper of its own, along with a handle that rotates a series of internal disks to count out the proper number of pellets.

Handloaders not wanting to buy the two-volume set of Hornady's *Reloading Manual*, 4th Edition, can now get an abridged edition. Containing the reloading data and ballistics tables for more than twenty-five of the most popular handgun and rifle calibers, this manual has been and is included with the Hornady reloading kits. Other new items are the *Hornady LoadNotes*. Available for twenty-four different handgun and rifle calibers from the 222 Remington to the 45-70 Government, and 9mm Luger to 45 RCP, the *LoadNotes* contain the reloading data and ballistics tables for a single caliber.

Corbin Mfg. & Supply, Inc., has several new items for handloaders, including custom dies to produce six- to eight-notch folds in ordinary bullet jackets. In this Sabr design, the jacket is not cut or notched, but folded inward upon itself. When the jacket begins to expand, it unfolds between these corrugations, tearing back cleanly to form six or eight little petals. All that's required to make the Sabr is a regular core swage and core seating die, hollowpoint punch, and the custom Sabr "star" punch. All sorts of bullet shapes can be formed, particularly if a point-forming die is used.

Corbin also has a new bullet jacket, the J-45-100, for producing big bore bullets. It has a .022-inch-thick forward wall tapering to a parallel .030-inch wall, 0.983-inch overall length and .456-inch diameter. Of 99.995 percent pure copper, these jackets are ductile enough to be drawn, using the correct dies, into virtually any of the more popular calibers down to 375, including 416, 404, 423, 429 and 451. Other bullet jackets, pure lead wire, and forming dies are available from Corbin, along with swaging presses and hand cannelure tools.

Handloading steel shot requires special wads, shot and suitable loading data for a start. **Ballistic Products, Inc.,** is a good place to start.

They have the special wads, several grades and sizes of steel shot, reliable loading data, and all sorts of accessories to make the loading process easier. In addition to steel shot components, Ballistic Products has components for loading shotshells with regular lead or copper-plated shot, including eight new G/BP plastic wads, mainly in 12-gauge, but also 32-gauge and 410-bore. New and once-fired hulls are available in gauges from the 8 down to the 410-bore, as are most of the powders, primers and equipment necessary for loading them.

A-Square recently introduced a new ballistics test service for serious handloaders. With more than 100 pressure barrels in stock, A-Square can provide a complete written report on the internal and external ballistics of a particular load, along with trajectories out to 600 yards. All at competitive prices per laboratory hour.

Readers may note the lack of mention of some time-honored manufacturers of handloading equipment. It is not intentional, but may be due to a lack of any new products or, simply, a lack of time and space. Time permitting, they will be included in the next edition, hopefully along with new firms bringing the handloader the best in equipment and components. ●

Hornady LoadNotes are available for 24 different rifle and handgun cartridges.

CUSTOM GUNS

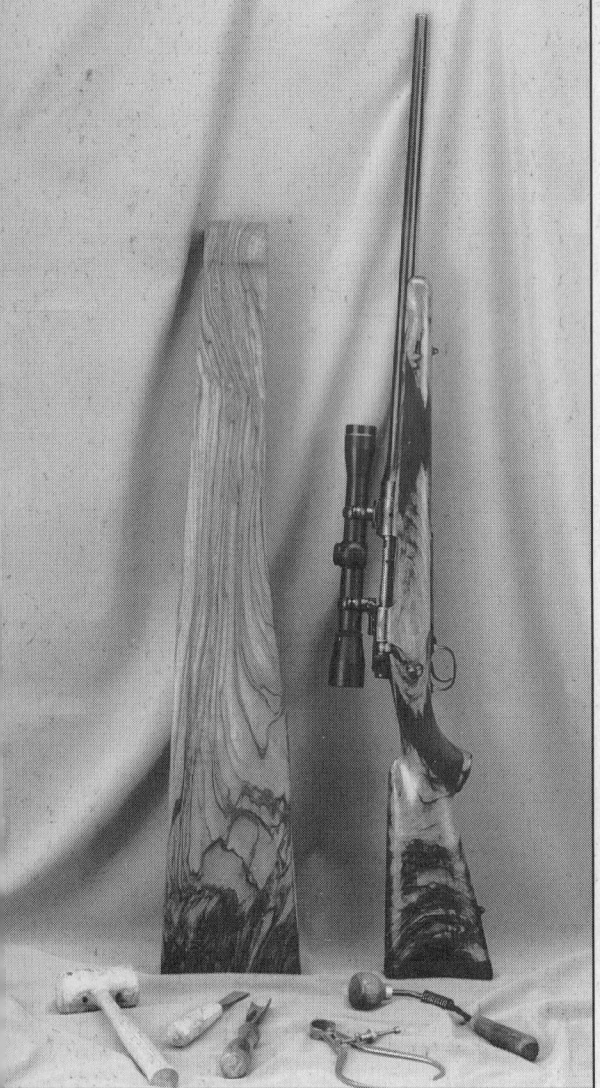

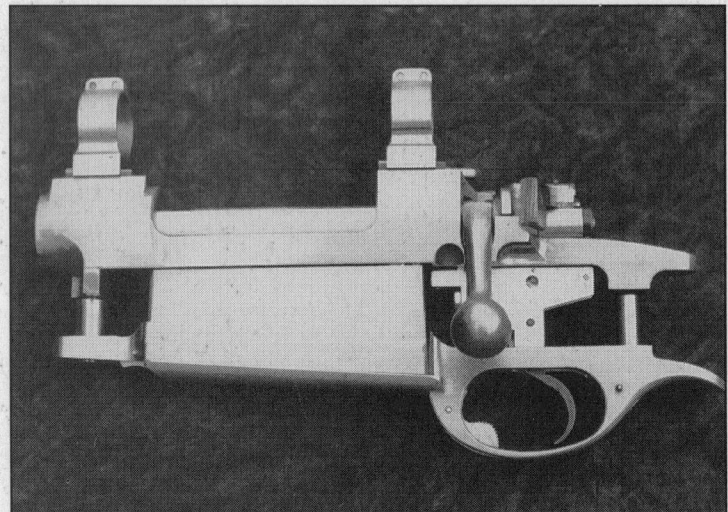

▲ FRED WELLS
Shop-made left-hand magnum Mauser with all the special Wells touches.

◀ KENT BOWERLY
What exhibition-grade California English walnut looks like in the block.

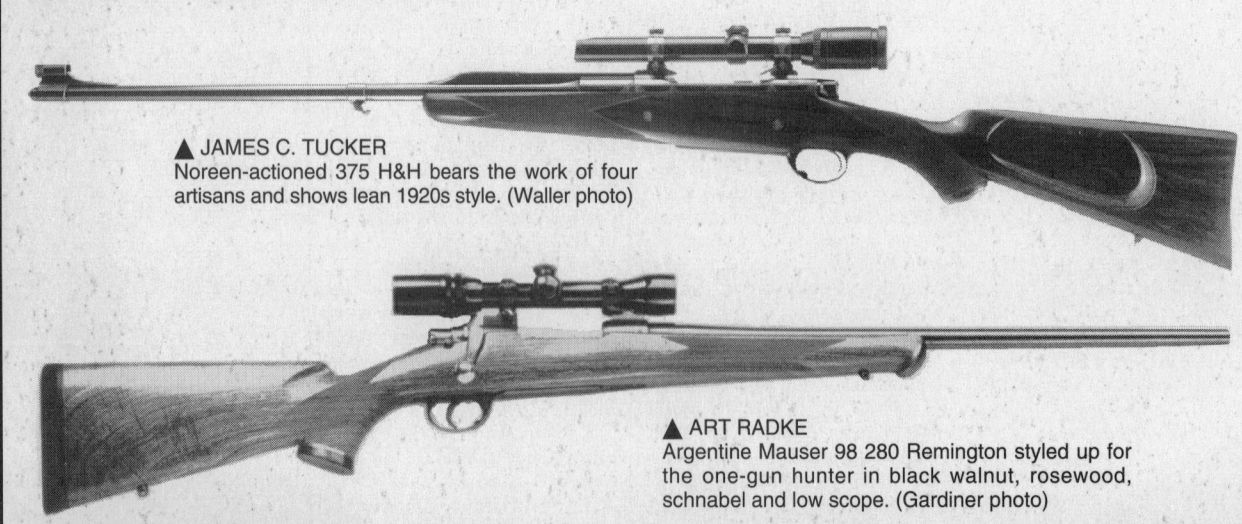

▲ JAMES C. TUCKER
Noreen-actioned 375 H&H bears the work of four artisans and shows lean 1920s style. (Waller photo)

▲ ART RADKE
Argentine Mauser 98 280 Remington styled up for the one-gun hunter in black walnut, rosewood, schnabel and low scope. (Gardiner photo)

▲ VIC OLSON
Deluxed low-wall Winchester in 22 Hornet has the old touches—octagonal barrel, color case-hardened receiver, ebony tip.

▶ FRED WELLS
Big rifle in 416 shows off Wells action; stocked with high comb in handsome straight-grained English walnut. (Gable photo)

▲ MAURICE OTTMAR
Hagn-actioned 17 Remington demonstrates Ottmar talent and Hehr engraving. Stock is Turkish walnut. (Bolster photo)

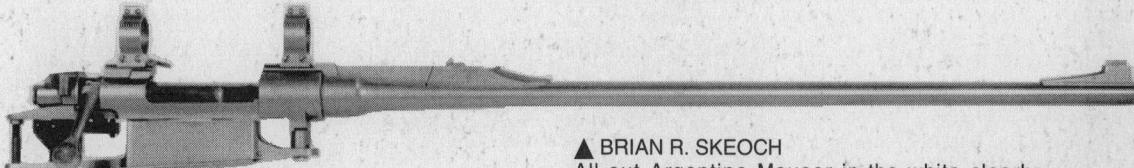

▲ BRIAN R. SKEOCH
All-out Argentine Mauser in the white clearly assembles good stuff around a Douglas 280 Remington barrel.

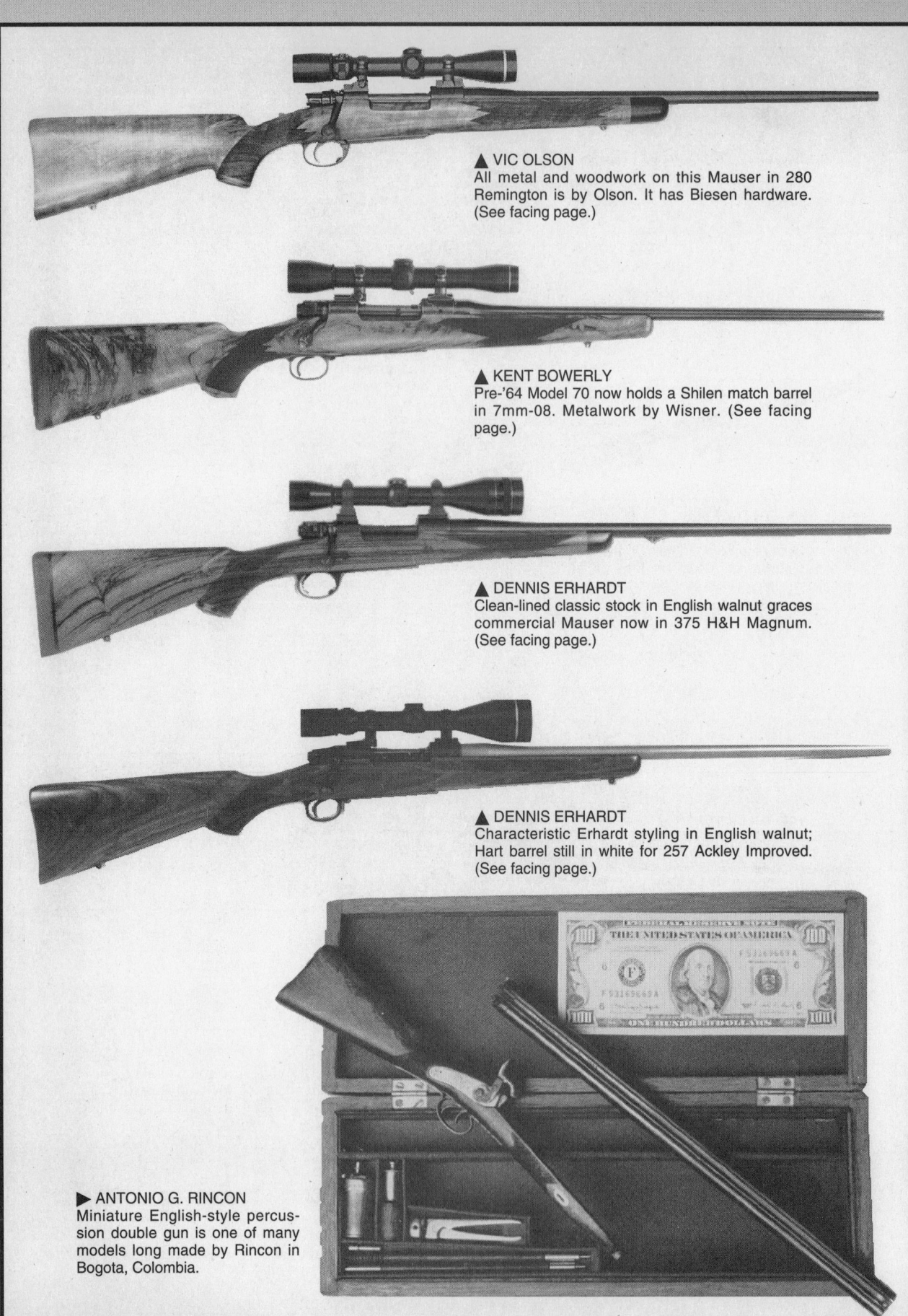

▲ VIC OLSON
All metal and woodwork on this Mauser in 280 Remington is by Olson. It has Biesen hardware. (See facing page.)

▲ KENT BOWERLY
Pre-'64 Model 70 now holds a Shilen match barrel in 7mm-08. Metalwork by Wisner. (See facing page.)

▲ DENNIS ERHARDT
Clean-lined classic stock in English walnut graces commercial Mauser now in 375 H&H Magnum. (See facing page.)

▲ DENNIS ERHARDT
Characteristic Erhardt styling in English walnut; Hart barrel still in white for 257 Ackley Improved. (See facing page.)

▶ ANTONIO G. RINCON
Miniature English-style percussion double gun is one of many models long made by Rincon in Bogota, Colombia.

▲ VIC OLSON
Claro walnut, elegant point-pattern checkering and special treatments all along the bottom.

▲ KENT BOWERLY
Evans engraving dresses up the pre-'64 Model 70 now seated in exhibition-grade California English walnut.

▲ DENNIS ERHARDT
Big recoil pad, big scope, no irons, open pistol grip and small forearm tip—a modern 375. (Third Eye photos)

▲ DENNIS ERHARDT
Model 70 set up for big scope, no irons. Walnut stock has *fleur-de-lis* checkering, plain forearm tip. (Third Eye photos)

▲ STEPHEN L. BILLEB
American Custom Gunmakers Guild No. 10 L.C. Smith 20-gauge stocked in English walnut by Billeb. Metalwork by Pete Mazur; engraved by Bob Evans. (Bilal photo)

A master hunter has little trouble coming to terms...

With a 25-20

Marlin's new Model 1894CL in 25-20 presents a most classic profile.

by FRANCIS SELL

I JUST TOOK A 25-20-caliber Marlin lever-action rifle out of its shipping box, expecting and getting a well-finished rifle in my hands. The action responded beautifully. Trigger pull was a bit heavy, but easily corrected. All in all, just about what I expected from previous experience with Marlin rifles. This 25-20 nicely rounds out my personal hunting rifles, each filling a niche, and each complementing the others—a 22 Marlin lever action, this 25-20 and a 25-35 wildcat caliber of my own design.

I never put this one on the scales, maintaining that if it feels light, it is too light, and if it feels heavy, it is too heavy, but if it comes into firing position without feeling either light or heavy, it carries the right weight. This Marlin responded beautifully.

The Marlin comes with a 24-inch barrel and open sights. These I removed. I sweated on a low ramp front sight base to hold my own front sight designed for the moist misty rain forests of coastal Oregon. The

rear sight slot was filled with a blank filed to the contour of the barrel, then blued. I mounted a rear receiver sight of the type used on all my rifles. Going from one rifle to another, I find the same type sights, same trigger pull, and very close to the same rifle weight.

In many ways, this rifle fills a special need—elk. In my reforesting, there are many abandoned logging roads. These are beautiful hiking and hunting trails I often use during the deer hunting season, and I have turned up many prime bucks along them. In addition, before and after these primary uses, these trails are used by elk, large primary bulls keeping an eye on their cows and looking for a battle if another bull intrudes.

I walk these trails winter, spring and summer, especially during the spring months, when deer fawns are being dropped, becoming easy prey for coyotes. All this I had in mind when I ordered the 25-20.

The 25-20 is no stranger. I once owned a Model 92 Winchester in this

caliber with a 25-inch barrel. I bought it when a coal company was updating their assets during the Big Depression of 1929-32, selling about forty 45-70 lever-action Winchesters and a sprinkling of 25-20 rifles for $5 apiece.

I remember the late Al Wyman telling me with tears in his eyes (tears brought about by drinking a bit of triple-run moonshine, aged in a glass gallon jug laced with oak sawdust), "You know, Spud, I wish I had worked steady before this Depression. I could have been a hundredaire by now, and I would latch onto one of them 45-70 rifles and a 25-20, especially that 25-20. It would make a good shining rifle for deer and blue grouse."

I knew what he had in mind when he talked of shining deer and blue grouse, and it wasn't spotlighting. Shining is always done during the daylight, with a bright sun out and a small hand mirror.

You still-hunt until you come to some shadowed cover, a likely spot for a deer. Then, using your mirror, you run a spot of light close to, but not directly on, the favored cover and work it back and forth. It's not difficult, though it takes skilled hunting to be effective.

And in the spring, when the blue grouse are hooting, they lay flat out on the large limbs of the old-growth spruce and fir. They hoot three tones, then pause. That third hoot, which is slightly lower in tone than the first two, gives the experienced still-hunter the correct location. Run a spot of light slowly toward it and the blue grouse will stand up to see what has disturbed him. The skilled hunter will have him dead to rights. The 25-20 is a good rifle choice for this, with the added advantage of

One had been roughed up by a wild hog, and had a nice soft moss bed of his own, and was covered with his master's jacket. Hanging by its lever from a cut-off limb was a 25-20 lever-action Marlin. Hanging from the same limb was a buckskin thong and an oiled cleaning patch of the same type I used afield. All this testified to a basic fact—this man was no tenderfoot.

He invited me to have my evening meal with him—roast venison, a large loaf of sourdough bread done to a turn in a light dutch oven, and a pot of black coffee. He was working for the state, taking predators. He told me that he had killed fifty-seven bear,

"Small deer" they used to call them and the 25-20 is still good medicine in the squirrel woods.

Marlin chose, Sell puts it, to go back to the 1893 action, scaled down, in their revival of the 1894 here lately.

Neither the rifle factory nor the ammo factory nor the Editor will recommend the 25-20 for deer, but Sell has eaten too much 25-20-bagged venison to go along with that.

having a rifle in hand that will take larger game.

During the Big Depression, starting in 1929 when stockbrokers were jumping out of top-story windows, the backwoods people—trappers, homesteaders and moonshiners—fared fairly well. I recall I had a job as a timber cruiser that paid $1.50 a day. I furnished all my own equipment including rifle and grubstake. I carried a 25-20 Winchester carbine. In my knapsack, I had a slab of bacon, flour and light shelter half. This was used only when I got too far from my base camp to return in the evening.

Once, coming to a sheltered hemlock grove, I decided to camp for the night and, looking farther along the sheltered section, I saw a man already camped. He nodded his head in welcome. He had four hounds.

seven cougar, and dozens of bobcats with this 25-20. He said he never kept track of the wild hog and deer killed for camp meat and to feed his hounds.

All of this is in the background of the 25-20 Marlin I recently purchased.

To get this in perspective, let's for a moment go back to the period when backwoods people were getting their hands on the 30-30 lever action and the benchresters were beginning to appear. Some were riflemen, such as Townsend Whelen, who spent a lot of time bringing the bolt action to the attention of all riflemen, so there would be a trained reserve of riflemen in the event of war. His efforts were quite successful, but by the time he had pushed aside the lever action in favor of the bolt, the military went all-out automatic.

The wooden ramrod gives much less wear on the barrel interior than a brass or steel rod. I made one for my 25-35 Tomcat, and straightaway I tried it in the 25-20 Marlin, but I found it a bit too snug, due to the difference in the rifling of the two calibers.

I sanded the rod down to a proper fit in the 25-20 and enlarged the slot for the cleaning patch. No problem. The rod took on a beautiful polish in the process of fitting. It is made long enough to do all cleaning from the breech, bolt removed.

This wood cleaning rod is never taken afield. For field cleaning, a special patch soaked in a good gun oil is standard among backwoods riflemen. This patch is placed in a slot cut in a buckskin thong long enough to reach through the barrel from the breech. Before use, the thong is rolled and stretched and

20 Marlin is good for all expected shooting out to a full 100 yards.

To confirm this, I turned to my record of deer killed with the 25-35 Tomcat, which stands at thirty deer killed with thirty-four shots. The four misses include two shots through the ear of a buck running directly away from me at about forty-five yards. When it stopped to look back, I clipped it behind the ear for a clean kill.

Going over the entire record, I found one doubtful shot at 150 yards. The deer was facing the gun in poor evening light, but the shot was well within the capabilities of the 25-20 Marlin lever action. In short, this 25-20 Marlin could have answered quite well for all my deer hunting requirements.

Beyond this, I had elk in mind, not so much as an elk rifle, if I were going out looking for elk, but as elk insurance. I felt that this light weight rifle would be nice to carry when I walked through the reforestings, reading sign as backwoods hunters say, but I had no intention of carrying it if I was going all out looking for elk. Still, I could have filled my elk license one day, while carrying my new 25-20.

I walked along an overgrown logging road, seeing a few elk tracks, most of them days old, but there was one fresh track at a turning in the trail. I sounded a low herd-calling note on my elk call and was immediately answered by a full-throated call from a herd bull, and he was taking no nonsense from an interloper.

I kept walking slowly toward my cabin, getting out of the woods, and I kept sounding a low herd call, trying to convince that big bull elk I wanted nothing to do with his cows. He followed me to the edge of the woods, his head lowered, shaking a beautiful set of antlers, then turned back to his immediate concern, his harem bedded in the thickets.

I came in and cleaned the Marlin, well pleased with my purchase. I never did get around to weighing it, but it felt neither light nor heavy, a very essential requirement in any rifle. ●

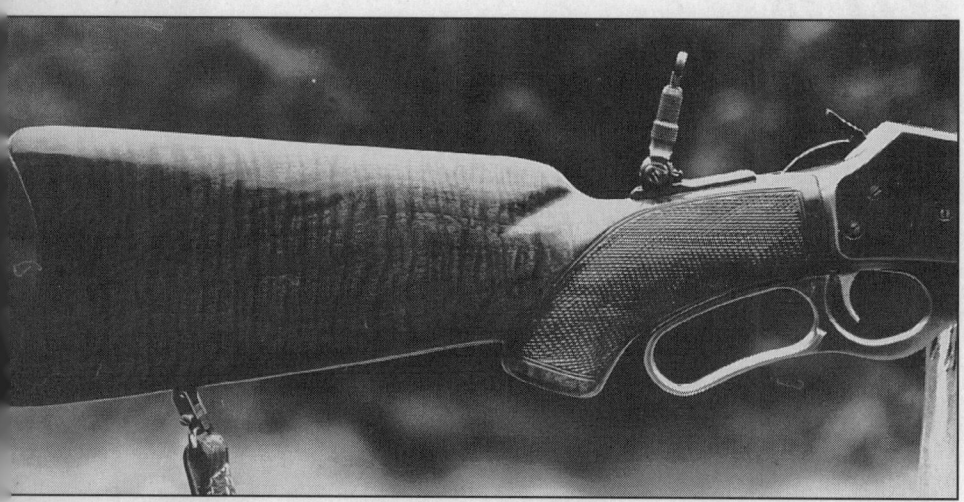

This is the Sell prescription for the back end of a serious hunter's gun—it worked for him for a half-century or more.

The shouting and screaming left deer hunters and backwoodsmen unimpressed. They stuck with the lever action come hell or high water.

When the benchresters discovered that the popular Sheard gold bead wasn't precise on paper and quit it, the backwoods continued to use this excellent front sight for the simple reason that it always gave a beautiful point of aim, well within one inch of the mark, top or bottom, left or right side of aim, depending on the light. It provided sufficiently accurate big game shooting at the usual 50 yards in the brush. Despite all the expert condemning, the Marble Sight Company still has this sight available for the backwoods rifleman.

Another backwoods item that is still standard is the wooden ramrod.

oiled to make it small enough to drop through the bore from the chamber end. The patch is pulled through the bore each night, leaving a well oiled and protected interior while afield.

I sighted in the new 25-20 at 40 yards, using standard Remington ammunition, standing for all shots, leaning against a maple for a bit of extra steadiness. Three shots printed in slightly less than an inch, a half-inch to the right of aim. I corrected for this and fired another three-shot group. This printed beautifully over the front sight. Moving the target back about 5 yards, I shot a tight group about one inch above point of aim over the front sight of my own design which has dead-white color.

I never fired any groups at longer range than this, feeling that the 25-

▲ CLAUS WILLIG

◄ HEIDEMARIE HIPTMAYER

▲ CLAUS WILLIG

ART OF THE ENGRAVER

◄ RONALD COLLINGS

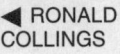

▼ FRANK MELE

◄ RONALD COLLINGS

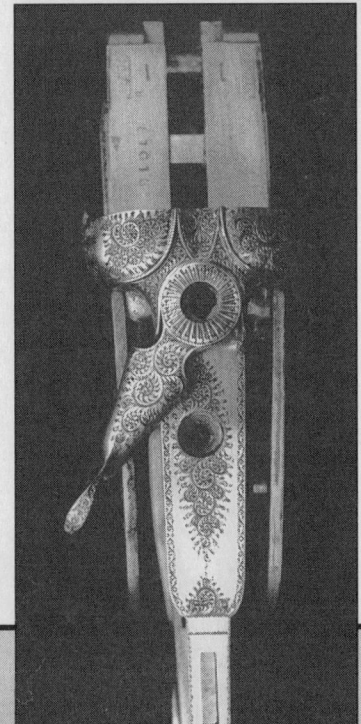

▲ ROGER L. KEHR

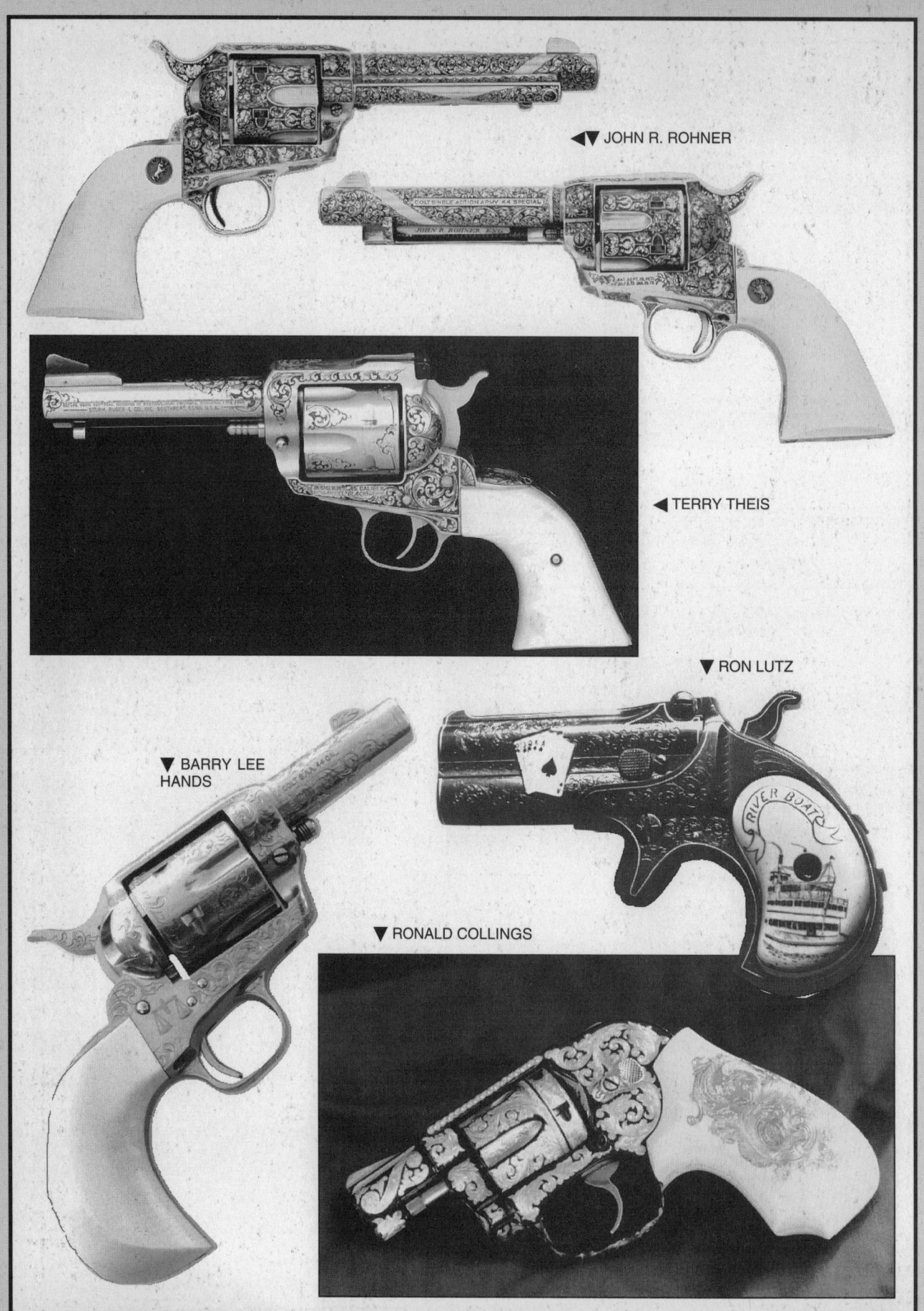

◄◄ JOHN R. ROHNER

◄ TERRY THEIS

▼ RON LUTZ

▼ BARRY LEE
HANDS

▼ RONALD COLLINGS

▲ BILL JOHNS

▲ JOHN M. KUDLAS

▲ ROGER SAMPSON   ▲ ED DELORGE

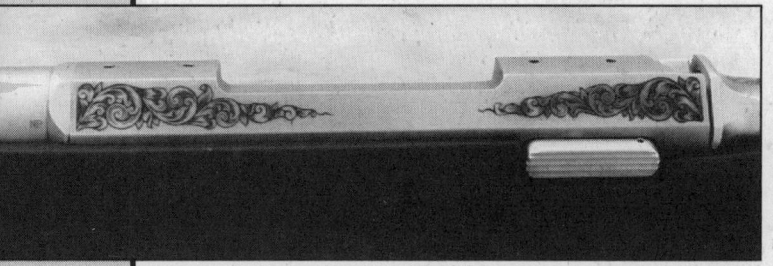

▲ BILLY BATES   ▲ GEOFFROY GOURNET

▶ RACHEL WELLS

by EDWARD A. MATUNAS

AMMUNITION, BALLISTICS AND COMPONENTS

A LOT HAS happened since we last wrote for these pages. A famous premium rifle bullet company has decided to make handgun bullets, a major ammo company has acquiesced to anti-gun media pressure and now will sell their finest handgun ammo only to police departments, a major arms and ammo company has been sold to a group never before in this business, and a number of new components have been made available to handloaders, to mention just some of the "news."

I had the opportunity to get to Wyoming with the folks from Nosler and Leupold. Seems there was a need to do some serious testing of a new bullet, and Nosler's Chub Eastman felt his Red Mist Society was the best gang to get the job done. On this trip, I got into the prairie dogs like never before, and hundreds of bullets received the ultimate test.

There is much to discuss, so let's get to the most newsworthy of the latest bids for our shooting dollars, presented in alphabetical order:

Bertram Co.

Bertram makes a heap of rare and unusual cartridge cases. There are ninety or so calibers listed in their current export catalog. All are made in Australia and available from either Huntington Die Specialties or Dixie Gun Works.

Included are a great many metrics from all corners of Europe (and even Japan). Plenty of the various English car-

tridges, with and without rims, as well as many of the early rimmed U.S. rounds are also included in the listing. Just a random sample are 5.6 Vom Hofe, 7x72Rmm, 9.3x82Rmm, 43 Mauser and Spanish, 8mm Nambu, 240 Flanged, 318 Rimless, 400/360 Westley Richards, 600 Nitro, 32 Ideal, 38-72, 405 Winchester and 50 3¼-inch Sharps. If you own an oddball and want brass, contact Huntington or Dixie.

Blount

Speer's Lawman ammo line has been revised to include only Totally Metal Jacket bullet loads, one each in 9mm Luger (115-grain), 38 Special +P (158-grain), 40 S&W (180-grain), and 45 ACP (230-grain). Modest pricing should make these attractive to plinkers and target shooters who want a brass case to reload.

Speer is now marketing handgun ammo under the "Gold Dot" logo. All of the loads in this line use high-performance Gold Dot hollowpoint bullets. Calibers and weights are 9mm Luger (115, 124, 147 grains); 38 Special +P (125 grains); 357 Magnum (125, 158 grains); 40 S&W (155, 180 grains); 41 Action Express (180 grains); 44 Magnum (270 grains); 45 ACP (185, 200, 230 grains); and 50 Action Express (325 grains). This ammo is loaded in re-usable brass cases and packed in twenty-round boxes.

Additionally, more Gold Dot bullets have been incorporated into the non-reloadable, but

inexpensive, Blazer line of handgun ammo. There will be a 90-grain load for the 9mm Makarov, a 124-grain 9mm Luger and a 155-grain in 40 S&W.

Component Gold Dot bullets new to the Speer line are 90-grain .355-inch, 125 and 158-grain .357-inch, and 90-grain .364-inch (9mm Makarov). New for the 9x18 is a 95-grain TMJ. There is also a 155-grain TMJ of .400-inch. Three component bullet additions are TNT varmint styles of .257-inch 87-

grain, .277-inch 90-grain, and .284-inch 110-grain.

Buffalo Bullets

Muzzle-loading shooters may find the 50-caliber "BALL-Et" bullet of interest. This is a 245-grain cross between a round ball and a conical bullet. Because it is relatively light, its recoil is rather light (ball-like). But, because it has a conical shape, it is loaded without the need for patching and will deliver better than ball-type accuracy. I have found it well suited to

Speer's Lawman ammo is now exclusively loaded with Totally Metal Jacketed bullets.

The high-performance Speer Gold Dot hollowpoint handgun bullets are available in Speer's factory load ammo.

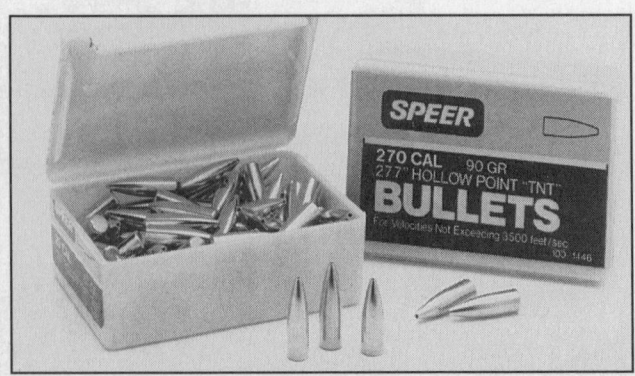

Among Speer's new rifle bullets is a highly explosive TNT 90-grain, .277-inch one.

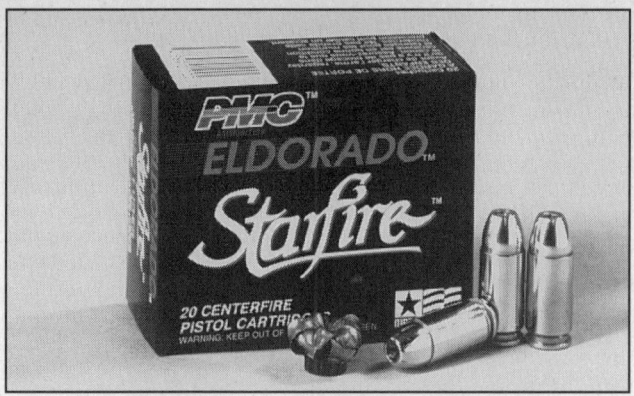

Eldorado's Starfire bullet is now loaded in a 95-grain 380 Auto version.

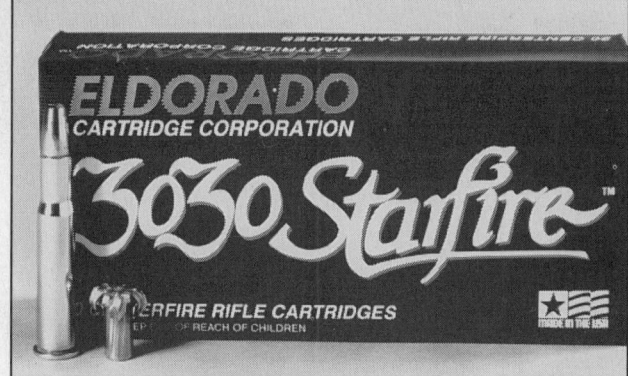

A solid 150-grain copper bullet with a Starfire-shaped hollowpoint is now loaded for the 30-30 Eldorado.

plinking and target shooting, and less expensive to use compared to traditional conical bullets.

New diameter swaged pure lead round balls include .310-inch (45 grains), .454-inch (142 grains), and .570-inch (280 grains). These bring the total number of Buffalo round ball diameters to ten. All of Buffalo's bullets now use a new lubricant called Eureka. It's said to be non-drying and to leave less barrel fouling.

Eldorado (PMC)

The high-performance Starfire bullet style is now available in 380 Auto. A good round to try if, like me, you prefer to carry a very light and compact pocket gun. It is a 95-grain load that appears to have a point of impact similar to several FMC loads, at least in my three 380s. There are two new 40 S&W loads available—one using a 155-grain Starfire bullet, the other of the same weight but with a truncated hollowpoint bullet.

A new rifle bullet design, of solid copper with a Starfire-shaped hollowpoint, is now available in 30-30 loaded ammo. It weighs 150 grains and has typical ballistics. Eldorado is also offering both 338 Winchester and 375 H&H Magnum ammo loaded with the Barnes X-Bullet. Weights are 225 grains for the Winchester cartridge, 270 grains for the Holland & Holland round.

Federal

Factory premium ammo, in some instances, has been taken to a performance level that the handloader cannot better or, sometimes, even duplicate. As an example, I recently acquired a second T/C Contender in 30-30 Winchester and began im-

mediately to look for the best load. When all is said and done, the very best load is Federal's Premium 170-grain Nosler Partition. This load—three different lots were tested—consistently provides MOA accuracy. Testing at 60 yards, some groups of five would see four shots into a ragged hole with the other not extending the group beyond a half-inch.

I am unable to duplicate this load's average velocity of 1980 fps from the 14-inch barrel without exceeding the pressure of the factory load. And no reload tested can duplicate the accuracy. In short, the factory Federal load has a premium bullet, high velocity, superb accuracy and relatively low chamber pressure, so I no longer reload for the 30-30 cartridge!

Using this load, I took several whitetails and some smaller plains game without a hitch, single shot kills all. Indeed, this load seems every bit as effective as the 180-grain Nosler Partition reload I have been using in my original Contender.

Another feather in Federal's cap is their 416 Rigby 410-grain ammo. I have yet to duplicate the accuracy of either the softpoint or solid loads with any of my favored component bullets. Results with Federal's 210- and 250-grain Premium loads (Nosler Partition bullets) for the 338 have been so close to my best handload performance as to make it meaningless whether I use one or the other.

There are now two new Federal Premium loads for the 416 Rigby: the 400-grain Trophy Bonded Sledgehammer solid and a Trophy Bonded Bearclaw softpoint. Plenty of other new Premium loads too, including 7mm Remington Magnum 175 grains, 165-grain

308 Winchester, 458 Winchester Magnum 400 and 500 grains, and 500-grain 470 Nitro Express. All use Trophy Bonded Bearclaw softpoints. New Sledgehammer solid loads include 400-grain 416 Rigby, 500-grain 458 Winchester Magnum, and 500-grain 470 Nitro Express. The Trophy Bonded Bearclaw softpoints and Sledgehammer solids have earned an enviable reputation among hunters who pursue the most dangerous of game.

It's not all about rifles at Federal. A newly designed shotshell wad is said to greatly enhance the accuracy of slug loads. They're claiming 2-inch 100-yard groups.

Fiocchi of America

Fiocchi's newest catalog shows a great many new shotshell offerings. Some of these are buckshot, steel pellet target, extra-light 7/8-ounce training loads, etc., all in 12-gauge. And not to be outdone by the others,

they now load for the 9mm Makarov.

If you own a handgun for an oddball cartridge, it just may be that one of Fiocchi's specialty cartridges could turn it into a shooter. While it is not "news," loads are available for such calibers as 7.62mm Nagant, 7.63mm Mauser, 30 Luger, 8mm Lebel (pistol), 8mm Gasser, 9mm Steyr, 44 S&W Russian, 10.4mm Italian, 450 Short Colt, 455 Webley, and a few others. Ditto for oddball shotguns such as 9mm Long Rimfire; 12-gauge 2⅝-inch; 16-, 20-, 24- and 32-gauge 2½-inch shells. And lead-free component pistol primers should appeal to indoor shooters. Large and small sizes are offered.

Some unusual law enforcement ammo is shown in the new listings. Not necessarily unique, but for the first time generally available are the plastic and rubber pellet and buckshot loads for 12-gauge. There is also a rubber slug load called

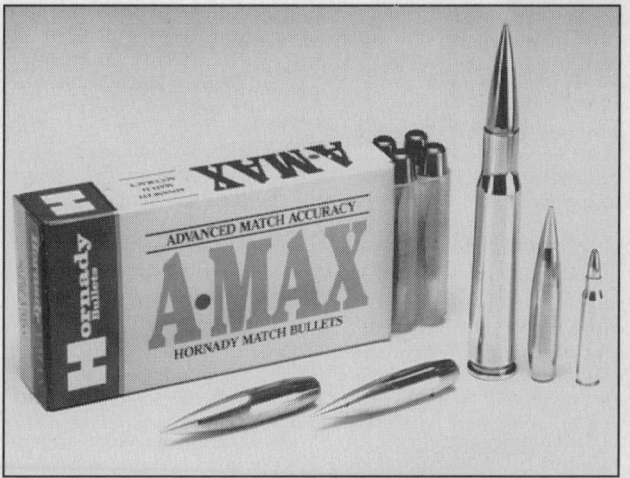

Hornady is now offering an affordable 50-caliber bullet for those who shoot the 50 BMG cartridge. It weighs 750 grains.

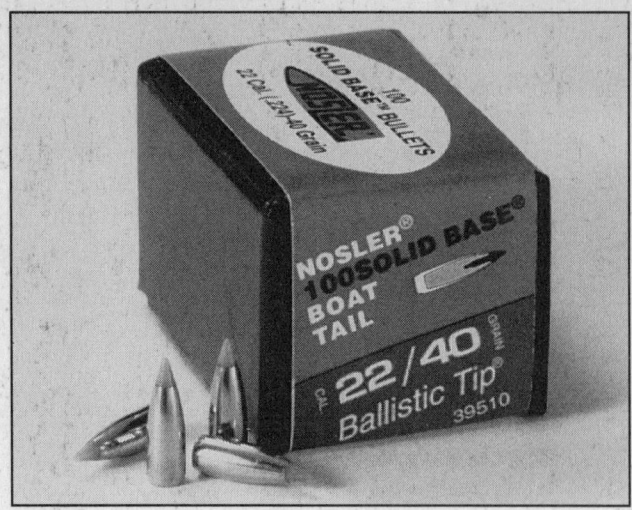

Nosler's newest Ballistic Tip bullet has proven itself on many hundreds of prairie dogs. It is a 40-grain 22-caliber.

the Baton. And how about a 12-gauge demolition load for knocking out door locks or what have you. Frangible light-bullet loads for the 38 Special and 9mm Luger use a plastic/metallic bullet. These loads are truly 100-percent lead-free. Interesting.

Hansen Cartridge Co.

Hansen has been supplying affordable ammo to shooters for a long time. In the past, much of their ammo was imported from Yugoslavia. The current political climate in that part of the world has brought an end to that relationship. Currently, all of Hansen's ammo is being imported from IMI (Israel), and I suspect this will mean an upgrade in performance. New Hansen/IMI handgun rounds include 125-grain JHP 38 Special, 158-grain JHP 357 Magnum, 180-grain FMC and JHP 40 S&W, 240-grain JHP 44 Remington Magnum, and 185-grain SWCFMC Match 45 ACP. New rifle loads are 308 Winchester in 125 and 165 grains, and 165-grain 30-06, softpoints all.

Hodgdon

For about three years now, all of Hodgdon's extruded propellants have been imported from ADI (Australian Defense Industries). Such powders are no longer of Scottish origin. I suspect this is no surprise as, unlike some other imports, Hodgdon powders are clearly marked to identify the country of origin. With the move to Australian manufacture has

come a beneficial change—short-cut propellants.

If you have used H-4831 of older manufacture, you may have found it excellent in every way except the uniformity of charges metered through a powder measure. Grains of the new short-cut H-4831 have the same diameter as the older type, but are only two-thirds as long. This length allows the powder to meter more uniformly. According to Bob Hodgdon, the new powder maintains the same ballistics as the older one and can be loaded with identical charges. Nice!

Hornady

There are a lot of new items for 1994 from this Nebraska manufacturer. Their 50-caliber BMG A-MAX (Advanced Match Accuracy) 750-grain bullet could be a real money saver to those with long-range 50-caliber guns like the AAO Model 2000. At about $1.15 per bullet, they are affordable. The bullet is designed solely for long-range accuracy and flat trajectory for 1000-yard shooting. It is a boattail type with a specially designed nose insert which should prove a lot easier on barrel life than many of the bullets commonly used. When one considers the cost of some of the 50-caliber guns, long barrel life is not something to be ignored.

Hornady is also now loading ammo for the many 9mm Makarov pistols being brought into the country. This ammo is loaded with a .365-inch XTP bullet of 95 grains. It is one of the best loads available for this cartridge. Owners of the German and Russian handguns so chambered will find the $10.85 per twenty-five rounds for this expanding bullet ammo a rather fair price.

Other new Hornady ammo includes the following loads: 7mm Weatherby with 154-grain softpoints, 300 Winchester Magnum with 150-grain boat-tail softpoints, and 44 Special with 180-grain XTP bullets. A new bullet board is also being offered for $165.

Sabots in 45-, 50-, 54- and 58-caliber are new items. These allow the muzzle-loading shooter to use various handgun bullets in the search for accuracy.

Of special interest are new loads which are being called "Light Magnum." These are standard cartridges loaded to noticeably higher velocities without any increase over standard chamber pressures. The first of these is a 150-grain 30-06 which delivers 30-caliber magnum velocities, or a gain of about 300 fps. Such an increase will have a real effect on flattening trajectories and adding a substantial increase in effective range. The second of the new light magnum loads is a 308 Winchester, also with a 150-grain bullet. This load delivers 30-06-like speeds. This type of loading is being accomplished, according to Hornady, by using non-canister-grade propellants. Pricing will be about fifty percent higher than standard Hornady ammunition. This certainly will be seen as an enhancement of specific cartridge capability by many shooters.

"Vector" is the name for another new style of ammo being offered by Hornady. As stated by the Grand Island folks, these light-emitting rounds might well be loosely called tracers and will first be available in 9mm Luger (115 grains), 40 S&W (180 grains), and 45 ACP (200 grains).

As normally understood, tracer rounds incorporate a

comparatively large amount of pyrotechnic material placed into the base of the bullet. This burns from the back end inward toward the bullet base. The Hornady bullet uses a rather minuscule amount of pyrotechnic material placed along the axis of the bullet. By keeping the necessary cavity small and centrally located, accuracy is not noticeably affected. Hornady says the carefully controlled pressures of the load are necessary to get the chemical compound to ignite and burn from the inside out. Because chamber pressures are critical to ignition, this bullet type will not be offered as a component. All Vector ammo will necessarily use full metal jacket bullets. This ammo is said to have specific applications for training new or poor shooters. It will allow errors in aiming (or pointing) to be discernible as each round is fired. Said to be at least 90-percent effective, the ammo will be priced at about one-and-a-half times the cost of similar but non-light-emitting loads.

Midway

Midway is a reloader's dream come true. They have uncountable items in stock at very competitive prepaid shipping prices. New in their monthly catalog are a line of extra-hard (92-6-2)

Solid copper slugs are now available in 12-gauge 3-inch and 20-gauge 2³/₄-inch lengths from Remington.

cast bullets. The various weights and profiles are in 32, 9mm, 38, 40, 41, 44 and 45 calibers. They are packed in 500- or 1000-count boxes.

Special personalized head-stamp brass handgun cases are available. Also they have a Jordan headstamp on 357 Magnum, Keith on 44 Magnum and Cooper on 45 ACP. A percentage of each sale on the "famous" headstamps goes to the NRA's ILA fund.

Those who prefer nickel-plated rifle cases will find that Midway has these in stock in almost every imaginable caliber. And loaded ammo, too, now.

Norma

In the recent past, to be a Norma powder user you had to know that it was exactly what you needed. Otherwise, its price made it a "designer" powder. A few years ago, Terry Paul (Paul Co.) took over the importation of all Norma products. Now, he has effected something almost unheard of: a reduction of the retail price of Norma propellants from about $33 to about $23 per can. In that there are

Going along with the trend to rid lead from ranges is Winchester's Super Unleaded handgun ammo. No exposed bullet lead and no lead in the primer—a wave from the future?

about 1¹⁄₈ pounds in a can, this brings the effective per pound cost to about $20. This is only a few dollars more than the retail price of some of the popular powders.

I'll bet a lot of the newer reloaders will now want a first-hand look at some of the special features of Norma propellants. Magnum rifle users may want a firsthand experience with MRP, and '06-size users will be looking hard at N-204. Also, many of the older reloaders will find that Norma powders are once again affordable.

Norma brass cases are now available in the 30 American, a benchrest redo of the 30-30 case with a small rifle primer pocket. Also, according to Terry Paul, Norma cases are now universally made of a very hard "watch-brass" alloy. For example, all

magnum calibers and the PPCs have a shoulder hardness of 80 Rockwell B reading and a head reading of 95. This should eliminate comments about "soft" cases. Because of the increased hardness of the PPC cases, Norma has been able to increase case capacity by about 1¹⁄₂ grains. This should please many benchrest and varmint shooters.

Norma will now be offering new "low drag" bullets in 6.5mm diameter; 30-caliber and then 7mm bullets will follow. There is some marketing consideration being given to returning Norma shotgun propellants to the U.S. market. Still, some Norma stuff is hard to get, as my unproductive

efforts to find some Norma 416 Rigby cases shows. (Terry Paul will also now be the exclusive importer for J.P. Sauer and Varberger firearms.)

Nosler

Nosler has, as I forecast, dropped their standard Solid Base bullets. They will continue to manufacture their premium-grade Partition hunting bullets and the very high ballistic coefficient Ballistic Tip numbers. Their marketing folks must believe that premium hunting bullets are Nosler's bag, so why compete in the popular priced bullet market?

New to the Ballistic Tip line is a 40-grain 22-caliber spitzer. These shot very well in a prairie dog field test. They were fired side by side with the super-accurate 55-grain bullet of the same type, and the field performance out to 200 yards was right on par with the heavier bullet. Superb! Among all the shooters, bunches and bunches of prairie dogs were cleanly done-in. There were no

complaints from any of the shooters or critters.

During the past year, I did manage to whack another few dozen big game critters with Nosler Partitions. All went as expected, and each was a one-shot kill, from tiny grysbok (20 pounds) to waterbuck (500 pounds) and kudu (580 pounds). Those bullets recovered averaged 65-percent weight retention. The Partition is premium priced, but still affordable for almost all hunters. Accuracy, shooter and rifle so capable, is usually minute-of-angle or less.

About half of Nosler's handgun bullets are now available only in a bulk 250-bullet pack. I bet that eventually all their handgun bullets will be so packed. And a new handgun bullet has been designed specifically for IPSC shooting. It is a 135-grain, non-cannelured .357-inch diameter bullet meant for the 38 Super. Just a tad of lead shows at the front end of the truncated cone nose. As expected, it is packed in a 250-bullet bulk pack. Should be ideal for "killing" steel.

Remington

A lot of this year's "new" from Remington is in the firearms area and is covered elsewhere in this book. Still, there are a few new items in the ammo line. There have been substantial design improvements in Golden Sabre handgun bullets, intended to enhance mushroom characteristics at lower velocities. Also, three new loads have been added to this high-perfor-

mance ammo, namely 124-grain 9mm, 165-grain 40 S&W, and 185-grain 45 ACP.

Remington has decided to add the 7x64mm Brenneke to their ammo offerings. Bullet weights are 140 and 175 grains. Also, there will be 6.5x55 Swedish Mauser ammo with a 140-grain Core Lokt bullet. And there's a 160-grain Swift A-Frame bullet in a 7mm Remington Magnum load.

Steel shotshell target loads are now a standard offering. More than a few ranges now insist on the use of non-toxic shot, and I would not be surprised to see steel pellets become mandatory in a great many areas. Both 12- and 20-gauge loadings are available. Twelve-gauge loads have 1¹⁄₈ ounces of #6¹⁄₂, #7 or #8 shot sizes. Twenty-gauge loads use ⁷⁄₈-ounce of #8 shot.

Sierra Bullets

There are seven new Sierra bullets for 1994, the first two for the 9mm Makarov. Others offer .364- to .365-inch bullets for this cartridge, but Sierra has opted for the .363-inch diameter. Reloaders will get to decide which diameter best fits their individual handguns. Sierra is building both a 95-grain hollow-point and a 100-grain solid.

A 300-grain .451-inch soft-point has been designed, so says Sierra, with the 45 Colt and 454 Casull in mind. This is a heavy-jacket, hard-core bullet. There is also a .356-inch diameter 150-grain target bullet for IPSC/USPSA competition.

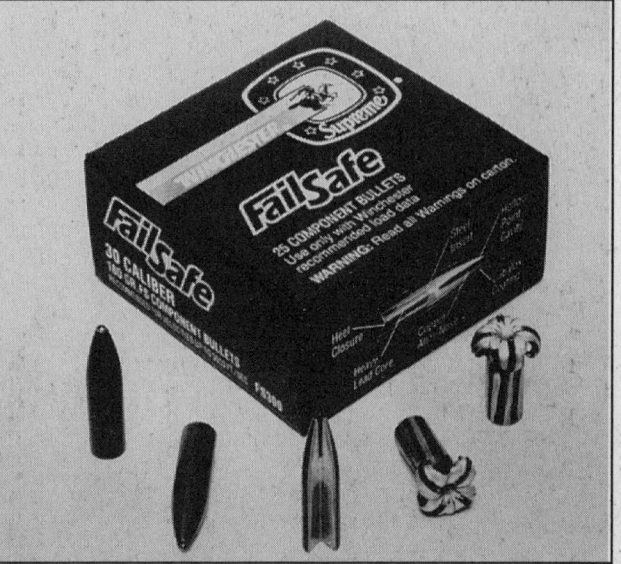

Winchester's new FailSafe bullets are being offered as components in a limited number of styles. Thirty-caliber ones have been accuracy tested successfully.

A Blitz varmint bullet is now available for 243 and weighs 80 grains. Explosive expansion is claimed for this one, which should make it ideal for long-range applications. A true match-grade bullet is now available in .277-inch diameter. It is 135 grains and of a boattail hollowpoint configuration. Methinks 27-caliber fans now may be on even footing with the 30-caliber target shooters. The new 215-grain .338-inch spitzer boattail bullet should please some shooters who would like to avoid the heavier recoil of Sierra's 250-grain 338 bullet.

Swift Bullet Co.

This outfit makes what may be the perfect hunting bullet. Accuracy is great, weight retention is phenomenal (90 to 95 percent), and expansion is at least double diameter. They will begin to expand on even very small big game, yet plow deep into the likes of even a 4000-pound hippo. I have taken both ends of this spectrum with Swift A-Frame bullets. They cost more than most premium bullets, but are well worth it.

Up to now, A-Frames were available only in 30-caliber or larger diameters. But Swift now makes .284-inch bullets of 140, 160 and 175 grains. I have loaded the two heavier weights in a 280 Remington, as well as a cartridge of my own design. These have accounted for a handful of game, and in one case again proved that Swift bullets can make any cartridge a lot more potent than might otherwise be expected. I killed game as small as 140-pound whitetail and bushbuck, as well as some critters too big to brag about. These new bonded dual-core bullets are about $1 each.

3-D Ammo and Bullets

3-D has completed a large internal expansion effort—more space, more machines, and more quality-assurance testing. This should make it possible for them to keep up with the demand for their remanufactured handgun ammo (3-D Brand) and their new ammo (Impact Brand).

Newly introduced rounds using all new components include 380 Auto, 100-grain JHP; 357 Magnum, 140-grain JHP; 44 Magnum, 240-grain JHP; and 45 Auto, 185-grain JHP. They also offer a large number of "lead-free" loads in 380 Auto, 38 Special, 357 Magnum, 9mm Luger, 40 S&W, 10mm Auto and 45 ACP.

Winchester

Winchester has introduced four handgun loadings that are referred to as "Super Unleaded." These are a 130-grain 38 Special, 115-grain 9mm Luger, 180-grain 40 S&W, and a bit down the road a 260-grain 45 Winchester Magnum load. These all feature a bullet that is fully metal cased. No exposed lead—none!

Further, the primer is a lead-free component as well. I long ago gave up shooting on indoor ranges, but ammo such as this Super Unleaded effort could make me change my mind. Of course, many indoor ranges do not allow the use of jacketed bullets, so we'll have to see how it works out.

There is soon to be a 45 Winchester Magnum round loaded with a 260-grain soft-point. This load has the possibility of supplying more punch than any 44 Magnum hunting load. Time will tell.

Winchester has announced a new 6.5x55 Swedish loading, a 140-grain softpoint. No down-range ballistics yet, as the load was still under development at this writing. Winchester also says there will be 270 Win-

Winchester has announced another new Ball Powder—WMR or Winchester Magnum Rifle—perhaps to replace the discontinued 785.

chester and 7mm Remington Magnum loads using FailSafe Black Talon bullets. Not even potential bullet weights were being published when this was put together.

There is a new Double A light international target load using 24 grams of shot at 1325 fps. Also new is another run of 22 WRF rimfire ammo. Wonder if most of this stuff gets shot up in old WRF rifles or in newer 22 Magnum rifles as a light load?

The same bullets as used in the factory-loaded FailSafe Black Talon rifle ammo loads are now being offered to reloaders. These are a premium-style bullet constructed with a solid copper alloy front section and a base section that has a lead core. These have a unique black coating which helps control the excess fouling associated with copper alloy bullets. I did try about 100 of these on group tests, and they appeared as good as many competitive bullets with respect to accuracy.

There are two 30-caliber FailSafe bullets, both of 180 grains. One is intended for 30-06 velocities (under 2700 fps), the other for 300 Magnum speeds. Methinks this is silly because if the magnum bullets will work at extended ranges, would they not also be suitable for closer ranges with the 30-06? There is also a 230-grain 33-caliber bullet. This one appears to optimize trajectory in the 338 Winchester Magnum.

VihtaVuori Oy

This Finnish manufacturer sells powder through Kaltron-Pettibone of Bensenville, Illinois, their U.S. importer. Their line of rifle and handgun powders has been expanded to include shotshell speeds N3SL, N3SM, and N3SH. Though data is not in the VO manual, they can supply data sheets free for the asking. (See New Data Sources which follows).

The new shotshell powders are not unlike the old Alcan propellants, in that, they are of a extruded ribbon geometry. At least one major American ammunition company is using this powder in their best target loads.

New Data Sources

Speer has announced they are publishing their Number 12 reloading manual. No copies were available at this writing, but it is sure to prove a must for Speer bullet users. Loads for

fifty-five bullets not included in the 1987 Number 11 manual are reported to be part of the new effort.

Lyman has two new publications. One is exclusively directed toward handgun cartridge reloaders. Calibers not found in the massive 47th reloading manual are included here, i.e. 9x18mm Makarov, 9x21mm, 41 Action Express, 454 Casull and 50 Action Express. This new 2nd Edition, Pistol And Revolver Handbook also includes a great deal of how-to information.

The second new Lyman book is *Big Game Cartridges & Rifles*. Lots of ballistics here—including an in-depth look at "Optimum Game Weight" ballistic tables. It would be hard to find a more detailed review of big game cartridges from 24- to 50-caliber. Included are detailed cartridge drawings of each cartridge and lots of good photos spread over 288 pages. Practical interpretations of actual field performance are also covered by the author, who has been lucky enough to take hundreds of head of dozens of species of big game. Lots of gun and sight info too. Quite a bargain at less than eighteen bucks. How do I know? I wrote it!

VihtaVuori Oy has a redo of their original European flavor data listing. Twenty-six pages of loading data for all of their new imports, as well as some truly interesting stuff on internal ballistics. Calibers covered are, of course, all of the popular ones as well as some difficult to find loads for metrics like 220 Russian, 5.6x50mm Magnum, 5.6x57mm, a ton of 6.5x55 Swedish data, 6.5x57mm, 6.5x68mm, 7x33mm Sako, etc. It is free at your VihtaVuori Oy powder outlet or from the importer.

Hercules is offering a free supplemental flyer on Sporting Clay loads, as well as the new Federal 209A primer. It is available from Hercules powder outlets. Some new high-velocity target loads are included for 7/8- and 1-ounce 12-gauge undertakings.

If you do not have the 13th edition of the Winchester Ball powder data booklet, you may be missing out on some really new loads. There is lots of data for the new WST, WSL and WSF shotshell powders. Also, handgun data has been extended to include many shotshell powders in 38 Super, 38 Special, 9mm Luger, 40 S&W and so on. ●

Caliber	Bullet weight grains	Muzzle	VELOCITY (fps) 100 yds.	200 yds.	300 yds.	400. yds.	Muzzle	ENERGY (ft. lbs.) 100 yds.	200 yds.	300 yds.	400 yds.	TRAJ. (in.) 100 yds.	200 yds.	300 yds.	400 yds.	Approx. Price per box
17																
17 Remington	25	4040	3284	2644	2086	1606	906	599	388	242	143	+2.0	+1.7	-4.0	-17.0	$17
22																
221 Fireball	50	2800	2137	1580	1180	988	870	507	277	155	109	0.0	-7.0	-28.0	NA	$14
22 Hornet	45	2690	2042	1502	1128	948	723	417	225	127	90	0.0	-7.7	-31.0	NA	$27**
218 Bee	46	2760	2102	1550	1155	961	788	451	245	136	94	0.0	-7.2	-29.0	NA	$46**
222 Remington	50	3140	2602	2123	1700	1350	1094	752	500	321	202	+2.0	-0.4	-11.0	-33.0	$11
222 Remington	55	3020	2562	2147	1773	1451	1114	801	563	384	257	+2.0	-0.4	-11.0	-33.0	$12
22 PPC	52	3400	2930	2510	2130	NA	1335	990	730	525	NA	+2.0	1.4	-5.0	NA	NA
223 Remington	40	3650	3010	2450	1950	1530	1185	805	535	340	265	+2.0	+1.0	-6.0	-22.0	$14
223 Remington	52/53	3330	2882	2477	2106	1770	1305	978	722	522	369	+2.0	+0.6	-6.5	-21.5	$14
223 Remington	55	3240	2748	2305	1906	1556	1282	922	649	444	296	+2.0	-0.2	-9.0	-27.0	$12
223 Remington	60	3100	2712	2355	2026	1726	1280	979	739	547	397	+2.0	+0.2	-8.0	-24.7	$16
223 Remington	64	3020	2621	2256	1920	1619	1296	977	723	524	373	+2.0	-0.2	-9.3	-23.0	$14
223 Remington	69	3000	2720	2460	2210	1980	1380	1135	925	750	600	+2.0	+0.8	-5.8	-17.5	$15
222 Rem. Mag.	55	3240	2748	2305	1906	1556	1282	922	649	444	296	+2.0	-0.2	-9.0	-27.0	$14
225 Winchester	55	3570	3066	2616	2208	1838	1556	1148	836	595	412	+2.0	+1.0	-5.0	-20.0	$19
224 Wea. Mag.	55	3650	3192	2780	2403	2057	1627	1244	943	705	516	+2.0	+1.2	-4.0	-17.0	$32
22-250 Rem.	40	4000	3320	2720	2200	1740	1420	980	660	430	265	+2.0	+1.8	-3.0	-16.0	$14
22-250 Rem.	52/55	3680	3137	2656	2222	1832	1654	1201	861	603	410	+2.0	+1.3	-4.0	-17.0	$13
22-250 Rem.	60	3600	3195	2826	2485	2169	1727	1360	1064	823	627	+2.0	+2.0	-2.4	-12.3	$19
220 Swift	50	3780	3158	2617	2135	1710	1586	1107	760	506	325	+2.0	+1.4	-4.4	-17.9	$20
220 Swift	55	3650	3194	2772	2384	2035	1627	1246	939	694	506	+2.0	+2.0	-2.6	-13.4	$19
220 Swift	60	3600	3199	2824	2475	2156	1727	1364	1063	816	619	+2.0	+1.6	-4.1	-13.1	$19
22 Savage H.P	71	2790	2340	1930	1570	1280	1225	860	585	390	190	+2.0	-1.0	-10.4	-35.7	NA
6mm (24)																
6mm BR Rem.	100	2550	2310	2083	1870	1671	1444	1185	963	776	620	+2.5	-0.6	-11.8	NA	$22
6mm PPC	70	3140	2750	2400	2070	NA	1535	1175	895	665	NA	+2.0	+1.4	-5.0	NA	NA
243 Winchester	60	3600	3110	2660	2260	1890	1725	1285	945	680	475	+2.0	+1.8	-3.3	-15.5	$17
243 Winchester	75/80	3350	2955	2593	2259	1951	1993	1551	1194	906	676	+2.0	+0.9	-5.0	-19.0	$16
243 Winchester	85	3320	3070	2830	2600	2380	2080	1770	1510	1280	1070	+2.0	+1.2	-4.0	-14.0	$18
243 Winchester*	100	2960	2697	2449	2215	1993	1945	1615	1332	1089	882	+2.5	+1.2	-6.0	-20.0	$16
243 Winchester	105	2920	2689	2470	2261	2062	1988	1686	1422	1192	992	+2.5	+1.6	-5.0	-18.4	$21
6mm Remington	80	3470	3064	2694	2352	2036	2139	1667	1289	982	736	+2.0	+1.1	-5.0	-17.0	$16
6mm Remington*	100	3100	2829	2573	2332	2104	2133	1777	1470	1207	983	+2.5	+1.6	-5.0	-17.0	$16
6mm Remington	105	3060	2822	2596	2381	2177	2105	1788	1512	1270	1059	+2.5	+1.1	-3.3	-15.0	$21
240 Wea. Mag.	87	3500	3202	2924	2663	2416	2366	1980	1651	1370	1127	+2.0	+2.0	-2.0	-12.0	$32
240 Wea. Mag.*	100	3395	3106	2835	2581	2339	2559	2142	1785	1478	1215	+2.5	+2.8	-2.0	-11.0	$43
25																
25-20 Win.	86	1460	1194	1030	931	858	407	272	203	165	141	0.0	-23.5	NA	NA	$32**
25-35 Win.	117	2230	1866	1545	1282	1097	1292	904	620	427	313	+2.5	-4.2	-26.0	NA	$24
250 Savage	100	2820	2504	2210	1936	1684	1765	1392	1084	832	630	+2.5	+0.4	-9.0	-28.0	$17
257 Roberts	100	2980	2661	2363	2085	1827	1972	1572	1240	965	741	+2.5	-0.8	-5.2	-21.6	$20
257 Roberts+P	117	2780	2411	2071	1761	1488	2009	1511	1115	806	576	+2.5	-0.2	-10.2	-32.6	$18
257 Roberts+P*	120	2780	2560	2360	2160	1970	2060	1750	1480	1240	1030	+2.5	+1.2	-6.4	-23.6	$22
257 Roberts	122	2600	2331	2078	1842	1625	1831	1472	1169	919	715	+2.5	0.0	-10.6	-31.4	$21
25-06 Rem.	87	3440	2995	2591	2222	1884	2286	1733	1297	954	686	+2.0	+1.1	-2.5	-14.4	$17
25-06 Rem.	90	3440	3043	2680	2344	2034	2364	1850	1435	1098	827	+2.0	+1.8	-3.3	-15.6	$17
25-06 Rem.	100	3230	2893	2580	2287	2014	2316	1858	1478	1161	901	+2.0	+0.8	-5.7	-18.9	$17
25-06 Rem.	117	2990	2770	2570	2370	2190	2320	2000	1715	1465	1246	+2.5	+1.0	-7.9	-26.6	$19
25-06 Rem.*	120	2990	2730	2484	2252	2032	2382	1985	1644	1351	1100	+2.5	+1.2	-5.3	-19.6	$17
25-06 Rem.	122	2930	2706	2492	2289	2095	2325	1983	1683	1419	1189	+2.5	+1.8	-4.5	-17.5	$23
257 Wea. Mag.	87	3825	3456	3118	2805	2513	2826	2308	1870	1520	1220	+2.0	+2.7	-0.3	-7.6	$32
257 Wea. Mag.	100	3555	3237	2941	2665	2404	2806	2326	1920	1576	1283	+2.5	+3.2	0.0	-8.0	$32
6.5																
6.5x50mm Jap.	139	2360	2160	1970	1790	1620	1720	1440	1195	985	810	+2.5	-1.0	-13.5	NA	NA
6.5x50mm Jap.	156	2070	1830	1610	1430	1260	1475	1155	900	695	550	+2.5	-4.0	-23.8	NA	NA
6.5x52mm Car.	139	2580	2360	2160	1970	1790	2045	1725	1440	1195	985	+2.5	0.0	-9.9	-29.0	NA
6.5x52mm Car.	156	2430	2170	1930	1700	1500	2045	1630	1285	1005	780	+2.5	-1.0	-13.9	NA	NA
6.5x55mm Swe.	140	2550	NA	NA	NA	NA	2020	NA	NA	NA	NA	NA	NA	NA	NA	$18
6.5x55mm Swe.*	139/140	2850	2640	2440	2250	2070	2525	2170	1855	1575	1330	+2.5	+1.6	-5.4	-18.9	$18
6.5x55mm Swe.	156	2650	2370	2110	1870	1650	2425	1950	1550	1215	945	+2.5	0.0	-10.3	-30.6	NA
6.5 Rem. Mag.	120	3210	2905	2621	2353	2102	2745	2248	1830	1475	1177	+2.5	+1.7	-4.1	-16.3	Disc.
264 Win. Mag.	140	3030	2782	2548	2326	2114	2854	2406	2018	1682	1389	+2.5	+1.4	-5.1	-18.0	$24

CAUTION: PRICES SHOWN ARE SUPPLIED BY THE MANUFACTURER OR IMPORTER. CHECK YOUR LOCAL GUNSHOP.

Caliber	Bullet weight grains	VELOCITY (fps) Muzzle	100 yds.	200 yds.	300 yds.	400. yds.	ENERGY (ft. lbs.) Muzzle	100 yds.	200 yds.	300 yds.	400 yds.	TRAJ. (in.) 100 yds.	200 yds.	300 yds.	400 yds.	Approx. Price per box
27 270 Winchester	100	3430	3021	2649	2305	1988	2612	2027	1557	1179	877	+2.0	+1.0	-4.9	-17.5	$17
270 Winchester	130	3060	2776	2510	2259	2022	2702	2225	1818	1472	1180	+2.5	+1.4	-5.3	-18.2	$17
270 Winchester	135	3000	2780	2570	2369	2178	2697	2315	1979	1682	1421	+2.5	+1.4	-6.0	-17.6	$23
270 Winchester*	140	2940	2700	2480	2260	2060	2685	2270	1905	1590	1315	+2.5	+1.8	-4.6	-17.9	$20
270 Winchester*	150	2850	2585	2336	2100	1879	2705	2226	1817	1468	1175	+2.5	+1.2	-6.5	-22.0	$17
270 Wea. Mag.	100	3760	3380	3033	2712	2412	3139	2537	2042	1633	1292	+2.0	+2.4	-1.2	-10.1	$32
270 Wea. Mag.	130	3375	3119	2878	2649	2432	3287	2808	2390	2026	1707	+2.5	+2.9	-0.9	-9.9	$32
270 Wea. Mag.*	150	3245	3036	2837	2647	2465	3507	3070	2681	2334	2023	+2.5	+2.6	-1.8	-11.4	$47
7mm 7mm BR	140	2215	2012	1821	1643	1481	1525	1259	1031	839	681	+2.0	-3.7	-20.0	NA	$23
7mm Mauser*	139/140	2660	2435	2221	2018	1827	2199	1843	1533	1266	1037	+2.5	0.0	-9.6	-27.7	$17
7mm Mauser	145	2690	2442	2206	1985	1777	2334	1920	1568	1268	1017	+2.5	+0.1	-9.6	-28.3	$18
7mm Mauser	154	2690	2490	2300	2120	1940	2475	2120	1810	1530	1285	+2.5	+0.8	-7.5	-23.5	$17
7mm Mauser	175	2440	2137	1857	1603	1382	2313	1774	1340	998	742	+2.5	-1.7	-16.1	NA	$17
7x30 Waters	120	2700	2300	1930	1600	1330	1940	1405	990	685	470	+2.5	-0.2	-12.3	NA	$18
7mm-08 Rem.	120	3000	2725	2467	2223	1992	2398	1979	1621	1316	1058	+2.0	0.0	-7.6	-22.3	$18
7mm-08 Rem.*	140	2860	2625	2402	2189	1988	2542	2142	1793	1490	1228	+2.5	+0.8	-6.9	-21.9	$18
7mm-08 Rem.	154	2715	2510	2315	2128	1950	2520	2155	1832	1548	1300	+2.5	+1.0	-7.0	-22.7	$23
7x64mm Bren.	140	Not Yet announced														$17
7x64mm Bren.	154	2820	2610	2420	2230	2050	2720	2335	1995	1695	1430	+2.5	+1.4	-5.7	-19.9	NA
7x64mm Bren.*	160	2850	2669	2495	2327	2166	2885	2530	2211	1924	1667	+2.5	+1.6	-4.8	-17.8	$24
7x64mm Bren.	175	Not yet announced														$17
284 Winchester	150	2860	2595	2344	2108	1886	2724	2243	1830	1480	1185	+2.5	+0.8	-7.3	-23.2	$24
280 Remington	120	3150	2866	2599	2348	2110	2643	2188	1800	1468	1186	+2.0	+0.6	-6.0	-17.9	$17
280 Remington	140	3000	2758	2528	2309	2102	2797	2363	1986	1657	1373	+2.5	+1.4	-5.2	-18.3	$17
280 Remington*	150	2890	2624	2373	2135	1912	2781	2293	1875	1518	1217	+2.5	+0.8	-7.1	-22.6	$17
280 Remington	160	2840	2637	2442	2556	2078	2866	2471	2120	1809	1535	+2.5	+0.8	-6.7	-21.0	$20
280 Remington	165	2820	2510	2220	1950	1701	2913	2308	1805	1393	1060	+2.5	+0.4	-8.8	-26.5	$17
7x61mm S&H Sup.	154	3060	2720	2400	2100	1820	3200	2520	1965	1505	1135	+2.5	+1.8	-5.0	-19.8	NA
7mm Rem. Mag.*	139/140	3150	2930	2710	2510	2320	3085	2660	2290	1960	1670	+2.5	+2.4	-2.4	-12.7	$21
7mm Rem. Mag.	150/154	3110	2830	2085	2320	2085	3221	2667	2196	1792	1448	+2.5	+1.6	-4.6	-16.5	$21
7mm Rem. Mag.*	160/162	2950	2730	2520	2320	2120	3090	2650	2250	1910	1600	+2.5	+1.8	-4.4	-17.8	$34
7mm Rem. Mag.	165	2900	2699	2507	2324	2147	3081	2669	2303	1978	1689	+2.5	+1.2	-5.9	-19.0	$28
7mm Rem. Mag.	175	2860	2645	2440	2244	2057	3178	2718	2313	1956	1644	+2.5	+1.0	-6.5	-20.7	$21
7mm Wea. Mag.	140	3225	2970	2729	2501	2283	3233	2741	2315	1943	1621	+2.5	+2.0	-3.2	-14.0	$35
7mm Wea. Mag.	154	3260	3023	2799	2586	2382	3539	3044	2609	2227	1890	+2.5	+2.8	-1.5	-10.8	$32
7mm Wea. Mag.*	160	3200	3004	2816	2637	2464	3637	3205	2817	2469	2156	+2.5	+2.7	-1.5	-10.6	$47
7mm Wea. Mag.	165	2950	2747	2553	2367	2189	3188	2765	2388	2053	1756	+2.5	+1.8	-4.2	-16.4	$43
7mm Wea. Mag.	175	2910	2693	2486	2288	2098	3293	2818	2401	2033	1711	+2.5	+1.2	-5.9	-19.4	$35
30 30 Carbine	110	1990	1567	1236	1035	923	977	600	373	262	208	0.0	-13.5	NA	NA	$28**
303 Savage	190	1890	1612	1372	1183	1055	1507	1096	794	591	469	+2.5	-7.6	NA	NA	$24
30 Remington	170	2120	1822	1555	1328	1153	1696	1253	913	666	502	+2.5	-4.7	-26.3	NA	$20
30-30 Win.	55	3400	2693	2085	1570	1187	1412	886	521	301	172	+2.0	0.0	-10.2	-35.0	$18
30-30 Win.	125	2570	2090	1660	1320	1080	1830	1210	770	480	320	+2.0	-2.6	-19.9	NA	$13
30-30 Win.	150	2390	1973	1605	1303	1095	1902	1296	858	565	399	+2.5	-3.2	-22.5	NA	$13
30-30 Win.	160	2300	1997	1719	1473	1268	1879	1416	1050	771	571	+2.5	-2.9	-20.2	NA	$18
30-30 Win.*	170	2200	1895	1619	1381	1191	1827	1355	989	720	535	+2.5	-5.8	-23.6	NA	$13
300 Savage	150	2630	2354	2094	1853	1631	2303	1845	1462	1143	886	+2.5	-0.4	-10.1	-30.7	$17
300 Savage	180	2350	2137	1935	1754	1570	2207	1825	1496	1217	985	+2.5	-1.6	-15.2	NA	$17
30-40 Krag	180	2430	2213	2007	1813	1632	2360	1957	1610	1314	1064	+2.5	-1.4	-13.8	NA	$18
7.65x53mm Arg.	180	2590	2390	2200	2010	1830	2685	2280	1925	1615	1345	+2.5	0.0	-27.6	NA	NA
307 Winchester	150	2760	2321	1924	1575	1289	2530	1795	1233	826	554	+2.5	-1.5	-13.6	NA	Disc.
307 Winchester	180	2510	2179	1874	1599	1362	2519	1898	1404	1022	742	+2.5	-1.6	-15.6	NA	$20
7.5x55 Swiss	180	2650	2450	2250	2060	1880	2805	2390	2020	1700	1415	+2.5	+0.6	-8.1	-24.9	NA
308 Winchester	55	3770	3215	2726	2286	1888	1735	1262	907	638	435	+2.0	+1.4	-3.8	-15.8	$22
308 Winchester	150	2820	2533	2263	2009	1774	2648	2137	1705	1344	1048	+2.5	+0.4	-8.5	-26.1	$17
308 Winchester	165	2700	2440	2194	1963	1748	2670	2180	1763	1411	1199	+2.5	0.0	-9.7	-28.5	$20
308 Winchester	168	2680	2493	2314	2143	1979	2678	2318	1998	1713	1460	+2.5	0.0	-8.9	-25.3	$18
308 Winchester	178	2620	2415	2220	2034	1857	2713	2306	1948	1635	1363	+2.5	0.0	-9.6	-27.6	$23
308 Winchester*	180	2620	2393	2178	1974	1782	2743	2288	1896	1557	1269	+2.5	-0.2	-10.2	-28.5	$17
308 Light Mag.*	150	2900	NA	NA	NA	NA	NA	NA	NA	NA	NA	NA	NA	NA	NA	NEW
30-06 Spfd.	55	4080	3485	2965	2502	2083	2033	1483	1074	764	530	+2.0	+1.9	-2.1	-11.7	$22
30-06 Spfd.	125	3140	2780	2447	2138	1853	2736	2145	1662	1279	953	+2.0	+1.0	-6.2	-21.0	$17
30-06 Spfd.	150	2910	2617	2342	2083	1853	2820	2281	1827	1445	1135	+2.5	+0.8	-7.2	-23.4	$17

CAUTION: PRICES SHOWN ARE SUPPLIED BY THE MANUFACTURER OR IMPORTER. CHECK YOUR LOCAL GUNSHOP.

AVERAGE CENTERFIRE RIFLE CARTRIDGE BALLISTICS AND PRICES (cont.)

Caliber	Bullet weight grains	VELOCITY (fps) Muzzle	100 yds.	200 yds.	300 yds.	400 yds.	ENERGY (ft. lbs.) Muzzle	100 yds.	200 yds.	300 yds.	400 yds.	TRAJ. (in.) 100 yds.	200 yds.	300 yds.	400 yds.	Approx. Price per box
30 (cont.) 30-06 Spfd.	152	2910	2654	2413	2184	1968	2858	2378	1965	1610	1307	+2.5	+1.0	-6.6	-21.3	$23
30-06 Spfd.*	165	2800	2534	2283	2047	1825	2872	2352	1909	1534	1220	+2.5	+0.4	-8.4	-25.5	$17
30-06 Spfd.	168	2710	2522	2346	2169	2003	2739	2372	2045	1754	1497	+2.5	+0.4	-8.0	-23.5	$18
30-06 Spfd.	178	2720	2511	2311	2121	1939	2924	2491	2111	1777	1486	+2.5	+0.4	-8.2	-24.6	$23
30-06 Spfd.*	180	2700	2469	2250	2042	1846	2913	2436	2023	1666	1362	+2.5	0.0	-9.3	-27.0	$17
30-06 Spfd.	220	2410	2130	1870	1632	1422	2837	2216	1708	1301	988	+2.5	-1.7	-16.0	NA	$17
30 Mag 30-06 Light Mag.	150	3000	NA	NA	NA	NA	NA	NA	NA	NA	NA	NA	NA	NA	NA	NEW
308 Norma Mag.	180	3020	2820	2630	2440	2270	3645	3175	2755	2385	2050	+2.5	+2.0	-3.5	-14.8	NA
300 H&H Magnum*	180	2880	2640	2412	2196	1990	3315	2785	2325	1927	1583	+2.5	+0.8	-6.8	-21.7	$24
300 H&H Magnum	220	2550	2267	2002	1757	NA	3167	2510	1958	1508	NA	+2.5	-0.4	-12.0	NA	NA
300 Win. Mag.	150	3290	2951	2636	2342	2068	3605	2900	2314	1827	1424	+2.5	+1.9	-3.8	-15.8	$22
300 Win. Mag.	165	3100	2877	2665	2462	2269	3522	3033	2603	2221	1897	+2.5	+2.4	-3.0	-16.9	$24
300 Win. Mag.	178	2980	2769	2568	2375	2191	3509	3030	2606	2230	1897	+2.5	+1.4	-5.0	-17.6	$29
300 Win. Mag.*	180	2960	2745	2540	2344	2157	3501	3011	2578	2196	1859	+2.5	+1.2	-5.5	-18.5	$22
300 Win. Mag.	190	2885	2691	2506	2327	2156	3511	3055	2648	2285	1961	+2.5	+1.2	-5.7	-19.0	$26
300 Win. Mag.*	200	2825	2595	2376	2167	1970	3545	2991	2508	2086	1742	+2.5	+1.6	-4.7	-17.2	$36
300 Win. Mag.	220	2680	2448	2228	2020	1823	3508	2927	2424	1993	1623	+2.5	0.0	-9.5	-27.5	$23
300 Wea. Mag.	110	3900	3441	3038	2652	2305	3714	2891	2239	1717	1297	+2.0	+2.6	-0.6	-8.7	$32
300 Wea. Mag.	150	3600	3307	3033	2776	2533	4316	3642	3064	2566	2137	+2.5	+3.2	0.0	-8.1	$32
300 Wea. Mag.	165	3450	3210	3000	2792	2593	4360	3796	3297	2855	2464	+2.5	+3.2	0.0	-7.8	NA
300 Wea. Mag.	178	3120	2902	2695	2497	2308	3847	3329	2870	2464	2104	+2.5	-1.7	-3.6	-14.7	$43
300 Wea. Mag.*	180	3120	2866	2667	2400	2184	3890	3284	2758	2301	1905	+2.5	+1.7	-3.8	-15.0	$35
300 Wea. Mag.	190	3030	2830	2638	2455	2279	3873	3378	2936	2542	2190	+2.5	+1.6	-4.3	-16.0	$38
300 Wea. Mag.	220	2850	2541	2283	1984	1736	3967	3155	2480	1922	1471	+2.5	+0.4	-8.5	-26.4	$35
31 32-20 Win.	100	1210	1021	913	834	769	325	231	185	154	131	0.0	-32.3	NA	NA	$23**
303 British	150	2685	2441	2210	1992	1787	2401	1984	1627	1321	1064	+2.5	+0.6	-8.4	-26.2	$18
303 British	180	2460	2124	1817	1542	1311	2418	1803	1319	950	687	+2.5	-1.8	-16.8	NA	$18
7.62x39mm Rus.	123/125	2300	2030	1780	1550	1350	1445	1125	860	655	500	+2.5	-2.0	-17.5	NA	$13
7.62x54mm Rus.	146	2950	2730	2520	2320	NA	2820	2415	2055	1740	NA	+2.5	+2.0	-4.4	-17.7	NA
7.62x54mm Rus.	180	2580	2370	2180	2000	1820	2650	2250	1900	1590	1100	+2.5	0.0	-9.8	-28.5	NA
7.7x58mm Jap.	180	2500	2300	2100	1920	1750	2490	2105	1770	1475	1225	+2.5	0.0	-10.4	-30.2	NA
8mm 8x57mm JS Mau.	165	2850	2520	2210	1930	1670	2965	2330	1795	1360	1015	+2.5	+1.0	-7.7	NA	NA
32 Win. Special	170	2250	1921	1626	1372	1175	1911	1393	998	710	521	+2.5	-3.5	-22.9	NA	$14
8mm Mauser	170	2360	1969	1622	1333	1123	2102	1464	993	671	476	+2.5	-3.1	-22.2	NA	$18
8mm Rem. Mag.	185	3080	2761	2464	2186	1927	3896	3131	2494	1963	1525	+2.5	+1.4	-5.5	-19.7	$30
8mm Rem. Mag.	220	2830	2581	2346	2123	1913	3912	3254	2688	2201	1787	+2.5	+0.6	-7.6	-23.5	Disc.
33 338 Win. Mag.	200	2960	2658	2375	2110	1862	3890	3137	2505	1977	1539	+2.5	+1.0	-6.7	-22.3	$27
338 Win. Mag.*	210	2830	2590	2370	2150	1940	3735	3130	2610	2155	1760	+2.5	+1.4	-6.0	-20.9	$33
338 Win. Mag.*	225	2785	2517	2266	2029	1808	3871	3165	2565	2057	1633	+2.5	+0.4	-8.5	-25.9	$27
338 Win. Mag.	230	2780	2573	2375	2186	2005	3948	3382	2881	2441	2054	+2.5	+1.2	-6.3	-21.0	$40
338 Win. Mag.*	250	2660	2456	2261	2075	1898	3927	3348	2837	2389	1999	+2.5	+0.2	-9.0	-26.2	$27
34 340 Wea. Mag.*	210	3250	2991	2746	2515	2295	4924	4170	3516	2948	2455	+2.5	1.9	-1.8	-11.8	$56
340 Wea. Mag.*	250	3000	2806	2621	2443	2272	4995	4371	3812	3311	2864	+2.5	+2.0	-3.5	-14.8	$56
35 338 A-Square	250	3120	2799	2500	2220	1958	5403	4348	3469	2736	2128	+2.5	+2.7	-1.5	-10.5	NA
348 Winchester	200	2520	2215	1931	1672	1443	2820	2178	1656	1241	925	+2.5	-1.4	-14.7	NA	$42
357 Magnum	158	1830	1427	1138	980	883	1175	715	454	337	274	0.0	-16.2	-33.1	NA	$25**
35 Remington	150	2300	1874	1506	1218	1039	1762	1169	755	494	359	+2.5	-4.1	-26.3	NA	$16
35 Remington	200	2080	1698	1376	1140	1001	1921	1280	841	577	445	+2.5	-6.3	-17.1	-33.6	$16
356 Winchester	200	2460	2114	1797	1517	1284	2688	1985	1434	1022	732	+2.5	-1.8	-17.1	NA	$31
356 Winchester	250	2160	1911	1682	1476	1299	2591	2028	1571	1210	937	+2.5	-3.7	-22.2	NA	$31
358 Winchester	200	2490	2171	1876	1619	1379	2753	2093	1563	1151	844	+2.5	-1.6	-15.6	NA	$31
350 Rem. Mag.	200	2710	2410	2130	1870	1631	3261	2579	2014	1553	1181	+2.5	-0.2	-10.0	-30.1	$33
35 Whelen	200	2675	2378	2100	1842	1606	3177	2510	1958	1506	1145	+2.5	-0.2	-10.3	-31.1	$20
35 Whelen	250	2400	2197	2005	1823	1652	3197	2680	2230	1844	1515	+2.5	-1.2	-13.7	NA	$20
358 Norma Mag.	250	2800	2510	2230	1970	1730	4350	3480	2750	2145	1655	+2.5	+1.0	-7.6	-25.2	NA
9.3 9.3x57mm Mau.	286	2070	1810	1590	1390	1110	2710	2090	1600	1220	955	+2.5	-2.6	-22.5	NA	NA
9.3 x 62mm Mau.	286	2360	2089	1844	1623	NA	3538	2771	2157	1670	1260	+2.5	-1.6	-21.0	NA	NA
9.3 x 64mm	286	2700	2505	2318	2139	1968	4629	3984	3411	2906	2460	+2.5	+2.7	-4.5	-19.2	NA
9.3 x 74Rmm	286	2360	2089	1844	1623	NA	3538	2771	2157	1670	NA	+2.5	-2.0	-11.0	NA	NA
375 38-55 Win.	255	1320	1190	1091	1018	963	987	802	674	587	525	0.0	-23.4	NA	NA	$25
375 Winchester	200	2200	1841	1526	1268	1089	2150	1506	1034	714	527	+2.5	-4.0	-26.2	NA	$27
375 Winchester	250	1900	1647	1424	1239	1103	2005	1506	1126	852	676	+2.5	-6.9	-33.3	NA	$27
375 N.E. 2½"	270	2000	1740	1507	1310	NA	2398	1815	1362	1026	NA	+2.5	-6.0	-30.0	NA	NA

Caliber	Bullet weight grains	-VELOCITY (fps)- Muzzle	100 yds.	200 yds.	300 yds.	400 yds.	-ENERGY (ft. lbs.)- Muzzle	100 yds.	200 yds.	300 yds.	400 yds.	-TRAJ. (in.)- 100 yds.	200 yds.	300 yds.	400 yds.	Approx. Price per box
375 (cont.)																
375 Flanged	300	2450	2150	1886	1640	NA	3998	3102	2369	1790	NA	+2.5	-2.4	-17.0	NA	NA
375 H&H Magnum	250	2670	2450	2240	2040	1850	3955	3335	2790	2315	1905	+2.5	-0.4	-10.2	-28.4	NA
375 H&H Magnum	270	2690	2420	2166	1928	1707	4337	3510	2812	2228	1747	+2.5	0.0	-10.0	-29.4	$28
375 H&H Magnum*	300	2530	2245	1979	1733	1512	4263	3357	2608	2001	1523	+2.5	-1.0	-10.5	-33.6	$28
375 Wea. Mag.	300	2700	2420	2157	1911	1685	4856	3901	3100	2432	1891	+2.5	-0.4	-10.7	-	NA
378 Wea. Mag.	270	3180	2976	2781	2594	2415	6062	5308	4635	4034	3495	+2.5	+2.6	-1.8	-11.3	$71
378 Wea. Mag.	300	2929	2576	2252	1952	1680	5698	4419	3379	2538	1881	+2.5	+1.2	-7.0	-24.5	$77
375 A-Square	300	2920	2626	2351	2093	1850	5679	4594	3681	2917	2281	+2.5	+1.4	-6.0	-21.0	NA
38-40 Win.	180	1160	999	901	827	764	538	399	324	273	233	0.0	-33.9	NA	NA	$42**
40																
450/400-3"	400	2150	1932	1730	1545	1379	4105	3316	2659	2119	1689	+2.5	-4.0	-9.5	-30.3	NA
416 Taylor	400	2350	2117	1896	1693	NA	4905	3980	3194	2547	NA	+2.5	-1.2	_15.0	NA	NA
41																
416 Hoffman	400	2380	2145	1923	1718	1529	5031	4087	3285	2620	2077	+2.5	-1.0	-14.1	NA	NA
416 Rigby	350	2600	2449	2303	2162	2026	5253	4661	4122	3632	3189	+2.5	-1.8	-10.2	-26.0	NA
416 Rigby	400	2370	2210	2050	1900	NA	4990	4315	3720	3185	NA	+2.5	-0.7	-12.1	NA	NA
416 Rigby	410	2370	2110	1870	1640	NA	5115	4050	3165	2455	NA	+2.5	-2.4	-17.3	NA	$110
416 Rem. Mag.*	350	2520	2270	2034	1814	1611	4935	4004	3216	2557	2017	+2.5	-0.8	-12.6	-35.0	$82
416 Rem. Mag.*	400	2400	2175	1962	1763	1579	5115	4201	3419	2760	2214	+2.5	-1.5	-14.6	NA	$80
416 Wea. Mag.*	400	2700	2397	2115	1852	1613	6474	5104	3971	3047	2310	+2.5	0.0	-10.1	-30.4	$96
404 Jeffrey	400	2150	1924	1716	1525	NA	4105	3289	2614	2064	NA	+2.5	-4.0	-22.1	NA	NA
425																
425 Express	400	2400	2160	1934	1725	NA	5115	4145	3322	2641	NA	+2.5	-1.0	-14.0	NA	NA
44-40 Win.	200	1190	1006	900	822	756	629	449	360	300	254	0.0	-33.3	NA	NA	$36**
44																
44 Rem. Mag.	210	1920	1477	1155	982	880	1719	1017	622	450	361	0.0	-17.6	NA	NA	$14
44 Rem. Mag.	240	1760	1380	1114	970	878	1650	1015	661	501	411	0.0	-17.6	NA	NA	$13
444 Marlin	240	2350	1815	1377	1087	941	2942	1753	1001	630	472	+2.5	-15.1	-31.0	NA	$22
444 Marlin	265	2120	1733	1405	1160	1012	2644	1768	1162	791	603	+2.5	-6.0	-32.2	NA	Disc.
45																
45-70 Govt.	300	1810	1497	1244	1073	969	2182	1492	1031	767	625	0.0	-14.8	NA	NA	$21
45-70 Govt.	405	1330	1168	1055	977	918	1590	1227	1001	858	758	0.0	-24.6	NA	NA	$21
458 Win. Magnum	350	2470	1990	1570	1250	1060	4740	3065	1915	1205	870	+2.5	-2.5	-21.6	NA	$43
458 Win. Magnum	400	2380	2170	1960	1770	NA	5030	4165	3415	2785	NA	+2.5	-0.4	-13.4	NA	$73
458 Win. Magnum	465	2220	1999	1791	1601	NA	5088	4127	3312	2646	NA	+2.5	-2.0	-17.7	NA	NA
458 Win. Magnum	500	2040	1823	1623	1442	1237	4620	3689	2924	2308	1839	+2.5	-3.5	-22.0	NA	$61
458 Win. Magnum	510	2040	1770	1527	1319	1157	4712	3547	2640	1970	1516	+2.5	-4.1	-25.0	NA	$41
450 N.E.-3¼"	465	2190	1970	1765	1577	NA	4952	4009	3216	2567	NA	+2.5	-3.0	-20.0	NA	NA
450 N.E.-3¼"	500	2150	1920	1708	1514	NA	5132	4093	3238	2544	NA	+2.5	-4.0	-22.9	NA	NA
450 No. 2	465	2190	1970	1765	1577	NA	4952	4009	3216	2567	NA	+2.5	-3.0	-20.0	NA	NA
450 No. 2	500	2150	1920	1708	1514	NA	5132	4093	3238	2544	NA	+2.5	-4.0	-22.9	NA	NA
458 Lott	465	2380	2150	1932	1730	NA	5848	4773	3855	3091	NA	+2.5	-1.0	-14.0	NA	NA
458 Lott	500	2300	2062	1838	1633	NA	5873	4719	3748	2960	NA	+2.5	-1.6	-16.4	NA	NA
450 Ackley Mag	465	2400	2169	1950	1747	NA	5947	4857	3927	3150	NA	+2.5	-1.0	-13.7	NA	NA
450 Ackley Mag.	500	2320	2081	1855	1649	NA	5975	4085	3820	3018	NA	+2.5	-1.2	-15.0	NA	NA
460 Short A-Sq.	500	2420	2175	1943	1729	NA	6501	5250	4193	3319	NA	+2.5	-0.8	-12.8	-	NA
460 Wea. Mag.	500	2700	2404	2128	1869	1635	8092	6416	5026	3878	2969	+2.5	+0.6	-8.9	-28.0	$72
475																
500/465 N.E.	480	2150	1917	1703	1507	NA	4926	3917	3089	2419	NA	+2.5	-4.0	-22.2	-	NA
470 Rigby	500	2150	1940	1740	1560	NA	5130	4170	3360	2695	NA	+2.5	-2.8	-19.4	NA	NA
470 Nitro Ex.	480	2190	1954	1735	1536	NA	5111	4070	3210	2515	NA	+2.5	-3.5	-20.8	NA	NA
470 Nitro Ex.	500	2150	1890	1650	1440	1270	5130	3965	3040	2310	1790	+2.5	-4.3	-24.0	NA	$177
475 No. 2	500	2200	1955	1728	1522	NA	5375	4243	3316	2573	NA	+2.5	-3.2	-20.9	NA	NA
50																
505 Gibbs	525	2300	2063	1840	1637	NA	6166	4922	3948	3122	NA	+2.5	-3.0	-18.0	NA	NA
500 N.E.-3"	570	2150	1928	1722	1533	NA	5850	4703	3752	2975	NA	+2.5	-3.7	-22.0	NA	NA
58																
500 N.E.-3"	600	2150	1927	1721	1531	NA	6158	4947	3944	3124	NA	+2.5	-4.0	-22.0	NA	NA
495 A-Square	570	2350	2117	1896	1693	NA	5850	4703	3752	2975	NA	+2.5	-1.0	-14.5	NA	NA
495 A-Square	600	2280	2050	1833	1635	NA	6925	5598	4478	3562	NA	+2.5	-2.0	-17.0	NA	NA
500 A-Square	600	2380	2144	1922	1766	NA	7546	6126	4920	3922	NA	+2.5	-3.0	-17.0	NA	NA
500 A-Square	707	2250	2040	1841	1567	NA	7947	6530	5318	4311	NA	+2.5	-2.0	-17.0	NA	NA
577 Nitro Ex.	750	2050	1793	1562	1360	NA	6990	5356	4065	3079	NA	+2.5	-5.0	-26.0	NA	NA

Notes: NA in vel. or eng. column = This data not available from manufacturer. NA in trajectory column = Bullet has fallen more than 3 feet below line of sight and further hold-over is not practical. Wea. Mag. = Weatherby Magnum. Spfd. = Springfield. A-Sq. = A-Square. N.E.= Nitro Express. Many manufacturer's do not supply suggested retail prices. Others did not get their pricing to us before press time. All pricing can vary dependent on the exact brand and style of ammo selected and/or the retail outlet from which you make your purchase. Pricing has been rounded to the nearest dollar and represent our best estimate of average pricing. An * after the bullet weight means these loads are available with Nosler Partition or Swift A-Frame bullets. Listed pricing may or may not reflect this bullet type. ** = these are packed 50 to box, all others are 20 to box.

CAUTION: PRICES SHOWN ARE SUPPLIED BY THE MANUFACTURER OR IMPORTER. CHECK YOUR LOCAL GUNSHOP.

CENTERFIRE HANDGUN CARTRIDGES—BALLISTICS AND PRICES

Caliber	Bullet Wgt. Grs.	Velocity (fps) MV	Velocity 50 yds.	Velocity 100 yds.	Energy (ft. lbs.) ME	Energy 50 yds.	Energy 100 yds.	Mid-Range Traj. (in.) 50 yds.	Mid-Range Traj. 100 yds.	Bbl. Lgth. (in.)	Est. Price /box
221 Rem. Fireball	50	2650	2380	2130	780	630	505	0.2	0.8	10.5"	$15
25 Automatic	35	900	813	742	63	51	43	NA	NA	2"	$18
25 Automatic	45	815	730	655	65	55	40	1.8	7.7	2"	$21
25 Automatic	50	760	705	660	65	55	50	2.0	8.7	2"	$17
7.5mm Swiss	107	1010	NA	NA	240	NA	NA	NA	NA	NA	NEW
7.62mm Tokarev	87	1390	NA	NA	365	NA	NA	0.6	NA	4.5"	NA
7.62mm Nagant	97	1080	NA	NA	350	NA	NA	NA	NA	NA	NEW
7.63mm Mauser	88	1440	NA	NA	405	NA	NA	NA	NA	NA	NEW
30 Luger	93†	1220	1110	1040	305	255	225	0.9	3.5	4.5"	$34
30 Carbine	110	1790	1600	1430	785	625	500	0.4	1.7	10"	$28
32 S&W	88	680	645	610	90	80	75	2.5	10.5	3"	$17
32 S&W Long	98	705	670	635	115	100	90	2.3	10.5	4"	$17
32 Short Colt	80	745	665	590	100	80	60	2.2	9.9	4"	$19
32 Long Colt	82	755	715	675	100	95	85	2.0	8.7	4"	Disc.
32 H&R Magnum	85	1100	1020	930	230	195	165	1.0	4.3	4.5"	$21
32 H&R Magnum	95	1030	940	900	225	190	170	1.1	4.7	4.5"	$19
32 Automatic	60	970	895	835	125	105	95	1.3	5.4	4"	$22
32 Automatic	71	905	855	810	130	115	95	1.4	5.8	4"	$19
8mm Lebel Pistol	111	850	NA	NA	180	NA	NA	NA	NA	NA	NEW
8mm Steyr	113	1080	NA	NA	290	NA	NA	NA	NA	NA	NEW
8mm Gasser	126	850	NA	NA	200	NA	NA	NA	NA	NA	NEW
380 Automatic	85/88	990	920	870	190	165	145	1.2	5.1	4"	$20
380 Automatic	90	1000	890	800	200	160	130	1.2	5.5	3.75"	$10
380 Automatic	95/100	955	865	785	190	160	130	1.4	5.9	4"	$20
38 Automatic	130	1040	980	925	310	275	245	1.0	4.7	4.5"	Disc.
38 Super Auto +P	115	1300	1145	1040	430	335	275	0.7	3.3	5"	$26
38 Super Auto +P	125/130	1215	1100	1015	425	350	300	0.8	3.6	5"	$26
9x18mm Makarov	95	1000	NA	NA	NA	NA	NA	NA	NA	NA	NEW
9x18mm Ultra	100	1050	NA	NA	240	NA	NA	NA	NA	NA	NEW
9mm Steyr	115	1180	NA	NA	350	NA	NA	NA	NA	NA	NEW
9mm Luger	88	1500	1190	1010	440	275	200	0.6	3.1	4"	$24
9mm Luger	90	1360	1112	978	370	247	191	NA	NA	4"	$26
9mm Luger	95	1300	1140	1010	350	275	215	0.8	3.4	4"	NA
9mm Luger	115	1155	1045	970	340	280	240	0.9	3.9	4"	$21
9mm Luger	123/125	1110	1030	970	340	290	260	1.0	4.0	4"	$23
9mm Luger	140	935	890	850	270	245	225	1.3	5.5	4"	$23
9mm Luger	147	990	940	900	320	290	265	1.1	4.9	4"	$26
9mm Luger +P	115	1250	1113	1019	399	316	265	0.8	3.5	4"	$27
9mm Federal	115	1280	1130	1040	420	330	280	0.7	3.3	4"V	$24
38 S&W	146	685	650	620	150	135	125	2.4	10.0	4"	$19
38 Short Colt	125	730	685	645	150	130	115	2.2	9.4	6"	$19
38 Special	110	945	895	850	220	195	175	1.3	5.4	4"V	$23
38 Special	130	775	745	710	175	160	120	1.9	7.9	4"V	$22
38 (Multi-Ball)	140	830	730	505	215	130	80	2.0	10.6	4"V	$10**
38 Special	148	710	635	565	165	130	105	2.4	10.6	4"V	$17
38 Special	158	755	725	690	200	185	170	2.0	8.3	4"V	$18
38 Special	200	635	615	595	180	170	155	2.8	11.5	4"V	Disc.
38 Special +P	95	1175	1045	960	290	230	195	0.9	3.9	4"V	$23
38 Special +P	110	995	925	870	240	210	185	1.2	5.1	4"V	$23
38 Special +P	125	945	900	860	250	225	205	1.3	5.4	4"V	$23
38 Special +P	129	945	910	870	255	235	215	1.3	5.3	4"V	$11
38 Special +P	147/150(c)	884	NA	NA	264	NA	NA	NA	NA	4"V	$27
38 Special +P	158	890	855	825	280	255	240	1.4	6.0	4"V	$20
357 Magnum	110	1295	1095	975	410	290	230	0.8	3.5	4"V	$25
357 (Med. Vel.)	125	1220	1075	985	415	315	270	0.8	3.7	4"V	$25
357 Magnum	125	1450	1240	1090	585	425	330	0.6	2.8	4"V	$25
357 (Multi-Ball)	140	1155	830	665	420	215	135	1.2	6.4	4"V	$11**
357 Magnum	140	1360	1195	1075	575	445	360	0.7	3.0	4"V	$25
357 Magnum	145	1290	1155	1060	535	430	360	0.8	3.5	4"V	$26
357 Magnum	150/158	1235	1105	1015	535	430	360	0.8	3.5	4"V	$25
357 Magnum	180	1145	1055	985	525	445	390	0.9	3.9	4"V	$25
357 Rem. Maximum	158	1825	1590	1380	1170	885	670	0.4	1.7	10.5"	$14**
40 S&W	155	1140	1026	958	447	362	309	0.9	4.1	4"	$14***
40 S&W	165	1150	NA	NA	485	NA	NA	NA	NA	4"	$18***
40 S&W	180	985	936	893	388	350	319	1.4	5.0	4"	$14***
10mm Automatic	155	1125	1046	986	436	377	335	0.9	3.9	5"	$26
10mm Automatic	170	1340	1165	1145	680	510	415	0.7	3.2	5"	$31
10mm Automatic	175	1290	1140	1035	650	505	420	0.7	3.3	5.5"	$11**
10mm Auto.(FBI)	180	950	905	865	361	327	299	1.5	5.4	4"	$16**
10mm Automatic	180	1030	970	920	425	375	340	1.1	4.7	5"	$16**
10mm Auto H.V.	180†	1240	1124	1037	618	504	430	0.8	3.4	5"	$27
10mm Automatic	200	1160	1070	1010	495	510	430	0.9	3.8	5"	$14**
10.4mm Italian	177	950	NA	NA	360	NA	NA	NA	NA	NA	NEW
41 Action Exp.	180	1000	947	903	400	359	326	0.5	4.2	5"	$13**
41 Rem. Magnum	170	1420	1165	1015	760	515	390	0.7	3.2	4"V	$33
41 Rem. Magnum	175	1250	1120	1030	605	490	410	0.8	3.4	4"V	$14**
41 (Med. Vel.)	210	965	900	840	435	375	330	1.3	5.4	4"V	$30
41 Rem. Magnum	210	1300	1160	1060	790	630	535	0.7	3.2	4"V	$33
44 S&W Russian	247	780	NA	NA	335	NA	NA	NA	NA	NA	NA
44 S&W Special	180	980	NA	NA	383	NA	NA	NA	NA	6.5"	NA
44 S&W Special	200†	875	825	780	340	302	270	1.2	6.0	6"	$13**
44 S&W Special	200	1035	940	865	475	390	335	1.1	4.9	6.5"	$13**
44 S&W Special	240/246	755	725	695	310	285	265	2.0	8.3	6.5"	$26
44 Rem. Magnum	180	1610	1365	1175	1035	745	550	0.5	2.3	4"V	$18***
44 Rem. Magnum	200	1400	1192	1053	870	630	492	0.6	NA	6.5"	$20
44 Rem. Magnum	210	1495	1310	1165	1040	805	635	0.6	2.5	6.5"	$18***
44 (Med. Vel.)	240	1000	945	900	535	475	435	1.1	4.8	6.5"	$17
44 R.M.(Jacketed)	240	1180	1080	1010	740	625	545	0.9	3.7	4"V	$18***
44 R.M. (Lead)	240	1350	1185	1070	970	750	610	0.7	3.1	4"V	$29
44 Rem. Magnum	250	1180	1100	1040	775	670	600	0.8	3.6	6.5"V	$21
44 Rem. Magnum	300	1200	1100	1026	959	806	702	NA	NA	7.5"	$17
450 Short Colt	226	830	NA	NA	350	NA	NA	NA	NA	NA	NEW
45 Automatic	185	1000	940	890	410	360	325	1.1	4.9	5"	$28
45 Auto. (Match)	185	770	705	650	245	204	175	2.0	8.7	5"	$28
45 Auto. (Match)	200	940	890	840	392	352	312	2.0	8.6	5"	$20
45 Automatic	200	975	917	860	421	372	328	1.4	5.0	5"	$18
45 Automatic	230	830	800	675	355	325	300	1.6	6.8	5"	$27
45 Automatic	Shot	This data not available									
45 Automatic +P	185	1140	1040	970	535	445	385	0.9	4.0	5"	$31
45 Win. Magnum	230	1400	1230	1105	1000	775	635	0.6	2.8	5"	$14**
45 Win. Magnum	260	Ballistics not yet announced by manufacturer								NA	$16**
45 Auto. Rim	230	810	775	730	335	305	270	1.8	7.4	5.5"	Disc.
455 Webley MKII	262	850	NA	NA	420	NA	NA	NA	NA	NA	NA
45 Colt	200	1000	938	889	444	391	351	1.3	4.8	5.5"	$21
45 Colt	225	960	890	830	460	395	345	1.3	5.5	5.5"	$22
45 Colt	250/255	860	820	780	410	375	340	1.6	6.6	5.5"	$27
50 Action Exp.	325	1400	1209	1075	1414	1055	835	0.2	2.3	6"	$24**

Notes: Blanks are available in 32 S&W, 38 S&W, and 38 Special. V after barrel length indicates test barrel was vented to produce ballistics similar to a revolver with a normal barrel-to-cylinder gap. Ammo prices are per 50 rounds except when marked with an ** which signifies a 20 round box; *** signifies a 25-round box. Not all loads are available from all ammo manufacturers. Listed loads are those made by Remington, Winchester, Federal, and others. DISC. is a discontinued load. Prices are rounded to nearest whole dollar and will vary with brand and retail outlet. †= new bullet weight this year; "c" indicates a change in data.

RIMFIRE AMMUNITION—BALLISTICS AND PRICES

Cartridge type	Bullet Wt. Grs.	Velocity (fps) 22½" Barrel Muzzle	50 Yds.	100 Yds.	Energy (ft. lbs.) 22½" Barrel Muzzle	50 Yds.	100 Yds.	Velocity (fps) 6" Barrel Muzzle	50 Yds.	Energy (ft. lbs) 6" Barrel Muzzle	50 Yds.	Approx. Price Per Box 50 Rds.	100 Rds.
22 Short Blank						Not applicable						$4	NA
22 CB Short	30	725	667	610	34	29	24	706	—	32	—	$2	NA
22 Short Match	29	830	752	695	44	36	31	786	—	39	—	—	NA
22 Short Std. Vel.	29	1045	—	810	70	—	42	865	—	48	—	Discontinued	
22 Short High Vel.	29	1095	—	903	77	—	53	—	—	—	—	$2	NA
22 Short H.V. H.P.	27	1120	—	904	75	—	49	—	—	—	—	—	NA
22 CB Long	30	725	667	610	34	29	24	706	—	32	—	$2	NA
22 Long Std. Vel.	29	1180	1038	946	90	69	58	1031	—	68	—	—	NA
22 Long High Vel.	29	1240	—	962	99	—	60	—	—	—	—	$2	NA
22 L.R. Sub Sonic	38/40	1070	970	890	100	80	70	940	—	—	—	$2	NA
22 L.R. Std. Vel.	40	1138	1047	975	116	97	84	1027	925	93	76	$2	NA
22 L.R. High Vel.	40	1255	1110	1017	140	109	92	1060	—	100	—	$2	NA
22 L.R. H.V. Sil.	42	1220	—	1003	139	—	94	1025	—	98	—	$2	NA
22 L.R. H.V. H.P.	36/38	1280	1126	1010	131	101	82	1089	—	95	—	$2	NA
22 L.R. Shot	#11 or #12	1047	—	—	—	—	—	950	—	—	—	$5	NA
22 L.R. Hyper Vel	36	1410	1187	1056	159	113	89	—	—	—	—	$2	NA
22 L.R. Hyper H.P	32/33/34	1500	1240	1075	165	110	85	—	—	—	—	$2	NA
22 WRF	45	1320	—	1055	175	—	111	—	—	—	—	NA	$5
22 Win. Mag.	30	2200	1750	1373	322	203	127	1610	—	—	—	—	NA
22 Win. Mag.	40	1910	1490	1326	324	197	156	1428	—	181	—	$6	NA
22 Win. Mag.	50	1650	—	1280	300	180	—	—	—	—	—	NA	NA
22 Win. Mag. Shot	#11	1126	—	—	—	—	—	—	—	—	—	NA	NA

Note: The actual ballistics obtained with your firearm can vary considerably from the advertised ballistics. Also ballistics can vary from lot to lot with the same brand and type load. Prices can vary with manufacturer and retail outlet. NA in the price column indicates this size packaging currently unavailable.

SHOTSHELL LOADS AND PRICES

Dram Equivalent	Shot Ozs.	Load Style	Shot Sizes	Brands	Avg.Nom. Price /box	Velocity (fps)
10 Gauge 3½" Magnum						
4½	2¼	premium	BB, 2, 4, 6	Win., Fed., Rem.	$33	1205
4½	2¼	premium	4, 6	Win., Fed.	$13*	1205
4¼	2	high velocity	BB, 2, 4	Rem.	$22	1210
4½	2¼	duplex	4x6	Rem.	$14*	1205
Max	18 pellets	premium	00 buck	Fed., Win.	$7**	1100
Max	54 pellets	premium	4 buck	Win.	Disc.	1100
4¼	1¾	steel	T, BBB, BB, 1, 2, 3	Win., Rem.	$27	1260
4¼	1¾	steel duplex	TxBB, BBBx1	Rem.	$12**	1260
Mag	1⅝	steel	T, BBB	Win.	$27	1285
4⅝	1⅝	steel	F, T, BBB	Fed.	$26	1350
Max	1¾	slug, rifled	slug	Fed.	NA	1280
12 Gauge 3½" Magnum						
Max	2¼	premium	4, 6	Fed., Rem., Win.	$13*	1150
Max	18 pellets	premium	00 buck	Fed., Win.	$7**	1100
4⅛	1 9/16	steel	F, T, BB, 1, 2	Win., Fed.	$22	1335
12 Gauge 3" Magnum						
4	2	premium	BB, 2, 4, 5, 6	Win., Fed., Rem.	$9*	1175
4	2	duplex	4x6	Rem.	$10	1175
4	1⅞	premium	BB, 2, 4, 6	Win., Fed., Rem.	$19	1210
4	1⅞	duplex	BBx4, 2x4, 2x6, 4x6	Rem.	$9*	1210
4	1⅝	premium	2, 4, 5, 6	Win., Fed., Rem.	$18	1290
4	24 pellets	buffered	1 buck	Win., Fed., Rem.	$5**	1040
4	15 pellets	buffered	00 buck	Win., Fed., Rem.	$6**	1210
4	10 pellets	buffered	000 buck	Win., Fed., Rem.	$6**	1225
4	41 pellets	buffered	4 buck	Win., Fed., Rem.	$6**	1210
Max	1¼	slug, rifled	slug	Fed.	NA	1600
Max	1	slug, rifled	slug, magnum	Win., Rem.	$5**	1760
Max	1	saboted slug	slug	Win.	$10**	1550
3⅝	1⅜	steel	F, T, BBB, BB, 1, 2, 3, 4	Win., Fed., Rem.	$19	1275
3⅝	1⅜	steel duplex	BBBx1, BBx2, 1x3	Rem.	$8*	1275
4	1¼	steel	F, T, BBB, BB, 1, 2, 3, 4, 6	Win., Fed., Rem.	$18	1375
4	1¼	steel duplex	BBx1, BBx2, BBx4, 1x3, 2x6	Rem.	$8*	1375
12 gauge 2¾"						
Max	1⅝	magnum	4, 5, 6	Win.	$8*	1250
3¾	1½	magnum	BB, 2, 4, 5, 6	Win., Fed., Rem.	$16	1260
3¾	1½	duplex	BBx4, 2x4, 2x6, 4x6	Rem.	$9*	1260
3¾	1¼	high velocity	BB, 2, 4, 5, 6, 7½, 8, 9	Win., Fed., Rem.	$13	1330
3½	1¼	mid velocity	7, 8, 9	Win.	Disc.	1275
3¼	1¼	standard velocity	6, 7½, 8, 9	Win., Fed., Rem.	$11	1220
3¼	1⅛	standard velocity	4, 6, 7½, 8, 9	Win., Fed., Rem.	$9	1255
3¼	1	standard velocity	6, 7½, 8	Rem., Fed.	$6	1290
3¼	1¼	target	7½, 8, 9	Win., Fed., Rem.	$10	1220
3	1⅛	target	7½, 8, 9, 7½x8	Win., Fed., Rem.	$7	1200
2¾	1⅛	target	7½, 8, 8½, 9, 7½x8	Win., Fed., Rem.	$7	1145
2¼	1⅛	target	7½, 8, 8½, 9	Rem., Fed.	$7	1080
3½	1	target	10	Fed.	NA	1350
3¼	28grams(1oz)	target	7½, 8, 9	Win., Fed., Rem.	$8	1290
2¾	1	target	8½	Fed.	NA	1180
3¼	24grams	target	7½, 8, 9	Win.	NA	1325
3¾	8 pellets	buffered	000 buck	Win., Fed., Rem.	$4**	1325
4	12 pellets	premium	00 buck	Win., Fed., Rem.	$5**	1290
3¾	9 pellets	buffered	00 buck	Win., Fed., Rem.	$19	1325
3¾	12 pellets	buffered	0 buck	Win., Fed., Rem.	$4**	1275
4	20 pellets	buffered	1 buck	Win., Fed., Rem.	$4**	1075
3¾	16 pellets	buffered	1 buck	Win., Fed., Rem.	$4**	1250
4	34 pellets	premium	4 buck	Fed., Rem.	$5**	1250
3¾	27 pellets	buffered	4 buck	Win., Fed., Rem.	$4**	1325
Max	1	saboted slug	slug	Win., Fed.	$10**	1450
Max	1¼	slug, rifled	slug	Fed.	NA	1520
Max	1	slug, rifled	slug, magnum	Rem.	$5**	1680
Max	1	slug, rifled	slug	Win., Fed., Rem.	$4**	1610
3	1#	steel	7	Win.	$11	1235
3½	1¼	steel	T, BBB, BB, 1, 2, 3, 4, 5, 6	Win., Fed., Rem.	$18	1275
3½	1¼	steel duplex	BBx2, 1x3	Rem.	$8*	1275
3¾	1⅛	steel	BB, 1, 2, 3, 4, 5, 6	Win., Fed., Rem.	$16	1365
3¾	1⅛	steel duplex	BBx1, BBx2, BBx4, 1x3, 2x6	Rem.	$7*	1365
3¾	1	steel	2, 4, 6	Win., Fed.	$13	1390
16 Gauge 2¾"						
3¼	1¼	magnum	2, 4, 6	Win., Fed., Rem.	$16	1260
3¼	1⅛	high velocity	4, 6, 7½	Win., Fed., Rem.	$12	1295
2¾	1⅛	standard velocity	6, 7½, 8	Fed., Rem.	$9	1185
2½	1	promotional	6, 7½, 8	Win., Fed., Rem.	$6	1165
Max	15/16	steel	2, 4	Fed.	NA	1300
Max	⅞	steel	2, 4	Win.	$16	1300
3	12 pellets	buffered	1 buck	Win., Fed., Rem.	$4**	1225
Max	⅘	slug, rifled	slug	Win., Fed., Rem.	$4**	1570
20 Gauge 3" Magnum						
3	1¼	premium	2, 4, 6, 7½	Win., Fed., Rem.	$15	1185
Max	18 pellets	buck shot	2 buck	Fed.	NA	1200
Max	24 pellets	buffered	3 buck	Win.	$5**	1150
2¾	20 pellets	buck	3 buck	Rem.	$4**	1200
3¼	1	steel	1, 2, 3, 4, 5, 6	Win., Fed., Rem.	$15	1330
20 Gauge 2¾"						
2¾	1⅛	magnum	4, 6, 7½	Win., Fed., Rem.	$14	1175
2¾	1	high velocity	4, 5, 6, 7½, 8, 9	Win., Fed., Rem.	$12	1220
2½	1	standard velocity	6, 7½, 8	Win., Rem., Fed.	$6	1165
2½	⅞	promotional	6, 7½, 8	Win., Rem.	$6	1210
2½	1#	target	8, 9	Win., Rem.	$8	1165
2½	⅞	target	8, 9	Win., Fed., Rem.	$8	1200
Max	20 pellets	buffered	3 buck	Win., Fed.	$4	1200
Max	⅝	slug, saboted	slug	Win.	$9**	1400
2¾	⅝	slug, rifled	slug	Rem.	$4**	1580
Max	¾	slug, rifled	slug	Win., Fed., Rem.	$4**	1570
Max	¾	steel	4, 6	Win., Fed.	$14	1425
28 Gauge 2¾"						
2	1	high velocity	6, 7½, 8	Win.	$12	1125
2¼	¾	high velocity	6, 7½, 8	Win., Fed., Rem.	$11	1295
2	¾	target	8, 9	Win., Fed., Rem.	$9	1200
410 Bore 3"						
Max	11/16	high velocity	4, 5, 6, 7½, 8, 9	Win., Fed., Rem.	$10	1135
410 Bore 2½"						
Max	½	high velocity	4, 6, 7½	Win., Fed., Rem.	$9	1245
Max	⅕	slug, rifled	slug	Win., Fed., Rem.	$4**	1815
1½	½	target	8½, 9	Win., Fed., Rem.	$8	1200

NOTES: * = 10 rounds per box. ** = 5 rounds per box. Pricing variations and number of rounds per box can occur with type and brand of ammunition. Listed pricing is the average nominal cost for load style and box quantity shown. Not every brand is available in all shot size variations. Some manufacturers do not provide suggested list prices. All prices rounded to nearest whole dollar. The price you pay will vary dependent upon outlet of purchase. # = new load spec this year; "C" indicates a change in data.

CAUTION: PRICES SHOWN ARE SUPPLIED BY THE MANUFACTURER OR IMPORTER. CHECK YOUR LOCAL GUNSHOP.

Put The Sport Back Into Your Sport.

With a hunting handgun from Magnum Research.

Around the world, people are putting the challenge back into their big game hunt by relying on the Magnum Research Desert Eagle and Lone Eagle pistols to supply their firepower. For the disciplined hunter, these magnificent hunting handguns rely on your skills at maneuvering the right shot, but never let you down once you fire. Both pistols deliver maximum accuracy, reliability, and impact, while they minimize recoil. These features allow hunters to execute clean, felling shots that are right on target.

What's more, both the Desert Eagle and Lone Eagle pistols come in a wide variety of calibers and finishes — to provide the look and load for any occasion. A wide selection of scopes and hunting accessories are also available.

Real hunting is at its best with a hunting handgun from Magnum Research. If you have a photo of yourself and a trophy you've taken with a Magnum Research firearm, send it in to Magnum Research and become a member of the MRI Handgun Trophy Club. In return for your entry, you'll receive a free MRI Handgun Trophy Club certificate and a Handgun Trophy t-shirt.

For more information about these handsome handguns or the MRI Handgun Trophy Club, call or write Magnum Research at (612) 574-1868, 7110 University Avenue, Minneapolis, MN 55432.

NORTH·AMERICAN·HUNTING·CLUB
FIELD TESTED RECOMMENDED TO MEMBERS

The Lone Eagle Single-Shot Pistol features field-interchangeable barreled actions in .22 Hornet, .223 Remington, .22/.250, .243 Winchester, 7mm-08, 7mm BR, .308 Winchester, .30-.30, .30-06 Springfield, .35 Remington, .357 Maximum, .358 Winchester, .44 Magnum, and .444 Marlin.

LONE EAGLE
SINGLE SHOT PISTOL

The gas-operated, semi-automatic Desert Eagle Pistol is available in .357, .41, .44 Magnum and the recently released .50 Magnum.

DESERT EAGLE®

MAGNUM RESEARCH, INC.
7110 University Avenue
Minneapolis, Minnesota 55432
(612) 574-1868

ACTUAL SIZE

THE COMPLETE GLOCK ARMORER'S KIT.

You can break down and reassemble every Glock handgun with one simple tool.
Which makes choosing your next handgun just as simple.

G̱LOCK®
PERFECTION

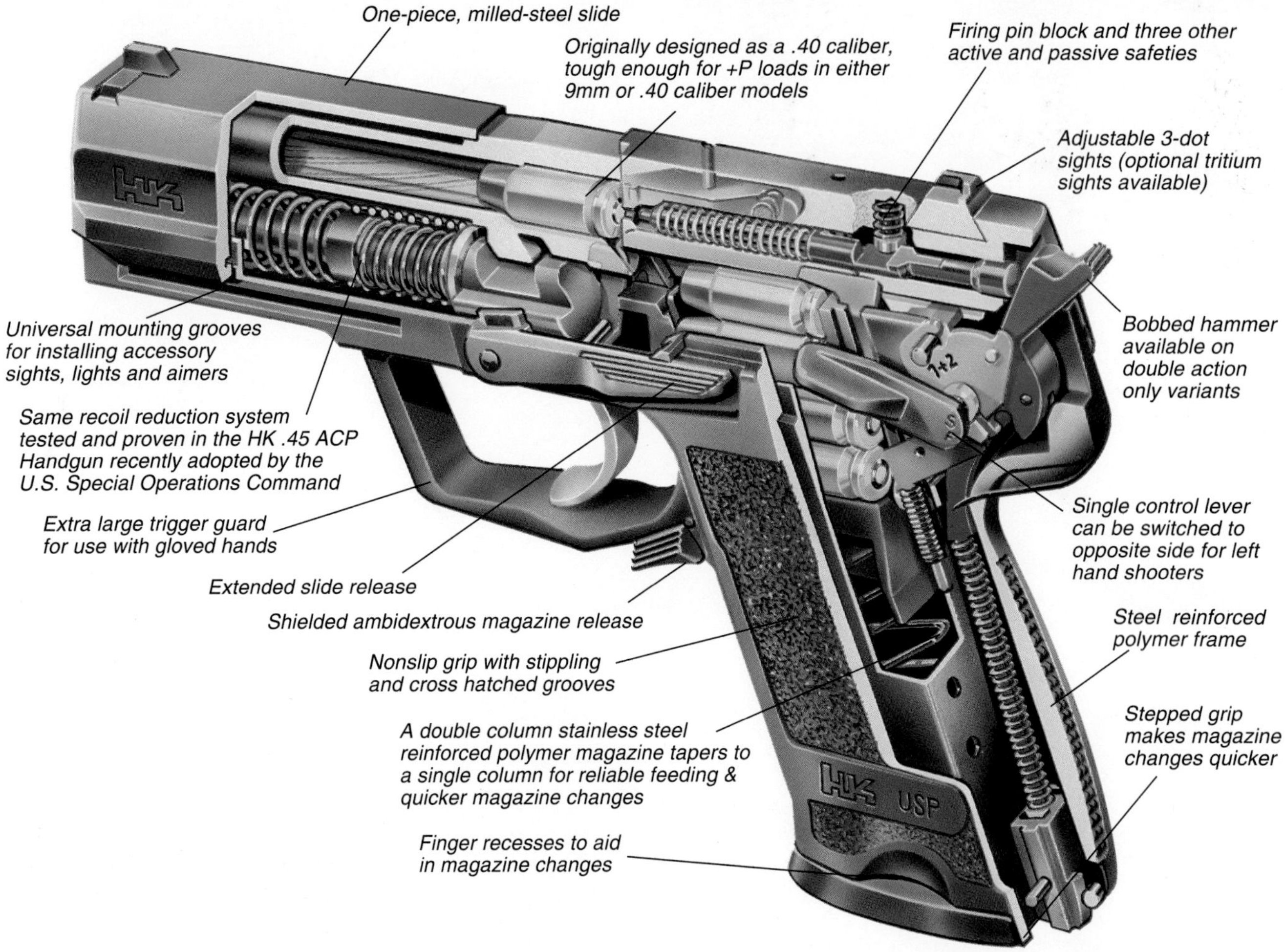

One-piece, milled-steel slide

Originally designed as a .40 caliber,
tough enough for +P loads in either
9mm or .40 caliber models

Firing pin block and three other
active and passive safeties

Adjustable 3-dot
sights (optional tritium
sights available)

Bobbed hammer
available on
double action
only variants

Universal mounting grooves
for installing accessory
sights, lights and aimers

Same recoil reduction system
tested and proven in the HK .45 ACP
Handgun recently adopted by the
U.S. Special Operations Command

Extra large trigger guard
for use with gloved hands

Extended slide release

Shielded ambidextrous magazine release

Nonslip grip with stippling
and cross hatched grooves

A double column stainless steel
reinforced polymer magazine tapers to
a single column for reliable feeding &
quicker magazine changes

Finger recesses to aid
in magazine changes

Single control lever
can be switched to
opposite side for left
hand shooters

Steel reinforced
polymer frame

Stepped grip
makes magazine
changes quicker

Form follows function.

In 1993, Heckler & Koch introduced a revolutionary new pistol — the USP. The HK USP (Universal Self-loading Pistol) represents the epitome of a modern pistol, designed especially for you, the American shooter. Each USP variant gives you a distinct choice. Choice of fire modes. Choice of controls. Choice of conditions of carry. Choice of calibers (.40 S&W or 9mm).

Special features favored by law enforcement, military, and civilian shooters provided the design criteria for the USP. Its controls are uniquely American — influenced by such famous pistols as the Government Model 1911. And like the Model 1911, the USP can be safely carried "cocked and locked".

The control lever, a combination safety and decocking lever, is frame mounted and quickly accessible, unlike the slide mounted safeties common on many other pistols.

A special "HE" (Hostile Environment) finish protects metal parts of the USP from the worst types of corrosion and wear, including prolonged exposure to salt water.

Another unique feature of the HK USP is its patented mechanical recoil reduction system incorporated into the recoil and buffer spring assembly located below the barrel. This recoil reduction system was tested and proven in the HK .45 ACP Handgun recently designed for the U.S. Special Operations Command (SOCOM). Using the same system as the USP, the "SOCOM pistol" fired more than 30,000 +P cartridges without damage to any major components.

At Heckler & Koch, form follows function. All HK pistols are designed and manufactured to meet the operational requirements of the most demanding users. And they're covered by a lifetime warranty.

In a world of compromise, some don't.

USP
Handgun innovation for the next century.

For more information and the location of your nearest Authorized Dealer, contact:
Heckler & Koch, Inc.
21480 Pacific Boulevard
Sterling, Virginia 20166 USA
Telephone (703) 450-1900

SHOOTER'S MARKETPLACE

ADJUSTABLE DISC APERTURE

Hunters are constantly faced with continually changing light conditions. A receiver sight with a fixed aperture is adequate for only one light condition.

The Merit Hunting Disc aperture is instantly adjustable from .025- to .155-inch in diameter, allowing a clear sight picture to be maintained under changing light conditions.

The aperture leaves are supported to withstand recoil from heavy calibers, and the shank is tapered to provide solid lockup of the disc to your receiver sight.

Contact Merit Corp. for a free copy of their brochure describing this and other sighting aids for shooters.

MERIT CORP.

ELECTRONIC CASELESS CARTRIDGE RIFLE

Introduced just over a year ago in the U.S., the VEC 91 from Voere in Austria offers benchrest accuracy in a hunting rifle and delivers hole-in-hole performance in 223-caliber.

This 6-pound rifle has a five-round magazine and is fired electronically using a trigger/micro switch for zero lock time. The UCC caseless propellant and primer are totally consumed on ignition, pushing a 55-grain 223 bullet out of the barrel at better than 3200 fps. Because of the stability of the propellant (it can be submersed in water with no effect), the velocity remains the same round after round, which means extreme accuracy with each shot.

Larger calibers such as 6mm will be introduced this year. Contact JägerSport for a brochure and more info.

VOERE/JÄGERSPORT

SHOOTING GLASSES APERTURE

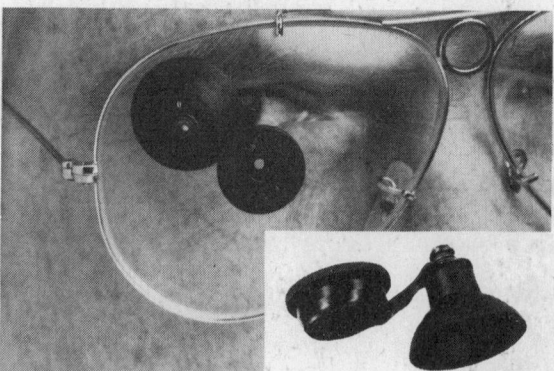

Pistol shooters are able to see their sights and target clearly with the Merit Optical Attachment and its instantly adjustable diameter aperture.

An aperture (pinhole) increases the eyes' depth of field (range of focus) dramatically.

The Merit Optical Attachment is instantly adjustable from .022- to .156-inch in diameter to accommodate different light conditions. Thus the sights and target remain in clear focus.

Additionally, using an aperture improves a shooter's concentration by helping maintain a consistent head position. This device works equally well with bifocals, trifocals and plain-lensed shooting glasses.

Contact Merit Corp. for a free brochure.

MERIT CORP.

See manufacturers' addresses on page 259.

SHOOTER'S MARKETPLACE

NEW RIMFIRE/CENTERFIRE TARGETS

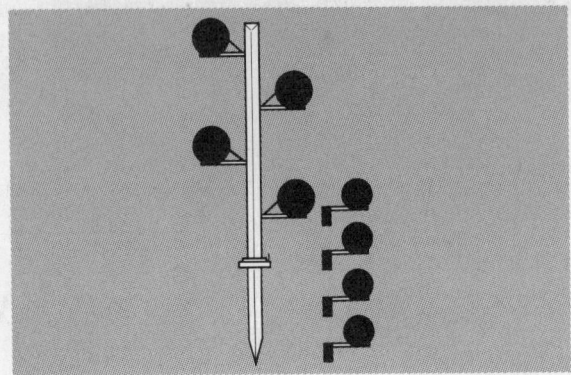

Birchwood Casey is offering an economical new target concept called the Challenger Dueling Post Combo. The Challenger is designed for both 22 rimfire handgun target work as well as centerfire handguns up to 44 Magnum.

It features a universal stand with spear tip and stop collar for positive, solid anchoring and two sets of round, removable target paddles. Each target paddle set includes four paddles—one set of four for rimfire and one set of four for centerfire. The 22 rimfire targets are 3/16" in size; the centerfire 3/8". Switching from rimfire to centerfire is easily accomplished—just lift one set out and drop in the other.

Call, write or fax Birchwood Casey for additional information.

BIRCHWOOD CASEY

SOMETHING FOR THE LADIES

TomBoy, Inc., was established for women interested in hunting and fishing sports.

The organization, which was founded by women, publishes *Tomboy*, the first magazine for women hunters and anglers.

The TomBoy Club is the first women's hunting and fishing club to be recognized nationally. It provides a much-needed resource for women who want to learn and experience these sports.

Learning resources, outdoor clothing and equipment for women have not been readily available until recently because women have not let their interest in these sports be known. Hence, Tomboy's logo: "We're Breaking the Silence."

Write or call TomBoy, Inc. for more information.

TOMBOY, INC.

EXTENDIBLE SPOTTING SCOPES

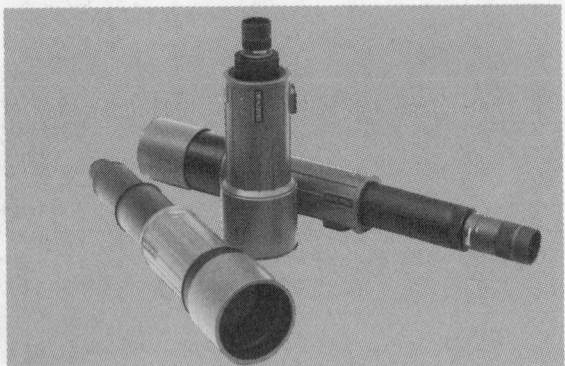

The Swarovski CT-75 and CT-85 extendible spotting scopes for big game hunters and naturalists were designed with strength, optical performance and portability in mind.

The bright, sharp optical images produced are due to a longer light path and the use of extra-large roof prisms with phase-correcting coatings. A new focusing system and a large built-in sun shade are other features.

The scopes use a variety of interchangeable eyepieces from 20x to 60x as well as a camera adapter, all from the Swarovski Spotting Scope System.

Like all Swarovski optics, the lens surfaces of the scopes and eyepieces are fully multi-coated using the patented Swarotop® coating system. For a color catalog and more information, contact Swarovski.

SWAROVSKI OPTIK NORTH AMERICA LTD.

SHOOTING GLASSES

New Randolph Ranger shooting glasses combine safety, comfort, visual acuity and flexibility. The standard shatter-proof interchangeable polycarbonate lenses are designed to withstand multiple 12-gauge shotgun blasts from 12 meters and offer 100% UV ray lens protection. Choose any three of the ten lens colors offered: clear, yellow, canary, orange, sunset, vermilion, purple, brown, bronze, or gray. Ranger shooting glasses now come in three sizes—small, medium and large—and in two finishes—23k gold-plate or matte black finish. The Ranger can be purchased with the three-lens system or as Rx frame only for prescription wearers. For more information, write, call or fax Randolph Engineering, or see your local gun dealer or sporting goods store.

RANDOLPH ENGINEERING, INC.

See manufacturers' addresses on page 259.

NEW LASER SIGHTS

Laseraim, the originator of the Hotdot daylight laser, offers an expanded line of laser sights and electronic red dot sights and mounts for 1994. Ideal for the handgunner, rifleman, shotgunner and archer, Laseraim sights feature 5 milliwatts of power, long battery life, microlock windage and elevation adjustments and secure mounting.

The new LA14 (pictured above) features an integral mount and laser in a single package. Mounting is quick and easy, requiring no gunsmithing or modification to the pistol. The LA14 is available for Glock, Beretta, Smith & Wesson, Ruger, Heckler & Koch and Sig Sauer pistols in black or satin finish.

For more information and free Laseraim color catalog, contact Emerging Technologies, Inc.

EMERGING TECHNOLOGIES, INC.

NEW SHOTGUN CLEANING SYSTEM

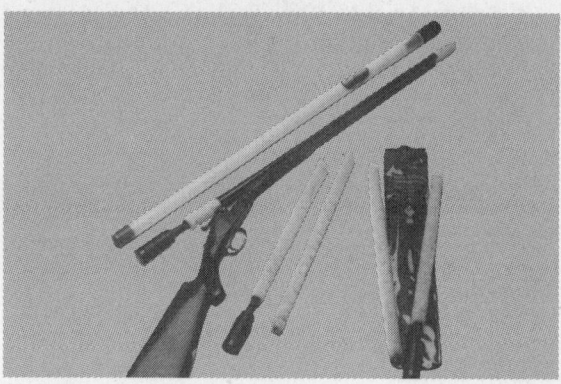

Silencio offers their Tico Tool Shotgun Cleaner System for cleaning and oiling your smoothbore thoroughly in about 30 seconds.

The Tico Tool is a one-piece, or two-piece takedown, cleaning bar with oiling bob attachment. The washable bar is run down the barrel for the cleaning and polishing operation, and then, with the oiling bob attached, a final stroke down the barrel prepares your shotgun for storage.

The standard one-piece model is available for 12-, 16-, 20-, 28-gauge and .410 bore; the two-piece takedown model is offered for 12-, 16- and 20-gauge.

For information on all Silencio products currently available, visit your local gun store or call, write or fax Silencio directly.

SILENCIO/SAFETY DIRECT

NEW STAINLESS STEEL PISTOLS

The Laseraim lineup of single-action pistols contains many of the standard features generally found only on customized "race guns." All pistols are of stainless steel construction with polished ramp barrel, integral dovetail mount, sculptured hammer and trigger, beveled magazine well and more.

Four Laseraim Series (I, II, III, IV) are available to the shooter, each Series offering its own special performance options. The Laseraim line is available in 45 ACP, 40 S&W, 10mm and 9mm calibers and can be equipped with optional sighting system packages—adjustable sights, laser sights, electronic red dot and telescopic sight options.

For more information, call Laseraim Arms, Inc. for a free four-color catalog.

LASERAIM ARMS, INC.

SHOOTER'S EAR MUFF

Silencio's CDS-80 Magnum Deluxe ear muff provides the competition shooter or plinker with quality hearing protection.

Each pair of muffs was designed with comfort, style, protection and affordability in mind. The CDS-80 features a padded, non-absorbent head cushion plus liquid-filled ear cushions, which provide an excellent seal for prescription glasses wearers and are extremely comfortable. Also featured are side-bar adjusters and rotating ear cups. The muffs are available in black, white or blue.

Silencio's CDS-80 noise reduction rating is one of the highest in the industry.

For information on all Silencio products check with your local gun dealer or contact Silencio directly.

SILENCIO/SAFETY DIRECT

See manufacturers' addresses on page 259.

SHOOTER'S MARKETPLACE

SHOTGUN SADDLE MOUNTS

B-Square Shotgun Saddle Mounts are now available for most popular 12-gauge guns. These newly designed mounts straddle the receiver and fit the top of the gun tightly. All mounts have a standard dovetail base and "see-thru" design, allowing for continued use of the gun's sight. Standard dovetail rings can be used.

B-Square shotgun mounts do not require gunsmithing, have a blued finish and attach to the gun's side with included hardware. Saddle mounts are available for Remington 870/1100; Mossberg 500, 5500 and 835; Winchester 1400/1300/1200; Ithaca 37/87; and Browning A-5 shotguns.

The mounts retail for $49.95 at your local dealer, or call B-Square toll-free. A catalog featuring the complete line of B-Square products is available upon request.

B-SQUARE COMPANY, INC.

CHOKE TUBE SPEED WRENCH

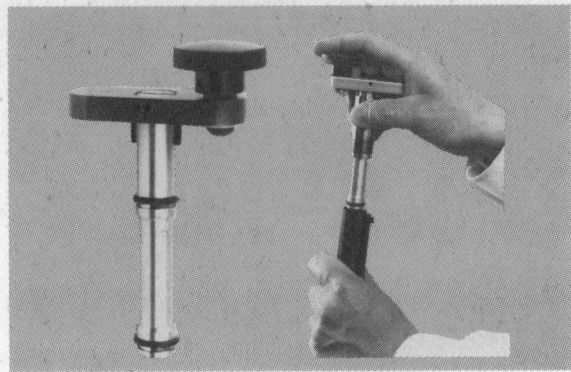

The Texas Twister© Choke Tube Speed Wrench from B-Square is currently available for most 12-gauge shotguns.

The wrench inserts into the choke tube so it can be cranked out of the bore and has a bore guide to prevent crooked starts and damaged threads. The T-handle is designed to break stubborn tubes loose so they can be cranked out quickly and easily.

Texas Twister wrenches are available for Briley, Beretta, Browning, Mossberg, Weatherby, Remington, Ruger, SKB and Winchester 12-gauge shotguns.

Retail price is $29.95 at your local dealer, or call B-Square toll-free. A catalog featuring the complete line of B-Square products is available upon request.

B-SQUARE COMPANY, INC.

COMPACT MINI LASERS

The Compact Mini Laser from B-Square is only 1.1"x1.1"x.6" and delivers 5mW of power (Class IIIa) while operating on common A76 size batteries (lithium or alkaline). Visibility with the Mini Laser is 1.0" at 25 yards.

The laser makes use of an omnidirectional screw-type aiming method with windage and elevation adjustments and has an "Aim-Lock" feature. Moisture-proof and shock-resistant, it comes with a lifetime warranty.

Mounting systems are available for long guns and handguns. Their vertical T-slot design makes them quick-detachable and ensures no change in zero.

For more information or a catalog, see your local dealer or call B-Square toll-free.

B-SQUARE COMPANY, INC.

SCREW KITS

B-Square has become known within the industry as the source for screws—especially those hard-to-find "must have" firearm screws needed at one time or another.

B-Square screws are available in a variety of sizes for a variety of uses. All screw kits include a wrench and the appropriate number of socket head screws plus one extra. Available screw kit categories include base screws, trigger guard/action screws, grip screws, ring screws, plug screws and Smith & Wesson sideplate screws.

B-Square screw kit display units for retailers are now available. For additional information about display units and/or screw kits, call B-Square Co. toll-free.

B-SQUARE COMPANY, INC.

See manufacturers' addresses on page 259.

SHOOTER'S MARKETPLACE

GUNSMITH TOOLS

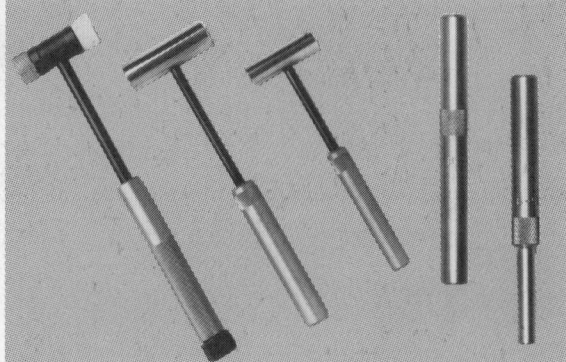

B-Square brass hammers and punches are known for their design and quality.

For the professional and hobby gunsmith, solid brass-headed hammers are perfect for dent removal and setting work in machine vises.

They provide the right sensitivity and feel for gunsmithing and other delicate jobs. Hammers are available in three weights: 2.5 ounces, 5 ounces and 10 ounces.

B-Square solid brass drifts are used for driving out gunsights and large pins without damage. The set of two knurled ¼" diameter and ⅜" diameter punches retails for $9.95 at your local dealer.

Call B-Square toll-free for a catalog featuring their complete line of tools and accessories.

B-SQUARE COMPANY, INC.

NO-GUNSMITHING SCOPE MOUNTS

B-Square offers a complete line of scope mounts for pistols, revolvers, shotguns, sporting rifles and military rifles. Installation of any B-Square scope mount is simple and requires no gunsmithing.

Most mounts feature a "see-thru" standard dovetail base which accepts all standard dovetail (Weaver) rings. Scope mounts are available in blued and stainless finish and come with socket head screws.

New mounts are always being developed at B-Square. For additional information, ask your dealer or call B-Square toll-free. A 32-page catalog featuring the complete line of products is available for $2.00.

B-SQUARE COMPANY, INC.

COMPETITION GEAR

B-Square has a shooting accessory line for competitive shooters.

Mounting systems are currently available for CZ 75/Tanfoglio and Colt/Para Ordnance 1911 handguns. The mounts attach to tapped holes on the side of the gun. All standard optical sight and dovetail rings can be used. Drill jigs for each model can be purchased to ensure perfect installation of the sight mount.

Slide pulls and magazine bumpers for race guns are also available from B-Square.

Competition mounts retail for $99.50 at your local dealer, or call B-Square toll-free. A catalog featuring the complete line of products is available for $2.00.

B-SQUARE COMPANY, INC.

NEW BIPOD MODELS

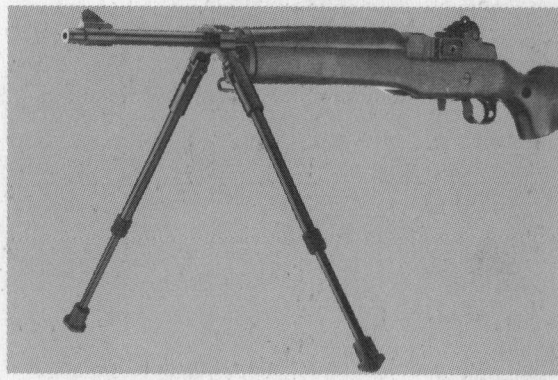

B-Square bipods are offered in several models.

The Rigid Bipod provides strong support and is available with swivel stud "Sporter" or barrel clamp "Service" attachment.

The Tilt Bipod offers rigid support and cants from side to side for fine tuning aim. Tilt Bipods are also available with swivel stud or barrel clamp attachment.

The Roto-Tilt provides that same support and side-to-side canting, but also swivels in a 30-degree angle, enabling shooters to follow perfectly aimed shots. It is available only with the swivel stud attachment.

All B-Square bipods are available in blue or stainless finish and feature an Unlimited Leg Extension System with 7" leg extenders, sold separately.

B-SQUARE COMPANY, INC.

See manufacturers' addresses on page 259.

FIREARM PROTECTORS AND LUBES

Chem-Pak's Gun Sav'r Firearms and Gun Sav'r Black Powder Protector & Lubricant are ozone friendly and specially formulated to provide the maximum in care for fine firearms.

Gun Sav'r Firearms Protector & Lubricant contains special disulfide additives to reduce wear and provide extreme pressure lubrication. It protects against corrosion, with good salt atmosphere protection, provides long-term rust protection and lubricates without penetrating the primer or causing build-up in the action.

New Gun Sav'r Black Powder protects blackpowder bores for three days when applied after shooting.

Available at your favorite gun supply shop. Write or call Chem-Pak for more information.

CHEM-PAK, INC.

CLAY TARGET TRAPS

Trius offers low-cost, easy-cocking mechanical clay target traps with lay-on loading. Singles, doubles and piggy-back doubles make it possible to put up to four birds in the air at one time.

For the casual shooter, Trius offers three models: the Birdshooter—quality at an affordable price; the Model 92 Trius Trap—with high-angle clip and can thrower; and the Trapmaster—with sit-down comfort and pivoting action.

For Sporting Clays/Hunter Clays, the Trius SC92, a heavy-duty trap designed for permanent installation, will throw all Sporting Clays targets except battue and rabbit. The Model BAT2 throws all targets except rabbit, and the Rabbitmaster throws "rabbit discs" along the ground. A free catalog is available.

TRIUS TRAPS

SPRAYABLE STOCK FINISHES

Custom-Oil and Pro-Custom Oil are two newly developed, environmentally friendly, urethane-oil stock finishes from Chem-Pak.

Available in high gloss or hunter satin, they come complete with instructions. Both finishes dry quickly to a transparent, long-lasting, hard finish tough enough to resist moisture, scuffs and scratches.

Custom-Oil stock finish is easy to apply, run resistant and requires no rubbing between coats. Pro-Custom Oil is a liquid formulation for the professional or first-time finisher willing to do the required sanding and rubbing. It has been tested and approved by members of the American Custom Gun Makers Guild.

Available at your local gun supply shop. Write or call Chem-Pak, Inc. for additional information.

CHEM-PAK, INC.

CATALOG AND PATCH OFFER

Here's an opportunity to receive a maroon and silver shoulder patch with the new 1994 Mitchell Arms gun catalog.

This fully illustrated catalog features Mitchell's extensive line of firearms including the new Mitchell High Standard rimfire Target Pistol, the 45 ACP Gold Series, the Pistol P-08 Parabellum, Bat Masterson revolvers and an extensive line of rifles—bolt-action, semi-automatic and combat—plus their pump-action shotguns.

Mitchell Arms offers some of the best in exciting guns from the old days, along with today's modern firearms.

Send $5.00 for your new 1994 Mitchell Arms catalog and shoulder patch.

MITCHELL ARMS, INC.

See manufacturers' addresses on page 259.

QUICK-CHANGE MUZZLE BRAKE

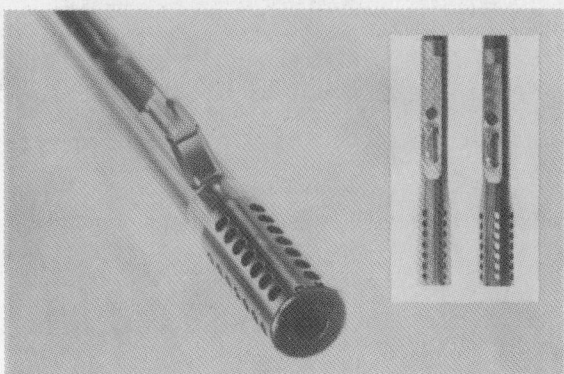

The Hastings Quick-Change Muzzle Brake is right at home on the range or in the woods.

The HQC tames recoil and muzzle jump by deflecting expanding gases perpendicular to the bore. This reduces the pounding taken during extended shooting sessions and helps eliminate flinching.

All effective muzzlebrakes do increase noise for the shooter (this is not a problem on the range when ear protection is worn, but can be a problem when hunting). The HQC is unique in that a quick rotation of the outer sleeve seals the gas ports deactivating the brake and returns noise levels to normal.

Hastings installs the HQC on most centerfire rifles. It's available in stainless steel or blued finish. Contact Hastings for complete details.

HASTINGS BARRELS

CHOKE TUBE INSTALLATION

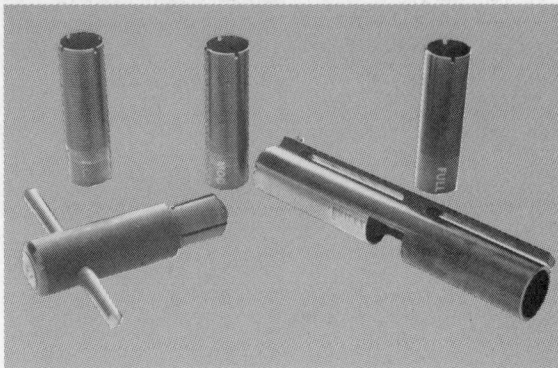

Everything from close-flushing woodcock to high-flying geese can be hunted with a single gun when shooters use the Briley Screw-In Choke System.

If outstanding patterns with target loads, turkey loads, steel or buckshot are important, there is a Briley System for the job. Briley tubes can be installed in nearly any shotgun of any gauge, including most single-barrel guns, plus thin-walled over/unders and side-by-sides.

Hastings is the master distributor and installer of Briley Chokes. They have perfected installation to ensure correct point of impact (tubes are concentric with the bore and fit to exacting tolerances).

Call for complete information.

HASTINGS BARRELS

RIFLED SHOTGUN BARRELS

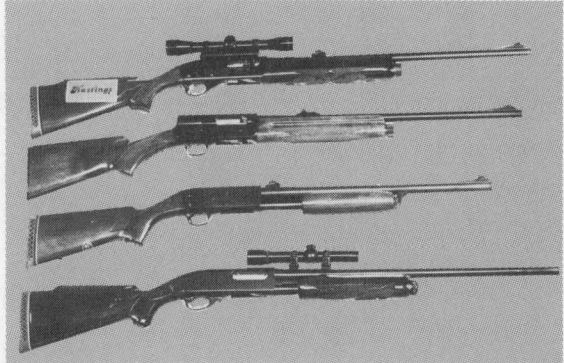

The Hastings Paradox Rifled Slug Barrel puts rifle-like accuracy within the reach and budget of every shotgun hunter. The rifled bore has a 1:34 twist for increased slug stability and superb accuracy. These are the only rifled slug barrels sold as exact replacement barrels for most popular single-barrel 12-gauge guns (no fitting required).

Barrels are offered in 20" and 24" lengths and are equipped with rifle sights or scope mount blocks. The popular Cantilever Scope Mount barrel has an extended mount to allow the use of a standard eye relief scope. All barrels have a high-polish blued finish and are proof-tested and serial-numbered.

Paradox barrels are available from select gunshops or directly from Hastings. Call for more information.

HASTINGS BARRELS

LINSEED RUBBING OIL

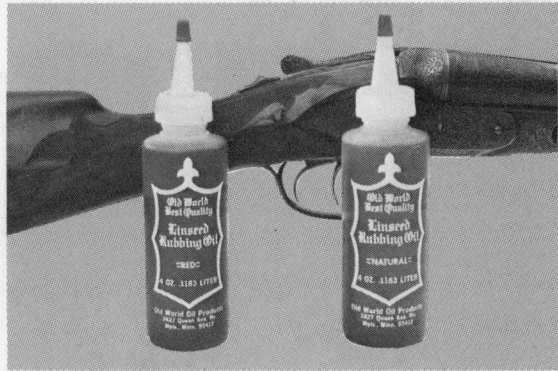

Old World Oil Products has been offering best-quality linseed oil for over a decade. Long recognized as *the* professional gun stock finish, linseed oil brings out the full character and quality of a walnut gun stock.

This linseed oil is available in red or amber shades and is perfect for the expert refinishing of old gun lumber or the complete and total enhancement of a brand new gun stock.

This product is also ideal for maintaining original, oil-finished stocks.

Each bottle of linseed oil comes complete with instructions. Simply send $7.50 for a 4-oz. bottle of red or amber Old World Linseed Oil. Catalogs are not available.

OLD WORLD OIL PRODUCTS

See manufacturers' addresses on page 259.

SHOOTER'S MARKETPLACE

FREE CATALOG OFFER

The 32-page catalog from Century International Arms contains hundreds of new and surplus rifles, handguns, ammunition, parts and accessories.

The catalog features Century's latest products, including the Deluxe Custom Sporter Rifle. Built from specially selected small-ring M98 actions, which have proven to be the most reliable, this low-recoil rifle is ideally suited for women, youth and recoil-sensitive shooters. It is also the perfect rifle for deer hunting.

Also featured in the catalog is an expanded sporting line of new optical accessories, as well as new replica swords.

Write Century International Arms for a free catalog.

CENTURY INTERNATIONAL ARMS, INC.

NEW SEE-THROUGH SCOPE MOUNT

J.B. Holden Co. introduced the patented Ironsighter® "See-Thru" scope mount line in 1967. Today, the Ironsighter two-way sighting option is accepted as standard. The Holden Wide Ironsighters are one of their most recent developments; the 700 series Ironsighters are now available for most centerfire, rimfire and muzzleloading rifles as well as many handguns and shotguns.

Holden offers a superior aluminum alloy which is as much as 60% stronger than the materials found in similar products. When combined with solid engineering designs, added metal thickness in high-stress areas, and precision-machined contact surfaces, Holden mounts will withstand the heaviest types of use.

J.B. HOLDEN CO.

CUSTOM SPORTING RIFLE

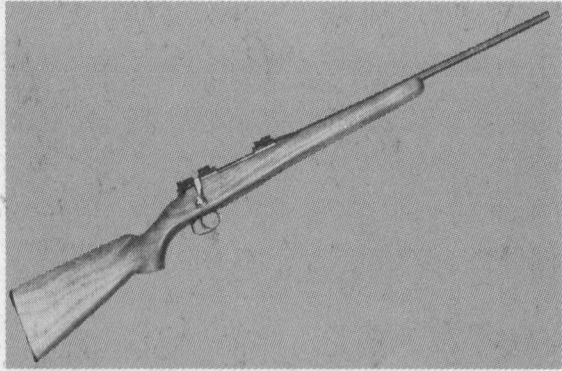

The Deluxe Custom Sporter rifle from Century International Arms is available in two calibers—7.62x39mm and 308 Winchester.

It is built from specially selected small-ring M98 actions, making it among the strongest, most accurate sporting rifles currently on the market.

This rifle is particularly interesting because there are very few bolt actions currently available chambered for the 7.62x39mm caliber, a round developed during World War II and traditionally used in semi-auto rifles like the popular Chinese SKS.

The 308 Winchester is available for those shooters looking for a rifle with a little more range.

Write for a free catalog describing this and other rifles available from Century.

CENTURY INTERNATIONAL ARMS, INC.

CLASSIC GUN SAFES

A classic series of gun safes is available from Treadlok for the safe and secure storage of your firearms.

All Treadlok safes feature the Posilok locking system, one of the finest in the industry. Posilok secures the safe door with large rectangular bolts and is backed up by a floating, drill-resistant, hardplate, remote relocking device and industry standard S&G lock.

Treadlok safes come in three sizes with the capacity to hold up to fifty guns and are offered in four designer colors with brass hardware and accents. All have an attractive high gloss finish.

Write or call Tread Corp. for additional information. Be sure to mention *Shooter's Marketplace*.

TREADLOK GUN SAFE, INC.

See manufacturers' addresses on page 259.

SHOOTER'S MARKETPLACE

ACCESSORY/SERVICE BROCHURE

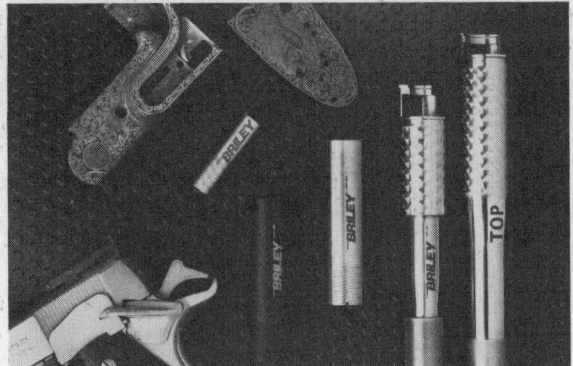

This Houston-based firm is well-known for providing precision products to the avid shotgunner. The Briley tradition of attention to detail and complete customer satisfaction keeps the hunter and competition shooter happy.

Their brochure describes Briley's line of shotgun and now pistol and revolver services. Briley has added a new division for the discerning handgun enthusiast.

Everything from screw-in chokes to competition Skeet tubes to pistol and revolver customizing and accessories is available. Briley offers an extensive line of products and services for the shotgunner and handgunner.

Write or call toll-free for a free brochure.

BRILEY MFG., INC.

SCREW-IN CHOKES

Briley screw-in chokes produce reliable, uniform patterns. This system allows the shooter the complete choke control necessary to utilize the full spectrum of ammunition available to today's shotgunner.

There are new innovations in chokes, as well. The unique "Comp-Choke" gives the shooter not only reliable patterns, but aids in second-shot recovery time by porting gases upward at the muzzle.

Total steel shot compatibility is also available with the screw-in choke system. Even the largest shot sizes are usable through their steel shot chokes. Briley also offers exclusive choke designs and constrictions for turkey hunters.

Write or call toll-free for a free brochure.

BRILEY MFG., INC.

PISTOL CUSTOMIZING/ACCESSORIES

Briley Mfg. has a new fully specialized Pistol Division. For the dedicated handgun enthusiast, Briley offers some of the finest modifications, customizing, repair parts and accessories currently available.

Compensators, extended slide releases, thumb guards, squared trigger guards and more are just some of the services currently available from the new division.

The Pistol Division is currently manufacturing custom slides, barrels, custom titanium compensators and other unique accessories for the discerning handgun shooter and competitor.

Briley also offers complete, conventional repair services for all makes of handguns.

BRILEY MFG., INC.

CUSTOM SHOTGUN REBARRELING

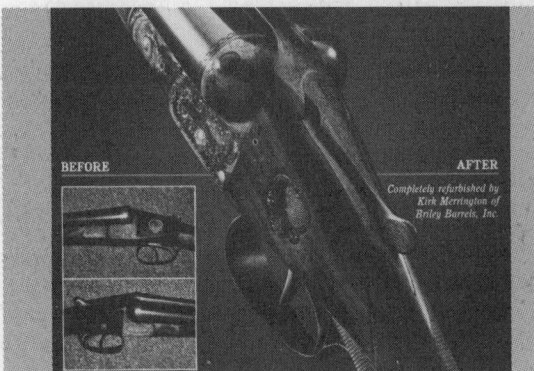

Briley has added a new custom department that is dedicated to the refurbishing of over/under and side-by-side shotgun barrels.

Briley can now fully restore a set of unshootable shotgun barrels. Barrels that have been severely dented, have rusted or have even burst during firing (due to a bore obstruction) can virtually all be saved.

Additionally, Briley can manufacture a set of new barrels (any make) for any gun, can provide new or custom ribs, and can completely strip, clean and/or repair the action.

This new Briley department also offers custom engraving services and complete stock repair and refinishing.

Write or call for more details.

BRILEY MFG., INC.

See manufacturers' addresses on page 259.

Shooter's Marketplace

SHOOTERS' NEWSPAPER

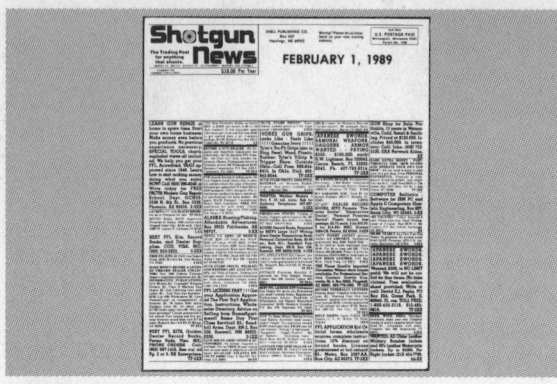

Established in 1946, *The Shotgun News* is a leader in its field.

It offers some of the finest gun buys in the United States. More than 160,000 people read, enjoy and profit from this newspaper, which is published three times a month.

The Shotgun News has helped thousands of gun enthusiasts locate firearms, both modern and antique—rifles, pistols, shotguns, scopes, etc...all at money-saving prices.

The money saved on the purchase of any of the 10,000 plus listings could more than pay for the $20.00 (36-issue) annual subscription cost.

As it says on the cover, it's "the trading post for anything that shoots."

THE SHOTGUN NEWS

TARGET RANGE EXPERTS

Action Target offers a broad range of services, specialized equipment and targets for the professional shooting facility as well as the individual shooter.

Action Target has the ability to travel to any location and construct a fully professional shooting range based on your requirements. Additionally, they currently offer a dozen different "reactive" targets specifically designed for law enforcement and self-defense purposes.

Action Target puts on a number of 5-day advanced law enforcement training camps throughout the country. Six to ten fully qualified instructors handle up to 120 students per class. For date, time and location in your area or more information, write, call or fax Action Target, Inc.

ACTION TARGET, INC.

CUSTOM RESTORATION/CASE COLORING

For over a decade, Doug Turnbull has been case-hardening and restoring firearms under the "Creekside Gun Shop" logo, in Upstate New York.

Now on his own, his new outfit, Doug Turnbull Restoration, continues to offer bone charcoal color case work plus nitre and rust bluing. Turnbull will match the original case colors produced by Winchester, Colt, Marlin, Parker, LC Smith, Ansley Fox and other noted manufacturers, without reassembly problems.

Also available is charcoal blue, known as Carbona or machine blue, a pre-war finish used by most makers.

Turnbull offers production work with single run control. He will restore partially or completely. Pre-polished parts can also be sent in for finish work.

DOUG TURNBULL RESTORATION

SIZING AND FORMING LUBE

Imperial Sizing Wax from E-Z-Way Systems was developed in the early 1970s to allow simple, easy and effective reloading and reforming.

A blend of two waxes and two oils, a thin film of high-lubricity Imperial applied to the outside of a rifle case with your fingertips will ensure smooth loading tool operation with no stuck or dented cases. The lube can be removed simply with a paper towel.

Because it is used sparingly, it is very economical—one tin will size several thousand cases. It is available in 1- and 2-ounce tins with suggested retail prices of $3.00 and $5.50, respectively.

See your local dealer or write directly to E-Z-Way Systems for more information.

E-Z-WAY SYSTEMS

See manufacturers' addresses on page 259.

14X BORESCOPE

Bald Eagle has introduced a new borescope with 14x magnification. The 360° panoramic view permits the user to see the entire inside of the bore at one time. When a glitch is found in the barrel, the eyepiece can be slid forward and the problem area viewed in the 90° mode. The depth of field is almost unlimited and it's 3 to 5 times clearer than fiber optics. In fact, the clarity is such that the user can actually distinguish the difference between a shadow and a stain.

These instruments were manufactured in Germany for the military to enable them to check aircraft gatling gun barrels. They are not surplus and are of current production having a full warranty. The borescopes are 5mm in diameter and 19.5 inches long and are sold exclusively by Bald Eagle.

BALD EAGLE PRECISION MACHINE CO.

RIMFIRE CARTRIDGE GAGE

The Rimfire Cartridge Gage from Bald Eagle Precision Machine Co. can improve overall group size by up to 25% by sorting rimfire ammo into uniform rim-thickness lots.

The more consistent the rim thickness, the more consistent the ignition of the primer and powder charge, and the firing pin travel remains uniform from shot-to-shot.

The Cartridge Gage is a snap to use—grab a box or two of rimfire ammo and start sorting. It is ideal for BR-50 benchrest competitors and serious small game hunters.

Normally $80.00, mention *Shooter's Marketplace* and it's only $74.95. Write Bald Eagle for a free brochure.

BALD EAGLE PRECISION MACHINE CO.

PROTECTIVE METAL CASES

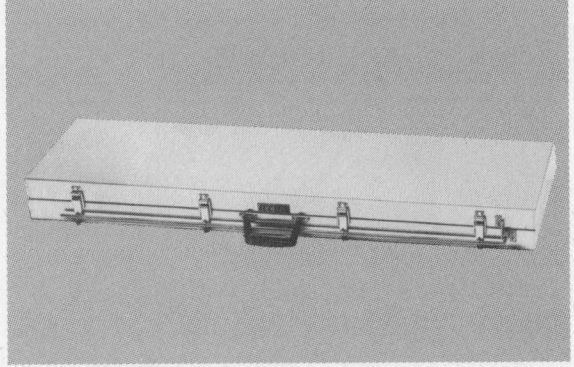

Impact Case Co. (ICC) offers a full line of standard-size pistol, shotgun, rifle and utility cases designed for the traveling sportsman who must subject his equipment to third-party handling (airlines, etc.).

These rugged, protective cases are constructed of .063 marine-grade aluminum. With an emphasis on strength and value, ICC cases have achieved wide acceptance by serious hunters and competition shooters. ICC, a product group of Knouff & Knouff, Inc., was introduced in 1985.

For special case requirements, Knouff & Knouff's KK Air International product line offers "one-of-a-kinds," along with a complete line of trunk-style cases.

Write or call for specification sheets and other details.

IMPACT CASE COMPANY

PRECISION RIFLE REST

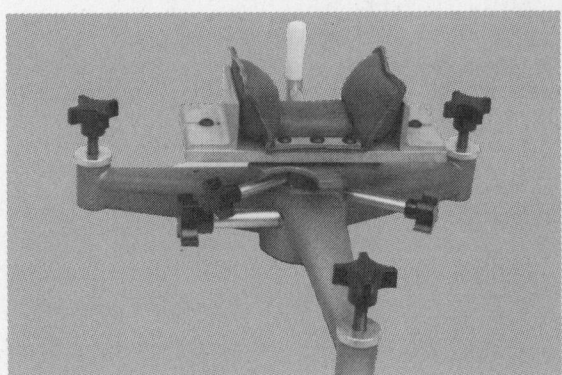

Bald Eagle Precision Machine Co. offers a rifle rest perfect for the serious benchrester or dedicated varminter.

The rest is constructed of aircraft-quality aluminum and weighs 7 pounds, 12 ounces. It's finished with three coats of Imron Clear. Height adjustments are made with a rack and pinion and a mariner wheel. A fourth leg allows lateral movement on the bench.

Bald Eagle offers approximately 56 rest models to choose from, including windage adjustments, right or left hand, cast aluminum or cast iron. The Standard Rest with rifle stop and bag is pictured above.

Prices: $99.95 to $260.00. For more information or a free brochure, contact Bald Eagle.

BALD EAGLE PRECISION MACHINE CO.

See manufacturers' addresses on page 259.

SHOOTER'S MARKETPLACE

SMALL ARMS PATENTS, 1855-1930

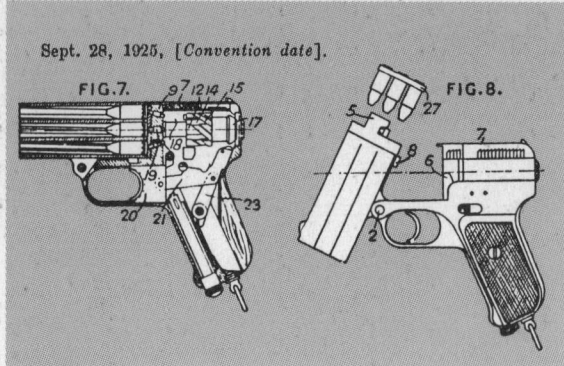

Firearms collectors, historians and authors can now have instant access to 74 years of small arms history, from 1855 through 1930. *Patents For Inventions, Class 119 (Small Arms)*, a now-rare British Patent Office publication, contains 7,980 abridged patent descriptions in English with their original drawings. It has been reprinted from a surviving original in seven 8½"x11" hardcover volumes with a separate alphabetical index of 6,050 inventors.

Patentees include the American, German, French, Italian, Scandinavian, Slavic, Spanish and other inventors who protected their ideas in Britain. Sold as a seven-volume set only—$350 postage-paid. Write, call or fax Armory for details and a list of other encyclopedic references.

ARMORY PUBLICATIONS

RIFLE/CARTRIDGE FAMILY

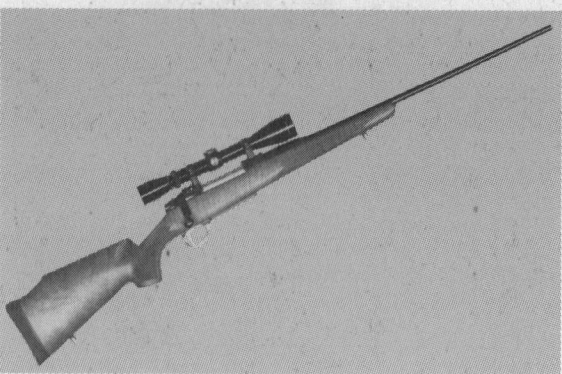

Imperial Magnum Corp. offers a family of rifles and cartridges designed to provide the highest velocities possible in each caliber.

These large-capacity, extra-strong cartridge cases are designed for handloaders only. The beltless cases provide for more accurate headspacing, smoother feeding and simpler reloading.

Imperial production rifles have barreled actions by Sako and fiberglass stocks by McMillan and Pacific Research.

Custom rifles, chambering reamers/gauges, loading dies and unprimed cartridge cases are also available from Imperial.

Write, phone or fax Imperial for free product information.

IMPERIAL MAGNUM CORPORATION

GUN PARTS CATALOG

The Gun Parts Corp., one of the world's largest suppliers of gun parts (formerly Numrich Arms Parts Div.), offers a newly updated 18th Edition Catalog—a standard reference for gunsmiths, shooters, collectors and military organizations worldwide.

Its 650-plus pages contain complete listings and prices for more than 400 million gun parts currently in stock.

Machinegun, military, U.S., foreign, commercial and antique gun parts are included, as well as hundreds of schematic drawings.

To order, U.S. customers send $5.95; foreign surface mail orders $10.95. Write The Gun Parts Corp. for airmail quote.

THE GUN PARTS CORP.

CUSTOM PISTOLS AND SERVICES

Les Baer Custom, Inc. offers custom pistols, accessories and services for the handgun enthusiast—from beginner to professional.

For the competitive shooter this custom gunsmith house handcrafts pistols for the Bullseye, I.P.S.C. and PPC shooter. The Match-grade frames and slides for these competition pistols are precision machined out of high-quality forgings with the final machine work completed after heat-treating.

Baer also stocks precision barrels, ambidextrous safeties, compensators plus many other parts for the 1911-style auto.

For more information on their complete product line and many gunsmithing services, call or write Les Baer Custom, Inc.

LES BAER CUSTOM, INC.

See manufacturers' addresses on page 259.

SHOOTER'S MARKETPLACE

CENTER-FOCUS BINOCULARS

The 7x42 and 10x42 SLC binoculars from Swarovski Optik have earned a reputation of excellence among hunters and outdoorsmen. These center-focus, premium binoculars are waterproof and submersible.

The patented SLC construction imbeds and anchors the binocular's optical core after it is laser-aligned during manufacture. This, combined with the armored exterior, makes misalignment virtually impossible.

Like all Swarovski optics, these binoculars have quality optical glass; all internal and external surfaces are multi-coated using the Swarotop® process. The roof prisms are extra large and phase-corrected for a brilliant, sharp image.

For a catalog and more information, contact Swarovski Optik.

SWAROVSKI OPTIK NORTH AMERICA LTD.

PREMIUM BULLET MOULDS

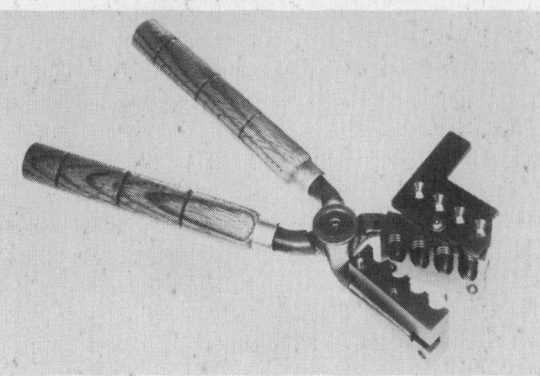

SAECO has long been regarded as one of the premier names in production bullet moulds by knowledgeable casters.

Several years ago, Redding Reloading purchased the remains of the old SAECO Reloading Company and is now producing the SAECO bullet mould line.

Redding has been constantly refining and adding to the lineup of sizes and styles to choose from and offers two-cavity and four-cavity blocks as standard items. Single-, three-, six- and eight-cavity moulds are also available on special order.

When you write or call Redding Reloading for a free catalog of SAECO products, be sure to mention you read about the SAECO lineup in *Shooter's Marketplace*.

REDDING RELOADING EQUIPMENT

CHECKERING TOOLS

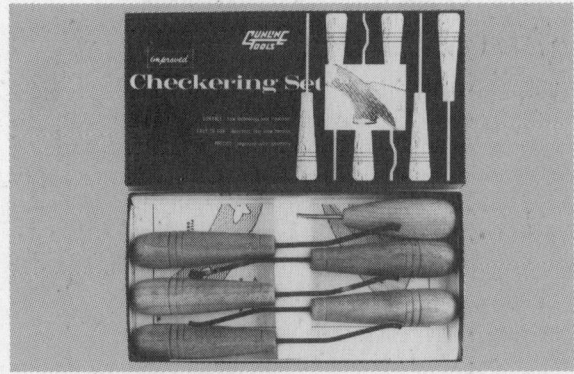

Gunline Checkering Tools are precisely made and come with illustrated instructions and easy-to-follow sample checkering patterns.

Easy to use, the cutting qualities and simple design of the checkering tools are useful for hobbyists and professional gunstockers.

Gunline offers a full line of medium and fine replaceable cutters from 16 to 32 lines per inch. They are available in 60° to 90°, in short or long sizes. Three types of handles are available, one with an offset rear-view feature.

Tool set prices start at $25.90 plus $3.50 shipping. The illustrated Camp Perry Set of six tools lists at $52.98 and provides everything needed. Send a stamped envelope for a brochure, price list and order blank.

GUNLINE TOOLS

SPECIALTY RELOADING DIES

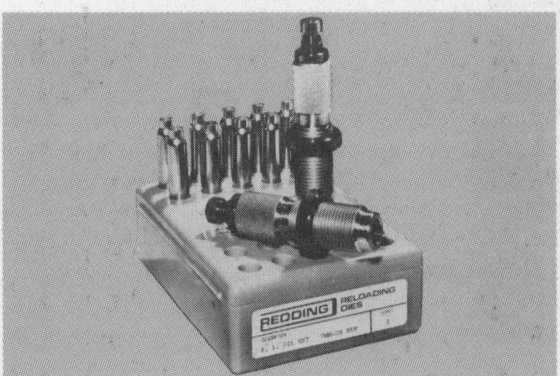

Redding Reloading has built a reputation equal to the quality of the reloading gear they produce, and they continue to expand their line of reloading dies that are available from stock.

The latest catalog from Redding lists dies for over 400 different calibers and a whole host of special-purpose dies. There are neck-sizing dies, benchrest competition dies, special-purpose crimping dies, trim dies, custom-made dies and a section on case forming that lists what is needed to form one caliber from another.

If you have something you've always wanted to shoot, or if you're contemplating building up a wildcat, contact Redding Reloading and they'll be happy to supply the dies.

REDDING RELOADING EQUIPMENT

See manufacturers' addresses on page 259.

49th EDITION, 1995 **237**

SHOOTER'S MARKETPLACE

DELUXE BLACK POWDER MEASURE

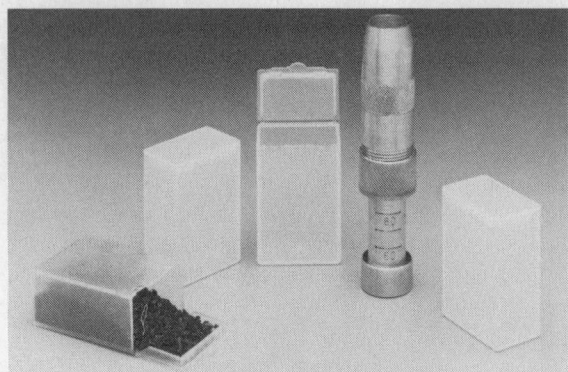

From Anderson Mfg. Co., Inc. comes the blackpowder Accra-Shot® Deluxe Powder Measure. Calibrated and numbered, the Accra-Shot is fully adjustable for any load between 50 and 120 grains of blackpowder or the volume equivalent of Pyrodex®.

The bottom of the measure is flat for easy filling, allowing hunters the complete use of both hands. The unit is compact and fits easily in any possibles bag or can be hung from the belt. Each measure comes with four plastic easy-pour powder packs to hold premeasured loads for instant access. The Accra-Shot sells for a suggested retail of $12.95. Pyrodex is a registered trademark of the Hodgdon Powder Company.

Call Anderson Mfg. Co., Inc.'s toll-free number for more information.

ANDERSON MANUFACTURING CO., INC.

SKS ACCESSORIES

GUNS, a division of D.C. Engineering, Inc., offers a full line of accessories for the SKS rifle. Blue steel magazines, scopes and mounts, rings, muzzlebrakes, competition trigger groups, ventilated handguards, bipods, buttpads, peep sight systems, five-round plugs, tools and gunstocks are some of the accessories available from this Detroit-based firm.

Many of their innovative accessories are patented designs and all are built with quality and function in mind. Twenty years of manufacturing experience combined with new and improved computer-aided design and manufacturing techniques ensure exact tolerances of all their products.

To order, call their toll-free line; for inquiries or catalog call GUNS direct.

GUNS, DIV. OF D.C. ENGINEERING, INC.

22 RIMFIRE ACCURACY GAUGE

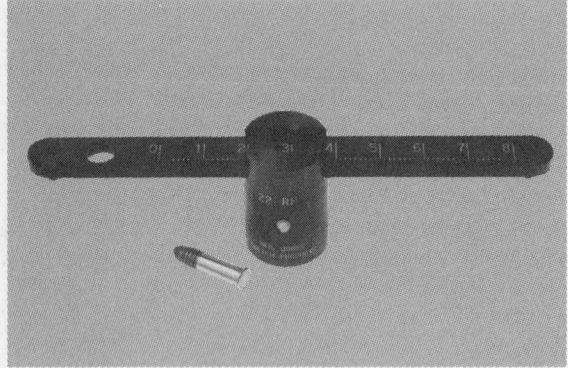

The 22 Rimfire Accuracy Gauge from Neil Jones Custom Products measures the thickness of the cartridge rim and enables ammunition to be sorted for consistent headspacing. The use of this gauge helps eliminate flyers, which results in smaller groups.

The rimfire gauge has been used for 15 years by thousands of satisfied customers. It is 100% safe, with nothing to wear out or break. It is easily modified for use with 22 Rimfire Magnum ammunition.

Shooter's Marketplace readers can send for a free catalog of prices and information on this and other Neil Jones accuracy products for shooters and handloaders.

NEIL JONES CUSTOM PRODUCTS

BULLET CASTING MACHINE

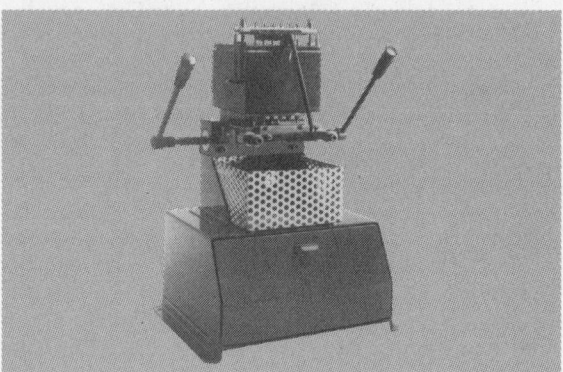

The MX 93 semi-automatic bullet casting machine from Policlips can cast up to 2,000 bullets per hour.

Its features include an electric alloy pot with six adjustable-flow nozzles and internal heating element for faster heat up; interchangeable six-cavity bronze moulds made with 0.002-grain precision for pistol and rifle calibers 224 to 458; an automatic single sprue cut for all six cavities of the mould; special Policlips adapters which allow the use of most standard moulds available; and automatic bullet ejection, six at a time.

The cost of the MX 93 including one mould is $850 f.o.b. Niagara Falls, NY. Extra moulds are $80 each for pistol bullets and $100 for rifle bullets. For ordering information, contact Policlips direct.

POLICLIPS NORTH AMERICA

See manufacturers' addresses on page 259.

SHOOTER'S MARKETPLACE

FREE CATALOG OFFER

MTM Case-Gard's catalog offers products for pistol and rifle enthusiasts, reloaders, shotgunners, small-bore shooters, law enforcement officers, benchresters and bowhunters.

The catalog features the BH-37, an oversized arrow case that holds up to 36 arrows and has compartments for extra accessories, and the SDB-2 sportsman's dry box, an oversized all-plastic ammo container with an O-ring seal to keep contents dry. The SBD-2 will float in water while housing up to 20 pounds of gear.

MTM Case-Gard is a leader in the field of manufacturing ammo boxes, gun cases and reloading aids.

Write MTM for a free catalog.

MTM MOLDED PRODUCTS CO., INC.

PORTABLE FIELD STAND

The new PRO-1 from MTM Case-Gard is a portable field stand which offers some of the advantages of an organized range regardless of the shooting location.

The special barrel grooves on the side of the stand are designed to hold single-barreled rifles and shotguns, but are large enough for doubles, too. The platform on top of the stand is large enough to hold several boxes of shells and tools.

The gull wing sides, which were designed for hanging a bow, will also hold a variety of shooting accessories such as eye and ear protection and even a handgun.

The PRO-1 comes with two plated steel stakes for anchoring to the ground. Write MTM for their free catalog.

MTM MOLDED PRODUCTS CO., INC.

CARTRIDGES FOR COLLECTORS

James Tillinghast's *Cartridges for Collectors List* contains over 1000 cartridges for sale: patent ignition, rimfire, pistol, rifle, shotgun. It also lists American and foreign books and catalogs available. Send $2.00 for a single cartridge list; $8.00 for the next five, a real "bargain."

Also offered is the *Antique Ammunition Price Guide #1*—8½x11, 64 pages, well illustrated. Regular price: $6.00; special price: $3.50 prepaid. The cartridge list is free with the purchase of the price guide.

Tillinghast is looking to buy cartridge collections, accumulations, box lots and rare singles of all types. He also purchases gun catalogs, gun powder tins, and gun and ammunition related advertising material.

JAMES C. TILLINGHAST

NEW BINOCULARS

Swarovski is offering a new generation of SLC binoculars—the 7x30 and 8x30 SCL MK III models.

Designed in Austria and based on the central-focus SLC MK II series, additional features include pop-up, pop-down eyecups for eyeglass wearers, fully nitrogen-purged housings which are waterproof/submersible and a new armored exterior design. The patented SLC construction stabilizes the optical core so that misalignment due to shock or heavy use is virtually impossible.

Bright, color-correct images with edge-to-edge sharpness are the result of decades of optical engineering. Use of the finest optical lens glass, extra-large phase-corrected roof prisms, multi-layered Swarotop® lens coatings and an affordable price are some of the exceptional features of the MK III models.

SWAROVSKI OPTIK NORTH AMERICA LTD.

See manufacturers' addresses on page 259.

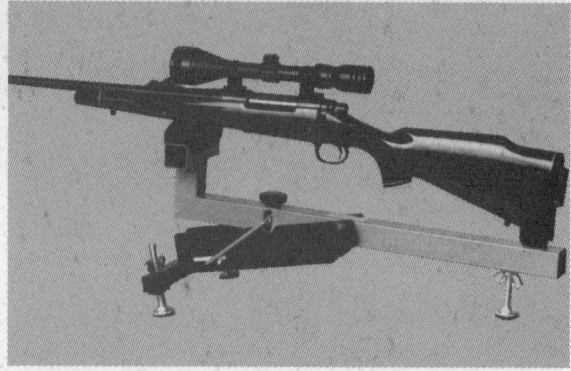

PROTECTIVE METAL CASES

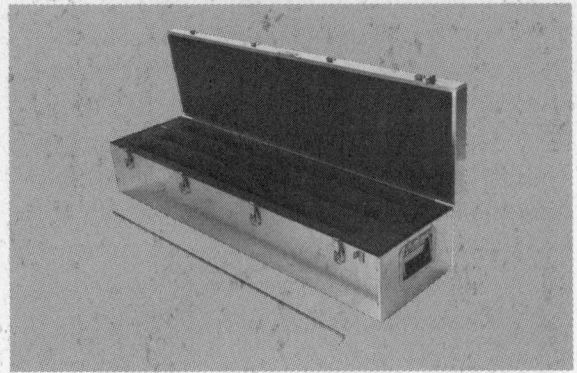

KK Air International offers "special" cases built to meet each customer's design and size requirements. KK Air can build one case or large quantities of cases.

They also offer standard .080" wall firearm transport cases (marine-grade aluminum) and .063" wall Safari model "trunk-style" cases. Seven Safari model sizes are offered for pistols, shotguns, rifles and miscellaneous.

KK Air products offer uncompromised quality and strength and are designed for the serious sportsman who must subject his equipment to third-party handling and where often the success of a trip depends upon the equipment arriving intact.

Write or call KK Air International, a product group of Knouff & Knouff, Inc., for detail sheets and pricing.

KK AIR INTERNATIONAL

BULLET SEATING DEPTH SYSTEM

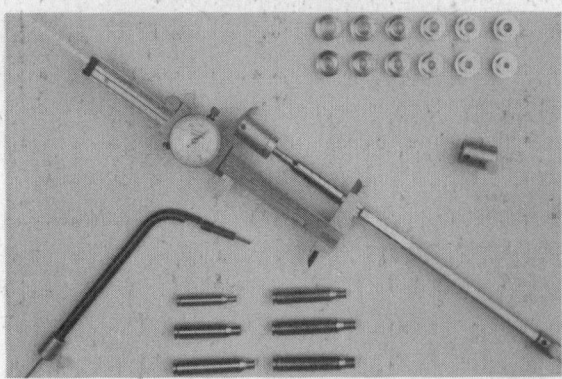

Stoney Point Products offers a versatile and affordable two-gauge system to improve accuracy by establishing proper bullet seating depth. Both gauges utilize special Modified Cases to effect depth measurements.

The Chamber-All OAL Gauge allows your bullet to contact the rifling and locks it at that position. Withdraw the assembly from the chamber and a special tool port allows caliper measurement from case base to bullet tip for exact seating die adjustment. Two models, the C-1000 (straight) and C-1550 (curved) fit all rifle actions including most lever actions. The Bullet Comparator attaches to a caliper with a thumb screw and is designed to circumvent bullet tip variations by measuring from the bullet's ogive using interchangeable inserts from 17- to 45-caliber. Call or write Stoney Point Products, Inc. for free information.

STONEY POINT PRODUCTS, INC.

MATCH GRADE 1911 MAGAZINES

The patented Shooting Star magazine design from Chip McCormick Corp. gives the shooter extra-capacity and performance. Manufactured to tolerances 50% tighter than other military specification magazines, this same patented design is being used by America's top 1911 pistol manufacturers for their products.

Shooting Star Government Model magazines are available in either silver or black stainless steel in 45 ACP, and silver stainless steel in 38 Super and 10mm. New for 1994 is the Officer's Model in silver or black stainless steel for 45 ACP with a carbon blue version due in mid-summer. Shooting Star also offers conversion kits for existing stock-capacity magazines.

Write or call Chip McCormick Corp. for more information.

CHIP McCORMICK CORP.

VERSATILE SHOOTING REST

Steady Stix™ from Stoney Point Products is a new concept in shooting rests. Its universal design makes it usable for the handgunner, rifleman and shotgunner.

The rest features rigid fiberglass legs with tough thermoplastic fittings and a slip-swivel-clamp system for adjusting the rest to any desired height in any shooting position—prone, sitting, kneeling or standing. Moving game can be tracked without changing shooting position.

It has a foam cushion to protect the gunstock finish and Quick Couplers for adding the two 18" extension legs (included). The lightweight rest is available in black or white and comes in a handy belt pouch for ease of carry and storage. Steady Stix retails for $29.99 plus $3.75 shipping and handling. Call or write Stoney Point Products for more information.

STONEY POINT PRODUCTS, INC.

See manufacturers' addresses on page 259.

SHOOTER'S MARKETPLACE

BIG GAME HUNTING GUIDE

Lyman's Guide to Big Game Cartridges and Rifles, by well-known firearms authority and hunting enthusiast Ed Matunas, is a new book for selecting the proper cartridge and rifle for hunting big game.

The guide reviews cartridges from the 243 Winchester to the 500 A-Square for their effectiveness on game from antelope and deer to elephants. Cartridge drawings and recommendations on the best factory cartridges and handloads are included with each review.

The rifle section includes profiles of all the popular action types, cartridge availability and the pluses and minuses of using each. Also incorporated is a discussion of some of the most popular shooting accessories, plus tips on getting the most from your rifle.

LYMAN PRODUCTS CORPORATION

SAKO TRIGGERS

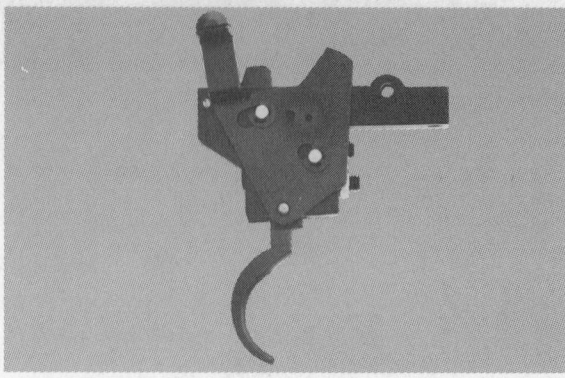

Timney's latest trigger, the Sako, joins a growing list of some of the world's finest triggers. The Sako fits all "A" actions—L461, L579, L61—and features a bolt-lock safety which, when on the "Safe" position, prevents the bolt handle from being lifted and blocks the trigger.

Precision-machined and handcrafted, all Timney triggers give the feel of a much lighter trigger pull. Each is fully adjustable for pull weight, creep and overtravel and is individually tested. Trigger adjustments are secured with lock nuts before shipping. Timney triggers come packaged complete with installation instructions.

Call or write Timney Mfg., Inc. for a free brochure describing all Timney trigger models.

TIMNEY MFG., INC.

NEW AMMUNITION SERVICE

New England Ammunition Co. offers a comprehensive selection of Hansen Cartridge Co. products.

All ammunition has been designed to fit the needs of avid American target shooters, plinkers, hunters and reloaders. It's all newly manufactured, non-corrosive, Boxer-primed and fully reloadable. There are over 70 items available.

New England Ammunition Co. offers many unique and specialty calibers at reasonable prices as well as such standbys as the 9mm Luger, full-metal jacket and hollowpoint 223 Rem. (5.56 NATO), and 30-06 softpoint.

Write New England Ammunition Co. for pricing information and ordering instructions.

NEW ENGLAND AMMUNITION CO.

RANGE-FINDING SCOPE

Shepherd Scope offers a German-design Speed Focus eyepiece that provides razor sharp images with a twist of the rear ring.

The eyepiece remains rock solid throughout focusing and zooming.

Also available is an adjustable objective lens housing which will accept Shepherd Scope's sunshade. The scopes have a scratch-resistant 340 hard matte finish.

All scopes have Shepherd's patented dual reticle system that provides one-shot zeroing, instant range finding, bullet drop and constant visual verification of the original zero.

Call, write or fax Shepherd Scope direct for a free brochure.

SHEPHERD SCOPE, LTD.

See manufacturers' addresses on page 259.

ADDITIONAL BARREL OFFERINGS

Owners of New England Firearms manufactured model SB-1 shotguns or SB-2 Handi-Rifles can now add barrels to their existing action through the New England Firearms Second Barrel Program.

For the SB-2 Handi-Rifle the selection includes four rifle calibers and 24 shotgun barrels. For the Pardner model SB-1 owner any of the 24 shotgun barrel offerings can be added. Selections include rifled and Cylinder-bore slug barrels with fully adjustable rifle sights; 3½" chamber 24" turkey and 28" goose barrels with screw-in chokes; fixed-choke barrels including 16- and 28-gauge and standard choke 22" youth length in .410 bore, 28-, 20-, and 12-gauge. Contact New England Firearms for additional information or an order form.

NEW ENGLAND FIREARMS

CLASSIC WESTERN REVOLVER

Harrington & Richardson is now offering the M949, a classic western-style revolver. With the renewed interest in cowboy shooting, the 100% American-made M949 fills a distinct void in the market.

The M949 double action features a nine-shot cylinder, windage-adjustable rear sight, two-piece walnut-stained hardwood grips and true Western styling with loading gate, shrouded ejector rod, and case-colored frame and backstrap. Made of high-quality ferrous metals, it reliably digests 22 Short, Long and Long Rifle cartridges. A transfer bar safety system virtually eliminates accidental discharge due to a blow on the hammer.

See your Harrington & Richardson dealer or write H&R 1871, Inc.

H&R 1871, INC.

YOUTH TURKEY GUN

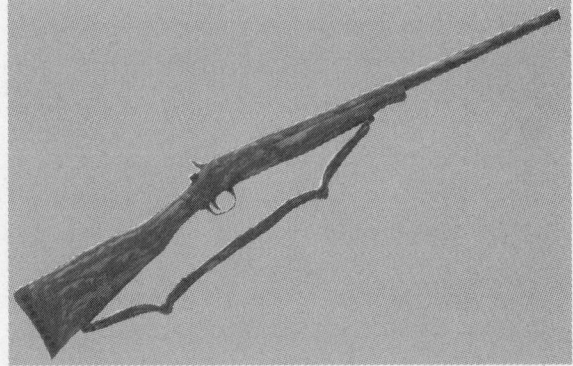

Harrington & Richardson offers a new National Wild Turkey Federation sponsored Youth Turkey Gun for 1994. This 20-gauge, 3" chambered single shot with 22" Full-choke barrel and Realtree® overall camo finish and sling is specially designed for young turkey hunters. It sports a new Thin Wrist™ stock with recoil pad, sling swivels and semi-beavertail forend. Lower recoil makes it perfect for short-range turkey hunting as well as for upland game and waterfowl. It is 100% American made and features the reliable H&R single shot action with transfer bar safety and automatic ejection. With each purchase, H&R 1871, Inc. will make a substantial contribution to the N.W.T.F. for their habitat restoration program.

See your Harrington & Richardson dealer.

H&R 1871, INC.

NEW .410 SHOTGUN

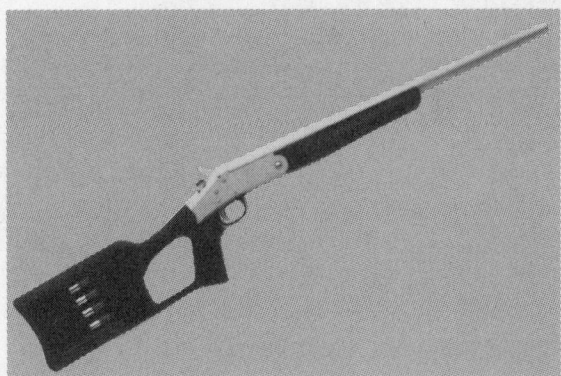

H&R 1871, Inc. announces a new short-barreled, .410 snake gun produced under the Harrington & Richardson trademark. Called the Tamer™, it features the H&R single shot action with their highly respected transfer bar safety. A specially designed synthetic stock with modified thumbhole and full pistol grip has a recessed open side with a shell-holder. The synthetic forend is of modified beavertail configuration. The matte, electroless nickel finish provides extra durability and the configuration is good for camping, hiking or use as a home defense gun. The Tamer sports 20" Full-choked barrels chambered for 3" shotshells for shooting commercial .410 loads including slugs. Contact an H&R dealer for more information or write H&R 1871, Inc.

H&R 1871, INC.

See manufacturers' addresses on page 259.

GUN REPAIR SCHOOL

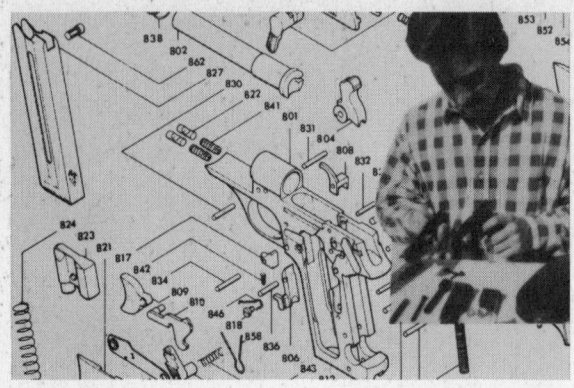

Modern Gun Repair School has taught gun repair the home-study way to more than 45,000 students since 1946. All courses are nationally accredited and approved for Veterans Training.

Courses include all lessons (including how to get your FFL), a custom tool kit, Powley Calculator and Powley Computer, a copy of GUN DIGEST, the Gun Parts Catalog and Brownell's Catalog, a mainspring vise, school binders, a pull and drop gauge and trigger pull gauge, two parchment diplomas ready for framing and free consultation service, plus much more.

You can enjoy your career; start your own business and make money in your spare time. No experience is needed. Write or call for free information; there is no obligation and no salesman will call.

MODERN GUN REPAIR SCHOOL

22 RIMFIRE FOR BIG GAME

Airrow's new 22 rimfire archery rifle combines patented archery barrel technology with the Ruger 77/22 action. This unique system uses Airrow 22-caliber blanks to propel 2512/16" fletched aluminum arrows or other special projectiles with accuracy. That means big game power with low noise, low recoil and 22 rimfire power. Features include three-position safety, simplified bolt stop, patented bolt-locking mechanism, floating barrel system and walnut stock. Velocities are in the 315-450 fps range with three power levels from which to choose. Archery barrels are available separately for current owners of either the 10/22 or 77/22 model Rugers. Suggested retail is $699.00; barrels only $299.00. For more information, send $3.00 for brochure; dealers send current FFL.

SWIVEL MACHINE WORKS, INC.

TOP-QUALITY BULLET LUBE

Rooster Laboratories offers consistently high performance, professional high-melt cannelure bullet lubricants in a choice of two hardnesses. Both are available in 2"x 6" sticks for the commercial reloader, and 1"x 4" hollow and solid sticks.

With a 230°F melting point, both are ideal for indoor and outdoor shooting. Both bond securely to the bullet, remaining intact during shipping.

Zambini is a hard, tough lubricant designed primarily for pistols. HVR is softer, but still firm. Designed primarily for high-velocity rifles, HVR is easier to apply, and also excellent for pistols. Application requires the lubesizer be heated.

Prices: 2"x 6" sticks $4.00; 1"x 4" sticks $135.00 per 100. Contact Rooster for more information.

ROOSTER LABORATORIES

10/22 TARGET HAMMER

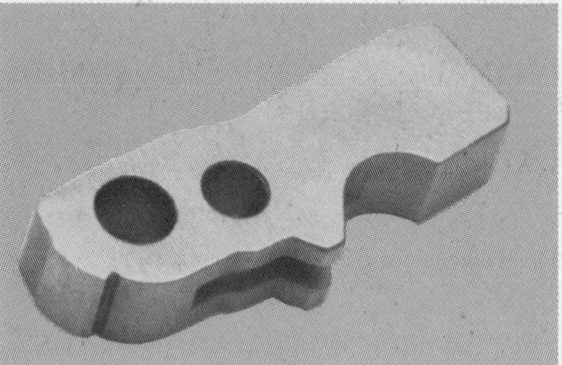

This new target hammer with replacement hammer spring from Volquartsen Custom is designed to give the stock Ruger 10/22 a superb "trigger job" by simply installing it in place of the factory hammer. No stoning or fitting is required to the sear or springs.

This hammer may appear similar to the production hammer, but is geometrically advanced in the sear engagement area. The hammers are heat-treated to achieve 60-61 Rc, then sapphire-honed for ultra smooth RMS. Trigger pull is reduced to $1\frac{1}{3}$ pounds to $1\frac{3}{4}$ pounds, depending on the gun.

The target hammer sells for $33.00 plus $4.00 shipping and handling, satisfaction guaranteed. To receive a 38-page catalog, send $4.00; mention *Shooter's Marketplace* and that catalog is yours for just $3.00.

VOLQUARTSEN CUSTOM LTD.

See manufacturers' addresses on page 259.

SHOOTER'S MARKETPLACE

STAINLESS-FINISH RIFLESCOPES

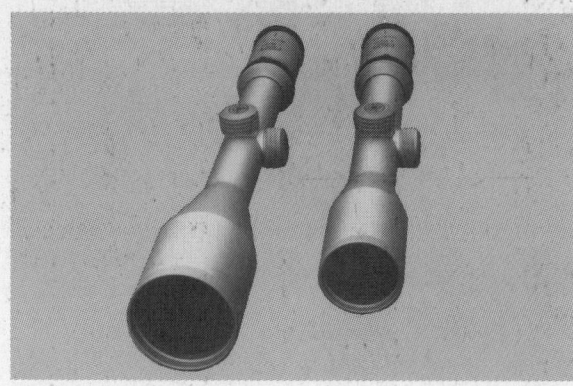

Rugged, brilliantly sharp 30mm riflescopes with a stainless steel finish are currently available from Kahles, one of the world's oldest manufacturers of precision riflescopes. Made in Austria, these scopes are recognized internationally by professional hunters and guides.

These new scopes mount easily on many of the better stainless steel rifles currently popular. When combined with a synthetic stock, this scope and rifle combination is ready for the most extreme hunting conditions where moisture and changing temperatures are the norm rather than the exception.

For more information on these scopes and their full line of hunting and law enforcement riflescopes, contact Kahles U.S.A.

KAHLES U.S.A.

EXTENDED MAGAZINE

Butler Creek Corp., known for its Hot Lips® magazine, has introduced a new 22 LR extended banana magazine—Steel Lips™. With precision-cast stainless steel lips based on exacting specifications, Steel Lips is a dependable and unique magazine for competitive-grade and serious shooters.

Guaranteed to feed all types of 22 LR ammunition, this magazine is precision-engineered to function in factory 10/22s and 77/22s as well as in selected custom and import versions, where its featured steel ejector point provides consistent performance. Two can be jungle-clipped together for 50-round capacity.

Steel Lips is available in clear and smoke and comes with a lifetime warranty. Send $2 for their catalog or mention *Shooter's Marketplace* and receive it free.

BUTLER CREEK CORP.

NEW SHOTSHELL POWDER

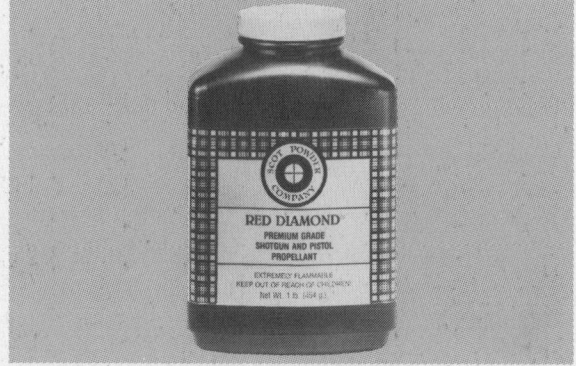

In conjunction with its recent acquisition of the Scot Powder Company, Accurate Arms announces the introduction of a new shotshell powder called Red Diamond.

Red Diamond is a canister-grade, sheet-cut, flake powder, a powder type that has long been popular in Europe but has not been available to U.S. shotgunners for many years.

This double-base, diamond-shaped propellant offers one of the most popular burning speeds on the market today. Suitable for 12-gauge target and light field loads from 1-oz. to 1⅛ oz., Red Diamond ignites easily, burns cleanly and offers low recoil.

Red Diamond has already been introduced into the shotshell ammunition manufacturing market and is available from your local Scot powder dealer.

SCOT POWDER

VERSATILE SYNTHETIC STOCK

Butler Creek Corp. now offers a new SKS Sporter Stock. This advanced-design, versatile stock will accept all SKS actions, scope mounts, ambidextrous safeties and fixed or detachable magazines.

The raised diamond cut checkering combined with double palm swells and slimmer pistol grip give right- and left-handed shooters excellent control. The comb design and recoil pad extends the trigger pull for comfortable shooting with sights or scope.

Manufactured with state-of-the-art polymers for maximum quietness and unsurpassed strength, the synthetic all-weather Sporter won't warp in adverse conditions.

American-made, the SKS Sporter comes with a lifetime warranty.

BUTLER CREEK CORP.

See manufacturers' addresses on page 259.

SHOOTER'S MARKETPLACE

REAMERS AND GAUGES

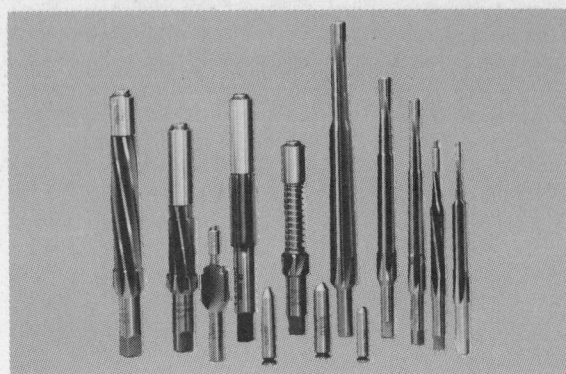

As a leader in the field of chambering reamers and headspace gauges for the gunsmith and serious shooter, Clymer Manufacturing continues to expand its line of tooling available from stock.

Reamers and gauges are offered in all popular rifle, pistol and shotgun calibers. Many other tools are also available to alter factory-standard firearms for each shooter's requirements.

Clymer Manufacturing will help the wildcatter design a new cartridge and provide technical assistance in design and manufacture of specialized tooling not normally carried in stock.

A 40-page catalog is available for $4.00 (refunded on first $20.00 order).

Call Clymer direct for more information.

CLYMER MANUFACTURING CO., INC.

FIBERGLASS STOCKS

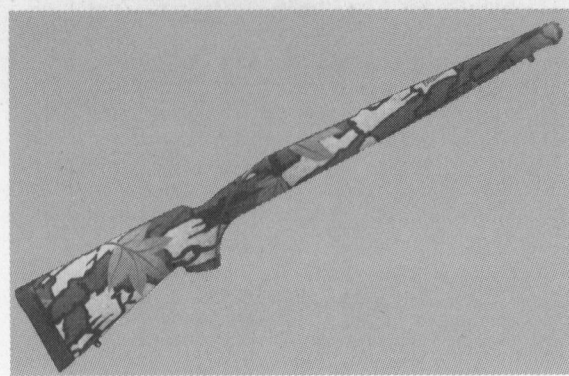

A recognized name in the industry, McMillan Fiberglass Stocks, Inc. offers a complete line of drop-in fiberglass stocks to fit most American-made actions as well as most popular European designs.

McMillan is well-known for their Fibergrain stock that combines the stability of fiberglass with the look of fine wood, and their Quiet Stock with flannel jacket to reduce noise and provide a positive grip. McMillan stocks are also available in textured painted polyurethane, molded-in color, camouflage or marbled finishes.

All McMillan fiberglass stocks carry an unconditional lifetime guarantee.

Write, call or fax McMillan direct for more information.

McMILLAN FIBERGLASS STOCKS, INC.

ANNIVERSARY CATALOG

Safariland celebrates their 30th anniversary with their 1994 Product Guide. The new catalog contains 64 pages of full-color graphics displaying their innovative, state-of-the-art law enforcement and competition gear. In addition to law enforcement duty holsters, belts and accessories, the catalog features concealment holsters and magazine carriers, tactical holsters and shoulder holsters.

Included is a Competition Products section devoted to Team Safariland filled with the latest holsters and accessories for IPSC, USPSA, PPC and Stock competitions, many of which were used to win most major USPSA/IPSC events including the U.S. Nationals and World Shoot. Write, call or fax Safariland for more information and a free copy of their catalog.

SAFARILAND LTD., INC.

PREMIUM RIFLESCOPES

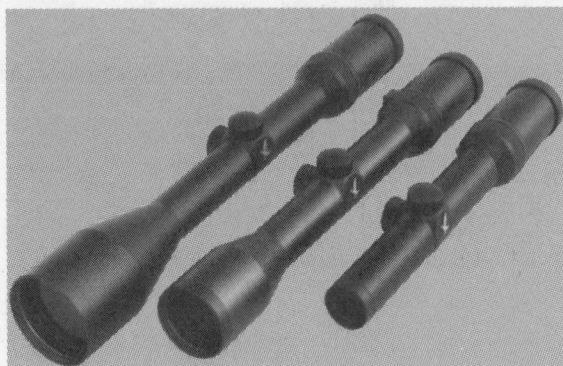

The engineers at Swarovski Optik in Austria started fresh when they designed their radically new 30mm Professional Hunter Series riflescopes.

The entire scope tube and central turret housing are machined from one solid bar of steel or aluminum alloy for incredible strength. The "zoom system" tube assembly and reticle are supported and cushioned by a unique "Four Point Coil Spring Suspension" to handle heavy recoil and maintain a consistently accurate zero.

Consistent with Swarovski's premium optical performance, these scopes are stronger, lighter and more dependable. They utilize the newest reticle technology and have shock-absorbing eyepieces, large fields of view, fine image quality and high light transmission.

For more information, contact Swarovski.

SWAROVSKI OPTIK NORTH AMERICA LTD.

See manufacturers' addresses on page 259.

SHOOTER'S MARKETPLACE

HOME-DEFENSE LASER SIGHT

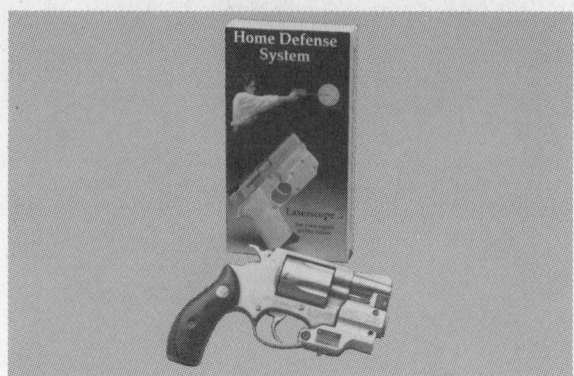

Laser Devices has recently introduced the latest in home defense—the below-the-barrel laser sight for the Smith & Wesson LadySmith and Taurus 85 revolvers.

This miniaturized BA-3 laser was designed with women in mind. Perfectly streamlined to the contour of the above revolvers, its cosmetic appearance is especially appealing to women.

Mounting requires no modifications to the revolver and its external windage and elevation adjustments make it easy to adjust. Convenient placement of the switch makes it practical for left- and right-handed shooters.

For a free instructional video and/or catalog, contact Laser Devices and mention *Shooter's Marketplace.*

LASER DEVICES, INC.

HANDGUN LASER SIGHTS

Laser Devices offers a large selection of below-the-barrel laser sights such as the BA-2 model.

Once the BA-2 is mounted onto a handgun, the laser and firearm become one. The patented trigger guard makes installation easy; the handgun does not require any modification. Since the laser is mounted under the barrel, it does not interfere with the open sights.

Along with 15 years of experience, Laser Devices offers their customers a lifetime warranty on all diode modules and a true 5mW output. All diode lasers are available with a daytime diode, which is 10x more powerful than standard laser diodes. They also offer a variety of accessories.

For a free instructional video and/or catalog, contact Laser Devices.

LASER DEVICES, INC.

SHOTGUN LASER SIGHTS

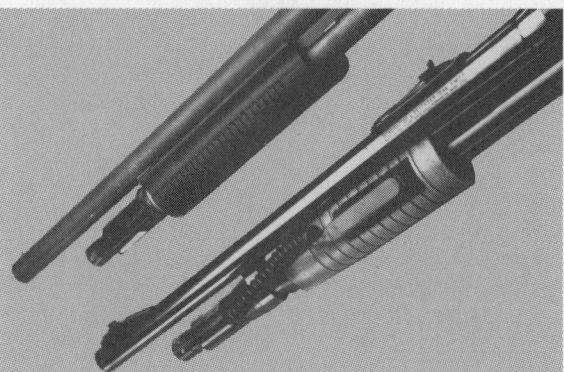

Laser Devices offers below-the-barrel laser sights for shotguns.

The SA-2 is mounted to the front of the magazine tube and does not require any modification to the shotgun. Each laser sight comes with a mounted magazine cap to fit a specific shotgun. The laser is activated by squeezing the tactical paddle switch, placed on the forend of the gun.

Laser Devices offers their customers 15 years of experience, a lifetime warranty on all diode modules and a true 5mW output. All diode lasers are also available with a daytime diode, which is 10x more powerful than standard laser diodes.

For a free instructional video and/or catalog, contact Laser Devices and mention *Shooter's Marketplace.*

LASER DEVICES, INC.

AMBIDEXTROUS HANDGUN LASER

The Duty Grade laser from Laser Devices was designed with the law enforcement customer in mind.

Upgraded, sophisticated and easy to install, the Duty Grade has been computer-designed to fit each handgun without any modification, while still remaining field-strippable.

The ambidextrous switch allows the user to turn the unit on and off from one side, or turn it on from the right side and off from the left, or vice versa.

The laser is a true 5mW and is also available with a daytime laser diode. In addition, Laser Devices offers leather duty holsters at a special price when laser and holster are purchased together.

For a free instructional video and/or catalog, contact Laser Devices and mention *Shooter's Marketplace.*

LASER DEVICES, INC.

Shooter's Marketplace

SPOTTING SCOPES

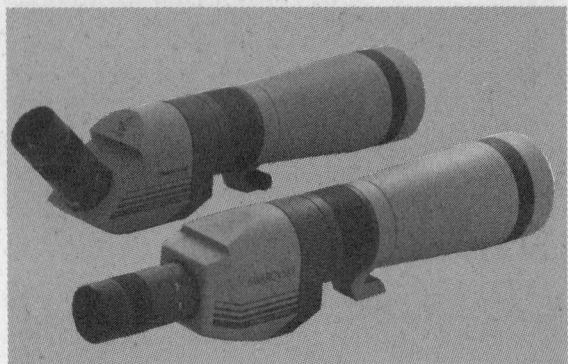

Swarovski's line of fixed-tube spotting scopes includes two regular models—the AT-80 and ST-80—and two models with high-density (low-dispersion) glass—the AT-80 HD and ST-80 HD.

These scopes have extra-large 80mm objective lenses for high light transmission and are part of a larger family of spotting scopes for hunting and wildlife observation. They share a variety of fixed and variable eyepieces from 20x to 60x, as well as 35mm camera adapters. They come with the finest optical glass, multi-layered lens coatings on all surfaces and extra-large, phase-corrected prisms.

These waterproof/submersible scopes outperform smaller, compact scopes by delivering high definition, edge-to-edge sharpness and color fidelity.

SWAROVSKI OPTIK NORTH AMERICA LTD.

FOLDING BIPODS

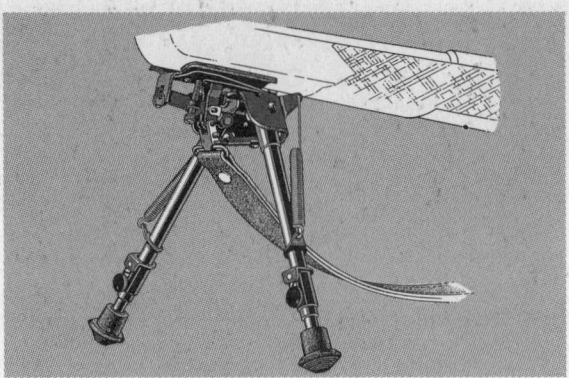

Harris Bipods clamp securely to most stud-equipped bolt-action rifles and are quick-detachable. With adapters, they will fit some other guns. On all models except the Model LM, folding legs have completely adjustable spring-return extensions. The sling swivel attaches to the clamp. This time-proven design is manufactured with heat-treated steel and hard alloys and has a black anodized finish.

Series S Bipods rotate 45° for instant leveling on uneven ground. Hinged base has tension adjustment and buffer springs to eliminate tremor or looseness in crotch area of bipod. They are otherwise similar to non-rotating Series 1A2.

Eleven models are available from Harris Engineering; literature is free.

HARRIS ENGINEERING, INC.

COMPLETE GUNSMITHING SERVICES

Walker Arms Company, Inc., one of the nation's oldest firearms service centers, provides factory authorized warranty service and general repair for many of the world's best known manufacturers—Bersa, Browning, Colt, Daewoo, Lakefield, Llama, Mossberg, Remington, Smith & Wesson, Stoeger, Thompson/Center, Weatherby and Winchester.

Walker Arms also provides warranty firearm service for major U.S. retailers, and is one of the Southeast's largest parts distributors. The almost 100 years combined experience of their professional gunsmiths is available to assist customers with any gunsmithing need. Services include screw-in choke systems, barrel, sight and action work, metal and wood refinishing, custom made guns, antique gun restoration plus many more.

WALKER ARMS CO., INC.

BORE BRUSHES

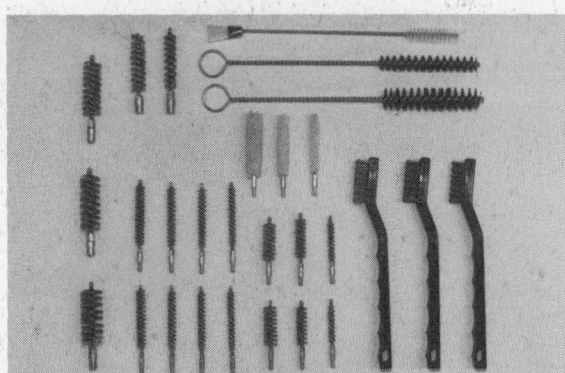

Faith Associates has expanded their line of bore brushes to meet a variety of gun cleaning needs.

Brushes are available in calibers 22 through 45 (including the new 40-caliber/10mm) and shotgun sizes .410-bore through 10-gauge.

Bristle materials are offered in phospher bronze or stainless steel; cotton swabs are also available. Stems are threaded in the standard $8/32$" for pistol and rifle calibers and $5/16$-27" for shotgun gauges.

Faith Associates carries a variety of shooter accessories such as cleaning rods, solvent, bore inspection lights and more.

For a copy of their current brochure, call or write the manufacturer. Mention *Shooter's Marketplace* and they'll send one free of charge.

FAITH ASSOCIATES, INC.

See manufacturers' addresses on page 259.

SHOOTER'S MARKETPLACE

NEW ELECTRONIC RED DOT SIGHT

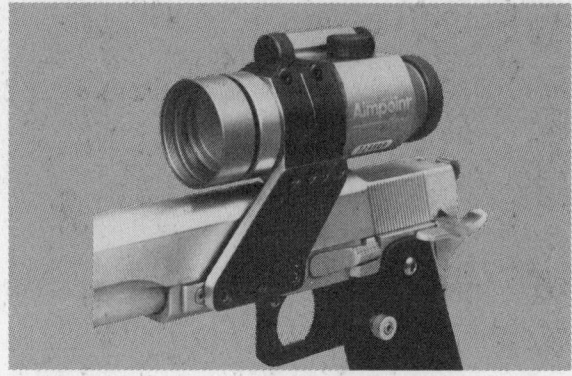

Aimpoint announces the introduction of the first electronic red dot sight developed specifically for the competitive shooter. Called the Aimpoint Comp, its design is based upon the requirements of competitive shooters from all over the world.

The Aimpoint Comp projects a small red dot into the parallax-free optical tube. Focusing and centering the dot is unnecessary. It has a true 30mm field of view and is the lightest red dot sight in its class, weighing a mere 4.7 ounces. In addition to the patented parallax-free system, the Aimpoint Comp features a new uni-body construction and choice of finishes, either stainless steel or Aimpoint's new medium blue finish.

The suggested retail price is $308.00. Call, fax or write Aimpoint for more information.

AIMPOINT, INC.

NEW 2X RED-DOT SIGHT

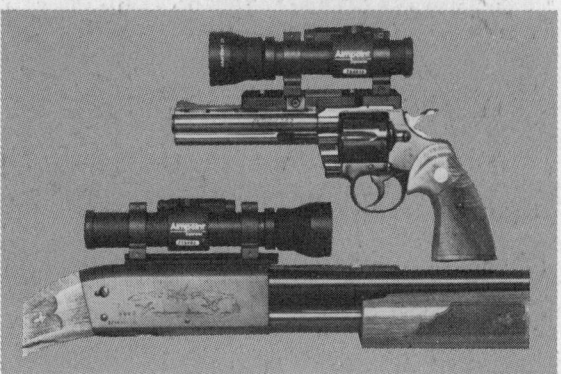

Aimpoint has developed a fixed, low-power electronic sight with floating red dot. The 30mm Aimpoint 5000 2-Power is one of the only sighting units with built-in magnification.

Shooters can now have the speed and accuracy of a red dot sight, combined with the advantages of a low-power scope.

Because the magnification is in the objective lens instead of the ocular lens (as with previous screw-in attachments), the dot covers only 1.5" at 200 yards.

The 5000 2-Power can be used on all types of firearms and is complete with 30mm rings and all accessories.

Suggested retail price for the Aimpoint 5000 2-Power is $399.95. Write Aimpoint for more information.

AIMPOINT, INC.

NEW FIXED-BLADE FIELD KNIFE

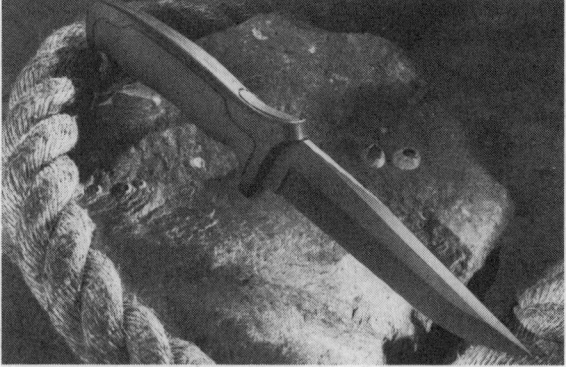

The Buck Nighthawk is a new heavy-duty field knife designed to perform reliably under virtually any conditions. It is 11" overall and weighs 10 ounces.

The 6¼-inch blade with non-reflective matte finish has been formed and honed from top-quality American-made 425 steel and black-oxided for protection.

Its black, ergonomically shaped handle is made of Kevlar-reinforced Zytel ST801 and has co-moulded Alcryn insets textured for a solid, comfortable grip. The formed thumbrest, for more effective cutting power, is co-moulded to the guard and handle to reduce moisture penetration.

The Model 650BK Nighthawk comes with a specially designed black sheath made of Cordura Plus. See your dealer or write to Buck Knives for more info.

BUCK KNIVES, INC.

NEW MODEL SHOTGUNS

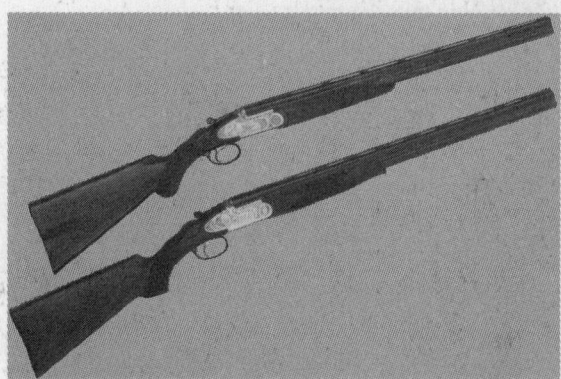

Master craftsmen at Rizzini are renown for building fine over/under sporting shotguns. Although new to the U.S., Rizzini guns are already available in a wide variety of gauges and specifications for trap, Skeet, Sporting Clays and field shooting.

All Rizzini guns have special steel barrels tested at Proof House 1200 BAR. They feature hand-engraved metal work, premium walnut stocks and excellent wood-to-metal fit. Interchangeable chokes and extra barrels are available depending on model and value range.

The new Models 2000 and 2000 SP pictured above are excellent examples of Sporting Clays guns suitable for field and all-round competition use.

For more information, contact Lou Alessandri & Son.

LOU ALESSANDRI & SON

See manufacturers' addresses on page 259.

LASER/ELECTRONIC SIGHT MOUNTS

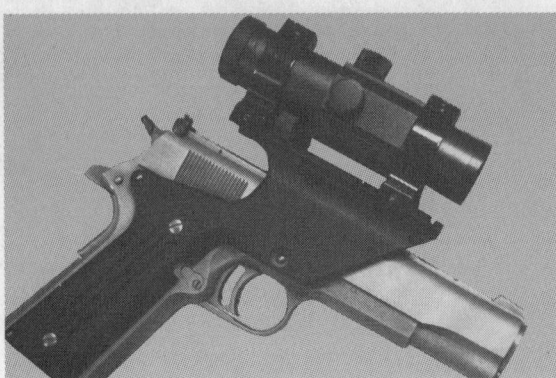

Aimtech offers a full line of unique scope, electronic sight and laser mounting systems. Right-side auto-pistol mounts, saddle shotgun mounts, double decker bow mounts, see-through solid rifle and muzzleloader mounts, as well as their patented revolver and Glock mount, were all designed with the convenience of the shooter in mind.

Highest-quality computer-aided design/manufacture and modern heat-treated alloy combine to make them among the best looking, best feeling mounts in the industry.

Aimtech products are available through all major distributors and quality gun dealers.

Write or call the manufacturer for more information or a free catalog.

AIMTECH MOUNT SYSTEMS

PROTECTIVE LUBRICANT

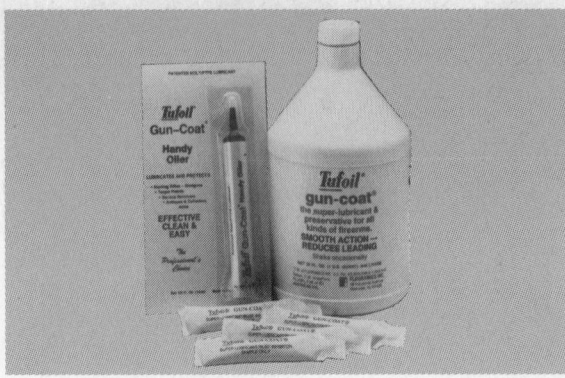

Gun-Coat®, a Tufoil® product from Fluoramics, is a unique protective film lubricant developed from a patented micro-miniature dispersion of PTFE (Teflon®) and molybdenum.

More slippery than Teflon, according to government tests, Gun-Coat fills the microscopic voids in the metal surface of any firearm to reduce leading, improve feeding, prevent powder build-up, reduce barrel heat and repel dirt and rust. It offers long-lasting protection.

Gun-Coat is available in 1/2-ounce oilers, or bulk in quart or gallon containers. Dealers can write to them on company letterhead to receive a 1/4-ounce sampler.

Distributor inquiries welcome.

Write, call or fax Fluoramics for additional information.

FLUORAMICS, INC.

BIG GAME RIFLES

The Express Model big game rifle from JägerSport is available in calibers 338 Lapua Magnum through 500 Nitro Express. This bolt action is built on the basic Mauser design and is noted for its strength, dependability and accuracy.

The Model 600 Express rifle, chambered for the 600 Nitro Express cartridge, delivers a 900-grain bullet from the muzzle at over 1950 fps.

The Models 88B and 88B Safari side-by-side double rifles are boxlock designs using a modified Anson & Deeley action with standing sears, plus Purdy-style underlocking lugs and Greener crossbolt. They are available in popular international calibers from 30-06 through 500 Nitro Express. For a brochure and more information contact JägerSport.

HEYM/JÄGERSPORT

SAFARI SLING

Boonie Packer's Safari Sling attaches easily to both 1" and 1 1/4" swivels interchangeably and allows rifles and shotguns to be carried upright in front of or at the side of the body. The patented design allows hunters to quickly bring their guns up and aim because there is nothing to undo or release.

The sling, which has been adopted by the U.S. military, stays securely on the shoulder and allows hunters' hands to be free, which reduces fatigue and permits them to perform other tasks, such as use binoculars. The sling also works well with backpacks.

The 2"-wide carrying strap is available in Black, Woodland Camo, Realtree™ Camo and Blaze Orange. Write or call for free literature.

BOONIE PACKER PRODUCTS

See manufacturers' addresses on page 259.

SHOOTER'S MARKETPLACE

COMPACT RIFLESCOPE

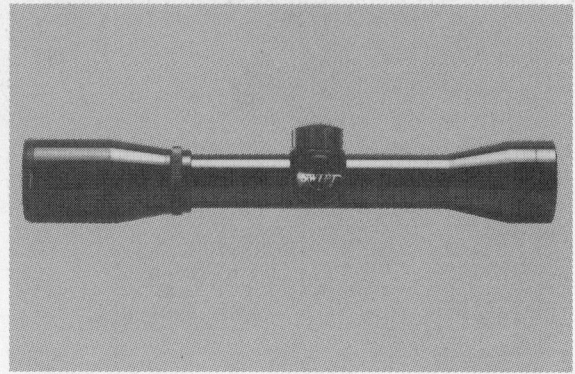

The 668 riflescope from Swift Instruments is a compact, general-purpose scope designed especially for 22-caliber rifles.

It has a 1-inch diameter tube, is 10 inches long and weighs just 8.9 ounces.

This 4x32mm lightweight scope has all the features of a full-sized Swift scope: it is fog-proof, waterproof and multi-coated.

The 668 is equipped with a self-centering Quadraplex reticle and is matte-finished.

The field of view of the 668 is 25 feet at 100 yards. It has an eye relief of 4 inches and a relative brightness reading of 64.

It is available from Swift Instruments attractively gift-boxed.

SWIFT INSTRUMENTS, INC.

VERSATILE BINOCULARS

The 815 Trilyte binocular from Swift Instruments has ruby coating on the objective lenses and is waterproofed on all other surfaces, making it equally functional for daytime marine use and all-weather hunting.

Its high 18mm eyepoint also makes it useful for eyeglass wearers.

Rubber-armored and nitrogen-purged, the Trilyte has a field of view of 300 feet at 1,000 yards.

This 8x24 binocular has a roof prism design with center focus, weighs 13.3 ounces and has a Relative Light Efficiency reading of 14.85.

The binoculars come complete with a Swift broadwoven neckstrap and padded polyurethane case.

Write Swift for more information on this and other products available.

SWIFT INSTRUMENTS, INC.

WIDE-FIELD RIFLESCOPE

The 649 Swift from Swift Instruments is a wide-field, multi-coated riflescope with a maximum effective objective lens diameter of 50mm.

The large objective lens on this scope makes it especially effective in poor light conditions. However, its 4-12x range also makes it useful under most hunting conditions.

The 649 is hard-anodized, fog- and waterproof, and is equipped with a self-centering quadraplex reticle.

Two finishes are available—regular (649) and matte (649M).

Shock tested by Swift, the 649 comes gift-boxed. For more information on this and other available products, write Swift Instruments.

SWIFT INSTRUMENTS, INC.

COMPACT RED DOT SCOPE

The 667 Fire-Fly scope from Swift Instruments has a variety of uses.

Because it has unlimited eye relief with no parallax, it permits shooting with both eyes open. Thus, its variable-intensity floating red dot sight is suitable for handguns, carbines, shotguns, paintball guns and bows. Under any light condition, it is a fast-aligning electronic sight which allows pinpoint accuracy.

This compact $5^{3}/_{8}$" 1x30mm scope with fog-proof, ruby-coated objective lens comes gift-boxed complete with a set of 30mm ring mounts to fit Weaver bases, an Allen wrench, lens caps with an elastic string, extension tubes, a polarizing filter, lithium battery Cr2032, an LED red dot with rheostat and instruction manual. Write Swift for more information.

SWIFT INSTRUMENTS, INC.

See manufacturers' addresses on page 259.

COMPOSITE GUN STOCKS

Bell & Carlson offers a most comprehensive line of quality gunstocks.

Their available stock line includes the entry-level-priced Duralite, a large selection of Carbelite™ stocks for rifles and shotguns, and the Premier line of Thumbhole and Sporter stocks for the discriminating sportsman.

All Bell & Carlson stocks are made with hand-placed layers of Kevlar, graphite and fiberglass. Each stock is bound with solid, structural urethane and chopped fiberglass throughout the entire cavity and is factory-fit to standard barrel contours as listed in their current catalog.

See your local dealer or write Bell & Carlson for a free brochure.

BELL & CARLSON, INC.

RELOADING/SHOOTING SUPPLY CATALOG

Midway Arms' 64-page monthly catalog contains one of the world's largest selections of reloading and shooting products.

The catalog features products from nearly every manufacturer of reloading equipment and shooting accessories. There are over 7,000 items offered for reloaders of every level.

Experienced shooters as well as beginners will find everything they need to perfect their reloading skills. Handloaders will find an extensive selection of bulk-packed bullets and brass at attractive prices.

Midway's staff has been providing fast, friendly service since 1977. For convenience, free shipping to the first 48 states is provided. Call or write for a free three-month catalog subscription.

MIDWAY ARMS, INC.

FLUORITE LENS SPOTTING SCOPE

Kowa Optimed's Prominar spotting scope features the only Fluorite 77mm lens on the market today. The Fluorite lens is unusual because it offers a sharper image, wider field of view and increased light-gathering capabilities of no less than 60% over conventional 60mm spotting scopes.

The Prominar is an ideal scope for the serious varmint hunter, big game hunter and dedicated benchrester.

The scope comes complete with bayonet mounting for easy eyepiece exchange. Seven fully interchangeable eyepieces are available from the manufacturer. An optional high-quality photo lens coupler is also offered.

Write or call Kowa for more information.

KOWA OPTIMED, INC.

MULTI-CALIBER ADAPTERS

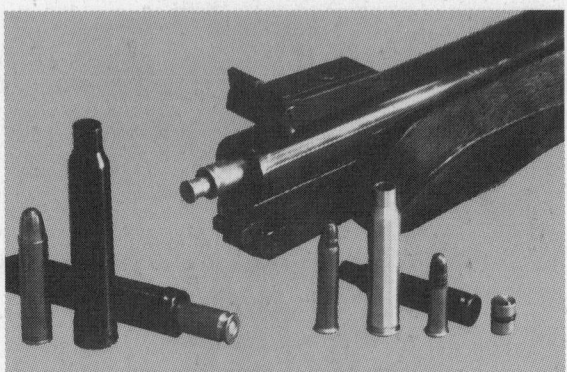

MCA Sports offers adapters and conversion devices for all types of firearms, including inserts for break-open shotguns and chamber adapters for rifles and pistols.

These inserts/adapters add versatility to any firearm. Big-bore shooters can practice on urban indoor ranges or take small game using the same rifle they used for big game hunting. For survival purposes, these adapters are unequaled, allowing a single rifle or pistol to fire a variety of ammunition. Wildcat and odd calibers are their specialty.

Write for prices; hundreds of combinations available. Offered in blue or stainless steel. Send self-addressed, stamped envelope (52¢ postage) to MCA Sports for information.

MCA SPORTS

See manufacturers' addresses on page 259.

SHOOTER'S MARKETPLACE

CUSTOM CHAMBERING

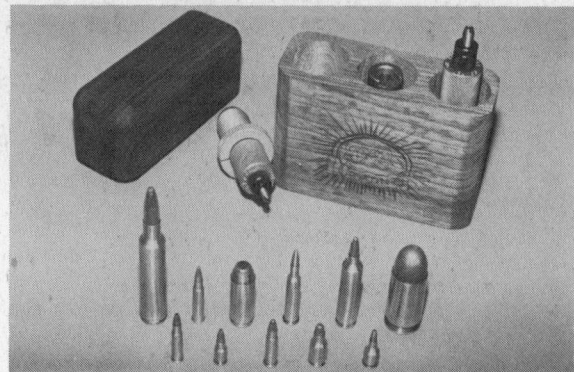

Competitor Corp., Inc.'s extensive line of services and products for the shooter and reloader includes custom chambering for over 300 calibers, ranging from 14-caliber to 18.4mm.

For the handloader, Competitor Corp. offers dies for reloading, caseforming, head sizing, belting and trimming, all custom-made to fill your needs. Solid shellholders for those heavy-duty forming and sizing chores are also available.

For the bullet swager, they offer bullet swaging dies and jacket drawing dies plus formed brass for wildcat calibers. Competitor's prices are reasonable and delivery is fast.

For information on pricing and delivery contact Competitor Corporation Inc. directly.

COMPETITOR CORP., INC.

SELF-ADHESIVE RECOIL PAD

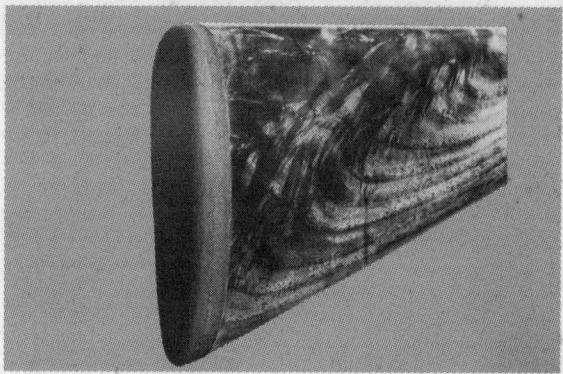

Add-A-Pad, for rifles or shotguns, can be installed in minutes by simply pressing a pad on the end of the butt, trimming it with a sharp knife and then sanding it to the exact shape of the stock.

Add-A-Pad is made from a shock-absorbent blended neoprene with a specially formulated adhesive backing.

The package includes two $1/4$" and one $1/2$" pads, allowing the use of any one pad or a combination of pads to build a recoil pad up to 1" thick. The result is an economical pad which looks professionally installed.

Add-A-Pad costs $10.95 and comes with complete installation instructions. Call or write Palsa Outdoor Products for more information.

PALSA OUTDOOR PRODUCTS

SINGLE SHOT PISTOL

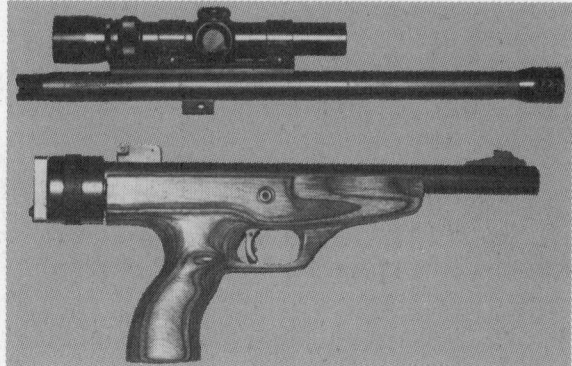

The Competitor® single shot pistol is completely ambidextrous with interchangeable barrels available in over 200 calibers, ranging from small rimfire to large belted magnum. Competitor barrels can be changed in three minutes and average accuracy exceeds most rifles.

Standard Competitor pistols come with a 14" barrel, adjustable sights, a choice of synthetic or laminated grips and have a black oxide finish. Other barrel lengths are available from $10^1/2$" to 23"; muzzlebrakes and nickel finish are optional.

All Competitor pistols are U.S.-made, feature a patented cammed rotary ejection system, are low in cost, strong, reliable and have a 100% lifetime guarantee. Contact your local dealer or distributor.

COMPETITOR CORP., INC.

SHOTGUN BARREL EXTENSIONS

New $2^1/2$", 4" and 6" L.A. Extensions will transform a double- or single-barrel shotgun into a 30", 32" or 34" competitor or fowling piece for a fraction of the cost of a new gun or extra set of barrels.

In many cases, the extensions will improve shotgun patterns and point of impact. The screw-in tubes are over-bored, made of tool steel and use threads from the existing choke system. They are designed to handle the softest targets and toughest steel loads.

To mount the system, remove the existing screw-in chokes, screw in the L.A. Extensions which are ordered to match the choke system, and then screw in a new L.A. Choke of your choice.

For more information, contact Lou Alessandri & Son.

LOU ALESSANDRI & SON

See manufacturers' addresses on page 259.

ADJUSTABLE BORE SAVER ROD GUIDES

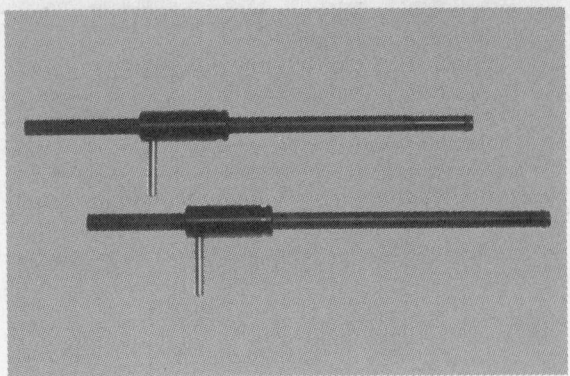

The Dewey Bore Saver cleaning rod guide replaces the bolt in your action while cleaning. The cleaning rod enters the bore straight, without harming the chamber or throat. Made from anodized aluminum in six bore sizes, the Delrin rod guide collar with threaded brass adjustment pin allows for quick adjustment to any bolt length. Chamber-sealing O-rings prohibit solvents from entering the action, trigger and magazine areas. On some rifles, the bolt stop will retain the rod guide by using the groove on the guide collar.

The guide can be used with all cleaning rods; all models fit .695- to .700-inch bolt diameter rifles. All guides allow brush clearance through tube I.D. and come with spare O-rings and O-ring assembly tool. Weatherby models available. Write for information.

J. DEWEY MFG. CO., INC.

NYLON COATED GUN CLEANING RODS

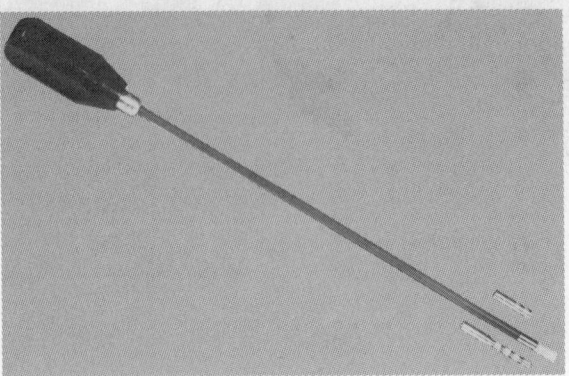

J. Dewey cleaning rods have been used by the U.S. Olympic shooting team and the benchrest community for over 20 years. These one-piece, spring-tempered, steel-base rods will not gall delicate rifling or damage the muzzle area of front-cleaned firearms. The nylon coating eliminates the problem of abrasives adhering to the rod during the cleaning operation. Each rod comes with a hard non-breakable plastic handle supported by ball-bearings, top and bottom, for ease of cleaning.

The brass cleaning jags are designed to pierce the center of the cleaning patch or wrap around the knurled end to keep the patch centered in the bore.

Coated rods are available from 17-caliber to shotgun bore size in several lengths to meet the needs of any shooter. Write for more information.

J. DEWEY MFG. CO., INC.

PELLET FIRING CONVERSIONS

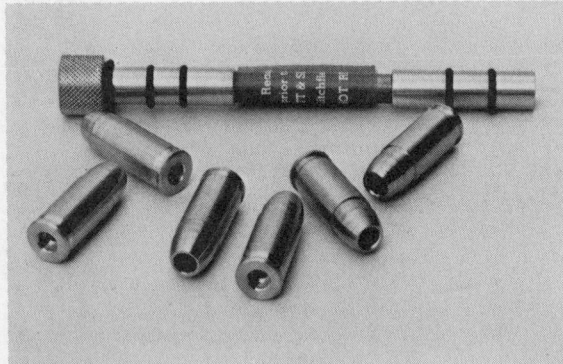

The Convert-A-Pell kit from Loch Leven Industries enables shooters to convert handguns to shoot inexpensive pellets.

Available for any caliber from 380 through 45LC, each kit contains a barrel adapter tube (to convert a bore to 177-caliber) and six brass "cartridges." Special tools, disassembly and reloading expertise is not required.

Convert-A-Pell will not harm the bore, action or component parts of any handgun. A 22 Centerfire rifle version of the kit and complete line of accessories is also available.

Practice all year, indoors or out, with Convert-A-Pell. Suggested retail price for the handgun kit is $39.95. Write Loch Leven for more information.

LOCH LEVEN INDUSTRIES

VARIABLE POWER SCOPES

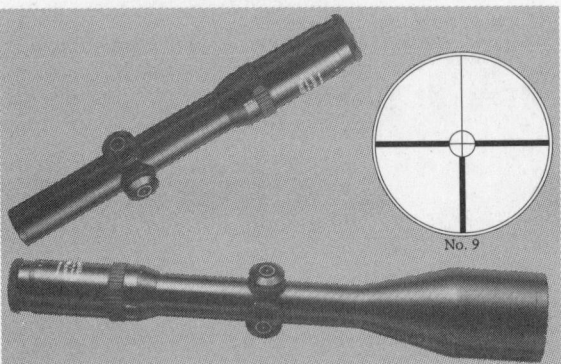

No. 9

Schmidt & Bender last year established their own subsidiary in the United States and continue to build a network of stocking dealers.

The 3-12x50 scope offered to U.S. consumers in 1993 is reported to perform as well in poor light as other scopes do with a 56mm objective. Available for 1994 are four of Schmidt & Bender's variable scopes featuring their new #9 reticle, a reticle similar to the #4 but with a circle that acts somewhat like a peep sight. Also back by popular demand is the 25x50 Extendible Spotting Scope which sheep hunters like for the compactness when closed, good balance when extended and the usual Schmidt & Bender quality.

Contact Schmidt & Bender for additional information and new product updates.

SCHMIDT & BENDER, INC.

See manufacturers' addresses on page 259.

SHOOTER'S MARKETPLACE

357 MAGNUM AUTOLOADER

Coonan Arms, manufacturer of one of the finest 357 semi-auto pistols currently on the market, is offering variations on their standard Model "B" 5-inch 357 (top)—a 6-inch model ideal for handgun hunters (middle); and the Factory Comp., a favorite with competitive shooters (bottom).

All models are handcrafted from high-quality stainless steel and are American-made. Features include a linkless barrel system plus extended slide catch and thumbblock for one-hand operation. Capacity is 8+1; all use standard 357 Magnum ammunition. A 38+P conversion kit is also offered.

Available through most major distributors and gun dealers; contact Coonan for more information or a free catalog. Be sure to mention *Shooter's Marketplace*.

COONAN ARMS, INC.

PERSONAL DEFENSE AMMUNITION

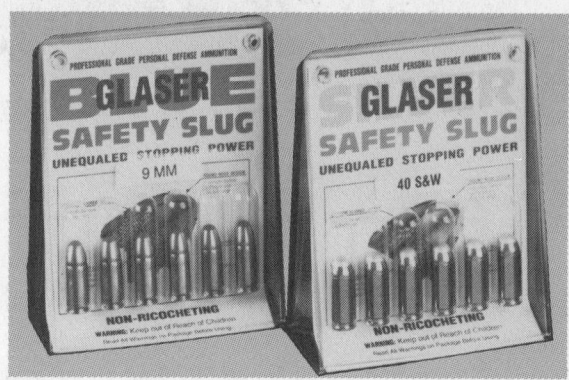

Glaser Safety Slug's state-of-the-art, professional-grade personal defense ammunition is offered in two bullet styles: Blue uses a #12 compressed shot core for maximum ricochet protection; and Silver uses a #6 compressed shot core for maximum penetration.

The Glaser Safety Slug manufacturing process results in outstanding accuracy with documented groups of less than 1" at 100 yards. This is one reason Glaser has been a top choice of professional and private law enforcement agencies worldwide for more than sixteen years.

Currently available in every caliber from 25 ACP through 30-06, plus 40 S&W, 10mm, 223 and 7.62x39.

Write Glaser Safety Slug for a free brochure.

GLASER SAFETY SLUG, INC.

COMPACT 357 AUTOLOADER

The Cadet from Coonan Arms is one of the only "compact" 357 semi-auto magnum pistols on the market today.

Handcrafted from high-quality stainless steel, the Cadet offers a 6+1 capacity, weighs 39 ounces and has a 3.9-inch barrel length. The Cadet is American-made and features a linkless bull barrel, full-length guide rod, and extended slide catch and thumbblock for one-hand operation.

Like all Coonan pistols, the reliable and accurate Cadet uses standard 357 Magnum ammunition. Other options available include porting for less felt recoil.

Available through most major distributors and gun dealers; contact Coonan for more information or a free catalog. Be sure to mention *Shooter's Marketplace*.

COONAN ARMS, INC.

MG-42 STOCK KIT

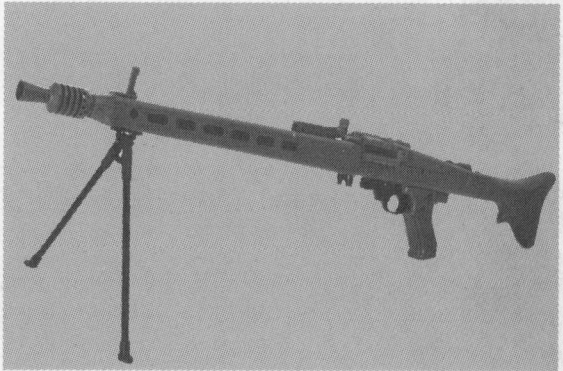

Dress up your Ruger 10/22™ with Glaser's MG-42 Stock Kit. With the simplest of tools, this 2/3 replica, WWII MG-42 can be assembled in less than 10 minutes.

The lightweight stock fully encloses the 10/22's receiver and barrel, maintaining an excellent balance and giving the feel and appearance of a completely new gun. Ventilation slots in the barrel shroud provide barrel cooling just like the original MG-42. Fully assembled, the new MG-42 weighs no more than the old 10/22.

This kit incorporates front and rear sights, with both windage and elevation adjustments. It requires no alterations to the gun and the old stock can easily be replaced. As an option, the Featherweight Bipod can be added to enhance accurate prone and bench shooting.

For a free brochure, contact Glaser Safety Slug.

GLASER SAFETY SLUG, INC.

See manufacturers' addresses on page 259.

FIXED AND DETACHABLE SCOPE MOUNTS

New England Custom Gun Service, Ltd. offers the hunter magnum fixed mounts and detachable "Quick-Loc" scope mounts for his hunting rifle. The Magnum Fixed Mount features oversize rotary and rear ring dovetails; four front ring extension lengths for proper eye relief; front ring leveling adjustment; three ring heights to accommodate various size scopes; and built-in windage adjustment for rear rings. Precision-machined in Germany, their patented E.A.W. "Quick-Loc" Detachable Pivot Mount allows switching to open sights or installing a different magnification back-up scope quickly and easily. The mount adjustments ensure stress-free mounting and perfect return to zero. Contact New England Custom Gun Service, Ltd. for more information.

NEW ENGLAND CUSTOM GUN SERVICE, LTD.

PREMIUM GUN CLEANING KITS

The gun cleaning kits from Lou Alessandri & Son are works of art. Each locking case is hand-crafted in cherry wood with a hand-rubbed finish. The machined bronze ferrules for the ebony cleaning rods and the bronze snap caps, cleaning brushes and jags are plated in 24 karat gold.

These fully functional kits are heirloom quality, meant to be passed from generation to generation. The canoe and retriever motif for the handle and the gold-plated oil bottle is crafted in bronze and sterling silver.

The kits come with 12- and 20-gauge accessories and are fully lined with felt. They are priced at about $1,300.

For a catalog and more information, contact Lou Alessandri & Son.

LOU ALESSANDRI & SON

GATLING GUN PLANS

Complete plans for the 22-caliber Long Rifle Gatling are now available and have been fully adapted to incorporate obtainable materials and makeable parts. No castings or FFL required.

The to-scale blueprints are fully dimensioned and toleranced. A 40-page instruction booklet lists materials and explains each part and how it is made.

The booklet includes drawings and instructions for making rifled barrels and all internal parts. The finished gun has 10 rifled barrels and is 20" in overall length.

Plans for a gun on a swivel mount are $44.96; plans for a wooden carriage $9.50, priority postage within the U.S. included. Materials kits also available. Only check or money order accepted. Include a self-addressed card.

R.G.-G., INC.

QUALITY GUNSTOCK BLANKS

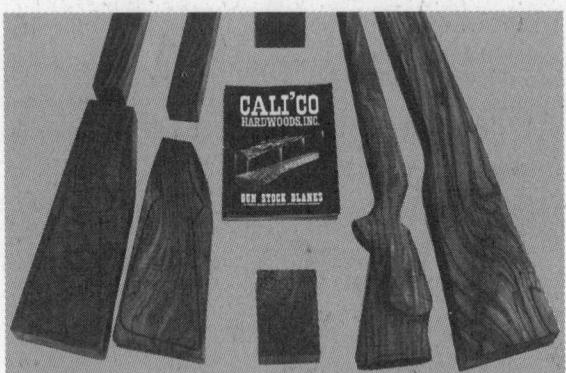

Cali'co Hardwoods has been cutting superior-quality shotgun and rifle blanks for more than 31 years. Cali'co supplies blanks to many of the major manufacturers—Browning, Weatherby, Ruger, Holland & Holland, to name a few—as well as custom gunsmiths the world over.

Profiled rifle blanks are available, ready for inletting and sanding. Cali'co sells superior California hardwoods in Claro walnut, French walnut, Bastogne, maple and myrtle.

Cali'co offers good, serviceable blanks and some of the finest exhibition blanks available. Satisfaction guaranteed.

Color catalog, retail and dealer price list (FFL required) free upon request.

CALI'CO HARDWOODS, INC.

See manufacturers' addresses on page 259.

A Trio Of High Performance .22s That Will Put Five Shots Inside A Nickel...

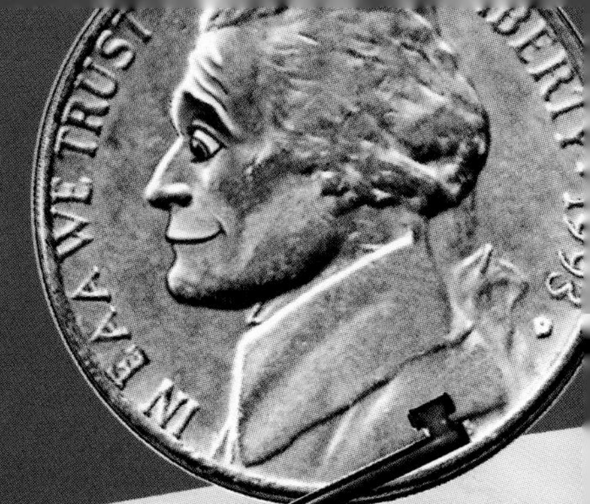

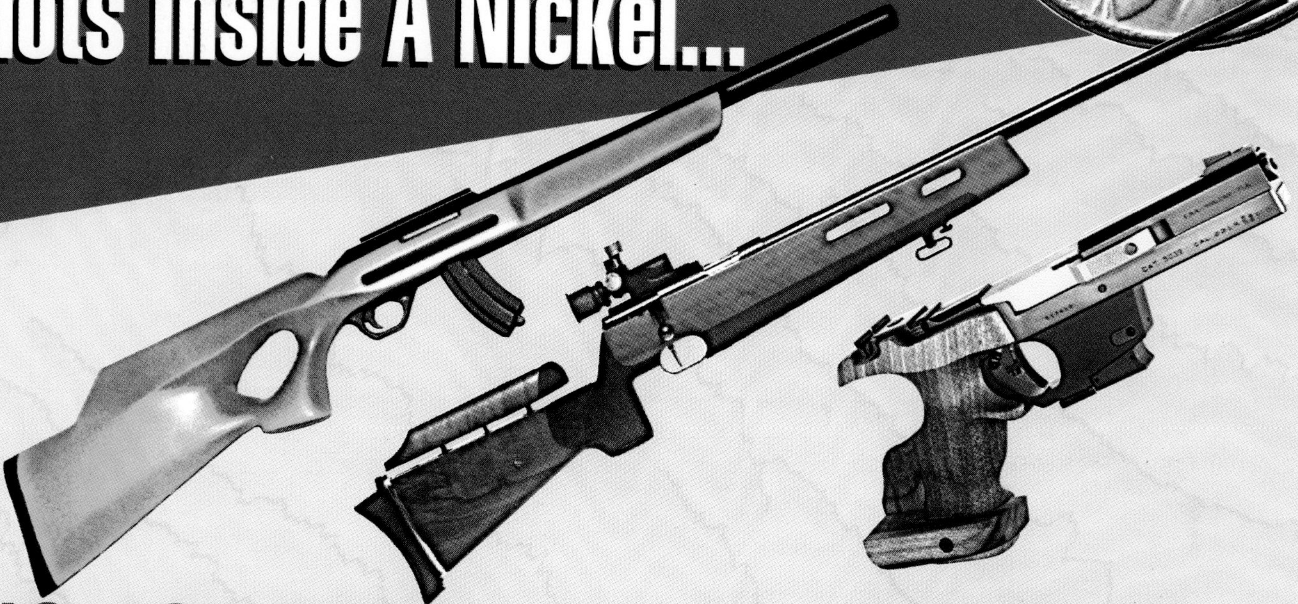

And Cost Only Pennies. If super accurate .22 rimfires are your game...or if you've always wanted them to be your game but couldn't afford the freight....*have we got the .22s for you!* Chances are, at least one of them will fit your shooting style like a glove...and fit your budget like a penny pinching old uncle.

SP-1822H Autoloading Sporter

Everybody needs a great semiauto .22, and this is one of the greatest. Because besides performing like a million bucks, it's priced for shooters who work for a living. Dressed in its exotic thumbhole stock, it looks and performs like the heavily customized .22s you've seen in big televised matches like the Sportsmen's Team Challenge. In its more traditional stock, it fills the bill as a tack driving plinker/squirrel rifle/competition rifle. There's no off-the-rack magazine-fed .22 anywhere that can compare to our HB/22 in performance, price or value.

Suggested Retail: $205 to $357

HW660 Single Shot Silhouette Rifle

In a gun shop, you would expect to see this competition rifle with a hefty four-figure price tag. If you saw it perform at a metallic silhouette match, you'd be willing to *pay* that much. **But your favorite firearms dealer can order you one for hundreds of dollars less than that.** Features include: *an adjustable match trigger...a match grade aperture rear sight and hooded ramp front sight...and a beautiful walnut stock with adjustable buttplate and cheekpiece and grooved forend rail.* **The HW660 even accepts most Anschutz Accessories!** Imagine that.

Suggested Retail: $795

Benelli MP90 Series Match Pistol

If Benelli's past reputation for excellence was earned by its rugged, reliable shotguns, its place in history will be guaranteed by this superior .22 match pistol. The MP90 Series is one of the world's finest small bore handguns. It comes with all the features you would expect from a world class performer: *adjustable grips...fully adjustable trigger... adjustable sights...and a winning tradition.* Now you can own one of the world's truly superior competitive firearms.

Calibers: 32WC or 22LR.

JULY '94 – The new MP95E will be available. This is the economical version of the MP90S (MP95E has a fixed S/A trigger and grip).

Suggested Retail: $553

See the complete line of EAA products at your local firearms dealer, or send $2 for our current color catalog. Dealers, send your current FFL, retail tax certificate *and your phone number* for a catalog.

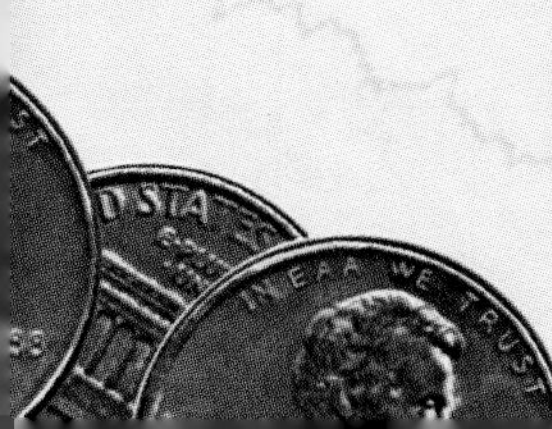

EUROPEAN AMERICAN ARMORY CORP.

P.O. Box 1299 ▪ Sharpes, FL 32959 ▪ 407/639-4842

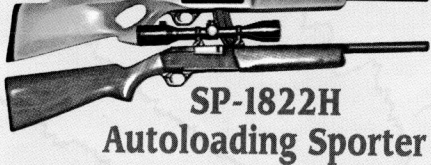

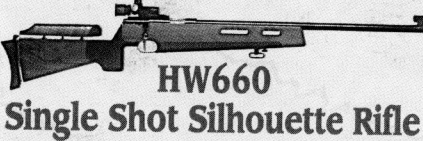

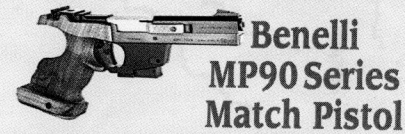

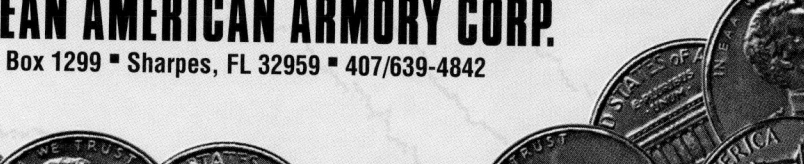

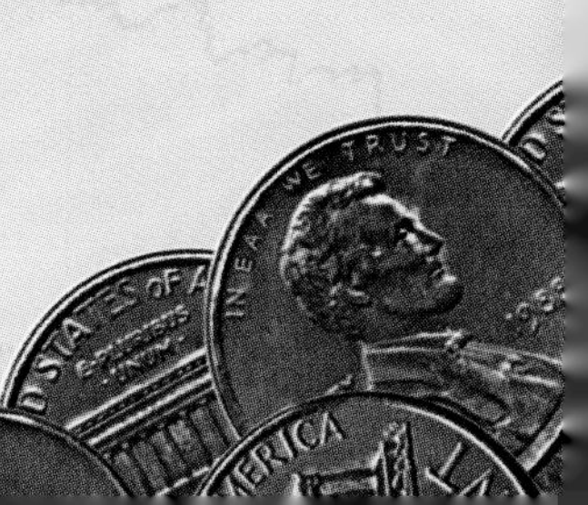

Exclusive steel insert protects the bullet's lead core.

The innovative Fail Safe bullet features a solid copper-alloy nose and a notched hollow-point cavity.

Patented, black Lubalox® coating reduces in-barrel friction and chamber pressure.

Corrosion-resistant, nickel-plated cases are engineered to precise tolerances to ensure smooth-feeding and positive chambering in all rifles.

Winchester's patented, clean-burning Ball Powder® propellant is custom-blended to maximize velocities and on-target energy.

Non-corrosive, all-weather primer delivers fast, dependable ignition under any hunting condition.

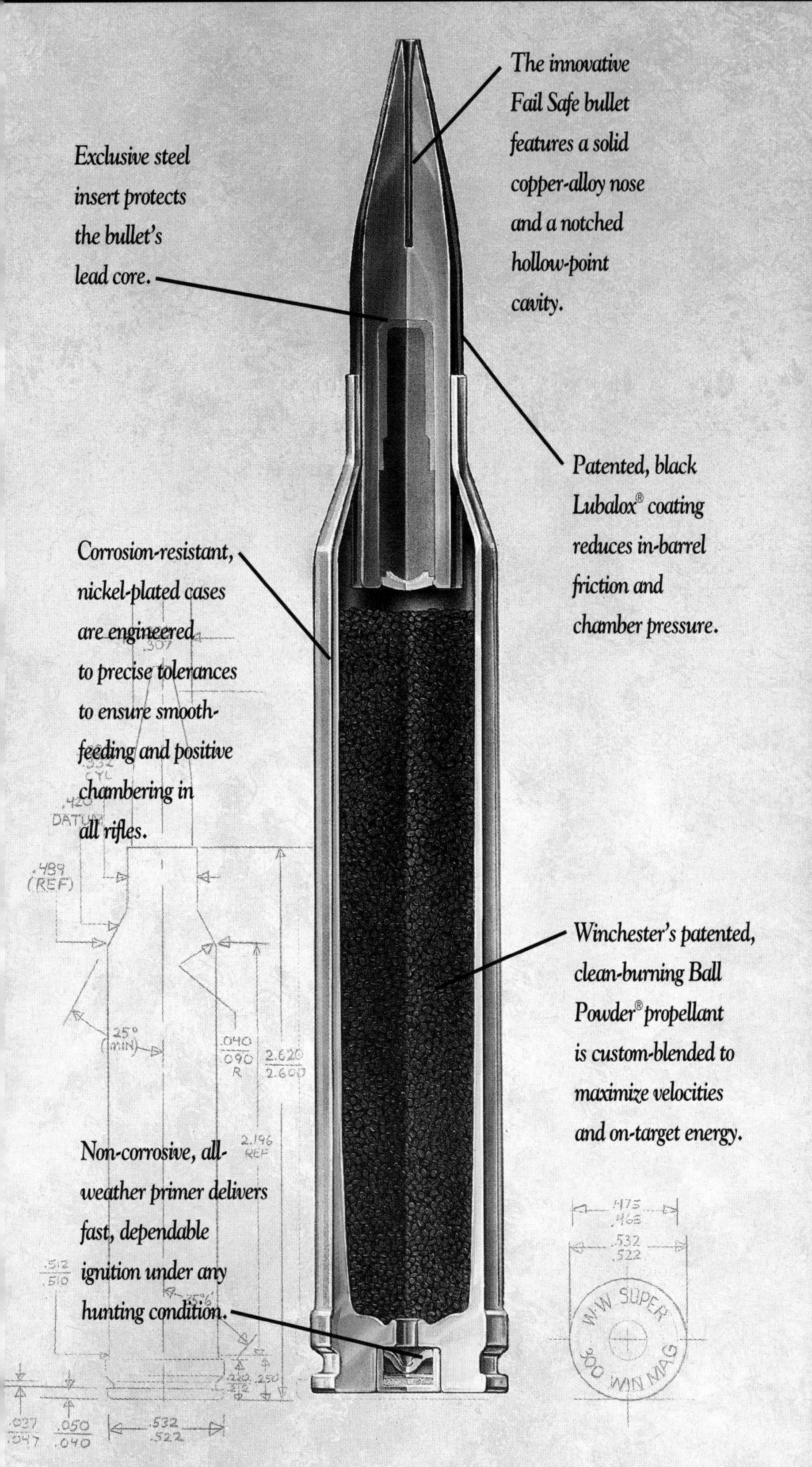

Supreme® Fail Safe® Centerfire Rifle Ammunition.

Load up with the ultimate performer –Winchester's Supreme **Fail Safe** Centerfire Rifle ammunition.

Fail Safe features:
- Technology So Innovative It's Covered By 6 Active and Pending Patents.
- Dramatic Expansion and Upset Performance
- Friction-Reducing Black Lubalox® Coating
- Virtual 100% Weight Retention
- Smooth-Feeding, Corrosion-Resistant Nickel-Plated Shellcase
- Exclusive Steel Insert Protects The Bullet's Lead Core

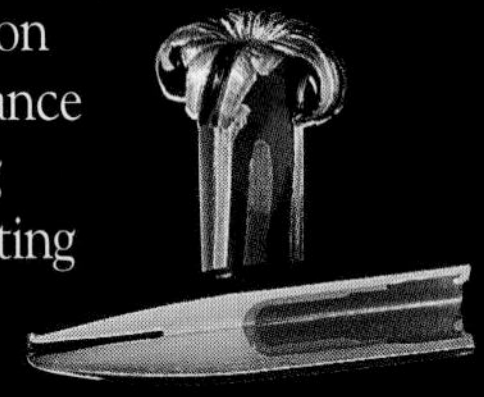

Available in:
308 Winchester 180 gr. FS
30-06 Springfield 180 gr. FS
300 Winchester Magnum 180 gr. FS
338 Winchester Magnum 230 gr. FS

New Caliber Offerings:
270 Winchester, 7mm Rem. Magnum.

Winchester's Supreme Fail Safe Centerfire Rifle Ammunition: Revolutionary, patented design giving you the ultimate in superior performance. Stop by your Winchester Ammunition Dealer - today!

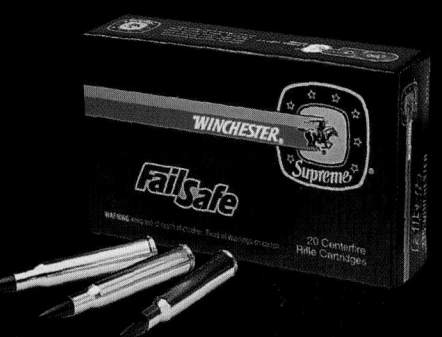

WINCHESTER
AMMUNITION

What America Shoots.™

Subscribe today by joining . . .

INTERNATIONAL Handloader ASSOCIATION

. . . and receive your $100 value New Member Pack

FREE!

Members also receive a TRADINGPLACE classified advertisment ($30 value) along with *Handloader* magazine and other exclusive offers!

Join handloaders around the world today as a new *International Handloader Association* member and receive a $100 new member value pack from our sponsors! Including:

Birchwood Casey's Anti-Rust Gun Cloth, target samples and catalog; **Lyman's** coupon for 1/2 off the Stubby Rachet Set or Camp Saw, $25 off any of their starter kits and the Lyman hat or lapel pin; **PACT's** $10 off coupon for the Electronic Powder Scale; a $25 off coupon on **Production Industries'** The Rock reloading bench; **Shiloh Creek Products'** discount coupon and sample offer; **Barnes Bullets'** 20% discount coupon on bore cleaner and load manual; **Wolfe Publishing's** 10% off coupon for any books and prints; **National Muzzle Loading Rifle Association's** free book with membership; $4 off the **Prairie Dog Digest**; $5 off **Accurate Arms'** loading guide; **Sierra Bullet's** key chain and catalog; **Vihtavouri's** reloading guide and a **Nosler** product catalog.

International Handloader Association sponsors are: Lyman • Birchwood Casey • PACT • Accurate Arms • Barnes Bullets • Production Industries • National Muzzle Loading Rifle Assoc. • Shiloh Creek Products • Prairie Dog Digest • Wolfe Publishing • Sierra Bullets • National Reloading Manufacturers Assoc. • Vihtavuori • Nosler

---

Send **$29.00** ($39.00 outside U.S.) for your annual **International Handloader Association** membership to: **HANDLOADER**, 6471 Airpark Drive, Prescott, Arizona 86301 or for fast service call 1-800-899-7810.

NAME _____ DAYTIME PHONE ( ) _____

ADDRESS _____

CITY _____ STATE _____ ZIP _____

CHARGE MY ☐ VISA ☐ MASTERCARD # _____ EXP. DATE _____

SIGNATURE _____

SHOOTER'S MARKETPLACE

NEW SEMI-AUTO SINGLE-ACTION PISTOL

    The new stainless-steel 22 semi-automatic, single-action pistol from Colt's provides high performance at a competitive price, making it an ideal choice for training a new shooter or as an affordable plinker for the experienced shooter.

    Reminiscent of the old Woodsman, this new generation Colt features a $4^1/_2$" barrel, an overall length of $8^5/_8$" and weighs only 33 ounces. Its ergonomic design and black composite grips provide shooting comfort for all ages and all sizes. The integral ventilated barrel rib gives this little 22 a "big gun" appearance. Other features include fixed sights with a sight radius of $5^3/_4$" and 10+1 magazine capacity.

    Call their toll-free number or write Colt's for more information.

COLT'S MFG. CO., INC.

TWO NEW CATALOGS

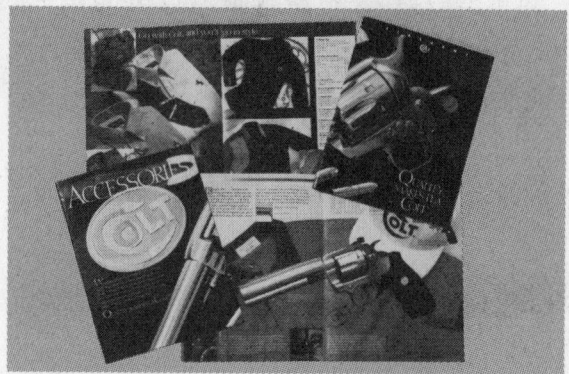

    Two catalogs from Colt's present detailed looks at the current firearm offerings from this company and all the available accessory items bearing the Colt name and insignia. The Firearms Catalog features a full-color, life-size photograph of each Colt revolver, pistol and rifle, even the Single Action Army, and a detailed specification chart for each model. Woven through the catalog is a storyline tracing the manufacturing process and explaining the handcraft involved in producing each gun. A section also highlights the special services and firearms offered through The Colt Custom Gun Shop. The Wearables Catalog itemizes over 100 Colt's wearables and accessories, ranging from leather or denim jackets to golf balls and drinking glasses. To order, call toll-free, fax or write Colt's for your free catalogs.

COLT'S MFG. CO., INC.

RIFLESCOPE LINE

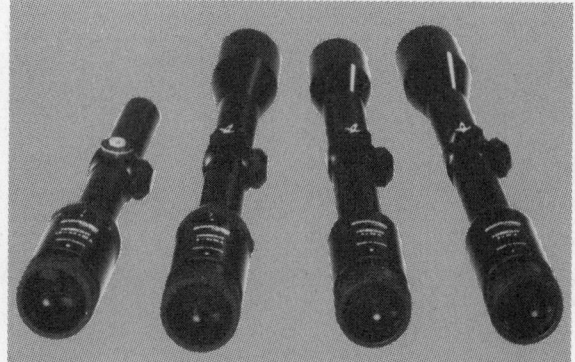

    Swarovski Optik assembles and reconditions riflescopes right here in the United States. Their most popular "A" or American line consists of four models in 1" tubes—4x32, 6x36, 1.5-4x20 and 3-9x36.

    These scopes are housed in alloy tubes for light weight, are compact in design for ease of mounting and balance and have telescoping eyepieces. The optical image is brilliantly clear and sharp to the edge of the wide field of view. This is due, primarily, to the use of quality optical glass and the full multi-coating of all surfaces using the patented Swarotop® process.

    The scopes are internally dry, nitrogen-filled and waterproof/submersible. For a color catalog and more information, contact Swarovski directly.

SWAROVSKI OPTIK NORTH AMERICA LTD.

RE-ENERGIZING SERRATED KNIVES

    Diamond Machining Technology (DMT) offers a pocket Serrated Knife Sharpener that quickly restores the edges of serrated knives and other cutting tools. The sharpener is a 4-inch cone that tapers in diameter from $1/_{16}$- to $1/_4$-inch, the most common serration sizes found on cutting tools.

    The knife sharpener is coated with micronized diamond crystals in coarse or fine grit. The diamond abrasive quickly sharpens one serration at a time, restoring knives and tools to peak efficiency.

    The sharpener is part of DMT's Diafold™ line of sharpening tools. Diafold sharpeners are housed in a plastic case that unfolds into a convenient handle.

    Contact DMT for a full-line catalog of precision Diamond products, all made in the United States.

DIAMOND MACHINING TECHNOLOGY, INC.

See manufacturers' addresses on page 259.

SHOOTER'S MARKETPLACE

REPLICA FIREARMS

Navy Arms Company, well-known in the industry for their blackpowder replica firearms, also offers a variety of cartridge reproductions to the collector and shooter. The newest addition to the Navy Arms product line is the 1875 Schofield, a replica of the S&W top-break revolver carried by Jesse James and Gen. George Armstrong Custer.

Their full-color catalog is packed with arms, accoutrements and accessories. Weapons represented range from replicas from the Revolutionary War period to reproductions from the Old West.

Mention *Shooter's Marketplace* and you'll receive their $2.00 catalog for only $1.00. Dealers send a copy of your F.F.L. for a free catalog and inclusion on Navy Arms' dealer special/military surplus mailing list.

NAVY ARMS COMPANY

PRECISION SHOOTING MAGAZINE

Precision Shooting is a 100-page monthly publication that deals exclusively with extreme rifle accuracy.

In each issue there is extensive coverage of the following subjects: benchrest shooting, big bores, small bores, lead bullets, Schuetzens, single shot rifles, precision reloading, wildcat cartridges, long-distance live-varmint shooting, rifle gunsmiths from 1870 to the present, and rifle nostalgia and personna. While the subject matter is somewhat technical in nature, much of the writing and editing is saucy and irreverent and spiced with editorial humor, quips and philosophy.

The annual subscription rate is $29.00; Visa and MasterCard accepted.

PRECISION SHOOTING, INC.

ECONOMICAL CLEANING KITS

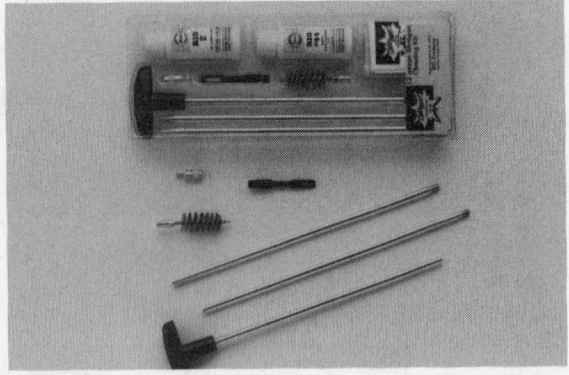

RIG Products, a leading manufacturer of gun cleaning gear since 1936, pays attention to detail and takes pride in their American-made products.

Their stainless steel RIG Rod™ is precision-machined, as are the products in their new Clean-Power™ line.

RIG's new lineup includes economical cleaning kits and aluminum rods. CleanPower patches, among the finest available, are made of densely woven 100 percent cotton twill fabric. Absorbing up to 10 times more than most patches, they come in six sizes to fit just about any gun.

The RIG Products line is available at sporting goods dealers and gun stores. Call, write or fax for a free brochure.

RIG PRODUCTS

MACHINE/TOOL CATALOG

The Blue Ridge Machinery & Tools, Inc. #17 Catalog offers a complete selection of lathes, milling machines, shop supplies, tools, accessories, books, metals—aluminum, stainless steel, sheet metal, brass, bronze, copper, tubing—and more for the gunsmithing and pistolsmithing trades.

Their catalog includes well-known names such as Emco Maier, Jet, Myford, South Bend, Sherline, Rusnok, Omatech, Wells Index and Toolmex. Products are also offered from Atlas Parts & Accessories, Baldor, Kalamazoo, Foredom, Palmgren, Royal, Trinco, Niagara and Norton.

Blue Ridge Machinery & Tools offers competitive prices and great service.

Call their toll-free number for a catalog.

BLUE RIDGE MACHINERY & TOOLS, INC.

ACCURATE ARMS CO., INC. *(Pg. 240)*
Attn: Dept. SM'95
1 Gunpowder Blvd.
McEwen, TN 37101
Phone: 615-729-4207
Fax: 615-729-4217

ACTION TARGET, INC. *(Pg. 234)*
Attn: Dept. SM'95
P.O. Box 636
Provo, UT 84603
Phone: 801-377-8033
Fax: 801-377-8096

AIMPOINT, INC. *(Pg. 249)*
Attn: Dept. SM'95
580 Herndon Parkway, Suite 500
Herndon, VA 22070
Phone: 703-471-6828
Fax: 703-689-0575

AIMTECH MOUNT SYSTEMS *(Pg. 250)*
Attn: Dept. SM'95
P.O. Box 223
Thomasville, GA 31799
Phone: 912-226-4313
Fax: 912-227-0222

LOU ALESSANDRI & SON *(Pgs. 249,253,256)*
Attn: Dept. SM'95
24 French St.
Rehoboth, MA 02769
Phone: 800-248-5652
Fax: 508-252-3436

ANDERSON MANUFACTURING CO., INC. *(Pg. 238)*
Attn: Dept. SM'95
P.O. Box 2640
Oak Harbor, WA 98277
Phone: 206-675-7300
Fax: 206-675-3939

ARMORY PUBLICATIONS *(Pg. 236)*
Attn: Dept. SM'95
P.O. Box 4206
Oceanside, CA 92052
Phone: 619-757-3930
Fax: 619-722-4108

B-SQUARE COMPANY, INC. *(Pgs. 228,229)*
Attn: Dept. SM'95
P.O. Box 11530
Fort Worth, TX 76110
Phone: 800-433-2909 or 817-923-0964
Fax: 817-926-7012

LES BAER CUSTOM, INC. *(Pg. 236)*
Attn: Dept. SM'95
29601 34th Ave.
Hillsdale, IL 61257
Phone: 309-794-1166
Fax: 309-794-9882

BALD EAGLE PRECISION MACHINE CO. *(Pg. 235)*
Attn: Dept. SM'95
101-K Allison Street
Lock Haven, PA 17745
Phone: 717-748-6772
Fax: 717-748-4443

BELL & CARLSON, INC. *(Pg. 252)*
Attn: Dept. SM'95
509 N. 5th Street
Atwood, KS 67730
Phone: 800-634-8586
Fax: 913-626-9602

BIRCHWOOD CASEY *(Pg. 226)*
Attn: Dept. SM'95
7900 Fuller Road
Eden Prairie, MN 55344
Phone: 800-328-6156
Fax: 612-937-7979

BLUE RIDGE MACHINERY & TOOLS, INC. *(Pg. 258)*
Attn: Dept. GD'95
P.O. Box 536
Hurricane, WV 25526
Phone: 800-872-6500
Fax: 304-562-5311

BOONIE PACKER PRODUCTS *(Pg. 250)*
Attn: Dept. SM'95
P.O. Box 12204
Salem, OR 97309
Phone: 800-477-3244
Fax: 503-581-3191

BRILEY MFG., INC. *(Pg. 233)*
Attn: Dept. SM'95
1230 Lumpkin
Houston, TX 77043
Phone: 713-932-6995 or 800-331-5718
Fax: 713-932-1043

BUCK KNIVES, INC. *(Pg. 249)*
Attn: Dept. SM'95
P.O. Box 1267
El Cajon, CA 92022
Phone: 619-449-1100

BUTLER CREEK CORP. *(Pg. 245)*
Attn: Dept. SM'95
290 Arden Drive
Belgrade, MT 59714
Phone: 800-423-8327 or 406-388-1356
Fax: 406-388-7204

CALI'CO HARDWOODS, INC. *(Pg. 256)*
Attn: Dept. SM'95
1648 Airport Blvd.
Windsor, CA 95492
Phone: 707-546-4045
Fax: 707-546-4027

CAPE OUTFITTERS *(Pg. 240)*
Attn: Dept. SM'95
599 County Road 206
Cape Girardeau, MO 63701
Phone: 314-335-4103

CENTURY INTERNATIONAL ARMS, INC. *(Pg. 232)*
Attn: Dept. SM'95
P.O. Box 714
St. Albans, VT 05478
Phone: 802-527-1252
Fax: 802-527-0470

CHEM-PAK, INC. *(Pg. 230)*
Attn: Dept. SM'95
11 Oates Ave.
Winchester, VA 22601
Phone: 800-336-9828
Fax: 703-722-3993

CLYMER MANUFACTURING CO., INC. *(Pg. 246)*
Attn: Dept. SM'95
1645 West Hamlin Road
Rochester Hills, MI 48309-3312
Phone: 810-853-5555
Fax: 810-853-1530

COLT'S MFG. CO., INC. *(Pg. 257)*
Attn: Dept. SM'95
P.O. Box 1868
Hartford, CT 06144-1868
Phone: 800-962-COLT
Fax: 203-244-1449

COMPETITOR CORP., INC. *(Pg. 253)*
Attn: Dept. SM'95
P.O. Box 244
West Groton, MA 01472-0244
Phone: 508-448-3521
Fax: 603-673-4540

COONAN ARMS, INC. *(Pg. 255)*
Attn: Dept. SM'95
1465 Selby Avenue
St. Paul, MN 55104
Phone: 612-646-6672
Fax: 612-646-0902

DESERT MOUNTAIN MFG. *(Pg. 240)*
Attn: Dept. SM'95
P.O. Box 130184
Coram, MT 59913
Phone: 406-387-5361 or 800-477-0762

J. DEWEY MFG. CO., INC. *(Pg. 254)*
Attn: Dept. SM'95
P.O. Box 2014
Southbury, CT 06488
Phone: 203-598-7912
Fax: 203-598-3119

DIAMOND MACHINING TECHNOLOGY, INC. (DMT)
(Pg. 257)
Attn: Dept. SM'95
85 Hayes Memorial Drive
Marlborough, MA 01752-1892
Phone: 508-481-5944
Fax: 508-485-3924

EMERGING TECHNOLOGIES, INC. *(Pg. 227)*
Attn: Dept. SM'95
P.O. Box 3548
Little Rock, AR 72203
Phone: 501-375-2227
Fax: 501-372-1445

E-Z-WAY SYSTEMS *(Pg. 234)*
Attn: Dept. SM'95
P.O. Box 700
Newark, OH 43058
Phone: 614-345-6645 or 800-848-2072
Fax: 614-345-6600

FAITH ASSOCIATES, INC. *(Pg. 248)*
Attn: Dept. SM'95
1139 South Greenville Highway
Hendersonville, NC 28739
Phone: 704-692-1916
Fax: 704-697-6827

FLUORAMICS, INC. *(Pg. 250)*
Attn: Dept. SM'95
18 Industrial Ave.
Mahwah, NJ 07430
Phone: 800-922-0075
Fax: 201-825-7035

GLASER SAFETY SLUG, INC. *(Pg. 255)*
Attn: Dept. SM'95
P.O. Box 8223
Foster City, CA 94404
Phone: 800-221-3489
Fax: 415-345-8217

GUNLINE TOOLS *(Pg. 237)*
Attn: Dept. SM'95
P.O. Box 478
Placentia, CA 92670
Phone: 714-528-5252
Fax: 714-572-4128

THE GUN PARTS CORP. *(Pg. 236)*
Attn: Dept. SM'95
226 Williams Lane
West Hurley, NY 12491
Phone: 914-679-2417
Fax: 914-679-5849

GUNS, DIV. OF D.C. ENGINEERING, INC. *(Pg. 238)*
Attn: Dept. SM'95
8633 Southfield Fwy.
Detroit, MI 48228,
Phone: 313-271-7111 or 800-886-7623 orders only
Fax: 313-271-7112

H&R 1871, INC. *(Pg. 243)*
Attn: Dept. SM'95
60 Industrial Rowe
Gardner, MA 01440
Phone: 508-632-9393
Fax: 508-632-2300

HARRIS ENGINEERING, INC. *(Pg. 248)*
Attn: Dept. SM'95
Route 1 Hwy. 60
Barlow, KY 42024
Phone: 502-334-3633
Fax: 502-334-3000

HASTINGS BARRELS *(Pg. 231)*
Attn: Dept. SM'95
P.O. Box 224
Clay Center, KS 67432
Phone: 913-632-3169
Fax: 913-632-6554

HEYM/JAGERSPORT *(Pg. 250)*
Attn: Dept. SM'95
One Wholesale Way
Cranston, RI 02920
Phone: 800-426-3089
Fax: 401-946-2587

J.B. HOLDEN CO. *(Pg. 232)*
Attn: Dept. SM'95
P.O. Box 700320
Plymouth, MI 48170
Phone: 313-455-4850
Fax: 313-455-4212

IMPACT CASE COMPANY *(Pg. 235)*
Attn: Dept. SM'95
P.O. Box 9912
Spokane, WA 99209
Phone: 800-262-3322
Fax: 509-326-5436

IMPERIAL MAGNUM CORPORATION *(Pg. 236)*
Attn: Dept. SM'95
1417 Main Street
Oroville, WA 98844
Phone: 604-495-3131
Fax: 604-495-2816

NEIL JONES CUSTOM PRODUCTS *(Pg. 238)*
Attn: Dept. SM'95
R.D. 1, Box 483-A
Saegertown, PA 16433
Phone: 814-763-2769
Fax: 814-763-4228

KAHLES U.S.A. *(Pg. 245)*
Attn: Dept. SM'95
P.O. Box 81071
Warwick, RI 02888
Phone: 800-7-KAHLES
Fax: 401-946-2587

KK AIR INTERNATIONAL *(Pg. 241)*
Attn: Dept. SM'95
P.O. Box 9912
Spokane, WA 99209
Phone: 800-262-3322
Fax: 509-326-5436

KOWA OPTIMED, INC. *(Pg. 252)*
Attn: Dept. SM'95
20001 S. Vermont Ave.
Torrance, CA 90502
Phone: 310-327-1913
Fax: 310-327-4177

LASERAIM ARMS, INC. *(Pg. 227)*
Attn: Dept. SM'95
P.O. Box 3548
Little Rock, AR 72203
Phone: 501-375-2227
Fax: 501-372-1445

LASER DEVICES, INC. *(Pg. 247)*
Attn: Dept. SM'95
2 Harris Court, A-4
Monterey, CA 93940
Phone: 408-373-0701
Fax: 408-373-0903

LOCH LEVEN INDUSTRIES *(Pg. 254)*
Attn: Dept. SM'95
P.O. Box 2751
Santa Rosa, CA 95405
Phone: 707-573-8735
Fax: 707-573-0369

LYMAN PRODUCTS CORPORATION *(Pg. 242)*
Attn: Dept. 635
Route 147
Middlefield, CT 06455
Phone: 800-22-LYMAN
Fax: 203-349-3586

MCA SPORTS *(Pg. 252)*
Attn: Dept. SM'95
P.O. Box 8868
Palm Springs, CA 92263
Phone: 619-770-2005

CHIP McCORMICK CORP. *(Pg. 241)*
Attn: Dept. SM'95
1825 Fortview Road, Suite 115
Austin, TX 78704
Phone: 800-328-CHIP
Fax: 512-462-0009

McMILLAN FIBERGLASS STOCKS, INC. *(Pg. 246)*
Attn: Dept. SM'95
21421 North 14th Ave.
Phoenix, AZ 85027
Phone: 602-582-9635
Fax: 602-581-3825

MERIT CORP. *(Pg. 225)*
Attn: Dept. SM'95
P.O. Box 9044
Schenectady, NY 12309
Phone: 518-346-1420

MIDWAY ARMS, INC. *(Pg. 252)*
Attn: Dept. SM'95
5875-E W. Van Horn Tavern Rd.
Columbia, MO 65203
Phone: 314-445-6363
Fax: 314-446-1018

MITCHELL ARMS, INC. *(Pg. 230)*
Attn: Dept. SM'95
3400-I W. MacArthur Blvd.
Santa Ana, CA 92704
Phone: 714-957-5711
Fax: 714-957-5732

MODERN GUN REPAIR SCHOOL *(Pg. 244)*
Attn: Dept. GNX'95
2538 North 8th St., P.O. Box 5338
Phoenix, AZ 85010
Phone: 602-990-8346

MTM MOLDED PRODUCTS CO., INC. *(Pg. 239)*
Attn: Dept. SM'95
P.O. Box 14117
Dayton, OH 45414
Phone: 513-890-7461
Fax: 513-890-1747

NAVY ARMS COMPANY *(Pg. 258)*
Attn: Dept. SM'95
689 Bergen Blvd.
Ridgefield, NJ 07657
Phone: 201-945-2500
Fax: 201-945-6859

NEW ENGLAND AMMUNITION CO. *(Pg. 242)*
Attn: Dept. SM'95
1771 Post Road East, Suite 223
Westport, CT 06880
Phone: 203-254-8048

NEW ENGLAND CUSTOM GUN SERVICE, LTD. *(Pg. 256)*
Attn: Dept. SM'95
Brook Road, RR 2, Box 122W
West Lebanon, NH 03784
Phone: 603-469-3450
Fax: 603-469-3471

NEW ENGLAND FIREARMS *(Pg. 243)*
Attn: Dept. SM'95
60 Industrial Rowe
Gardner, MA 01440
Phone: 508-632-9393
Fax: 508-632-2300

OLD WORLD OIL PRODUCTS *(Pg. 231)*
Attn: Dept. SM'95
3827 Queen Ave. North
Minneapolis, MN 55412
Phone: 612-522-5037

PALSA OUTDOOR PRODUCTS *(Pg. 253)*
Attn: Dept. SM'95
P.O. Box 81336
Lincoln, NE 68501-1336
Phone: 800-456-9281
Fax: 402-488-2321

POLICLIPS NORTH AMERICA *(Pg. 238)*
Attn: Dept. SM'95
59 Douglas Crescent
Toronto, Ontario
Canada M4W 2E6
Phone: 416-924-0383 or 800-229-5089
Fax: 416-924-4375

PRECISION SHOOTING, INC. *(Pg. 258)*
Attn: Dept. SM'95
5735 Sherwood Forest Dr.
Akron, OH 44319
Phone: 216-882-2515
Fax: 216-882-2214

RANDOLPH ENGINEERING, INC. *(Pg. 226)*
Attn: Dept. SM'95
26 Thomas Patten Drive
Randolph, MA 02368
Phone: 800-541-1405
Fax: 617-986-0337

REDDING RELOADING EQUIPMENT *(Pg. 237)*
Attn: Dept. SM'95
1095 Starr Road
Cortland, NY 13045
Phone: 607-753-3331
Fax: 607-756-8445

R.G.-G., INC. *(Pg. 256)*
Attn: Dept. SM'95, Plans Coordinator
P.O. Box 1261
Conifer, CO 80433-1261
Phone: 303-697-4154
Fax: 303-697-4154

RIG PRODUCTS *(Pg. 258)*
Attn: Dept. SM'95
87 Coney Island Drive
Sparks, NV 89431
Phone: 702-331-5666
Fax: 702-331-5669

ROOSTER LABORATORIES *(Pg. 244)*
Attn: Dept. SM'95
P.O. Box 412514
Kansas City, MO 64141
Phone: 816-474-1622
Fax: 816-474-1307

SAFARILAND LTD., INC. *(Pg. 246)*
Attn: Dept. SM'95
3120 E. Mission Blvd.
Ontario, CA 91761
Phone: 909-923-7300
Fax: 909-923-7400

SCHMIDT & BENDER, INC. *(Pg. 254)*
Attn: Dept. SM'95
P.O. Box 134, Brook Road
Meriden, NH 03770
Phone: 800-468-3450 or 603-469-3565
Fax: 603-469-3471

SCOT POWDER *(Pg. 245)*
Attn: Dept. SM'95
Rt. 1, Box 167
McEwen, TN 37101
Phone: 615-729-4207
Fax: 615-729-4217

SHEPHERD SCOPE, LTD. *(Pg. 242)*
Attn: Dept. GDA-2
Box 189
Waterloo, NE 68069
Phone: 402-779-2424
Fax: 402-779-4010

THE SHOTGUN NEWS *(Pg. 234)*
Attn: Dept. SM'95, S. Hoffman
P.O. Box 669
Hastings, NE 68901

SILENCIO/SAFETY DIRECT *(Pg. 227)*
Attn: Dept. SM'95
56 Coney Island Dr., Bldg. 22
Sparks, NV 89431
Phone: 800-648-1812
Fax: 702-359-1074

STONEY POINT PRODUCTS, INC. *(Pg. 241)*
Attn: Dept. SM'95
P.O. Box 5
Courtland, MN 56021-0005
Phone: 507-354-3360
Fax: 507-354-7236

SWAROVSKI OPTIK NORTH AMERICA LTD.
(Pgs. 226,237,239,246,248,257)
Attn: Dept. SM'95
One Wholesale Way
Cranston, RI 02920
Phone: 800-426-3089
Fax: 401-946-2587

SWIFT INSTRUMENTS, INC. *(Pg. 251)*
Attn: Dept. SM'95
952 Dorchester Ave.
Boston, MA 02125
Phone: 617-436-2960
Fax: 617-436-3232

SWIVEL MACHINE WORKS, INC. *(Pg. 244)*
Attn: Dept. SM'95
167 Cherry St., Suite 286
Milford, CT 06460
Phone: 203-926-1840
Fax: 203-874-9212

JAMES C. TILLINGHAST *(Pg. 239)*
Attn: Dept. SM'95
P.O. Box 19AG
Hancock, NH 03449-19AG
Phone: 603-525-4049

TIMNEY MFG., INC. *(Pg. 242)*
Attn: Dept. SM'95
3065 W. Fairmount Ave.
Phoenix, AZ 85017
Phone: 602-274-2999
Fax: 602-241-0361

TOMBOY, INC. *(Pg. 226)*
Attn: Dept. SM'95, Brandy Church
P.O. Box 846
Dallas, OR 97338
Phone: 503-623-6955

TREADLOK GUN SAFE, INC. *(Pg. 232)*
Attn: Dept. SM'95
1764 Granby St., N.E.
Roanoke, VA 24012
Phone: 800-729-8732
Fax: 703-982-1059

TRIUS TRAPS *(Pg. 230)*
Attn: Dept. SM'95
221 South Miami Ave.
Cleves, OH 45002
Phone: 513-941-5682
Fax: 513-941-7970

DOUG TURNBULL RESTORATION *(Pg. 234)*
Attn: Dept. SM'95
P.O. Box 471
Bloomfield, NY 14469
Phone: 716-657-6338

VOERE/JAGERSPORT *(Pg. 225)*
Attn: Dept. SM'95
One Wholesale Way
Cranston, RI 02920
Phone: 800-426-3089
Fax: 401-946-2587

VOLQUARTSEN CUSTOM LTD. *(Pg. 244)*
Attn: Dept. SM'95
P.O. Box 271
Carroll, IA 51401
Phone: 712-792-4238
Fax: 712-792-2542

WALKER ARMS CO., INC. *(Pg. 248)*
Attn: Dept. SM'95
499 County Road 820
Selma, AL 36701
Phone: 205-872-6231

1995
GUN DIGEST
Complete Compact
CATALOG

Includes models suitable for several forms of competition and other sporting purposes.

ACCU-TEK MODEL AT-9 AUTO PISTOL
Caliber: 9mm Para., 7-shot magazine.
Barrel: 3.2".
Weight: 28 oz. **Length:** 6.25" overall.
Stocks: Black checkered nylon.
Sights: Blade front, rear adjustable for windage; three-dot system.
Features: Stainless steel construction. Double action only. Firing pin block with no external safeties. Lifetime warranty. Introduced 1992. Made in U.S. by Accu-Tek.
Price: Satin stainless **$270.00**
Price: Black finish over stainless **$275.00**

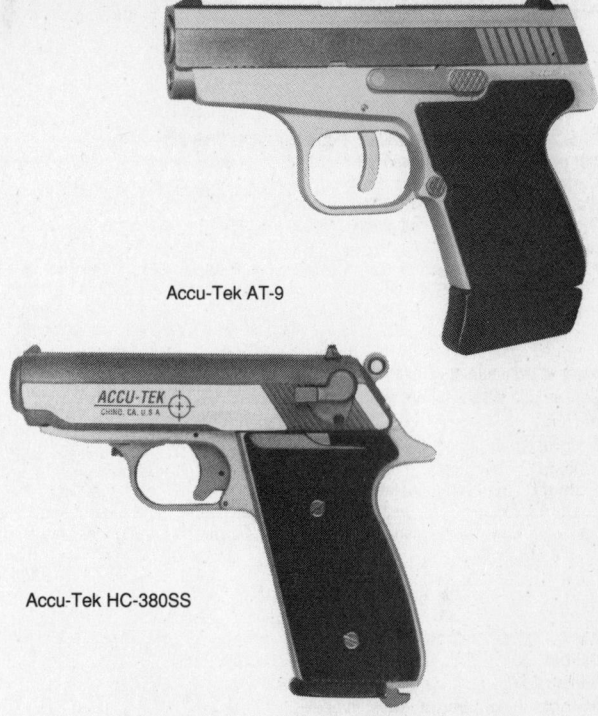

Accu-Tek AT-9

Accu-Tek AT-40 Auto Pistol
Same as the Model AT-9 except chambered for 40 S&W. Introduced 1992.
Price: Stainless **$270.00**
Price: Black finish over stainless (AT-40B) **$275.00**

ACCU-TEK MODEL HC-380SS AUTO PISTOL
Caliber: 380 ACP, 13-shot magazine.
Barrel: 2.75".
Weight: 28 oz. **Length:** 6" overall.
Stocks: Checkered black composition.
Sights: Blade front, rear adjustable for windage.
Features: External hammer; manual thumb safety with firing pin and trigger disconnect; bottom magazine release. Stainless finish. Introduced 1993. Made in U.S. by Accu-Tek.
Price: **$230.00**

Accu-Tek HC-380SS

Accu-Tek Model AT-32SS Auto Pistol
Same as the AT-380SS except chambered for 32 ACP. Introduced 1990.
Price: Satin stainless **$176.00**
Price: Black finish over stainless (AT-32SSB) **$181.00**

ACCU-TEK MODEL AT-380SS AUTO PISTOL
Caliber: 380 ACP, 5-shot magazine.
Barrel: 2.75".
Weight: 20 oz. **Length:** 5.6" overall.
Stocks: Grooved black composition.
Sights: Blade front, rear adjustable for windage.
Features: Stainless steel frame and slide. External hammer; manual thumb safety; firing pin block, trigger disconnect. Lifetime warranty. Introduced 1992. Made in U.S. by Accu-Tek.
Price: Satin stainless **$182.00**
Price: Black finish over stainless (AT-380SSB) **$187.00**

Accu-Tek AT-380SS

Accu-Tek Model AT-25SS Auto Pistol
Similar to the AT-380SS except chambered for 25 ACP with 7-shot magazine. Also available with aluminum frame and slide with 11-oz. weight. Introduced 1991.
Price: Satin stainless **$158.00**
Price: Black finish over stainless (AT-25SSB) **$163.00**

American Arms PK22

AMERICAN ARMS MODEL CX-22 DA AUTO PISTOL
Caliber: 22 LR, 8-shot magazine.
Barrel: 3⅓".
Weight: 22 oz. **Length:** 6⅓" overall.
Stocks: Checkered black polymer.
Sights: Blade front, rear adjustable for windage.
Features: Double action with manual hammer-block safety, firing pin safety. Alloy frame. Has external appearance of Walther PPK. Blue/black finish. Introduced 1990. Made in U.S. by American Arms, Inc.
Price: **$209.00**

AMERICAN ARMS MODEL PK22 DA AUTO PISTOL
Caliber: 22 LR, 8-shot magazine.
Barrel: 3.3".
Weight: 22 oz. **Length:** 6.3" overall.
Stocks: Checkered plastic.
Sights: Fixed.
Features: Double action. Polished blue finish. Slide-mounted safety. Made in the U.S. by American Arms, Inc.
Price: **$209.00**

AMERICAN ARMS MODEL P-98 AUTO PISTOL
Caliber: 22 LR, 8-shot magazine.
Barrel: 5".
Weight: 25 oz. **Length:** 8⅛" overall.
Stocks: Grooved black polymer.
Sights: Blade front, rear adjustable for windage.
Features: Double action with hammer-block safety, magazine disconnect safety. Alloy frame. Has external appearance of the Walther P-38 pistol. Introduced 1989. Made in U.S. by American Arms, Inc.
Price: $219.00

American Arms P-98

AMERICAN ARMS MODEL PX-22 AUTO PISTOL
Caliber: 22 LR, 7-shot magazine.
Barrel: 2.85".
Weight: 15 oz. **Length:** 5.39" overall.
Stocks: Black checkered plastic.
Sights: Fixed.
Features: Double action; 7-shot magazine. Polished blue finish. Introduced 1989. Made in U.S. From American Arms, Inc.
Price: $198.00

American Arms PX-22

AMT AUTOMAG II AUTO PISTOL
Caliber: 22 WMR, 9-shot magazine (7-shot with 3⅜" barrel).
Barrel: 3⅜", 4½", 6".
Weight: About 23 oz. **Length:** 9⅜" overall.
Stocks: Grooved carbon fiber.
Sights: Blade front, adjustable rear.
Features: Made of stainless steel. Gas-assisted action. Exposed hammer. Slide flats have brushed finish, rest is sandblast. Squared trigger guard. Introduced 1986. From AMT.
Price: $385.95

AMT AUTOMAG III PISTOL
Caliber: 30 Carbine, 9mm Win. Mag., 8-shot magazine.
Barrel: 6⅜".
Weight: 43 oz. **Length:** 10½" overall.
Stocks: Carbon fiber.
Sights: Blade front, adjustable rear.
Features: Stainless steel construction. Hammer-drop safety. Slide flats have brushed finish, rest is sandblasted. Introduced 1989. From AMT.
Price: $459.99

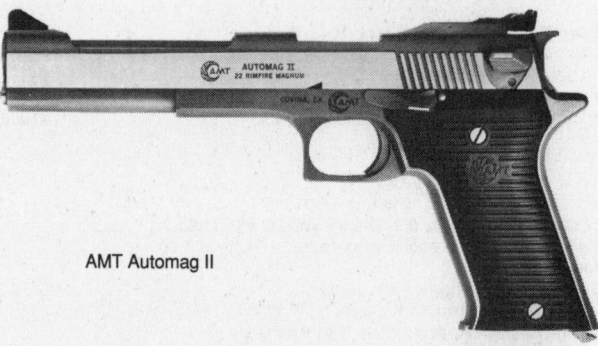

AMT Automag II

AMT AUTOMAG IV PISTOL
Caliber: 10mm Magnum, 45 Winchester Magnum, 6-shot magazine.
Barrel: 6.5" (45), 8⅝" (10mm only).
Weight: 46 oz. **Length:** 10.5" overall with 6.5" barrel.
Stocks: Carbon fiber.
Sights: Blade front, adjustable rear.
Features: Made of stainless steel with brushed finish. Introduced 1990. Made in U.S. by AMT.
Price: $679.99
Price: Automag V (50 A.E.) $899.00

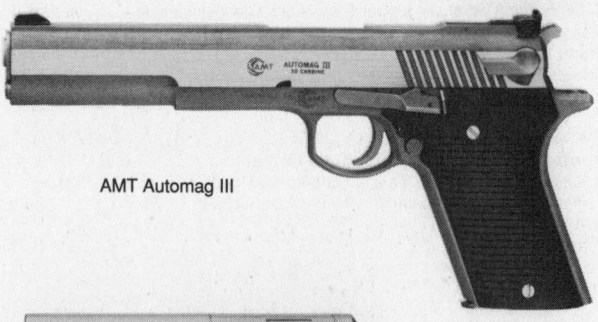

AMT Automag III

AMT BACKUP II AUTO PISTOL
Caliber: 380 ACP, 5-shot magazine.
Barrel: 2½".
Weight: 18 oz. **Length:** 5" overall.
Stocks: Carbon fiber.
Sights: Fixed, open, recessed.
Features: Concealed hammer, blowback operation; manual and grip safeties. All stainless steel construction. Smallest domestically-produced pistol in 380. From AMT.
Price: $295.99

Consult our Directory pages for the location of firms mentioned.

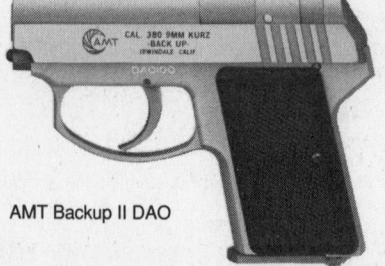

AMT Backup II DAO

AMT Backup II Double Action Only Pistol
Similar to the standard Backup except has double-action-only mechanism, enlarged trigger guard, slide is rounded ar rear. Has 6-shot magazine. Introduced 1992. From AMT.
Price: $309.99

AMT ON DUTY DA PISTOL
Caliber: 9mm Para., 15-shot; 40 S&W, 11-shot; 45 ACP, 9-shot magazine.
Barrel: 4½".
Weight: 32 oz. **Length:** 7¾" overall.
Stocks: Smooth carbon fiber.
Sights: Blade front, rear adjustable for windage; three-dot system.
Features: Choice of DA with decocker or double action only. Inertia firing pin, trigger disconnector safety. Aluminum frame with steel recoil shoulder, stainless steel slide and barrel. Introduced 1991. Made in the U.S. by AMT.
Price: 9mm, 40 S&W **$469.99**
Price: 45 ACP **$529.99**

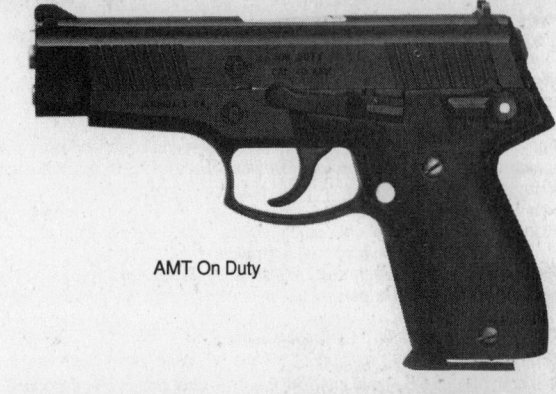
AMT On Duty

AMT 45 ACP HARDBALLER
Caliber: 45 ACP.
Barrel: 5".
Weight: 39 oz. **Length:** 8½" overall.
Stocks: Wrap-around rubber.
Sights: Adjustable.
Features: Extended combat safety, serrated matte slide rib, loaded chamber indicator, long grip safety, beveled magazine well, adjustable target trigger. All stainless steel. From AMT.
Price: **$529.99**
Price: Government model (as above except no rib, fixed sights) . . **$475.95**

AMT 45 ACP HARDBALLER LONG SLIDE
Caliber: 45 ACP.
Barrel: 7". **Length:** 10½" overall.
Stocks: Wrap-around rubber.
Sights: Fully adjustable rear sight.
Features: Slide and barrel are 2" longer than the standard 45, giving less recoil, added velocity, longer sight radius. Has extended combat safety, serrated matte rib, loaded chamber indicator, wide adjustable trigger. From AMT.
Price: **$575.95**

Argentine Hi-Power

ARGENTINE HI-POWER 9MM AUTO PISTOL
Caliber: 9mm Para., 13-shot magazine.
Barrel: 4²¹⁄₃₂".
Weight: 32 oz. **Length:** 7¾" overall.
Stocks: Checkered walnut.
Sights: Blade front, adjustable rear.
Features: Produced in Argentina under F.N. Browning license. Introduced 1990. Imported by Century International Arms, Inc.
Price: About **$299.95**

Argentine Hi-Power Detective Model
Similar to the standard model except has 3.8" barrel, 6.9" overall length and weighs 33 oz. Grips are finger-groove, checkered soft rubber. Matte black finish. Introduced 1994. Imported by Century International Arms, Inc.
Price: About **$310.00**

Astra A-75

ASTRA A-100 AUTO PISTOL
Caliber: 9mm Para., 17-shot; 40 S&W, 13-shot; 45 ACP, 9-shot magazine.
Barrel: 3.9".
Weight: 29 oz. **Length:** 7.1" overall.
Stocks: Checkered black plastic.
Sights: Blade front, interchangeable rear blades for elevation, screw adjustable for windage.
Features: Selective double action. Decocking lever permits lowering hammer onto locked firing pin. Automatic firing pin block. Side button magazine release. Introduced 1993. Imported from Spain by European American Armory.
Price: Blue, 9mm, 40 S&W, 45 ACP **$425.00**
Price: As above, nickel **$450.00**

Astra A-100

ASTRA A-70 AUTO PISTOL
Caliber: 9mm Para., 8-shot; 40 S&W, 7-shot magazine.
Barrel: 3.5".
Weight: 29.3 oz. **Length:** 6.5" overall.
Stocks: Checkered black plastic.
Sights: Blade front, rear adjustable for windage.
Features: All steel frame and slide. Checkered grip straps and trigger guard. Nickel or blue finish. Introduced 1992. Imported from Spain by European American Armory.
Price: Blue, 9mm Para. **$350.00**
Price: Blue, 40 S&W **$350.00**
Price: Nickel, 9mm Para. **$375.00**
Price: Nickel, 40 S&W **$375.00**
Price: Stainless steel, 9mm **$425.00**
Price: Stainless steel, 40 S&W **$425.00**

Astra A-75 Decocker Auto Pistol
Same as the A-70 except has decocker system, different trigger, contoured pebble-grain grips. Introduced 1993. Imported from Spain by European American Armory.
Price: Blue, 9mm or 40 S&W **$395.00**
Price: Nickel, 9mm or 40 S&W **$425.00**
Price: Blue, 45 ACP **$425.00**
Price: Nickel, 45 ACP **$455.00**
Price: Stainless steel, 9mm, 40 S&W **$475.00**
Price: Stainless steel, 45 ACP **$505.00**
Price: Airweight (23.5 oz.), 9mm, blue **$425.00**

AUTO-ORDNANCE 1911A1 AUTOMATIC PISTOL
Caliber: 9mm Para., 38 Super, 9-shot; 10mm, 45 ACP, 7-shot magazine.
Barrel: 5".
Weight: 39 oz. **Length:** 8½" overall.
Stocks: Checkered plastic with medallion.
Sights: Blade front, rear adjustable for windage.
Features: Same specs as 1911A1 military guns—parts interchangeable. Frame and slide blued; each radius has non-glare finish. Made in U.S. by Auto-Ordnance Corp.
Price: 45 cal. **$388.95**
Price: 9mm, 38 Super **$415.00**
Price: 10mm (has three-dot combat sights, rubber wrap-around grips) **$420.95**
Price: 45 ACP General Model (Commander style) **$427.95**
Price: Duo Tone (nickel frame, blue slide, three-dot sight system, textured black wrap-around grips) **$405.00**

Auto-Ordnance ZG-51 Pit Bull Auto
Same as the 1911A1 except has 3½" barrel, weighs 36 oz. and has an over-all length of 7¼". Available in 45 ACP only; 7-shot magazine. Introduced 1989.
Price: **$420.95**

Auto-Ordnance 1911A1

Auto-Ordnance 1911A1 Competition Model
Similar to the standard Model 19911A1 except has barrel compensator. Commander hammer, flat mainspring housing, three-dot sight system, low-profile magazine funnel, Hi-Ride beavertail grip safety, full-length recoil spring guide system, black-textured rubber, wrap-around grips, and extended slide stop, safety and magazine catch. Introduced 1994. Made in U.S. by Auto-Ordnance Corp.
Price: **$615.00**

BABY EAGLE AUTO PISTOL
Caliber: 9mm Para., 40 S&W, 41 A.E.
Barrel: 4.37".
Weight: 35 oz. **Length:** 8.14" overall.
Stocks: High-impact black polymer.
Sights: Combat.
Features: Double-action mechanism; polygonal rifling; ambidextrous safety. Model 9mm F has frame-mounted safety on left side of pistol; Model 9mm FS has frame-mounted safety and 3.62" barrel. Introduced 1992. Imported by Magnum Research.
Price: 9mm Para., 40 S&W, 41 A.E., black finish **$569.00**
Price: Conversion kit, 9mm Para. to 41 A.E. **$239.00**
Price: Matte or brushed chrome, add **$149.00**

Baby Eagle FS

BAIKAL IJ-70 AUTO PISTOL
Caliber: 9x18mm Makarov, 380 ACP, 8-shot magazine.
Barrel: 4".
Weight: 25 oz. **Length:** 6.25" overall.
Stocks: Checkered composition.
Sights: Blade front, rear adjustable for windage and elevation.
Features: Double action; all-steel construction; frame-mounted safety with decocker. Comes with two magazines, cleaning rod, universal tool and leather holster. Introduced 1994. Imported from Russia by K.B.I., Inc.
Price: 9x18mm, blue **$199.00**
Price: 380 ACP, blue **$219.00**
Price: 380 ACP, nickel **$234.00**

Baikal IJ-70

BERETTA MODEL 80 CHEETAH SERIES DA PISTOLS
Caliber: 380 ACP, 13-shot magazine (M84); 8-shot (M85); 22 LR, 7-shot (M87), 22 LR, 8-shot (M89).
Barrel: 3.82".
Weight: About 23 oz. (M84/85); 20.8 oz. (M87). **Length:** 6.8" overall.
Stocks: Glossy black plastic (wood optional at extra cost).
Sights: Fixed front, drift-adjustable rear.
Features: Double action, quick takedown, convenient magazine release. Introduced 1977. Imported from Italy by Beretta U.S.A.
Price: Model 84 Cheetah, plastic grips **$525.00**
Price: Model 84 Cheetah, wood grips **$555.00**
Price: Model 84 Cheetah, wood grips, nickel finish **$600.00**
Price: Model 85 Cheetah, plastic grips, 8-shot **$485.00**
Price: Model 85 Cheetah, wood grips, 8-shot **$510.00**
Price: Model 85 Cheetah, wood grips, nickel, 8-shot **$550.00**
Price: Model 87 Cheetah wood, 22 LR, 7-shot **$490.00**

Beretta Model 86 Cheetah
Similar to the 380-caliber Model 85 except has tip-up barrel for first-round loading. Barrel length is 4.33", overall length of 7.33". Has 8-shot magazine, walnut or plastic grips. Introduced 1989.
Price: **$510.00**

Beretta 84 Cheetah

CAUTION: PRICES SHOWN ARE SUPPLIED BY THE MANUFACTURER OR IMPORTER. CHECK YOUR LOCAL GUNSHOP.

BERETTA MODEL 92FS PISTOL

Caliber: 9mm Para., 15-shot magazine.
Barrel: 4.9".
Weight: 34 oz. **Length:** 8.5" overall.
Stocks: Checkered black plastic; wood optional at extra cost.
Sights: Blade front, rear adjustable for windage. Tritium night sights available.
Features: Double action. Extractor acts as chamber loaded indicator, squared trigger guard, grooved front- and backstraps, inertia firing pin. Matte finish. Introduced 1977. Made in U.S. and imported from Italy by Beretta U.S.A.
Price: With plastic grips $625.00
Price: With wood grips $645.00
Price: Tritium night sights, add $85.00

Beretta Model 92FS

Beretta Models 92FS/96 Centurion Pistols

Identical to the Model 92FS and 96F except uses shorter slide and barrel (4.3"). Trijicon or three-dot sight systems. Plastic or wood grips. Available in 9mm or 40 S&W. Also available in D Models (double action only). Introduced 1992.
Price: Model 92FS Centurion, three-dot sights, plastic grips $625.00
Price: Model 92FS Centurion, wood grips $645.00
Price: Model 96 Centurion, three-dot sights, plastic grips $640.00
Price: Model 92D Centurion $585.00
Price: Model 96D Centurion $605.00
Price: For Trijicon sights, add $65.00

Beretta Model 92F Stainless Pistol

Same as the Model 92FS except has stainless steel barrel and slide, and frame of aluminum-zirconium alloy. Has three-dot sight system. Introduced 1992.
Price: $755.00
Price: Model 92F-EL Stainless (gold trim, engraved barrel, slide, frame, gold-finished safety-levers, trigger, magazine release, grip screws) $1,240.00
Price: For Trijicon sights, add $65.00

Beretta Model 96

Beretta Model 96F Auto Pistol

Same as the Model 92F except chambered for 40 S&W. Ambidextrous safety mechanism with passive firing pin catch, slide safety/decocking lever, trigger bar disconnect. Has 10-shot magazine. Available with Trijicon or three-dot sights. Introduced 1992.
Price: Model 96F, plastic grips $640.00
Price: Model 96D, double action only, three-dot sights $605.00
Price: For Trijicon sights, add . . . . $80.00 to $90.00

Beretta Model 92D Pistol

Same as the Model 92FS except double action only and has bobbed hammer, no external safety. Introduced 1992.
Price: With plastic grips, three-dot sights $585.00
Price: As above with Trijicon sights $680.00

Beretta 950BS Jetfire

BERETTA MODEL 950BS JETFIRE AUTO PISTOL

Caliber: 25 ACP, 8-shot.
Barrel: 2.5".
Weight: 9.9 oz. **Length:** 4.5" overall.
Stocks: Checkered black plastic or walnut.
Sights: Fixed.
Features: Single action, thumb safety; tip-up barrel for direct loading/unloading, cleaning. From Beretta U.S.A.
Price: Jetfire wood, blue $180.00
Price: Jetfire wood, nickel $210.00
Price: Jetfire wood, engraved $260.00
Price: Jetfire plastic, matte blue $150.00

Beretta Model 8000 Cougar

Beretta Model 21 Bobcat Pistol

Similar to the Model 950 BS. Chambered for 22 LR or 25 ACP. Both double action. Has 2.5" barrel, 4.9" overall length; 7-round magazine on 22 cal.; available in nickel, matte, engraved or blue finish. Plastic or walnut grips. Introduced in 1985.
Price: Bobcat wood, 22-cal. $235.00
Price: Bobcat wood, nickel, 22-cal. $247.00
Price: Bobcat wood, 25-cal. $235.00
Price: Bobcat wood, nickel, 25-cal. $247.00
Price: Bobcat wood, engraved, 22 or 25 . . . . $285.00
Price: Bobcat plastic matte, 22 or 25 . . . . $185.00

BERETTA MODEL 8000/8040 COUGAR PISTOL

Caliber: 9mm Para., 15-shot, 40 S&W, 11-shot magazine.
Barrel: 3.5".
Weight: 33.5 oz. **Length:** NA.
Stocks: Textured composition.
Sights: Blade front, rear drift adjustable for windage.
Features: Slide-mounted safety; exposed hammer. Matte black Bruniton finish. Announced 1994. Imported from Italy by Beretta U.S.A.
Price: . . . . NA

HANDGUNS—AUTOLOADERS, SERVICE & SPORT

BERNARDELLI PO18 DA AUTO PISTOL
Caliber: 9mm Para., 16-shot magazine.
Barrel: 4.8".
Weight: 34.2 oz. **Length:** 8.23" overall.
Stocks: Checkered plastic; walnut optional.
Sights: Blade front, rear adjustable for windage and elevation; low profile, three-dot system.
Features: Manual thumb half-cock, magazine and auto-locking firing pin safeties. Thumb safety decocks hammer. Reversible magazine release. Imported from Italy by Armsport.
Price: Blue $505.00
Price: Chrome $568.00

Bernardelli PO 18

Bernardelli PO18 Compact DA Auto Pistol
Similar to the PO18 except has 4" barrel, 7.44" overall length, 14-shot magazine. Weighs 31.7 oz. Imported from Italy by Armsport.
Price: Blue $552.00
Price: Chrome $600.00

Bernardelli P. One Practical VB Pistol
Similar to the P. One except chambered for 9x21mm, two- or four-port compensator, straight trigger, micro-adjustable rear sight. Introduced 1994. Imported from Italy by Armsport.
Price: Blue/black, two-port compensator $1,425.00
Price: As above, four-port compensator $1,475.00
Price: Chrome, two-port compensator $1,498.00
Price: As above, four-port compensator $1,540.00
Price: Customized VB, four-plus-two-port compensator $2,150.00
Price: As above, chrome $2,200.00

BERNARDELLI P. ONE DA AUTO PISTOL
Caliber: 9mm Para., 16-shot, 40 S&W, 12-shot magazine.
Barrel: 4.8".
Weight: 34 oz. **Length:** 8.35" overall.
Stocks: Checkered black plastic.
Sights: Blade front, rear adjustable for windage and elevation; three dot system.
Features: Forged steel frame and slide; full-length slide rails; reversible magazine release; thumb safety/decocker; squared trigger guard. Introduced 1994. Imported from Italy by Armsport.
Price: 9mm Para., blue/black $530.00
Price: 9mm Para., chrome $580.00
Price: 40 S&W, blue/black $530.00
Price: 40 S&W, chrome $580.00

BERNARDELLI MODEL USA AUTO PISTOL
Caliber: 22 LR, 10-shot, 380 ACP, 7-shot magazine.
Barrel: 3.5".
Weight: 26.5 oz. **Length:** 6.5" overall.
Stocks: Checkered plastic with thumbrest.
Sights: Ramp front, white outline rear adjustable for windage and elevation.
Features: Hammer-block slide safety; loaded chamber indicator; dual recoil buffer springs; serrated trigger; inertia-type firing pin. Imported from Italy by Armsport.
Price: Blue, either caliber $387.00
Price: Chrome, either caliber $412.00
Price: Model AMR (6" barrel, target sights) $440.00

Bernardelli Model USA

BERSA MODEL 23 AUTO PISTOL
Caliber: 22 LR, 10-shot magazine.
Barrel: 3.5".
Weight: 24.5 oz. **Length:** 6.6" overall.
Stocks: Walnut with stippled panels.
Sights: Blade front, notch rear adjustable for windage; three-dot system.
Features: Double action; firing pin and magazine safeties. Available in blue or nickel. Introduced 1989. Distributed by Eagle Imports, Inc.
Price: Blue $287.95
Price: Nickel $321.95

CONSULT
Shooter's Marketplace
Page 225, This Issue

BERSA MODEL 83, 85 AUTO PISTOLS
Caliber: 380 ACP, 7-shot (M83), 13-shot magazine (M85).
Barrel: 3.5".
Weight: 25.75 oz. **Length:** 6.6" overall.
Stocks: Walnut with stippled panels.
Sights: Blade front, notch rear adjustable for windage; three-dot system.
Features: Double action; firing pin and magazine safeties. Available in blue or nickel. Introduced 1989. Distributed by Eagle Imports, Inc.
Price: Model 85, blue $339.95
Price: Model 85, nickel $386.95
Price: Model 83 (as above, except 7-shot magazine), blue $287.95
Price: Model 83, nickel $321.95

BERSA MODEL 86 AUTO PISTOL
Caliber: 380 ACP, 13-shot magazine.
Barrel: 3.5".
Weight: 22 oz. **Length:** 6.6" overall.
Stocks: Wraparound textured rubber.
Sights: Blade front, rear adjustable for windage; three-dot system.
Features: Double action; firing pin and magazine safeties; combat-style trigger guard. Matte blue or satin nickel. Introduced 1992. Distributed by Eagle Imports, Inc.
Price: Matte blue $374.95
Price: Satin nickel $403.95

Bersa Model 85

BERSA THUNDER 9 AUTO PISTOL
Caliber: 9mm Para., 15-shot magazine.
Barrel: 4".
Weight: 30 oz. **Length:** 7⅜" overall.
Stocks: Checkered black polymer.
Sights: Blade front, rear adjustable for windage and elevation; three-dot system.
Features: Double action. Ambidextrous safety, decocking levers and slide release; internal automatic firing pin safety; reversible extended magazine release; adjustable trigger stop; alloy frame. Link-free locked breech design. Matte blue finish. Introduced 1993. Imported from Argentina by Eagle Imports, Inc.
Price: Blue only $414.95

Bersa Thunder 9

Browning BDA-380

BROWNING BDM DA AUTO PISTOL
Caliber: 9mm Para., 15-shot magazine.
Barrel: 4.73"
Weight: 31 oz. **Length:** 7.85" overall.
Stocks: Moulded black composition; checkered, with thumbrest on both sides.
Sights: Low profile removable blade front, rear screw adjustable for windage.
Features: Mode selector allows switching from DA pistol to "revolver" mode via a switch on the slide. Decocking lever/safety on the frame. Two redundant, passive, internal safety systems. All steel frame; matte black finish. Introduced 1991. Made in the U.S. From Browning.
Price: $573.95

BROWNING BDA-380 DA AUTO PISTOL
Caliber: 380 ACP, 13-shot magazine.
Barrel: 3¹³⁄₁₆".
Weight: 23 oz. **Length:** 6¾" overall.
Stocks: Smooth walnut with inset Browning medallion.
Sights: Blade front, rear drift-adjustable for windage.
Features: Combination safety and de-cocking lever will automatically lower a cocked hammer to half-cock and can be operated by right- or left-hand shooters. Inertia firing pin. Introduced 1978. Imported from Italy by Browning.
Price: Blue $592.95
Price: Nickel $624.95

Browning BDM

Browning Hi-Power HP

BROWNING HI-POWER 9mm AUTOMATIC PISTOL
Caliber: 9mm Para., 13-shot magazine.
Barrel: 4²¹⁄₃₂".
Weight: 32 oz. **Length:** 7¾" overall.
Stocks: Walnut, hand checkered, or black Polyamide.
Sights: ⅛" blade front; rear screw-adjustable for windage and elevation. Also available with fixed rear (drift-adjustable for windage).
Features: External hammer with half-cock and thumb safeties. A blow on the hammer cannot discharge a cartridge; cannot be fired with magazine removed. Fixed rear sight model available. Ambidextrous safety available only with matte finish, moulded grips. Imported from Belgium by Browning.
Price: Fixed sight model, walnut grips $537.95
Price: 9mm with rear sight adj. for w. and e., walnut grips $585.95
Price: Mark III, standard matte black finish, fixed sight, moulded grips, ambidextrous safety $506.95
Price: Silver chrome, adjustable sight, Pachmayr grips $596.95

Browning 40 S&W Hi-Power Pistol
Similar to the standard Hi-Power except chambered for 40 S&W, 10-shot magazine, weighs 35 oz., and has 4¾" barrel. Comes with matte blue finish, low profile front sight blade, drift-adjustable rear sight, ambidextrous safety, moulded polyamide grips with thumb rest. Introduced 1993. Imported from Belgium by Browning.
Price: $506.95

Browning Capitan Hi-Power Pistol
Similar to the standard Hi-Power except has adjustable tangent rear sight authentic to the early-production model. Also has Commander-style hammer. Checkered walnut grips, polished blue finish. Reintroduced 1993. Imported from Belgium by Browning.
Price: $634.95

Consult our Directory pages for the location of firms mentioned.

Browning Hi-Power HP-Practical Pistol
Similar to the standard Hi-Power except has silver-chromed frame with blued slide, wrap-around Pachmayr rubber grips, round-style serrated hammer and removable front sight, fixed rear (drift-adjustable for windage). Introduced 1991.
Price: $579.95
Price: With fully adjustable rear sight $627.95

CAUTION: PRICES SHOWN ARE SUPPLIED BY THE MANUFACTURER OR IMPORTER. CHECK YOUR LOCAL GUNSHOP.

49th EDITION, 1995 **277**

HANDGUNS—AUTOLOADERS, SERVICE & SPORT

Browning Mico Buck Mark

Browning Buck Mark Varmint

BROWNING BUCK MARK 22 PISTOL
Caliber: 22 LR, 10-shot magazine.
Barrel: 5½".
Weight: 32 oz. **Length:** 9½" overall.
Stocks: Black moulded composite with skip-line checkering.
Sights: Ramp front, Browning Pro Target rear adjustable for windage and elevation.
Features: All steel, matte blue finish or nickel, gold-colored trigger. Buck Mark Plus has laminated wood grips. Made in U.S. Introduced 1985. From Browning.
Price: Buck Mark, blue $241.95
Price: Buck Mark, nickel finish with contoured rubber stocks $282.95
Price: Buck Mark Plus $293.95

Browning Micro Buck Mark
Same as the standard Buck Mark and Buck Mark Plus except has 4" barrel. Available in blue or nickel. Has 16-click Pro Target rear sight. Introduced 1992.
Price: Blue $241.95
Price: Nickel $282.95
Price: Micro Buck Mark Plus $293.95

Browning Buck Mark Varmint
Same as the Buck Mark except has 9⅞" heavy barrel with .900" diameter and full-length scope base (no open sights); walnut grips with optional forend, or finger-groove walnut. Overall length is 14", weight is 48 oz. Introduced 1987.
Price: $365.95

BRYCO MODEL 38 AUTO PISTOLS
Caliber: 22 LR, 32 ACP, 380 ACP, 6-shot magazine.
Barrel: 2.8".
Weight: 15 oz. **Length:** 5.3" overall.
Stocks: Polished resin-impregnated wood.
Sights: Fixed.
Features: Safety locks sear and slide. Choice of satin nickel, bright chrome or black Teflon finishes. Introduced 1988. From Jennings Firearms.
Price: 22 LR, 32 ACP, about $109.95
Price: 380 ACP, about $129.95

BRYCO MODEL 48 AUTO PISTOLS
Caliber: 22 LR, 32 ACP, 380 ACP, 6-shot magazine.
Barrel: 4".
Weight: 19 oz. **Length:** 6.7" overall.
Stocks: Polished resin-impregnated wood.
Sights: Fixed.
Features: Safety locks sear and slide. Choice of satin nickel, bright chrome or black Teflon finishes. Announced 1988. From Jennings Firearms.
Price: 22 LR, 32 ACP, about $139.00
Price: 380 ACP, about $139.00

CALICO MODEL 110 AUTO PISTOL
Caliber: 22 LR, 100-shot magazine.
Barrel: 6".
Weight: 3.7 lbs. (loaded). **Length:** 17.9" overall.
Stocks: Moulded composition.
Sights: Adjustable post front, notch rear.
Features: Aluminum alloy frame; flash suppressor; pistol grip compartment; ambidextrous safety. Uses same helical-feed magazine as M-100 Carbine. Introduced 1986. Made in U.S. From Calico.
Price: $268.30

Bryco Mdel 48

CALICO MODEL M-950 AUTO PISTOL
Caliber: 9mm Para., 50- or 100-shot magazine.
Barrel: 7.5".
Weight: 2.25 lbs. (empty). **Length:** 14" overall (50-shot magazine).
Stocks: Glass-filled polymer.
Sights: Post front adjustable for windage and elevation, fixed notch rear.
Features: Helical feed 50- or 100-shot magazine. Ambidextrous safety, static cocking handle. Retarded blowback action. Glass-filled polymer grip. Introduced 1989. From Calico.
Price: $518.80

BRYCO MODEL 59 AUTO PISTOL
Caliber: 9mm Para., 13-shot magazine.
Barrel: 4".
Weight: 33 oz. **Length:** 6.5" overall.
Stocks: Black composition.
Sights: Blade front, fixed rear.
Features: Striker-fired action; manual thumb safety; polished blue finish. Comes with two magazines. Introduced 1994. From Jennings Firearms.
Price: About $169.00
Price: Model 58 (5.5" overall length, 30 oz.) $169.00

Calico M-950

Century FEG P9RK Auto Pistol
Similar to the P9R except has 4.12" barrel, 7.5" overall length and weighs 33.6 oz. Checkered walnut grips, fixed sights, 15-shot magazine. Introduced 1994. Imported from Hungary by Century International Arms, Inc.
Price: About $290.00

CENTURY FEG P9R PISTOL
Caliber: 9mm Para., 15-shot magazine.
Barrel: 4.6".
Weight: 35 oz. **Length:** 8" overall.
Stocks: Checkered walnut.
Sights: Blade front, rear drift adjustable for windage.
Features: Double action with hammer-drop safety. Polished blue finish. Comes with spare magazine. Imported from Hungary by Century International Arms.
Price: About $263.00
Price: Chrome finish, about $375.00

COLT'S 22 AUTOMATIC PISTOL
Caliber: 22 LR, 11-shot magazine.
Barrel: 4.5".
Weight: 33 oz. **Length:** 8.62" overall.
Stocks: Textured black polymer.
Sights: Blade front, rear drift adjustable for windage.
Features: Stainless steel construction; ventilated barrel rib; single action mechanism; cocked striker indicator; push-button safety. Introduced 1994. Made in U.S. by Colt.
Price: . . . . **NA**

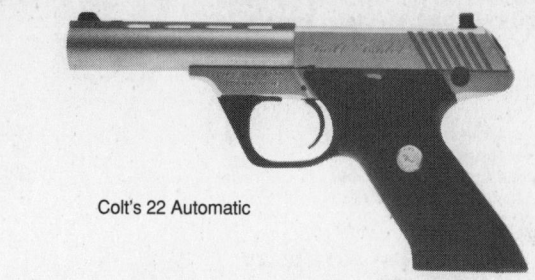

Colt's 22 Automatic

COLT COMBAT COMMANDER AUTO PISTOL
Caliber: 38 Super, 9-shot; 45 ACP, 8-shot.
Barrel: 4¼".
Weight: 36 oz. **Length:** 7¾" overall.
Stocks: Rubber combat.
Sights: Fixed, glare-proofed blade front, square notch rear; three-dot system.
Features: Long trigger; arched housing; grip and thumb safeties.
Price: 45, blue **$707.00**
Price: 45, stainless **$759.00**
Price: 38 Super, stainless **$759.00**

Colt Lightweight Commander MK IV/Series 80
Same as Commander except high strength aluminum alloy frame, rubber combat grips, weight 27½ oz. 45 ACP only.
Price: Blue **$707.00**

COLT DOUBLE EAGLE MKII/SERIES 90 DA PISTOL
Caliber: 45 ACP, 8-shot magazine.
Barrel: 4½", 5".
Weight: 39 ozs. **Length:** 8½" overall.
Stocks: Black checkered Xenoy thermoplastic.
Sights: Blade front, rear adjustable for windage. High profile three-dot system. Colt Accro adjustable sight optional.
Features: Made of stainless steel with matte finish. Checkered and curved extended trigger guard, wide steel trigger; decocking lever on left side; traditional magazine release; grooved frontstrap; bevelled magazine well; extended grip guard; rounded, serrated combat-style hammer. Announced 1989.
Price: **$697.00**
Price: Combat Comm., 45, 4½" bbl. **$697.00**

Colt Double Eagle Combat

Colt Double Eagle Officer's ACP
Similar to the regular Double Eagle except 45 ACP only, 3½" barrel, 34 oz., 7¼" overall length. Has 5¼" sight radius. Also offered in Lightweight version weighing 25 oz. Introduced 1991.
Price: Standard or Lightweight **$697.00**

COLT GOVERNMENT MODEL MK IV/SERIES 80
Caliber: 38 Super, 9-shot; 45 ACP, 8-shot magazine.
Barrel: 5".
Weight: 38 oz. **Length:** 8½" overall.
Stocks: Rubber combat.
Sights: Ramp front, fixed square notch rear; three-dot system.
Features: Grip and thumb safeties and internal firing pin safety, long trigger.
Price: 45 ACP, blue **$707.00**
Price: 45 ACP, stainless **$759.00**
Price: 45 ACP, bright stainless **$829.00**
Price: 38 Super, blue **$707.00**
Price: 38 Super, stainless **$759.00**
Price: 38 Super, bright stainless **$829.00**

Colt Government Model

Colt 10mm Delta Elite
Similar to the Government Model except chambered for 10mm auto cartridge. Has three-dot high profile front and rear combat sights, rubber combat stocks with Delta medallion, internal firing pin safety, and new recoil spring/buffer system. Introduced 1987.
Price: Blue **$774.00**

Colt Combat Elite MK IV/Series 80
Similar to the Government Model except has stainless frame with ordnance steel slide and internal parts. High profile front, rear sights with three-dot system, extended grip safety, beveled magazine well, rubber combat stocks. Introduced 1986.
Price: 45 ACP, STS/B **$860.00**
Price: 38 Super, STS/B **$860.00**

Colt Government Model 380

COLT GOVERNMENT MODEL 380
Caliber: 380 ACP, 7-shot magazine.
Barrel: 3¼".
Weight: 21¾ oz. **Length:** 6" overall.
Stocks: Checkered composition.
Sights: Ramp front, square notch rear, fixed.
Features: Scaled-down version of the 1911A1 Colt G.M. Has thumb and internal firing pin safeties. Introduced 1983.
Price: Blue **$443.00**
Price: Nickel **$504.00**
Price: Stainless **$473.00**
Price: Pocketlite 380, blue **$443.00**

Colt Mustang Plus II
Similar to the 380 Government Model except has the shorter barrel and slide of the Mustang. Introduced 1988.
Price: Blue **$443.00**
Price: Stainless **$473.00**

CAUTION: PRICES SHOWN ARE SUPPLIED BY THE MANUFACTURER OR IMPORTER. CHECK YOUR LOCAL GUNSHOP.

49th EDITION, 1995 **279**

Colt Mustang 380, Mustang Pocketlite

Similar to the standard 380 Government Model. Mustang has steel frame (18.5 oz.), Pocketlite has aluminum alloy (12.5 oz.). Both are ½" shorter than 380 G.M., have 2¾" barrel. Introduced 1987.

Price: Mustang 380, blue $443.00
Price: As above, nickel $504.00
Price: As above, stainless $473.00
Price: Mustang Pocketlite, blue $443.00
Price: Mustang Pocketlite STS/N $473.00

Colt Mustang 380

COLT MODEL 1991 A1 AUTO PISTOL

Caliber: 45 ACP, 7-shot magazine.
Barrel: 5".
Weight: 38 oz. Length: 8.5" overall.
Stocks: Checkered black composition.
Sights: Ramped blade front, fixed square notch rear, high profile.
Features: Parkerized finish. Continuation of serial number range used on original G.I. 1911-A1 guns. Comes with one magazine and moulded carrying case. Introduced 1991.
Price: $517.00

Colt Model 1991 A1 Commander Auto Pistol

Similar to the Model 1991 A1 except has 4¼" barrel. Parkerized finish. 7-shot magazine. Comes in moulded case. Introduced 1993.
Price: $517.00

Colt Model 1991 A1 Compact Auto Pistol

Similar to the Model 1991 A1 except has 3½" barrel. Overall length is 7", and gun is ⅜" shorter in height. Comes with one 6-shot magazine, moulded case. Introduced 1993.
Price: $517.00

Colt 1991A1 Compact

COLT OFFICER'S ACP MK IV/SERIES 80

Caliber: 45 ACP, 6-shot magazine.
Barrel: 3½".
Weight: 34 oz. (steel frame); 24 oz. (alloy frame). Length: 7¼" overall.
Stocks: Rubber combat.
Sights: Ramp blade front with white dot, square notch rear with two white dots.
Features: Trigger safety lock (thumb safety), grip safety, firing pin safety; long trigger; flat mainspring housing. Also available with lightweight alloy frame and in stainless steel. Introduced 1985.
Price: Blue $707.00
Price: L.W., blue finish $707.00
Price: Stainless $759.00
Price: Bright stainless $829.00

COONAN 357 MAGNUM PISTOL

Caliber: 357 Mag., 7-shot magazine.
Barrel: 5".
Weight: 42 oz. Length: 8.3" overall.
Stocks: Smooth walnut.
Sights: Interchangeable ramp front, rear adjustable for windage.
Features: Stainless and alloy steel construction. Unique barrel hood improves accuracy and reliability. Linkless barrel. Many parts interchange with Colt autos. Has grip, hammer, half-cock safeties, extended slide latch. Made in U.S. by Coonan Arms, Inc.
Price: 5" barrel $720.00
Price: 6" barrel $755.00
Price: With 6" compensated barrel $1,400.00

Coonan 357 Magnum

Coonan Compact 357 Magnum Cadet Pistol

Similar to the 357 Magnum full-size gun except has 3.9" barrel, shorter frame, 6-shot magazine. Weight is 39 oz., overall length 7.8". Linkless bull barrel, full-length recoil spring guide rod, extended slide latch. Introduced 1993. Made in U.S. by Coonan Arms, Inc.
Price: $841.00

CZ 75 AUTO PISTOL

Caliber: 9mm Para., 40 S&W, 15-shot magazine.
Barrel: 4.7".
Weight: 34.3 oz. Length: 8.1" overall.
Stocks: High impact checkered plastic.
Sights: Square post front, rear adjustable for windage; three-dot system.
Features: Single action/double action design; choice of black polymer, matte or high-polish blue finishes. All-steel frame. Imported from the Czech Republic by Action Arms, Ltd.
Price: 9mm, black polymer finish $479.00
Price: 40 S&W, SA/DA or DAO, black polymer finish $519.00
Price: 9mm, matte blue $499.00
Price: 40 S&W, SA/DA or DAO, matte blue $539.00
Price: High-polish blue $519.00
Price: 40 S&W, SA/DA or DAO, high-polish blue $559.00

CZ 75 Compact

CZ 75 Compact Auto Pistol

Similar to the CZ 75 except has 13-shot magazine, 3.9" barrel and weighs 32 oz. Has removable front sight, non-glare ribbed slide top. Trigger guard is squared and serrated; combat hammer. Introduced 1993. Imported from the Czech Republic by Action Arms, Ltd.
Price: Black polymer finish $519.00
Price: Matte blue $539.00
Price: High-polish blue $559.00

CZ 75 Semi-Compact Auto Pistol

Uses the shorter slide and barrel of the CZ 75 Compact with the full-size frame of the standard CZ 75. Has 15-shot magazine; 9mm Para. only. Introduced 1994. Imported from the Czech Republic by Action Arms Ltd.

Price: Black polymer finish $519.00
Price: Matte blue finish $539.00
Price: High-polish blue finish $559.00

CZ 85 Combat Auto Pistol

Same as the CZ 85 except has walnut grips, round combat hammer, fully adjustable rear sight, extended magazine release. Trigger parts coated with friction-free beryllium copper. Introduced 1992. Imported from the Czech Republic by Action Arms, Ltd.

Price: Black polymer finish $619.00
Price: Matte blue $645.00
Price: High-polish blue $669.00

CZ 83 DA

DAEWOO DP51 FASTFIRE AUTO PISTOL

Caliber: 9mm Para., 13-shot magazine.
Barrel: 4.25".
Weight: 28.2 oz. **Length:** 7" overall.
Stocks: Checkered composition.
Sights: 1/8" blade front, square notch rear drift adjustable for windage. Three dot system.
Features: Patented Fastfire mechanism. Ambidextrous manual safety and magazine catch, automatic firing pin block. No magazine safety. Alloy frame, squared trigger guard. Matte black finish. Introduced 1991. Imported from Korea by Nationwide Sports Dist.

Price: DP51 . . . . $390.00
Price: DH40 (40 S&W, 12-shot magazine) $420.00

DAEWOO DP52 AUTO PISTOL

Caliber: 22 LR, 10-shot magazine.
Barrel: 3.8".
Weight: 23 oz. **Length:** 6.7" overall.
Stocks: NA.
Sights: 1/8" blade front, rear drift adjustable for windage; three-dot system.
Features: Polished blue finish. Comes with two magazines. Introduced 1994. Imported from Korea by Nationwide Sports Distributors.

Price: $320.00

DAVIS P-32 AUTO PISTOL

Caliber: 32 ACP, 6-shot magazine.
Barrel: 2.8".
Weight: 22 oz. **Length:** 5.4" overall.
Stocks: Laminated wood.
Sights: Fixed.
Features: Choice of black Teflon or chrome finish. Announced 1986. Made in U.S. by Davis Industries.

Price: $87.50

DAVIS P-380 AUTO PISTOL

Caliber: 380 ACP, 5-shot magazine.
Barrel: 2.8".
Weight: 22 oz. **Length:** 5.4" overall.
Stocks: Black composition.
Sights: Fixed.
Features: Choice of chrome or black Teflon finish. Introduced 1991. Made in U.S. by Davis Industries.

Price: $98.00

CZ 85 Auto Pistol

Same gun as the CZ 75 except has ambidextrous slide release and safety-levers; non-glare, ribbed slide top; squared, serrated trigger guard; trigger stop to prevent overtravel. Introduced 1986. Imported from the Czech Republic by Action Arms, Ltd.

Price: Black polymer finish $515.00
Price: Matte blue $537.00
Price: High-polish blue $559.00

CZ 83 DOUBLE-ACTION PISTOL

Caliber: 32, 380 ACP, 12-shot magazine.
Barrel: 3.8".
Weight: 26.2 oz. **Length:** 6.8" overall.
Stocks: High impact checkered plastic.
Sights: Removable square post front, rear adjustable for windage; three-dot system.
Features: Single action/double action; ambidextrous magazine release and safety. Blue finish; non-glare ribbed slide top. Imported from the Czech Republic by Action Arms Ltd.

Price: $389.00

DAEWOO DH45 HIGH CAPACITY PISTOL

Caliber: 45 ACP, 13-shot magazine.
Barrel: 5".
Weight: 35 oz. **Length:** 8.1" overall.
Stocks: NA.
Sights: 1/8" blade front, rear drift adjustable for windage; three-dot system.
Features: Short-stroke double-action mechanism; hammerless striker design; ambidextrous external safety with internal firing pin lock. Announced 1994. Imported from Korea by Nationwide Sports Distributors.

Price: $500.00

Daewoo DP51 Fastfire

Daewoo DP52

Davis P-32

Desert Eagle Magnum

Desert Industries War Eagle

Desert Industries Double Deuce

DESERT EAGLE MAGNUM PISTOL
Caliber: 357 Mag., 9-shot; 41 Mag., 44 Mag., 8-shot; 50 Magnum, 7-shot.
Barrel: 6", 10", 14" interchangeable.
Weight: 357 Mag.—62 oz.; 41 Mag., 44 Mag.—69 oz.; 50 Mag.—72 oz.
Length: 10¼" overall (6" bbl.).
Stocks: Wraparound plastic.
Sights: Blade on ramp front, combat-style rear. Adjustable available.
Features: Rotating three-lug bolt; ambidextrous safety; combat-style trigger guard; adjustable trigger optional. Military epoxy finish. Satin, bright nickel, hard chrome, polished and blued finishes available. Imported from Israel by Magnum Research, Inc.

Price: 357, 6" bbl., standard pistol	$789.00
Price: As above, stainless steel frame	$839.00
Price: 41 Mag., 6", standard pistol	$799.00
Price: 41 Mag., stainless steel frame	$849.00
Price: 44 Mag., 6", standard pistol	$899.00
Price: As above, stainless steel frame	$949.00
Price: 50 Magnum, 6" bbl., standard pistol	$1,249.00

DESERT INDUSTRIES WAR EAGLE PISTOL
Caliber: 380 ACP, 8- or 13-shot; 9mm Para., 14-shot; 10mm, 13-shot; 40 S&W, 14-shot; 45 ACP, 12-shot.
Barrel: 4".
Weight: 35.5 oz. **Length:** 7.5" overall.
Stocks: Rosewood.
Sights: Fixed.
Features: Double action; matte-finished stainless steel; slide mounted ambidextrous safety. Announced 1986. From Desert Industries, Inc.

Price:	$795.00
Price: 380 ACP	$725.00

DESERT INDUSTRIES DOUBLE DEUCE, TWO BIT SPECIAL PISTOLS
Caliber: 22 LR, 6-shot; 25 ACP, 5-shot.
Barrel: 2½".
Weight: 15 oz. **Length:** 5½" overall.
Stocks: Rosewood.
Sights: Special order.
Features: Double action; stainless steel construction with matte finish; ambidextrous slide-mounted safety. From Desert Industries, Inc.

Price: 22	$399.95
Price: 25 (Two-Bit Special)	$399.95

E.A.A. EUROPEAN MODEL AUTO PISTOLS
Caliber: 32 ACP or 380 ACP, 7-shot magazine.
Barrel: 3.88".
Weight: 26 oz. **Length:** 7⅜" overall.
Stocks: European hardwood.
Sights: Fixed blade front, rear drift-adjustable for windage.
Features: Chrome or blue finish; magazine, thumb and firing pin safeties; external hammer; safety-lever takedown. Imported from Italy by European American Armory.

Price: Blue	$150.00
Price: Blue/chrome	$165.00
Price: Chrome	$165.00
Price: Ladies Model	$225.00

E.A.A. European 380/DA Pistol
Similar to the standard European except in 380 ACP only, with double-action trigger mechanism. Available in blue, chrome or blue/chrome finish. Introduced 1992. From European American Armory.

Price: Blue	$185.00
Price: Chrome	$199.00
Price: Blue/chrome	$199.00

E.A.A. WITNESS DA AUTO PISTOL
Caliber: 9mm Para., 16-shot magazine; 10mm Auto, 10-shot magazine; 38 Super, 40 S&W, 12-shot magazine; 45 ACP, 10-shot magazine.
Barrel: 4.50".
Weight: 35.33 oz. **Length:** 8.10" overall.
Stocks: Checkered rubber.
Sights: Undercut blade front, open rear adjustable for windage.
Features: Double-action trigger system; round trigger guard; frame-mounted safety. Introduced 1991. Imported from Italy by European American Armory.

Price: 9mm, blue	$399.00
Price: 9mm, satin chrome	$425.00
Price: 9mm, blue slide, chrome frame	$425.00
Price: 9mm Compact, blue, 13-shot	$399.00
Price: As above, blue slide, chrome frame, or all-chrome	$425.00
Price: 40 S&W, blue	$425.00
Price: As above, blue slide, chrome frame, or all-chrome	$450.00
Price: 40 S&W Compact, 8-shot, blue	$425.00
Price: As above, blue slide, chrome frame, or all-chrome	$450.00
Price: 45 ACP, blue	$495.00
Price: As above, blue slide, chrome frame, or all-chrome	$525.00
Price: 45 ACP Compact, 8-shot, blue	$495.00
Price: As above, blue slide, chrome frame or all-chrome	$525.00
Price: 9mm/40 S&W Combo, blue, compact or full size	$560.00
Price: As above, blue/chrome, compact or full size	$585.00
Price: 9mm or 40 S&W Carry Comp, blue	$550.00
Price: As above, blue/chrome	$575.00

E.A.A. Witness

CAUTION: PRICES SHOWN ARE SUPPLIED BY THE MANUFACTURER OR IMPORTER. CHECK YOUR LOCAL GUNSHOP.

ERMA KGP68 AUTO PISTOL
Caliber: 32 ACP, 6-shot, 380 ACP, 5-shot.
Barrel: 4".
Weight: 22½ oz. **Length:** 7⅜" overall.
Stocks: Checkered plastic.
Sights: Fixed.
Features: Toggle action similar to original "Luger" pistol. Action stays open after last shot. Has magazine and sear disconnect safety systems. Imported from Germany by Mandall Shooting Supplies.
Price: **$795.00**

FEG B9R AUTO PISTOL
Caliber: 380 ACP, 15-shot magazine.
Barrel: 4".
Weight: 25 oz. **Length:** 7" overall.
Stocks: Hand-checkered walnut.
Sights: Blade front, drift-adjustable rear.
Features: Hammer-drop safety; grooved backstrap; squared trigger guard. Comes with spare magazine. Introduced 1993. Imported from Hungary by Century International Arms.
Price: About **$312.00**

FEG FP9 AUTO PISTOL
Caliber: 9mm Para., 14-shot magazine.
Barrel: 5".
Weight: 35 oz. **Length:** 7.8" overall.
Stocks: Checkered walnut.
Sights: Blade front, windage-adjustable rear.
Features: Full-length ventilated rib. Polished blue finish. Comes with extra magazine. Introduced 1993. Imported from Hungary by Century International Arms.
Price: About **$269.00**

FEG GKK-45

FEG GKK-45 DA AUTO PISTOL
Caliber: 45 ACP, 8-shot magazine.
Barrel: 4.6".
Weight: 34 oz. **Length:** 8.06" overall.
Stocks: Hand-checkered walnut.
Sights: Blade front, rear adjustable for windage; three-dot system.
Features: Combat-type trigger guard. Polished blue or hard chrome finish. Comes with two magazines, cleaning rod. Introduced 1994. Imported from Hungary by K.B.I., Inc.
Price: Blue **$449.00**
Price: Hard chrome **$499.00**

FEG PJK-9HP

FEG PJK-9HP AUTO PISTOL
Caliber: 9mm Para., 13-shot magazine.
Barrel: 4.75".
Weight: 32 oz. **Length:** 8" overall.
Stocks: Hand-checkered walnut.
Sights: Blade front, rear adjustable for windage; three dot system.
Features: Single action; polished blue or hard chrome finish; rounded combat-style serrated hammer. Comes with two magazines and cleaning rod. Imported from Hungary by K.B.I., Inc.
Price: Blue **$349.00**
Price: Hard chrome **$429.00**

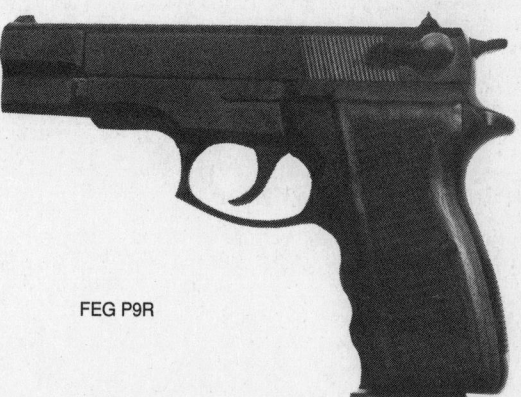

FEG P9R

FEG P9R AUTO PISTOL
Caliber: 9mm Para., 15-shot magazine.
Barrel: 4.6".
Weight: 35 oz. **Length:** 7.9" overall.
Stocks: Checkered walnut.
Sights: Blade front, rear adjustable for windage.
Features: Double-action mechanism; slide-mounted safety. All-Steel construction with polished blue finish. Comes with extra magazine. Introduced 1993. Imported from Hungary by Century International Arms.
Price: About **$262.00**

FEG SMC-22

FEG SMC-22 DA AUTO PISTOL
Caliber: 22 LR, 8-shot magazine.
Barrel: 3.5".
Weight: 18.5 oz. **Length:** 6.12" overall.
Stocks: Checkered composition with thumbrest.
Sights: Blade front, rear adjustable for windage.
Features: Patterned after the PPK pistol. Alloy frame, steel slide; blue finish. Comes with two magazines, cleaning rod. Introduced 1994. Imported from Hungary by K.B.I., Inc.
Price: **$299.00**

FEG SMC-380 AUTO PISTOL
Caliber: 380 ACP, 6-shot magazine.
Barrel: 3.5".
Weight: 18.5 oz. **Length:** 6.1" overall.
Stocks: Checkered composition with thumbrest.
Sights: Blade front, rear adjustable for windage.
Features: Patterned after the PPK pistol. Alloy frame, steel slide; double action. Blue finish. Comes with two magazines, cleaning rod. Imported from Hungary by K.B.I.
Price: **$279.00**

CAUTION: PRICES SHOWN ARE SUPPLIED BY THE MANUFACTURER OR IMPORTER. CHECK YOUR LOCAL GUNSHOP.

49th EDITION, 1995 **283**

Glock 19

Glock 21

GLOCK 17 AUTO PISTOL

Caliber: 9mm Para., 17-shot magazine.
Barrel: 4.49".
Weight: 21.9 oz. (without magazine). **Length:** 7.28" overall.
Stocks: Black polymer.
Sights: Dot on front blade, white outline rear adjustable for windage.
Features: Polymer frame, steel slide; double-action trigger with "Safe Action" system; mechanical firing pin safety, drop safety; simple takedown without tools; locked breech, recoil operated action. Adopted by Austrian armed forces 1983. NATO approved 1984. Imported from Austria by Glock, Inc.
Price: With extra magazine, magazine loader, cleaning kit **$608.95**
Price: Model 17L (6" barrel) **$806.67**

Glock 19 Auto Pistol

Similar to the Glock 17 except has a 4" barrel, giving an overall length of 6.85" and weight of 20.99 oz. Magazine capacity is 15 rounds. Fixed or adjustable rear sight. Introduced 1988.
Price: **$608.95**

Glock 20 10mm Auto Pistol

Similar to the Glock Model 17 except chambered for 10mm Automatic cartridge. Barrel length is 4.60", overall length is 7.59", and weight is 26.3 oz. (without magazine). Magazine capacity is 15 rounds. Fixed or adjustable rear sight. Comes with an extra magazine, magazine loader, cleaning rod and brush. Introduced 1990. Imported from Austria by Glock, Inc.
Price: **$670.41**

Glock 21 Auto Pistol

Similar to the Glock 17 except chambered for 45 ACP, 13-shot magazine. Overall length is 7.59", weight is 25.2 oz. (without magazine). Fixed or adjustable rear sight. Introduced 1991.
Price: **$670.41**

Glock 23 Auto Pistol

Similar to the Glock 19 except chambered for 40 S&W, 13-shot magazine. Overall length is 6.85", weight is 20.6 oz. (without magazine). Fixed or adjustable rear sight. Introduced 1990.
Price: **$608.95**

Glock 22 Auto Pistol

Similar to the Glock 17 except chambered for 40 S&W, 15-shot magazine. Overall length is 7.28", weight is 22.3 oz. (without magazine). Fixed or adjustable rear sight. Introduced 1990.
Price: **$670.41**

GRENDEL P-12 AUTO PISTOL

Caliber: 380 ACP, 11-shot magazine.
Barrel: 3".
Weight: 13 oz. **Length:** 5.3" overall.
Stocks: Checkered DuPont ST-800 polymer.
Sights: Fixed.
Features: Double action only with inertia safety hammer system. All steel frame; grip forms magazine well and trigger guard. Introduced 1992. Made in U.S. by Grendel, Inc.
Price: Blue **$175.00**
Price: Electroless nickel **$195.00**

Grendel P-12

GRENDEL P-30 AUTO PISTOL

Caliber: 22 WMR, 30-shot magazine.
Barrel: 5", 8".
Weight: 21 oz. (5" barrel). **Length:** 8.5" overall (5" barrel).
Stocks: Checkered Zytel.
Sights: Blade front, fixed rear.
Features: Blowback action with fluted chamber; ambidextrous safety, reversible magazine catch. Scope mount available. Introduced 1990.
Price: With 5" barrel **$225.00**
Price: With removable muzzlebrake (Model P-30M) **$235.00**
Price: With 8" barrel (Model P-30L) **$280.00**

Grendel P-30

Hammerli Model 212

HAMMERLI MODEL 212 AUTO PISTOL

Caliber: 22 LR, 8-shot magazine.
Barrel: 4.9".
Weight: 31 oz.
Stocks: Checkered walnut.
Sights: Blade front, rear adjustable for windage only.
Features: Polished blue finish. Imported from Switzerland by Mandall Shooting Supplies and Hammerli Pistols USA.
Price: About **$1,395.00**

CAUTION: PRICES SHOWN ARE SUPPLIED BY THE MANUFACTURER OR IMPORTER. CHECK YOUR LOCAL GUNSHOP.

Heckler & Koch P7M10

Heckler & Koch P7K3 Auto Pistol

Similar to the P7M8 and P7M13 except chambered for 22 LR or 380 ACP, 8-shot magazine. Uses an oil-filled buffer to decrease recoil. Introduced 1988.

Price: **$1,100.00**
Price: 22 LR conversion unit **$525.00**
Price: 32 ACP conversion unit **$228.00**

Heckler & Koch USP

HELWAN "BRIGADIER" AUTO PISTOL

Caliber: 9mm Para., 8-shot magazine.
Barrel: 4.5".
Weight: 32 oz. **Length:** 8" overall.
Stocks: Grooved plastic.
Sights: Blade front, rear adjustable for windage.
Features: Polished blue finish. Single-action design. Cross-bolt safety. Imported by Interarms.
Price: **$260.00**

HERITAGE MODEL HA25 AUTO PISTOL

Caliber: 25 ACP, 6-shot magazine.
Barrel: 2½".
Weight: 12 oz. **Length:** 4⅝" overall.
Stocks: Smooth or checkered walnut.
Sights: Fixed.
Features: Exposed hammer, manual safety; open-top slide. Polished blue or blue/gold finish. Introduced 1993. Made in U.S. by Heritage Mfg., Inc.
Price: Blue **$64.95**
Price: Blue/gold **$79.95**

HI-POINT FIREARMS MODEL JS-9MM COMPACT PISTOL

Caliber: 380 ACP, 9mm Para., 8-shot magazine.
Barrel: 3.5".
Weight: 35 oz. **Length:** 6.7" overall.
Stocks: Textured acetal plastic.
Sights: Combat-style fixed three-dot system; low profile.
Features: Single-action design; frame-mounted magazine release. Scratch-resistant matte finish. Introduced 1993. From MKS Supply, Inc.
Price: **$124.95**
Price: With polymer frame (32 oz.) **$132.95**
Price: 380 ACP . . . . **NA**

HECKLER & KOCH P7M8 AUTO PISTOL

Caliber: 9mm Para., 8-shot magazine.
Barrel: 4.13".
Weight: 29 oz. **Length:** 6.73" overall.
Stocks: Stippled black plastic.
Sights: Blade front, adjustable rear; three dot system.
Features: Unique "squeeze cocker" in frontstrap cocks the action. Gas-retarded action. Squared combat-type trigger guard. Blue finish. Compact size. Imported from Germany by Heckler & Koch, Inc.
Price: P7M8, blued **$1,100.00**
Price: P7M13 (13-shot capacity, ambidextrous magazine release, forged steel frame), blued **$1,330.00**
Price: P7M13, nickel **$1,330.00**

Heckler & Koch P7M10 Auto Pistol

Similar to the P7M8 except chambered for 40 S&W with 10-shot magazine. Weighs 43 oz., overall length is 6.9". Introduced 1992. Imported from Germany by Heckler & Koch, Inc.
Price: Blue **$1,315.00**
Price: Nickel **$1,315.00**

HECKLER & KOCH USP AUTO PISTOL

Caliber: 9mm Para., 15-shot magazine, 40 S&W, 13-shot magazine.
Barrel: 4.25".
Weight: 28 oz. (USP40). **Length:** 6.9" overall.
Stocks: Non-slip stippled black polymer.
Sights: Blade front, rear adjustable for windage.
Features: New HK design with polymer frame, modified Browning action with recoil reduction system, single control lever. Special "hostile environment" finish on all metal parts. Available in SA/DA, DAO, left- and right-hand versions. Introduced 1993. Imported from Germany by Heckler & Koch, Inc.
Price: Right-hand **$635.00**
Price: Left-hand **$655.00**

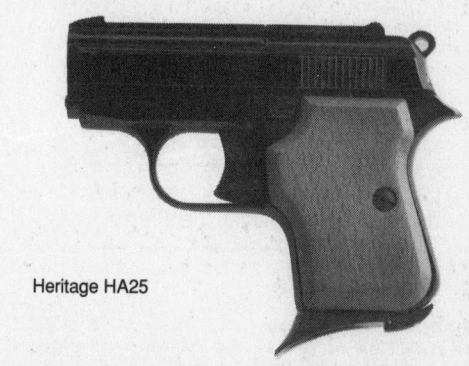

Heritage HA25

Hi-Point JS-9MM

HI-POINT FIREARMS JS-45 CALIBER PISTOL

Caliber: 45 ACP, 7-shot magazine.
Barrel: 4.5".
Weight: 44 oz. **Length:** 7.95" overall.
Stocks: Checkered acetal resin.
Sights: Fixed; low profile.
Features: Internal drop-safe mechanism; all aluminum frame. Introduced 1991. From MKS Supply, Inc.
Price: Matte black **$148.95**

HI-POINT FIREARMS JS-40 S&W AUTO
Caliber: 40 S&W, 8-shot magazine.
Barrel: 4.5".
Weight: 44 oz. **Length:** 7.95" overall.
Stocks: Checkered acetal resin.
Sights: Fixed; low profile.
Features: Internal drop-safe mechansim; all aluminum frame. Introduced 1991. From MKS Supply, Inc.
Price: Matte black **$148.95**

HI-POINT FIREARMS JS-9MM AUTO PISTOL
Caliber: 9mm Para., 9-shot magazine.
Barrel: 4.5".
Weight: 41 oz. **Length:** 7.72" overall.
Stocks: Textured acetal plastic.
Sights: Fixed, low profile.
Features: Single-action design. Scratch-resistant, non-glare blue finish. Introduced 1990. From MKS Supply, Inc.
Price: Matte black **$139.95**

HUNGARIAN T-58 AUTO PISTOL
Caliber: 7.62mm and 9mm Para., 8-shot magazine.
Barrel: 4.5".
Weight: 31 oz. **Length:** 7.68" overall.
Stocks: Grooved composition.
Sights: Blade front, rear adjustable for windage.
Features: Comes with both barrels and magazines. Thumb safety locks hammer. Blue finish. Imported by Century International Arms.
Price: About **$187.00**

INTRATEC CATEGORY 9 AUTO PISTOL
Caliber: 9mm Para., 8-shot magazine.
Barrel: 3".
Weight: 21 oz. **Length:** 5.5" overall.
Stocks: Textured black polymer.
Sights: Fixed channel.
Features: Black polymer frame. Announced 1993. Made in U.S. by Intratec.
Price: About **$225.00**

> Consult our Directory pages for the location of firms mentioned.

Intratec TEC-DC9M Auto Pistol
Similar to the TEC-DC9 except smaller. Has 3" barrel, weighs 44 oz.; 20-shot magazine. Made in U.S. by Intratec.
Price: **$245.00**
Price: TEC-DC9MS (as above, stainless) **$339.00**
Price: TEC-DC9MK (finished with TEC-KOTE) **$277.00**

Jennings J-25

KAHR K9 DA AUTO PISTOL
Caliber: 9mm Para., 7-shot magazine.
Barrel: 3.5".
Weight: 24 oz. **Length:** 6" overall.
Stocks: Smooth wood; wrap-around design.
Sights: Blade front, rear drift adjustable for windage; bar-dot combat style.
Features: Trigger-cocking double-action mechanism with passive firing pin block. Made of 4140 ordnance steel with blue finish. Introduced 1994. Made in U.S. by Kahr Arms.
Price: **$595.00**

Hi-Point JS-40

INTRATEC PROTEC-22, 25 AUTO PISTOLS
Caliber: 22 LR, 10-shot; 25 ACP, 8-shot magazine.
Barrel: 2½".
Weight: 14 oz. **Length:** 5" overall.
Stocks: Wraparound composition in gray, black or driftwood color.
Sights: Fixed.
Features: Double-action only trigger mechanism. Choice of black, satin or TEC-KOTE finish. Announced 1991. Made in U.S. by Intratec.
Price: 22 or 25, black finish **$102.00**
Price: 22 or 25, satin or TEC-KOTE finish **$107.95**

INTRATEC TEC-DC9 AUTO PISTOL
Caliber: 9mm Para., 32-shot magazine.
Barrel: 5".
Weight: 50 oz. **Length:** 12½" overall.
Stock: Moulded composition.
Sights: Fixed.
Features: Semi-auto, fires from closed bolt; firing pin block safety; matte blue finish. Made in U.S. by Intratec.
Price: **$269.00**
Price: TEC-DC9S (as above, except stainless) **$362.00**
Price: TEC-DC9K (finished with TEC-KOTE) **$297.00**

INTRATEC TEC-22T AUTO PISTOL
Caliber: 22 LR, 30-shot magazine.
Barrel: 4".
Weight: 30 oz. **Length:** 11³⁄₁₆" overall.
Stocks: Moulded composition.
Sights: Protected post front, front and rear adjustable for windage and elevation.
Features: Ambidextrous cocking knobs and safety. Matte black finish. Accepts any 10/22-type magazine. Introduced 1988. Made in U.S. by Intratec.
Price: **$161.00**
Price: TEC-22TK (as above, TEC-KOTE finish) **$183.50**

JENNINGS J-22, J-25 AUTO PISTOLS
Caliber: 22 LR, 25 ACP, 6-shot magazine.
Barrel: 2½".
Weight: 13 oz. (J-22). **Length:** 4¹⁵⁄₁₆" overall (J-22).
Stocks: Walnut on chrome or nickel models; grooved black Cycolac or resin-impregnated wood on Teflon model.
Sights: Fixed.
Features: Choice of bright chrome, satin nickel or black Teflon finish. Introduced 1981. From Jennings Firearms.
Price: J-22, about **$79.95**
Price: J-25, about **$79.95**

Kahr K9

Kareen Mk II

KAREEN MK II AUTO PISTOL
Caliber: 9mm Para., 13-shot magazine.
Barrel: 4.75".
Weight: 32 oz. **Length:** 8" overall.
Stocks: Textured composition.
Sights: Blade front, rear adjustable for windage.
Features: Single-action mechanism; external hammer safety; magazine safety; combat trigger guard. Blue finish standard, optional two-tone or matte black. Optional Meprolight sights, improved rubberized grips. Introduced 1969. Imported from Israel by J.O. Arms & Ammunition.
Price: . . . . $425.00 to $575.00
Price: Barak 9mm (3.25" barrel, 28 oz., 6.5" overall length) $425.00 to $575.00

KIMEL AP9 AUTO PISTOL
Caliber: 9mm Para., 20-shot magazine.
Barrel: 5".
Weight: 3.5 lbs. **Length:** 11.8" overall.
Stocks: Checkered plastic.
Sights: Adjustable post front in ring, fixed open rear.
Features: Matte blue/black or nickel finish. Lever safety blocks trigger and sear. Fires from closed bolt. Introduced 1988. Made in U.S. Available from Kimel Industries.
Price: Matte blue/black $264.00
Price: Nickel finish $274.00
Price: Mini AP9 (3" barrel) $258.00
Price: Nickel finish $268.00
Price: Target AP9 (12" bbl., grooved forend), blue $279.00

L.A.R. GRIZZLY WIN MAG MK I PISTOL
Caliber: 357 Mag., 357/45, 10mm, 44 Mag., 45 Win. Mag., 45 ACP, 7-shot magazine.
Barrel: 5.4", 6.5".
Weight: 51 oz. **Length:** 10½" overall.
Stocks: Checkered rubber, non-slip combat-type.
Sights: Ramped blade front, fully adjustable rear.
Features: Uses basic Browning/Colt 1911A1 design; interchangeable calibers; beveled magazine well; combat-type flat, checkered rubber mainspring housing; lowered and back-chamfered ejection port; polished feed ramp; throated barrel; solid barrel bushings. Available in satin hard chrome, matte blue, Parkerized finishes. Introduced 1983. From L.A.R. Mfg., Inc.
Price: 45 Win. Mag. $920.00
Price: 357 Mag. $933.00
Price: Conversion units (357 Mag.) $228.00
Price: As above, 45 ACP, 10mm, 45 Win. Mag., 357/45 Win. Mag. . . $214.00

Laseraim Arms Series III

L.A.R. Grizzly Win Mag

L.A.R. Grizzly Win Mag 8" & 10"
Similar to the standard Grizzly Win Mag except has lengthened slide and either 8" or 10" barrel. Available in 45 Win. Mag., 45 ACP, 357/45 Grizzly Win. Mag., 10mm or 357 Magnum. Introduced 1987.
Price: 8", 45 ACP, 45 Win. Mag., 357/45 Grizzly Win. Mag. $1,313.00
Price: As above, 10" $1,375.00
Price: 8", 357 Magnum $1,337.50
Price: As above, 10" $1,400.00

L.A.R. Grizzly 50 Mark V Pistol
Similar to the Grizzly Win Mag Mark I except chambered for 50 Action Express with 6-shot magazine. Weight, empty, is 56 oz., overall length 10⅝". Choice of 5.4" or 6.5" barrel. Has same features as Mark I, IV pistols. Introduced 1993. From L.A.R. Mfg., Inc.
Price: $1,060.00

L.A.R. Grizzly 44 Mag MK IV
Similar to the Win. Mag. Mk I except chambered for 44 Magnum, has beavertail grip safety. Matte blue finish only. Has 5.4" or 6.5" barrel. Introduced 1991. From L.A.R. Mfg., Inc.
Price: $933.00

LASERAIM ARMS SERIES I AUTO PISTOL
Caliber: 10mm Auto, 8-shot, 45 ACP, 7-shot magazine.
Barrel: 6", with compensator.
Weight: 46 oz. **Length:** 9.75" overall.
Stocks: Pebble-grained black composite.
Sights: Blade front, fully adjustable rear.
Features: Single action; barrel compensator; stainless steel construction; ambidextrous safety-levers; extended slide release; matte black Teflon finish; integral mount for laser sight. Introduced 1993. Made in U.S. by Emerging Technologies, Inc.
Price: Standard, fixed sight $552.95
Price: Standard, Compact (4⅜" barrel), fixed sight $552.95
Price: Adjustable sight $579.95
Price: Standard, fixed sight, Auto Illusion red dot sight system . . . $649.95
Price: Standard, fixed sight, Laseraim Laser with Hotdot $694.95

Laseraim Arms Series II Auto Pistol
Similar to the Series I except without compensator, has matte stainless finish. Standard Series II has 5" barrel, weighs 43 oz., Compact has 3⅜" barrel, weighs 37 oz. Blade front sight, rear adjustable for windage or fixed. Introduced 1993. Made in U.S. by Emerging Technologies, Inc.
Price: Standard or Compact (3⅜" barrel), fixed sight $399.95
Price: Adjustable sight, 5" only $429.95
Price: Standard, fixed sight, Auto Illusion red dot sight $499.95
Price: Standard, fixed sight, Laseraim Laser $499.95

Laseraim Arms Series III Auto Pistol
Similar to the Series I except has 5" barrel only, with dual-port compensator; weighs 43 oz.; overall length is 7⅝". Choice of fixed or adjustable rear sight. Introduced 1994. Made in U.S. by Emerging Technologies, Inc.
Price: Fixed sight $533.95
Price: Adjustable sight $559.95
Price: Fixed sight Dream Team Laseraim laser sight $629.95

LLAMA COMPACT FRAME AUTO PISTOL
Caliber: 45 ACP, 7-shot.
Barrel: $4^{5}/_{16}$".
Weight: 37 oz.
Stocks: Checkered polymer.
Sights: Blade front, rear adjustable for windage.
Features: Scaled-down version of the Large Frame gun. Locked breech mechanism; manual and grip safeties. Introduced 1985. Imported from Spain by SGS Importers Int'l., Inc.
Price: Model IX-B, blue $299.95
Price: As above, nickel $363.95

Llama Large Frame

LLAMA LARGE FRAME AUTO PISTOL
Caliber: 45 ACP.
Barrel: 5".
Weight: 40 oz. **Length:** $8\frac{1}{2}$" overall.
Stocks: Checkered polymer.
Sights: Fixed.
Features: Grip and manual safeties, ventilated rib. Imported from Spain by SGS Importers Int'l., Inc.
Price: Model IX-A, blue $299.95
Price: As above, nickel $363.95

Llama New Generation Auto Pistols
Similar to the Large and Compact frame 45 automatics except has 13-shot magazine, anatomically designed rubber grips, three-dot combat sights, non-glare matte finish. Chambered only for 45 ACP. Introduced 1994. Imported from Spain by SGS Importers International, Inc.
Price: Compact or Large frame $391.95
Price: Max-I (7-shot magazine) $324.95

Llama New Generation

LLAMA XV, III-A SMALL FRAME AUTO PISTOLS
Caliber: 22 LR, 380.
Barrel: $3^{11}/_{16}$".
Weight: 23 oz. **Length:** $6\frac{1}{2}$" overall.
Stocks: Checkered polymer, thumbrest.
Sights: Fixed front, adjustable notch rear.
Features: Ventilated rib, manual and grip safeties. Imported from Spain by SGS Importers International, Inc.
Price: Blue $248.95
Price: Satin Chrome $341.95

Llama Small Frame

LORCIN L9MM AUTO PISTOL
Caliber: 9mm Para., 13-shot magazine.
Barrel: 4.5".
Weight: 31 oz. **Length:** 7.5" overall.
Stocks: Grooved black composition.
Sights: Fixed; three-dot system.
Features: Matte black finish; hooked trigger guard; grip safety. Introduced 1994. Made in U.S. by Lorcin Engineering.
Price: $159.00

LORCIN L-22 AUTO PISTOL
Caliber: 22 LR, 9-shot magazine.
Barrel: 2.5".
Weight: 16 oz. **Length:** 5.25" overall.
Stocks: Black combat, or pink or pearl.
Sights: Fixed three-dot system.
Features: Available in chrome or black Teflon finish. Introduced 1989. From Lorcin Engineering.
Price: About $89.00

Lorcin L9MM

Lorcin L-25

LORCIN L-25, LT-25 AUTO PISTOLS
Caliber: 25 ACP, 7-shot magazine.
Barrel: 2.4".
Weight: 14.5 oz. **Length:** 4.8" overall.
Stocks: Smooth composition.
Sights: Fixed.
Features: Available in choice of finishes: chrome, black Teflon or camouflage. Introduced 1989. From Lorcin Engineering.
Price: L-25 . . . . $69.00
Price: LT-25 . . . . $79.00

LORCIN L-32, L-380 AUTO PISTOLS
Caliber: 32 ACP, 380 ACP, 7-shot magazine.
Barrel: 3.5".
Weight: 27 oz. **Length:** 6.6" overall.
Stocks: Grooved composition.
Sights: Fixed.
Features: Black Teflon or chrome finish with black grips. Introduced 1992. From Lorcin Engineering.
Price: L-32 32 ACP $89.00
Price: L-380 380 ACP $100.00

CAUTION: PRICES SHOWN ARE SUPPLIED BY THE MANUFACTURER OR IMPORTER. CHECK YOUR LOCAL GUNSHOP.

Mitchell American Eagle

Mitchell Arms Citation II Auto Pistol
Same as the Trophy II except has nickel-plated trigger, safety and magazine release, and has silver-filled roll marks. Available in stainless steel. Announced 1992. From Mitchell Arms, Inc.
Price: Stainless steel **$468.00**

MITCHELL ARMS SPORT-KING II AUTO PISTOL
Caliber: 22 LR, 10-shot magazine.
Barrel: 4.5", 6.75".
Weight: 39 oz. (4.5" barrel). **Length:** 9" overall (4.5" barrel).
Stocks: Checkered black plastic.
Sights: Blade front, rear adjustable for windage.
Features: Military grip; standard trigger; push-button barrel takedown. All stainless steel. Announced 1992. From Mitchell Arms, Inc.
Price: **$312.00**

MITCHELL HIGH STANDARD 45 SIGNATURE SERIES
Caliber: 45 ACP, 8-shot magazine.
Barrel: 5".
Weight: NA. **Length:** 8.75" overall.
Stocks: Checkered American walnut.
Sights: Interchangeable blade front, drift adjustable combat rear or fully adjustable rear.
Features: Royal blue or stainless steel. Introduced 1994. Made in U.S. From Mitchell Arms, Inc.
Price: Blue, drift adjustable sight **$529.00**
Price: As above, stainless **$559.00**
Price: Blue, fully adjustable sight **$569.00**
Price: As above, stainless **$599.00**
Price: Blue, drift adjustable sight, 13-shot magazine **$679.00**
Price: As above, stainless **$709.00**
Price: Blue, fully adjustable sight, 13-shot magazine **$719.00**
Price: As above, stainless **$749.00**

MITCHELL ARMS SHARPSHOOTER II AUTO PISTOL
Caliber: 22 LR, 10-shot magazine.
Barrel: 5.5" bull.
Weight: 45 oz. **Length:** 10.25" overall.
Stocks: Checkered walnut with thumbrest.
Sights: Ramp front, slide-mounted square notch rear adjustable for windage and elevation.
Features: Military grip. Slide lock; smooth gripstraps; push-button takedown. Announced 1992. From Mitchell Arms, Inc.
Price: Stainless steel **$379.00**

Mountain Eagle Target

MITCHELL ARMS AMERICAN EAGLE AUTO
Caliber: 9mm Para., 7-shot magazine.
Barrel: 4".
Weight: 29.6 oz. **Length:** 9.6" overall.
Stocks: Checkered walnut.
Sights: Blade front, fixed rear.
Features: Recreation of the American Eagle Parabellum pistol in stainless steel. Chamber loaded indicator. Made in U.S. From Mitchell Arms, Inc.
Price: **$695.00**

MITCHELL ARMS TROPHY II AUTO PISTOL
Caliber: 22 LR, 10-shot magazine.
Barrel: 5.5" bull, 7.25" fluted.
Weight: 44.5 oz. (5.5" barrel). **Length:** 9.75" overall (5.5" barrel).
Stocks: Checkered walnut with thumbrest.
Sights: Undercut ramp front, click-adjustable frame-mounted rear.
Features: Grip duplicates feel of military 45; positive action magazine latch; front- and backstraps stippled. Trigger adjustable for pull, over-travel; gold-filled roll marks, gold-plated trigger, safety, magazine release; push-button barrel takedown. Available in stainless steel. Announced 1992. From Mitchell Arms, Inc.
Price: Stainless steel **$494.00**

Mitchell Sport King II

Mitchell High Standard 45

Mitchell Sharpshooter II

MOUNTAIN EAGLE AUTO PISTOL
Caliber: 22 LR, 15-shot magazine.
Barrel: 6.5", 8".
Weight: 21 oz., 23 oz. **Length:** 10.6" overall (with 6.5" barrel).
Stocks: One-piece impact-resistant polymer in "conventional contour"; checkered panels.
Sights: Serrated ramp front with interchangeable blades, rear adjustable for windage and elevation; interchangeable blades.
Features: Injection moulded grip frame, alloy receiver; hybrid composite barrel replicates shape of the Desert Eagle pistol. Flat, smooth trigger. Introduced 1992. From Magnum Research.
Price: Mountain Eagle Standard **$239.00**
Price: Mountain Eagle Target Edition (8" barrel) **$279.00**

NAVY ARMS TT-OLYMPIA PISTOL
Caliber: 22 LR.
Barrel: 4.6".
Weight: 28 oz. **Length:** 8" overall.
Stocks: Checkered hardwood.
Sights: Blade front, rear adjsutable for windage.
Features: Reproduction of the Walther Olympia pistol. Polished blue finish. Introduced 1992. Imported by Navy Arms.
Price: **$290.00**

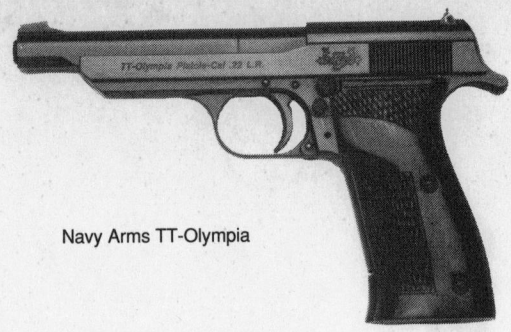

Navy Arms TT-Olympia

NORINCO MODEL 59 MAKAROV DA PISTOL
Caliber: 9x18mm, 380 ACP, 8-shot magazine.
Barrel: 3.5".
Weight: 21 oz. **Length:** 6.3" overall.
Stocks: Checkered plastic.
Sights: Blade front, adjustable rear.
Features: Blue finish. Double action. Introduced 1990. Imported from China by China Sports, Inc.
Price: . . . . **NA**

NORINCO NP-15 TOKAREV AUTO PISTOL
Caliber: 7.62x25mm, 8-shot magazine.
Barrel: 4.5".
Weight: 29 oz. **Length:** 7.7" overall.
Stocks: Grooved black plastic.
Sights: Fixed.
Features: Matte blue finish. Imported from China by China Sports, Inc.
Price: . . . . **NA**

Norinco 77B

NORINCO MODEL 77B AUTO PISTOL
Caliber: 9mm Para., 8-shot magazine.
Barrel: 5".
Weight: 34 oz. **Length:** 7.5" overall.
Stocks: Checkered wood.
Sights: Blade front, adjustable rear.
Features: Uses trigger guard cocking, gas-retarded recoil action. Front of trigger guard can be used to cock the action with the trigger finger. Introduced 1989. Imported from China by China Sports, Inc.
Price: . . . . **NA**

NORINCO M93 SPORTSMAN AUTO PISTOL
Caliber: 22 LR, 10-shot magazine.
Barrel: 4.6".
Weight: 26 oz. **Length:** 8.6" overall.
Stocks: Checkered composition.
Sights: Blade front, rear adjustable for windage.
Features: All steel construction with blue finish, Introduced 1992. Imported from China by Interarms.
Price: . . . . **NA**

NORINCO M1911A1 AUTO PISTOL
Caliber: 45 ACP, 7-shot magazine.
Barrel: 5".
Weight: 39 oz. **Length:** 8.5" overall.
Stocks: Checkered wood.
Sights: Blade front, rear adjustable for windage.
Features: Matte blue finish. Comes with two magazines. Imported from China by China Sports, Inc.
Price: . . . . **NA**

PARA-ORDNANCE P14.45 AUTO PISTOL
Caliber: 45 ACP, 14-shot magazine.
Barrel: 5".
Weight: 28 oz. (alloy frame). **Length:** 8.5" overall.
Stocks: Textured composition.
Sights: Blade front, rear adjustable for windage. High visibility three-dot system.
Features: Available with alloy, steel or stainless steel frame with black finish (silver or stainless gun). Steel and stainless steel frame guns weigh 38 oz. (P14.45), 35 oz. (P13.45), 33 oz. (P12.45). Grooved match trigger, rounded combat-style hammer. Double column, high-capacity magazine gives 15-shot total capacity (P14.45), Beveled magazine well. Manual thumb, grip and firing pin lock safeties. Solid barrel bushing. Introduced 1990. Made in Canada by Para-Ordnance.
Price: P14.45E (steel) **$716.25**
Price: P12.45R (12-shot magazine, 3½" bbl., 24 oz., alloy) **$650.00**
Price: P13.45R (13-shot magazine, 4¼" barrel, 28 oz., alloy) **$650.00**
Price: P14.45E steel frame **$716.25**
Price: P12.45E steel frame **$708.75**

Para-Ordnance P14.45

PHOENIX ARMS MODEL RAVEN AUTO PISTOL
Caliber: 25 ACP, 6-shot magazine.
Barrel: 2⁷/₁₆".
Weight: 15 oz. **Length:** 4¾" overall.
Stocks: Ivory-colored or black slotted plastic.
Sights: Ramped front, fixed rear.
Features: Available in blue, nickel or chrome finish. Made in U.S. Available from Phoenix Arms.
Price: **$69.95**

Phoenix Arms Raven

HANDGUNS—AUTOLOADERS, SERVICE & SPORT

PHOENIX ARMS HP22, HP25 AUTO PISTOLS
Caliber: 22 LR, 11-shot (HP22), 25 ACP, 10-shot (HP25).
Barrel: 3".
Weight: 20 oz. **Length:** 5½" overall.
Stocks: Checkered composition.
Sights: Blade front, adjustable rear.
Features: Single action, exposed hammer; manual hold-open; button magazine release. Available in satin nickel, polished blue finish. Introduced 1993. Made in U.S. by Phoenix Arms.
Price: $99.95

PSP-25 AUTO PISTOL
Caliber: 25 ACP, 6-shot magazine.
Barrel: 2⅛".
Weight: 9.5 oz. **Length:** 4⅛" overall.
Stocks: Checkered black plastic.
Sights: Fixed.
Features: All steel construction with polished finish. Introduced 1990. Made in the U.S. under F.N. license; distributed by K.B.I., Inc.
Price: Blue $249.00
Price: Hard chrome $299.00

Phoenix Arms HP22

Ram-Line Ram-Tech

RUGER P89 AUTOMATIC PISTOL
Caliber: 9mm Para., 15-shot magazine.
Barrel: 4.50".
Weight: 32 oz. **Length:** 7.84" overall.
Stocks: Grooved black Xenoy composition.
Sights: Square post front, square notch rear adjustable for windage, both with white dot inserts.
Features: Double action with ambidextrous slide-mounted safety-levers. Slide is 4140 chrome moly steel or 400-series stainless steel, frame is a lightweight aluminum alloy. Ambidextrous magazine release. Blue or stainless steel. Introduced 1986; stainless introduced 1990.
Price: P89, blue, with extra magazine and magazine loading tool, plastic case $410.00
Price: KP89, stainless, with extra magazine and magazine loading tool, plastic case $452.00
Price: KP89X Convertible 30 Luger/9mm Para. $497.00

Ruger P89 Double-Action Only Automatic Pistol
Same as the KP89 except operates only in the double-action mode. Has a bobbed, spurless hammer, gripping grooves on each side of the rear of the slide; no external safety or decocking lever. An internal safety prevents forward movement of the firing pin unless the trigger is pulled. Available in 9mm Para., stainless steel only. Introduced 1991.
Price: With lockable case, extra magazine, magazine loading tool . $452.00

Ruger P89D Decocker Automatic Pistol
Similar to the standard P89 except has ambidextrous decocking levers in place of the regular slide-mounted safety. The decocking levers move the firing pin inside the slide where the hammer can not reach it, while simultaneously blocking the firing pin from forward movement—allows shooter to decock a cocked pistol without manipulating the trigger. Conventional thumb decocking procedures are therefore unnecessary. Blue or stainless steel. Introduced 1990.
Price: P89D, blue with extra magazine and loader, plastic case . . . $410.00
Price: KP89D, stainless, with extra magazine, plastic case $452.00

Ruger P93 Compact Automatic Pistol
Similar to the P89 except has 3.9" barrel, 7.3" overall length, and weighs 31 oz. The forward third of the slide is tapered and polished to the muzzle. Front of the slide is crowned with a convex curve. Slide has seven finger grooves. Trigger guard bow is higher for better grip. Square post front sight, square notch rear drift adjustable for windage, both with white dot inserts. Slide is 400-series stainless steel, black-finished alloy frame. Available as decocker-only or double action-only. Introduced 1993.
Price: KP93DAO (double action only), KP93 (decocker) $452.00

RAM-LINE RAM-TECH AUTO PISTOL
Caliber: 22 LR, 15-shot magazine.
Barrel: 4.5".
Weight: 19.3 oz. **Length:** NA.
Stocks: One-piece injection moulded with checkered panels.
Sights: Ramp front, rear adjustable for windage.
Features: Compact frame; easy takedown. Injection moulded grip frame, alloy receiver; hybrid composite barrel. Constant force sear spring gives 3-lb. trigger pull. Comes with carrying case. Introduced 1994. Made in U.S. by Ram-Line, Inc.
Price: $179.00

ROCKY MOUNTAIN ARMS PATRIOT PISTOL
Caliber: 223, 5- , 20- , 30-shot magazine.
Barrel: 7", with Max Dynamic muzzle brake.
Weight: 5 lbs. **Length:** 20.5" overall.
Stocks: Black composition.
Sights: None furnished.
Features: Milled upper receiver with enhanced Weaver base; milled lower receiver from billet plate; machined aluminum National Match handguard. Finished in DuPont Teflon-S matte black or NATO green. Comes with black nylon case, one magazine. Introduced 1993. From Rocky Mountain Arms, Inc.
Price: $1,995.00

Ruger KP89D

Ruger KP93DC

RUGER P90 AUTOMATIC PISTOL

Caliber: 45 ACP, 7-shot magazine.
Barrel: 4.50".
Weight: 33.5 oz. **Length:** 7.87" overall.
Stocks: Grooved black Xenoy composition.
Sights: Square post front, square notch rear adjustable for windage, both with white dot inserts.
Features: Double action with ambidextrous slide-mounted safety-levers which move the firing pin inside the slide where the hammer can not reach it, while simultaneously blocking the firing pin from forward movement. Stainless steel only. Introduced 1991.
Price: KP90 with lockable case, extra magazine **$488.65**

Ruger P90 Decocker Automatic Pistol

Similar to the P90 except has a manual decocking system. The ambidextrous decocking levers move the firing pin inside the slide where the hammer can not reach it, while simultaneously blocking the firing pin from forward movement—allows shooter to decock a cocked pistol without manipulating the trigger. Available only in stainless steel. Overall length 7.87", weight 34 oz. Introduced 1991.
Price: P90D with lockable case, extra magazine, and magazine loading tool **$488.65**

RUGER P91 DECOCKER AUTOMATIC PISTOL

Caliber: 40 S&W, 11-shot magazine.
Barrel: 4.50".
Weight: 33 oz. **Length:** 7.87" overall.
Stocks: Grooved black Xenoy composition.
Sights: Square post front, square notch rear adjustable for windage, both with white dot inserts.
Features: Ambidextrous slide-mounted decocking levers move the firing pin inside the slide where the hammer can not reach it while simultaneously blocking the firing pin from forward movement. Allows shooter to decock a cocked pistol without manipulating the trigger. Conventional thumb decocking procedures are therefore unnecessary. Stainless steel only. Introduced 1991.
Price: KP91D with lockable case, extra magazine, and magazine loading tool **$488.65**

Ruger KP94 Automatic Pistol

Sized midway between the full-size P-Series and the compact P93. Has 4.25" barrel, 7.5" overall length and weighs about 33 oz. KP94 is manual safety model; KP94DAO is double-action-only (both 9mm Para., 15-shot magazine); KP94D is decocker-only in 40 S&W with 11-shot magazine. Slide gripping grooves roll over top of slide. KP94 has ambidextrous safety-levers; KP94DAO has no external safety, full-cock hammer position or decocking lever; KP94D has ambidextrous decocking levers. Matte finish stainless slide, barrel, alloy frame. Introduced 1994. Made in U.S. by Sturm, Ruger & Co.
Price: KP94 (9mm), KP944 (40 S&W) **$520.00**
Price: KP94DAO (9mm), KP944DAO (40 S&W) **$520.00**
Price: KP94D (40 S&W) **$520.00**

Ruger KP90C

Ruger P91 Double-Action-Only Automatic Pistol

Same as the KP91D except operates only in the double-action mode. Has a bobbed, spurless hammer, gripping grooves on each side at the rear of the slide, no external safety or decocking levers. An internal safety prevents forward movement of the firing pin unless the trigger is pulled. Available in 40 S&W, stainless steel only. Introduced 1992.
Price: KP91DAO with lockable case, extra magazine, and magazine loading tool **$488.65**

Ruger KP94

Ruger P94L Automatic Pistol

Same as the KP94 except mounts a laser sight in a housing cast integrally with the frame. Allen-head screws control windage and elevation adjustments. Announced 1994. Made in U.S. by Sturm, Ruger & Co.
Price: . . . . **NA**

> Consult our Directory pages for the location of firms mentioned.

Ruger 22/45 Mark II

SAFARI ARMS CREST SERIES PISTOLS

Caliber: 9mm Para., 38 Super, 45 ACP, 7-shot magazine (standard), 6-shot (4-Star).
Barrel: 5" (standard), 4.5" (4-Star); 416 stainless steel.
Weight: 39 oz. (standard), 35.7 oz. (4-Star). **Length:** 8.5" overall (standard).
Stocks: Checkered walnut.
Sights: Ramped blade front, fully adjustable rear.
Features: Right- or left-hand models available. Long aluminum trigger, long recoil spring guide, extended safety and slide stop. Stainless steel. Introduced 1993. Made in U.S. by Safari Arms, Inc.
Price: Right-hand, standard **$740.00**
Price: Left-hand, standard **$880.00**
Price: Right-hand, 4-Star **$770.00**
Price: Left-hand, 4-Star **$910.00**

RUGER MARK II STANDARD AUTO PISTOL

Caliber: 22 LR, 10-shot magazine.
Barrel: 4¾" or 6".
Weight: 36 oz. (4¾" bbl.). **Length:** 8⁵⁄₁₆" (4¾" bbl.).
Stocks: Checkered plastic.
Sights: Fixed, wide blade front, square notch rear adjustable for windage.
Features: Updated design of the original Standard Auto. Has new bolt hold-open latch. 10-shot magazine, magazine catch, safety, trigger and new receiver contours. Introduced 1982.
Price: Blued (MK 4, MK 6) **$252.00**
Price: In stainless steel (KMK 4, KMK 6) **$330.25**

Ruger 22/45 Mark II Pistol

Similar to the other 22 Mark II autos except has grip frame of Zytel that matchs the angle and magazine latch of the Model 1911 45 ACP pistol. Available in 4¾" standard, 5¼" tapered and 5½" bull barrel. Introduced 1992.
Price: KP4 (4¾" barrel) **$280.00**
Price: KP514 (5¼" barrel) **$330.00**
Price: KP512 (5½" bull barrel) **$330.00**

CAUTION: PRICES SHOWN ARE SUPPLIED BY THE MANUFACTURER OR IMPORTER. CHECK YOUR LOCAL GUNSHOP.

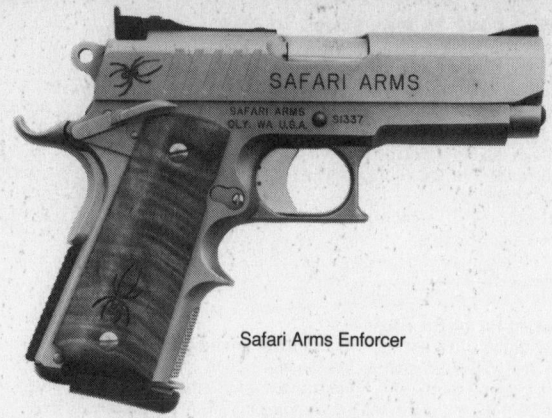

Safari Arms Enforcer

SEECAMP LWS 32 STAINLESS DA AUTO
Caliber: 32 ACP Win. Silvertip, 6-shot magazine.
Barrel: 2", integral with frame.
Weight: 10.5 oz. **Length:** 4⅛" overall.
Stocks: Glass-filled nylon.
Sights: Smooth, no-snag, contoured slide and barrel top.
Features: Aircraft quality 17-4 PH stainless steel. Inertia-operated firing pin. Hammer fired double-action only. Hammer automatically follows slide down to safety rest position after each shot—no manual safety needed. Magazine safety disconnector. Polished stainless. Introduced 1985. From L.W. Seecamp.
Price: $375.00

CONSULT

SHOOTER'S MARKETPLACE
Page 225, This Issue

SIG P-210-6 AUTO PISTOL
Caliber: 9mm Para., 8-shot magazine.
Barrel: 4¾".
Weight: 36.2 oz. **Length:** 8½" overall.
Stocks: Checkered black plastic; walnut optional.
Sights: Blade front, micro. adjustable rear for windage and elevation.
Features: Adjustable trigger stop; target trigger; ribbed frontstrap; sandblasted finish. Conversion unit for 22 LR consists of barrel, recoil spring, slide and magazine. Imported from Switzerland by Mandall Shooting Supplies.
Price: P-210-6 . . . . $3,500.00
Price: P-210-5 Target $3,700.00

SIG SAUER P220 "AMERICAN" AUTO PISTOL
Caliber: 38 Super, 45 ACP, (9-shot in 38 Super, 7 in 45).
Barrel: 4⅜".
Weight: 28¼ oz. (9mm). **Length:** 7¾" overall.
Stocks: Checkered black plastic.
Sights: Blade front, drift adjustable rear for windage.
Features: Double action. De-cocking lever permits lowering hammer onto locked firing pin. Squared combat-type trigger guard. Slide stays open after last shot. Imported from Germany by SIGARMS, Inc.
Price: "American," blue (side-button magazine release, 45 ACP only) $805.00
Price: 45 ACP, blue, Siglite night sights $905.00
Price: K-Kote finish $850.00
Price: K-Kote, Siglite night sights $950.00

SIG SAUER P225 DA AUTO PISTOL
Caliber: 9mm Para., 8-shot magazine.
Barrel: 3.8".
Weight: 26 oz. **Length:** 7³⁄₃₂" overall.
Stocks: Checkered black plastic.
Sights: Blade front, rear adjustable for windage. Optional Siglite night sights.
Features: Double action. De-cocking lever permits lowering hammer onto locked firing pin. Square combat-type trigger guard. Shortened, lightened version of P220. Imported from Germany by SIGARMS, Inc.
Price: $780.00
Price: With Siglite night sights $880.00
Price: K-Kote finish $850.00
Price: K-Kote with Siglite night sights $950.00

SAFARI ARMS ENFORCER PISTOL
Caliber: 45 ACP, 6-shot magazine.
Barrel: 3.8".
Weight: 36 oz. **Length:** 7.5" overall.
Stocks: Smooth walnut with etched black widow spider logo.
Sights: Ramped blade front, rear adjustable for windage and elevation.
Features: Extended safety, extended slide release; Commander-style hammer; beavertail grip safety; throated, ported, tuned, with cone-shaped barrel, no bushing. Parkerized matte black or satin stainless steel. From Safari Arms, Inc.
Price: $690.00

Safari Arms Enforcer Carrycomp II Pistol
Similar to the Enforcer except has Wil Schueman-designed hybrid compensator system. Introduced 1993. Made in U.S. by Safari Arms, Inc.
Price: $1,010.00

SAFARI ARMS G.I. SAFARI PISTOL
Caliber: 45 ACP, 7-shot magazine.
Barrel: 5".
Weight: 39.9 oz. **Length:** 8.5" overall.
Stocks: Checkered walnut.
Sights: Blade front, fixed rear.
Features: Beavertail grip safety, extended safety and slide release, Commander-style hammer. Barrel is chrome-lined 4140 steel; National Match 416 stainless optional. Parkerized matte black finish. Introduced 1991. Made in U.S. by Safari Arms, Inc.
Price: $430.00

SIG P-210-2 AUTO PISTOL
Caliber: 7.65mm or 9mm Para., 8-shot magazine.
Barrel: 4¾".
Weight: 31¾ oz. (9mm). **Length:** 8½" overall.
Stocks: Checkered black composition.
Sights: Blade front, rear adjustable for windage.
Features: Lanyard loop; matte finish. Conversion unit for 22 LR available. Imported from Switzerland by Mandall Shooting Supplies.
Price: P-210-2 Service Pistol $3,500.00

SIG Sauer P220 American

SIG Sauer P226 DA Auto Pistol
Similar to the P220 pistol except has 15-shot magazine, 4.4" barrel, and weighs 26½ oz. 9mm only. Imported from Germany by SIGARMS, Inc.
Price: Blue $825.00
Price: With Siglite night sights $930.00
Price: Blue, double-action only $825.00
Price: Blue, double-action only, Siglite night sights $930.00
Price: K-Kote finish $875.00
Price: K-Kote, Siglite night sights $975.00
Price: K-Kote, double-action only $875.00
Price: K-Kote, double-action only, Siglite night sights $975.00

CAUTION: PRICES SHOWN ARE SUPPLIED BY THE MANUFACTURER OR IMPORTER. CHECK YOUR LOCAL GUNSHOP.

SIG Sauer P228

SIG SAUER P230 DA AUTO PISTOL

Caliber: 380 ACP, 7-shot.
Barrel: 3¾".
Weight: 16 oz. **Length:** 6½" overall.
Stocks: Checkered black plastic.
Sights: Blade front, rear adjustable for windage.
Features: Double action. Same basic action design as P220. Blowback operation, stationary barrel. Introduced 1977. Imported from Germany by SIGARMS, Inc.

Price: Blue **$510.00**
Price: In stainless steel (P230 SL) **$595.00**

Smith & Wesson .356 TSW Compact

SMITH & WESSON MODEL 422, 622 AUTO

Caliber: 22 LR, 12-shot magazine.
Barrel: 4½", 6".
Weight: 22 oz. (4½" bbl.). **Length:** 7½" overall (4½" bbl.).
Stocks: Checkered simulated woodgrain polymer.
Sights: Field—serrated ramp front, fixed rear; Target— serrated ramp front, adjustable rear.
Features: Aluminum frame, steel slide, brushed stainless steel or blue finish; internal hammer. Introduced 1987. Model 2206 introduced 1990.

Price: Blue, 4½", 6", fixed sight **$235.00**
Price: As above, adjustable sight **$290.00**
Price: Stainless (Model 622), 4½", 6", fixed sight **$284.00**
Price: As above, adjustable sight **$337.00**

Smith & Wesson Model 2214 Sportsman Auto

Similar to the Model 422 except has 3" barrel, 8-shot magazine; dovetail Patridge front sight with white dot, fixed rear with two white dots; matte blue finish, black composition grips with checkered panels. Overall length 6⅛", weight 18 oz. Introduced 1990.

Price: **$269.00**
Price: Model 2213 (stainless steel) **$314.00**

Smith & Wesson Model 2206 Target Auto

Same as the Model 2206 except 6" barrel only; Millett Series 100 fully adjustable sight system; Patridge front sight; smooth contoured Herrett walnut target grips with thumbrest; serrated trigger with adjustable stop. Frame is bead-blasted along sighting plane, drilled and tapped for optics mount. Introduced 1994. Made in U.S. by Smith & Wesson.

Price: **$433.00**

SIG Sauer P228 DA Auto Pistol

Similar to the P226 except has 3.86" barrel, with 7.08" overall length and 3.35" height. Chambered for 9mm Para. only, 13-shot magazine. Weight is 29.1 oz. with empty magazine. Introduced 1989. Imported from Germany by SIGARMS, Inc.

Price: Blue **$825.00**
Price: Blue, with Siglite night sights **$930.00**
Price: Blue, double-action only **$825.00**
Price: Blue, double-action only, Siglite night sights . . . **$930.00**
Price: K-Kote finish **$875.00**
Price: K-Kote, Siglite night sights **$975.00**
Price: K-Kote, double-action only **$875.00**
Price: K-Kote, double-action only, Siglite night sights . . **$975.00**

SIG Sauer P229 DA Auto Pistol

Similar to the P228 except chambered for 9mm Para., 40 S&W with 12-shot magazine. Has 3.86" barrel, 7.08" overall length and 3.35" height. Weight is 30.5 oz. Introduced 1991. Frame made in Germany, stainless steel slide assembly made in U.S.; pistol assembled in U.S. From SIGARMS, Inc.

Price: Blue **$875.00**
Price: Blue, double-action only **$875.00**
Price: With Siglite night sights **$975.00**

Sig Sauer P230

SMITH & WESSON MODEL .356 TSW LIMITED PISTOL

Caliber: 356 TSW, 15-shot magazine.
Barrel: 5".
Weight: 44 oz. **Length:** 8.5" overall.
Stocks: Checkered black composition.
Sights: Blade front drift adjustable for windage, fully adjustable Bo-Mar rear.
Features: Single action trigger. Stainless steel frame and slide, hand-fitted titanium-coated stainless steel bushing, match grade barrel. Extended magazine well and oversize release; magazine pads; extended safety. Checkered front strap. Introduced 1993. Available from Lew Horton Dist.

Price: About **$1,349.00**

Smith & Wesson Model .356 TSW Compact Pistol

Similar to the .356 TSW Limited except has 3½" barrel, 12-shot magazine, Novak LoMount combat sights. Overall length 7", weight 37 oz. Introduced 1993. Available from Lew Horton Dist.

Price: **$999.00**

24D
Smith & Wesson Model 2214

Smith & Wesson Model 2206 Auto

Similar to the Model 422/622 except made entirely of stainless steel with non-reflective finish. Weight is 35 oz. with 4½" barrel, 39 oz. with 6" barrel. Introduced 1990.

Price: With fixed sight **$327.00**
Price: With adjustable sight **$385.00**

CAUTION: PRICES SHOWN ARE SUPPLIED BY THE MANUFACTURER OR IMPORTER. CHECK YOUR LOCAL GUNSHOP.

SMITH & WESSON MODEL 915 DA AUTO PISTOL
Caliber: 9mm Para., 15-shot magazine.
Barrel: 4".
Weight: 28.5 oz. **Length:** 7.5" overall.
Stocks: One-piece Xenoy, wraparound with straight backstrap.
Sights: Post front with white dot, fixed rear.
Features: Alloy frame, blue carbon steel slide. Slide-mounted decocking lever. Introduced 1992.
Price: **$467.00**

Smith & Wesson Model 411 DA Auto Pistol
Same as the Model 915 except chambered for 40 S&W, 11-shot magazine. Alloy frame, blue carbon steel slide. Introduced 1994. Made in U.S. by Smith & Wesson.
Price: **$525.00**

Smith & Wesson Model 915

SMITH & WESSON MODEL 3913/3914 DOUBLE ACTIONS
Caliber: 9mm Para., 8-shot magazine.
Barrel: 3½".
Weight: 26 oz. **Length:** 6¹³⁄₁₆" overall.
Stocks: One-piece Delrin wraparound, textured surface.
Sights: Post front with white dot, Novak LoMount Carry with two dots, adjustable for windage.
Features: Aluminum alloy frame, stainless slide (M3913) or blue steel slide (M3914). Bobbed hammer with no half-cock notch; smooth .304" trigger with rounded edges. Straight backstrap. Extra magazine included. Introduced 1989.
Price: Model 3913 . . . . **$622.00**
Price: Model 3914 . . . . **$562.00**

Smith & Wesson Model 3953DA Pistol
Same as the Models 3913/3914 except double-action only. Model 3953 has stainless slide with alloy frame. Overall length 7"; weight 25.5 oz. Extra magazine included. Introduced 1990.
Price: **$622.00**

Smith & Wesson Model 3913-NL Pistol
Same as the 3913/3914 LadySmith autos except without the LadySmith logo and it has a slightly modified frame design. Right-hand safety only. Has stainless slide on alloy frame; extra magazine included. Introduced 1990.
Price: **$622.00**

Smith & Wesson 3913 LadySmith

Smith & Wesson Model 3913 LadySmith Auto
Similar to the standard Model 3913/3914 except has frame that is upswept at the front, rounded trigger guard. Comes in frosted stainless steel with matching gray grips. Grips are ergonomically correct for a woman's hand. Novak LoMount Carry rear sight adjustable for windage, smooth edges for snag resistance. Extra magazine included. Introduced 1990.
Price: **$640.00**

SMITH & WESSON MODEL 4013, 4053 AUTOS
Caliber: 40 S&W, 8-shot magazine.
Barrel: 3½".
Weight: 26 oz. **Length:** 7" overall.
Stocks: One-piece Xenoy wraparound with straight backstrap.
Sights: Post front with white dot, fixed Novak LoMount Carry rear with two white dots.
Features: Model 4013 is traditional double action; Model 4053 is double-action only; stainless slide on alloy frame. Introduced 1991.
Price: Model 4013 . . . . **$722.00**
Price: Model 4053 . . . . **$722.00**

Smith & Wesson Model 4506

SMITH & WESSON MODEL 4006 DA AUTO
Caliber: 40 S&W, 11-shot magazine.
Barrel: 4".
Weight: 38.5 oz. **Length:** 7⅞" overall.
Stocks: Xenoy wraparound with checkered panels.
Sights: Replaceable post front with white dot, Novak LoMount Carry fixed rear with two white dots, or micro. click adjustable rear with two white dots.
Features: Stainless steel construction with non-reflective finish. Straight backstrap. Extra magazine included. Introduced 1990.
Price: With adjustable sights **$775.00**
Price: With fixed sight **$745.00**
Price: With fixed night sights **$855.00**

Smith & Wesson Model 4046 DA Pistol
Similar to the Model 4006 except is double-action only. Has a semi-bobbed hammer, smooth trigger, 4" barrel; Novak LoMount Carry rear sight, post front with white dot. Overall length is 7½", weight 28 oz. Extra magazine included. Introduced 1991.
Price: **$745.00**
Price: With fixed night sights **$855.00**

SMITH & WESSON MODEL 4500 SERIES AUTOS
Caliber: 45 ACP, 7-shot (M4516), 8-shot magazine for M4506, 4566/4586.
Barrel: 3¾" (M4516), 5" (M4506).
Weight: 41 oz. (4506). **Length:** 7⅛" overall (4516).
Stocks: Xenoy one-piece wraparound, arched or straight backstrap on M4506, straight only on M4516.
Sights: Post front with white dot, adjustable or fixed Novak LoMount Carry on M4506.
Features: M4506 has serrated hammer spur. Extra magazine included. Contact Smith & Wesson for complete data. Introduced 1989.
Price: Model 4506, fixed sight **$774.00**
Price: Model 4506, adjustable sight **$806.00**
Price: Model 4516, fixed sight **$774.00**
Price: Model 4566 (stainless, 4¼", traditional DA, ambidextrous safety, fixed sight) **$774.00**
Price: Model 4586 (stainless, 4¼", DA only) **$774.00**

SMITH & WESSON MODEL 5900 SERIES AUTO PISTOLS

Caliber: 9mm Para., 15-shot magazine.
Barrel: 4".
Weight: 28½ to 37½ oz. (fixed sight); 38 oz. (adj. sight). **Length:** 7½" overall.
Stocks: Xenoy wraparound with curved backstrap.
Sights: Post front with white dot, fixed or fully adjustable with two white dots.
Features: All stainless, stainless and alloy or carbon steel and alloy construction. Smooth .304" trigger, .260" serrated hammer. Extra magazine included. Introduced 1989.
Price: Model 5903 (stainless, alloy frame, traditional DA, fixed sight, ambextrous safety) **$690.00**
Price: Model 5904 (blue, alloy frame, traditional DA, adjustable sight, ambidextrous safety) **$642.00**
Price: Model 5906 (stainless, traditional DA, adjustable sight, ambidextrous safety) **$742.00**
Price: As above, fixed sight **$707.00**
Price: With fixed night sights **$817.00**
Price: Model 5946 (as above, stainless frame and slide) **$707.00**

Smith & Wesson Model 6904

Smith & Wesson Model 6904/6906 Double-Action Autos

Similar to the Models 5904/5906 except with 3½" barrel, 12-shot magazine (20-shot available), fixed rear sight, .260" bobbed hammer. Extra magazine included. Introduced 1989.
Price: Model 6904, blue **$614.00**
Price: Model 6906, stainless **$677.00**
Price: Model 6906 with fixed night sights **$788.00**
Price: Model 6946 (stainless, DA only, fixed sights) **$677.00**

SMITH & WESSON SIGMA SERIES PISTOLS

Caliber: 9mm Para., 17-shot, 40 S&W, 15-shot magazine.
Barrel: 4.5".
Weight: 26 oz. **Length:** 7.4" overall.
Stocks: Integral.
Sights: White dot front, fixed rear; three-dot system. Tritium night sights available.
Features: Ergonomic polymer frame; low barrel centerline; internal striker firing system; corrosion-resistant slide; Teflon-filled, electroless-nickel coated magazine. Introduced 1994. Made in U.S. by Smith & Wesson.
Price: Model SW9F (9mm Para.) **$593.00**
Price: Model SW40F (40 S&W) **$593.00**

Smith & Wesson Sigma

SPHINX AT-380M AUTO PISTOL

Caliber: 380 ACP, 10-shot magazine.
Barrel: 3.27".
Weight: 25 oz. **Length:** 6.03" overall.
Stocks: Checkered plastic.
Sights: Fixed.
Features: Double-action-only mechanism, Chamber loaded indicator; ambidextrous magazine release and slide latch. Blued slide, bright Palladium frame, or bright Palladium overall. Introduced 1993. Imported from Switzerland by Sile Distributors, Inc.
Price: Two-tone **$499.95**
Price: Palladium finish **$594.95**

Sphinx AT-380M

SPHINX AT-2000S DOUBLE-ACTION PISTOL

Caliber: 9mm Para., 9x21mm, 15-shot, 40 S&W, 11-shot magazine.
Barrel: 4.53".
Weight: 36.3 oz. **Length:** 8.03" overall.
Stocks: Checkered neoprene.
Sights: Fixed, three-dot system.
Features: Double-action mechanism changeable to double-action-only. Stainless frame, blued slide. Ambidextrous safety, magazine release, slide latch. Introduced 1993. Imported from Switzerland by Sile Distributors, Inc.
Price: 9mm, two-tone **$902.95**
Price: 9mm, Palladium finish **$989.95**
Price: 40 S&W, two-tone **$911.95**
Price: 40 S&W, Palladium finish **$998.95**

Sphinx AT-2000S

Sphinx AT-2000P, AT-2000PS Auto Pistols

Same as the AT-2000S except AT-2000P has shortened frame (13-shot magazine), 3.74" barrel, 7.25" overall length, and weighs 34 oz. Model AT-2000PS has full-size frame. Both have stainless frame with blued slide or bright Palladium finish. Introduced 1993. Imported from Switzerland by Sile Distributors, Inc.
Price: 9mm, two-tone **$858.95**
Price: 9mm, Palladium finish **$945.95**
Price: 40 S&W, two-tone **$867.95**
Price: 40 S&W, Palladium finish **$954.95**

Sphinx AT-2000H Auto Pistol

Similar to the AT-2000P except has shorter slide with 3.54" barrel, shorter frame, 10-shot magazine, with 7" overall length. Weight 32.2 oz. Stainless frame with blued slide, or overall bright Palladium finish. Introduced 1993. Imported from Switzerland by Sile Distributors, Inc.
Price: 9mm, two-tone **$858.95**
Price: 9mm, Palladium finish **$945.95**
Price: 40 S&W, two-tone **$867.95**
Price: 40 S&W, Palladium **$954.95**

CAUTION: PRICES SHOWN ARE SUPPLIED BY THE MANUFACTURER OR IMPORTER. CHECK YOUR LOCAL GUNSHOP.

HANDGUNS—AUTOLOADERS, SERVICE & SPORT

Springfield XM4

Springfield Inc. XM4 Champion Auto Pistol

Similar to the XM4 except has 4.25" barrel, weighs 26 oz.; overall length 7.75". Has 18-shot magazine in 9mm, 13-shot in 45 ACP. Introduced 1994. From Springfield, Inc.
Price: **$699.00**

Springfield 1911A1 Mil-Spec

Springfield Inc. 1911A1 Custom Carry Gun

Similar to the standard 1911A1 except has fixed three-dot low profile sights, Videki speed trigger, match barrel and bushing; extended thumb safety, beavertail grip safety; beveled, polished magazine well, polished feed ramp and throated barrel; match Commander hammer and sear, tuned extractor; lowered and flared ejection port; recoil buffer system, full-length spring guide rod; walnut grips. Comes with two magazines with slam pads, plastic carrying case. Available in all popular calibers. Introduced 1992. From Springfield Inc.
Price: . . . . **P.O.R.**

Springfield 1911A1 Factory Comp

Springfield 1911A1 Champion

SPORTARMS TOKAREV MODEL 213
Caliber: 9mm Para., 8-shot magazine.
Barrel: 4.5".
Weight: 31 oz. **Length:** 7.6" overall.
Stocks: Grooved plastic.
Sights: Fixed.
Features: Blue finish, hard chrome optional. 9mm version of the famous Russian Tokarev pistol. Made in China by Norinco. Imported by Sportarms of Florida. Introduced 1988.
Price: Blue, about **$150.00**
Price: Hard chrome, about **$179.00**

SPRINGFIELD INC. XM4 AUTO PISTOL
Caliber: 9mm Para., 18-shot magazine, 45 ACP, 13-shot magazine.
Barrel: 5".
Weight: 29.25 oz. **Length:** 8.75" overall.
Stocks: Xanex.
Sights: Three-dot combat style.
Features: Frame made of Xanex synthetic polymer; slide machined from stainless steel. Hammer-forged rifling; serrated top rib; lowered and flared ejection port; heavy duty extractor; recessed hammer beavertail grip safety; combat-style trigger tuned to 5-6 lbs.; extended combat-style slide stop. Introduced 1994. From Springfield, Inc.
Price: **$689.00**

SPRINGFIELD INC. 1911A1 AUTO PISTOL
Caliber: 9mm Para., 9-shot; 38 Super, 10-shot; 45 ACP, 8-shot.
Barrel: 5".
Weight: 35.06 oz. **Length:** 8.59" overall.
Stocks: Checkered plastic.
Sights: Fixed low-profile combat-style.
Features: Beveled magazine well. All forged parts, including frame, barrel, slide. All new production. Introduced 1990. From Springfield Inc.
Price: Basic, 45 ACP, Parkerized **$449.00**
Price: Standard, 45 ACP, blued **$489.00**
Price: Basic, 45 ACP, stainless **$532.00**
Price: Mil-spec (Parkerized), 38 Super **$489.00**

Springfield Inc. 1911A1 High Capacity Pistol
Similar to the Standard 1911A1 except available in 45 ACP and 9x21mm with 10-shot magazine (45 ACP), 16-shot magazine (9x21mm). Has Commander-style hammer, walnut grips, ambidextrous thumb safety, beveled magazine well, plastic carrying case. Blue finish only. Introduced 1993. From Springfield, Inc.
Price: 45 ACP **$999.00**
Price: 9x21mm **$1,099.00**
Price: 45 ACP Factory Comp **$1,225.00**

Springfield Inc. 1911A1 Factory Comp
Similar to the standard 1911A1 except comes with bushing-type dual-port compensator, adjustable rear sight, extended thumb safety, Videki speed trigger, and beveled magazine well. Checkered walnut grips standard. Available in 38 Super or 45 ACP, blue only. Introduced 1992.
Price: 38 Super **$929.00**
Price: 45 ACP **$869.00**

Springfield Inc. 1911A1 Champion Pistol
Similar to the standard 1911A1 except slide is 4.25". Has low-profile three-dot sight system. Comes with Commander hammer and walnut stocks. Available in 45 ACP only; blue or stainless. Introduced 1989.
Price: Blue **$529.00**
Price: Stainless **$558.00**
Price: Blue, comp **$829.00**
Price: Mil-Spec **$449.00**

Springfield Inc. Product Improved 1911A1 Defender Pistol
Similar to the 1911A1 Champion except has tapered cone dual-port compensator system, rubberized grips. Has reverse recoil plug, full-length recoil spring guide, serrated frontstrap, extended thumb safety, Commander-style hammer with modified grip safety to match and a Videki speed trigger. Bi-Tone finish. Introduced 1991.
Price: 45 ACP **$959.00**

Springfield Inc. 1911A1 Compact Pistol
Similar to the Champion model except has a shortened slide with 4.025" barrel, 7.75" overall length. Magazine capacity is 7 shots. Has Commander hammer, checkered walnut grips. Available in 45 ACP only. Introduced 1989.
Price: Blued **$529.00**
Price: Bi-Tone Comp (blue slide, stainless frame) **$829.00**
Price: Stainless **$558.00**
Price: Compact Lightweight **$499.00**

STAR FIRESTAR AUTO PISTOL
Caliber: 9mm Para., 7-shot; 40 S&W, 6-shot.
Barrel: 3.39".
Weight: 30.35 oz. **Length:** 6.5" overall.
Stocks: Checkered rubber.
Sights: Blade front, fully adjustable rear; three-dot system.
Features: Low-profile, combat-style sights; ambidextrous safety. Available in blue or weather-resistant Starvel finish. Introduced 1990. Imported from Spain by Interarms.

Price: Blue, 9mm	$453.00
Price: Starvel finish 9mm	$480.00
Price: Blue, 40 S&W	$471.00
Price: Starvel finish, 40 S&W	$497.00

Star Firestar

Star Firestar Plus

Star Firestar Plus Auto Pistol
Same as the standard Firestar except has 13-shot magazine in 9mm. Also available in 40 S&W and 45 ACP. Introduced 1994. Imported from Spain by Interarms.

Price: Blue	$494.00
Price: Starvel	$521.00

Star Firestar M45 Auto Pistol
Similar to the standard Firestar except chambered for 45 ACP with 6-shot magazine. Has 3.6" barrel, weighs 35 oz., 6.85" overall length. Reverse-taper Acculine barrel. Introduced 1992. Imported from Spain by Interarms.

Price: Blue	$494.00
Price: Starvel finish	$521.00

Star Megastar

STAR MEGASTAR 45 ACP AUTO PISTOL
Caliber: 10mm, 14-shot, 45 ACP, 12-shot magazine.
Barrel: 4.6".
Weight: 47.6 oz. **Length:** 8.44" overall.
Stocks: Checkered composition.
Sights: Blade front, adjustable rear.
Features: Double-action mechanism; steel frame and slide; reverse-taper Acculine barrel. Introduced 1992. Imported from Spain by Interarms.

Price: Blue, 10mm	$653.00
Price: Starvel finish, 10mm	$682.00
Price: Blue, 45 ACP	$653.00
Price: Starvel finish, 45 ACP	$682.00

Star Ultrastar

STAR ULTRASTAR DOUBLE-ACTION PISTOL
Caliber: 9mm Para., 9-shot magazine.
Barrel: 3.57".
Weight: 26 oz. **Length:** 7" overall.
Stocks: Checkered black polymer.
Sights: Blade front, rear adjustable for windage; three-dot system.
Features: Polymer frame with inside steel slide rails; ambidextrous two-position safety (Safe and Decock). Introduced 1994. Imported from Spain by Interarms.

Price:	$504.00

Stoeger American Eagle Luger

STOEGER AMERICAN EAGLE LUGER
Caliber: 9mm Para., 7-shot magazine.
Barrel: 4", 6".
Weight: 32 oz. **Length:** 9.6" overall.
Stocks: Checkered walnut.
Sights: Blade front, fixed rear.
Features: Recreation of the American Eagle Luger pistol in stainless steel. Chamber loaded indicator. Introduced 1994. From Stoeger Industries.

Price:	$695.00
Price: Navy Model, 6" barrel	$695.00

SUNDANCE MODEL A-25 AUTO PISTOL
Caliber: 25 ACP, 7-shot magazine.
Barrel: 2.5".
Weight: 16 oz. **Length:** 4⅞" overall.
Stocks: Grooved black ABS or simulated smooth pearl; optional pink.
Sights: Fixed.
Features: Manual rotary safety; button magazine release. Bright chrome or black Teflon finish. Introduced 1989. Made in U.S. by Sundance Industries, Inc.

Price:	$79.95

CAUTION: PRICES SHOWN ARE SUPPLIED BY THE MANUFACTURER OR IMPORTER. CHECK YOUR LOCAL GUNSHOP.

Sundance BOA

TAURUS MODEL PT58 AUTO PISTOL
Caliber: 380 ACP, 12-shot magazine.
Barrel: 4.01".
Weight: 30 oz. **Length:** 7.2" overall.
Stocks: Brazilian hardwood.
Sights: Integral blade on slide front, notch rear adjustable for windage. Three-dot system.
Features: Double action with exposed hammer; inertia firing pin. Introduced 1988. Imported by Taurus International.
Price: Blue $445.00
Price: Satin nickel $477.00
Price: Stainless steel $506.00

Taurus PT 92AFC Compact Pistol
Similar to the PT-92 except has 4.25" barrel, 13-shot magazine, weighs 31 oz. and is 7.5" overall. Available in stainless steel, blue or satin nickel. Introduced 1991. Imported by Taurus International.
Price: Blue $492.00
Price: Blue, Deluxe Shooter's Pak (extra magazine, case) $521.00
Price: Stainless steel $559.00
Price: Stainless, Deluxe Shooter's Pak (extra magazine and case) . $587.00

TAURUS PT 100 AUTO PISTOL
Caliber: 40 S&W, 11-shot magazine.
Barrel: 5".
Weight: 34 oz.
Stocks: Smooth Brazilian hardwood.
Sights: Fixed front, drift-adjustable rear. Three-dot combat.
Features: Double action, exposed hammer. Ambidextrous hammer-drop safety; inertia firing pin; chamber loaded indicator. Introduced 1991. Imported by Taurus International.
Price: Blue $502.00
Price: Blue, Deluxe Shooter's Pak (extra magazine, case) $530.00
Price: Nickel $542.00
Price: Nickel, Deluxe Shooter's Pak (extra magazine, case) $570.00
Price: Stainless $569.00
Price: Stainless, Deluxe Shooter's Pak (extra magazine, case) . . . $595.00

Taurus PT 101 Auto Pistol
Same as the PT 100 except has micro-click rear sight adjustable for windage and elevation, three-dot combat-style. Introduced 1991.
Price: Blue $542.00
Price: Blue, Deluxe Shooter's Pak (extra magazine, case) $571.00
Price: Nickel $587.00
Price: Nickel, Deluxe Shooter's Pak (extra magazine, case) $615.00
Price: Stainless $619.00
Price: Stainless, Deluxe Shooter's Pak (extra magazine, case) . . . $648.00

> Consult our Directory pages for the location of firms mentioned.

TAURUS MODEL PT-908 AUTO PISTOL
Caliber: 9mm Para., 8-shot magazine.
Barrel: 3.8".
Weight: 30 oz. **Length:** 7.05" overall.
Stocks: Checkered black composition.
Sights: Drift-adjustable front and rear; three-dot combat.
Features: Double action, exposed hammer; manual ambidextrous hammer-drop; inertia firing pin; chamber loaded indicator. Introduced 1993. Imported by Taurus International.
Price: Blue $492.00
Price: Stainless steel $559.00

SUNDANCE BOA AUTO PISTOL
Caliber: 25 ACP, 7-shot magazine.
Barrel: 2½".
Weight: 16 oz. **Length:** 4⅞".
Stocks: Grooved ABS or smooth simulated pearl; optional pink.
Sights: Fixed.
Features: Patented grip safety, manual rotary safety; button magazine release; lifetime warranty. Bright chrome or black Teflon finish. Introduced 1991. Made in the U.S. by Sundance Industries, Inc.
Price: $95.00

TAURUS MODEL PT 22/PT 25 AUTO PISTOLS
Caliber: 22 LR, 9-shot (PT 22); 25 ACP, 8-shot (PT 25).
Barrel: 2.75".
Weight: 12.3 oz. **Length:** 5.25" overall.
Stocks: Smooth Brazilian hardwood.
Sights: Blade front, fixed rear.
Features: Double action. Tip-up barrel for loading, cleaning. Blue only. Introduced 1992. Made in U.S. by Taurus International.
Price: 22 LR or 25 ACP $193.00

TAURUS MODEL PT 92AF AUTO PISTOL
Caliber: 9mm Para., 15-shot magazine.
Barrel: 4.92".
Weight: 34 oz. **Length:** 8.54" overall.
Stocks: Brazilian hardwood.
Sights: Fixed notch rear. Three-dot sight system.
Features: Double action, exposed hammer, chamber loaded indicator. Inertia firing pin. Imported by Taurus International.
Price: Blue $492.00
Price: Blue, Deluxe Shooter's Pak (extra magazine, case) $521.00
Price: Nickel $532.00
Price: Nickel, Deluxe Shooter's Pak (extra magazine, case) $561.00
Price: Stainless steel $559.00
Price: Stainless, Deluxe Shooter's Pak (extra magazine, case) . . . $587.00

Taurus PT 99AF Auto Pistol
Similar to the PT-92 except has fully adjustable rear sight, smooth Brazilian walnut stocks and is available in stainless steel, polished blue or satin nickel. Introduced 1983.
Price: Blue $532.00
Price: Blue, Deluxe Shooter's Pak (extra magazine, case) $562.00
Price: Nickel $577.00
Price: Nickel, Deluxe Shooter's Pak (extra magazine, case) $606.00
Price: Stainless steel $606.00
Price: Stainless, Deluxe Shooter's Pak (extra magazine, case) . . . $633.00

Taurus PT92C

Taurus PT-908

CAUTION: PRICES SHOWN ARE SUPPLIED BY THE MANUFACTURER OR IMPORTER. CHECK YOUR LOCAL GUNSHOP.

49th EDITION, 1995 **299**

WALTHER PP AUTO PISTOL
Caliber: 22 LR, 15-shot; 32 ACP, 380 ACP, 7-shot magazine.
Barrel: 3.86".
Weight: 23½ oz. **Length:** 6.7" overall.
Stocks: Checkered plastic.
Sights: Fixed, white markings.
Features: Double action; manual safety blocks firing pin and drops hammer; chamber loaded indicator on 32 and 380; extra finger rest magazine provided. Imported from Germany by Interarms.
Price: 22 LR $783.00
Price: 32 . . . . $1,206.00
Price: 380 . . . . $1,206.00
Price: Engraved models . . . . **On Request**

Walther PPK/S American Auto Pistol
Similar to Walther PP except made entirely in the United States. Has 3.27" barrel with 6.1" length overall. Introduced 1980.
Price: 380 ACP only, blue $610.00
Price: As above, stainless $610.00

WALTHER P-38 AUTO PISTOL
Caliber: 9mm Para., 8-shot.
Barrel: 4¹⁵⁄₁₆".
Weight: 28 oz. **Length:** 8½" overall.
Stocks: Checkered plastic.
Sights: Fixed.
Features: Double action; safety blocks firing pin and drops hammer. Matte finish standard, polished blue, engraving and/or plating available. Imported from Germany by Interarms.
Price: $824.00
Price: Engraved models . . . . **On Request**

Walther P-5 Auto Pistol
Latest Walther design that uses the basic P-38 double-action mechanism. Caliber 9mm Para., barrel length 3½"; weight 28 oz., overall length 7".
Price: $1,096.00
Price: P-5 Compact $1,096.00

Walther P-88 Compact

WALTHER MODEL TPH AUTO PISTOL
Caliber: 22 LR, 25 ACP, 6-shot magazine.
Barrel: 2¼".
Weight: 14 oz. **Length:** 5⅜" overall.
Stocks: Checkered black composition.
Sights: Blade front, rear drift-adjustable for windage.
Features: Made of stainless steel. Scaled-down version of the Walther PP/PPK series. Made in U.S. Introduced 1987. From Interarms.
Price: Blue or stainless steel, 22 or 25 . . . . $458.00

Wildey Auto

Walther PPK/S American

Walther PPK American Auto Pistol
Similar to Walther PPK/S except weighs 21 oz., has 6-shot capacity. Made in the U.S. Introduced 1986.
Price: Stainless, 380 ACP only $610.00
Price: Blue, 380 ACP only $610.00

Walther P-38

WALTHER P-88 COMPACT AUTO PISTOL
Caliber: 9mm Para., 14-shot magazine.
Barrel: 4".
Weight: 31½ oz. **Length:** 7⅜" overall.
Stocks: Checkered black composition.
Sights: Blade front, rear adjustable for windage and elevation.
Features: Double action with ambidextrous decocking lever and magazine release; alloy frame; loaded chamber indicator; matte finish. Imported from Germany by Interarms.
Price: $1,725.00

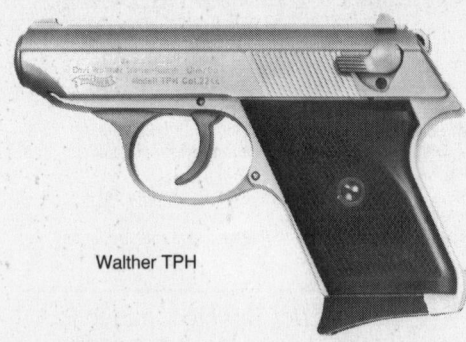

Walther TPH

WILDEY AUTOMATIC PISTOL
Caliber: 10mm Wildey Mag., 11mm Wildey Mag., 30 Wildey Mag., 357 Peterbuilt, 45 Win. Mag., 475 Wildey Mag., 7-shot magazine.
Barrel: 5", 6", 7", 8", 10", 12", 14" (45 Win. Mag.); 8", 10", 12", 14" (all other cals.). Interchangeable.
Weight: 64 oz. (5" barrel). **Length:** 11" overall (7" barrel).
Stocks: Hardwood.
Sights: Ramp front (interchangeable blades optional), fully adjustable rear. Scope base available.
Features: Gas-operated action. Made of stainless steel. Has three-lug rotary bolt. Double or single action. Polished and matte finish. Made in U.S. by Wildey, Inc.
Price: . . . . $1,175.00 to $1,495.00

CAUTION: PRICES SHOWN ARE SUPPLIED BY THE MANUFACTURER OR IMPORTER. CHECK YOUR LOCAL GUNSHOP.

Wilkinson Sherry

WILKINSON "SHERRY" AUTO PISTOL
Caliber: 22 LR, 8-shot magazine.
Barrel: 2⅛".
Weight: 9¼ oz. **Length:** 4⅜" overall.
Stocks: Checkered black plastic.
Sights: Fixed, groove.
Features: Cross-bolt safety locks the sear into the hammer. Available in all blue finish or blue slide and trigger with gold frame. Introduced 1985.
Price: $179.95

WILKINSON "LINDA" AUTO PISTOL
Caliber: 9mm Para., 31-shot magazine.
Barrel: 8⁵⁄₁₆".
Weight: 4 lbs., 13 oz. **Length:** 12¼" overall.
Stocks: Checkered black plastic pistol grip, maple forend.
Sights: Protected blade front, aperture rear.
Features: Fires from closed bolt. Semi-auto only. Straight blowback action. Cross-bolt safety. Removable barrel. From Wilkinson Arms.
Price: $484.84

HANDGUNS—COMPETITION HANDGUNS

Includes models suitable for several forms of competition and other sporting purposes.

AUTO-ORDNANCE 1911A1 COMPETITION MODEL
Caliber: 45 ACP.
Barrel: 5".
Weight: NA. **Length:** NA.
Stocks: Black textured rubber wrap-around.
Sights: Blade front, rear adjustable for windage; three-dot system.
Features: Machined compensator, combat Commander hammer; flat mainspring housing; low profile magazine funnel; metal form magazine bumper; high-ride beavertail grip safety; full-length recoil spring guide system; extended slide stop, safety and magazine catch; Videcki adjustable speed trigger; extended combat ejector. Introduced 1994. Made in U.S. by Auto-Ordnance Corp.
Price: $615.00

Auto-Ordnance competition Model

Benelli MP95SE

BENELLI MP95SE MATCH PISTOL
Caliber: 22 LR, 10-shot magazine.
Barrel: 4.33".
Weight: 38.8 oz. **Length:** 11.81" overall.
Stocks: Stippled walnut match type; anatomically shaped.
Sights: Match type. Blade front, click-adjustable rear for windage and elevation.
Features: Fully adjustable trigger for pull and position, and is removable. Special internal weight box on sub-frame below barrel. Cut for scope rails. Introduced 1993. Imported from Italy by European American Armory.
Price: Blue $550.00
Price: Chrome $625.00

BERNARDELLI MODEL 69 TARGET PISTOL
Caliber: 22 LR, 10-shot magazine.
Barrel: 5.9".
Weight: 38 oz. **Length:** 9" overall.
Stocks: Wrap-around, hand-checkered walnut with thumbrest.
Sights: Fully adjustable and interchangeable target type.
Features: Conforms to U.I.T. regulations. Has 7.1" sight radius, .27" wide grooved trigger. Manual thumb safety and magazine safety. Introduced 1987. Imported from Italy by Armsport.
Price: $612.00

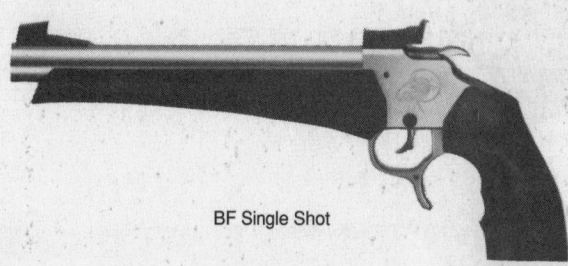

BF Single Shot

BF SINGLE SHOT PISTOL
Caliber: 22 LR, 357 Mag., 44 Mag., 7-30 Waters, 30-30 Win., 375 Win., 45-70; custom chamberings from 17 Rem. through 45-cal.
Barrel: 10", 10.75", 12", 15+".
Weight: 52 oz. **Length:** NA.
Stocks: Custom Herrett finger-groove grip and forend.
Sights: Undercut Patridge front, ½-MOA match-quality fully adjustable RPM Iron Sight rear; barrel or receiver mounting. Drilled and tapped for scope mounting.
Features: Rigid barrel/receiver; falling block action with short lock time; automatic ejection; air-gauged match barrels by Wilson or Douglas; matte black oxide finish standard, electroless nickel optional. Barrel has 11-degree recessed target crown. Introduced 1988. Made in U.S. by E.A. Brown Mfg.
Price: 10", no sights $499.95
Price: 10", RPM sights $564.95

Price: 10.75", no sights $529.95
Price: 10.75", RPM sights $594.95
Price: 12", no sights $562.95
Price: 12", RPM sights $643.75
Price: 15", no sights $592.95
Price: 15", RPM sights $675.00
Price: 10.75" Ultimate Silhouette (heavy barrel, special forend, RPM rear sight with hooded front, gold-plated trigger) $687.95

BERETTA MODEL 89 WOOD SPORT GOLD STANDARD PISTOL

Caliber: 22 LR, 8-shot magazine.
Barrel: 6"
Weight: 41 oz. **Length:** 9.5" overall.
Stocks: Target-type walnut with thumbrest.
Sights: Interchangeable blade front, fully adjustable rear.
Features: Single-action target pistol. Matte blue finish. Imported from Italy by Beretta U.S.A.
Price: **$735.00**

BROWNING BUCK MARK SILHOUETTE

Caliber: 22 LR, 10-shot magazine.
Barrel: 9⅞".
Weight: 53 oz. **Length:** 14" overall.
Stocks: Smooth walnut stocks and forend, or finger-groove walnut.
Sights: Post-type hooded front adjustable for blade width and height; Pro Target rear fully adjustable for windage and elevation.
Features: Heavy barrel with .900" diameter; 12½" sight radius. Special sighting plane forms scope base. Introduced 1987. Made in U.S. From Browning.
Price: **$401.95**

Browning Buck Mark Unlimited Match

Same as the Buck Mark Silhouette except has 14" heavy barrel. Conforms to IHMSA 15" maximum sight radius rule. Introduced 1991.
Price: **$499.95**

Browning Buck Mark Target 5.5

Same as the Buck Mark Silhouette except has a 5½" barrel with .900" diameter. Has hooded sights mounted on a scope base that accepts an optical or reflex sight. Rear sight is a Browning fully adjustable Pro Target, front sight is an adjustable post that customizes to different widths, and can be adjusted for height. Contoured walnut grips with thumbrest, or finger-groove walnut. Matte blue finish. Overall length is 9⅝", weight is 35½ oz. Has 10-shot magazine. Introduced 1990. From Browning.
Price: **$385.95**
Price: Target 5.5 Gold (as above with gold anodized frame and top rib) **$434.95**
Price: Target 5.5 Nickel (as above with nickel frame and top rib) . . **$434.95**

CONSULT
Shooter's
MARKETPLACE
Page 225, This Issue

COLT GOLD CUP NATIONAL MATCH MK IV/SERIES 80

Caliber: 45 ACP, 8-shot magazine.
Barrel: 5", with new design bushing.
Weight: 39 oz. **Length:** 8½".
Stocks: Rubber combat with silver-plated medallion.
Sights: Patridge-style front, Colt-Elliason rear adjustable for windage and elevation, sight radius 6¾".
Features: Arched or flat housing; wide, grooved trigger with adjustable stop; ribbed-top slide, hand fitted, with improved ejection port.
Price: Blue **$899.00**
Price: Stainless **$963.00**
Price: Bright stainless **$1,032.00**
Price: Delta Gold Cup (10mm, stainless) **$987.00**

Competitor Single Shot

Beretta Model 89

Browning Buck Mark Target 5.5

Browning Buck Mark Field 5.5

Same as the Target 5.5 except has hoodless ramp-style front sight and low profile rear sight. Matte blue finish, contoured or finger-groove walnut stocks. Introduced 1991.
Price: **$385.95**

Colt Gold Cup National Match

COMPETITOR SINGLE SHOT PISTOL

Caliber: 22 LR through 50 Action Express, including belted magnums.
Barrel: 14" standard; 10.5" silhouette; 16" optional.
Weight: About 59 oz. (14" bbl.). **Length:** 15.12" overall.
Stocks: Ambidextrous; synthetic (standard) or laminated or natural wood.
Sights: Ramp front, adjustable rear.
Features: Rotary canon-type action cocks on opening; cammed ejector; interchangeable barrels, ejectors. Adjustable single stage trigger, sliding thumb safety and trigger safety. Matte blue finish. Introduced 1988. From Competitor Corp., Inc.
Price: 14", standard calibers, synthetic grip **$379.90**
Price: Extra barrels, from **$132.95**

E.A.A. WINDICATOR TARGET GRADE REVOLVERS

Caliber: 22 LR, 8-shot, 38 Special, 357 Mag., 6-shot.
Barrel: 6".
Weight: 50.2 oz. **Length:** 11.8" overall.
Stocks: Walnut, competition style.
Sights: Blade front with three interchangeable blades, fully adjustable rear.
Features: Adjustable trigger with trigger stop and trigger shoe; frame drilled and tapped for scope mount; target hammer. Comes with barrel weights, plastic carrying box. Introduced 1991. Imported from Germany by European American Armory.
Price: **$299.00**

CAUTION: PRICES SHOWN ARE SUPPLIED BY THE MANUFACTURER OR IMPORTER. CHECK YOUR LOCAL GUNSHOP.

HANDGUNS—COMPETITION HANDGUNS

E.A.A. WITNESS GOLD TEAM AUTO
Caliber: 9mm Para., 9x21, 10mm Auto, 38 Super, 40 S&W, 45 ACP.
Barrel: 5.1".
Weight: 41.6 oz. **Length:** 9.6" overall.
Stocks: Checkered walnut, competition style.
Sights: Square post front, fully adjustable rear.
Features: Triple-chamber compensator; competition SA trigger; extended safety and magazine release; competition hammer; beveled magazine well; beavertail grip. Hand-fitted major components. Hard chrome finish. Match-grade barrel. From E.A.A. Custom Shop. Introduced 1992. From European American Armory.
Price: **$2,195.00**

E.A.A. Witness Gold Team

E.A.A. Witness Silver Team Auto
Similar to the Wittness Gold Team except has double-chamber compensator, paddle magazine release, checkered walnut grips, double-dip blue finish. Comes with Super Sight or drilled and tapped for scope mount. Built for the intermediate competition shooter. Introduced 1992. From European American Armory Custom Shop.
Price: 9mm Para., 9x21, 10mm Auto, 38 Super, 40 S&W, 45 ACP . . . **$1,195.00**

ERMA ER MATCH REVOLVERS
Caliber: 22 LR, 32 S&W Long, 6-shot.
Barrel: 6".
Weight: 47.3 oz. **Length:** 11.2" overall.
Stocks: Stippled walnut, adjustable match-type.
Sights: Blade front, micrometer rear adjustable for windage and elevation.
Features: Polished blue finish. Introduced 1989. Imported from Germany by Precision Sales International.
Price: 22 LR or 32 S&W Long **$1,371.00**

Erma Golden Target

ERMA ESP 85A MATCH PISTOL
Caliber: 22 LR, 8-shot; 32 S&W, 5-shot magazine.
Barrel: 6".
Weight: 39 oz. **Length:** 10" overall.
Stocks: Match-type of stippled walnut; adjustable.
Sights: Interchangeable blade front, micrometer adjustable rear with interchangeable leaf.
Features: Five-way adjustable trigger; exposed hammer and separate firing pin block allow unlimited dry firing practice. Blue or matte chrome; right- or left-hand. Introduced 1988. Imported from Germany by Precision Sales International.
Price: 22 LR **$1,645.00**
Price: 22 LR, left-hand **$1,675.00**
Price: 22 LR, matte chrome **$1,753.00**
Price: 32 S&W **$1,714.00**
Price: 32 S&W, left-hand **$1,744.00**
Price: 32 S&W, matte chrome **$1,822.00**
Price: 32 S&W, matte chrome, left-hand **$1,852.00**

Erma ESP 85A Golden Target Pistol
Similar to the ESP-85A Match except has high-polish gold finish on the slide, different adjustable match stocks with finger grooves. Comes with fully interchangeable 6" barrels for 22 LR and 32 S&W. Introduced 1994. Imported from Germany by Precision Sales International.
Price: **$2,100.00**

FAS 601 Match Pistol
Similar to Model 602 except has different match stocks with adjustable palm shelf, 22 Short only for rapid fire shooting; weighs 40 oz., 5.6" bbl.; has gas ports through top of barrel and slide to reduce recoil; slightly different trigger and sear mechanisms. Imported from Italy by Nygord Precision Products.
Price: **$1,095.00**

FAS 603 Match Pistol
Similar to the FAS 602 except chambered for 32 S&W with 5-shot magazine; 5.3" barrel; 8.66" sight radius; overall length 11.0"; weighs 42.3 oz. Imported from Italy by Nygord Precision Products.
Price: **$1,050.00**

FAS 602 MATCH PISTOL
Caliber: 22 LR, 5-shot.
Barrel: 5.6".
Weight: 37 oz. **Length:** 11" overall.
Stocks: Walnut wraparound; sizes small, medium or large, or adjustable.
Sights: Match. Blade front, open notch rear fully adjustable for windage and elevation. Sight radius is 8.66".
Features: Line of sight is only $^{11}/_{32}$" above centerline of bore; magazine is inserted from top; adjustable and removable trigger mechanism; single lever takedown. Full 5-year warranty. Imported from Italy by Nygord Precision Products.
Price: **$995.00**

Freedom Arms Casull 252 Varmint

FREEDOM ARMS CASULL MODEL 252 SILHOUETTE
Caliber: 22 LR, 5-shot cylinder.
Barrel: 9.95".
Weight: 63 oz. **Length:** NA
Stocks: Black micarta, western style.
Sights: $^{1}/_{8}$" Patridge front, Iron Sight Gun Works silhouette rear, click adjustable for windage and elevation.
Features: Stainless steel. Built on the 454 Casull frame. Two-point firing pin, lightened hammer for fast lock time. Trigger pull is 3 to 5 lbs. with pre-set overtravel screw. Introduced 1991. From Freedom Arms.
Price: Silhouette Class **$1,350.00**
Price: Extra fitted 22 WMR cylinder **$233.00**

Freedom Arms Casull Model 252 Varmint
Similar to the Silhouette Class revolver except has 7.5" barrel, weighs 59 oz., has black and green laminated hardwood grips, and comes with brass bead front sight, express shallow V rear sight with windage and elevation adjustments. Introduced 1991. From Freedom Arms.
Price: Varmint Class **$1,295.00**
Price: Extra fitted 22 WMR cylinder **$233.00**

GAUCHER GP SILHOUETTE PISTOL
Caliber: 22 LR, single shot.
Barrel: 10".
Weight: 42.3 oz. **Length:** 15.5" overall.
Stocks: Stained hardwood.
Sights: Hooded post on ramp front, open rear adjustable for windage and elevation.
Features: Matte chrome barrel, blued bolt and sights. Other barrel lengths available on special order. Introduced 1991. Imported by Mandall Shooting Supplies.
Price: $323.00

GLOCK 24 COMPETITION MODEL PISTOL
Caliber: 40 S&W, 15-shot magazine.
Barrel: 6.02".
Weight: 29.5 oz. **Length:** 8.85" overall.
Stocks: Black polymer.
Sights: Blade front with dot, white outline rear adjustable for windage.
Features: Long-slide competition model available as compensated or non-compensated gun. Factory-installed competition trigger; drop-free magazine. Introduced 1994. Imported from Austria by Glock, Inc.
Price: $806.67

Consult our Directory pages for the location of firms mentioned.

HAMMERLI MODEL 160/162 FREE PISTOLS
Caliber: 22 LR, single shot.
Barrel: 11.30".
Weight: 46.94 oz. **Length:** 17.52" overall.
Stocks: Walnut; full match style with adjustable palm shelf. Stippled surfaces.
Sights: Changeable blade front, open, fully adjustable match rear.
Features: Model 160 has mechanical set trigger; Model 162 has electronic trigger; both fully adjustable with provisions for dry firing. Introduced 1993. Imported from Switzerland by Hammerli Pistols USA.
Price: Model 160, about $1,910.00
Price: Model 162, about $2,095.00

HAMMERLI MODEL 208s PISTOL
Caliber: 22 LR, 8-shot magazine.
Barrel: 5.9".
Weight: 37.5 oz. **Length:** 10" overall.
Stocks: Walnut, target-type with thumbrest.
Sights: Blade front, open fully adjustable rear.
Features: Adjustable trigger, including length; interchangeable rear sight elements. Imported from Switzerland by Hammerli Pistols USA, Mandall Shooting Supplies.
Price: About $1,695.00

GLOCK 17L COMPETITION AUTO
Caliber: 9mm Para., 17-shot magazine.
Barrel: 6.02".
Weight: 23.3 oz. **Length:** 8.85" overall.
Stocks: Black polymer.
Sights: Blade front with white dot, fixed or adjustable rear.
Features: Polymer frame, steel slide; double-action trigger with "Safe Action" system; mechanical firing pin safety, drop safety; simple takedown without tools; locked breech, recoil operated action. Introduced 1989. Imported from Austria by Glock, Inc.
Price: $806.67

Glock 24 Competition

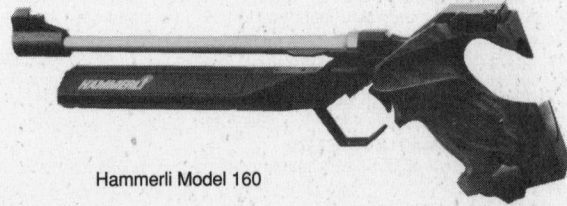

Hammerli Model 160

Hammerli Model 208s

Hammerli Model 280

McMILLAN SIGNATURE JR. LONG RANGE PISTOL
Caliber: Any suitable caliber.
Barrel: To customer specs.
Weight: 5 lbs.
Stock: McMillan fiberglass.
Sights: None furnished; comes with scope rings.
Features: Right- or left-hand McMillan benchrest action of titanium or stainless steel; single shot or repeater. Comes with bipod. Introduced 1992. Made in U.S. by McMillan Gunworks, Inc.
Price: $2,400.00

HAMMERLI MODEL 280 TARGET PISTOL
Caliber: 22 LR, 6-shot; 32 S&W Long WC, 5-shot.
Barrel: 4.5".
Weight: 39.1 oz. (32). **Length:** 11.8" overall.
Stocks: Walnut match-type with stippling, adjustable palm shelf.
Sights: Match sights, micrometer adjustable; interchangeable elements.
Features: Has carbon-reinforced synthetic frame and bolt/barrel housing. Trigger is adjustable for pull weight, take-up weight, let-off, and length, and is interchangeable. Interchangeable metal or carbon fiber counterweights. Sight radius of 8.8". Comes with barrel weights, spare magazine, loading tool, cleaning rods. Introduced 1990. Imported from Switzerland by Hammerli Pistols USA and Mandall Shooting Supplies.
Price: 22-cal., about $1,465.00
Price: 32-cal., about $1,650.00

McMILLAN WOLVERINE AUTO PISTOL
Caliber: 9mm Para., 10mm Auto, 38 Wadcutter, 38 Super, 45 Italian, 45 ACP.
Barrel: 6".
Weight: 45 oz. **Length:** 9.5" overall.
Stocks: Pachmayr rubber.
Sights: Blade front, fully adjustable rear; low profile.
Features: Integral compensator; round burr-style hammer; extended grip safety; checkered backstrap; skeletonized aluminum match trigger. Many finish options. Announced 1992. Made in U.S. by McMillan Gunworks, Inc.
Price: Combat or Competition Match $1,700.00

CAUTION: PRICES SHOWN ARE SUPPLIED BY THE MANUFACTURER OR IMPORTER. CHECK YOUR LOCAL GUNSHOP.

MITCHELL ARMS OLYMPIC II I.S.U. AUTO PISTOL
Caliber: 22 Short, 10-shot magazine.
Barrel: 6.75" round tapered, with stabilizer.
Weight: 40 oz. **Length:** 11.25" overall.
Stocks: Checkered walnut with thumbrest.
Sights: Undercut ramp front, frame-mounted click adjustable square notch rear.
Features: Integral stabilizer with two removable weights. Trigger adjustable for pull and over-travel; blue finish; stippled front and backstraps; push-button barrel takedown. Announced 1992. From Mitchell Arms.
Price: **$599.00**

Mitchell Olympic II I.S.U.

MITCHELL VICTOR II AUTO PISTOL
Caliber: 22 LR, 10-shot magazine.
Barrel: 4.5" vent rib, 5.5" vent, dovetail or Weaver ribs.
Weight: 44 oz. **Length:** 9.75" overall.
Stocks: Military-type checkered walnut with thumbrest.
Sights: Blade front, fully adjustable rear mounted on rib.
Features: Push-button takedown for barrel interchangeability. Bright stainless steel combo or royal blue finish. Introduced 1994. Made in U.S. From Mitchell Arms.
Price: Vent rib, 4.5" barrel **$569.00**
Price: Dovetail rib, 5.5" barrel **$599.00**
Price: Weaver rib, 5.5" barrel **$648.00**

Mitchell Victor II

Remington XP-100 Silhouette

REMINGTON XP-100 SILHOUETTE PISTOL
Caliber: 7mm BR Rem., single shot.
Barrel: 10½".
Weight: 3⅞ lbs. **Length:** 17¼" overall.
Stock: American walnut.
Sights: Blade front, fully adjustable square notch rear.
Features: Mid-handle grip with scalloped contours for left- or right-handed shooters; match-type trigger; two-position thumb safety. Matte blue finish.
Price: **$625.00**

RUGER MARK II TARGET MODEL AUTO PISTOL
Caliber: 22 LR, 10-shot magazine.
Barrel: 5¼", 6⅞".
Weight: 42 oz. **Length:** 11⅛" overall.
Stocks: Checkered hard plastic.
Sights: .125" blade front, micro-click rear, adjustable for windage and elevation. Sight radius 9⅜".
Features: Introduced 1982.
Price: Blued (MK-514, MK-678) **$310.50**
Price: Stainless (KMK-514, KMK-678) **$389.00**

Ruger Mark II Government Target Model
Same gun as the Mark II Target Model except has 6⅞" barrel, higher sights and is roll marked "Government Target Model" on the right side of the receiver below the rear sight. Identical in all aspects to the military model used for training U.S. armed forces except for markings. Comes with factory test target. Introduced 1987.
Price: Blued (MK-678G) **$356.50**
Price: Stainless (KMK-678G) **$427.29**

Ruger Stainless Government Competition Model 22 Pistol
Similar to the Mark II Government Target Model stainless pistol except has 6⅞" slab-sided barrel; the receiver top is drilled and tapped for a Ruger scope base adaptor of blued, chromemoly steel; comes with Ruger 1" stainless scope rings with integral bases for mounting a variety of optical sights; has checkered laminated grip panels with right-hand thumbrest. Has blued open sights with 9¼" radius. Overall length is 11⅛", weight 44 oz. Introduced 1991.
Price: KMK-678GC **$441.00**

Ruger Government Target

Ruger Mark II Bull Barrel
Same gun as the Target Model except has 5½" or 10" heavy barrel (10" meets all IHMSA regulations). Weight with 5½" barrel is 42 oz., with 10" barrel, 52 oz.
Price: Blued (MK-512) **$310.50**
Price: Blued (MK-10) **$294.50**
Price: Stainless (KMK-10) **$373.00**
Price: Stainless (KMK-512) **$389.00**

SAFARI ARMS MATCHMASTER PISTOL
Caliber: 45 ACP, 7-shot magazine.
Barrel: 5"; National Match, stainless steel.
Weight: 38 oz. **Length:** 8.5" overall.
Stocks: Smooth walnut with etched scorpion logo.
Sights: Ramped blade front, rear adjustable for windage and elevation.
Features: Beavertail grip safety, extended safety, extended slide release, Commander-style hammer; throated, ported, tuned. Finishes: Parkerized matte black, or satin stainless steel. Available from Safari Arms, Inc.
Price: **$670.00**

Safari Arms Matchmaster Carrycomp I Pistol
Similar to the Matchmaster except has Wil Schueman-designed hybrid compensator system. Introduced 1993. Made in U.S. by Safari Arms, Inc.
Price: **$1,010.00**

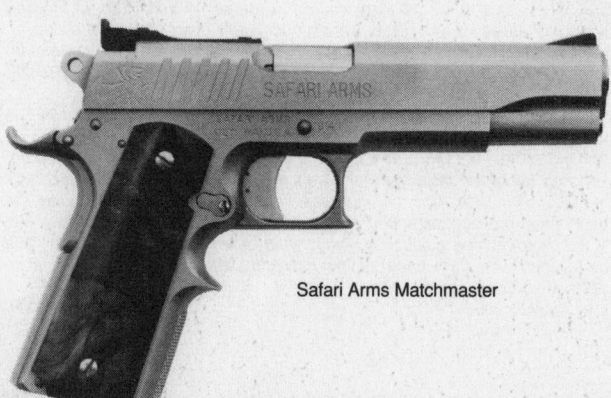

Safari Arms Matchmaster

CAUTION: PRICES SHOWN ARE SUPPLIED BY THE MANUFACTURER OR IMPORTER. CHECK YOUR LOCAL GUNSHOP.

49th EDITION, 1995   **305**

SMITH & WESSON MODEL 41 TARGET
Caliber: 22 LR, 12-shot clip.
Barrel: 5½", 7".
Weight: 44 oz. (5½" barrel). **Length:** 9" overall (5½" barrel).
Stocks: Checkered walnut with modified thumbrest, usable with either hand.
Sights: ⅛" Patridge on ramp base; micro-click rear adjustable for windage and elevation.
Features: ⅜" wide, grooved trigger; adjustable trigger stop.
Price: S&W Bright Blue, either barrel $753.00

SPHINX AT-2000C COMPETITOR PISTOL
Caliber: 9mm Para., 9x21mm, 15-shot, 40 S&W, 11-shot.
Barrel: 5.31".
Weight: 40.56 oz. **Length:** 9.84" overall.
Stocks: Checkered neoprene.
Sights: Fully adjustable Bo-Mar or Tasco Pro-Point dot sight in Sphinx mount.
Features: Extended magazine release. Competition slide with dual-port compensated barrel. Two-tone finish only. Introduced 1993. Imported from Switzerland by Sile Distributors, Inc.
Price: With Bo-Mar sights (AT-2000CS) $1,902.00
Price: With Tasco Pro-Point and mount $2,189.00

Sphinx AT-2000GM Grand Master Pistol
Similar to the AT-2000C except has single-action-only trigger mechanism, squared trigger guard, extended beavertail grip, safety and magazine release; notched competition slide for easier cocking. Two-tone finish only. Has dual-port compensated barrel. Available with fully adjustable Bo-Mar sights or Tasco Pro-Point and Sphinx mount. Introduced 1993. Imported from Switzerland by Sile Distributors, Inc.
Price: With Bo-Mar sights (AT-2000GMS) $2,893.00
Price: With Tasco Pro-Point and mount (AT-2000GM) $2,971.00

SPRINGFIELD INC. 1911A1 BULLSEYE WADCUTTER PISTOL
Caliber: 45 ACP.
Barrel: 5".
Weight: 45 oz. **Length:** 8.59" overall (5" barrel).
Stocks: Checkered walnut.
Sights: Bo-Mar rib with undercut blade front, fully adjustable rear.
Features: Built for wadcutter loads only. Has full-length recoil spring guide rod, fitted Videki speed trigger with 3.5-lb. pull; match Commander hammer and sear; beavertail grip safety; lowered and flared ejection port; tuned extractor; fitted slide to frame; recoil buffer system; beveled and polished magazine well; checkered front strap and steel mainspring housing (flat housing standard); polished and throated National Match barrel and bushing. Comes with two magazines with slam pads, plastic carrying case, test target. Introduced 1992. From Springfield Inc.
Price: . . . . P.O.R.

Springfield Inc. 1911A1 N.M. Hardball Pistol
Has Bo-Mar adjustable rear sight with undercut front blade; fitted match Videki trigger with 4-lb. pull; fitted slide to frame; throated National Match barrel and bushing, polished feed ramp; recoil buffer system; tuned extractor; Herrett walnut grips. Comes with two magazines, plastic carrying case, test target. Introduced 1992. From Springfield Inc.
Price: 45 ACP, blue . . . . P.O.R.

Springfield 1911A1 Trophy Match

Springfield Inc. Trophy Master Distinguished Pistol
Has all the features of the 1911A1 Trophy Master Expert except is full-house pistol with Bo-Mar low-mounted adjustable rear sight; full-length recoil spring guide rod and recoil spring retainer; beveled and polished magazine well; walnut grips. Hard chrome finish. Comes with two magazines with slam pads, plastic carrying case. From Springfield Inc.
Price: 45 ACP . . . . P.O.R.
Price: Trophy Master Distinguished Limited . . . . P.O.R.

Sphinx AT 2000C Competitor

Sphinx AT 2000 GM Grand Master

Springfield Inc. Basic Competition Pistol
Has low-mounted Bo-Mar adjustable rear sight, undercut blade front; match throated barrel and bushing; polished feed ramp; lowered and flared ejection port; fitted Videki speed trigger with tuned 3.5-lb. pull; fitted slide to frame; recoil buffer system; Pachmayr mainspring housing; Pachmayr grips. Comes with two magazines with slam pads, plastic carrying case. Introduced 1992. From Springfield Inc.
Price: 45 ACP, blue, 5" only . . . . P.O.R.

Springfield Inc. Trophy Master Expert Pistol
Similar to the 1911A1 Trophy Master Competition Pistol except has triple-chamber tapered cone compensator on match barrel with dovetailed front sight; lowered and flared ejection port; fully tuned for reliability. Comes with two magazines, plastic carrying case. Introduced 1992. From Springfield Inc.
Price: 45 ACP, Duotone finish . . . . P.O.R.
Price: Trophy Master Expert Ltd. . . . . P.O.R.

Springfield Inc. 1911A1 Trophy Match Pistol
Similar to the 1911A1 except factory accurized, has 4- to 5½-lb. trigger pull, click adjustable rear sight, match-grade barrel and bushing. Comes with checkered walnut grips. Introduced 1994. From Springfield, Inc.
Price: Blue $899.00
Price: Stainless steel $936.00

Springfield Inc. Trophy Master Competition Pistol
Similar to the 1911A1 Entry Level Wadcutter Pistol except has brazed, serrated improved ramp front sight; extended ambidextrous thumb safety; match Commander hammer and sear; serrated rear slide; Pachmay flat mainspring housing; extended magazine release; beavertail grip safety; full-length recoil spring guide; Pachmayr wrap-around grips. Comes with two magazines with slam pads, plastic carrying case. Introduced 1992. From Springfield Inc.
Price: 45 ACP, blue . . . . P.O.R.

CAUTION: PRICES SHOWN ARE SUPPLIED BY THE MANUFACTURER OR IMPORTER. CHECK YOUR LOCAL GUNSHOP.

Thompson/Center Super 14 Contender

THOMPSON/CENTER SUPER 14 CONTENDER
Caliber: 22 LR, 222 Rem., 223 Rem., 7mm TCU, 7-30 Waters, 30-30 Win., 35 Rem., 357 Rem. Maximum, 44 Mag., 10mm Auto, 445 Super Mag., single shot.
Barrel: 14".
Weight: 45 oz. **Length:** 17¼" overall.
Stocks: T/C "Competitor Grip" (walnut and rubber).
Sights: Fully adjustable target-type.
Features: Break-open action with auto safety. Interchangeable barrels for both rimfire and centerfire calibers. Introduced 1978.
Price: **$445.00**
Price: Extra barrels, blued **$210.00**

Thompson/Center Super 16 Contender
Same as the T/C Super 14 Contender except has 16¼" barrel. Rear sight can be mounted at mid-barrel position (10¾" radius) or moved to the rear (using scope mount position) for 14¾" radius. Overall length is 20¼". Comes with T/C Competitor Grip of walnut and rubber. Available in 22 LR, 22 WMR, 223 Rem., 7-30 Waters, 30-30 Win., 35 Rem., 44 Mag., 45-70 Gov't. Also available with 16" vent rib barrel with internal choke, caliber 45 Colt/410 shotshell.
Price: **$450.00**
Price: 45-70 Gov't **$455.00**
Price: Extra 16" barrels (blued) **$215.00**
Price: As above, 45-70 . . . . **$220.00**
Price: Super 16 Vent Rib (45-410) **$490.00**
Price: Extra vent rib barrel **$245.00**

UNIQUE D.E.S. 32U RAPID FIRE MATCH
Caliber: 32 S&W Long wadcutter.
Barrel: 5.9".
Weight: 40.2 oz.
Stocks: Anatomically shaped, adjustable stippled French walnut.
Sights: Blade front, micrometer click rear.
Features: Trigger adjustable for weight and position; dry firing mechanism; slide stop catch. Optional sleeve weights. Introduced 1990. Imported from France by Nygord Precision Products.
Price: Right-hand, about **$1,295.00**
Price: Left-hand, about **$1,345.00**

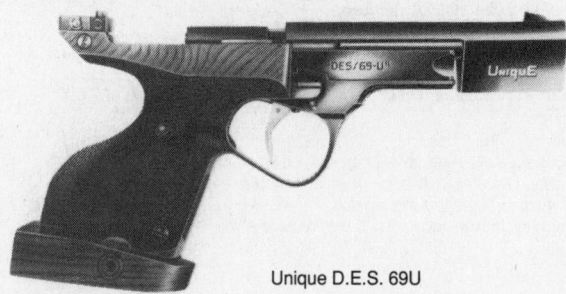

Unique D.E.S. 69U

UNIQUE D.E.S. 69U TARGET PISTOL
Caliber: 22 LR, 5-shot magazine.
Barrel: 5.91".
Weight: 35.3 oz. **Length:** 10.5" overall.
Stocks: French walnut target-style with thumbrest and adjustable shelf; hand-checkered panels.
Sights: Ramp front, micro. adj. rear mounted on frame; 8.66" sight radius.
Features: Meets U.I.T. standards. Comes with 260-gram barrel weight; 100, 150, 350-gram weights available. Fully adjustable match trigger; dry-firing safety device. Imported from France by Nygord Precision Products.
Price: Right-hand, about **$1,195.00**
Price: Left-hand, about **$1,245.00**

UNIQUE MODEL 2000-U MATCH PISTOL
Caliber: 22 Short, 5-shot magazine.
Barrel: 5.9".
Weight: 43 oz. **Length:** 11.3" overall.
Stocks: Anatomically shaped, adjustable, stippled French walnut.
Sights: Blade front, fully adjustable rear; 9.7" sight radius.
Features: Light alloy frame, steel slide and shock absorber; five barrel vents reduce recoil, three of which can be blocked; trigger adjustable for position and pull weight. Comes with 340-gram weight housing, 160-gram available. Introduced 1984. Imported from France by Nygord Precision Products.
Price: Right-hand, about **$1,350.00**
Price: Left-hand, about **$1,400.00**

Unique Model 2000-U

Wesson Firearms Model 40

WESSON FIREARMS MODEL 40 SILHOUETTE
Caliber: 357 Maximum, 6-shot.
Barrel: 4", 6", 8", 10".
Weight: 64 oz. (8" bbl.). **Length:** 14.3" overall (8" bbl.).
Stocks: Smooth walnut, target-style.
Sights: ⅛" serrated front, fully adjustable rear.
Features: Meets criteria for IHMSA competition with 8" slotted barrel. Blue or stainless steel. Made in U.S. by Wesson Firearms Co., Inc.
Price: Blue, 4" **$488.00**
Price: Blue, 6" **$508.00**
Price: Blue, 8" **$550.94**
Price: Blue, 10" **$579.20**
Price: Stainless, 4" **$550.00**
Price: Stainless, 6" **$569.00**
Price: Stainless, 8" slotted **$625.83**
Price: Stainless, 10" **$651.16**

Wesson Firearms Model 445 Supermag Revolver
Similar size and weight as the Model 40 revolvers. Chambered for the 445 Supermag cartridge, a longer version of the 44 Magnum. Barrel lengths of 4", 6", 8", 10". Contact maker for complete price list. Introduced 1989. From Wesson Firearms Co., Inc.
Price: 4", vent heavy, blue **$539.00**
Price: As above, stainless **$615.00**
Price: 8", vent heavy, blue **$594.00**
Price: As above, stainless **$662.00**
Price: 10", vent heavy, blue **$615.00**
Price: As above, stainless **$683.00**
Price: 8", vent slotted, blue **$575.00**
Price: As above, stainless **$632.00**
Price: 10", vent slotted, blue **$597.00**
Price: As above, stainless **$657.00**

Wesson Pin Gun

WESSON FIREARMS 45 PIN GUN
Caliber: 45 ACP, 6-shot.
Barrel: 5" with 1:14" twist; Taylor two-stage forcing cone; compensated shroud.
Weight: 54 oz. **Length:** 12.5" overall.
Stocks: Finger-groove Hogue Monogrip.
Sights: Pin front, fully adjustable rear. Has 8.375" sight radius.
Features: Based on 44 Magnum frame. Polished blue or brushed stainless steel. Uses half-moon clips with 45 ACP, or 45 Auto Rim ammunition. Introduced 1994. Made in U.S. by Wesson Firearms Co., Inc.
Price: Blue, regular vent **$654.00**
Price: Blue, vent heavy **$663.00**
Price: Stainless, regular vent **$713.00**
Price: Stainless vent heavy **$762.00**

WICHITA SILHOUETTE PISTOL
Caliber: 308 Win. F.L., 7mm IHMSA, 7mm-308.
Barrel: 14¹⁵⁄₁₆".
Weight: 4½ lbs. **Length:** 21⅜" overall.
Stock: American walnut with oil finish. Glass bedded.
Sights: Wichita Multi-Range sight system.
Features: Comes with left-hand action with right-hand grip. Round receiver and barrel. Fluted bolt, flat bolt handle. Wichita adjustable trigger. Introduced 1979. From Wichita Arms.
Price: Center grip stock **$1,207.00**
Price: As above except with Rear Position Stock and target-type Lightpull trigger **$1,207.00**

WICHITA INTERNATIONAL PISTOL
Caliber: 22 LR, 22 WMR, 32 H&R Mag., 357 Super Mag., 357 Mag., 7R, 7mm Super Mag., 7-30 Waters, 30-30 Win., single shot.
Barrel: 10", 10½", 14".
Weight: 3 lbs. 2 oz. (with 10", 10½" barrels).
Stocks: Walnut grip and forend.
Sights: Patridge front, adjustable rear. Wichita Multi-Range sight system optional.
Features: Made of stainless steel. Break-open action. Grip dimensions same as Colt 45 Auto. Drilled and tapped for furnished see-thru rings. Extra barrels are factory fitted. Introduced 1983. Available from Wichita Arms.
Price: International 10" $595.00
Price: International 14" $645.00
Price: Extra barrels, 10" $365.00
Price: Extra barrels, 14" $395.00

WESSON FIREARMS MODEL 22 SILHOUETTE REVOLVER
Caliber: 22 LR, 6-shot.
Barrel: 10", regular vent or vent heavy.
Weight: 53 oz.
Stocks: Combat style.
Sights: Patridge-style front, .080" narrow notch rear.
Features: Single action only. Available in blue or stainless. Introduced 1989. From Wesson Firearms Co., Inc.
Price: Blue, regular vent $459.72
Price: Blue, vent heavy $478.10
Price: Stainless, regular vent $488.84
Price: Stainless, vent heavy $516.40

WESSON FIREARMS MODEL 322/7322 TARGET REVOLVER
Caliber: 32-20, 6-shot.
Barrel: 2.5", 4", 6", 8", standard, vent, vent heavy.
Weight: 43 oz. (6" VH). **Length:** 11.25" overall.
Stocks: Checkered walnut.
Sights: Red ramp interchangeable front, fully adjustable rear.
Features: Brigh blue or stainless. Introduced 1991. From Wesson Firearms Co., Inc.
Price: 6", blue $355.00
Price: 6", stainless $384.00
Price: 8", vent, blue $404.55
Price: 8", stainless $434.71
Price: 6", vent heavy, blue $412.20
Price: 6", vent heavy, stainless $441.32
Price: 8", vent heavy, blue $422.94
Price: 8", vent heavy, stainless $459.72

WICHITA CLASSIC SILHOUETTE PISTOL
Caliber: All standard calibers with maximum overall length of 2.800".
Barrel: 11¼".
Weight: 3 lbs., 15 oz.
Stocks: AAA American walnut with oil finish, checkered grip.
Sights: Hooded post front, open adjustable rear.
Features: Three locking lug bolt, three gas ports; completely adjustable Wichita trigger. Introduced 1981. From Wichita Arms.
Price: $2,950.00

Wichita Silhouette

HANDGUNS—DOUBLE-ACTION REVOLVERS, SERVICE & SPORT

Includes models suitable for hunting and competitive courses for fire, both police and international.

CHARTER BULLDOG PUG REVOLVER
Caliber: 44 Spec., 5-shot.
Barrel: 2½".
Weight: 19½ oz. **Length:** 7" overall.
Stocks: Checkered walnut Bulldog.
Sights: Ramp-style front, fixed rear.
Features: Blue or stainless steel construction. Fully shrouded barrel. Reintroduced 1993. Made in U.S. by Charco, Inc.
Price: Blue $267.60
Price: Nickel $289.51

Charter Pug

CAUTION: PRICES SHOWN ARE SUPPLIED BY THE MANUFACTURER OR IMPORTER. CHECK YOUR LOCAL GUNSHOP.

CHARTER OFF-DUTY REVOLVER

Caliber: 22 LR, 22 WMR, 6-shot, 38 Spec., 5-shot.
Barrel: 2".
Weight: 17 oz. (38 Spec.). **Length:** 6¼" overall.
Stocks: Checkered walnut.
Sights: Ramp-style front, fixed rear.
Features: Available in blue, stainless or electroless nickel. Fully shrouded barrel. Introduced 1993. Made in U.S. by Charco, Inc.
Price: Blue, 22 or 38 Spec. **$199.00**
Price: Electroless nickel, 22 or 38 Spec. **$239.68**
Price: Blue, DA only **$207.98**
Price: Electroless nickel, DA only **$247.18**

Charter Off-Duty

CHARTER POLICE UNDERCOVER REVOLVER

Caliber: 32 H&R Mag., 38 Spec., 6-shot.
Barrel: 2½".
Weight: 16 oz. (38 Spec.). **Length:** 6¼" overall.
Stocks: Checkered walnut.
Sights: Ramp-style front, fixed rear.
Features: Blue or stainless steel. Fully shrouded barrel. Reintroduced 1993. Made in U.S. by Charco, Inc.
Price: Blue **$237.75**
Price: Electroless nickel **$252.00**

COLT ANACONDA REVOLVER

Caliber: 44 Rem. Magnum, 45 Colt, 6-shot.
Barrel: 4", 6", 8".
Weight: 53 oz. (6" barrel). **Length:** 11⅝" overall.
Stocks: Combat-style black neoprene with finger grooves.
Sights: Red insert front, adjustable white outline rear.
Features: Stainless steel; full-length ejector rod housing; ventilated barrel rib; offset bolt notches in cylinder; wide spur hammer. Introduced 1990.
Price: **$587.00**
Price: 45 Colt, 6" barrel only **$587.00**

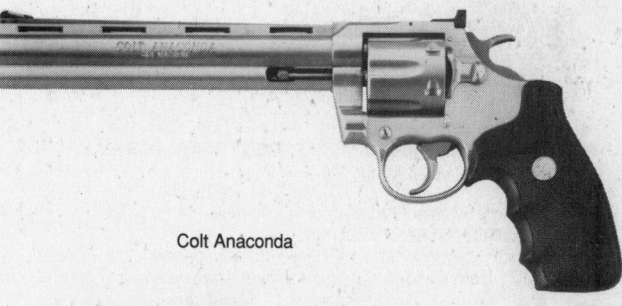

Colt Anaconda

COLT DETECTIVE SPECIAL REVOLVER

Caliber: 38 Special, 6-shot.
Barrel: 2".
Weight: 22 oz. **Length:** 6⅝" overall.
Stocks: Black composition.
Sights: Fixed. Ramp front, square notch rear.
Features: Glare-proof sights, grooved trigger, shrouded ejector rod. Colt blue finish. Reintroduced 1993.
Price: **$384.00**

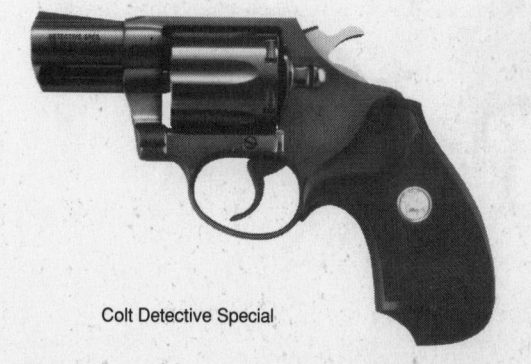

Colt Detective Special

COLT KING COBRA REVOLVER

Caliber: 357 Magnum, 6-shot.
Barrel: 4", 6".
Weight: 42 oz. (4" bbl.). **Length:** 9" overall (4" bbl.).
Stocks: Checkered rubber.
Sights: Red insert ramp front, adjustable white outline rear.
Features: Full-length contoured ejector rod housing, barrel rib. Introduced 1986.
Price: Stainless **$437.00**

COLT PYTHON REVOLVER

Caliber: 357 Magnum (handles all 38 Spec.), 6-shot.
Barrel: 4", 6" or 8", with ventilated rib.
Weight: 38 oz. (4" bbl.). **Length:** 9¼" (4" bbl.).
Stocks: Rubber wraparound.
Sights: ⅛" ramp front, adjustable notch rear.
Features: Ventilated rib; grooved, crisp trigger; swing-out cylinder; target hammer.
Price: Royal blue, 4", 6", 8" **$798.00**
Price: Stainless, 4", 6", 8" **$885.00**
Price: Bright stainless, 4", 6", 8" **$917.00**

Colt Python

E.A.A. STANDARD GRADE REVOLVERS

Caliber: 22 LR, 22 LR/22 WMR, 8-shot; 38 Special, 6-shot.
Barrel: 4", 6" (22 rimfire); 2", 4" (38 Special).
Weight: 38 oz. (22 rimfire, 4"). **Length:** 8.8" overall (4" bbl.).
Stocks: Rubber with finger grooves.
Sights: Blade front, fixed or adjustable on rimfires; fixed only on 32, 38.
Features: Swing-out cylinder; hammer block safety; blue finish. Introduced 1991. Imported from Germany by European American Armory.
Price: 38 Special 2" **$180.00**
Price: 38 Special, 4" **$199.00**
Price: 22 LR, 6" **$199.00**
Price: 22 LR/22 WMR combo, 4" **$200.00**
Price: As above, 6" **$200.00**

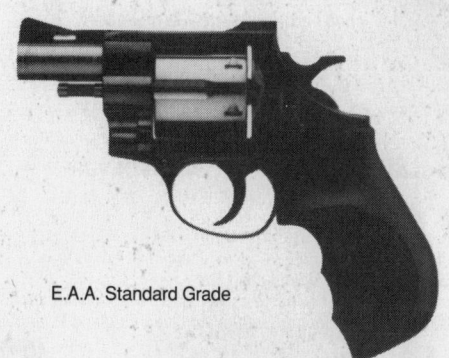

E.A.A. Standard Grade

CAUTION: PRICES SHOWN ARE SUPPLIED BY THE MANUFACTURER OR IMPORTER. CHECK YOUR LOCAL GUNSHOP.

49th EDITION, 1995 **309**

ERMA ER-777 SPORTING REVOLVER
Caliber: 357 Mag., 6-shot.
Barrel: 5½".
Weight: 43.3 oz. **Length:** 9½" overall (4" barrel).
Stocks: Stippled walnut service-type.
Sights: Interchangeable blade front, micro-adjustable rear for windage and elevation.
Features: Polished blue finish. Adjustable trigger. Imported from Germany by Precision Sales Int'l. Introduced 1988.
Price: **$1,420.00**

Erma ER-777

Harrington & Richardson 949

HARRINGTON & RICHARDSON 949 WESTERN REVOLVER
Caliber: 22 LR, 9-shot cylinder.
Barrel: 5½".
Weight: 36 oz. **Length:** NA.
Stocks: Walnut-stained hardwood.
Sights: Blade front, adjustable rear.
Features: Color case-hardened frame and backstrap, traditional loading gate and ejector rod. Introduced 1994. Made in U.S. by Harrington & Richardson.
Price: About **$174.95**

HARRINGTON & RICHARDSON SPORTSMAN 999 REVOLVER
Caliber: 22 Short, Long, Long Rifle, 9-shot.
Barrel: 4", 6".
Weight: 30 oz. (4" barrel). **Length:** 8.5" overall.
Stocks: Walnut-finished hardwood.
Sights: Blade front adjustable for elevation, rear adjustable for windage.
Features: Top-break loading; polished blue finish; automatic shell ejection. Reintroduced 1992. From Harrington & Richardson.
Price: **$279.95**

Harrington & Richardson Sportsman 999

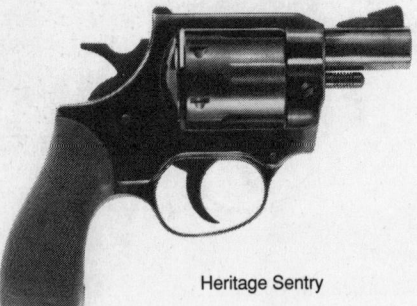

Heritage Sentry

HERITAGE SENTRY DOUBLE-ACTION REVOLVERS
Caliber: 22 LR, 22 WMR, 32 H&R Mag., 9mm Para., 38 Spec., 6-shot.
Barrel: 2", 4".
Weight: 23 oz. (2" barrel). **Length:** 6¼" overall (2" barrel).
Stocks: Magnum-style round butt; checkered plastic.
Sights: Ramp front, fixed rear.
Features: Pill-pin-type ejection; serrated hammer and trigger. Polished blue or nickel finish. Introduced 1993. Made in U.S. by Heritage Mfg., Inc.
Price: . . . . **$109.95 to $119.95**

NEW ENGLAND FIREARMS STANDARD REVOLVERS
Caliber: 22 LR, 9-shot; 32 H&R Mag., 5-shot.
Barrel: 2½", 4".
Weight: 26 oz. (22 LR, 2½"). **Length:** 8½" overall (4" bbl.).
Stocks: Walnut-finished American hardwood with NEF medallion.
Sights: Fixed.
Features: Choice of blue or nickel finish. Introduced 1988. From New England Firearms Co.
Price: 22 LR, 32 H&R Mag., blue **$124.95**
Price: 22 LR, 2½", 4", nickel, 32 H&R Mag. 2½" nickel **$134.95**

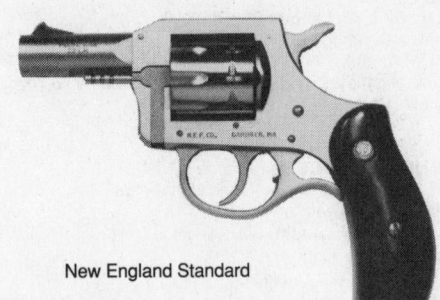

New England Standard

NEW ENGLAND FIREARMS LADY ULTRA REVOLVER
Caliber: 32 H&R Mag., 5-shot.
Barrel: 3".
Weight: 31 oz. **Length:** 7.25" overall.
Stocks: Walnut-finished hardwood with NEF medallion.
Sights: Blade front, fully adjustable rear.
Features: Swing-out cylinder; polished blue finish. Comes with lockable storage case. Introduced 1992. From New England Firearms Co.
Price: **$149.95**

NEW ENGLAND FIREARMS ULTRA REVOLVER
Caliber: 22 LR, 9-shot; 22 WMR, 6-shot.
Barrel: 4", 6".
Weight: 36 oz. **Length:** 10⅝" overall (6" barrel).
Stocks: Walnut-finished hardwood with NEF medallion.
Sights: Blade front, fully adjustable rear.
Features: Blue finish. Bull-style barrel with recessed muzzle, high "Lustre" blue/black finish. Introduced 1989. From New England Firearms.
Price: **$149.95**
Price: Ultra Mag 22 WMR **$149.95**

New England Lady Ultra

CAUTION: PRICES SHOWN ARE SUPPLIED BY THE MANUFACTURER OR IMPORTER. CHECK YOUR LOCAL GUNSHOP.

ROSSI MODEL 68 REVOLVER
Caliber: 38 Spec.
Barrel: 2", 3".
Weight: 22 oz.
Stocks: Checkered wood and rubber.
Sights: Ramp front, low profile adjustable rear.
Features: All-steel frame, thumb latch operated swing-out cylinder. Introduced 1978. Imported from Brazil by Interarms.
Price: 38, blue, 3", both wood and rubber grips **$218.00**
Price: M68/2 (2" barrel), wood and rubber grips **$231.00**
Price: 3", nickel **$223.00**

ROSSI MODEL 515, 518 REVOLVERS
Caliber: 22 LR (Model 518), 22 WMR (Model 515), 6-shot.
Barrel: 4".
Weight: 30 oz. **Length:** 9" overall.
Stocks: Checkered wood and finger-groove wrap-around rubber.
Sights: Blade front with red insert, rear adjustable for windage and elevation.
Features: Small frame; stainless steel construction; solid integral barrel rib. Introduced 1994. Imported from Brazil by Interarms.
Price: Model 518, 22 LR **$275.00**
Price: Model 515, 22 WMR **$290.00**

ROSSI MODEL 720 REVOLVER
Caliber: 44 Special, 5-shot.
Barrel: 3".
Weight: 27.5 oz. **Length:** 8" overall.
Stocks: Checkered rubber, combat style.
Sights: Red insert front on ramp, fully adjustable rear.
Features: All stainless steel construction; solid barrel rib; full ejector rod shroud. Introduced 1992. Imported from Brazil by Interarms.
Price: **$312.00**
Price: Model 720C, spurless hammer, DA only **$312.00**

ROSSI MODEL 971 REVOLVER
Caliber: 357 Mag., 6-shot.
Barrel: 2½", 4", 6", heavy.
Weight: 36 oz. **Length:** 9" overall.
Stocks: Checkered Brazilian hardwood. Stainless models have checkered, contoured rubber.
Sights: Blade front, fully adjustable rear.
Features: Full-length ejector rod shroud; matted sight rib; target-type trigger, wide checkered hammer spur. Introduced 1988. Imported from Brazil by Interarms.
Price: 4", stainless **$301.00**
Price: 6", stainless **$301.00**
Price: 4", blue **$270.00**
Price: 2½", stainless **$301.00**

Rossi Model 971 Comp

ROSSI MODEL 88 STAINLESS REVOLVER
Caliber: 32 S&W, 38 Spec., 5-shot.
Barrel: 2", 3".
Weight: 22 oz. **Length:** 7.5" overall.
Stocks: Checkered wood, service-style, and rubber.
Sights: Ramp front, square notch rear drift adjustable for windage.
Features: All metal parts except springs are of 440 stainless steel; matte finish; small frame for concealability. Introduced 1983. Imported from Brazil by Interarms.
Price: 3" barrel, wood and rubber grips **$249.00**
Price: M88/2 (2" barrel), wood and rubber grips **$265.00**

Rossi Model 518

Rossi Model 720C

ROSSI MODEL 851 REVOLVER
Caliber: 38 Special, 6-shot.
Barrel: 3" or 4".
Weight: 27.5 oz. (3" bbl.). **Length:** 8" overall (3" bbl.).
Stocks: Checkered Brazilian hardwood.
Sights: Blade front with red insert, rear adjustable for windage.
Features: Medium-size frame; stainless steel construction; ventilated barrel rib. Introduced 1991. Imported from Brazil by Interarms.
Price: **$270.00**

Rossi Model 971 Comp Gun
Same as the Model 971 stainless except has 3¼" barrel with integral compensator. Overall length is 9", weight 32 oz. Has red insert front sight, fully adjustable rear. Checkered, contoured rubber grips. Introduced 1993. Imported from Brazil by Interarms.
Price: **$301.00**

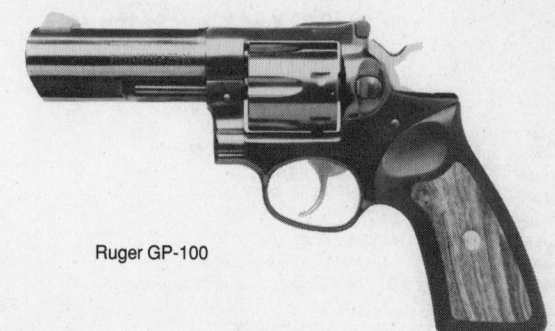

Ruger GP-100

RUGER GP-100 REVOLVERS
Caliber: 38 Special, 357 Magnum, 6-shot.
Barrel: 3", 3" heavy, 4", 4" heavy, 6", 6" heavy.
Weight: 3" barrel—35 oz., 3" heavy barrel—36 oz., 4" barrel—37 oz., 4" heavy barrel—38 oz.
Sights: Fixed; adjustable on 4" heavy, 6", 6" heavy barrels.
Stocks: Ruger Santoprene Cushioned Grip with Goncalo Alves inserts.
Features: Uses action and frame incorporating improvements and features of both the Security-Six and Redhawk revolvers. Full length and short ejector shroud. Satin blue and stainless steel. Introduced 1988.
Price: GP-141 (357, 4" heavy, adj. sights, blue) **$413.50**
Price: GP-160 (357, 6", adj. sights, blue) **$413.50**
Price: GP-161 (357, 6" heavy, adj. sights, blue) **$413.50**
Price: GPF-330 (357, 3"), GPF-830 (38 Spec.) **$397.00**

Price: GPF-331 (357, 3" heavy), GPF-831 (38 Spec.) **$397.00**
Price: GPF-340 (357, 4"), GPF-840 (38 Spec.) **$397.00**
Price: GPF-341 (357, 4" heavy), GPF-841 (38 Spec.) **$397.00**
Price: KGP-141 (357, 4" heavy, adj. sights, stainless) **$446.50**
Price: KGP-160 (357, 6", adj. sights, stainless) **$446.50**
Price: KGP-161 (357, 6" heavy, adj. sights, stainless) **$446.50**
Price: KGPF-330 (357, 3", stainless), KGPF-830 (38 Spec.) **$430.00**
Price: KGPF-331 (357, 3" heavy, stainless), KGPF-831 (38 Spec.) . . **$430.00**
Price: KGPF-340 (357, 4", stainless), KGPF-840 (38 Spec.) **$430.00**
Price: KGPF-341 (357, 4" heavy, stainless), KGPF-841 (38 Spec.) . . **$430.00**

Ruger Redhawk

Ruger SP101 DAO

RUGER REDHAWK
Caliber: 44 Rem. Mag., 6-shot.
Barrel: 5½", 7½".
Weight: About 54 oz. (7½" bbl.). **Length:** 13" overall (7½" barrel).
Stocks: Square butt Goncalo Alves.
Sights: Interchangeable Patridge-type front, rear adjustable for windage and elevation.
Features: Stainless steel, brushed satin finish, or blued ordnance steel. Has a 9½" sight radius. Introduced 1979.
Price: Blued, 44 Mag., 5½", 7½" **$458.50**
Price: Blued, 44 Mag., 7½", with scope mount, rings **$496.50**
Price: Stainless, 44 Mag., 5½", 7½" **$516.75**
Price: Stainless, 44 Mag., 7½", with scope mount, rings **$557.25**

Ruger Super Redhawk Revolver
Similar to the standard Redhawk except has a heavy extended frame with the Ruger Integral Scope Mounting System on the wide topstrap. The wide hammer spur has been lowered for better scope clearance. Incorporates the mechanical design features and improvements of the GP-100. Choice of 7½" or 9½" barrel, both with ramp front sight base with Redhawk-style Interchangeable Insert sight blades, adjustable rear sight. Comes with Ruger "Cushioned Grip" panels of Santoprene with Goncalo Alves wood panels. Satin polished stainless steel, 44 Magnum only. Introduced 1987.
Price: KSRH-7 (7½"), KSRH-9 (9½") **$557.25**

RUGER SP101 REVOLVERS
Caliber: 22 LR, 32 H&R Mag., 6-shot, 9mm Para., 38 Special +P, 357 Mag., 5-shot.
Barrel: 2¼", 3 1/16", 4".
Weight: 2¼"—25 oz.; 3 1/16"—27 oz.
Sights: Adjustable on 22, 32, fixed on others.
Stocks: Ruger Santoprene Cushioned Grip with Xenoy inserts.
Features: Incorporates improvements and features found in the GP-100 revolvers into a compact, small frame, double-action revolver. Full-length ejector shroud. Stainless steel only. Introduced 1988.
Price: KSP-821 (2½", 38 Spec.) **$408.00**
Price: KSP-831 (3 1/16", 38 Spec.) **$408.00**
Price: KSP-221 (2¼", 22 LR) **$408.00**
Price: KSP-240 (4", 22 LR) **$408.00**
Price: KSP-241 (4" heavy bbl., 22 LR) **$408.00**
Price: KSP-3231 (3 1/16", 32 H&R) **$408.00**
Price: KSP-921 (2¼", 9mm Para.) **$408.00**
Price: KSP-931 (3 1/16", 9mm Para.) **$408.00**
Price: KSP-321 (2¼", 357 Mag.) **$408.00**
Price: KSP-331 (3 1/16", 357 Mag.) **$408.00**

Ruger SP101 Double-Action-Only Revolver
Similar to the standard SP101 except is double action only with no single-action sear notch. Has spurless hammer for snag-free handling, floating firing pin and Ruger's patented transfer bar safety system. Available with 2½" barrel in 38 Special +P and 357 Magnum only. Weight is 25½ oz., overall length 7.06". Natural brushed satin stainless steel. Introduced 1993.
Price: KSP821L (38 Spec.), KSP321XL (357 Mag.) **$408.00**

Smith & Wesson Model 65

Smith & Wesson Model 15

SMITH & WESSON MODEL 10 M&P REVOLVER
Caliber: 38 Special, 6-shot.
Barrel: 2", 4".
Weight: 30 oz. **Length:** 9 5/16" overall.
Stocks: Soft rubber; round or square butt. Wood optional.
Sights: Fixed, ramp front, square notch rear.
Price: Blue **$368.00**
Price: With square butt grips **$375.00**

Smith & Wesson Model 10 38 M&P Heavy Barrel
Same as regular M&P except has heavy ribbed barrel with square butt grips. Weighs 33½ oz.
Price: Blue **$375.00**

SMITH & WESSON MODEL 13 H.B. M&P
Caliber: 357 and 38 Special, 6-shot.
Barrel: 3" or 4".
Weight: 34 oz. **Length:** 9 5/16" overall (4" bbl.).
Stocks: Soft rubber; wood optional.
Sights: 1/8" serrated ramp front, fixed square notch rear.
Features: Heavy barrel, K-frame, square butt (4"), round butt (3").
Price: Blue **$386.00**
Price: Model 65, as above in stainless steel **$423.00**

SMITH & WESSON MODEL 14 FULL LUG REVOLVER
Caliber: 38 Special, 6-shot.
Barrel: 6", full lug.
Weight: 47 oz. **Length:** 11 1/8" overall.
Stocks: Soft rubber; wood optional.
Sights: Pinned Patridge front, adjustable micrometer click rear.
Features: Has .500" target hammer, .312" smooth combat trigger. Polished blue finish. Reintroduced 1991. Limited production.
Price: **$461.00**

SMITH & WESSON MODEL 15 COMBAT MASTERPIECE
Caliber: 38 Special, 6-shot.
Barrel: 4".
Weight: 32 oz. **Length:** 9 5/16" (4" bbl.).
Stocks: Soft rubber; wood optional.
Sights: Front, Baughman Quick Draw on ramp, micro-click rear, adjustable for windage and elevation.
Price: Blued **$407.00**

SMITH & WESSON MODEL 19 COMBAT MAGNUM
Caliber: 357 Magnum and 38 Special, 6-shot.
Barrel: 2½", 4", 6".
Weight: 36 oz. **Length:** 9⁹⁄₁₆" (4" bbl.).
Stocks: Soft rubber; wood optional.
Sights: Serrated ramp front 2½" or 4" bbl., red ramp on 4", 6" bbl., micro-click rear adjustable for windage and elevation.
Price: S&W Bright Blue, adj. sights . . . . $408.00 to $443.00

SMITH & WESSON MODEL 29, 629 REVOLVERS
Caliber: 44 Magnum, 6-shot.
Barrel: 6", 8⅜".
Weight: 47 oz. (6" bbl.). **Length:** 11⅜" overall (6" bbl.).
Stocks: Soft rubber; wood optional.
Sights: ⅛" red ramp front, micro-click rear, adjustable for windage and elevation.
Price: S&W Bright Blue, 6" $549.00
Price: S&W Bright Blue, 8⅜" $560.00
Price: Model 629 (stainless steel), 4" $581.00
Price: Model 629, 6" $586.00
Price: Model 629, 8⅜" barrel $600.00

Smith & Wesson Model 29, 629 Classic Revolvers
Similar to the standard Model 29 and 629 except has full-lug 5", 6½" or 8⅜" barrel; chamfered front of cylinder; interchangable red ramp front sight with adjustable white outline rear; Hogue round butt Santoprene grips with S&W monogram; the frame is drilled and tapped for scope mounting. Factory accurizing and endurance packages. Overall length with 5" barrel is 10½"; weight is 51 oz. Introduced 1990.
Price: Model 29 Classic, 5", 6½" $591.00
Price: As above, 8⅜", (blue) $603.00
Price: Model 629 Classic (stainless), 5", 6½" $623.00
Price: As above, 8⅜" $643.00

Smith & Wesson Model 629 Classic DX Revolver
Similar to the Classic Hunters except offered only with 6½" or 8⅜" full-lug barrel; comes with five front sights: 50-yard red ramp; 50-yard black Patridge; 100-yard black Patridge with gold bead; 50-yard black ramp; and 50-yard black Patridge with white dot. Comes with Hogue combat-style round butt grip. Introduced 1991.
Price: Model 629 Classic DX, 6½" $803.00
Price: As above, 8⅜" $829.00

> Consult our Directory pages for
> the location of firms mentioned.

SMITH & WESSON MODEL 36, 37 CHIEFS SPECIAL & AIR-WEIGHT
Caliber: 38 Special, 5-shot.
Barrel: 2", 3".
Weight: 19½ oz. (2" bbl.); 13½ oz. (Airweight). **Length:** 6½" (2" bbl. and round butt).
Stocks: Round butt soft rubber; wood optional.
Sights: Fixed, serrated ramp front, square notch rear.
Price: Blue, standard Model 36, 2" $374.00
Price: As above, 3" $374.00
Price: Blue, Airweight Model 37, 2" only $408.00
Price: As above, nickel, 2" only $424.00

Smith & Wesson Model 36LS, 60LS LadySmith
Similar to the standard Model 36. Available with 2" barrel. Comes with smooth, contoured rosewood grips with the S&W monogram. Has a speedloader cutout. Comes in a fitted carry/storage case. Introduced 1989.
Price: Model 36LS $404.00
Price: Model 60LS (as above except in stainless) . . . $456.00

Smith & Wesson Model 60 3" Full-Lug Revolver
Similar to the Model 60 Chief's Special except has 3" full-lug barrel, adjustable micrometer click black blade rear sight; rubber Uncle Mike's Custom Grade Boot Grip. Overall length 7½"; weight 24½ oz. Introduced 1991.
Price: $453.00

Smith & Wesson Model 60 Chiefs Special Stainless
Same as Model 36 except all stainless construction, 2" bbl. and round butt only.
Price: Stainless steel $427.00

SMITH & WESSON MODEL 27 REVOLVER
Caliber: 357 Magnum and 38 Special, 6-shot.
Barrel: 6".
Weight: 45½ oz. **Length:** 11⁵⁄₁₆" overall.
Stocks: Soft rubber; wood optional. Grooved tangs and trigger.
Sights: Patridge front, micro-click rear adjustable for windage and elevation.
Price: $486.00

Smith & Wesson Model 19

Smith & Wesson Model 27

Smith & Wesson Model 629

Smith & Wesson Model 36LS LadySmith

Smith & Wesson Model 60 3"

SMITH & WESSON MODEL 38 BODYGUARD
Caliber: 38 Special, 5-shot.
Barrel: 2".
Weight: 14½ oz. **Length:** 6⁵⁄₁₆" overall.
Stocks: Soft rubber; wood optional.
Sights: Fixed serrated ramp front, square notch rear.
Features: Alloy frame; internal hammer.
Price: Blue $440.00
Price: Nickel $455.00

Smith & Wesson Model 49, 649 Bodyguard Revolvers
Same as Model 38 except steel construction, weight 20½ oz.
Price: Blued, Model 49 . . . . $405.00
Price: Stainless, Model 649 . . . . $464.00

Smith & Wesson Model 49

SMITH & WESSON MODEL 63 KIT GUN
Caliber: 22 LR, 6-shot.
Barrel: 2", 4".
Weight: 24 oz. (4" bbl.). **Length:** 8³⁄₈" (4" bbl. and round butt).
Stocks: Round butt soft rubber; wood optional.
Sights: Red ramp front, micro-click rear adjustable for windage and elevation.
Features: Stainless steel construction.
Price: 2" $453.00
Price: 4" $458.00

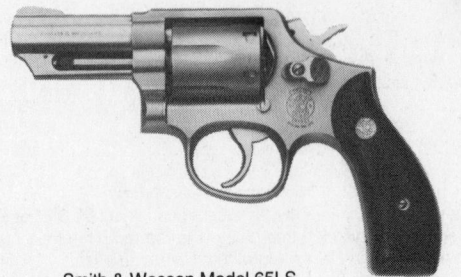

Smith & Wesson Model 65LS

SMITH & WESSON MODEL 65LS LADYSMITH
Caliber: 357 Magnum, 6-shot.
Barrel: 3".
Weight: 31 oz. **Length:** 7.94" overall.
Stocks: Rosewood, round butt.
Sights: Serrated ramp front, fixed notch rear.
Features: Stainless steel with frosted finish. Smooth combat trigger, service hammer, shrouded ejector rod. Comes with soft case. Introduced 1992.
Price: $456.00

SMITH & WESSON MODEL 66 STAINLESS COMBAT MAGNUM
Caliber: 357 Magnum and 38 Special, 6-shot.
Barrel: 2½", 4", 6".
Weight: 36 oz. (4" barrel). **Length:** 9⁹⁄₁₆" overall.
Stocks: Soft rubber; wood optional.
Sights: Red ramp front, micro-click rear adjustable for windage and elevation.
Features: Satin finish stainless steel.
Price: 2½" $461.00
Price: 4", 6" $467.00

SMITH & WESSON MODEL 64 STAINLESS M&P
Caliber: 38 Special, 6-shot.
Barrel: 2", 3", 4".
Weight: 34 oz. **Length:** 9⁵⁄₁₆" overall.
Stocks: Soft rubber; wood optional.
Sights: Fixed, ⅛" serrated ramp front, square notch rear.
Features: Satin finished stainless steel, square butt.
Price: 2" $411.00
Price: 3", 4" $419.00

SMITH & WESSON MODEL 586, 686 DISTINGUISHED COMBAT MAGNUMS
Caliber: 357 Magnum.
Barrel: 4", 6", full shroud.
Weight: 46 oz. (6"), 41 oz. (4").
Stocks: Soft rubber, wood optional.
Sights: Baughman red ramp front, four-position click-adjustable front, S&W micrometer click rear (or fixed).
Features: Uses new L-frame, but takes all K-frame grips. Full-length ejector rod shroud. Smooth combat-type trigger, semi-target type hammer. Trigger stop on 6" models. Also available in stainless as Model 686. Introduced 1981.
Price: Model 586, blue, 4", from $457.00
Price: Model 586, blue, 6" $461.00
Price: Model 686, 6", adjustable front sight $525.00
Price: Model 686, 8³⁄₈" $510.00
Price: Model 686, 2½" $476.00

SMITH & WESSON MODEL 67 COMBAT MASTERPIECE
Caliber: 38 Special, 6-shot.
Barrel: 4".
Weight: 32 oz. **Length:** 9⁵⁄₁₆" overall.
Stocks: Soft rubber; wood optional.
Sights: Red ramp front, micro-click rear adjustable for windage and elevation.
Features: Stainless steel with satin finish. Smooth combat trigger, semi-target hammer. Introduced 1994.
Price: $462.00

Smith & Wesson Model 648 K-22 Masterpiece MRF
Similar to the Model 617 except chambered for 22 WMR cartridge. Available with 6" full-lug barrel only, combat-style square butt grips, combat trigger and semi-target hammer. Introduced 1991.
Price: $464.00

SMITH & WESSON MODEL 617 FULL LUG REVOLVER
Caliber: 22 LR, 6-shot.
Barrel: 4", 6", 8³⁄₈".
Weight: 42 oz. (4" barrel). **Length:** NA.
Stocks: Soft rubber; wood optional.
Sights: Patridge front, adjustable rear.
Features: Stainless steel with satin finish; 4" has .312" smooth trigger, .375" semi-target hammer; 6" has either .312" combat or .400" serrated trigger, .375" semi-target or .500" target hammer; 8³⁄₈" with .400" serrated trigger, .500" target hammer. Introduced 1990.
Price: 4" $455.00
Price: 6", semi-target hammer, combat trigger $460.00
Price: 6", target hammer, target trigger $485.00
Price: 8³⁄₈" $496.00

SMITH & WESSON MODEL 625 REVOLVER
Caliber: 45 ACP, 6-shot.
Barrel: 5".
Weight: 46 oz. **Length:** 11.375" overall.
Stocks: Soft rubber; wood optional.
Sights: Patridge front on ramp, S&W micrometer click rear adjustable for windage and elevation.
Features: Stainless steel construction with .400" semi-target hammer, .312" smooth combat trigger; full lug barrel. Introduced 1989.
Price: $591.00

Smith & Wesson Model 625

CAUTION: PRICES SHOWN ARE SUPPLIED BY THE MANUFACTURER OR IMPORTER. CHECK YOUR LOCAL GUNSHOP.

SMITH & WESSON MODEL 640, 940 CENTENNIAL
Caliber: 38 Special, 9mm Para., 5-shot.
Barrel: 2", 3".
Weight: 20 oz. **Length:** 6⁵⁄₁₆" overall.
Stocks: Soft rubber; wood optional.
Sights: Serrated ramp front, fixed notch rear.
Features: Stainless steel version of the original Model 40 but without the grip safety. Fully concealed hammer, snag-proof smooth edges. Model 640 introduced 1990; Model 940 introduced 1991.
Price: Model 640 (38 Special) **$464.00**
Price: Model 940 (9mm Para., rubber grips) **$470.00**

Smith & Wesson Model 640 Centennial

Smith & Wesson Model 442 Centennial Airweight
Similar to the Model 640 Centennial except has alloy frame giving weight of 15.8 oz. Chambered for 38 Special, 2" carbon steel barrel; carbon steel cylinder; concealed hammer; Uncle Mike's Custom Grade Santoprene grips. Fixed square notch rear sight, serrated ramp front. Introduced 1993.
Price: Blue **$423.00**
Price: Nickel **$438.00**

Smith & Wesson Model 651

SMITH & WESSON MODEL 651 REVOLVER
Caliber: 22 WMR, 6-shot cylinder.
Barrel: 4".
Weight: 24½ oz. **Length:** 8¹¹⁄₁₆" overall.
Stocks: Soft rubber; wood optional.
Sights: Red ramp front, adjustable micrometer click rear.
Features: Stainless steel construction with semi-target hammer, smooth combat trigger. Reintroduced 1991. Limited production.
Price: **$455.00**

SMITH & WESSON MODEL 657 REVOLVER
Caliber: 41 Magnum, 6-shot.
Barrel: 6".
Weight: 48 oz. **Length:** 11⅜" overall.
Stocks: Soft rubber; wood optional.
Sights: Pinned ⅛" red ramp front, micro-click rear adjustable for windage and elevation.
Features: Stainless steel construction.
Price: **$523.00**

TAURUS MODEL 44 REVOLVER
Caliber: 44 Magnum, 6-shot.
Barrel: 4", 6½", 8⅜".
Weight: 44¾ oz. (4" barrel). **Length:** NA.
Stocks: Checkered Brazilian hardwood.
Sights: Serrated ramp front, micro-click rear adjustable for windage and elevation.
Features: Heavy solid rib on 4", vent rib on 6½", 8⅜". Compensated barrel. Blued model has color case-hardened hammer and trigger. Introduced 1994. Imported by Taurus International.
Price: Blue, 4" **$418.00**
Price: Blue, 6½", 8⅜" **$435.00**
Price: Stainless, 4" **$480.00**
Price: Stainless, 6½", 8⅜" **$500.00**

Taurus Model 66

SPORTARMS MODEL HS38S REVOLVER
Caliber: 38 Special, 6-shot.
Barrel: 3", 4".
Weight: 31.3 oz. **Length:** 8" overall (3" barrel).
Stocks: Checkered hardwood; round butt on 3" model, target-style on 4".
Sights: Blade front, adjustable rear.
Features: Polished blue finish; ventilated rib on 4" barrel. Made in Germany by Herbert Schmidt; Imported by Sportarms of Florida.
Price: About **$150.00**

TAURUS MODEL 66 REVOLVER
Caliber: 357 Magnum, 6-shot.
Barrel: 2.5", 4", 6".
Weight: 35 oz.(4" barrel).
Stocks: Checkered Brazilian hardwood.
Sights: Serrated ramp front, micro-click rear adjustable for windage and elevation. Red ramp front with white outline rear on stainlees models only.
Features: Wide target-type hammer spur, floating firing pin, heavy barrel with shrouded ejector rod. Introduced 1978. Imported by Taurus International.
Price: Blue, 2.5" **$313.00**
Price: Blue, 4", 6" **$313.00**
Price: Blue, 4", 6" compensated **$323.00**
Price: Stainless, 2.5" **$393.00**
Price: Stainless, 4", 6" **$393.00**
Price: Stainless, 4", 6" compensated **$463.00**

Taurus Model 65 Revolver
Same as the Model 66 except has fixed rear sight and ramp front. Available with 2.5" or 4" barrel only, round butt grip. Imported by Taurus International.
Price: Blue, 2.5", 4" **$285.00**
Price: Stainless, 2.5", 4" **$355.00**

TAURUS MODEL 80 STANDARD REVOLVER
Caliber: 38 Spec., 6-shot.
Barrel: 3" or 4".
Weight: 30 oz. (4" bbl.). **Length:** 9¼" overall (4" bbl.).
Stocks: Checkered Brazilian hardwood.
Sights: Serrated ramp front, square notch rear.
Features: Imported by Taurus International.
Price: Blue **$248.00**
Price: Stainless **$299.00**

TAURUS MODEL 82 HEAVY BARREL REVOLVER
Caliber: 38 Spec., 6-shot.
Barrel: 3" or 4", heavy.
Weight: 34 oz. (4" bbl.). **Length:** 9¼" overall (4" bbl.).
Stocks: Checkered Brazilian hardwood.
Sights: Serrated ramp front, square notch rear.
Features: Imported by Taurus International.
Price: Blue $248.00
Price: Stainless $299.00

Taurus Model 82

TAURUS MODEL 83 REVOLVER
Caliber: 38 Spec., 6-shot.
Barrel: 4" only, heavy.
Weight: 34 oz.
Stocks: Oversize checkered Brazilian hardwood.
Sights: Ramp front, micro-click rear adjustable for windage and elevation.
Features: Blue or nickel finish. Introduced 1977. Imported by Taurus International.
Price: Blue $260.00
Price: Stainless $309.00

TAURUS MODEL 85 REVOLVER
Caliber: 38 Spec., 5-shot.
Barrel: 2", 3".
Weight: 21 oz.
Stocks: Checkered Brazilian hardwood.
Sights: Ramp front, square notch rear.
Features: Blue, satin nickel finish or stainless steel. Introduced 1980. Imported by Taurus International.
Price: Blue, 2", 3" $276.00
Price: Stainless steel $337.00

Taurus Model 85CH

Taurus Model 85CH Revolver
Same as the Model 85 except has 2" barrel only and concealed hammer. Smooth Brazilian hardwood stocks. Introduced 1991. Imported by Taurus International.
Price: Blue $276.00
Price: Stainless $337.00

TAURUS MODEL 86 REVOLVER
Caliber: 38 Spec., 6-shot.
Barrel: 6" only.
Weight: 34 oz. **Length:** 11¼" overall
Stocks: Oversize target-type, checkered Brazilian hardwood.
Sights: Patridge front, micro-click rear adjustable for windage and elevation.
Features: Blue finish with non-reflective finish on barrel. Imported by Taurus International.
Price: $352.00

Taurus Model 86

TAURUS MODEL 96 REVOLVER
Caliber: 22 LR, 6-shot.
Barrel: 6".
Weight: 34 oz. **Length:** NA.
Stocks: Checkered Brazilian hardwood.
Sights: Patridge-type front, micrometer click rear adjustable for windage and elevation.
Features: Heavy solid barrel rib; target hammer; adjustable target trigger. Blue only. Imported by Taurus International.
Price: $352.00

TAURUS MODEL 669 REVOLVER
Caliber: 357 Mag., 6-shot.
Barrel: 4", 6".
Weight: 37 oz., (4" bbl.).
Stocks: Checkered Brazilian hardwood.
Sights: Serrated ramp front, micro-click rear adjustable for windage and elevation.
Features: Wide target-type hammer, floating firing pin, full-length barrel shroud. Introduced 1988. Imported by Taurus International.
Price: Blue, 4", 6" $322.00
Price: Blue, 4", 6" compensated $340.00
Price: Stainless, 4", 6" $402.00
Price: Stainless, 4", 6" compensated $421.00

Taurus Model 689 Revolver
Same as the Model 669 except has full-length ventilated barrel rib. Available in blue or stainless steel. Introduced 1990. From Taurus International.
Price: Blue, 4" or 6" $335.00
Price: Stainless, 4" or 6" $416.00

TAURUS MODEL 94 REVOLVER
Caliber: 22 LR, 9-shot cylinder.
Barrel: 3", 4".
Weight: 25 oz.
Stocks: Checkered Brazilian hardwood.
Sights: Serrated ramp front, click-adjustable rear for windage and elevation.
Features: Floating firing pin, color case-hardened hammer and trigger. Introduced 1989. Imported by Taurus International.
Price: Blue $288.00
Price: Stainless $339.00

TAURUS MODEL 441/431 REVOLVERS
Caliber: 44 Special, 5-shot.
Barrel: 3", 4", 6".
Weight: 40.4 oz. (6" barrel). **Length:** NA.
Stocks: Checkered Brazilian hardwood.
Sights: Serrated ramp front, micrometer click rear adjustable for windage and elevation.
Features: Heavy barrel with solid rib and full-length ejector shroud. Introduced 1992. Imported by Taurus International.
Price: Blue, 3", 4", 6" $307.00
Price: Stainless, 3", 4", 6" $386.00
Price: Model 431 (fixed sights), blue $281.00
Price: Model 431 (fixed sights), stainless $351.00

TAURUS MODEL 761 REVOLVER
Caliber: 32 H&R Magnum, 6-shot.
Barrel: 6", heavy, solid rib.
Weight: 34 oz.
Stocks: Checkered Brazilian hardwood.
Sights: Patridge-type front, micro-click rear adjustable for windage and elevation.
Features: Target hammer, adjustable target trigger. Blue only. Introduced 1991. Imported by Taurus International.
Price: $326.00

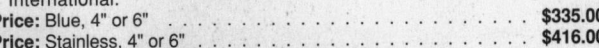

Taurus Model 741 Revolver

Same as the Model 761 except with 3" or 4" heavy barrel only, serrated ramp front sight, micro click rear adjustable for windage and elevation. Introduced 1991. Imported by Taurus International.

Price: Blue, 3", 4" **$254.00**
Price: Stainless, 3", 4" **$342.00**

TAURUS MODEL 941 REVOLVER

Caliber: 22 WMR, 8-shot.
Barrel: 3", 4".
Weight: 27.5 oz. (4" barrel). **Length:** NA.
Stocks: Checkered Brazilian hardwood.
Sights: Serrated ramp front, rear adjustable for windage and elevation.
Features: Solid rib heavy barrel with full-length ejector rod shroud. Blue or stainless steel. Introduced 1992. Imported by Taurus International.

Price: Blue **$310.00**
Price: Stainless **$367.00**

THUNDER FIVE REVOLVER

Caliber: 45 Colt/410 shotshell, 2" and 3"; 5-shot cylinder.
Barrel: 2".
Weight: 48 oz. **Length:** 9" overall.
Stocks: Pachmayr checkered rubber.
Sights: Fixed.
Features: Double action with ambidextrous hammer-block safety; squared trigger guard; internal draw bar safety. Made of chrome moly steel, with matte blue finish. Announced 1991. From Holston Ent.

Price: **$549.00**
Price: Model T-70, 45-70 Gov't. (from Dragun Ent.) **$599.00**

Wesson Firearms Model 9, 15 & 32M Revolvers

Same as Models 8 and 14 except they have adjustable sight. Model 9 chambered for 38 Special, Model 15 for 357 Magnum. Model 32M is chambered for 32 H&R Mag. Same specs and prices as for Model 15 guns. Available in blue or stainless. Contact Wesson Firearms for complete price list.

Price: Model 9-2 or 15-2, 2½", blue **$338.00**
Price: As above except in stainless **$366.00**

Wesson Firearms Model 15 Gold Series

Similar to the Model 15 except has smoother action to reduce DA pull to 8-10 lbs.; comes with either 6" or 8" vent heavy slotted barrel shroud with bright blue barrel. Shroud is stamped "Gold Series" with the Wesson signature engraved and gold filled. Hammer and trigger are polished bright; rosewood grips. New sights with orange dot Patridge front, white triangle on rear blade. Introduced 1989.

Price: 6" . . . . **NA**
Price: 8" . . . . **NA**

WESSON FIREARMS FB44, FB744 REVOLVERS

Caliber: 44 Magnum, 6-shot.
Barrel: 4", 5", 6", 8".
Weight: 50 oz. (4" barrel). **Length:** 9¾" overall (4" barrel).
Stocks: Hogue finger-groove rubber.
Sights: Interchangeable blade front, fully adjustable rear.
Features: Fixed, non-vented heavy barrel shrouds, but other features same as other Wesson revolvers. Brushed stainless or polished blue finish. Introduced 1994. Made in U.S. by Wesson Firearms Co., Inc.

Price: FB44-4 (4", blue) **$400.00**
Price: As above, stainless (FB744-4) **$442.00**
Price: FB44-5 (5", blue) **$403.00**
Price: As above, stainless (FB744-5) **$444.00**
Price: FB44-6 (6", blue) **$407.00**
Price: As above, stainless (FB744-6) **$448.00**
Price: FB44-8 (8", blue) **$414.00**
Price: As above, stainless (FB744-8) **$455.00**

Wesson FB15

Taurus Model 741

WESSON FIREARMS MODEL 8 & MODEL 14

Caliber: 38 Special (Model 8); 357 (Model 14), both 6-shot.
Barrel: 2½", 4", 6"; interchangeable.
Weight: 30 oz. (2½"). **Length:** 9¼" overall (4" bbl.).
Stocks: Checkered, interchangeable.
Sights: ⅛" serrated front, fixed rear.
Features: Interchangeable barrels and grips; smooth, wide trigger; wide hammer spur with short double-action travel. Available in stainless or Brite blue. Contact Wesson Firearms for complete price list.

Price: Model 8-2, 2½", blue **$267.00**
Price: As above except in stainless **$311.00**
Price: Model 714-2 Pistol Pac, stainless **$522.00**

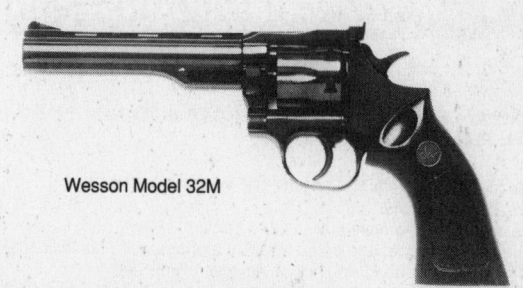

Wesson Model 32M

WESSON FIREARMS MODEL 22 REVOLVER

Caliber: 22 LR, 22 WMR, 6-shot.
Barrel: 2½", 4", 6", 8"; interchangeable.
Weight: 36 oz. (2½"), 44 oz. (6"). **Length:** 9¼" overall (4" barrel).
Stocks: Checkered; undercover, service or over-size target.
Sights: ⅛" serrated, interchangeable front, white outline rear adjustable for windage and elevation.
Features: Built on the same frame as the Wesson 357; smooth, wide trigger with over-travel adjustment, wide spur hammer, with short double-action travel. Available in Brite blue or stainless steel. Contact Wesson Firearms for complete price list.

Price: 2½" bbl., blue **$349.00**
Price: As above, stainless **$391.00**
Price: With 4", vent. rib, blue **$381.00**
Price: As above, stainless **$423.00**
Price: Blue Pistol Pac, 22 LR **$637.00**

WESSON FIREARMS FB15, FB715 REVOLVERS

Caliber: 357 Magnum, 6-shot.
Barrel: 2½", 4" (Service models), 3", 4", 5", 6" (target models).
Weight: 40 oz. (4" barrel). **Length:** 9¾" overall (4" barrel).
Stocks: Service style or Hogue rubber.
Sights: Blade front, adjustable rear (Target); fixed rear on Service.
Features: Fixed barrels, but other features same as other Wesson revolvers. Service models in brushed stainless, satin blue, Target in brushed stainless or polished blue. Introduced 1993. Made in U.S. by Wesson Firearms Co., Inc.

Price: FB14-2 (Service, 2½", blue) **$249.00**
Price: As above, 4" **$254.00**
Price: FB714-2 (Service, 2½", stainless) **$268.00**
Price: As above, 4" **$274.00**
Price: FB15-3 (Target, 3", blue) **$259.00**
Price: As above, 5" **$272.00**
Price: FB715 (Target, 4", stainless) **$284.00**
Price: As above, 6" **$298.00**

CAUTION: PRICES SHOWN ARE SUPPLIED BY THE MANUFACTURER OR IMPORTER. CHECK YOUR LOCAL GUNSHOP.

49th EDITION, 1995 **317**

WESSON FIREARMS HUNTER SERIES REVOLVERS
Caliber: 357 Supermag, 41 Mag., 44 Mag., 445 Supermag, 6-shot.
Barrel: 6", 7½", depending upon model.
Weight: About 64 oz. **Length:** 14" overall.
Stocks: Hogue finger-groove rubber, wood presentation.
Sights: Blade front, dovetailed Iron Sight Gunworks rear.
Features: Fixed barrel revolvers. Barrels have 1:18.75" twist, Alan Taylor two-stage forcing cone; non-fluted cylinder; bright blue or satin stainless. Introduced 1994. Made in U.S. by Wesson Firearms Co., Inc.
Price: Open Hunter (open sights, 7½" barrel), blue **$804.94**
Price: As above, stainless **$848.63**
Price: Compensated Open Hunter (6" compensated barrel, 7" shroud), blue **$836.98**
Price: As above, stainless **$880.65**
Price: Scoped Hunter (7½" barrel, no sights, comes with scope rings on shroud), blue **$837.97**
Price: As above, stainless **$880.96**
Price: Compensated Scoped Hunter (6" barrel, 7" shroud, scope rings on shroud), blue **$870.73**
Price: As above, stainless **$913.72**

WESSON FIREARMS MODEL 738P REVOLVER
Caliber: 38 Special +P, 5-shot.
Barrel: 2".
Weight: 24.6 oz. **Length:** 6.5" overall.
Stocks: Pauferro wood or rubber.
Sights: Blade front, fixed notch rear.
Features: Designed for +P ammunition. Stainless steel construction. Introduced 1992. Made in U.S. by Wesson Firearms Co., Inc.
Price: **$285.00**

WESSON FIREARMS MODEL 41V, 44V, 45V REVOLVERS
Caliber: 41 Mag., 44 Mag., 45 Colt, 6-shot.
Barrel: 4", 6", 8", 10"; interchangeable.
Weight: 48 oz. (4"). **Length:** 12" overall (6" bbl.).
Stocks: Smooth.
Sights: ⅛" serrated front, white outline rear adjustable for windage and elevation.
Features: Available in blue or stainless steel. Smooth, wide trigger with adjustable over-travel; wide hammer spur. Available in Pistol Pac set also. Contact Wesson Firearms for complete price list.
Price: 41 Mag., 4", vent **$433.55**
Price: As above except in stainless **$508.30**
Price: 44 Mag., 4", blue **$433.55**
Price: As above except in stainless **$508.30**
Price: 45 Colt, 4", vent **$433.55**
Price: As above except in stainless **$508.30**

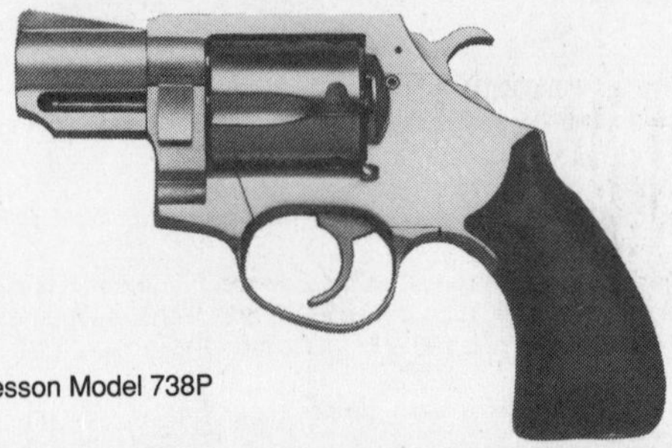

Wesson Model 738P

HANDGUNS—SINGLE-ACTION REVOLVERS

Both classic six-shooters and modern adaptations for hunting and sport.

AMERICAN ARMS REGULATOR SINGLE ACTIONS
Caliber: 357 Mag. 44-40, 45 Colt.
Barrel: 4¾", 5½", 7½".
Weight: 32 oz. (4¾" barrel) **Length:** 8⅙" overall (4¾" barrel).
Stocks: Smooth walnut.
Sights: Blade front, groove rear.
Features: Blued barrel and cylinder, brass trigger guard and backstrap. Introduced 1992. Imported from Italy by American Arms, Inc.
Price: Regulator, single cylinder **$305.00**
Price: Regulator, dual cylinder (44-40/44 Spec. or 45 Colt/45 ACP) . **$349.00**
Price: Regulator DLX (all steel) **$349.00**

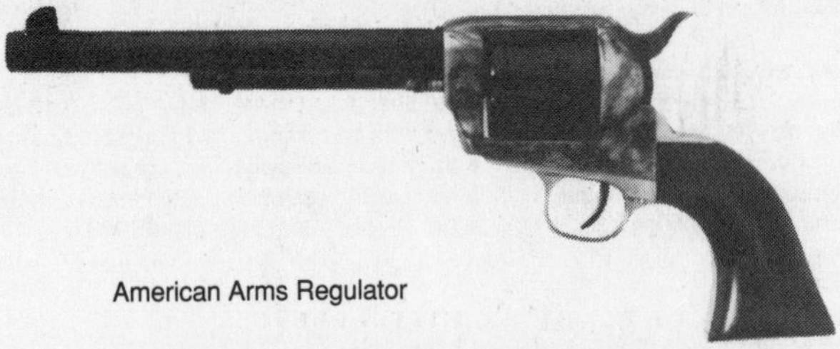

American Arms Regulator

American Arms Buckhorn Single Action
Similar to the Regulator single action except chambered for 44 Magnum. Available with 4¾", 6" or 7½" barrel. Overall length 11¾", weight is 44 oz. with 6" barrel. Introduced 1993. Imported from Italy by American Arms, Inc.
Price: **$339.00**
Price: Buckhorn Target (with target sights) **$349.00**

CONSULT
SHOOTER'S MARKETPLACE
Page 225, This Issue

CENTURY GUN DIST. MODEL 100 SINGLE ACTION
Caliber: 30-30, 375 Win., 444 Marlin, 45-70, 50-70.
Barrel: 6½" (standard), 8", 10", 12".
Weight: 6 lbs. (loaded). **Length:** 15" overall (8" bbl.).
Stocks: Smooth walnut.
Sights: Ramp front, Millett adjustable square notch rear.
Features: Highly polished high tensile strength manganese bronze frame, blue cylinder and barrel; coil spring trigger mechanism. Calibers other than 45-70 start at $2,000.00. Contact maker for full price information. Introduced 1975. Made in U.S. From Century Gun Dist., Inc.
Price: 6½" barrel, 45-70 . . . . **$1,250.00**

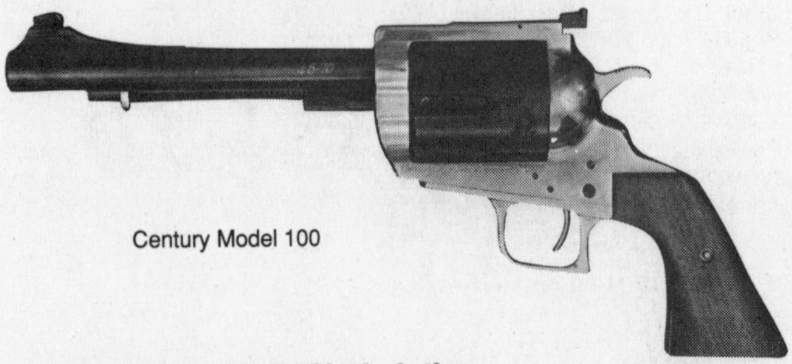

Century Model 100

CIMARRON U.S. CAVALRY MODEL SINGLE ACTION
Caliber: 45 Colt
Barrel: 7½".
Weight: 42 oz. **Length:** 13½" overall.
Stocks: Walnut.
Sights: Fixed.
Features: Has "A.P. Casey" markings; "U.S." plus patent dates on frame, serial number on backstrap, trigger guard, frame and cylinder, "APC" cartouche on left grip; color case-hardened frame and hammer, rest charcoal blue. Exact copy of the original. Imported by Cimarron Arms.
Price: . . . . **$459.00.**

Cimarron Artillery Model Single Action
Similar to the U.S. Cavalry model except has 5½" barrel, weighs 39 oz., and is 11½" overall. U.S. markings and cartouche, case-hardened frame and hammer; 45 Colt only.
Price: **$459.00**

CAUTION: PRICES SHOWN ARE SUPPLIED BY THE MANUFACTURER OR IMPORTER. CHECK YOUR LOCAL GUNSHOP.

CIMARRON 1873 PEACEMAKER REPRO
Caliber: 38 WCF, 357 Mag., 44 WCF, 44 Spec., 45 Colt.
Barrel: 4¾", 5½", 7½".
Weight: 39 oz. **Length:** 10" overall (4" barrel).
Stocks: Walnut.
Sights: Blade front, fixed or adjustable rear.
Features: Uses "old model" blackpowder frame with "Bullseye" ejector or New Model frame. Imported by Cimarron Arms.
Price: Peacemaker, 4¾" barrel $429.95
Price: Frontier Six Shooter, 5½" barrel $429.95
Price: Single Action Army, 7½" barrel $429.95

Cimarron Peacemaker

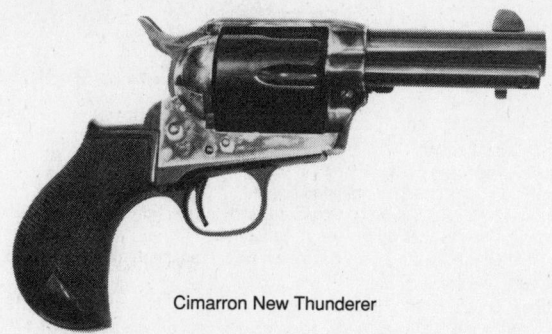

Cimarron New Thunderer

CIMARRON NEW THUNDERER REVOLVER
Caliber: 357 Mag., 44 WCF, 44 Spec., 45 Colt, 6-shot.
Barrel: 3½", 4¾", with ejector.
Weight: 38 oz. (3½" barrel). **Length:** NA.
Stocks: Hand-checkered walnut.
Sights: Blade front, notch rear.
Features: Thunderer grip; color case-hardened frame with balance blued, or nickel finish. Introduced 1993. Imported by Cimarron Arms.
Price: Color case-hardened $429.95
Price: Nickeled $529.95

COLT SINGLE ACTION ARMY REVOLVER
Caliber: 44-40, 45 Colt, 6-shot.
Barrel: 4¾", 5½", 7½".
Weight: 40 oz. (4¾" barrel). **Length:** 10¼" overall (4¾" barrel).
Stocks: American walnut.
Sights: Blade front, notch rear.
Features: Available in full nickel finish with nickel grip medallions, or Royal Blue with color case-hardened frame, gold grip medallions. Reintroduced 1992.
Price: $1,213.00

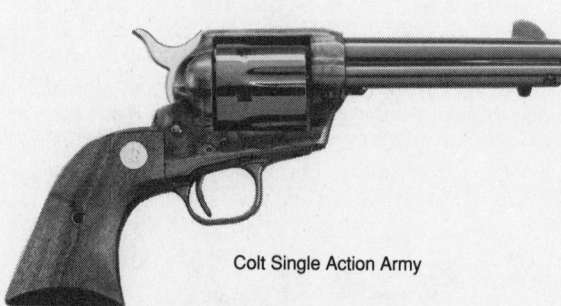

Colt Single Action Army

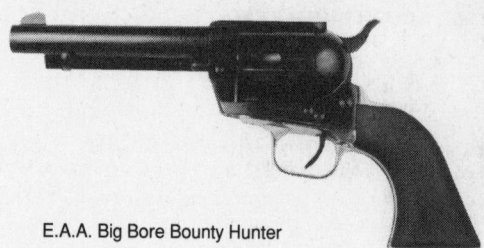

E.A.A. Big Bore Bounty Hunter

E.A.A. BIG BORE BOUNTY HUNTER SA REVOLVERS
Caliber: 357 Mag., 41 Mag., 44-40, 44 Mag., 45 Colt, 6-shot.
Barrel: 4⅝", 7½".
Weight: 2.5 lbs. **Length:** 11" overall (4⅝" barrel).
Stocks: Smooth walnut.
Sights: Blade front, grooved topstrap rear.
Features: Transfer bar safety; three position hammer; hammer forged barrel. Introduced 1992. Imported by European American Armory.
Price: Blue $299.00
Price: Color case-hardened frame $310.00
Price: Chrome-plated $350.00

E.A.A. BOUNTY HUNTER REVOLVER
Caliber: 22 LR, 22 WMR, 6-shot cylinder.
Barrel: 4¾", 6", 9".
Weight: 32 oz. **Length:** 10" overall (4¾" barrel).
Stocks: European hardwood.
Sights: Blade front, adjustable rear.
Features: Available in blue finish only. Introduced 1991. From European American Armory Corp.
Price: 4¾", blue $80.00
Price: 4¾", blue, 22 LR/22 WMR combo $99.00
Price: 6", blue, 22 LR/22 WMR combo $125.00
Price: 9", blue, 22 LR/22 WMR combo $110.00

E.A.A. Bounty Hunter

EMF Dakota 1890 Police Revolver
Similar to the 1875 Outlaw except has 5½" barrel, weighs 40 oz., with 12½" overall length. Has lanyard ring in butt. No web under barrel. Calibers 357, 44-40, 45 Colt. Imported by E.M.F.
Price: All calibers $470.00
Price: Nickel $560.00
Price: Engraved $620.00
Price: Engraved nickel $725.00

EMF DAKOTA 1875 OUTLAW REVOLVER
Caliber: 357, 44-40, 45 Colt.
Barrel: 7½".
Weight: 46 oz. **Length:** 13½" overall.
Stocks: Smooth walnut.
Sights: Blade front, fixed groove rear.
Features: Authentic copy of 1875 Remington with firing pin in hammer; color case-hardened frame, blue cylinder, barrel, steel backstrap and brass trigger guard. Also available in nickel, factory engraved. Imported by E.M.F.
Price: All calibers $465.00
Price: Nickel $550.00
Price: Engraved $600.00
Price: Engraved Nickel $710.00

CAUTION: PRICES SHOWN ARE SUPPLIED BY THE MANUFACTURER OR IMPORTER. CHECK YOUR LOCAL GUNSHOP.

HANDGUNS—SINGLE-ACTION REVOLVERS

EMF DAKOTA HARTFORD SINGLE-ACTION REVOLVERS
Caliber: 22 LR, 357 Mag., 32-20, 38-40, 44-40, 44 Spec., 45 Colt.
Barrel: 4¾", 5½", 7½".
Weight: 45 oz. **Length:** 13" overall (7½" barrel).
Stocks: Smooth walnut.
Sights: Blade front, fixed rear.
Features: Identical to the origianl Colts with inspector cartouche on left grip, original patent dates and U.S. markings. All major parts serial numbered using original Colt-style lettering, numbering. Bullseye ejector head and color case-hardening on frame and hammer. Introduced 1990. From E.M.F.
Price: $600.00
Price: Cavalry or Artillery $655.00
Price: Nickel plated $725.00
Price: Pinkerton (bird's-head grip), 45 Colt, 4" barrel ... $680.00
Price: Bisley Model (45 Colt) $680.00
Price: Nickel plated $805.00

EMF Dakota New Model Single-Action Revolvers
Similar to the standard Dakota except has color case-hardened forged steel frame, black nickel backstrap and trigger guard. Calibers 357 Mag., 44-40, 45 Colt only.
Price: $460.00
Price: Nickel $585.00

Freedom Arms Casull Model 353 Revolver
Similar to the Premier 454 Casull except chambered for 357 Magnum with 5-shot cylinder; 4¾", 6", 7½" or 9" barrel. Weighs 59 oz. with 7½" barrel. Standard model has adjustable sights, matte finish, Pachmayr grips, 7½" or 9" barrel; Silhouette has 9" barrel, Patridge front sight, Iron Sight Gun Works Silhouette adjustable rear, Pachmayr grips, trigger over-travel adjustment screw. All stainless steel. Introduced 1992.
Price: Field Grade $1,175.00
Price: Premier Grade (brushed finish, impregnated hardwood grips, Premier Grade sights) $1,480.00
Price: Silhouette $1,267.05

HERITAGE ROUGH RIDER REVOLVER
Caliber: 22 LR, 22 LR/22 WMR combo, 6-shot.
Barrel: 3", 4¾", 6½", 9".
Weight: 31 to 38 oz. **Length:** NA
Stocks: Goncolo Alves.
Sights: Blade front, fixed rear.
Features: Hammer block safety. High polish blue finish, gold-tone screws, polished hammer. Introduced 1993. Made in U.S. by Heritage Mfg., Inc.
Price: .... $89.95 to $129.95

MITCHELL SINGLE-ACTION ARMY REVOLVERS
Caliber: 357 Mag., 45 ACP, 45 Colt, 6-shot.
Barrel: 4¾", 5½", 7½".
Weight: NA. **Length:** NA.
Stocks: One-piece walnut.
Sights: Serrated ramp front, fixed or adjustable rear.
Features: Color case-hardened frame, brass or steel backstrap/trigger guard; hammer-block safety. Bright nickel-plated model and dual cylinder models available. Contact importer for complete price list. Imported by Mitchell Arms, Inc.
Price: Cowboy, 4¾", Army 5½", Cavalry 7½", blue, 357, 45 Colt, 45 ACP $399.00
Price: As above, nickel $439.00
Price: 45 Colt/45 ACP dual cyl., blue $549.00
Price: As above, nickel $588.00
Price: Bat Masterson model, 45 Colt, 4¾", nickel $439.00

Freedom 454 Field Grade

FREEDOM ARMS PREMIER 454 CASULL
Caliber: 44 Mag., 454 Casull with 45 Colt, 45 ACP, 45 Win. Mag. optional cylinders, 5-shot.
Barrel: 4¾", 6", 7½", 10".
Weight: 50 oz. **Length:** 14" overall (7½" bbl.).
Stocks: Impregnated hardwood.
Sights: Blade front, notch or adjustable rear.
Features: All stainless steel construction; sliding bar safety system. Lifetime warranty. Made in U.S. by Freedom Arms, Inc.
Price: Field Grade (matte finish, Pachmayr grips), adjustable sights, 4¾", 6", 7½", 10" $1,175.00
Price: Field Grade, fixed sights, 4¾" only $1,119.00
Price: Field Grade, 44 Rem. Mag., adjustable sights, all lengths ... $1,175.00
Price: Premier Grade (brush finish, impregnated hardwood grips) adjustable sights, 4¾", 6", 7½", 10" $1,480.00
Price: Premier Grade, fixed sights, 7½" only $1,396.00
Price: Premier Grade, 44 Rem. Mag., adjustable sights, all lengths ... $1,480.00
Price: Fitted 45 ACP or 45 Colt cylinder, add $233.00

Freedom Arms Model 555 Revolver
Same as the 454 Casull except chambered for the 50 A.E. (Action Express) cartridge. Offered in Premier and Field Grades with adjustable sights, 4¾", 6", 7½" or 10" barrel. Introduced 1994. Made in U.S. by Freedom Arms, Inc.
Price: Premier Grade $1,480.00
Price: Field Grade $1,175.00

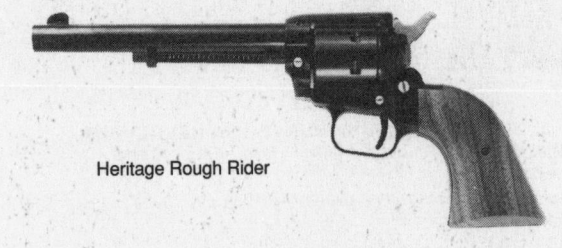

Heritage Rough Rider

Mitchell Single Action

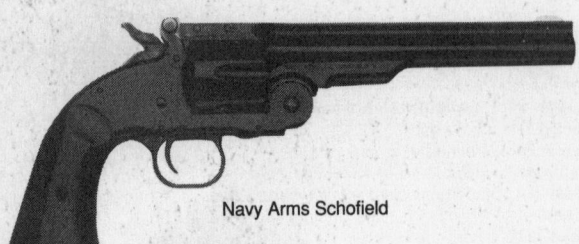

Navy Arms Schofield

NAVY ARMS 1875 SCHOFIELD REVOLVER
Caliber: 44-40, 45 Colt, 6-shot cylinder.
Barrel: 5", 7".
Weight: 39 oz. **Length:** 10¾" overall (5" barrel).
Stocks: Smooth walnut.
Sights: Blade front, notch rear.
Features: Replica of Smith & Wesson Model 3 Schofield. Single-action, top-break with automatic ejection. Polished blue finish. Introduced 1994. Imported by Navy Arms.
Price: Wells Fargo (5" barrel, Wells Fargo markings) $795.00
Price: U.S. Cavalry model (7" barrel, military markings $795.00

CAUTION: PRICES SHOWN ARE SUPPLIED BY THE MANUFACTURER OR IMPORTER. CHECK YOUR LOCAL GUNSHOP.

HANDGUNS—SINGLE-ACTION REVOLVERS

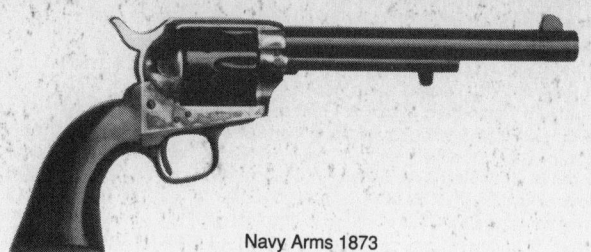

Navy Arms 1873

North American Mini

North American Mini-Master

Phelps Heritage I

Ruger Blackhawk

NAVY ARMS 1873 SINGLE-ACTION REVOLVER
Caliber: 44-40, 45 Colt, 6-shot cylinder.
Barrel: 3", 4¾", 5½", 7½".
Weight: 36 oz. **Length:** 10¾" overall (5½" barrel).
Stocks: Smooth walnut.
Sights: Blade front, groove in topstrap rear.
Features: Blue with color case-hardened frame, or nickel. Introduced 1991. Imported by Navy Arms.
Price: Blue $390.00
Price: Nickel $455.00
Price: Economy model with brass backstrap and trigger guard . . . $340.00
Price: 1873 U.S. Cavalry Model (7½", 45 Colt, arsenal markings) . . $480.00
Price: 1895 U.S. Artillery Model (as above, 5½" barrel) $480.00

NORTH AMERICAN MINI-REVOLVERS
Caliber: 22 LR, 22 WMR, 5-shot.
Barrel: 1⅛", 1⅝".
Weight: 4 to 6.6 oz. **Length:** 3⅝" to 6⅛" overall.
Stocks: Laminated wood.
Sights: Blade front, notch fixed rear.
Features: All stainless steel construction. Polished satin and matte finish. Engraved models available. From North American Arms.
Price: 22 LR, 1⅛" bbl. $157.00
Price: 22 LR, 1⅝" bbl. $157.00
Price: 22 WMR, 1⅝" bbl. $178.00
Price: 22 WMR, 1⅛" or 1⅝" bbl. with extra 22 LR cylinder $210.00

NORTH AMERICAN MINI-MASTER
Caliber: 22 LR, 22 WMR, 5-shot cylinder.
Barrel: 4".
Weight: 10.7 oz. **Length:** 7.75" overall.
Stocks: Checkered hard black rubber.
Sights: Blade front, white outline rear adjustable for elevation, or fixed.
Features: Heavy vent barrel; full-size grips. Non-fluted cylinder. Introduced 1989.
Price: Adjustable sight, 22 WMR or 22 LR $279.00
Price: As above with extra WMR/LR cylinder $317.00
Price: Fixed sight, 22 WMR or 22 LR $264.00
Price: As above with extra WMR/LR cylinder $302.00

North American Black Widow Revolver
Similar to the Mini-Master except has 2" Heavy Vent barrel. Built on the 22 WMR frame. Non-fluted cylinder, black rubber grips. Available with either Millett Low Profile fixed sights or Millett sight adjustable for elevation only. Overall length 5⅞", weight 8.8 oz. From North American Arms.
Price: Adjustable sight, 22 LR or 22 WMR $249.00
Price: As above with extra WMR/LR cylinder $285.00
Price: Fixed sight, 22 LR or 22 WMR $235.00
Price: As above with extra WMR/LR cylinder $270.00

PHELPS HERITAGE I, EAGLE I, GRIZZLY REVOLVERS
Caliber: 444 Marlin, 45-70, 50-70, 6-shot.
Barrel: 8", 12", 16" (45-70).
Weight: 5½ lbs. **Length:** 19½" overall (12" bbl.).
Stocks: Smooth walnut.
Sights: Ramp front, adjustable rear.
Features: Single action; polished blue finish; safety bar. From Phelps Mfg. Co.
Price: 8", 45-70 or 444 Marlin, about $1,185.00
Price: 12", 45-70 or 444 Marlin, about $1,265.00
Price: 8", 50-70, about $1,550.00

RUGER BLACKHAWK REVOLVER
Caliber: 30 Carbine, 357 Mag./38 Spec., 41 Mag., 45 Colt, 6-shot.
Barrel: 4⅝" or 6½", either caliber; 7½" (30 Carbine, 45 Colt only).
Weight: 42 oz. (6½" bbl.). **Length:** 12¼" overall (6½" bbl.).
Stocks: American walnut.
Sights: ⅛" ramp front, micro-click rear adjustable for windage and elevation.
Features: Ruger interlock mechanism, independent firing pin, hardened chrome moly steel frame, music wire springs throughout.
Price: Blue, 30 Carbine (7½" bbl.), BN31 . . . . $328.00
Price: Blue, 357 Mag. (4⅝", 6½"), BN34, BN36 . . . . $328.00
Price: Blue, 357/9mm Convertible (4⅝", 6½"), BN34X, BN36X $343.50
Price: Blue, 41 Mag., 45 Colt (4⅝", 6½"), BN41, BN42, BN45 . . . . $328.00
Price: Stainless, 357 Mag. (4⅝", 6½"), KBN34, KBN36 . . . . $404.00
Price: High-gloss stainless, 357 Mag. (4⅝", 6½"), GKBN34, GKBN36 . . . . $404.00
Price: High-gloss stainless, 45 Colt (4⅝", 7½"), GKBN44, GKBN45 . . . . $404.00

Ruger Bisley Single-Action Revolver
Similar to standard Blackhawk except the hammer is lower with a smoothly curved, deeply checkered wide spur. The trigger is strongly curved with a wide smooth surface. Longer grip frame has a hand-filling shape. Adjustable rear sight, ramp-style front. Has an unfluted cylinder and roll engraving, adjustable sights. Chambered for 357, 41, 44 Mags. and 45 Colt; 7½" barrel; overall length of 13". Introduced 1985.
Price: $391.00

CAUTION: PRICES SHOWN ARE SUPPLIED BY THE MANUFACTURER OR IMPORTER. CHECK YOUR LOCAL GUNSHOP.

49th EDITION, 1995 **321**

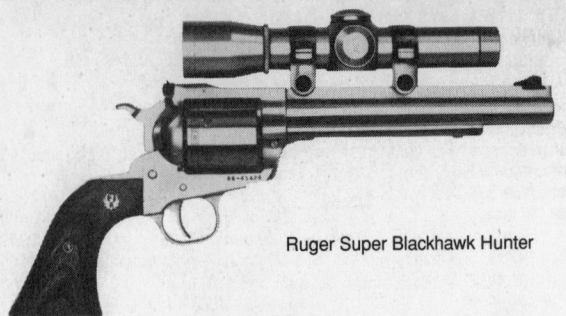

Ruger Super Blackhawk Hunter

Ruger New Super Bearcat

Ruger SSM Single-Six

Ruger Bisley

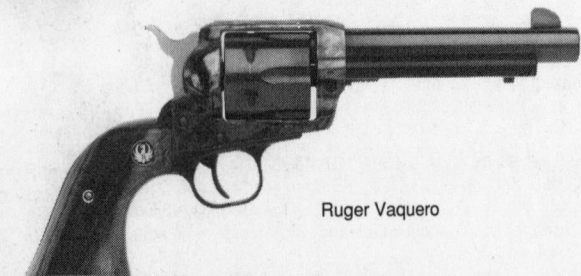

Ruger Vaquero

RUGER SUPER BLACKHAWK

Caliber: 44 Magnum, 6-shot. Also fires 44 Spec.
Barrel: 4⅝", 5½", 7½", 10½".
Weight: 48 oz. (7½" bbl.), 51 oz. (10½" bbl.). **Length:** 13⅜" overall (7½" bbl.).
Stocks: American walnut.
Sights: ⅛" ramp front, micro-click rear adjustable for windage and elevation.
Features: Ruger interlock mechanism, non-fluted cylinder, steel grip and cylinder frame, square back trigger guard, wide serrated trigger and wide spur hammer.
Price: Blue (S45N, S47N, S411N) **$378.50**
Price: Stainless (KS45N, KS47N, KS411N) **$413.75**
Price: Stainless KS47NH Hunter with scope rings, 7½" **$479.50**
Price: High-gloss stainless (4⅝", 5½", 7½"), GKS458N, GKS45N, GKS47N **$413.75**

RUGER NEW SUPER BEARCAT SINGLE ACTION

Caliber: 22 LR/22 WMR, 6-shot.
Barrel: 4".
Weight: 23 oz. **Length:** 8⅞" overall.
Stocks: Smooth rosewood with Ruger medallion.
Sights: Blade front, fixed notch rear.
Features: Reintroduction of the Ruger Super Bearcat with slightly lengthened frame, Ruger patented transfer bar safety system. Comes with two cylinders. Available in blue or stainless steel. Introduced 1993. From Sturm, Ruger & Co.
Price: SBC4, blue **$298.00**
Price: KSBC4, stainless **$325.00**

RUGER SUPER SINGLE-SIX CONVERTIBLE

Caliber: 22 LR, 6-shot; 22 WMR in extra cylinder.
Barrel: 4⅝", 5½", 6½", or 9½" (6-groove).
Weight: 34½ oz. (6½" bbl.). **Length:** 11¹³⁄₁₆" overall (6½" bbl.).
Stocks: Smooth American walnut.
Sights: Improved Patridge front on ramp, fully adjustable rear protected by integral frame ribs; or fixed sight.
Features: Ruger interlock mechanism, transfer bar ignition, gate-controlled loading, hardened chrome moly steel frame, wide trigger, music wire springs throughout, independent firing pin.
Price: 4⅝", 5½", 6½", 9½" barrel, blue, fixed or adjustable sight (5½", 6½") **$281.00**
Price: 5½", 6½" bbl. only, high-gloss stainless steel, fixed or adjustable sight **$354.00**

Ruger SSM Single-Six Revolver

Similar to the Super Single-Six revolver except chambered for 32 H&R Magnum (also handles 32 S&W and 32 S&W Long). Weight is about 34 oz. with 6½" barrel. Barrel lengths: 4⅝", 5½", 6½", 9½". Introduced 1985.
Price: **$281.00**

Ruger Bisley Small Frame Revolver

Similar to the Single-Six except frame is styled after the classic Bisley "flat-top." Most mechanical parts are unchanged. Hammer is lower and smoothly curved with a deeply checkered spur. Trigger is strongly curved with a wide smooth surface. Longer grip frame designed with a hand-filling shape, and the trigger guard is a large oval. Adjustable dovetail rear sight; front sight base accepts interchangeable square blades of various heights and styles. Has an unfluted cylinder and roll engraving. Weight about 41 oz. Chambered for 22 LR and 32 H&R Mag., 6½" barrel only. Introduced 1985.
Price: **$328.75**

> Consult our Directory pages for the location of firms mentioned.

SPORTARMS MODEL HS21S SINGLE ACTION

Caliber: 22 LR or 22 LR/22 WMR combo, 6-shot.
Barrel: 5½".
Weight: 33.5 oz. **Length:** 11" overall.
Stocks: Smooth hardwood.
Sights: Blade front, rear drift adjustable for windage.
Features: Available in blue with imitation stag or wood stocks. Made in Germany by Herbert Schmidt; Imported by Sportarms of Florida.
Price: 22 LR, blue, "stag" grips, about **$100.00**
Price: 22 LR/22 WMR combo, blue, wood stocks, about **$120.00**

RUGER VAQUERO SINGLE-ACTION REVOLVER

Caliber: 44-40, 44 Magnum, 45 Colt, 6-shot.
Barrel: 4⅝", 5½", 7½".
Weight: 41 oz. **Length:** 13⅜" overall (7½" barrel).
Stocks: Smooth rosewood with Ruger medallion.
Sights: Blade front, fixed notch rear.
Features: Uses Ruger's patented transfer bar safety system and loading gate interlock with classic styling. Blued model has color case-hardened finish on the frame, the rest polished and blued. Stainless model is polished. Introduced 1993. From Sturm, Ruger & Co.
Price: BNV44 (4⅝"), BNV445 (5½"), BNV45 (7½"), blue **$394.00**
Price: KBNV44 (4⅝"), KBNV455 (5½"), KBNV45 (7½"), stainless . **$394.00**

CAUTION: PRICES SHOWN ARE SUPPLIED BY THE MANUFACTURER OR IMPORTER. CHECK YOUR LOCAL GUNSHOP.

TEXAS LONGHORN ARMS GROVER'S IMPROVED NO. FIVE
Caliber: 44 Magnum, 6-shot.
Barrel: 5½".
Weight: 44 oz. **Length:** NA.
Stocks: Fancy AAA walnut.
Sights: Square blade front on ramp, fully adjustable rear.
Features: Music wire coil spring action with double locking bolt; polished blue finish. Handmade in limited 1,200-gun production. Grip contour, straps, oversized base pin, lever latch and lockwork identical copies of Elmer Keith design. Lifetime warranty to original owner. Introduced 1988.
Price: **$985.00**

Texas Longhorn Grover's No. Five

TEXAS LONGHORN ARMS RIGHT-HAND SINGLE ACTION
Caliber: All centerfire pistol calibers.
Barrel: 4¾".
Weight: NA. **Length:** NA.
Stocks: One-piece fancy walnut, or any fancy AAA wood.
Sights: Blade front, grooved topstrap rear.
Features: Loading gate and ejector housing on left side of gun. Cylinder rotates to the left. All steel construction; color case-hardened frame; high polish blue; music wire coil springs. Lifetime guarantee to original owner. Introduced 1984. From Texas Longhorn Arms.
Price: South Texas Army Limited Edition—handmade, only 1,000 to be produced; "One of One Thousand" engraved on barrel **$1,500.00**

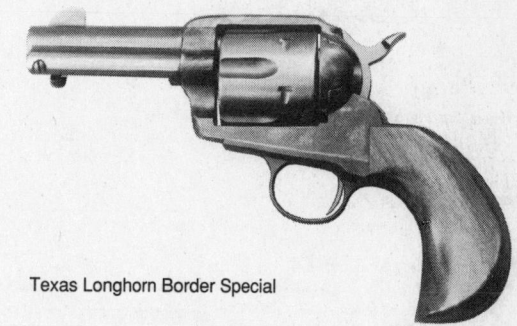

Texas Longhorn Border Special

Texas Longhorn Arms Texas Border Special
Similar to the South Texas Army Limited Edition except has 3½" barrel, bird's-head style grip. Same special features. Introduced 1984.
Price: **$1,500.00**

Texas Longhorn Arms Sesquicentennial Model Revolver
Similar to the South Texas Army Model except has ¾-coverage Nimschke-style engraving, antique golden nickel plate finish, one-piece elephant ivory grips. Comes with handmade solid walnut presentation case, factory letter to owner. Limited edition of 150 units. Introduced 1986.
Price: **$2,500.00**

Texas Longhorn Arms West Texas Flat Top Target
Similar to the South Texas Army Limited Edition except choice of barrel length from 7½" through 15"; flat-top style frame; ⅛" contoured ramp front sight, old model steel micro-click rear adjustable for windage and elevation. Same special features. Introduced 1984.
Price: **$1,500.00**

UBERTI 1873 CATTLEMAN SINGLE ACTIONS
Caliber: 38 Spec., 357 Mag., 44 Spec., 44-40, 45 Colt/45 ACP, 6-shot.
Barrel: 4¾", 5½", 7½"; 44-40, 45 Colt also with 3".
Weight: 38 oz. (5½" bbl.). **Length:** 10¾" overall (5½" bbl.).
Stocks: One-piece smooth walnut.
Sights: Blade front, groove rear; fully adjustable rear available.
Features: Steel or brass backstrap, trigger guard; color case-hardened frame, blued barrel, cylinder. Imported from Italy by Uberti USA.
Price: Steel backstrap, trigger guard, fixed sights **$410.00**
Price: Brass backstrap, trigger guard, fixed sights **$365.00**

UBERTI 1875 SA ARMY OUTLAW REVOLVER
Caliber: 357 Mag., 44-40, 45 Colt, 6-shot.
Barrel: 7½".
Weight: 44 oz. **Length:** 13¾" overall.
Stocks: Smooth walnut.
Sights: Blade front, notch rear.
Features: Replica of the 1875 Remington S.A. Army revolver. Brass trigger guard, color case-hardened frame, rest blued. Imported by Uberti USA.
Price: **$405.00**
Price: 45 Colt/45 ACP convertible **$450.00**

UBERTI 1890 ARMY OUTLAW REVOLVER
Caliber: 357 Mag., 44-40, 45 Colt, 6-shot.
Barrel: 5½".
Weight: 37 oz. **Length:** 12½" overall.
Stocks: American walnut.
Sights: Blade front, groove rear.
Features: Replica of the 1890 Remington single action. Brass trigger guard, rest is blued. Imported by Uberti USA.
Price: **$410.00**
Price: 45 Colt/45 ACP convertible **$415.00**

Texas Longhorn Arms Cased Set
Set contains one each of the Texas Longhorn Right-Hand Single Actions, all in the same caliber, same serial numbers (100, 200, 300, 400, 500, 600, 700, 800, 900). Ten sets to be made (#1000 donated to NRA museum). Comes in hand-tooled leather case. All other specs same as Limited Edition guns. Introduced 1984.
Price: **$5,750.00**
Price: With ¾-coverage "C-style" engraving **$7,650.00**

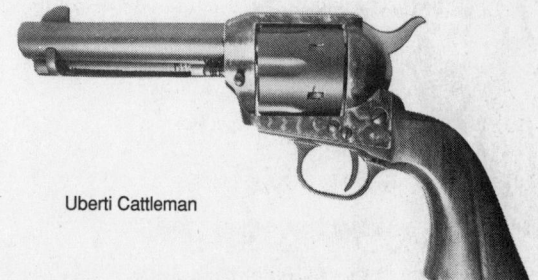

Uberti Cattleman

Uberti 1873 Buckhorn Single Action
A slightly larger version of the Cattleman revolver. Available in 44 Magnum or 44 Magnum/44-40 convertible, otherwise has same specs.
Price: Steel backstrap, trigger guard, fixed sights **$410.00**
Price: Convertible (two cylinders) **$460.00**

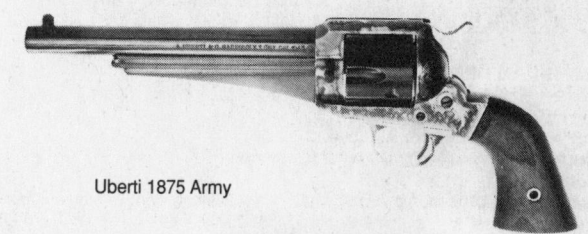

Uberti 1875 Army

CAUTION: PRICES SHOWN ARE SUPPLIED BY THE MANUFACTURER OR IMPORTER. CHECK YOUR LOCAL GUNSHOP.

49th EDITION, 1995 **323**

Specially adapted single-shot and multi-barrel arms.

American Derringer Model 1

American Derringer Texas Commemorative

A Model 1 Derringer with solid brass frame, stainless steel barrel and rosewood grips. Available in 38 Speical, 44-40 Win., or 45 Colt. Introduced 1987.

Price: 38 Spec.	**$225.00**
Price: 44-40 or 45 Colt	**$320.00**

American Derringer Model 4

Similar to the Model 1 except has 4.1" barrel, overall length of 6", and weighs 16½ oz.; chambered for 3" 410-bore shotshells or 45 or 44 Magnum Colt. Can be had with 45-70 upper barrel and 3" 410-bore or 45 Colt bottom barrel. Made of stainless steel. Manual hammer block safety. Introduced 1985.

Price: 3" 410/45 Colt (either barrel)	**$352.00**
Price: 3" 410/45 Colt or 45-70 (Alaskan Survival model)	**$387.50**
Price: 44 Magnum with oversize grips	**$422.00**
Price: Alaskan Survival model (45-70 upper, 410-45 Colt lower)	**$387.50**

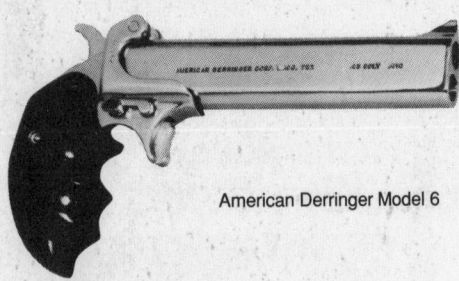

American Derringer Model 6

AMERICAN DERRINGER DA 38 MODEL

Caliber: 9mm Para., 38 Spec.
Barrel: 3".
Weight: 14.5 oz. **Length:** 4.8" overall.
Stocks: Rosewood, walnut or other hardwoods.
Sights: Fixed.
Features: Double-action only; two-shots. Manual safety. Made of satin-finished stainless steel and aluminum. Introduced 1989. From American Derringer Corp.

Price: 38 Spec.	**$250.00**
Price: 9mm Para.	**$275.00**

AMERICAN DERRINGER MODEL 1

Caliber: 22 LR, 22 WMR, 30 Luger, 30-30 Win., 32 ACP, 380 ACP, 38 Spec., 9mm Para., 357 Mag., 357 Maximum, 10mm, 40 S&W, 41 Mag., 38-40, 44-40 Win., 44 Spec., 44 Mag., 45 Colt, 45 ACP, 410-bore (2½").
Barrel: 3".
Weight: 15½ oz. (38 Spec.). **Length:** 4.82" overall.
Stocks: Rosewood, Zebra wood.
Sights: Blade front.
Features: Made of stainless steel with high-polish or satin finish. Two-shot capacity. Manual hammer block safety. Introduced 1980. Available in almost any pistol caliber. Contact the factory for complete list of available calibers and prices. From American Derringer Corp.

Price: 22 LR or WMR	**$312.00 to $375.00**
Price: 38 Spec.	**$225.00**
Price: 357 Maximum	**$265.00**
Price: 357 Mag.	**$250.00**
Price: 9mm, 380,	**$224.00**
Price: 10mm, 40 S&W	**$257.00**
Price: 44 Spec.,	**$320.00**
Price: 44-40 Win., 45 Colt, 45 Auto Rim	**$320.00**
Price: 30-30, 41, 44 Mags., 45 Win. Mag.	**$375.00**
Price: 45-70, single shot	**$312.00**
Price: 45 Colt, 410, 2½"	**$320.00**
Price: 45 ACP, 10mm Auto	**$257.00**
Price: 125th Anniversary model (brass frame, stainless bbl., 44-40, 45 Colt, 38 Spec.)	**$320.00**

American Derringer Lady Derringer

Same as the Model 1 except has tuned action, is fitted with scrimshawed synthetic ivory grips; chambered for 32 H&R Mag. and 38 Spec.; 22 LR, 22 WMR, 380 ACP, 357 Mag., 9mm Para., 45 ACP, 45 Colt/410 shotshell available at extra cost. Deluxe Grade is highly polished; Deluxe Engraved is engraved in a pattern similar to that used on 1880s derringers. All come in a French fitted jewelry box. Introduced 1991.

Price: Deluxe Grade	**$235.00**
Price: Deluxe Engraved Grade	**$750.00**

American Derringer Model 6

Similar to the Model 1 except has 6" barrels chambered for 3" 410 shotshells or 45 Colt, rosewood stocks, 8.2" o.a.l. and weighs 21 oz. Shoots either round for each barrel. Manual hammer block safety. Introduced 1986.

Price: High polish or satin finish	**$387.50**
Price: Gray matte finish	**$362.50**

American Derringer Model 7 Ultra Lightweight

Similar to Model 1 except made of high strength aircraft aluminum. Weighs 7½ oz., 4.82" o.a.l., rosewood stocks. Available in 22 LR, 32 H&R Mag., 380 ACP, 38 Spec., 44 Spec. Introduced 1986.

Price: 22 LR	**$220.00**
Price: 38 Spec.	**$220.00**
Price: 380 ACP	**$220.00**
Price: 32 H&R Mag.	**$220.00**
Price: 44 Spec.	**$500.00**

American Derringer Model 10 Lightweight

Similar to the Model 1 except frame is of aluminum, giving weight of 10 oz. Available in 45 Colt or 45 ACP only. Matte gray finish. Introduced 1989.

Price: 45 Colt	**$320.00**
Price: 45 ACP	**$257.00**
Price: Model 11 (38 Spec., aluminum bbls., wgt. 11 oz.)	**$205.00**

American Derringer Semmerling

AMERICAN DERRINGER SEMMERLING LM-4

Caliber: 9mm Para., 7-shot magazine; 45 ACP, 5-shot magazine.
Barrel: 3.625".
Weight: 24 oz. **Length:** 5.2" overall.
Stocks: Checkered plastic on blued guns, rosewood on stainless guns.
Sights: Open, fixed.
Features: Manually-operated repeater. Height is 3.7", width is 1". Comes with manual, leather carrying case, spare stock screws, wrench. From American Derringer Corp.

Price: Blued	**$1,750.00**
Price: Stainless steel	**$1,875.00**

CAUTION: PRICES SHOWN ARE SUPPLIED BY THE MANUFACTURER OR IMPORTER. CHECK YOUR LOCAL GUNSHOP.

AMERICAN DERRINGER COP 357 DERRINGER
Caliber: 38 Spec. or 357 Mag., 4-shot.
Barrel: 3.14".
Weight: 16 oz. **Length:** 5.53" overall.
Stocks: Rosewood.
Sights: Fixed.
Features: Double-action only. Four shots. Made of stainless steel. Introduced 1990. Made in U.S. by American Derringer Corp.
Price: $375.00

American Derringer Mini COP Derringer
Similar to the COP 357 except chambered for 22 WMR. Barrel length of 2.85", overall length of 4.95", weight is 16 oz. Double action with automatic hammer-block safety. Made of stainless steel. Grips of rosewood, walnut or other hardwoods. Introduced 1990. Made in U.S. by American Derringer Corp.
Price: $312.50

ANSCHUTZ EXEMPLAR BOLT-ACTION PISTOL
Caliber: 22 LR, 5-shot; 22 Hornet, 5-shot.
Barrel: 10", 14".
Weight: 3½ lbs. **Length:** 17" overall.
Stock: European walnut with stippled grip and forend.
Sights: Hooded front on ramp, open notch rear adjustable for windage and elevation.
Features: Uses Match 64 action with left-hand bolt; Anschutz #5091 two-stage trigger set at 9.85 oz. Receiver grooved for scope mounting; open sights easily removed. The 22 Hornet version uses Match 54 action with left-hand bolt, Anschutz #5099 two-stage trigger set at 19.6 oz. Introduced 1987. Imported from Germany by Precision Sales International.
Price: 22 LR $499.50
Price: 22 LR, left-hand $499.50
Price: 22 LR, 14" barrel $522.00
Price: 22 Hornet (no sights, 10" bbl.) $899.00

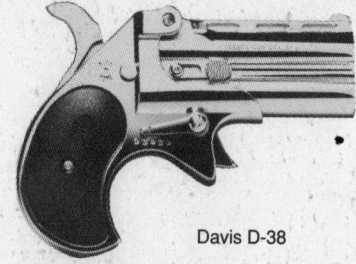

Davis D-38

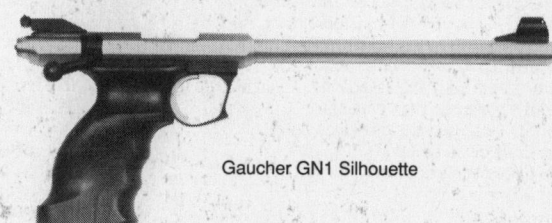

Gaucher GN1 Silhouette

HIGH STANDARD DERRINGER
Caliber: 22 LR, 22 WMR, 2-shot.
Barrel: 3.5".
Weight: 11 oz. **Length:** 5.12" overall.
Stocks: Black composition.
Sights: Fixed.
Features: Double action, dual extraction. Hammer-block safety. Blue finish. Introduced 1990. Made in U.S. by American Derringer Corp.
Price: $169.50

HJS LONE STAR DERRINGER
Caliber: 380 ACP.
Barrel: 2".
Weight: 6 oz. **Length:** 3¹⁵⁄₁₆" overall.
Stocks: Brown plastic.
Sights: Groove.
Features: Stainless steel Construction. Beryllium copper firing pin. Button-rifled barrel. Introduced 1993. Made in U.S. by HJS Arms, Inc.
Price: $185.00

Anschutz Exemplar

DAVIS DERRINGERS
Caliber: 22 LR, 22 WMR, 25 ACP, 32 ACP.
Barrel: 2.4".
Weight: 9.5 oz. **Length:** 4" overall.
Stocks: Laminated wood.
Sights: Blade front, fixed notch rear.
Features: Choice of black Teflon or chrome finish; spur trigger. Introduced 1986. Made in U.S. by Davis Industries.
Price: $65.00

DAVIS D-38 DERRINGER
Caliber: 32 H&R, 38 Special.
Barrel: 2.75".
Weight: 11.5 oz. **Length:** 4.65" overall.
Stocks: Textured black synthetic.
Sights: Blade front, fixed notch rear.
Features: Alloy frame, steel-lined barrels, steel breech block. Plunger-type safety with integral hammer block. Chrome or black Teflon finish. Introduced 1992. Made in U.S. by Davis Industries.
Price: $98.00

FEATHER GUARDIAN ANGEL PISTOL
Caliber: 22 LR/22 WMR.
Barrel: 2".
Weight: 12 oz. **Length:** 5" overall.
Stocks: Black composition.
Sights: Fixed.
Features: Uses a pre-loaded two-shot drop-in "magazine." Stainless steel construction; matte finish. From Feather Industries. Introduced 1988.
Price: $119.95

GAUCHER GN1 SILHOUETTE PISTOL
Caliber: 22 LR, single shot.
Barrel: 10".
Weight: 2.4 lbs. **Length:** 15.5" overall.
Stock: European hardwood.
Sights: Blade front, open adjustable rear.
Features: Bolt action, adjustable trigger. Introduced 1990. Imported from France by Mandall Shooting Supplies.
Price: About $289.95
Price: Model GP Silhouette $259.95

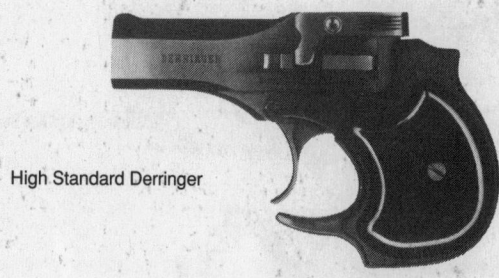

High Standard Derringer

CAUTION: PRICES SHOWN ARE SUPPLIED BY THE MANUFACTURER OR IMPORTER. CHECK YOUR LOCAL GUNSHOP.

49th EDITION, 1995 **325**

HJS FRONTIER FOUR DERRINGER
Caliber: 22 LR.
Barrel: 2".
Weight: 5½ oz. **Length:** 3¹⁵⁄₁₆" overall.
Stocks: Brown plastic.
Sights: None.
Features: Four barrels fire with rotating firing pin. Stainless steel construction. Introduced 1993. Made in U.S. by HJS Arms, Inc.
Price: $165.00

HJS Antigua Derringer
Same as the Frontier Four except blued stainess barrel, brass frame, brass pivot pins. Brown plastic grips. Introduced 1994. Made in U.S. by HJS Arms, Inc.
Price: $180.00

ITHACA MODEL 20 SINGLE SHOT
Caliber: 22 LR, 44 Mag.
Barrel: 10", 12".
Weight: 3¼ lbs. **Length:** 15" overall (10" barrel).
Stocks: American walnut with satin finish.
Sights: Ithaca Gun Raybar Deerslayer sights or drilled and tapped for scope mounting.
Features: Single firing pin for RF/CF use. Comes with both barrels matched to one frame. Matte blue finish.
Price: 22 LR/44 Mag. combo, 10" and 12" barrels $348.65

MAGNUM RESEARCH LONE EAGLE SINGLE SHOT PISTOL
Caliber: 22 Hornet, 223, 22-250, 243, 7mm BR, 7mm-08, 30-30, 308, 30-06, 357 Max., 35 Rem., 358 Win., 44 Mag., 444 Marlin.
Barrel: 14", interchangable.
Weight: 4lbs., 3 oz. to 4 lbs., 7 oz. **Length:** 15" overall.
Stocks: Composition, with thumbrest.
Sights: None furnished; drilled and tapped for scope mounting and open sights. Open sights optional.
Features: Cannon-type rotating breech with spring-activated ejector. Ordnance steel with matte blue finish. Cross-bolt safety. External cocking lever on left side of gun. Introduced 1991. Available from Magnum Research, Inc.
Price: Complete pistol $344.00
Price: Barreled action only $254.00
Price: Scope base $14.00
Price: Adjustable open sights $35.00

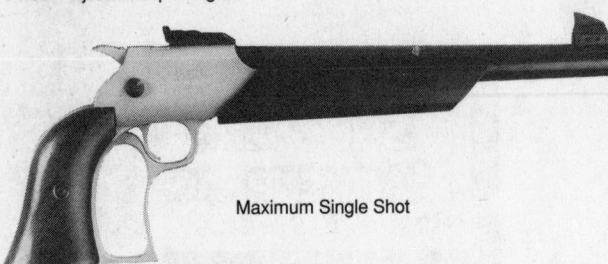

Maximum Single Shot

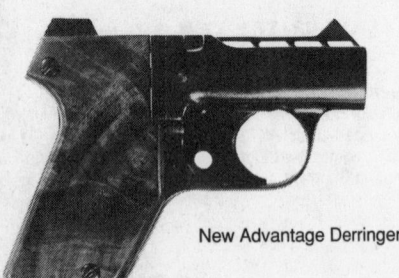

New Advantage Derringer

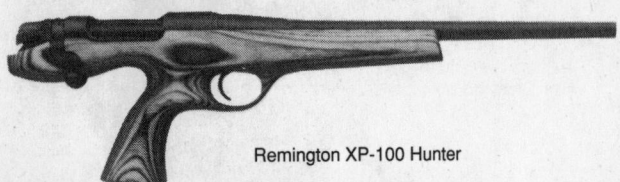

Remington XP-100 Hunter

HJS Fronteir Four

MANDALL/CABANAS PISTOL
Caliber: 177, pellet or round ball; single shot.
Barrel: 9".
Weight: 51 oz. **Length:** 19" overall.
Stock: Smooth wood with thumbrest.
Sights: Blade front on ramp, open adjustable rear.
Features: Fires round ball or pellets with 22 blank cartridge. Automatic safety; muzzlebrake. Imported from Mexico by Mandall Shooting Supplies.
Price: $139.95

Magnum Research Lone Eagle

MAXIMUM SINGLE SHOT PISTOL
Caliber: 22 LR, 22 Hornet, 22 BR, 22 PPC, 223 Rem., 22-250, 6mm BR, 6mm PPC, 243, 250 Savage, 6.5mm-35M, 270 MAX, 270 Win., 7mm TCU, 7mm BR, 7mm-35, 7mm INT-R, 7mm-08, 7mm Rocket, 7mm Super Mag., 30 Herrett, 30 Carbine, 30-30, 308 Win., 30x39, 32-20, 357 Mag., 357 Maximum, 358 Win., 44 Mag., 454 Casull.
Barrel: 8¾", 10½", 14".
Weight: 61 oz. (10½" bbl.); 78 oz. (14" bbl.). **Length:** 15", 18½" overall (with 10½" and 14" bbl., respectively).
Stocks: Smooth walnut stocks and forend.
Sights: Ramp front, fully adjustable open rear.
Features: Falling block action; drilled and tapped for M.O.A. scope mounts; integral grip frame/receiver; adjustable trigger; Douglas barrel (interchangeable). Introduced 1983. Made in U.S. by M.O.A. Corp.
Price: Stainless receiver, blue barrel $622.00
Price: Stainless receiver, stainless barrel $677.00
Price: Extra blued barrel $164.00
Price: Extra stainless barrel $222.00
Price: Scope mount $52.00

NEW ADVANTAGE ARMS DERRINGER
Caliber: 22 LR, 22 WMR, 4-shot.
Barrel: 2½".
Weight: 15 oz. **Length:** 4½" overall.
Stocks: Smooth walnut.
Sights: Fixed.
Features: Double-action mechanism, four barrels, revolving firing pin. Rebounding hammer. Blue or stainless. Reintroduced 1989. From New Advantage Arms Corp.
Price: 22 LR, 22 WMR, blue, about $199.00
Price: As above, stainless, about $229.00

REMINGTON XP-100 HUNTER PISTOL
Caliber: 223 Rem., 7mm BR Rem., 7mm-08 Rem., 35 Rem., single shot.
Barrel: 14½".
Weight: 4½ lbs. **Length:** 21¼" overall.
Stocks: Laminated wood with contoured grip.
Sights: None furnished. Drilled and tapped for scope mounting.
Features: Mid-handle grip design with scalloped contours for right- or left-handed shooters; two-position safety. Matte blue finish. Introduced 1993.
Price: $548.00

CAUTION: PRICES SHOWN ARE SUPPLIED BY THE MANUFACTURER OR IMPORTER. CHECK YOUR LOCAL GUNSHOP.

Remington XP-100 KS

Remington XP-100 Custom HB Long Range Pistol

Chambered for 223 Rem., 22-250 Rem., 7mm-08 Rem., 35 Rem., 250 Savage, 6mm BR, 7mm BR, 308. Offered with standard 14½" barrel with adjustable rear leaf and front bead sights, or with heavy 15½" barrel without sights. Custom Shop 14½" barrel, Custom Shop English walnut stock in right- or left-hand configuration. Action tuned in Custom Shop. Weight is under 4½ lbs. (heavy barrel, 5½ lbs.). Introduced 1986.

Price: Right- or left-hand **$945.00**

RPM XL SINGLE SHOT PISTOL

Caliber: 22 LR, 22 WMR, 225 Win., 25 Rocket, 6.5 Rocket, 32 H&R Mag., 357 Max., 357 Mag., 30-30 Win., 30 Herrett, 357 Herrett, 41 Mag., 44 Mag., 454 Casull, 375 Win., 7mm UR, 7mm Merrill, 30 Merrill, 7mm Rocket, 270 Ren, 270 Rocket, 270 Max., 45-70.
Barrel: 8" slab, 10¾", 12", 14" bull; .450" wide rib, matted to prevent glare.
Weight: About 60 oz. **Length:** 12¼" overall (10¾" bbl.).
Stocks: Smooth Goncalo with thumb and heel rest.
Sights: Front .100" blade, rear adjustable for windage and elevation. Hooded front with interchangeable post optional.
Features: Blue finish, hard chrome optional. Barrel is drilled and tapped for scope mounting. Cocking indicator visible from rear of gun. Has spring-loaded barrel lock, positive hammer block thumb safety. Trigger adjustable for weight of pull and over-travel. For complete price list contact RPM.
Price: Regular ¾" frame, right-hand action **$807.50**
Price: As above, left-hand action **$832.50**
Price: Wide ⅞" frame, right-hand action **$857.50**
Price: Extra barrel, 8", 10¾" **$287.50**
Price: Extra barrel, 12", 14" **$357.50**

SUNDANCE POINT BLANK O/U DERRINGER

Caliber: 22 LR, 2-shot.
Barrel: 3".
Weight: 8 oz. **Length:** 4.6" overall.
Stocks: Grooved composition.
Sights: Blade front, fixed notch rear.
Features: Double-action trigger, push-bar safety, automatic chamber selection. Fully enclosed hammer. Matte black finish. Introduced 1994. Made in U.S. by Sundance Industries.
Price: **$99.00**

TEXAS ARMS DEFENDER DERRINGER

Caliber: 9mm Para., 357 Mag., 44 Mag., 45 ACP, 45 Colt/410.
Barrel: 3".
Weight: 21 oz. **Length:** 5" overall.
Stocks: Smooth wood.
Sights: Blade front, fixed rear.
Features: Interchangeable barrels; retracting firing pins; rebounding hammer; cross-bolt safety; removable trigger guard; automatic extractor. Blasted finish stainless steel. Introduced 1993. Made in U.S. by Texas Arms.
Price: **$310.00**
Price: Extra barrel **$100.00**

T/C Contender

Remington XP-100R KS Repeater Pistol

Similar to the Custom Long Range Pistol except chambered for 223 Rem., 22-250, 7mm-08 Rem., 250 Savage, 308, 350 Rem. Mag., and 35 Rem., and has a blind magazine holding 5 rounds (7mm-08 and 35), or 6 (223 Rem.). Comes with a rear-handle, synthetic stock of Du Pont Kevlar to eliminate the transfer bar between the forward trigger and rear trigger assembly. Fitted with front and rear sling swivel studs. Has standard-weight 14½" barrel with adjustable leaf rear sight, bead front. The receiver is drilled and tapped for scope mounts. Weight is about 4½ lbs. Introduced 1990. From Remington Custom Shop.
Price: **$840.00**

RPM XL Pistol

Sundance Point Blank

Texas Arms Defender

TEXAS LONGHORN "THE JEZEBEL" PISTOL

Caliber: 22 Short, Long, Long Rifle, single shot.
Barrel: 6".
Weight: 15 oz. **Length:** 8" overall.
Stocks: One-piece fancy walnut grip (right- or left-hand), walnut forend.
Sights: Bead front, fixed rear.
Features: Handmade gun. Top-break action; all stainless steel; automatic hammer block safety; music wire coil springs. Barrel is half-round, half-octagon. Announced 1986. From Texas Longhorn Arms.
Price: About **$250.00**

THOMPSON/CENTER CONTENDER

Caliber: 7mm TCU, 30-30 Win., 22 LR, 22 WMR, 22 Hornet, 223 Rem., 270 Ren, 7-30 Waters, 32-20 Win., 357 Mag., 357 Rem. Max., 44 Mag., 10mm Auto, 445 Super Mag., 45/410, single shot.
Barrel: 10", tapered octagon, bull barrel and vent. rib.
Weight: 43 oz. (10" bbl.). **Length:** 13¼" (10" bbl.).
Stocks: T/C "Competitor Grip." Right or left hand.
Sights: Under-cut blade ramp front, rear adjustable for windage and elevation.
Features: Break-open action with automatic safety. Single-action only. Interchangeable bbls., both caliber (rim & centerfire), and length. Drilled and tapped for scope. Engraved frame. See T/C catalog for exact barrel/caliber availability.
Price: Blued (rimfire cals.) **$435.00**
Price: Blued (centerfire cals.) **$435.00**
Price: Extra bbls. (standard octagon) **$200.00**
Price: 45/410, internal choke bbl. **$205.00**

HANDGUNS—MISCELLANEOUS

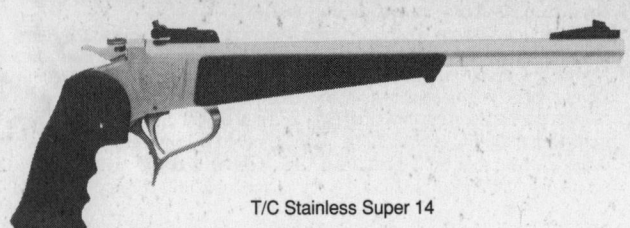

T/C Stainless Super 14

Thompson/Center Contender Hunter Package
Package contains the Contender pistol in 223, 7-30 Waters, 30-30, 375 Win., 357 Rem. Maximum, 35 Rem., 44 Mag. or 45-70 with 14" barrel with T/C's Muzzle Tamer, a 2.5x Recoil Proof Long Eye Relief scope with lighted reticle, q.d. sling swivels with a nylon carrying sling. Comes with a suede leather case with foam padding and fleece lining. Introduced 1990. From Thompson/Center Arms.
Price: 14" barrel $740.00

UBERTI ROLLING BLOCK TARGET PISTOL
Caliber: 22 LR, 22 WMR, 22 Hornet, 357 Mag., single shot.
Barrel: 9⅞", half-round, half-octagon.
Weight: 44 oz. **Length:** 14" overall.
Stocks: Walnut grip and forend.
Sights: Blade front, fully adjustable rear.
Features: Replica of the 1871 rolling block target pistol. Brass trigger guard, color case-hardened frame, blue barrel. Imported by Uberti USA.
Price: $380.00

ULTRA LIGHT ARMS MODEL 20 REB HUNTER'S PISTOL
Caliber: 22-250 thru 308 Win. standard. Most silhouette calibers and others on request. 5-shot magazine.
Barrel: 14", Douglas No. 3.
Weight: 4 lbs.
Stock: Composite Kevlar, graphite reinforced. Du Pont Imron paint in green, brown, black and camo.
Sights: None furnished. Scope mount included.
Features: Timney adjustable trigger; two-position, three-function safety; benchrest quality action; matte or bright stock and metal finish; right- or left-hand action. Shipped in hard case. Introduced 1987. From Ultra Light Arms.
Price: $1,600.00

WICHITA MASTER PISTOL
Caliber: 6mm BR, 7mm BR, 243, 7mm-08, 22-250, 308, 3-shot magazine.
Barrel: 13", 14.875".
Weight: 4.5 lbs. (13" barrel). **Length:** NA.
Stock: American walnut with oil finish; glass bedded.
Sights: Hooded post front, open adjustable rear.
Features: Comes with left-hand action with right-hand grip. round receiver and barrel. Wichita adjustable trigger. Introduced 1991. From Wichita Arms.
Price: $1,550.00

Thompson/Center Stainless Super 14, Super 16 Contender
Same as the standard Super 14 and Super 16 except they are made of stainless steel with blued sights. Both models have black Rynite forend and finger-groove, ambidextrous grip with a built-in rubber recoil cushion that has a sealed-in air pocket. Receiver has a different cougar etching. Available in 22 LR, 22 LR Match, 22 Hornet, 223 Rem., 30-30 Win., 35 Rem. (Super 14), 45-70 (Super 16 only), 45 Colt/410. Introduced 1993.
Price: 14" bull barrel $475.00
Price: 16¼" bull barrel $480.00
Price: 45 Colt/410, 14" $505.00
Price: 45 Colt/410, 16" $510.00

Thompson/Center Stainless Contender
Same as the standard Contender except made of stainless steel with blued sights, black Rynite forend and ambidextrous finger-groove grip with a built-in rubber recoil cushion that has a sealed-in air pocket. Receiver has a different cougar etching. Available with 10" bull barrel in 22 LR, 22 LR Match, 22 Hornet, 223 Rem., 30-30 Win., 357 Mag., 44 Mag., 45 Colt/410. Introduced 1993.
Price: $465.00
Price: 45 Colt/410 . . . . $470.00

Uberti Rolling Block

Ultra Light Model 20

Wichita Master

CENTERFIRE RIFLES—AUTOLOADERS

Both classic arms and recent designs in American-style repeaters for sport and field shooting.

Thompson M1

Auto-Ordnance Thompson M1
Similar to the Model 27 A-1 except is in the M-1 configuration with side cocking knob, horizontal forend, smooth unfinned barrel, sling swivels on butt and forend. Matte black finish. Introduced 1985.
Price: $747.50

AUTO-ORDNANCE 27 A-1 THOMPSON
Caliber: 45 ACP, 30-shot magazine.
Barrel: 16".
Weight: 11½ lbs. **Length:** About 42" overall (Deluxe).
Stock: Walnut stock and vertical forend.
Sights: Blade front, open rear adjustable for windage.
Features: Recreation of Thompson Model 1927. Semi-auto only. Deluxe model has finned barrel, adjustable rear sight and compensator; Standard model has plain barrel and military sight. From Auto-Ordnance Corp.
Price: Deluxe $770.00
Price: 1927A5 Pistol (M27A1 without stock; wgt. 7 lbs.) $740.00
Price: 1927A1C Lightweight model $742.00

CAUTION: PRICES SHOWN ARE SUPPLIED BY THE MANUFACTURER OR IMPORTER. CHECK YOUR LOCAL GUNSHOP.

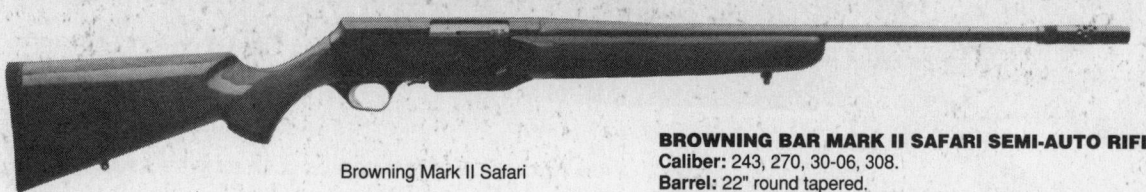

Browning Mark II Safari

Browning BAR Mark II Safari Magnum Rifle

Same as the standard caliber model, except weighs 8⅜ lbs., 45" overall, 24" bbl., 3-round mag. Cals. 7mm Mag., 270 Wea. Mag., 300 Win. Mag., 338 Win. Mag. BOSS barrel vibration modulator and muzzle brake system available only on models without sights. Introduced 1993.

Price: Safari, with sights **$731.95**
Price: Safari, no sights **$714.95**
Price: Safari, no sights, BOSS **$794.95**

BARRETT LIGHT-FIFTY MODEL 82 A-1 AUTO

Caliber: 50 BMG, 10-shot detachable box magazine.
Barrel: 29".
Weight: 28.5 lbs. **Length:** 57" overall.
Stock: Composition with Sorbothane recoil pad.
Sights: Open, iron; scope optional.
Features: Semi-automatic, recoil operated with recoiling barrel. Three-lug locking bolt; muzzlebrake. Self-leveling bipod. Fires same 50-cal. ammunition as the M2HB machinegun. Introduced 1985. From Barrett Firearms.
Price: From **$6,750.00**

CALICO MODEL M-951 TACTICAL CARBINE

Caliber: 9mm Para., 50- or 100-shot magazine.
Barrel: 16.1" (long compensator).
Weight: 3.7 lbs. (empty). **Length:** 28.75" overall (stock collapsed).
Stock: Sliding steel buttstock, adjustable forward grip.
Sights: Post front adjustable for windage and elevation, fixed notch rear.
Feature: Helical feed 50- or 100-shot magazine. Ambidextrous safety, static cocking handle. Retarded blowback action. Glass-filled polymer grip. Introduced 1989. From Calico.
Price: **$555.60**
Price: M-951S (fixed stock) **$566.90**

BROWNING BAR MARK II SAFARI SEMI-AUTO RIFLE

Caliber: 243, 270, 30-06, 308.
Barrel: 22" round tapered.
Weight: 7⅜ lbs. **Length:** 43" overall.
Stock: French walnut p.g. stock and forend, hand checkered.
Sights: Gold bead on hooded ramp front, click adjustable rear, or no sights.
Features: Has new bolt release lever; removable trigger assembly with larger trigger guard; redesigned gas and buffer systems. Detachable 4-round box magazine. Scroll-engraved receiver is tapped for scope mounting. BOSS barrel vibration modulator and muzzle brake system available only on models without sights. Mark II Safari introduced 1993. Imported from Belgium by Browning.
Price: Safari, with sights **$681.95**
Price: Safari, no sights **$664.95**
Price: Safari, no sights, BOSS **$794.95**

> Consult our Directory pages for the location of firms mentioned.

Calico Model M-951

Century FAL Sporter

CENTURY INTERNATIONAL FAL SPORTER RIFLE

Caliber: 308 Win.
Barrel: 20.75".
Weight: 9 lbs., 13 oz. **Length:** 41.125" overall.
Stock: Bell & Carlson thumbhole sporter.
Sights: Protected post front, adjustable aperture rear.
Features: Matte blue finish; rubber butt pad. From Century International Arms.
Price: About **$625.00**

CENTURY INTERNATIONAL M-14 SEMI-AUTO RIFLE

Caliber: 308 Win., 20-shot magazine.
Barrel: 22".
Weight: 8.25 lbs. **Length:** 40.8" overall.
Stock: Walnut with rubber recoil pad.
Sights: Protected blade front, fully adjustable aperture rear.
Features: Gas-operated; forged receiver; Parkerized finish. Imported from China by Century International Arms.
Price: About **$468.95**

Colt Sporter Lightweight

COLT SPORTER LIGHTWEIGHT RIFLE

Caliber: 9mm Para., 223 Rem., 7.62x39mm, 5-shot magazine.
Barrel: 16".
Weight: 6.7 lbs. (223); 7.1 lbs. (9mm Para.). **Length:** 34.5" overall extended.
Stock: Composition stock, grip, forend.
Sights: Post front, rear adjustable for windage and elevation.
Features: 5-round detachable box magazine, flash suppressor, sling swivels. Forward bolt assist included. Introduced 1991.
Price: **$939.00**
Price: 7.62x39mm **$939.00**

Eagle Arms EA-15

Eagle Arms EA-15 E2 H-BAR Auto Rifle
Same as the EA-15 Golden Eagle except has 20" heavy match barrel with 1:9" twist. Weighs about 9 lbs. Introduced 1989. Made in U.S. by Eagle Arms, Inc.
Price: **$895.00**
Price: With NM sights **$945.00**

Eagle Arms EA-15 E2 Carbine
Collapsible carbine-type buttstock, 16" heavy carbine barrel. Weighs about 7 lbs., 3 oz. Introduced 1989. Made in U.S. by Eagle Arms, Inc.
Price: **$895.00**

Feather Model F9

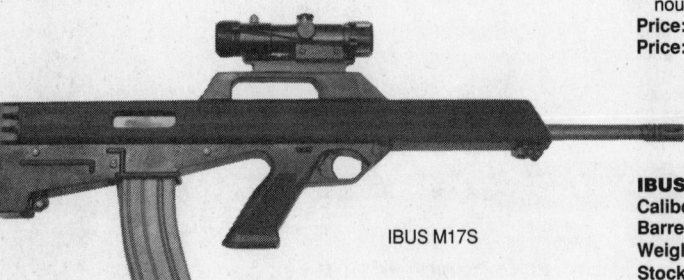

IBUS M17S

Marlin Model 45

NORINCO MAK 90 SEMI-AUTO RIFLE
Caliber: 7.62x39, 5-shot magazine.
Barrel: 16.25".
Weight: 8 lbs., 3 oz. **Length:** 35.5" overall.
Stock: Walnut-finished thumbhole with recoil pad.
Sights: Adjustable post front, open adjustable rear.
Features: Chrome-lined barrel; forged receiver; black oxide finish. Comes with extra magazine, oil bottle, cleaning kit, sling. Imported from China by Century International Arms.
Price: About **$312.00**

EAGLE ARMS EA-15E2 H-BAR GOLDEN EAGLE MATCH RIFLE
Caliber: 223 Rem., 30-shot magazine.
Barrel: 20", premium, extra-heavy NM; 1:8" twist.
Weight: About 12 lbs. **Length:** 39" overall.
Stock: Black composition; weighted.
Sights: Elevation-adjustable, extra-fine front, E-2-style NM rear with ½-MOA adjustments, NM aperture.
Features: Upper and lower receivers have push-type pivot pin for easy take-down. Receivers hard coat anodized. E2-style forward assist mechanism. Integral raised M-16A2-type fence around magazine release button. Introduced 1989. Made in U.S. by Eagle Arms, Inc.
Price: **$1,075.00**

Eagle Arms EA-15 Action Master Auto Rifle
One-piece international-style upper receiver for scope mounting, no front sight; solid aluminum handguard tube; free-floating 20" premium barrel; muzzle compensator; NM trigger group. Weighs about 8 lbs., 9 oz. Introduced 1991. Made in U.S. by Eagle Arms, Inc.
Price: **$1,075.00**
Price: Eagle Spirit (16" premium air-gauged barrel, weighs 8 lbs.) **$1,075.00**

FEATHER AT-9 SEMI-AUTO CARBINE
Caliber: 9mm Para., 25-shot magazine.
Barrel: 17".
Weight: 5 lbs. **Length:** 35" overall (stock extended); 26½" (closed).
Stock: Telescoping wire, composition pistol grip.
Sights: Hooded post front, adjustable aperture rear.
Features: Semi-auto only. Matte black finish. From Feather Industries. Announced 1988.
Price: **$499.95**
Price: Model F9 (fixed stock) **$534.95**

IBUS M17S 223 BULLPUP RIFLE
Caliber: 223, 20-shot magazine.
Barrel: 22".
Weight: 8.8 lbs. **Length:** 31½" overall.
Stock: Zytel glass-filled nylon.
Sights: None furnished. Comes with scope mount for Weaver-type rings.
Features: Gas-operated, short-stroke piston system. Ambidextrous magazine release. Introduced 1993. Made in U.S. by Quality Parts Co.
Price: **$975.00**

MARLIN MODEL 9 CAMP CARBINE
Caliber: 9mm Para., 12-shot magazine.
Barrel: 16½", Micro-Groove® rifling.
Weight: 6¾ lbs. **Length:** 35½" overall.
Stock: Walnut-finished hardwood; rubber buttpad; Mar-Shield® finish; swivel studs.
Sights: Ramp front with orange post, cutaway Wide-Scan™ hood, adjustable open rear.
Features: Manual bolt hold-open; Garand-type safety, magazine safety; loaded chamber indicator; receiver drilled, tapped for scope mounting. Introduced 1985.
Price: **$384.95**

Marlin Model 45 Carbine
Similar to the Model 9 except chambered for 45 ACP, 7-shot magazine. Introduced 1986.
Price: **$384.95**

CAUTION: PRICES SHOWN ARE SUPPLIED BY THE MANUFACTURER OR IMPORTER. CHECK YOUR LOCAL GUNSHOP.

CENTERFIRE RIFLES—AUTOLOADERS

Olympic CAR-310

OLYMPIC ARMS CAR SERIES CARBINES
Caliber: 223, 20- or 30-shot; 9mm Para., 34-shot; 45 ACP, 16-shot; 10mm, 40 S&W, 41 A.E., 15-shot; 7.62x39mm, 5- or 30-shot.
Barrel: 16".
Weight: 7 lbs. **Length:** 34" overall (stock extended).
Stock: Telescoping butt.
Sights: Post front adjustable for elevation, rear adjustable for windage.
Features: Based on the AR-15 rifle. Has A2 Stowaway pistol grip and stock. Introduced 1982. Made in U.S. by Olympic Arms, Inc.
Price: CAR-15, 223 caliber $650.00
Price: CAR-9, 9mm Para. $700.00
Price: CAR-45, 45 ACP $730.00
Price: CAR-40, 40 S&W $780.00
Price: CAR-41, 41 A.E. $780.00
Price: CAR-310, 10mm $850.00
Price: 7.62x39mm $700.00

Quality Parts E-2 Dissipator

QUALITY PARTS SHORTY E-2 CARBINE
Caliber: 223, 30-shot magazine.
Barrel: 16".
Weight: NA. **Length:** NA.
Stock: Telescoping buttstock.
Sights: Adjustable post front, adjustable aperture rear.
Features: Patterned after Colt M-16A2. Chrome-lined barrel with manganese phosphate finish. Has E-2 lower receiver with push-pin. From Quality Parts Co.
Price: $850.00
Price: E-2 Carbine Dissipator (M-16A2 handguard, E-2 sight, fixed or telescoping stock) $895.00
Price: As above with A-1 sight, fixed or telescoping stock $875.00

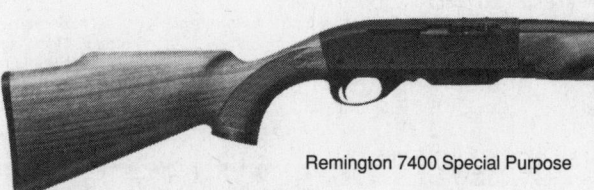

Remington 7400 Special Purpose

REMINGTON MODEL 7400 AUTO RIFLE
Caliber: 243 Win., 270 Win., 280 Rem., 308 Win., 30-06, 35 Whelan, 4-shot magazine.
Barrel: 22" round tapered.
Weight: 7½ lbs. **Length:** 42" overall.
Stock: Walnut, deluxe cut checkered p.g. and forend. Satin or high-gloss finish.
Sights: Gold bead front sight on ramp; step rear sight with windage adjustable.
Features: Redesigned and improved version of the Model 742. Positive cross-bolt safety. Receiver tapped for scope mount. Comes with green Remington hard case. Introduced 1981.
Price: About $524.00
Price: Carbine (18½" bbl., 30-06 only) $524.00

Remington Model 7400 Special Purpose Auto Rifle
Similar to the standard Model 7400 except chambered only for 270 and 30-06, non-glare finish on the American walnut stock. All exposed metal has non-reflective matte black finish. Comes with quick-detachable sling swivels and camo-pattern Cordura carrying sling. Introduced 1993.
Price: $524.00

Ruger Mini-14/5R

RUGER MINI-14/5 AUTOLOADING RIFLE
Caliber: 223 Rem., 5-shot detachable box magazine.
Barrel: 18½". Rifling twist 1:7".
Weight: 6.4 lbs. **Length:** 37¼" overall.
Stock: American hardwood, steel reinforced.
Sights: Ramp front, fully adjustable rear.
Features: Fixed piston gas-operated, positive primary extraction. New buffer system, redesigned ejector system. Ruger S100RH scope rings included. 20-, 30-shot magazine available to police departments and government agencies only.
Price: Mini-14/5R, Ranch Rifle, blued, scope rings $530.00
Price: K-Mini-14/5R, Ranch Rifle, stainless, scope rings . . . $580.00
Price: Mini-14/5, blued, no scope rings $491.50
Price: K-Mini-14/5, stainless, no scope rings $542.00

Ruger Mini Thirty Rifle
Similar to the Mini-14 Ranch Rifle except modified to chamber the 7.62x39 Russian service round. Weight is about 7 lbs., 3 oz. Has 6-groove barrel with 1-10" twist, Ruger Integral Scope Mount bases and folding peep rear sight. Detachable 5-shot staggered box magazine. Blued finish. Introduced 1987.
Price: Blue $530.00
Price: Stainless $580.00

Springfield M-1A

SPRINGFIELD INC. M-1A RIFLE

Caliber: 7.62mm NATO (308), 5-, 10- or 20-shot box magazine.
Barrel: 25¹⁄₁₆" with flash suppressor, 22" without suppressor.
Weight: 8¾ lbs. **Length:** 44¼" overall.
Stock: American walnut with walnut-colored heat-resistant fiberglass handguard. Matching walnut handguard available. Also available with fiberglass stock.
Sights: Military, square blade front, full click-adjustable aperture rear.
Features: Commercial equivalent of the U.S. M-14 service rifle with no provision for automatic firing. From Springfield Inc.
Price: Standard M-1A rifle, about **$1,269.00**
Price: National Match, about **$1,598.00**
Price: Super Match (heavy premium barrel), about **$1,929.00**
Price: M1A-A1 Bush Rifle, walnut stock, about **$1,289.00**

Stoner SR-25

VOERE MODEL 2185 SEMI-AUTO RIFLE

Caliber: 7x64, 308, 30-06, 2-shot detachable magazine.
Barrel: 20".
Weight: 7¾ lbs. **Length:** 43½" overall.
Stock: European walnut with checkered grip and forend, ventilated rubber recoil pad. Oil finish.
Sights: Blade on ramp front, open adjustable rear. Receiver drilled and tapped for scope mounting.
Features: Gas-operated with three forward locking lugs; hammer-forged free-floating barrel; two-stage trigger; cocking indicator inside trigger guard. Imported from Austria by JagerSports, Ltd.
Price: About **$1,950.00**
Price: With Mannlicher-style full stock, about **$2,015.00**

STONER SR-25 STANDARD RIFLE

Caliber: 7.62 NATO, 20-shot steel magazine, 5- and 10-shot optional.
Barrel: 20".
Weight: 8.8 lbs. **Length:** 40.75" overall.
Stock: Black synthetic AR-15A2 design, synthetic round forend.
Sights: AR-15-style front adjustable for elevation, rear is adjustable for windage.
Features: Merges designs of the AR-10 and AR-15 rifles. Upper and lower receivers made of lightweight aircraft aluminum alloy. Quick-detachable carrying handle/rear sight assembly. Introduced 1993. Made in U.S. by Knight's Mfg. Co.
Price: **$2,495.00**

WILKINSON TERRY CARBINE

Caliber: 9mm Para., 31-shot magazine.
Barrel: 16³⁄₁₆".
Weight: 6 lbs., 3 oz. **Length:** 30" overall.
Stock: Maple stock and forend.
Sights: Protected post front, aperture rear.
Features: Semi-automatic blowback action fires from a closed breech. Bolt-type safety and magazine catch. Ejection port has automatic trap door. Receiver equipped with dovetail for scope mounting. Made in U.S. From Wilkinson Arms.
Price: $578.43

CENTERFIRE RIFLES—LEVER & SLIDE

Both classic arms and recent designs in American-style repeaters for sport and field shooting.

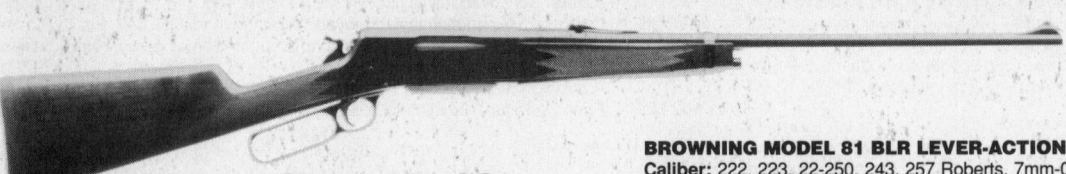

Browning Long Action BLR

Browning Model 81 Long Action BLR

Similar to the standard Model 81 BLR except has long acton to accept 30-06, 270 and 7mm Rem. Mag. Barrel lengths are 22" for 30-06 and 270, 24" for 7mm Rem. Mag. Has six-lug rotary bolt; bolt and receiver are full-length fluted. Fold-down hammer at half-cock. Weight about 8½ lbs., overall length 42½" (22" barrel). Introduced 1991.
Price: $561.95

CIMARRON 1860 HENRY REPLICA

Caliber: 44 WCF, 13-shot magazine.
Barrel: 24¼" (rifle), 22" (carbine).
Weight: 9½lbs. **Length:** 43" overall (rifle).
Stock: European walnut.
Sights: Bead front, open adjustable rear.
Features: Brass receiver amd buttplate. Uses original Henry loading system. Faithful to the original rifle. Introduced 1991. Imported by Cimarron Arms.
Price: $799.95

BROWNING MODEL 81 BLR LEVER-ACTION RIFLE

Caliber: 222, 223, 22-250, 243, 257 Roberts, 7mm-08, 308 Win. or 358 Win., 4-shot detachable magazine.
Barrel: 20" round tapered.
Weight: 6 lbs., 15 oz. **Length:** 39¾" overall.
Stock: Walnut. Checkered straight grip and forend, high-gloss finish.
Sights: Gold bead on hooded ramp front; low profile square notch adj. rear.
Features: Wide, grooved trigger; half-cock hammer safety; fold-down hammer. Receiver tapped for scope mount. Recoil pad installed. Imported from Japan by Browning.
Price: With sights $529.95

CIMARRON 1866 WINCHESTER REPLICAS

Caliber: 22 LR, 22 WMR, 38 Spec., 44 WCF.
Barrel: 24¼" (rifle), 19" (carbine).
Weight: 9 lbs. **Length:** 43" overall (rifle).
Stock: European walnut.
Sights: Bead front, open adjustable rear.
Features: Solid brass receiver, buttplate, forend cap. Octagonal barrel. Faithful to the original Winchester '66 rifle. Introduced 1991. Imported by Cimarron Arms.
Price: Rifle $689.95

CAUTION: PRICES SHOWN ARE SUPPLIED BY THE MANUFACTURER OR IMPORTER. CHECK YOUR LOCAL GUNSHOP.

CENTERFIRE RIFLES—LEVER & SLIDE

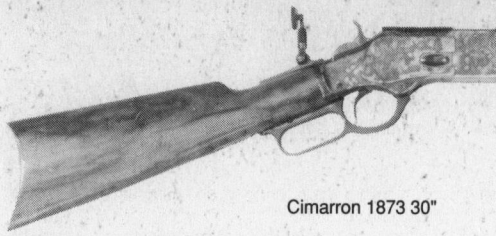

Cimarron 1873 30"

CIMARRON 1873 SHORT RIFLE
Caliber: 22 LR, 22 WMR, 357 Magnum, 44-40, 45 Colt.
Barrel: 20" tapered octagon.
Weight: 7.5 lbs. **Length:** 39" overall.
Stock: Walnut.
Sights: Bead front, adjustable semi-buckhorn rear.
Features: Has half "button" magazine. Original-type markings, including caliber, on barrel and elevator and "Kings" patent. From Cimarron Arms.
Price: $799.95

CIMARRON 1873 30" EXPRESS RIFLE
Caliber: 22 LR, 22 WMR, 357 Mag., 38-40, 44-40, 45 Colt.
Barrel: 30", octagonal.
Weight: 8½ lbs. **Length:** 48" overall.
Stock: Walnut.
Sights: Blade front, semi-buckhorn ramp rear. Tang sight optional.
Features: Color case-hardened frame; choice of modern blue-black or charcoal blue for other parts. Barrel marked "Kings improvement." From Cimarron Arms.
Price: $819.95

Cimarron 1873 Sporting Rifle
Similar to the 1873 Express except has 24" barrel with half-magazine.
Price: $799.95
Price: 1873 Saddle Ring Carbine, 19" barrel $799.95

Dixie 1873

DIXIE ENGRAVED 1873 RIFLE
Caliber: 44-40, 11-shot magazine.
Barrel: 20", round.
Weight: 7¾ lbs. **Length:** 39" overall.
Stock: Walnut.
Sights: Blade front, adjustable rear.
Features: Engraved and case-hardened frame. Duplicate of Winchester 1873. Made in Italy. From Dixie Gun Works.
Price: $1,250.00
Price: Plain, blued carbine $895.00

E.M.F. 1860 HENRY RIFLE
Caliber: 44-40 or 44 rimfire.
Barrel: 24.25".
Weight: About 9 lbs. **Length:** About 43.75" overall.
Stock: Oil-stained American walnut.
Sights: Blade front, rear adjustable for elevation.
Features: Reproduction of the original Henry rifle with brass frame and buttplate, rest blued. From E.M.F.
Price: Standard $1,100.00

E.M.F. 1866 YELLOWBOY LEVER ACTIONS
Caliber: 38 Spec., 44-40.
Barrel: 19" (carbine), 24" (rifle).
Weight: 9 lbs. **Length:** 43" overall (rifle).
Stock: European walnut.
Sights: Bead front, open adjustable rear.
Features: Solid brass frame, blued barrel, lever, hammer, buttplate. Imported from Italy by E.M.F.
Price: Rifle $848.00
Price: Carbine $825.00

CONSULT
Shooter's Marketplace
Page 225, This Issue

E.M.F. MODEL 73 LEVER-ACTION RIFLE
Caliber: 357 Mag., 44-40, 45 Colt.
Barrel: 24".
Weight: 8 lbs. **Length:** 43¼" overall.
Stock: European walnut.
Sights: Bead front, rear adjustable for windage and elevation.
Features: Color case-hardened frame (blue on carbine). Imported by E.M.F.
Price: Rifle $1,050.00
Price: Carbine, 19" barrel $1,020.00

Marlin Model 336CS

MARLIN MODEL 444SS LEVER-ACTION SPORTER
Caliber: 444 Marlin, 5-shot tubular magazine.
Barrel: 22" Micro-Groove®.
Weight: 7½ lbs. **Length:** 40½" overall.
Stock: Checkered American black walnut, capped p.g. with white line spacers, rubber rifle buttpad. Mar-Shield® finish; swivel studs.
Sights: Hooded ramp front, folding semi-buckhorn rear adjustable for windage and elevation.
Features: Hammer-block safety. Receiver tapped for scope mount; offset hammer spur.
Price: $490.25

MARLIN MODEL 336CS LEVER-ACTION CARBINE
Caliber: 30-30 or 35 Rem., 6-shot tubular magazine.
Barrel: 20" Micro-Groove®.
Weight: 7 lbs. **Length:** 38½" overall.
Stock: Checkered select American black walnut, capped p.g. with white line spacers. Mar-Shield® finish; rubber buttpad; swivel studs.
Sights: Ramp front with Wide-Scan™ hood, semi-buckhorn folding rear adjustable for windage and elevation.
Features: Hammer-block safety. Receiver tapped for scope mount, offset hammer spur; top of receiver sand blasted to prevent glare.
Price: $416.00

Marlin Model 30AS Lever-Action Carbine
Same as the Marlin 336CS except has walnut-finished hardwood p.g. stock, 30-30 only, 6-shot. Hammer-block safety. Adjustable rear sight, brass bead front.
Price: $354.95

Marlin Model 1894CS

Marlin Model 1894CS Carbine

Similar to the standard Model 1894S except chambered for 38 Special/357 Magnum with full-length 9-shot magazine, 18½" barrel, hammer-block safety, brass bead front sight. Introduced 1983.
Price: **$454.85**

MARLIN MODEL 1894S LEVER-ACTION CARBINE

Caliber: 44 Special/44 Magnum, 10-shot tubular magazine.
Barrel: 20" Micro-Groove®.
Weight: 6 lbs. **Length:** 37½" overall.
Stock: Checkered American black walnut, straight grip and forend. Mar-Shield® finish. Rubber rifle buttpad; swivel studs.
Sights: Wide-Scan™ hooded ramp front, semi-buckhorn folding rear adjustable for windage and elevation.
Features: Hammer-block safety. Receiver tapped for scope mount, offset hammer spur, solid top receiver sand blasted to prevent glare.
Price: **$454.85**

Marlin 1894 Century Limited

MARLIN MODEL 1895SS LEVER-ACTION RIFLE

Caliber: 45-70, 4-shot tubular magazine.
Barrel: 22" round.
Weight: 7½ lbs. **Length:** 40½" overall.
Stock: Checkered American black walnut, full pistol grip. Mar-Shield® finish; rubber buttpad; q.d. swivel studs.
Sights: Bead front with Wide-Scan™ hood, semi-buckhorn folding rear adjustable for windage and elevation.
Features: Hammer-block safety. Solid receiver tapped for scope mounts or receiver sights; offset hammer spur.
Price: **$490.25**

MITCHELL 1866 WINCHESTER REPLICA

Caliber: 44-40, 13-shot.
Barrel: 24¼".
Weight: 9 lbs. **Length:** 43" overall.
Stock: European walnut.
Sights: Bead front, open adjustable rear.
Features: Solid brass receiver, buttplate, forend cap. Octagonal barrel. Faithful to the original Winchester '66 rifle. Introduced 1990. Imported by Mitchell Arms, Inc.
Price: **$829.00**

MARLIN MODEL 1894 CENTURY LIMITED RIFLE

Caliber: 44-40, 12-shot magazine.
Barrel: 24", tapered octagon with conventional rifling.
Weight: 6½ lbs. **Length:** 40¾" overall.
Stock: Semi-fancy American black walnut with straight grip, brass crescent buttplate.
Sights: Carbine front, adjustable semi-buckhorn folding rear.
Features: Celebrates 100th anniversary of this model. Receiver, bolt and lever engraved by Giovanelli of Italy, and color case-hardened by the traditional bone and charcoal method. Wood is checkered in an authentic early Marlin pattern. Introduced 1994. Made in U.S. by Marlin Firearms Co.
Price: **$1,087.90**

MITCHELL 1858 HENRY REPLICA

Caliber: 44-40, 13-shot magazine.
Barrel: 24¼".
Weight: 9.5 lbs. **Length:** 43" overall.
Stock: European walnut.
Sights: Bead front, open adjustable rear.
Features: Brass receiver and buttplate. Uses original Henry loading system. Faithful to the original rifle. Introduced 1990. Imported by Mitchell Arms, Inc.
Price: **$999.00**

MITCHELL 1873 WINCHESTER REPLICA

Caliber: 45 Colt, 13-shot.
Barrel: 24¼".
Weight: 9.5 lbs. **Length:** 43" overall.
Stock: European walnut.
Sights: Bead front, open adjustable rear.
Features: Color case-hardened steel receiver. Faithful to the original Model 1873 rifle. Introduced 1990. Imported by Mitchell Arms, Inc.
Price: **$950.00**

NAVY ARMS MILITARY HENRY RIFLE

Caliber: 44-40, 12-shot magazine.
Barrel: 24¼".
Weight: 9 lbs., 4 oz.
Stock: European walnut.
Sights: Blade front, adjustable ladder-type rear.
Features: Recreation of the model used by cavalry units in the Civil War. Has full-length magazine tube, sling swivels; no forend. Introduced 1991. Imported from Italy by Navy Arms.
Price: **$875.00**

Navy Arms Military Henry

Consult our Directory pages for the location of firms mentioned.

Navy Arms Iron Frame Henry

Similar to the Military Henry Rifle except receiver is blued or color case-hardened steel. Introduced 1991. Imported by Navy Arms.
Price: **$895.00**

Navy Arms Henry Carbine

Similar to the Military Henry rifle except has 22" barrel, weighs 8 lbs., 12 oz., is 41" overall; no sling swivels. Caliber 44-40. Introduced 1992. Imported from Italy by Navy Arms.
Price: **$875.00**

Navy Arms Henry Trapper

Similar to the Military Henry Rifle except has 16½" barrel, weighs 7½ lbs. Brass frame and buttplate, rest blued. Introduced 1991. Imported from Italy by Navy Arms.
Price: **$875.00**

CENTERFIRE RIFLES—LEVER & SLIDE

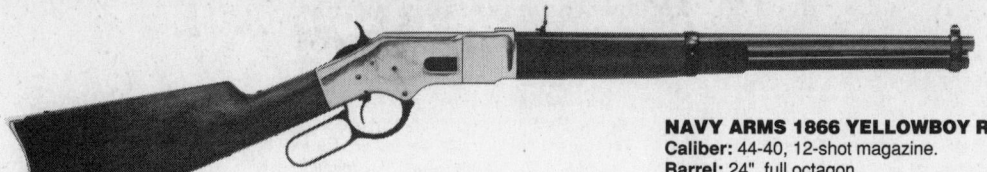

Navy Arms 1866 Yellowboy

NAVY ARMS 1866 YELLOWBOY RIFLE
Caliber: 44-40, 12-shot magazine.
Barrel: 24", full octagon.
Weight: 8½ lbs. **Length:** 42½" overall.
Stock: European walnut.
Sights: Blade front, adjustable ladder-type rear.
Features: Brass frame, forend tip, buttplate, blued barrel, lever, hammer. Introduced 1991. Imported from Italy by Navy Arms.
Price: **$695.00**
Price: Carbine, 19" barrel **$680.00**

Navy Arms 1873 Sporting

Navy Arms 1873 Sporting Rifle
Similar to the 1873 Winchester-Style rifle except has checkered pistol grip stock, 30" octagonal barrel (24" available). Introduced 1992. Imported by Navy Arms.
Price: **$895.00**

NAVY ARMS 1873 WINCHESTER-STYLE RIFLE
Caliber: 44-40, 45 Colt, 12-shot magazine.
Barrel: 24".
Weight: 8¼ lbs. **Length:** 43" overall.
Stock: European walnut.
Sights: Blade front, buckhorn rear.
Features: Color case-hardened frame, rest blued. Full-octagon barrel. Introduced 1991. Imported by Navy Arms.
Price: **$820.00**
Price: Carbine, 19" barrel **$795.00**

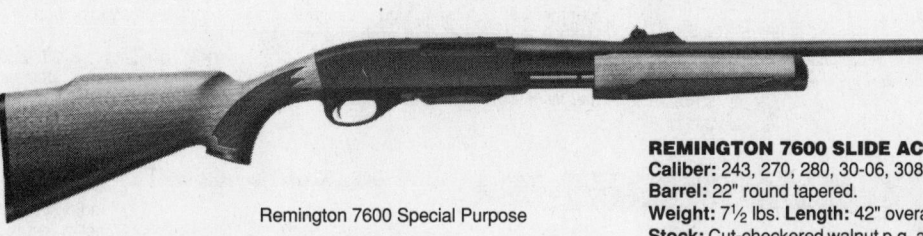

Remington 7600 Special Purpose

Remington 7600 Special Purpose Slide Action
Similar to the standard Model 7600 except chambered only for 270 and 30-06, non-glare finish on the American walnut stock. All exposed metal has non-reflective matte black finish. Comes with quick-detachable sling swivels and camo-pattern Cordura carrying sling. Introduced 1993.
Price: **$496.00**

REMINGTON 7600 SLIDE ACTION
Caliber: 243, 270, 280, 30-06, 308, 35 Whelen.
Barrel: 22" round tapered.
Weight: 7½ lbs. **Length:** 42" overall.
Stock: Cut-checkered walnut p.g. and forend, Monte Carlo with full cheekpiece. Satin or high-gloss finish.
Sights: Gold bead front sight on matted ramp, open step adjustable sporting rear.
Features: Redesigned and improved version of the Model 760. Detachable 4-shot clip. Cross-bolt safety. Receiver tapped for scope mount. Also available in high grade versions. Comes with green Remington hard case. Introduced 1981.
Price: About **$496.00**
Price: Carbine (18½" bbl., 30-06 only) **$496.00**

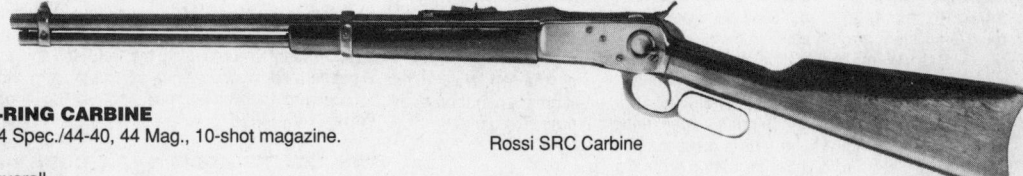

Rossi SRC Carbine

ROSSI M92 SRC SADDLE-RING CARBINE
Caliber: 38 Spec./357 Mag., 44 Spec./44-40, 44 Mag., 10-shot magazine.
Barrel: 20".
Weight: 5¾ lbs. **Length:** 37" overall.
Stock: Walnut.
Sights: Blade front, buckhorn rear.
Features: Recreation of the famous lever-action carbine. Handles 38 and 357 interchangeably. Has high-relief puma medallion inlaid in the receiver. Introduced 1978. Imported by Interarms.
Price: **$334.00**
Price: 44 Spec./44 Mag. (Model 65) **$350.00**

Rossi M92 SRS Short Carbine
Similar to the standard M92 except has 16" barrel, overall length of 33", in 38/357 only. Puma medallion on side of receiver. Introduced 1986.
Price: **$334.00**

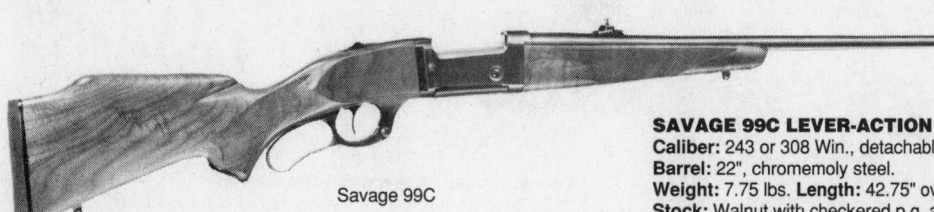

Savage 99C

SAVAGE 99C LEVER-ACTION RIFLE
Caliber: 243 or 308 Win., detachable 4-shot magazine.
Barrel: 22", chromemoly steel.
Weight: 7.75 lbs. **Length:** 42.75" overall.
Stock: Walnut with checkered p.g. and forend, Monte Carlo comb.
Sights: Hooded ramp front, adjustable ramp rear sight. Tapped for scope mounts.
Features: Grooved trigger, top tang slide safety locks trigger and lever. Brown rubber buttpad, q.d. swivel studs, push-button magazine release.
Price: **$629.00**

CENTERFIRE RIFLES—LEVER & SLIDE

UBERTI HENRY RIFLE
Caliber: 44-40.
Barrel: 24¼", half-octagon.
Weight: 9.2 lbs. **Length:** 43¾" overall.
Stock: American walnut.
Sights: Blade front, rear adjustable for elevation.
Features: Frame, elevator, magazine follower, buttplate are brass, balance blue (also available in polished steel). Imported by Uberti USA.
Price: **$895.00**
Price: Henry Carbine (22¼" bbl.) **$900.00**
Price: Henry Trapper (16", 18" bbl.) **$900.00**

UBERTI 1866 SPORTING RIFLE
Caliber: 22 LR, 22 WMR, 38 Spec., 44-40, 45 Colt.
Barrel: 24¼", octagonal.
Weight: 8.1 lbs. **Length:** 43¼" overall.
Stock: Walnut.

Winchester 94 Side Eject

Winchester Model 94 Trapper Side Eject
Same as the Model 94 except has 16" barrel, 5-shot magazine in 30-30, 9-shot in 44 Magnum/44 Special, 45 Colt. Has stainless steel claw extractor, saddle ring, hammer spur extension, walnut wood. Specially inscribed with "1894-1994" on the receiver.
Price: 30-30 . . . . **$342.00**
Price: 44 Mag./44 Spec., 45 Colt **$361.00**

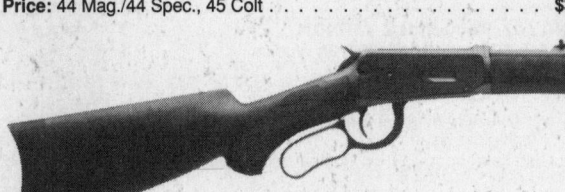

Winchester 94 Limited Grade I

Winchester Model 94 Custom Limited Edition Centennial Rifle
Similar to the 30-30 Model 94 Side Eject except has top ejection action; hand-engraved, grayed action with inking in the same #5 style as on early Model 94s. Within gold-inlaid ovals on each side are engraved game scenes: a pair of pronghorns on the right, caribou on the left. Has 26" half-round/half-octagon barrel with half-magazine tube, crescent buttplate, pistol grip stock, carved spade design checkering patterns. Tang rear sight with micrometer-like adjustment is a replica of the original Lyman No. 2. Introduced 1994. From U.S. Repeating Arms Co., Inc.
Price: **$4,684.00**

Winchester Model 94 Ranger Side Eject Lever-Action Rifle
Same as Model 94 Side Eject except has 5-shot magazine, American hardwood stock and forend, post front sight. Specially inscribed with "1894-1994" on the receiver. Introduced 1985.
Price: **$302.00**
Price: With 4x32 Bushnell scope, mounts **$355.00**

UBERTI 1873 SPORTING RIFLE
Caliber: 22 LR, 22 WMR, 38 Spec., 357 Mag., 44-40, 45 Colt.
Barrel: 24¼", 30", octagonal.
Weight: 8.1 lbs. **Length:** 43¼" overall.
Stock: Walnut.
Sights: Blade front adjustable for windage, open rear adjustable for elevation.
Features: Color case-hardened frame, blued barrel, lever, buttplate, brass elevator. Also available with pistol grip stock ($100.00 extra). Imported from Italy by Uberti USA.
Price: **$900.00**
Price: 1873 Carbine (19" round barrel) **$890.00**

Sights: Blade front adjustable for windage, rear adjustable for elevation.
Features: Frame, buttplate, forend cap of polished brass, balance charcoal blued. Imported by Uberti USA.
Price: **$780.00**
Price: Yellowboy Carbine (19" round bbl.) **$720.00**

WINCHESTER MODEL 94 SIDE EJECT LEVER-ACTION RIFLE
Caliber: 30-30, 7x30 Waters, 32 Win. Spec., 6-shot tubular magazine.
Barrel: 20".
Weight: 6½ lbs. **Length:** 37¾" overall.
Stock: Straight grip walnut stock and forend.
Sights: Hooded blade front, semi-buckhorn rear. Drilled and tapped for scope mount. Post front sight on Trapper model.
Features: Solid frame, forged steel receiver; side ejection, exposed rebounding hammer with automatic trigger-activated transfer bar. Specially inscribed with "1894-1994" on the receiver. Introduced 1984.
Price: Checkered walnut **$370.00**
Price: No checkering, walnut **$342.00**
Price: With WinTuff laminated hardwood stock, 30-30 only **$381.00**

Winchester Model 94 Limited Edition Grade I
Similar to the Model 94 Limited Edition High Grade rifle except uses a close reproduction of the turn-of-the-century #9 factory engraving, diamond-style "H" checkering pattern on the pistol grip stock and forend. Engraving on receiver sides shows whitetail deer profiles. Top tang drilled and tapped for a tang sight. Has half-round/half-octagon barrel with half-magazine tube. Introduced 1994. From U.S. Repeating Arms Co., Inc.
Price: **$811.00**

Winchester Model 94 Limited Edition High Grade Rifle
Similar to the Model 94 Custom Limited Edition except has blued receiver with gold inlays and #6-style engraving pattern showing a gold deer on the right, gold mountain sheep on the left. Has the replica Lyman No. 2 tang sight, spade-pattern checkering on pistol grip stock. Only 3,000 of this grade produced. Introduced 1994. From U.S. Repeating Arms Co., Inc.
Price: **$1,272.00**

WINCHESTER MODEL 94 BIG BORE SIDE EJECT
Caliber: 307 Win., 356 Win., 6-shot magazine.
Barrel: 20".
Weight: 7 lbs. **Length:** 38⅝" overall.
Stock: American walnut. Satin finish.
Sights: Hooded ramp front, semi-buckhorn rear adjustable for windage and elevation.
Features: All external metal parts have Winchester's deep blue finish. Rifling twist 1:12". Rubber recoil pad fitted to buttstock. Specially inscribed with "1894-1994" on the receiver. Introduced 1983. From U.S. Repeating Arms Co.
Price: **$381.00**

Winchester 94 Wrangler

Winchester Model 94 Wrangler Side Eject
Same as the Model 94 except has 16" barrel and large loop lever for large and/or gloved hands. Has 9-shot capacity (5-shot for 30-30), stainless steel claw extractor. Available in 30-30, 44 Magnum/44 Special. Specially inscribed with "1894-1994" on the receiver. Reintroduced 1992.
Price: 30-30 . . . . **$361.00**
Price: 44 Magnum/44 Special **$381.00**

CAUTION: PRICES SHOWN ARE SUPPLIED BY THE MANUFACTURER OR IMPORTER. CHECK YOUR LOCAL GUNSHOP.

Includes models for a wide variety of sporting and competitive purposes and uses.

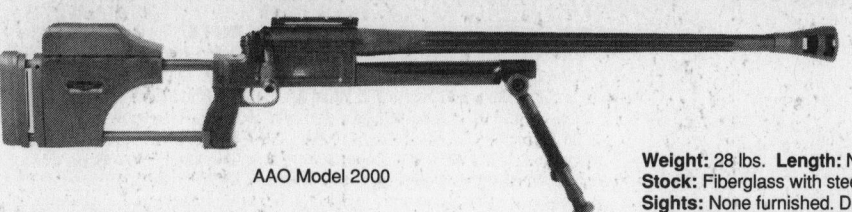

AAO Model 2000

AAO MODEL 2000 50-CALIBER RIFLE
Caliber: 50 BMG, 5-shot magazine.
Barrel: 30"; 1:15" twist; muzzle brake.

Weight: 28 lbs. **Length:** NA.
Stock: Fiberglass with steel reinforcing plates, Kick-Ease recoil pad.
Sights: None furnished. Drilled and tapped for scope base.
Features: Controlled feeding via rotating enclosed claw extractor; 90-degree bolt rotation; cone bolt face and barrel; trigger-mounted safety blocks sear; fully adjustable, detachable tripod. Introduced 1994. From Ithaca Acquisition Corp.
Price: $4,595.00

Alpine Rifle

ALPINE BOLT-ACTION RIFLE
Caliber: 22-250, 243 Win., 270, 30-06, 308, 7mm Rem. Mag., 8mm, 5-shot magazine (3 for magnum).
Barrel: 23" (std. cals.), 24" (mag.).

Weight: 7½ lbs.
Stock: European walnut. Full p.g. and Monte Carlo; checkered p.g. and forend; rubber recoil pad; white line spacers; sling swivels.
Sights: Ramp front, open rear adjustable for windage and elevation.
Features: Made by Firearms Co. Ltd. in England. Imported by Mandall Shooting Supplies.
Price: Custom Grade $395.00
Price: Supreme Grade $425.00

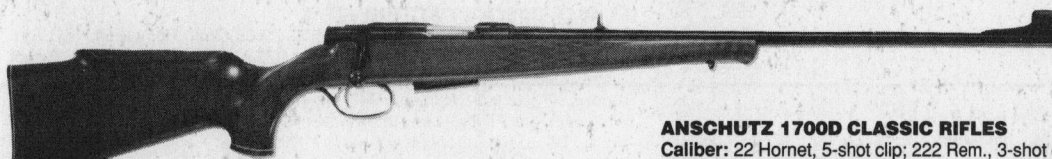

Anschutz 1700D Classic

ANSCHUTZ 1700D CLASSIC RIFLES
Caliber: 22 Hornet, 5-shot clip; 222 Rem., 3-shot clip.
Barrel: 24", $^{13}/_{16}$" dia. heavy.
Weight: 7¾ lbs. **Length:** 43" overall.
Stock: Select European walnut with checkered pistol grip and forend.
Sights: Hooded ramp front, folding leaf rear; drilled and tapped for scope mounting.
Features: Adjustable single stage trigger. Receiver drilled and tapped for scope mounting. Introduced 1988. Imported from Germany by Precision Sales International.
Price: $1,395.00
Price: Meistergrade (select stock, gold engraved trigger guard) . . $1,594.00

Anschutz 1700D Custom Rifles
Similar to the Classic models except have roll-over Monte Carlo cheekpiece, slim forend with Schnabel tip, Wundhammer palm swell on pistol grip, rosewood grip cap with white diamond insert. Skip-line checkering on grip and forend. Introduced 1988. Imported from Germany by PSI.
Price: $1,426.00
Price: Meistergrade (select stock, gold engraved trigger guard) . . $1,625.00

Anschutz 1733D

ANSCHUTZ 1700D BAVARIAN BOLT-ACTION RIFLE
Caliber: 22 Hornet, 222 Rem., detachable clip.
Barrel: 24".
Weight: 7¼ lbs. **Length:** 43" overall.
Stock: European walnut with Bavarian cheek rest. Checkered p.g. and forend.
Sights: Hooded ramp front, folding leaf rear.
Features: Uses the improved 1700 Match 54 action with adjustable trigger. Drilled and tapped for scope mounting. Introduced 1988. Imported from Germany by Precision Sales International.
Price: $1,426.00
Price: Meistergrade (select stock, gold engraved trigger guard) . . $1,625.00

Anschutz 1733D Mannlicher Rifle
Similar to the 1700D Bavarian except chambered only for 22 Hornet and has Mannlicher stock. Uses improved Match 54 action with #5096 single-stage trigger with 2.6 lb. adjustable pull weight. Has 19.75" barrel, overall length of 39". Comes with sling swivels, Lyman folding rear sight and hooded ramp front, 4-shot magazine. Introduced 1993. Imported from Germany by Precision Sales International.
Price: $1,539.00

A-SQUARE CAESAR BOLT-ACTION RIFLE
Caliber: 7mm Rem. Mag., 7mm STW, 30-06, 300 Win. Mag., 300 H&H, 300 Wea. Mag., 8mm Rem. Mag., 338 Win. Mag., 340 Wea. Mag., 338 A-Square, 9.3x62, 9.3x64, 375 Wea. Mag., 375 H&H, 375 JRS, 375 A-Square, 416 Hoffman, 416 Rem. Mag., 416 Taylor, 404 Jeffery, 425 Express, 458 Win. Mag., 458 Lott, 450 Ackley, 460 Short A-Square, 470 Capstick, 495 A-Square.
Barrel: 20" to 26" (no-cost customer option).
Weight: 8½ lbs.
Stock: Claro walnut with hand-rubbed oil finish; classic style with A-Square Coil-Chek® features for reduced recoil; flush detachable swivels. Customer

choice of length of pull.
Sights: Choice of three-leaf express, forward or normal-mount scope, or combination (at extra cost).
Features: Matte non-reflective blue, double cross-bolts, steel and fiberglass reinforcement of wood from tang to forend tip; three-position positive safety; three-way adjustable trigger; expanded magazine capacity. Right- or left-hand. Introduced 1984. Made in U.S. by A-Square Co., Inc.
Price: Walnut stock $2,550.00
Price: Synthetic stock $2,800.00

A-Square Hannibal

A-SQUARE HANNIBAL BOLT-ACTION RIFLE
Caliber: 7mm Rem. Mag., 7mm STW, 30-06, 300 Win. Mag., 300 H&H, 300 Wea. Mag., 8mm Rem. Mag., 338 Win. Mag., 340 Wea. Mag., 338 A-Square Mag., 9.3x62, 9.3x64, 375 H&H, 375 Wea. Mag., 375 JRS, 375 A-Square Mag., 378 Wea. Mag., 416 Taylor, 416 Rem. Mag., 416 Hoffman, 416 Rigby, 416 Wea. Mag., 404 Jeffery, 425 Express, 458 Win. Mag., 458 Lott, 450 Ackley, 460 Short A-Square Mag., 460 Wea. Mag., 470 Capstick, 495 A-Square Mag., 500 A-Square Mag.
Barrel: 20" to 26" (no-cost customer option).
Weight: 9 to 11¾ lbs.
Stock: Claro walnut with hand-rubbed oil finish; classic style with A-Square Coil-Chek® features for reduced recoil; flush detachable swivels. Customer choice of length of pull. Available with synthetic stock.
Sights: Choice of three-leaf express, forward or normal-mount scope, or combination (at extra cost).
Features: Matte non-reflective blue, double cross-bolts, steel and fiberglass reinforcement of wood from tang to forend tip; Mauser-style claw extractor; expanded magazine capacity; two-position safety; three-way target trigger. Right-hand only. Introduced 1983. Made in U.S. by A-Square Co., Inc.
Price: Walnut stock **$2,495.00**
Price: Synthetic stock **$2,645.00**

BARRETT MODEL 90 BOLT-ACTION RIFLE
Caliber: 50 BMG, 5-shot magazine.
Barrel: 29".
Weight: 22 lbs. **Length:** 45" overall.
Stock: Sorbothane recoil pad.
Sights: Scope optional.
Features: Bolt-action, bullpup design. Disassembles without tools; extendable bipod legs; match-grade barrel; high efficiency muzzlebrake. Introduced 1990. From Barrett Firearms Mfg., Inc.
Price: From **$3,650.00**

Blaser R93

BLASER R93 BOLT-ACTION RIFLE
Caliber: 222, 243, 6.5x55, 270, 7x57, 308, 30-06, 7mm Rem. Mag., 300 Win. Mag., 300 Wea. Mag., 338 Win. Mag., 375 H&H, 416 Rem. Mag., 3-shot magazine.
Barrel: 22" (standard calibers), 24" (magnum calibers).
Weight: 6.5 to 7.5 lbs. **Length:** 40" overall (22" barrel).
Stock: Two-piece European walnut.
Sights: Blade front on ramp, open rear, or no sights.
Features: Straight-pull bolt action with thumb-activated safety slide/cocking mechanism. Interchangeable barrels and bolt heads. Introduced 1994. Imported from Germany by Autumn Sales, Inc.
Price: Standard **$2,800.00**
Price: Safari, standard grade, 375 H&H, 416 Rem. Mag. **$3,200.00**

BLASER R84 BOLT-ACTION RIFLE
Caliber: Std. cals.—22-250, 243, 6mm Rem., 25-06, 270, 280, 30-06; magnum cals.—257 Wea., 264 Win. Mag., 7mm Rem. Mag., 300 Win. Mag., 300 Wea., 338 Win. Mag., 375 H&H.
Barrel: 23" (24" in magnum cals.).
Weight: 7-7¼ lbs. **Length:** Std. cals.—41" overall (23" barrel).
Stock: Two-piece Turkish walnut. Solid black buttpad.
Sights: None furnished. Comes with low-profile Blaser scope mountings.
Features: Interchangeable barrels (scope mountings on barrel), and magnum/standard caliber bolt assemblies. Left-hand models available in all calibers. Imported from Germany by Autumn Sales, Inc.
Price: Right-hand, standard or magnum calibers **$2,300.00**
Price: Left-hand, standard or magnum calibers **$2,350.00**
Price: Interchangeable barrels, standard or magnum calibers **$600.00**

BRNO ZKB 527 Fox

BRNO ZKB 527 FOX BOLT-ACTION RIFLE
Caliber: 22 Hornet, 222 Rem., 223 Rem., detachable 5-shot magazine.
Barrel: 23½"; standard or heavy barrel.
Weight: 6 lbs., 1 oz. **Length:** 42½" overall.
Stock: European walnut with Monte Carlo.
Sights: Hooded front, open adjustable rear.
Features: Improved mini-Mauser action with non-rotating claw extractor; grooved receiver. Imported from the Czech Republic by Action Arms Ltd.
Price: **$665.00**

BRNO ZKK 600, 601, 602 BOLT-ACTION RIFLES
Caliber: 7x57, 30-06, 270 (M600); 243, 308 (M601); 300 Win. Mag., 375 H&H, 458 Win. Mag. (M602), 5-shot magazine.
Barrel: 23½" (M600, 601); 25" (M602).
Weight: 7 lbs., 3 oz. to 9 lbs., 9 oz. **Length:** 43" overall (M601).
Stock: Classic-style checkered walnut.
Sights: Hooded ramp front, open folding leaf adjustable rear.
Features: Improved Mauser action with controlled feed, claw extractor; safety blocks trigger and locks bolt; sling swivels. Imported from the Czech Republic by Action Arms Ltd.
Price: Model 600, 601 . . . . **$609.00**
Price: Model 602 . . . . **$835.00**
Price: Model 602, synthetic stock (300 Win. Mag. 375 H&H, 458 Win. Mag.) **$745.00**

BRNO 537 SPORTER BOLT-ACTION RIFLE
Caliber: 243, 270, 30-06 (internal 5-shot magazine), 308 (detachable 5-shot magazine).
Barrel: 23.6".
Weight: 7 lbs., 9 oz. **Length:** 44.7" overall.
Stock: Checkered walnut.
Sights: Hooded ramp front, adjustable folding leaf rear.
Features: Improved standard size Mauser-style action with non-rotating claw extractor; externally adjustable trigger, American-style safety; streamlined bolt shroud with cocking indicator. Introduced 1992. Imported from the Czech Republic by Action Arms Ltd.
Price: **$669.00**
Price: Mountain Carbine (19" barrel with ring mounts, 243 Win.) . . **$669.00**

Browning A-Bolt II Medallion

Browning A-Bolt II Stainless Stalker

Similar to the Hunter model A-Bolt except receiver and barrel are made of stainless steel; the rest of the exposed metal surfaces are finished with a durable matte silver-gray. Graphite-fiberglass composite textured stock. No sights are furnished. Available in 270, 30-06, 7mm Rem. Mag., 375 H&H. BOSS barrel vibration modulator and muzzle brake system not available in 375 H&H. Introduced 1987.

Price:	**$726.95**
Price: With BOSS	**$806.95**
Price: Left-hand, no sights	**$749.95**
Price: With BOSS	**$829.95**
Price: 375 H&H, with sights	**$827.95**
Price: 375 H&H, left-hand, with sights	**$856.95**

Browning A-Bolt II Composite Stalker

Similar to the A-Bolt II Hunter except has black graphite-fiberglass stock with textured finish. Matte blue finish on all exposed metal surfaces. Available in 223, 22-250, 243, 7mm-08, 308, 30-06, 270, 280, 25-06, 7mm Rem. Mag., 300 Win. Mag., 338 Win. Mag. BOSS barrel vibration modulator and muzzle brake system offered in all calibers. Introduced 1994.

Price: No sights	**$576.95**
Price: No sights, BOSS	**$656.95**

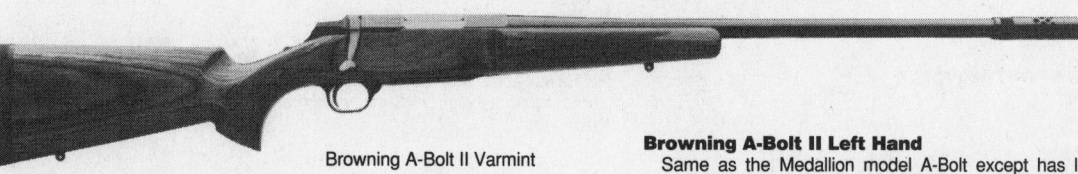

Browning A-Bolt II Varmint

Browning A-Bolt II Varmint Rifle

Same as the A-Bolt II Hunter except has heavy varmint/target barrel, laminated wood stock with special dimensions, flat forend and palm swell grip. Chambered only for 223, 22-250. Comes with BOSS barrel vibration modulator and muzzle brake system. Introduced 1994.

Price: With BOSS	**$856.95**

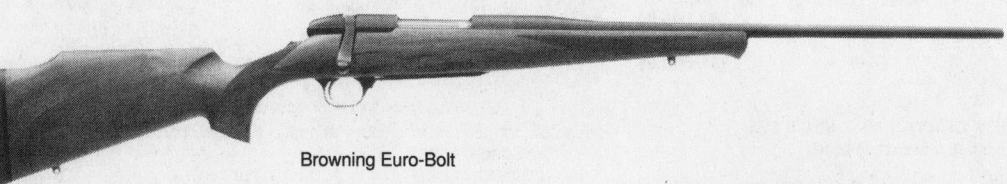

Browning Euro-Bolt

Browning A-Bolt II Gold Medallion

Similar to the standard A-Bolt except has select walnut stock with brass spacers between rubber recoil pad and between the rosewood grip cap and forend tip; gold-filled barrel inscription; palm-swell pistol grip, Monte Carlo comb, 22 lpi checkering with double borders; engraved receiver flats. In 270, 30-06, 7mm Rem. Mag. only. Introduced 1988.

Price:	**$876.95**
Price: For BOSS, add	**$80.00**

BROWNING A-BOLT II RIFLE

Caliber: 25-06, 270, 30-06, 280, 7mm Rem. Mag., 300 Win. Mag., 338 Win. Mag., 375 H&H Mag.
Barrel: 22" medium sporter weight with recessed muzzle; 26" on mag. cals.
Weight: 6½ to 7½ lbs. **Length:** 44¾" overall (magnum and standard); 41¾" (short action).
Stock: Classic style American walnut; recoil pad standard on magnum calibers.
Features: Short-throw (60°) fluted bolt, three locking lugs, plunger-type ejector; adjustable trigger is grooved and gold-plated. Hinged floorplate, detachable box magazine (4 rounds std. cals., 3 for magnums). Slide tang safety. Medallion has glossy stock finish, rosewood grip and forend caps, high polish blue. BOSS barrel vibration modulator and muzzle brake system not available in 375 H&H. Introduced 1985. Imported from Japan by Browning.

Price: Medallion, no sights	**$652.95**
Price: Hunter, no sights	**$559.95**
Price: Hunter, with sights	**$629.95**
Price: Medallion, 375 H&H Mag., with sights	**$756.95**
Price: For BOSS (except 375 H&H), add	**$80.00**

Browning A-Bolt II Short Action

Similar to the standard A-Bolt except has short action for 22 Hornet, 223, 22-250, 243, 257 Roberts, 7mm-08, 284 Win., 308 chamberings. Available in Hunter or Medallion grades. Weighs 6½ lbs. Other specs essentially the same. BOSS barrel vibration modulator and muzzle brake system optional. Introduced 1985.

Price: Medallion, no sights	**$652.95**
Price: Hunter, no sights	**$559.95**
Price: Hunter, with sights	**$629.95**
Price: Composite, no sights	**$576.95**
Price: For BOSS, add	**$80.00**

Browning A-Bolt II Left Hand

Same as the Medallion model A-Bolt except has left-hand action and is available only in 270, 30-06, 7mm Rem. Mag., 375 H&H. BOSS barrel vibration modulator and muzzle brake system not available in 375 H&H. Introduced 1987.

Price:	**$679.95**
Price: With BOSS	**$759.95**
Price: 375 H&H, with sights	**$782.95**

Browning Euro-Bolt II Rifle

Similar to the A-Bolt II Hunter except has satin-finished walnut stock with Continental-style cheekpiece, palm-swell grip and schnabel forend, rounded bolt shroud and Mannlicher-style flattened bolt handle. Available in 30-06 and 270 with 22" barrel, 7mm Rem. Mag. with 26" barrel. Weighs about 6 lbs., 11 oz. BOSS barrel vibration modulator and muzzle brake system optional. Introduced 1993.

Price:	**$762.95**
Price: For BOSS, add	**$80.00**

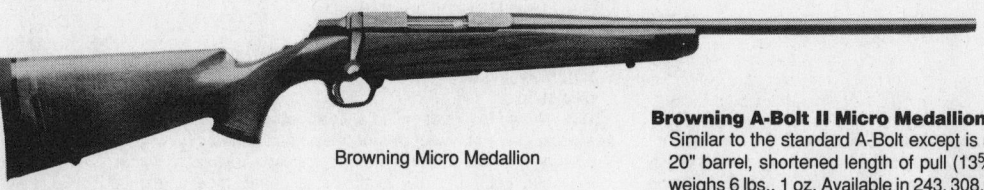

Browning Micro Medallion

Browning A-Bolt II Micro Medallion

Similar to the standard A-Bolt except is a scaled-down version. Comes with 20" barrel, shortened length of pull (13⅝"); three-shot magazine capacity; weighs 6 lbs., 1 oz. Available in 243, 308, 7mm-08, 257 Roberts, 223, 22-250. BOSS feature not available for this model. Introduced 1988.

Price: No sights	**$652.95**

CAUTION: PRICES SHOWN ARE SUPPLIED BY THE MANUFACTURER OR IMPORTER. CHECK YOUR LOCAL GUNSHOP.

49th EDITION, 1995 **339**

Century Centurion 14

CENTURY DELUXE CUSTOM SPORTER
Caliber: 243, 270, 308, 30-06.
Barrel: 24".
Weight: NA. **Length:** 44" overall.
Stock: Black synthetic.
Sights: None furnished. Scope base installed.
Features: Mauser 98 action; bent bolt handle for scope use; low-swing safety; matte black finish; blind magazine. Introduced 1992. From Century International Arms.
Price: About **$288.00**

> Consult our Directory pages for the location of firms mentioned.

CENTURY CENTURION 14 SPORTER
Caliber: 7mm Rem. Mag., 300 Win. Mag., 5-shot magazine.
Barrel: 24".
Weight: NA. **Length:** 43.3" overall.
Stock: Walnut-finished European hardwood. Checkered p.g. and forend. Monte Carlo comb.
Sights: None furnished.
Features: Uses modified Pattern 14 Enfield action. Drilled and tapped; scope base mounted. Blue finish. From Century International Arms.
Price: About **$275.00**

CENTURY ENFIELD SPORTER #4
Caliber: 303 British, 10-shot magazine.
Barrel: 25.2".
Weight: 8 lbs., 5 oz. **Length:** 44.5" overall.
Stock: Beechwood with checkered p.g. and forend, Monte Carlo comb.
Sights: Blade front, adjustable aperture rear.
Features: Uses Lee-Enfield action; blue finish. Trigger pinned to receiver. Introduced 1987. From Century International Arms.
Price: About **$156.00**

Century Custom Sporting Rifle

CENTURY CUSTOM SPORTING RIFLE
Caliber: 308, 7.62x39mm.
Barrel: 22".

COOPER ARMS MODEL 21 VARMINT EXTREME RIFLE
Caliber: 17 Rem., 17 Mach IV, 221 Fireball, 222, 223, 6x45, 6x47, single shot.
Barrel: 24"; stainless steel, with competition step crown; free-floated.
Weight: NA. **Length:** NA.
Stock: AAA Claro walnut with flared oval forend, ambidextrous palm swell, 22 lpi checkering, oil finish, Pachmayr buttpad.
Sights: None furnished; drilled and tapped for scope mounting.
Features: Action has three mid-bolt locking lugs; adjustable trigger; glass bedded; swivel studs. Introduced 1994. Made in U.S. by Cooper Arms.
Price: **$1,295.00**
Price: Custom Classic (ebony forend tip, steel grip cap, beaded cheekpiece) **$1,350.00**

COOPER ARMS MODEL 36CF CENTERFIRE SPORTER
Caliber: 17 CCM, 22 CCM, 22 Hornet, 5-shot magazine.
Barrel: 23".
Weight: 7 lbs. **Length:** 42½" overall.
Stock: AA Claro walnut with 22 lpi checkering, oil finish; Custom has AAA Claro or AA French walnut.
Sights: None furnished.
Features: Action has three mid-bolt locking lugs, 45-degree bolt rotation; fully

Weight: 6.7 lbs. **Length:** 43.75".
Stock: Walnut-finished hardwood.
Sights: None furnished; comes with two-piece Weaver-type base.
Features: Uses small ring Model 98 action; low-swing safety; blue finish. Introduced 1994. From Century International Arms.
Price: About **$275.00**

CENTURY SWEDISH SPORTER #38
Caliber: 6.5x55 Swede, 5-shot magazine.
Barrel: 24".
Weight: NA. **Length:** 44.1" overall.
Stock: Walnut-finished European hardwood with checkered p.g. and forend; Monte Carlo comb.
Sights: Blade front, adjustable rear.
Features: Uses M38 Swedish Mauser action; comes with Holden Ironsighter see-through scope mount. Introduced 1987. From Century International Arms.
Price: About **$237.50**

adjustable trigger; swivel studs. Pachmayr butt pad. Introduced 1994. Made in U.S. by Cooper Arms.
Price: Standard **$1,125.00**
Price: Classic **$1,350.00**
Price: Custom (AAA Claro walnut, Monte Carlo beaded cheekpiece, oil finish) **$1,250.00**
Price: Custom Classic (as above with ebony forend tip, steel grip cap, Brownell No. 1 checkering pattern) **$1,350.00**

Dakota 76 Classic

Dakota 76 Short Action Rifles
A scaled-down version of the standard Model 76. Standard chamberings are 22-250, 243, 6mm Rem., 250-3000, 7mm-08, 308, others on special order. Short Classic Grade has 21" barrel; Alpine Grade is lighter (6½ lbs.), has a blind magazine and slimmer stock. Introduced 1989.
Price: Short Classic **$2,300.00**

DAKOTA 76 CLASSIC BOLT-ACTION RIFLE
Caliber: 257 Roberts, 270, 280, 30-06, 7mm Rem. Mag., 338 Win. Mag., 300 Win. Mag., 375 H&H, 458 Win. Mag.
Barrel: 23".
Weight: 7½ lbs. **Length:** NA.
Stock: Medium fancy grade walnut in classic style. Checkered p.g. and forend; solid buttpad.
Sights: None furnished; drilled and tapped for scope mounts.
Features: Has many features of the original Model 70 Winchester. One-piece rail trigger guard assembly; steel grip cap. Adjustable trigger. Many options available. Left-hand rifle available at same price. Introduced 1988. From Dakota Arms, Inc.
Price: **$2,300.00**

Dakota 416 Rigby

Dakota 76 Varmint Rifle

Similar to the Dakota 76 except is a single shot with heavy barrel contour and special stock dimensions for varmint shooting. Chambered for 17 Rem., 22 BR, 22 Hornet, 222 Rem., 22-250, 220 Swift, 223, 6mm BR, 6mm PPC. Introduced 1994. Made in U.S. by Dakota Arms, Inc.

Price: **$2,300.00**

Dakota 416 Rigby African

Similar to the 76 Safari except chambered for 404 Jeffery, 416 Rigby, 416 Dakota, 450 Dakota, 4-round magazine, select wood, two stock cross-bolts. Has 24" barrel, weight of 9-10 lbs. Ramp front sight, standing leaf rear. Introduced 1989.

Price: **$3,500.00**

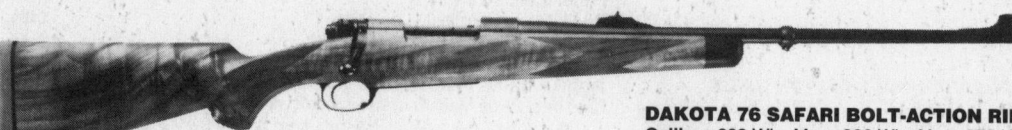

Dakota 76 Safari

AUGUSTE FRANCOTTE BOLT-ACTION RIFLES

Caliber: 243, 270, 7x64, 30-06, 308, 300 Win. Mag., 338, 7mm Rem. Mag., 375 H&H, 458 Win. Mag.; others on request.
Barrel: 23½" to 26½".
Weight: 8 to 10 lbs.
Stock: Fancy European walnut. To customer specs.
Sights: To customer specs.
Features: Basically a custom gun, Francotte offers many options. Imported from Belgium by Armes de Chasse.

Price: . . . . **$6,000.00 to $10,000.00**

DAKOTA 76 SAFARI BOLT-ACTION RIFLE

Caliber: 338 Win. Mag., 300 Win. Mag., 375 H&H, 458 Win. Mag.
Barrel: 23".
Weight: 8½ lbs. **Length:** NA.
Stock: Fancy walnut with ebony forend tip; point-pattern with wraparound forend checkering.
Sights: Ramp front, standing leaf rear.
Features: Has many features of the original Model 70 Winchester. Barrel band front swivel, inletted rear. Cheekpiece with shadow line. Steel grip cap. Introduced 1988. From Dakota Arms, Inc.

Price: Wood stock **$3,000.00**

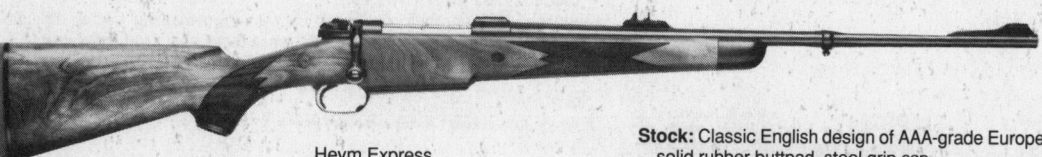

Heym Express

HEYM MAGNUM EXPRESS SERIES RIFLE

Caliber: 338 Lapua Mag., 375 H&H, 378 Wea. Mag., 416 Rigby, 500 Nitro Express 3", 460 Wea. Mag., 500 A-Square, 450 Ackley, 600 N.E.
Barrel: 24".
Weight: About 9.9 lbs. **Length:** 45¼" overall.

Stock: Classic English design of AAA-grade European walnut with cheekpiece, solid rubber buttpad, steel grip cap.
Sights: Adjustable post front on ramp, three-leaf express rear.
Features: Modified magnum Mauser action, Timney single trigger; special hinged floorplate; barrel-mouted q.d. swivel, q.d. rear; vertical double recoil lug in rear of stock. Double square bridge, three-position safety and 5-shot magazine in 416 Rigby. Introduced 1989. Imported from Germany by Jager-Sport, Ltd.

Price: **$6,500.00**
Price: 600 Nitro Express **$11,350.00**

Howa Lightning

HOWA LIGHTNING BOLT-ACTION RIFLE

Caliber: 223, 22-250, 243, 270, 308, 30-06, 7mm Rem. Mag., 300 Win. Mag., 338 Win. Mag.
Barrel: 22", 24" magnum calibers.
Weight: 7½ lbs. **Length:** 42" overall (22" barrel).

Stock: Black Bell & Carlson Carbelite composite with Monte Carlo comb; checkered grip and forend.
Sights: None furnished. Drilled and tapped for scope mounting.
Features: Sliding thumb safety; hinged floorplate; polished blue/black finish. Introduced 1993. From Interarms.

Price: Standard calibers **$498.00**
Price: Magnum calibers **$517.00**

Howa Realtree

HOWA REALTREE CAMO RIFLE

Caliber: 270, 30-06, 5-shot magazine.
Barrel: 22".

Weight: 8 lbs. **Length:** 42¼" overall.
Stock: Bell & Carlson Carbelite composite. Straight comb; checkered grip and forend.
Sights: None furnished. Drilled and tapped for scope mouting.
Features: Completely covered with Realtree camo finish, except bolt. Sliding thumb safety, hinged floorplate; sling swivel studs, recoil pad. Introduced 1993. From Interarms.

Price: **$620.00**

CAUTION: PRICES SHOWN ARE SUPPLIED BY THE MANUFACTURER OR IMPORTER. CHECK YOUR LOCAL GUNSHOP.

49th EDITION, 1995   **341**

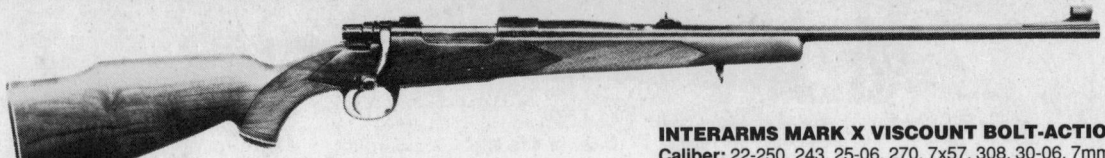

Interarms Mark X Viscount

Interarms Mini-Mark X Rifle

Scaled-down version of the Mark X Viscount. Uses miniature M98 Mauser-system action, chambered for 223 Rem. and 7.62x39; 20" barrel. Overall length of 39¾", weight 6.35 lbs. Drilled and tapped for scope mounting. Checkered hardwood stock. Adjustable trigger. Introduced 1987. Imported from Yugoslavia by Interarms.
Price: Either caliber **$455.00**

INTERARMS MARK X WHITWORTH BOLT-ACTION RIFLE

Caliber: 22-250, 243, 25-06, 270, 7x57, 308, 30-06, 7mm Rem. Mag., 300 Win. Mag., 5-shot magazine (3-shot for 300 Win. Mag.).
Barrel: 24".
Weight: 7 lbs. **Length:** 44" overall.
Stock: European walnut with checkered grip and forend, straight comb.

INTERARMS MARK X VISCOUNT BOLT-ACTION RIFLE

Caliber: 22-250, 243, 25-06, 270, 7x57, 308, 30-06, 7mm Rem. Mag., 300 Win. Mag.
Barrel: 24".
Weight: 7 lbs. **Length:** 44" overall.
Stock: European hardwood with Monte Carlo comb, checkered grip and forend.
Sights: Blade on ramp front, open fully adjustable rear. Drilled and tapped for scope mounting.
Features: Polished blue finish. Uses Mauser system action with sliding thumb safety, hinged floorplate, adjustable trigger. Reintroduced 1987. Imported from Yugoslavia by Interarms.
Price: Standard calibers **$471.00**
Price: Magnum calibers **$486.00**

Sights: Hooded blade on ramp front, open fully adjustable rear.
Features: Uses Mauser system action with sliding thumb safety, hinged floor-plate, adjustable trigger. Polished blue finish. Swivel studs. Imported from Yugoslavia by Interarms.
Price: Standard calibers **$565.00**
Price: Magnum calibers **$584.00**

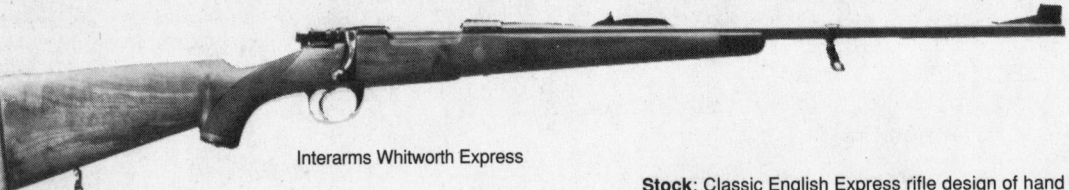

Interarms Whitworth Express

INTERARMS WHITWORTH EXPRESS RIFLE

Caliber: 375 H&H, 458 Win. Mag.
Barrel: 24".
Weight: 7½-8 lbs. **Length:** 44".

Stock: Classic English Express rifle design of hand checkered, select European walnut.
Sights: Ramp front with removable hood, three-leaf open sight calibrated for 100, 200, 300 yards on ¼-rib.
Features: Solid rubber recoil pad, barrel-mounted sling swivel, adjustable trigger, hinged floorplate, solid steel recoil cross bolt. From Interarms.
Price: 375, 458, with express sights **$703.00**

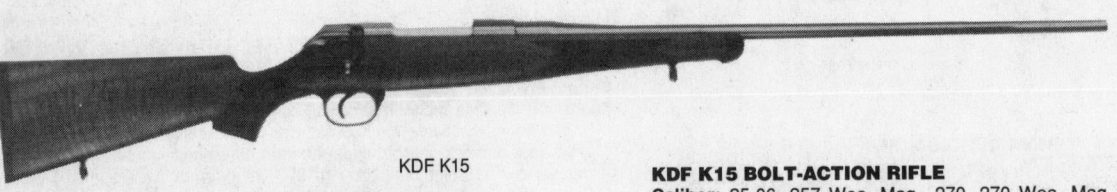

KDF K15

KDF K15 BOLT-ACTION RIFLE

Caliber: 25-06, 257 Wea. Mag., 270, 270 Wea. Mag., 7mm Rem. Mag., 30-06, 300 Win. Mag., 300 Wea. Mag., 338 Win. Mag., 340 Wea. Mag., 375 H&H, 411 KDF Mag., 416 Rem. Mag., 458 Win. Mag.; 4-shot magazine for standard calibers, 3-shot for magnums.
Barrel: 22" standard, 24" optional.
Weight: About 8 lbs. **Length:** 44" overall (24" barrel).
Stock: Laminated standard; Kevlar composite or AAA walnut in Monte Carlo, classic, schnabel or thumbhole styles optional.
Sights: None furnished; optional. Drilled and tapped for scope mounting.
Features: Three-lug locking design with 60° bolt lift; ultra-fast lock time; fully adjustable trigger. Options available. Introduced 1976. From KDF, Inc.
Price: Standard calibers **$1,950.00**
Price: Magnum calibers **$2,000.00**

CONSULT **Shooter's Marketplace** Page 225, This Issue

Krico Model 700

KRICO MODEL 600 BOLT-ACTION RIFLE

Caliber: 222, 223, 22-250, 243, 308, 5.6x50 Mag., 4-shot magazine.
Barrel: 23.6".
Weight: 7.9 lbs. **Length:** 43.7" overall.
Stock: European walnut with Monte Carlo comb.
Sights: None furnished; drilled and tapped for scope mounting.
Features: Rubber recoil pad, sling swivels, checkered grip and forend. Polished blue finish. Imported from Germany by Mandall Shooting Supplies.
Price: **$1,295.00**

KRICO MODEL 700 BOLT-ACTION RIFLES

Caliber: 17 Rem., 222, 222 Rem. Mag., 223, 5.6x50 Mag., 243, 308, 5.6x57 RWS, 22-250, 6.5x55, 6.5x57, 7x57, 270, 7x64, 30-06, 9.3x62, 6.5x68, 7mm Rem. Mag., 300 Win. Mag., 8x68S, 7.5 Swiss, 9.3x64, 6x62 Freres.
Barrel: 23.6" (std. cals.); 25.5" (mag. cals.).
Weight: 7 lbs. **Length:** 43.3" overall (23.6" bbl.).
Stock: European walnut, Bavarian cheekpiece.
Sights: Blade on ramp front, open adjustable rear.
Features: Removable box magazine; sliding safety. Drilled and tapped for scope mounting. Imported from Germany by Mandall Shooting Supplies.
Price: Model 700 . . . . **$995.00**
Price: Model 700 Deluxe S **$1,495.00**
Price: Model 700 Deluxe **$1,025.00**
Price: Model 700 Stutzen (full stock) **$1,249.00**

CENTERFIRE RIFLES—BOLT ACTION

L.A.R. Grizzly 50

L.A.R. GRIZZLY 50 BIG BOAR RIFLE
Caliber: 50 BMG, single shot.
Barrel: 36".
Weight: 28.4 lbs. **Length:** 45.5" overall.
Stock: Integral. Ventilated rubber recoil pad.
Sights: None furnished; scope mount.
Features: Bolt-action bullpup design; thumb safety. All-steel construction. Introduced 1994. Made in U.S. by L.A.R. Mfg., Inc.
Price: **$2,400.00**

McMILLAN SIGNATURE CLASSIC SPORTER
Caliber: 22-250, 243, 6mm Rem., 7mm-08, 284, 308 (short action); 25-06, 270, 280 Rem., 30-06, 7mm Rem. Mag., 300 Win. Mag., 300 Wea. (long action); 338 Win. Mag., 340 Wea., 375 H&H (magnum action).
Barrel: 22", 24", 26".
Weight: 7 lbs. (short action).
Stock: McMillan fiberglass in green, beige, brown or black. Recoil pad and 1" swivels installed. Length of pull up to 14¼".
Sights: None furnished. Comes with 1" rings and bases.
Features: Uses McMillan right- or left-hand action with matte black finish. Trigger pull set at 3 lbs. Four-round magazine for standard calibers; three for magnums. Aluminum floorplate. Fibergrain and wood stocks optional. Introduced 1987. From McMillan Gunworks, Inc.
Price: **$2,400.00**

McMillan Alaskan

McMillan Signature Super Varminter
Similar to the Classic Sporter except has heavy contoured barrel, adjustable trigger, field bipod and special hand-bedded fiberglass stock (Fibergrain optional). Chambered for 223, 22-250, 220 Swift, 243, 6mm Rem., 25-06, 7mm-08 and 308. Comes with 1" rings and bases. Introduced 1989.
Price: **$2,400.00**

McMillan Signature Titanium Mountain Rifle
Similar to the Classic Sporter except action made of titanium alloy, barrel of chromemoly steel. Stock is of graphite reinforced fiberglass. Weight is 5½ lbs. Chambered for 270, 280 Rem., 30-06, 7mm Rem. Mag., 300 Win. Mag. Fibergrain stock optional. Introduced 1989.
Price: **$3,000.00**

McMillan Signature Alaskan
Similar to the Classic Sporter except has match-grade barrel with single leaf rear sight, barrel band front, 1" detachable rings and mounts, steel floorplate, electroless nickel finish. Has wood Monte Carlo stock with cheekpiece, palm-swell grip, solid buttpad. Chambered for 270, 280 Rem., 30-06, 7mm Rem. Mag., 300 Win. Mag., 300 Wea., 358 Win., 340 Wea., 375 H&H. Introduced 1989.
Price: **$3,300.00**

McMillan Classic Stainless

McMillan Classic Stainless Sporter
Similar to the Classic Sporter except barrel and action made of stainless steel. Same calibers, in addition to 416 Rem. Mag. Comes with fiberglass stock, right- or left-hand action in natural stainless, glass bead or black chrome sulfide finishes. Introduced 1990. From McMillan Gunworks, Inc.
Price: **$2,500.00**

McMILLAN TALON SAFARI RIFLE
Caliber: 300 Win. Mag., 300 Wea. Mag., 338 Win. Mag., 300 H&H, 340 Wea. Mag., 375 H&H, 404 Jeffery, 416 Rem. Mag., 458 Win. Mag. (Safari Magnum); 378 Wea. Mag., 416 Rigby, 416 Wea. Mag., 460 Wea. Mag. (Safari Super Magnum).
Barrel: 24".
Weight: About 9-10 lbs. **Length:** 43" overall.
Stock: McMillan fiberglass Safari.
Sights: Barrel band front ramp, multi-leaf express rear.
Features: Uses McMillan Safari action. Has q.d. 1" scope mounts, positive locking steel floorplate, barrel band sling swivel. Match-grade barrel. Matte black finish standard. Introduced 1989. From McMillan Gunworks, Inc.
Price: Talon Safari Magnum **$3,600.00**
Price: Talon Safari Super Magnum **$4,200.00**

McMILLAN TALON SPORTER RIFLE
Caliber: 25-06, 270, 280 Rem., 30-06 (Long Action); 7mm Rem. Mag., 300 Win. Mag., 300 Wea. Mag., 300 H&H, 338 Win. Mag., 340 Wea. Mag., 375 H&H, 416 Rem. Mag.
Barrel: 24" (standard).
Weight: About 7½ lbs. **Length:** NA.
Stock: Choice of walnut or McMillan fiberglass.
Sights: None furnished; comes with rings and bases. Open sights optional.
Features: Uses pre-'64 Model 70-type action with cone breech, controlled feed, claw extractor and three-position safety. Barrel and action are of stainless steel; chromemoly optional. Introduced 1991. From McMillan Gunworks, Inc.
Price: **$2,600.00**

MIDLAND 1500S SURVIVOR RIFLE
Caliber: 308, 5-shot magazine.
Barrel: 22".
Weight: 7 lbs. **Length:** 43" overall.
Stock: Black composite with recoil pad, Monte Carlo cheekpiece.
Sights: Hooded ramp front, open rear adjustable for windage.
Features: Stainless steel barreled action with satin chromed bolt. Introduced 1993. Made by Gibbs Rifle Co.
Price: **$450.00**
Price: Model 1500C clip model **$480.00**

NAVY ARMS TU-33/40 CARBINE
Caliber: 7.62x39mm, 4-shot magazine.
Barrel: 20.75".
Weight: 9 lbs. **Length:** NA.
Stock: Hardwood.
Sights: Hooded barleycorn front, military V-notch adjustable rear.
Features: Miniature Mauser-style action. Comes with leather sling. Introduced 1992. Imported by Navy Arms.
Price: . . . . **NA**

CAUTION: PRICES SHOWN ARE SUPPLIED BY THE MANUFACTURER OR IMPORTER. CHECK YOUR LOCAL GUNSHOP. 49th EDITION, 1995 **343**

CENTERFIRE RIFLES—BOLT ACTION

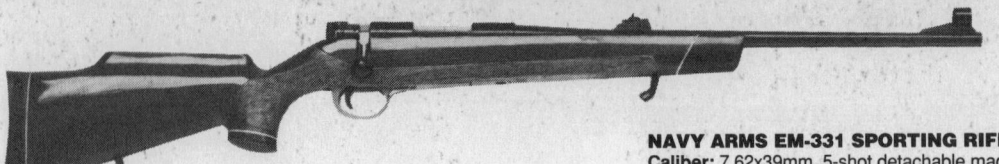

Navy Arms EM-331

NAVY ARMS EM-331 SPORTING RIFLE
Caliber: 7.62x39mm, 5-shot detachable magazine.
Barrel: 21".
Weight: 7.5 lbs. **Length:** 42" overall.
Stock: Monte Carlo style with sling swivels, rubber recoil pad.
Sights: Hooded ramp front, open adjustable rear.
Features: Receiver dovetailed for scope rings. Polished blue finish. Contrasting forend tip. Introduced 1994. Imported by Navy Arms.
Price: **$350.00**

Parker-Hale 81 Classic

PARKER-HALE MODEL 81 CLASSIC RIFLE
Caliber: 22-250, 243, 6mm Rem., 270, 6.5x55, 7x57, 7x64, 308, 30-06, 300 Win. Mag., 7mm Rem. Mag., 4-shot magazine.
Barrel: 24".
Weight: About 7¾ lbs. **Length:** 44½" overall.
Stock: European walnut in classic style with oil finish, hand-cut checkering; palm-swell pistol grip, rosewood grip cap.
Sights: Drilled and tapped for open sights and scope mounting. Scope bases included.
Features: Uses Mauser-style action; one-piece steel, Oberndorf-style trigger guard with hinged floorplate; rubber buttpad; quick-detachable sling swivels. Introduced 1984. Made by Gibbs Rifle Co.
Price: **$900.00**

Parker-Hale Model 81 Classic African Rifle
Similar to the Model 81 Classic except chambered only for 375 H&H and 9.3x62. Has adjustable trigger, barrel band front swivel, African express rear sight, engraved receiver. Classic-style stock has a solid buttpad, checkered pistol grip and forend. Introduced 1986. Made by Gibbs Rifle Co.
Price: **$1,050.00**

Parker-Hale Model 1000 Rifle
Similar to the Model 81 Classic except has walnut Monte Carlo stock, 22" barrel (24" in 22-250), weighs 7.25 lbs. Not available in 300 Win. Mag. Introduced 1992. Made by Gibbs Rifle Co.
Price: **$495.00**
Price: Model 1000 Clip (detachable magazine) **$535.00**

Parker-Hale Model 1100 Lightweight Rifle
Similar to the Model 81 Classic except has slim barrel profile, hollow bolt handle, alloy trigger guard/floorplate. The Monte Carlo stock has a schnabel forend, hand-cut checkering, swivel studs, palm-swell pistol grip. Comes with hooded ramp front sight, open Williams rear adjustable for windage and elevation. Same calibers as Model 81. Overall length is 43", weight 6½ lbs., with 22" barrel. Introduced 1984. Made by Gibbs Rifle Co.
Price: **$510.00**

PARKER-HALE MODEL 2100 MIDLAND RIFLE
Caliber: 22-250, 243, 6mm, 270, 6.5x55, 7x57, 7x64, 308, 30-06, 300 Win. Mag., 7mm Rem. Mag.
Barrel: 22".
Weight: About 7 lbs. **Length:** 43" overall.
Stock: European walnut, cut-checkered pistol grip and forend; sling swivels.
Sights: Hooded post front, flip-up open rear.
Features: Mauser-type action has twin front locking lugs, rear safety lug, and claw extractor; hinged floorplate; adjustable single-stage trigger; silent side safety. Introduced 1984. Made by Gibbs Rifle Co.
Price: **$390.00**
Price: Model 2600 (hardwood stock, no white spacers) **$375.00**

Parker-Hale Midland Model 2700 Lightweight Rifle
Similar to the Model 2100 Midland except has tapered lightweight barrel, aluminum trigger guard, lightened stock. Receiver drilled and tapped for scope mounting. Weighs 6.5 lbs. Not available in 300 Win. Mag. Introduced 1992. Made by Gibbs Rifle Co.
Price: **$415.00**

Parker-Hale Model 2800 Midland Rifle
Similar to the Model 2100 Midland except has Monte Carlo stock of laminated birch. Not available in 300 Win. Mag. Made by Gibbs Rifle Co.
Price: **$405.00**

Parker-Hale 1100M

PARKER-HALE MODEL 1200 SUPER RIFLE
Caliber: 22-250, 243, 6mm, 25-06, 270, 6.5x55, 7x57, 7x64, 308, 30-06, 8mm Mauser (standard action); 7mm Rem. Mag., 300 Win. Mag. (1200M Super Magnum).
Barrel: 24".
Weight: About 7½ lbs. **Length:** 44½" overall.
Stock: European walnut, rosewood grip and forend tips, hand-cut checkering; roll-over cheekpiece; palm-swell pistol grip; ventilated recoil pad; wraparound checkering.
Sights: Hooded post front, open rear.
Features: Uses Mauser-style action with claw extractor; gold-plated adjustable trigger; silent side safety locks trigger, sear and bolt; aluminum trigger guard. Introduced 1984. Made by Gibbs Rifle Co.
Price: **$595.00**

PARKER-HALE MODEL 1100M AFRICAN MAGNUM
Caliber: 375 H&H, 458 Win. Mag.
Barrel: 24".
Weight: 9.5 lbs. **Length:** NA.
Stock: Checkered walnut with reinforcing lugs.
Sights: Hooded ramp front, shallow V open rear.
Features: Mauser-style 98 action with steel trigger guard, special lengthened steel magazine. Drilled and tapped for scope mounts. Made by Gibbs Rifle Co.
Price: **$930.00**

Parker-Hale Model 1200 Super Clip Rifle
Same as the Model 1200 Super except has a detachable steel box magazine and steel trigger guard. Introduced 1984. Made by Gibbs Rifle Co.
Price: **$640.00**

CAUTION: PRICES SHOWN ARE SUPPLIED BY THE MANUFACTURER OR IMPORTER. CHECK YOUR LOCAL GUNSHOP.

Parker-Hale 1300C

PARKER-HALE MODEL 1300C SCOUT RIFLE
Caliber: 243, 308, 10-shot magazine.
Barrel: 20".

Weight: 8.5 lbs. Length: 41" overall.
Stock: Checkered laminated birch.
Sights: None furnished. Drilled and tapped for scope mounting.
Features: Detachable magazine; muzzle brake; polished blue finish. Introduced 1992. Made by Gibbs Rifle Co.
Price: $525.00
Price: With fixed 5-shot magazine $495.00

Remington Model Seven

Remington Model Seven Youth Rifle
Similar to the Model Seven except has hardwood stock with 12³⁄₁₆" length of pull and chambered for 6mm Rem., 243, 7mm-08. Introduced 1993.
Price: About $439.00

REMINGTON MODEL SEVEN BOLT-ACTION RIFLE
Caliber: 17 Rem., 223 Rem. (5-shot); 243, 6mm Rem., 7mm-08, 6mm, 308 (4-shot).
Barrel: 18½".
Weight: 6¼ lbs. Length: 37½" overall.
Stock: Walnut, with modified schnabel forend. Cut checkering.
Sights: Ramp front, adjustable open rear.
Features: Short-action design; silent side safety; free-floated barrel except for single pressure point at forend tip. Introduced 1983.
Price: About $532.00
Price: 17 Rem., about $559.00

Remington Model Seven SS

Remington Model Seven Custom KS
Similar to the standard Model Seven except has custom finished stock of lightweight Kevlar aramid fiber and chambered for 223 Rem., 7mm-08, 308, 35 Rem. and 350 Rem. Mag. Barrel length is 20", weight 5¾ lbs. Comes with iron sights and is drilled and tapped for scope mounting. Special order through Remington Custom Shop. Introduced 1987.
Price: $1,017.00

Remington Model Seven SS
Similar to the Model Seven except has stainless steel barreled action and black synthetic stock, 20" barrel. Chambered for 243, 7mm-08, 308. Introduced 1994.
Price: $585.00

Remington Model Seven Custom MS Rifle
Similar to the Model Seven except has full-length Mannlicher-style stock of laminated wood with straight comb, solid black recoil pad, black steel forend tip, cut checkering, gloss finish. Barrel length 20", weight 6¾ lbs. Availabloe in 222 Rem., 223, 22-250, 243, 6mm Rem., 7mm-08 Rem., 308, 350 Rem. Mag. Calibers 250 Savage, 257 Roberts, 35 Rem. available on special order. Polished blue finish. Introduced 1993. From Remington Custom Shop.
Price: About $999.00

REMINGTON 700 ADL BOLT-ACTION RIFLE
Caliber: 243, 270, 308, 30-06 and 7mm Rem. Mag.
Barrel: 22" or 24" round tapered.
Weight: 7 lbs. Length: 41½" to 43½" overall.
Stock: Walnut. Satin-finished p.g. stock with fine-line cut checkering, Monte Carlo.
Sights: Gold bead ramp front; removable, step-adj. rear with windage screw.
Features: Side safety, receiver tapped for scope mounts.
Price: About $452.00
Price: 7mm Rem. Mag., about $479.00

> Consult our Directory pages for the location of firms mentioned.

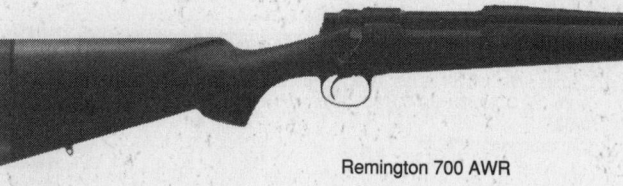

Remington 700 AWR

Remington 700 AWR Alaskan Wilderness Rifle
Similar to the Model 700 BDL except has stainless barreled action with satin blue finish; special 24" Custom Shop barrel profile; matte gray stock of fiberglass and graphite, reinforced with DuPont Kevlar, straight comb with raised cheekpiece, magnum-grade black rubber recoil pad. Chambered for 7mm Rem. Mag., 300 Win. Mag., 300 Wea. Mag., 338 Win. Mag., 375 H&H. Introduced 1994.
Price: $1,232.00

Remington 700 BDL Bolt-Action Rifle
Same as the 700 ADL except chambered for 222, 223 (short action, 24" barrel), 22-250, 25-06, 6mm Rem. (short action, 22" barrel), 243, 270, 7mm-08, 280, 300 Savage, 30-06, 308; skip-line checkering; black forend tip and grip cap with white line spacers. Matted receiver top, quick-release floorplate. Hooded ramp front sight; q.d. swivels.
Price: About $532.00
Also available in 17 Rem., 7mm Rem. Mag., 300 Win. Mag. (long action, 24" barrel), 338 Win. Mag., 35 Whelen (long action, 22" barrel). Overall length 44½", weight about 7½ lbs.
Price: About $559.00
Price: Custom Grade, about $2,341.00

CAUTION: PRICES SHOWN ARE SUPPLIED BY THE MANUFACTURER OR IMPORTER. CHECK YOUR LOCAL GUNSHOP.

49th EDITION, 1995 **345**

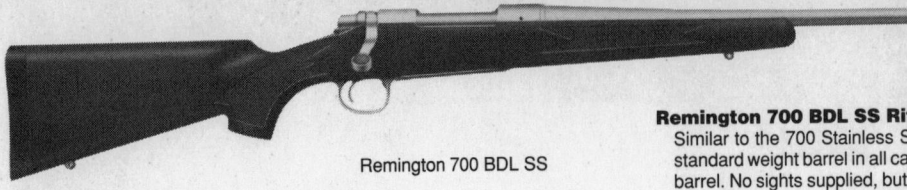

Remington 700 BDL SS

Remington 700 APR African Plains Rifle
Similar to the Model 700 BDL except has magnum receiver and specially contoured 26" Custom Shop barrel with satin finish, laminated wood stock with raised cheekpiece, satin finish, black buttpad, 20 lpi cut checkering. Chambered for 7mm Rem. Mag., 300 Win. Mag., 300 Wea. Mag., 338 Win. Mag., 375 H&H. Introduced 1994.
Price: **$1,475.00**

Remington 700 BDL Varmint Special
Same as 700 BDL, except 24" heavy bbl., 43½" overall, weighs 9 lbs. Cals. 222, 223, 22-250, 243, 6mm Rem., 7mm-08 Rem. and 308. No sights.
Price: About **$565.00**

Remington 700 BDL SS Rifle
Similar to the 700 Stainless Synthetic rifle except has hinged floorplate, 24" standard weight barrel in all calibers; magnum calibers have magnum-contour barrel. No sights supplied, but comes drilled and tapped. Has corrosion-resistant follower and fire control, stainless BDL-style barreled action with fine matte finish. Synthetic stock has straight comb and cheekpiece, textured finish, positive checkering, plated swivel studs. Short action calibers—223, 243, 6mm Rem., 7mm-08 Rem., 308; standard long action—25-06, 270, 280 Rem., 30-06; magnums—7mm Rem. Mag., 7mm Wea. Mag., 300 Win. Mag., 300 Wea. Mag., 338 Win. Mag. Weighs 6¾-7 lbs. Introduced 1993.
Price: Standard calibers, about **$585.00**
Price: Magnum calibers, about **$612.00**

Remington 700 BDL European Bolt-Action Rifle
Same as the 700 BDL except has oil-finished walnut stock and is chambered for 243, 270, 7mm-08, 280 Rem., 30-06 (22" barrel), 7mm Rem. Mag. (24" barrel). Introduced 1993.
Price: Standard calibers, about **$532.00**
Price: 7mm Rem. Mag., about **$559.00**

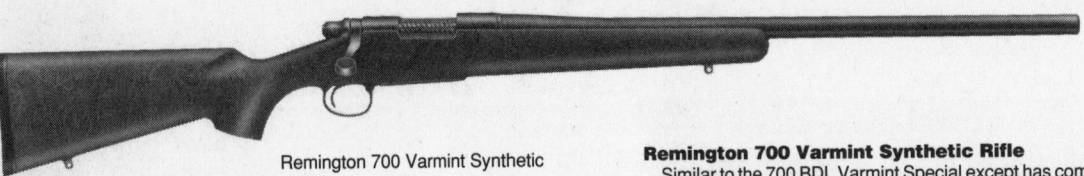

Remington 700 Varmint Synthetic

Remington 700 BDL Left Hand
Same as 700 BDL except mirror-image left-hand action, stock. Available in 22-250, 243, 308, 270, 30-06 only.
Price: About **$559.00**
Price: 7mm Rem. Mag., 338 Win. Mag., about **$585.00**

Remington 700 VS SF Rifle
Similar to the Model 700 Varmint Synthetic except has satin-finish stainless barreled action with 26" fluted barrel, spherical concave muzzle crown. Chambered for 223, 220 Swift, 22-250, 308. Introduced 1994.
Price: **$799.00**

Remington 700 Varmint Synthetic Rifle
Similar to the 700 BDL Varmint Special except has composite stock reinforced with DuPont Kevlar, fiberglass and graphite. Has aluminum bedding block that runs the full length of the receiver. Free-floating 26" barrel. Metal has black matte finish; stock has textured black and gray finish and swivel studs. Available in 220 Swift, 223, 22-250, 308. Introduced 1992.
Price: **$652.00**

Remington 700 Safari
Similar to the 700 BDL except custom finished and tuned. In 8mm Rem. Mag., 375 H&H, 416 Rem. Mag. or 458 Win. Magnum calibers only with heavy barrel. Hand checkered, oil-finished stock in classic or Monte Carlo style with recoil pad installed. Delivery time is about 5 months.
Price: About **$1,021.00**
Price: Classic stock, left-hand **$1,084.00**
Price: Safari Custom KS (Kevlar stock), right-hand **$1,176.00**
Price: As above, left-hand **$1,238.00**

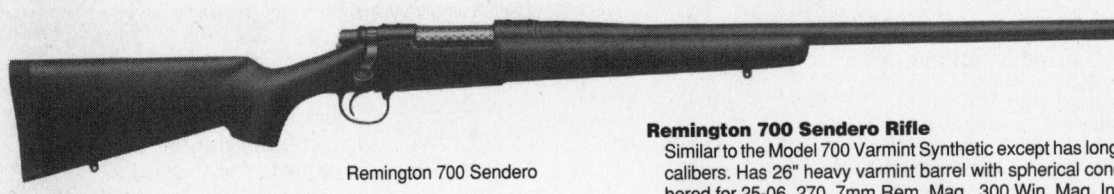

Remington 700 Sendero

REMINGTON 700 CLASSIC RIFLE
Caliber: 6.5x55 Swedish only, 5-shot magazine.
Barrel: 24".
Weight: About 7¾ lbs. **Length:** 44½" overall.
Stock: American walnut, 20 lpi checkering on p.g. and forend. Classic styling. Satin finish.
Sights: None furnished. Receiver drilled and tapped for scope mounting.
Features: A "classic" version of the M700 ADL with straight comb stock. Fitted with rubber recoil pad. Sling swivel studs installed. Hinged floorplate. Limited production in 1994 only.
Price: About **$532.00**

Remington 700 Mountain Rifle
Similar to the 700 BDL except weighs 6¾ lbs., has a 22" tapered barrel. Redesigned pistol grip, straight comb, contoured cheekpiece, satin stock finish, fine checkering, hinged floorplate and magazine follower, two-position thumb safety. Chambered for 243, 257 Roberts, 270 Win., 7x57, 7mm-08, 25-06, 280 Rem., 30-06, 308, 4-shot magazine. Overall length is 42½". Introduced 1986.
Price: About **$532.00**

Remington 700 Sendero Rifle
Similar to the Model 700 Varmint Synthetic except has long action for magnum calibers. Has 26" heavy varmint barrel with spherical concave crown. Chambered for 25-06, 270, 7mm Rem. Mag., 300 Win. Mag. Introduced 1994.
Price: 25-06, 270 .... **$652.00**
Price: 7mm Rem. Mag., 300 Win. Mag. **$679.00**

Remington 700 Camo Synthetic Rifle
Similar to the 700 BDL except has synthetic stock and the stock and metal (except bolt and sights) are fully camouflaged in Mossy Oak Bottomland camo. Comes with swivel studs, open adjustable sights. Available in 22-250, 243, 7mm-08, 270, 280, 30-06, 308, 7mm Rem. Mag., 300 Wea. Mag. Introduced 1992.
Price: Standard calibers **$581.00**
Price: Magnum calibers **$608.00**

Remington 700 Custom KS Mountain Rifle
Similar to the 700 "Mountain Rifle" except custom finished with Kevlar reinforced resin synthetic stock. Available in both left- and right-hand versions. Chambered for 270 Win., 280 Rem., 30-06, 7mm Rem. Mag., 300 Win. Mag., 300 Wea. Mag., 35 Whelen, 338 Win. Mag., 8mm Rem. Mag., 375 H&H, all with 24" barrel only. Weight is 6 lbs., 6 oz. Introduced 1986.
Price: Right-hand **$1,017.00**
Price: Left-hand **$1,080.00**
Price: Stainless **$1,160.00**

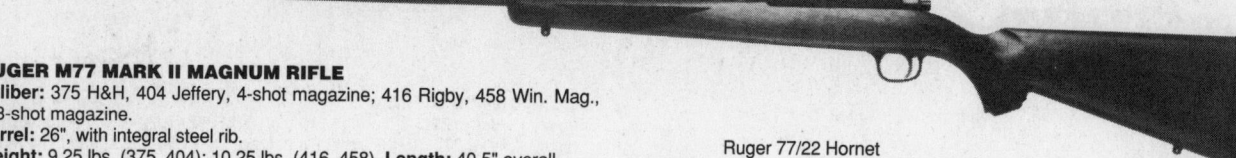

RUGER M77 MARK II MAGNUM RIFLE

Caliber: 375 H&H, 404 Jeffery, 4-shot magazine; 416 Rigby, 458 Win. Mag., 3-shot magazine.
Barrel: 26", with integral steel rib.
Weight: 9.25 lbs. (375, 404); 10.25 lbs. (416, 458). **Length:** 40.5" overall.
Stock: Circassian walnut with hand-cut checkering, swivel studs, steel grip cap, rubber butt pad.
Sights: Ramp front, three leaf express on serrated integral steel rib. Rib also serves as base for front scope ring.
Features: Uses an enlarged Mark II action with three-position safety, stainless bolt, steel trigger guard and hinged steel floorplate. Controlled feed. Introduced 1989.
Price: M77MKIIRSM $1,550.00

Ruger 77/22 Hornet

RUGER 77/22 HORNET BOLT-ACTION RIFLE

Caliber: 22 Hornet, 6-shot rotary magazine.
Barrel: 20".
Weight: About 6 lbs. **Length:** 39¾" overall.
Stock: Checkered American walnut, black rubber buttpad.
Sights: Brass bead front, open adjustable rear; also available without sights.
Features: Same basic features as the rimfire model except has slightly lengthened receiver. Uses Ruger rotary magazine. Three-position safety. Comes with 1" Ruger scope rings. Introduced 1994.
Price: 77/22RH (rings only) $452.00
Price: 77/22RSH (with sights) $469.00

Ruger M77 All-Weather

Ruger M77 Mark II All-Weather Stainless Rifle

Similar to the wood-stock M77 Mark II except all metal parts are of stainless steel, and has an injection-moulded, glass-fiber-reinforced Du Pont Zytel stock. Chambered for 223, 243, 270, 308, 30-06, 7mm Rem. Mag., 300 Win. Mag., 338 Win. Mag. Has the fixed-blade-type ejector, three-position safety, and new trigger guard with patented floorplate latch. Comes with integral Scope Base Receiver and 1" Ruger scope rings, built-in sling swivel loops. Introduced 1990.
Price: KM77MKIIRP $558.00

RUGER M77 MARK II RIFLE

Caliber: 223, 243, 6mm Rem., 257 Roberts, 25-06, 6.5x55 Swedish, 270, 280 Rem., 308, 30-06, 7mm Rem. Mag., 300 Win. Mag., 338 Win. Mag., 4-shot magazine.
Barrel: 20", 22"; 24" (magnums).
Weight: About 7 lbs. **Length:** 39¾" overall.
Stock: Hand-checkered American walnut; swivel studs, rubber butt pad.
Sights: None furnished. Receiver has Ruger integral scope mount base, comes with Ruger 1" rings. Some models have iron sights.
Features: Short action with new trigger and three-position safety. New trigger guard with redesigned floorplate latch. Left-hand model available. Introduced 1989.
Price: M77MKIIR (no sights $558.00
Price: M77MKIIRS (open sights) $617.00
Price: M77MKIILR (left-hand, 270, 30-06,
7mm Rem. Mag., 300 Win. Mag.) $558.00

Ruger M77RSI International

Ruger M77RL Ultra Light

Similar to the standard M77 except weighs only 6 lbs., chambered for 223, 243, 308, 270, 30-06, 257; barrel tapped for target scope blocks; has 20" Ultra Light barrel. Overall length 40". Ruger's steel 1" scope rings supplied. Introduced 1983.
Price: M77MKIIRL $592.50

Ruger M77RSI International Carbine

Same as the standard Model 77 except has 18½" barrel, full-length Mannlicher-style stock, with steel forend cap, loop-type steel sling swivels. Integral-base receiver, open sights, Ruger 1" steel rings. Improved front sight. Available in 243, 270, 308, 30-06. Weighs 7 lbs. Length overall is 38⅜".
Price: M77MKIIRSI $623.50

Ruger M77VT Target

RUGER M77 MARK II EXPRESS RIFLE

Caliber: 270, 30-06, 7mm Rem. Mag., 300 Win. Mag., 4-shot magazine.
Barrel: 22", with integral steel rib; barrel-mounted front swivel stud.
Weight: 7.5 lbs. **Length:** 42.125" overall.
Stock: Hand-checkered medium quality walnut with steel grip cap, black rubber butt pad, swivel studs.
Sights: Ramp front, open rear adjustable for windage and elevation mounted on rib.
Features: Mark II action with three-position safety, stainless steel bolt, steel trigger guard, hinged steel floorplate. Introduced 1991.
Price: M77EXPMKII $1,550.00

RUGER M77VT TARGET RIFLE

Caliber: 22 PPC, 22-250, 220 Swift, 223, 243,6mm PPC, 25-06, 308.
Barrel: 26" heavy stainless steel with matte finish.
Weight: Approx. 9.25 lbs. **Length:** Approx. 44" overall.
Stock: Laminated American hardwood with flat forend, steel swivel studs; no checkering or grip cap.
Sights: Integral scope mount bases in receiver.
Features: Ruger diagonal bedding system. Ruger steel 1" scope rings supplied. Fully adjustable trigger. Steel floorplate and trigger guard. New version introduced 1992.
Price: KM77MKIIVT $665.00

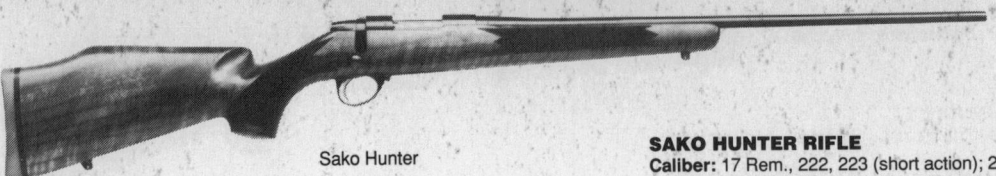

Sako Hunter

SAKO HUNTER RIFLE
Caliber: 17 Rem., 222, 223 (short action); 22-250, 243, 7mm-08, 308 (medium action); 25-06, 270, 30-06, 7mm Rem. Mag., 300 Win. Mag., 338 Win. Mag., 375 H&H Mag., 300 Wea. Mag., 416 Rem. Mag. (long action).
Barrel: 22" to 24" depending on caliber.
Weight: 5¾ lbs. (short); 6¼ lbs. (med.); 7¼ lbs. (long).
Stock: Hand-checkered European walnut.
Sights: None furnished.
Features: Adj. trigger, hinged floorplate. Imported from Finland by Stoeger.
Price: 17 Rem., 222, 223 . . . . **$1,000.00**
Price: 22-250, 243, 308, 7mm-08 . . . . **$1,000.00**
Price: Long action cals. (except magnums) **$1,025.00**
Price: Magnum cals. **$1,055.00**
Price: 375 H&H, 416 Rem. Mag., from **$1,070.00**
Price: 300 Wea. **$1,070.00**

Sako Hunter LS Rifle
Same gun as the Sako Hunter except has laminated stock with dull finish. Chambered for same calibers. Also available in left-hand version. Introduced 1987.
Price: Medium action **$1,195.00**
Price: Long action, from **$1,210.00**
Price: Magnum cals., from **$1,230.00**
Price: 375 H&H, 416 Rem. Mag., from **$1,230.00**

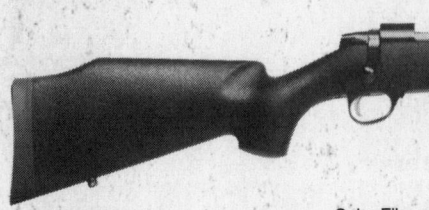

Sako Fiberclass

Sako Fiberclass Sporter
Similar to the Hunter except has a black fiberglass stock in the classic style, with wrinkle finish, rubber buttpad. Barrel length is 23", weight 7 lbs., 2 oz. Introduced 1985.
Price: 25-06, 270, 280 Rem., 30-06 . . . . **$1,355.00**
Price: 7mm Rem. Mag., 300 Win. Mag., 338 Win. Mag. **$1,370.00**
Price: 375 H&H, 416 Rem. Mag. **$1,390.00**

Sako Safari Grade

Sako Hunter Left-Hand Rifle
Same gun as the Sako Hunter except has left-hand action, stock with dull finish. Available in medium, long and magnum actions. Introduced 1987.
Price: Standard calibers, 22-250 to 7mm-08 . . . . **$1,085.00**
Price: Magnum calibers **$1,135.00**
Price: 375 H&H, 416 Rem. Mag. **$1,150.00**
Price: Deluxe, standard calibers, 25-06, 30-06 . . . . **$1,475.00**
Price: Deluxe, magnum calibers **$1,490.00**
Price: Deluxe, 375 H&H, 416 Rem. Mag. **$1,500.00**
Price: Long action, 25-06, 270, 280, 30-06 . . . . **$1,120.00**

Sako Safari Grade Bolt Action
Similar to the Hunter except available in long action, calibers 338 Win. Mag. or 375 H&H Mag. or 416 Rem. Mag. only. Stocked in French walnut, checkered 20 lpi, solid rubber buttpad; grip cap and forend tip; quarter-rib "express" rear sight, hooded ramp front. Front sling swivel band-mounted on barrel.
Price: **$2,715.00**

Sako Classic Bolt Action
Similar to the Hunter except has classic-style stock with straight comb. Has 21¾" barrel, weighs 6 lbs. Matte finish wood. Introduced 1993. Imported from Finland by Stoeger.
Price: 243 . . . . **$1,000.00**
Price: 270, 30-06 . . . . **$1,025.00**
Price: 7mm Rem. Mag. **$1,055.00**
Price: Left-hand, 270 . . . . **$1,120.00**
Price: Left-hand, 7mm Rem. Mag. **$1,135.00**

Sako Super Deluxe Sporter
Similar to Hunter except has select European walnut with high-gloss finish and deep-cut oak leaf carving. Metal has super high polish, deep blue finish. Special order only.
Price: **$2,895.00**

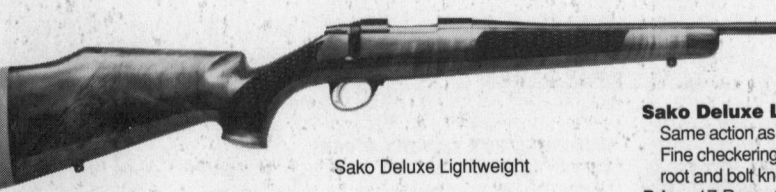

Sako Deluxe Lightweight

Sako Deluxe Lightweight
Same action as Hunter except has select wood, rosewood p.g. cap and forend tip. Fine checkering on top surfaces of integral dovetail bases, bolt sleeve, bolt handle root and bolt knob. Vent. recoil pad, skip-line checkering, mirror finish bluing.
Price: 17 Rem., 222, 223, 22-250, 243, 308, 7mm-08 . . . . **$1,325.00**
Price: 25-06, 270, 280 Rem., 30-06 . . . . **$1,410.00**
Price: 7mm Rem. Mag., 300 Win. Mag., 338 Win. Mag. **$1,425.00**
Price: 300 Wea., 375 H&H, 416 Rem. Mag. **$1,440.00**

Sako Mannlicher-Style Carbine
Same as the Hunter except has full "Mannlicher" style stock, 18½" barrel, weighs 7½ lbs., chambered for 243, 25-06, 270, 308 and 30-06, 7mm Rem. Mag., 300 Win. Mag., 338 Win. Mag., 375 H&H. Introduced 1977. From Stoeger.
Price: 243, 308 . . . . **$1,190.00**
Price: 270, 30-06 . . . . **$1,225.00**
Price: 338 Win. Mag., 375 H&H **$1,245.00**
Price: 375 H&H **$1,260.00**

Sako Varmint Heavy Barrel
Same as std. Super Sporter except has beavertail forend; available in 17 Rem., 222, 223 (short action), 22 PPC, 6mm PPC (single shot), 22-250, 243, 308, 7mm-08 (medium action). Weight from 8¼ to 8½ lbs., 5-shot magazine capacity.
Price: 17 Rem., 222, 223 (short action) **$1,155.00**
Price: 22-250, 243, 308 (medium action) **$1,155.00**
Price: 22 PPC, 6mm PPC (single shot) **$1,155.00**

    CAUTION: PRICES SHOWN ARE SUPPLIED BY THE MANUFACTURER OR IMPORTER. CHECK YOUR LOCAL GUNSHOP.

Sako TRG-S

SAKO TRG-S BOLT-ACTION RIFLE
Caliber: 243, 7mm-08, 270, 30-06, 7mm Rem. Mag., 300 Win. Mag., 338 Win. Mag., 375 H&H, 416 Rem. Mag., 5-shot magazine (4-shot for 375 H&H).
Barrel: 22", 24" (magnum calibers).

SAUER 90 BOLT-ACTION RIFLE
Caliber: Standard—222, 22-250, 243, 25-06, 6.5x55, 6.5x57, 270, 7x64, 308, 30-06, 9.3x62, 4-shot magazine; magnum—6.5x68, 7mm Rem. Mag., 300 Win. Mag., 300 Wea. Mag., 8x68S, 338 Win. Mag., 375 H&H, 458 Win. Mag., 3-shot magazine.
Barrel: 21" (Stutzen), 24" (standard calibers), 26" (magnum calibers).
Weight: 7.25 lbs. (standard and Stutzen). **Length:** 44" overall (24" barrel).
Stock: Monte Carlo style with sculptured cheekpiece, Wundhammar palm swell, hand-checkered grip and forend, rosewood grip cap and forend tip. Lux is French walnut with hand-rubbed oil finish, Supreme is fancy Claro walnut with high-gloss epoxy finish.

Weight: 7.75 lbs. **Length:** 45.5" overall.
Stock: Reinforced polyurethane with Monte Carlo comb.
Sights: None furnished.
Features: Resistance-free bolt with 60-degree lift. Recoil pad adjustable for length. Free-floating barrel, detachable magazine, fully adjustable trigger. Matte blue metal. Introduced 1993. Imported from Finland by Stoeger.
Price: 243, 7mm-08, 270, 30-06 . . . . $759.00
Price: Magnum calibers $799.00

Sights: None furnished; drilled and tapped for scope mounting. Safari model has iron sights.
Features: Bolt has rear-cam activated locking lugs, 65-degree lift; fully adjustable gold-plated trigger; chamber loaded and cocking indicators; tang safety; push-button bolt release; hammer-forged barrel; detachable box magazine. Introduced 1986. Imported from Germany by Paul Co.
Price: Lux, Supreme or Stutzen $1,495.00
Price: With Grade I engraving $2,495.00
Price: With Grade II engraving $3,095.00
Price: With Grade III engraving $3,495.00
Price: With Grade IV engraving $3,995.00
Price: Safari model, 458 Win. Mag. $1,995.00

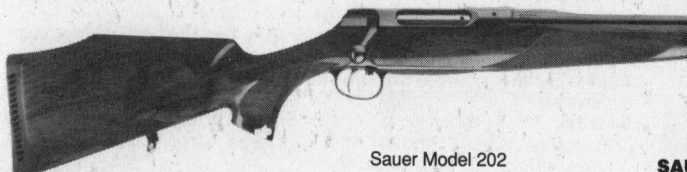

Sauer Model 202

Sauer Model 202 Alaska Bolt-Action Rifle
Similar to the standard Model 202 except chambered for 300 Wea. Mag. or 300 Win. Mag. only, with 26" barrel; laminated brown stock; metal coated with "Ilaflon" for protection. Accepts any Model 202 magnum barrel. Weighs 8.4 lbs. Introduced 1994. Imported from Germany by Paul Co.
Price: $1,335.00

Sauer Model 202 Hunter-Match Rifle
Similar to the standard Model 202 except has 26" or 28.5" match-grade heavy barrel, chambered for 6.5x55 or 308 Win. French walnut, two-piece stock has a wide, flat target-type forend, target-type alloy rail for swivels or bipod; butt has Monte Carlo comb. Drilled and tapped for scope mounting. Accepts standard-caliber Model 202 interchangeable barrels, including 22 LR conversion unit. Weighs 10.1 lbs. Matte black metal finish. Introduced 1994. Imported from Germany by Paul Co.
Price: $1,495.00

Consult our Directory pages for the location of firms mentioned.

SAUER MODEL 202 BOLT-ACTION RIFLE
Caliber: Standard—22 LR, 243, 6.5x55, 6.5x57, 25-06, 270, 280, 7x64, 308, 30-06, 9,3x62; magnum—6.5x68, 8x68S, 7mm Rem. Mag., 300 Win. Mag., 300 Wea. Mag., 338 Win. Mag., 375 H&H.
Barrel: 24" (standard calibers), 26" (magnum calibers).
Weight: 7.5 lbs. (steel), 6.5 lbs. (alloy). **Length:** NA.
Stock: Standard—fancy Claro walnut, two-piece, with Monte Carlo comb, palm swell grip, semi-schnabel forend tip; Super Grade has extra-fancy Claro walnut with rosewood grip cap, forend tip, high-gloss epoxy finish. French walnut Eurostock available (oil finish).
Sights: Optional; drilled and tapped for scope mounting.
Features: Modular receiver accepts interchangeable barrels. Steel or alloy receiver; right- or left-hand bolt; tang safety; fully adjustable trigger; cocking indicator; detachable magazine. Introduced 1994. Imported from Germany by Paul Co.
Price: Standard $899.00
Price: Magnum $949.00
Price: Super Grade Standard $1,025.00
Price: Super Grade Magnum $1,060.00
Price: 375 H&H Magnum $1,075.00
Price: 375 H&H Magnum Super Grade $1,185.00
Price: Extra barrel, standard calibers $240.00
Price: Extra barrel, magnum calibers $250.00
Price: 22 LR conversion unit $585.00

SAVAGE MODEL 110FP TACTICAL RIFLE
Caliber: 223, 308, 4-shot magazine.
Barrel: 24", heavy; recessed target muzzle.
Weight: 8½ lbs. **Length:** 45.5" overall.
Stock: Black graphite/fiberglass composition; positive checkering.
Sights: None furnished. Receiver drilled and tapped for scope mounting.
Features: Black matte finish on all metal parts. Double swivel studs on the forend for sling and/or bipod mount. Introduced 1990. From Savage Arms.
Price: $409.00

SAVAGE MODEL 110GXP3, 110GCXP3 PACKAGE GUNS
Caliber: 223, 22-250, 243, 250 Savage, 25-06, 270, 300 Sav., 30-06, 308, 7mm Rem. Mag., 7mm-08, 300 Win. Mag. (Model 110GXP3); 270, 30-06, 7mm Rem. Mag., 300 Win. Mag. (Model 110GCXP3).
Barrel: 22" (standard calibers), 24" (magnum calibers).
Weight: 7.25-7.5 lbs. **Length:** 43.5" overall (22" barrel).
Stock: Monte Carlo-style hardwood with walnut finish, rubber buttpad, swivel studs.

SAVAGE MODEL 110CY LADIES/YOUTH RIFLE
Caliber: 223, 243, 270, 300 Sav., 308, 5-shot magazine.
Barrel: 22".
Weight: About 6.5 lbs. **Length:** 42.5" overall.
Stock: Walnut-stained hardwood with high comb, cut checkering.
Sights: Ramp front, fully adjustable rear.
Features: Length of pull is 12.5", with red rubber buttpad. Drilled and tapped for scope mounting. Uses standard Model 110 barreled action. Introduced 1991. Made in U.S. by Savage Arms, Inc.
Price: $362.00

Sights: None furnished.
Features: Model 110GXP3 has fixed, top-loading magazine, Model 110GCXP3 has detachable box magazine. Rifles come with a factory-mounted and bore-sighted 3-9x32 scope, rings and bases, quick-detachable swivels, sling. Left-hand models available in all calibers. Introduced 1991 (GXP3); 1994 (GCXP3). Made in U.S. by Savage Arms, Inc.
Price: Model 110GXP3, right- or left-hand $418.00
Price: Model 110GCXP3, right- or left-hand $480.00

Savage Model 111FCXP3

Savage Model 111FXP3, 111FCXP3 Package Guns

Similar to the Model 110 Series Package Guns except with lightweight, black graphite/fiberglass composite stock with non-glare finish, positive checkering. Same calibers as Model 110 rifles, plus 338 Win. Mag. Model 111FXP3 has fixed top-loading magazine; Model 111FCXP3 has detachable box. Both come with mounted 3-9x32 scope, quick-detachable swivels, sling. Introduced 1994. Made in U.S. by Savage Arms, Inc.

Price: Model 111FXP3, right- or left-hand **$447.00**
Price: Model 111FCXP3, right- or left-hand **$488.00**

Savage Model 111G

SAVAGE MODEL 111 CLASSIC HUNTER RIFLES

Caliber: 223, 22-250, 243, 250 Sav., 25-06, 270, 300 Sav., 30-06, 308, 7mm Rem. Mag., 7mm-08, 300 Win. Mag., 338 Win. Mag. (Models 111G, GL, GNS, F, FL, FNS); 270, 30-06, 7mm Rem. Mag., 300 Win. Mag. (Models 111GC, GLC, FC, FLC).
Barrel: 22", 24" (magnum calibers).
Weight: 6.3 to 7 lbs. **Length:** 43.5" overall (22" barrel).
Stock: Walnut-finished hardwood (M111G, GC); graphite/fiberglass filled composite.
Sights: Ramp front, open fully adjustable rear; drilled and tapped for scope mounting.
Features: Three-position top tang safety, double front locking lugs, free-floated button-rifled barrel. Comes with trigger lock, target, ear puffs. Introduced 1994. Made in U.S. by Savage Arms, Inc.
Price: Model 111FC (detachable magazine, composite stock, right- or left-hand) **$418.00**
Price: Model 111F (top-loading magazine, composite stock, right- or left-hand) **$376.00**
Price: Model 111FNS (as above, no sights, right-hand only) **$372.00**
Price: Model 111G (wood stock, top-loading magazine, right- or left-hand) **$362.00**
Price: Model 111GC (as above, detachable magazine) **$407.00**
Price: Model 111GNS (wood stock, top-loading magzine, no sights, right-hand only) **$353.00**

SAVAGE MODEL 112 VARMINT RIFLES

Caliber: 220 Swift (single shot), 22-250, 223, 5-shot magazine.
Barrel: 26" heavy.
Weight: 8.8 lbs. **Length:** 47.5" overall.
Stock: Black graphite/fiberglass filled composite with positive checkering.
Sights: None furnished; drilled and tapped for scope mounting.
Features: Blued barrel with recessed target-style muzzle. Double front swivel studs for attaching bipod. Introduced 1991. Made in U.S. by Savage Arms, Inc.
Price: Model 112FV **$392.00**
Price: Model 112FVSS (stainless barrel, bolt handle, trigger guard) . **$495.00**
Price: Model 112FVSS-S (as above, single shot) **$495.00**
Price: Model 112BVSS (heavy-prone laminated stock with high comb, Wund-hammer swell, stainless barrel, bolt handle, trigger guard) **$509.00**
Price: Model 112BVSS-S (as above, single shot) **$509.00**

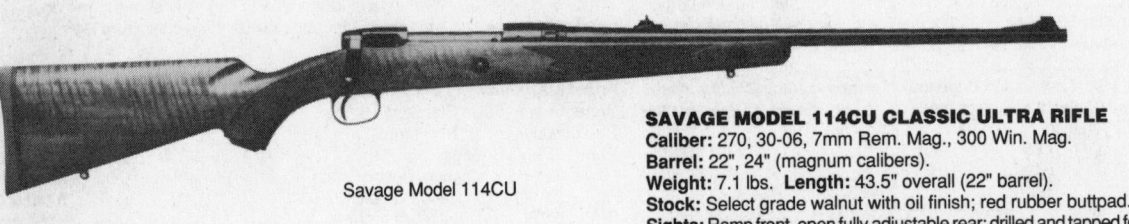

Savage Model 114CU

SAVAGE MODEL 114CU CLASSIC ULTRA RIFLE

Caliber: 270, 30-06, 7mm Rem. Mag., 300 Win. Mag.
Barrel: 22", 24" (magnum calibers).
Weight: 7.1 lbs. **Length:** 43.5" overall (22" barrel).
Stock: Select grade walnut with oil finish; red rubber buttpad.
Sights: Ramp front, open fully adjustable rear; drilled and tapped for scope mounting.
Features: Barrel, receiver and bolt handle have high-lustre blue finish, bolt body has laser-etched Savage logo. Detachable box magazine. Introduced 1991. Made in U.S. by Savage Arms, Inc.
Price: **$501.00**

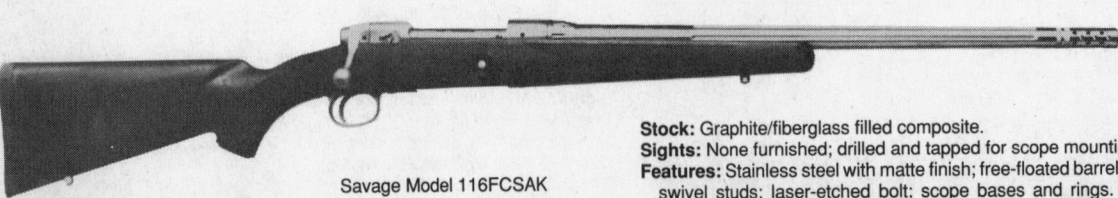

Savage Model 116FCSAK

Stock: Graphite/fiberglass filled composite.
Sights: None furnished; drilled and tapped for scope mounting.
Features: Stainless steel with matte finish; free-floated barrel; quick-detachable swivel studs; laser-etched bolt; scope bases and rings. Left-hand models available in all models, calibers at same price. Models 116FCS, 116FSS introduced 1991; Model 116FSK introduced 1993; Model 116FCSAK, 116FSAK introduced 1994. Made in U.S. by Savage Arms, Inc.
Price: Model 116FSS (top-loading magazine) **$489.00**
Price: Model 116FCS (detachable box magazine) **$552.00**
Price: Model 116FCSAK (as above with Savage Adjustable Muzzle Brake system) **$644.00**
Price: Model 116FSAK (top-loading magazine, Savage Adjustable Muzzle Brake system) **$581.00**
Price: Model 116FSK Kodiak (as above with 22" Shock -Suppressor barrel) **$552.00**

SAVAGE MODEL 116 WEATHER WARRIORS

Caliber: 223, 243, 270, 30-06, 7mm Rem. Mag., 300 Win. Mag., 338 Win. Mag. (Model 116FSS); 270, 30-06, 7mm Rem. Mag., 300 Win. Mag. (Models 116FCSAK, 116FCS); 270, 30-06, 7mm Rem. Mag., 300 Win. Mag., 338 Win. Mag. (Models 116FSAK, 116FSK).
Barrel: 22", 24" for 7mm Rem. Mag., 300 Win. Mag. (M116FSS only).
Weight: 6.25 to 6.5 lbs. **Length:** 43.5" overall (22" barrel).

CENTERFIRE RIFLES—BOLT ACTION

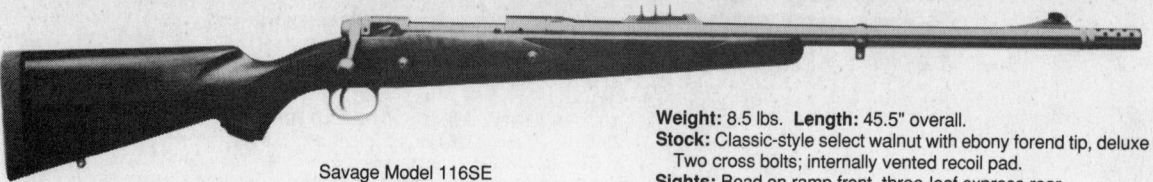

Savage Model 116SE

SAVAGE MODEL 116SE SAFARI EXPRESS RIFLE
Caliber: 300 Win. Mag., 338 Win. Mag., 458 Win. Mag.
Barrel: 24".

Weight: 8.5 lbs. **Length:** 45.5" overall.
Stock: Classic-style select walnut with ebony forend tip, deluxe cut checkering. Two cross bolts; internally vented recoil pad.
Sights: Bead on ramp front, three-leaf express rear.
Features: Controlled-round feed design; adjustable muzzle brake; one-piece barrel band stud. Satin-finished stainless steel barreled action. Introduced 1994. Made in U.S. by Savage Arms, Inc.
Price: $893.00

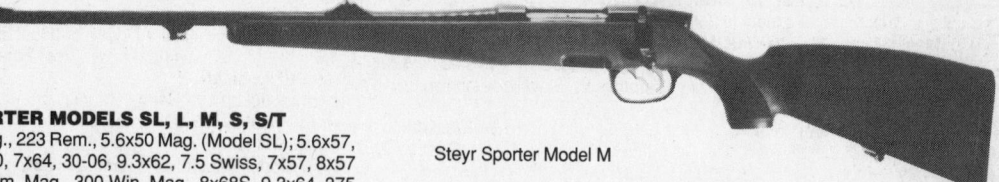

STEYR-MANNLICHER SPORTER MODELS SL, L, M, S, S/T
Caliber: 222 Rem., 222 Rem. Mag., 223 Rem., 5.6x50 Mag. (Model SL); 5.6x57, 243, 308 (Model L); 6.5x57, 270, 7x64, 30-06, 9.3x62, 7.5 Swiss, 7x57, 8x57 JS (Model M); 6.5x68, 7mm Rem. Mag., 300 Win. Mag., 8x68S, 9.3x64, 375 H&H, 458 Win. Mag. (Model S).
Barrel: 20" (full-stock), 23.6" (half-stock), 26" (magnums).
Weight: 6.8 to 7.5 lbs. **Length:** 39" (full-stock), 43" (half-stock).
Stock: Hand-checkered European walnut. Full Mannlicher or standard half-stock with Monte Carlo comb and rubber recoil pad.
Sights: Ramp front, open adjustable rear.
Features: Choice of single- or double-set triggers. Detachable 5-shot rotary magazine. Drilled and tapped for scope mounting. Model M actions available in left-hand models; S (magnum) actions available in half-stock only. Imported by GSI, Inc.

Steyr Sporter Model M

Price: Models SL, L, M, half-stock $2,023.00
Price: As above, full-stock, 20" barrel $2,179.00
Price: Models SL, L Varmint, 26" heavy barrel ... $2,179.00
Price: Model M left-hand, half-stock (270, 30-06, 7x64) ... $2,179.00
Price: As above, full-stock (270, 7x57, 7x64, 30-06) ... $2,335.00
Price: Model S Magnum $2,179.00
Price: Model S/T, 26" heavy barrel (375 H&H, 9.3x64, 458 Win. Mag.) $2,335.00

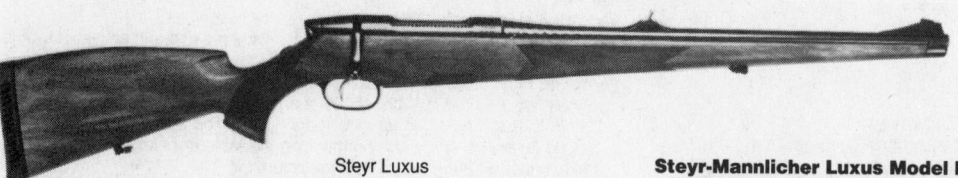

Steyr Luxus

Steyr-Mannlicher MIII Professional Rifle
Similar to the Sporter series except has black ABS Cycolac half-stock, 23.6" barrel, no sights. Available in 270, 30-06, 7x64. Single trigger or optional double-set triggers. Weighs about 7 lbs., 5 oz. Introduced 1994. Imported by GSI, Inc.
Price: $995.00
Price: With stipple-checkered walnut stock $1,125.00

Steyr-Mannlicher Luxus Model L, M, S
Similar to the Sporter series except has single set trigger, detachable steel 3-shot, in-line magazine, rear tang slide safety. Calibers: 5.6x57, 243, 308 (Model L); 6.5x57, 270, 7x64, 30-06, 9.3x62, 7.5 Swiss (Model M); 6.5x68, 7mm Rem. Mag., 300 Win. Mag., 8x68S (Model S). S (magnum) calibers available in half-stock only. Imported by GSI, Inc.
Price: Model L, M, half-stock $2,648.00
Price: As above, full-stock $2,804.00
Price: Model S (magnum) $2,804.00

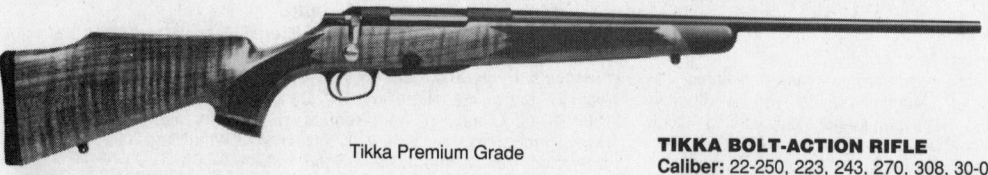

Tikka Premium Grade

Tikka Premium Grade Rifles
Similar to the standard grade Tikka except has stock with roll-over cheekpiece, select walnut, rosewood grip and forend caps. Hand-checkered grip and forend. Highly polished and blued barrel. Introduced 1990. Imported from Finland by Stoeger.
Price: Standard calibers $825.00
Price: Magnum calibers $850.00

Tikka Varmint/Continental Rifle
Similar to the standard Tikka rifle except has heavy barrel, extra-wide forend. Chambered for 22-250, 223, 243, 308. Introduced 1991. Made in Finland by Sako. Imported by Stoeger.
Price: $935.00

Tikka Whitetail/Battue Rifle
Similar to the standard Tikka rifle except has 20½" barrel with raised quarter-rib with wide V-shaped sight for rapid sighting. Chambered for 308, 270, 30-06, 7mm Rem. Mag., 300 Win. Mag., 338 Win. Mag. Made in Finland by Sako. Introduced 1991. Imported by Stoeger.
Price: 308, 270, 30-06 .... $715.00
Price: 7mm Rem. Mag., 300 Win. Mag., 338 Win. Mag. ... $740.00

TIKKA BOLT-ACTION RIFLE
Caliber: 22-250, 223, 243, 270, 308, 30-06, 7mm Rem. Mag., 300 Win. Mag., 338 Win. Mag.
Barrel: 22½" (std. cals.), 24½" (magnum cals.).
Weight: 7⅛ lbs. **Length:** 43" overall (std. cals.).
Stock: European walnut with Monte Carlo comb, rubber buttpad, checkered grip and forend.
Sights: None furnished.
Features: Detachable four-shot magazine (standard calibers), three-shot in magnums. Receiver dovetailed for scope mounting. Introduced 1988. Imported from Finland by Stoeger Industries.
Price: Standard calibers $675.00
Price: Magnum calibers $700.00

ULTIMATE ACCURACY MODEL 5100A1 LONG-RANGE RIFLE
Caliber: 50 BMG.
Barrel: 29", fully fluted, free-floating.
Weight: 36 lbs. **Length:** 51.5" overall.
Stocks: Composition. Adjustable drop and comb.
Sights: None furnished. Optional Leupold Ultra M1 16x scope.
Features: Bolt-action long-range rifle. Adjustable trigger. Rifle breaks down for transport, storage. From Ultimate Accuracy.
Price: $3,250.00
Price: M5100A1 Improved Model (receiver drilled and tapped for scope mount, manual safety, one-piece muzzle brake) $3,750.00

CAUTION: PRICES SHOWN ARE SUPPLIED BY THE MANUFACTURER OR IMPORTER. CHECK YOUR LOCAL GUNSHOP.

49th EDITION, 1995 **351**

CENTERFIRE RIFLES—BOLT ACTION

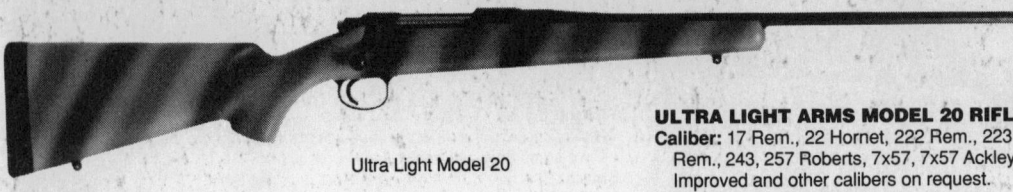

Ultra Light Model 20

Ultra Light Arms Model 28, Model 40 Rifles

Similar to the Model 20 except in 264, 7mm Rem. Mag., 300 Win. Mag., 338 Win. Mag. (Model 28), 300 Wea. Mag., 416 Rigby (Model 40). Both use 24" Douglas Premium No. 2 contour barrel. Weight 5½ lbs., 45" overall length. KDF or ULA recoil arrestor built in. Any custom feature available on any ULA product can be incorporated.
Price: Right-hand, Model 28 or 40 . . . . $2,900.00
Price: Left-hand, Model 28 or 40 . . . . $3,000.00

ULTRA LIGHT ARMS MODEL 20 RIFLE

Caliber: 17 Rem., 22 Hornet, 222 Rem., 223 Rem. (Model 20S); 22-250, 6mm Rem., 243, 257 Roberts, 7x57, 7x57 Ackley, 7mm-08, 284 Win., 308 Savage. Improved and other calibers on request.
Barrel: 22" Douglas Premium No. 1 contour.
Weight: 4½ lbs. Length: 41½" overall.
Stock: Composite Kevlar, graphite reinforced. Du Pont imron paint colors— green, black, brown and camo options. Choice of length of pull.
Sights: None furnished. Scope mount included.
Features: Timney adjustable trigger; two-position three-function safety. Benchrest quality action. Matte or bright stock and metal finish. 3" magazine length. Shipped in a hard case. From Ultra Light Arms, Inc.
Price: Right-hand $2,400.00
Price: Model 20 Left Hand (left-hand action and stock) $2,500.00
Price: Model 24 (25-06, 270, 280 Rem., 30-06, 3⅜" magazine length) $2,500.00
Price: Model 24 Left Hand (left-hand action and stock) $2,600.00

Voere VEC 91

VOERE MODEL 2165 BOLT-ACTION RIFLE

Caliber: 22-250, 243, 270, 7x57, 7x64, 308, 30-06 (standard), 7mm Rem. Mag., 300 Win. Mag., 9,3x64; 5-shot magazine for standard calibers, 3-shot for magnums.
Barrel: 22" (standard calibers), 24" (magnums).
Weight: 7-7½ lbs. Length: 44½" overall (22" barrel).
Stock: European walnut with Bavarian cheekpiece; schnabel forend tip; rosewood grip cap.
Sights: Ramp front, open adjustable rear.
Features: Built on Mauser 98-type action; tang safety; detachable box magazine. Comes with extra magazine. Imported from Austria by JagerSport, Ltd.
Price: Standard calibers, about $1,425.00
Price: Magnum calibers (Model 2165M), about $1,495.00

Weatherby Mark V Crown Custom Rifles

Uses hand-honed, engraved Mark V barreled action with fully-checkered bolt knob, damascened bolt and follower. Floorplate is engraved "Weatherby Custom." Super fancy walnut stock with inlays and stock carving. Gold monogram with name or initials. Right-hand only. Available in 240, 257, 270, 7mm, 300 Wea. Mag. or 30-06. Introduced 1989.
Price: From $4,933.00
Price: For 340 Wea. Mag., add $20.00

VOERE VEC 91 LIGHTNING BOLT-ACTION RIFLE

Caliber: 5.7x26mm UCC (223-cal.) caseless, 5-shot magazine.
Barrel: 20".
Weight: 6 lbs. Length: 39' Overall.
Stock: European walnut with cheekpiece, checkered grip and schnabel forend.
Sights: Blade on ramp front, open adjustable rear.
Features: Fires caseless ammunition via electric ignition; two batteries housed in the pistol grip last for about 5000 shot. Trigger is adjustable from 5 oz. to 7 lbs. Bolt action has twin forward locking lugs. Top tang safety. Drilled and tapped for scope mounting. Ammunition available from importer. Introduced 1991. Imported from Austria by JagerSport, Ltd.
Price: About $2,730.00

Voere Model 2155 Bolt-Action Rifle

Has conventional non-removable magazine, comes without sights (drilled and tapped); 22" barrel in standard calibers, 24" magnums. Imported from Austria by JagerSport, Ltd.
Price: Standard calibers—243, 270, 30-06, about $910.00

Voere Model 2150 Bolt-Action Rifle

Uses K-98 Mauser action with hinged floorplate; adjustable open rear sight, ramp front. Deluxe walnut stock with hand-rubbed oil finish, hand-checkered grip and forend; barrel-mounted front sling swivel. Standard calibers with 22" barrel, magnums have 24". Calibers 22-250, 243, 270, 7x57, 7x64, 308, 30-06 (standard); 7mm Rem. Mag., 300 Win. Mag., 9.3x64, 338 Win. Mag. (magnum). Available in 375 H&H, 458 Win. Mag. on special order. Imported from Austria by JagerSport, Ltd.
Price: Model 2150 (standard calibers) $1,795.00
Price: Model 2150M (magnum calibers) $1,845.00

Weatherby Mark V

WEATHERBY MARK V DELUXE BOLT-ACTION RIFLE

Caliber: All Weatherby cals., plus 22-250, 270, 30-06, 7mm Rem. Mag., 375 H&H, 460 Wea. Mag.
Barrel: 24" or 26" round tapered.
Weight: 6½-10½ lbs. Length: 43¼"-46½" overall.
Stock: Walnut, Monte Carlo with cheekpiece, high luster finish, checkered p.g. and forend, recoil pad.

Sights: Optional (extra).
Features: Cocking indicator, adjustable trigger, hinged floorplate, thumb safety, quick detachable sling swivels.
Price: 22-250, 26" $1,245.00
Price: 240, 257, 270, 7mm, 300 Wea. Mag., 30-06, right-hand, left-hand available, 24" $1,275.00
Price: 240, 257, 270, 7mm Wea. Mag., 30-06, right-hand, 26" . . $1,289.00
Price: 300 Wea. Mag., left-hand available, 340 Wea. Mag., right-hand, 26" $1,322.00
Price: 378 Wea. Mag., right-hand, 26" $1,358.00
Price: 416 Wea. Mag., right-hand, 26" $1,401.00
Price: 460 Wea. Mag., right-hand, 26", left-hand, 24" $1,727.00

CAUTION: PRICES SHOWN ARE SUPPLIED BY THE MANUFACTURER OR IMPORTER. CHECK YOUR LOCAL GUNSHOP.

Weatherby Mark V Sporter

Weatherby Lazermark V Rifle

Same as standard Mark V except stock has extensive laser carving under cheekpiece on butt, p.g. and forend. Introduced 1981.

Price: 240, 257, 270, right-hand, 7mm, 300 Wea. Mag., right- or
left-hand, 24" **$1,395.00**
Price: 240, 257, 270, 7mm Wea. Mag., 30-06, right-hand, 26" . . **$1,409.00**
Price: 300 Wea. Mag., 340 Wea. Mag., right- or left-hand, 26" . . **$1,445.00**
Price: 378 Wea. Mag., right-hand, 26" **$1,486.00**
Price: 416 Wea. Mag., right-hand, 26" **$1,533.00**
Price: 460 Wea. Mag., right-hand, 26" **$1,899.00**

Weatherby Mark V Custom Bolt-Action Rifle

Similar to the Mark V Deluxe except has super-fancy walnut stock with buttstock inlay, two forend inlays, gold monogram inlay engraved with name or initials, and stock carving with stained background. Fully checkered bolt knob, damascened bolt and follower, hand-honed action, floorplate engraved "Weatherby Custom."

Price: 240, 257, 270, 7mm, 300 Wea. Mags., 30-06, right-hand, 24" **$3,533.00**
Price: For 340 Wea. Mag., 26", add **$20.00**

Weatherby Weathermark Rifle

Similar to the Mark V rifle except has impregnated-color black composite stock with raised point checkering. Uses the Mark V action. Weighs 7.5 lbs. Right-hand only. Introduced 1992.

Price: 257, 270, 7mm, 300 Wea. Mag., 7mm Rem. Mag., 300 Win. Mag., 300
Win. Mag., right-hand, 24" **$675.00**
Price: 257, 270, 7mm Wea. Mag., right-hand, 26" **$705.00**
Price: 375 H&H, right-hand, 24" **$802.00**
Price: 270 Win., 30-06, right-hand, 22" **$675.00**
Price: 300, 340 Wea. Mag., right-hand, 26" **$705.00**

WICHITA VARMINT RIFLE

Caliber: 222 Rem., 222 Rem. Mag., 223 Rem., 22 PPC, 6mm PPC, 22-250, 243, 6mm Rem., 308 Win.; other calibers on special order.
Barrel: 20⅛".
Weight: 9 lbs. **Length:** 40⅛" overall.
Stock: AAA Fancy American walnut. Hand-rubbed finish, hand checkered, 20 lpi pattern. Hand-inletted, glass bedded, steel grip cap. Pachmayr rubber recoil pad.
Sights: None. Drilled and tapped for scope mounts.
Features: Right- or left-hand Wichita action with three locking lugs. Available as a single shot only. Checkered bolt handle. Bolt is hand fitted, lapped and jeweled. Side thumb safety. Firing pin fall is ³⁄₁₆". Non-glare blue finish. From Wichita Arms.
Price: Single shot **$2,275.00**

Weatherby Mark V Sporter Rifle

Same as the Mark V Deluxe without the embellishments. Metal has low-luster blue, Stock is Claro walnut with high-gloss epoxy finish, Monte Carlo comb, recoil pad. Introduced 1993.

Price: 257 270, 7mm, 300 Wea. Mag., 7mm Rem. Mag., 300, 338 Win. Mag.,
right-hand, 24" **$799.00**
Price: 375 H&H, right-hand, 24" **$909.00**
Price: 270 Win., 30-06, right-hand, 22" **$799.00**
Price: 300, 340 Wea. Mag., right-hand, 26" **$852.00**

Weatherby Mark V Safari Grade Custom Rifles

Uses the Mark V barreled action. Stock is of European walnut with satin oil finish, rounded ebony tip and cap, black presentation recoil pad, no white spacers, and pattern #16 fine-line checkering. Matte finish bluing, floorplate is engraved "Weatherby Safari Grade"; 24" barrel. Standard rear stock swivel, barrel band front swivel. Has quarter-rib rear sight with a stationary leaf and one folding shallow V leaf. Front sight is a hooded ramp with brass bead. Right- or left-hand. Allow 8-10 months delivery. Introduced 1985.

Price: 300 W.M. **$3,301.00**
Price: 340 W.M. **$3,321.00**
Price: 378 W.M. **$3,481.00**
Price: 416 W.M. **$3,534.00**
Price: 460 W.M. **$3,574.00**

Weatherby Weathermark Alaskan Rifle

Same as the Weathermark except all metal plated with electroless nickel. Available in right-hand only. Introduced 1992.

Price: 257, 270, 7mm, 300 Wea. Mag., 7mm Rem. Mag., 300 Win. Mag., 338
Win. Mag., right-hand, 24" **$875.00**
Price: 257, 270, 7mm Wea. Mag., right-hand, 26" **$912.00**
Price: 375 H&H, right-hand, 24" **$1,039.00**
Price: 270 Win., 30-06, right-hand, 22" **$875.00**
Price: 300, 340 Wea. Mag., right-hand, 26" **$912.00**

WICHITA CLASSIC RIFLE

Caliber: 17-222, 17-222 Mag., 222 Rem., 222 Rem. Mag., 223 Rem., 6x47; other calibers on special order.
Barrel: 21⅛".
Weight: 8 lbs. **Length:** 41" overall.
Stock: AAA Fancy American walnut. Hand-rubbed and checkered (20 lpi). Hand-inletted, glass bedded, steel grip cap. Pachmayr rubber recoil pad.
Sights: None. Drilled and tapped for scope mounting.
Features: Available as single shot only. Octagonal barrel and Wichita action, right- or left-hand. Checkered bolt handle. Bolt is hand-fitted, lapped and jeweled. Adjustable trigger is set at 2 lbs. Side thumb safety. Firing pin fall is ³⁄₁₆". Non-glare blue finish. From Wichita Arms.
Price: Single shot **$2,975.00**

Winchester Model 70 Sporter

WINCHESTER MODEL 70 SPORTER

Caliber: 25-06, 270 Win., 270 Wea., 30-06, 264 Win. Mag., 7mm Rem. Mag., 300 Win. Mag., 300 Wea. Mag., 338 Win. Mag., 3-shot magazine.

Barrel: 24".
Weight: 7¾ lbs. **Length:** 44½" overall.
Stock: American walnut with Monte Carlo cheekpiece. Cut checkering and satin finish.
Sights: Optional hooded ramp front, adjustable folding leaf rear. Drilled and tapped for scope mounting.
Features: Three-position safety, stainless steel magazine follower; rubber buttpad; epoxy bedded receiver recoil lug. From U.S. Repeating Arms Co.
Price: With sights **$590.00**
Price: Without sights **$556.00**

CAUTION: PRICES SHOWN ARE SUPPLIED BY THE MANUFACTURER OR IMPORTER. CHECK YOUR LOCAL GUNSHOP.

49th EDITION, 1995 **353**

WINCHESTER MODEL 70 CLASSIC SUPER EXPRESS MAGNUM
Caliber: 375 H&H Mag., 416 Rem. Mag., 458 Win. Mag., 3-shot magazine.
Barrel: 24" (375); 22" (458).
Weight: 8½ lbs.
Stock: American walnut with Monte Carlo cheekpiece. Wraparound checkering and finish.
Sights: Hooded ramp front, open rear.
Features: Controlled round feeding. Two steel cross bolts in stock for added strength. Front sling swivel stud mounted on barrel. Contoured rubber buttpad. From U.S. Repeating Arms Co.
Price: $816.00

WINCHESTER MODEL 70 CLASSIC CUSTOM SHARPSHOOTER
Caliber: 223, 22-250, 308 Win., 300 Win. Mag.
Barrel: 24" (308), 26" (223, 22-250, 300 Win. Mag.).
Weight: 11 lbs. **Length:** 44.5" overall (24" barrel).
Stock: McMillan A-2 target style; glass bedded; recoil pad, swivel studs.
Sights: None furnished; comes with bases and rings.
Features: Hand-honed and fitted action, Schneider barrel. Matte blue finish. Introduced 1992. From U.S. Repeating Arms Co.
Price: $1,747.00
Price: With standard push-feed action, 220 Swift $1,711.00

WINCHESTER MODEL 70 CLASSIC SUPER GRADE
Caliber: 270, 30-06, 5-shot magazine; 7mm Rem. Mag., 300 Win. Mag., 338 Win. Mag., 3-shot magazine.
Barrel: 24".
Weight: About 7¾ lbs. **Length:** 44½" overall.
Stock: Walnut with straight comb, sculptured cheekpiece, wraparound cut checkering, tapered forend, solid rubber buttpad.
Sights: None furnished; comes with scope bases and rings.
Features: Controlled round feeding with stainless steel claw extractor, bolt guide rail, three-position safety; all steel bottom metal, hinged floorplate, stainless magazine follower. Introduced 1994. From U.S. Repeating Arms Co.
Price: $792.00

Winchester Model 70 Classic Custom Sporting Sharpshooter
Similar to the Custom Sharpshooter except has pre-64-style action with controlled round feed, McMillan sporter-style, gray-finished composite stock, stainless steel Schneider barrel with natural matte finish, blued receiver. Available in 270, (24"), 7mm STW and 300 Win. Mag. (26"). Comes with rings and bases. Introduced 1994.
Price: $1,685.00
Price: 220 Swift $1,654.00
Price: With standard push-feed action, 220 Swift $1,654.00

Winchester Model 70 Classic SM

Winchester Model 70 Classic SM
Same as the Model 70 Sporter except has pre-64 controlled feed action, black composite, graphite-impregnated stock and matte-finished metal. Available in 270, 308, 30-06, 7mm Rem. Mag., 300 Win. Mag., 338 Win. Mag., 375 H&H. Weighs about 7.8 lbs. Introduced 1994.
Price: $585.00
Price: 375 H&H, with sights $634.00

Winchester Model 70 DBM Rifle
Same as the Model 70 Sporter except has detachable box magazine. Available in 243, 270, 30-06, 7mm Rem. Mag., 300 Win. Mag. with 24" barrel. Introduced 1992.
Price: With sights $634.00
Price: Model 70 Classic DBM without sights (as above except has pre-64-style action with controlled round feed, same calibers as above, but also 22-250, 284 Win., 308; introduced 1994) $619.00
Price: As above, with sights $671.00

Winchester Model 70 Classic DBM-S Rifle
Same as the Model 70 DBM except has pre-64-type controlled round action, fiberglass/graphite composite stock. Available in 270, 30-06, 7mm Rem. Mag., 300 Win. Mag. Detachable box magazine, 24" barrel. Introduced 1994.
Price: $619.00

Winchester Model 70 Classic Sporter
Similar to the Model 70 Sporter except uses pre-64-type action with controlled round feeding. Has classic-style stock with straight comb. Introduced 1994. From U.S. Repeating Arms Co.
Price: Without sights $577.00
Price: With sights $613.00

Winchester Model 70 Stainless Rifle
Same as the Model 70 Sporter except has stainless steel barrel and action with matte gray finish, black composite stock impregnated with fiberglass and graphite, contoured rubber recoil pad. Available in 270, 30-06, 7mm Rem. Mag., 300 Win. Mag., 338 Win. Mag. (24" barrel), 3- or 5-shot magazine. Weighs 6.75 lbs. Introduced 1992.
Price: $616.00
Price: Model 70 Classic Stainless (as above except has pre-64-style action with controlled round feeding; introduced 1994) $634.00

Winchester Model 70 Heavy Varmint

Winchester Model 70 Heavy Varmint
Similar to the Model 70 Sporter except has heavy 26" stainless barrel with counter-bored muzzle. Available in 220 Swift, 22-250, 223, 243 and 308. Receiver bedded in special stock with full-length Pillar Plus Accu Block; beavertail forend. Has rubber buttpad. Receiver drilled and tapped for scope mounting. Weight about 10¾ lbs., overall length 46". Introduced 1989.
Price: $720.00

Winchester Model 70 Synthetic Heavy Varmint Rifle
Similar to the Model 70 Varmint except has fiberglass/graphite stock, 26" heavy stainless steel barrel, blued receiver. Weighs about 10¾ lbs. Available in 220 Swift, 223, 22-250, 243, 308. Uses full-length Pillar Plus Accu Block bedding system. Introduced 1993.
Price: $720.00

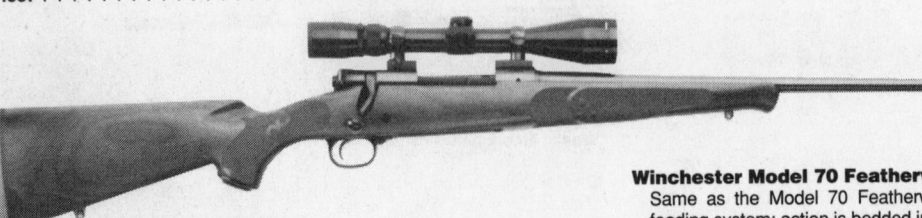

Winchester Model 70 Featherweight Classic

Winchester Model 70 Featherweight Classic
Same as the Model 70 Featherweight except has claw controlled-round feeding system; action is bedded in a standard-grade walnut stock. Available in 223, 22-250, 243, 308, 7mm-08. Drilled and tapped for scope mounts. Weighs 7.25 lbs. Introduced 1992.
Price: $585.00

CENTERFIRE RIFLES—BOLT ACTION

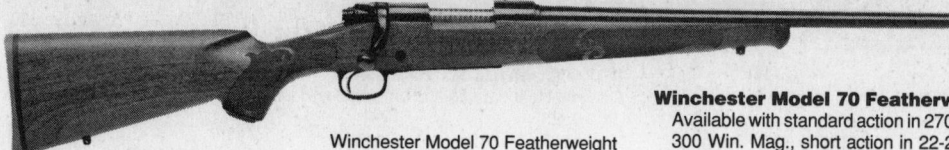

Winchester Model 70 Featherweight

WINCHESTER MODEL 70 LIGHTWEIGHT RIFLE
Caliber: 270, 280, 30-06 (standard action); 22-250, 223, 243, 308 (short action), both 5-shot magazine, except 6-shot in 223.
Barrel: 22".
Weight: 6¼ lbs. **Length:** 40½" overall (std.), 40" (short).
Stock: American walnut with satin finish, deep-cut checkering.
Sights: None furnished. Drilled and tapped for scope mounting.
Features: Three position safety; stainless steel magazine follower; hinged floorplate; sling swivel studs. Introduced 1984.
Price: Walnut **$498.00**

Winchester Model 70 Featherweight
Available with standard action in 270 Win., 280 Rem., 30-06, 7mm Rem. Mag., 300 Win. Mag., short action in 22-250, 223, 243, 6.5x55, 7mm-08, 308; 22" tapered. Featherweight barrel; classic-style American walnut stock with Schnabel forend, wraparound checkering fashioned after early Model 70 custom rifle patterns. Red rubber buttpad, sling swivel studs. Weighs 6¾ lbs. (standard action), 6½ lbs. (short action). Introduced 1984.
Price: **$562.00**

Winchester Ranger Rifle
Similar to Model 70 Lightweight except chambered only for 223, 243, 270, 30-06, with 22" barrel. American hardwood stock, no checkering, composition butt-plate. Metal has matte blue finish. Introduced 1985.
Price: **$455.00**
Price: Ranger Ladies/Youth, 243, 308 only, scaled-down stock . . . **$455.00**

CENTERFIRE RIFLES—SINGLE SHOT

Classic and modern designs for sporting and competitive use.

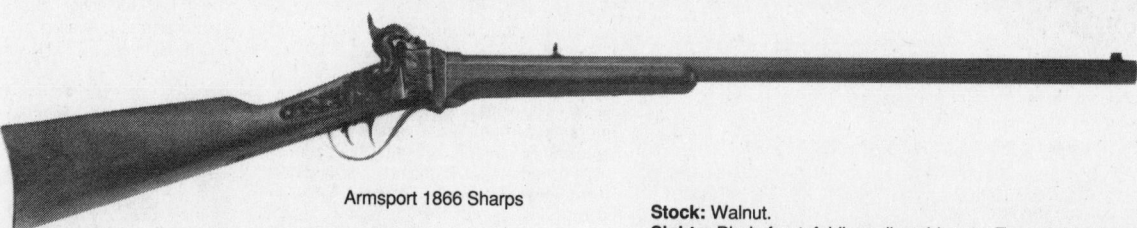

Armsport 1866 Sharps

ARMSPORT 1866 SHARPS RIFLE, CARBINE
Caliber: 45-70.
Barrel: 28", round or octagonal.
Weight: 8.10 lbs. **Length:** 46" overall.

Stock: Walnut.
Sights: Blade front, folding adjustable rear. Tang sight set optionally available.
Features: Replica of the 1866 Sharps. Color case-hardened frame, rest blued. Imported by Armsport.
Price: **$860.00**
Price: With octagonal barrel **$880.00**
Price: Carbine, 22" round barrel **$830.00**

Brown Model One

BROWN MODEL ONE SINGLE SHOT RIFLE
Caliber: 22 LR, 357 Mag., 44 Mag., 7-30 Waters, 30-30 Win., 375 Win., 45-70; custom chamberings from 17 Rem. through 45-caliber available.
Barrel: 22" or custom, bull or tapered.
Weight: 6 lbs. **Length:** NA.
Stock: Smooth walnut; custom takedown design by Woodsmith. Palm swell for right- or left-hand; rubber butt pad.
Sights: Optional. Drilled and tapped for scope mounting.
Features: Rigid barrel/receiver; falling block action with short lock time, automatic case ejection; air-gauged barrels by Wilson and Douglas. Muzzle has 11-degree target crown. Matte black oxide finish standard, polished and electroless nickel optional. Introduced 1988. Made in U.S. by E.A. Brown Mfg.
Price: **$750.00**

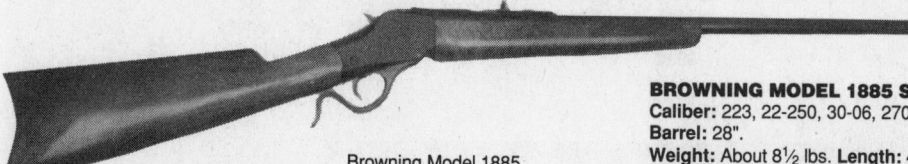

Browning Model 1885

CUMBERLAND MOUNTAIN ELK RIVER RIFLE
Caliber: 22 through 300 Win. Mag.; 32-40, 40-65, 45-70.
Barrel: 24", 26", 28", round or octagon.
Weight: 6.25 lbs. **Length:** 44" overall (28" barrel).
Stock: American walnut.
Sights: Marble's bead front, Marble's adjustable open rear.
Features: Falling block action with underlever. Blued barrel and receiver. Introduced 1993. Made in U.S. by Cumberland Mountain Arms, Inc.
Price: **$925.00**

BROWNING MODEL 1885 SINGLE SHOT RIFLE
Caliber: 223, 22-250, 30-06, 270, 7mm Rem. Mag., 45-70.
Barrel: 28".
Weight: About 8½ lbs. **Length:** 43½" overall.
Stock: Walnut with straight grip, schnabel forend.
Sights: None furnished; drilled and tapped for scope mounting.
Features: Replica of J.M. Browning's high-wall falling block rifle. Octagon barrel with recessed muzzle. Imported from Japan by Browning. Introduced 1985.
Price: **$853.95**

Cumberland Mountain Plateau Silhouette Rifle
Similar to the Elk River rifle except has heavy barrel in 32-40, 40-65 or 45-70; up to 34" octagon, 28" for round style. Stock dimensioned for silhouette shooting; has Neidner-style buttplate. Weight about 11.5 lbs. Furnished with or without Lyman tang sight ($70). Introduced 1993. Made in U.S. by Cumberland Mountain Arms, Inc.
Price: **$1,015.00**

CAUTION: PRICES SHOWN ARE SUPPLIED BY THE MANUFACTURER OR IMPORTER. CHECK YOUR LOCAL GUNSHOP.

49th EDITION, 1995 **355**

Dakota Single Shot

DAKOTA SINGLE SHOT RIFLE
Caliber: Most rimmed and rimless commercial calibers.
Barrel: 23".
Weight: 6 lbs. **Length:** 39½" overall.
Stock: Medium fancy grade walnut in classic style. Checkered grip and forend.
Sights: None furnished. Drilled and tapped for scope mounting.
Features: Falling block action with under-lever. Top tang safety. Removable trigger plate for conversion to single set trigger. Introduced 1990. Made in U.S. by Dakota Arms.
Price: $2,500.00
Price: Barreled action $1,650.00
Price: Action only $1,400.00

DESERT INDUSTRIES G-90 SINGLE SHOT RIFLE
Caliber: 22-250, 220 Swift, 223, 6mm, 243, 25-06, 257 Roberts, 270 Win., 270 Wea. Mag., 280, 7x57, 7mm Rem. Mag., 30-06, 300 Win. Mag., 300 Wea. Mag., 338 Win. Mag., 375 H&H, 45-70, 458 Win. Mag.
Barrel: 20", 22", 24", 26"; light, medium, heavy.
Weight: About 7.5 lbs.
Stock: Walnut.
Sights: None furnished. Drilled and tapped for scope mounting.
Features: Cylindrical falling block action. All steel construction. Blue finish. Announced 1990. From Desert Industries, Inc.
Price: $795.00

> Consult our Directory pages for the location of firms mentioned.

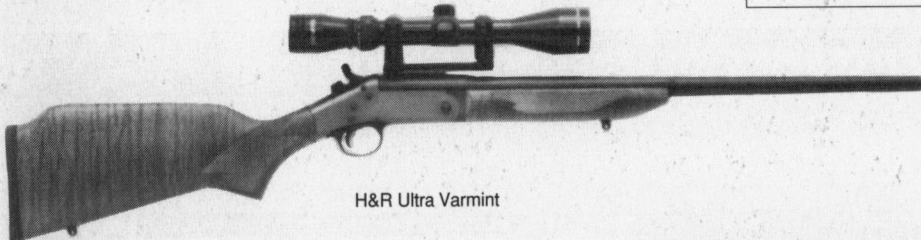

H&R Ultra Varmint

Stock: Hand-checkered curly maple with Monte Carlo comb.
Sights: None furnished. Drilled and tapped for scope mounting.
Features: Break-open action with side-lever release, positive ejection. Comes with scope mount. Blued receiver and barrel. Swivel studs. Introduced 1993. From H&R 1971, Inc.
Price: $249.95

HARRINGTON & RICHARDSON ULTRA VARMINT RIFLE
Caliber: 223, 22-250.
Barrel: 22", heavy.
Weight: About 7.5 lbs. **Length:** NA.

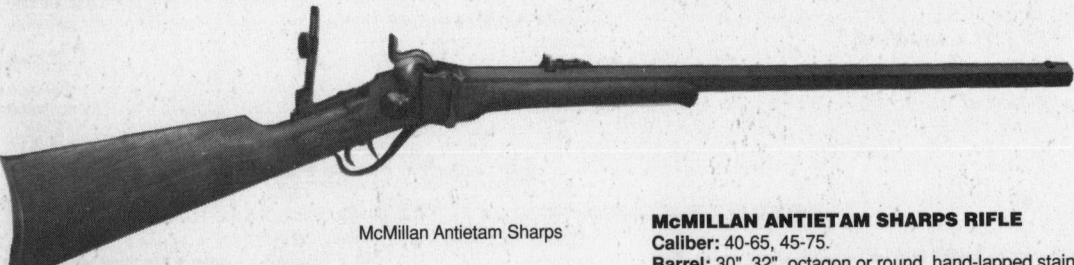

McMillan Antietam Sharps

McMILLAN ANTIETAM SHARPS RIFLE
Caliber: 40-65, 45-75.
Barrel: 30", 32", octagon or round, hand-lapped stainless or chrome moly.
Weight: 11.25 lbs. **Length:** 47" overall.
Stock: Choice of straight grip, pistol grip or Creedmoor with schnabel forend; pewter tip optional. Standard wood is A Fancy; higher grades available.
Sights: Montana Vintage Arms #111 Low Profile Spirit Level front, #108 mid-range tang rear with windage adjustments.
Features: Recreation of the 1874 Sharps sidehammer. Action is color case-hardened, barrel satin black. Chrome moly barrel optionally blued. Optional sights include #112 Spirit Level Globe front with windage, #107 Long Range rear with windage. Introduced 1994. Made in U.S. by McMillan Gunworks.
Price: $1,800.00

MODEL 1885 HIGH WALL RIFLE
Caliber: 30-40 Krag, 32-40, 38-55, 40-65 WCF, 45-70.
Barrel: 26" (30-40), 28" all others. Douglas Premium #3 tapered octagon.
Weight: NA. **Length:** NA.
Stock: Premium American black walnut.
Sights: Marble's standard ivory bead front, #66 long blade top rear with reversible notch and elevator.
Features: Recreation of early octagon top, thick-wall High Wall with Coil spring action. Tand drilled, tapped for High Wall tand sight. Receiver, lever, hammer and breechblock color case-hardened. Introduced 1991. Avaiable from Montana Armory, Inc.
Price: $1,095.00

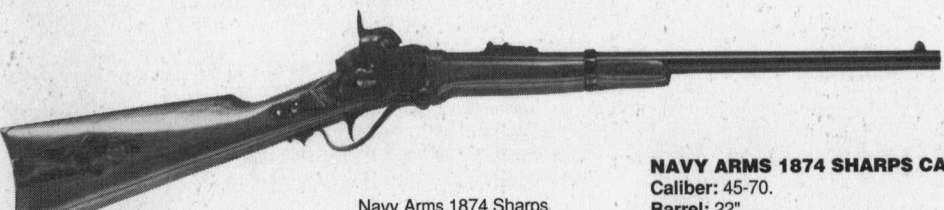

Navy Arms 1874 Sharps

NAVY ARMS 1874 SHARPS CAVALRY CARBINE
Caliber: 45-70.
Barrel: 22".
Weight: 7lbs., 12 oz. **Length:** 39" overall.
Stock: Walnut.
Sights: Blade front, military ladder-type rear.
Features: Replica of the 1874 Sharps miltary carbine. Color case-hardened receiver, patchbox and furniture. Introduced 1991. Imported by Navy Arms.
Price $775.00

NAVY ARMS 1874 SHARPS SNIPER RIFLE
Similar to the Navy Arms Sharps Carbine except has 30" barrel, double-set triggers; weighs 8 lbs., 8 oz., overall length 46¾". Introduced 1984. Imported by Navy Arms.
Price: $920.00
Price: 1874 Sharps Infantry Rifle (three-band) $875.00

CAUTION: PRICES SHOWN ARE SUPPLIED BY THE MANUFACTURER OR IMPORTER. CHECK YOUR LOCAL GUNSHOP.

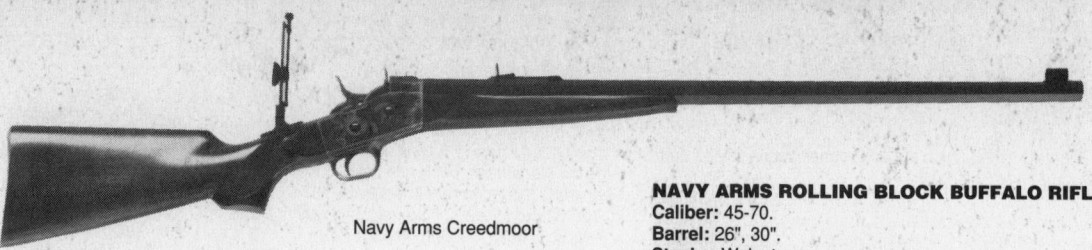

Navy Arms Creedmoor

Navy Arms #2 Creedmoor Rifle
Similar to the Navy Arms Buffalo Rifle except has 30" tapered octagon barrel, checkered full-pistol grip stock, blade front sight, open adjustable rear sight and Creedmoor tang sight. Introduced 1991. Imported by Navy Arms.
Price: **$775.00**

NAVY ARMS ROLLING BLOCK BUFFALO RIFLE
Caliber: 45-70.
Barrel: 26", 30".
Stocks: Walnut.
Sights: Blade front, adjustable rear.
Features: Reproduction of classic rolling block action. Available with full-octagon or half-octagon-half-round barrel. Color case-hardened action. From Navy Arms.
Price: **$530.00**

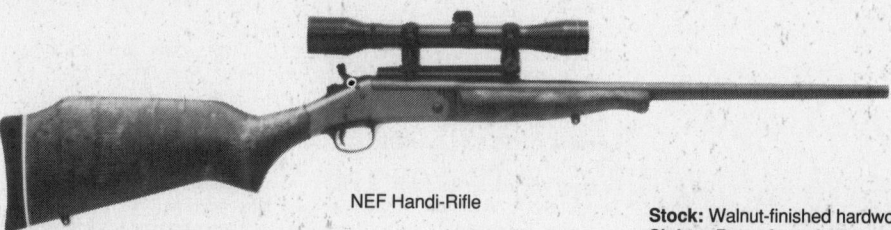

NEF Handi-Rifle

NEW ENGLAND FIREARMS HANDI-RIFLE
Caliber: 22 Hornet, 22-250, 223, 243, 30-30, 270, 30-06, 45-70.
Barrel: 22".
Weight: 7 lbs.
Stock: Walnut-finished hardwood.
Sights: Ramp front, folding rear. Drilled and tapped for scope mount; 22-250, 223, 243, 270, 30-06 have no open sights, come with scope mounts.
Features: Break-open action with side-lever release. The 243, 270 and 30-06 have recoil pad and Monte Carlo stock for shooting with scope. Swivel studs on all models. Blue finish. Introduced 1989. From New England Firearms.
Price: 22-250, 243, 270, 30-06 . . . . **$199.95**
Price: 22 Hornet, 223, 30-30, 45-70 . . . . **$199.95**

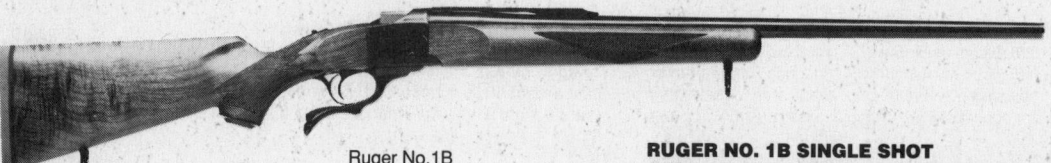

Ruger No.1B

Ruger No. 1A Light Sporter
Similar to the No. 1B Standard Rifle except has lightweight 22" barrel, Alexander Henry-style forend, adjustable folding leaf rear sight on quarter-rib, dovetailed ramp front with gold bead. Calibers 243, 30-06, 270 and 7x57. Weight about 7¼ lbs.
Price: No. 1A **$634.00**
Price: Barreled action **$429.50**

Ruger No. 1H Tropical Rifle
Similar to the No. 1B Standard Rifle except has Alexander Henry forend, adjustable folding leaf rear sight on quarter-rib, ramp front with dovetail gold bead, 24" heavy barrel. Calibers 375 H&H, 404 Jeffery, 416 Rem. Mag. (weight about 8¼ lbs.), 416 Rigby, and 458 Win. Mag. (weight about 9 lbs.).
Price: No. 1H **$634.00**
Price: Barreled action **$429.50**

RUGER NO. 1B SINGLE SHOT
Caliber: 218 Bee, 22 Hornet, 220 Swift, 22-250, 223, 243, 6mm Rem., 25-06, 257 Roberts, 270, 280, 30-06, 7mm Rem. Mag., 300 Win. Mag., 338 Win. Mag., 270 Wea., 300 Wea.
Barrel: 26" round tapered with quarter-rib; with Ruger 1" rings.
Weight: 8 lbs. **Length:** 43⅜" overall.
Stock: Walnut, two-piece, checkered p.g. and semi-beavertail forend.
Sights: None, 1" scope rings supplied for integral mounts.
Features: Under-lever, hammerless falling block design has auto ejector, top tang safety.
Price: **$634.00**
Price: Barreled action **$429.50**

Ruger No. 1S Medium Sporter
Similar to the No. 1B Standard Rifle except has Alexander Henry-style forend, adjustable folding leaf rear sight on quarter-rib, ramp front sight base and dovetail-type gold bead front sight. Calibers 218 Bee, 7mm Rem. Mag., 338 Win. Mag., 300 Win. Mag. with 26" barrel, 45-70 with 22" barrel. Weight about 7½ lbs. In 45-70.
Price: No. 1S **$634.00**
Price: Barreled action **$429.50**

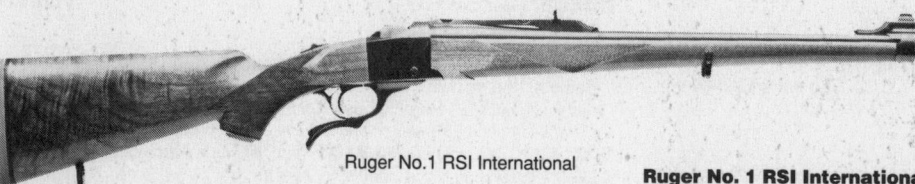

Ruger No.1 RSI International

Ruger No. 1V Special Varminter
Similar to the No. 1B Standard Rifle except has 24" heavy barrel. Semi-beavertail forend, barrel tapped for target scope block, with 1" Ruger scope rings. Calibers 22 PPC, 22-250, 220 Swift, 223, 6mm PPC, 25-06. Weight about 9 lbs.
Price: No. 1V **$634.00**
Price: Barreled action **$429.50**

Ruger No. 1 RSI International
Similar to the No. 1B Standard Rifle except has lightweight 20" barrel, full-length Mannlicher-style forend with loop sling swivel, adjustable folding leaf rear sight on quarter-rib, ramp front with gold bead. Calibers 243, 30-06, 270 and 7x57. Weight is about 7¼ lbs.
Price: No. 1 RSI **$656.00**
Price: Barreled action **$429.50**

SHARPS 1874 OLD RELIABLE

Caliber: 45-70.
Barrel: 28", octagonal.
Weight: 9¼ lbs. **Length:** 46" overall.
Stock: Checkered walnut.
Sights: Blade front, adjustable rear.
Features: Double set triggers on rifle. Color case-hardened receiver and butt-plate, blued barrel. Imported from Italy by E.M.F.

Price: Rifle or carbine	$950.00
Price: Military rifle, carbine	$860.00
Price: Sporting rifle	$860.00

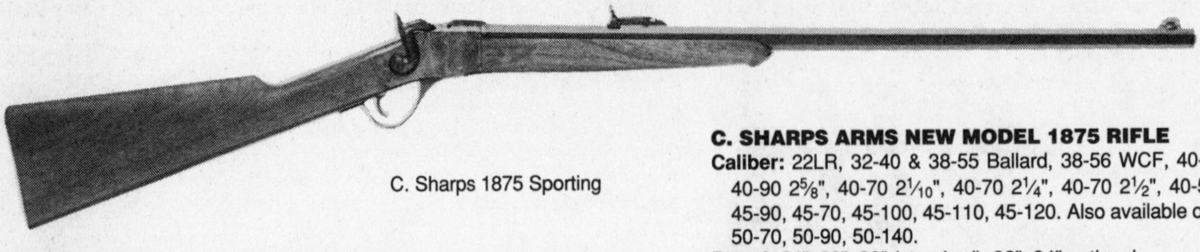

C. SHARPS ARMS NEW MODEL 1874 OLD RELIABLE

Caliber: 40-50, 40-70, 40-90, 45-70, 45-90, 45-100, 45-110, 45-120, 50-70, 50-90, 50-140.
Barrel: 26", 28", 30" tapered octagon.
Weight: About 10 lbs. **Length:** NA.
Stock: American black walnut; shotgun butt with checkered steel buttplate; straight grip, heavy forend with schnabel tip.
Sights: Blade front, buckhorn rear. Drilled and tapped for tang sight.
Features: Recreation of the Model 1874 Old Reliable Sharps Sporting Rifle. Double set triggers. Reintroduced 1991. Made in U.S. by C. Sharps Arms. Available from Montana Armory, Inc.

Price:	$995.00

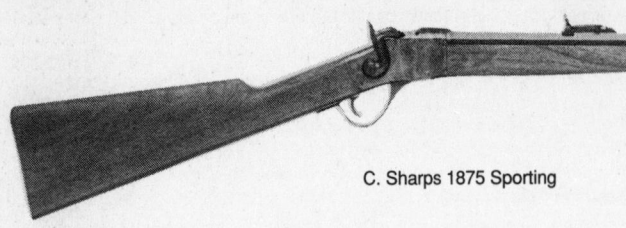

C. Sharps 1875 Sporting

Shiloh Sharps 1874 Montana Roughrider

Similar to the No. 1 Sporting Rifle except available with half-octagon or full-octagon barrel in 24", 26", 28", 30", 34" lengths; standard supreme or semi-fancy wood, shotgun, pistol grip or military-style butt. Weight about 8½ lbs. Calibers 30-40, 30-30, 40-50x1¹¹⁄₁₆" BN, 40-70x2¹⁄₁₀" BN, 45-70x2¹⁄₁₀" ST. Globe front and tang sight optional.

Price: Standard supreme	$904.00
Price: Semi-fancy	$988.00

C. Sharps Arms New Model 1875 Target & Long Range

Similar to the New Model 1875 except available in all listed calibers except 22 LR; 34" tapered octagon barrel; globe with post front sight, Long Range Vernier tang sight with windage adjustments. Pistol grip stock with cheek rest; checkered steel buttplate. Introduced 1991. From C. Sharps Arms Co. and Montana Armory, Inc.

Price:	$1,165.00

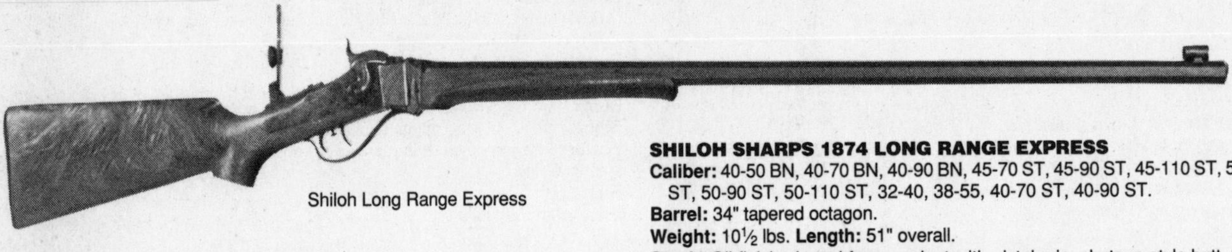

C. SHARPS ARMS NEW MODEL 1875 RIFLE

Caliber: 22LR, 32-40 & 38-55 Ballard, 38-56 WCF, 40-65 WCF, 40-90 3¼", 40-90 2⅝", 40-70 2¹⁄₁₀", 40-70 2¼", 40-70 2½", 40-50 1¹¹⁄₁₆", 40-50 1⅞", 45-90, 45-70, 45-100, 45-110, 45-120. Also available on special order only in 50-70, 50-90, 50-140.
Barrel: 24", 26", 30" (standard); 32", 34" optional.
Weight: 8-12 lbs.
Stocks: Walnut, straight grip, shotgun butt with checkered steel buttplate.
Sights: Silver blade front, Rocky Mountain buckhorn rear.
Features: Recreation of the 1875 Sharps rifle. Production guns will have case colored receiver. Available in Custom Sporting and Target versions upon request. Announced 1986. From C. Sharps Arms Co. and Montana Armory, Inc.

Price: 1875 Carbine (24" tapered round bbl.)	$725.00
Price: 1875 Saddle Rifle (26" tapered oct. bbl.)	$825.00
Price: 1875 Sporting Rifle (30" tapered oct. bbl.)	$850.00
Price: 1875 Business Rifle (28" tapered round bbl.)	$775.00

C. Sharps Arms 1875 Classic Sharps

Similar to the New Model 1875 Sporting Rifle except has 26", 28" or 30" full octagon barrel, crescent buttplate with toe plate, Hartford-style forend with cast German silver nose cap. Blade front sight, Rocky Mountain buckhorn rear. Weight is 10 lbs. Introduced 1987. From C. Sharps Arms Co. and Montana Armory, Inc.

Price:	$1,075.00

Shiloh Long Range Express

Shiloh Sharps 1874 Business Rifle

Similar to No. 3 Rifle except has 28" heavy round barrel, military-style buttstock and steel buttplate. Weight about 9½ lbs. Calibers 40-50 BN, 40-70 BN, 40-90 BN, 45-70 ST, 45-90 ST, 50-70 ST, 50-100 ST, 32-40, 38-55, 40-70 ST, 40-90 ST.

Price:	$910.00
Price: 1874 Saddle Rifle (similar to Carbine except has 26" octagon barrel, semi-fancy shotgun butt)	$962.00

THOMPSON/CENTER CONTENDER CARBINE

Caliber: 22 LR, 22 Hornet, 223 Rem., 7mm T.C.U., 7x30 Waters, 30-30 Win., 357 Rem. Maximum, 35 Rem., 44 Mag., 410, single shot.
Barrel: 21".
Weight: 5 lbs., 2 oz. **Length:** 35" overall.
Stock: Checkered American walnut with rubber buttpad. Also with Rynite stock and forend.
Sights: Blade front, open adjustable rear.
Features: Uses the T/C Contender action. Eleven interchangeable barrels available, all with sights, drilled and tapped for scope mounting. Introduced 1985. Offered as a complete Carbine only.

Price: Rifle calibers	$485.00
Price: Extra barrels, rifle calibers, each	$220.00
Price: 410 shotgun	$505.00
Price: Extra 410 barrel	$245.00

SHILOH SHARPS 1874 LONG RANGE EXPRESS

Caliber: 40-50 BN, 40-70 BN, 40-90 BN, 45-70 ST, 45-90 ST, 45-110 ST, 50-70 ST, 50-90 ST, 50-110 ST, 32-40, 38-55, 40-70 ST, 40-90 ST.
Barrel: 34" tapered octagon.
Weight: 10½ lbs. **Length:** 51" overall.
Stock: Oil-finished semi-fancy walnut with pistol grip, shotgun-style butt, traditional cheek rest and accent line. Schnabel forend.
Sights: Globe front, sporting tang rear.
Features: Recreation of the Model 1874 Sharps rifle. Double set triggers. Made in U.S. by Shiloh Rifle Mfg. Co.

Price:	$1,034.00
Price: Sporting Rifle No. 1 (similar to above except with 30" bbl., blade front, buckhorn rear sight)	$1,008.00
Price: Sporting Rifle No. 3 (similar to No. 1 except straight-grip stock, standard wood)	$904.00
Price: 1874 Hartford model	$1,074.00

Thompson/Center Contender Carbine Youth Model

Same as the standard Contender Carbine except has 16¼" barrel, shorter buttstock with 12" length of pull. Comes with fully adjustable open sights. Overall length is 29", weight about 4 lbs., 9 oz. Available in 22 LR, 22 WMR, 223 Rem., 7x30 Waters, 30-30, 35 Rem., 44 Mag. Also available with 16¼", rifled vent. rib barrel chambered for 45/410.

Price:	$450.00
Price: With 45/410 barrel	$480.00
Price: Extra barrels	$215.00
Price: Extra 45/410 barrel	$245.00
Price: Extra 45-70 barrel	$220.00

CAUTION: PRICES SHOWN ARE SUPPLIED BY THE MANUFACTURER OR IMPORTER. CHECK YOUR LOCAL GUNSHOP.

CENTERFIRE RIFLES—SINGLE SHOT

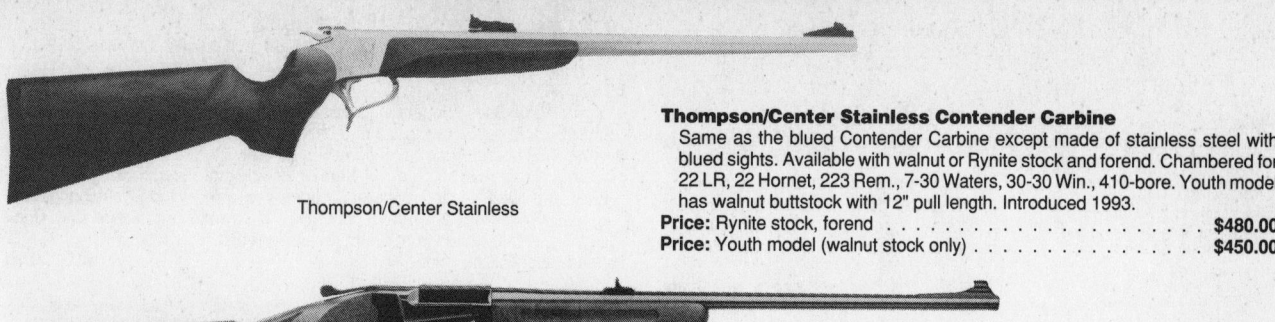

Thompson/Center Stainless

Thompson/Center Stainless Contender Carbine

Same as the blued Contender Carbine except made of stainless steel with blued sights. Available with walnut or Rynite stock and forend. Chambered for 22 LR, 22 Hornet, 223 Rem., 7-30 Waters, 30-30 Win., 410-bore. Youth model has walnut buttstock with 12" pull length. Introduced 1993.
Price: Rynite stock, forend **$480.00**
Price: Youth model (walnut stock only) **$450.00**

Thompson/Center TCR '87

THOMPSON/CENTER CUSTOM SHOP TCR '87 SINGLE SHOT

Caliber: 22 Hornet, 222 Rem., 223 Rem., 22-250, 243 Win., 270, 308, 7mm-08, 30-06, 32-40 Win., 12-ga. slug. Also 10-ga. and 12-ga. field barrels.
Barrel: 23" (standard), 25⅞" (heavy).
Weight: About 6¾ lbs. **Length:** 39½" overall.
Stock: American black walnut, checkered p.g. and forend.
Sights: None furnished.
Features: Break-open design with interchangeable barrels. Single-stage trigger. Cross-bolt safety. Introduced 1983. Made in U.S. by T/C. Available only through the T/C custom shop.
Price: With Medium Sporter barrel (223, 22-250, 7mm-08, 308, 32-40 Win.), about **$540.00**
Price: With Light Sporter barrel (22 Hornet, 222, 223, 22-250, 243, 270, 7mm-08, 308, 30-06), about **$540.00**
Price: 12-ga. slug barrel, about **$220.00**
Price: Extra Medium or Light Sporter barrel, about **$220.00**
Price: 10-, 12-ga. field barrels **$220.00**

UBERTI ROLLING BLOCK BABY CARBINE

Caliber: 22 LR, 22 WMR, 22 Hornet, 357 Mag., single shot.
Barrel: 22".
Weight: 4.8 lbs. **Length:** 35½" overall.
Stock: Walnut stock and forend.
Sights: Blade front, fully adjustable open rear.
Features: Resembles Remington New Model No. 4 carbine. Brass trigger guard and buttplate; color case-hardened frame, blued barrel. Imported by Uberti USA.
Price: **$460.00**

DRILLINGS, COMBINATION GUNS, DOUBLE RIFLES

Designs for sporting and utility purposes worldwide.

Beretta 455EELL Express

BERETTA EXPRESS SSO O/U DOUBLE RIFLES

Caliber: 375 H&H, 458 Win. Mag., 9.3x74R.
Barrel: 25.5".
Weight: 11 lbs.
Stock: European walnut with hand-checkered grip and forend.
Sights: Blade front on ramp, open V-notch rear.
Features: Sidelock action with color case-hardened receiver (gold inlays on SSO6 Gold). Ejectors, double triggers, recoil pad. Introduced 1990. Imported from Italy by Beretta U.S.A.
Price: SSO6 . . . . **$22,500.00**
Price: SSO6 Gold **$24,600.00**

AUGUSTE FRANCOTTE BOXLOCK MOUNTAIN RIFLE

Caliber: 5.6x57R, 5.6x65R, 6.5x57R, 7x57R, 7x65R.
Barrel: 24.5".
Weight: NA. **Length:** NA.
Stock: Deluxe walnut to customer specifications.
Sights: Ramp front, quarter-rib fixed rear.
Features: Anson & Deeley boxlock action; many options available. Made to customer specifications. Imported from Belgium by Armes de Chasse.
Price: From about **$10,000.00**

AUGUSTE FRANCOTTE SIDELOCK MOUNTAIN RIFLE

Caliber: Rimmed calibers from 5mm to 9mm.
Barrel: 23" to 26"; chopper lump.
Weight: NA. **Length:** NA.
Stock: Deluxe walnut to customer specifications.
Sights: Ramp front, quarter-rib fixed rear.
Features: True Holland & Holland system; many options available. Made to customer specifications. Imported from Belgium by Armes de Chasse.
Price: From about **$20,000.00**

BERETTA MODEL 455 SxS EXPRESS RIFLE

Caliber: 375 H&H, 458 Win. Mag., 470 NE, 500 NE 3", 416 Rigby.
Barrel: 23½" or 25½".
Weight: 11 lbs.
Stock: European walnut with hand-checkered grip and forend.
Sights: Blade front, folding leaf V-notch rear.
Features: Sidelock action with easily removable sideplates; color case-hardened finish (455), custom big game or floral motif engraving (455EELL). Double triggers, recoil pad. Introduced 1990. Imported from Italy by Beretta U.S.A.
Price: Model 455 . . . . **$38,500.00**
Price: Model 455EELL **$50,800.00**

CONSULT
SHOOTER'S MARKETPLACE
Page 225, This Issue

AUGUSTE FRANCOTTE BOXLOCK DOUBLE RIFLE

Caliber: 243, 270, 30-06, 7x64, 7x65R, 8x57JRS, 9.3x74R, 375 H&H, 470 N.E.; other calibers on request.
Barrel: 23.5" to 26".
Weight: NA. **Length:** NA.
Stock: Deluxe European walnut to customer specs; pistol grip or straight grip with Francotte cheekpiece; checkered butt; oil finish.
Sights: Bead front on long ramp, quarter-rib with fixed V rear.
Features: Side-by-side barrels; Anson & Deeley boxlock action with double triggers (front hinged), manual safety, floating firing pins and gas vent safety screws. Splinter or beavertail forend. English scroll engraving; coin finish or color case-hardening. Many options available. Made to customer specs. Imported from Belgium by Armes de Chasse.
Price: From about . . . . **$20,000.00 to $25,000.00**

CAUTION: PRICES SHOWN ARE SUPPLIED BY THE MANUFACTURER OR IMPORTER. CHECK YOUR LOCAL GUNSHOP.

DRILLINGS, COMBINATION GUNS, DOUBLE RIFLES

AUGUSTE FRANCOTTE SIDELOCK DOUBLE RIFLES
Caliber: 243, 7x64, 7x65R, 8x57JRS, 270, 30-06, 9.3x74R, 375 H&H, 470 N.E.; others on request.
Barrel: 23½" to 26".
Weight: 7.61 lbs. (medium calibers), 11.1 lbs. (mag. calibers).
Stock: Fancy European walnut; dimensions to customer specs. Straight or pistol grip style. Checkered butt, oil finish.
Sights: Bead on ramp front, leaf rear on quarter-rib; to customer specs.
Features: Custom made to customer's specs. Special extractor for rimless cartridges; back-action sidelocks; double trigger with hinged front trigger. Automatic or free safety. Wide range of options available. Imported from Belgium by Armes de Chasse.
Price: . . . . $30,000.00 to $36,000

HEYM MODEL 55B O/U DOUBLE RIFLE
Caliber: 7x65R, 308, 30-06, 8x57JRS, 8x75 RS, 9.3x74R, 375 H&H, 458 Win. Mag., 470 N.E.
Barrel: 25".
Weight: About 8 lbs., depending upon caliber. **Length:** 42" overall.
Stock: Dark European walnut, hand-checkered p.g. and forend. Oil finish.
Sights: Silver bead ramp front, open V-type rear.
Features: Boxlock or full sidelock; Kersten double cross bolt, cocking indicators; hand-engraved hunting scenes. Options available include interchangeable barrels, Swarovski scopes in claw mounts, deluxe engravings and stock carving, etc. Imported from Germany by JagerSport, Ltd.
Price: Model 55B boxlock $10,800.00

Heym 88B Safari

HEYM MODEL 88B SIDE-BY-SIDE DOUBLE RIFLE
Caliber: 30-06, 8x57JRS, 9.3x74R, 375 H&H.
Barrel: 25".
Weight: 7½ lbs. (std. cals.), 8½ lbs. (mag.). **Length:** 42" overall.
Stock: Fancy French walnut, classic North American design.
Sights: Silver bead post on ramp front, fixed or three-leaf express rear.
Features: Action has complete coverage hunting scene engraving. Available as boxlock or with q.d. sidelocks. Imported from Germany by JagerSport, Ltd.
Price: Boxlock . . . . $12,500.00 to $18,950.00
Price: Sidelock, Model 88B-SS, from $16,600.00
Price: Model 88B Safari (boxlock with ejectors, large frame, weighs about 10 lbs.; 375 H&H, 458 Win. Mag., 470 NE, 500 NE) $16,400.00

MERKEL OVER/UNDER COMBINATION GUNS
Caliber/Gauge: 12, 16, 20 (2¾" chamber) over 22 Hornet, 5.6x50R, 5.6x52R, 222 Rem., 243 Win., 6.5x55, 6.5x57R, 7x57R, 7x65R, 308 Win., 30-06, 8x57JRS, 9.3x74R, 375 H&H.
Barrel: 25.6".
Weight: About 7.6 lbs. **Length:** NA.
Stock: Oil-finished walnut; pistol grip, cheekpiece.
Sights: Bead front, fixed rear.
Features: Kersten double cross-bolt lock; scroll-engraved, color case-hardened receiver; Blitz action; double triggers. Imported from Germany by GSI.
Price: Model 210E $6,195.00
Price: Model 211E (silver-grayed receivcer, fine hunting scene engraving) $7,895.00
Price: Model 213E (sidelock action, English-style, large scroll Arabesque engraving) $14,695.00
Price: Model 313E (as above, medium-scroll engraving) $23,395.00

MERKEL MODEL 160 SIDE-BY-SIDE DOUBLE RIFLE
Caliber: 22 Hornet, 5.6x50R Mag., 5.6x52R, 222 Rem., 243 Win., 6.5x55, 6.5x57R, 7x57R, 7x65R, 308, 30-06, 8x57JRS, 9.3x74R, 375 H&H.
Barrel: 25.6".
Weight: About 7.7 lbs, depending upon caliber. **Length:** NA.
Stock: Oil-finished walnut with pistol grip, cheekpiece.
Sights: Blade front on ramp, fixed rear.
Features: Sidelock action. Double barrel locking lug with Greener cross-bolt; fine engraved hunting scenes on sideplates; Holland & Holland ejectors; double triggers. Imported from Germany by GSI.
Price: From $10,995.00

Savage 24F-12T Turkey Gun

MERKEL DRILLINGS
Caliber/Gauge: 12, 20, 3" chambers, 16, 2¾" chambers; 22 Hornet, 5.6x50R Mag., 5.6x52R, 222 Rem., 243 Win., 6.5x55, 6.5x57R, 7x57R, 7x65R, 308, 30-06, 8x57JRS, 9.3x74R, 375 H&H.
Barrel: 25.6".
Weight: 7.9 to 8.4 lbs. depending upon caliber. **Length:** NA.
Stock: Oil-finished walnut with pistol grip; cheekpiece on 12- , 16-gauge.
Sights: Blade front, fixed rear.
Features: Double barrel locking lug with Greener cross-bolt; scroll-engraved, case-hardened receiver; automatic trigger safety; Blitz action; double triggers. Imported from Germany by GSI.
Price: Model 90 . . . . $6,895.00
Price: Model 90S (as above except has selective sear safety) . . . $7,195.00
Price: Model 90K (manually cocked rifle system) $7,595.00
Price: Model 95 (silver-grayed receiver with fine hunting scene engraving) $7,895.00
Price: Model 95S (selective sear safety) $8,195.00
Price: Model 95K (manually cocked rifle system) $8,595.00

MERKEL OVER/UNDER DOUBLE RIFLES
Caliber: 22 Hornet, 5.6x50R Mag., 5.6x52R, 222 Rem., 243 Win., 6.5x55, 6.5x57R, 7x57R, 7x65R, 308, 30-06, 8x57JRS, 9.3x74R, 375 H&H.
Barrel: 25.6".
Weight: About 7.7 lbs, depending upon caliber. **Length:** NA.
Stock: Oil-finished walnut with pistol grip, cheekpiece.
Sights: Blade front, fixed rear.
Features: Kersten double cross-bolt lock; scroll-engraved, case-hardened receiver; Blitz action with double triggers. Imported from Germany by GSI.
Price: Model 220E $10,795.00
Price: Model 221 E (silver-grayed receiver finish, hunting scene engraving) $12,295.00
Price: Model 223E (sidelock action, English-style large-scroll Arabesque engraving) $18,395.00
Price: Model 323E (as above with medium-scroll engraving) . . . $27,595.00

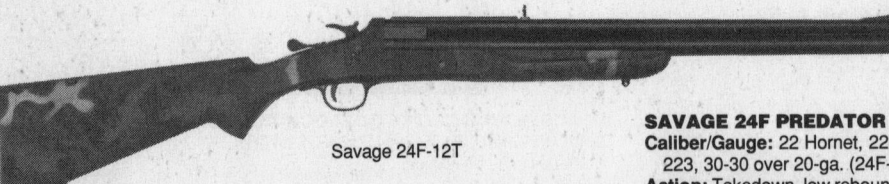

Savage 24F-12T

Similar to Model 24F except has camouflage Rynite stock. Available only in 22 Hornet (fixed Full) or 223 over 12-gauge (Mod., Imp. Cyl. choke tubes) with 3" chamber. Introduced 1989.
Price: $414.00

SAVAGE 24F PREDATOR O/U COMBINATION GUN
Caliber/Gauge: 22 Hornet, 223, 30-30 over 12 (24F-12) or 22 LR, 22 Hornet, 223, 30-30 over 20-ga. (24F-20); 3" chambers.
Action: Takedown, low rebounding visible hammer. Single trigger, barrel selector spur on hammer.
Barrel: 24" separated barrels; 12-ga. has Full, Mod., Imp. Cyl. choke tubes, 20-ga. has fixed Mod. choke.
Weight: 8 lbs. **Length:** 40½" overall.
Stock: Black Rynite composition.
Sights: Ramp front, rear open adjustable for elevation. Grooved for tip-off scope mount.
Features: Removable butt cap for storage and accessories. Introduced 1989.
Price: 24F-12 . . . . $400.00
Price: 24F-20 . . . . $400.00

CAUTION: PRICES SHOWN ARE SUPPLIED BY THE MANUFACTURER OR IMPORTER. CHECK YOUR LOCAL GUNSHOP.

DRILLINGS, COMBINATION GUNS, DOUBLE RIFLES

SAUER DRILLING
Caliber/Gauge: 12, 2¾" chambers/243, 6.5x57R, 7x57R, 7x65R, 30-06, 9.3x74R; 16, 2¾" chambers/6.5x57R, 7x57R, 7x65R, 30-06.
Barrel: 25".
Weight: 7.5 lbs. **Length:** 46" overall.
Stock: Fancy French walnut with checkered grip and forend, hog-back comb, sculptured cheekpiece, hand-rubbed oil finish.
Sights: Bead front, automatic pop-up rifle rear.
Features: Greener boxlock cross-bolt action with double underlugs, Greener side safety; separate rifle cartridge extractor. Side-by-side shotgun barrels over rifle barrel. Nitride-coated, hand-engraved receiver available with English Arabesque or relief game animal scene engraving. Lux has profuse relief-engraved game scenes, extra-fancy stump wood. Imported from Germany by Paul Co.
Price: Standard $4,600.00
Price: Lux $6,100.00

TIKKA MODEL 512S COMBINATION GUN
Caliber/Gauge: 12 over 222, 308.
Barrel: 24" (Imp. Mod.).
Weight: 7⅝ lbs.
Stock: American walnut, with recoil pad. Monte Carlo style. Standard measurements 14"x1⅗"x2"x2⅗".
Sights: Blade front, flip-up-type open rear.
Features: Barrel selector on trigger. Hand-checkered stock and forend. Barrels are screw-adjustable to change bullet point of impact. Barrels are interchangeable. Introduced 1980. Imported from Italy by Stoeger.
Price: $1,350.00
Price: Extra barrels, from $725.00

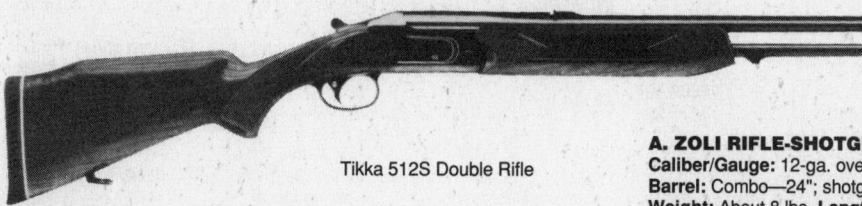

Tikka 512S Double Rifle

A. ZOLI RIFLE-SHOTGUN O/U COMBO
Caliber/Gauge: 12-ga. over 222, 308 or 30-06.
Barrel: Combo—24"; shotgun—28" (Mod. & Full).
Weight: About 8 lbs. **Length:** 41" overall (24" bbl.).
Stock: European walnut.
Sights: Blade front, flip-up rear.
Features: Available with German claw scope mounts on rifle/shotgun barrels. Comes with set of 12/12 (Mod. & Full) barrels. Imported from Italy by Mandall Shooting Supplies.
Price: With two barrel sets $1,695.00
Price: As above with claw mounts, scope$2,495.00

TIKKA MODEL 512S DOUBLE RIFLE
Caliber: 9.3x74R.
Barrel: 24".
Weight: 8⅝ lbs.
Stock: American walnut with Monte Carlo style.
Sights: Ramp front, adjustable open rear.
Features: Barrel selector mounted in trigger. Cocking indicators in tang. Recoil pad. Valmet scope mounts available. Introduced 1980. Imported from Italy by Stoeger.
Price: With ejectors $1,525.00

RIMFIRE RIFLES—AUTOLOADERS

Designs for hunting, utility and sporting purposes, including training for competition.

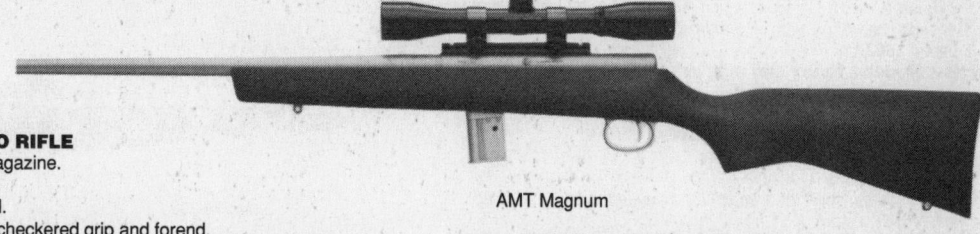

AMT Magnum

AMT MAGNUM HUNTER AUTO RIFLE
Caliber: 22 WMR, 10-shot rotary magazine.
Barrel: 22".
Weight: 6 lbs. **Length:** 40½" overall.
Stock: Black fiberglass-filled nylon; checkered grip and forend.
Sights: None furnished; grooved for scope mounting.
Features: Stainless steel construction. Free-floating target-weight barrel. Removable recoil pad for storage of ammo, knife, etc. Introduced 1993. Made in U.S. by AMT.
Price: $459.99

Consult our Directory pages for the location of firms mentioned.

Anschutz 525

ARMSCOR MODEL 1600 AUTO RIFLE
Caliber: 22 LR, 15-shot magazine.
Barrel: 19.5".
Weight: 6 lbs. **Length:** 38" overall.
Stock: Mahogany.
Sights: Post front, aperture rear.
Features: Resembles Colt AR-15. Matte black finish. Introduced 1987. Imported from the Philippines by Ruko Products.
Price: About $199.00
Price: M1600R (as above except has retractable buttstock, ventilated forend), about $199.00

ANSCHUTZ 525 DELUXE AUTO
Caliber: 22 LR, 10-shot clip.
Barrel: 24".
Weight: 6½ lbs. **Length:** 43" overall.
Stock: European hardwood; checkered pistol grip, Monte Carlo comb, beavertail forend.
Sights: Hooded ramp front, folding leaf rear.
Features: Rotary safety, empty shell deflector, single stage trigger. Receiver grooved for scope mounting. Introduced 1982. Imported from Germany by Precision Sales International.
Price: $508.00

Armscor Model 2000SC

ARMSCOR MODEL AK22 AUTO RIFLE
Caliber: 22 LR, 15- and 30-shot magazine.
Barrel: 18.5".
Weight: 7 lbs. **Length:** 36" overall.
Stock: Plain mahogany.
Sights: Post front, open rear adjustable for windage and elevation.
Features: Resembles the AK-47. Matte black finish. Introduced 1987. Imported from the Philippines by Ruko Products.
Price: About **$269.00**
Price: With folding steel stock, about **$299.00**

AUTO-ORDNANCE 1927A-3
Caliber: 22 LR, 10-, 30- or 50-shot magazine.
Barrel: 16", finned.
Weight: About 7 lbs.
Stock: Walnut stock and forend.

ARMSCOR MODEL 20P AUTO RIFLE
Caliber: 22 LR, 15-shot magazine.
Barrel: 21".
Weight: 6.5 lbs. **Length:** 39.75" overall.
Stock: Walnut-finished mahogany.
Sights: Hooded front, rear adjustable for elevation.
Features: Receiver grooved for scope mounting. Blued finish. Introduced 1990. Imported from the Philippines by Ruko Products.
Price: About **$129.00**
Price: With checkered stock **$159.00**
Price: Model 20C (carbine-style stock, steel barrel band, buttplate) . **$149.00**
Price: Model 2000SC (as above except has checkered stock, fully adjustable sight, rubber buttpad, forend tip), about . . . . **NA**
Price: Model 50S (similar to Model 20P except has ventilated barrel shroud, and 30-shot magazine) **$209.00**

Sights: Blade front, open rear adjustable for windage and elevation.
Features: Recreation of the Thompson Model 1927, only in 22 Long Rifle. Alloy receiver, finned barrel.
Price: **$510.00**

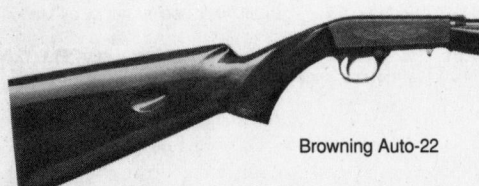

Browning Auto-22

Browning Auto-22 Grade VI
Same as the Grade I Auto-22 except available with either grayed or blued receiver with extensive engraving with gold-plated animals: right side pictures a fox and squirrel in a woodland scene; left side shows a beagle chasing a rabbit. On top is a portrait of the beagle. Stock and forend are of high-grade walnut with a double-bordered cut checkering design. Introduced 1987.
Price: Grade VI, blue or gray receiver **$747.95**

BROWNING AUTO-22 RIFLE
Caliber: 22 LR, 11-shot.
Barrel: 19¼".
Weight: 4¾ lbs. **Length:** 37" overall.
Stock: Checkered select walnut with p.g. and semi-beavertail forend.
Sights: Gold bead front, folding leaf rear.
Features: Engraved receiver with polished blue finish; cross-bolt safety; tubular magazine in buttstock; easy takedown for carrying or storage. Imported from Japan by Browning.
Price: Grade I **$363.95**

CALICO MODEL M-100 CARBINE
Caliber: 22 LR, 100-shot magazine.
Barrel: 16".
Weight: 5.7 lbs. (loaded). **Length:** 35.8" overall (stock extended).
Stock: Folding steel.
Sights: Post front adjustable for elevation, notch rear adjustable for windage.
Features: Uses alloy frame and helical-feed magazine; ambidextrous safety; removable barrel assembly; pistol grip compartment; flash suppressor; bolt stop. Made in U.S. From Calico.
Price: **$308.30**

Calico M-105

Calico Model M-105 Sporter
Similar to the M-100 except has hand-rubbed wood buttstock and forend. Weight is 4¾ lbs. Introduced 1987.
Price: **$335.00**

ERMA EM1 CARBINE
Caliber: 22 LR, 10-shot magazine.
Barrel: 18".
Weight: 5.6 lbs. **Length:** 35.5" overall.
Stock: Polished beech or oiled walnut.
Sights: Blade front, fully adjustable aperture rear.
Features: Blowback action. Receiver grooved for scope mounting. Imported from Germany by Mandall Shooting Supplies.
Price: **$499.95**

```
┌─────────────────────────────────┐
│ Consult our Directory pages for │
│ the location of firms mentioned.│
└─────────────────────────────────┘
```

FEATHER AT-22 SEMI-AUTO CARBINE
Caliber: 22 LR, 20-shot magazine.
Barrel: 17".
Weight: 3.25 lbs. **Length:** 35" overall (stock extended).
Stock: Telescoping wire; composition pistol grip.
Sights: Protected post front, adjustable aperture rear.
Features: Removable barrel. Length when folded is 26". Matte black finish. From Feather Industries. Introduced 1986.
Price: **$249.95**
Price: Model F2 (fixed stock) **$279.95**

E.A.A./SABATTI MODEL 1822 AUTO RIFLE
Caliber: 22 LR, 10-shot magazine.
Barrel: 18½" round tapered; bull barrel on Heavy and Thumbhole Heavy models.
Weight: 5¼ lbs. (Sporter). **Length:** 37" overall.
Stock: Stained hardwood; Thumbhole model has one-piece stock.
Sights: Bead front, folding leaf rear adjustable for elevation on Sporter model. Heavy and Thumbhole models only dovetailed for scope mount.
Features: Cross-bolt safety. Blue finish. Lifetime warranty. Introduced 1993. Imported from Italy by European American Armory.
Price: Sporter **$190.00**
Price: Heavy **$205.00**
Price: Thumbhole Heavy **$350.00**

CAUTION: PRICES SHOWN ARE SUPPLIED BY THE MANUFACTURER OR IMPORTER. CHECK YOUR LOCAL GUNSHOP.

FEDERAL ENGINEERING XC222 AUTO CARBINE
Caliber: 22 LR, 30-shot magazine.
Barrel: 16.5" (with flash hider).
Weight: 7.25 lbs. **Length:** 34.5" overall.
Stock: Quick-detachable tube steel.
Sights: Hooded post front, Williams adjustable rear; sight bridge grooved for scope mounting.
Features: Quick takedown; all-steel heli-arc welded construction; internal parts industrial hard chromed. Made in U.S. by Federal Engineering Corp.
Price: Includes receiver cap, sling, swivels **$459.00**

Federal XC222

Grendel R-31

GRENDEL R-31 AUTO CARBINE
Caliber: 22 WMR, 30-shot magazine.
Barrel: 16".
Weight: 4 lbs. **Length:** 23.5" overall (stock collapsed).
Stock: Telescoping tube, Zytel forend.
Sights: Post front adustable for windage and elevation, aperture rear.
Features: Blowback action with fluted chamber; ambidextrous safety. Steel receiver. Matte black finish. Muzzle brake. Scope mount optional. Introduced 1991. Made in U.S. by Grendel, Inc.
Price: **$385.00**

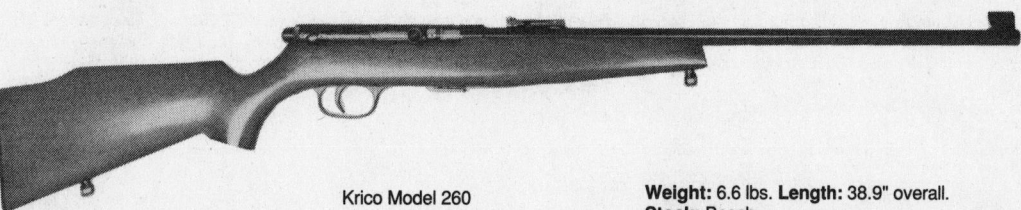

Krico Model 260

KRICO MODEL 260 AUTO RIFLE
Caliber: 22 LR, 5-shot magazine.
Barrel: 19.6".

Weight: 6.6 lbs. **Length:** 38.9" overall.
Stock: Beech.
Sights: Blade on ramp front, open adjustable rear.
Features: Receiver grooved for scope mounting. Sliding safety. Imported from Germany by Mandall Shooting Supplies.
Price: **$700.00**

Lakefield Arms Model 64B

LAKEFIELD ARMS MODEL 64B AUTO RIFLE
Caliber: 22 LR, 10-shot magazine.
Barrel: 20".
Weight: 5½ lbs. **Length:** 40" overall.
Stock: Walnut-finished hardwood with Monte Carlo-type comb, checkered grip and forend.
Sights: Bead front, open adjustable rear. Receiver grooved for scope mounting.
Features: Thumb-operated rotating safety. Blue finish. Side ejection, bolt hold-open device. Introduced 1990. Made in Canada by Lakefield Arms Ltd.
Price: About **$138.45**

MARLIN MODEL 60 SELF-LOADING RIFLE
Caliber: 22 LR, 14-shot tubular magazine.
Barrel: 22" round tapered.
Weight: About 5½ lbs. **Length:** 40½" overall.
Stock: Walnut-finished Monte Carlo, full pistol grip; Mar-Shield® finish.
Sights: Ramp front, open adjustable rear.
Features: Matted receiver is grooved for scope mount. Manual bolt hold-open; automatic last-shot bolt hold-open.
Price: **$153.05**

Marlin Model 990L Self-Loading Rifle
Similar to the Model 60 except has laminated hardwood stock with black rubber rifle butt pad and swivel studs, gold-plated steel trigger. Ramp front sight with brass bead and Wide-Scan hood, adjustable semi-buckhorn folding rear. Weighs 5.75 lbs. Introduced 1992. From Marlin.
Price: **$223.10**

Marlin Model 60SS Self-Loading Rifle
Same as the Model 60 except breech bolt, barrel and outer magazine tube are made of stainless steel; most other parts are either nickel-plated or coated to match the stainless finish. Monte Carlo stock is of black/gray Main birch laminate, and has nickel-plated swivel studs, rubber butt pad. Introduced 1993.
Price: **$229.05**

Marlin Model 60SS

MARLIN MODEL 70 HC AUTO
Caliber: 22 LR, 7-shot clip magazine.
Barrel: 18" (16-groove rifling).
Weight: 5 lbs. **Length:** 36¾" overall.
Stock: Walnut-finished hardwood with Monte Carlo, full p.g. Mar-Shield® finish.
Sights: Ramp front, adjustable open rear. Receiver grooved for scope mount.
Features: Receiver top has serrated, non-glare finish; cross-bolt safety; manual bolt hold-open. Comes with two magazines.
Price: **$161.70**

CAUTION: PRICES SHOWN ARE SUPPLIED BY THE MANUFACTURER OR IMPORTER. CHECK YOUR LOCAL GUNSHOP.

49th EDITION, 1995   **363**

Marlin Model 70P Papoose

Marlin Model 70P Papoose

Similar to the Model 70 HC except is a takedown model with easily removable barrel—no tools needed. Has 16¼" Micro-Groove® barrel, walnut-finished hardwood stock, ramp front, adjustable open rear sights, cross-bolt safety. Takedown feature allows removal of barrel without tools. Overall length is 35¼", weight is 3¼ lbs. Receiver grooved for scope mounting. Comes with zippered case. Introduced 1986.
Price: **$200.15**

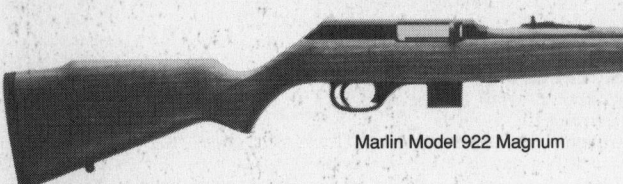

Marlin Model 922 Magnum

MARLIN MODEL 922 MAGNUM SELF-LOADING RIFLE

Caliber: 22 WMR, 7-shot magazine.
Barrel: 20.5".
Weight: 6.5 lbs. **Length:** 39.75" overall.
Stock: Checkered American black walnut with Monte Carlo comb, swivel studs, rubber buttpad.
Sights: Ramp front with bead and removable Wide-Scan® hood, adjustable folding semi-buckhorn rear.
Features: Action based on the centerfire Model 9 Carbine. Receiver drilled and tapped for scope mounting. Automatic last-shot bolt holdopen; magazine safety. Introduced 1993.
Price: **$377.95**

MARLIN MODEL 995 SELF-LOADING RIFLE

Caliber: 22 LR, 7-shot clip magazine.
Barrel: 18" Micro-Groove®.
Weight: 5 lbs. **Length:** 36¾" overall.
Stock: American black walnut, Monte Carlo-style, with full pistol grip. Checkered p.g. and forend; white buttplate spacer; Mar-Shield® finish.
Sights: Ramp bead front with Wide-Scan™ hood; adjustable folding semi-buckhorn rear.
Features: Receiver grooved for scope mount; bolt hold-open device; cross-bolt safety. Introduced 1979.
Price: **$205.75**

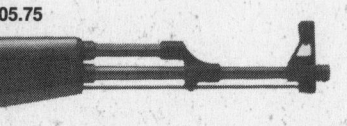

Mitchell AK-22

MITCHELL AK-22 SEMI-AUTO RIFLE

Caliber: 22 LR, 20-shot magazine; 22 WMR, 10-shot magazine.
Barrel: 18".
Weight: 6½ lbs. **Length:** 36" overall.
Stock: European walnut.
Sights: Post front, open adjustable rear.
Features: Replica of the AK-47 rifle. Wide magazine to maintain appearance. Imported from Italy by Mitchell Arms, Inc.
Price: 22 LR **$359.00**
Price: 22 WMR **$359.00**

MITCHELL GALIL/22 AUTO RIFLE

Caliber: 22 LR, 20-shot magazine; 22 WMR, 10-shot magazine.
Barrel: 18".
Weight: 6.5 lbs. **Length:** 36" overall.
Stock: European walnut grip and forend with metal folding stock.
Sights: Post front adjustable for elevation, rear adjustable for windage.
Features: Replica of the Israeli Galil rifle. Introduced 1987. Imported by Mitchell Arms, Inc.
Price: 22 LR, fixed or folding stock **$359.00**
Price: 22 WMR, fixed or folding stock **$359.00**

Mitchell High Standard 15/22

MITCHELL HIGH STANDARD 15/22 RIFLES

Caliber: 22 LR, 15-shot magazine; 30-shot available.
Barrel: 20.5".
Weight: 6.25 lbs. **Length:** 37.5" overall.
Stock: American walnut.
Sights: Blade on ramp front, open adjustable rear.
Features: Polished blue finish; barrel band on forend. Introduced 1994. Imported from Philippines by Mitchell Arms.
Price: **$159.95**
Price: Model 15/22D (fancy walnut stock with checkering, rosewood grip and forend caps) **$199.95**

MITCHELL MAS/22 AUTO RIFLE

Caliber: 22 LR, 20-shot magazine.
Barrel: 18".
Weight: 7½ lbs. **Length:** 28.5" overall.
Stock: Walnut butt, grip and forend.
Sights: Adjustable post front, flip-type aperture rear.
Features: Bullpup design resembles French armed forces rifle. Top cocking lever, flash hider. Introduced 1987. Imported by Mitchell Arms, Inc.
Price: **$359.00**

Mitchell CAR-15/22 Semi-Auto Rifle

Similar to the M-16 A-1/22 rifle except has 16¾" barrel, telescoping butt, giving an overall length of 32" when collapsed. Adjustable post front sight, adjustable aperture rear. Scope mount available. Has 15-shot magazine. Replica of the CAR-15 rifle. Introduced 1990. Imported by Mitchell Arms, Inc.
Price: **$359.00**

MITCHELL M-16A-1/22 RIFLE

Caliber: 22 LR, 15-shot magazine.
Barrel: 20.5".
Weight: 7 lbs. **Length:** 38.5" overall.
Stock: Black composition.
Sights: Adjustable post front, adjustable aperture rear.
Features: Replica of the AR-15 rifle. Full width magazine. Comes with military-type sling. Introduced 1990. Imported by Mitchell Arms, Inc.
Price: **$359.00**

RIMFIRE RIFLES—AUTOLOADERS

MITCHELL PPS/50 RIFLE
Caliber: 22 LR, 20-shot magazine (50-shot drum optional).
Barrel: 16½".
Weight: 5½ lbs. **Length:** 33½" overall.
Stock: Walnut.
Sights: Blade front, adjustable rear.

Features: Full-length perforated barrel shroud. Matte finish. Introduced 1989. Imported by Mitchell Arms, Inc.
Price: With 20-shot "banana" magazine $359.00
Price: With 50-shot drum magazine $459.00

Norinco Model 22 ATD

NORINCO MODEL 22 ATD RIFLE
Caliber: 22 LR, 11-shot magazine.
Barrel: 19.4".

Weight: 4.6 lbs. **Length:** 36.6" overall.
Stock: Checkered hardwood.
Sights: Blade front, open adjustable rear.
Features: Browning-design takedown action for storage, transport. Cross-bolt safety. Tube magazine loads through buttplate. Blue finish with engraved receiver. Introduced 1987. Imported from China by Interarms.
Price: $166.00

Remington 522 Viper

REMINGTON 552 BDL SPEEDMASTER RIFLE
Caliber: 22 S (20), L (17) or LR (15) tubular mag.
Barrel: 21" round tapered.
Weight: About 5¾ lbs. **Length:** 40" overall.
Stock: Walnut. Checkered grip and forend.
Sights: Bead front, step open rear adjustable for windage and elevation.
Features: Positive cross-bolt safety, receiver grooved for tip-off mount.
Price: About $265.00

REMINGTON MODEL 522 VIPER AUTOLOADING RIFLE
Caliber: 22 LR, 10-shot magazine.
Barrel: 20".
Weight: 4⅝ lbs. **Length:** 40" overall.
Stock: Black synthetic with positive checkering, beavertail forend.
Sights: Bead on ramp front, fully adjustable open rear. Integral grooved rail for scope mounting.
Features: Synthetic stock and receiver with overall matte black finish. Has magazine safety, cocking indicator; manual and last-shot hold-open; trigger mechanism has primary and secondary sears; integral ejection port shield. Introduced 1993.
Price: $165.00

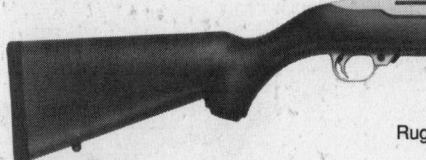

Ruger 10/22 International

Ruger 10/22 International Carbine
Similar to the Ruger 10/22 Carbine except has full-length Mannlicher stock of American hardwood, no checkering; comes with rubber buttpad, sling swivels. Reintroduced 1994.
Price: Blue (10/22RBI) $249.50
Price: Stainless (K10/22RBI) $269.00

Ruger 10/22 Deluxe Sporter
Same as 10/22 Carbine except walnut stock with hand checkered p.g. and forend; straight buttplate, no barrel band, has sling swivels.
Price: Model 10/22 DSP $254.50

RUGER 10/22 AUTOLOADING CARBINE
Caliber: 22 LR, 10-shot rotary magazine.
Barrel: 18½" round tapered.
Weight: 5 lbs. **Length:** 37¼" overall.
Stock: American hardwood with p.g. and bbl. band.
Sights: Brass bead front, folding leaf rear adjustable for elevation.
Features: Detachable rotary magazine fits flush into stock, cross-bolt safety, receiver tapped and grooved for scope blocks or tip-off mount. Scope base adaptor furnished with each rifle.
Price: Model 10/22 RB (blue) $201.50
Price: Model K10/22RB (bright finish stainless barrel) $236.00

SURVIVAL ARMS AR-7 EXPLORER RIFLE
Caliber: 22 LR, 8-shot magazine.
Barrel: 16".
Weight: 2.5 lbs. **Length:** 34.5" overall; 16.5" stowed.
Stock: Moulded Cycolac; snap-on rubber butt cap.
Sights: Square blade front, aperture rear adjustable for elevation.

Features: Takedown design stores barrel and action in hollow stock. Light enough to float. Black, Silvertone or camouflage finish. Reintroduced 1992. From Survival Arms, Inc.
Price: Silver or camo $150.00
Price: Sporter (black finish with telescoping stock, 25-shot magazine) $200.00
Price: Wildcat (black finish with wood stock) $150.00

Voere Model 2115

VOERE MODEL 2115 AUTO RIFLE
Caliber: 22 LR, 10-shot magazine.
Barrel: 18.1"; hammer forged.

Weight: 5.75 lbs. **Length:** 37.7" overall.
Stock: Walnut-finished beechwood with cheekpiece; checkered pistol grip and forend.
Sights: Post front with hooded ramp, leaf rear.
Features: Clip-fed autoloader with single stage trigger, wing-type safety. Introduced 1984. Imported from Austria by JagerSport, Ltd.
Price: About $585.00

CAUTION: PRICES SHOWN ARE SUPPLIED BY THE MANUFACTURER OR IMPORTER. CHECK YOUR LOCAL GUNSHOP.

Classic and modern models for sport and utility, including training.

Browning BL 22

BROWNING BL-22 LEVER-ACTION RIFLE
Caliber: 22 S (22), L (17) or LR (15), tubular magazine.
Barrel: 20" round tapered.
Weight: 5 lbs. **Length:** 36¾" overall.
Stock: Walnut, two-piece straight grip Western style.
Sights: Bead post front, folding-leaf rear.
Features: Short throw lever, half-cock safety, receiver grooved for tip-off scope mounts. Imported from Japan by Browning.
Price: Grade I **$317.95**
Price: Grade II (engraved receiver, checkered grip and forend) . . . **$361.95**

Marlin Model 39AS

MARLIN MODEL 39AS GOLDEN LEVER-ACTION RIFLE
Caliber: 22 S (26), L (21), LR (19), tubular magazine.
Barrel: 24" Micro-Groove®.
Weight: 6½ lbs. **Length:** 40" overall.
Stock: Checkered American black walnut with white line spacers at p.g. cap and buttplate; Mar-Shield® finish. Swivel studs; rubber buttpad.
Sights: Bead ramp front with detachable Wide-Scan™ hood, folding rear semi-buckhorn adjustable for windage and elevation.
Features: Hammer-block safety; rebounding hammer. Takedown action, receiver tapped for scope mount (supplied), offset hammer spur; gold-plated steel trigger.
Price: **$417.25**

MARLIN 39TDS CARBINE
Caliber: 22 S (16), 22 L (12), 22 LR (11).
Barrel: 16½" Micro-Groove®.
Weight: 5¼ lbs. **Length:** 32⅝" overall.
Stock: Checkered American black walnut with straight grip; short forend with blued tip. Mar-Shield® finish.
Sights: Ramp front with Wide-Scan™ hood, adjustable semi-buckhorn folding rear.
Features: Takedown style, comes with carrying case. Hammer-block safety, rebounding hammer; blued metal, gold-plated steel trigger. Introduced 1988.
Price: With case **$430.25**

Norinco Pioneer

NORINCO PIONEER LEVER-ACTION RIFLE
Caliber: 22 LR, 15-shot magazine.
Barrel: 20.25".
Weight: 6.1 lbs. **Length:** 37.5" overall.
Stock: Checkered hardwood.
Sights: Bead front, rear drift adjustable for windage.
Features: Sliding tang safety; polished blue finish. Announced 1994. Imported from China by Interarms.
Price: . . . . **NA**

REMINGTON 572 BDL FIELDMASTER PUMP RIFLE
Caliber: 22 S (20), L (17) or LR (14), tubular magazine.
Barrel: 21" round tapered.
Weight: 5½ lbs. **Length:** 42" overall.
Stock: Walnut with checkered p.g. and slide handle.
Sights: Blade ramp front; sliding ramp rear adjustable for windage and elevation.
Features: Cross-bolt safety; removing inner magazine tube converts rifle to single shot; receiver grooved for tip-off scope mount.
Price: About **$279.00**

NORINCO EM-321 PUMP RIFLE
Caliber: 22 LR, 9-shot magazine.
Barrel: 19.5".
Weight: 6 lbs. **Length:** 37" overall.
Stock: Hardwood.
Sights: Blade front, open folding rear.
Features: Blue finish; grooved slide handle. Imported from China by China Sports, Inc.
Price: . . . . **NA**

Rossi Model 62 SAC

ROSSI MODEL 62 SA PUMP RIFLE
Caliber: 22 LR, 22 WMR.
Barrel: 23", round or octagonal.
Weight: 5¾ lbs. **Length:** 39¼" overall.
Stock: Walnut, straight grip, grooved forend.
Sights: Fixed front, adjustable rear.
Features: Capacity 20 Short, 16 Long or 14 Long Rifle. Quick takedown. Imported from Brazil by Interarms.
Price: Blue **$218.00**
Price: Nickel **$235.00**
Price: Blue, with octagonal barrel **$243.00**
Price: 22 WMR, as Model 59 . . . . **$267.00**

Rossi Model 62 SAC Carbine
Same as standard model except 22 LR only, has 16¼" barrel. Magazine holds slightly fewer cartridges.
Price: Blue **$218.00**
Price: Nickel **$235.00**

CAUTION: PRICES SHOWN ARE SUPPLIED BY THE MANUFACTURER OR IMPORTER. CHECK YOUR LOCAL GUNSHOP.

Winchester Model 9422

Winchester Model 9422 Magnum Lever-Action Rifle

Same as the 9422 except chambered for 22 WMR cartridge, has 11-round mag. capacity.

Price: Walnut **$400.00**
Price: With WinCam green stock **$400.00**
Price: With WinTuff brown laminated stock **$400.00**

WINCHESTER MODEL 9422 LEVER-ACTION RIFLE

Caliber: 22 S (21), L (17), LR (15), tubular magazine.
Barrel: 20½".
Weight: 6¼ lbs. **Length:** 37⅛" overall.
Stock: American walnut, two-piece, straight grip (no p.g.).
Sights: Hooded ramp front, adjustable semi-buckhorn rear.
Features: Side ejection, receiver grooved for scope mounting, takedown action. From U.S. Repeating Arms Co.
Price: Walnut **$384.00**
Price: With WinTuff laminated stock **$384.00**

RIMFIRE RIFLES—BOLT ACTIONS & SINGLE SHOTS

Includes models for a variety of sports, utility and competitive shooting.

ANSCHUTZ ACHIEVER BOLT-ACTION RIFLE

Caliber: 22 LR, single shot adaptor.
Barrel: 19½".
Weight: 5 lbs. **Length:** 35½" to 36⅔" overall.
Stock: Walnut-finished hardwood with adjustable buttplate, vented forend, stippled pistol grip. Length of pull adjustable from 11⅞" to 13".
Sights: Hooded front, open rear adjustable for windage and elevation.
Features: Uses Mark 2000-type action with adjustable two-stage trigger. Receiver grooved for scope mounting. Designed for training in junior rifle clubs and for starting young shooters. Introduced 1987. Imported from Germany by Precision Sales International.
Price: **$395.00**
Price: Sight Set #1 . . . . **$70.00**

ANSCHUTZ 1416D/1516D CLASSIC RIFLES

Caliber: 22 LR (1416D), 5-shot clip; 22 WMR (1516D), 4-shot clip.
Barrel: 22½".
Weight: 6 lbs. **Length:** 41" overall.
Stock: European walnut; Monte Carlo with cheekpiece, schnabel forend, checkered pistol grip and forend.
Sights: Hooded ramp front, folding leaf rear.
Features: Uses Model 1403 target rifle action. Adjustable single stage trigger. Receiver grooved for scope mounting. Imported from Germany by Precision Sales International.
Price: 1416D, 22 LR **$695.00**
Price: 1516D, 22 WMR **$708.00**
Price: 1416D Classic left-hand **$729.00**

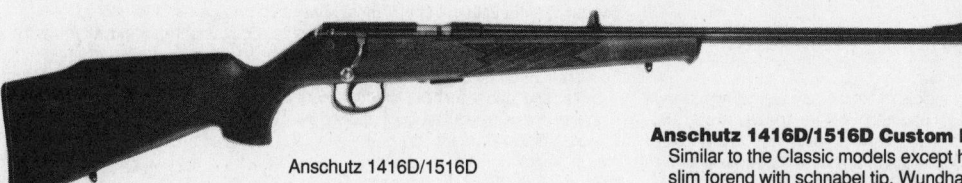

Anschutz 1416D/1516D

Anschutz 1416D/1516D Custom Rifles

Similar to the Classic models except have roll-over Monte Carlo cheekpiece, slim forend with schnabel tip, Wundhammer swell on grip, rosewood grip cap with white diamond insert. Fine cut checkering on grip and forend. Introduced 1988. Imported from Germany by Precision Sales International.
Price: 1416D (22 LR) **$730.00**
Price: 1516D (22 WMR) **$744.00**

Anschutz 1418D/1518D Mannlicher Rifles

Similar to the 1416D/1516D rifles except has full-length Mannlicher-style stock, shorter 19¾" barrel. Weighs 5½ lbs. Stock has mahogany schnabel tip. Model 1418D chambered for 22 LR, 1518D for 22 WMR. Imported from Germany by Precision Sales International.
Price: 1418D **$1,076.00**
Price: 1518D **$1,087.00**

Anschutz 1700 FWT Bolt-Action Rifle

Similar to the Anschutz Custom except has McMillan fiberglass stock with Monte Carlo, roll-over cheekpiece, Wundhammer swell, and checkering. Comes without sights but the receiver is drilled and tapped for scope mounting. Has 22" barrel, single stage #5095 trigger. Weighs 6.25 lbs. Introduced 1989.
Price: With fiberglass stock **$1,163.00**
Price: As above, with Fibergrain stock **$1,392.00**

ANSCHUTZ 1700D BAVARIAN BOLT-ACTION RIFLE

Caliber: 22 LR, 5-shot clip.
Barrel: 24".
Weight: 7¼ lbs. **Length:** 43" overall.
Stock: European walnut with Bavarian cheek rest. Checkered p.g. and forend.
Sights: Hooded ramp front, folding leaf rear.
Features: Uses the Improved 1700 Match 54 action with adjustable 5096 trigger. Drilled and tapped for scope mounting. Introduced in 1988. Imported from Germany by Precision Sales International.
Price: 22 LR **$1,267.00**
Price: Custom 1700D Meistergrade (select walnut, gold engraved trigger guard), add **$199.00**

ANSCHUTZ 1700D CLASSIC RIFLES

Caliber: 22 LR, 5-shot clip.
Barrel: 23½", ¹³/₁₆" dia. heavy.
Weight: 7¾ lbs. **Length:** 42½" overall.
Stock: Select European walnut with checkered pistol grip and forend.
Sights: Hooded ramp front, folding leaf rear; drilled and tapped for scope mounting.
Features: Adjustable single stage trigger. Receiver drilled and tapped for scope mounting. Introduced 1988. Imported from Germany by Precision Sales International.
Price: 22 LR **$1,236.00**
Price: As above, Meistergrade (select walnut, gold engraved trigger guard), add **$199.00**

Anschutz 1700D Custom Rifles

Similar to the Classic models except have roll-over Monte Carlo cheekpiece, slim forend with schnabel tip, Wundhammer palm swell on pistol grip, rosewood grip cap with white diamond insert. Skip-line checkering on grip and forend. Introduced 1988. Imported from Germany by Precision Sales International.
Price: 22 LR **$1,267.00**
Price: Custom 1700 Meistergrade (select walnut, gold engraved trigger guard), add **$199.00**

Anschutz 1700D Graphite Custom Rifle

Similar to the Model 1700D Custom except has McMillan graphite reinforced stock with roll-over cheekpiece. Has 22" barrel. No sights furnished, but drilled and tapped for scope mounting. Comes with embroidered sling, Michael's quick-detachable swivels. Introduced 1991.
Price: **$1,233.00**

Armscor Model 14D

Armscor Model 1500 Rifle

Similar to the Model 14P except chambered for 22 WMR. Has 21.5" barrel, double lug bolt, checkered stock, weighs 6.5 lbs. Introduced 1987.

Price: About **$199.00**

ARMSCOR MODEL 14P BOLT-ACTION RIFLE

Caliber: 22 LR, 10-shot magazine.
Barrel: 23".
Weight: 7 lbs. **Length:** 41.5" overall.
Stock: Walnut-finished mahogany.
Sights: Bead front, rear adjustable for elevation.
Features: Receiver grooved for scope mounting. Blued finish. Introduced 1987. Imported from the Philippines by Ruko Products.
Price: About **$129.00**
Price: Model 14D Deluxe (checkered stock) **$149.00**

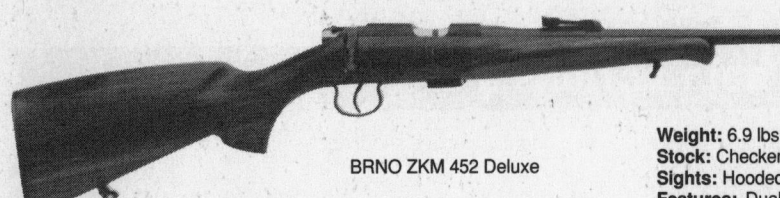

BRNO ZKM 452 Deluxe

BRNO ZKM-452 DELUXE BOLT-ACTION RIFLE

Caliber: 22 LR, detachable 5-shot magazine.
Barrel: 23.6".

Weight: 6.9 lbs. **Length:** 43.5" overall.
Stock: Checkered walnut.
Sights: Hooded bead front, open rear adjustable for windage and elevation.
Features: Dual claw extractors, safety locks firing pin. Blue finish; grooved receiver; oiled stock; sling swivels. Introduced 1992. Imported from the Czech Republic by Action Arms Ltd.
Price: **$349.00**
Price: With beechwood stock **$305.00**

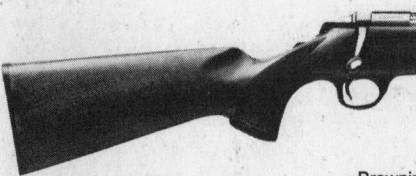

Browning A-Bolt 22

Browning A-Bolt Gold Medallion

Similar to the standard A-Bolt except stock is of high-grade walnut with brass spacers between stock and rubber recoil pad and between the rosewood grip cap and forend. Medallion-style engraving covers the receiver flats, and the words "Gold Medallion" are engraved and gold filled on the right side of the barrel. High gloss stock finish. Introduced 1988.

Price: No sights **$521.95**

BROWNING A-BOLT 22 BOLT-ACTION RIFLE

Caliber: 22 LR, 22 WMR, 5-shot magazines standard.
Barrel: 22".
Weight: 5 lbs., 9 oz. **Length:** 40¼" overall.
Stock: Walnut with cut checkering, rosewood grip cap and forend tip.
Sights: Offered with or without open sights. Open sight model has ramp front and adjustable folding leaf rear.
Features: Short 60-degree bolt throw. Top tang safety. Grooved for 22 scope mount. Drilled and tapped for full-size scope mounts. Detachable magazines. Gold-colored trigger preset at about 4 lbs. Imported from Japan by Browning. Introduced 1986.
Price: A-Bolt 22, no sights **$393.95**
Price: A-Bolt 22, with open sights **$403.95**
Price: A-Bolt 22 WMR, no sights **$454.95**
Price: As above, with sights **$464.95**

Cabanas Master

Cabanas Leyre Bolt-Action Rifle

Similar to Master model except 44" overall, has sport/target stock.
Price: **$149.95**
Price: Model R83 (17" barrel, hardwood stock, 40" o.a.l.) **$79.95**
Price: Mini 82 Youth (16½" barrel, 33" o.a.l., 3½ lbs.) **$69.95**
Price: Pony Youth (16" barrel, 34" o.a.l., 3.2 lbs.) **$69.95**

Cabanas Espronceda IV Bolt-Action Rifle

Similar to the Leyre model except has full sporter stock, 18¾" barrel, 40" overall length, weighs 5½ lbs.
Price: **$134.95**

CABANAS TASER RIFLE

Caliber: 177.
Barrel: 19".
Weight: 6 lbs., 12 oz. **Length:** 42" overall.
Stock: Target-type thumbhole.
Sights: Blade front, open fully adjustable rear.
Features: Fires round ball or pellets with 22 blank cartridge. Imported from Mexico by Mandall Shooting Supplies.
Price: **$159.95**

CABANAS MASTER BOLT-ACTION RIFLE

Caliber: 177, round ball or pellet; single shot.
Barrel: 19½".
Weight: 8 lbs. **Length:** 45½" overall.
Stocks: Walnut target-type with Monte Carlo.
Sights: Blade front, fully adjustable rear.
Features: Fires round ball or pellet with 22-cal. blank cartridge. Bolt action. Imported from Mexico by Mandall Shooting Supplies. Introduced 1984.
Price: **$189.95**
Price: Varmint model (has 21½" barrel, 4½ lbs., 41" o.a.l., varmint-type stock) **$119.95**

CAUTION: PRICES SHOWN ARE SUPPLIED BY THE MANUFACTURER OR IMPORTER. CHECK YOUR LOCAL GUNSHOP.

RIMFIRE RIFLES—BOLT ACTIONS & SINGLE SHOTS

Chipmunk Rifle

CHIPMUNK SINGLE SHOT RIFLE
Caliber: 22, S, L, LR, single shot.

COOPER ARMS MODEL 36RF SPORTER RIFLE
Caliber: 22 LR, 5-shot magazine.
Barrel: 23" Shilen match.
Weight: 7 lbs. **Length:** 42½" overall.
Stock: AA Claro walnut with 22 lpi checkering, oil finish; Custom has AAA Claro or AA French walnut.
Sights: None furnished.
Features: Action has three mid-bolt locking lugs, 45-degree bolt rotation; fully

Barrel: 16⅛".
Weight: About 2½ lbs. **Length:** 30" overall.
Stocks: American walnut, or camouflage.
Sights: Post on ramp front, peep rear adjustable for windage and elevation.
Features: Drilled and tapped for scope mounting using special Chipmunk base ($9.95). Made in U.S. Introduced 1982. From Oregon Arms.
Price: Standard **$174.95**
Price: Deluxe (better wood, checkering) **$225.00**

adjustable single stage match trigger; swivel studs. Pachmayr butt pad. Introduced 1991. Made in U.S. by Cooper Arms.
Price: Standard **$1,125.00**
Price: Custom (AAA Claro walnut, Monte Carlo beaded cheekpiece, oil finish) **$1,250.00**
Price: Custom Classic (as above with ebony forend tip, steel grip cap, Brownell No. 1 checkering pattern) **$1,350.00**
Price: Model 36RF Featherweight (custom stock shape, black textured finish) **$1,195.00**

Dakota 22 Sporter

DAKOTA 22 SPORTER BOLT-ACTION RIFLE
Caliber: 22 LR, 5-shot magazine.
Barrel: 22".

Weight: About 6.5 lbs. **Length:** NA.
Stock: Claro or English walnut in classic design; 13.6" length of pull. Choice of grade. Point panel hand checkering. Swivel studs. Black buttpad.
Sights: None furnished; comes with mount bases.
Features: Combines features of Winchester 52 and Dakota 76 rifles. Full-sized receiver; rear locking lug and bolt machined from bar stock. Trigger and striker-blocking safety; adjustable trigger. Introduced 1992. From Dakota Arms, Inc.
Price: **$1,500.00**

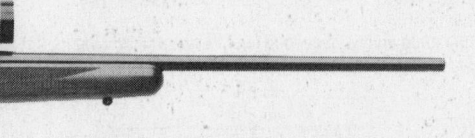

Kimber Model 82C

Kimber Model 82C SuperAmerica Bolt-Action Rifle
Similar to the Model 82C except has AAA fancy grade Claro walnut with beaded cheekpiece, ebony forend cap; hand-checkered 22 lpi patterns with wrap-around coverage; black rubber buttpad. Reintroduced 1994. Made in U.S. by Kimber of America, Inc.
Price: **$1,175.00**

Kimber Model 82C Custom Shop SuperAmerica
Similar to standard SuperAmerica except has Neidner-style buttplate. Available options include: steel skeleton grip cap and buttplate; quarter-rib and open express sights; jewelled bolt; checkered bolt knob; special length of pull; rust blue finish. Reintroduced 1994. Made in U.S. by Kimber of America, Inc.
Price: Basic Custom Shop SuperAmerica **$1,250.00**

KRICO MODEL 300 BOLT-ACTION RIFLES
Caliber: 22 LR, 22 WMR, 22 Hornet.
Barrel: 19.6" (22 RF), 23.6" (Hornet).
Weight: 6.3 lbs. **Length:** 38.5" overall (22 RF).
Stock: Walnut-stained beech.
Sights: Blade on ramp front, open adjustable rear.
Features: Double triggers, sliding safety. Checkered grip and forend. Imported from Germany by Mandall Shooting Supplies.
Price: Model 300 Standard **$700.00**
Price: Model 300 Deluxe **$795.00**
Price: Model 300 Stutzen (walnut full-length stock) **$825.00**
Price: Model 300 SA (walnut Monte Carlo stock) **$750.00**

LAKEFIELD ARMS MARK II BOLT-ACTION RIFLE
Caliber: 22 LR, 10-shot magazine.
Barrel: 20½".
Weight: 5½ lbs. **Length:** 39½" overall.
Stock: Walnut-finished hardwood with Monte Carlo-type comb, checkered grip and forend.

KIMBER MODEL 82C CLASSIC BOLT-ACTION RIFLE
Caliber: 22 LR, 4-shot magazine (10-shot available).
Barrel: 21"; premium air-gauged.
Weight: 6.5 lbs. **Length:** 40.5" overall.
Stock: Classic style of Claro walnut; 13.5" length of pull; hand-checkered; red rubber buttpad; polished steel grip cap.
Sights: None furnished; drilled and tapped for Warne scope mounts (optionally available from factory).
Features: Action uses aluminum pillar bedding for consistent accuracy; single-set trigger with 2.5-lb. pull is fully adjustable. Reintroduced 1994. Made in U.S. by Kimber of America, Inc.
Price: **$696.00**

LAKEFIELD ARMS MARK I BOLT-ACTION RIFLE
Caliber: 22 LR, single shot.
Barrel: 20½".
Weight: 5½ lbs. **Length:** 39½" overall.
Stock: Walnut-finished hardwood with Monte Carlo-type comb, checkered grip and forend.
Sights: Bead front, open adjustable rear. Receiver grooved for scope mounting.
Features: Thumb-operated rotating safety. Blue finish. Rifled or smooth bore. Introduced 1990. Made in Canada by Lakefield Arms Ltd.
Price: Mark I, rifled or smooth bore **$124.95**
Price: Mark I left-hand **$137.95**
Price: Mark IY (Youth), 19" barrel, 37" overall, 5 lbs. **$124.95**
Price: Mark IY left-hand **$137.95**
Price: Mark I left-hand, smooth bore **$137.95**
Price: Mark IY left-hand, smooth bore **$137.95**

Sights: Bead front, open adjustable rear. Receiver grooved for scope mounting.
Features: Thumb-operated rotating safety. Blue finish. Introduced 1990. Made in Canada by Lakefield Arms Ltd.
Price: About **$133.95**
Price: Mark II-Y (youth), 19" barrel, 37" overall, 5 lbs. **$133.95**
Price: Mark II left-hand **$146.95**
Price: Mark II-Y (youth) left-hand **$146.95**

CAUTION: PRICES SHOWN ARE SUPPLIED BY THE MANUFACTURER OR IMPORTER. CHECK YOUR LOCAL GUNSHOP.

Lakefield Model 93M

LAKEFIELD ARMS MODEL 93M BOLT-ACTION RIFLE
Caliber: 22 WMR, 5-shot magazine.
Barrel: 20.75".

Weight: 5.75 lbs. **Length:** 39.5" overall.
Stock: Walnut-finished hardwood with Monte Carlo-type comb, checkered grip and forend.
Sights: Bead front, adjustable open rear. Receiver grooved for scope mount.
Features: Thumb-operated rotary safety. Blue finish. Introduced 1994. Made in Canada by Lakefield Arms Ltd.
Price: About **$162.95**

Magtech Model 122.2R

MAGTECH MODEL 122.2 BOLT-ACTION RIFLES
Caliber: 22 S, L, LR, 6- and 10-shot magazines.
Barrel: 24" (six-groove).

Weight: 6.5 lbs. **Length:** 43" overall.
Stock: Brazilian hardwood.
Sights: Blade front, open rear adjustable for windage and elevation.
Features: Sliding safety; double extractors; receiver grooved for scope mount. Introduced 1994. Imported from Brazil by Magtech Recreational Products, Inc.
Price: Model 122.2S (no sights) **$139.95**
Price: Model 122.2R (open sights) **$149.95**
Price: Model 122.2T (ramp front, micro-type open rear) **$169.95**

MARLIN MODEL 15YN "LITTLE BUCKAROO"
Caliber: 22 S, L, LR, single shot.
Barrel: 16¼" Micro-Groove;rm.
Weight: 4¼ lbs. **Length:** 33¼" overall.
Stock: One-piece walnut-finished hardwood with Monte Carlo; Mar-Shield® finish.
Sights: Ramp front, adjustable open rear.
Features: Beginner's rifle with thumb safety, easy-load feed throat, red cocking indicator. Receiver grooved for scope mounting. Introduced 1989.
Price: **$156.55**

> Consult our Directory pages for the location of firms mentioned.

Marlin Model 880

MARLIN MODEL 880 BOLT-ACTION RIFLE
Caliber: 22 LR; 7-shot clip magazine.
Barrel: 22" Micro-Groove®.
Weight: 5½ lbs. **Length:** 41".
Stock: Checkered Monte Carlo American black walnut with checkered p.g. and forend. Rubber buttpad, swivel studs. Mar-Shield® finish.
Sights: Wide-Scan™ ramp front, folding semi-buckhorn rear adjustable for windage and elevation.
Features: Receiver grooved for scope mount. Introduced 1989.
Price: **$225.35**

Marlin Model 881 Bolt-Action Rifle
Same as the Marlin 880 except tubular magazine, holds 17 Long Rifle, 19 Long, 25 Short cartridges. Weighs 6 lbs.
Price: **$234.75**

Marlin Model 880SS

Marlin Model 880SS Stainless Steel Bolt-Action Rifle
Same as the Model 880 except barrel, receiver, front breech bolt, striker knob, trigger stud, cartridge lifter stud and outer magazine tube are made of stainless steel. Most other parts are nickel-plated to match the stainless finish. Has black fiberglass-filled AKZO synthetic stock with moulded-in checkering, stainless steel swivel studs. Introduced 1994. Made in U.S. by Marlin Firearms Co.
Price: **$240.80**

Marlin Model 882 Bolt-Action Rifle
Same as the Marlin 880 except 22 WMR cal. only with 7-shot clip magazine; weight about 6 lbs. Comes with swivel studs.
Price: **$248.50**
Price: Model 882L (laminated hardwood stock) **$263.45**

Marlin Model 883SS Bolt-Action Rifle
Same as the Model 883 except front breech bolt, striker knob, trigger stud, cartridge lifter stud and outer magazine tube are of stainless steel; other parts are nickel-plated. Has two-tone brown laminated Monte Carlo stock with swivel studs, rubber butt pad. Introduced 1993.
Price: **$274.25**

Marlin Model 883 Bolt-Action Rifle
Same as Marlin 882 except tubular magazine holds 12 rounds of 22 WMR ammunition.
Price: **$257.60**

Marlin Model 25N Bolt-Action Repeater
Similar to Marlin 880, except walnut-finished p.g. stock, adjustable open rear sight, ramp front.
Price: **$162.60**

Marlin Model 25MN Bolt-Action Rifle
Similar to the Model 25N except chambered for 22 WMR. Has 7-shot clip magazine, 22" Micro-Groove® barrel, checkered walnut-finished hardwood stock. Introduced 1989.
Price: **$185.90**

CAUTION: PRICES SHOWN ARE SUPPLIED BY THE MANUFACTURER OR IMPORTER. CHECK YOUR LOCAL GUNSHOP.

Mitchell High Standard 9302

MITCHELL HIGH STANDARD BOLT-ACTION RIFLES

Caliber: 22 LR, 10-shot magazine; 22 WMR, 5-shot magazine.
Barrel: 22.5".
Weight: About 6.5 lbs. **Length:** 40.75" overall.

Stock: American walnut (Models 9301, 9302 have rosewood grip and forend caps, checkering).
Sights: Bead on ramp front, open adjustable rear.
Features: Polished blue finish. Introduced 1994. Imported from the Philippines by Mitchell Arms.
Price: Model 9301 (22 LR, checkering, rosewood caps) **$312.50**
Price: Model 9302 (as above, 22 WMR) **$317.50**
Price: Model 9303 (22 LR, no checkering or rosewood caps) **$275.00**
Price: Model 9304 (as above, 22 WMR) **$280.00**

Navy Arms Sniper Trainer

Navy Arms TU-KKW Sniper Trainer

Same as the TU-33/40 except comes with Type 89 2.75x scope with quick-detachable mount system. Weighs 7 lbs., 6 oz. with scope. Comes with bayonet lug, sling, cleaning rod. Introduced 1992. Imported by Navy Arms.
Price: **$310.00**

Navy Arms TU-33/40 Carbine

Similar to the TU-KKW Training Rifle except has 20.75" barrel, weighs 6.5 lbs., 38" overall. Based on Mauser G.33/40 mountain carbine. Comes with bayonet lug, sling, cleaning rod. Introduced 1992. Imported by Navy Arms.
Price: **$210.00**

NAVY ARMS TU-KKW TRAINING RIFLE

Caliber: 22 LR, 5-shot detachable magazine.
Barrel: 26".
Weight: 8 lbs. **Length:** 44" overall.
Stock: 98k-style walnut-stained hardwood.
Sights: Blade front, open rear adjustable for elevation; military style.
Features: Replica of the German WWII training rifle. Polished blue metal. Bayonet lug, cleaning rod, takedown disk in butt. Introduced 1991. Imported by Navy Arms.
Price: **$210.00**

NORINCO JW-15 BOLT-ACTION RIFLE

Caliber: 22 LR, 5-shot detachable magazine.
Barrel: 24".
Weight: 5 lbs., 12 oz. **Length:** 41¾" overall.
Stock: Walnut-stained hardwood.
Sights: Hooded blade front, open rear drift adjustable for windage.
Features: Polished blue finish; sling swivels; wing-type safety. Introduced 1991. Imported by Interarms, Navy Arms.
Price: About . . . . **$110.00 to $118.00**

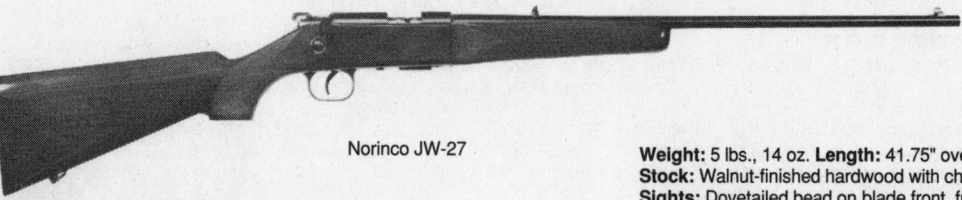

Norinco JW-27

NORINCO JW-27 BOLT-ACTION RIFLE

Caliber: 22 LR, 5-shot magazine.
Barrel: 22.75".

Weight: 5 lbs., 14 oz. **Length:** 41.75" overall.
Stock: Walnut-finished hardwood with checkered grip and forend.
Sights: Dovetailed bead on blade front, fully adjustable rear.
Features: Receiver grooved for scope mounting. Blued finish. Introduced 1992. Imported from China by Century International Arms.
Price: About **$106.95**

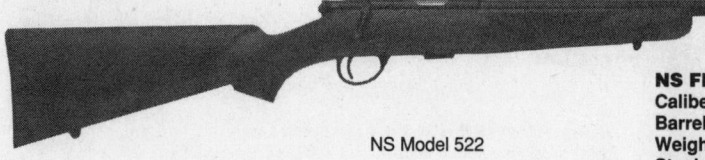

NS Model 522

NS FIREARMS MODEL 522 RIFLE

Caliber: 22 LR, 5-shot magazine.
Barrel: 21".
Weight: 7.75 lbs. **Length:** 39.5" overall.
Stock: Walnut with cut-checkered grip and forend; satin finish.
Sights: None furnished. Receiver grooved for scope mount.
Features: Free-floated hammer-forged heavy barrel; forged receiver and bolt with two locking lugs, dual extractors. Safety locks bolt and trigger. Introduced 1993. Imported by Keng's Firearms Specialty.
Price: About **$299.95**

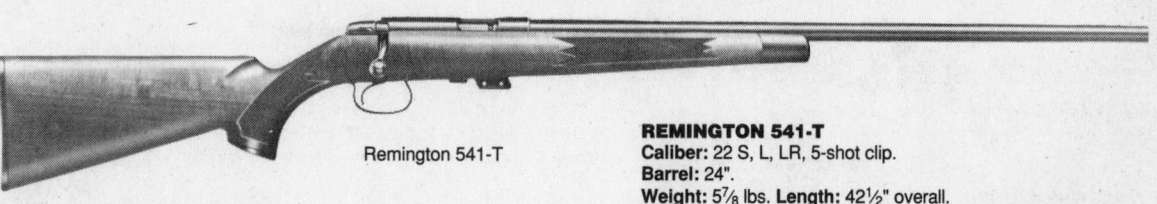

Remington 541-T

REMINGTON 541-T

Caliber: 22 S, L, LR, 5-shot clip.
Barrel: 24".
Weight: 5⅞ lbs. **Length:** 42½" overall.
Stock: Walnut, cut-checkered p.g. and forend. Satin finish.
Sights: None. Drilled and tapped for scope mounts.
Features: Clip repeater. Thumb safety. Reintroduced 1986.
Price: About **$399.00**

CAUTION: PRICES SHOWN ARE SUPPLIED BY THE MANUFACTURER OR IMPORTER. CHECK YOUR LOCAL GUNSHOP.

49th EDITION, 1995 **371**

RIMFIRE RIFLES—BOLT ACTIONS & SINGLE SHOTS

Remington 541-T HB Bolt-Action Rifle
Similar to the 541-T except has a heavy target-type barrel without sights. Receiver is drilled and tapped for scope mounting. American walnut stock with straight comb, satin finish, cut checkering, black checkered buttplate, black grip cap and forend tip. Weight is about 6½ lbs. Introduced 1993.
Price: **$425.00**

REMINGTON 40-XR RIMFIRE CUSTOM SPORTER
Caliber: 22 LR.
Barrel: 24".
Weight: 10 lbs. **Length:** 42½" overall.
Stock: Full-sized walnut, checkered p.g. and forend.
Sights: None furnished; drilled and tapped for scope mounting.
Features: Custom Shop gun. Duplicates Model 700 centerfire rifle.
Price: Grade I **$2,341.00**

REMINGTON 581-S SPORTSMAN RIFLE
Caliber: 22 S, L or LR, 5-shot clip magazine.
Barrel: 24" round.
Weight: 4¾ lbs. **Length:** 42⅜" overall.
Stock: Walnut-finished hardwood, Monte Carlo with p.g.
Sights: Bead post front, screw adjustable open rear.
Features: Sliding side safety, wide trigger, receiver grooved for tip-off scope mounts. Comes with single shot adaptor. Reintroduced 1986.
Price: About **$212.00**

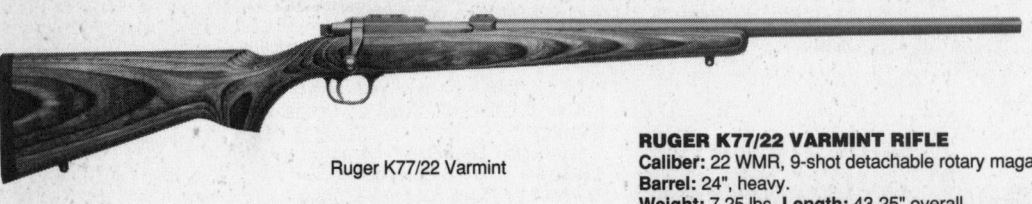

Ruger K77/22 Varmint

RUGER K77/22 VARMINT RIFLE
Caliber: 22 WMR, 9-shot detachable rotary magazine.
Barrel: 24", heavy.
Weight: 7.25 lbs. **Length:** 43.25" overall.
Stock: Laminated hardwood with rubber butt pad, quick-detachable swivel studs. No checkering or grip cap.
Sights: None furnished. Comes with Ruger 1" scope rings.
Features: Made of stainless steel with matte finish. Three-position safety, dual extractors. Stock has wide, flat forend. Introduced 1993.
Price: K77/22VBZ **$485.00**

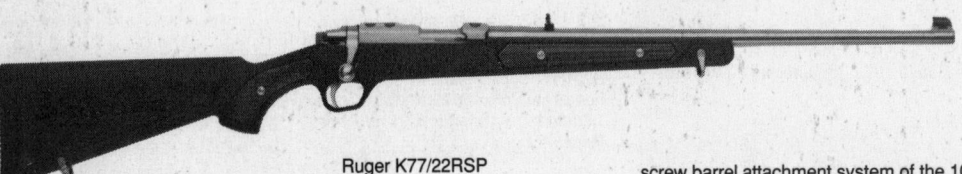

Ruger K77/22RSP

RUGER 77/22 RIMFIRE BOLT-ACTION RIFLE
Caliber: 22 LR, 10-shot rotary magazine; 22 WMR, 9-shot rotary magazine.
Barrel: 20".
Weight: About 5¾ lbs. **Length:** 39¾" overall.
Stock: Checkered American walnut or injection-moulded fiberglass-reinforced Du Pont Zytel with Xenoy inserts in forend and grip, stainless sling swivels.
Sights: Brass bead front, adjustable folding leaf rear or plain barrel with 1" Ruger rings.
Features: Mauser-type action uses Ruger's 10-shot rotary magazine. Three-position safety, simplified bolt stop, patented bolt locking system. Uses the dual-

screw barrel attachment system of the 10/22 rifle. Integral scope mounting system with 1" Ruger rings. Blued model introduced in 1983. Stainless steel model and blued model with the synthetic stock introduced in 1989.
Price: 77/22R (no sights, rings, walnut stock) **$402.00**
Price: 77/22RS (open sights, rings, walnut stock) **$424.00**
Price: K77/22RP (stainless, no sights, rings, synthetic stock) **$419.00**
Price: K77/22RSP (stainless, open sights, rings, synthetic stock) .. **$445.00**
Price: 77/22RM (22 WMR, blue, walnut stock) **$402.00**
Price: K77/22RSMP (22 WMR, stainless, open sights, rings, synthetic stock) **$445.00**
Price: K77/22RMP (22 WMR, stainless, synthetic stock) **$419.00**
Price: 77/22RSM (22 WMR, blue, open sights, rings, walnut stock) . **$424.00**

Sako Finnfire

SAKO FINNFIRE BOLT-ACTION RIFLE
Caliber: 22 LR, 5-shot magazine.
Barrel: 22".
Weight: 5.25 lbs. **Length:** 40" overall.
Stock: European walnut with checkered grip and forend.
Sights: Hooded blade front, open adjustable rear.
Features: Adjustable single-stage trigger; has 50-degree bolt lift. Introduced 1994. Imported from Finland by Stoeger Industries.
Price: **$685.00**

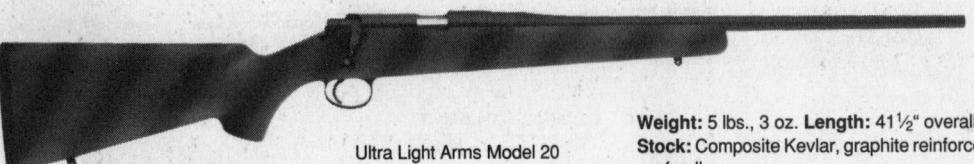

Ultra Light Arms Model 20

Weight: 5 lbs., 3 oz. **Length:** 41½" overall.
Stock: Composite Kevlar, graphite reinforced. Du Pont Imron paint; 13½" length of pull.
Sights: None furnished. Drilled and tapped for scope mounting.
Features: Available as either single shot or repeater with 5-shot removable magazine. Comes with scope mounts. Introduced 1993. Made in U.S. by Ultra Light Arms, Inc.
Price: **$800.00**

ULTRA LIGHT ARMS MODEL 20 RF BOLT-ACTION RIFLE
Caliber: 22 LR, single shot or 5-shot repeater.

CAUTION: PRICES SHOWN ARE SUPPLIED BY THE MANUFACTURER OR IMPORTER. CHECK YOUR LOCAL GUNSHOP.

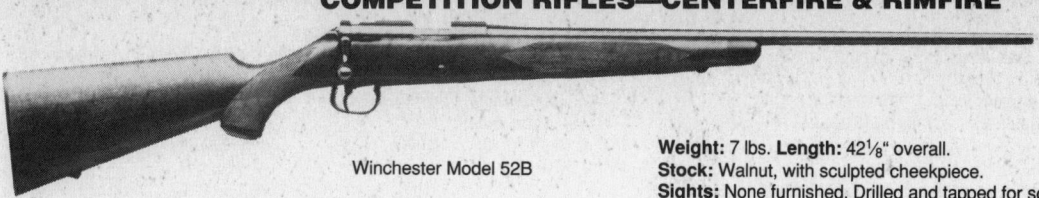

Winchester Model 52B

WINCHESTER MODEL 52B SPORTING RIFLE
Caliber: 22 LR, 5-shot magazine.
Barrel: 24".

Weight: 7 lbs. **Length:** 42⅛" overall.
Stock: Walnut, with sculpted cheekpiece.
Sights: None furnished. Drilled and tapped for scope mounting.
Features: Uses the Model 52C mechanism with stock configuration of the Model 52B. Has Micro-Motion trigger system of the original. Production limited to 6000 rifles. Reintroduced 1993. From U.S. Repeating Arms Co.
Price: **$576.00**

COMPETITION RIFLES—CENTERFIRE & RIMFIRE

Includes models for classic American and ISU target competition and other sporting and competitive shooting.

Anschutz Achiever ST

ANSCHUTZ ACHIEVER ST-SUPER TARGET RIFLE
Caliber: 22 LR, single shot.
Barrel: 22", .75" diameter.
Weight: About 6.5 lbs. **Length:** 38.75" to 39.75" overall.

Stock: Walnut-finished European hardwood with hand-stippled panels on grip and forend; 13.5" accessory rail on forend.
Sights: Optional. Anschutz #1 or #2 Sight Set. Receiver grooved for scope mounting.
Features: Designed for the advanced junior shooter with adjustable length of pull from 13.25" to 14.25" via removable butt spacers. Two-stage #5066 adjustable trigger factory set at 2.6 lbs. Introduced 1994. Imported from Germany by Precision Sales International.
Price: **$485.00**

Anschutz BR-50

ANSCHUTZ BR-50 BENCHREST RIFLE
Caliber: 22 LR, single shot.
Barrel: 19.75" (without 11-oz. muzzle weight).
Weight: About 11 lbs. **Length:** 37.75" to 42.5" overall.

Stock: Benchrest style of European hardwood with stippled grip. Cheekpiece vertically adjustable to 1". Stock length adjustable via spacers and buttplate. Finished with glossy blue-black paint.
Sights: None furnished. Receiver grooved for mounts, barrel drilled and tapped for target mounts.
Features: Uses the Anschutz 2013 target action, #5015 two-stage adjustable target trigger factory set at 3.9 oz. Introduced 1994. Imported from Germany by Precision Sales International.
Price: **$3,075.00**

ANSCHUTZ 1827B BIATHLON RIFLE
Caliber: 22 LR, 5-shot magazine.
Barrel: 21½".
Weight: 8½ lbs. with sights. **Length:** 42½" overall.
Stock: Walnut-finished hardwood; cheekpiece, stippled pistol grip and forend.
Sights: Globe front specially designed for Biathlon shooting, micrometer rear with hinged snow cap.
Features: Uses Match 54 action and nine-way adjustable trigger; adjustable wooden buttplate, Biathlon butthook, adjustable hand-stop rail. **Special Order Only.** Introduced 1982. Imported from Germany by Precision Sales International.
Price: Right-hand **$2,233.00**
Price: With Fortner straight-pull bolt **$3,449.00**
Price: As above, left-hand **$3,794.00**

ANSCHUTZ 1808D RT SUPER MATCH 54 TARGET
Caliber: 22 LR, single shot.
Barrel: 32½".
Weight: 9.4 lbs. **Length:** 50½" overall.
Stock: Walnut-finished European hardwood. Heavy beavertail forend; adjustable cheekpiece and buttplate. Stippled grip and forend.
Sights: None furnished. Grooved for scope mounting.
Features: Designed for Running Target competition. Nine-way adjustable single-stage trigger, slide safety. Introduced 1991. Imported from Germany by Precision Sales International.
Price: Right-hand **$1,760.00**

ANSCHUTZ 1903D MATCH RIFLE
Caliber: 22 LR, single shot.
Barrel: 25", ¾" diameter.
Weight: 8.6 lbs. **Length:** 43¾" overall.
Stock: Walnut-finished hardwood with adjustable cheekpiece; stippled grip and forend.
Sights: None furnished.
Features: Uses Anschutz Match 64 action and #5091 two-stage trigger. A medium weight rifle for intermediate and advanced Junior Match competition. Introduced 1987. Imported from Germany by Precision Sales International.
Price: Right-hand **$1,039.00**
Price: Left-hand **$1,193.00**
Price: #6823 sight set **$300.53**

ANSCHUTZ 64-MS, 64-MS LEFT SILHOUETTE
Caliber: 22 LR, single shot.
Barrel: 21½", medium heavy; ⅞" diameter.
Weight: 8 lbs. **Length:** 39½" overall.
Stock: Walnut-finished hardwood, silhouette-type.
Sights: None furnished. Receiver drilled and tapped for scope mounting.
Features: Uses Match 64 action. Designed for metallic silhouette competition. Stock has stippled checkering, contoured thumb groove with Wundhammer swell. Two-stage #5091 trigger. Slide safety locks sear and bolt. Introduced 1980. Imported from Germany by Precision Sales International.
Price: 64-MS **$916.00**
Price: 64-MS Left **$960.00**

COMPETITION RIFLES—CENTERFIRE & RIMFIRE

ANSCHUTZ 1911 PRONE MATCH RIFLE
Caliber: 22 LR, single shot.
Barrel: 27¼" round (1" dia.).
Weight: 11 lbs. **Length:** 46" overall.
Stock: Walnut-finished European hardwood; American prone style with Monte Carlo, cast-off cheekpiece, checkered p.g., beavertail forend with swivel rail and adjustable swivel, adjustable rubber buttplate.
Sights: None. Receiver grooved for Anschutz sights (extra). Scope blocks.
Features: Two-stage #5018 trigger adjustable from 2.1 to 8.6 oz. Extremely fast lock time. Imported from Germany by Precision Sales International.
Price: Right-hand, no sights **$2,134.00**

Anschutz 1907 ISU Standard Match Rifle
Same action as Model 1913 but with ⅞" diameter 26" barrel. Length is 44½" overall, weight 10 lbs. Blonde wood finish with vented forend. Designed for prone and position shooting ISU requirements; suitable for NRA matches.
Price: Right-hand, no sights **$1,827.00**
Price: With walnut stock **$1,897.00**
Price: M1907-L (true left-hand action and stock) **$1,916.00**

Anschutz 1913 Super Match Rifle
Same as the Model 1911 except European walnut International-type stock with adjustable cheekpiece, adjustable aluminum hook buttplate, adjustable hand stop, weight 15½ lbs., 46" overall. Imported from Germany by Precision Sales International.
Price: Right-hand, no sights **$3,212.00**
Price: M1913 left-hand **$3,182.00**

CONSULT **SHOOTER'S MARKETPLACE** Page 225, This Issue

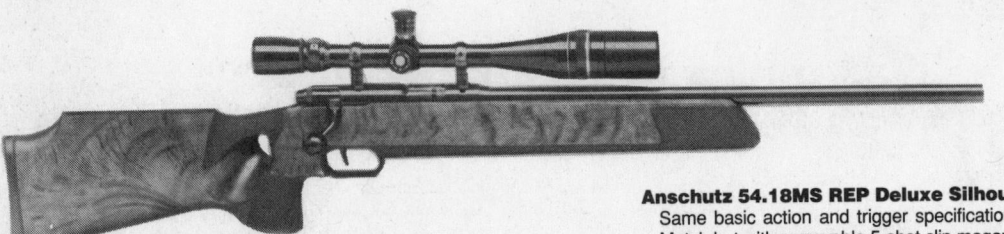
Anschutz 54.18MS REP

Anschutz 54.18MS REP Deluxe Silhouette Rifle
Same basic action and trigger specifications as the Anschutz 1913 Super Match but with removable 5-shot clip magazine, 22" barrel extendable to 30" using optional extension and weight set. Receiver drilled and tapped for scope mounting. Silhouette stock with thumbhole grip is of fiberglass with walnut wood Fibergrain finish. Introduced 1990. Imported from Germany by Precision Sales International.
Price: 54.18MS REP Deluxe **$2,280.00**
Price: 54.18MS Standard with fiberglass stock **$1,896.00**

Anschutz 1910 Super Match II
Similar to the Super Match 1913 rifle except has a stock of European hardwood with tapered forend and deep receiver area. Hand and palm rests not included. Uses Match 54 action. Adjustable hook buttplate and cheekpiece. Sights not included. Introduced 1982. Imported from Germany by Precision Sales International.
Price: Right-hand **$2,709.00**
Price: Left-hand **$2,843.00**

Anschutz 54.18MS Silhouette Rifle
Same basic features as Anschutz 1913 Super Match but with special metallic silhouette European hardwood stock and two-stage trigger. Has 22" barrel; receiver drilled and tapped.
Price: **$1,488.00**
Price: 54.18MSL (true left-hand version of above) **$1,670.00**

Anschutz 2013

ANSCHUTZ SUPER MATCH 54 TARGET MODEL 2013
Caliber: 22 LR.
Barrel: 19.75" (26" with tube installed).
Weight: 15.5 lbs. **Length:** NA.
Stock: European walnut; target adjustable.
Sights: Optional. Uses #6820 sight set.
Features: Improved Super Match 54 action, #5018 trigger give fastest consistent lock time for a production target rifle. Barrel is micro-honed; trigger has nine points of adjustment, two stages. Slide safety. Comes with test target. Introduced 1992. Imported from Germany by Precision Sales International.
Price: **$3,812.00**
Price: M2013 left-hand **$4,004.00**

Anschutz Super Match 54 Target Model 2007
Similar to the Model 2013 except has ISU Standard design European walnut stock. Sights optional. Introduced 1992. Imported from Germany by Precision Sales International.
Price: **$2,675.00**
Price: M2007 left-hand **$2,807.00**

Colt Sporter Competition HBAR

COLT SPORTER TARGET MODEL RIFLE
Caliber: 223 Rem., 5-shot magazine.
Barrel: 20".
Weight: 7.5 lbs. **Length:** 39" overall.
Stock: Composition stock, grip, forend.
Sights: Post front, aperture rear adjustable for windage and elevation.
Features: Five-round detachable box magazine, standard-weight barrel, flash suppressor, sling swivels. Has forward bolt assist. Military matte black finish. Model introduced 1991.
Price: **$970.00**

CAUTION: PRICES SHOWN ARE SUPPLIED BY THE MANUFACTURER OR IMPORTER. CHECK YOUR LOCAL GUNSHOP.

Colt Sporter Competition HBAR Rifle
Similar to the Sporter Target except has flat-top receiver with integral Weaver-type base for scope mounting. Counter-bored muzzle, 1:9" rifling twist. Introduced 1991.
Price: Model R6700 . . . . **$1,020.00**

Colt Sporter Competition HBAR Range Selected Rifle
Same as the Sporter Competition HBAR #R6700 except is range selected for accuracy, and comes with 3-9x rubber armored scope, scope mount, carrying handle with iron sights, Cordura nylon carrying case. Introduced 1992.
Price: Model R6700CH **$1,527.00**

Colt Sporter Match HBAR Rifle
Similar to the Target Model except has heavy barrel, 800-meter rear sight adjustable for windage and elevation. Introduced 1991.
Price: **$1,014.00**

COOPER ARMS MODEL BR-50
Caliber: 22 LR, single shot.
Barrel: 22"; .860" straight.
Weight: 10 lbs. **Length:** 40.5" overall.
Stock: Benchrest style synthetic; smooth flat black finish.
Sights: None furnished.
Features: Action has three mid-bolt locking lugs; fully adjustable match grade trigger; stainless barrel. Introduced 1994. Made in U.S. by Cooper Arms.
Price: **$1,295.00**

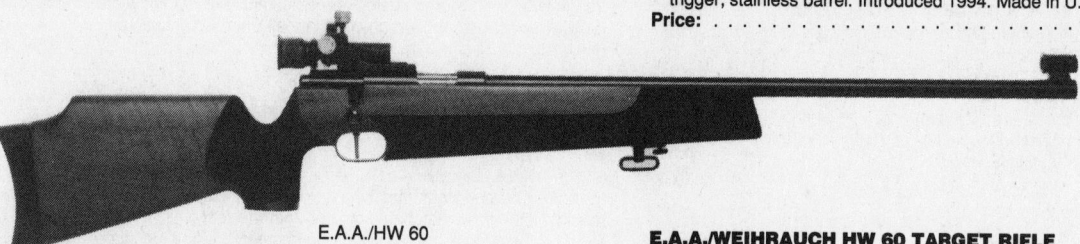

E.A.A./HW 60

E.A.A./HW 660 MATCH RIFLE
Caliber: 22 LR.
Barrel: 26".
Weight: 10.7 lbs. **Length:** 45.3" overall.
Stock: Match-type walnut with adjustable cheekpiece and buttplate.
Sights: Globe front, match aperture rear.
Features: Adjustable match trigger; stippled p.g. and forend; forend accessory rail. Introduced 1988. Imported from Germany by European American Armory.
Price: About **$795.00**

Eagle Arms EA-15E2 H-BAR Rifle
Similar to the Golden Eagle except has 20" slightly lighter and smaller heavy match barrel with 1:9" twist; weighs about 9 lbs. Introduced 1989. Made in U.S. by Eagle Arms, Inc.
Price: **$895.00**
Price: With NM sights **$945.00**

Eagle Arms EA-15E2 Eagle Eye Match Rifle
Has 24", 1" diameter, stainless, heavy match barrel that is air-gauged, free-floating. Weighted buttstock to counterbalance the barrel. Has match-type hand-stop on handguard. Match sights available on special order. Weighs about 14 lbs. Introduced 1994. Made in U.S. by Eagle Arms, Inc.
Price: **$1,495.00**

E.A.A./WEIHRAUCH HW 60 TARGET RIFLE
Caliber: 22 LR, single shot.
Barrel: 26.8".
Weight: 10.8 lbs. **Length:** 45.7" overall.
Stock: Walnut with adjustable buttplate. Stippled p.g. and forend. Rail with adjustable swivel.
Sights: Hooded ramp front, match-type aperture rear.
Features: Adjustable match trigger with push-button safety. Left-hand version also available. Introduced 1981. Imported from Germany by European American Armory.
Price: Right-hand **$695.00**

EAGLE ARMS EA-15E2 GOLDEN EAGLE MATCH RIFLE
Caliber: 223 Rem.
Barrel: 20" extra-heavy NM; 1:8" twist.
Weight: About 12 lbs. **Length:** 39" overall.
Stock: Black composition; weighted.
Sights: Elevation-adjustable NM extra-fine front with set screw, E2-style NM rear with ½-min. adjustments for windage and elevation; NM aperture.
Features: Upper and lower receivers have push-type pivot pin for easy takedown. Receivers hard coat anodized. Fence-type magazine release. Introduced 1989. Made in U.S. by Eagle Arms, Inc.
Price: **$1,075.00**

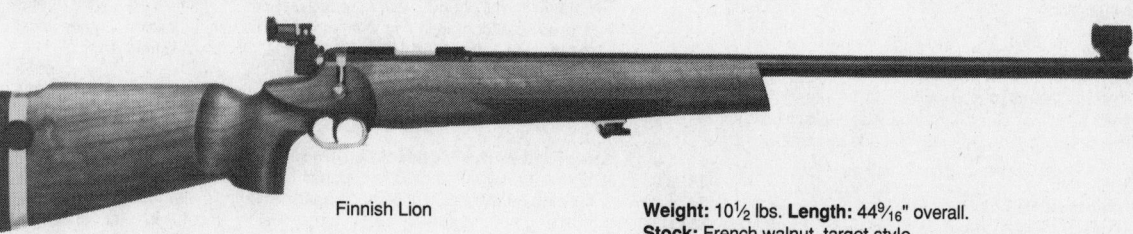

Finnish Lion

FINNISH LION STANDARD TARGET RIFLE
Caliber: 22 LR, single shot.
Barrel: 27⅝".

HECKLER & KOCH PSG-1 MARKSMAN RIFLE
Caliber: 308, 5- and 20-shot magazines.
Barrel: 25.6", heavy.
Weight: 17.8 lbs. **Length:** 47.5" overall.
Stock: Matte black high impact plastic, adjustable for length, pivoting butt cap, vertically-adjustable cheekpiece; target-type pistol grip with adjustable palm shelf.
Sights: Hendsoldt 6x42 scope.
Features: Uses HK-91 action with low-noise bolt closing device, special Marksman trigger group; special forend with T-way rail for sling swivel or tripod. Gun comes in special foam-fitted metal transport case with tripod, two 20-shot and two 5-shot magazines, tripod. Imported from Germany by Heckler & Koch, Inc. Introduced 1986.
Price: **$9,750.00**

Weight: 10½ lbs. **Length:** 44⁹/₁₆" overall.
Stock: French walnut, target style.
Sights: Globe front, International micrometer rear.
Features: Optional accessories: palm rest, hook buttplate, forend stop and swivel assembly, buttplate extension, five front sight aperture inserts, three rear sight apertures, Allen wrench. Adjustable trigger. Imported from Finland by Mandall Shooting Supplies.
Price: Without sights **$695.00**
Price: Sight set **$195.00**

KRICO MODEL 360 S2 BIATHLON RIFLE
Caliber: 22 LR, 5-shot magazine.
Barrel: 21.25".
Weight: 9 lbs., 15 oz. **Length:** 40.55" overall.
Stock: Biathlon design of black epoxy-finished walnut with pistol grip.
Sights: Globe front, fully adjustable Diana 82 match peep rear.
Features: Pistol-grip-activated action. Comes with five magazines (four stored in stock recess), muzzle/sight snow cap. Introduced 1991. Imported from Germany by Mandall Shooting Supplies.
Price: **$1,595.00**

CAUTION: PRICES SHOWN ARE SUPPLIED BY THE MANUFACTURER OR IMPORTER. CHECK YOUR LOCAL GUNSHOP.

49th EDITION, 1995 **375**

Krico Model 360S Biathlon

KRICO MODEL 400 MATCH RIFLE
Caliber: 22 LR, 22 Hornet, 5-shot magazine.
Barrel: 23.2" (22 LR), 23.6" (22 Hornet).
Weight: 8.8 lbs. **Length:** 42.1" overall (22 RF).
Stock: European walnut, match type.
Sights: None furnished; receiver grooved for scope mounting.
Features: Heavy match barrel. Double-set or match trigger. Imported from Germany by Mandall Shooting Supplies.
Price: $950.00

KRICO MODEL 600 SNIPER RIFLE
Caliber: 222, 223, 22-250, 243, 308, 4-shot magazine.
Barrel: 23.6".
Weight: 9.2 lbs. **Length:** 45.2" overall.
Stock: European walnut with adjustable rubber buttplate.
Sights: None supplied; drilled and tapped for scope mounting.
Features: Match barrel with flash hider; large bolt knob; wide trigger shoe. Parkerized finish. Imported from Germany by Mandall Shooting Supplies.
Price: $2,645.00

KRICO MODEL 360S BIATHLON RIFLE
Caliber: 22 LR, 5-shot magazine.
Barrel: 21.25".
Weight: 9.26 lbs. **Length:** 40.55" overall.
Stock: Walnut with high comb, adjustable buttplate.
Sights: Globe front, fully adjustable Diana 82 match peep rear.
Features: Straight-pull action with 17.6-oz. match trigger. Comes with five magazines (four stored in stock recess), muzzle/sight snow cap. Introduced 1991. Imported from Germany by Mandall Shooting Supplies.
Price: $1,695.00

KRICO MODEL 500 KRICOTRONIC MATCH RIFLE
Caliber: 22 LR, single shot.
Barrel: 23.6".
Weight: 9.4 lbs. **Length:** 42.1" overall.
Stock: European walnut, match type with adjustable butt.
Sights: Globe front, match micrometer aperture rear.
Features: Electronic ignition system for fastest possible lock time. Completely adjustable trigger. Barrel has tapered bore. Imported from Germany by Mandall Shooting Supplies.
Price: $3,950.00

KRICO MODEL 600 MATCH RIFLE
Caliber: 222, 223, 22-250, 243, 308, 5.6x50 Mag., 4-shot magazine.
Barrel: 23.6".
Weight: 8.8 lbs. **Length:** 43.3" overall.
Stock: Match stock of European walnut with cheekpiece.
Sights: None furnished; drilled and tapped for scope mounting.
Features: Match stock with vents in forend for cooling, rubber recoil pad, sling swivels. Imported from Germany by Mandall Shooting Supplies.
Price: $1,250.00

Lakefield Model 92S

LAKEFIELD ARMS MODEL 91T TARGET RIFLE
Caliber: 22 LR, single shot.
Barrel: 25".
Weight: 8 lbs. **Length:** 43⅝" overall.
Stock: Target-type, walnut-finished hardwood.
Sights: Target front with inserts, peep rear with ¼-minute click adjustments.
Features: Comes with shooting rail and hand stop. Also available as 5-shot repeater as Model 91-TR. Introduced 1991. Made in Canada by Lakefield Arms.
Price: Model 91T $445.95
Price: Model 91T left-hand $489.95
Price: Model 91-TR (repeater) $474.95
Price: Model 91-TR left-hand $521.95

LAKEFIELD ARMS MODEL 90B TARGET RIFLE
Caliber: 22 LR, 5-shot magazine.
Barrel: 21".
Weight: 8¼ lbs. **Length:** 39⅝" overall.
Stock: Natural finish hardwood with clip holder, carrying and shooting rails, butt hook, hand stop.
Sights: Target front with inserts, peep rear with ¼-minute click adjustments.
Features: Biathlon-style rifle with snow cap muzzle protector. Comes with five magazines. Introduced 1991. Made in Canada by Lakefield Arms.
Price: About $558.95
Price: left-hand, about $614.95

Lakefield Arms Model 92S Silhouette Rifle
Similar to the Model 90B except has high-comb target-type stock of walnut-finished hardwood, one 5-shot magazine. Comes without sights, but receiver is drilled and tapped for scope base. Weight about 8 lbs. Introduced 1992. Made in Canada by Lakefield Arms.
Price: $379.95
Price: left-hand $417.95

Marlin Model 2000A

Marlin Model 2000A Target Rifle
Same as the Model 2000 except has an adjustable comb, ambidextrous pistol grip and the Marlin logo moulded into the blue Carbelite stock. Weight is 8.5 lbs. Introduced 1994. Made in U.S. by Marlin Firearms Co.
Price: $625.00

MARLIN MODEL 2000 TARGET RIFLE
Caliber: 22 LR, single shot.
Barrel: 22" heavy, Micro-Groove® rifling, match chamber, recessed muzzle.
Weight: 8 lbs. **Length:** 41" overall.
Stock: High-comb fiberglass/Kevlar with stipple finish grip and forend.
Sights: Hooded front with seven aperture inserts, fully adjustable target rear peep.
Features: Stock finished with royal blue enamel. Buttplate adjustable for length of pull, height and angle. Aluminum forend rail with stop and quick-detachable swivel. Two-stage target trigger; red cocking indicator. Five-shot adaptor kit available. Introduced 1991. From Marlin.
Price: $581.90

CAUTION: PRICES SHOWN ARE SUPPLIED BY THE MANUFACTURER OR IMPORTER. CHECK YOUR LOCAL GUNSHOP.

McMillan M-86

McMILLAN COMBO M-87/M-88 50-CALIBER RIFLE
Caliber: 50 BMG, single shot.
Barrel: 29", with muzzlebrake.
Weight: About 21½ lbs. **Length:** 53" overall.
Stock: McMillan fiberglass.
Sights: None furnished.
Features: Right-handed McMillan stainless steel receiver, chromemoly barrel with 1:15 twist. Introduced 1987. From McMillan Gunworks, Inc.
Price: **$4,000.00**
Price: M-87R (5-shot repeater) "Combo" **$4,300.00**

McMILLAN 300 PHOENIX LONG RANGE RIFLE
Caliber: 300 Phoenix.
Barrel: 28".
Weight: 12.5 lbs. **Length:** NA.
Stock: Fiberglass with adjustable cheekpiece, adjustable butt plate.
Sights: None furnished; comes with rings and bases.
Features: Matte black finish; textured stock. Introduced 1992. Made in U.S. by McMillan Gunworks, Inc.
Price: **$2,995.00**

McMILLAN NATIONAL MATCH RIFLE
Caliber: 7mm-08, 308, 5-shot magazine.
Barrel: 24", stainless steel.
Weight: About 11 lbs. (std. bbl.). **Length:** 43" overall.
Stock: Modified ISU fiberglass with adjustable buttplate.
Sights: Barrel band and Tompkins front; no rear sight furnished.
Features: McMillan repeating action with clip slot, Canjar trigger. Match-grade barrel. Available in right-hand only. Fibergrain stock, sight installation, special machining and triggers optional. Introduced 1989. From McMillan Gunworks, Inc.
Price: **$2,600.00**

McMILLAN M-86 SNIPER RIFLE
Caliber: 308, 30-06, 4-shot magazine; 300 Win. Mag., 300 Phoenix, 3-shot magazine.
Barrel: 24", McMillan match-grade in heavy contour.
Weight: 11¼ lbs. (308), 11½ lbs. (30-06, 300). **Length:** 43½" overall.
Stock: Specially designed McHale fiberglass stock with textured grip and forend, recoil pad.
Sights: None furnished.
Features: Uses McMillan repeating action. Comes with bipod. Matte black finish. Sling swivels. Introduced 1989. From McMillan Gunworks, Inc.
Price: **$1,900.00**
Price: 300 Phoenix **$2,100.00**

McMILLAN M-89 SNIPER RIFLE
Caliber: 308 Win., 5-shot magazine.
Barrel: 28" (with suppressor).
Weight: 15 lbs., 4 oz.
Stock: McMillan fiberglass; adjustable for length; recoil pad.
Sights: None furnished. Drilled and tapped for scope mounting.
Features: Uses McMillan repeating action. Comes with bipod. Introduced 1990. From McMillan Gunworks, Inc.
Price: Standard (non-suppressed) **$2,300.00**

> Consult our Directory pages for the location of firms mentioned.

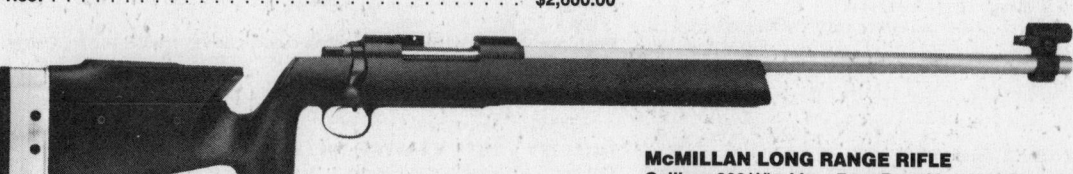

McMillan Long Range

McMILLAN LONG RANGE RIFLE
Caliber: 300 Win. Mag., 7mm Rem. Mag., 300 Phoenix, 338 Lapua, single shot.
Barrel: 26", stainless steel, match-grade.
Weight: 14 lbs. **Length:** 46½" overall.
Stock: Fiberglass with adjustable buttplate and cheekpiece. Adjustable for length of pull, drop, cant and cast-off.
Sights: Barrel band and Tompkins front; no rear sight furnished.
Features: Uses McMillan solid bottom single shot action and Canjar trigger. Barrel twist 1:12". Introduced 1989. From McMillan Gunworks, Inc.
Price: **$2,600.00**

Olympic International

OLYMPIC ARMS ULTRAMATCH/INTERNATIONAL MATCH RIFLES
Caliber: 223, 20- or 30-shot magazine.
Barrel: 20", 24", stainless steel.
Weight: 10 lbs., 3 oz. **Length:** 39½" overall (20" barrel).
Stock: A2 stowaway butt and grip.
Sights: Cut-off carrying handle with scope rail attached (Ultramatch); target peep on International Match.
Features: Based on the AR-15 rifle. Broach-cut, free-floating barrel with 1:10" or 1:8.5" twist; fluting optional. Introduced 1985. Made in U.S. by Olympic Arms, Inc.
Price: Ultramatch **$1,120.00**
Price: International Match **$1,200.00**

Olympic Arms Intercontinental Match Rifle
Similar to the Ultramatch/International Match except 20" barrel only, has woodgrain thumbhole buttstock, magazine well floorplate, 5-shot magazine. Introduced 1992. Made in U.S. by Olympic Arms, Inc.
Price: **$1,330.00**

CAUTION: PRICES SHOWN ARE SUPPLIED BY THE MANUFACTURER OR IMPORTER. CHECK YOUR LOCAL GUNSHOP.

49th EDITION, 1995 **377**

COMPETITION RIFLES—CENTERFIRE & RIMFIRE

Olympic Service Match

OLYMPIC ARMS SERVICE MATCH RIFLE
Caliber: 223, 20- or 30-shot magazine.
Barrel: 20" stainless.
Weight: 8¾ lbs. **Length:** 39½" overall.
Stock: Black composition A2 standard stock.
Sights: Post front, fully adjustable aperture rear.
Features: Based on the AR-15 rifle. Conforms to all DCM standards. Barrel is broach-cut and free-floating with 1:10" or 1:8.5" twist; fluting optional. Introduced 1989. Made in U.S. by Olympic Arms, Inc.
Price: **$875.00**

OLYMPIC ARMS MULTIMATCH RIFLES
Caliber: 223, 20- or 30-shot magazine.
Barrel: 16" stainless steel.
Weight: 8 lbs., 2 oz. **Length:** 36" overall.
Stock: Telescoping or A2 stowaway butt and grip.
Sights: Post front, E2 rear (ML1); cut front, cut-off carrying handle with scope rail attached (ML2).
Features: Based on the AR-15 rifle. Barrel is broach-cut and free-floating with 1:10" or 1:8.5" twist. Introduced 1991. Made in U.S. by Olympic Arms, Inc.
Price: **$890.00**

Olympic Arms AR-15 Match Rifle
Similar to the Service Match except has cut-off carrying handle with scope rail attached, button-rifled 4140 ordnance steel or 416 stainless barrel with 1:9" twist standard, 1:7", 1:12", 1:14" twists optional. Weighs 8 lbs, 5 oz. Introduced 1993. Made in U.S. by Olympic Arms, Inc.
Price: **$690.00**

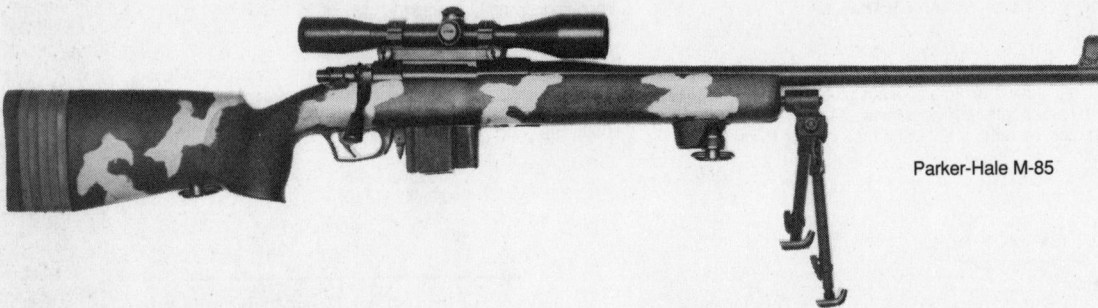

Parker-Hale M-85

PARKER-HALE M-87 TARGET RIFLE
Caliber: 308 Win., 243, 6.5x55, 308, 30-06, 300 Win. Mag. (other calibers on request), 5-shot detachable box magazine.
Barrel: 26" heavy.
Weight: About 10 lbs. **Length:** 45" overall.
Stock: Walnut target-style, adjustable for length of pull; solid buttpad; accessory rail with hand-stop. Deeply stippled grip and forend.
Sights: None furnished. Receiver dovetailed for Parker-Hale "Roll-Off" scope mounts.
Features: Mauser-style action with large bolt knob. Parkerized finish. Introduced 1987. Made by Gibbs Rifle Co.
Price: **$1,500.00**

PARKER-HALE M-85 SNIPER RIFLE
Caliber: 308 Win., 10-shot magazine.
Barrel: 24¼".
Weight: 12½ lbs (with scope). **Length:** 45" overall.
Stock: McMillan fiberglass (several color patterns available).
Sights: Post front adjustable for windage, fold-down rear adjustable for elevation.
Features: Comes with quick-detachable bipod, palm stop with rail; sling swivels; matte finish. Made by Gibbs Rifle Co.
Price: Less scope **$1,950.00**

QUALITY PARTS XM-15-E2 TARGET MODEL RIFLE
Caliber: 223, 30-shot magazine.
Barrel: 20", 24", 26"; 1:7" or 1:9" twist; heavy.
Weight: NA. **Length:** NA.
Stock: Black composition.
Sights: Adjustable post front, adjustable aperture rear.
Features: Patterned after Colt M-16A2. Chrome-lined barrel with manganese phosphate exterior. Has E-2 lower receiver with push-pin. From Quality Parts Co.
Price: 20" match heavy barrel **$895.00**
Price: 24" match heavy barrel **$905.00**
Price: 26" match heavy barrel **$915.00**

QUALITY PARTS V MATCH RIFLE
Caliber: 223, 30-shot magazine.
Barrel: 20", 24", 26"; 1:9" twist.
Weight: NA. **Length:** NA.
Stock: Composition.
Sights: None furnished; comes with scope mount base installed.
Features: Hand-built match gun. Barrel is .950" outside diameter with counter-bored crown; integral flash suppressor; upper receiver has brass deflector; free-floating steel handguard accepts laser sight, flashlight, bipod; 5-lb. trigger pull. From Quality Parts Co.
Price: From **$1,200.00**

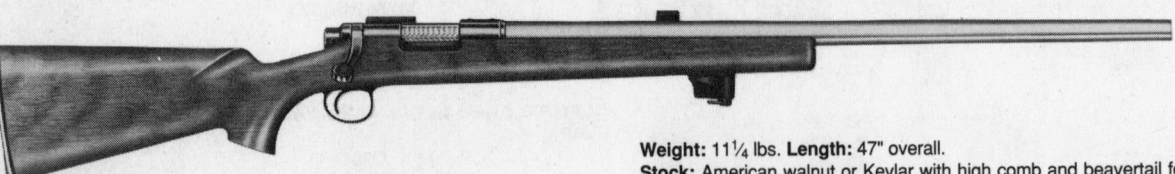

Remington 40-XB

REMINGTON 40-XB RANGEMASTER TARGET CENTERFIRE
Caliber: 222 Rem., 222 Rem. Mag., 223, 220 Swift, 22-250, 6mm Rem., 243, 25-06, 7mm BR Rem., 7mm Rem. Mag., 30-338 (30-7mm Rem. Mag.), 300 Win. Mag., 7.62 NATO (308 Win.), 30-06, single shot.
Barrel: 27¼".

Weight: 11¼ lbs. **Length:** 47" overall.
Stock: American walnut or Kevlar with high comb and beavertail forend stop. Rubber non-slip buttplate.
Sights: None. Scope blocks installed.
Features: Adjustable trigger. Stainless barrel and action. Receiver drilled and tapped for sights.
Price: Standard single shot, stainless steel barrel, about **$1,232.00**
Price: Repeater model **$1,325.00**
Price: Model 40-XB KS **$1,390.00**
Price: Repeater model (KS) **$1,484.00**
Price: Extra for 2-oz. trigger **$155.00**

CAUTION: PRICES SHOWN ARE SUPPLIED BY THE MANUFACTURER OR IMPORTER. CHECK YOUR LOCAL GUNSHOP.

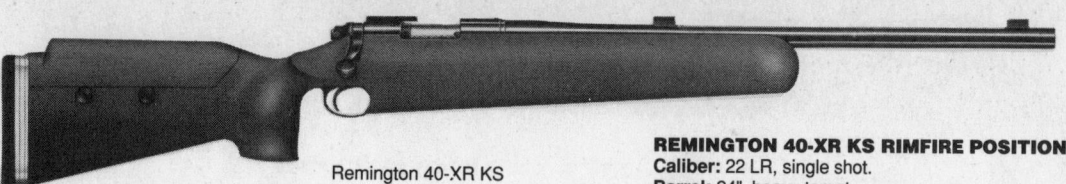

Remington 40-XR KS

REMINGTON 40-XBBR KS
Caliber: 22 BR Rem., 222 Rem., 222 Rem. Mag., 223, 6mmx47, 6mm BR Rem., 7.62 NATO (308 Win.).
Barrel: 20" (light varmint class), 24" (heavy varmint class).
Weight: 7¼ lbs. (light varmint class); 12 lbs. (heavy varmint class).
Length: 38" (20" bbl.), 42" (24" bbl.).
Stock: Kevlar.
Sights: None. Supplied with scope blocks.
Features: Unblued stainless steel barrel, trigger adjustable from 1½ lbs. to 3½ lbs. Special 2-oz. trigger at extra cost. Scope and mounts extra.
Price: With Kevlar stock **$1,345.00**
Price: Extra for 2-oz. trigger, about **$155.00**

REMINGTON 40-XR KS RIMFIRE POSITION RIFLE
Caliber: 22 LR, single shot.
Barrel: 24", heavy target.
Weight: 10 lbs. **Length:** 43" overall.
Stock: Kevlar. Position-style with front swivel block on forend guide rail.
Sights: Drilled and tapped. Furnished with scope blocks.
Features: Meets all ISU specifications. Deep forend, buttplate vertically adjustable, wide adjustable trigger.
Price: About **$1,265.00**

REMINGTON 40-XC KS NATIONAL MATCH COURSE RIFLE
Caliber: 7.62 NATO, 5-shot.
Barrel: 24", stainless steel.
Weight: 11 lbs. without sights. **Length:** 43½" overall.
Stock: Kevlar, position-style, with palm swell, handstop.
Sights: None furnished.
Features: Designed to meet the needs of competitive shooters firing the national match courses. Position-style stock, top loading clip slot magazine, anti-bind bolt and receiver, stainless steel barrel and action. Meets all ISU Army Rifle specifications. Adjustable buttplate, adjustable trigger.
Price: About **$1,480.00**

Sako TRG-21

SAUER 202 TR TARGET RIFLE
Caliber: 6.5x55mm, 308 Win., 5-shot magazine.
Barrel: 26" or 28.5", heavy match target.
Weight: 12.1 lbs. **Length:** 44.5" overall.
Stock: One-piece true target type of laminated beechwood/epoxy; adjustable buttplate and cheekpiece.
Sights: Globe front, Sauer-Busk 200-600m diopter rear. Drilled and tapped for scope mounting.
Features: Interchangeable free-floating, hammer-forged barrel; two-stage adjustable trigger; vertical slide safety; 3 millisecond lock time; rail for swivel, bipod; right- or left-hand; Converts to 22 rimfire. Introduced 1994. Imported from Germany by Paul Co.
Price: **$1,900.00**
Price: Spare Match-Target barrel **$425.00**

SAKO TRG-21 BOLT-ACTION RIFLE
Caliber: 308 Win., 10-shot magazine.
Barrel: 25.75".
Weight: 10.5 lbs. **Length:** 46.5" overall.
Stock: Reinforced polyurethane with fully adjustable cheekpiece and buttplate.
Sights: None furnished. Optional quick-detachable, one-piece scope mount base, 1" or 30mm rings.
Features: Resistance-free bolt, free-floating heavy stainless barrel, 60-degree bolt lift. Two-stage trigger is adjustable for length, pull, horizontal or vertical pitch. Introduced 1993. Imported from Finland by Stoeger.
Price: **$4,000.00**

SAVAGE MODEL 112BT COMPETITION GRADE RIFLE
Caliber: 223, 308.
Barrel: 26", heavy contour stainless with black finish; 1:9" twist (223), 1:10" (308).
Weight: 10.8 lbs. **Length:** 47.5" overall.
Stock: Laminated wood with straight comb, adjustable cheek rest, Wundhammer palm swell, ventilated forend. Recoil pad is adjustable for length of pull.
Sights: None furnished; drilled and tapped for scope mounting and aperture target-style sights. Recessed target-style muzzle has .812" diameter section for universal target sight base.
Features: Matte black alloy receiver. Bolt has black titanium nitride coating, large handle ball. Has alloy accessory rail on forend. Comes with safety gun lock, target and ear puffs. Introduced 1994. Made in U.S. by Savage Arms, Inc.
Price: **$1,000.00**

Springfield M-1A Match

SPRINGFIELD INC. M-1A SUPER MATCH
Caliber: 243, 7mm-08, 308 Win.
Barrel: 22", heavy Douglas Premium, or Hart stainless steel.
Weight: About 10 lbs. **Length:** 44.31" overall.
Stock: Heavy walnut competition stock with longer pistol grip, contoured area behind the rear sight, thicker butt and forend, glass bedded.
Sights: National Match front and rear.
Features: Has figure-eight-style operating rod guide. Introduced 1987. From Springfield, Inc.
Price: About **$1,929.00**

STEYR-MANNLICHER MATCH SPG-UIT RIFLE
Caliber: 308 Win.
Barrel: 25.5".
Weight: 10 lbs. **Length:** 44" overall.
Stock: Laminated and ventilated. Special UIT Match design.
Sights: Steyr globe front, Steyr peep rear.
Features: Double-pull trigger adjustable for let-off point, slack, weight of first-stage pull, release force and length; buttplate adjustable for height and length. Meets UIT specifications. Introduced 1992. Imported from Austria by GSI, Inc.
Price: **$3,995.00**
Price: SPG-CISM **$4,295.00**
Price: SPG-T **$3,695.00**

CAUTION: PRICES SHOWN ARE SUPPLIED BY THE MANUFACTURER OR IMPORTER. CHECK YOUR LOCAL GUNSHOP.

Steyr-Mannlicher SSG P-IV

Steyr-Mannlicher SSG P-IV Rifle

Similar to the SSG P-I except has 16.75" heavy barrel with flash hider. Available in 308 only. ABS Cycolac synthetic stock in green or black. Introduced 1992. Imported from Austria by GSI, Inc.

Price: **$2,660.00**

STEYR-MANNLICHER SSG P-I RIFLE

Caliber: 243, 308 Win.
Barrel: 25.6".
Weight: 8.6 lbs. **Length:** 44.5" overall.
Stock: ABS Cycolac synthetic half-stock. Removable spacers in butt adjusts length of pull from 12¾" to 14".
Sights: Hooded blade front, folding leaf rear.
Features: Parkerized finish. Choice of interchangeable single- or double-set triggers. Detachable 5-shot rotary magazine (10-shot optional). Receiver grooved for Steyr and Bock Quick Detach mounts. Imported from Austria by GSI, Inc.
Price: Synthetic half-stock **$1,995.00**
Price: SSG-PII (as above except has large bolt knob, heavy bbl., no sights, forend rail). **$1,995.00**

STONER SR-25 MATCH RIFLE

Caliber: 7.62 NATO, 20-shot steel magazine, 5- and 10-shot optional.
Barrel: 24" heavy match; 1:11.25" twist.
Weight: 10.75 lbs. **Length:** 44" overall.
Stock: Black synthetic AR-15A2 design. Full floating forend of Mil-spec synthetic attaches to upper receiver at a single point.
Sights: None furnished. Has integral Weaver-style rail.
Features: Modified AR-15 trigger; AR-15-style seven-lug rotating bolt. Gas block rail takes detachable front sight. Introduced 1993. Made in U.S. by Knight's Mfg. Co.
Price: **$2,495.00**

Stoner SR-25 Match

TANNER 300 METER FREE RIFLE

Caliber: 308 Win., 7.5 Swiss, single shot.
Barrel: 27.58".
Weight: 15 lbs. **Length:** 45.3" overall.
Stock: Seasoned walnut, thumbhole style, with accessory rail, palm rest, adjustable hook butt.
Sights: Globe front with interchangeable inserts, Tanner-design micrometer-diopter rear with adjustable aperture.
Features: Three-lug revolving-lock bolt design; adjustable set trigger; short firing pin travel; supplied with 300-meter test target. Imported from Switzerland by Mandall Shooting Supplies. Introduced 1984.
Price: About **$4,900.00**

Tanner 300 Meter

TANNER 50 METER FREE RIFLE

Caliber: 22 LR, single shot.
Barrel: 27.7".
Weight: 13.9 lbs. **Length:** 44.4" overall.
Stock: Seasoned walnut with palm rest, accessory rail, adjustable hook buttplate.
Sights: Globe front with interchangeable inserts, Tanner micrometer-diopter rear with adjustable aperture.
Features: Bolt action with externally adjustable set trigger. Supplied with 50-meter test target. Imported from Switzerland by Mandall Shooting Supplies. Introduced 1984.
Price: About **$3,900.00**

WICHITA SILHOUETTE RIFLE

Caliber: All standard calibers with maximum overall cartridge length of 2.800".
Barrel: 24" free-floated Matchgrade.
Weight: About 9 lbs.
Stock: Metallic gray fiberthane with ventilated rubber recoil pad.
Sights: None furnished. Drilled and tapped for scope mounts.
Features: Legal for all NRA competitions. Single shot action. Fluted bolt, 2-oz. Canjar trigger; glass-bedded stock. Introduced 1983. From Wichita Arms.
Price: **$2,275.00**
Price: Left-hand **$2,400.00**

TANNER STANDARD UIT RIFLE

Caliber: 308, 7.5mm Swiss, 10-shot.
Barrel: 25.9".
Weight: 10.5 lbs. **Length:** 40.6" overall.
Stock: Match style of seasoned nutwood with accessory rail; coarsely stippled pistol grip; high cheekpiece; vented forend.
Sights: Globe front with interchangeable inserts, Tanner micrometer-diopter rear with adjustable aperture.
Features: Two locking lug revolving bolt encloses case head. Trigger adjustable from ½ to 6½ lbs.; match trigger optional. Comes with 300-meter test target. Imported from Switzerland by Mandall Shooting Supplies. Introduced 1984.
Price: About **$4,700.00**

CAUTION: PRICES SHOWN ARE SUPPLIED BY THE MANUFACTURER OR IMPORTER. CHECK YOUR LOCAL GUNSHOP.

SHOTGUNS—AUTOLOADERS

Includes a wide variety of sporting guns and guns suitable for various competitions.

American Arms/Franchi 48/AL

AMERICAN ARMS/FRANCHI BLACK MAGIC 48/AL
Gauge: 12 or 20, 2¾" chamber.

Barrel: 24" rifled, 24", 26", 28" (Franchoke Imp. Cyl., Mod., Full choke tubes). Vent. rib.
Weight: 5.2 lbs. (20-gauge). **Length:** NA
Stock: 14¼"x1⅝"x2½". Walnut with checkered grip and forend.
Features: Recoil-operated action. Chrome-lined bore; cross-bolt safety. Imported from Italy by American Arms, Inc.
Price: $609.00
Price: 12-ga., 24" rifled slug, open sights $640.00

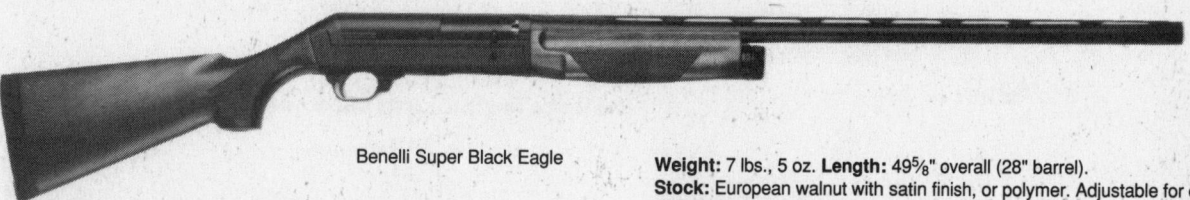

Benelli Super Black Eagle

BENELLI SUPER BLACK EAGLE SHOTGUN
Gauge: 12, 3½" chamber.
Barrel: 24", 26", 28" (Imp. Cyl., Mod., Imp. Mod., Full choke tubes).

Weight: 7 lbs., 5 oz. **Length:** 49⅝" overall (28" barrel).
Stock: European walnut with satin finish, or polymer. Adjustable for drop.
Sights: Bead front.
Features: Uses Montfeltro inertia recoil bolt system. Fires all 12-gauge shells from 2¾" to 3½" magnums. Introduced 1991. Imported from Italy by Heckler & Koch, Inc.
Price: $1,115.00

Benelli Super Black Eagle Slug Gun
Similar to the Benelli Super Black Eagle except has 24" E.R. Shaw Custom rifled barrel with 3" chamber, and comes with scope mount base. Uses the Montefeltro inertia recoil bolt system. Matte-finish receiver. Weight is 7.5 lbs.,

overall length 45.5". Wood or polymer stocks available. Introduced 1992. Imported from Italy by Heckler & Koch, Inc.
Price: $1,140.00
Price: With polymer stock $1,125.00

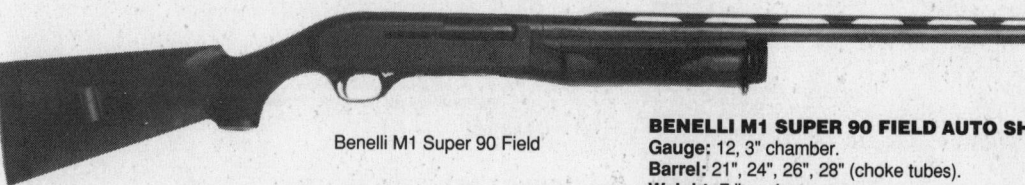

Benelli M1 Super 90 Field

Benelli Montefeltro Super 90 Shotgun
Similar to the M1 Super 90 except has checkered walnut stock with high-gloss finish. Uses the Montefeltro rotating bolt system with a simple inertia recoil design. Full, Imp. Mod, Mod., Imp. Cyl. choke tubes. Weight is 7-7½ lbs. Finish is matte black. Introduced 1987.
Price: 21", 24", 26", 28" $840.00
Price: Left-hand, 26", 28" $860.00
Price: 20-ga., Montefeltro Super 90, 26", 5¾ lbs. $840.00

Benelli Montefeltro Super 90 20-Gauge Shotgun
Similar to the 12-gauge Montefeltro Super 90 except chambered for 3" 20-gauge, 26" barrel (choke tubes), weighs 5 lbs., 12 oz. Has drop-adjustable walnut stock with gloss finish, blued receiver. Overall length 47.5". Introduced 1993. Imported from Italy by Heckler & Koch, Inc.
Price: $840.00

BENELLI M1 SUPER 90 FIELD AUTO SHOTGUN
Gauge: 12, 3" chamber.
Barrel: 21", 24", 26", 28" (choke tubes).
Weight: 7 lbs., 4 oz.
Stock: High impact polymer; wood on 26", 28".
Sights: Metal bead front.
Features: Sporting version of the military & police gun. Uses the rotating Montefeltro bolt system. Ventilated rib; blue finish. Comes with set of five choke tubes. Imported from Italy by Heckler & Koch, Inc.
Price: $825.00
Price: Wood stock version $840.00

BENELLI M1 SPORTING SPECIAL AUTO SHOTGUN
Gauge: 12, 3" chamber.
Barrel: 18.5" (Imp. Cyl. Mod., Full choke tubes).
Weight: 6 lbs., 8 oz. Length: 39.75" overall.
Stock: Sporting-style polymer with drop adjustment.
Sights: Ghost ring.
Features: Uses Montefeltro inertia recoil bolt system. Matte-finish receiver. Introduced 1993. Imported from Italy by Heckler & Koch, Inc.
Price: $845.00

Benelli Black Eagle Competition

BENELLI BLACK EAGLE COMPETITION AUTO SHOTGUN
Gauge: 12, 3" chamber.
Barrel: 26", 28" (Full, Mod., Imp. Cyl., Imp. Mod., Skeet choke tubes). Mid-bead sight.
Weight: 7.1 to 7.6 lbs. Length: 49⅝" overall (26" barrel).

Stock: European walnut with high-gloss finish. Special competition stock comes with drop adjustment kit.
Features: Uses the Montefeltro rotating bolt inertia recoil operating system with a two-piece steel/aluminum etched receiver (bright on lower, blue upper). Drop adjustment kit allows the stock to be custom fitted without modifying the stock. Black lower receiver finish, blued upper. Introduced 1989. Imported from Italy by Heckler & Koch, Inc.
Price: $1,125.00
Price: Limited Edition model (gold inlays, high grade wood, special serial numbers) $2,000.00

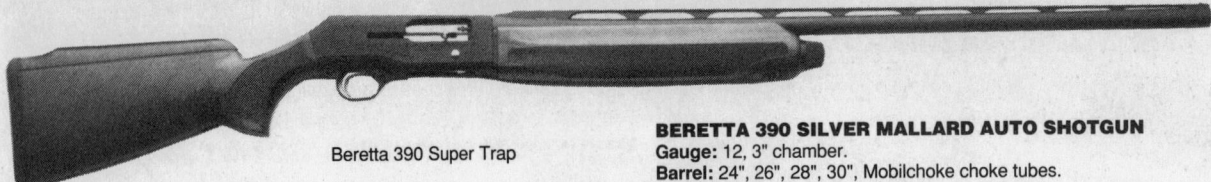

Beretta 390 Super Trap

Beretta 390 Super Trap, Super Skeet Shotguns
Similar to the 390 Field except have adjustable-comb stocks that allow height adjustments via interchangeable comb inserts. Rounded recoil pad system allows adjustments for length of pull. Wide ventilated rib with orange front sight. Factory ported barrels in 28" (fixed Skeet), 30", 32" Trap (Mobilchoke tubes). Weight 7 lbs., 10 oz. In 12-gauge only, with 3" chamber. Introduced 1993. Imported from Italy by Beretta U.S.A.
Price: 390 Super Trap $1,210.00
Price: 390 Super Skeet $1,160.00

BERETTA 390 SILVER MALLARD AUTO SHOTGUN
Gauge: 12, 3" chamber.
Barrel: 24", 26", 28", 30", Mobilchoke choke tubes.
Weight: About 7 lbs.
Stock: Select walnut. Adjustable drop and cast.
Features: Gas-operated action with self-compensating valve allows shooting all loads without adjustment. Alloy receiver, reversible safety; chrome-plated bore; floating vent. rib. Matte-finish models for turkey/waterfowl and Deluxe with gold, engraving also available. Introduced 1992. Imported from Italy by Beretta U.S.A.
Price: $775.00
Price: Waterfowl/Turkey (matte finish) $775.00
Price: Gold Mallard $935.00

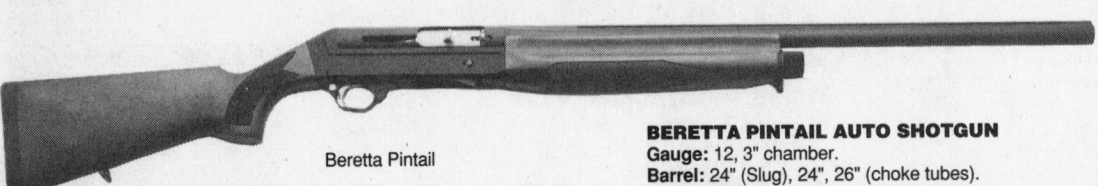

Beretta Pintail

BERETTA A-303 AUTO SHOTGUN
Gauge: 12, 20, 2¾" or 3" chamber.
Barrel: 24". 26", 28", 30", Mobilchoke choke tubes.
Weight: About 6½ lbs., 20-gauge; about 7½ lbs., 12-gauge.
Stock: American walnut; hand-checkered grip and forend.
Features: Gas-operated action, alloy receiver, magazine cut-off, push-button safety. Mobilchoke models come with three interchangeable flush-mounted screw-in choke tubes. Imported from Italy by Beretta U.S.A. Introduced 1983.
Price: Mobilchoke, 20-ga. $755.00
Price: 12-ga. trap with standard trap stock $735.00
Price: 12- or 20-ga., Skeet $735.00
Price: A-303 Youth Gun, 20-ga., 3" chamber, 24" barrel $735.00
Price: A-303 Sporting Clays with Mobilchoke, 12 or 20 . . . . . . $835.00

BERETTA PINTAIL AUTO SHOTGUN
Gauge: 12, 3" chamber.
Barrel: 24" (Slug), 24", 26" (choke tubes).
Weight: 7 lbs.
Stock: Checkered walnut.
Features: Montefeltro-type short recoil action. Matte finish on wood and metal. Slug version has rifle sights and rifled choke tube. Comes with sling swivels. Introduced 1993. Imported from Italy by Beretta U.S.A.
Price: $700.00

Beretta A-303 Upland Model
Similar to the field A-303 except has straight English-style stock, 26" vent. rib barrel with Mobilchoke choke tubes, 3" chamber. Introduced 1989.
Price: $735.00

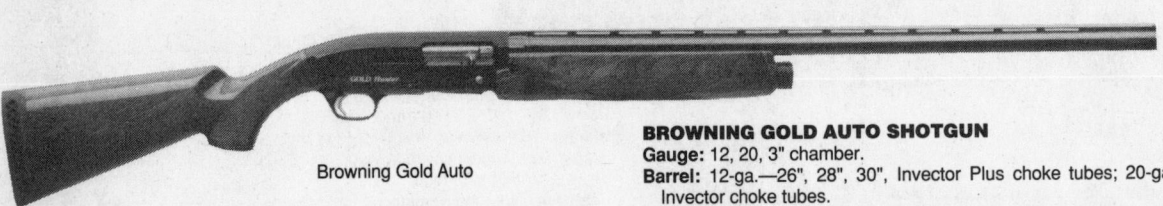

Browning Gold Auto

Consult our Directory pages for the location of firms mentioned.

BROWNING GOLD AUTO SHOTGUN
Gauge: 12, 20, 3" chamber.
Barrel: 12-ga.—26", 28", 30", Invector Plus choke tubes; 20-ga.—26", 30", Invector choke tubes.
Weight: 7 lbs., 9 oz. (12-ga.), 6 lbs., 12 oz. (20-ga.) Length: 46¼" overall (20-ga., 26" barrel).
Stock: 14"x1½"x2⅓"; select walnut with gloss finish; palm swell grip.
Features: Self-regulating, self-cleaning gas system shoots all loads; lightweight receiver with special non-glare deep black finish; large reversible safety button; large rounded trigger guard, gold trigger. The 20-gauge has slightly smaller dimensions; 12-gauge have back-bored barrels, Invector Plus tube system. Introduced 1994. Imported by Browning.
Price: 12- or 20-gauge $687.95
Price: Extra barrels $254.95

Browning Gold 10 Auto

Browning Gold 10 Stalker Auto Shotgun
Same as the standard BSA 10 except has non-glare metal finish and black graphite-fiberglass composite stock with dull finish and checkering. Introduced 1993. Imported by Browning.
Price: $934.95
Price: Extra barrel $239.95

BROWNING GOLD 10 AUTO SHOTGUN
Gauge: 10, 3½" chamber, 5-shot magazine.
Barrel: 26", 28", 30" (Imp. Cyl., Mod., Full standard Invector).
Weight: 10 lbs., 7 oz. (28" barrel).
Stock: 14⅜"x1½"x2⅜". Select walnut with gloss finish, cut checkering, recoil pad.
Features: Short-stroke , gas-operated action, cross-bolt safety. Forged steel receiver with polished blue finish. Introduced 1993. Imported by Browning.
Price: $934.95
Price: Extra barrel $239.95

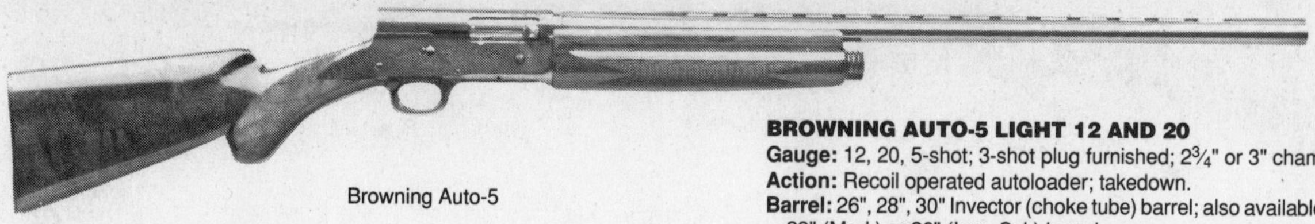

SHOTGUNS—AUTOLOADERS

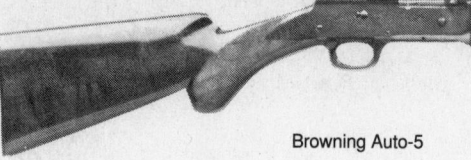

Browning Auto-5

Browning Auto-5 Stalker
Similar to the Auto-5 Light and Magnum models except has matte blue metal finish and black graphite-fiberglass stock and forend. Stock is scratch and impact resistant and has checkered panels. Light Stalker has 2¾" chamber, 26" or 28" vent. rib barrel with Invector choke tubes, weighs 8 lbs., 1 oz. (26"). Magnum Stalker has 3" chamber, 28" or 30" back-bored vent. rib barrel with Invector choke tubes, weighs 8 lbs., 11 oz. (28"). Introduced 1992.
Price: Light Stalker $772.95
Price: Magnum Stalker $795.95

Browning Auto-5 Magnum 12
Same as standard Auto-5 except chambered for 3" magnum shells (also handles 2¾" magnum and 2¾" HV loads). 28" Mod., Full; 30" and 32" (Full) bbls. Back-bored barrel comes with Invector choke tubes. 14"x1⅝"x2½" stock. Recoil pad. Wgt. 8¾ lbs.
Price: With back-bored barrel, Invector Plus $795.95
Price: Extra standard Invector barrel $282.95
Price: Extra Invector Plus barrel $282.95

COSMI AUTOMATIC SHOTGUN
Gauge: 12 or 20, 2¾" or 3" chamber.
Barrel: 22" to 34". Choke (including choke tubes) and length to customer specs. Boehler steel.
Weight: About 6¼ lbs. (20-ga.).
Stock: Length and style to customer specs. Hand-checkered exhibition grade circassian walnut standard.
Features: Hand-made, essentially a custom gun. Recoil-operated auto with tip-up barrel. Made completely of stainless steel (lower receiver polished); magazine tube in buttstock holds 7 rounds. Double ejectors, double safety system. Comes with fitted leather case. Imported from Italy by Incor, Inc.
Price: From $7,400.00

BROWNING AUTO-5 LIGHT 12 AND 20
Gauge: 12, 20, 5-shot; 3-shot plug furnished; 2¾" or 3" chamber.
Action: Recoil operated autoloader; takedown.
Barrel: 26", 28", 30" Invector (choke tube) barrel; also available with Light 20-ga. 28" (Mod.) or 26" (Imp. Cyl.) barrel.
Weight: 12-, 16-ga. 7¼ lbs.; 20-ga. 6⅜ lbs.
Stock: French walnut, hand checkered half-p.g. and forend. 14¼"x1⅝"x2½".
Features: Receiver hand engraved with scroll designs and border. Double extractors, extra bbls. Interchangeable without factory fitting; mag. cut-off; cross-bolt safety. All models except Buck Special and game guns have back-bored barrels with Invector Plus choke tubes. Imported from Japan by Browning.
Price: Light 12, 20, vent. rib., Invector Plus $772.95
Price: Extra Invector barrel $282.95
Price: Light 12 Buck Special $762.95
Price: Extra fixed-choke barrel (Light 20 only) $194.95
Price: 12, 12 magnum, 20 Buck Special barrel $272.95
Price: Light 12, Hunting, Invector Plus $772.95

Browning Auto-5 Magnum 20
Same as Magnum 12 except 20-gauge, 26" or 28" barrel with Invector Plus choke tubes with back-bored barrels. With ventilated rib, 7½ lbs.
Price: Invector Plus $795.95
Price: Standard Invector $704.05
Price: Extra Invector barrel $282.95

CHURCHILL TURKEY AUTOMATIC SHOTGUN
Gauge: 12, 3" chamber, 5-shot magazine.
Barrel: 25" (Mod., Full, Extra Full choke tubes).
Weight: 7 lbs.. **Length:** NA.
Stock: Walnut with satin finish, hand checkering.
Features: Gas-operated action, magazine cut-off, non-glare metal finish. Gold-colored trigger. Introduced 1990. Imported by Ellett Bros.
Price: $569.95

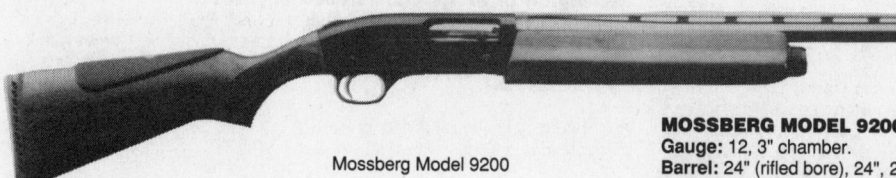

Mossberg Model 9200

Mossberg Model 9200 USST Autoloading Shotgun
Same as the Model 9200 Crown Grade except has "United States Shooting Team" custom engraved receiver. Comes with 26" vent rib barrel with Accu-Choke tubes (including Skeet), cut-checkered walnut-finish stock and forend. Introduced 1993.
Price: $457.00

MOSSBERG MODEL 9200 CROWN GRADE AUTO SHOTGUN
Gauge: 12, 3" chamber.
Barrel: 24" (rifled bore), 24", 28" (Accu-Choke tubes); vent. rib.
Weight: About 7.5 lbs. **Length:** 48" overall (28" bbl.).
Stock: Walnut with high-gloss finish, cut checkering.
Features: Shoots all 2¾" or 3" loads without adjustment. Alloy receiver, ambidextrous top safety. Introduced 1992.
Price: 28", vent rib $457.00
Price: Turkey, 24" vent rib $457.00
Price: Trophy, 24" with scope base, rifled bore, Dual-Comb stock . . $478.00
Price: 24", rifle sights, rifled bore $457.00

Mossberg Model 9200 Camo

Mossberg Model 9200 Camo Shotgun
Same as the Model 9200 Crown Grade except completely covered with Mossy Oak Tree Stand or OFM camouflage finish. Available with 24" barrel with Accu-Choke tubes. Has synthetic stock and forend. Introduced 1993.
Price: Turkey, 24" vent rib, Mossy Oak finish $538.00
Price: 28" vent rib, Accu-Chokes, OFM camo finish $443.00

Mossberg Model 9200 NWTF Edition
Same as the Model 9200 Crown Grade except has black matte receiver etched on both sides with turkey scenes; rest of gun has Realtree camo finish. Introduced 1994. From Mossberg.
Price: $538.00

REMINGTON SP-10 MAGNUM AUTO SHOTGUN
Gauge: 10, 3½" chamber, 3-shot magazine.
Barrel: 26", 30" (Full and Mod. Rem Chokes).
Weight: 11 to 11¼ lbs. **Length:** 47½" overall (26" barrel).
Stock: Walnut with satin finish. Checkered grip and forend.
Sights: Metal bead front.
Features: Stainless steel gas system with moving cylinder; ⅜" ventilated rib. Receiver and barrel have matte finish. Brown recoil pad. Comes with padded Cordura nylon sling. Introduced 1989.
Price: $993.00

Remington SP-10 Magnum Turkey Combo
Combines the SP 10 with 26" or 30" vent. rib barrel, plus extra 22" rifle-sighted barrel with Mod., Full, Extra-Full Turkey Rem Choke tubes. Comes with camo sling, swivels. Introduced 1991.
Price: $1,132.00

CAUTION: PRICES SHOWN ARE SUPPLIED BY THE MANUFACTURER OR IMPORTER. CHECK YOUR LOCAL GUNSHOP.

CAUTION: PRICES SHOWN ARE SUPPLIED BY THE MANUFACTURER OR IMPORTER. CHECK YOUR LOCAL GUNSHOP.

49th EDITION, 1995   383

Remington SP-10 Magnum-Camo

Remington SP-10 Magnum-Camo Auto Shotgun
Similar to the SP-10 Magnum except buttstock, forend, receiver, barrel and magazine cap are covered with Mossy Oak Bottomland camo finish; bolt body

and trigger guard have matte black finish. Comes with Extra-Full Turkey Rem Choke tube, 23" vent rib barrel with mid-rib bead and Bradley-style front sight, swivel studs and quick-detachable swivels, and a non-slip Cordura carrying sling in the same camo pattern. Introduced 1993.
Price: **$1,078.00**

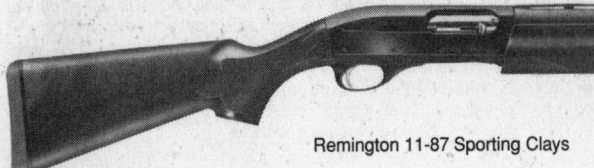

Remington 11-87 Sporting Clays

REMINGTON 11-87 SPORTING CLAYS
Gauge: 12, 2¾" chamber.
Barrel: 26", 28", vent. rib, Rem Choke (Skeet, Imp. Cyl., Mod., Full); Light Contour barrel. Medium height rib.
Weight: 7.5 lbs. **Length:** 46.5" overall (26" barrel).
Stock: 14³⁄₁₆"x1½"x2¼". Walnut, with cut checkering; sporting clays butt pad.
Features: Top of receiver, barrel and rib have matte finish; shortened magazine tube and forend; lengthened forcing cone; ivory bead front sight; competition trigger. Special no-wrench choke tubes marked on the outside. Comes in two-barrel fitted hard case. Introduced 1992.
Price: **$725.00**

Remington 11-87 Premier Trap
Similar to 11-87 Premier except trap dimension stock with straight or Monte Carlo combs; select walnut with satin finish and Tournament-grade cut checkering; 30" barrel with Rem Chokes (Trap Full, Trap Extra Full, Trap Super Full). Gas system set for 2¾" shells only. Introduced 1987.
Price: With straight stock, Rem Choke **$708.00**
Price: With Monte Carlo stock **$725.00**
Price: Left-hand, straight stock **$745.00**
Price: Left-hand, Monte Carlo stock **$761.00**

Remington 11-87 Special Purpose Synthetic Camo
Similar to the 11-87 Special Purpose Magnum except has synthetic stock and all metal (except bolt and trigger guard) and stock covered with Mossy Oak Bottomland camo finish. In 12-gauge only, 26", 28" vent. rib, Rem Choke. Comes with camo sling, swivels. Introduced 1992.
Price: **$693.00**

REMINGTON 11-87 PREMIER SHOTGUN
Gauge: 12, 3" chamber.
Barrel: 26", 28", 30" Rem Choke tubes. Light Contour barrel.
Weight: About 8¼ lbs. **Length:** 46" overall (26" bbl.).
Stock: Walnut with satin or high-gloss finish; cut checkering; solid brown buttpad; no white spacers.
Sights: Bradley-type white-faced front, metal bead middle.
Features: Pressure compensating gas system allows shooting 2¾" or 3" loads interchangeably with no adjustments. Stainless magazine tube; redesigned feed latch, barrel support ring on operating bars; pinned forend. Introduced 1987.
Price: **$644.00**
Price: Left-hand **$692.00**
Price: Premier Cantilever Deer Barrel, scope rings, sling, swivels, Monte Carlo stock **$699.00**

Remington 11-87 Premier Skeet
Similar to 11-87 Premier except Skeet dimension stock with cut checkering, satin finish, two-piece buttplate; 26" barrel with Skeet or Rem Chokes (Skeet, Imp. Skeet). Gas system set for 2¾" shells only. Introduced 1987.
Price: **$700.00**
Price: Left-hand **$735.00**

Remington 11-87 Special Purpose Magnum
Similar to the 11-87 Premier except has dull stock finish, Parkerized exposed metal surfaces. Bolt and carrier have dull blackened coloring. Comes with 26" or 28" barrel with Rem Chokes, padded Cordura nylon sling and q.d. swivels. Introduced 1987.
Price: **$625.00**
Price: With synthetic stock and forend (SPS) **$625.00**
Price: Magnum-Turkey with synthetic stock (SPS-T) **$639.00**

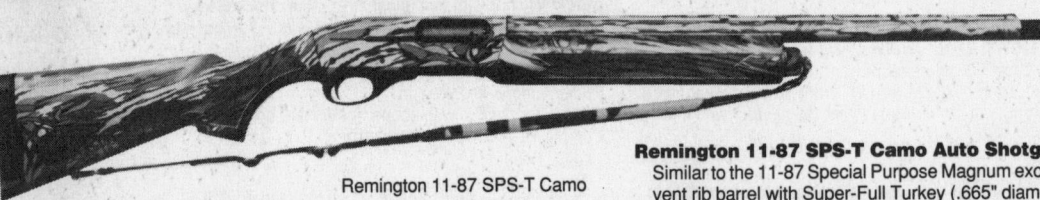

Remington 11-87 SPS-T Camo

Remington 11-87 SPS-Deer Shotgun
Similar to the 11-87 Special Purpose Deer except has fully-rifled 21" barrel with rifle sights, black non-reflective, synthetic stock and forend, black carrying sling. Introduced 1993.
Price: **$633.00**

Remington 11-87 SPS-T Camo Auto Shotgun
Similar to the 11-87 Special Purpose Magnum except with synthetic stock, 21" vent rib barrel with Super-Full Turkey (.665" diameter with knurled extension) and Imp. Cyl. Rem Choke tubes. Completely covered with Mossy Oak Green Leaf camouflage. Bolt body, trigger guard and recoil pad are non-reflective black. Introduced 1993.
Price: **$707.00**

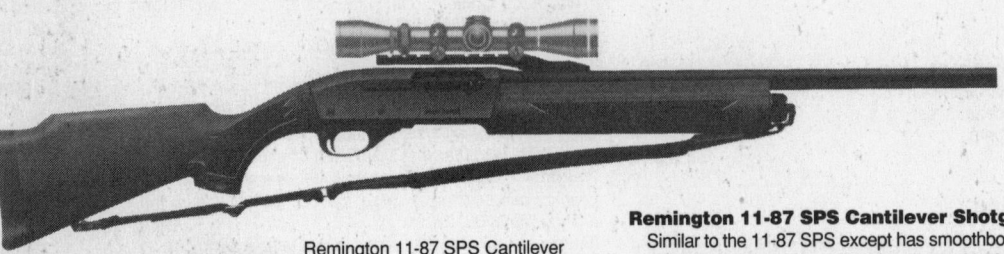

Remington 11-87 SPS Cantilever

Remington 11-87 SPS Cantilever Shotgun
Similar to the 11-87 SPS except has smoothbore barrel with Imp. Cyl. and 3½" Rifled Rem Choke tubes; synthetic stock with Monte Carlo comb; cantilever scope mount deer barrel. Comes with sling and swivels. Introduced 1994.
Price: **$665.00**

    CAUTION: PRICES SHOWN ARE SUPPLIED BY THE MANUFACTURER OR IMPORTER. CHECK YOUR LOCAL GUNSHOP.

SHOTGUNS—AUTOLOADERS

Remington 11-87 Special Purpose Deer Gun
Similar to the 11-87 Special Purpose Magnum except has 21" barrel with rifle sights, rifled and Imp. Cyl. choke tubes. Gas system set to handle all 2¾" and 3" slug, buckshot, high velocity field and magnum loads. Not designed to function with light 2¾" field loads. Introduced 1987.
Price: **$605.00**
Price: With cantilever scope mount, rings **$699.00**

REMINGTON 1100 LT-20 AUTO
Gauge: 20, 28, 410.
Barrel: 25" (Full, Mod.), 26", 28" with Rem Chokes.
Weight: 7½ lbs.
Stock: 14"x1½"x2½". American walnut, checkered p.g. and forend.
Features: Quickly interchangeable barrels. Matted receiver top with scroll work on both sides of receiver. Cross-bolt safety.
Price: With Rem Chokes, 20-ga. about **$605.00**
Price: 28 and 410 . . . . **$647.00**
Price: Youth Gun LT-20 (21" Rem Choke) **$605.00**
Price: 20-ga., 3" magnum **$605.00**

Remington 11-87 SPS-BG-Camo Deer/Turkey Shotgun
Similar to the 11-87 Special Purpose Deer Gun except completely covered with Mossy Oak Bottomland camouflage, comes with Super-Full Turkey Rem Choke tube of .665" diameter with knurled end-ring, Rifled choke tube insert, and an Imp. Cyl. tube. Synthetic stock and forend, quick-detachable swivels, camo Cordura carrying sling. Barrel is 21" with rifle sights, 3" chamber. Introduced 1993.
Price: **$692.00**

Remington 1100 Special Field
Similar to Standard Model 1100 except 12- and 20-ga. only, comes with 23" Rem Choke barrel. LT-20 version 6½ lbs.; has straight-grip stock, shorter forend, both with cut checkering. Comes with vent. rib only; matte finish receiver without engraving. Introduced 1983.
Price: 12- and 20-ga., 21" Rem Choke, about **$605.00**

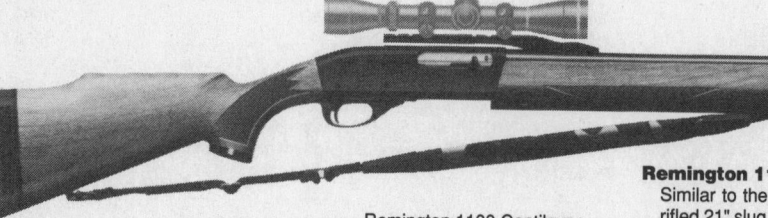

Remington 1100 Cantilever

Remington 1100 20-Gauge Deer Gun
Same as 1100 except 20-ga. only, 21" barrel (Imp. Cyl.), rifle sights adjustable for windage and elevation; recoil pad with white spacer. Weight 7¼ lbs.
Price: About **$545.00**

Remington 1100 Cantilever 20-Gauge Deer
Similar to the 1100 LT-20 except comes with cantilever scope mount, fully rifled 21" slug barrel. Walnut stock and forend. Comes with sling and swivels. Introduced 1994.
Price: **$652.00**

Remington 1100 LT-20 Tournament Skeet
Same as the 1100 except 26" barrel, special Skeet boring, vent. rib, ivory bead front and metal bead middle sights. 14"x1½"x2½" stock. 20-, 28-gauge, 410-bore. Weight 7½ lbs., cut checkering, walnut, new receiver scroll.
Price: Tournament Skeet (28, 410), about **$692.00**
Price: Tournament Skeet (20), about **$692.00**

Winchester Model 1400

WINCHESTER MODEL 1400 SEMI-AUTO SHOTGUN
Gauge: 12 and 20, 2¾" chamber.
Barrel: 22", 26", 28" vent. rib with Winchoke tubes (Imp. Cyl., Mod., Full).
Weight: 7¾ lbs. **Length:** 48⅝" overall.

Stock: Walnut-finished hardwood, finger-grooved forend with deep cut checkering. Also available with walnut stock.
Sights: Metal bead front.
Features: Cross-bolt safety, front-locking rotary bolt, black serrated buttplate, gas-operated action. From U.S. Repeating Arms Co., Inc.
Price: Ranger, vent. rib with Winchoke **$377.00**
Price: As above with walnut stock (1400 Walnut) **$419.00**
Price: Ranger Deer barrel combo **$430.00**

SHOTGUNS—SLIDE ACTIONS

Includes a wide variety of sporting guns and guns suitable for competitive shooting.

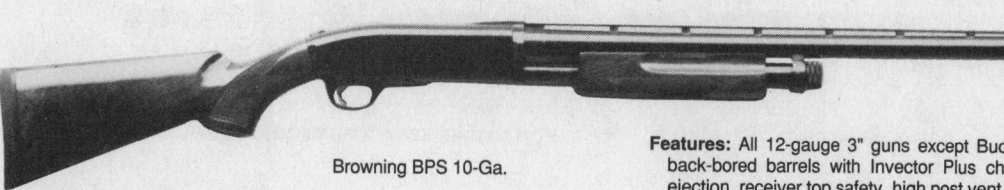

Browning BPS 10-Ga.

BROWNING BPS PUMP SHOTGUN
Gauge: 10, 12, 3½" chamber; 12 or 20, 3" chamber (2¾" in target guns), 28, 2¾" chamber, 5-shot magazine.
Barrel: 10-ga.—24" Buck Special, 28", 30", 32" Invector; 12-, 20- ga.—22", 24", 26", 28", 30", 32" (Imp. Cyl., Mod. or Full). Also available with Invector choke tubes, 12- or 20-ga.; Upland Special has 22" barrel with Invector tubes. BPS 3" and 3½" have back-bored barrel.
Weight: 7 lbs., 8 oz. (28" barrel). **Length:** 48¾" overall (28" barrel).

Features: All 12-gauge 3" guns except Buck Special and game guns have back-bored barrels with Invector Plus choke tubes. Bottom feeding and ejection, receiver top safety, high post vent. rib. Double action bars eliminate binding. Vent. rib barrels only. All 12- and 20-gauge guns with 3" chamber available with fully engraved receiver flats at no extra cost. Each gsuge has its own unique game scene. Introduced 1977. Imported from Japan by Browning.
Price: 10-ga., Hunting, Invector **$615.95**
Price: 12-ga., 3½" Mag., Hunting, Invector Plus **$615.95**
Price: 12-, 20-ga., Hunting, Invector Plus **$489.95**
Price: 12-, 20-ga., Upland Special, Invector Plus **$489.95**
Price: 10-ga. Buck Special **$620.95**
Price: 12-ga. Buck Special **$474.95**
Price: 28-ga., Hunting, Invector **$489.95**

Browning BPS Game Deer

Browning BPS Game Gun Turkey Special
Similar to the standard BPS except has satin-finished walnut stock and dull-finished barrel and receiver. Receiver is drilled and tapped for scope mounting. Rifle-style stock dimensions and swivel studs. Has Extra-Full Turkey choke tube. Introduced 1992.
Price: $524.95

Browning BPS Pigeon Grade Pump Shotgun
Same as the standard BPS except has select high grade walnut stock and forend, and gold-trimmed receiver. Available in 12-gauge only with 26" or 28" vent. rib barrels. Introduced 1992.
Price: $651.95
Price: 10-gauge Waterfowl Model $787.95

Browning BPS Game Gun Deer Special
Similar to the standard BPS except has newly designed receiver/magazine tube/barrel mounting system to eliminate play, heavy 20.5" barrel with rifle-type sights with adjustable rear, solid receiver scope mount, "rifle" stock dimensions for scope or open sights, sling swivel studs. Gloss-finish wood with checkering, polished blue metal. Introduced 1992.
Price: $554.95

Browning BPS Stalker Pump Shotgun
Same gun as the standard BPS except all exposed metal parts have a matte blued finish and the stock has a durable black finish with a black recoil pad. Available in 10-ga. (3½") and 12-ga. with 3" or 3½" chamber, 22", 28", 30" barrel with Invector choke system. Introduced 1987.
Price: 12-ga., 3" chamber, Invector Plus $489.95
Price: 10-, 12-ga., 3½" chamber $615.95

Browning BPS Pump Shotgun Ladies and Youth Model
Same as BPS Upland Special except 20-ga. only, 22" Invector barrel, stock has pistol grip with recoil pad. Length of pull is 13¼". Introduced 1986.
Price: $489.95

Ithaca Model 87 Supreme

Ithaca Model 87 Turkey Gun
Similar to the Model 87 Supreme except comes with 22" or 24" (fixed Full or Full choke tube) barrel, either Camoseal camouflage or matte blue finish, oiled wood, blued trigger.
Price: With fixed choke, blue $465.75
Price: With choke tube, blue $508.25
Price: With fixed choke, green camo $508.25
Price: With choke tube, green camo $550.75

Ithaca Model 87 Deluxe Pump Shotgun
Similar to the Model 87 Supreme Vent. Rib except comes with three choke tubes in 26", 28", 30". Standard-grade walnut.
Price: $533.25

Ithaca Deerslayer II Rifled Shotgun
Similar to the Deerslayer except has rifled 25" barrel and checkered American walnut stock and forend with high-gloss finish and Monte Carlo comb. Solid frame construction. Introduced 1988.
Price: 12 or 20 . . . . $566.50

ITHACA MODEL 87 SUPREME PUMP SHOTGUN
Gauge: 12, 20, 3" chamber, 5-shot magazine.
Barrel: 26", 28", 30" (Imp. Cyl., Mod., Full tubes); vent. rib.
Weight: 6¾ to 7 lbs.
Stock: 14"x1½"x2¼". Full fancy-grade walnut, checkered p.g. and slide handle.
Sights: Raybar front.
Features: Bottom ejection, cross-bolt safety. Polished and blued engraved receiver. Reintroduced 1988. From Ithaca Acquisition Corp.
Price: $808.50
Price: M87 green or brown Camo Vent. (28", Mod. choke tube, camouflage finish) $542.00
Price: M87 English (20-ga., 24", 26", choke tubes) $545.50

ITHACA MODEL 87 DEERSLAYER SHOTGUN
Gauge: 12, 20, 3" chamber.
Barrel: 20", 25" (Special Bore), or rifled bore.
Weight: 6 to 6¾ lbs.
Stock: 14"x1½"x2¼". American walnut. Checkered p.g. and slide handle.
Sights: Raybar blade front on ramp, rear adjustable for windage and elevation, and grooved for scope mounting.
Features: Bored for slug shooting. Bottom ejection, cross-bolt safety. Reintroduced 1988. From Ithaca Acquisition Corp.
Price: $464.75
Price: Deluxe $498.25
Price: Field Deerslayer, Basic $424.50
Price: Smooth Bore Basic $424.50
Price: Smooth Bore Deluxe $464.75

Magtech Model 586-VR

MAVERICK MODEL 91 ULTI-MAG PUMP SHOTGUN
Gauge: 12, 3½" chamber.
Barrel: 28" (ACCU-MAG Mod. tube); vent. rib.
Weight: 7¾ lbs. **Length:** 48½" overall.
Stock: Black synthetic.
Sights: Brass bead front.
Features: Dual slide bars; cross-bolt safety; rubber recoil pad. Accessories interchangeable with Mossberg Model 835. Cablelock included. Introduced 1993. From Mossberg.
Price: $259.00

MAGTECH MODEL 586-VR PUMP SHOTGUN
Gauge: 12, 3" chamber.
Barrel: 26", 28", choke tubes.
Weight: 8.5 lbs. **Length:** 46.5" overall (26" barrel).
Stock: Brazilian hardwood.
Features: Double action slide bars. Ventilated rib with bead front sight. Polished blue finish. Introduced 1993. Imported from Brazil by Magtech Recreational Products.
Price: Model 586-VR, about $255.00
Price: Model 586 (as above, plain barrel), about $225.00
Price: Model 586-S (24" barrel, rifle sights), about $235.00

CAUTION: PRICES SHOWN ARE SUPPLIED BY THE MANUFACTURER OR IMPORTER. CHECK YOUR LOCAL GUNSHOP.

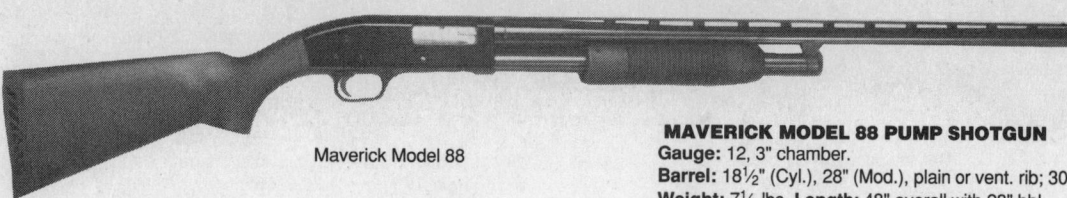

Maverick Model 88

MITCHELL HIGH STANDARD PUMP SHOTGUNS
Gauge: 12, 2¾" chamber.
Barrel: 18½", 20" (Imp. Cyl., Mod., Full choke tubes).
Weight: 7½ lbs.
Stock: Walnut.
Features: Polished blue finish. Introduced 1994. Imported from the Philippines by Mitchell Arms.
Price: 20", 5- or 7-shot, walnut $269.00
Price: 20", 5- or 7-shot, rifle sights, walnut $289.00
Price: 18½", 6-shot, bead sight, walnut $269.00
Price: 18½", 6-shot, rifle sights, walnut $289.00
Price: 18½", 6-shot, fiberglass stock $335.00

MAVERICK MODEL 88 PUMP SHOTGUN
Gauge: 12, 3" chamber.
Barrel: 18½" (Cyl.), 28" (Mod.), plain or vent. rib; 30" (Full), plain or vent. rib.
Weight: 7¼ lbs. **Length:** 48" overall with 28" bbl.
Stock: Black synthetic with ribbed synthetic forend.
Sights: Bead front.
Features: Alloy receiver with blue finish; dual slide bars; cross-bolt safety in trigger guard; interchangeable barrels. Rubber recoil pad. Mossberg Cablelock included. Introduced 1989. From Maverick Arms, Inc.
Price: Model 88, synthetic stock, 28", 30" plain bbl. $219.00
Price: Model 88, synthetic stock, 28", 30" vent. rib $229.00
Price: Model 88, synthetic stock, 24" with rifle sights $236.00
Price: Model 88, synthetic stock, Combo 18½", 28" plain bbl. $254.00
Price: Model 88, synthetic stock, Combo 18½" (plain), 28" (vent. rib) $265.00
Price: Model 88, synthetic stock, 28" vent. rib, ACCU-TUBE set . . . $249.00

Mossberg Model 500

Mossberg Model 500 Camo Pump
Same as the Model 500 Sporting Pump except 12-gauge only and entire gun is covered with special camouflage finish. Receiver drilled and tapped for scope mounting. Comes with q.d. swivel studs, swivels, camouflage sling, Mossberg Cablelock.
Price: From about $282.00
Price: Camo Combo (as above with extra Slugster barrel), from about $385.00

Mossberg Model 500 Muzzleloader Combo
Same as the Model 500 Sporting Pump except comes with 24" rifled bore, rifle-sighted Slugster barrel and 24" fully rifled 50-caliber muzzle-loading barrel and ramrod. Uses #209 standard primer. Introduced 1992.
Price: $418.00

MOSSBERG MODEL 500 TROPHY SLUGSTER
Gauge: 12, 3" chamber.
Barrel: 24", rifled bore. Plain (no rib).
Weight: 7¼ lbs. **Length:** 44" overall.
Stock: 14" pull, 1⅜" drop at heel. Walnut; Dual Comb design for proper eye positioning with or without scoped barrels. Recoil pad and swivel studs.
Features: Ambidextrous thumb safety, twin extractors, dual slide bars. Comes with scope mount. Mossberg Cablelock included. Introduced 1988.
Price: Rifled bore, with scope mount $340.00
Price: Rifled bore, rifle sights $312.00
Price: Cyl. bore, rifle sights $276.00

MOSSBERG MODEL 500 SPORTING PUMP
Gauge: 12, 20, 410, 3" chamber.
Barrel: 18½" to 28" with fixed or Accu-Choke, with Accu-II tubes or Accu-Steel tubes for steel shot, plain or vent. rib.
Weight: 6¼ lbs. (410), 7¼ lbs. (12). **Length:** 48" overall (28" barrel).
Stock: 14"x1½"x2½". Walnut-stained hardwood. Cut-checkered grip and forend.
Sights: White bead front, brass mid-bead.
Features: Ambidextrous thumb safety, twin extractors, disconnecting safety, dual action bars. Quiet Carry forend. Mossberg Cablelock included. From Mossberg.
Price: From about $269.00
Price: Sporting Combos (field barrel and Slugster barrel), from . . . $318.00

Mossberg Model 500 Bantam Pump
Same as the Model 500 Sporting Pump except 20-gauge only, 22" vent. rib Accu-Choke barrel with Mod. choke tube; has 1" shorter stock, reduced length from pistol grip to trigger, reduced forend reach. Introduced 1992.
Price: $269.00

Mossberg Turkey Model 500 Pump
Same as the Model 500 Sporting Pump except has overall OFM camo finish, Ghost-Ring sights, Accu-Choke barrel with Imp. Cyl., Mod., Full, Extra-Full lead shot choke tubes, 24" barrel, swivel studs, camo sling. Introduced 1992.
Price: $368.00

Mossberg Field Grade Model 835 Pump Shotgun
Same as the Model 835 Crown Grade except has walnut-stained hardwood stock and comes only with Modified choke tube, 28" barrel. Introduced 1992.
Price: $294.00

Mossberg Model 835 Crown Grade

MOSSBERG MODEL 835 CROWN GRADE ULTI-MAG PUMP
Gauge: 12, 3½" chamber.
Barrel: 24" rifled bore, 24", 28", Accu-Mag with four choke tubes for steel or lead shot.
Weight: 7¾ lbs. **Length:** 48½" overall.
Stock: 14"x1½"x2½". Dual Comb. Cut-checkered walnut or camo synthetic; both have recoil pad.
Sights: White bead front, brass mid-bead.
Features: Shoots 2¾", 3" or 3½" shells. Backbored barrel to reduce recoil, improve patterns. Ambidextrous thumb safety, twin extractors, dual slide bars.

Mossberg Cablelock included. Introduced 1988.
Price: 28" vent rib, Dual-Comb stock $400.00
Price: As above, standard stock $393.00
Price: 24" Trophy Slugster, rifled bore, scope base, Dual-Comb stock $421.00
Price: Combo, 24" rifled bore, rifle sights, 28" vent rib, Accu-Mag choke tubes, Dual-Comb stock $463.00
Price: Combo, 24" Trophy Slugster rifled bore, 28" vent rib, Accu-Mag choke tubes, Dual-Comb stock $472.00
Price: Realtree or Mossy Oak Camo Turkey, 24" vent rib, Accu-Mag Extra-Full tube, synthetic stock $468.00
Price: Realtree Camo, 28" vent rib, Accu-Mag tubes, synthetic stock $468.00
Price: Realtree Camo Combo, 24" rifled bore, rifle sights, 24" vent rib, Accu-Mag choke tubes, synthetic stock, hard case $571.00
Price: OFM Camo, 28" vent rib, Accu-Mag tubes, wood stock $428.00
Price: OFM Camo Combo, 24" rifled bore, rifle sights, 28" vent rib, Accu-Mag tubes, wood stock $490.00

Remington 870 Wingmaster

REMINGTON 870 WINGMASTER
Gauge: 12, 3" chamber.
Barrel: 26", 28", 30" (Rem Chokes). Light Contour barrel.
Weight: 7¼ lbs. **Length:** 46½" overall (26" bbl.).
Stock: 14"x2½"x1". American walnut with satin or high-gloss finish, cut-checkered p.g. and forend. Rubber buttpad.
Sights: Ivory bead front, metal mid-bead.
Features: Double action bars; cross-bolt safety; blue finish. Available in right- or left-hand style. Introduced 1986.
Price: $479.00
Price: Left-hand (28" only) $527.00
Price: Deer Gun (rifle sights, 20" bbl.) $452.00
Price: Deer Gun, left-hand, Monte Carlo stock $495.00
Price: LW-20 20-ga., vent. rib, 26", 28" (Rem Choke) $467.00
Price: Fully rifled Cantilever, 20" $532.00

Remington 870 TC Trap
Same as the Model 870 except 12-ga. only, 30" Rem Choke, vent. rib barrel, Ivory front and white metal middle beads. Special sear, hammer and trigger assembly. 14⅜"x1½"x1⅞" stock with recoil pad. Hand fitted action and parts. Weight 8 lbs.
Price: Model 870TC Trap, Rem Choke, about $613.00
Price: TC Trap with Monte Carlo stock, about $628.00

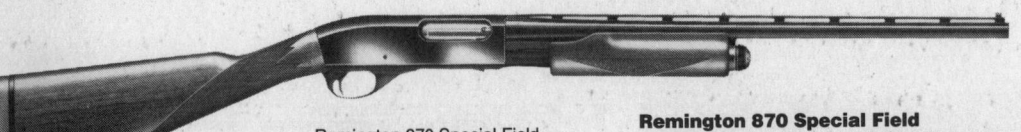

Remington 870 Special Field

Remington 870 Special Field
Similar to the standard Model 870 except comes with 23" barrel only, 3" chamber, choked Imp. Cyl., Mod., Full and Rem Choke; 12-ga. weighs 6¾ lbs., LW-20 weighs 6 lbs.; has straight-grip stock, shorter forend, both with cut checkering. Vent. rib barrel only. Introduced 1984.
Price: 12- or 20-ga., Rem Choke, about $473.00

Remington 870 Marine Magnum
Similar to the 870 Wingmaster except all metal is plated with electroless nickel and has black synthetic stock and forend. Has 18" plain barrel (Cyl.), bead front sight, 7-shot magazine. Introduced 1992.
Price: $465.00

Remington 870 Wingmaster Small Gauges
Same as the standard Model 870 Wingmaster except chambered for 20-ga. (2¾" and 3"), 28-ga., and 410-bore. The 20-ga. available with 26", 28" vent. rib barrel with Rem Choke tubes, high-gloss or satin wood finish; 28 and 410 available with 25" Full or Mod. fixed choke, satin finish only.
Price: 20-ga. $467.00
Price: 20-ga. Deer Gun, rifle sights $432.00
Price: 28 and 410 . . . . $504.00

Remington 870 Special Purpose Deer Gun
Similar to the 870 Wingmaster except available with 20" barrel with rifled and Imp. Cyl. choke tubes; rifle sights or cantilever scope mount with rings. Metal has black, non-glare finish, satin finish on wood. Recoil pad, detachable sling of camo Cordura nylon. Introduced 1989.
Price: With rifle sights, Monte Carlo stock $432.00
Price: With scope mount and rings, Monte Carlo stock $532.00

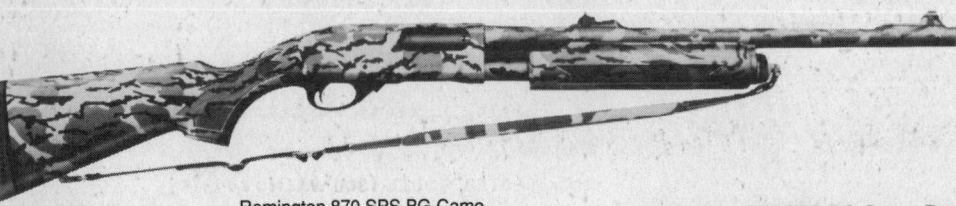

Remington 870 SPS-BG-Camo

Remington 870 SPS-BG-Camo Deer/Turkey Shotgun
Similar to the 870 Special Purpose Deer Gun except completely covered with Mossy Oak Bottomland camouflage, comes with Super-Full Turkey Rem Choke tube of .665" diameter with knurled end-ring, Rifled choke tube insert, and an Imp. Cyl. tube. Synthetic stock and forend, quick-detachable swivels, camo Cordura carrying sling. Barrel is 20" with rifle sights, 3" chamber. Introduced 1993.
Price: $452.00

Remington 870 SPS Cantilever Shotgun
Similar to the 870 SPS-Deer except has smoothbore barrel with Imp. Cyl. and 3½" Rifled Rem Choke tubes; synthetic stock with Monte Carlo comb; cantilever scope mount deer barrel. Comes with sling and swivels. Introduced 1994.
Price: $419.00

Remington 870 SPS-Deer Shotgun
Similar to the 870 Special Purpose Deer excet has fully-rifled 20" barrel with rifle sights, black non-reflective, synthetic stock and forend, black carrying sling. Introduced 1993.
Price: $395.00

Remington 870 Express
Similar to the 870 Wingmaster except has a walnut-toned hardwood stock with solid, black recoil pad and pressed checkering on grip and forend. Outside metal surfaces have a black oxide finish. Comes with 26" or 28" vent. rib barrel with a Mod. Rem Choke tube. Introduced 1987.
Price: 12 or 20 . . . . $292.00
Price: Express Combo (with extra 20" Deer barrel), 12 or 20 . . . . $395.00
Price: Express 20-ga., 28" with Mod. Rem Choke tubes $292.00
Price: 410-bore $307.00
Price: 28-gauge $307.00

Remington 870 Express Rifle-Sighted Deer Gun
Same as the Model 870 Express except comes with 20" barrel with fixed Imp. Cyl. choke, open iron sights, Monte Carlo stock. Introduced 1991.
Price: $287.00
Price: With fully rifled barrel $320.00

Remington Model 870 Express Youth Gun
Same as the Model 870 Express except comes with 12½" length of pull, 21" barrel with Mod. Rem Choke tube. Hardwood stock with low-luster finish. Introduced 1991.
Price: $292.00
Price: 20-ga. Express Youth (1" shorter stock) $307.00
Price: 20-ga. Express Youth Deer (rifle sights, fully rifled barrel) . . $320.00

Remington 870 Express Turkey
Same as the Model 870 Express except comes with 3" chamber, 21" vent. rib turkey barrel and Extra-Full Rem Choke Turkey tube; 12-ga. only. Introduced 1991.
Price: $305.00

Remington 870 Express Synthetic
Similar to the 870 Express with 26", 28" barrel except has synthetic stock and forend. Introduced 1994.
Price: **$299.00**

Remington 870 SPS-T Special Purpose Magnum
Similar to the Model 870 except chambered only for 12-ga., 3" shells, 26" or 28" Rem Choke barrel. All exposed metal surfaces are finished in dull, non-reflective black. Black synthetic stock and forend. Comes with padded Cordura 2" wide sling, quick-detachable swivels. Chrome-lined bores. Dark recoil pad. Introduced 1985.
Price: **$399.00**

Remington 870 SPS Camo

Remington 870 Special Purpose Synthetic Camo
Similar to the 870 Special Purpose Magnum except has synthetic stock and all metal (except bolt and trigger guard) and stock covered with Mossy Oak Bottomland camo finish. In 12-gauge only, 26", 28" vent. rib, Rem Choke. Comes with camo sling, swivels. Introduced 1992.
Price: **$440.00**

Remington 870 SPS-T Camo Pump Shotgun
Similar to the 870 Special Purpose Magnum except with synthetic stock, 21" vent rib barrel with Super-Full Turkey (.665" diameter with knurled extension) and Imp. Cyl. Rem Choke tubes. Completely covered with Mossy Oak Green Leaf camouflage. Bolt body, trigger guard and recoil pad are non-reflective black. Introduced 1993.
Price: **$453.00**

Remington 870 High Grades
Same as 870 except better walnut, hand checkering. Engraved receiver and barrel. Vent. rib. Stock dimensions to order.
Price: 870D, about **$2,509.00**
Price: 870F, about **$5,169.00**
Price: 870F with gold inlay, about **$7,752.00**

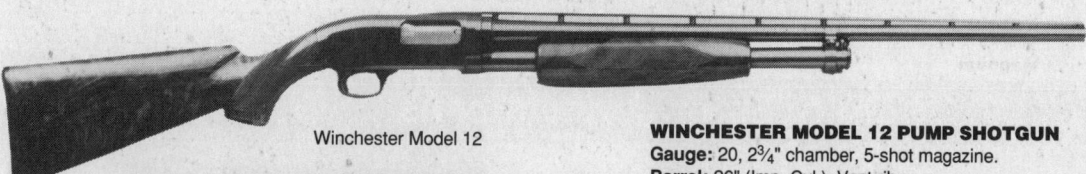

Winchester Model 12

WINCHESTER MODEL 12 PUMP SHOTGUN
Gauge: 20, 2¾" chamber, 5-shot magazine.
Barrel: 26" (Imp. Cyl.). Vent rib.
Weight: 7 lbs. **Length:** 45" overall.
Stock: 14"x2½"x1½". Select walnut with satin finish. Checkered grip and forend.
Features: Grade I has plain blued receiver; production limited to 4000 guns. Grade IV receiver has engraved game scenes and gold highlights identical to traditional Grade IV, and is limited to 1000 guns. Introduced 1993. From U.S. Repeating Arms Co.
Price: Grade I **$879.00**
Price: Grade IV **$1,431.00**

Winchester 1300 Turkey

Winchester Model 1300 Realtree® Turkey Gun
Similar to the standard Model 1300 except has synthetic Realtree® camo stock and forend, matte finished barrel and receiver, 22" barrel with Extra Full, Full and Mod. WinChoke tubes. Drilled and tapped for scope mounting. Comes with padded, adjustable sling. In 12-gauge only, 3" chamber; weight about 7 lbs. Introduced 1994. From U.S. Repeating Arms Co., Inc.
Price: **$359.00**

WINCHESTER MODEL 1300 WALNUT PUMP
Gauge: 12 and 20, 3" chamber, 5-shot capacity.
Barrel: 22", 26", 28" vent. rib, with Full, Mod., Imp. Cyl. Winchoke tubes.
Weight: 6⅜ lbs. **Length:** 42⅝" overall.
Stock: American walnut, with deep cut checkering on pistol grip, traditional ribbed forend; high luster finish.
Sights: Metal bead front.
Features: Twin action slide bars; front-locking rotary bolt; roll-engraved receiver; blued, highly polished metal; cross-bolt safety with red indicator. Introduced 1984. From U.S. Repeating Arms Co., Inc.
Price: **$331.00**
Price: Model 1300 Ladies/Youth, 20-ga., 22" vent. rib **$300.00**

Winchester 1300 Black Shadow Turkey

Winchester Model 1300 Black Shadow Turkey Gun
Similar to the Model 1300 Realtree® Turkey except synthetic stock and forend are matte black, and all metal surfaces finished matte black. Drilled and tapped for scope mounting. In 12-gauge only, 3" chamber, 22" vent. rib barrel; comes with one Full WinChoke tube. Introduced 1994. From U.S. Repeating Arms Co., Inc.
Price: **$287.00**

Winchester Model 1300 Black Shadow Deer Gun
Similar to the Model 1300 Black Shadow Turkey Gun except has ramp-type front sight, fully adjustable rear, drilled and tapped for scope mounting. Black composite stock and forend, matte black metal. Smoothbore 22" barrel with one Imp. Cyl. WinChoke tube; 12-gauge only, 3" chamber. Weighs 7¼ lbs. Introduced 1994. From U.S. Repeating Arms Co., Inc.
Price: **$287.00**

SHOTGUNS—SLIDE ACTIONS

Winchester 1300 Slug Hunter Deer

Winchester 1300 Ranger

Winchester Model 1300 Slug Hunter Deer Gun
Same as the Model 1300 except has rifled 22" barrel, walnut stock, rifle-type sights. Introduced 1990.
Price: Walnut stock **$445.00**

Winchester Model 1300 Ranger Pump Gun Combo & Deer Gun
Similar to the standard Ranger except comes with two barrels: 22" (Cyl.) deer barrel with rifle-type sights and an interchangeable 28" vent. rib Winchoke barrel with Full, Mod. and Imp. Cyl. choke tubes. Drilled and tapped; comes with rings and bases. Available in 12- and 20-gauge 3" only, with recoil pad. Introduced 1983.
Price: Deer Combo with two barrels **$368.00**
Price: 12-ga., 22" rifled barrel **$333.00**
Price: 12-ga., 22" (Imp. Cyl., rifled sabot tubes) **$345.00**
Price: Combo 12-ga. with 18" (Cyl.) and 28" (Mod. tube) . . **$368.00**
Price: Rifled Deer Combo (22" rifled and 28" vent. rib barrels, 12 or 20-ga.) **$390.00**

WINCHESTER MODEL 1300 RANGER PUMP GUN
Gauge: 12 or 20, 3" chamber, 5-shot magazine.
Barrel: 26", 28" vent. rib with Full, Mod., Imp. Cyl. Winchoke tubes.
Weight: 7 to 7¼ lbs.
Length: 48⅝" to 50⅝" overall.
Stock: Walnut-finished hardwood with ribbed forend.
Sights: Metal bead front.
Features: Cross-bolt safety, black rubber recoil pad, twin action slide bars, front-locking rotating bolt. From U.S. Repeating Arms Co., Inc.
Price: Vent. rib barrel, Winchoke **$300.00**

SHOTGUNS—OVER/UNDERS

Includes a variety of game guns and guns for competitive shooting.

American Arms Silver I

American Arms Silver II Shotgun
Similar to the Silver I except 26" barrel (Imp. Cyl., Mod., Full choke tubes, 12- and 20-ga.), 28" (Imp. Cyl., Mod., Full choke tubes, 12-ga. only), 26" (Imp. Cyl. & Mod. fixed chokes, 28 and 410), 26" two-barrel set (Imp. Cyl. & Mod., fixed, 28 and 410); automatic selective ejectors. Weight is about 6 lbs., 15 oz. (12-ga., 26").
Price: **$719.00**
Price: 28, 410 . . . . **$739.00**

American Arms Silver II Lite
Similar to the Silver II except weighs 6 lbs., 4 oz. (12-gauge), 5 lbs., 12 oz. (20-gauge), 6 lbs. (28-gauge). Single selective trigger, automatic selective ejectors. Franchoke tubes on 12- and 20-gauge, fixed chokes on 28. Vent. rib, engraved frame with antique silver finish. Introduced 1994. Imported by American Arms, Inc.
Price: 12-, 20-ga., 3" chambers, 26" **$959.00**
Price: 28-gauge, 2¾", 26" (Imp. Cyl. & Mod.) **$959.00**

AMERICAN ARMS SILVER I O/U
Gauge: 12, 20, 28, 410, 3" chamber (28 has 2¾").
Barrel: 26" (Imp. Cyl. & Mod., all gauges), 28" (Mod. & Full, 12, 20).
Weight: About 6¾ lbs.
Stock: 14⅛"x1⅜"x2⅜". Checkered walnut.
Sights: Metal bead front.
Features: Boxlock action with scroll engraving, silver finish. Single selective trigger, extractors. Chrome-lined barrels. Manual safety. Rubber recoil pad. Introduced 1987. Imported from Italy and Spain by American Arms, Inc.
Price: 12- or 20-gauge **$569.00**
Price: 28 or 410 . . . . **$629.00**

AMERICAN ARMS SILVER SPORTING O/U
Gauge: 12, 2¾" chambers.
Barrel: 28", 30" (Skeet, Imp. Cyl., Mod., Full choke tubes).
Weight: 7⅜ lbs. **Length:** 45½" overall.
Stock: 14⅜"x1½"x2⅜". Figured walnut, cut checkering; Sporting Clays quick-mount buttpad.
Sights: Target bead front.
Features: Boxlock action with single selective mechanical trigger, automatic selective ejectors; special broadway channeled rib; vented barrel rib; chrome bores. Chrome-nickel finish on frame, with engraving. Introduced 1990. Imported from Italy by American Arms, Inc.
Price: **$899.00**

American Arms WS/OU 12

American Arms WT/OU 10 Shotgun
Similar to the WS/OU 12 except chambered for 10-gauge 3½" shell, 26" (Full & Full, choke tubes) barrel. Single selective trigger, extractors. Non-reflective finish on wood and metal. Imported by American Arms, Inc.
Price: **$989.00**

AMERICAN ARMS WS/OU 12, TS/OU 12 SHOTGUNS
Gauge: 12, 3½" chambers.
Barrel: WS/OU—28" (Imp. Cyl., Mod., Full choke tubes); TS/OU—24" (Imp. Cyl., Mod., Full choke tubes).
Weight: 6 lbs., 15 oz. **Length:** 46" overall.
Stock: 14⅛"x1⅛"x2⅜". European walnut with cut checkering, black vented recoil pad, matte finish.
Features: Boxlock action with single selective trigger, automatic selective ejectors; chrome bores. Matte metal finish. Imported by American Arms, Inc.
Price: **$739.00**

    CAUTION: PRICES SHOWN ARE SUPPLIED BY THE MANUFACTURER OR IMPORTER. CHECK YOUR LOCAL GUNSHOP.

SHOTGUNS—OVER/UNDERS

ARMSPORT 2700 SERIES O/U
Gauge: 10, 12, 20, 28, 410.
Barrel: 26" (Imp. Cyl. & Mod.); 28" (Mod. & Full); vent. rib.
Weight: 8 lbs.
Stock: European walnut, hand-checkered p.g. and forend.
Features: Single selective trigger, automatic ejectors, engraved receiver. Imported by Armsport. Contact Armsport for complete list of models.
Price: M2733/2735 (Boss-type action, 12, 20, extractors) $790.00
Price: M2741 (as above with ejectors) $825.00
Price: M2730/2731 (as above with single trigger, screw-in chokes) . $975.00
Price: M2705 (410 bore, 26" Imp. & Mod., double triggers) $785.00
Price: M2742 Sporting Clays (12-ga., 28", choke tubes) $930.00
Price: M2744 Sporting Clays (20-ga., 26", choke tubes) $930.00
Price: M2750 Sporting Clays (12-ga., 28", choke tubes, sideplates) $1,050.00
Price: M2751 Sporting Clays (20-ga., 26", choke tubes, sideplates) $1,050.00

ARMSPORT 2700 O/U GOOSE GUN
Gauge: 10, 3½" chambers.
Barrel: 28" (Full & Imp. Mod.), 32" (Full & Full).
Weight: About 9.8 lbs.
Stock: European walnut.
Features: Boss-type action; double triggers; extractors. Introduced 1986. Imported from Italy by Armsport.
Price: Fixed chokes $1,190.00
Price: With choke tubes $1,299.00

ARMSPORT 2900 TRI-BARREL SHOTGUN
Gauge: 12, 3" chambers.
Barrel: 28" (Imp., Mod., Full).
Weight: 7¾ lbs.
Stock: European walnut.
Features: Has three barrels. Top-tang barrel selector; double triggers; silvered, engraved frame. Introduced 1986. Imported from Italy by Armsport.
Price: $3,400.00

> Consult our Directory pages for the location of firms mentioned.

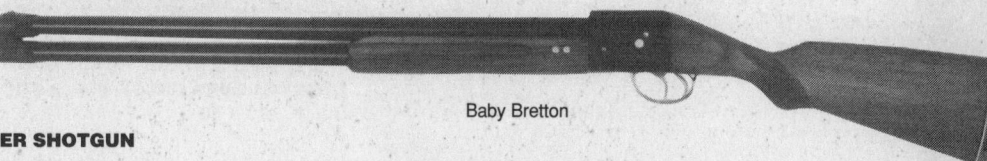

Baby Bretton

BABY BRETTON OVER/UNDER SHOTGUN
Gauge: 12 or 20, 2¾" chambers.
Barrel: 27½" (Cyl., Imp. Cyl., Mod., Full choke tubes).
Weight: About 5 lbs.
Stock: Walnut, checkered pistol grip and forend, oil finish.
Features: Receiver slides open on two guide rods, is locked by a large thumb lever on the right side. Extractors only. Light alloy barrels. Imported from France by Mandall Shooting Supplies.
Price: Sprint Standard $895.00
Price: Sprint Deluxe $975.00
Price: Model Fairplay $1,025.00

BAIKAL IJ-27 OVER/UNDER SHOTGUN
Gauge: 12, 2¾" chambers.
Barrel: 28" (Mod. & Full).
Weight: 7 lbs.
Stock: Checkered walnut.
Features: Double triggers; extractors; blued receiver with engraving. Reintroduced 1994. Imported from Russia by K.B.I., Inc.
Price: $429.00
Price: IJ-27 EIC (single trigger, automatic ejectors) $469.00

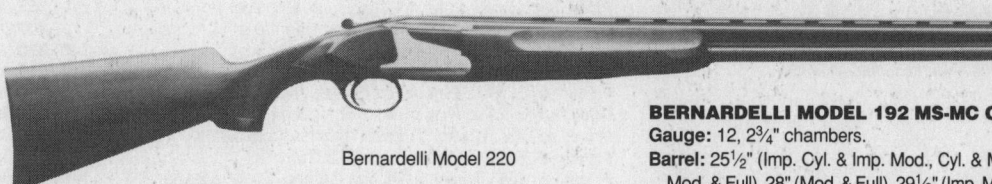

Bernardelli Model 220

Bernardelli Model 115 Over/Under Shotgun
Similar to the Model 192 except designed for competition shooting with thicker barrel walls, specially designed stock with anatomical grip. Leather-faced recoil pad and schnabel forend on Sporting Clays and Skeet guns. Concave top rib, ventilated middle rib. Imported from Italy by Armsport.
Price: Model 115 S (inclined-plane locking, ejectors, selective or non-selective trigger, Multichoke standard on Sporting Clays) $2,895.00
Price: Model 115 S Trap/Skeet $2,799.00

BERNARDELLI MODEL 192 MS-MC O/U SHOTGUN
Gauge: 12, 2¾" chambers.
Barrel: 25½" (Imp. Cyl. & Imp. Mod., Cyl. & Mod.), 26¾" (Imp. Cyl. & Imp. Mod., Mod. & Full), 28" (Mod. & Full), 29½" (Imp. Mod. & Full); or with Multichoke tubes.
Weight: About 7 lbs.
Stock: 14"x1⅜"x2⅜". Hand-checkered European walnut. English or pistol grip style.
Features: Boxlock action; single selective trigger. Silvered, engraved action. Imported from Italy by Armsport.
Price: With Multichokes $1,340.00
Price: Model 192 Waterfowler (3½" chambers, three Multichoke tubes) $1,460.00
Price: Model 192 MS (Sporting Clays, non-selective or selective trigger) $2,140.00
Price: Model 220 MS (similar to M192 except 20-ga., different frame) $1,490.00
Price: Model 220 (20-ga., 3" chambers) $1,420.00

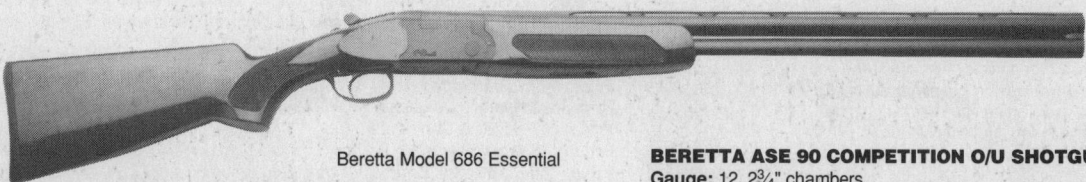

Beretta Model 686 Essential

BERETTA MODEL 686 ESSENTIAL O/U
Gauge: 12, 3" chambers.
Barrel: 26", 28", Mobilchoke tubes (Imp. Cyl., Mod., Full).
Weight: 6.7 lbs. **Length:** 45.7" overall (28" barrels).
Stock: 14.5"x2.2"x1.4". American walnut; radiused black buttplate.
Features: Matte finish on receiver and barrels; hard-chrome bores; low-profile receiver with dual conical locking lugs; single selective trigger, ejectors. Introduced 1994. Imported from Italy by Beretta U.S.A.
Price: $1,215.00

BERETTA ASE 90 COMPETITION O/U SHOTGUN
Gauge: 12, 2¾" chambers.
Barrel: 28" (Pigeon, Sporting Clays, Skeet), 30" (Sporting Clays, Trap), Mobilchoke tubes on Sporting Clays, Trap; fixed chokes on Trap, Skeet, Pigeon. Trap model also available as Top Combo (30", 32" barrels or 30", 34").
Weight: About 8 lbs., 6 oz.
Stock: High grade walnut.
Features: Has drop-out trigger assembly, wide ventilated top and side ribs, hard-chrome bores. Comes with hard case. Introduced 1992. Imported from Italy by Beretta U.S.A.
Price: Pigeon, Trap, Skeet $8,070.00
Price: Sporting Clays $8,140.00

CAUTION: PRICES SHOWN ARE SUPPLIED BY THE MANUFACTURER OR IMPORTER. CHECK YOUR LOCAL GUNSHOP.

49th EDITION, 1995 **391**

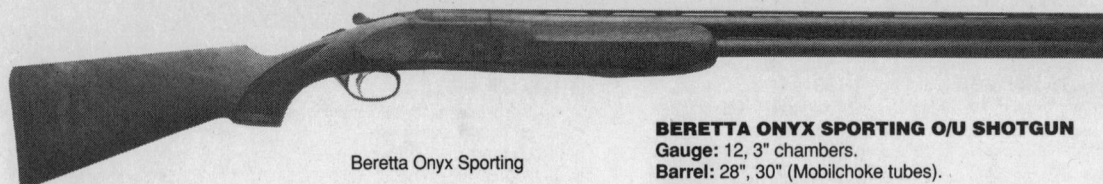

Beretta Onyx Sporting

BERETTA MODEL 686 ULTRALIGHT ONYX O/U

Gauge: 12, 2¾" chambers.
Barrel: 26", 28", Mobilchoke choke tubes.
Weight: About 5 lbs., 13 oz.
Stock: Select American walnut with checkered grip and forend.
Features: Low-profile aluminum alloy receiver with titanium breech face insert. Matte black receiver finish with gold P. Beretta signature inlay. Single selective trigger; automatic safety. Introduced 1992. Imported from Italy by Beretta U.S.A.
Price: $1,525.00

BERETTA ONYX SPORTING O/U SHOTGUN

Gauge: 12, 3" chambers.
Barrel: 28", 30" (Mobilchoke tubes).
Weight: 6 lbs., 13 oz.
Stock: Checkered American walnut.
Features: Intended for the beginning sporting clays shooter. Has wide, vented 12.5mm target rib, radiused recoil pad. Matte black finish on receiver and barrels. Introduced 1993. Imported from Italy by Beretta U.S.A.
Price: $1,385.00
Price: 686 Silver Perdiz Sporting (as above except coin silver receiver with scroll engraving; 12- or 20-ga.) $1,425.00

Beretta 686EL

BERETTA OVER/UNDER FIELD SHOTGUNS

Gauge: 12, 20, 28, and 410 bore, 2¾", 3" and 3½" chambers.
Barrel: 26" and 28" (Mobilchoke tubes).
Stock: Close-grained walnut.
Features: Highly-figured, American walnut stocks and forends, and a unique, weather-resistant finish on barrels. The 686 Onyx bears a gold P. Beretta signature on each side of the receiver. Silver designates standard 686, 687 models with silver receivers; Gold indicates higher grade 686EL, 687EL models with full sideplates; Diamond is for 687EELL models with highest grade wood, engraving. Case provided with Gold and Diamond grades. Silver Gold, Diamond grades introduced 1994. Imported from Italy by Beretta U.S.A.

CONSULT

Shooter's Marketplace

Page 225, This Issue

Price: 686 Onyx $1,355.00
Price: 686 two bbl. set $2,085.00
Price: 686 Silver Perdiz $1,385.00
Price: 686L Silver Perdiz (12-ga., polished silver receiver) $1,355.00
Price: 686EL Gold Perdiz (engraved sideplates, hard case) $2,200.00
Price: 687L Silver Perdiz $1,870.00
Price: 687L Silver Pigeon $1,870.00
Price: 687EL Gold Pigeon (gold inlays, sideplates) . $3,180.00 to $3,320.00
Price: 687EL Gold Pigeon, 410, 26", 28-ga., 28" $3,320.00
Price: 687EELL Diamond Pigeon (engraved sideplates) . $4,625.00 to $5,130.00
Price: 687EELL Diamond Pigeon, 28-ga., 28" $4,625.00
Price: 687EELL Diamond Pigeon Combo, 20- and 28-ga., 26" . . $5,130.00

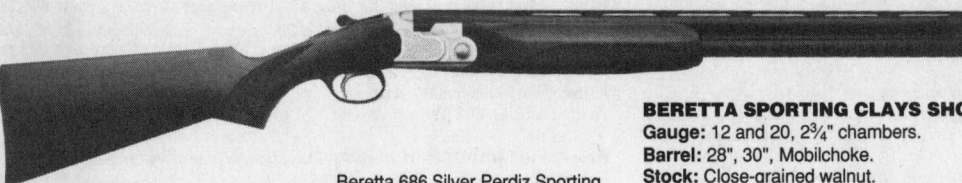

Beretta 686 Silver Perdiz Sporting

Beretta 687EL Gold Pigeon Sporting O/U

Similar to the 687 Silver Pigeon Sporting except has sideplates with gold inlay game scene, vent side and top ribs, bright orange front sight. Stock and forend are of high grade walnut with fine-line checkering. Available in 12-gauge only with 28" or 30" barrels and Mobilchoke tubes. Weight is 6 lbs., 13 oz. Introduced 1993. Imported from Italy by Beretta U.A.S.
Price: $3,225.00

Beretta 682 Super Sporting O/U

Similar to the 682 Sporting except has stock with adjustable comb that allows height adjustments via interchangeable inserts. Accessory recoil pad system and adjustable trigger allow length of pull changes. Factory ported barrels, raised tapered top rib with mid-rib bead, bright orange front sight. Available in 12-gauge only, 2¾" chambers, 28" 30", Mobilchoke tubes. Introduced 1993. Imported from Italy by Beretta U.S.A.
Price: $2,925.00

BERETTA SPORTING CLAYS SHOTGUNS

Gauge: 12 and 20, 2¾" chambers.
Barrel: 28", 30", Mobilchoke.
Stock: Close-grained walnut.
Features: Equipped with Beretta Mobilchoke flush-mounted screw-in choke tube system. Dual-purpose O/U for hunting and Sporting Clays. 12- or 20-gauge, 28", 30" Mobilchoke tubes (four, Skeet, Imp. Cyl., Mod., Full). Wide 12.5mm top rib with 2.5mm center groove; 686 Onyx models have matte black receiver, 686 Silver Perdiz has silver receiver with scroll engraving; 687 Silver Pigeon Sporting has silver receiver, highly figured walnut; 687 EL Pigeon Sporting has game scene engraving with gold inlaid animals on full sideplate. Introduced 1994. Imported from Italy by Beretta U.S.A.
Price: 682 Sporting, 30" (with case) $2,605.00
Price: 682 Super Sporting, 28", 30", ported, adj. l.o.p. $2,925.00
Price: 682 Sporting 20-gauge $2,605.00
Price: 682 Sporting Combo, 28" and 30" $3,470.00
Price: 686 Onyx Sporting $1,385.00
Price: 686 Continental Course Sporting, 2¾" chambers, 28", 30" . $2,715.00
Price: 686 Silver Perdiz Sporting $1,425.00
Price: 686 Silver Perdiz Sporting Combo, 28" and 30" $2,600.00
Price: 687 Silver Perdiz Sporting $2,285.00
Price: 687 Silver Pigeon Sporting $2,285.00
Price: 687 Silver Pigeon Sporting (20 gauge) $2,285.00
Price: 687 Diamond Pigeon EELL Sporter (hand engraved sideplates, deluxe wood) $4,700.00
Price: 687 Silver Pigeon Sporting Combo, 28" and 30" $3,405.00
Price: 687EL Pigeon Sporting $3,225.00
Price: ASE 90 Gold Sporting Clay $8,140.00

Beretta 682 Competition

BERETTA SERIES 682 COMPETITION OVER/UNDERS
Gauge: 12, 2¾" chambers.
Barrel: Skeet—26" and 28"; trap—30" and 32", Imp. Mod. & Full and Mobilchoke; trap mono shotguns—32" and 34" Mobilchoke; trap top single guns—32" and 34" Full and Mobilchoke; trap combo sets—from 30" O/U, to 32" O/U, 34" top single.
Stock: Close-grained walnut, hand checkered.
Sights: White Bradley bead front sight and center bead.
Features: Trap Monte Carlo stock has deluxe trap recoil pad. Various grades

BERETTA MODEL SO5, SO6, SO9 SHOTGUNS
Gauge: 12, 2¾" chambers.
Barrel: To customer specs.
Stock: To customer specs.
Features: SO5—Trap, Skeet and Sporting Clays models SO5; SO6—SO6 and SO6 EELL are field models. SO6 has a case-hardened or silver receiver with contour hand engraving. SO6 EELL has hand-engraved receiver in a fine floral or "fine English" pattern or game scene, with bas-relief chisel work and gold

available; contact Beretta U.S.A. for details. Imported from Italy by Beretta U.S.A.
Price: 682 Skeet $2,520.00
Price: 682 Trap $2,495.00
Price: 682 Trap Mono shotguns $3,400.00
Price: 682 Trap Top Single shotguns $2,650.00
Price: 682 Trap Combo sets . . . . $3,340.00 to $3,400.00
Price: 686 Silver Perdiz Skeet (28") $1,390.00
Price: 686 Silver Perdiz Trap (30") $1,300.00
Price: 682 Pigeon Silver $2,760.00
Price: 687 EELL Diamond Pigeon Trap . . . . . . $4,610.00 to $5,815.00
Price: 687 EELL Diamond Pigeon Skeet (4-bbl. set) $8,040.00
Price: 682 Super Diamond Pigeon Skeet (adjustable comb and butt pads, bbl. porting) $2,915.00
Price: 682 Super Trap (adjustable comb and butt pad, barrel porting) . . . . $2,885.00 to $3,865.00

inlays. SO6 and SO6 EELL are available with sidelocks removable by hand. Imported from Italy by Beretta U.S.A.
Price: SO5 Trap, Skeet, Sporting $12,900.00
Price: SO5 Combo, two-bbl. set $16,600.00
Price: SO6 Trap, Skeet, Sporting $17,400.00
Price: SO6 EELL Field, custom specs $26,000.00
Price: SO9 (12, 20, 28, 410, 26", 28", 30", any choke) $30,500.00

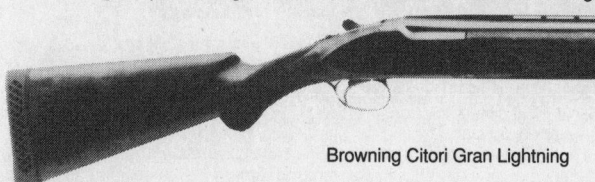

Browning Citori Gran Lightning

Browning Superlight Citori Over/Under
Similar to the standard Citori except available in 12, 20 with 24", 26" or 28" Invector barrels, 28 or 410 with 26" barrels choked Imp. Cyl. & Mod. or 28" choked Mod. & Full. Has straight grip stock, schnabel forend tip. Superlight 12 weighs 6 lbs., 9 oz. (26" barrels); Superlight 20, 5 lbs., 12 oz. (26" barrels). Introduced 1982.
Price: Grade I only, 28 or 410, Invector $1,325.00
Price: Grade III, Invector, 12 or 20 . . . . $1,835.00
Price: Grade III, 28 or 410, Invector $2,050.00
Price: Grade VI, Invector, 12 or 20 . . . . $2,672.00
Price: Grade VI, 28 or 410, Invector $2,880.00
Price: Grade I Invector, 12 or 20 . . . . $1,278.00
Price: Grade I Invector, Upland Special (24" bbls.), 12 or 20 . . . $1,278.00

Browning Lightning Sporting Clays
Similar to the Citori Lightning with rounded pistol grip and classic forend. Has high post tapered rib or lower hunting-style rib with 30" back-bored Invector Plus barrels, ported or non-ported, 3" chambers. Gloss stock finish, radiused recoil pad. Has "Lightning Sporting Clays Edition" engraved and gold filled on receiver. Introduced 1989.
Price: Low-rib, ported $1,370.00
Price: High-rib, ported $1,430.00
Price: Pigeon Grade, low rib, ported $1,566.00
Price: Pigeon Grade, high rib, ported $1,630.00
Price: Golden Clays, low rib, ported $2,830.00
Price: Golden Clays, high rib, ported $2,930.00

BROWNING CITORI O/U SHOTGUN
Gauge: 12, 20, 28 and 410.
Barrel: 26", 28" in 28 and 410. Offered with Invector choke tubes. All 12- and 20-gauge models have back-bored barrels and Invector Plus choke system.
Weight: 6 lbs., 8 oz. (26" 410) to 7 lbs., 13 oz. (30" 12-ga.).
Length: 43" overall (26" bbl.).
Stock: Dense walnut, hand checkered, full p.g., beavertail forend. Field-type recoil pad on 12-ga. field guns and trap and Skeet models.
Sights: Medium raised beads, German nickel silver.
Features: Barrel selector integral with safety, automatic ejectors, three-piece takedown. Imported from Japan by Browning. Contact Browning for complete list of models and prices.
Price: Grade I, Hunting, Invector, 12 and 20 . . . . $1,228.00
Price: Grade III, Hunting, Invector, 12 and 20 . . . . $1,802.00
Price: Grade VI, Hunting, Invector, 12 and 20 . . . . $2,610.00
Price: Grade I, Lightning, 28 and 410, Invector $1,305.00
Price: Grade III, Lightning, 28 and 410, Invector $2,050.00
Price: Grade VI, 28 and 410 Lightning, Invector $2,880.00
Price: Grade I, Lightning, Invector Plus, 12, 20 . . . . $1,263.00
Price: Grade I, Hunting, 28", 30" only, 3½", Invector Plus $1,303.00
Price: Grade III, Lightning, Invector, 12, 20 . . . . $1,838.00
Price: Grade VI, Lightning, Invector, 12, 20 . . . . $2,672.00
Price: Gran Lightning, 26", 28", Invector, 12 ,20 . . . . $1,712.00
Price: Gran Lightning, 28, 410 . . . . $1,800.00

Browning Micro Citori Lightning
Similar to the standard Citori 20-ga. Lightning except scaled down for smaller shooter. Comes with 24" Invector Plus back-bored barrels, 13¾" length of pull. Weighs about 6 lbs., 3 oz. Introduced 1991.
Price: Grade I $1,315.00
Price: Grade III $1,850.00
Price: Grade VI $2,680.00

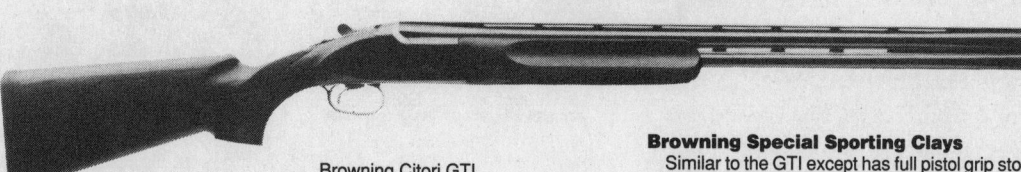

Browning Citori GTI

Browning Citori GTI Sporting Clays
Similar to the Citori Hunting except has semi-pistol grip with slightly grooved, semi-beavertail forend, satin-finish stock, radiused rubber buttpad. Has three interchangeable trigger shoes, trigger has three length of pull adjustments. Wide 13mm vent. rib, 28" or 30" barrels (ported or non-ported) with Invector Plus choke tubes. Ventilated side ribs. Introduced 1989.
Price: With ported barrels $1,450.00
Price: Golden Clays $2,930.00

Browning Special Sporting Clays
Similar to the GTI except has full pistol grip stock with palm swell, gloss finish, 28", 30" or 32" barrels with back-bored Invector Plus chokes (ported or non-ported); high post tapered rib. Also available as 28" and 30" two-barrel set. Introduced 1989.
Price: With ported barrels $1,430.00
Price: As above, adjustable comb $1,550.00
Price: Golden Clays $2,930.00

CAUTION: PRICES SHOWN ARE SUPPLIED BY THE MANUFACTURER OR IMPORTER. CHECK YOUR LOCAL GUNSHOP.

49th EDITION, 1995 **393**

SHOTGUNS—OVER/UNDERS

Browning Citori O/U Skeet Models

Similar to standard Citori except 26", 28", 12-gauge, Invector choke tubes; stock dimensions of 14⅜"x1½"x2", fitted with Skeet-style recoil pad; conventional target rib and high post target rib.

Price: Grade I Invector, 12-ga., Invector Plus (high post rib)	**$1,450.00**
Price: Grade I, 20, 28 and 410 (high post rib)	**$1,450.00**
Price: Grade III, 20, 28, 410 (high post rib)	**$1,995.00**
Price: Grade VI, 20, 28, 410 (high post rib)	**$2,518.00**
Price: Four barrel Skeet set—12, 20, 28, 410 barrels, with case, Grade I only	**$4,275.00**
Price: Grade III, four-barrel set (high post rib)	**$4,617.00**
Price: Grade VI, four-barrel set (high post rib)	**$5,225.00**
Price: Grade I, three-barrel set	**$2,975.00**
Price: Grade III, three-barrel set	**$3,750.00**
Price: Golden Clays, three-barrel set	**$4,875.00**
Price: Golden Clays	**$2,969.00**
Price: Golden Clays, four-barrel set	**$6,480.00**
Price: Grade III, 12-ga. Invector Plus	**$1,995.00**
Price: Grade VI, 12-ga., Invector Plus	**$2,555.00**

Browning Citori O/U Trap Models

Similar to standard Citori except 12 gauge only; 30", 32" ported or non-ported (Full & Full, Imp. Mod. & Full, Mod. & Full) or Invector Plus, 34" single barrel in Combo Set (Full, Imp. Mod., Mod.), or Invector model; Monte Carlo cheek piece (14⅜"x1⅜"x1⅜"x2"); fitted with trap-style recoil pad; conventional

Browning Citori Plus Trap Gun

Similar to the Grade I Citori Trap except comes only with 30" barrels with .745" over-bore, Invector Plus choke system with Full, Imp. Mod. and Mod. choke tubes; high post, ventilated, tapered, target rib for adjustable impact from 3" to 12" above point of aim. Available with or without ported barrels. Select walnut stock has high-gloss finish, Monte Carlo comb, modified beavertail forend and is fully adjustable for length of pull, drop at comb and drop at Monte Carlo. Has Browning Recoil Reduction System. Introduced 1989.

Price: Grade I, with ported barrel	**$2,030.00**
Price: Grade I, non-ported barrel	**$2,005.00**
Price: Pigeon Grade, ported barrel	**$2,225.00**
Price: Golden Clays, Invector Plus, ported	**$3,435.00**

Browning Citori Plus Trap Combo

Same as the Citori Plus Trap except comes with 34" single barrel with the 32" O/U model, or 32" or 34" single with the 30" O/U model. Introduced 1992.

Price: With fitted luggage case	**$3,435.00**
Price: Golden Clays	**$5,200.00**

target rib and high post target rib.

Price: Grade I, Invector Plus, ported bbls.	**$1,450.00**
Price: Grade III, Invector Plus Ported	**$1,995.00**
Price: Grade IV, Invector Plus Ported	**$2,555.00**
Price: Golden Clays	**$2,965.00**

Browning 325 Sporting Clays

BROWNING 325 SPORTING CLAYS

Gauge: 12, 20, 2¾" chambers.
Barrel: 12-ga.—28", 30", 32" (Invector Plus tubes), back-bored; 20-ga.—28", 30" (Imp. Mod. & Imp. Cyl.).

Weight: 7 lbs., 13 oz. (12-ga., 28").
Stock: 14¹³⁄₁₆" (+/-⅛")x1⁷⁄₁₆"x2³⁄₁₆" (12-ga.). Select walnut with gloss finish, cut checkering, schnabel forend.
Features: Grayed receiver with engraving, blued barrels. Barrels are ported on 12-gauge guns. Has 10mm wide vent rib. Comes with three interchangeable trigger shoes to adjust length of pull. Introduced in U.S. 1993. Imported by Browning.

Price: 12-, 20-ga., Invector Plus	**$1,625.00**
Price: Golden Clays, 12-, 20-ga., Invector Plus	**$3,030.00**

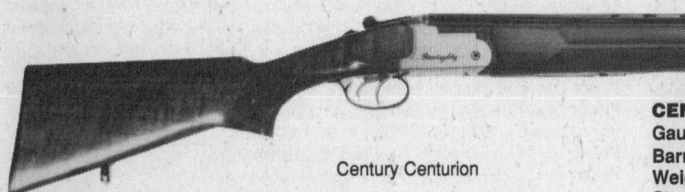

Century Centurion

CENTURY CENTURION OVER/UNDER SHOTGUN

Gauge: 12, 2¾" chambers.
Barrel: 28" (Mod. & Full).
Weight: 7.3 lbs. **Length:** 44.5" overall (26" barrels).
Stock: European walnut.
Features: Double triggers; extractors. Polished blue finish. Introduced 1993. Imported by Century International Arms.
Price: About $250.00

CHAPUIS OVER/UNDER SHOTGUN

Gauge: 12, 16, 20.
Barrel: 22", 23.6", 26.8", 27.6", 31.5", chokes to customer specs.
Weight: 5 to 8 lbs. **Length:** NA.
Stock: French walnut, straight English or pistol grip.
Features: Double hook blitz system boxlock action with automatic ejectors or extractors. Long trigger guard (most models), choice of raised solid rib, vent. rib or ultra light rib. Imported from France by Armes de Chasse.
Price: About . . . . $4,000.00 to $5,000.00

> Consult our Directory pages for the location of firms mentioned.

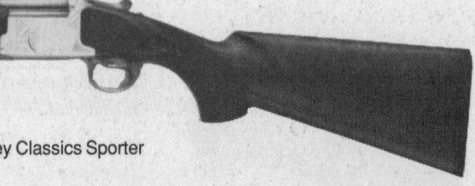

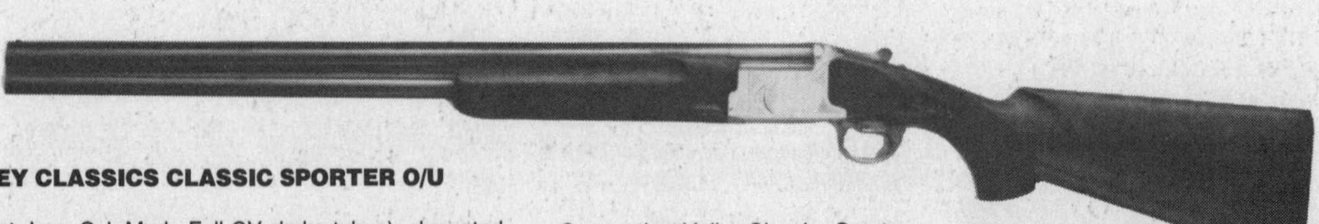

Connecticut Valley Classics Sporter

CONNECTICUT VALLEY CLASSICS CLASSIC SPORTER O/U

Gauge: 12, 3" chambers.
Barrel: 28", 30", 32" (Skeet, Imp. Cyl. Mod., Full CV choke tubes); elongated forcing cones.
Weight: 7¾ lbs. **Length:** 44⅞" overall (28" barrels).
Stock: 14½"x1½"x2⅛". American black walnut with hand-checkered grip and forend.
Features: Receiver duplicates Classic Doubles M101 specifications. Nitrided grayed or stainless receiver with fine engraving. Chrome-lined bores and chambers suitable for steel shot. Optionally available are CV Plus (2⅜" tubes) or Competition (2¾" Briley) choke tubes. Introduced 1993. Made in U.S. by Connecticut Valley Classics.

Price: Classic Sporter	**$2,750.00**
Price: Classic Sporter Stainless	**$2,750.00**

Connecticut Valley Classics Classic Field Waterfowler

Similar to the Classic Sporter except with 30" barrel only, blued, non-reflective overall finish. Interchangeable CV choke tube system includes Skeet, Imp. Cyl., Mod. Full tubes. Introduced 1993. Made in U.S. by Connecticut Valley Classics.
Price: $2,195.00

CAUTION: PRICES SHOWN ARE SUPPLIED BY THE MANUFACTURER OR IMPORTER. CHECK YOUR LOCAL GUNSHOP.

SHOTGUNS—OVER/UNDERS

CHARLES DALY FIELD GRADE O/U

Gauge: 12 or 20, 3" chambers.
Barrel: 12- and 20- ga.—26" (Imp. Cyl. & Mod.), 12-ga.—28" (Mod. & Full).
Weight: 6 lbs., 15 oz. (12-ga.); 6 lbs., 10 oz. (20-ga.). **Length:** 43½" overall (26" bbl.).
Stock: 14⅛"x1⅜"x2⅜". Walnut with cut-checkered grip and forend. Black, vent. rubber recoil pad. Semi-gloss finish.
Features: Boxlock action with manual safety; extractors; single selective trigger. Color case-hardened receiver with engraving. Introduced 1989. Imported from Europe by Outdoor Sports Headquarters.
Price: **$545.00**
Price: Sporting Clays model (12-ga., 30", choke tubes) **$895.00**

Charles Daly Deluxe Over/Under

Similar to the Field Grade except available in 12 and 20 gauge, has automatic selective ejectors, antique silver finish on frame, and has choke tubes for Imp. Cyl., Mod. and Full. Introduced 1989.
Price: **$770.00**

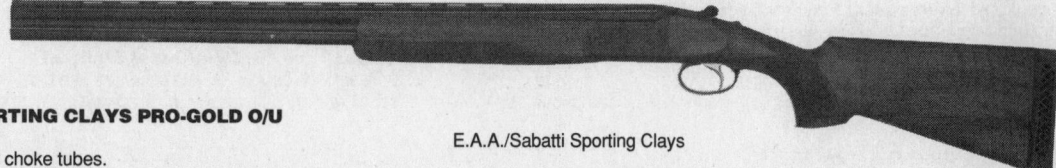

E.A.A./Sabatti Sporting Clays

E.A.A./SABATTI SPORTING CLAYS PRO-GOLD O/U

Gauge: 12, 3" chambers.
Barrel: 28" or 30" with six choke tubes.
Weight: 7¼ lbs.
Stock: European walnut with gloss finish, checkered grip and forend. Special sporting clays recoil pad.
Features: Boxlock action with gold-plated single selective trigger, automatic ejectors. Engraved, blued receiver with gold inlays. Target-style flourescent bar front sight. Comes with lockable hard shell plastic case. Introduced 1993. Imported from Italy by European American Armory.
Price: **$999.00**

HATFIELD UPLANDER OVER/UNDER SHOTGUN

Gauge: 20, 28, 3" chambers.
Barrel: 26" (Imp. Cyl. & Mod.).
Weight: 5 lbs., 4 oz.
Stock: Straight English grip of special select XXX fancy walnut; hand-checkered grip and forend; hand-rubbed oil finish.
Features: Boxlock action with single selective trigger; half-coverage hand engraving; French gray finish. Comes with English-style oxblood leather luggage case with billiard felt interior. Special engraving, stock dimensions, metal finish available. Introduced 1994. From Hatfield Gun Co.
Price: Grade I **$3,749.00**

Kemen KM-4

KEMEN OVER/UNDER SHOTGUNS

Gauge: 12, 2¾" or 3" chambers.
Barrel: 27⅝" (Hunting, Pigeon, Sporting Clays, Skeet), 30", 32" (Sporting Clays, Trap).
Weight: 7.25 to 8.5 lbs.
Stock: Dimensions to customer specs. High grade walnut.

Features: Drop-out trigger assembly; ventilated flat or step top rib, ventilated, solid or no side ribs. Low-profile receiver with black finish on Standard model, antique silver on sideplate models and all engraved, gold inlaid models. Barrels, forend, trigger parts interchangeable with Perazzi. Comes with hard case, accessory tools, spares. Introduced 1989. Imported from Spain by USA Sporting, Inc.
Price: KM-4 Standard **$4,388.00**
Price: KM-4 Luxe-A (engraved scroll), Luxe-B (game scenes) . . . **$6,879.00**
Price: KM-4 Super Luxe (engraved game scene) **$7,819.00**
Price: KM-4 Extra Luxe-A (scroll engraved sideplates) **$8,792.00**
Price: KM-4 Extra Luxe-B (game scene sideplates) **$10,026.00**
Price: KM-4 Extra Gold (inlays, game scene) **$11,771.00**

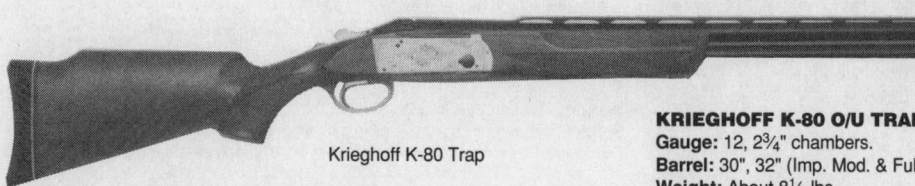

Krieghoff K-80 Trap

KRIEGHOFF K-80 SKEET SHOTGUN

Gauge: 12, 2¾" chambers.
Barrel: 28" (Skeet & Skeet, optional Tula or choke tubes).
Weight: About 7¾ lbs.
Stock: American Skeet or straight Skeet stocks, with palm-swell grips. Walnut.
Features: Satin gray receiver finish. Selective mechanical trigger adjustable for position. Choice of ventilated 8mm parallel flat rib or ventilated 8-12mm tapered flat rib. Introduced 1980. Imported from Germany by Krieghoff International, Inc.
Price: Standard, Skeet chokes **$6,450.00**
Price: As above, Tula chokes **$6,750.00**
Price: Lightweight model (weighs 7 lbs.), Standard **$6,450.00**
Price: Two-Barrel Set (tube concept), 12-ga., Standard **$11,135.00**
Price: Skeet Special (28", tapered flat rib, Skeet & Skeet choke tubes) **$7,110.00**

Krieghoff K-80 Four-Barrel Skeet Set

Similar to the Standard Skeet except comes with barrels for 12, 20, 28, 410. Comes with fitted aluminum case.
Price: Standard grade **$14,625.00**

KRIEGHOFF K-80 O/U TRAP SHOTGUN

Gauge: 12, 2¾" chambers.
Barrel: 30", 32" (Imp. Mod. & Full or choke tubes).
Weight: About 8½ lbs.
Stock: Four stock dimensions or adjustable stock available; all have palm-swell grips. Checkered European walnut.
Features: Satin nickel receiver. Selective mechanical trigger, adjustable for position. Ventilated step rib. Introduced 1980. Imported from Germany by Krieghoff International, Inc.
Price: K-80 O/U (30", 32", Imp. Mod. & Full), from **$6,895.00**
Price: K-80 Unsingle (32", 34", Full), Standard, from **$7,595.00**
Price: K-80 Combo (two-barrel set), Standard, from **$9,595.00**

Krieghoff K-80 International Skeet

Similar to the Standard Skeet except has ½" ventilated Broadway-style rib, special Tula chokes with gas release holes at muzzle. International Skeet stock. Comes in fitted aluminum case.
Price: Standard grade **$7,200.00**

Krieghoff K-80/RT Shotguns

Same as the standard K-80 shotguns except has a removable internally selective trigger mechanism. Can be considered an option on all K-80 guns of any configuration. Introduced 1990.
Price: RT (removable trigger) option on K-80 guns, add **$1,000.00**
Price: Extra pull trigger mechanisms **$1,275.00**

CAUTION: PRICES SHOWN ARE SUPPLIED BY THE MANUFACTURER OR IMPORTER. CHECK YOUR LOCAL GUNSHOP.

Krieghoff K-80 Sporting Clays

KRIEGHOFF K-80 SPORTING CLAYS O/U
Gauge: 12.
Barrel: 28" or 30" with choke tubes.
Weight: About 8 lbs.
Stock: #3 Sporting stock designed for gun-down shooting.
Features: Choice of standard or lightweight receiver with satin nickel finish and classic scroll engraving. Selective mechanical trigger adjustable for position. Choice of tapered flat or 8mm parallel flat barrel rib. Free-floating barrels. Aluminum case. Imported from Germany by Krieghoff International, Inc.
Price: Standard grade with five choke tubes $7,550.00

LANBER 82 OVER/UNDER SHOTGUN
Gauge: 12, 20, 3" chamber.
Barrel: 26" (Imp. Cyl. & Mod.), 28" (Mod. & Full).
Weight: About 7 lbs., 2 oz.
Stock: 14⅜"x1½"x2½". European walnut.
Features: Double triggers; silvered, engraved receiver. Introduced 1994. Imported from Spain by Eagle Imports, Inc.
Price: $584.95

Lanber 87 Deluxe Over/Under Shotgun
Similar to the Lanber 82 except comes with Lanberchoke choke tubes, single selective trigger, better wood. Introduced 1994. Imported from Spain by Eagle Imports, Inc.
Price: $914.95
Price: Sporting Clays (12-ga., 28", 2¾" chambers) $964.95

Laurona Super 85 MS Pigeon

LAURONA SUPER MODEL OVER/UNDERS
Gauge: 12, 20, 2¾" or 3" chambers.
Barrel: 26", 28" (Multichoke), 29" (Multichokes and Full).
Weight: About 7 lbs.
Stock: European walnut. Dimensions may vary according to model. Full pistol grip.
Features: Boxlock action, silvered with engraving. Automatic selective ejectors; choke tubes available on most models; single selective or twin single triggers; clack chrome barrels. Has 5-year warranty, including metal finish. Imported from Spain by Galaxy Imports.
Price: Model 83 MG, 12- or 20-ga. $1,215.00
Price: Model 84S Super Trap (fixed chokes) $1,340.00
Price: Model 85 Super Game, 12- or 20-ga. $1,215.00
Price: Model 85 MS Super Trap (Full/Multichoke) $1,390.00
Price: Model 85 MS Super Pigeon $1,370.00
Price: Model 85 S Super Skeet, 12-ga. $1,300.00

Laurona Silhouette 300 Trap
Same gun as the Silhouette 300 Sporting Clays except has 29" barrels, trap stock dimensions of 14⅜"x1⁷⁄₁₆"x1⅝", weighs 7 lbs., 15 oz. Available with flush or knurled Multichokes.
Price: $1,310.00

LAURONA SILHOUETTE 300 SPORTING CLAYS
Gauge: 12, 2¾" or 3" chambers.
Barrel: 28", 29" (Multichoke tubes, flush-type or knurled).
Weight: 7 lbs., 12 oz.
Stock: 14⅜"x1⅜"x2½". European walnut with full pistol grip, beavertail forend. Rubber buttpad.

Features: Selective single trigger, automatic selective ejectors. Introduced 1988. Imported from Spain by Galaxy Imports.
Price: $1,250.00
Price: Silhouette Ultra-Magnum, 3½" chambers $1,265.00

Ljutic LM-6

LJUTIC LM-6 DELUXE O/U SHOTGUN
Gauge: 12.
Barrel: 28" to 34", choked to customer specs for live birds, trap, International Trap.

Weight: To customer specs.
Stock: To customer specs. Oil finish, hand checkered.
Features: Custom-made gun. Hollow-milled rib, pull or release trigger, pushbutton opener in front of trigger guard. From Ljutic Industries.
Price: Super Deluxe LM-6 O/U $19,995.00
Price: Over/under Combo (interchangeable single barrel, two trigger guards, one for single trigger, one for doubles) $21,995.00
Price: Extra over/under barrel sets, 29"-32" $5,995.00

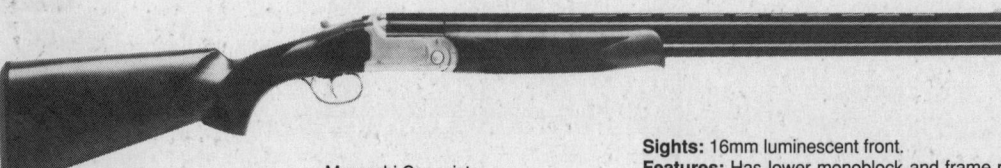

Marocchi Conquista

MAROCCHI CONQUISTA SPORTING CLAYS O/U SHOTGUNS
Gauge: 12, 2¾" chambers.
Barrel: 28", 30", 32" (Contrechoke tubes).
Weight: About 8 lbs.
Stock: 14½"-14⅞"x2³⁄₁₆"x1⁷⁄₁₆"; American walnut with checkered grip and forend; sporting clays butt pad.

Sights: 16mm luminescent front.
Features: Has lower monoblock and frame profile. Fast lock time. Ergonomically-shaped trigger is adjustable for pull length and weight. Automatic selective ejectors. Coin-finished receiver, blued barrels. Comes with five choke tubes, hard case, stock wrench. Also available as left-hand model—opening lever operates from left to right; stock has left-hand cast. Introduced 1994. Imported from Italy by Precision Sales International.
Price: Grade I, right- or left-hand $1,885.00
Price: Grade II $2,250.00
Price: Grade III, from $3,550.00

CAUTION: PRICES SHOWN ARE SUPPLIED BY THE MANUFACTURER OR IMPORTER. CHECK YOUR LOCAL GUNSHOP.

SHOTGUNS—OVER/UNDERS

Marocchi Conquista Trap Over/Under Shotgun
Similar to the Conquista Sporting Clays model except has 30" or 32" barrels choked Imp. Cyl. & Full, stock dimensions of 14½"-14⅞"x1¹¹⁄₁₆"x1⁹⁄₃₂"; weighs about 8¼ lbs. Introduced 1994. Imported from Italy by Precision Sales International.

Price: Grade I $1,885.00
Price: Grade II $2,250.00
Price: Grade III, from $3,550.00

Marocchi Conquista Skeet Over/Under Shotgun
Similar to the Conquista Sporting Clays except has 28" (Skeet & Skeet) barrels, stock dimensions of 14⅜"-14¾"x2³⁄₁₆"x1½". Weighs about 7¾ lbs. Introduced 1994. Imported from Italy by Precision Sales International.

Price: Grade I $1,885.00
Price: Grade II $2,250.00
Price: Grade III, from $3,550.00

MAROCCHI AVANZA O/U SHOTGUN
Gauge: 12 and 20, 3" chambers.
Barrel: 26" (Imp. Cyl. & Mod. or Imp. Cyl., Mod., Full Interchokes); 28" (Mod. & Full or Imp. Cyl. Mod., Full Interchokes).
Weight: 6 lbs., 6 oz. to 6 lbs., 13 oz.
Stock: 14"x2¼"x1½". Select walnut with cut checkering. Recoil pad.
Features: Single selective trigger, auto-mechanical barrel cycling, automatic selective ejectors, unbreakable firing pins. Ventilated top and middle ribs. Automatic safety. Introduced 1990. Imported from Italy by Precision Sales International.

Price: 12-ga., 26" or 28", fixed chokes $769.00
Price: As above, with Interchokes $829.00

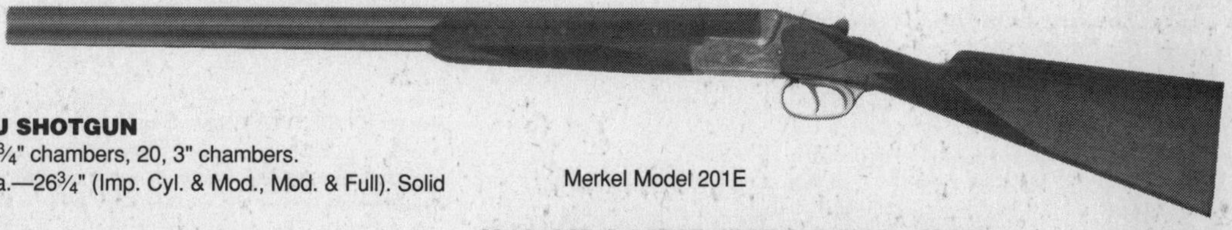

Merkel Model 201E

MERKEL MODEL 200E O/U SHOTGUN
Gauge: 12, 3" chambers, 16, 2¾" chambers, 20, 3" chambers.
Barrel: 12-, 16-ga.—28"; 20-ga.—26¾" (Imp. Cyl. & Mod., Mod. & Full). Solid rib.
Weight: About 7 lbs. (12-ga.).
Stock: Oil-finished walnut; straight English or pistol grip.
Features: Scroll engraved, color case-hardened receiver. Single selective or double triggers; ejectors. Imported from Germany by GSI.

Price: Model 200E $3,395.00
Price: Model 201E (as above except silver-grayed receiver with engraved hunting scenes) $4,195.00
Price: Model 202E (as above except has false sideplates, fine hunting scenes with Arabesque engraving) $7,995.00

Merkel Model 200E Skeet, Trap Over/Unders
Similar to the Model 200E except in 12-gauge only with 2¾" chambers, tapered ventilated rib, competition stock with full pistol grip, half-coverage Arabesque engraving on silver-grayed receiver. Single selective trigger only. Model 200ES has 26¾" (Skeet & Skeet) barrels; Model 200ET has 30" (Full & Full) barrles. Imported from Germany by GSI.

Merkel Model 203E, 303E Over/Under Shotguns
Similar to the Model 200E except with Holland & Holland-style sidelocks, both quick-detachable: Model 203E with cranked screw, 303E with integral retracting hook. Model 203E has coil spring ejectors; 303E H&H ejectors. Both have silver-grayed receiver with English-style Arabesque engraving—large scrolls on 203E, medium on 303E. Imported from Germany by GSI.

Price: Model 203E $9,695.00
Price: Model 303E $21,295.00

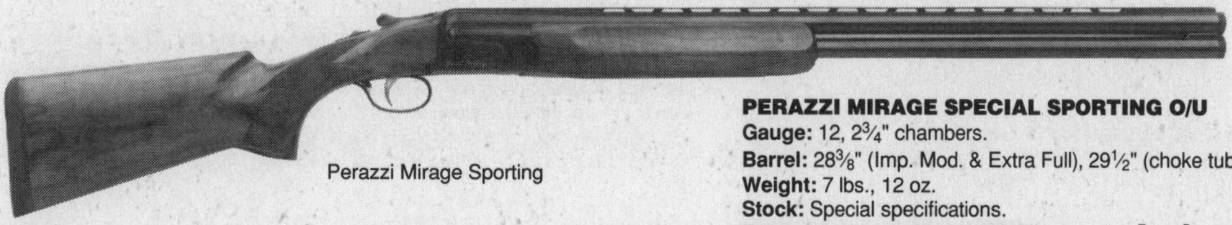

Price: Model 200ES $4,995.00
Price: Model 200ET $4,795.00
Price: Model 201ES (full-coverage engraving) $5,595.00
Price: Model 201ET (full-coverage engraving) $5,395.00
Price: Model 203ES (sidelock action, Skeet) $9,795.00
Price: Model 203ET (sidelock action, Trap) $9,795.00

Perazzi Mirage Sporting

PERAZZI MIRAGE SPECIAL SPORTING O/U
Gauge: 12, 2¾" chambers.
Barrel: 28⅜" (Imp. Mod. & Extra Full), 29½" (choke tubes).
Weight: 7 lbs., 12 oz.
Stock: Special specifications.
Features: Has single selective trigger; flat ⁷⁄₁₆"x⁵⁄₁₆" vent. rib. Many options available. Imported from Italy by Perazzi U.S.A., Inc.
Price: $8,500.00

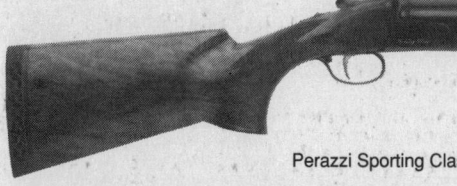

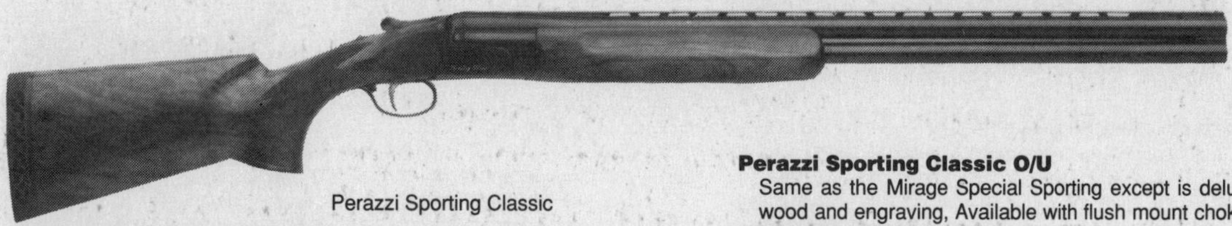

Perazzi Sporting Classic

Perazzi Sporting Classic O/U
Same as the Mirage Special Sporting except is deluxe version with select wood and engraving, Available with flush mount choke tubes, 29.5" barrels. Introduced 1993.
Price: From $9,500.00

Perazzi Mirage Special Four-Gauge Skeet
Similar to the Mirage Sporting model except has Skeet dimensions, interchangeable, adjustable four-position trigger assembly. Comes with four barrel sets in 12, 20, 28, 410, flat ⁵⁄₁₆"x⁵⁄₁₆" rib.
Price: From $18,200.00

Perazzi MX8/20 Over/Under Shotgun
Similar to the MX8 except has smaller frame and has a removable trigger mechanism. Available in trap, Skeet, sporting or game models with fixed chokes or choke tubes. Stock is made to customer specifications. Introduced 1993.
Price: From $7,550.00

Perazzi Mirage Special Skeet Over/Under
Similar to the MX8 Skeet except has adjustable four-position trigger, Skeet stock dimensions.
Price: $8,000.00

PERAZZI MX8/MX8 SPECIAL TRAP, SKEET
Gauge: 12, 2¾" chambers.
Barrel: Trap—29½" (Imp. Mod. & Extra Full), 31½" (Full & Extra Full). Choke tubes optional. Skeet—27⅝" (Skeet & Skeet).
Weight: About 8½ lbs. (Trap); 7 lbs., 15 oz. (Skeet).
Stock: Interchangeable and custom made to customer specs.
Features: Has detachable and interchangeable trigger group with flat V springs. Flat ⁷⁄₁₆" ventilated rib. Many options available. Imported from Italy by Perazzi U.S.A., Inc.

Price: From $7,550.00
Price: MX8 Special (adj. four-position trigger), from $8,000.00
Price: MX8 Special Single (32" or 34" single barrel, step rib), from $7,600.00
Price: MX8 Special Combo (o/u and single barrel sets), from . . $10,550.00

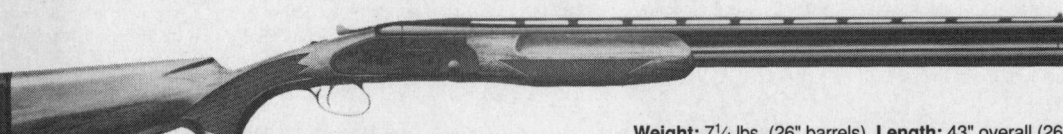

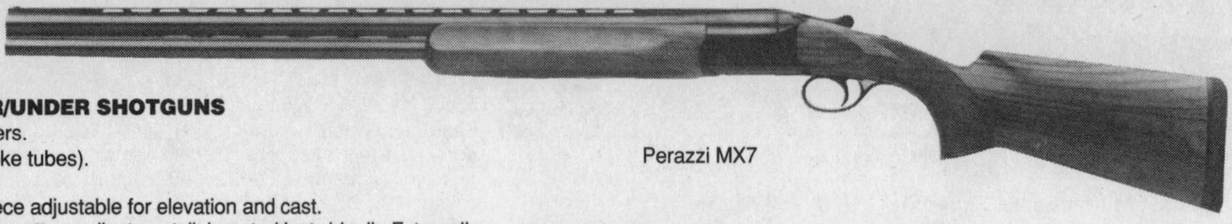

Perazzi MX7

PERAZZI MX9 OVER/UNDER SHOTGUNS

Gauge: 12, 2¾" chambers.
Barrel: 29.5", 31.5" (choke tubes).
Weight: NA.
Stock: Walnut; cheekpiece adjustable for elevation and cast.
Features: Comes with six pattern adjustment rib inserts. Vent side rib. Externally selective trigger. Available in single barrel, combo, over/under trap, Skeet, pigeon and sporting models. Introduced 1993. Imported from Italy by Perazzi U.S.A.
Price: From **$9,900.00**
Price: MX10 (fixed chokes, different rib), from **$10,300.00**

PERAZZI MX12 HUNTING OVER/UNDER

Gauge: 12, 2¾" chambers.
Barrel: 26", 27⅝", 28⅜", 29½" (Mod. & Full); choke tubes available in 27⅝", 29½" only (MX12C).
Weight: 7 lbs., 4 oz.
Stock: To customer specs; Interchangeable.
Features: Single selective trigger; coil springs used in action; schnabel forend tip. Imported from Italy by Perazzi U.S.A., Inc.
Price: From **$7,550.00**
Price: MX12C (with choke tubes), from **$8,050.00**

PERAZZI MX28, MX410 GAME O/U SHOTGUNS

Gauge: 28, 2¾" chambers, 410, 3" chambers.
Barrel: 26" (Imp. Cyl. & Full).
Weight: NA.
Stock: To customer specifications.
Features: Made on scaled-down frames proportioned to the gauge. Introduced 1993. Imported from Italy by Perazzi U.S.A.
Price: From **$15,100.00**

PERAZZI MX7 OVER/UNDER SHOTGUNS

Gauge: 12, 2¾" chambers.
Barrel: 29.5", 31.5", fixed or choke tubes.
Weight: NA.
Stock: To customer specifications.
Features: Has fixed coil spring trigger mechanism; selective firing order. Available in combo or over/under configurations. Introduced 1992. Imported from Italy by Perazzi U.S.A.
Price: From **$7,450.00**

Perazzi MX20 Hunting Over/Under

Similar to the MX12 except 20-ga. frame size. Available in 20, 28, 410 with 2¾" or 3" chambers. 26" standard, and choked Mod. & Full. Weight is 6 lbs., 6 oz.
Price: From **$7,550.00**
Price: MX20C (as above, 20-ga. only, choke tubes), from **$8,050.00**

PIOTTI BOSS OVER/UNDER SHOTGUN

Gauge: 12, 20.
Barrel: 25" to 32", chokes as specified.
Weight: 6.5 to 8 lbs.
Stock: Dimensions to customer specs. Best quality figured walnut.
Features: Essentially a custom-made gun with many options. Introduced 1993. Imported from Italy by Wm. Larkin Moore.
Price: From **$31,200.00**

Remington Peerless

REMINGTON PEERLESS OVER/UNDER SHOTGUN

Gauge: 12, 3" chambers.
Barrel: 26", 28", 30" (Imp. Cyl., Mod., Full Rem Chokes).

Weight: 7¼ lbs. (26" barrels). **Length:** 43" overall (26" barrels).
Stock: 14³⁄₁₆"x1½"x2¼". American walnut with Imron gloss finish, cut-checkered grip and forend. Black, ventilated recoil pad.
Features: Boxlock action with removable sideplates. Gold-plated, single selective trigger, automatic safety, automatic ejectors. Fast lock time. Mid-rib bead, Bradley-type front. Polished blue finish with light scrollwork on sideplates, Remington logo on bottom of receiver. Introduced 1993.
Price: **$1,172.00**

RUGER RED LABEL O/U SHOTGUN

Gauge: 12 and 20, 3" chambers.
Barrel: 26", 28" (Skeet, Imp. Cyl., Full, Extra-Full, Mod. screw-in choke tubes). Proved for steel shot.
Weight: About 7 lbs. (20-ga.); 7½ lbs. (12-ga.). **Length:** 43" overall (26" barrels).
Stock: 14"x1½"x2½". Straight grain American walnut. Checkered pistol grip and forend, rubber butt pad.
Features: Choice of blue or stainless receiver. Single selective mechanical trigger, selective automatic ejectors; serrated free-floating vent. rib. Comes with two Skeet, one Imp. Cyl., one Mod., one Full choke tube and wrench; Extra-Full tube available at extra cost. Made in U.S. by Sturm, Ruger & Co.
Price: Red Label with pistol grip stock **$1,157.50**
Price: English Field with straight-grip stock **$1,157.50**

Ruger English Field

Ruger 20-Gauge Sporting Clays O/U Shotgun

Similar to the 12-gauge Sporting Clays except chambered for 3" 20-gauge shells; 30" barrels back-bored to .631"-.635". No barrel side spacers. Comes with four special longer, 2", interchangeable, screw-in choke tubes: two Skeet, one Mod., one Imp. Cyl.; Full and Extra-Full tubes available. Introduced 1994.
Price: **$1,285.00**

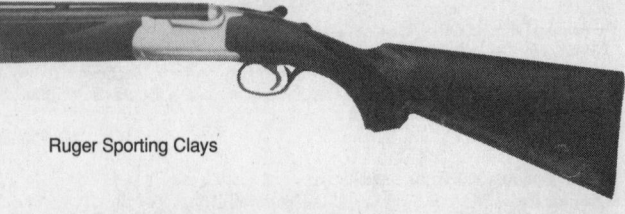

Ruger Sporting Clays

Ruger Sporting Clays O/U Shotgun

Similar to the Red Label except 12-gauge only, 30" barrels back-bored to .744" diameter with stainless steel choke tubes. Weight is 7.75 lbs., overall length 47". Stock dimensions of 14⅛"x1½"x2½". Free-floating serrated vent. rib with brass front and mid-rib beads. No barrel side spacers. Comes with two Skeet, one Imp. Cyl., one Mod. choke tubes. Full and Extra-Full available at extra cost. Introduced 1992.
Price: **$1,285.00**

CAUTION: PRICES SHOWN ARE SUPPLIED BY THE MANUFACTURER OR IMPORTER. CHECK YOUR LOCAL GUNSHOP.

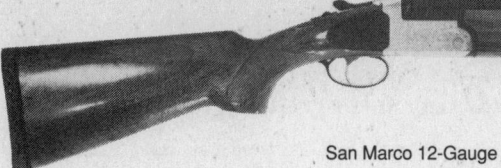

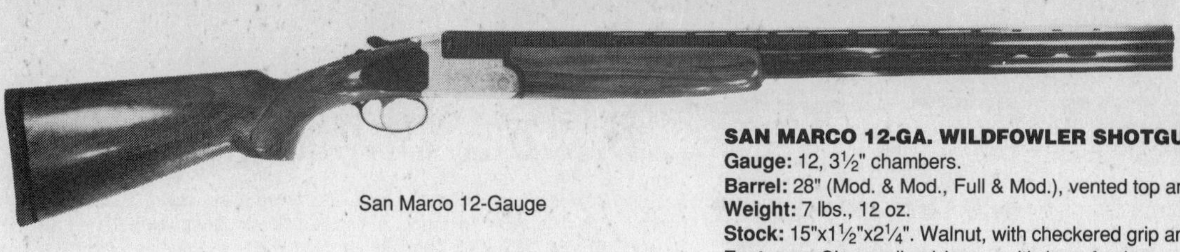

San Marco 12-Gauge

SAN MARCO 10-GAUGE O/U SHOTGUN
Gauge: 10, 3½" chambers.
Barrel: 28" (Mod. & Mod.), 32" (Mod. & Full). Chrome lined.
Weight: 9 to 9½ lbs.
Stock: 15"x1⅜"x2⅛". Walnut.
Features: Solid ⅜" barrel rib. Long forcing cones. Double triggers, extractors; Deluxe grade has automatic ejectors. Engraved receiver with game scenes, matte finish. Waterproof finish on wood. Introduced 1990. Imported from Italy by Cape Outfitters.
Price: Standard grade **$795.00**
Price: Deluxe grade **$895.00**

SKB Model 685 Over/Under Shotgun
Similar to the Model 585 Deluxe except has gold-plated trigger, semi-fancy American walnut stock, jeweled barrel block and fine engraving in silvered receiver, top lever, and trigger guard. Gold inlay on receiver, better walnut, ventilated side ribs. All 12-gauge barrels are back-bored, have lengthened forcing cones and longer choke tube system. Sporting Clays models in 12-gauge with 28" or 30" barrels available with optional ⅜" step-up target-style rib, with matte finish, nickel center bead, white front bead.
Price: Field **$1,649.00**
Price: Two-barrel Field Set (12 & 20, 20 & 28 or 28 & 410) **$2,395.00**
Price: Trap, Skeet **$1,695.00**
Price: Two-barrel trap combo **$2,349.00**
Price: Sporting Clays **$2,495.00**
Price: Sporting Clays two-barrel set **$2,495.00**
Price: Skeet Set (20, 28, 410) **$3,449.00**

SKB Model 885 Over/Under Field, Trap, Skeet, Sporting Clays
Similar to the Model 685 except has engraved sideplates, top lever and trigger guard, select American walnut stock. All 12-gauge barrels are back-bored, have lengthened forcing cones and longer choke tube system. Sporting Clays models in 12-gauge with 28", 30" barrels available with optional ⅜" step-up target-style rib, matte finish, nickel center bead, white front bead.
Price: Field, 12, 20 . . . . **$2,049.00**
Price: Field, 28, 410 . . . . **$2,095.00**
Price: Skeet Set (20, 28, 410) **$3,895.00**
Price: Trap **$2,095.00**
Price: Trap Combo **$2,995.00**
Price: Field Set, 12, 20 . . . . **$3,049.00**
Price: Field Set, 20 & 28, 28 & 410 . . . . **$3,095.00**
Price: Sporting Clays **$2,149.00**

SAN MARCO 12-GA. WILDFOWLER SHOTGUN
Gauge: 12, 3½" chambers.
Barrel: 28" (Mod. & Mod., Full & Mod.), vented top and middle ribs.
Weight: 7 lbs., 12 oz.
Stock: 15"x1½"x2¼". Walnut, with checkered grip and forend.
Features: Chrome-lined bores with long forcing cones; single non-selective trigger; extractors on Standard, automatic ejectors on Deluxe; silvered, engraved action. Waterproof wood finish. Introduced 1990. Imported from Italy by Cape Outfitters.
Price: Standard **$595.00**
Price: Deluxe **$695.00**

San Marco Field Special O/U Shotgun
Similar to the 12-ga. Wildfowler except in 12-, 20- and 28-gauge with 3" chambers, 26" (Imp. Cyl. & Mod.) or 28" (Full & Mod.) barrels. Stock dimensions of 14¼"x1½"x1½". Weight of 5½ to 6 lbs. Engraved, silvered receiver, vented top and middle ribs, single trigger. Introduced 1990. Imported from Italy by Cape Outfitters.
Price: **$695.00**

SKB MODEL 585 OVER/UNDER SHOTGUN
Gauge: 12, or 3"; 20, 3"; 28, 2¾"; 410, 3".
Barrel: 12-ga.—26", 28", 30", 32", 34" (Inter-Choke tube); 20-ga.—26", 28" (Inter-Choke tube); 28—26", 28" (Inter-Choke tube); 410—26", 28" (Imp. Cyl. & Mod., Mod. & Full). Ventilated side ribs.
Weight: 6.6 to 8.5 lbs. **Length:** 43" to 51⅜" overall.
Stock: 14⅛"x1½"x2³⁄₁₆". Hand checkered walnut with high-gloss finish. Target stocks available in standard and Monte Carlo.
Sights: Metal bead front (field), target style on Skeet, trap, Sporting Clays.
Features: Boxlock action; silver nitride finish with Field or Target pattern engraving; manual safety, automatic ejectors, single selective trigger. All 12-gauge barrels are back-bored, have lengthened forcing cones and longer choke tube system. Sporting Clays models in 12-gauge with 28" or 30" barrels available with optional ⅜" step-up target-style rib, matte finish, nickel center bead, white front bead. Introduced 1992. Imported from Japan by G.U., Inc.
Price: Field **$1,149.00**
Price: Two-barrel Field Set, 12 & 20 . . . . **$1,849.00**
Price: Two-barrel Field Set, 20 & 28 or 28 & 410) . . . **$1,895.00**
Price: Trap, Skeet **$1,195.00**
Price: Two-barrel trap combo **$1,849.00**
Price: Sporting Clays model . . . . **$1,249.00-$1,295.00**
Price: Skeet Set (20, 28, 410) **$2,849.00**

SKB Model 585 Youth Model Shotgun
Similar to the Field Model 585 except has 13½" length of pull. Available in 12-gauge with 26" or 28", or 20-gauge with 26" barrels. The 12-gauge has .755" bores, lengthened forcing cones and competition series choke tubes. Introduced 1994. Imported from Japan by G.U., Inc.
Price: **$1,149.00**

Tikka 512S Sporting Clays

STOEGER/IGA CONDOR I OVER/UNDER SHOTGUN
Gauge: 12, 20, 3" chambers.
Barrel: 26" (Full & Full, Imp. Cyl. & Mod.), 28" (Mod. & Full), or with choke tubes.
Weight: 6¾ to 7 lbs.
Stock: 14½"x1½"x2½". Oil-finished hardwood with checkered pistol grip and forend.
Features: Manual safety, single trigger, extractors only, ventilated top rib. Introduced 1983. Imported from Brazil by Stoeger Industries.
Price: **$558.00**
Price: With choke tubes **$600.00**
Price: Condor II (sames as Condor I except has double triggers, moulded buttplate) **$458.00**
Price: Condor Supreme (same as Condor I with single trigger, choke tubes, but with auto. ejectors), 12- or 20-ga., 26", 28" . . . **$689.00**

> Consult our Directory pages for the location of firms mentioned.

TIKKA MODEL 512S FIELD GRADE OVER/UNDER
Gauge: 12, 20, 3" chambers.
Barrel: 26", 28", with stainless steel screw-in chokes (Imp. Cyl, Mod., Imp. Mod., Full); 20-ga.—28" only.
Weight: About 7¼ lbs.
Stock: American walnut. Standard dimensions—13⁹⁄₁₀"x1½"x2⅖". Checkered p.g. and forend.
Features: Free interchangeability of barrels, stocks and forends into double rifle model, combination gun, etc. Barrel selector in trigger; auto. top tang safety; barrel cocking indicators. Introduced 1980. Imported from Italy by Stoeger.
Price: Model 512S (ejectors), Standard Grade **$1,225.00**
Price: Model 512S Premier Grade **$1,275.00**
Price: Model 512S Sporting Clays, 12-ga., 28", choke tubes . . . **$1,315.00**

CAUTION: PRICES SHOWN ARE SUPPLIED BY THE MANUFACTURER OR IMPORTER. CHECK YOUR LOCAL GUNSHOP.

49th EDITION, 1995 **399**

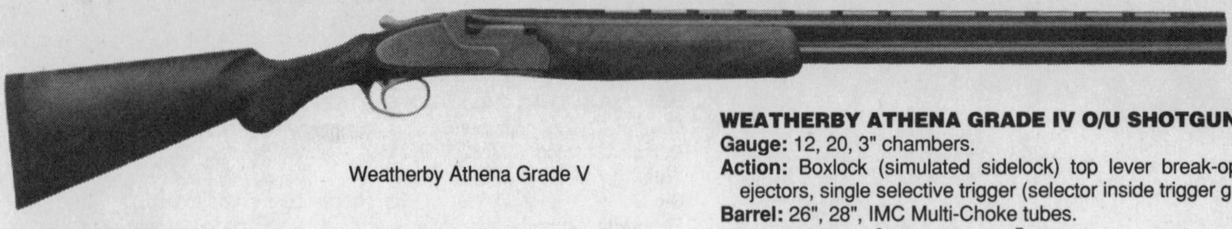

Weatherby Athena Grade V

Weatherby Athena Grade V Classic Field O/U

Similar to the Athena Grade IV except has rounded pistol grip, slender forend, oil-finished Claro walnut stock with fine-line checkering, Old English recoil pad. Sideplate receiver has rose and scroll engraving. Available in 12-gauge, 26", 28", 30", 20-gauge, 26", 28", all with 3" chambers. Introduced 1993.
Price: **$2,575.00**

WEATHERBY ORION O/U SHOTGUNS

Gauge: 12, 20, 3" chambers.
Barrel: 12-gauge—26", 28", 30"; 20-gauge— 26", 30"; IMC Multi-Choke tubes.
Weight: 6½ to 9 lbs.
Stock: American walnut, checkered grip and forend. Rubber recoil pad. Dimensions for Field and Skeet models, 14¼"x1½"x2½".
Features: Selective automatic ejectors, single selective mechanical trigger. Top tang safety, Greener cross bolt. Orion I has plain blued receiver, no engraving; Orion III has silver-gray receiver with engraving. Imported from Japan by Weatherby.
Price: Orion I, Field, 12, IMC, 26", 28", 30" **$1,165.00**
Price: Orion I, Field, 20, IMC, 26", 28" **$1,165.00**
Price: Orion III, Field, 12, IMC, 26", 28", 30" **$1,470.00**
Price: Orion III, Field, 20, IMC, 26", 28" **$1,470.00**

WEATHERBY ATHENA GRADE IV O/U SHOTGUNS

Gauge: 12, 20, 3" chambers.
Action: Boxlock (simulated sidelock) top lever break-open. Selective auto ejectors, single selective trigger (selector inside trigger guard).
Barrel: 26", 28", IMC Multi-Choke tubes.
Weight: 12-ga., 7⅜ lbs.; 20-ga. 6⅞ lbs.
Stock: American walnut, checkered p.g. and forend (14¼"x1½"x2½").
Features: Mechanically operated trigger. Top tang safety, Greener cross bolt, fully engraved receiver, recoil pad installed. IMC models furnished with three interchangeable flush-fitting choke tubes. Imported from Japan by Weatherby. Introduced 1982.
Price: 12-ga., IMC, 26", 28" **$2,200.00**
Price: 20-ga., IMC, 26", 28" **$2,200.00**

Weatherby Orion II, III Classic Field O/Us

Similar to the Orion II, Orion III except with rounded pistol grip, slender forend, oil-finished Claro walnut stock with fine-line checkering, Old English recoil pad. Sideplate receiver has rose and scroll engraving. Available in 12-gauge, 26", 28", 30" (IMC tubes), 20-gauge, 26", 28" (IMC tubes), 28-gauge, 26" (IMC tubes), 3" chambers. Introduced 1993.
Price: Orion II Classic Field **$1,235.00**
Price: Orion III Classic Field (12 and 20 only) **$1,470.00**

Weatherby Orion II Sporting Clays O/U

Similar to the Orion II Field except in 12-gauge only with 2¾" chambers, 28", 30" barrels with Imp. Cyl., Mod., Full chokes. Stock dimensions are 14¼"x1½"x2¼"; weight 7.5 to 8 lbs. Matte finish, competition center vent. rib, mid-barrel and enlarged front beads. Rounded recoil pad. Receiver finished in silver nitride with acid-etched, gold-plate clay pigeon monogram. Barrels have lengthened forcing cones. Introduced 1992.
Price: **$1,335.00**

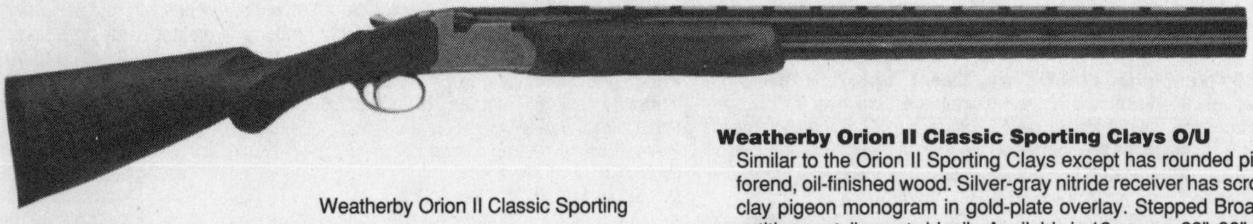

Weatherby Orion II Classic Sporting

Weatherby Orion II Classic Sporting Clays O/U

Similar to the Orion II Sporting Clays except has rounded pistol grip, slender forend, oil-finished wood. Silver-gray nitride receiver has scroll engraving with clay pigeon monogram in gold-plate overlay. Stepped Broadway-style competition vent rib, vent side rib. Available in 12-gauge, 28", 30" with choke tubes. Introduced 1993.
Price: **$1,335.00**

Winchester Model 1001 Field

WINCHESTER MODEL 1001 O/U SHOTGUN

Gauge: 12, 3" chambers.
Barrel: 28" (Imp. Cyl., Mod., Imp. Mod., Skeet WinPlus choke tubes).
Weight: 7 lbs. **Length:** 45" overall.
Stock: 14¼"x1½"x2". Select walnut with checkered grip and forend.
Features: Single selective inertia trigger; automatic ejectors; wide vent rib; back-bored barrels; matte-finished receiver top; receiver is blued and has scroll engraving. Introduced 1993. From U.S. Repeating Arms Co.
Price: **$1,099.00**

Winchester Model 1001 Sporting Clays

Winchester Model 1001 Sporting Clays O/U

Similar to the Field 1001 except has silver nitrate-finished receiver with special engraving incorporating a flying target, fuller pistol grip and radiused recoil pad. Ventilated rib is 10mm wide with mid-rib bead, white front bead. Available with 28" or 30" barrels with four WinPlus choke tubes. Stock dimensions are 14⅜"x1⅜"x2⅛"; weight 7¾ lbs. Introduced 1993.
Price: **$1,253.00**

PIETRO ZANOLETTI MODEL 2000 FIELD O/U

Gauge: 12 only.
Barrel: 28" (Mod. & Full).
Weight: 7 lbs.
Stock: European walnut, checkered grip and forend.
Sights: Gold bead front.
Features: Boxlock action with auto ejectors, double triggers; engraved receiver. Introduced 1984. Imported from Italy by Mandall Shooting Supplies.
Price: **$895.00**

CAUTION: PRICES SHOWN ARE SUPPLIED BY THE MANUFACTURER OR IMPORTER. CHECK YOUR LOCAL GUNSHOP.

Variety of models for utility and sporting use, including some competitive shooting.

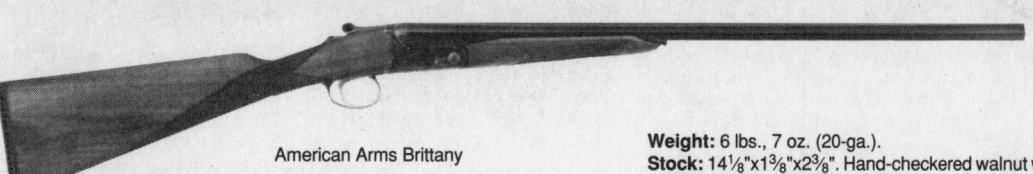

American Arms Brittany

AMERICAN ARMS BRITTANY SHOTGUN
Gauge: 12, 20, 3" chambers.
Barrel: 12-ga.—27"; 20-ga.—25" (Imp. Cyl., Mod., Full choke tubes).

Weight: 6 lbs., 7 oz. (20-ga.).
Stock: 14⅛"x1⅜"x2⅜". Hand-checkered walnut with oil finish, straight English-style with semi-beavertail forend.
Features: Boxlock action with case-color finish, engraving; single selective trigger, automatic selective ejectors; rubber recoil pad. Introduced 1989. Imported from Spain by American Arms, Inc.
Price: $809.00

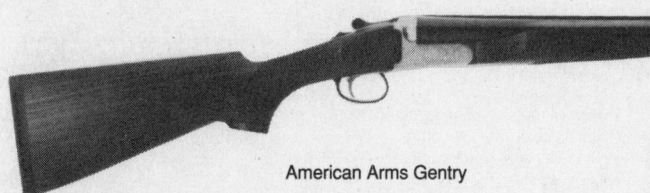

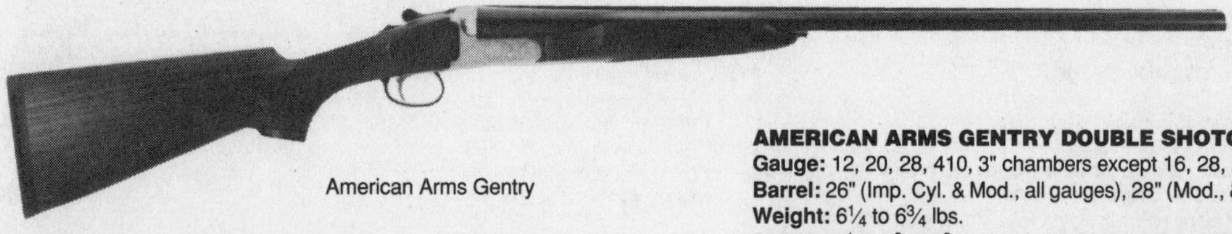

American Arms Gentry

American Arms Derby Side-by-Side
Has sidelock action with English-style engraving on the sideplates. Straight-grip, hand-checkered walnut stock with splinter forend, hand-rubbed oil finish. Single non-selective trigger, automatic selective ejectors. Same chokes, rib, barrel lengths as the Gentry. Has 5-year warranty. From American Arms, Inc.
Price: 12- or 20-ga. $1,039.00

American Arms TS/SS 12 Side-by-Side
Similar to the WS/SS 10 except in 12-ga. with 3½" chambers, 26" barrels with Imp. Cyl., Mod., Full choke tubes, single selective trigger, extractors. Comes with camouflage sling, swivels, 5-year warranty. From American Arms, Inc.
Price: $669.00

AMERICAN ARMS GENTRY DOUBLE SHOTGUN
Gauge: 12, 20, 28, 410, 3" chambers except 16, 28, 2¾".
Barrel: 26" (Imp. Cyl. & Mod., all gauges), 28" (Mod., & Full, 12 and 20 gauges).
Weight: 6¼ to 6¾ lbs.
Stock: 14⅛"x1⅜"x2⅜". Hand-checkered walnut with semi-gloss finish.
Sights: Metal bead front.
Features: Boxlock action with English-style scroll engraving, color case-hardened finish. Double triggers, extractors. Independent floating firing pins. Manual safety. Five-year warranty. Introduced 1987. Imported from Spain by American Arms, Inc.
Price: 12 or 20 . . . . $659.00
Price: 28 or 410 . . . . $689.00

AMERICAN ARMS TS/SS 10
Gauge: 10, 3½" chambers.
Barrel: 26", choke tubes.
Weight: 10 lbs., 13 oz.
Stock: 14⁵⁄₁₆"x1⅜"x2⅜". Hand-checkered walnut with beavertail forend, full pistol grip, dull finish, rubber recoil pad.
Features: Boxlock action with double triggers and extractors. All metal has Parkerized finish. Comes with camouflaged sling, sling swivels, 5-year warranty. Introduced 1987. Imported from Spain by American Arms, Inc.
Price: $669.00

Consult our Directory pages for the location of firms mentioned.

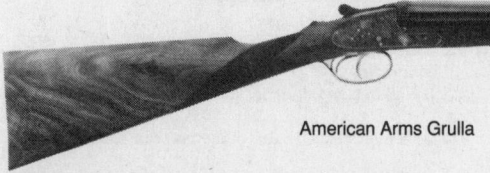

American Arms Grulla

ARMSPORT 1050 SERIES DOUBLE SHOTGUNS
Gauge: 12, 20, 410, 28, 3" chambers.
Barrel: 12-ga.—28" (Mod. & Full); 20-ga.—26" (Imp. & Mod.); 410—26" (Full & Full); 28-ga.—26" (Mod. & Full).
Weight: About 6¾ lbs.
Stock: European walnut.
Features: Chrome-lined barrels. Boxlock action with engraving. Imported from Italy by Armsport.
Price: 12, 20 . . . . $785.00
Price: 28, 410 . . . . $860.00

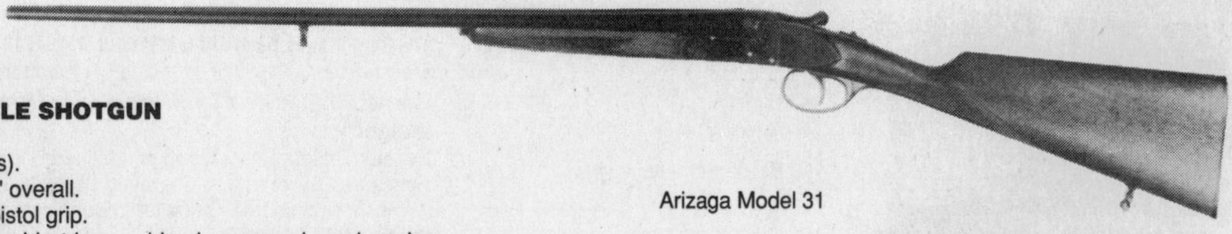

AMERICAN ARMS GRULLA #2 DOUBLE SHOTGUN
Gauge: 12, 20, 28, 410.
Barrel: 12-ga.—28" (Mod. & Full); 26" (Imp. Cyl. & Mod.), all gauges.
Weight: 5 lbs., 13 oz. to 6 lbs., 4 oz.
Stock: Select walnut with straight English grip, splinter forend; hand-rubbed oil finish; checkered grip, forend, butt.
Features: True sidelock action with double triggers, detachable locks, automatic selective ejectors, cocking indicators, gas escape valves. Color case-hardened receiver with scroll engraving. English-style concave rib. Introduced 1989. Imported from Spain by American Arms, Inc.
Price: 12, 20, 28, 410 . . . . $3,099.00
Price: Two-barrel sets $4,219.00

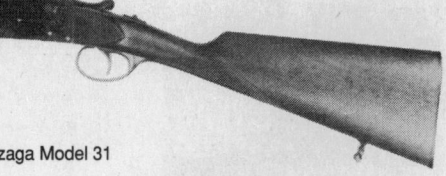

Arizaga Model 31

ARIZAGA MODEL 31 DOUBLE SHOTGUN
Gauge: 12, 16, 20, 28, 410.
Barrel: 26", 28" (standard chokes).
Weight: 6 lbs., 9 oz. **Length:** 45" overall.
Stock: Straight English style or pistol grip.
Features: Boxlock action with double triggers; blued, engraved receiver. Imported by Mandall Shooting Supplies.
Price: $550.00

CAUTION: PRICES SHOWN ARE SUPPLIED BY THE MANUFACTURER OR IMPORTER. CHECK YOUR LOCAL GUNSHOP.

49th EDITION, 1995 **401**

SHOTGUNS—SIDE BY SIDES

ARRIETA SIDELOCK DOUBLE SHOTGUNS
Gauge: 12, 16, 20, 28, 410.
Barrel: Length and chokes to customer specs.
Weight: To customer specs.
Stock: 14½"x1½"x2½" (standard dimensions), or to customer specs. Straight English with checkered butt (standard), or pistol grip. Select European walnut with oil finish.
Features: Essentially a custom gun with myriad options. Holland & Holland-pattern hand-detachable sidelocks, selective automatic ejectors, double triggers (hinged front) standard. Some have self-opening action. Finish and engraving to customer specs. Imported from Spain by Wingshooting Adventures.
Price: Model 557, auto ejectors, from $2,750.00
Price: Model 570, auto ejectors, from $3,380.00

Price: Model 578, auto ejectors, from $3,740.00
Price: Model 600 Imperial, self-opening, from $4,990.00
Price: Model 601 Imperial Tiro, self-opening, from $5,750.00
Price: Model 801, from $7,950.00
Price: Model 802, from $7,950.00
Price: Model 803, from $5,850.00
Price: Model 871, auto ejectors, from $4,290.00
Price: Model 872, self-opening, from $9,790.00
Price: Model 873, self-opening, from $6,850.00
Price: Model 874, self-opening, from $7,950.00
Price: Model 875, self-opening, from $12,950.00

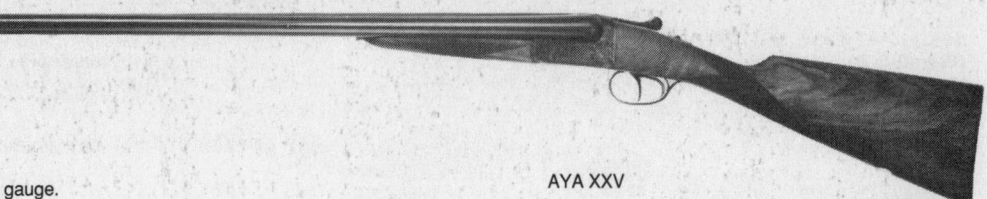

AYA XXV

AYA BOXLOCK SHOTGUNS
Gauge: 12, 16, 20, 28, 410.
Barrel: 26", 27", 28", depending upon gauge.
Weight: 5 to 7 lbs.
Stock: European walnut.
Features: Anson & Deeley system with double locking lugs; chopper lump barrels; bushed firing pins; automatic safety and ejectors; articulated front trigger. Imported by Armes de Chasse.

Price: Model 931, self-opening, from $14,500.00
Price: Model XXV, 12 or 20 . . . . $3,000.00
Price: Model 4 Deluxe, 12, 16, 20, 28, 410 . . . . $3,000.00
Price: Model 4, 12, 16, 20, 28, 410 . . . . $1,700.00

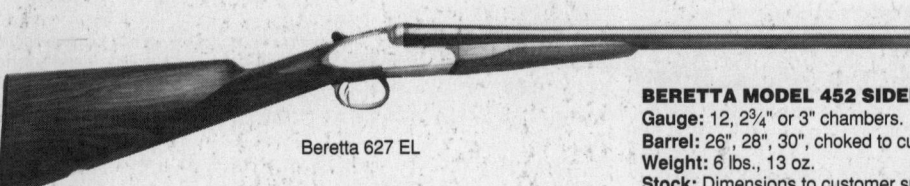

AYA Model 2

AYA SIDELOCK DOUBLE SHOTGUNS
Gauge: 12, 16, 20, 28, 410.
Barrel: 26", 27", 28", 29", depending upon gauge.
Weight: NA.
Stock: Figured European walnut; cut checkering; oil finish.
Features: Sidelock actions with double triggers (articulated front), automatic safety, automatic ejectors, cocking indicators, bushed firing pins, replaceable hinge pins, chopper lump barrels. Many options available. Imported by Armes de Chasse.
Price: Model 1, 12 or 20, exhibition-quality wood $6,000.00
Price: Model 2, 12, 16, 20, 28, 410 . . . . $3,500.00
Price: Model 53, 12, 16, 20 . . . . $5,000.00
Price: Model 56, 12 only $8,000.00
Price: Model XXV, 12 or 20, Churchill-type rib $4,000.00

BAIKAL IJ-43 DOUBLE SHOTGUN
Gauge: 12, 2¾" chambers.
Barrel: 20" (Cyl. & Cyl.), 28" (Mod. & Full).
Weight: About 6.75 lbs.
Stock: Checkered walnut.
Features: Double triggers; extractors; blued, engraved receiver. Introduced 1994. Imported from Russia by K.B.I., Inc.
Price: 28" $349.00
Price: 20" $369.00

Beretta 627 EL

BERETTA MODEL 452 SIDELOCK SHOTGUN
Gauge: 12, 2¾" or 3" chambers.
Barrel: 26", 28", 30", choked to customer specs.
Weight: 6 lbs., 13 oz.
Stock: Dimensions to customer specs. Highly figured walnut; Model 452 EELL has walnut briar.
Features: Full sidelock action with English-type double bolting; automatic selective ejectors, manual safety; double triggers, single or single non-selective trigger on request. Essentially custom made to specifications. Model 452 is coin finished without engraving; 452 EELL is fully engraved. Imported from Italy by Beretta U.S.A.
Price: 452 . . . . $23,500.00
Price: 452 EELL $33,600.00

BERETTA SIDE-BY-SIDE FIELD SHOTGUNS
Gauge: 12, 3" chambers.
Barrel: 26" and 28" (Mobilchoke tubes).
Stock: Close-grained American walnut.
Features: Front and center beads on a raised ventilated rib. Comes with case. Imported from Italy by Beretta U.S.A.
Price: 627 EL (gold inlays, sideplates) $3,270.00
Price: 627 EELL (engraved sideplates, pistol grip or straight English stock) $5,405.00

Bernardelli Hemingway

BERNARDELLI HEMINGWAY LIGHTWEIGHT DOUBLES
Gauge: 12, 20, 2¾" or 3", 16, 2¾" chambers.
Barrel: 23½" to 28" (Cyl. & Imp. Cyl. to Mod. & Full).
Weight: 6¼ lbs.
Stock: Straight English grip of checkered European walnut.
Features: Silvered and engraved boxlock action. Folding front trigger on double-trigger models. Ejectors. Imported from Italy by Armsport.
Price: 12 or 20 . . . . $1,750.00
Price: With single trigger $1,800.00
Price: Deluxe, double trigger $1,900.00
Price: As above, single trigger $2,000.00

CAUTION: PRICES SHOWN ARE SUPPLIED BY THE MANUFACTURER OR IMPORTER. CHECK YOUR LOCAL GUNSHOP.

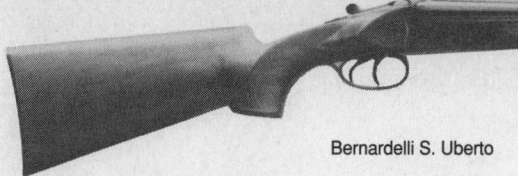

Bernardelli S. Uberto

Bernardelli Series Roma Shotguns

Similar to the Series S. Uberto models except with dummy sideplates to simulate sidelock action. In 12-, 16-, 20-, 28-gauge, 25½", 26¾", 28", 29" barrels. Straight English or pistol grip stock. Chrome-lined barrels, boxlock action, double triggers, ejectors, automatic safety. Checkered butt. Special choke combinations, barrel lengths available. Imported from Italy by Armsport.

Price: Roma 3, extractors, about **$1,470.00**
Price: Roma 4, about **$1,800.00**
Price: Roma 6, about **$1,970.00**
Price: Roma 7M, ejectors, about **$2,750.00**
Price: Roma 8M, ejectors, about **$3,250.00**
Price: Roma 9M, ejectors, about **$3,850.00**
Price: Las Palomas, 12, 20, about **$3,350.00**

AUGUSTE FRANCOTTE BOXLOCK SHOTGUN

Gauge: 12, 16, 20, 28 and 410-bore, 2¾" or 3" chambers.
Barrel: 26" to 29", chokes to customer specs.
Weight: NA. **Length:** NA.
Stock: Deluxe European walnut to customer specs. Straight or pistol grip; checkered butt; oil finish; splinter or beavertail forend.
Sights: Bead front.
Features: Anson & Deeley boxlock action with double locks, double triggers (front hinged), manual or automatic safety, Holland & Holland ejectors. English scroll engraving, coin finish or color case-hardening. Custom made to customer's specs. Many options available. Imported from Belgium by Armes de Chasse.
Price: From about . . . . **$10,000.00 to $20,000.00**

BERNARDELLI SERIES S. UBERTO DOUBLES

Gauge: 12, 20, 28, 2¾" or 3" chambers.
Barrel: 25⅝", 26¾", 28", 29½" (Mod. & Full).
Weight: 6 to 6½ lbs.
Stock: 14³⁄₁₆"x2³⁄₈"x1⁹⁄₁₆" standard dimensions. Select walnut with hand checkering.
Features: Anson & Deeley boxlock action with Purdey locks, choice of extractors or ejectors. Custom options available. Imported from Italy by Armsport.
Price: With ejectors **$1,555.00**
Price: With extractors **$1,435.00**
Price: F.S. model, ejectors **$1,750.00**

CONSULT
Shooter's Marketplace
Page 225, This Issue

AUGUSTE FRANCOTTE SIDELOCK SHOTGUN

Gauge: 12, 16, 20, 28 and 410-bore, 2¾" or 3" chambers.
Barrel: 26" to 29", chokes to customer specs.
Weight: NA. **Length:** NA.
Stock: Deluxe European walnut to customer specs. Straight or pistol grip; checkered butt; oil finish; splinter or beavertail forend.
Sights: Bead front.
Features: True Holland & Holland sidelock action with double locks, double triggers (front hinged), manual or automatic safety, Holland & Holland ejectors. English scroll engraving, coin finish or color case-hardening. Many options available. Imported from Belgium by Armes de Chasse.
Price: From about . . . . **$20,000.00 to $25,000.00**

A.H. Fox DE Grade

A.H. FOX SIDE-BY-SIDE SHOTGUNS

Gauge: 20, 2¾" chambers.
Barrel: Length and chokes to customer specifications. Rust-blued Chromox or Krupp steel.
Weight: 5½ to 7 lbs.

Stock: Dimensions to customer specifications. Hand-checkered Turkish Circassian walnut with hand-rubbed oil finish. Straight semi- or full pistol grip; splinter, schnabel or beavertail forend; traditional pad, hard rubber buttplate or skeleton butt.
Features: Boxlock action with automatic ejectors; double or Fox single selective trigger. Scalloped, rebated and color case-hardened receiver; hand finished and hand-engraved. Grades differ in engraving, inlays, grade of wood, amount of hand finishing. Introduced 1993. Made in U.S. by Connecticut Shotgun Mfg.
Price: CE Grade **$5,650.00**
Price: XE Grade **$8,500.00**
Price: DE Grade **$12,500.00**
Price: FE Grade **$17,500.00**
Price: Exhibition Grade **$25,000.000**

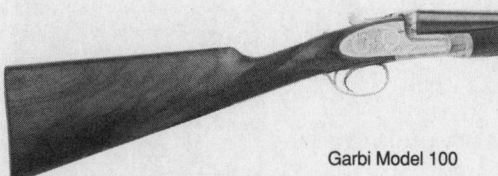

Garbi Model 100

Garbi Model 101 Side-by-Side

Similar to the Garbi Model 100 except is hand engraved with scroll engraving, select walnut stock. Better overall quality than the Model 100. Imported from Spain by Wm. Larkin Moore.
Price: From **$5,750.00**

Garbi Model 103A, B Side-by-Side

Similar to the Garbi Model 100 except has Purdey-type fine scroll and rosette engraving. Better overall quality than the Model 101. Model 103B has nickel-chrome steel barrels, H&H-type easy opening mechanism; other mechanical details remain the same. Imported from Spain by Wm. Larkin Moore.
Price: Model 103A, from **$7,100.00**
Price: Model 103B, from **$9,900.00**

GARBI MODEL 100 DOUBLE

Gauge: 12, 16, 20, 28.
Barrel: 26", 28", choked to customer specs.
Weight: 5½ to 7½ lbs.
Stock: 14½"x2¼"x1½". European walnut. Straight grip, checkered butt, classic forend.
Features: Sidelock action, automatic ejectors, double triggers standard. Color case-hardened action, coin finish optional. Single trigger; beavertail forend, etc. optional. Five other models are available. Imported from Spain by Wm. Larkin Moore.
Price: From **$4,500.00**

Garbi Model 200 Side-by-Side

Similar to the Garbi Model 100 except has heavy-duty locks, magnum proofed. Very fine Continental-style floral and scroll engraving, well figured walnut stock. Other mechanical features remain the same. Imported from Spain by Wm. Larkin Moore.
Price: **$9,400.00**

CAUTION: PRICES SHOWN ARE SUPPLIED BY THE MANUFACTURER OR IMPORTER. CHECK YOUR LOCAL GUNSHOP.

49th EDITION, 1995 **403**

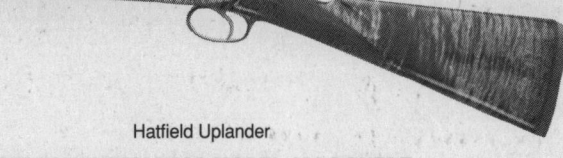

HATFIELD UPLANDER SHOTGUN
Gauge: 20, 3" chambers.
Barrel: 26" (Imp. Cyl. & Mod.).
Weight: 5¾ lbs.
Stock: Straight English style, special select XXX fancy maple. Hand-rubbed oil finish. Splinter forend.
Features: Double locking under-lug boxlock action; color case-hardened frame; single non-selective trigger. Grades differ in engraving, finish, gold work. Introduced 1988. From Hatfield.
Price: Grade I $2,249.00
Price: Grade II $2,995.00

Hatfield Uplander

CRUCELEGUI HERMANOS MODEL 150 DOUBLE
Gauge: 12, 16 or 20, 2¾" chambers.
Action: Greener triple cross bolt.
Barrel: 20", 26", 28", 30", 32" (Cyl. & Cyl., Full & Full, Mod. & Full, Mod. & Imp. Cyl., Imp. Cyl. & Full, Mod. & Mod.).
Weight: 5 to 7¼ lbs.
Stock: Hand-checkered walnut, beavertail forend.
Features: Double triggers; color case-hardened receiver; sling swivels; chrome-lined bores. Imported from Spain by Mandall Shooting Supplies.
Price: $450.00

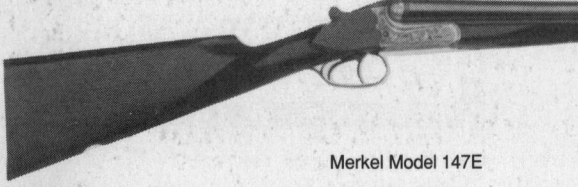

Merkel Model 147E

Merkel Model 47S, 147S Side-by-Sides
Similar to the Model 122 except with Holland & Holland-style sidelock action with cocking indicators, ejectors. Silver-grayed receiver and sideplates have Arabesque engraving, engraved border and screws (Model 47S), or fine hunting scene engraving (Model 147S). Imported from Germany by GSI.
Price: Model 47S $4,195.00
Price: Model 147S $5,195.00
Price: Model 247S (English-style engraving, large scrolls) . . . $6,895.00
Price: Model 347S (English-style engraving, medium scrolls) . . . $7,895.00
Price: Model 447S (English-style engraving, small scrolls) $8,995.00

MERKEL MODEL 47LSC SPORTING CLAYS DOUBLE
Gauge: 12, 3" chambers.
Barrel: 28" with Briley choke tubes.
Weight: 7.2 lbs.
Stock: Fancy figured walnut with pistol grip, recoil pad. Beavertail forend.
Features: Anson & Deeley boxlock action with single selective trigger adjsutable for length of pull; H&H-type ejectors; white front sight with mid-rib bead; manual safety; cocking indicators; lengthened forcing cones; color case-hardened receiver with Arabesque engraving. Comes with fitted leather luggage case. Introduced 1993. Imported from Germany by GSI.
Price: $2,995.00

MERKEL MODEL 8, 47E SIDE-BY-SIDE SHOTGUNS
Gauge: 12, 3" chambers, 16, 2¾" chambers, 20, 3" chambers.
Barrel: 12-, 16-ga.—28"; 20-ga.—26¾" (Imp. Cyl. & Mod., Mod. & Full).
Weight: About 6¾ lbs. (12-ga.).
Stock: Oil-finished walnut; straight English or pistol grip.
Features: Anson & Deeley-type boxlock action with single selective or double triggers, automatic safety, cocking indicators. Color case-hardened receiver with standard Arabesque engraving. Imported from Germany by GSI.
Price: Model 8 (extractors only) $1,295.00
Price: Model 47E (H&H ejectors) $1,595.00
Price: Model 147 (extractors, silver-grayed receiver with hunting scenes) $1,795.00
Price: Model 147E (as above with ejectors) $1,995.00
Price: Model 122 (as above with false sideplates, fine engraving) . $3,195.00

PARKER REPRODUCTIONS SIDE-BY-SIDE SHOTGUN
Gauge: 12, 16/20 combo, 20, 28, 2¾" and 3" chambers.
Barrel: 26" (Skeet 1 & 2, Imp. Cyl. & Mod.), 28" (Mod. & Full, 2¾" and 3", 12, 20, 28; Skeet 1 & 2, Imp. Cyl. & Mod., Mod. & Full 16-ga. only).
Weight: 6¾ lbs. (12-ga.)
Stock: Checkered (26 lpi) AAA fancy California English or Claro walnut, skeleton steel and checkered butt. Straight or pistol grip, splinter or beavertail forend.
Features: Exact reproduction of the original Parker—parts interchange. Double or single selective trigger, selective ejectors, hard-chromed bores, designed for steel shot. One, two or three (16-20, 20) barrel sets available. Hand-engraved snap caps included. Introduced 1984. Made by Winchester. Imported from Japan by Parker Division, Reagent Chemical.
Price: D Grade, one-barrel set $3,370.00
Price: Two-barrel set, same gauge $4,200.00
Price: Two-barrel set, 16/20 . . . . $4,870.00
Price: Three-barrel set, 16/20/20 . . . . $5,630.00
Price: A-1 Special two-barrel set $11,200.00
Price: A-1 Special three-barrel set $13,200.00

Piotti King No.1

Piotti Lunik Side-by-Side
Similar to the Piotti King No. 1 except better overall quality. Has Renaissance-style large scroll engraving in relief, gold crown in top lever, gold name and gold crest in forend. Best quality Holland & Holland-pattern sidelock ejector double with chopper lump (demi-bloc) barrels. Other mechanical specifications remain the same. Imported from Italy by Wm. Larkin Moore.
Price: From $18,800.00

Piotti King Extra Side-by-Side
Similar to the Piotti King No. 1 except highest quality wood and metal work. Choice of either bulino game scene engraving or game scene engraving with gold inlays. Engraved and signed by a master engraver. Exhibition grade wood. Other mechanical specifications remain the same. Imported from Italy by Wm. Larkin Moore.
Price: From $21,200.00

PIOTTI KING NO. 1 SIDE-BY-SIDE
Gauge: 12, 16, 20, 28, 410.
Barrel: 25" to 30" (12-ga.), 25" to 28" (16, 20, 28, 410). To customer specs. Chokes as specified.
Weight: 6½ lbs. to 8 lbs. (12-ga. to customer specs.).
Stock: Dimensions to customer specs. Finely figured walnut; straight grip with checkered butt with classic splinter forend and hand-rubbed oil finish standard. Pistol grip, beavertail forend, satin luster finish optional.
Features: Holland & Holland pattern sidelock action, automatic ejectors. Double trigger with front trigger hinged standard; non-selective single trigger optional. Coin finish standard; color case-hardened optional. Top rib; level, file-cut standard; concave, ventilated optional. Very fine, full coverage scroll engraving with small floral bouquets, gold crown in top lever, name in gold, and gold crest in forend. Imported from Italy by Wm. Larkin Moore.
Price: From $17,400.00

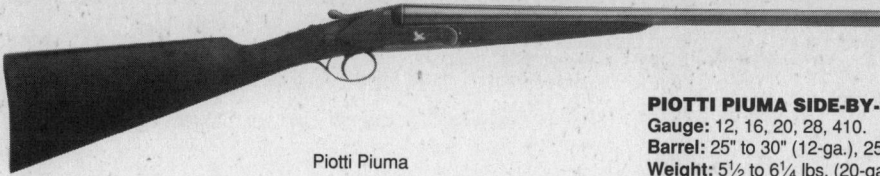

Piotti Piuma

RIZZINI BOXLOCK SIDE-BY-SIDE
Gauge: 12, 16, 20, 28, 410.
Barrel: 25" to 30" (12-, 16-, 20-ga.), 25" to 28" (28, 410).
Weight: 5½ to 6¼ lbs. (20-ga.).
Stock: Dimensions to customer specs. Straight grip stock with checkered butt, classic splinter forend, hand-rubbed oil finish are standard; pistol grip, beavertail forend; satin luster finish optional.
Features: Anson & Deeley boxlock ejector double with chopper lump barrels. Level, file-cut rib, scalloped frame. Double triggers with hinged front optional, single non-selective standard. Coin finish standard. Imported from Italy by Wm. Larkin Moore.
Price: 12-, 20-ga., from **$23,000.00**
Price: 28, 410 bore, from **$25,000.00**

RIZZINI SIDELOCK SIDE-BY-SIDE
Gauge: 12, 16, 20, 28, 410.
Barrel: 25" to 30" (12-, 16-, 20-ga.), 25" to 28" (28, 410). To customer specs. Chokes as specified.
Weight: 6½ lbs. to 8 lbs. (12-ga. to customer specs).
Stock: Dimensions to customer specs. Finely figured walnut; straight grip with checkered butt with classic splinter forend and hand-rubbed oil finish standard.

PIOTTI PIUMA SIDE-BY-SIDE
Gauge: 12, 16, 20, 28, 410.
Barrel: 25" to 30" (12-ga.), 25" to 28" (16, 20, 28, 410).
Weight: 5½ to 6¼ lbs. (20-ga.).
Stock: Dimensions to customer specs. Straight grip stock with walnut checkered butt, classic splinter forend, hand-rubbed oil finish are standard; pistol grip, beavertail forend, satin luster finish optional.
Features: Anson & Deeley boxlock ejector double with chopper lump barrels. Level, file-cut rib, light scroll and rosette engraving, scalloped frame. Double triggers with hinged front standard, single non-selective optional. Coin finish standard, color case-hardened optional. Imported from Italy by Wm. Larkin Moore.
Price: From **$10,000.00**

Pistol grip, beavertail forend, satin luster finish optional.
Features: Holland & Holland pattern sidelock action, auto ejectors. Double triggers with front trigger hinged optional; non-selective single trigger standard. Coin finish standard. Top rib level, file cut standard; concave optional. Imported from Italy by Wm. Larkin Moore.
Price: 12-, 20-ga., from $38,500.00
Price: 28, 410 bore, from $43,500.00

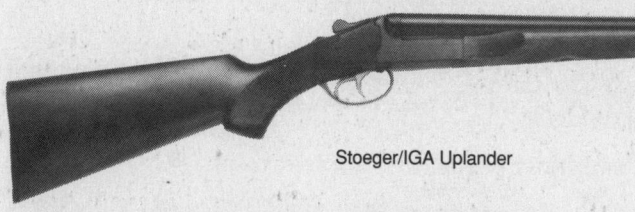

Stoeger/IGA Uplander

STOEGER/IGA UPLANDER SIDE-BY-SIDE SHOTGUN
Gauge: 12, 20, 28, 2¾" chambers; 410, 3" chambers.
Barrel: 26" (Full & Full, 410 only, Imp. Cyl. & Mod.), 28" (Mod. & Full).

Weight: 6¾ to 7 lbs.
Stock: 14½"x1½"x2½". Oil-finished hardwood. Checkered pistol grip and forend.
Features: Automatic safety, extractors only, solid matted barrel rib. Double triggers only. Introduced 1983. Imported from Brazil by Stoeger Industries.
Price: **$398.00**
Price: With choke tubes **$442.00**
Price: Coach Gun, 12, 20, 410, 20" bbls. **$382.00**

Ugartechea 10-Gauge

Consult our Directory pages for the location of firms mentioned.

UGARTECHEA 10-GAUGE MAGNUM SHOTGUN
Gauge: 10, 3½" chambers.
Action: Boxlock.
Barrel: 32" (Full).
Weight: 11 lbs.
Stock: 14½"x1½"x2⅝". European walnut, checkered at pistol grip and forend.
Features: Double triggers; color case-hardened action, rest blued. Front and center metal beads on matted rib; ventilated rubber recoil pad. Forend release has positive Purdey-type mechanism. Imported from Spain by Mandall Shooting Supplies.
Price: **$699.50**

SHOTGUNS—BOLT ACTIONS & SINGLE SHOTS

Variety of designs for utility and sporting purposes, as well as for competitive shooting.

ARMSPORT SINGLE BARREL SHOTGUN
Gauge: 20, 3" chamber.
Barrel: 26" (Mod.).
Weight: About 6½ lbs.
Stock: Hardwood with oil finish.
Features: Chrome-lined barrel, manual safety, cocking indicator. Opening lever behind trigger guard. Imported by Armsport.
Price: **$100.00**

BAIKAL IJ-18M SHOTGUN
Gauge: 12, 16, 2¾", 20, 410, 3" chamber.
Barrel: 12, 20-ga.—26" (Imp. Cyl.), 410 (Full); 12, 20-ga.—28" (Full, Mod.).
Weight: 5.5 to 6 lbs.
Stock: Stained hardwood.
Features: Internal hammer with cocking indicator; trigger block safety; engraved, blued receiver. Re-introduced 1994. Imported from Russia by K.B.I., Inc.
Price: **$79.00**

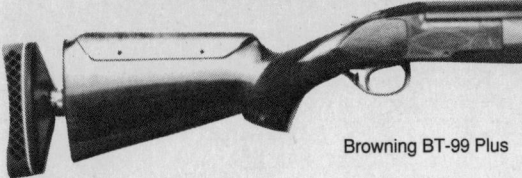

Browning BT-99 Plus

Browning BT-99 Plus Trap Gun

Similar to the Grade I BT-99 except comes with 32" or 34" barrel with .745" over bore, Invector Plus choke system with Full, Imp. Mod. and Mod. choke tubes; high post, ventilated, tapered, target rib adjustable from 3" to 12" above point of aim. Available with or without ported barrel. Select walnut stock has high-gloss finish, Monte Carlo comb, modified beavertail forend and is fully adjustable for length of pull, drop at comb and drop at Monte Carlo. Has Browning Recoil Reduction System. Introduced 1989.

Price: Grade I, with ported barrel $1,855.00
Price: Grade I, non-ported barrel $1,835.00
Price: Stainless, ported $2,240.00
Price: Pigeon Grade, ported $2,065.00
Price: Signature Painted, ported $1,890.00
Price: Golden Clays $3,205.00

Browning BT-99 Plus Micro

Similar to the standard BT-99 Plus except scaled down for smaller shooters. Comes with 28", 30", 32" or 34" barrel with adjustable rib system and buttstock with adjustable length of pull range of 13½" to 14". Also has Browning's recoil reducer system, ported barrels, Invector Plus choke system and back-bored barrel. Weight is about 8 lbs., 6 oz. Introduced 1991.

Price: With ported barrel $1,855.00
Price: With non-ported barrel : $1,835.00
Price: Stainless, ported $2,240.00
Price: Pigeon Grade, ported $2,065.00
Price: Signature Painted $1,890.00
Price: Golden Clays $3,205.00

BROWNING BT-99 COMPETITION TRAP SPECIAL

Gauge: 12, 2¾" chamber.
Action: Top lever break-open, hammerless.
Barrel: 32" or 34" with ¹¹⁄₃₂" wide high post floating vent. rib. Comes with Invector Plus choke tubes; .745" overbore.
Weight: 8 lbs. (32" bbl.).
Stock: French walnut; hand-checkered, full pistol grip, full beavertail forend; recoil pad. Trap dimensions with M.C. 14³⁄₈"x1³⁄₈"x1³⁄₈"x2".
Sights: Ivory front and middle beads.
Features: Gold-plated trigger with 3½-lb. pull, deluxe trap-style recoil pad, automatic ejector, no safety. Available with either Monte Carlo or standard stock. Imported from Japan by Browning.

Price: Grade I Invector, Plus Ported barrels $1,288.00
Price: Stainless, ported $1,738.00
Price: Pigeon Grade, ported $1,505.00
Price: Signature Painted $1,323.00
Price: Golden Clays $2,800.00

CONSULT Shooter's Marketplace Page 225, This Issue

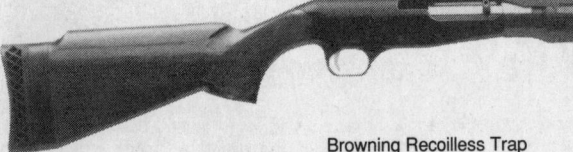

Browning Recoilless Trap

Browning Micro Recoilless Trap Shotgun

Same as the standard Recoilless Trap except has 27" barrel, weighs 8 lbs., 10 oz., and stock length of pull adjustable from 13" to 13¾", Overall length 47⅝". Introduced 1993. Imported by Browning.

Price: $1,850.00
Price: Signature Painted $1,900.00

BROWNING RECOILLESS TRAP SHOTGUN

Gauge: 12, 2¾" chamber.
Barrel: Back-bored 30" (Invector Plus tubes).
Weight: 9 lbs., 1 oz. **Length:** 51⅝" overall.
Stock: 14"-14¾"x1⅜"-1¾"x1⅛"-1¾". Select walnut with high gloss finish, cut checkering.
Features: Eliminates up to 72 percent of recoil. Mass of the inner mechansim (barrel, receiver and inner bolt) is driven forward when trigger is pulled, cancelling most recoil. Forend is used to cock action when the action is forward. Ventilated rib adjusts to move point of impact; drop at comb and length of pull adjustable. Introduced 1993. Imported by Browning.

Price: $1,850.00
Price: Signature Painted $1,900.00

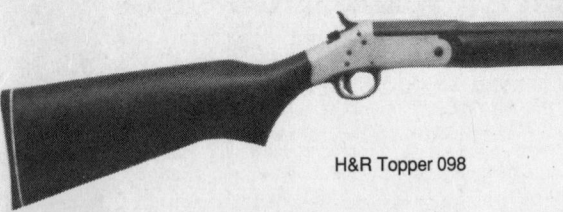

H&R Topper 098

DESERT INDUSTRIES BIG TWENTY SHOTGUN

Gauge: 20, 2¾" chamber.
Barrel: 19" (Cyl.).
Weight: 4¾ lbs. **Length:** 31¾" overall.
Stock: Fixed wire, with buttplate. Walnut forend and grip.
Sights: Bead front.
Features: Single shot action of all steel construction. Blue finish. Announced 1990. From Desert Industries, Inc.

Price: $189.95

Harrington & Richardson Topper Deluxe Model 098

Similar to the standard Topper 098 except 12-gauge only with 3½" chamber, 28" barrel with choke tube (comes with Mod. tube, others optional). Satin nickel frame, blued barrel, black-finished wood. Introduced 1992. From H&R 1871, Inc.

Price: $124.95

HARRINGTON & RICHARDSON TOPPER MODEL 098

Gauge: 12, 20, 410, 3" chamber.
Barrel: 12 ga.—28" (Mod.); 20 ga.—26" (Mod.); 410 bore—26" (Full).
Weight: 5-6 lbs.
Stock: Black-finish hardwood with full pistol grip; semi-beavertail forend.
Sights: Gold bead front.
Features: Break-open action with side-lever release, automatic ejector. Satin nickel frame, blued barrel. Reintroduced 1992. From H&R 1871, Inc.

Price: $109.95
Price: Topper Junior 098 (as above except 22" barrel, 20-ga. (Mod.), 410-bore (Full), 12½" length of pull) $114.95

Harrington & Richardson Topper Classic Youth Shotgun

Similar to the Topper Junior 098 except available in 20-gauge (3", Mod.), 410-bore (Full) with 3" chamber; 28-gauge, 2¾" chamber (Mod.); all have 22" barrel. Stock is American black walnut with cut-checkered pistol grip and forend. Ventilated rubber recoil pad with white line spacers. Blued barrel, blued frame. Introduced 1992. From H&R 1871, Inc.

Price: $139.95

SHOTGUNS—BOLT ACTIONS & SINGLE SHOTS

Harrington & Richardson N.W.T.F Turkey Mag
Similar to the Topper 098 except covered with Mossy Oak camouflage. Chambered for 12-gauge 3½" chamber, 24" barrel (comes with Turkey Full choke tube, others available); weighs 6 lbs., overall length 40". Comes with Mossy Oak sling, swivels, studs. Introduced 1992. From H&R 1871, Inc.
Price: **$169.95**
Price: N.W.T.F. Youth Turkey (3" 20-ga., 22", Full choke, recoil pad) **$154.95**

HARRINGTON & RICHARDSON TAMER SHOTGUN
Gauge: 410, 3" chamber.
Barrel: 19½" (Full).
Weight: 5-6 lbs. **Length:** 33" overall.
Stock: Thumbhole grip of high density black polymer.
Features: Uses H&R Topper action with matte electroless nickel finish. Stock holds four spare shotshells. Introduced 1994. From H&R 1871, Inc.
Price: **$149.95**

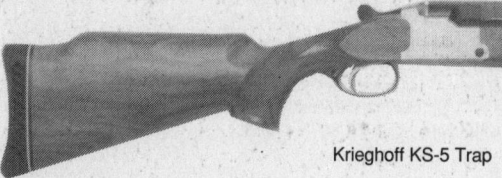

Krieghoff KS-5 Trap

KRIEGHOFF KS-5 TRAP GUN
Gauge: 12, 2¾" chamber.
Barrel: 32", 34"; Full choke or choke tubes.
Weight: About 8½ lbs.
Stock: Choice of high Monte Carlo (1½"), low Monte Carlo (1⅜") or factory adjustable stock. European walnut.
Features: Ventilated tapered step rib. Adjustable trigger or optional release trigger. Satin gray electroless nickel receiver. Comes with fitted aluminum case. Introduced 1988. Imported from Germany by Krieghoff International, Inc.
Price: Fixed choke, cased **$3,575.00**
Price: With choke tubes **$3,975.00**

Krieghoff KS-5 Special
Same as the KS-5 except the barrel has a fully adjustable rib and adjustable stock. Rib allows shooter to adjust point of impact from 50%/50% to nearly 90%/10%. Introduced 1990.
Price: **$4,480.00**

KRIEGHOFF K-80 SINGLE BARREL TRAP GUN
Gauge: 12, 2¾" chamber.
Barrel: 32" or 34" Unsingle; 34" Top Single. Fixed Full or choke tubes.
Weight: About 8¾ lbs.
Stock: Four stock dimensions or adjustable stock available. All hand-checkered European walnut.

Features: Satin nickel finish with K-80 logo. Selective mechanical trigger adjustable for finger position. Tapered step vent. rib. Adjustable point of impact on Unsingle.
Price: Standard grade full Unsingle **$7,595.00**
Price: Standard grade full Top Single combo (special order), from **$9,595.00**
Price: RT (removable trigger) option, add **$1,000.00**

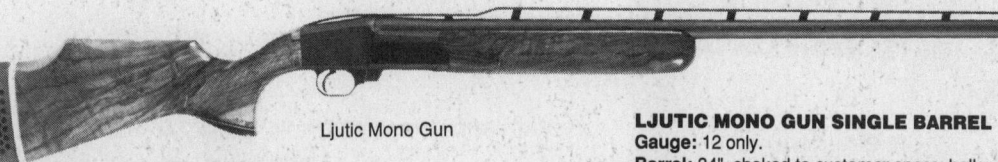

Ljutic Mono Gun

LJUTIC MONO GUN SINGLE BARREL
Gauge: 12 only.
Barrel: 34", choked to customer specs; hollow-milled rib, 35½" sight plane.
Weight: Approx. 9 lbs.
Stock: To customer specs. Oil finish, hand checkered.
Features: Totally custom made. Pull or release trigger; removable trigger guard contains trigger and hammer mechanism; Ljutic pushbutton opener on front of trigger guard. From Ljutic Industries.
Price: With standard, medium or Olympic rib, custom 32"-34" bbls. **$4,495.00**
Price: As above with screw-in choke barrel **$4,695.00**

Ljutic LTX Super Deluxe Mono Gun
Super Deluxe version of the standard Mono Gun with high quality wood, extra-fancy checkering pattern in 24 lpi, double recessed choking. Available in two weights: 8¼ lbs. or 8¾ lbs. Extra light 33" barrel; medium-height rib. Introduced 1984. From Ljutic Industries.
Price: **$5,595.00**
Price: With three screw-in choke tubes **$5,995.00**

LJUTIC RECOILLESS SPACE GUN SHOTGUN
Gauge: 12 only, 2¾" chamber.
Barrel: 30" (Full). Screw-in or fixed-choke barrel.
Weight: 8½ lbs.
Stock: 14½" to 15" pull length; universal comb; medium or large p.g.

Sights: Vent. rib.
Features: Pull trigger standard, release trigger available; anti-recoil mechanism. Revolutionary design. Introduced 1981. From Ljutic Industries.
Price: From **$5,995.00**

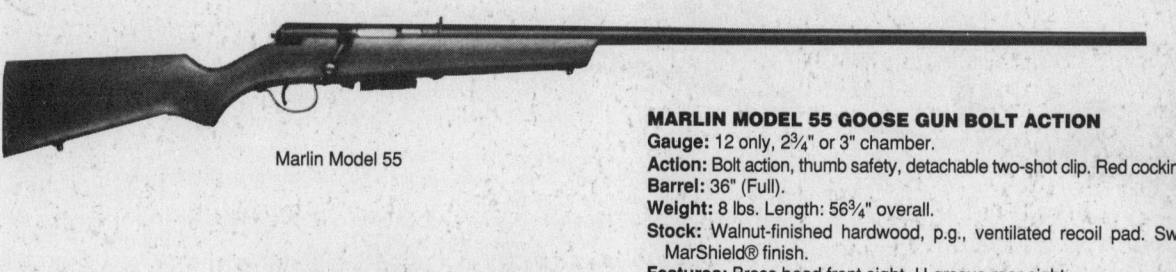

Marlin Model 55

MARLIN MODEL 55 GOOSE GUN BOLT ACTION
Gauge: 12 only, 2¾" or 3" chamber.
Action: Bolt action, thumb safety, detachable two-shot clip. Red cocking indicator.
Barrel: 36" (Full).
Weight: 8 lbs. **Length:** 56¾" overall.
Stock: Walnut-finished hardwood, p.g., ventilated recoil pad. Swivel studs, MarShield® finish.
Features: Brass bead front sight, U-groove rear sight.
Price: **$284.40**

Marlin Model 512

Weight: 8 lbs. **Length:** 44¾" overall.
Stock: Walnut-finished, press-checkered Maine birch with Mar-Shield® finish, ventilated recoil pad.
Sights: Ramp front with brass bead and removable Wide-Scan™ hood, adjustable folding semi-buckhorn rear. Drilled and tapped for scope mounting.
Features: Uses Model 55 action with thumb safety. Designed for shooting saboted slugs. Comes with special Weaver scope mount. Introduced 1994. Made in U.S. by Marlin Firearms Co.
Price: **$343.05**

MARLIN MODEL 512 SLUGMASTER SHOTGUN
Gauge: 12, 3" chamber; 2-shot detachable box magazine.
Barrel: 21", rifled (1:28" twist).

CAUTION: PRICES SHOWN ARE SUPPLIED BY THE MANUFACTURER OR IMPORTER. CHECK YOUR LCOAL GUNSHOP.

NEW ENGLAND FIREARMS TURKEY AND GOOSE GUN

Gauge: 10, 3½" chamber.
Barrel: 28" (Full).
Weight: 9.5 lbs. **Length:** 44" overall.
Stock: American hardwood with walnut, or matte camo finish; ventilated rubber recoil pad.
Sights: Bead front.
Features: Break-open action with side-lever release; ejector. Matte finish on metal. Introduced 1992. From New England Firearms.
Price: Walnut-finish wood $149.95
Price: Camo finish, sling and swivels $159.95

New England Turkey

New England Firearms Turkey Special

Similar to the Turkey and Goose gun except 12-gauge, 3" chamber, 24" (fixed Full Turkey choke). Full coverage Realtree camouflage. Weighs 5-6 lbs, overall length 40". Stock has modified pistol grip, recoil pad, swivel studs. Introduced 1994. From New England Firearms.
Price: About $115.00

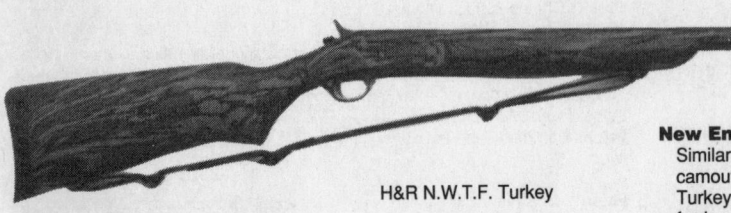

H&R N.W.T.F. Turkey

New England Firearms N.W.T.F. Shotgun

Similar to the Turkey/Goose Gun except completely covered with Mossy Oak camouflage finish; 24" barrel with interchangeable choke tubes (comes with Turkey Full, others optional); comes with Mossy Oak sling. Drilled and tapped for long eye relief scope mount. Introduced 1992. From New England Firearms.
Price: $199.95
Price: 20-ga., 24" (Mod.), Mossy Oak camo $149.95

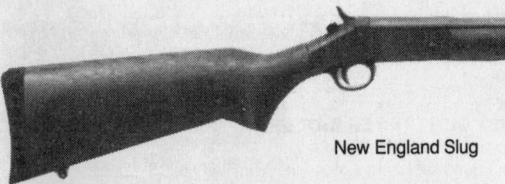

New England Slug

NEW ENGLAND FIREARMS STANDARD PARDNER

Gauge: 12, 20, 410, 3" chamber; 16, 28, 2¾" chamber.
Barrel: 12-ga.—28" (Full, Mod.); 16-ga.—28" (Full); 20-ga.—26" (Full, Mod.); 28-ga.—26" (Mod.); 410-bore—26" (Full).
Weight: 5-6 lbs. **Length:** 43" overall (28" barrel).
Stock: Walnut-finished hardwood with full pistol grip.
Sights: Bead front.
Features: Transfer bar ignition; break-open action with side-lever release. Introduced 1987. From New England Firearms.
Price: $99.95
Price: Youth model (20-, 28-ga., 410, 22" barrel, recoil pad) $104.95

NEW ENGLAND FIREARMS TRACKER SLUG GUN

Gauge: 12, 20, 3" chamber.
Barrel: 24" (Cyl.).
Weight: 6 lbs. **Length:** 40" overall.
Stock: Walnut-finished hardwood with full pistol grip, recoil pad.
Sights: Blade front, fully adjustable rifle-type rear.
Features: Break-open action with side-lever release; blued barrel, color case-hardened frame. Introduced 1992. From New England Firearms.
Price: Tracker $124.95
Price: Tracker II (as above except fully rifled bore) $129.95

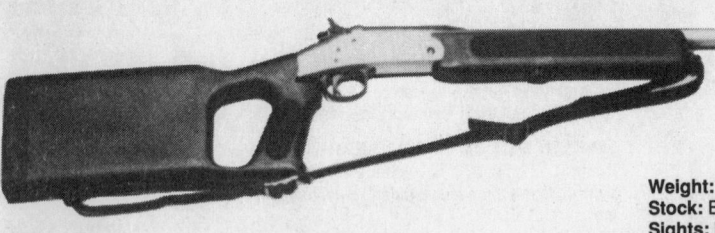

New England Survivor

NEW ENGLAND FIREARMS SURVIVOR

Gauge: 12, 20, 3" chamber.
Barrel: 22" (Mod.).

Weight: 6 lbs. **Length:** 36" overall.
Stock: Black polymer with thumbhole/pistol grip, sling swivels.
Sights: Bead front.
Features: Buttplate swings open to expose storage for extra ammunition. Blue or nickel finish. Introduced 1993. From New England Firearms.
Price: Blue $129.95
Price: Nickel $149.95

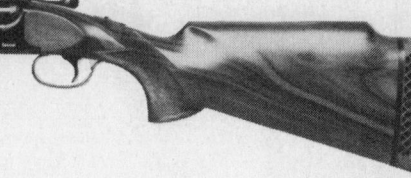

PERAZZI TM1 SPECIAL SINGLE TRAP

Gauge: 12, 2¾" chambers.
Barrel: 32" or 34" (Extra Full).
Weight: 8 lbs., 6 oz.
Stock: To customer specs; interchangeable.
Features: Tapered and stepped high rib; adjustable four-position trigger. Also available with choke tubes. Imported from Italy by Perazzi U.S.A., Inc.
Price: From $5,950.00
Price: TMX Special Single (as above except special high rib), from $6,150.00

Perazzi TM1

SHOTGUNS—BOLT ACTIONS & SINGLE SHOTS

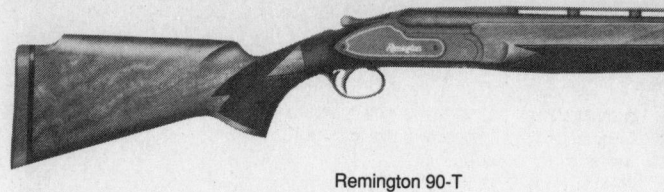

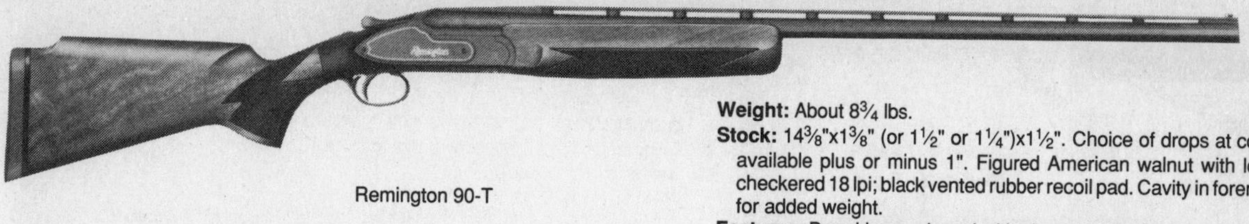

Remington 90-T

REMINGTON 90-T SUPER SINGLE SHOTGUN
Gauge: 12, 2¾" chamber.
Barrel: 30", 32", 34", fixed choke or Rem Choke tubes; ported or non-ported. Medium-high tapered, ventilated rib; white Bradley-type front bead, stainless center bead.

Weight: About 8¾ lbs.
Stock: 14⅜"x1⅜" (or 1½" or 1¼")x1½". Choice of drops at comb, pull length available plus or minus 1". Figured American walnut with low-luster finish, checkered 18 lpi; black vented rubber recoil pad. Cavity in forend and buttstock for added weight.
Features: Barrel is over-bored with elongated forcing cones. Removable side-plates can be ordered with engraving; drop-out trigger assembly. Metal has non-glare matte finish. Available with extra barrels in different lengths, chokes, extra trigger assemblies and sideplates, porting, stocks. Introduced 1990. From Remington.
Price: Depending on options $2,995.00
Price: With high post adjustable rib $3,595.00

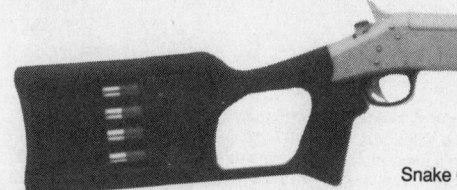

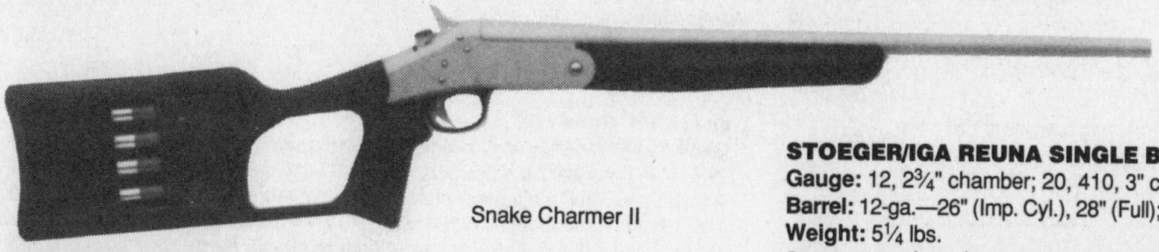

Snake Charmer II

SNAKE CHARMER II SHOTGUN
Gauge: 410, 3" chamber.
Barrel: 18¼".
Weight: About 3½ lbs. **Length:** 28⅝" overall.
Stock: ABS grade impact resistant plastic.
Features: Thumbhole-type stock holds four extra rounds. Stainless steel barrel and frame. Reintroduced 1989. From Sporting Arms Mfg., Inc.
Price: $149.00
Price: New Generation Snake Charmer (as above except with black carbon steel bbl.) $139.00

STOEGER/IGA REUNA SINGLE BARREL SHOTGUN
Gauge: 12, 2¾" chamber; 20, 410, 3" chamber.
Barrel: 12-ga.—26" (Imp. Cyl.), 28" (Full); 20-ga.—26" (Full); 410 bore—26" (Full).
Weight: 5¼ lbs.
Stock: 14"x1½"x2½". Brazilian hardwood.
Sights: Metal bead front.
Features: Exposed hammer with half-cock safety; extractor; blue finish. Introduced 1987. Imported from Brazil by Stoeger Industries.
Price: $120.00
Price: 12-, 20-ga., Full choke tube $142.00
Price: Youth model (20-ga., 410, 22" Full) $132.00

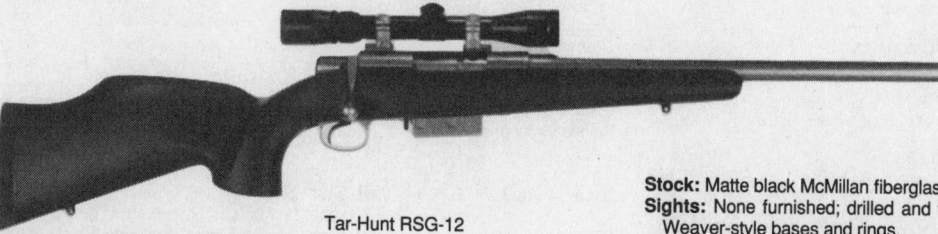

Tar-Hunt RSG-12

TAR-HUNT RSG-12 RIFLED SLUG GUN
Gauge: 12, 20, 2¾" chamber.
Barrel: 21½"; fully rifled, with muzzle brake.
Weight: 7¾ lbs. **Length:** 41½" overall.

Stock: Matte black McMillan fiberglass with Pachmayr Decelerator pad.
Sights: None furnished; drilled and tapped for scope mounting; comes with Weaver-style bases and rings.
Features: Uses Fritz/McMillan bolt action with two locking lugs; two-position safety; single-stage, adjustable rifle trigger; muzzle brake. Many options available. Introduced 1991. Made in U.S. by Tar-Hunt Custom Rifles, Inc.
Price: 12-gauge, right- or left-hand action $1,395.00
Price: 20-gauge, right-hand only $1,395.00

THOMPSON/CENTER CUSTOM SHOP TCR '87 HUNTER SHOTGUN
Gauge: 10, 12, 3½".
Barrel: 25" (Full).
Weight: 8 lbs.
Stock: Uncheckered walnut.

Sights: Bead front.
Features: Uses same receiver as TCR '87 rifle models, and stock has extra 7/16" drop at heel. Choke designed for steel shot. Available only through the T/C custom shop. Introduced 1989. From Thompson/Center.
Price: About $540.00

SHOTGUNS— MILITARY & POLICE

Designs for utility, suitable for and adaptable to competitions and other sporting purposes.

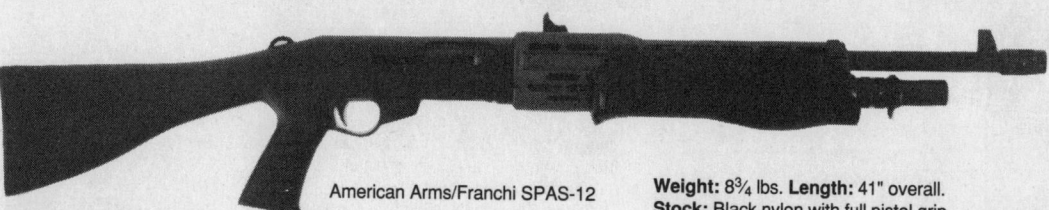

American Arms/Franchi SPAS-12

AMERICAN ARMS/FRANCHI SPAS-12 SHOTGUN
Gauge: 12, 2¾" chamber.
Barrel: 21½" (Cyl.), with muzzle protector.

Weight: 8¾ lbs. **Length:** 41" overall.
Stock: Black nylon with full pistol grip.
Sights: Blade front, aperture rear.
Features: Gas-operated semi-auto converts instantly to pump action; cross-bolt safety and secondary tactical lever safety; 7-shot tubular magazine; matte phosphate finish. Choke tubes available as accessories. Imported from Italy by American Arms, Inc.
Price: $769.00
Price: LAW-12 (as above except gas-operated action only) $719.00

CAUTION: PRICES SHOWN ARE SUPPLIED BY THE MANUFACTURER OR IMPORTER. CHECK YOUR LCOAL GUNSHOP.

49th EDITION, 1995 **409**

Benelli M1 Super 90 Tactical

Benelli M1 Super 90 Tactical Shotgun
Similar to the M1 Super 90 except has 18.5" barrel with Imp. Cyl., Mod., Full choke tubes, rifle sights of Ghost Ring system (tritium night sights optional), 7-shot magazine. In 12-gauge (3" chamber) only, matte-finish receiver. Overall length 39.75". Introduced 1993. Imported from Italy by Heckler & Koch, Inc.
Price: With rifle sights, standard stock $800.00
Price: As above, pistol grip stock $835.00
Price: With Ghost Rifle sights, standard stock $840.00
Price: As above, pistol grip stock $875.00

Consult our Directory pages for the location of firms mentioned.

BENELLI M3 SUPER 90 PUMP/AUTO SHOTGUN
Gauge: 12, 3" chamber, 7-shot magazine.
Barrel: 19¾" (Cyl.).
Weight: 7 lbs., 8 oz. **Length:** 41" overall.
Stock: High-impact polymer with sling loop in side of butt; rubberized pistol grip on stock.
Sights: Post front, buckhorn rear adjustable for windage. Ghost ring system available.
Features: Combination pump/auto action. Alloy receiver with inertia recoil rotating locking lug bolt; matte finish; automatic shell release lever. Introduced 1989. Imported by Heckler & Koch, Inc.
Price: $972.00
Price: With Ghost Ring sight system $1,008.00
Price: With standard stock $936.00

Benelli M1 Super 90
Similar to the M3 Super 90 except is semi-automatic only, has overall length of 41" and weighs 7 lbs. Introduced 1986.
Price: Slug Gun with standard stock $745.00
Price: With pistol grip stock (Defense) $780.00
Price: With ghost ring sight system (standard stock) $785.00
Price: With ghost ring sight system, pistol grip stock (Defense) . . . $820.00

Beretta Model 1201FP3

ITHACA MODEL 87 M&P DSPS SHOTGUNS
Gauge: 12, 3" chamber, 5- or 8-shot magazine.
Barrel: 18½", 20" (Cyl.).
Weight: 7 lbs.
Stock: Walnut.
Sights: Bead front on 5-shot, rifle sights on 8-shot.
Features: Parkerized finish; bottom ejection; cross-bolt safety. Reintroduced 1988. From Ithaca Acquisition Corp.
Price: M&P, 5-shot $428.75
Price: DSPS, 8-shot $428.75
Price: DSPS, 5-shot, rifled $462.75
Price: DSPS, rifled, 20", 25" $583.25

BERETTA MODEL 1201FP3 AUTO SHOTGUN
Gauge: 12, 3" chamber.
Barrel: 20" (Cyl.).
Weight: 7.3 lbs. **Length:** NA
Stock: Special strengthened technopolymer, matte black finish.
Stock: Fixed rifle type.
Features: Has 6-shot magazine. Introduced 1988. Imported from Italy by Beretta U.S.A.
Price: $660.00
Price: Pistol grip model $705.00

Ithaca Model 87 Hand Grip Shotgun
Similar to the Model 87 M&P except has black polymer pistol grip and slide handle. In 12- or 20-gauge, 18½" barrel (Cyl.), 5-shot magazine. Reintroduced 1988.
Price: $430.50

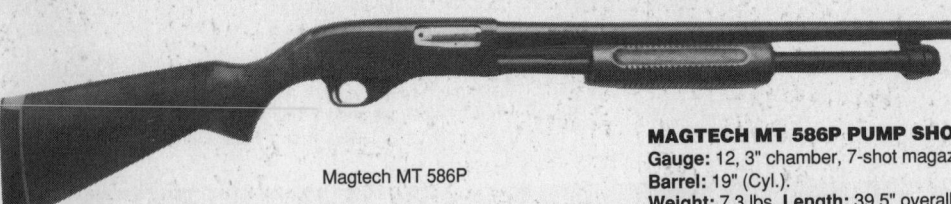

Magtech MT 586P

MAGTECH MT 586P PUMP SHOTGUN
Gauge: 12, 3" chamber, 7-shot magazine (8-shot with 2¾" shells).
Barrel: 19" (Cyl.).
Weight: 7.3 lbs. **Length:** 39.5" overall.
Stock: Brazilian hardwood.
Sights: Bead front.
Features: Dual action slide bars, cross-bolt safety. Blue finish. Introduced 1991. Imported from Brazil by Magtech Recreational Products.
Price: About $219.00

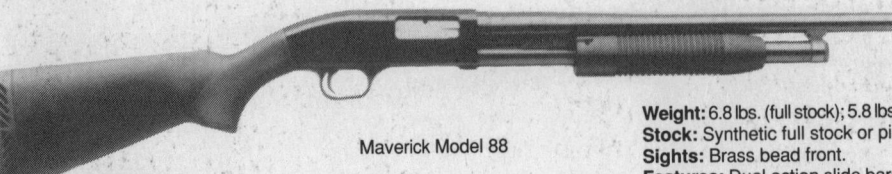

Maverick Model 88

Weight: 6.8 lbs. (full stock); 5.8 lbs. (pistol grip model). **Length:** 40" overall (full stock).
Stock: Synthetic full stock or pistol grip only.
Sights: Brass bead front.
Features: Dual action slide bars; cross-bolt safety; optional heat shield. Accessories interchangeable with Mossberg Model 500. Cablelock included. Introduced 1993. From Maverick Arms, Inc.
Price: 6-shot, full stock $217.00
Price: 8-shot, full stock $234.00
Price: 8-shot, full stock with pistol grip kit $249.00
Price: 8-shot pistol grip model $234.00
Price: 8-shot, pistol grip, heat shield $249.00

MAVERICK MODEL 88 PUMP SECURITY SHOTGUN
Gauge: 12, 3" chamber.
Barrel: 18½", 20" (Cyl.).

SHOTGUNS—MILITARY & POLICE

Maverick Model 88 Bullpup

MAVERICK MODEL 88 BULLPUP SHOTGUN
Gauge: 12, 3" chamber; 6- or 9-shot magazine.
Barrel: 18½" (Cyl.), 6-shot; 20" (Cyl.), 9-shot.
Weight: 9½ lbs. **Length:** 26½" overall.
Stock: Bullpup design of high-impact plastics.
Sights: Fixed, mounted in carrying handle.
Features: Uses the Model 88 pump shotgun action. Cross-bolt and grip safeties. Mossberg Cablelock included. Introduced 1991. From Maverick Arms.
Price: 6- or 9-shot $317.00

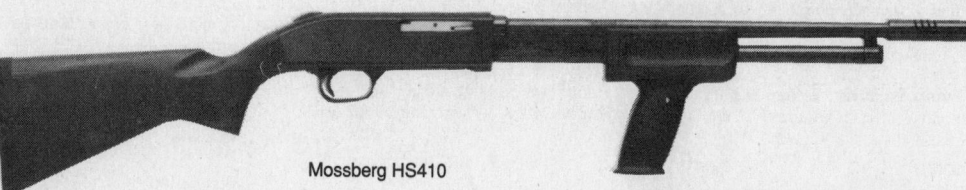

Mossberg Model 500

MOSSBERG MODEL 500 PERSUADER/CRUISER SECURITY SHOTGUNS
Gauge: 12, 20, 410, 3" chamber.
Barrel: 18½", 20" (Cyl.).
Weight: 7 lbs.
Stock: Walnut-finished hardwood or synthetic field.
Sights: Metal bead front.
Features: Available in 6- or 8-shot models. Top-mounted safety, double action slide bars, swivel studs, rubber recoil pad. Blue, Parkerized, Marinecote finishes. Pistol grip kit and Mossberg Cablelock included. From Mossberg.
Price: 12- or 20-ga., 18½", blue, wood or synthetic stock, 6-shot . . $272.00
Price: As above, Parkerized finish, synthetic stock, 6-shot $304.00
Price: Cruiser, 12- or 20-ga., 18½", blue, pistol grip, heat shield . . . $265.00
Price: As above, 410-bore $271.00
Price: 12-ga., 8-shot, blue, wood or synthetic stock $272.00
Price: As above with rifle sights $296.00

Mossberg Model 500, 590 Ghost-Ring Shotguns
Similar to the Model 500 Security except has adjustable blade front, adjustable Ghost-Ring rear sight with protective "ears." Model 500 has 18.5" (Cyl.) barrel, 6-shot capacity; Model 590 has 20" (Cyl.) barrel, 9-shot capacity. Both have synthetic field stock. Mossberg Cablelock included. Introduced 1990. From Mossberg.
Price: Model 500, blue $321.00
Price: As above, Parkerized $374.00
Price: Model 590, blue $376.00
Price: As above, Parkerized $426.00

Mossberg HS410

Mossberg Model HS410 Shotgun
Similar to the Model 500 Security pump except chambered for 410 with 3" chamber; has pistol grip forend, thick recoil pad, muzzle brake and has special spreader choke on the 18.5" barrel. Overall length is 37.5", weight is 6.25 lbs. Blue finish; synthetic field stock. Mossberg Cablelock and video included. Introduced 1990.
Price: HS 410 . . . . $284.00

Mossberg Model 500, 590 Mariner Pump
Similar to the Model 500 or 590 Security except all metal parts finished with Marinecote metal finish to resist rust and corrosion. Synthetic field stock; pistol grip kit included. Mossberg Cablelock included.
Price: 6-shot, 18½" barrel $396.00
Price: 9-shot, 20" barrel $406.00

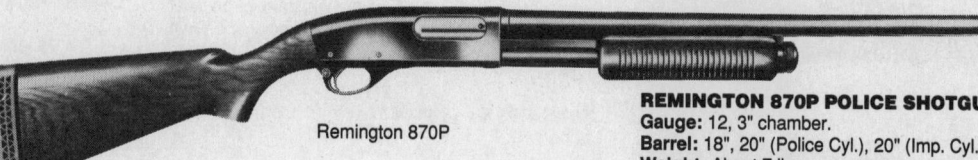

Mossberg Model 590

Stock: Synthetic field or Speedfeed.
Sights: Metal bead front.
Features: Top-mounted safety, double slide action bars. Comes with heat shield, bayonet lug, swivel studs, rubber recoil pad. Blue, Parkerized or Marinecote finish. Mossberg Cablelock included. From Mossberg.
Price: Blue, synthetic stock $322.00
Price: Parkerized, synthetic stock $371.00
Price: Blue, Speedfeed stock $351.00
Price: Parkerized, Speedfeed stock $403.00

MOSSBERG MODEL 590 SHOTGUN
Gauge: 12, 3" chamber.
Barrel: 20" (Cyl.).
Weight: 7¼ lbs.

Remington 870P

REMINGTON 870P POLICE SHOTGUN
Gauge: 12, 3" chamber.
Barrel: 18", 20" (Police Cyl.), 20" (Imp. Cyl.).
Weight: About 7 lbs.
Stock: Lacquer-finished hardwood.
Sights: Metal bead front or rifle sights.
Features: Solid steel receiver, double action slide bars. Blued or Parkerized finish.
Price: 18" or 20", bead sight, about $372.00
Price: As above, Parkerized $385.00
Price: 20", rifle sights, about $399.00

CAUTION: PRICES SHOWN ARE SUPPLIED BY THE MANUFACTURER OR IMPORTER. CHECK YOUR LCOAL GUNSHOP.

49th EDITION, 1995 **411**

SHOTGUNS—MILITARY & POLICE

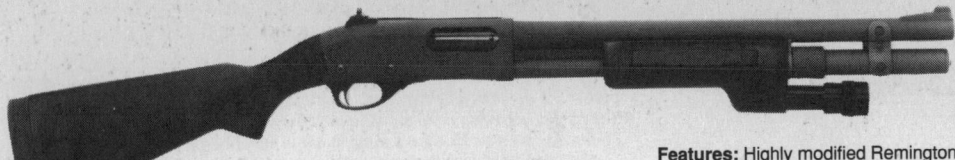

Tactical Response TR-870

TACTICAL RESPONSE TR-870 SHOTGUN
Gauge: 12, 3" chamber, 7-shot magazine.
Barrel: 18" (Cyl.).
Weight: 9 lbs. **Length:** 38" overall.
Stock: Fiberglass-filled polypropolene with non-snag recoil absorbing butt pad. Nylon tactical forend houses flashlight.
Sights: Trak-Lock ghost ring sight system. Front sight has tritium insert.

Features: Highly modified Remington 870P with Parkerized finish. Comes with nylon three-way adjustable sling, high visibility non-binding follower, high performance magazine spring, Jumbo Head safety, and Side Saddle extended 6-shot shell carrier on left side of receiver. Introduced 1991. From Scattergun Technologies, Inc.
Price: Standard model $695.00
Price: FBI model, 5-shot $665.00
Price: Patrol model, 5-shot, no Side Saddle $525.00
Price: Border Patrol model, 7-shot, standard forend $555.00
Price: Military model, 7-shot, bayonet lug $655.00
Price: K-9 model, 7-shot (Rem. 11-87 action) $755.00
Price: Urban Sniper, 7-shot, rifled bbl., Burris Scout scope, Rem. 11-87 action $1,095.00

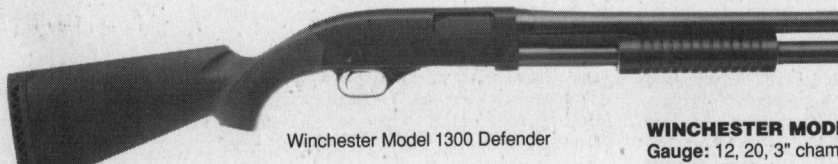

Winchester Model 1300 Defender

Winchester Model 1300 Stainless Marine Pump Gun
Same as the Defender except has bright chrome finish, stainless steel barrel, rifle-type sights only. Phosphate coated receiver for corrosion resistance.
Price: **$440.00**

Winchester 8-Shot Pistol Grip Pump Security Shotguns
Same as regular Defender Pump but with pistol grip and forend of high-impact resistant ABS plastic with non-glare black finish. Introduced 1984.
Price: Pistol Grip Defender **$277.00**

WINCHESTER MODEL 1300 DEFENDER PUMP GUN
Gauge: 12, 20, 3" chamber, 5- or 8-shot capacity.
Barrel: 18" (Cyl.).
Weight: 6¾ lbs. **Length:** 38⅝" overall.
Stock: Walnut-finished hardwood stock and ribbed forend, or synthetic; or pistol grip.
Sights: Metal bead front.
Features: Cross-bolt safety, front-locking rotary bolt, twin action slide bars. Black rubber buttpad. From U.S. Repeating Arms Co.
Price: 8-shot, wood or synthetic stock $277.00
Price: 5-shot, wood stock $277.00
Price: Defender Field Combo with pistol grip $381.00

BLACKPOWDER SINGLE SHOT PISTOLS—FLINT & PERCUSSION

Dixie Charleville

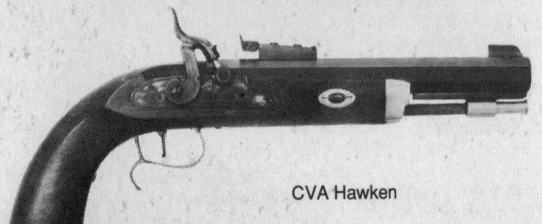

CVA Hawken

BLACK WATCH SCOTCH PISTOL
Caliber: 577 (.500" round ball).
Barrel: 7", smoothbore.
Weight: 1½ lbs. **Length:** 12" overall.
Stock: Brass.
Sights: None.
Features: Faithful reproduction of this military flintlock. From Dixie Gun Works.
Price: **$175.00**

CHARLEVILLE FLINTLOCK PISTOL
Caliber: 69 (.680" round ball).
Barrel: 7½".
Weight: 48 oz. **Length:** 13½" overall.
Stock: Walnut.
Sights: None.
Features: Brass frame, polished steel barrel, iron belt hook, brass buttcap and backstrap. Replica of original 1777 pistol. Imported by Dixie Gun Works.
Price: **$195.00**

CVA HAWKEN PISTOL
Caliber: 50.
Barrel: 9¾"; ¹⁵⁄₁₆" flats.
Weight: 50 oz. **Length:** 16½" overall.
Stock: Select hardwood.
Sights: Beaded blade front, fully adjustable open rear.
Features: Color case-hardened lock, polished brass wedge plate, nose cap, ramrod thimble, trigger guard, grip cap. Imported by CVA.
Price: **$149.95**
Price: Kit **$109.95**

CAUTION: PRICES SHOWN ARE SUPPLIED BY THE MANUFACTURER OR IMPORTER. CHECK YOUR LOCAL GUNSHOP.

BLACKPOWDER PISTOLS—SINGLE SHOT, FLINT & PERCUSSION

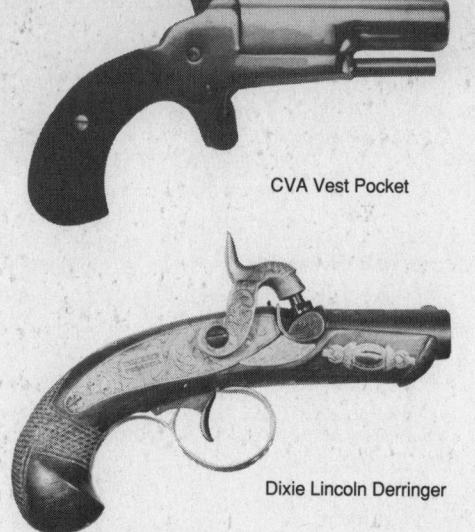

CVA Vest Pocket

CVA VEST POCKET DERRINGER
Caliber: 31.
Barrel: 2½", brass.
Weight: 16 oz.
Stock: Two-piece walnut.
Features: All brass frame and barrel. A muzzle-loading version of the Colt No. 3 derringer. Imported by CVA.
Price: Finished **$69.95**

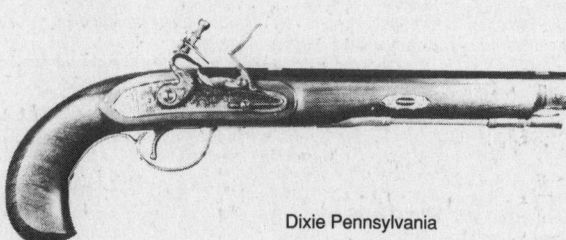

Dixie Lincoln Derringer

DIXIE LINCOLN DERRINGER
Caliber: 41.
Barrel: 2", 8 lands, 8 grooves.
Weight: 7 oz. **Length:** 5½" overall.
Stock: Walnut finish, checkered.
Sights: Fixed.
Features: Authentic copy of the "Lincoln Derringer." Shoots .400" patched ball. German silver furniture includes trigger guard with pineapple finial, wedge plates, nose, wrist, side and teardrop inlays. All furniture, lockplate, hammer, and breech plug engraved. Imported from Italy by Dixie Gun Works.
Price: With wooden case **$285.95**

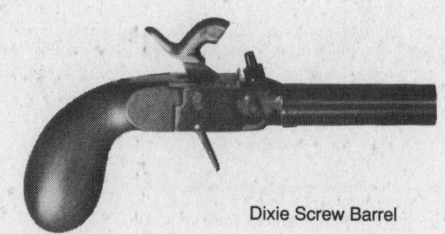

Dixie Pennsylvania

DIXIE PENNSYLVANIA PISTOL
Caliber: 44 (.430" round ball).
Barrel: 10" (⅞" octagon).
Weight: 2½ lbs.
Stock: Walnut-stained hardwood.
Sights: Blade front, open rear drift-adjustable for windage; brass.
Features: Available in flint only. Brass trigger guard, thimbles, nosecap, wedgeplates; high-luster blue barrel. Imported from Italy by Dixie Gun Works.
Price: Finished **$149.95**
Price: Kit **$119.95**

DIXIE SCREW BARREL PISTOL
Caliber: .445".
Barrel: 2½".
Weight: 8 oz. **Length:** 6½" overall.
Stock: Walnut.
Features: Trigger folds down when hammer is cocked. Close copy of the originals once made in Belgium. Uses No. 11 percussion caps. From Dixie Gun Works.
Price: **$89.00**
Price: Kit **$74.95**

Dixie Screw Barrel

DIXIE TORNADO TARGET PISTOL
Caliber: 44 (.430" round ball).
Barrel: 10", octagonal, 1:22 twist.
Stocks: Walnut, target-style. Left unfinished for custom fitting. Walnut forend.
Sights: Blade on ramp front, micro-type open rear adjustable for windage and elevation.
Features: Grip frame style of 1860 Colt revolver. Improved model of the Tingle and B.W. Southgate pistol. Trigger adjustable for pull. Frame, barrel, hammer and sights in the white, brass trigger guard. Comes with solid brass, walnut-handled cleaning rod with jag and nylon muzzle protector. Introduced 1983. From Dixie Gun Works.
Price: **$215.50**

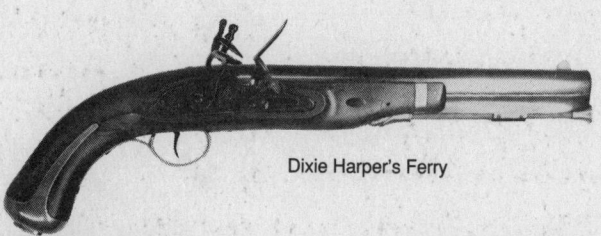

Dixie Tornado

FRENCH-STYLE DUELING PISTOL
Caliber: 44.
Barrel: 10".
Weight: 35 oz. **Length:** 15¾" overall.
Stock: Carved walnut.
Sights: Fixed.
Features: Comes with velvet-lined case and accessories. Imported by Mandall Shooting Supplies.
Price: **$295.00**

Dixie Harper's Ferry

HARPER'S FERRY 1806 PISTOL
Caliber: 58 (.570" round ball).
Barrel: 10".
Weight: 40 oz. **Length:** 16" overall.
Stock: Walnut.
Sights: Fixed.
Features: Case-hardened lock, brass-mounted browned barrel. Replica of the first U.S. Gov't.-made flintlock pistol. Imported by Navy Arms, Dixie Gun Works.
Price: . . . . **$249.95 to $405.00**
Price: Kit (Dixie) **$199.95**

CAUTION: PRICES SHOWN ARE SUPPLIED BY THE MANUFACTURER OR IMPORTER. CHECK YOUR LCOAL GUNSHOP.

49th EDITION, 1995 **413**

BLACKPOWDER PISTOLS—SINGLE SHOT, FLINT & PERCUSSION

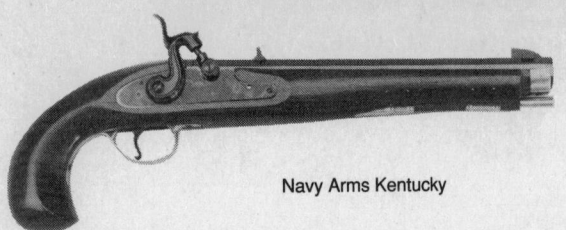

Navy Arms Kentucky

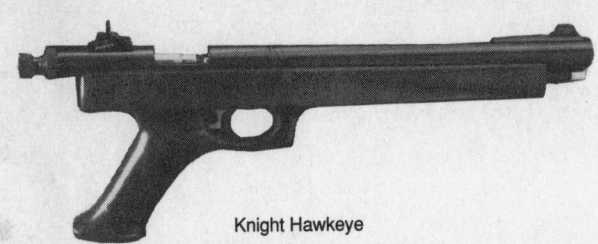

Knight Hawkeye

LE PAGE PERCUSSION DUELING PISTOL
Caliber: 45.
Barrel: 10", rifled.
Weight: 40 oz. **Length:** 16" overall.
Stock: Walnut, fluted butt.
Sights: Blade front, notch rear.
Features: Double-set triggers. Blued barrel; trigger guard and buttcap are polished silver. Imported by Dixie Gun Works.
Price: $259.95

Lyman Plains Pistol

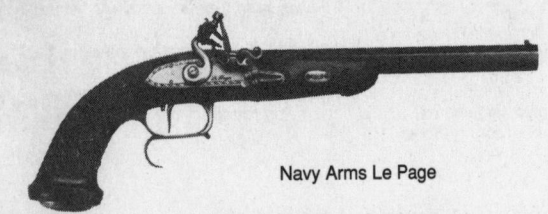

Navy Arms Le Page

> Consult our Directory pages for the location of firms mentioned.

W. PARKER FLINTLOCK PISTOL
Caliber: 45.
Barrel: 11", rifled.
Weight: 40 oz. **Length:** 16½" overall.
Stock: Walnut.
Sights: Blade front, notch rear.
Features: Browned barrel, silver-plated trigger guard, finger rest, polished and engraved lock. Double-set triggers. Imported by Dixie Gun Works.
Price: $310.00

KENTUCKY FLINTLOCK PISTOL
Caliber: 44, 45.
Barrel: 10⅛".
Weight: 32 oz. **Length:** 15½" overall.
Stock: Walnut.
Sights: Fixed.
Features: Specifications, including caliber, weight and length may vary with importer. Case-hardened lock, blued barrel; available also as brass barrel flint Model 1821. Imported by Cabela's, Navy Arms (44 only), The Armoury.
Price: . . . . **$145.00 to $207.00**
Price: In kit form, from . . . . **$90.00 to $112.00**
Price: Single cased set (Navy Arms) **$300.00**
Price: Double cased set (Navy Arms) **$515.00**

Kentucky Percussion Pistol
Similar to flint version but percussion lock. Imported by The Armoury, Cabela's, Navy Arms, CVA (50-cal.).
Price: . . . . **$129.95 to $250.00**
Price: Steel barrel (Armoury) **$179.00**
Price: Single cased set (Navy Arms) **$290.00**
Price: Double cased set (Navy Arms) **$495.00**

KNIGHT HAWKEYE PISTOL
Caliber: 50.
Barrel: 12", 1:20" twist.
Weight: 3¼ lbs. **Length:** 20" overall.
Stock: Black composite, autumn brown or shadow black laminate.
Sights: Bead front on ramp, open fully adjustable rear.
Features: In-line ignitiion design; patented double safety system; removeable breech plug; fully adjustable trigger; receiver drilled and tapped for scope mounting. Made in U.S. by Modern Muzzle Loading, Inc.
Price: Blued **$374.95**
Price: Stainless **$424.50**

LYMAN PLAINS PISTOL
Caliber: 50 or 54.
Barrel: 8", 1:30 twist, both calibers.
Weight: 50 oz. **Length:** 15" overall.
Stock: Walnut half-stock.
Sights: Blade front, square notch rear adjustable for windage.
Features: Polished brass trigger guard and ramrod tip, color case-hardened coil spring lock, spring-loaded trigger, stainless steel nipple, blackened iron furniture. Hooked patent breech, detachable belt hook. Introduced 1981. From Lyman Products.
Price: Finished **$219.95**
Price: Kit **$179.95**

MOORE & PATRICK FLINT DUELING PISTOL
Caliber: 45.
Barrel: 10", rifled.
Weight: 32 oz. **Length:** 14½" overall.
Stock: European walnut, checkered.
Sights: Fixed.
Features: Engraved, silvered lockplate, blue barrel. German silver furniture. Imported from Italy by Dixie Gun Works.
Price: **$335.00**

NAVY ARMS LE PAGE DUELING PISTOL
Caliber: 44.
Barrel: 9", octagon, rifled.
Weight: 34 oz. **Length:** 15" overall.
Stock: European walnut.
Sights: Adjustable rear.
Features: Single-set trigger. Polished metal finish. From Navy Arms.
Price: Percussion **$475.00**
Price: Single cased set, percussion **$685.00**
Price: Double cased set, percussion **$1,290.00**
Price: Flintlock, rifled **$550.00**
Price: Flintlock, smoothbore (45-cal.) **$550.00**
Price: Flintlock, single cased set **$760.00**
Price: Flintlock, double cased set **$1,430.00**

CAUTION: PRICES SHOWN ARE SUPPLIED BY THE MANUFACTURER OR IMPORTER. CHECK YOUR LOCAL GUNSHOP.

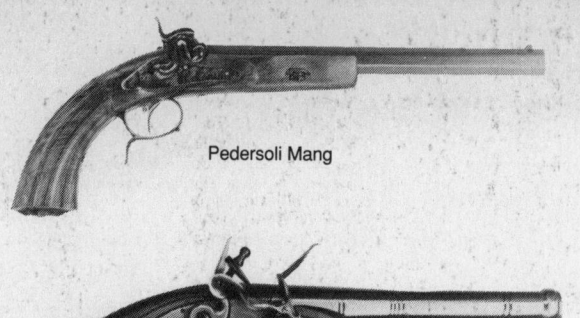

Pedersoli Mang

Dixie Queen Anne

PEDERSOLI MANG TARGET PISTOL
Caliber: 38.
Barrel: 10.5", octagonal; 1:15" twist,
Weight: 2.5 lbs. **Length:** 17.25" overall.
Stock: Walnut with fluted grip.
Sights: Blade front, open rear adjustable for windage.
Features: Browned barrel, polished breech plug, rest color case-hardened. Imported from Italy by Dixie Gun Works.
Price: **$749.00**

QUEEN ANNE FLINTLOCK PISTOL
Caliber: 50 (.490" round ball).
Barrel: 7½", smoothbore.
Stock: Walnut.
Sights: None.
Features: Browned steel barrel, fluted brass trigger guard, brass mask on butt. Lockplate left in the white. Made by Pedersoli in Italy. Introduced 1983. Imported by Dixie Gun Works.
Price: **$189.95**
Price: Kit **$138.50**

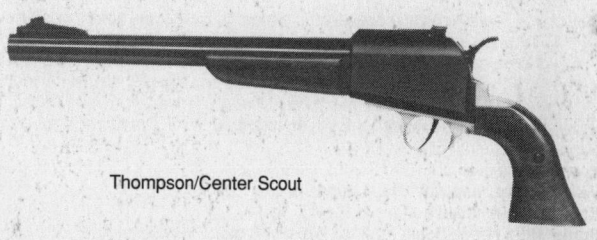

Thompson/Center Scout

THOMPSON/CENTER SCOUT PISTOL
Caliber: 45, 50 and 54.
Barrel: 12", interchangeable.
Weight: 4 lbs., 6 oz. **Length:** NA.
Stocks: American black walnut stocks and forend.
Sights: Blade on ramp front, fully adjustable Patridge rear.
Features: Patented in-line ignition system with special vented breech plug. Patented trigger mechanism consists of only two moving parts. Interchangeable barrels. Wide grooved hammer. Brass trigger guard assembly. Introduced 1990. From Thompson/Center.
Price: 45-, 50- or 54-cal. **$340.00**
Price: Extra barrel, 45-, 50- or 54-cal. **$145.00**

TRADITIONS BUCKSKINNER PISTOL
Caliber: 50.
Barrel: 10" octagonal, 15/16" flats.
Weight: 40 oz. **Length:** 15" overall.
Stocks: Stained beech or laminated wood.
Sights: Blade front, rear adjustable for windage.
Features: Percussion ignition. Blackened furniture. Imported by Traditions, Inc.
Price: Beech stocks **$157.00**
Price: Laminated stocks **$182.00**

TRADITIONS PHILADELPHIA DERRINGER
Caliber: 45.
Barrel: 3¼" octagonal, 7/8" flats.
Weight: 16 oz. **Length:** 7⅛" overall.
Stock: Stained beech.
Sights: Blade front.
Features: Color case-hardened percussion lock has coil mainspring. Brass furniture, engraved wedge plate. Imported by Traditions, Inc.
Price: **$109.00**
Price: Kit **$82.00**

Traditions Pioneer

TRADITIONS PIONEER PISTOL
Caliber: 45.
Barrel: 9⅝", 13/16" flats.
Weight: 36 oz. **Length:** 15" overall.
Stock: Beech.
Sights: Blade front, fixed rear.
Features: V-type mainspring; 1:18" twist. Single trigger. German silver furniture, blackened hardware. From Traditions, Inc.
Price: **$169.00**
Price: Kit **$119.00**

TRADITIONS WILLIAM PARKER PISTOL
Caliber: 45 and 50.
Barrel: 10⅜", 15/16" flats; polished steel.
Weight: 40 oz. **Length:** 17½" overall.
Stock: Walnut with checkered grip.
Sights: Brass blade front, fixed rear.
Features: Replica dueling pistol with 1:18" twist, hooked breech. Brass wedge plate, trigger guard, cap guard; separate ramrod. Double-set triggers. Polished steel barrel, lock. Imported by Traditions, Inc.
Price: **$265.00**

TRADITIONS VEST POCKET DERRINGER
Caliber: 31.
Barrel: 2½", round.
Weight: 16 oz. **Length:** 5" overall.
Stocks: White composite.
Sights: Post front.
Features: Polished brass barrel and frame, blued trigger and screws. Imported by Traditions, Inc.
Price: **$75.00**

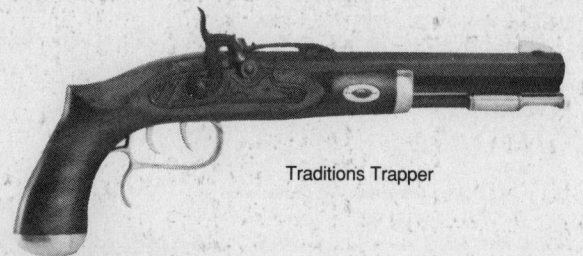

Traditions Trapper

TRADITIONS TRAPPER PISTOL
Caliber: 50.
Barrel: 9¾", 7/8" flats.
Weight: 2¾ lbs. **Length:** 16" overall.
Stock: Beech.
Sights: Blade front, adjustable rear.
Features: Double-set triggers; brass buttcap, trigger guard, wedge plate, forend tip, thimble. From Traditions, Inc.
Price: **$170.00**
Price: Kit **$130.00**

Army 1851

ARMY 1860 PERCUSSION REVOLVER
Caliber: 44, 6-shot.
Barrel: 8".
Weight: 40 oz. **Length:** 13⅝" overall.
Stocks: Walnut.
Sights: Fixed.
Features: Engraved Navy scene on cylinder; brass trigger guard; case-hardened frame, loading lever and hammer. Some importers supply pistol cut for detachable shoulder stock, have accessory stock available. Imported by American Arms, Cabela's (1860 Lawman), E.M.F., Navy Arms, The Armoury, Cimarron, Dixie Gun Works (half-fluted cylinder, not roll engraved), Euroarms of America (brass or steel model), Armsport, Mitchell, Traditions, Inc. (brass or steel), Uberti USA.
Price: About . . . . **$92.95 to $300.00**
Price: Single cased set (Navy Arms) **$265.00**
Price: Double cased set (Navy Arms) **$430.00**
Price: 1861 Navy: Same as Army except 36-cal., 7½" bbl., wgt. 41 oz., cut for shoulder stock; round cylinder (fluted avail.), from CVA (brass frame, 44-cal.), Mitchell . . . . **$99.95 to $249.00**
Price: Steel frame kit (E.M.F., Mitchell, Navy, Euroarms) **$125.00 to $216.25**
Price: Colt Army Police, fluted cyl., 5½", 36-cal. (Cabela's) **$124.95**

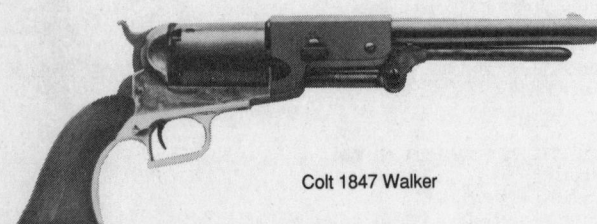

Colt 1847 Walker

COLT 1849 POCKET DRAGOON REVOLVER
Caliber: 31.
Barrel: 4".
Weight: 24 oz. **Length:** 9½" overall.
Stocks: One-piece walnut.
Sights: Fixed. Brass pin front, hammer notch rear.
Features: Color case-hardened frame. No loading lever. Unfluted cylinder with engraved scene. Exact reproduction of original. From Colt Blackpowder Arms Co.
Price: **$390.00**

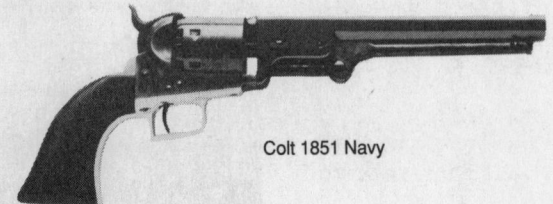

Colt 1851 Navy

CVA Colt Sheriff's Model
Similar to the Uberti 1861 Navy except has 5½" barrel, brass or steel frame, semi-fluted cylinder. In 36-caliber only.
Price: Brass frame, finished **$149.95**
Price: Brass frame (Armsport) **$155.00**
Price: Steel frame (Armsport) **$193.00**

ARMY 1851 PERCUSSION REVOLVER
Caliber: 44, 6-shot.
Barrel: 7½".
Weight: 45 oz. **Length:** 13" overall.
Stocks: Walnut finish.
Sights: Fixed.
Features: 44-caliber version of the 1851 Navy. Imported by The Armoury, Armsport.
Price: **$129.00**

American Arms 1860 Army

BABY DRAGOON 1848, 1849 POCKET, WELLS FARGO
Caliber: 31.
Barrel: 3", 4", 5", 6"; seven-groove, RH twist.
Weight: About 21 oz.
Stock: Varnished walnut.
Sights: Brass pin front, hammer notch rear.
Features: No loading lever on Baby Dragoon or Wells Fargo models. Unfluted cylinder with stagecoach holdup scene; cupped cylinder pin; no grease grooves; one safety pin on cylinder and slot in hammer face; straight (flat) mainspring. From Armsport, Dixie Gun Works, Uberti USA, Cabela's.
Price: 6" barrel, with loading lever (Dixie Gun Works) **$254.00**
Price: 4" (Cabela's, Uberti USA) **$179.95**

COLT 1847 WALKER PERCUSSION REVOLVER
Caliber: 44.
Barrel: 9", 7 groove, right-hand twist.
Weight: 73 oz.
Stocks: One-piece walnut.
Sights: German silver front sight, hammer notch rear.
Features: Made in U.S. Faithful reproduction of the original gun, including markings. Color case-hardened frame, hammer, loading lever and plunger. Blue steel backstrap, brass square-back trigger guard. Blue barrel, cylinder, trigger and wedge. From Colt Blackpowder Arms Co.
Price: **$442.50**

CABELA'S PATERSON REVOLVER
Caliber: 36, 5-shot cylinder.
Barrel: 7½".
Weight: 24 oz. **Length:** 11½" overall.
Stocks: One-piece walnut.
Sights: Fixed.
Features: Recreation of the 1836 gun. Color case-hardened frame, steel backstrap; roll-engraved cylinder scene. Imported by Cabela's.
Price: **$199.95**

COLT 1851 NAVY PERCUSSION REVOLVER
Caliber: 36.
Barrel: 7½", octagonal, 7 groove left-hand twist.
Weight: 40½ oz.
Stocks: One-piece oiled American walnut.
Sights: Brass pin front, hammer notch rear.
Features: Faithful reproduction of the original gun. Color case-hardened frame, loading lever, plunger, hammer and latch. Blue cylinder, trigger, barrel, screws, wedge. Silver-plated brass backstrap and square-back trigger guard. From Colt Blackpowder Arms Co.
Price: **$427.50**

Uberti 1861 Navy Percussion Revolver
Similar to 1851 Navy except has round 7½" barrel, rounded trigger guard, German silver blade front sight, "creeping" loading lever. Available with fluted or round cylinder. Imported by Uberti USA.
Price: Steel backstrap, trigger guard, cut for stock **$300.00**

BLACKPOWDER REVOLVERS

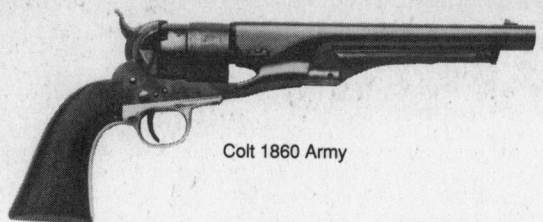

Colt 1860 Army

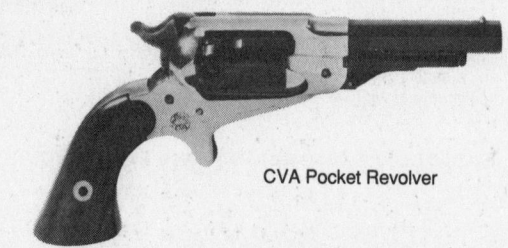

CVA Pocket Revolver

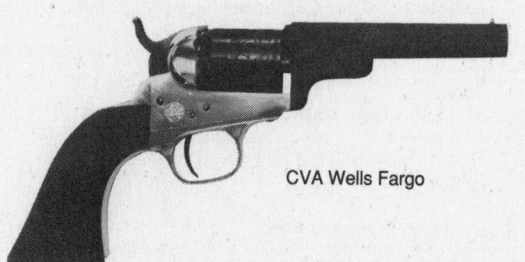

CVA Wells Fargo

Dixie Third Model Dragoon

Griswold & Gunnison

COLT 1860 ARMY PERCUSSION REVOLVER
Caliber: 44.
Barrel: 8", 7 groove, left-hand twist.
Weight: 42 oz.
Stocks: One-piece walnut.
Sights: German silver front sight, hammer notch rear.
Features: Steel backstrap cut for shoulder stock; brass trigger guard. Cylinder has Navy scene. Color case-hardened frame, hammer, loading lever. Reproduction of original gun with all original markings. From Colt Blackpowder Arms Co.
Price: **$427.50**

CVA POCKET REVOLVER
Caliber: 31, 5-shot.
Barrel: 4", octagonal.
Weight: 15 oz. **Length:** 7½" overall.
Stocks: Two-piece walnut.
Sights: Post front, grooved topstrap rear.
Features: Spur trigger, brass frame with blued barrel and cylinder. Introduced 1984. Imported by CVA.
Price: Finished **$129.95**

CVA WELLS FARGO MODEL
Caliber: 31, 5-shot.
Barrel: 4", octagonal.
Weight: 28 oz. (with extra cylinder). **Length:** 9" overall.
Stocks: Walnut.
Sights: Post front, hammer notch rear.
Features: Brass frame and backstrap; blue finish. Comes with extra cylinder. Imported by CVA.
Price: Brass frame, finished **$129.95**

DIXIE THIRD MODEL DRAGOON
Caliber: 44 (.454" round ball).
Barrel: 7⅜".
Weight: 4 lbs., 2½ oz.
Stocks: One-piece walnut.
Sights: Brass pin front, hammer notch rear, or adjustable folding leaf rear.
Features: Cylinder engraved with Indian fight scene. This is the only Dragoon replica with folding leaf sight. Brass backstrap and trigger guard; color case-hardened steel frame, blue-black barrel. Imported by Dixie Gun Works.
Price: **$199.95**

DIXIE WYATT EARP REVOLVER
Caliber: 44.
Barrel: 12" octagon.
Weight: 46 oz. **Length:** 18" overall.
Stocks: Two-piece walnut.
Sights: Fixed.
Features: Highly polished brass frame, backstrap and trigger guard; blued barrel and cylinder; case-hardened hammer, trigger and loading lever. Navy-size shoulder stock ($45) will fit with minor fitting. From Dixie Gun Works.
Price: **$130.00**

GRISWOLD & GUNNISON PERCUSSION REVOLVER
Caliber: 36 or 44, 6-shot.
Barrel: 7½".
Weight: 44 oz. (36-cal.). **Length:** 13" overall.
Stocks: Walnut.
Sights: Fixed.
Features: Replica of famous Confederate pistol. Brass frame, backstrap and trigger guard; case-hardened loading lever; rebated cylinder (44-cal. only). Rounded Dragoon-type barrel. Imported by Navy Arms (as Reb Model 1860).
Price: About **$229.00**
Price: Single cased set (Navy Arms) **$205.00**
Price: Double cased set (Navy Arms) **$335.00**
Price: As above, kit **$90.00**

LE MAT REVOLVER
Caliber: 44/65.
Barrel: 6¾" (revolver); 4⅞" (single shot).
Weight: 3 lbs., 7 oz.
Stocks: Hand-checkered walnut.
Sights: Post front, hammer notch rear.
Features: Exact reproduction with all-steel construction; 44-cal. 9-shot cylinder, 65-cal. single barrel; color case-hardened hammer with selector; spur trigger guard; ring at butt; lever-type barrel release. From Navy Arms.
Price: Cavalry model (lanyard ring, spur trigger guard) **$595.00**
Price: Army model (round trigger guard, pin-type barrel release) . . **$595.00**
Price: Naval-style (thumb selector on hammer) **$595.00**
Price: Engraved 18th Georgia cased set **$795.00**
Price: Engraved Beauregard cased set **$1,000.00**

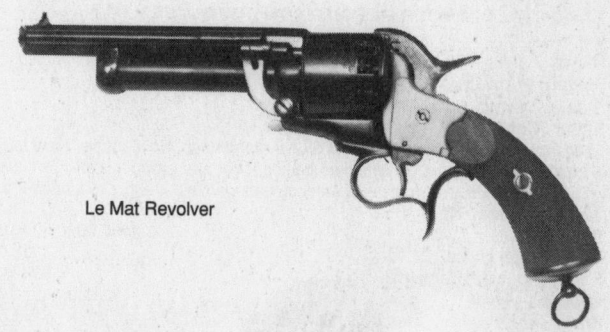

Le Mat Revolver

CAUTION: PRICES SHOWN ARE SUPPLIED BY THE MANUFACTURER OR IMPORTER. CHECK YOUR LCOAL GUNSHOP.

49th EDITION, 1995 **417**

Uberti 1851 Squareback

CONSULT
Shooter's Marketplace
Page 225, This Issue

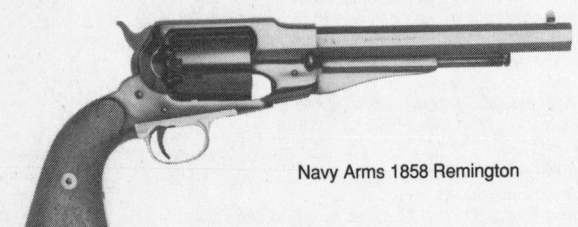

Navy Arms 1858 Remington

CVA 1858 Target Revolver

Similar to the New Model 1858 Army revolver except has ramp-mounted blade front sight on 8" barrel, adjustable rear sight, overall blue finish. Imported by CVA.
Price: **$204.95**

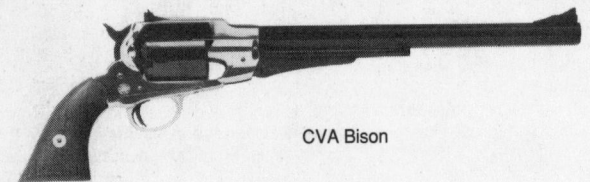

CVA Bison

POCKET POLICE 1862 PERCUSSION REVOLVER

Caliber: 36, 5-shot.
Barrel: 4½", 5½", 6½", 7½".
Weight: 26 oz. **Length:** 12" overall (6½" bbl.).
Stocks: Walnut.
Sights: Fixed.
Features: Round tapered barrel; half-fluted and rebated cylinder; case-hardened frame, loading lever and hammer; silver or brass trigger guard and backstrap. Imported by CVA (7½" only), Navy Arms (5½" only), Uberti USA (5½", 6½" only).
Price: About . . . . **$139.95 to $310.00**
Price: Single cased set with accessories (Navy Arms) **$360.00**

ROGERS & SPENCER PERCUSSION REVOLVER

Caliber: 44.
Barrel: 7½".
Weight: 47 oz. **Length:** 13¾" overall.
Stocks: Walnut.
Sights: Cone front, integral groove in frame for rear.
Features: Accurate reproduction of a Civil War design. Solid frame; extra large nipple cut-out on rear of cylinder; loading lever and cylinder easily removed for cleaning. From Euroarms of America (standard blue, engraved, burnished, target models), Navy Arms.
Price: . . . . **$160.00 to $276.00**
Price: Nickel-plated **$215.00**
Price: Engraved (Euroarms) **$349.00**
Price: Kit version . . . . **$245.00–$252.00**
Price: Target version (Euroarms, Navy Arms) **$291.00**
Price: Burnished London Gray (Euroarms, Navy Arms) . . . **$299.00**

NAVY MODEL 1851 PERCUSSION REVOLVER

Caliber: 36, 44, 6-shot.
Barrel: 7½".
Weight: 44 oz. **Length:** 13" overall.
Stocks: Walnut finish.
Sights: Post front, hammer notch rear.
Features: Brass backstrap and trigger guard; some have 1st Model square-back trigger guard, engraved cylinder with navy battle scene; case-hardened frame, hammer, loading lever. Imported by American Arms, The Armoury, Cabela's, Mitchell, Navy Arms, E.M.F., Dixie Gun Works, Euroarms of America, Armsport, CVA (36-cal. only), Traditions, Inc., Uberti USA.
Price: Brass frame . . . . **$99.95 to $280.00**
Price: Steel frame . . . . **$130.00 to $285.00**
Price: Kit form . . . . **$110.00 to $123.95**
Price: Engraved model (Dixie Gun Works) **$139.95**
Price: Single cased set, steel frame (Navy Arms) **$245.00**
Price: Double cased set, steel frame (Navy Arms) **$405.00**
Price: Confederate Navy (Cabela's) **$69.95**

NAVY ARMS DELUXE 1858 REMINGTON-STYLE REVOLVER

Caliber: 44.
Barrel: 8".
Weight: 2 lbs., 13 oz.
Stocks: Smooth walnut.
Sights: Dovetailed blade front.
Features: First exact reproduction—correct in size and weight to the original, with progressive rifling; highly polished with blue finish, silver-plated trigger guard. From Navy Arms.
Price: Deluxe model **$365.00**

NEW MODEL 1858 ARMY PERCUSSION REVOLVER

Caliber: 36 or 44, 6-shot.
Barrel: 6½" or 8".
Weight: 38 oz. **Length:** 13½" overall.
Stocks: Walnut.
Sights: Blade front, groove-in-frame rear.
Features: Replica of Remington Model 1858. Also available from some importers as Army Model Belt Revolver in 36-cal., a shortened and lightened version of the 44. Target Model (Uberti USA, Navy Arms) has fully adjustable target rear sight, target front, 36 or 44. Imported by American Arms, Cabela's, Cimarron, CVA (as 1858 Army), Dixie Gun Works, Navy Arms, The Armoury, E.M.F., Euroarms of America (engraved, stainless and plain), Armsport, Mitchell, Traditions, Inc., Uberti USA.
Price: Steel frame, about . . . . **$99.95 to $280.00**
Price: Steel frame kit (Euroarms, Navy Arms) . . . . . **$115.95 to $242.00**
Price: Single cased set (Navy Arms) **$255.00**
Price: Double cased set (Navy Arms) **$420.00**
Price: Stainless steel Model 1858 (American Arms, Euroarms, Uberti USA, Cabela's, Navy Arms, Armsport, Traditions) . . . . . . **$169.95 to $380.00**
Price: Target Model, adjustable rear sight (Cabela's, Euroarms, Uberti USA, Navy Arms) . . . . **$95.95 to $399.00**
Price: Brass frame (CVA, Cabela's, Traditions, Navy Arms) **$79.95 to $212.95**
Price: As above, kit (CVA, Dixie Gun Works, Navy Arms) **$145.00 to $188.95**
Price: Remington "Texas" (Mitchell) **$199.00**
Price: Buffalo model, 44-cal. (Cabela's) **$129.95**

CVA Bison Revolver

Similar to the CVA 1858 Target except has 10¼" octagonal barrel, 44-caliber, brass frame.
Price: Finished **$194.95**
Price: From Armsport **$222.00**

Euroarms Rogers & Spencer

CAUTION: PRICES SHOWN ARE SUPPLIED BY THE MANUFACTURER OR IMPORTER. CHECK YOUR LOCAL GUNSHOP.

BLACKPOWDER REVOLVERS

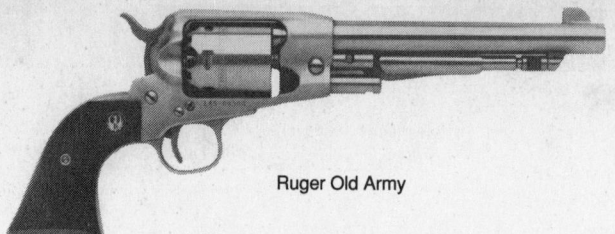

Ruger Old Army

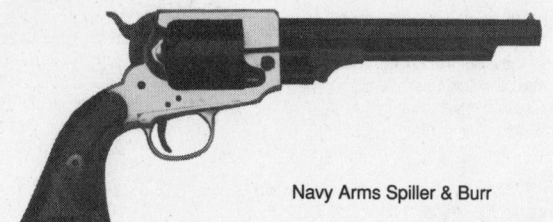

Navy Arms Spiller & Burr

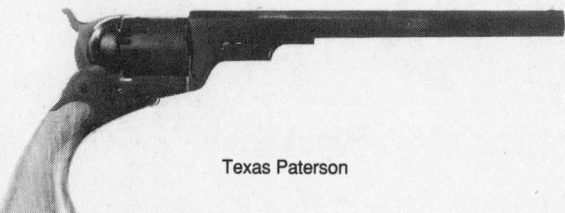

Texas Paterson

TEXAS PATERSON 1836 REVOLVER
Caliber: 36 (.375" round ball).
Barrel: 7½".
Weight: 42 oz.
Stocks: One-piece walnut.
Sights: Fixed.
Features: Copy of Sam Colt's first commercially-made revolving pistol. Has no loading lever but comes with loading tool. From Dixie Gun Works, Navy Arms, Uberti USA.
Price: About . . . . $335.00 to $395.00
Price: With loading lever (Uberti USA) $450.00
Price: Engraved (Navy Arms) $465.00

UBERTI 1862 POCKET NAVY PERCUSSION REVOLVER
Caliber: 36, 5-shot.
Barrel: 5½", 6½", octagonal, 7-groove, LH twist.
Weight: 27 oz. (5½" barrel). **Length:** 10½" overall (5½" bbl.).
Stocks: One-piece varnished walnut.
Sights: Brass pin front, hammer notch rear.
Features: Rebated cylinder, hinged loading lever, brass or silver-plated backstrap and trigger guard, color-cased frame, hammer, loading lever, plunger and latch, rest blued. Has original-type markings. From Uberti USA.
Price: With brass backstrap, trigger guard $310.00

UBERTI 1st MODEL DRAGOON
Caliber: 44.
Barrel: 7½", part round, part octagon.
Weight: 64 oz.
Stocks: One-piece walnut.
Sights: German silver blade front, hammer notch rear.
Features: First model has oval bolt cuts in cylinder, square-back flared trigger guard, V-type mainspring, short trigger. Ranger and Indian scene roll-engraved on cylinder. Color case-hardened frame, loading lever, plunger and hammer; blue barrel, cylinder, trigger and wedge. Available with old-time charcoal blue or standard blue-black finish. Polished brass backstrap and trigger guard. From Uberti USA.
Price: $325.00

Uberti 2nd Model Dragoon Revolver
Similar to the 1st Model except distinguished by rectangular bolt cuts in the cylinder.
Price: $325.00

RUGER OLD ARMY PERCUSSION REVOLVER
Caliber: 45, 6-shot. Uses .457" dia. lead bullets.
Barrel: 7½" (6-groove, 16" twist).
Weight: 46 oz. **Length:** 13¾" overall.
Stocks: Smooth walnut.
Sights: Ramp front, rear adjustable for windage and elevation; or fixed (groove).
Features: Stainless steel; standard size nipples, chrome-moly steel cylinder and frame, same lockwork as in original Super Blackhawk. Also available in stainless steel. Made in USA. From Sturm, Ruger & Co.
Price: Stainless steel (Model KBP-7) $428.00
Price: Blued steel (Model BP-7) $378.50
Price: Stainless steel, fixed sight (KBP-7F) $428.00
Price: Blued steel, fixed sight (BP-7F) $378.50

SHERIFF MODEL 1851 PERCUSSION REVOLVER
Caliber: 36, 44, 6-shot.
Barrel: 5".
Weight: 40 oz. **Length:** 10½" overall.
Stocks: Walnut.
Sights: Fixed.
Features: Brass backstrap and trigger guard; engraved navy scene; case-hardened frame, hammer, loading lever. Imported by E.M.F.
Price: Steel frame $172.00
Price: Brass frame $140.00

SPILLER & BURR REVOLVER
Caliber: 36 (.375" round ball).
Barrel: 7", octagon.
Weight: 2½ lbs. **Length:** 12½" overall.
Stocks: Two-piece walnut.
Sights: Fixed.
Features: Reproduction of the C.S.A. revolver. Brass frame and trigger guard. Also available as a kit. From Cabela's, Dixie Gun Works, Mitchell, Navy Arms.
Price: . . . . $89.95 to $199.00
Price: Kit form $95.00
Price: Single cased set (Navy Arms) $230.00
Price: Double cased set (Navy Arms) $370.00

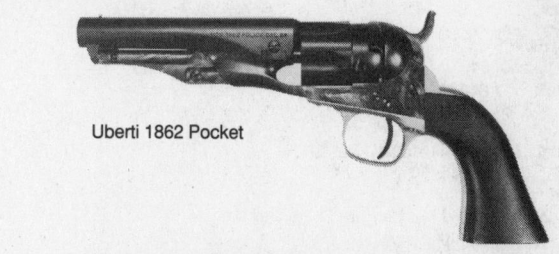

Uberti 1862 Pocket

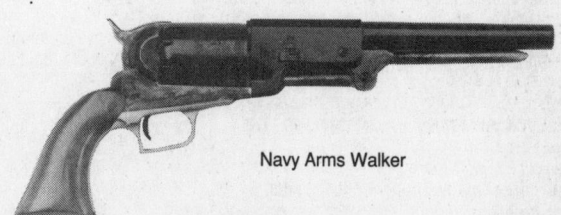

Navy Arms Walker

WALKER 1847 PERCUSSION REVOLVER
Caliber: 44, 6-shot.
Barrel: 9".
Weight: 84 oz. **Length:** 15½" overall.
Stocks: Walnut.
Sights: Fixed.
Features: Case-hardened frame, loading lever and hammer; iron backstrap; brass trigger guard; engraved cylinder. Imported by American Arms, Cabela's, CVA, Navy Arms, Dixie Gun Works, Uberti USA, E.M.F., Cimarron, Traditions, Inc.
Price: About . . . . $225.00 to $360.00
Price: Single cased set (Navy Arms) $385.00
Price: Deluxe Walker with French fitted case (Navy Arms) $505.00

Uberti 3rd Model Dragoon Revolver
Similar to the 2nd Model except for oval trigger guard, long trigger, modifications to the loading lever and latch. Imported by Uberti USA.
Price: Military model (frame cut for shoulder stock, steel backstrap) . $330.00
Price: Civilian (brass backstrap, trigger guard) $325.00

CAUTION: PRICES SHOWN ARE SUPPLIED BY THE MANUFACTURER OR IMPORTER. CHECK YOUR LCOAL GUNSHOP.

49th EDITION, 1995 **419**

Armoury R140 Hawken

ARMSPORT 1863 SHARPS RIFLE, CARBINE
Caliber: 45, 54.
Barrel: 28", round.
Weight: 8.4 lbs. **Length:** 46" overall.
Stock: Walnut.
Sights: Blade front, folding adjustable rear. Tang sight set optionally available.
Features: Replica of the 1863 Sharps. Color case-hardened frame, rest blued. Imported by Armsport.
Price: **$740.00**
Price: Carbine, 54 caliber, 22" barrel **$640.00**

ARMOURY R140 HAWKEN RIFLE
Caliber: 45, 50 or 54.
Barrel: 29".
Weight: 8¾ to 9 lbs. **Length:** 45¾" overall.
Stock: Walnut, with cheekpiece.
Sights: Dovetail front, fully adjustable rear.
Features: Octagon barrel, removable breech plug; double set triggers; blued barrel, brass stock fittings, color case-hardened percussion lock. From Armsport, The Armoury.
Price: . . . . **$225.00 to $245.00**

BOSTONIAN PERCUSSION RIFLE
Caliber: 45.
Barrel: 30", octagonal
Weight: 7¼ lbs. **Length:** 46" overall.
Stock: Walnut.
Sights: Blade front, fixed notch rear.
Features: Color case-hardened lock, brass trigger guard, buttplate, patchbox. Imported from Italy by E.M.F.
Price: **$285.00**

Cabela's Accura 9000

CABELA'S ACCURA 9000 MUZZLELOADER
Caliber: 50, 54.
Barrel: 27"; 1:54 twist.

CABELA'S BLUE RIDGE RIFLE
Caliber: 32, 36, 45, 50, 54.
Barrel: 39", octagonal.
Weight: About 7¾ lbs. **Length:** 55" overall.
Stock: American black walnut.
Sights: Blade front, rear drift adjustable for windage.
Features: Color case-hardened lockplate and cock/hammer, brass trigger guard and buttplate, double set, double-phased triggers. From Cabela's.
Price: Percussion **$299.95**
Price: Flintlock **$329.95**

CABELA'S SHARPS SPORTING RIFLE
Caliber: 45, 54.
Barrel: 31", octagonal.
Weight: About 10 lbs. **Length:** 49" overall.
Stock: American walnut with checkered grip and forend.
Sights: Blade front, ladder-type adjustable rear.
Features: Color case-hardened lock and buttplate. Adjustable double set, double-phased triggers. From Cabela's.
Price: **$595.00**

Weight: About 7½ lbs. **Length:** 44" overall.
Stock: European walnut with Monte Carlo cheekpiece, checkered grip and forend.
Sights: Hooded front with interchangeable blades, open rear adjustable for windage and elevation.
Features: In-line ignition system with removable breech plug. Automatic safety and half-cock. Quick detachable sling swivels, schnabel forend tip, recoil pad. From Cabela's.
Price: Right or left-hand **$359.95**

CABELA'S ROLLING BLOCK MUZZLELOADER
Caliber: 50, 54.
Barrel: 26½" octagonal; 1:32" (50), 1:48" (54) twist.
Weight: About 9¼ lbs. **Length:** 43½" overall.
Stock: American walnut, rubber butt pad.
Sights: Blade front, adjustable buckhorn rear.
Features: Uses in-line ignition system, Brass trigger guard, color case-hardened hammer, block and buttplate; black-finished, engraved receiver; easily removable screw-in breech plug; black ramrod and thimble. From Cabela's.
Price: **$269.95**

Cabela's Rolling Block Muzzleloader Carbine
Similar to the rifle version except has 22¼" barrel, weighs 8¼ lbs. Has bead on ramp front sight, modern fully adjustable rear. From Cabela's.
Price: **$249.95**

CABELA'S SWIVEL-BARREL RIFLE

Cabela's Swivel Barrel

Caliber: 50, 54.
Barrel: 23.75".
Weight: 10 lbs. **Length:** 40" overall.
Stock: Checkered American walnut.
Sights: Blade front, open rear adjustable for windage and elevation; one set for each barrel.
Features: Barrel assembly rotates for second shot. Back action mechanism. Monte Carlo comb, rubber butt pad; checkered pistol grip and forend panels. Introduced 1992. From Cabela's.
Price: **$379.95**

BLACKPOWDER MUSKETS & RIFLES

CABELA'S TAOS RIFLE
Caliber: 45, 50.
Barrel: 28¼".
Weight: 6 lbs., 11 oz. **Length:** 43¼" overall.
Stock: Oil-finished walnut.
Sights: Blade front, rear adjustable for windage.
Features: Carbine version of the Pennsylvania rifle. Adjustable double-set triggers. Imported by Cabela's.
Price: Percussion $259.95
Price: Flintlock $244.95

Cabela's Sporterized Hawken Hunter Rifle
Similar to the Traditional Hawken's except has more modern stock style with rubber recoil pad, blued furniture, sling swivels. Percussion only, in 45-, 50-, 54- or 58-caliber.
Price: Carbine or rifle, right-hand $189.95
Price: Carbine or rifle, left-hand $199.95

Cabela's Ranger Hawken
Similar to the Traditional Hawken except has hardwood stock with matte finish, rubber buttpad, 28" barrel with brass-plated front sight, adjustable buckhorn rear. Has single trigger with pioneer-style brass trigger guard, color case-hardened lockplate. From Cabela's.
Price: Right-hand only $129.95

CABELA'S TRADITIONAL HAWKEN
Caliber: 45, 50, 54, 58.
Barrel: 29".
Weight: About 9 lbs.
Stock: Walnut.
Sights: Blade front, open adjustable rear.
Features: Flintlock or percussion. Adjustable double-set triggers. Polished brass furniture, color case-hardened lock. Imported by Cabela's.
Price: Percussion, right-hand $174.95
Price: Percussion, right-hand, kit $144.95
Price: Percussion, left-hand $179.95
Price: Flintlock, right-hand $199.95
Price: Flintlock kit $159.95

CONSULT **Shooter's Marketplace** Page 225, This Issue

Cook & Brother

COOK & BROTHER CONFEDERATE CARBINE
Caliber: 58.
Barrel: 24".

Weight: 7½ lbs. **Length:** 40½" overall.
Stock: Select walnut.
Features: Recreation of the 1861 New Orleans-made artillery carbine. Color case-hardened lock, browned barrel. Buttplate, trigger guard, barrel bands, sling swivels and nose cap of polished brass. From Euroarms of America.
Price: $504.00
Price: Cook & Brother rifle (33" barrel) $549.00

Cumberland Mountain

CUMBERLAND MOUNTAIN BLACKPOWDER RIFLE
Caliber: 50.
Barrel: 26", round.

Weight: 9½ lbs. **Length:** 43" overall.
Stock: American walnut.
Sights: Bead front, open rear adjustable for windage.
Features: Falling block action fires with shotshell primer. Blued receiver and barrel. Introduced 1993. Made in U.S. by Cumberland Mountain Arms, Inc.
Price: $865.00

CVA Apollo Classic

CVA APOLLO CARBELITE RIFLE
Caliber: 50.
Barrel: 27", blued, round; 1:32" rifling.
Weight: 7½ lbs. **Length:** 43" overall.
Stock: Black Carbelite composite with fluted Monte Carlo comb, cheekpiece, full pistol grip. Sling swivel studs.
Sights: Bead on ramp front, fully adjustable click rear. Drilled and tapped for scope mounting or peep sight.
Features: In-line percussion system with push-pull bolt block safety system. One-piece blued barrel/receiver. Has loading window and foul weather cover. Vented for gas escape. From CVA.
Price: $349.95

CVA APOLLO SHADOW SS, CLASSIC RIFLES
Caliber: 50, 54.
Barrel: 24"; round with octagon integral receiver; 1:32" twist.
Weight: 9 lbs. **Length:** 42" overall.
Stock: Hardwood with black textured DuraGrip finish (Shadow SS); brown laminate with swivel studs (Classic); pistol grip, solid rubber buttpad.
Sights: Blade on ramp front, fully adjustable rear; drilled and tapped for scope mounting.
Features: In-line ignition, modern-style trigger with automatic safety; oversize trigger guard; synthetic ramrod. From CVA.
Price: Shadow SS $219.95
Price: Classic $266.95

CVA BUSHWACKER RIFLE
Caliber: 50.
Barrel: 26", octagonal; ¹⁵⁄₁₆" flats; 1:48" twist.
Weight: 7.5 lbs. **Length:** 40" overall.
Stock: Walnut-stained hardwood.
Sights: Brass blade front, adjustable open rear.
Features: Color case-hardened lockplate; single trigger with oversize blackened trigger guard; blued barrel, wedge plates. From CVA.
Price: Percussion only $159.95

CAUTION: PRICES SHOWN ARE SUPPLIED BY THE MANUFACTURER OR IMPORTER. CHECK YOUR LCOAL GUNSHOP.

49th EDITION, 1995 **421**

BLACKPOWDER MUSKETS & RIFLES

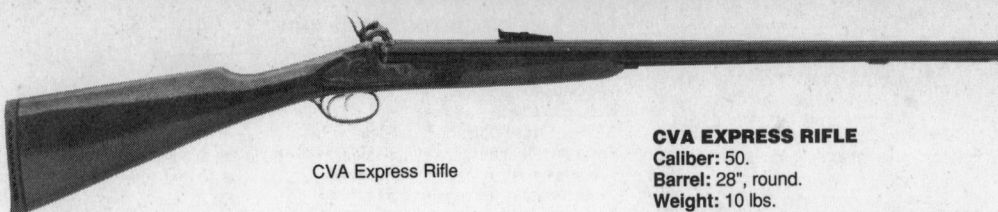

CVA Express Rifle

CVA FRONTIER CARBINE
Caliber: 50.
Barrel: 24" octagon; $^{15}/_{16}$" flats.
Weight: 6¾ lbs. **Length:** 40" overall.
Stock: Selected hardwood.
Sights: Steel bead front, click adjustable rear.
Features: Color case-hardened lockplate, V-type mainspring. Early style brass trigger with tension spring. Brass buttplate, trigger guard, wedge plate, nose cap, thimble, synthetic ramrod. From CVA.
Price: Percussion $189.95
Price: Flintlock rifle $199.95
Price: Percussion Carbine kit (fixed sight, wood ramrod) . . . $129.95

CVA St. Louis Hawken

CVA KENTUCKY RIFLE
Caliber: 50.
Barrel: 33½", rifled, octagon; ⅞" flats.
Weight: 7½ lbs. **Length:** 48" overall.
Stock: Select hardwood.
Sights: Brass Kentucky blade-type front, fixed open rear.
Features: Available in percussion only. Color case-hardened lockplate. Stainless steel nipple included. From CVA.
Price: Percussion $279.95
Price: Percussion kit $189.95

CVA TRACKER CARBINE LS
Caliber: 50.
Barrel: 21", half round, half octagon with $^{15}/_{16}$" flats; 1:32" twist.
Weight: 6.5 lbs. **Length:** 37" overall.
Stock: Laminated hardwood.
Sights: Beaded blade front on ramp, fully adjustable click rear.
Features: Color case-hardened lockplate, synthetic ramrod, offset hammer, black-chromed furniture; drilled and tapped for scope mounting. From CVA.
Price: $229.95

CVA Timber Wolf

CVA VARMINT RIFLE
Caliber: 32.
Barrel: 24" octagonal; ⅞" flats; 1:48" rifling.
Weight: 6¾ lbs. **Length:** 40" overall.
Stock: Select hardwood.
Sights: Blade front, Patridge-style click adjustable rear.
Features: Brass trigger guard, nose cap, wedge plate, thimble and buttplate. Drilled and tapped for scope mounting. Color case-hardened lock. Single trigger. Aluminum ramrod. Imported by CVA.
Price: $219.95

CVA Woodsman LS Rifle
Similar to the Wolf Series except has straight-grip stock of stained, laminated hardwood, traditional blade front sight. Has 1:48" twist barrel. From CVA.
Price: $169.95

CVA EXPRESS RIFLE
Caliber: 50.
Barrel: 28", round.
Weight: 10 lbs.
Stock: Select hardwood; ventilated rubber recoil pad.
Sights: Bead and blade front, adjustable rear.
Features: Double rifle with twin percussion locks and triggers, adjustable barrels. Button breech. Introduced 1989. From CVA.
Price: Finished $419.95

CVA Frontier Hunter Carbine LS
Similar to the CVA Frontier Carbine except has conventional-style black rubber butt pad, black chrome furniture. Laminated stock. Offset hammer. Has 1:32" twist. Barrel is drilled and tapped for scope mounting. Fully adjustable rear sight. Overall length 40", weight 7.5 lbs. From CVA.
Price: 50- and 54-caliber $209.95

CVA HAWKEN RIFLE
Caliber: 50, 54.
Barrel: 28", octagon; $^{15}/_{16}$" across flats; 1:48" twist.
Weight: 8 lbs. **Length:** 44" overall.
Stock: Select hardwood.
Sights: Beaded blade front, fully adjustable open rear.
Features: Fully adjustable double-set triggers; synthetic ramrod (kits have wood); brass patch box, wedge plates, nosecap, thimbles, trigger guard and buttplate; blued barrel; color case-hardened, engraved lockplate. V-type mainspring. Button breech. Introduced 1981. From CVA.
Price: St. Louis Hawken, finished (50-, 54-cal.) . . . $209.95
Price: As above, combo kit (50-, 54-cal. bbls.) . . . $229.95
Price: Left-hand, percussion $234.95
Price: Flintlock, 50-cal. only $234.95
Price: Flintlock, left-hand $249.95
Price: Percussion kit (50-cal., blued, wood ramrod) . . . $169.95

CVA TROPHY CARBINE
Caliber: 50, 54.
Barrel: 24", half round, half octagon with $^{15}/_{16}$" flats; 1:32" twist.
Weight: 6.75 lbs. **Length:** 40" overall.
Stock: Walnut with Monte Carlo comb, cheekpiece, pistol grip.
Sights: White bead on blade front, fully adjustable click rear. **Features:** Color case-hardened lockplate, blued barrel, thimble. Modern-style stock; modern rifle trigger with over-sized guard; synthetic ramrod; offset hammer; drilled and tapped for scope mounting. From CVA.
Price: $259.95

CVA WOLF SERIES RIFLES
Caliber: 50, 54.
Barrel: 26" octagonal; 1:32" twist; $^{15}/_{16}$" flats; blue finish.
Weight: 6½ lbs. **Length:** 40" overall.
Stock: Tuff-Lite polymer—gray finish, solid buttplate (Grey Wolf); black finish, ventilated recoil pad, swivel studs (Lone Wolf); Realtree All Purpose camo finish, solid buttplate (Timber Wolf); checkered grip.
Sights: Blade front on ramp, fully adjustable open rear; drilled and tapped for scope mounting.
Features: Oversize trigger guard; synthetic ramrod; offset hammer. From CVA.
Price: Grey Wolf $199.95
Price: Lone Wolf (50-cal. only) $219.95
Price: Timber Wolf (50-cal. only) $229.95

CVA Panther Carbine
Similar to the CVA Wolf Series except has 24" barrel, textured black Dura Grip hardwood stock with Monte Carlo comb, formed cheekpiece; ventilated rubber recoil pad. Weighs 7½ lbs. Matte finish on barrel, color case-hardened lock. From CVA.
Price: $189.95
Price: Left-hand (50-cal. only) $204.95

BLACKPOWDER MUSKETS & RIFLES

Dixie English Matchlock

DIXIE DELUX CUB RIFLE
Caliber: 40.
Barrel: 28".
Weight: 6½ lbs.
Stock: Walnut.
Sights: Fixed.
Features: Short rifle for small game and beginning shooters. Brass patchbox and furniture. Flint or percussion. From Dixie Gun Works.
Price: Finished **$335.00**
Price: Kit **$205.00**

DIXIE ENGLISH MATCHLOCK MUSKET
Caliber: 72.
Barrel: 44".
Weight: 8 lbs. **Length:** 57.75" overall.
Stock: Walnut with satin oil finish.
Sights: Blade front, open rear adjustable for windage.
Features: Replica of circa 1600-1680 English matchlock. Getz barrel with 11" octagonal area at rear, rest is round with cannon-type muzzle. All steel finished in the white. Imported by Dixie Gun Works.
Price: **$895.00**

DIXIE HAWKEN RIFLE
Caliber: 45, 50, 54.
Barrel: 30".
Weight: 8 lbs. **Length:** 46½" overall.
Stock: Walnut.
Sights: Blade front, adjustable rear.
Features: Blued barrel, double-set triggers, steel crescent buttplate. Imported by Dixie Gun Works.
Price: Finished **$250.00**
Price: Kit **$220.00**

Dixie Inline Carbine

DIXIE TENNESSEE MOUNTAIN RIFLE
Caliber: 32 or 50.
Barrel: 41½", 6-groove rifling, brown finish. **Length:** 56" overall.
Stock: Walnut, oil finish; Kentucky-style.
Sights: Silver blade front, open buckhorn rear.
Features: Recreation of the original mountain rifles. Early Schultz lock, interchangeable flint or percussion with vent plug or drum and nipple. Tumbler has fly. Double-set triggers. All metal parts browned. From Dixie Gun Works.
Price: Flint or percussion, finished rifle, 50-cal. **$525.00**
Price: Kit, 50-cal. **$446.25**
Price: Left-hand model, flint or percussion **$525.00**
Price: Left-hand kit, flint or perc., 50-cal. **$525.00**
Price: Squirrel Rifle (as above except in 32-cal. with ¹³⁄₁₆" barrel flats), flint or percussion **$525.00**
Price: Kit, 32-cal., flint or percussion **$525.00**

DIXIE INLINE CARBINE
Caliber: 50, 54.
Barrel: 24"; 1:32" twist.
Weight: 6.5 lbs. **Length:** 41" overall.
Stock: Walnut-finished hardwood with Monte Carlo comb.
Sights: Ramp front with red insert, open fully adjustable rear.
Features: Sliding "bolt" fully encloses cap and nipple. Fully adjustable trigger, automatic safety. Aluminum ramrod. Imported from Italy by Dixie Gun Works.
Price: **$349.95**

DIXIE U.S. MODEL 1861 SPRINGFIELD
Caliber: 58.
Barrel: 40".
Weight: About 8 lbs. **Length:** 55¹³⁄₁₆" overall.
Stock: Oil-finished walnut.
Sights: Blade front, step adjustable rear.
Features: Exact recreation of original rifle. Sling swivels attached to trigger guard bow and middle barrel band. Lockplate marked "1861" with eagle motif and "U.S. Springfield" in front of hammer; "U.S." stamped on top of buttplate. From Dixie Gun Works.
Price: **$525.00**
Price: Kit **$446.25**

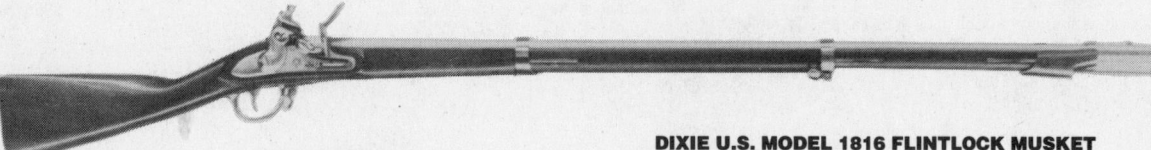

Dixie Model 1816

> Consult our Directory pages for the location of firms mentioned.

DIXIE 1863 SPRINGFIELD MUSKET
Caliber: 58 (.570" patched ball or .575" Minie).
Barrel: 50", rifled.
Stocks: Walnut stained.
Sights: Blade front, adjustable ladder-type rear.
Features: Bright-finish lock, barrel, furniture. Reproduction of the last of the regulation muzzleloaders. Imported from Japan by Dixie Gun Works.
Price: Finished **$525.00**
Price: Kit **$446.25**

DIXIE U.S. MODEL 1816 FLINTLOCK MUSKET
Caliber: 69.
Barrel: 42", smoothbore.
Weight: 9.75 lbs. **Length:** 56.5" overall.
Stock: Walnut with oil finish.
Sights: Blade front.
Features: All metal finished "National Armory Bright"; three barrel bands with springs; steel ramrod with buttom-shaped head. Imported by Dixie Gun Works.
Price: **$725.00**

EUROARMS BUFFALO CARBINE
Caliber: 58.
Barrel: 26", round.
Weight: 7¾ lbs. **Length:** 42" overall.
Stock: Walnut.
Sights: Blade front, open adjustable rear.
Features: Shoots .575" round ball. Color case-hardened lock, blue hammer, barrel, trigger; brass furniture. Brass patchbox. Imported by Euroarms of America.
Price: **$515.45**

BLACKPOWDER MUSKETS & RIFLES

Euroarms Volunteer

EUROARMS 1861 SPRINGFIELD RIFLE
Caliber: 58.
Barrel: 40".
Weight: About 10 lbs. **Length:** 55.5" overall.
Stock: European walnut.
Sights: Blade front, three-leaf military rear.
Features: Reproduction of the original three-band rifle. Lockplate marked "1861" with eagle and "U.S. Springfield." Metal left in the white. Imported by Euroarms of America.
Price: $647.00

EUROARMS VOLUNTEER TARGET RIFLE
Caliber: .451.
Barrel: 33" (two-band), 36" (three-band).
Weight: 11 lbs. (two-band). **Length:** 48.75" overall (two-band).
Stock: European walnut with checkered wrist and forend.
Sights: Hooded bead front, adjustable rear with interchangeable leaves.
Features: Alexander Henry-type rifling with 1:20" twist. Color case-hardened hammer and lockplate, brass trigger guard and nose cap, rest blued. Imported by Euroarms of America.
Price: Two-band $870.00
Price: Three-band $935.00

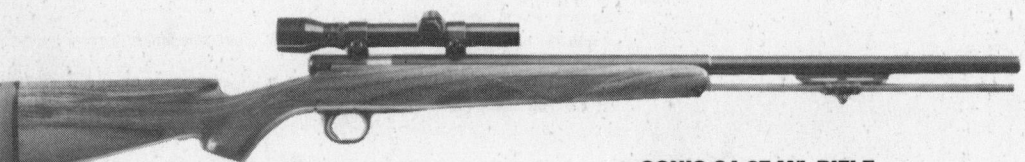

Gonic GA-87

Gonic GA-93 Magnum M/L Rifle
Similar to the GA-87 except has open bolt mechanism, single safety, 22" barrel and comes only in 50-caliber. Stock is black wrinkle-finish wood or gray or brown, standard or thumbhole laminate. Introduced 1993. From Gonic Arms, Inc.

Price: Black stock, blue, no sights	$442.00
Price: As above, stainless	$521.00
Price: Laminated stock, blue, no sights	$505.00
Price: As above, stainless	$597.00
Price: Thumbhole stock, blue, no sights	$754.00
Price: As above, stainless	$833.00
Price: Black stock, blue, no sights	$484.57
Price: As above, stainless	$563.57
Price: Laminated stock, blue, open sights	$547.57
Price: As above, stainless	$642.03
Price: Thumbhole stock, blue, open sights	$796.57
Price: As above, stainless	$875.57

HATFIELD MOUNTAIN RIFLE
Caliber: 50, 54.
Barrel: 32".
Weight: 8 lbs. **Length:** 49" overall.
Stock: Select American fancy maple. Half-stock with nose cap.
Sights: Silver blade front on brass base, fixed buckhorn rear.
Features: Traditional leaf spring and fly lock with extra-wide tumbler of 4140 steel. Slow rust brown metal finish. Double-set triggers. From Hatfield Gun Co.
Price: $950.00

GONIC GA-87 M/L RIFLE
Caliber: 30, 38, 44, 45, 50, 54, 20-ga.
Barrel: 26".
Weight: 6 to 6½ lbs. **Length:** 43" overall (Carbine).
Stock: American walnut with checkered grip and forend, or laminated stock.
Sights: Optional bead front, open or peep rear adjustable for windage and elevation; drilled and tapped for scope bases (included).
Features: Closed-breech action with straight-line ignition. Modern trigger mechanism with ambidextrous safety. Satin blue finish on metal, satin stock finish. Introduced 1989. From Gonic Arms, Inc.

Price: Standard rifle, no sights	$547.00
Price: As above, with sights, from	$595.00
Price: Walnut stock, no sights	$547.00
Price: Laminated stock, no sights	$595.00
Price: Walnut stock, open sights	$593.00
Price: Laminated stock, open sights	$640.00
Price: Walnut stock, peep sight	$597.00
Price: Laminated stock, peep sight	$644.00

HARPER'S FERRY 1803 FLINTLOCK RIFLE
Caliber: 54 or 58.
Barrel: 35".
Weight: 9 lbs. **Length:** 59½" overall.
Stock: Walnut with cheekpiece.
Sights: Brass blade front, fixed steel rear.
Features: Brass trigger guard, sideplate, buttplate; steel patch box. Imported by Euroarms of America, Navy Arms (54-cal. only).
Price: $512.00
Price: 54-cal. (Navy Arms) $555.00

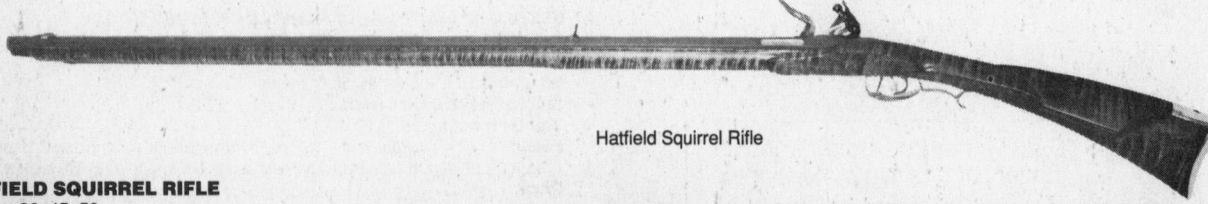

Hatfield Squirrel Rifle

HATFIELD SQUIRREL RIFLE
Caliber: 36, 45, 50.
Barrel: 39½", octagon, 32" on half-stock.
Weight: 7½ lbs. (32-cal.).
Stock: American fancy maple.
Sights: Silver blade front, buckhorn rear.
Features: Recreation of the traditional squirrel rifle. Available in flint or percussion with brass trigger guard and buttplate. From Hatfield Rifle Works. Introduced 1983.
Price: Full stock, percussion, Grade II $819.00
Price: As above, flintlock $819.00
Price: As above, Grade III, flint or percussion $969.00

HAWKEN RIFLE
Caliber: 45, 50, 54 or 58.
Barrel: 28", blued, 6-groove rifling.
Weight: 8¾ lbs. **Length:** 44" overall.
Stock: Walnut with cheekpiece.
Sights: Blade front, fully adjustable rear.
Features: Coil mainspring, double-set triggers, polished brass furniture. From Armsport, Navy Arms, E.M.F.
Price: . . . . $220.00 to $345.00

    CAUTION: PRICES SHOWN ARE SUPPLIED BY THE MANUFACTURER OR IMPORTER. CHECK YOUR LOCAL GUNSHOP.

BLACKPOWDER MUSKETS & RIFLES

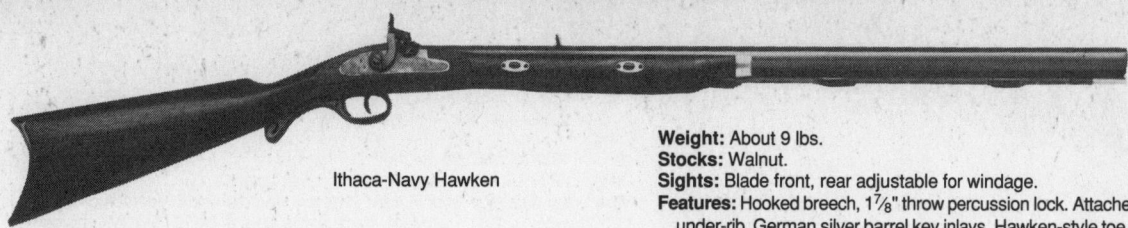

Ithaca-Navy Hawken

ITHACA-NAVY HAWKEN RIFLE
Caliber: 50.
Barrel: 32" octagonal, 1" dia.

Weight: About 9 lbs.
Stocks: Walnut.
Sights: Blade front, rear adjustable for windage.
Features: Hooked breech, 1⅞" throw percussion lock. Attached twin thimbles and under-rib. German silver barrel key inlays, Hawken-style toe and buttplates, lock bolt inlays, barrel wedges, entry thimble, trigger guard, ramrod and cleaning jag, nipple and nipple wrench. Introduced 1977. From Navy Arms.
Price: Complete, percussion $400.00
Price: Kit, percussion $360.00

Navy Arms Kentucky

Kentucky Percussion Rifle
Similar to flintlock except percussion lock. Finish and features vary with importer. Imported by Navy Arms, The Armoury, CVA.
Price: About $259.95
Price: 45- or 50-cal. (Navy Arms) $330.00
Price: Kit, 50-cal. (CVA) $189.95

KENTUCKY FLINTLOCK RIFLE
Caliber: 44, 45, or 50.
Barrel: 35".
Weight: 7 lbs. **Length:** 50" overall.
Stock: Walnut stained, brass fittings.
Sights: Fixed.
Features: Available in carbine model also, 28" bbl. Some variations in detail, finish. Kits also available from some importers. Imported by Navy Arms, The Armoury.
Price: About . . . . $217.95 to $345.00
Price: Flintlock, 45 or 50-cal. (Navy Arms) $345.00

KENTUCKIAN RIFLE & CARBINE
Caliber: 44.
Barrel: 35" (Rifle), 27½" (Carbine).
Weight: 7 lbs. (Rifle), 5½ lbs. (Carbine). **Length:** 51" overall (Rifle), 43" (Carbine).
Stock: Walnut stain.

Sights: Brass blade front, steel V-ramp rear.
Features: Octagon barrel, case-hardened and engraved lockplates. Brass furniture. Imported by Dixie Gun Works.
Price: Rifle or carbine, flint, about $269.95
Price: As above, percussion, about $259.95

Knight MK-85

Knight MK-85 Grand American Rifle
Similar to the MK-85 Hunter except comes with Shadow Black or Shadow Brown thumbhole stock. Hand-selected barrel and components. Comes with test target, hard gun case. Blue finish.
Price: $995.00
Price: As above except in stainless steel $1,095.00

KNIGHT MK-85 RIFLE
Caliber: 50, 54.
Barrel: 24".
Weight: 6¾ lbs.
Stock: Walnut, laminated or composition.
Sights: Hooded blade front on ramp, open adjustable rear.
Features: Patented double safety; Sure-Fire in-line percussion ignition; Timney Featherweight adjustable trigger; aluminum ramrod; receiver drilled and tapped for scope bases. Made in U.S. by Modern Muzzleloading, Inc.
Price: Hunter, walnut stock $529.95
Price: Stalker, laminated or composition stock $579.95
Price: Predator (stainless steel), laminated or composition stock $649.95
Price: Knight Hawk, blued, composition thumbhole stock $689.95
Price: As above, stainless steel $759.95

Knight MK-95 Magnum

KNIGHT BK-92 BLACK KNIGHT RIFLE
Caliber: 50, 54.
Barrel: 24", blued.
Weight: 6½ lbs.
Stock: Prolight synthetic coated hardwood or composition.
Sights: Blade front on ramp, open adjustable rear.
Features: Patented double safety system; removeable breech plug for cleaning; adjustable Accu-Lite trigger; Green Mountain barrel; receiver drilled and tapped for scope bases. Made in U.S. by Modern Muzzleloading, Inc.
Price: With Prolight stock $379.95
Price: With composition stock $429.95

KNIGHT MK-95 MAGNUM ELITE RIFLE
Caliber: 50, 54.
Barrel: 24", stainless.
Weight: 6¾ lbs.
Stock: Composition; black or Realtree All-Purpose camouflage.
Sights: Hooded blade front on ramp, open adjustable rear.
Features: Enclosed Posi-Fire ignition system uses large rifle primers; Timney Featherweight adjustable trigger; Green Mountain barrel; receiver drilled and tapped for scope bases. Made in U.S. by Modern Muzzleloading, Inc.
Price: Black composition stock $783.66
Price: Realtree camouflage composition stock $849.95

CAUTION: PRICES SHOWN ARE SUPPLIED BY THE MANUFACTURER OR IMPORTER. CHECK YOUR LCOAL GUNSHOP.

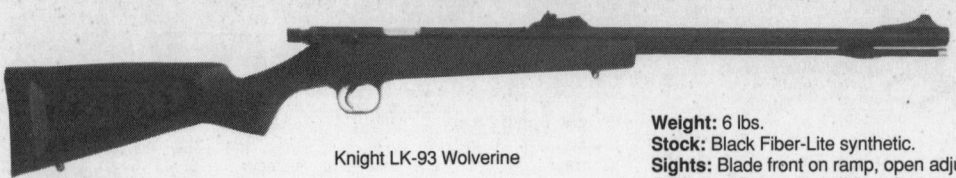

Knight LK-93 Wolverine

KNIGHT LK-93 WOLVERINE RIFLE
Caliber: 50.
Barrel: 22", blued.

KODIAK MK. III DOUBLE RIFLE
Caliber: 54x54, 58x58, 50x50.
Barrel: 28", 5-groove, 1:48 twist.
Weight: 9½ lbs. **Length:** 43¼" overall.
Stock: Czechoslovakian walnut, hand-checkered.
Features: Hooked breech allows interchangeability of barrels. Comes with sling, swivels, bullet mould and bullet starter. Engraved lockplates, top tang and trigger guard. Locks and top tang polished, rest browned. Introduced 1976. Imported from Italy by Navy Arms.
Price: 50-, 54-, 58-cal. SxS $650.00
Price: Spare barrels, all calibers $395.50
Price: Spare barrels, 12-ga.x12-ga. $295.50

Weight: 6 lbs.
Stock: Black Fiber-Lite synthetic.
Sights: Blade front on ramp, open adjustable rear.
Features: Patented double safety system; removeable breech plug; Sure-Fire in-line percussion ignition system. Made in U.S. by Modern Muzzleloading, Inc.
Price: $249.95
Price: LK-93 Legend (as above, hardwood stock) $349.95

LONDON ARMORY 2-BAND 1858 ENFIELD
Caliber: .577" Minie, .575" round ball.
Barrel: 33".
Weight: 10 lbs. **Length:** 49" overall.
Stock: Walnut.
Sights: Folding leaf rear adjustable for elevation.
Features: Blued barrel, color case-hardened lock and hammer, polished brass buttplate, trigger guard, nosecap. From Navy Arms, Euroarms of America, Dixie Gun Works.
Price: . . . . $385.00 to $531.00
Price: Assembled kit (Euroarms of America) $481.00

London Armory 1861

LONDON ARMORY 1861 ENFIELD MUSKETOON
Caliber: 58, Minie ball.
Barrel: 24", round.
Weight: 7-7½ lbs. **Length:** 40½" overall.
Stock: Walnut, with sling swivels.
Sights: Blade front, graduated military-leaf rear.
Features: Brass trigger guard, nose cap, buttplate; blued barrel, bands, lockplate, swivels. Imported by Euroarms of America, Navy Arms.
Price: . . . . $300.00 to $496.00
Price: Kit $448.00

LONDON ARMORY 3-BAND 1853 ENFIELD
Caliber: 58 (.577" Minie, .575" round ball, .580" maxi ball).
Barrel: 39".
Weight: 9½ lbs. **Length:** 54" overall.
Stock: European walnut.
Sights: Inverted "V" front, traditional Enfield folding ladder rear.
Features: Recreation of the famed London Armory Company Pattern 1853 Enfield Musket. One-piece walnut stock, brass buttplate, trigger guard and nose cap. Lockplate marked "London Armoury Co." and with a British crown. Blued Baddeley barrel bands. From Dixie Gun Works, Euroarms of America, Navy Arms.
Price: About . . . . $350.00 to $565.00
Price: Assembled kit (Dixie, Euroarms of America) . . . $425.00 to $504.00

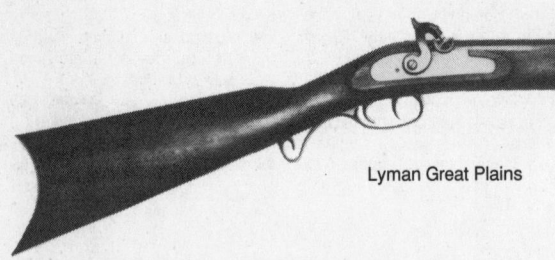

Lyman Great Plains

┌─────────────────────────────────────┐
│ Consult our Directory pages for   │
│ the location of firms mentioned.   │
└─────────────────────────────────────┘

LYMAN DEERSTALKER RIFLE
Caliber: 50, 54.
Barrel: 24", octagonal; 1:48 rifling.
Weight: 7½ lbs.
Stock: Walnut with black rubber buttpad.
Sights: Lyman #37MA beaded front, fully adjustable fold-down Lyman #16A rear.
Features: Stock has less drop for quick sighting. All metal parts are blackened, with color case-hardened lock; single trigger. Comes with sling and swivels. Available in flint or percussion. Introduced 1990. From Lyman.
Price: 50- or 54-cal., percussion $304.95
Price: 50- or 54-cal., flintlock $324.95
Price: 50- or 54-cal., percussion, left-hand $304.95
Price: 50-cal., flintlock, left-hand $324.95

LYMAN GREAT PLAINS RIFLE
Caliber: 50- or 54-cal.
Barrel: 32", 1:66 twist.
Weight: 9 lbs.
Stock: Walnut.
Sights: Steel blade front, buckhorn rear adjustable for windage and elevation and fixed notch primitive sight included.
Features: Blued steel furniture. Stainless steel nipple. Coil spring lock, Hawken-style trigger guard and double-set triggers. Round thimbles recessed and sweated into rib. Steel wedge plates and toe plate. Introduced 1979. From Lyman.
Price: Percussion $409.95
Price: Flintlock $439.95
Price: Percussion kit $329.95
Price: Flintlock kit $359.95
Price: Left-hand percussion $409.95
Price: Left-hand flintlock $439.95

Lyman Deerstalker Custom Carbine
Similar to the Deerstalker rifle except in 50-caliber only with 21" stepped octagon barrel; 1:24 twist for optimum performance with conical projectiles. Comes with Lyman 37MA front sight, Lyman 16A folding rear. Weighs 6¾ lbs., measures 38½" overall. Percussion or flintlock. Comes with Delrin ramrod, modern sling and swivels. Introduced 1991.
Price: Percussion $314.95
Price: Flintlock $339.95
Price: Percussion, left-hand $314.95

    CAUTION: PRICES SHOWN ARE SUPPLIED BY THE MANUFACTURER OR IMPORTER. CHECK YOUR LOCAL GUNSHOP.

BLACKPOWDER MUSKETS & RIFLES

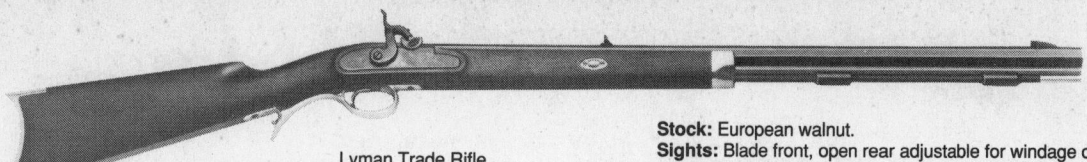

Lyman Trade Rifle

Stock: European walnut.
Sights: Blade front, open rear adjustable for windage or optional fixed sights.
Features: Fast twist rifling for conical bullets. Polished brass furniture with blue steel parts, stainless steel nipple. Hook breech, single trigger, coil spring percussion lock. Steel barrel rib and ramrod ferrules. Introduced 1980. From Lyman.
Price: Percussion **$289.95**
Price: Kit, percussion **$249.95**
Price: Flintlock **$319.95**
Price: Kit, flintlock **$284.95**

LYMAN TRADE RIFLE
Caliber: 50 or 54.
Barrel: 28" octagon, 1:48 twist.
Weight: 8¾ lbs. **Length:** 45" overall.

Mowrey Squirrel Rifle

MOWREY SQUIRREL RIFLE
Caliber: 32, 36 or 45.
Barrel: 28"; ¹³⁄₁₆" flats; 1:66" twist.
Weight: About 7.5 lbs. **Length:** 43" overall.
Stock: Curly maple; crescent buttplate.
Sights: German silver blade front, semi-buckhorn rear.
Features: Brass or steel boxlock action; cut-rifled barrel. Steel rifles have browned finish, brass have browned barrel. Adjustable sear and trigger pull. Made in U.S. by Mowrey Gun Works.
Price: Brass or steel **$350.00**
Price: Kit **$300.00**

Mowrey 1 N 30 Conical Rifle
Similar to the Squirrel Rifle except in steel frame only, 45-, 50- or 54-caliber. Has special 1:24" twist barrel for conical- and sabot-style bullets. The 50- and 54-caliber barrels have 1" flats.
Price: **$350.00**
Price: Kit **$300.00**

Mowrey Plains Rifle
Similar to the Squirrel Rifle except in 50- or 54-caliber with 32" barrel. Available in brass or steel frame.
Price: Brass frame **$350.00**
Price: Steel frame **$350.00**
Price: Rocky Mountain Hunter (as above except 28" bbl.), brass . . **$350.00**
Price: As above, steel frame **$350.00**
Price: All above in kit form **$300.00**

Mowrey Silhouette Rifle
Similar to the Squirrel Rifle except in 40-caliber with 32" barrel. Available in brass or steel frame.
Price: Brass frame **$350.00**
Price: Steel frame **$350.00**
Price: Kit, brass or steel **$300.00**

Navy Arms J.P. Murray

J.P. MURRAY 1862-1864 CAVALRY CARBINE
Caliber: 58 (.577" Minie).
Barrel: 23".
Weight: 7 lbs., 9 oz. **Length:** 39" overall.
Stock: Walnut.
Sights: Blade front, rear drift adjustable for windage.
Features: Browned barrel, color case-hardened lock, blued swivel and band springs, polished brass buttplate, trigger guard, barrel bands. From Navy Arms, Euroarms of America.
Price: . . . . **$300.00 to $459.95**

NAVY ARMS 1777 CHARLEVILLE MUSKET
Caliber: 69.
Barrel: 44⅝".
Weight: 10 lbs., 4 oz. **Length:** 59¾" overall.
Stock: Walnut.
Sights: Brass blade front.
Features: Exact copy of the musket used in the French Revolution. All steel is polished, in the white. Brass flashpan. Introduced 1991. Imported by Navy Arms.
Price: **$690.00**
Price: 1816 M.T. Wickham Musket **$690.00**

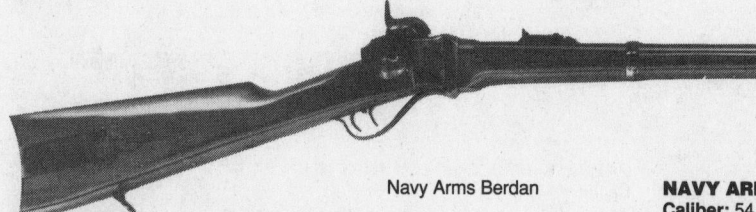

Navy Arms Berdan

NAVY ARMS BERDAN 1859 SHARPS RIFLE
Caliber: 54.
Barrel: 30".
Weight: 8 lbs., 8 oz. **Length:** 46¾" overall.
Stock: Walnut.
Sights: Blade front, folding military ladder-type rear.
Features: Replica of the Union sniper rifle used by Berdan's 1st and 2nd Sharpshooter regiments. Color case-hardened receiver, patch box, furniture. Double-set triggers. Imported by Navy Arms.
Price: **$895.00**
Price: 1859 Sharps Infantry Rifle (three-band) **$850.00**

NAVY ARMS 1863 SHARPS CAVALRY CARBINE
Caliber: 54.
Barrel: 22".
Weight: 7¾ lbs. **Length:** 39" overall.
Stock: Walnut.
Sights: Blade front, military ladder-type rear.
Features: Color case-hardened action, blued barrel. Has saddle ring. Introduced 1991. Imported from Navy Arms.
Price: **$750.00**

CAUTION: PRICES SHOWN ARE SUPPLIED BY THE MANUFACTURER OR IMPORTER. CHECK YOUR LCOAL GUNSHOP.

49th EDITION, 1995   **427**

BLACKPOWDER MUSKETS & RIFLES

Navy Arms 1863

NAVY ARMS 1862 C.S. RICHMOND RIFLE
Caliber: 58.
Barrel: 40".
Weight: 10 lbs. **Length:** NA.
Stock: Walnut.
Sights: Blade front, adjustable rear.
Features: Copy of the three-band rifle musket made at Richmond Armory for the Confederacy. All steel polished bright. Imported by Navy Arms, Euroarms.
Price: $550.00
Price: From Euroarms $647.15

NAVY ARMS 1863 SPRINGFIELD
Caliber: 58, uses .575" Minie.
Barrel: 40", rifled.
Weight: 9½ lbs. **Length:** 56" overall.
Stock: Walnut.
Sights: Open rear adjustable for elevation.
Features: Full-size three-band musket. Polished bright metal, including lock. From Navy Arms.
Price: Finished rifle $550.00
Price: Kit $450.00

Navy Arms Mortimer Match

NAVY ARMS MORTIMER FLINTLOCK RIFLE
Caliber: 54.
Barrel: 36".
Weight: 9 lbs. **Length:** 52¼" overall.
Stock: Checkered walnut.
Sights: Bead front, rear adjustable for windage.
Features: Waterproof pan, roller frizzen; sling swivels; browned barrel; external safety. Introduced 1991. Imported by Navy Arms.
Price: $690.00
Price: Mortimer Match Rifle (hooded globe front sight, fully adjustable target aperture rear, color case-hardened lock) $850.00

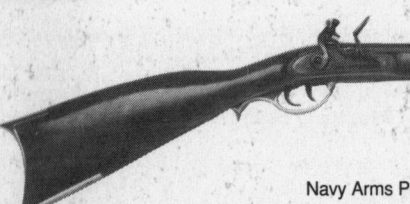

Navy Arms Pennsylvania

NAVY ARMS PENNSYLVANIA LONG RIFLE
Caliber: 32, 45.
Barrel: 40½".
Weight: 7½ lbs. **Length:** 56½" overall.
Stock: Walnut.
Sights: Blade front, fully adjustable rear.
Features: Browned barrel, brass furniture, polished lock with double-set triggers. Introduced 1991. Imported by Navy Arms.
Price: Percussion $395.00
Price: Flintlock $410.00

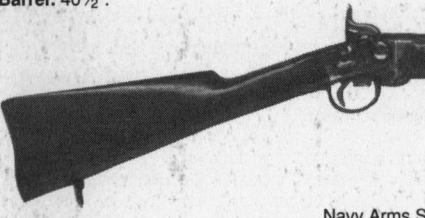

Navy Arms Smith Carbine

NAVY ARMS SMITH CARBINE
Caliber: 50.
Barrel: 21½".
Weight: 7¾ lbs. **Length:** 39" overall.
Stock: American walnut.
Sights: Brass blade front, folding ladder-type rear.
Features: Replica of the breech-loading Civil War carbine. Color case-hardened receiver, rest blued. Cavalry model has saddle ring and bar, Artillery model has sling swivels. Introduced 1991. Imported by Navy Arms.
Price: Cavalry model $600.00
Price: Artillery model $600.00

Parker-Hale 1853

PARKER-HALE ENFIELD PATTERN 1858 NAVAL RIFLE
Caliber: .577".
Barrel: 33".
Weight: 8½ lbs. **Length:** 48½" overall.
Stock: European walnut.
Sights: Blade front, step adjustable rear.
Features: Two-band Enfield percussion rifle with heavy barrel. Five-groove progressive depth rifling, solid brass furniture. All parts made exactly to original patterns. Made by Gibbs Rifle Co., distributed by Navy Arms.
Price: $550.00

PARKER-HALE ENFIELD 1853 MUSKET
Caliber: .577".
Barrel: 39", 3-groove cold-forged rifling.
Weight: About 9 lbs. **Length:** 55" overall.
Stock: Seasoned walnut.
Sights: Fixed front, rear step adjustable for elevation.
Features: Three-band musket made to original specs from original gauges. Solid brass stock furniture, color hardened lockplate, hammer; blued barrel, trigger. Made by Gibbs Rifle Co., distributed by Navy Arms.
Price: $585.00

CAUTION: PRICES SHOWN ARE SUPPLIED BY THE MANUFACTURER OR IMPORTER. CHECK YOUR LOCAL GUNSHOP.

BLACKPOWDER MUSKETS & RIFLES

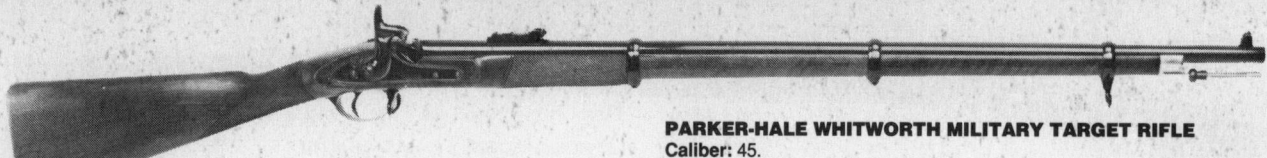

Parker-Hale Whitworth

Parker-Hale Limited Edition Whitworth Sniping Rifle
Same as the Parker-Hale Whitworth Military Target Rifle except has replica of the Model 1860 brass telescope sight in fully adjustable mount. Made by Gibbs Rifle Co., distributed by Navy Arms.
Price: **$995.00**

PARKER-HALE ENFIELD 1861 MUSKETOON
Caliber: 58.
Barrel: 24".
Weight: 7 lbs. **Length:** 40½" overall.
Stock: Walnut.
Sights: Fixed front, adjustable rear.
Features: Percussion muzzleloader, made to original 1861 English patterns. Made by Gibbs Rifle Co., distributed by Navy Arms.
Price: **$450.00**

PENNSYLVANIA FULL-STOCK RIFLE
Caliber: 45 or 50.
Barrel: 32" rifled, 15/16" dia.
Weight: 8½ lbs.
Stock: Walnut.

PARKER-HALE WHITWORTH MILITARY TARGET RIFLE
Caliber: 45.
Barrel: 36".
Weight: 9¼ lbs. **Length:** 52½" overall.
Stock: Walnut. Checkered at wrist and forend.
Sights: Hooded post front, open step-adjustable rear.
Features: Faithful reproduction of the Whitworth rifle, only bored for 45-cal. Trigger has a detented lock, capable of being adjusted very finely without risk of the sear nose catching on the half-cock bent and damaging both parts. Introduced 1978. Made by Gibbs Rifle Co., distributed by Navy Arms.
Price: **$815.00**

PARKER-HALE VOLUNTEER RIFLE
Caliber: .451".
Barrel: 32".
Weight: 9½ lbs. **Length:** 49" overall.
Stock: Walnut, checkered wrist and forend.
Sights: Globe front, adjustable ladder-type rear.
Features: Recreation of the type of gun issued to volunteer regiments during the 1860s. Rigby-pattern rifling, patent breech, detented lock. Stock is glass bedded for accuracy. Made by Gibbs Rifle Co., distributed by Navy Arms.
Price: **$750.00**
Price: Three-band Volunteer **$815.00**

Sights: Fixed.
Features: Available in flint or percussion. Blued lock and barrel, brass furniture. Offered complete or in kit form. From The Armoury.
Price: Flint **$250.00**
Price: Percussion **$225.00**

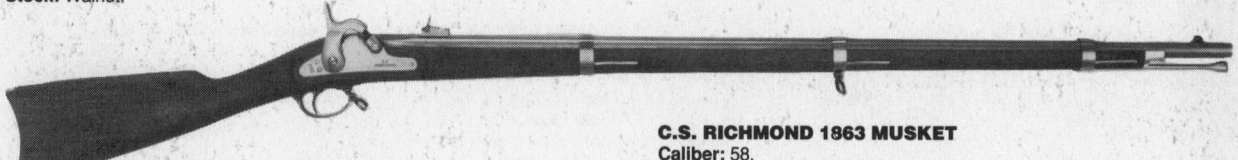

C.S. Richmond

ROBERTS 98 MAUSER MUZZLE LOADER
Caliber: 45, 50, 54.
Barrel: 26".
Weight: 8 lbs. **Length:** 46" overall.
Stock: Walnut-finished hardwood.
Sights: None furnished; comes with Weaver-style one-piece scope mount.
Features: Uses 98 Mauser bolt action. Wilson #3 tapered barrel; Mark II low profile safety. Announced 1993. Made in U.S. Available from Sile Distributors.
Price: About **$336.00**

C.S. RICHMOND 1863 MUSKET
Caliber: 58.
Barrel: 40".
Weight: 11 lbs. **Length:** 56¼" overall.
Stock: European walnut with oil finish.
Sights: Blade front, adjustable folding leaf rear.
Features: Reproduction of the three-band Civil War musket. Sling swivels attached to trigger guard and middle barrel band. Lock plate marked "1863" and "C.S. Richmond." All metal left in the white. Brass buttplate and forend cap. Imported by Euroarms of America.
Price: **$647.00**

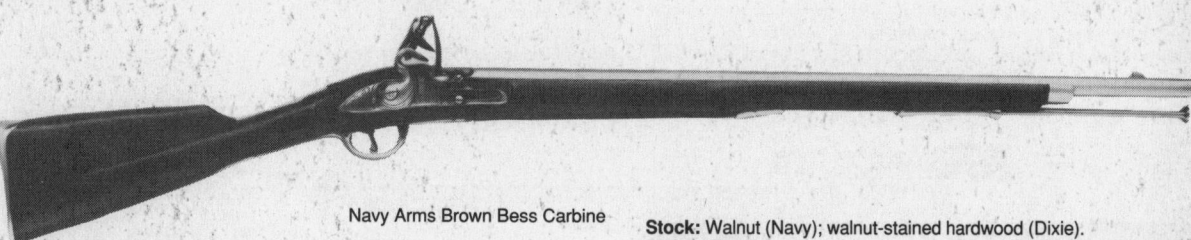

Navy Arms Brown Bess Carbine

SECOND MODEL BROWN BESS MUSKET
Caliber: 75, uses .735" round ball.
Barrel: 42", smoothbore.
Weight: 9½ lbs. **Length:** 59" overall.

Stock: Walnut (Navy); walnut-stained hardwood (Dixie).
Sights: Fixed.
Features: Polished barrel and lock with brass trigger guard and buttplate. Bayonet and scabbard available. From Navy Arms, Dixie Gun Works.
Price: Finished .... **$475.00 to $850.00**
Price: Kit (Dixie Gun Works, Navy Arms) ...... **$495.00 to $510.00**
Price: Carbine (Navy Arms) **$675.00**

T/C Big Boar

THOMPSON/CENTER BIG BOAR RIFLE
Caliber: 58.

Barrel: 26" octagon; 1:48 twist.
Weight: 7¾ lbs. **Length:** 42½" overall.
Stock: American black walnut; rubber buttpad; swivels.
Sights: Bead front, fullt adjustable open rear.
Features: Percussion lock; single trigger with wide bow trigger guard. Comes with soft leather sling. Introduced 1991. From Thompson/Center.
Price: **$355.00**

BLACKPOWDER MUSKETS & RIFLES

T/C Hawken

Thompson/Center Hawken Custom Rifle

Same as the standard Hawken except has select grade American walnut stock; barrel and all hardware polished to a high luster and deeply blued. Does not have patch box in stock. From Thompson/Center Arms.
Price: **$475.00**

THOMPSON/CENTER NEW ENGLANDER RIFLE

Caliber: 50, 54.
Barrel: 28", round.
Weight: 7 lbs., 15 oz.
Stock: American walnut or Rynite.
Sights: Open, adjustable.
Features: Color case-hardened percussion lock with engraving, rest blued. Also accepts 12-ga. shotgun barrel. Introduced 1987. From Thompson/Center.
Price: Right-hand model **$285.00**
Price: As above, Rynite stock **$270.00**
Price: Left-hand model **$305.00**
Price: Accessory 12-ga. barrel, right-hand **$160.00**

THOMPSON/CENTER HAWKEN RIFLE

Caliber: 45, 50 or 54.
Barrel: 28" octagon, hooked breech.
Stock: American walnut.
Sights: Blade front, rear adjustable for windage and elevation.
Features: Solid brass furniture, double-set triggers, button rifled barrel, coil-type mainspring. From Thompson/Center.
Price: Percussion model (45-, 50- or 54-cal.) **$395.00**
Price: Flintlock model (50-cal.) **$405.00**
Price: Percussion kit **$290.00**
Price: Flintlock kit **$310.00**

THOMPSON/CENTER GREY HAWK PERCUSSION RIFLE

Caliber: 50, 54.
Barrel: 24"; 1:48" twist.
Weight: 7 lbs. **Length:** 41" overall.
Stock: Black Rynite with rubber recoil pad.
Sights: Bead front, fully adjustable open hunting rear.
Features: Stainless steel barrel, lock, hammer, trigger guard, thimbles; blued sights. Percussion only. Introduced 1993. From Thompson/Center Arms.
Price: **$310.00**

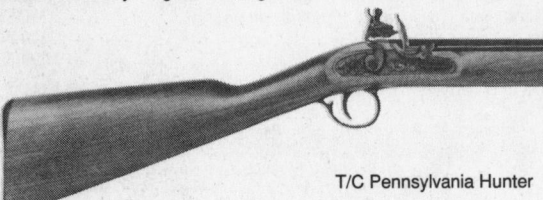

T/C Pennsylvania Hunter

Thompson/Center Pennsylvania Hunter Carbine

Similar to the Pennsylvania Hunter except has 21" barrel, weighs 6.5 lbs., and has an overall length of 38". Designed for shooting patched round balls. Available in percussion or flintlock styles. Introduced 1992. From Thompson/Center.
Price: Percussion **$330.00**
Price: Flintlock **$345.00**

Thompson/Center Renegade Hunter

Similar to standard Renegade except has single trigger in a large-bow shotgun-style trigger guard, no brass trim. Available in 50- or 54-caliber. Color case-hardened lock, rest blued. Introduced 1987. From Thompson/Center.
Price: **$325.00**

THOMPSON/CENTER PENNSYLVANIA HUNTER RIFLE

Caliber: 50.
Barrel: 31", half-octagon, half-round.
Weight: About 7½ lbs. **Length:** 48" overall.
Stock: Black walnut.
Sights: Open, adjustable.
Features: Rifled 1:66 for round ball shooting. Available in flintlock or percussion. From Thompson/Center.
Price: Percussion **$340.00**
Price: Flintlock **$355.00**

THOMPSON/CENTER RENEGADE RIFLE

Caliber: 50 and 54.
Barrel: 26", 1" across the flats.
Weight: 8 lbs.
Stock: American walnut.
Sights: Open hunting (Patridge) style, fully adjustable for windage and elevation.
Features: Coil spring lock, double-set triggers, blued steel trim. From Thompson/Center.
Price: Percussion model **$350.00**
Price: Flintlock model, 50-cal. only **$360.00**
Price: Percussion kit **$258.00**
Price: Flintlock kit **$258.00**
Price: Left-hand percussion, 50- or 54-cal. **$360.00**

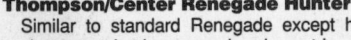

T/C Thunder Hawk

THOMPSON/CENTER THUNDER HAWK RIFLE

Caliber: 50, 54.
Barrel: 21"; 1:38" twist.
Weight: 6.75 lbs. **Length:** 38.75" overall.
Stock: American walnut or black Rynite with rubber recoil pad.
Sights: Bead on ramp front, adjustable leaf rear.
Features: Uses modern in-line ignition system, adjustable trigger. Knurled striker handle indicators for Safe and Fire. Black wood ramrod, Drilled and tapped for T/C scope mounts. Introduced 1993. From Thompson/Center Arms.
Price: Blue, walnut stock **$290.00**
Price: SST, Rynite stock **$290.00**

THOMPSON/CENTER SCOUT RIFLE

Caliber: 50 and 54.
Barrel: 21", interchangeable, 1:20 twist.
Weight: 7 lbs., 4 oz. **Length:** 38⅝" overall.
Stocks: American black walnut stock and forend.
Sights: Bead front, adjustable semi-buckhorn rear.
Features: Patented in-line ignition system with special vented breech plug. Patented trigger mechanism consists of only two moving parts. Interchangeable barrels. Wide grooved hammer. Brass trigger guard assembly, brass barrel band and buttplate. Ramrod has blued hardware. Comes with q.d. swivels and suede leather carrying sling. Drilled and tapped for standard scope mounts. Introduced 1990. From Thompson/Center.
Price: 50- or 54-cal. **$415.00**
Price: With black Rynite stock **$325.00**
Price: Extra barrel, 50- or 54-cal. **$165.00**

BLACKPOWDER MUSKETS & RIFLES

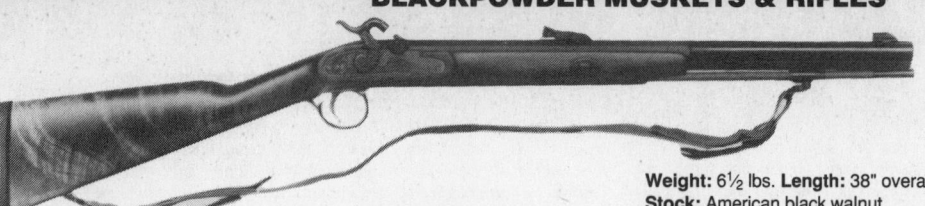

T/C White Mountain

THOMPSON/CENTER WHITE MOUNTAIN CARBINE
Caliber: 50, 54.
Barrel: 21", half-octagon, half-round.

Weight: 6½ lbs. **Length:** 38" overall.
Stock: American black walnut.
Sights: Open hunting (Patridge) style, fully adjustable rear.
Features: Percussion or flintlock. Single trigger, large trigger guard; rubber buttpad; rear q.d. swivel, front swivel mounted on thimble; comes with sling. Introduced 1989. From Thompson/Center.
Price: Percussion $350.00

Traditions Buckskinner

TRADITIONS DEERHUNTER RIFLE
Caliber: 50.
Barrel: 26", octagonal, 15/16" flats; 1:48" or 1:66" twist.
Weight: 5 lbs., 14 oz. **Length:** 39¼" overall.
Stock: Stained beech with rubber buttpad, sling swivels.
Sights: Blade front, rear adjustable for windage.
Features: Flint or percussion with color case-hardened lock. Hooked breech, oversized trigger guard, blackened furniture, wood ramrod. Imported by Traditions, Inc.
Price: Percussion, 1:48" twist $165.00
Price: Flintlock, 1:66" twist $182.00
Price: Percussion kit $149.00

TRADITIONS BUCKSKINNER CARBINE
Caliber: 50.
Barrel: 21", 15/16" flats, half octagon, half round.
Weight: 6 lbs. **Length:** 36¼" overall.
Stock: Beech or black laminated.
Sights: Beaded blade front, hunting-style open rear click adjustable for windage and elevation.
Features: Uses V-type mainspring, single trigger. Non-glare hardware. Comes with leather sling. From Traditions, Inc.
Price: Flintlock $290.00
Price: Flintlock, laminated stock $337.00
Price: Percussion $274.00
Price: Percussion, laminated stock $320.00
Price: Percussion, left-hand $290.00

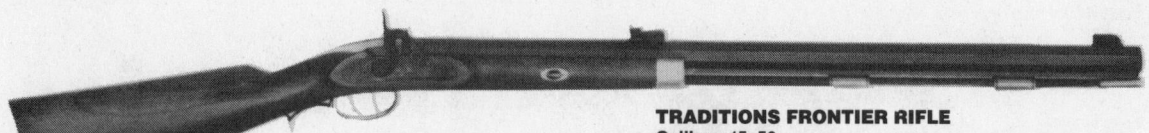

Traditions Frontier

Traditions Frontier Carbine
Similar to the Frontier Rifle except has 24" barrel, is 40½" overall, weighs 6½ lbs. Available in 50-caliber percussion only. From Traditions, Inc.
Price: $254.00

TRADITIONS FRONTIER SCOUT RIFLE
Caliber: 36, 45, 50.
Barrel: 24" (36-cal.), 26" (45, 50); 7/8" flats.
Weight: 6 lbs. **Length:** 39⅛" overall (24" barrel).
Stock: Beech.
Sights: Blade Front, primitive-style adjustable rear.
Features: Scaled-down version of the Frontier rifle for smaller shooters. Percussion only. Color case-hardened lock plate. From Traditions, Inc.
Price: $232.00

TRADITIONS FRONTIER RIFLE
Caliber: 45, 50.
Barrel: 28", 15/16" flats.
Weight: 8 lbs. **Length:** 44¾" overall.
Stock: Beech.
Sights: Beaded blade front, hunting-style rear click adjustable for windage and elevation.
Features: Adjustable sear engagement with fly and bridle, V-type mainspring; double-set triggers. Brass furniture. From Traditions, Inc.
Price: Percussion $254.00
Price: Flintlock $274.00
Price: Kit, 50-caliber percussion $165.00

TRADITIONS HAWKEN RIFLE
Caliber: 50, 54.
Barrel: 32¼"; 1" flats.
Weight: 9 lbs. **Length:** 50" overall.
Stock: Walnut with cheekpiece.
Sights: Hunting style, click adjustable for windage and elevation.
Features: Fiberglass ramrod, double-set triggers, polished brass furniture. From Traditions, Inc.
Price: Percussion $412.00

Traditions Pennsylvania

TRADITIONS PENNSYLVANIA RIFLE
Caliber: 45, 50.
Barrel: 40¼", 7/8" flats.
Weight: 9 lbs. **Length:** 57½" overall.
Stock: Walnut.
Sights: Blade front, adjustable rear.
Features: Brass patchbox and ornamentation. Double-set triggers. From Traditions, Inc.
Price: Flintlock $495.00
Price: Percussion $467.00

TRADITIONS HAWKEN WOODSMAN RIFLE
Caliber: 50 and 54.
Barrel: 28"; 15/16" flats.
Weight: 7 lbs. **Length:** 45.75" overall.
Stock: Walnut-stained hardwood.
Sights: Beaded blade front, hunting-style open rear adjustable for windage and elevation.
Features: Percussion only. Brass patchbox and furniture. Double triggers. From Traditions, Inc.
Price: 50 or 54 . . . . $292.00
Price: 50-cal., left-hand $309.00
Price: Kit $210.00

BLACKPOWDER MUSKETS & RIFLES

TRADITIONS PIONEER RIFLE/CARBINE
Caliber: 50, 54.
Barrel: 27¼"; ¹⁵⁄₁₆" flats.
Weight: 7 lbs. **Length:** 44" overall.
Stock: Beech with pistol grip, recoil pad.
Sights: German silver blade front, buckhorn rear with elevation ramp.
Features: V-type mainspring, adjustable single trigger; blackened furniture; color case-hardened lock; large trigger guard. From Traditions, Inc.
Price: Percussion only, rifle **$227.00**
Price: Carbine. 24" barrel, 50-cal. only **$227.00**

TRADITIONS T93 CUSTOM IN-LINE RIFLE, CARBINE
Caliber: 50.
Barrel: 21", 28", round.
Weight: 7 lbs., 14 oz. (rifle). **Length:** 44¼" overall (rifle).
Stock: Stained beech.
Sights: Beaded blade front, click adjustable rear.
Features: Closed breech in-line percussion action, ambidextrous and half-cock safety. Comes with blackened furniture, swivel studs, unbreakable ramrod, oversized trigger guard. Polished blue finish. From Traditions, Inc.
Price: Rifle or carbine **$432.00**

TRADITIONS WHITETAIL SERIES RIFLES
Caliber: 50, 54 (percussion only).
Barrel: 21", 26", ¹⁵⁄₁₆" flats.
Weight: 5 lbs., 14 oz. (rifle). **Length:** 39¼" overall (rifle).
Stock: Walnut-stained hardwood, rubber recoil pad; or synthetic.
Sights: Beaded blade front with flourescent dot, fully adjustable hunting-style rear.
Features: Flint or percussion. Color case-hardened, engraved lock with V-type mainspring, offset hammer. Barrel drilled and tapped for scope mounting (percussion only). Oversized trigger guard, sling swivels, blackened furniture, inletted wedge plates. Imported by Traditions, Inc.
Price: Flintlock, wood stock, rifle or carbine **$274.00**
Price: Flintlock, synthetic stock, stainless barrel **$337.00**
Price: Percussion, wood stock, 50 or 54 . . . . **$257.00**
Price: As above, synthetic stock **$290.00**
Price: Carbine, percussion, wood stock **$257.00**
Price: As above, synthetic stock **$290.00**
Price: Carbine, percussion, synthetic stock, stainless barrel **$320.00**

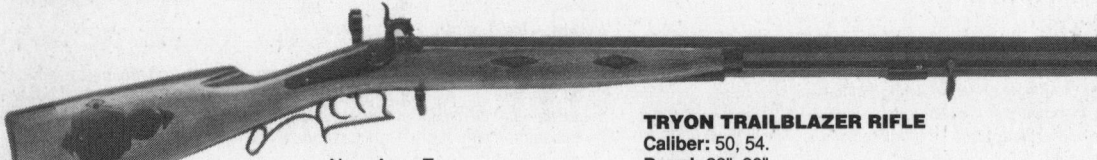

Navy Arms Tryon

TRYON TRAILBLAZER RIFLE
Caliber: 50, 54.
Barrel: 28", 30".
Weight: 9 lbs. **Length:** 48" overall.
Stock: European walnut with cheekpiece.
Sights: Blade front, semi-buckhorn rear.
Features: Reproduction of a rifle made by George Tryon about 1820. Double-set triggers, back action lock, hooked breech with long tang. From Armsport.
Price: About **$825.00**

Navy Arms Tryon Creedmoor Target Model
Similar to the standard Tryon rifle except 45-caliber only, 33" octagon barrel, globe front sight with inserts, fully adjustable match rear. Has double-set triggers, sling swivels. Imported by Navy Arms.
Price: **$680.00**

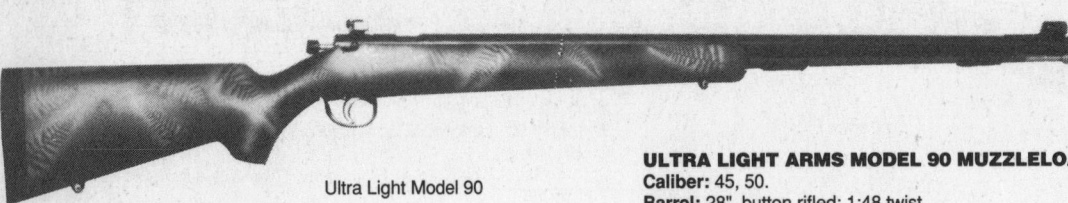

Ultra Light Model 90

ULTRA LIGHT ARMS MODEL 90 MUZZLELOADER
Caliber: 45, 50.
Barrel: 28", button rifled; 1:48 twist.
Weight: 6 lbs.
Stock: Kevlar/graphite, colors optional.
Sights: Hooded blade front on ramp, Williams aperture rear adjustable for windage and elevation.
Features: In-line ignition system with top loading port. Timney trigger; integral side safety. Comes with recoil pad, sling swivels and hard case. Introduced 1990. Made in U.S. by Ultra Light Arms.
Price: **$950.00**

UBERTI SANTA FE HAWKEN RIFLE
Caliber: 50 or 54.
Barrel: 32", octagonal.
Weight: 9.8 lbs. **Length:** 50" overall.
Stock: Walnut, with beavertail cheekpiece.
Sights: German silver blade front, buckhorn rear.
Features: Browned finish, color case-hardened lock, double triggers, German silver ferrule, wedge plates. Imported by Uberti USA.
Price: **$495.00**

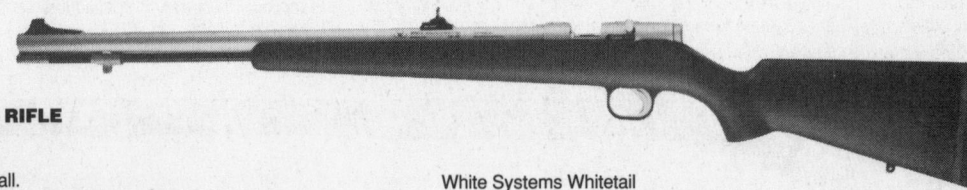

White Systems Whitetail

WHITE SYSTEMS WHITETAIL RIFLE
Caliber: 41, 45 or 50.
Barrel: 22".
Weight: 6.5 lbs. **Length:** 39.5" overall.
Stock: Black composite; classic style; recoil pad, swivel studs.
Sights: Bead front on ramp, fully adjustable open rear.
Features: Insta-Fire straight-line ignition; action and trigger safeties; adjustable trigger; stainless steel. Introduced 1992. Made in U.S. by White Systems, Inc.
Price: Blue, composite stock **$399.00**
Price: Stainless, composite stock **$499.00**

White Systems Bison Blackpowder Rifle
Similar to the blued Whitetail model except in 50-caliber (1:24" twist) or 54-caliber (1:28" twist) with 22" ball barrel. Uses Insta-Fire in-line percussion system, double safety. Adjustable sight, black-finished hardwood stock, matte blue metal finish, Delron ramrod, swivel studs. Drilled and tapped for scope mounting. Weighs 7¼ lbs. Introduced 1993. From White Systems, Inc.
Price: **$299.00**

WHITE SYSTEMS SPORTING RIFLE
Caliber: 41, 45, 50.
Barrel: 26".
Weight: 8¾ lbs. **Length:** NA.
Stock: Figured crotchwood fiber composite.
Sights: Bead front on ramp, fully adjustable open rear.
Features: Traditional sidelock action; Delron ramrod; swivel studs; matte blue finish. Introduced 1994. From White Systems, Inc.
Price: **$699.00**

BLACKPOWDER MUSKETS & RIFLES

White Systems Super 91

White Systems Super Safari Rifle
Same as the stainless Super 91 except has Mannlicher-style stock of black composite. Introduced 1993. From White Systems, Inc.
Price: **$799.00**

WHITE SYSTEMS SUPER 91 BLACKPOWDER RIFLE
Caliber: 41, 45 or 50.
Barrel: 26".
Weight: 7½ lbs. **Length:** 43.5" overall.
Stock: Black laminate or black composite; recoil pad, swivel studs.
Sights: Bead front on ramp, fully adjustable open rear.
Features: Insta-Fire straight-line ignition system; all stainless steel construction; side-swing safety; fully adjustable trigger; full barrel under-rib with two ramrod thimbles. Introduced 1991. Made in U.S. by White Systems, Inc.
Price: Blue **$599.00**
Price: Stainless **$699.00**

Navy Arms 1841 Mississippi

Mississippi Model 1841 Percussion Rifle
Similar to Zouave rifle but patterned after U.S. Model 1841. Imported by Dixie Gun Works, Euroarms of America, Navy Arms.
Price: . . . . **$430.00 to $569.00**

ZOUAVE PERCUSSION RIFLE
Caliber: 58, 59.
Barrel: 32½".
Weight: 9½ lbs. **Length:** 48½" overall.
Stock: Walnut finish, brass patchbox and buttplate.
Sights: Fixed front, rear adjustable for elevation.
Features: Color case-hardened lockplate, blued barrel. From Navy Arms, Dixie Gun Works, Euroarms of America (M1863), E.M.F.
Price: About . . . . **$325.00 to $540.00**
Price: Kit (Euroarms 58-cal. only) **$388.00**

BLACKPOWDER SHOTGUNS

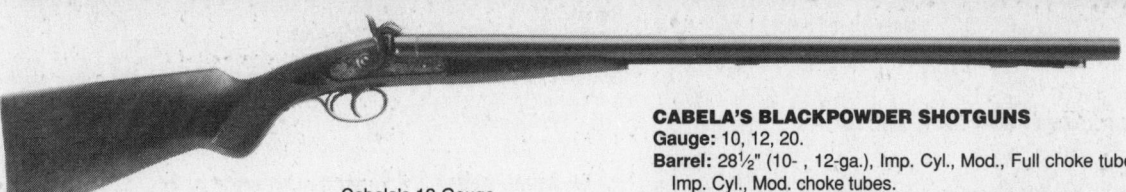

Cabela's 12-Gauge

CABELA'S BLACKPOWDER SHOTGUNS
Gauge: 10, 12, 20.
Barrel: 28½" (10-, 12-ga.), Imp. Cyl., Mod., Full choke tubes; 27½" (20-ga.), Imp. Cyl., Mod. choke tubes.
Weight: 6½ to 7 lbs. **Length:** 45" overall (28½" barrel).
Stock: American walnut with checkered grip; 12- and 20-gauge have straight stock, 10-gauge has pistol grip.
Features: Blued barrels, engraved, color case-hardened locks and hammers, brass ramrod tip. From Cabela's.
Price: 10-gauge **$374.95**
Price: 12-gauge **$369.95**

CVA TRAPPER PERCUSSION
Gauge: 12.
Barrel: 28". Choke tubes (Imp. Cyl., Mod., Full).
Weight: 6 lbs.
Length: 46" overall.
Stock: English-style checkered straight grip of walnut-finished hardwood.
Sights: Brass bead front.
Features: Single blued barrel; color case-hardened lockplate and hammer; screw adjustable sear engagements, V-type mainspring; brass wedge plates; color case-hardened and engraved trigger guard and tang. From CVA.
Price: Finished **$229.95**

CONSULT
Shooter's Marketplace
Page 225, This Issue

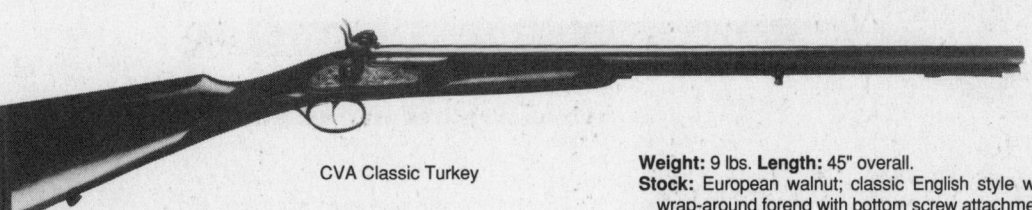

CVA Classic Turkey

CVA CLASSIC TURKEY DOUBLE SHOTGUN
Gauge: 12.
Barrel: 28" (Imp. & Imp.).

Weight: 9 lbs. **Length:** 45" overall.
Stock: European walnut; classic English style with checkered straight grip, wrap-around forend with bottom screw attachment.
Sights: Bead front.
Features: Hinged double triggers; color case-hardened and engraved lockplates, trigger guard and tang. Polymer-coated fiberglass ramrod. Rubber recoil pad. Not suitable for steel shot. Introduced 1990. Imported by CVA.
Price: **$409.95**

CAUTION: PRICES SHOWN ARE SUPPLIED BY THE MANUFACTURER OR IMPORTER. CHECK YOUR LCOAL GUNSHOP.

49th EDITION, 1995 **433**

BLACKPOWDER SHOTGUNS

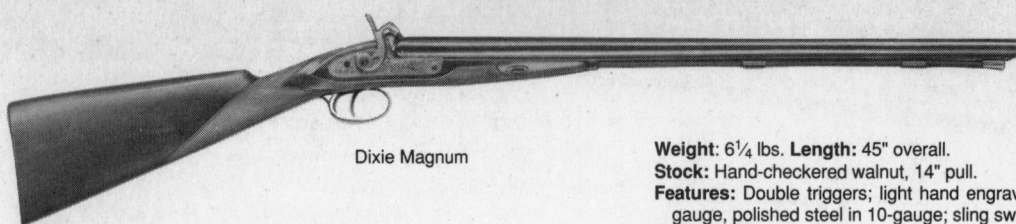

Dixie Magnum

DIXIE MAGNUM PERCUSSION SHOTGUN
Gauge: 10, 12, 20.
Barrel: 30" (Imp. Cyl. & Mod.) in 10-gauge; 28" in 12-gauge.

Weight: 6¼ lbs. **Length:** 45" overall.
Stock: Hand-checkered walnut, 14" pull.
Features: Double triggers; light hand engraving; case-hardened locks in 12-gauge, polished steel in 10-gauge; sling swivels. From Dixie Gun Works.
Price: Upland **$399.00**
Price: 12-ga. kit **$350.00**
Price: 10-ga. **$495.00**
Price: 10-ga. kit **$375.00**

Mowrey Shotgun

MOWREY SHOTGUN
Gauge: 12, 28.
Barrel: 28" (28-gauge, Cyl.); 32" (12-gauge, Cyl.); octagonal.
Weight: About 8 lbs. **Length:** 48" overall (32" barrel).
Stock: Curly maple.
Sights: Bead front.
Features: Brass or steel frame; shotgun butt. Made in U.S. by Mowrey Gun Works.
Price: Finished **$350.00**
Price: Kit **$300.00**

Navy Arms Fowler

NAVY ARMS MORTIMER FLINTLOCK SHOTGUN
Gauge: 12.
Barrel: 36".
Weight: 7 lbs. **Length:** 53" overall.
Stock: Walnut, with cheekpiece.
Features: Waterproof pan, roller frizzen, external safety. Color case-hardened lock, rest blued. Introduced 1991. Imported by Navy Arms.
Price: **$670.00**

NAVY ARMS FOWLER SHOTGUN
Gauge: 12.
Barrel: 28".
Weight: 7 lbs., 12 oz. **Length:** 45" overall.
Stock: Walnut-stained hardwood.
Features: Color case-hardened lockplates and hammers; checkered stock. Imported by Navy Arms.
Price: Fowler model, 12-ga. only **$325.00**

NAVY ARMS STEEL SHOT MAGNUM SHOTGUN
Gauge: 10.
Barrel: 28" (Cyl. & Cyl.).
Weight: 7 lbs., 9 oz. **Length:** 45½" overall.
Stock: Walnut, with cheekpiece.
Features: Designed specifically for steel shot. Engraved, polished locks; sling swivels; blued barrels. Introduced 1991. Imported by Navy Arms.
Price: **$510.00**

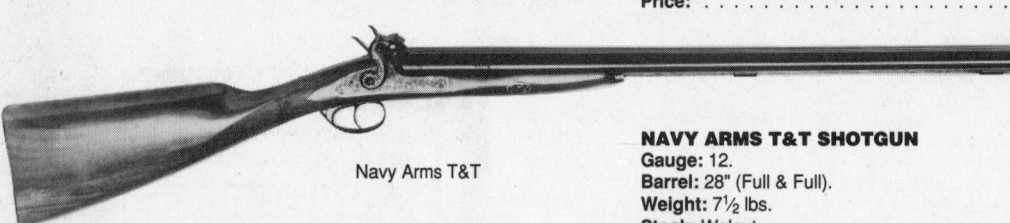

Navy Arms T&T

NAVY ARMS T&T SHOTGUN
Gauge: 12.
Barrel: 28" (Full & Full).
Weight: 7½ lbs.
Stock: Walnut.
Sights: Bead front.
Features: Color case-hardened locks, double triggers, blued steel furniture. From Navy Arms.
Price: **$500.00**

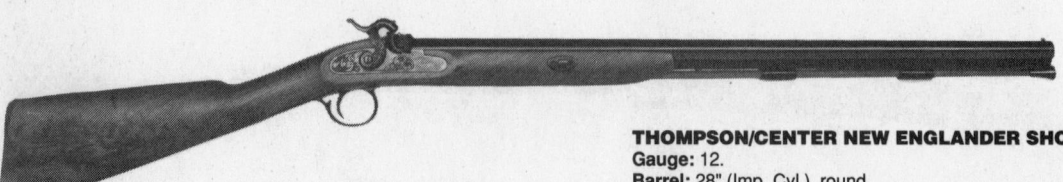

T/C New Englander

THOMPSON/CENTER NEW ENGLANDER SHOTGUN
Gauge: 12.
Barrel: 28" (Imp. Cyl.), round.
Weight: 5 lbs., 2 oz.
Stock: Select American black walnut with straight grip.
Features: Percussion lock is color case-hardened, rest blued. Also accepts 26" round 50- and 54-cal. rifle barrel. Introduced 1986. From Thompson/Center.
Price: Right-hand **$305.00**
Price: Accessory rifle barrel, right-hand, 50 or 54 . . . . **$130.00**
Price: As above, left-hand **$140.00**

AIRROW MODEL 6A AIR PISTOL

Caliber: #2512 10.75" arrow.
Barrel: 10.75".
Weight: 1.75 lbs. **Length:** 16.5" overall.
Power: CO_2 or compressed air.
Stocks: Checkered composition.
Sights: Bead front, fully adjustable Williams rear.
Features: Velocity to 375 fps. Pneumatic air trigger. Floating barrel. All aircraft aluminum and stainless steel construction; Mil-spec materials and finishes. Announced 1993. From Swivel Machine Works, Inc.
Price: About **$597.00**

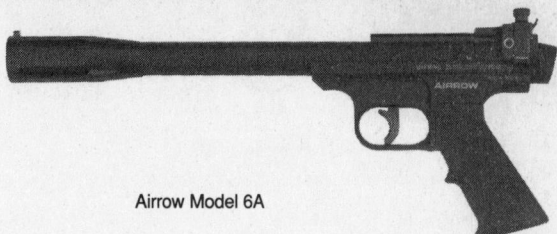

Airrow Model 6A

BEEMAN P1 MAGNUM AIR PISTOL

Caliber: 177, 5mm, 22, single shot.
Barrel: 8.4".
Weight: 2.5 lbs. **Length:** 11" overall.
Power: Top lever cocking; spring piston.
Stocks: Checkered walnut.
Sights: Blade front, square notch rear with click micrometer adjustments for windage and elevation. Grooved for scope mounting.
Features: Dual power for 177 and 20-cal.: low setting gives 350-400 fps; high setting 500-600 fps. Rearward expanding mainspring simulates firearm recoil. All Colt 45 auto grips fit gun. Dry-firing feature for practice. Optional wooden shoulder stock. Introduced 1985. Imported by Beeman.
Price: 177, 5mm, 22-cal. **$390.00**
Price: 177, 5mm, stainless/blue finish **$440.00**

Beeman P1

BEEMAN/FEINWERKBAU C20 CO_2 PISTOL

Caliber: 177, single shot.
Barrel: 10.1", 12-groove rifling.
Weight: 2.5 lbs. **Length:** 16" overall.
Power: Special CO_2 cylinder.
Stock: Stippled walnut with adjustable palm shelf.
Sights: Blade front, open rear adjustable for windage and elevation. Notch size adjustable for width. Interchangeable front blades.
Features: Fully adjustable trigger; can be set for dry firing. Separate gas chamber for uniform power. Cylinders interchangeable even when full. Short-barrel model also available. Introduced 1988. Imported by Beeman.
Price: Right-hand, regular or Mini **$1,130.00**
Price: Left-hand **$1,195.00**

Beeman P2 Match Air Pistol

Similar to the Beeman P1 Magnum except shoots only 177 or 5mm pellets; completely recoilless single-stroke pnuematic action. Weighs 2.2 lbs. Choice of thumbrest match grips or standard style. Introduced 1990.
Price: 177, 5mm, standard grip **$430.00**
Price: 177, match grip **$460.00**

Beeman/Feinwerkbau 102

BEEMAN/FEINWERKBAU C25 CO_2 PISTOL

Caliber: 177, single shot.
Barrel: 10.1"; 12-groove rifling.
Weight: 2.5 lbs. **Length:** 16.5" overall.
Power: Vertical, interchangeable CO_2 bottles.
Stocks: Stippled walnut with adjustable palm shelf.
Sights: Blade front, rear micrometer adjustable. Notch size adjustable for width; interchangeable front blades.
Features: Fully adjustable trigger; can be set for dry firing. Has special vertical CO_2 cylinder and weight rail for balance. Short-barrel model (C25 Mini) also available. Introduced 1992. Imported by Beeman.
Price: Right-hand **$1,295.00**
Price: Left-hand **$1,295.00**
Price: C25 Mini **$1,285.00**

BEEMAN/FEINWERKBAU 65 MKII AIR PISTOL

Caliber: 177, single shot.
Barrel: 6.1" or 7.5", removable bbl. wgt. available.
Weight: 42 oz. **Length:** 13.3" or 14.1" overall.
Power: Spring, sidelever cocking.
Stocks: Walnut, stippled thumbrest; adjustable or fixed.
Sights: Front, interchangeable post element system, open rear, click adjustable for windage and elevation and for sighting notch width. Scope mount available.
Features: New shorter barrel for better balance and control. Cocking effort 9 lbs. Two-stage trigger, four adjustments. Quiet firing, 525 fps. Programs instantly for recoil or recoilless operation. Permanently lubricated. Steel piston ring. Special switch converts trigger from 17.6-oz. pull to 42-oz. let-off. Imported by Beeman.
Price: Right-hand **$1,090.00**
Price: Left-hand, 6.1" barrel **$1,160.00**
Price: Model 65 Mk. I (7.5" bbl.) **$1,160.00**

BEEMAN/FEINWERKBAU 102 PISTOL

Caliber: 177, single shot.
Barrel: 10.1", 12-groove rifling.
Weight: 2.5 lbs. **Length:** 16.5" overall.
Power: Single-stroke pneumatic, underlever cocking.
Stocks: Stippled walnut with adjustable palm shelf.
Sights: Blade front, open rear adjustable for windage and elevation. Notch size adjustable for width. Interchangeable front blades.
Features: Velocity 460 fps. Fully adjustable trigger. Cocking effort 12 lbs. Introduced 1988. Imported by Beeman.
Price: Right-hand **$1,360.00**

Beeman/FWB C55

BEEMAN/FWB C55 CO$_2$ RAPID FIRE PISTOL
Caliber: 177, single shot or 5-shot magazines.
Barrel: 7.3".
Weight: 2.5 lbs. **Length:** 15" overall.
Power: Special CO$_2$ cylinder.
Stocks: Anatomical, adjustable.
Sights: Interchangeable front, fully adjustable open micro-click rear with adjustable notch size.
Features: Velocity 510 fps. Has 11.75" sight radius. Built-in muzzle brake. Introduced 1993. Imported by Beeman Precision Airguns.
Price: Right-hand **$1,590.00**
Price: Left-hand **$1,665.00**

BEEMAN HW70A AIR PISTOL
Caliber: 177, single shot.
Barrel: 6¼", rifled.
Weight: 38 oz. **Length:** 12¾" overall.
Power: Spring, barrel cocking.
Stocks: Plastic, with thumbrest.
Sights: Hooded post front, square notch rear adjustable for windage and elevation. Comes with scope base.
Features: Adjustable trigger, 24-lb. cocking effort, 410 fps MV; automatic barrel safety. Imported by Beeman.
Price: **$200.00**

Beeman HW70A

Benjamin Sheridan Pneumatic

BENJAMIN SHERIDAN PNEUMATIC PELLET PISTOLS
Caliber: 177, 20, 22, single shot.
Barrel: 9⅜", rifled brass.
Weight: 38 oz. **Length:** 13⅛" overall.
Power: Under-lever pnuematic, hand pumped.
Stocks: Walnut stocks and pump handle.
Sights: High ramp front, fully adjustable notch rear.
Features: Velocity to 525 fps (variable). Bolt action with cross-bolt safety. Choice of black or nickel finish. Made in U.S. by Benjamin Sheridan Co.
Price: Black finish, HB17 (177), HB20 (20), HB22 (22) **$104.95**
Price: Nickel finish, H17 (177), H20 (20), H22 (22) **$111.50**

Benjamin Sheridan CO$_2$

BENJAMIN SHERIDAN CO$_2$ PELLET PISTOLS
Caliber: 177, 20, 22, single shot.
Barrel: 6⅜", rifled brass.
Weight: 29 oz. **Length:** 9.8" overall.
Power: 12-gram CO$_2$ cylinder.
Stocks: Walnut.
Sights: High ramp front, fully adjustable notch rear.
Features: Velocity to 500 fps. Turn-bolt action with cross-bolt safety. Gives about 40 shots per CO$_2$ cylinder. Black or nickel finish. Made in U.S. by Benjamin Sheridan Co.
Price: Black finish, EB17 (177), EB20 (20), EB22 (22) **$96.50**
Price: Nickel finish, E17 (177), E20 (20), E22 (22) **$109.50**

BRNO AERON-TAU CO$_2$ PISTOL
Caliber: 177.
Barrel: 10".
Weight: 37 oz. **Length:** 12.5" overall.
Power: 12.5-gram CO$_2$ cartridges.
Stocks: Stippled hardwood with palm rest.
Sights: Blade front, open fully adjustable rear.
Features: Comes with extra seals and counterweight. Blue finish. Imported by Century International Arms.
Price: About **$299.00**

Crosman Auto Air II

CROSMAN MODEL 357 AIR PISTOL
Caliber: 177, 6- and 10-shot pellet clips.
Barrel: 4" (Model 357-4), 6" (Model 357-6), rifled steel; 8" (Model 357-8), rifled brass.
Weight: 32 oz. (6"). **Length:** 11⅜" overall (357-6).
Power: CO$_2$ Powerlet.
Stocks: Checkered wood-grain plastic.
Sights: Ramp front, fully adjustable rear.
Features: Average 430 fps (Model 357-6). Break-open barrel for easy loading. Single or double action. Vent. rib barrel. Wide, smooth trigger. Two cylinders come with each gun. Model 357-8 has matte gray finish, black grips. From Crosman.
Price: 4" or 6", about **$45.00**
Price: 8", about **$50.00**
Price: Model 1357 (same gun as above, except shoots BBs, has 6-shot clip), about **$45.00**

CROSMAN AUTO AIR II PISTOL
Caliber: BB, 17-shot magazine, 177 pellet, single shot.
Barrel: 8⅝" steel, smoothbore.
Weight: 13 oz. **Length:** 10¾" overall.
Power: CO$_2$ Powerlet.
Stocks: Grooved plastic.
Sights: Blade front, adjustable rear; highlighted system.
Features: Velocity to 480 fps (BBs), 430 fps (pellets). Semi-automatic action with BBs, single shot with pellets. Silvered finish. Introduced 1991. From Crosman.
Price: About **$28.00**

Crosman Model 1008

CROSMAN MODEL 1008 REPEAT AIR
Caliber: 177, 8-shot pellet clip
Barrel: 4.25", rifled steel.
Weight: 17 oz. **Length:** 8.625" overall.
Power: CO_2 Powerlet.
Stocks: Checkered plastic.
Sights: Post front, adjustable rear.
Features: Velocity about 430 fps. Break-open barrel for easy loading; single or double semi-automatic action; two 8-shot clips included. Optional carrying case available. Introduced 1992. From Crosman.
Price: About **$43.00**
Price: With case, about **$50.00**

Crosman 1322

CROSMAN MODEL 1322, 1377 AIR PISTOLS
Caliber: 177 (M1377), 22 (M1322), single shot.
Barrel: 8", rifled steel.
Weight: 39 oz. **Length:** 13⅝".
Power: Hand pumped.
Sights: Blade front, rear adjustable for windage and elevation.
Features: Moulded plastic grip, hand size pump forearm. Cross-bolt safety. Model 1377 also shoots BBs. From Crosman.
Price: About **$50.00**

Crosman SSP 250

CROSMAN MODEL SSP 250 PISTOL
Caliber: 177, 20, 22, single shot.
Barrel: 9⅞", rifled steel.
Weight: 3 lbs., 1 oz. **Length:** 14" overall.
Power: CO_2 Powerlet.
Stocks: Composition; black, with checkering.
Sights: Hooded front, fully adjustable rear.
Features: Velocity about 560 fps. Interchangeable accessory barrels. Two-stage trigger. High/low power settings. From Crosman.
Price: About **$48.00**

DAISY MODEL 91 MATCH PISTOL
Caliber: 177, single shot.
Barrel: 10.25", rifled steel.
Weight: 2.5 lbs. **Length:** 16.5" overall.
Power: CO_2, 12-gram cylinder.
Stocks: Stippled hardwood; anatomically shaped and adjustable.
Sights: Blade and ramp front, changeable-width rear notch with full micrometer adjustments.
Features: Velocity to 476 fps. Gives 55 shots per cylinder. Fully adjustable trigger. Imported by Daisy Mfg. Co.
Price: About **$670.00**

CZ MODEL 3 AIR PISTOL
Caliber: 177, single shot.
Barrel: 7.25".
Weight: 44 oz. **Length:** 13.75" overall.
Power: Spring piston, barrel cocking.
Stocks: High-impact plastic; ambidextrous, with thumbrest.
Sights: Hooded front, fully adjustable rear.
Features: Velocity about 420 fps. Externally adjustable trigger; removable screwdriver threaded into receiver. Imported from the Czech Republic by Action Arms.
Price: **$79.00**

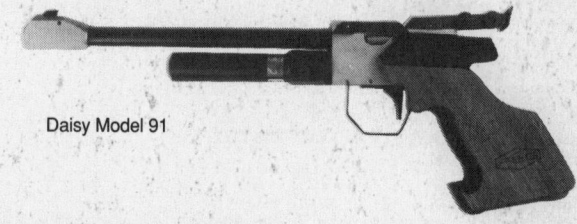

Daisy Model 91

Daisy Model 288

DAISY MODEL 288 AIR PISTOL
Caliber: 177 pellets, 24-shot.
Barrel: Smoothbore steel.
Weight: .8 lb. **Length:** 12.1" overall.
Power: Single stroke spring air.
Stocks: Moulded resin with checkering and thumbrest.
Sights: Blade and ramp front, open fixed rear.
Features: Velocity to 215 fps. Cross-bolt trigger block safety. Black finish. From Daisy Mfg. Co.
Price: About **$26.00**

Daisy Model 500

DAISY MODEL 500 RAVEN AIR PISTOL
Caliber: 177 pellets, single shot.
Barrel: Rifled steel.
Weight: 36 oz. **Length:** 8.5" overall.
Power: CO_2.
Stocks: Moulded plastic with checkering.
Sights: Blade front, fixed rear.
Features: Velocity up to 500 fps. Hammer-block safety. Resembles semi-auto centerfire pistol. Barrel tips up for loading. Introduced 1993. From Daisy Mfg. Co.
Price: About **$65.00**

CAUTION: PRICES SHOWN ARE SUPPLIED BY THE MANUFACTUER OR IMPORTER. CHECK YOUR LOCAL GUNSHOP.

49th EDITION, 1995 **437**

Daisy/Power Line 45

Daisy/Power Line 93

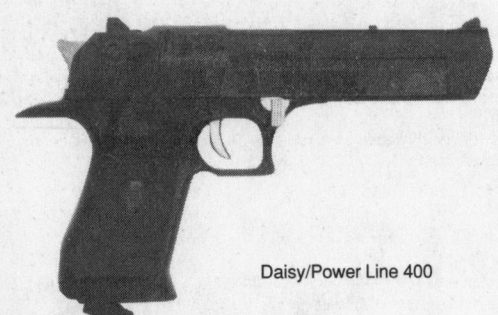

Daisy/Power Line 400

DAISY/POWER LINE 44 REVOLVER
Caliber: 177 pellets, 6-shot.
Barrel: 6", rifled steel; interchangeable 4" and 8".
Weight: 2.7 lbs.
Power: CO_2.
Stocks: Moulded plastic with checkering.
Sights: Blade on ramp front, fully adjustable notch rear.
Features: Velocity up to 400 fps. Replica of 44 Magnum revolver. Has swingout cylinder and interchangeable barrels. Introduced 1987. From Daisy Mfg. Co.
Price: **$70.00**

DAISY/POWER LINE 45 AIR PISTOL
Caliber: 177, 13-shot clip.
Barrel: 5", rifled steel.
Weight: 1.25 lbs. **Length:** 8.5" overall.
Power: CO_2.
Stocks: Checkered plastic.
Sights: Fixed.
Features: Velocity 400 fps. Semi-automatic repeater with double-action trigger. Manually operated lever-type trigger block safety; magazine safety. Introduced 1990. From Daisy Mfg. Co.
Price: About **$80.00**
Price: Model 645 (nickel-chrome plated), about **$85.00**

DAISY/POWER LINE 93 PISTOL
Caliber: 177, BB, 15-shot clip.
Barrel: 5", steel.
Weight: 17 oz. **Length:** NA.
Power: CO_2.
Stocks: Checkered plastic.
Sights: Fixed.
Features: Velocity to 400 fps. Semi-automatic repeater. Manual lever-type trigger-block safety. Introduced 1991. From Daisy Mfg. Co.
Price: About **$80.00**
Price: Model 693 (nickel-chrome plated), about **$85.00**

DAISY/POWERLINE 400 BB PISTOL
Caliber: BB, 20-shot magazine.
Barrel: Smoothbore steel.
Weight: 1.4 lbs. **Length:** 10.7" overall.
Power: 12-gram CO_2.
Stocks: Moulded black checkered plastic.
Sights: Blade front, fixed open rear.
Features: Velocity to 420 fps. Blowback slide cycles automatically on firing. Rotary trigger block safety. Introduced 1994. From Daisy Mfg. Co.
Price: About **$83.00**

DAISY/POWER LINE 717 PELLET PISTOL
Caliber: 177, single shot.
Barrel: 9.61".
Weight: 2.8 lbs. **Length:** 13½" overall.
Stocks: Moulded wood-grain plastic, with thumbrest.
Sights: Blade and ramp front, micro-adjustable notch rear.
Features: Single pump pneumatic pistol. Rifled steel barrel. Cross-bolt trigger block. Muzzle velocity 385 fps. From Daisy Mfg. Co. Introduced 1979.
Price: About **$80.00**

Daisy/Power Line 747 Pistol
Similar to the 717 pistol except has a 12-groove rifled steel barrel by Lothar Walther, and adjustable trigger pull weight. Velocity of 360 fps. Manual cross-bolt safety.
Price: About **$160.00**

DAISY/POWER LINE MATCH 777 PELLET PISTOL
Caliber: 177, single shot.
Barrel: 9.61" rifled steel by Lothar Walther.
Weight: 32 oz. **Length:** 13½" overall.
Power: Sidelever, single pump pneumatic.
Stocks: Smooth hardwood, fully contoured with palm and thumbrest.
Sights: Blade and ramp front, match-grade open rear with adjustable width notch, micro. click adjustments.
Features: Adjustable trigger; manual cross-bolt safety. MV of 385 fps. Comes with cleaning kit, adjustment tool and pellets. From Daisy Mfg. Co.
Price: About **$335.00**

Daisy/Power Line 717

Daisy/Power Line 777

Daisy/Power Line 1200

Daisy/Power Line 1700

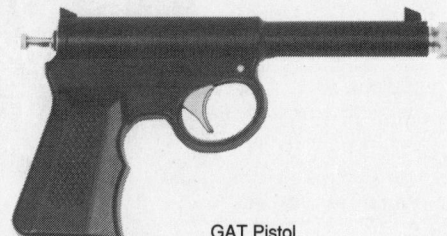

GAT Pistol

DAISY/POWER LINE CO₂ 1200 PISTOL
Caliber: BB, 177.
Barrel: 10½", smooth.
Weight: 1.6 lbs. **Length:** 11.1" overall.
Power: Daisy CO₂ cylinder.
Stocks: Contoured, checkered moulded wood-grain plastic.
Sights: Blade ramp front, fully adjustable square notch rear.
Features: 60-shot BB reservoir, gravity feed. Cross-bolt safety. Velocity of 420-450 fps for more than 100 shots. From Daisy Mfg. Co.
Price: About **$37.50**

DAISY/POWERLINE 1700 AIR PISTOL
Caliber: 177 BB, 60-shot magazine.
Barrel: Smoothbore steel.
Weight: 1.4 lbs. **Length:** 11.2" overall.
Power: CO₂
Stocks: Moulded checkered plastic.
Sights: Blade front, adjustable rear.
Features: Velocity to 420 fps. Cross-bolt trigger block safety; matte finish. Has ⅜" dovetail mount for scope or point sight. Introduced 1994. From Daisy Mfg. Co.
Price: About **$40.00**

"GAT" AIR PISTOL
Caliber: 177, single shot.
Barrel: 7½" cocked, 9½" extended.
Weight: 22 oz.
Power: Spring piston.
Stocks: Cast checkered metal.
Sights: Fixed.
Features: Shoots pellets, corks or darts. Matte black finish. Imported from England by Stone Enterprises, Inc.
Price: **$21.95**

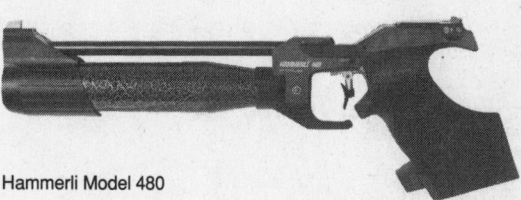

Hammerli Model 480

HAMMERLI 480 COMPETITION AIR PISTOL
Caliber: 177, single shot.
Barrel: 9.8".
Weight: 37 oz. **Length:** 16.5" overall.
Power: Air or CO₂.
Stocks: Walnut with 7-degree rake adjustment. Stippled grip area.
Sights: Undercut blade front, fully adjustable open match rear.
Features: Under-barrel cannister charges with air or CO₂ for power supply; gives 320 shots per filling. Trigger adjustable for position. Introduced 1994. Imported from Switzerland by Hammerli Pistols USA.
Price: **$1,295.00**

MARKSMAN 1015 SPECIAL EDITION AIR PISTOL
Caliber: 177, 24-shot repeater.
Barrel: 3.8", rifled.
Weight: 22 oz. **Length:** 10.3" overall.
Power: Spring-air.
Stocks: Checkered brown composition.
Sights: Fixed.
Features: Velocity about 230 fps. Skeletonized trigger, extended barrel with "ported compensator." Shoots BBs, pellets, darts or bolts. From Marksman Products.
Price: **$30.95**

MARKSMAN 1010 REPEATER PISTOL
Caliber: 177, 18-shot repeater.
Barrel: 2½", smoothbore.
Weight: 24 oz. **Length:** 8¼" overall.
Power: Spring.
Features: Velocity to 200 fps. Thumb safety. Black finish. Uses BBs, darts or pellets. Repeats with BBs only. From Marksman Products.
Price: Matte black finish **$24.95**
Price: Model 1010X (as above except nickel-plated) **$33.50**

Marksman 1015

Record Jumbo

Consult our Directory pages for the location of firms mentioned.

RECORD JUMBO DELUXE AIR PISTOL
Caliber: 177, single shot.
Barrel: 6", rifled.
Weight: 1.9 lbs. **Length:** 7.25" overall.
Power: Spring-air, lateral cocking lever.
Stocks: Smooth walnut.
Sights: Blade front, fully adjustable open rear.
Features: Velocity to 322 fps. Thumb safety. Grip magazine compartment for extra pellet storage. Introduced 1983. Imported from Germany by Great Lakes Airguns.
Price: **$110.50**

AIRGUNS—HANDGUNS

RWS/DIANA MODEL 5G AIR PISTOL
Caliber: 177, single shot.
Barrel: 7".
Weight: 2¾ lbs. **Length:** 16" overall.
Power: Spring-air, barrel cocking.
Stocks: Plastic, thumbrest design.
Sights: Tunnel front, micro-click open rear.
Features: Velocity of 410 fps. Two-stage trigger with automatic safety. Imported from Germany by Dynamit Nobel-RWS, Inc.
Price: $200.00

RWS/Diana Model 5G

RWS/DIANA MODEL 6M MATCH AIR PISTOL
Caliber: 177, single shot.
Barrel: 7".
Weight: 3 lbs. **Length:** 16" overall.
Power: Spring-air, barrel cocking.
Stocks: Walnut-finished hardwood with thumbrest.
Sights: Adjustable front, micro. click open rear.
Features: Velocity of 410 fps. Recoilless double piston system, movable barrel shroud to protect from sight during cocking. Imported from Germany by Dynamit Nobel-RWS, Inc.
Price: Right-hand $475.00
Price: Left-hand $530.00

RWS/Diana Model 6G Air Pistols
Similar to the Model 6M except does not have the movable barrel shroud. Has click micrometer rear sight, two-stage adjustable trigger, interchangeable tunnel front sight. Available in right- or left-hand models.
Price: Right-hand $350.00
Price: Left-hand $390.00

RWS GAMO PR-45 AIR PISTOL
Caliber: 177, single shot.
Barrel: 8.3".
Weight: 25 oz. **Length:** 11" overall.
Power: Pre-compressed air.
Stocks: Composition.
Sights: Blade front, adjustable rear.
Features: Velocity to 430 fps. Recoilless and vibration free. Manual safety. Imported from Spain by Dynamit Nobel-RWS, Inc.
Price: $130.00
Price: Compact model (adjustable walnut grips, adjustable trigger, swiveling trigger shoe) $200.00

Sharp Model U-FP

SHARP MODEL U-FP CO_2 PISTOL
Caliber: 177, single shot.
Barrel: 8", rifled steel.
Weight: 2.4 lbs. **Length:** 11.6" overall.
Power: 12-gram CO_2 cylinder.
Stocks: Smooth hardwood. Walnut target stocks available.
Sights: Post front, fully adjustable target rear.
Features: Variable power adjustment up to 545 fps. Adjustable trigger. Also available with adjustable field sight. Imported from Japan by Great Lakes Airguns.
Price: $199.50
Price: With walnut target grips $228.50

STEYR LP5 MATCH PISTOL
Caliber: 177, 5-shot magazine.
Barrel: NA.
Weight: 40.2 oz. **Length:** 13.39" overall.
Power: Pre-compressed CO_2 cylinders.
Stocks: Adjustable Morini match with palm shelf; stippled walnut.
Sights: Movable 2.5mm blade front; 2-3mm interchangeable in .2mm increments; fully adjustable open match rear.
Features: Velocity about 500 fps. Fully adjustable trigger; has dry-fire feature. Barrel and grip weights available. Introduced 1993. Imported from Austria by Nygord Precision Products.
Price: About $1,250.00

STEYR CO_2 MATCH 91 PISTOL
Caliber: 177, single shot.
Barrel: 9".
Weight: 38.7 oz. **Length:** 15.3" overall.
Power: Pre-compressed CO_2 cylinders.
Stocks: Fully adjustable Morini match with palm shelf; stippled walnut.
Sights: Interchangeable blade in 4mm, 4.5mm or 5mm widths, fully adjustable open rear with interchangeable 3.5mm or 4mm leaves.
Features: Velocity about 500 fps. Adjustable trigger, adjustable sight radius from 12.4" to 13.2". Imported from Austria by Nygord Precision Products.
Price: About $1,050.00

AIRGUNS—LONG GUNS

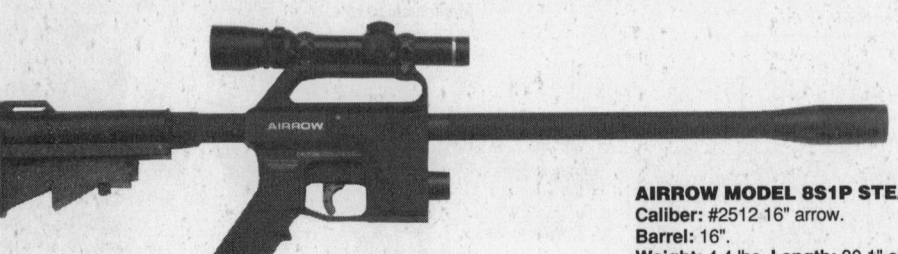
Airrow Model 8S1P

AIRROW MODEL 8S1P STEALTH AIR GUN
Caliber: #2512 16" arrow.
Barrel: 16".
Weight: 4.4 lbs. **Length:** 30.1" overall.
Power: CO_2 or compressed air; variable power.
Stock: Telescoping CAR-15-type.
Sights: 1.5-5x variable power scope.
Features: Velocity to 650 fps with 260-grain arrow. Pneumatic air trigger. All aircraft aluminum and stainless steel construction. Mil-spec materials and finishes. Waterproof case. Introduced 1991. From Swivel Machine Works, Inc.
Price: About $1,699.00

AIRGUNS—LONG GUNS

AIRROW MODEL 8SRB STEALTH AIR GUN
Caliber: 177, 22, 25, 38, 9-shot.
Barrel: 19.7"; rifled.
Weight: 6 lbs. **Length:** 34" overall.
Power: CO_2 or compressed air; variable power.
Stock: Telescoping CAR-15-type.
Sights: 3.5-10x A.O. variable power scope.
Features: Velocity 1100 fps in all calibers. Pneumatic air trigger. All aircraft aluminum and stainless steel construction. Mil-spec materials and finishes. Introduced 1992. From Swivel Machine Works, Inc.
Price: About **$2,599.00**

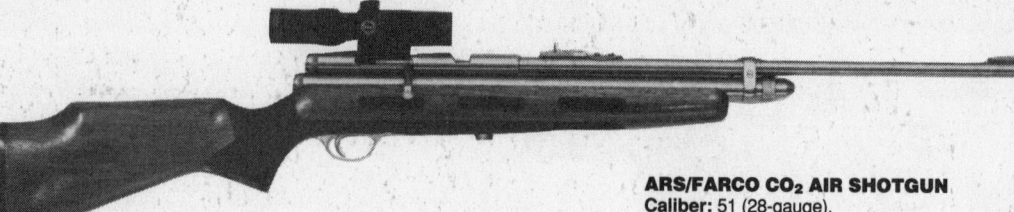

ARS/Farco CO_2 Stainless

ARS/Farco CO_2 Stainless Steel Air Rifle
Similar to the ARS/Farco CO_2 shotgun except in 22- or 25-caliber with 21½" barrel; weighs 6¾ lbs, 42½" overall; Philippine hardwood stock with stippled grip and forend; blade front sight, adjustable rear, grooved for scope mount. Uses 10-oz. refillable CO_2 cylinder. Made of stainless steel. Imported from Korea by Air Rifle Specialists.
Price: Including CO_2 cylinder **$395.00**

ARS/King Hunting Master

ARS/AR6 AIR RIFLE
Caliber: 22, 6-shot repeater.
Barrel: 25½".
Weight: 7 lbs. **Length:** 41¼" overall.
Power: Pre-compressed air from 3000 psi diving tank.
Stock: Indonesian walnut with checkered grip; rubber buttpad.
Sights: Blade front, adjustable peep rear.
Features: Velocity over 1000 fps with 32-grain pellet. Receiver grooved for scope mounting. Has 6-shot rotary magazine. Imported by Air Rifle Specialists.
Price: **$550.00**

ARS/Magnum 6 Air Rifle
Similar to the king Hunting Master except is 6-shot repeater with 23¾" barrel, weighs 8¼ lbs. Stock is walnut-stained hardwood with checkered grip and forend; rubber buttpad. Velocity of 1000+ fps with 32-grain pellet. Imported from Korea by Air Rifle Specialists.
Price: **$500.00**

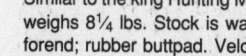

Anschutz 2002

ARS/QB77 DELUXE AIR RIFLE
Caliber: 177, 22, single shot.
Barrel: 21½".
Weight: 5½ lbs. **Length:** 40" overall.
Power: Two 12-oz. CO_2 cylinders.
Stock: Walnut-stained hardwood.
Sights: Blade front, adjustable rear.
Features: Velocity to 625 fps (22), 725 fps (177). Receiver grooved for scope mounting. Imported by Air Rifle Specialists.
Price: **$199.00**

ARS/FARCO FP SURVIVAL AIR RIFLE
Caliber: 22, 25, single shot.
Barrel: 22¾".
Weight: 5¾ lbs. **Length:** 42¾" overall.
Power: Multi-pump foot pump.
Stock: Philippine hardwood.
Sights: Blade front, fixed rear.
Features: Velocity to 850 fps (22 or 25). Receiver grooved for scope mounting. Imported from Korea by Air Rifle Specialists.
Price: **$295.00**

ARS/FARCO CO_2 AIR SHOTGUN
Caliber: 51 (28-gauge).
Barrel: 30".
Weight: 7 lbs. **Length:** 48½" overall.
Power: 10-oz. refillable CO_2 tank.
Stock: Hardwood.
Sights: Blade front, fixed rear.
Features: Gives over 100 ft. lbs. energy for taking small game. Imported from Korea by Air Rifle Specialists.
Price: **$395.00**

ARS/KING HUNTING MASTER AIR RIFLE
Caliber: 22, 5-shot repeater.
Barrel: 22¾".
Weight: 7¾ lbs. **Length:** 42" overall.
Power: Pre-compressed air from 3000 psi diving tank.
Stock: Indonesian walnut with checkered grip and forend; rubber buttpad.
Sights: Blade front, fully adjustable open rear. Receiver grooved for scope mounting.
Features: Velocity over 1000 fps with 32-grain pellet. High and low power switch for hunting or target velocities. Side lever cocks action and inserts pellet. Rotary magazine. Imported from Korea by Air rifle Specialists.
Price: **$550.00**
Price: Hunting Master 900 (9mm, limited production) **$1,000.00**

> Consult our Directory pages for the location of firms mentioned.

ANSCHUTZ 2002 MATCH AIR RIFLE
Caliber: 177, single shot.
Barrel: 26".
Weight: 10½ lbs. **Length:** 44½" overall.
Stock: European walnut; stippled grip and forend.
Sights: Globe front, #6824 Micro Peep rear.
Features: Balance, weight match the 1907 ISU smallbore rifle. Uses #5019 match trigger. Recoil and vibration free. Fully adjustable cheekpiece and buttplate. Introduced 1988. Imported from Germany by Precision Sales International.
Price: Right-hand **$1,800.00**
Price: Left-hand, hardwood stock **$1,889.00**
Price: Model 2002D RT (Running Target) **$1,929.00**

CAUTION: PRICES SHOWN ARE SUPPLIED BY THE MANUFACTUER OR IMPORTER. CHECK YOUR LOCAL GUNSHOP.

49th EDITION, 1995 **441**

BEEMAN CARBINE MODEL C1
Caliber: 177, single shot.
Barrel: 14", 12-groove rifling.
Weight: 6¼ lbs. **Length:** 38" overall.
Power: Spring-piston, barrel cocking.
Stock: Walnut-stained beechwood with rubber buttpad.
Sights: Blade front, rear click-adjustable for windage and elevation.

Beeman C1

Features: Velocity 830 fps. Adjustable trigger. Receiver grooved for scope mounting. Imported by Beeman.
Price: **$285.00**

Beeman Crow Magnum

BEEMAN CROW MAGNUM AIR RIFLE
Caliber: 20, 25, single shot.
Barrel: 16"; 10-groove rifling.

Weight: 8.5 lbs. **Length:** 46" overall.
Power: Gas-spring; adjustable power to 32 foot pounds muzzle energy. Barrel-cocking.
Stock: Classic-style walnut; hand checkered.
Sights: For scope use only; built-in base and 1" rings included.
Features: Adjustable two-stage trigger. Automatic safety. Also available in 22-caliber on special order. Introduced 1992. Imported by Beeman.
Price: **$1,195.00**

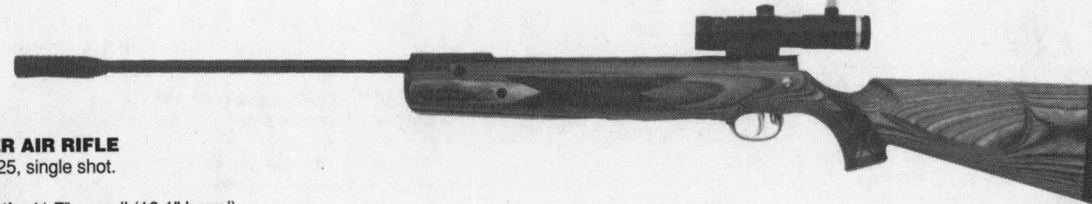

Beeman/HW 97

BEEMAN KODIAK AIR RIFLE
Caliber: 25, single shot.
Barrel: 17.6".
Weight: 9 lbs. **Length:** 45.6" overall.
Power: Barrel cocking.
Stock: Stained hardwood.
Sights: Blade front, open fully adjustable rear.
Features: Velocity to 820 fps. Up to 30 foot pounds muzzle energy. Introduced 1993. Imported by Beeman.
Price: **$560.00**

BEEMAN/HW 97 AIR RIFLE
Caliber: 177, 20, single shot.
Barrel: 17.75".
Weight: 9.2 lbs. **Length:** 44.1" overall.
Power: Spring-piston, underlever cocking.
Stock: Walnut-stained beech; rubber buttpad.
Sights: None. Receiver grooved for scope mounting.
Features: Velocity 830 fps (177). Fixed barrel with fully opening, direct loading breech. Adjustable trigger. Imported by Beeman Precision Airguns.
Price: Right-hand only . . . . **NA**

BEEMAN R1 AIR RIFLE
Caliber: 177, 20 or 22, single shot.
Barrel: 19.6", 12-groove rifling.
Weight: 8.5 lbs. **Length:** 45.2" overall.
Power: Spring-piston, barrel cocking.
Stock: Walnut-stained beech; cut-checkered pistol grip; Monte Carlo comb and cheekpiece; rubber buttpad.
Sights: Tunnel front with interchangeable inserts, open rear click-adjustable for windage and elevation. Grooved for scope mounting.
Features: Velocity of 940-1050 fps (177), 860 fps (20), 800 fps (22). Non-drying nylon piston and breech seals. Adjustable metal trigger. Milled steel safety. Right- or left-hand stock. Available with adjustable cheekpiece and buttplate at extra cost. Custom and Super Laser versions available. Imported by Beeman.
Price: Right-hand, 177, 20, 22 . . . . **$485.00**
Price: Left-hand, 177, 20, 22 . . . . **$550.00**

BEEMAN R1 CARBINE
Caliber: 177, 20, 22, 25, single shot.
Barrel: 16.1".
Weight: 8.6 lbs. **Length:** 41.7" overall.
Power: Spring-piston, barrel cocking.
Stock: Stained beech; Monte Carlo comb and checkpiece; cut checkered p.g.; rubber buttpad.
Sights: Tunnel front with interchangeable inserts, open adjustable rear; receiver grooved for scope mounting.
Features: Velocity up to 1050 fps (177). Non-drying nylon piston and breech seals. Adjustable metal trigger. Machined steel receiver end cap and safety. Right- or left-hand stock. Imported by Beeman.
Price: 177, 20, 22, 25, right-hand **$485.00**
Price: As above, left-hand **$550.00**

Beeman R1 Laser

BEEMAN R1 LASER AIR RIFLE
Caliber: 177, 20, 22, 25, single shot.
Barrel: 16.1" or 19.6".
Weight: 8.4 lbs. **Length:** 41.7" overall (16.1" barrel).
Power: Spring-piston, barrel cocking.
Stock: Laminated wood with Monte Carlo comb and cheekpiece; checkered p.g. and forend; rubber buttpad.
Sights: Tunnel front with interchangeable inserts, open adjustable rear.
Features: Velocity up to 1150 fps (177). Special powerplant components. Built from the Beeman R1 rifle by Beeman.
Price: 177, 20, 22, 25 . . . . **$975.00**

BEEMAN R8 AIR RIFLE

Caliber: 177, single shot.
Barrel: 18.3".
Weight: 7.2 lbs. **Length:** 43.1" overall.
Power: Barrel cocking, spring-piston.
Stock: Walnut with Monte Carlo cheekpiece; checkered pistol grip.
Sights: Globe front, fully adjustable rear; interchangeable inserts.
Features: Velocity of 735 fps. Similar to the R1. Nylon piston and breech seals. Adjustable match-grade, two-stage, grooved metal trigger. Milled steel safety. Rubber buttpad. Imported by Beeman.
Price: $375.00

Beeman R7 Air Rifle

Similar to the R8 model except has lighter ambidextrous stock, match-grade trigger block; velocity of 680-700 fps; barrel length 17"; weight 5.8 lbs. Milled steel safety. Imported by Beeman.
Price: 177, 20 . . . . $300.00

BEEMAN R10 AIR RIFLES

Caliber: 177, 20, 22, single shot.
Barrel: 16.1"; 12-groove rifling.
Weight: 7.9 lbs. **Length:** 46" overall.
Power: Spring-piston, barrel cocking.
Stock: Standard—walnut-finished hardwood with Monte Carlo comb, rubber buttplate; Deluxe has white spacers at grip cap, buttplate, checkered grip, rubber buttplate.
Sights: Tunnel front with interchangeable inserts, open rear click adjustable for windage and elevation. Receiver grooved for scope mounting.
Features: Over 1000 fps in 177-cal. only; 26-lb. cocking effort; milled steel safety and body tube. Right- and left-hand models. Similar in appearance to the Beeman R8. Introduced 1986. Imported by Beeman.
Price: 177, 20 or 22 Standard $395.00
Price: 177, 20, 22, Deluxe, right-hand $450.00
Price: 177, 20, 22, Deluxe, left-hand $500.00

Beeman R11

BEEMAN R11 AIR RIFLE

Caliber: 177, single shot.
Barrel: 19.6".

BEEMAN SUPER 7 AIR RIFLE

Caliber: 22, 7-shot repeater.
Barrel: 19"; 12-groove rifling.
Weight: 7.2 lbs. **Length:** 41" overall.
Power: Pre-charged pneumatic, external air reservoir.
Stock: Walnut; high cheekpiece; rubber buttpad.
Sights: None furnished; drilled and tapped; 1" ring scope mounts included.
Features: Two-stage adjustable trigger; 7-shot rotary magazine. Receiver of anodized aircraft aluminum. All working parts either hardened or stainless steel. Imported by Beeman.
Price: $1,575.00

Weight: 8.8 lbs. **Length:** 47" overall.
Power: Spring-piston, barrel cocking.
Stock: Walnut-stained beech; adjustable buttplate and cheekpiece.
Sights: None furnished. Has dovetail for scope mounting.
Features: Velocity 910-940 fps. All-steel barrel sleeve. Imported by Beeman.
Price: $490.00

BEEMAN RX-1 GAS-SPRING MAGNUM AIR RIFLE

Caliber: 177, 20, 22, 25, single shot.
Barrel: 19.6"; 12-groove rifling.
Weight: 8.8 lbs.
Power: Gas-spring piston air; single stroke barrel cocking.
Stock: Walnut-finished hardwood, hand checkered, with cheekpiece. Adjustable cheekpiece and buttplate.
Sights: Tunnel front, click-adjustable rear.
Features: Velocity adjustable to about 1200 fps. Uses special sealed chamber of air as a mainspring. Gas-spring cannot take a set. Introduced 1990. Imported by Beeman.
Price: 177 or 22, regular, right-hand $540.00
Price: 20 or 25, regular, right hand $540.00
Price: 177, 20, 22, 25, left-hand $600.00

Beeman/FWB C60

BEEMAN/FEINWERKBAU C60 CO₂ RIFLE

Caliber: 177.
Barrel: 16.9". With barrel sleeve, 25.4".

Weight: 10 lbs. **Length:** 42.6" overall.
Stock: Laminated hardwood and hard rubber.
Sights: Tunnel front with interchangeable inserts, quick release micro. click match aperture rear.
Features: Similar features, performance as Beeman/FWB 601. Virtually no cocking effort. Right- or left-hand. Running target version available. Introduced 1987. Imported from Germany by Beeman.
Price: Right-hand $1,550.00
Price: Left-hand $1,770.00
Price: Running Target, right-hand $1,550.00
Price: Running Target, left-hand $1,700.00
Price: Mini C60, right-hand $1,550.00

BEEMAN/FEINWERKBAU 300-S SERIES MATCH RIFLE

Caliber: 177, single shot.
Barrel: 19.9", fixed solid with receiver.
Weight: Approx. 10 lbs. with optional bbl. sleeve. **Length:** 42.8" overall.
Power: Single stroke sidelever, spring piston.
Stock: Match model—walnut, deep forend, adjustable buttplate.
Sights: Globe front with interchangeable inserts. Click micro. adjustable match aperture rear. Front and rear sights move as a single unit.
Features: Recoilless, vibration free. Five-way adjustable match trigger. Grooved for scope mounts. Permanent lubrication, steel piston ring. Cocking effort 9 lbs. Optional 10-oz. barrel sleeve. Available from Beeman.
Price: Right-hand $1,215.00
Price: Left-hand $1,315.00

BEEMAN/FEINWERKBAU 300-S MINI-MATCH

Caliber: 177, single shot.
Barrel: 17⅛".
Weight: 8.8 lbs. **Length:** 40" overall.
Power: Spring piston, single stroke sidelever cocking.
Stock: Walnut. Stippled grip, adjustable buttplate. Scaled-down for youthful or slightly built shooters.
Sights: Globe front with interchangeable inserts, micro. adjustable rear. Front and rear sights move as a single unit.
Features: Recoilless, vibration free. Grooved for scope mounts. Steel piston ring. Cocking effort about 9½ lbs. Barrel sleeve optional. Left-hand model available. Introduced 1978. Imported by Beeman.
Price: Right-hand $1,215.00
Price: Left-hand $1,315.00

CAUTION: PRICES SHOWN ARE SUPPLIED BY THE MANUFACTUER OR IMPORTER. CHECK YOUR LOCAL GUNSHOP.

49th EDITION, 1995 **443**

BEEMAN/FEINWERKBAU MODEL 601 AIR RIFLE

Caliber: 177, single shot.
Barrel: 16.6".
Weight: 10.8 lbs. **Length:** 43" overall.
Power: Single stroke pneumatic.
Stock: Special laminated hardwoods and hard rubber for stability.
Sights: Tunnel front with interchangeable inserts, click micrometer match apperture rear.
Features: Recoilless action; double supported barrel; special, short rifled area frees pellet from barrel faster so shooter's motion has minimum effect on accuracy. Fully adjustable match trigger. Trigger and sights blocked when loading latch is open. Imported by Beeman. Introduced 1984.
Price: Right-hand **$1,615.00**
Price: Left-hand **$1,775.00**
Price: Right-hand, walnut stock **$1,615.00**

Beeman/Feinwerkbau 601 Running Target

Similar to the standard Model 601. Has 16.9" barrel (33.7" with barrel sleeve); special match trigger, short loading gate which allows scope mounting. No sights—built for scope use only. Introduced 1987.
Price: Right-hand **$1,615.00**
Price: Left-hand **$1,725.00**

Benjamin Sheridan CO2

BENJAMIN SHERIDAN CO₂ AIR RIFLES

Caliber: 177, 20 or 22, single shot.
Barrel: 19⅜", rifled brass.
Weight: 5 lbs. **Length:** 36½" overall.

BRNO Aeron-Tau

BRNO AERON-TAU-2000 AIR RIFLE

Caliber: 177, single shot
Barrel: 23".
Weight: 6 lbs., 8 oz. **Length:** 40" overall.

BRNO 630 SERIES AIR RIFLES

Caliber: 177 single shot.
Barrel: 20.75".
Weight: 6 lbs., 15 oz. **Length:** 45.75" overall.
Power: Spring piston, barrel cocking.
Stock: Beechwood (Model 630); checkered, walnut stained (Model 631).

Crosman Model 664X

BEEMAN/HW30 AIR RIFLE

Caliber: 177, 22, single shot.
Barrel: 17" (177), 16.9" (20); 12-groove rifling.
Weight: 5.5 lbs.
Power: Spring piston; single-stroke barrel cocking.
Stock: Walnut-finished hardwood.
Sights: Blade front, adjustable rear.
Features: Velocity about 660 fps (177). Double-jointed cocking lever. Cast trigger guard. Synthetic non-drying breech and piston seals. Introduced 1990. Imported by Beeman.
Price: 177 . . . . **$196.50**

BENJAMIN SHERIDAN PNEUMATIC (PUMP-UP) AIR RIFLES

Caliber: 177 or 22, single shot.
Barrel: 19⅜", rifled brass.
Weight: 5½ lbs. **Length:** 36¼" overall.
Power: Under-lever pneumatic, hand pumped.
Stock: American walnut stock and forend.
Sights: High ramp front, fully adjustable notch rear.
Features: Variable velocity to 800 fps. Bolt action with ambidextrous push-pull safety. Black or nickel finish. Introduced 1991. Made in the U.S. by Benjamin Sheridan Co.
Price: Black finish, Model 397 (177), Model 392 (22) **$125.50**
Price: Nickel finish, Model S397 (177), Model S392 (22) **$134.00**

Power: 12-gram CO₂ cylinder.
Stock: American walnut with buttplate.
Sights: High ramp front, fully adjustable notch rear.
Features: Velocity to 680 fps (177). Bolt action with ambidextrous push-pull safety. Gives about 40 shots per cylinder. Black or nickel finish. Introduced 1991. Made in the U.S. by Benjamin Sheridan Co.
Price: Black finish, Model G397 (177), Model G392 (22) **$114.50**
Price: Nickel finish, Model GS397 (177), Model GS392 (22) **$122.00**
Price: Black finish, Model FB9 (20) **$124.00**
Price: Nickel finish, Model F9 (20) **$131.95**

Power: 12.5-gram CO₂ cartridges.
Stock: Synthetic match style with adjustable comb and buttplate.
Sights: Globe front with interchangeable inserts, fully adjustable open rear.
Features: Adjustable trigger. Rear sight converts to aperture on receiver. Comes with sling, extra seals, CO₂ cartridges, large CO₂ bottle, counterweight. Introduced 1993. Imported by Century International Arms.
Price: About **$312.00**

Sights: Hooded front, fully adjustable rear; grooved for scope mount.
Features: Velocity about 600 fps. Automatic safety; externally adjustable trigger; sling swivels. Imported from the Czech Republic by Action Arms, Ltd.
Price: Model 630 (Standard) **$79.00**
Price: Model 631 (Deluxe) **$95.00**

CROSMAN MODEL 66 POWERMASTER

Caliber: 177 (single shot pellet) or BB, 200-shot reservoir.
Barrel: 20", rifled steel.
Weight: 3 lbs. **Length:** 38½" overall.
Power: Pneumatic; hand pumped.
Stock: Wood-grained ABS plastic; checkered p.g. and forend.
Sights: Ramp front, fully adjustable open rear.
Features: Velocity about 645 fps. Bolt action, cross-bolt safety. Introduced 1983. From Crosman.
Price: About **$42.00**
Price: Model 66RT (as above with Realtree camo finish), about **$50.00**
Price: Model 664X (as above, with 4x scope) **$50.00**

CAUTION: PRICES SHOWN ARE SUPPLIED BY THE MANUFACTURER OR IMPORTER. CHECK YOUR LOCAL GUNSHOP.

AIRGUNS—LONG GUNS

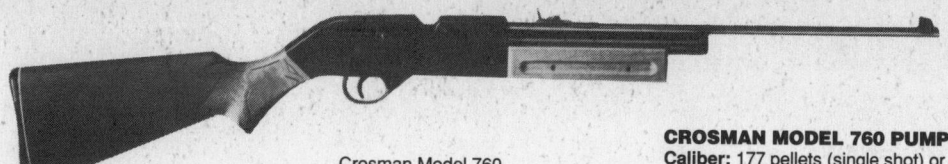

Crosman Model 760

CROSMAN MODEL 781 SINGLE PUMP
Caliber: 177 pellets (5-shot pellet clip) or BB (195-shot BB reservoir).
Barrel: 19½"; steel.
Weight: 2 lbs., 14 oz. **Length:** 35.8" overall.
Power: Pneumatic, single pump.
Stock: Wood-grained ABS plastic; checkered pistol grip and forend.
Sights: Blade front, open adjustable rear.
Features: Velocity of 405 fps (pellets). Uses only one pump. Hidden BB reservoir holds 195 shots; pellets loaded via 5-shot clip. Introduced 1984. From Crosman.
Price: About $35.00

CONSULT
Shooter's Marketplace
Page 225, This Issue

CROSMAN MODEL 782 BLACK DIAMOND AIR RIFLE
Caliber: 177 pellets (5-shot clip) or BB (195-shot reservoir).
Barrel: 18", rifled steel.
Weight: 3 lbs.
Power: CO₂ Powerlet.
Stock: Wood-grained ABS plastic; checkered grip and forend.
Sights: Blade front, open adjustable rear.
Features: Velocity up to 595 fps (pellets), 650 fps (BB). Black finish with white diamonds. Introduced 1990. From Crosman.
Price: About $40.00

CROSMAN MODEL 2100 CLASSIC AIR RIFLE
Caliber: 177 pellets (single shot), or BB (200-shot BB reservoir).
Barrel: 21", rifled.
Weight: 4 lbs., 13 oz. **Length:** 39¾" overall.
Power: Pump-up, pneumatic.
Stock: Wood-grained checkered ABS plastic.
Features: Three pumps give about 450 fps, 10 pumps about 755 fps (BBs). Cross-bolt safety; concealed reservoir holds over 200 BBs. From Crosman.
Price: About $55.00

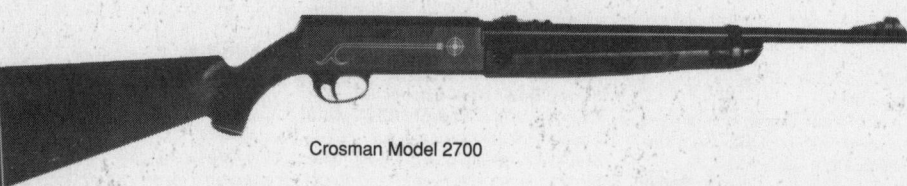

Crosman Model 2700

CROSMAN MODEL 2200 MAGNUM AIR RIFLE
Caliber: 22, single shot.
Barrel: 19", rifled steel.
Weight: 4 lbs., 12 oz. **Length:** 39" overall.

Daisy Model 225

DAISY MODEL 225 AMERICAN LEGEND
Caliber: 177 BB, 650-shot magazine.
Barrel: Smoothbore steel.

CROSMAN MODEL 760 PUMPMASTER
Caliber: 177 pellets (single shot) or BB (200-shot reservoir).
Barrel: 19½", rifled steel.
Weight: 2 lbs., 12 oz. **Length:** 33.5" overall.
Power: Pneumatic, hand pumped.
Stock: Walnut-finished ABS plastic stock and forend
Features: Velocity to 590 fps (BBs, 10 pumps). Short stroke, power determined by number of strokes. Post front sight and adjustable rear sight. Cross-bolt safety. Introduced 1966. From Crosman.
Price: About $32.00

CROSMAN MODEL 788 BB SCOUT RIFLE
Caliber: BB only, 20-shot magazine.
Barrel: 14", steel.
Weight: 2 lbs. 7 oz. **Length:** 31½" overall.
Power: Pneumatic; hand pumped.
Stock: Wood-grained ABS plastic, checkered p.g. and forend.
Sights: Blade front, open adjustable rear.
Features: Variable pump power—three pumps give MV of 330 fps, six pumps 437 fps, 10 pumps 465 fps (BBs, average). Steel barrel, cross-bolt safety. Introduced 1978. From Crosman.
Price: About $25.00

CROSMAN MODEL 1077 REPEATAIR RIFLE
Caliber: 177 pellets, 12-shot clip
Barrel: 20.3", rifled steel.
Weight: 3 lbs., 11 oz. **Length:** 38.8" overall.
Power: CO₂ Powerlet.
Stock: Textured synthetic.
Sights: Blade front, fully adjustable rear.
Features: Velocity 590 fps. Removable 12-shot clip. True semi-automatic action. Introduced 1993. From Crosman.
Price: About $60.00

CROSMAN MODEL 1389 BACKPACKER RIFLE
Caliber: 177, single shot.
Barrel: 14", rifled steel.
Weight: 3 lbs. 3 oz. **Length:** 31" overall.
Power: Hand pumped, pneumatic.
Stock: Composition, skeletal type.
Sights: Blade front, rear adjustable for windage and elevation.
Features: Velocity to 560 fps. Detachable stock. Receiver grooved for scope mounting. Metal parts blued. From Crosman.
Price: About $54.00

Stock: Full-size, wood-grained ABS plastic with checkered grip and forend.
Sights: Ramp front, open step-adjustable rear.
Features: Variable pump power—three pumps give 395 fps, six pumps 530 fps, 10 pumps 595 fps (average). Full-size adult air rifle. Has white line spacers at pistol grip and buttplate. Introduced 1978. From Crosman.
Price: About $55.00

Weight: 2.8 lbs. **Length:** 37.2" overall.
Power: Single-pump spring air.
Stock: Moulded woodgrain plastic.
Sights: Blade and ramp front, adjustable open rear.
Features: Velocity to 330 fps. Grooved pump handle; Monte Carlo-style stock with cheekpiece and checkered grip. Cross-bolt trigger block safety. Introduced 1994. From Daisy.
Price: About $50.00

CAUTION: PRICES SHOWN ARE SUPPLIED BY THE MANUFACTUER OR IMPORTER. CHECK YOUR LOCAL GUNSHOP.

49th EDITION, 1995 **445**

AIRGUNS—LONG GUNS

Daisy Model 840

DAISY MODEL 840
Caliber: 177 pellet single shot; or BB 350-shot.
Barrel: 19", smoothbore, steel.

Weight: 2.7 lbs. **Length:** 36.8" overall.
Stock: Moulded wood-grain stock and forend.
Sights: Ramp front, open, adjustable rear.
Features: Single pump pneumatic rifle. Muzzle velocity 335 fps (BB), 300 fps (pellet). Steel buttplate; straight pull bolt action; cross-bolt safety. Forend forms pump lever. Introduced 1978. From Daisy Mfg. Co.
Price: About $40.00

Daisy Model 1894C

DAISY MODEL 1894C COMMEMORATIVE
Caliber: BB, 40-shot magazine.
Barrel: 17.5". Octagon shroud.

Weight: 2.2 lbs. **Length:** 39.5" overall.
Power: Spring air.
Stock: Moulded woodgrain plastic.
Sights: Blade on ramp front, adjustable open rear.
Features: Velocity 300 fps. Side loading port; sliding sear-block safety; silk screened die-cast receiver. Has commemorative foil medallion in the stock. Made in U.S. From Daisy Mfg. Co.
Price: $52.00

Daisy Red Ryder

DAISY 1938 RED RYDER CLASSIC
Caliber: BB, 650-shot repeating action.
Barrel: Smoothbore steel with shroud.

Weight: 2.2 lbs. **Length:** 35.4" overall.
Stock: Walnut stock burned with Red Ryder lariat signature.
Sights: Post front, adjustable V-slot rear.
Features: Walnut forend. Saddle ring with leather thong. Lever cocking. Gravity feed. Controlled velocity. One of Daisy's most popular guns. From Daisy Mfg. Co.
Price: About $45.00

DAISY/POWER LINE 853
Caliber: 177 pellets.
Barrel: 20.9"; 12-groove rifling, high-grade solid steel by Lothar Walther™, precision crowned; bore size for precision match pellets.
Weight: 5.08 lbs. **Length:** 38.9" overall.
Power: Single-pump pneumatic.
Stock: Full-length, select American hardwood, stained and finished; black buttplate with white spacers.
Sights: Globe front with four aperture inserts; precision micrometer adjustable rear peep sight mounted on a standard 3/8" dovetail receiver mount.
Features: Single shot. From Daisy Mfg. Co.
Price: About $245.00

DAISY/POWER LINE 880 PUMP-UP AIRGUN
Caliber: 177 pellets, BB.
Barrel: Rifled steel with shroud.
Weight: 4.5 lbs. **Length:** 37¾" overall.
Power: Pneumatic pump-up.
Stock: Wood-grain moulded plastic with Monte Carlo cheekpiece.
Sights: Ramp front, open rear adjustable for elevation.
Features: Crafted by Daisy. Variable power (velocity and range) increase with pump strokes. 10 strokes for maximum power. 100-shot BB magazine. Cross-bolt trigger safety. Positive cocking valve. From Daisy Mfg. Co.
Price: About $60.00

> Consult our Directory pages for the location of firms mentioned.

DAISY/POWER LINE 922
Caliber: 22, 5-shot clip.
Barrel: Rifled steel with shroud.
Weight: 4.5 lbs. **Length:** 37¾" overall.
Stock: Moulded wood-grained plastic with checkered p.g. and forend, Monte Carlo cheekpiece.
Sights: Ramp front, fully adjustable open rear.
Features: Muzzle velocity from 270 fps (two pumps) to 530 fps (10 pumps). Straight-pull bolt action. Separate buttplate and grip cap with white spacers. Introduced 1978. From Daisy Mfg. Co.
Price: About $85.00
Price: Models 970/920 (same as Model 922 except with hardwood stock and forend), about $120.00

DAISY/POWER LINE 753 TARGET RIFLE
Caliber: 177, single shot.
Barrel: 20.9", Lothar Walther.
Weight: 6.4 lbs. **Length:** 39.75" overall.
Power: Recoilless pneumatic, single pump.
Stock: Walnut with adjustable cheekpiece and buttplate.
Sights: Globe front with interchangeable inserts, diopter rear with micro. click adjustments.
Features: Includes front sight reticle assortment, web shooting sling. From Daisy Mfg. Co.
Price: About $400.00

DAISY/POWER LINE 856 PUMP-UP AIRGUN
Caliber: 177 pellets (single shot) or BB (100-shot reservoir).
Barrel: Rifled steel with shroud.
Weight: 2.7 lbs. **Length:** 37.4" overall.
Power: Pneumatic pump-up.
Stock: Moulded wood-grain with Monte Carlo cheekpiece.
Sights: Ramp and blade front, open rear adjustable for elevation.
Features: Velocity from 315 fps (two pumps) to 650 fps (10 pumps). Shoots BBs or pellets. Heavy die-cast metal receiver. Cross-bolt trigger-block safety. Introduced 1984. From Daisy Mfg. Co.
Price: About $45.00

DAISY MODEL 990 DUAL-POWER AIR RIFLE
Caliber: 177 pellets (single shot) or BB (100-shot magazine).
Barrel: Rifled steel.
Weight: 4.1 lbs. **Length:** 37.4" overall.
Power: Pneumatic pump-up and 12-gram CO_2.
Stock: Moulded woodgrain.
Sights: Ramp and blade front, adjustable open rear.
Features: Velocity to 650 fps (BB), 630 fps (pellet). Choice of pump or CO_2 power. Shoots BBs or pellets. Heavy die-cast receiver dovetailed for scope mount. Cross-bolt trigger block safety. Introduced 1993. From Daisy Mfg. Co.
Price: About $68.00

CAUTION: PRICES SHOWN ARE SUPPLIED BY THE MANUFACTURER OR IMPORTER. CHECK YOUR LOCAL GUNSHOP.

AIRGUNS—LONG GUNS

DAISY/POWER LINE 2001 AIR RIFLE
Caliber: 177 pellets, 35-shot helical magazine.
Barrel: Rifled steel.
Weight: 3.1 lbs. **Length:** 37.4" overall.
Power: CO_2.
Stock: Moulded woodgrain with Monte Carlo comb.
Sights: Ramp and blade front, fully adjustable open rear.
Features: Velocity to 625 fps. Bolt-action repeater with cross-bolt trigger block safety; checkered grip and forend; white buttplate spacer. Introduced 1994. From Daisy Mfg. Co.
Price: About $95.00

DAISY/POWER LINE EAGLE 7856 PUMP-UP AIRGUN
Caliber: 177 (pellets), BB, 100-shot BB magazine.
Barrel: Rifled steel with shroud.
Weight: 2¾ lbs. **Length:** 37.4" overall.
Power: Pneumatic pump-up.
Stock: Moulded wood-grain plastic.
Sights: Ramp and blade front, open rear adjustable for elevation.
Features: Velocity from 315 fps (two pumps) to 650 fps (10 pumps). Finger grooved forend. Cross-bolt trigger-block safety. Introduced 1985. From Daisy Mfg. Co.
Price: With 4x scope, about $60.00

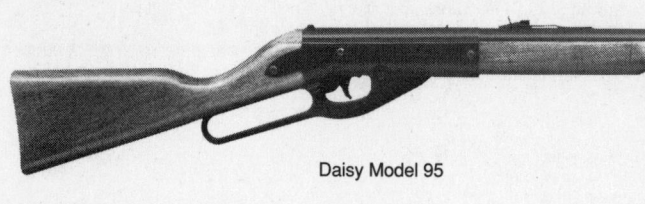

Daisy Model 95

DAISY/YOUTH LINE RIFLES

Model:	95	111	105
Caliber:	BB	BB	BB
Barrel:	18"	18"	13½"
Length:	35.2"	34.3"	29.8"
Power:	Spring	Spring	Spring
Capacity:	700	650	400
Price: About	$45.00	$35.00	$29.00

Features: Model 95 stock and forend are wood; 105 and 111 have plastic stocks. From Daisy Mfg. Co.

El Gamo 126

EL GAMO 126 SUPER MATCH TARGET RIFLE
Caliber: 177, single shot.
Barrel: Match grade, precision rifled.

Weight: 10.6 lbs. **Length:** 43.8" overall.
Power: Single pump pneumatic.
Stock: Match-style, hardwood, with stippled grip and forend.
Sights: Hooded front with interchangeable elements, fully adjustable match rear.
Features: Velocity of 590 fps. Adjustable trigger; easy loading pellet port; adjustable buttpad. Introduced 1984. Imported from Spain by Daisy Mfg. Co.
Price: About $750.00

FAMAS SEMI-AUTO AIR RIFLE
Caliber: 177, 10-shot magazine.
Barrel: 19.2".
Weight: About 8 lbs. **Length:** 29.8" overall.
Power: 12 gram CO_2.
Stock: Synthetic bullpup design.
Sights: Adjustable front, aperture rear.
Features: Velocity of 425 fps. Duplicates size, weight and feel of the centerfire MAS French military rifle in caliber 223. Introduced 1988. Imported from France by Century International Arms.
Price: About $275.00

"GAT" AIR RIFLE
Caliber: 177, single shot.
Barrel: 17¼" cocked, 23¼" extended.
Weight: 3 lbs.
Power: Spring piston.
Stock: Composition.
Sights: Fixed.
Features: Velocity about 450 fps. Shoots pellets, darts, corks. Imported from England by Stone Enterprises, Inc.
Price: $34.95

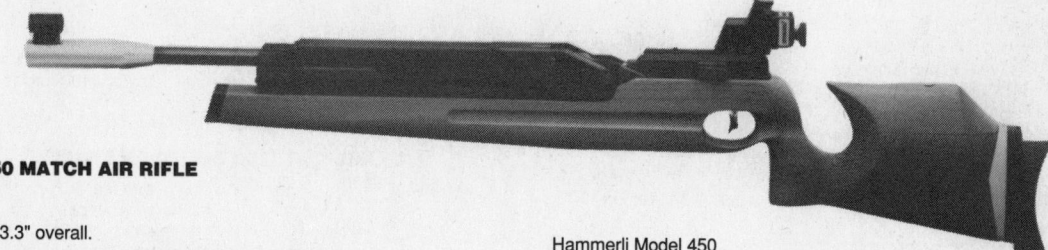

Hammerli Model 450

HAMMERLI MODEL 450 MATCH AIR RIFLE
Caliber: 177, single shot.
Barrel: 19.5".
Weight: 9.8 lbs. **Length:** 43.3" overall.
Power: Pneumatic.
Stock: Match style with stippled grip, rubber buttpad. Beach or walnut.
Sights: Match tunnel front, Hammerli diopter rear.
Features: Velocity about 560 fps. Removeable sights; forend sling rail; adjustable trigger; adjustable comb. Introduced 1994. Imported from Switzerland by Hammerli USA.
Price: $1,295.00

MARKSMAN 28 INTERNATIONAL AIR RIFLE
Caliber: 177, single shot.
Barrel: 17".
Weight: 5¾ lbs.
Power: Spring-air, barrel cocking.
Stock: Hardwood.
Sights: Hooded front, adjustable rear.
Features: Velocity of 580-620 fps. Introduced 1989. Imported from Germany by Marksman Products.
Price: $210.00

MARKSMAN 40 INTERNATIONAL AIR RIFLE
Caliber: 177, single shot.
Barrel: 18⅜".
Weight: 7⅓ lbs.
Power: Spring-air, barrel cocking.
Stock: Hardwood.
Sights: Hooded front, adjustable rear.
Features: Velocity of 700-720 fps. Introduced 1989. Imported from Germany by Marksman Products.
Price: $235.00

CAUTION: PRICES SHOWN ARE SUPPLIED BY THE MANUFACTUER OR IMPORTER. CHECK YOUR LOCAL GUNSHOP.

49th EDITION, 1995 **447**

AIRGUNS—LONG GUNS

Marksman Model 45

MARKSMAN MODEL 60 AIR RIFLE
Caliber: 177, single shot.
Barrel: 18.5", rifled.
Weight: 8.9 lbs. **Length:** 44.75" overall.
Power: Spring piston, under-lever cocking.
Stock: Walnut-stained beech with Monte Carlo comb, hand-checkered pistol grip, rubber butt pad.
Sights: Blade front, open, micro. adjustable rear.
Features: Velocity of 810-840 fps. Automatic button safety on rear of receiver. Receiver grooved for scope mounting. Fully adjustable Rekord trigger. Introduced 1990. Imported from Germany by Marksman Products.
Price: $490.00

Marksman 55 Air Rifle
Similar to the Model 70T except has uncheckered hardwood stock, no cheekpiece, plastic buttplate. Adjustable Rekord trigger. Overall length is 45.25", weight is 7½ lbs. Available in 177-caliber only.
Price: $289.00
Price: Model 59T (as above, carbine) $289.00

MARKSMAN MODEL 45 AIR RIFLE
Caliber: 177, single shot.
Barrel: 19.1".
Weight: 7.3 lbs. **Length:** 46.75" overall.
Power: Spring-air, barrel cocking.
Stock: Stained hardwood with Monte Carlo cheekpiece, butt pad.
Sights: Hooded front, fully adjustable micrometer rear.
Features: Velocity 900-930 fps. Adjustable trigger; automatic safety. Introduced 1993. Imported from Spain by Marksman Products.
Price: $189.00

MARKSMAN 70 AIR RIFLE
Caliber: 177, 20 or 22, single shot.
Barrel: 19.75".
Weight: 8 lbs. **Length:** 45.5" overall.
Power: Spring air, barrel cocking.
Stock: Stained hardwood with Monte Carlo cheekpiece, rubber buttpad, cut checkered p.g.
Sights: Hooded front, open fully adjustable rear.
Features: Velocity of 910-940 fps (177), 810-840 fps (20), 740-780 fps (22); adjustable Rekord trigger. Introduced 1988. Imported from Germany by Marksman Products.
Price: 177 (Model 70T) $350.00
Price: 20 (Model 72) $360.00
Price: 22 (Model 71) $350.00

Marksman 1710

MARKSMAN 1710 PLAINSMAN AIR RIFLE
Caliber: BB, 20-shot repeater.
Barrel: Smoothbore steel with shroud.
Weight: 2.25 lbs. **Length:** 34" overall.
Power: Spring-air.
Stock: Stained hardwood.
Sights: Blade on ramp front, adjustable V-slot rear.
Features: Velocity about 275 fps. Positive feed; automatic safety. Introduced 1994. Made in U.S. From Marksman Products.
Price: $35.00

MARKSMAN 1740 AIR RIFLE
Caliber: 177 or 18-shot BB repeater.
Barrel: 15½", smoothbore.
Weight: 5 lbs., 1 oz. **Length:** 36½" overall.
Power: Spring, barrel cocking.
Stock: Moulded high-impact ABS plastic.
Sights: Ramp front, open rear adjustable for elevation.
Features: Velocity about 450 fps. Automatic safety; fixed front, adjustable rear sight; positive feed BB magazine; shoots 177-cal. BBs, pellets and darts. From Marksman Products.
Price: $48.50
Price: Model 1780 (deluxe sights, rifled barrel, shoots only pellets) . . $63.50

Marksman 1790

> Consult our Directory pages for the location of firms mentioned.

MARKSMAN 1750 BB BIATHLON REPEATER RIFLE
Caliber: BB, 18-shot magazine.
Barrel: 15", smoothbore.
Weight: 4.7 lbs.
Power: Spring piston, barrel cocking.
Stock: Moulded composition.
Sights: Tunnel front, open adjustable rear.
Features: Velocity of 450 fps. Automatic safety. Positive Feed System loads a BB each time gun is cocked. Introduced 1990. From Marksman Products.
Price: $55.50

MARKSMAN 1790 BIATHLON TRAINER
Caliber: 177, single shot.
Barrel: 15", rifled.
Weight: 4.7 lbs.
Power: Spring-air, barrel cocking.
Stock: Synthetic.
Sights: Hooded front, match-style diopter rear.
Features: Velocity of 450 fps. Endorsed by the U.S. Shooting Team. Introduced 1989. From Marksman Products.
Price: $66.95

MARKSMAN 1792 COMPETITION TRAINER AIR RIFLE
Caliber: 177, single shot.
Barrel: 15", rifled.
Weight: 4.7 lbs.
Power: Spring-air, barrel cocking.
Stock: Synthetic.
Sights: Hooded front, match-style diopter rear.
Features: Velocity about 450 fps. Automatic safety. Introduced 1993. More economical version of the 1790 Biathlon Trainer. Made in U.S. From Marksman Products.
Price: $58.95

Parker-Hale Dragon Field

PARKER-HALE DRAGON SPORTER AIR RIFLE
Caliber: 22, single shot.
Barrel: 23".
Weight: 8.6 lbs. **Length:** 37.75" overall.
Power: Single stroke pneumatic.
Stock: European walnut; checkered grip and forend; rubber buttpad.
Sights: None furnished. Action and front sight base dovetailed for scope or iron sights.
Features: Velocity about 520 fps. Very moderate cocking effort; recoilless, vibration free. Constant power. Imported from England by Beeman.
Price: About **$675.00**

RWS/DIANA MODEL 24 AIR RIFLE
Caliber: 177, 22, single shot.
Barrel: 17", rifled.
Weight: 6 lbs. **Length:** 42" overall.
Power: Spring air, barrel cocking.
Stock: Beech.
Sights: Hooded front, adjustable rear.
Features: Velocity of 700 fps (177). Easy cocking effort; blue finish. Imported from Germany by Dynamit Nobel-RWS, Inc.
Price: **$200.00**
Price: Model 24C **$200.00**

RWS/Diana Model 34 Air Rifle
Similar to the Model 24 except has 19" barrel, weighs 7.5 lbs. Gives velocity of 1000 fps (177), 800 fps (22). Adjustable trigger, synthetic seals. Comes with scope rail.
Price: 177 or 22 . . . . **$245.00**

PARKER-HALE DRAGON FIELD TARGET AIR RIFLE
Caliber: 177, single shot.
Barrel: 25".
Weight: 10.7 lbs. **Length:** 40" overall.
Power: Single stroke pneumatic.
Stock: European walnut; high comb thumbhole with adjustable rubber buttpad. Right- or left-hand versions available.
Sights: None furnished. Action and front sight base dovetailed for scope or iron sights.
Features: Velocity about 800 fps. Very moderate cocking effort. Fully adjustable target trigger. Recoilless; vibration free. Imported from England by Beeman.
Price: About **$850.00**

RWS/DIANA MODEL 36 AIR RIFLE
Caliber: 177, 22, single shot.
Barrel: 19", rifled.
Weight: 8 lbs. **Length:** 45" overall.
Power: Spring air, barrel cocking.
Stock: Beech.
Sights: Hooded front (interchangeable inserts avail.), adjustable rear.
Features: Velocity of 1000 fps (177-cal.). Comes with scope mount; two-stage adjustable trigger. Imported from Germnay by Dynamit Nobel-RWS, Inc.
Price: **$360.00**
Price: Model 36 Carbine (same as Model 36 except has 15" barrel) . **$360.00**

RWS/DIANA MODEL 45 AIR RIFLE
Caliber: 177, single shot.
Weight: 7¾ lbs. **Length:** 46" overall.
Power: Spring air, barrel cocking.
Stock: Walnut-finished hardwood with rubber recoil pad.
Sights: Globe front with interchangeable inserts, micro. click open rear with four-way blade.
Features: Velocity of 820 fps. Dovetail base for either micrometer peep sight or scope mounting. Automatic safety. Imported from Germany by Dynamit Nobel-RWS, Inc.
Price: **$280.00**

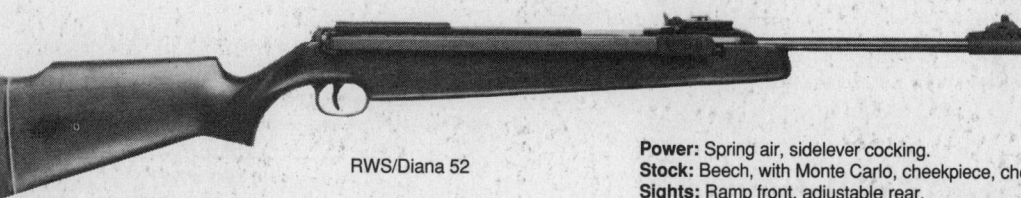

RWS/Diana 52

RWS/DIANA MODEL 52 AIR RIFLE
Caliber: 177, 22, single shot.
Barrel: 17", rifled.
Weight: 8½ lbs. **Length:** 43" overall.

Power: Spring air, sidelever cocking.
Stock: Beech, with Monte Carlo, cheekpiece, checkered grip and forend.
Sights: Ramp front, adjustable rear.
Features: Velocity of 1100 fps (177). Blue finish. Solid rubber buttpad. Imported from Germany by Dynamit Nobel-RWS, Inc.
Price: **$465.00**
Price: Model 48 (same as Model 52 except no Monte Carlo, cheekpiece or checkering) **$415.00**
Price: Model 54, recoilless action **$650.00**

RWS/Diana 75 T01

RWS/Diana Model 75S T01 Air Rifle
Similar to the Model 75 T01 except has beech stock specially shaped for standing and three-position shooting. Buttplate is vertically adjustable with curved and straight spacers for individual fit, adjustable cheekpiece. Introduced 1990.
Price: Right-hand **$1,315.00**
Price: Left-hand **$1,405.00**

RWS/DIANA MODEL 75 T01 MATCH AIR RIFLE
Caliber: 177, single shot.
Barrel: 19".
Weight: 11 lbs. **Length:** 43.7" overall.
Power: Spring air, sidelever cocking.
Stock: Oil-finished beech with stippled grip, adjustable buttplate, accessory rail. Conforms to ISU rules.
Sights: Globe front with five inserts, fully adjustable match peep rear.
Features: Velocity of 574 fps. Fully adjustable trigger. Model 75 HV has stippled forend, adjustable cheekpiece. Uses double opposing piston system for recoilless operation. Imported from Germany by Dynamit Nobel-RWS, Inc.
Price: Model 75 T01 . . . . **$1,200.00**

CAUTION: PRICES SHOWN ARE SUPPLIED BY THE MANUFACTUER OR IMPORTER. CHECK YOUR LOCAL GUNSHOP.

49th EDITION, 1995 **449**

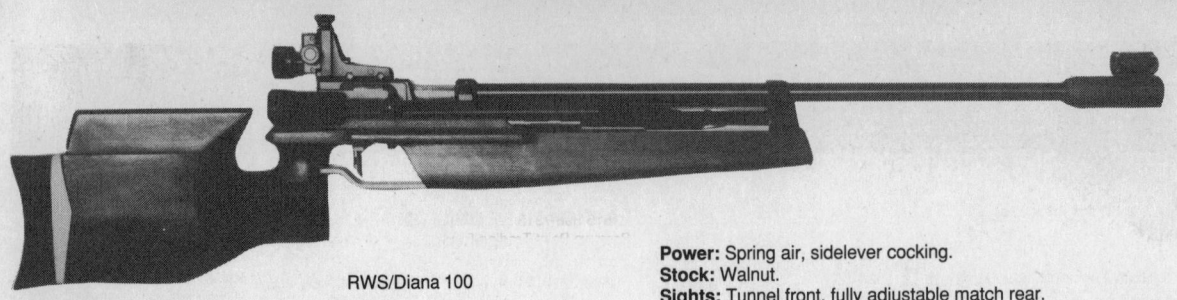

RWS/Diana 100

RWS/DIANA MODEL 100 MATCH AIR RIFLE
Caliber: 177, single shot.
Barrel: 19".
Weight: 11 lbs. **Length:** 43" overall.
Power: Spring air, sidelever cocking.
Stock: Walnut.
Sights: Tunnel front, fully adjustable match rear.
Features: Velocity of 580 fps. Single-stroke cocking; cheekpiece adjustable for height and length; recoilless operation. Cocking lever secured against rebound. Introduced 1990. Imported from Germany by Dynamit Nobel-RWS, Inc.
Price: Right-hand only $1,500.00

RWS Gamo Delta

RWS GAMO DELTA AIR RIFLE
Caliber: 177.
Barrel: 15.73".
Weight: 5.3 lbs. **Length:** 37" overall.
Power: Barrel cocking, spring piston.
Stock: Carbon fiber.
Sights: Blade front, fully adjustable open rear.
Features: Velocity to 565 fps. Has 20-lb. cocking effort. Synthetic seal; dual safeties; grooved for scope mounting. Imported from Spain by Dynamit Nobel-RWS, Inc.
Price: $115.00

RWA GAMO HUNTER 440 AIR RIFLE
Caliber: 177, single shot.
Barrel: 18".
Weight: 6.75 lbs. **Length:** 43" overall.
Power: Spring piston, barrel cocking.
Stock: Hardwood.
Sights: Hooded blade on ramp front, fully adjustable rear.
Features: Velocity 1000 fps. Monte Carlo stock with cheekpiece; scope rail; dual safeties. Imported from Spain by Dynamit Nobel-RWS.
Price: $210.00

RWS SM 100 AIR RIFLE
Caliber: 177, 22, single shot.
Barrel: 22", 12-groove Lothar Walther.
Weight: 8½ lbs. **Length:** 39½" overall.
Power: Pre-charged compressed air from diving tank.
Stock: Walnut-finished beech.
Sights: None furnished.
Features: Velocity to 1000 fps (177), 800 fps (22). PFTE-coated lightweight striker for consistent shots. Blued barrel and air chamber. Imported from England by Dynamit Nobel-RWS.
Price: $750.00
Price: Model XM 100 (same as SM100 except walnut stock) $970.00

RWS TM 100 Air Rifle
Similar to the SM 100 except is target model with hand-picked barrel for best accuracy. Target-type walnut stock with adjustable cheekpiece and adjustable buttplate. Stippled grip and forend. Available in 177 or 22 (special order), right- or left-hand models. Variable power settings. Two-stage adjustable trigger; 22" barrel. Imported from England by Dynamit Nobel-RWS.
Price: $1,250.00

RWS NJR 100 Air Rifle
Similar to the SM 100 except designed for Field Target competition. Hand-picked Walther barrel for best accuracy. Walnut Field Target thumbhole stock has adjustable forend, cheekpiece and buttpad. Has lever-type bolt, straight blade trigger. Imported from England by Dynamit Nobel-RWS.
Price: $2,000.00

CONSULT Shooter's MARKETPLACE *Page 225, This Issue*

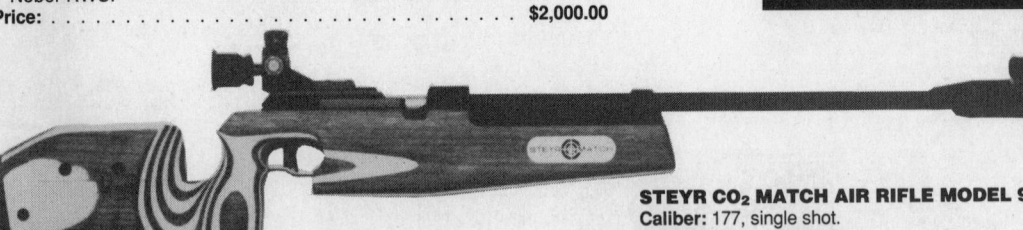

Steyr CO₂ Match

SHERIDAN PNEUMATIC (PUMP-UP) AIR RIFLES
Caliber: 20 (5mm), single shot.
Barrel: 19⅜", rifled brass.
Weight: 6 lbs. **Length:** 36½" overall.
Power: Under-lever pneumatic, hand pumped.
Stock: Walnut with buttplate and sculpted forend.
Sights: High ramp front, fully adjustable notch rear.
Features: Variable velocity to 675 fps. Bolt action with ambidextrous push-pull safety. Blue finish (Blue Streak) or nickel finish (Silver Streak). Introduced 1991. Made in the U.S. by Benjamin Sheridan Co.
Price: Blue Streak, Model CB9 . . . . $139.95
Price: Silver streak, Model C9 . . . . $148.50

STEYR CO₂ MATCH AIR RIFLE MODEL 91
Caliber: 177, single shot.
Barrel: 23.75", (13.75" rifled).
Weight: 10.5 lbs. **Length:** 51.7" overall.
Power: CO₂.
Stock: Match. Laminated wood. Adjustable buttplate and cheekpiece.
Sights: None furnished; comes with scope mount.
Features: Velocity 577 fps. CO₂ cylinders are refillable; about 320 shots per cylinder. Designed for 10-meter shooting. Introduced 1990. Imported from Austria by Nygord Precision Products.
Price: About $1,300.00
Price: Left-hand, about $1,400.00
Price: Running Target Rifle, right-hand, about $1,325.00
Price: As above, left-hand, about $1,425.00

CAUTION: PRICES SHOWN ARE SUPPLIED BY THE MANUFACTURER OR IMPORTER. CHECK YOUR LOCAL GUNSHOP.

A

A&M Sales, 23 W. North Ave., North Lake, IL 60264/708-562-8190

A-Square Co., Inc., One Industrial Park, Bedford, KY 40006-9667/502-255-7456; FAX: 502-255-7657

Accu-Tek, 4525 Carter Ct., Chino, CA 91710/909-627-2404; FAX: 909-627-7817

Accuracy Gun Shop, 1240 Hunt Ave., Columbus, GA 31907/706-561-6386

Accuracy Gun Shop, Inc., 5903 Boulder Highway, Las Vegas, NV 89122/702-458-3330

Action Arms Ltd., P.O. Box 9573, Philadelphia, PA 19124/215-744-0100; FAX: 215-533-2188

Adventure A.G.R., 2991 St. Jude, Waterford, MI 48329/313-673-3090

Ahlman's Custom Gun Shop, Inc., Rt. 1, Box 20, Morristown, MN 55052/507-685-4244

Aimpoint, Inc., 580 Herndon Parkway, Suite 500, Herndon, VA 22070/703-471-6828; FAX: 703-689-0575

Aimtech Mount Systems, P.O. Box 223, Thomasville, GA 31799/912-226-4313; FAX: 912-227-0222

Air Arms (See U.S. importer—Air Rifle Specialists)

Air Gun Rifle Repair, 6420 1st Ave. W., Sebring, FL 33870/813-655-0516

Air Gun Shop, The, 2312 Elizabeth St., Billings, MT 59102/406-656-2983

Air Guns Unlimited, 15866 Main St., La Puente, CA 91744/818-333-4991

Air Rifle Specialists, 311 East Water St., Elmira, NY 14901/607-734-7340; FAX: 607-733-3261

Air Venture, 9752 E. Flower St., Bellflower, CA 90706/310-867-6355

Airgun Repair Centre, 3227 Garden Meadows, Lawrenceburg, IN 47025/812-637-1463

Airgun Repair Centre, Ltd., P.O. Box 6249, Cincinnati, OH 45206-0249/812-637-1463

Alessandri & Son, Lou, 24 French St., Rehoboth, MA 02769/508-252-5590, 800-248-5652; FAX: 508-3436

Alexander, Gunsmith, W.R., 1406 Capitol Circle N.E. #D, Tallahassee, FL 32308/904-656-6176

All Game Sport Center, 6076 Guinea Pike, Milford, OH 45150/513-575-0134

Allison & Carey Gun Works, 17311 S.E. Stark, Portland, OR 97233/503-256-5166

Alpine Arms Corp., 6716 Fort Hamilton Pkwy., Brooklyn, NY 11219/718-833-2228

Alpine Range, 5482 Shelby Rd., Fort Worth, TX 76140/817-478-6613

American Arms & Ordnance, Inc., P.O. Box 2691, 1303 S. College Ave., Bryan, TX 77805/409-822-4983

American Arms, Inc., 715 E. Armour Rd., N. Kansas City, MO 64116/816-474-3161; FAX: 816-474-1225

American Derringer Corp., 127 N. Lacy Dr., Waco, TX 76705/800-642-7817, 817-799-9111; FAX: 817-799-7935

Ammo Load, Inc., 1560 East Edinger, Suite G., Santa Ana, CA 92705/714-558-8858; FAX: 714-569-0319

AMT, 6226 Santos Diaz St., Irwindale, CA 91702/818-334-6629; FAX: 818-969-5247

Andersen Gunsmithing, 2485 Petaluma Blvd. N.,Petaluma, CA 94952/707-763-3852

Anderson Manufacturing Co., Inc., P.O. Box 2640, 2741 N. Crosby Rd., Oak Harbor, WA 98277/206-675-7300; FAX: 206-675-3939

Anschutz GmbH (See U.S. importer—PSI, Inc.)

Antonowicz, Frank, 8349 Kentucky Ave. North, Minneapolis, MN 55445

Apple Town Gun Shop, Rt. 104, Williamson, NY 14589/315-589-3311

Argonaut Gun Shop, 607 McHenry Ave., Modesto, CA 95350/209-522-5876

Arizaga (See U.S. importer—Mandall Shooting Supplies, Inc.)

Armadillo Air Gun Repair, 5892 Hampshire Rd., Corpus Christi, TX 78408/512-289-5458

Armes de Chasse, P.O. Box 827, Chadds Ford, PA 19317/215-388-1146; FAX: 215-388-1147

Armoury, Inc., The, Rt. 202, Box 2340, New Preston, CT 06777/203-868-0001

Armscor (See U.S. importer—Ruko Products)

Armscorp USA, Inc., 4424 John Ave., Baltimore, MD 21227/410-247-6200

Armsport, Inc., 3950 NW 49th St., Miami, FL 33142/305-635-7850; FAX: 305-633-2877

Armurie De L'Outaouqis, 28 Rue Bourque, Hull, Quebec, CANADA J8Y 1X1/819-777-9824

Arrieta, S.L. (See U.S. importers—Hi-Grade Imports; Jack J. Jansma; New England Arms Co.; The Orvis Co., Inc.; Quality Arms, Inc.)

ASI, 6226 Santos Dias St., Irwindale, CA 91706/818-334-6629

Astra-Unceta Y Cia, S.A. (See U.S. importer—E.A.A. Corp.)

Atlantic & Pacific Guns, 4859 Virginia Beach Blvd., Virginia Beach, VA 23462/804-490-1618

Atlantic Guns, Inc., 944 Bonifant St., Silver Springs, MD 20910/301-585-4448/301-279-7963

Atlas Gun Repair, 4908 E. Judge Perez Dr., Violet, LA 70092/504-277-4229

Auto-Ordnance Corp., Williams Lane, West Hurley, NY 12491/914-679-7225; FAX: 914-679-2698

Autumn Sales, Inc. (Blaser), 1320 Lake St., Fort Worth, TX 76102/817-335-1634; FAX: 817-338-0119

AYA (See U.S. importer—Armes de Chasse)

B

B&B Supply Co., 4501 Minnehaha Ave., Minneapolis, MN 55406/612-724-5230

B&T, Inc., 1777 Central Ave., Albany, NY 12205/518-869-7934

B&W Gunsmithing, 505 Main Ave. N.W., Cullman, AL 35055/205-737-9595

B-Square Co., P.O. Box 11281, 2708 St. Louis Ave., Ft. Worth, TX 76110/817-923-0964, 800-433-2909; FAX: 817-926-7012

Bachelder Custom Arms, 1229 Michigan N.E., Grand Rapids, MI 49503/616-459-3636

Badger Shooters Supply, Inc., 202 N. Harding, Owen, WI 54460/715-229-2101; FAX: 715-229-2332

Baikal (See U.S. importer—K.B.I., Inc.)

Bain & Davis, Inc., 307 E. Valley Blvd., San Gabriel, CA 91776-3522/818-573-4241, 213-283-7449

Bait & Tackle Shop, The, Rt. 1, Box 5B, Fairmont, WV 26554/304-363-0183

Baity's Custom Gunworks, Rt. 4 Box 409-A (old Hwy. 421), North Wilkesboro, NC 28659/919-667-8785

Baltimore Gunsmiths, 218 South Broadway, Baltimore, MD 21231/301-276-6908

Barrett Firearms Mfg., Inc., P.O. Box 1077, Murfreesboro, TN 37133/615-896-2938; FAX: 615-896-7313

Barrows Point Trading Post, Rt. 4 West, Quechee, VT 05059/802-295-1050

Bausch & Lomb, Inc., 42 East Ave., Rochester, NY 14603/800-828-5423

Beard's Sport Shop, 811 Broadway, Cape Girardeau, MO 63701/314-334-2266

Beauchamp & Son, Inc., 160 Rossiter Rd., Richmond, MA 01254/413-698-3822; FAX: 413-698-3866

Bedlan's Sporting Goods, Inc., 1318 E. Street, P.O. Box 244, Fairbury, NE 68352/402-729-6112

Beeman Precision Airguns, Inc., 5454 Argosy Dr., Huntington Beach, CA 92649/714-890-4800; FAX: 714-890-4808

Bell's Legendary Country Wear, 22 Circle Dr., Bellmore, NY 11710/516-679-1158

Belleplain Supply, Inc., Box 346, Handsmill Rd., Belleplain, NJ 08270/609-861-2345

Bellrose & Son, L.E., 21 Forge Pond Rd., Granby, MA 01033-0184/413-467-3637

Ben's Gun Shop, 1151 S. Cedar Ridge, Duncanville, TX 75137/214-780-1807

Benelli Armi S.p.A. (See U.S. importers—E.A.A. Corp.; Heckler & Koch, Inc.; Sile Distributors)

Benjamin/Sheridan Co., Crossman, Rts. 5 and 20, E. Bloomfield, NY 14443/716-657-6161; FAX: 716-657-5405

Benson Gun Shop, 35 Middle Country Rd., Coram L.I., NY 11727/516-736-0065

Beretta Firearms, Pietro (See U.S. importer—Beretta U.S.A. Corp.)

Beretta, Dr. Franco (See U.S. importer—Nevada Cartridge Co.)

Beretta U.S.A. Corp., 17601 Beretta Drive, Accokeek, MD 20607/301-283-2191

Bernardelli Vincenzo S.p.A., Via Matteotti 125, Gardone V.T., ITALY I-25063/30-8912851-2-3

Bersa S.A. (See U.S. importer—Eagle Imports, Inc.)

Bertuzzi (See U.S. importers—Moore & Co.; Wm. Larkin; New England Arms Co.)

Bickford's Gun Repair, 426 N. Main St., Joplin, MO 64801/417-781-6440

Bill Barton Sport Center, 7414 N. Milwaukee Ave., Niles, IL 60648/708-647-8585

Billings Gunsmiths, Inc., 1940 Grand Ave., Billings, MT 59102/406-652-3104

Billy Freds, P.O. Box 7646, 2465 I-40, Amarillo, TX 79109/806-352-2519

Blaser Jagdwaffen GmbH (See U.S. importer—Autumn Sales, Inc.)

Blount, Inc., Sporting Equipment Div., 2299 Snake River Ave., P.O. Box 856, Lewiston, ID 83501/800-627-3640, 208-746-2351

Blue Ridge Outdoor Sports, Inc., 2314 Spartansburg Hwy., E. Flat Rock, NC 28726/704-697-3006

Blythe's Sport Shop, Inc., 2810 N. Calmut Ave., Valparaiso, IN 46383/219-462-4412

Bob's Crosman Repair, 2510 E. Henry Ave., Cudahy, WI 53110/414-769-8256

Bob's Gun & Tackle Shop, (Blaustein & Reich, Inc.), 746 Granby St., Norfolk, VA 23510/804-627-8311/804-622-9786

Bob's Repair, 3127 E. 650 N., Menan, ID 83434/208-754-4664

Boggus Gun Shop, 1402 W. Hopkins St., San Marcos, TX 78666/512-392-3513

Bohemia Arms Co., 17101 Los Modelos, Fountain Valley, CA 92708/714-963-0809; FAX: 714-963-0809

Bolsa Gunsmithing, 7404 Bolsa Ave., Westminster, CA 92683/714-894-9100

Boracci, E. John, Village Sport Center, 38-10 Merrick Rd., Seaford L.I., NY 11783/516-785-7110

Borgheresi, Enrique, 106 E. Tallalah, P.O. Box 8063, Greenville, SC 29604/803-271-2664

Boudreaux, Gunsmith, Preston, 412 W. School St., Lake Charles, LA 70605/318-478-0640

Bradys Sportsmans Surplus, P.O. Box 4166, Missoula, MT 59806/460-721-5500

Braverman Arms Co., 912 Penn Ave., Wilkinsburg, PA 15221/412-241-1344

Brazdas Top Guns, 307 Bertrand Dr., Lafayette, LA 70506/318-233-4137

Brenner Sport Shop, Charlie, 344 St. George Ave., Rahway, NJ 07065/908-382-4066

Bretton (See U.S. importer—Mandall Shooting Supplies, Inc.)

Bridge Sportsmen's Center, 1319 Spring St., Paso Robles, CA 93446/805-238-4407

British Sporting Arms, RR1, Box 130, Millbrook, NY 12545/914-677-8303

BRNO (See U.S. importers—Action Arms Ltd.; Bohemia Arms Co.)

Broadway Arms, 4116 E. Broadway, N. Little Rock, AR 72117/501-945-9348

Brock's Gunsmithing, Inc., North 2104 Division St., Spokane, WA 99207/509-328-9788

Brown Co., E. Arthur, 3404 Pawnee Dr., Alexandria, MN 56308/612-762-8847

Browning Arms Co. (See page 457)

Brunswick Gun Shop, 31 Bath Rd., Brunswick, ME 04011/207-729-8322

Bryan & Associates, 209 Rushton Rd., Belton, SC 29627/803-338-4786

Bryco Arms (See U.S. distributor—Jennings Firearms, Inc.)

BSA Guns Ltd. (See U.S. importer—Air Rifle Specialists)

Buffalo Gun Center, Inc., 3385 Harlem Rd., Buffalo, NY 14225/716-833-2581

Bullseye Gun Works, 7949 E. Frontage Rd.. Overland Park, KS 66204/913-648-4867

Burby, Inc. Guns & Gunsmithing, Rt. 7 South RR #3, Box 345, Middlebury, VT 05753/802-388-7365

Burgins Gun Shop, RD #1 Box 66, Mericksville Rd., Sidney Center, NY 13839/607-829-8668

Burris, P.O. Box 1747, Greeley, CO 80631/303-356-1670; FAX: 303-356-8702

Burton Hardware, 200 N. Huntington, Sulphur, LA 70663/318-527-8651

Bushnell, Bausch & Lomb Sports Optics Div., 9200 Cody, Overland Park, KS 66214/913-888-0220

C

C-H Tool & Die Corp. (See 4-D Custom Die Co.)

Cabanas (See U.S. importer—Mandall Shooting Supplies, Inc.)

Cabela's, 812-13th Ave., Sidney, NE 69160/308-254-5505; FAX: 308-254-7809

Caddo Arms & Cycle, 1400 Fairfield Ave., Shreveport, LA 71101/318-424-9011

Cal's Customs, 110 E. Hawthorne, Fallbrook, CA 92028/619-728-5230

Calico Light Weapon Systems, 405 E. 19th St., Bakersfield, CA 93305/805-323-1327; FAX: 805-323-7844

Camdex, Inc., 2330 Alger, Troy, MI 48083/313-528-2300

Cape Outfitters, Rt. 2, Box 437C, Cape Girardeau, MO 63701/314-335-4103; FAX: 314-335-1555

Capitol Sports & Western Wear, 1092 Helena Ave., Helena, MT 59601/406-443-2978

Carl's Gun Shop, Route 1, Box 131, El Dorado Springs, MO 64744/417-876-4168

Carpenters Gun Works, RD 1 Box 43D, Newton Rd., Proctorsville, VT 05153/802-226-7690

Carroll's Gun Shop, Inc., 1610 N. Alabama Rd., Wharton, TX 77488/409-532-3175

Carter's Country, 8925 Katy Freeway, Houston, TX 77024/713-461-1844

Casey's Gun Shop, 59 Des E Rables, P.O. Box 100, Rogersville, New Brunswick E0A 2T0 CANADA/506-775-6822

Catfish Guns, 900 Jeffco-Executive Park, Imperial, MO 63052/314-464-1217

CBC (See U.S. importer—MAGTECH Recreational Products, Inc.)

Central Ohio Police Supply, c/o Wammes Guns, 225 South Main St., Bellefontaine, OH 43311

Centre Firearms Co., Inc., 10 West 37th St., New York City, NY 10018/212-244-4040

Century Gun Dist., Inc., 1467 Jason Rd., Greenfield, IN 46140/317-462-4524

Century International Arms, Inc., 48 Lower Newton St., St. Albans, VT 05478/802-527-1252; FAX: 802-527-0470

Cervera, Albert J., Rt. 1 Box 808, Hanover, VA 23069/804-994-5783

Chalmette Jewelry & Guns, 507 W. St. Bernard Hwy., Chalmette, LA 70043/504-271-2538

Chapuis Armes (See U.S. importer—Chapuis USA)

Chapuis USA, 416 Business Park, Bedford, KY 40006

CHARCO, 26 Beaver St., Ansonia, CT 06401/203-735-4686; 203-735-6569

Charlie's Sporting Goods, Inc., 7401 Menaul Blvd. N.E., Albuquerque, NM 87110/505-884-4545

Charlton Co., Ltd., M.D., Box 153, Brentwood Bay, B.C., CANADA V0S 1A0/604-652-5266

Charter Arms (See CHARCO)

Cherry Corners, Inc., 11136 Congress Rd., P.O. Box 38, Lodi, OH 44254/216-948-1238

Cherry's Gun Shop, 302 S. Farmerville St., Ruston, LA 71270/318-255-5678

Chet Paulson Outfitters, 1901 South 72nd St., Suite A-14, Tacoma, WA 98408/206-475-8831

ChinaSports, Inc., 2010 S. Lynx Place, Ontario, CA 91761/714-923-1411; FAX: 714-923-0775

Christopher Firearms Co., Inc., E., Route 128 & Ferry St., Miamitown, OH 45041/513-353-1321

Chuck's Gun Shop, Box 9112 Espinosa Rd., Ranchos De Taos, NM 87557/505-758-8594

Chung, Gunsmith, Mel, 8 Ing Rd., P.O. Box 1008, Kaunakakai, HI 96748/808-553-5888

Churchill (See U.S. importer—Ellett Bros.)

Cimarron Arms, P.O. Box 906, Fredericksburg, TX 78624-0906/210-997-9090; FAX: 210-997-0802

Clapps Gun Shop, P.O. Box 578, Brattleboro, VT 05302-0578/802-254-4663

Claridge Hi-Tec, Inc., 19350 Business Center Dr., Northridge, CA 91324/818-700-9093; FAX: 818-700-0026

Clark Custom Guns, Inc., P.O. Box 530, 11462 Keatchie Rd., Keithville, LA 71047/318-925-0836; FAX: 318-925-9425

Clifton Arms, Inc., P.O. Box 1471, Medina, TX 78055/210-589-2666; FAX: 210-589-2661

Cogdell's, Inc., 615 N. Valley Mills Dr., Waco, TX 76710/817-772-8224

Colabaugh Gunsmith, Inc., Craig, R.D. 4, Box 4168 Gumm St., Stroudsburg, PA 18360/717-992-4499

Coleman, Inc., Ron, 1600 North I-35 #106, Carrollton, TX 75006/214-245-3030

Coliseum Gun Traders, Ltd., 1180 Hempstead Turnpike, Uniondale, NY 11553/516-481-3593

Colt Blackpowder Arms Co., 5 Centre Market Place, New York, NY 10013/212-925-2159; FAX: 212-966-4986

Colt's Mfg. Co., Inc., P.O. Box 1868, Hartford, CT 06144-1868/203-236-6311; FAX: 203-244-1449

Competitor Corp., Inc., P.O. Box 244, 293 Townsend Rd., West Groton, MA 01472/508-448-3521; FAX: 603-673-4540

Connecticut Valley Classics, P.O. Box 2068, 12 Taylor Lane, Westport, CT 06880/203-435-4600

Coonan Arms, Inc., 1465 Selby Ave., St. Paul, MN 55104/612-646-0902; FAX: 612-646-0902

Cooper Arms, P.O. Box 114, Stevensville, MT 59870/406-777-5534

Corbin, Inc., 600 Industrial Circle, P.O. Box 2659, White City, OR 97503/503-826-5211; FAX: 503-826-8669

Cosmi Americo & Figlio s.n.c. (See U.S. importer—New England Arms Co.)

Covey's Precision Gunsmith, 700 N. Main St., Roswell, NM 88201/505-623-6565

CR Specialty, 1701 Baltimore Ave., Kansas City, MO 64108/816-221-3550

Creekside Gun Shop, Inc., P.O. Box 100 Main St., Holcomb, NY 14469/716-657-6338; FAX: 716-657-7900

Crosman Airguns (See page 457)

Crucelegui Hermanos (See U.S. importer—Mandall Shooting Supplies, Inc.)

Cumberland Arms, Rt. I, Box 1150 Shafer Rd., Blantons Chapel, Manchester, TN 37355

Cumberland Knife & Gun Works, 5661 Bragg Blvd., Fayetteville, NC 28303/919-867-0009

Custom Firearms Shop, The, 1133 Indiana Ave., Sheboygan, WI 53081/414-457-3320

Custom Gun Service, 1104 Upas Ave., McAllen, TX 78501/512-686-4670

Custom Gun Shop, 12505 97th St., Edmonton, Alberta, CANADA T5G 1Z8/403-477-3737

Custom Gun Works, 4952 Johnston St., Lafayette, LA 70503/318-984-0721

CVA, 5988 Peachtree Corners East, Norcross, GA 30071/404-449-4687; FAX: 404-242-8546

CZ (See U.S. importer—Action Arms Ltd.)

D

D&D Sporting Goods, 108 E. Main, Tishomingo, OK 73460/405-371-3571

D&J Coleman Service, 4811 Guadalupe Ave., Hobbs, NM 88240/505-392-5318

D&L Gunsmithing/Guns & Ammo, 3615 Summer Ave., Memphis, TN 38122/901-327-4384

D&L Shooting Supplies, 2663 W. Shore Rd., Warwick, RI 02886/401-738-1889

Daenzer, Charles E., 142 Jefferson Ave., Otisville, MI 48463/313-631-2415

Daewoo Precision Industries Ltd., (See U.S. importer—Nationwide Sports Distributors)

Daisy Mfg. Co., P.O. Box 220, Rogers, AR 72756/501-636-1200; FAX: 501-636-1601

Dakota (See U.S. importer—EMF Co., Inc.)

Dakota Arms, HC55, Box 326, Sturgis, SD 57785/605-347-4686; FAX: 605-347-4459

Dale's Guns & Archery Center, 3915 Eighteenth Ave., S.W., Rochester, MN 55902/507-289-8308

Damiano's Field & Stream, 172 N. Highland Ave., Ossining, NY 10562/914-941-6005

Danny's Gun Repair, Inc., 811 East Market St., Louisville, KY 40206/502-583-7100

Darnall's Gun Works, RR #3, Box 274, Bloomington, IL 61704/309-379-4331

Daryl's Gun Shop, Inc., R.R. #2 Highway 30 West, Box 145, State Center, IA 50247/515-483-2656

Davco Stores, 305 Broadway, Box 152, Monticello, NY 12701/914-794-5225

Davidson's of Canada, 584 Neal Dr., Box 479, Peterborough, Ontario, CANADA K9J 6X7/705-742-5408; 800-461-7663

Davis Industries, 11186 Venture Dr., Mira Loma, CA 91752/909-360-5598

Dayton Traister, P.O. Box 593, Oak Harbor, WA 98277/206-679-4657; FAX: 206-675-1114

Delhi Small Arms, 22B Argyle Ave., Delhi, Ontario, CANADA N4B 1J3/519-582-0522

Delisle Thompson Sporting Goods, Ltd., 1814A Loren Ave., Saskatoon, Saskatchewan, CANADA S7H 1Y4/306-653-2171

Denver Arms, Ltd., P.O. Box 4640, Pagosa Springs, CO 81157/303-731-2295

Denver Instrument Co., 6542 Fig St., Arvada, CO 80004/800-321-1135, 303-431-7255; FAX: 303-423-4831

Desert Industries, Inc., 3245 E. Patrick Ln., Suite H, Las Vegas, NV 89120/702-597-1066; FAX: 702-434-9495

Diana (See U.S. importer—Dynamit Nobel-RWS, Inc.)

Dixie Gun Works, Hwy. 51 South, Union City, TN 38261/901-885-0700, order 800-238-6785; FAX: 901-885-0440

Dillon Precision Products, Inc., 7442 E. Butherus Dr., Scottsdale, AZ 85260/602-948-8009, 800-762-3845; FAX: 602-998-2786

Dollar Drugs, Inc., 15A West 3rd, Lee's Summit, MO 64063/816-524-7600

Don & Tim's Gun Shop, 3724 Northwest Loop 410 and Fredricksburg, San Antonio, TX 78229/512-736-0263

Don's Gun Shop, 1085 Tunnel Rd., Ashville, NC 28805/704-298-4867

Don's Sport Shop, Inc., 7803 E. McDowell Rd., Scottsdale, AZ 85257/602-945-4051

Don's Sporting Goods, 120 Second Ave. South, Lewiston, MT 59457/406-538-9408

Dorn's Outdoor Center, 4388 Mercer University Drive, Macon, GA 31206/912-471-0304

Down Under Gunsmiths, 318 Driveway, Fairbanks, AK 99701/907-456-8500

Dragun Enterprises, P.O. Box 222, Murfreesboro, TN 37133-2222/615-895-7373, 800-467-7375; FAX: 800-829-7536

Dubbs, Gunsmith, Dale R., 32616 U.S. Hwy. 90, Seminole, AL 36574/205-946-3245

Duncan Gun Shop, Inc., 414 Second St., North Wilksboro, NC 28659/919-838-4851

Duncan's Gun Works, Inc., 1619 Grand Ave., San Marcos, CA 92069/619-727-0515

Dynamit Nobel-RWS, Inc., 81 Ruckman Rd., Closter, NJ 07624/201-767-1995; FAX: 201-767-1589

E

E.A.A. Corp., P.O. Box 1299, Sharpes, FL 32959/407-639-7006

Eagle Arms, Inc., 128 E. 23rd Ave., Coal Valley, IL 61240/309-799-5619; FAX: 309-799-5150

Eagle Imports, Inc., 1750 Brielle Ave., Unit B1, Wanamassa, NJ 07712/908-493-0333; FAX: 908-493-0301

Ed's Gun & Tackle Shop, Inc., Suite 90, 2727 Canton Rd. (Hwy. 5), Marietta, GA 30066/404-425-8461

Efinger Sporting Goods, 513 W. Union Ave. Rt. 28, Bound Brook, NJ 08805/908-356-0604

Elbe Arms Co., Inc., 610 East 27th St., Cheyenne, WY 82001/307-634-5731

Ellett Bros., P.O. Box 128, Columbia, SC 29036/803-345-3751, 800-845-3711; FAX: 803-345-1820

EMF Co., Inc., 1900 E. Warner Ave. Suite 1-D, Santa Ana, CA 92705/714-261-6611; FAX: 714-956-0133

Enstad & Douglas, 211 Hedges, Oregon City, OR 97045/503-655-3751

Epps "Orillia" Ltd., Ellwood, RR 3, Hwy. 11 North, Orillia, Ont. L3V 6H3, CANADA/705-689-5333

Erma Werke GmbH (See U.S. importers—Mandall Shooting Supplies, Inc.; PSI, Inc.)

Ernie's Gun Shop, Ltd., 1031 Marion St., Winnipeg, Manitoba, CANADA R2J 0L1/204-233-1928

Essex Arms, P.O. Box 345, Island Pond, VT 05846/802-723-4313

Euroarms of America, Inc., 208 E. Piccadilly St., Winchester, VA 22601/703-662-1863; FAX: 703-662-4464

Europtik Ltd., P.O. Box 319, Dunmore, PA 18512/717-347-6049, 800-873-5362; FAX: 717-969-4330

Ewell Cross Gun Shop, Inc., 8240 Interstate 30W, Ft. Worth, TX 76108/817-246-4622

Eyster Heritage Gunsmiths, Inc., Ken, 6441 Bishop Rd., Centerburg, OH 43011/614-625-6131

F

F&D Guns, 5140 Westwood Drive, St. Charles, MO 63304/314-441-5897

Fabarm S.p.A. (See U.S. importer—Ithaca Acquisition Corp.)

Fabrica D'Armi Sabatti S.R.L. (See U.S. importer—E.A.A. Corp.)

Famas (See U.S. importer—Century International Arms, Inc.)

FAS (See U.S. importer—Nygord Precision Products)

Fausti & Figlie s.n.c., Stefano (See U.S. importer—American Arms, Inc.)

Feather Industries, Inc., 2300 Central Ave. K, Boulder, CO 80301/303-442-7021; FAX: 303-447-0944

Federal Engineering Corp., 1090 Bryn Mawr, Bensenville, IL 60106/708-860-1938

Federal Firearms Co., Inc., Box 145, Thom's Run Rd., Oakdale, PA 15071/412-221-0300

FEG (See U.S. importers—Century International Arms, Inc.; K.B.I., Inc.)

Felton, James, Custom Gunsmith, 1033 Elizabeth St., Eugene, OR 97402/503-689-1687

FERLIB (See U.S. importers—Wm. Larkin Moore & Co.; New England Arms Co., Pachmayr Co.; Quality Arms, Inc.)

Firearms Co. Ltd./Alpine (See U.S. importer—Mandall Shooting Supplies, Inc.)

Firearms Repair & Refinish Shoppe, 639 Hoods Mill Rd., Woodbine, MD 21797/410-795-5859

Firearms Service Center, 2140 Old Shepherdsville Rd., Louisville, KY 40218/502-458-1148

Firearms Unlimited, Inc., 4360 Corporate Square, Naples, FL 33942/813-643-2922

Fix Gunshop, Inc., Michael D., R.D. 11, Box 192, Reading, PA 19607/215-775-2067

Flaig's Inc., 2200 Evergreen Rd., Pittsburgh, PA 15209/412-821-1717

Flintrop Arms Corp., 4034 W. National Ave., Milwaukee, WI 53215/414-383-2626

Foothills Shooting Center, 7860 W. Jewell Ave., Lakewood, CO 80226/303-985-4417

Forster Products, 82 E. Lanark Ave., Lanark, IL 61046/815-493-6360; FAX: 815-493-2371

Four Seasons, 76 R Winn St., Woburn, MA 01801/617-932-3133/3255

4-D Custom Die Co., 711 N. Sandusky St., P.O. Box 889, Mt. Vernon, OH 43050-0889/614-397-7214; FAX: 614-397-6600

Fox & Company, 2211 Dutch Valley Rd., Knoxville, TN 37918/615-687-7411

Franchi S.p.A., Luigi (See U.S. importer—American Arms, Inc.)

Francotte & Cie S.A., Auguste (See U.S. importer—Armes de Chasse)

Franklin Sports, Inc., 3941 Atlanta Hwy., Bogart, GA 30622/706-543-7803

Fred's Gun Shop, 1364 Ridgewood Dr., Mobile, AL 36608/205-344-1079

Freedom Arms, Inc., P.O. Box 1776, Freedom, WY 83120/307-883-2468; FAX: 307-883-2005

Freer's Gun Shop, Building B-1, 8928 Spring Branch Dr., Houston, TX 77080/713-467-3016

Fremont Tool Works, 1214 Prairie, Ford, KS 67842/316-369-2338

Fricano, Gunsmith, J., 15258 Moreland, Grand Haven, MI 49417/616-846-4458

Friedman's Army Surplus, 2617 Nolenville Rd., Nashville, TN 37211/615-244-1653

Frontiersman's Sports, 6925 Wayzata Blvd., Minneapolis, MN 55426/612-544-3775

FWB (See U.S. importer—Beeman Precision Airguns, Inc.)

G

G&S Gunsmithing, 220 N. Second St., Eldridge, IA 52748/319-285-4153

G.H. Gun Shop, 520 W. "B" St., McCook, NE 69001/308-345-1250

G.I. Loan Shop, 1004 W. Second St., Grand Island, NE 68801/308-382-9573

G.U., Inc., 4325 S. 120th St., Omaha, NE 68137/402-330-4492

Galaxy Imports Ltd., Inc., P.O. Box 3361, Victoria, TX 77903/512-573-4867; FAX: 512-576-9622

Galazan, Div. of Connecticut Shotgun Mfg. Co., P.O. Box 622, 35 Woodland St., New Britain, CT 06051-0622/203-225-6581; FAX: 203-832-8707

Gamba S.p.A., Renato, (See U.S. importers—Giacomo Sporting, Inc.; New England Arms Co.)

Gamo (See U.S. importers—Daisy Mfg. Co.; Dynamit Nobel-RWS, Inc.)

Gander Mountain, Inc., P.O. Box 128, Hwy. "W", Wilmot, WI 53192/414-862-2331,Ext. 6425

Gander Mt. Inc., 1307 Miller Trunk Highway, Duluth, MN 55811/218-726-1100

Garber & Sams Gunsmithing, 1821 Maytown Rd., Elizabethtown, PA 17022/717-361-7875

Garbi, Armas Urki (See U.S. importer—Moore & Co., Wm. Larkin)

Garfield Gunsmithing, 237 Wessington Ave., Garfield, NJ 07026/201-478-0171

Garrett Gunsmiths, Inc., Peter, 838 Monmouth St., Newport, KY 41071-1821/606-261-1855

Gart Brothers Sporting Goods, 1000 Broadway, Denver, CO 80203/303-861-1122

Gary's Gun Shop, 905 W. 41st St., Sioux Falls, SD 57104/605-332-6119

Gat Guns, 14N 915 Route 25, East Dundee, IL 60118/708-428-4867

Gaucher Armes, S.A. (See U.S. importer—Mandall Shooting Supplies, Inc.)

Geake & Son, Inc., 23510 Woodward Ave., Ferndale MI 48220/313-542-0498

Gemini Arms Ltd., 79 Broadway, Hicksville, NY 11801/516-931-2641

Gene's Gunsmithing, Box 34 GRP 326 R.R. 3, Selkirk, Manitoba, CANADA R1A 2A8/204-757-4413

GFR Corp., P.O. Box 430, Andover, NH 03216/603-735-5300

Giacomo Sporting, Inc., Delta Plaza, Rt. 26N, Rome, NY 13440

Gibbs Rifle Co., Inc., Cannon Hill Industrial Park, Rt. 2, Box 214 Hoffman, Rd./Martinsburg, WV 25401/304-274-0458; FAX: 304-274-0078

Gilbert Equipment Co., Inc., 960 Downtowner Rd., Mobile, AL 36609/205-344-3322

Girard, Florent, Gunsmith, 598 Verreault, Chicoutimi, Quebec, CANADA G7H 2B8/418-696-3329

Glenn's Reel & Rod Repair, 2210 E. 9th St., Des Moines, IA 50316/515-262-2990

Glock GmbH (See U.S. importer—Glock, Inc.)

Glock, Inc., 6000 Highlands Parkway, Smyrna, GA 30082/404-433-8719

Gonic Arms, Inc., 134 Flagg Rd., Gonic, NH 03839/603-332-8456, 603-332-8457

Gordon's Wigwam, 501 S. St. Francis, Wichita, KS 67202/316-264-5891

Gorenflo Gunsmithing, 1821 State St., Erie, PA 16501/814-452-4855

Great Lakes Airguns, 6175 S. Park Ave., Hamburg, NY 14075/716-648-6666; FAX: 716-648-5279

Green Acres Sporting Goods, Inc., 8774 Normandy Blvd., Jacksonville, FL 32221/904-786-5166

Greene's Gun Shop, 4778 Monkey Hill Rd., Oak Harbor, WA 98277/206-675-3421

Grenada Gun Works, Hwy. 8 East, Grenada, MS 38901/601-226-9272

Grendel, Inc., P.O. Box 560909, Rockledge, FL 32956-0909/800-274-7427, 407-636-1211; FAX: 407-633-6710

Grice Gun Shop, Inc., 216 Reed St., P.O. 1028, Clearfield, PA 16830/814-765-9273

Griffin & Howe, Inc., 33 Claremont Rd., Bernardsville, NJ 07924/908-766-2287; FAX: 908-766-1068

Griffiths & Sons, E.J., 1014 N. McCullough St., Lima OH 45801/419-228-2141

Grulla Armes (See U.S. importer—American Arms, Inc.)

Grundman's, Inc., 75 Wildwood Ave., Rio Dell, CA 95562/707-764-5744

GSI, Inc., 108 Morrow Ave., P.O. Box 129, Trussville, AL 35173/205-655-8299; FAX: 205-655-7078

G.U., Inc., 4325 S. 120th St., Omaha, NE 68137/402-330-4492

Gun & Tackle Store, The, 6041 Forrest Ln., Dallas, TX 75230/214-239-8181

Gun Ace Gunsmithing, 3395 So. 5175 West, P.O. Box 1606, Cedar City, UT 84721/801-586-7421

Gun Center, The, 5831 Buckeystown Pike, Frederick, MD 21701/301-694-6887

Gun City USA Inc., 573 Murfreesboro Rd., Nashville, TN 37210/615-256-6127

Gun City, 212 W. Main Ave., Bismarck, ND 58501/701-223-2304

Gun Corral, Inc., 2827 East College Ave., Decatur, GA 30030/404-299-0288

Gun Doc, Inc., 5405 N.W. 82nd Ave., Miami, FL 33166/305-477-2777

Gun Exchange, Inc., 5317 W. 65th St., Little Rock, AR 72209/501-562-4668

Gun Hospital, The, 45 Vineyard Ave., E. Providence, RI 02914/401-438-3495

Gun Rack, Inc., The, 213 Richland Ave., Aiken, SC 29801/803-648-7100

Gun Room, The, 201 Clark St., Chapin, SC 29036/803-345-2199

Gun Shop, Inc., The, 8945 Biscayne Blvd., Miami Shores, FL 33138/305-757-1422

Gun Shop, The, 5550 S. 900 East St., Salt Lake City, UT 84117/801-263-3633

Gun Shop, The, 5567 Manitou Rd., Excelsior, MN 55331/612-474-2646

Gun Works, The, 8540 I St., Omaha, NE 68127/402-339-2249

Gun World, 392 Fifth Street, Elko, NV 89801/702-738-2666

Guns & Stuff, Inc., 3055 N. Broadway, Wichita, KS 67219/316-838-2448

Gunshop, Inc., The, 44633 N. Sierra Hwy., Lancaster CA 93534/805-942-8377

Gunsmith Co., The, 3435 S. State St., Salt Lake City, UT 84115/801-467-8949

Gunsmith, Inc., The, 1410 Sunset Blvd., West Columbia, SC 29169/803-791-0250

Gunsmith, The, 2205 Nord Ave., Chico, CA 95926/916-343-4550

Gunsmithing Ltd., 57 Unquowa Rd., Fairfield, CT 06430/203-254-0436

Gunsmithing Specialties, Co., 110 North Washington St., Papillion, NE 68046/402-339-1222

H

H&R 1871, Inc., 60 Industrial Rowe, Gardner, MA 01440/508-632-9393; FAX: 508-632-2300

Hagstrom, E.G., 2008 Janis Dr., Memphis, TN 38116/901-398-5333

Hammerli Ltd. (See U.S. importers—Beeman Precision Ariguns, Inc.; Hammerli USA; Mandall Shooting Supplies, Inc.)

Hammerli USA, 19296 Oak Grove Circle, Groveland, CA 95321/209-962-5311

Hampel's, Inc., 710 Randolph, Traverse City, MI 49684/616-946-5485

Harry's Army & Navy Store, 691 NJSH Rt. 130, Yardville, NJ 08620/609-585-5450

Hart & Son, Inc., Robert W., 401 Montgomery St., Nescopeck, PA 18635/717-752-3655; FAX: 717-752-1088

Hart's Gun Supply, Ed, U.S. Route 415, Bath, NY 14810/607-776-4228

Hatfield Gun Co., Inc., 224 N. 4th St., St. Joseph, MO 64501/816-279-8688; FAX: 816-279-2716

Hawken Shop, The (See Dayton Traister)

Heckler & Koch GmbH (See U.S. importer—Heckler & Koch, Inc.)

Heckler & Koch, Inc., 21480 Pacific Blvd., Sterling, VA 20166/703-450-1900; FAX: 703-450-8160

Heckman Arms Company, 1736 Skyline Dr., Richmond Heights, OH 44143

Helwan (See U.S. importer—Interarms)

Hemlock Gun Shop, Box 149, Rt. 590 & Crane Rd., Lakeville, PA 18438/717-226-9410

Henry's Airguns, 1204 W. Locust, Belvidere, IL 61008/815-547-5091

Herold's Gun Shoppe, 1498 E. Main Street, Box 350, Waynesboro, PA 17268/717-762-4010

Heym GmbH & Co. KG, Friedrich Wilh. (See U.S. importers—JägerSport, Ltd.; Swarovski Optik North America Ltd.)

Hi-Grade Imports, 8655 Monterey Rd., Gilroy, CA 95021/408-842-9301; FAX: 408-842-2374

Hill Top Gunsmithing, Rt. 3, Box 85, Canton, NY 13617/315-386-1165

Hill's Hardware & Sporting Goods, 1234 S. Second St., Union City, TN 38261/901-885-1510

Hill's, Inc., 1720 Capital Blvd., Raleigh, NC 27604/919-833-4884

HJS Arms, Inc., 1515 Oriole Ln., Brownsville, TX 78521·H-S Precision, Inc., 1301 Turbine Dr., Rapid City, SD 57701/605-341-3006; FAX: 605-342-8964

Hobb's Bicycle & Gun Sales, 406 E. Broadway, Hobbs, NM 88240/505-393-9815

Hodson & Son Pell Gun Repair, 4500 S. 100 E., Anderson, IN 46013/317-643-2055

Hoffman's Gun Center, Inc., 2600 Berlin Turnpike, Newington, CT 06111/203-666-8827

Hollywood Engineering, 10642 Arminta St., Sun Valley, CA 91352/818-842-8376

Horchler's Gun Shop, 100 Ratlum Rd. RFD, Collinsville, CT 06022/203-379-1977

Hornady Mfg. Co., P.O. Box 1848, Grand Island, NE 68801/800-338-3220, 308-382-1390

Houma Gun Works, 1520 Grand Caillou Rd., Houma, LA 70363/504-872-2782

Howa Machinery, Ltd. (See U.S. importer—Interarms)

Hunter's Den, 4000 McLain Rd., North Little Rock, AR 72116-8026/501-771-1675

Huntington Die Specialties, 601 Oro Dam Blvd., Oroville, CA 95965/916-534-1210; FAX: 916-534-1212

Huntington Sportsman's Store, 601 Oro Dam Blvd., P.O. Box 991, Oroville, CA 95965/916-534-8000

Hutch's, 50 E. Main St., Lehi, UT 84043/801-768-3461

Hutchinson's Gun Repair, 507 Clifton St., Pineville, LA 71360/318-640-4315

I

IAI, 6226 Santos Diaz St., Irwindale, CA 91702/818-334-1200

IGA (See U.S. importer—Stoeger Industries)

Imbert & Smithers, Inc., 1144 El Camino Real, San Carlos, CA 94070/415-593-4207

IMI (See U.S. importer—Magnum Research, Inc.)

INDESAL (See U.S. importer—American Arms, Inc.)

Interarms, 10 Prince St., Alexandria, VA 22314/703-548-1400

Intermountain Arms & Tackle, Inc., 105 E. Idaho St., Meridian, ID 83642/208-888-4911; FAX: 208-888-4381

Intratec, 12405 SW 130th St., Miami, FL 33186/305-232-1821; FAX: 305-253-7207

Ithaca Acquisition Corp., Ithaca Gun Co., 891 Route 34B, King Ferry, NY 13081/315-364-7171; FAX: 315-364-5134

J

J&G Gunsmithing, 625 Vernon St., Roseville, CA 95678/916-782-7075

J.O. Arms & Ammunition Co., 5709 Hartsdale, Houston, TX 77036/713-789-0745; FAX: 713-789-7513

J.T. Gunshop, Inc., d/b/a Carolina Gun & Sports, 1697 Robert C. Byrd Dr., Beckley, WV 25801/304-255-1217

Jack's Lock & Gun Shop, 32 4th St., Fond Du Lac, WI 54935/414-922-4420

Jackalope Gun Shop, 1048 S. 5th St., Douglas, WY 82633/307-358-3441

Jackson, Inc., Bill, 9501 U.S. 19 N., Pinellas Park, FL 34666/813-576-4169

Jaeger, Inc. Paul, /Dunn's, P.O. Box 449, 1 Madison Ave., Grand Junction, TN 38039/901-764-6909; FAX: 901-764-6503

JagerSport, Ltd., One Wholesale Way, Cranston, RI 02920/401-944-9682; FAX: 401-946-2587

Jansma, Jack J., 4320 Kalamazoo Ave., Grand Rapids, MI 49508/616-455-7810; FAX: 616-455-5212

Jason Empire, Inc., 9200 Cody, Overland Park, KS 66214-3259/913-888-0220; FAX: 913-888-0222

Jay's Sports, Inc., North 88 West 15263 Main St., Menomonee Falls, WI 53051/414-251-0550

Jennings Firearms, Inc., 17692 Cowan, Irvine, CA 92714/714-252-7621; FAX: 714-252-7626

Jensen's Custom Ammunition, 5146 E. Pima, Tucson, AZ 85712/602-325-3346; FAX: 602-322-5704

Jim's Gun & Service Center, 514 Tenth Ave. S.E., Aberdeen, SD 57401/605-225-9111

Jim's Sporting Goods, 1307 Malcolm Ave., Newport, AR 72112/501-523-5165

Jim's Trading Post, #10 Southwest Plaza, Pine Bluff, AR 71603/501-534-8591

Joe's Gun Shop, 4430 14th St., Dorr, MI 49323/616-877-4615

Joe's Gun Shop, 5215 W. Edgemont Ave., Phoenix, AZ 85035/602-233-0694

John Q's Quality Gunsmithing, 5165 Auburn Blvd., Sacramento, CA 95841/916-344-7669

Johnson Gunsmithing, Don, N15515 Country Rd. 566, Powers, MI 49874/906-497-5757

Johnson Service, Inc., W., 3654 N. Adrian Rd., Adrian, MI 49221/517-265-2545

Jordan Gun Shop, 28 Magnolia Dr., Tifton, GA 31794/912-382-4251

Jovino Co., Inc., John, 5 Center Market Pl., New York, NY 10013/212-925-4881

JSL (Hereford) Ltd. (See U.S. importer—Specialty Shooters Supply, Inc.)

Junior's Gun & Lock Shop, 100 E. Grand St., Ponca City, OK 74601/405-762-4553

K

K&M Services, 5430 Salmon Run Rd., Dover, PA 17315

K-Sports Imports, Inc., 2755 Thompson Creek Rd., Pomona, CA 91767/909-392-2345; FAX: 909-392-2354

K.B.I., Inc., P.O. Box 5440, Harrisburg, PA 17110-0440/717-540-8518; FAX: 717-540-8567

Kahles USA, P.O. Box 81071, Warwick, RI 02888/800-752-4537; FAX: 717-540-8567

Kahr Arms, P.O. Box 220, Blauvelt, NY 10913/914-353-5996; FAX: 914-353-7833/800-453-2767, 210-542-2767

Karrer's Gunatorium, 5323 N. Argonne Rd., Spokane, WA 99212/509-924-3030

Kassnar (See U.S. importer—K.B.I., Inc.)

Keeley, John L., 671 Ridge Rd., Spring City, PA 19475/215-469-6874

Keidel's Gunsmithing Service, 927 Jefferson Ave., Washington, PA 15301/412-222-6379

Keller Gunsmithing, 147 N. Miami Ave., Bradford, OH 45308/513-448-2424

Keller's Co., Inc., Rt. 4, Box 1257, Burlington, CT 06013/203-583-2220

Keng's Firearms Specialty, Inc., 875 Wharton Dr. SW, Atlanta, GA 30336/404-691-7611; FAX: 404-505-8445

Kesselring Gun Shop, 400 Hwy. 99 North, Burlington, WA 98233/206-724-3113; FAX: 206-724-7003

Kick's Sport Center, 300 Goodge St., Claxton, GA 30417/912-739-1734

Kimber of America, Inc., 9039 SE Jannsen Rd., Clackamas, OR 97015/503-656-1704; FAX: 503-657-5695

Kimel Industries, 3800 Old Monroe Rd., P.O. Box 335, Matthews, NC 28105/800-438-9288; FAX: 704-821-6339

King's Gun Shop, Inc., 32301 Walter's Hwy., Franklin, VA 23851/804-562-4725
King's Gun Works, 1837 W. Glenoaks Blvd., Glendale, CA 91201/818-956-6010
Kirkpatrick, Gunsmith, Larry, 707 79th St., Lubbock, TX 79404/806-745-5308
Klelon, Gunsmith, Dave, 57 Kittleberger Park, Webster, NY 14580/716-872-2256
Knight's Mfg. Co., 7750 9th St. SW, Vero Beach, FL 32968/407-778-3700; FAX: 407-569-2955
Kopp, Terry K., 1301 Franklin, Lexington, MO 64067/816-259-2636
Korth (See U.S. importer—Mandall Shooting Supplies, Inc.)
Kotila Gun Shop, Rt. #2, Box 212, Cokato, MN 55321/612-286-5636
Kowa Optimed, Inc., 20001 S. Vermont Ave., Torrance, CA 90502/310-327-1913; FAX: 310-327-4177
Krebs Gunsmithing, 7417 N. Milwaukee Ave., Niles, IL 60714/708-647-6994
Krico/Kriegeskorte GmbH, A. (See U.S. importer—Mandall Shooting Supplies, Inc.)
Krieghoff Gun Co., H. (See U.S. importer—Krieghoff International, Inc.)
Krieghoff International, Inc., 7528 Easton Rd., Ottsville, PA 18942/215-847-5173; FAX: 215-847-8691

L

L&M Firing Line, Inc., 20 S. Potomac St., Aurora, CO 80012/303-363-0041
L&S Technologies, Inc. (See Aimtech Mount Systems)
L'Armurier Alain Bouchard, Inc., 420 Route 143, Ulverton, Quebec CANADA J0B 2J0/819-826-6611
L.A.R. Manufacturing, Inc., 4133 W. Farm Rd., West Jordan, UT 84088/801-255-7106; FAX: 801-569-1972
Labs Air Gun Shop, 2307 N. 62nd St., Omaha, NE 68104/402-553-0990
Lafayette Shooters, 3530 Amb Caffrey Parkway, Lafayette, LA 70503/318-988-1191
Laibs Gunsmithing, North Hwy. 23, R.R. 1, Spicer, MN 56288/612-796-2686
Lakefield Arms Ltd., 248 Water St., Lakefield, Ont. K0L 2H0, CANADA/705-652-6735, 705-652-8000; FAX: 705-652-8431
Laser Devices, Inc., 2 Harris Ct. A-4, Monterey, CA 93940/408-373-0701; FAX: 408-373-0903
Laseraim Arms, Sub. of Emerging Technologies, Inc., P.O. Box 3548, Little Rock, AR 72203/501-375-2227; FAX: 501-372-1445
Laurona Armas S.A. (See U.S. importer—Galaxy Imports Ltd., Inc.)
Lawson's Custom Firearms, Inc., Art, 313 S. Magnolia Ave., Ocala, FL 32671/904-629-7793
Lebeau-Courally (See U.S. importer—New England Arms Co.)
Lee Precision, Inc., 4275 Hwy. U, Hartford, WI 53027/414-673-3075
LeFever & Sons, Inc., Frank, RD 1, Box 31, Lee Center, NY 13363/315-337-6722
Leica USA, Inc., 156 Ludlow Ave., Northvale, NJ 07647/201-767-7500; FAX: 201-767-8666
Leo's Custom Stocks, 1767 Washington Ave., Library, PA 15129/412-835-4126
Les Gun & Pawn Shop, 1423 New Boston Rd., Texarkana, TX 75501/903-793-2201
Leupold, P.O. Box 688, Beaverton, OR 97075/503-526-1491; FAX: 503-526-1475
Levan's Sport Goods, 433 N. Ninth St., Lebanon, PA 17042/717-273-3148
Lew's Mountaineer Gunsmithing, Route 2, Box 330A, Charleston, WV 25314/304-344-3745
Lewis Arms, 1575 Hooksett Rd., Hooksett, NH 03106/603-485-7334
Ljutic Industries, Inc., 732 N. 16th Ave., Yakima, WA 98902/509-248-0476; FAX: 509-457-5141
Llama Gabilondo Y Cia (See U.S. importer—SGS Importers International, Inc.)
Lock Stock & Barrel, 775 S.E. 6th St. (rear), Grants Pass, OR 97526/503-474-0775
Loftin & Taylor, 2619 N. Main St., Jacksonville, FL 32206/904-353-9634
Log Cabin Sport Shop, 8010 Lafayette Rd., Lodi, OH 44254/216-948-1082
Lolo Sporting Goods, 1026 Main St., Lewiston, ID 83501/208-743-1031
Lone Star Guns, Inc., 2452 Avenue "K", Plano, TX 75074/214-424-4501; 800-874-7923
Long Beach Uniform Co., Inc., 2789 Long Beach Blvd., Long Beach, CA 90806/310-424-0220
Long Gunsmithing Ltd., W.R., 2007 Brook Rd. North, Cobourg, Ontario CANADA K9A 4S3/416-372-5955
Longacres, Inc., 358 Chestnut St., Abilene, TN 79602/915-672-9521
Lorcin Engineering Co., Inc., 10427 San Sevaine Way, Ste. A, Mira Loma, CA 91752/909-360-1406; FAX: 909-360-0623
Lounsbury Sporting Goods, Bob, 104 North St., Middletown, NY 10940/914-343-1808
Lusignant Armurier, A. Richard, 15820 St. Michel, St. Hyacinthe, Quebec, CANADA, J2T 3R7/514-773-7997
Lutter, Robert E., 3547 Auer Dr., Ft. Wayne, IN 46835/219-485-8319
Lyman Products Corp., Rt. 147 West St., Middlefield, CT 06455/203-349-3421; FAX: 203-349-3586

M

M.O.A. Corp., 2451 Old Camden Pike, Eaton, OH 45320/513-456-3669
Mac-1 Distributors, 13974 Van Ness Ave., Gardena, CA 90249/310-327-3582
Magasin Latulippe, Inc., 637 St. Vallier O, P.O. Box 395, Quest, Quebec, CANADA G1K 6W8/418-529-0024
Magma Engineering Co., P.O. Box 161, Queen Creek, AZ 85242/602-987-9008; FAX: 602-987-0148
Magnum Gun Service, 357 Welsh Track Rd., Newark, DE 19702/302-454-0141
Magnum Research, Inc., 7110 University Ave., Minneapolis, MN 55432/612-574-1868; FAX: 612-574-0109
Mandall Shooting Supplies, Inc., 3616 N. Scottsdale Rd., Scottsdale, AZ 85252/602-945-2553; FAX: 602-949-0734
Magnum Research, Inc., 7110 University Ave., Minneapolis, MN 55432/612-574-1868; FAX: 612-574-0109
Manufacture D'Armes Des Pyrenees Francaises (See Unique/M.A.P.F.)
Marksman Products, 5482 Argosy Dr., Huntington Beach, CA 92649/714-898-7535, 800-822-8005; FAX: 714-891-0782
Marlin Firearms Co., 100 Kenna Dr., New Haven, CT 06473/203-239-5621; FAX: 203-234-7991
Marocchi F.lli S.p.A. (See U.S. importers—PSI, Inc.; Sile Distributors)
Marshall Gun Shop, 1345 Chambers Rd., Dellwood, MO 63135/314-522-8359
Martin Gun Shop, Henry, 206 Kay Lane, Shreveport, LA 71115/318-797-1119
Martin's Gun Shop, 3600 Laurel Ave., Natchez, MS 39120/601-442-0784
Mashburn Arms Co., Inc., 1218 North Pennsylvania Ave., Oklahoma City, OK 73107/405-236-5151
Master Gunsmiths, Inc., 21621 Ticonderoga, Houston, TX 77044/713-459-1631
Matt's 10X Gunsmithing, Inc., 5906 Castle Rd., Duluth, MN 55803/218-721-4210
Maverick Arms, Inc., 7 Grasso Ave., P.O. Box 497, North Haven, CT 06473/203-230-5300; FAX: 203-230-5420
May & Company, Inc., P.O. Box 1111, 838 W. Capitol St., Jackson, MS 39209/601-354-5781
McBride's Guns, Inc., 2915 San Gabriel, Austin, TX 78705/512-472-3532

McClelland Gun Shop, 1533 Centerville Rd., Dallas, TX 75228-2597/214-321-0231
McDaniel Co., Inc., B., 8880 Pontiac Tr., P.O. Box 119, South Lyon, MI 48178/313-437-8989
McGuns, W.H., N. 22nd Ave. at Osborn St., Humboldt, TN 38343/901-784-5742
McMillan Bros. Rifle Co., Inc., P.O. Box 86549, Phoenix, AZ 85080/602-780-2115; FAX: 602-581-3825
McMillan Gunworks, Inc., 302 W. Melinda Lane, Phoenix, AZ 85027/602-582-9627; FAX: 602-582-5178
MCS, Inc., 34 Delmar Dr., Brookfield, CT 06804/203-775-1013; FAX: 203-775-9462
MEC, Inc., 715 South St., Mayville, WI 53050/414-387-4500
MEC-Gar S.R.L. (See U.S. importer—MEC-Gar U.S.A., Inc.)
MEC-Gar U.S.A., Inc., Box 112, 500B Monroe Turnpike, Monroe, CT 06468/203-635-8662; FAX: 203-635-8662
Merkel Freres (See U.S. importer—GSI, Inc.)
Metro Rod & Reel, 236 S.E. Grand Ave., Portland, OR 97214/503-232-3193
Meydag, Peter, 12114 East 16th, Tulsa, OK 74128/918-437-1928
Miclean, Bill, 499 Theta Ct., San Jose, CA 95123/408-224-1445
Midwest Sporting Goods Co., Inc., 8565 Plainfield Rd., Lyons, IL 60534/708-447-4848
Midwestern Shooters Supply, Inc., 150 Main St., Lomira, WI 53048/414-269-4995
Mike's Crosman Service, 5995 Renwood Dr., Winston-Salem, NC 27106/919-922-1031
Mill Creek Sport Center, 8180 Main St., Dexter, MI 48104/313-426-3445
Miller Arms, Inc., P.O. Box 260 Purl St., St. Onge, SD 57779/605-642-5160; FAX: 605-642-5160
Miller's Sport Shop, 2 Summit View Dr., Mountaintop, PA 18707/717-474-6931
Millers Gun Shop, 915 23rd St., Gulfport, MS 39501/601-684-1765
Millie "D" Enterprises, 1241 W. Calle Concordia, Tucson, AZ 85737/602-297-4887
Milliken's Gun Shop, Rt. 4, Box 167, Elm Grove, WV 26003/304-242-0827
Mines Gun Shack, Rt. 4 Box 4623, Tullahoma, TN 37388/615-455-1414
Mirador Optical Corp., P.O. Box 11614, Marina Del Rey, CA 90295-7614/310-821-5587; FAX: 310-305-0386
Miroku, B.C./Daly, Charles (See U.S. importers—Bell's Legendary Country Wear; British Sporting Arms; U.S. distributor—Outdoor Sports Headquarters, Inc.)
Mitchell Arms, Inc., 3400 W. MacArthur Blvd., Ste. 1, Santa Ana, CA 92704/714-957-5711; FAX: 714-957-5732
MKS Supply, Inc., 174 S. Mulberry St., Mansfield, OH 44902/419-522-8330
Moates Sport Shop, Bob, 10418 Hull St. Rd., Midlothian, VA 23112/804-276-2293
Modern Guncraft, 148 N. Branford Rd., Collinsville, CT 06492/203-265-1015
Modern MuzzleLoading, Inc., 234 Airport Rd., P.O. Box 130, Centerville, IA 52544/515-856-2626; FAX: 515-856-2628
Moneymaker Guncraft Corp., 1420 Military Ave., Omaha, NE 68131/402-556-0226
Montana Armory, Inc., 100 Centennial Dr., Big Timber, MT 59011/406-932-4353
Montana Gun Works, 3017 10th Ave. S., Great Falls, MT 59405/406-761-4346
Moore & Co., Wm. Larkin, 31360 Via Colinas, Suite 109, Westlake Village, CA 91361/818-889-4160; FAX: 818-889-1986
Moreau, Gunsmith, Pete, 1807 S. Erie, Bay City, MI 48706/517-893-7106
Morini (See U.S. importer—Mandall Shooting Supplies, Inc.)
Morrison, Carl Bill, Middle Rd., Bradford, ME 04410/207-327-1116
Mossberg & Sons, Inc., O.F. (See page 457)
Mowrey Gun Works, P.O. Box 246, Waldron, IN 46182/317-525-6181; FAX: 317-525-6181
Mueschke Manufacturing Co., 1003 Columbia St., Houston, TX 77008/713-869-7073
Mulvey's Marine & Sport Shop, 994 E. Broadway, Monticello, NY 12701/914-794-2000

N

N.A. Guns, Inc., 10220 Florida Blvd., Baton Rouge, LA 70815/504-272-3620
Nagel Gun Shop, Inc., 6201 San Pedro Ave., San Antonio, TX 78216/210-342-5420; 210-342-9893
Nationwide Sports Distributors, 70 James Way, Southampton, PA 18966/215-322-2050; FAX: 215-322-5972
Navy Arms Co., 689 Bergen Blvd., Ridgefield, NJ 07657/201-945-2500; FAX: 201-945-6859
Nelson's Engine Shop, 620 State St., Cedar Falls, IA 50613/319-266-4497
Nesika Bay Precision, 22239 Big Valley Rd., Poulsbo, WA 98370/206-697-3830
Nevada Air Guns, 3297 "J" Las Vegas Blvd. N., N. Las Vegas, NV 89115/702-643-8532
Nevada Cartridge Co., 44 Montgomery St., Suite 500, San Francisco, CA 94104/415-925-9394; FAX: 415-925-9396
New Advantage Arms Corp., 2843 N. Alvernon Way, Tucson, AZ 85712/602-881-7444; FAX: 602-323-0949
New England Arms Co., Box 278, Lawrence Lane, Kittery Point, ME 03905/207-439-0593; FAX: 207-439-6726
New England Firearms, 60 Industrial Rowe, Gardner, MA 01440/508-632-9393; FAX: 508-632-2300
Newby, Stewart, Gunsmith, Main & Cross Streets, Newburgh, Ontario CANADA K0K 2S0/613-378-6613
Nichols Sports Optics, P.O. Box 37669, Omaha, NE 68137/402-339-3530; FAX: 402-330-8029
Nicholson's Gunsmithing, 33 Hull St., Shelton, CT 06484/203-924-5635
Nikon, Inc., 1300 Walt Whitman Rd., Melville, NY 11747/516-547-4200
Norica (See U.S. importers—American Arms, Inc.)
Norinco (See U.S. importers—Century International Arms, Inc.; ChinaSports, Inc.; Interarms)
North American Arms, 2150 South 950 East, Provo, UT 84606-6285/800-821-5783, 801-374-9990; FAX: 801-374-9998
Northern Precision Airguns, 1161 Grove St., Tawas City, MI 48763/517-362-6949
Northern Virginia Gun Works, Inc., 7518-K Fullerton Road, Springfield, VA 22150/703-644-6504
Northland Sport Center, 1 Mile W. on U.S. 2, Bagley, MN 56621/218-694-2464
Northwest Arms Service, 720 S. Second St., Atwood, KS 67730/913-626-3700
Nu-Line Guns, Inc., 1053 Caulks Hill Rd., Harvester, MO 63304/314-441-4500; FAX: 314-447-5018
Nusbaum Enterprises, Inc., 1364 Ridgewood Dr., Mobile, AL 38808/205-344-1079
Nygord Precision Products, P.O. Box 8394, La Crescenta, CA 91224/818-352-3027; FAX: 818-352-3378

O

Oakland Custom Arms, Inc., 4690 W. Walton Blvd., Waterford, MI 48329/810-674-8261
Old Dominion Engravers, 100 Progress Drive, Lynchburg, VA 24502/804-237-4450
Old Western Scrounger, Inc., 12924 Hwy. A-I2, Montague, CA 96064/916-459-5445; FAX: 916-459-3944

Olympic Arms, Inc., 624 Old Pacific Hwy. SE, Olympia, WA 98503/206-456-3471; FAX: 206-491-3447

On Target Gunshop, Inc., 6984 West Main St., Kalamazoo, MI 49009/616-375-4570

Oregon Arms, Inc., 790 Stevens St., Medford, OR 97504-6746/503-560-4040

Orvis Co., The, Rt. 7, Manchester, VT 05254/802-362-3622 ext. 283; FAX: 802-362-3525

Oshman's Sporting Goods, Inc., 975 Gessner, Houston, TX 77024/713-467-1155

Ott's Gun Service, Rt. 2, Box 169A, Atmore, AL 36502/205-862-2588

Ott's Gunsmith Service, RR 1, Box 259, Decatur, IL 62526/217-875-3468

Outdoor America Store, 1925 N. MacArthur Blvd., Oklahoma City, OK 73127/405-789-0051

Outdoorsman Sporting Goods Co., The, 1707 Radner Ct., Geneva, IL 60134/708-232-9518

Outdoorsman, Inc., Village West Shopping Center, Fargo, ND 58103/701-282-0131

Outpost, The, 2451 E. Maple Rapids Rd., Eureka, MI 48833/517-224-9562

Ozark Shooters, Inc., P.O. Box 6518, Branson, MO 65616/417-587-3093

P

Pachmayr Ltd., 1875 S. Mountain Ave., Monrovia, CA 91016/818-357-7771, 800-423-9704; FAX: 818-358-7251

Pacific International Service Co., Mountain Way, P.O. Box 3, Janesville, CA 96114/916-253-2218

Paducah Shooters Supply, Inc., 3919 Cairo St., Paducah, KY 42001/502-443-3758

Para-Ordnance Mfg., Inc. (See U.S. importer—Para-Ordnance, Inc.)

Pardini Armi Commerciale Srl (See U.S. importers—MCS, Inc.; Nygord Precision Products)

Pasadena Gun Center, 206 E. Shaw, Pasadena, TX 77506/713-472-0417; FAX: 713-472-1322

Paul Co., The, 27385 Pressonville Rd., Wellsville, KS 66092/913-883-4444; FAX: 913-883-2525

Pecatonica River Longrifle, 5205 Noddingham Dr., Rockford, IL 61111/815-968-1995; FAX: 815-968-1996

Pedersen & Son, 2717 S. Pere Marquette Hwy., Ludington, MI 49431/616-843-2061

Pedersoli Davide & C. (See U.S. importers—Beauchamp & Son, Inc.; Cabela's; Dixie Gun Works; EMF Co., Inc.; Navy Arms Co.)

Pekin Gun & Sporting Goods, 1304 Derby St., Pekin, IL 61554/309-347-6060

Pentax Corp., 35 Inverness Dr. E., Englewood, CO 80112/303-799-8000

Perazzi USA, Inc., 1207 S. Shamrock Ave., Monrovia, CA 91016/818-303-0068

Perazzi m.a.p. S.P.A. (See U.S. importer—Perazzi USA, Inc.)

Perry's of Wendell, Inc., P.O. Box 826, Wendell, NC 27591/919-365-6391

Pete's Gun Shop, 31 Columbia St., Adams, MA 01220/413-743-0780

Peters Stahl GmbH (See U.S. importers—McMillan Gunworks, Inc.; Olympic Arms)

Phelps Mfg. Co., Box 2266, Evansville, IN 47714/812-476-8791

Phillips, D.J., Gunsmith, Rt. 1, N31-W22087 Shady Ln., Pewaukee, WI 53072/414-691-2165

Phoenix Armoury, Inc., 248 Miami Ave., Norristown, PA 19403/215-539-0733

Phoenix Arms, 1420 S. Archibald Ave., Ontario, CA 91761/909-947-4843; FAX: 909-947-6798

PHOXX Shooters Supply, 5813 Watt Ave., N. Highlands, CA 95660/916-348-9827

Pintos Gun Shop, 835 N. Central Bldg. B, Kent, WA 98032/206-859-6333

Pioneer Arms Co., 355 Lawrence Rd., Broomall, OA 19008/215-356-5203

Piotti (See U.S. importer—Moore & Co., Wm. Larkin)

Plaza Gunworks, Inc., 983 Gasden Highway, Birmingham, AL 35235/205-836-6206

Poly Technologies, Inc. (See U.S. importer—Keng's Firearms Specialty, Inc.)

Ponsness/Warren, P.O. Box 8, Rathdrum, ID 83858/208-687-2231; FAX: 208-687-2232

Poor Borch's, Inc., 1204 E. College Dr., Marshall, MN 56258/507-532-4880

Potter Gunsmithing, 13960 Boxhorn Dr., Muskego, WI 53150/414-425-4830

Powell & Son Ltd., William (See U.S. importer—Bell's Legendary Country Wear)

Precision Airgun Sales, Inc., 5139 Warrensville Center Rd., Maple Hts., OH 44137-1906/216-587-5005

Precision Arms & Gunsmithing Ltd., Hwy. 27 & King Road Box 809, Nobleton, Ontario, CANADA L0G 1N0/416-859-0965

Precision Gun Works, 4717 State Rd. 44, Oshkosh, WI 54904/414-233-2274

Precision Gunsmithing, 2723 W. 6th St., Amarillo, TX 79106/806-376-7223

Precision Pellet, 1018 Erwin Dr., Joppa, MD 21085/410-679-8179

Precision Reloading, Inc., P.O. Box 122, Stafford Springs, CT 06076/203-684-7979; FAX: 203-684-6788

Precision Sales International, Inc., P.O. Box 1776, Westfield, MA 01086/413-562-5055; FAX: 413-562-5056

Precision Sport Optics, 15571 Producer Lane, Unit G, Huntington Beach, CA 92649/714-891-1309; FAX: 714-892-6920

Preuss Gun Shop, 4545 E. Shepherd, Clovis, CA 93612/209-299-6248

Princess Anne Marine & Sport Center, 2371 Virginia Beach Blvd., Virginia Beach, VA 23454/804-340-6269

Professional Armaments, Inc., 4555 S. 300 West, Murray, UT 84107/801-268-2598

Q

Quality Arms, Inc., Box 19477, Dept. GD, Houston, TX 77224/713-870-8377; FAX: 713-870-8524

Quality Firearms of Idaho, Inc., 114 13th Ave. S., Nampa, ID 83651/208-466-1631

Quality Firearms, Inc., 4530 NW 135 Street, Opa Locka, FL 33054

Quality Parts Co./Bushmaster Firearms, 999 Roosevelt Trail, Bldg. 3, Windham, ME 04062/800-998-7928, 207-892-2005; FAX: 207-892-8068

R

R&R Shooters Supply, W6553 North Rd., Mauston, WI 53948/608-847-4562

R.D.P. Tool Co., Inc., 49162 McCoy Ave., East Liverpool, OH 43920/216-385-5129

Rajo Corporation, 2027 W. Franklin St., Evansville, IN 47712/812-422-6945

Ralph's Gun Shop, 200 Fourth St., South, Niverville, Manitoba, CANADA R0A 1E0/204-338-4581

Ram-Line, Inc., 545 Thirty-One Rd., Grand Junction, CO 81504/303-434-4500; FAX: 303-434-4004

Randy's Gun Repair, P.O. Box 106, Tabustinac, N.B. CANADA E0C 2A0/506-779-4768

Ranging, Inc., Routes 5 & 20, East Bloomfield, NY 14443/716-657-6161

Rapids Gun Shop, 7811 Buffalo Ave., Niagara Falls, NY 14304/716-283-7873

Ray's Gunsmith Shop, 3199 Elm Ave., Grand Junction, CO 81504/303-434-6162

Ray's Liquor and Sporting Goods, 1956 Solano St., Box 677, Corning, CA 96021/916-824-5625

Ray's Rod & Reel Service, 414 Pattie St., Wichita, KS 67211/316-267-9462

Ray's Sport Shop, Inc., 559 Route 22, North Plainfield, NJ 07060/908-561-4400

Ray's Sporting Goods, 730 Singleton Blvd., Dallas, TX 75212/214-747-7916

RCBS, Div. of Blount, Inc., 605 Oro Dam Blvd., Oroville, CA 95965/800-533-5000, 916-533-5191

Red's Gunsmithing, P.O. Box 1251, Chickaloon, AK 99674/907-745-4500

Redding Reloading, Inc., 1089 Starr Rd., Cortland, NY 13045/607-753-3331; FAX: 607-756-8445

Redfield, Inc., 5800 E. Jewell Ave., Denver, CO 80224/303-757-6411; FAX: 303-756-2338

Reliable Gun & Tackle, Ltd., 3227 Fraser St., Vancouver, British Columbia CANADA V5V 4B8/604-874-4710

Reloading Center, 515 W. Main St., Burley, ID 83318/208-678-5053

Remington Arms Co., Inc. (See page 457)

Reynolds Gun Shop, Inc., 3502A S. Broadway, Tyler, TX 75702/903-592-1531

Rice Hardware, 15 S.W. First Ave., Gainesville, FL 32601/904-377-0892

Richland Gun Shop, 207 Park St., Richland, PA 17087/717-866-4246

Richmond Gun Shop, 517 E. Main St., Richmond, VA 23219/804-644-7207

Rigby & Co., John (See U.S. importer—Griffin & Howe, Inc.)

River Bend Sport Shop, 230 Grand Seasons Dr., Waupaca, WI 54981/715-258-3583

Rizzini, Battista (See U.S. importer—Alessandri & Son, Lou)

Rizzini, F.LLI (See U.S. importers—Moore & Co. Wm. Larkin; New England Arms Co.)

Robinson's Sporting Goods, Ltd., 1307 Broad St., Victoria, British Columbia CANADA V8W 2A8/604-385-3429

Ron's Gun Repair, 1212 Benson Rd., Sioux Falls, SD 57104/605-338-7398

Ross Sporting Goods, 204 W. Main St, Farmington, NM 87401/505-325-1062

Rossi S.A., Amadeo (See U.S. importer—Interarms)

Roy's Antiques & Things, Route 1 Box 303, Mountain Rest, SC 29664/803-638-5340

Roy's Sport Shop, 10 Second St. NE, Watertown, SD 57201/605-886-7508

RPM, 15481 N. Twin Lakes Dr., Tucson, AZ 85737/602-825-1233; FAX: 602-825-3333

Rue's Gunsmithing, 664 S. Magnolia, El Cajon, CA 92020/619-447-2169

Ruko Products, Inc., P.O. Box 1181, Buffalo, NY 14240-1181/905-874-2707; FAX: 905-826-1353

Rusk Gun Shop, Inc., 6904 Watts Rd., Madison, WI 53719/608-274-8740

Russel's Sporting Goods, 8228 Macleod Trail SE, Calgary, Alberta, CANADA T2M 2B8/403-276-9222

Rutko Corp. d/b/a Stonewall Range, 100 Ken-Mar Dr., Broadview Heights, OH 44147/216-526-0029

RWS (See U.S. importer—Dynamit Nobel-RWS, Inc.)

S

S.E.M. Gun Works, 3204 White Horse Rd., Greenville, SC 29611/803-295-2948

S.K. Guns, Inc., 3041A Main Ave., Fargo, ND 58103/701-293-4867; FAX: 701-232-0001

Safari Arms/SGW (See Olympic Arms, Inc.)

Saffle Repair Service, 312 Briar Wood Dr., Jackson, MS 39206/601-956-4968

Sako Ltd. (See U.S. importer—Stoeger Industries)

San Marco (See U.S. importers—Cape Outfitters; EMF Co., Inc.)

Sanders Custom Gun Shop, P.O. Box 5967-2031, Bloomingdale Ave., Augusta, GA 30906/706-798-5220

Sanders Gun Shop, 3001 Fifth St., P.O. Box 4181, Meridian, MS 39301/601-485-5301

Saskatoon Gunsmith Shoppe, Ltd., 2310 Avenue "C" N., Saskatoon, Saskatchewan, CANADA S7L 5X5/306-244-2023

Sauer (See U.S. importer—Paul Co., The)

Savage Arms, Inc., Springdale Rd., Westfield, MA 01085/413-568-7001; FAX: 413-562-7764

Scalzo's Sporting Goods, 207 Odell Ave., Endicott, NY 13760/607-746-7586

Scattergun Technologies, Inc., 518 3rd Ave. S., Nashville, TN 37210/615-254-1441

Scharch Mfg., Inc., 10325 Co. Rd. 120, Unit C, Salida, CO 81201/719-539-7242

Schmidt & Bender, Inc., Brook Rd., P.O. Box 134, Meriden, NH 03770/603-469-3565, 800-468-3450; FAX: 603-469-3471

Schmidt, Herbert (See U.S. importer—Sportarms of Florida)

Schultheis Sporting Goods, 6 Main St., Arkport, NY 14807/607-295-7485

Sea Gull Marina, 1400 Lake, Two Rivers, WI 54241/414-794-7533

Seecamp Co., Inc., L.W., P.O. Box 255, New Haven, CT 06502/203-877-3429

Selin Gunsmith, Ltd., Del, 2803 28th Street, Vernon, British Columbia, CANADA V1T 4Z5/604-545-6413

SGS Importers International, Inc., 1750 Brielle Ave., Unit B1, Wanamassa, NJ 07712/908-493-0302; FAX: 908-493-0301

Shaler Eagle, 192 Arrow Wood, Jonesbrough, TN 37659/615-753-7620

Shamburg's Wholesale Spt. Gds., 403 Frisco Ave., Clinton, OK 73601/405-323-0209

Shapel's Gun Shop, 1708 N. Liberty, Boise, ID 83704/208-375-6159

Sharps Arms Co., Inc., C. (See Montana Armory, Inc.)

Shepherd Scope Ltd., Box 189, Waterloo, NE 68069/402-779-2424; FAX: 402-779-4010

Sheridan USA, Inc., Austin, P.O. Box 577, Durham, CT 06422

Shiloh Rifle Mfg., P.O. Box 279, Big Timber, MT 59011/406-932-4454; FAX: 406-932-5627

Shooters Supply, 1120 Tieton Dr., Yakima, WA 98902

Shooting Gallery, The, 1619 Penna, Weirton, WV 26062/304-723-3298

Siegle's Gunshop, Inc., 508 W. MacArthur Blvd., Oakland, CA 94609/415-655-8789

Sievert's Guns 4107 W. Northern, Pueblo, CO 81005/719-564-0035

SIG (See U.S. importer—Mandall Shooting Supplies, Inc.)

SIG-Sauer (See U.S. importer—Sigarms, Inc.)

Sigarms, Inc., Industrial Drive, Corporate Park, Exeter, NH 03833/603-772-2302; FAX: 603-772-9082

Sile Distributors, Inc., 7 Centre Market Pl., New York, NY 10013/212-925-4389; FAX: 212-925-3149

Sillman, Hal, Associated Services, 1514 NE 205 Terrace, Miami, FL 33179/305-651-4450

Simmons Enterprises, Ernie, 709 East Elizabethtown Rd., Manheim, PA 17545/717-664-4040

Simmons Gun Repair/Sauer, 700 S. Rodgers Rd., Olathe, KS 66062/913-782-3131

Simmons Outdoor Corp., 2120 Killearney Way, Tallahassee, FL 32308-3402/904-878-5100; FAX: 904-878-0300

Sipes Gun Shop, 7415 Asher Ave., Little Rock, AR 72204/501-565-8480

SKB Arms Co. (See U.S. importers—G.U., Inc.)

Skeet's Gun Shop, Rt. 3, Box 235, Tahlequah, OK 74464/918-456-4749

Smith & Smith Gun Shop, Inc., 2589 Oscar Johnson Drive, Charleston Heights, SC 29405/803-744-2024

Smith & Wesson (See page 457)
Smith's Lawn & Marine Svc., 9100 Main St., Clarence, NY 14031/716-633-7868
Societa Armi Bresciane Srl (See U.S. importer—Cape Outfitters)
Sodak Sport & Bait, 850 South Hwy 281, Aberdeen, SD 57401/605-225-2737
Solothurn (See U.S. importer—Sile Distributors)
Solvay Home & Outdoor Center, 102 First St., Solvay, NY 13209/315-468-6285
Somerset Sports Shop, 140 W. Sanner St., Somerset, PA 15501/814-445-6214
Southland Gun Works, Inc., 1134 Hartsville Rd., Darlington, SC 29532/803-393-6291
Southwest Airguns, Box 132 Route 8, Lake Charles, LA 70605-9304/318-474-6038
Southwest Shooters Supply, Inc., 1940 Linwood Blvd., Oklahoma City, OK 73106/405-235-4476
Specialty Shooters Supply, Inc., 3325 Griffin Rd., Suite 9mm, Fort Lauderdale, FL 33317
Speer Products, Div. of Blount, Inc., P.O. Box 856, Lewiston, ID 83501/208-746-2351; FAx: 208-746-2915
Sport Shop, The, 100 Will Roger Dr., Kingfisher, OK 73750/405-375-5130
Sportarms of Florida, 5555 NW 36 Ave., Miami, FL 33142/305-635-2411; FAX: 305-634-4536
Sporting Arms Mfg., Inc., 801 Hall Ave., Littlefield, TX 79339/806-385-5665; FAX: 806-385-3394
Sporting Goods, Inc., 232 North Lincoln St., Hastings, NE 68901/402-462-6132
Sports Mart, The, 828 Ford St., Ogdensburg, NY 13669/315-393-2865
Sports World, Inc., 5800 S. Lewis Ave., Suite 154, Tulsa, OK 74105/918-742-4027
Sportsman's Center, U.S. Hwy. 130, Box 731, Bordentown, NJ 08505/609-298-5300
Sportsman's Depot, 644 Miami St., Urban, OH 43078/513-653-4429
Sportsman's Haven, RR 4, Box 541, 14695 E. Pike Rd., Cambridge, OH 43725/614-432-7243
Sportsman's Paradise Gunsmith, 640 Main St., Pineville, LA 71360/318-443-6041
Sportsman's Shop, 101 W. Main St., New Holland, PA 17557/717-354-4311
Sportsmen's Exchange & Western Gun Traders, Inc., 560 S. "C" St., Oxnard, CA 93030/805-483-1917
Sportsmen's Repair Ctr., Inc., 106 S. High St., Box 134, Columbus Groves, OH 45830/419-659-5818
Spradlin's, 113 Arthur St., Pueblo, CO 81004/719-543-9462
Springfield, Inc., 420 W. Main St., Geneseo, IL 61254/309-944-5631; FAX: 309-944-3676
Stalwart Corp., P.O. Box 357, Pocatello, ID 83204/208-232-7899; FAX: 208-232-0815
Stan's Gun Repair, RR #2 Box 48, Westbrook, MN 56183-9521/507-274-5649
Star Bonifacio Echeverria S.A. (See U.S. importer—Interarms)
Star Machine Works, 418 10th Ave., San Diego, CA 92101/619-232-3216
Starnes, Ken, 32900 SW Laurelview Rd., Hillsboro, OR 97123/503-628-0705
Steyr Airguns (See U.S. importers—GSI, Inc./Nygord Presion Products)
Steyr Mannlicher AG (See U.S. importer—GSI, Inc.)
Steyr-Daimler-Puch (See U.S. importer—GSI, Inc.)
Stocker's Shop, 5199 Mahoning Ave., Warren, OH 44483/216-847-9579
Stoeger Industries (See page 457)
Stratemeyer, H.P., Winch Hill Rd., P.O. Box 489, Langdon, NH 03602/603-835-6130
Sturm, Ruger & Co., Inc., Lacey Place, Southport, CT 06490/203-259-7843
Sundance Industries, Inc., 25163 W. Avenue Stanford, Valencia, CA 91355/805-257-4807
Surplus Center, 621 S.E. Cass, Roseburg, OR 97470/503-672-4312
Survival Arms, Inc., 4500 Pine Cone Place, Cocoa, FL 32922/407-633-4880; FAX: 407-633-4975
Swarovski Optik North America Ltd., One Wholesale Way, Cranston, RI 02920/401-946-2220, 800-426-3089; FAX: 401-946-2587
Swift Instruments, Inc., 952 Dorchester Ave., Boston, MA 02125/617-436-2960; FAX: 617-436-3232
Swivel Machine Works, Inc., 167 Cherry St., Suite 286, Milford, CT 06460/203-926-1840; FAX: 203-726-9431

T

Tanfoglio S.r.l., Fratelli (See U.S. importer—E.A.A. Corp.)
Tanner (See U.S. importer—Mandall Shooting Supplies, Inc.)
Tapco, Inc., P.O. Box 818, Smyrna, GA 30081/404-435-9782, 800-359-6195; FAX: 404-333-9798
Tar-Hunt Custom Rifles, Inc., RR3, Box 572, Bloomsburg, PA 17815/717-784-6368; FAX: 717-784-6368
Tasco Sales, Inc., 7600 NW 84th Ave., Miami, FL 33122/305-591-3670; FAX: 305-592-5895
Taurus Firearms, Inc., 16175 NW 49th Ave., Miami, FL 33014/305-624-1115; FAX: 305-623-7506
Taurus International Firearms (See U.S. importer—Taurus Firearms, Inc.)
Taylor & Vadney, Inc., 303 Central Ave., Albany, NY 12206/518-472-9183
Taylor's Sporting Goods, Gene, 445 W. Gunnison Ave., Grand Junction, CO 81505/303-242-8165
Taylor's Technical Gunsmithing Co., 14 Stalwart Industrial Drive, P.O. Box 508, Gormely, Ontario CANADA L0H 1G0/416-888-9391
Techni-Mec (See U.S. importer—Mandall Shooting Supplies, Inc.)
Ted's Gun & Reel Repair, 311 Natchitoches St. Box 1635, W. Monroe, LA 71291/318-323-0661
Ten Ring Service, 2227 West Lou Dr., Jacksonville, FL 32216/904-724-7419
Texas Arms, P.O. Box 154906, Waco, TX 76715/817-867-6972
Texas Gun Shop, Inc., 4518 S. Padre Island Dr., Corpus Christi, TX 78411/512-854-4424
Texas Longhorn Arms, Inc., 5959 W. Loop South, Suite 424, Bellaire, TX 77401/713-660-6323; FAX: 713-660-0493
Theoben Engineering (See U.S. importer—Air Rifle Specialists)
Thompson's Gunshop, Inc., 10254-84th St., Alto, MI 49302/616-891-0440
Thompson/Center Arms (See page 457)
300 Gunsmith Service, Inc. (Wichita Guncraft), 6850 S. Yosemite Ct., Englewood, CO 80112/303-773-0300
Thunder Mountain Arms, P.O. Box 593, Oak Harbor, WA 98277/206-679-4657; FAX: 206-675-1114
Tikka (See U.S. importer—Stoeger Industries)
Traders, The, 685 E. 14th St., San Leandro, CA 94577/510-569-0555
Trading Post, The, 412 Erie St. S., Massillon, OH 44646/216-833-7761
Traditions, P.O. Box 235, Deep River, CT 06417/203-526-9555; FAX: 203-526-4564
Treaster, Inc., Verne, 3604 West 16th St., Indianapolis, IN 46222/317-638-6921
Treptow, Inc., Herman, 209 S. Main St., Milltown, NJ 08850/908-828-0184
Trijicon, Inc., P.O. Box 6029, Wixom, MI 48393-6029/810-960-7700; FAX: 810-960-7725

U

U.F.A., Inc., 7655 E. Evans Rd., Scottsdale, AZ 85260
Ultimate Accuracy, 121 John Shelton Rd., Jacksonville, AR 72076/501-985-2530
U.S. General Technologies, Inc., 145 Mitchell Ave., South San Francisco, CA 94080/415-634-8440; FAX: 415-634-8452

U.S. Repeating Arms Co., Inc., 275 Winchester Ave., New Haven, CT 06511/203-789-5000; FAX: 203-789-5071
Uberti USA, Inc., 362 Limerock Rd., P.O. Box 469, Lakeville, CT 06039/203-435-8068; FAX: 203-435-8146
Uberti, Aldo (See U.S. importers—American Arms, Inc.; E. Christopher Firearms Co., Inc.; Cimarron Arms; Dixie Gun Works; EMF Co., Inc.; Mitchell Arms, Inc.; Navy Arms Co; Uberti USA, Inc.)
Ugartechea S.A., Ignacio (See U.S. importer—Mandall Shooting Supplies, Inc.)
Ultra Light Arms, Inc., P.O. Box 1270, 214 Price St., Granville, WV 26534/304-599-5687
Unertl Optical Co., John, Inc., 308 Clay Ave., P.O. Box 818, Mars, PA 16046-0818/412-625-3810
Unique Sporting Goods, Rd. 1 Box 131 E., Lorreto, PA 15940/814-674-8889
Unique/M.A.P.F. (See U.S. importer—Nygord Precision Products)
Upper Missouri Trading Co., 304 Harold St., Crofton, NE 68730/402-388-4844
Upton's Gun Shop, 810 Croghan St., Fremont, OH 43420/419-332-1326

V

Valley Gun Shop, 7719 Hartford Rd., Baltimore, MD 21234/410-668-2171
Valley Gunsmithing, John A. Foster, 619 Second St., Webster City, IA 50595/515-832-5102
Valmet (See Tikka/U.S. importer—Stoeger Industries)
Van Burens Gun Shop, 2706 Sylvania Ave., Toledo, OH 43613/419-475-9526
Van's Gunsmith Service, Rt. 69A, Parish, NY 13131/315-625-7251
Voere-KGH m.b.H. (See U.S. importers—JägerSport, Ltd.; Swarovski Optik North America Ltd.)

W

Walker Arms Co., Inc., 499 County Rd. 820, Selma, AL 36701/205-872-6231
Wallace Gatlin Gun Repair, Rt. 2, Box 73, Oxford, AL 36203/205-831-6993
Walther GmbH, Carl (See U.S. importer—Interarms)
Warren's Sports Hdqts., 240 W. Main St., Washington, NC 27889/919-946-0960
Way It Was Sporting, The, 620 Chestnut Street, Moorestown, NJ 08057/609-231-0111
Weatherby, Inc. (See page 457)
Weaver Scope Repair Service, 1121 Larry Mahan Dr., Suite B, El Paso, TX 79925/915-593-1005
Webley & Scott Ltd. (See U.S. importer—Beeman Precision Airguns, Inc.)
Weihrauch KG, Hermann (See U.S. importers—Beeman Precision Airguns; E.A.A. Corp.)
Weinberger Gunsmithing, Herbert, 30 W. Prospect St., Waldwick, NJ 07436/201-447-0025
Wessel Gun Service, 4000 E. 9-Mile Rd., Warren, MI 48091/313-756-2660
Wesson Firearms Co., Inc., Maple Tree Industrial Center, Rt. 20, Wilbraham, Rd./Palmer, MA 01069/413-267-4081; FAX: 413-267-3601
West Gate Gunsports, Inc., 10116-175th Street, Edmonton, Alberta, CANADA T5S 1A1/403-489-9633
West Luther Gun Repair, R.R. #1, Conn, Ontario, CANADA N0G 1N0/519-848-6260
Westley Richards & Co. (See U.S. importer—Cape Outfitters)
Wheeler Gun Shop, C., 1908 George Washington Way Bldg. F, Richland, WA 99352/509-946-4634
White Dog Gunsmithing, 62 Central Ave., Ilion, NY 13357/315-894-6211
White Shooting Systems, Inc., P.O. Box 277, Roosevelt, UT 84066/801-722-3085; FAX: 801-722-3054
Wholesale Shooters Supplies, 751 W. Brubaker Valley Rd., Lititz, PA 17543/717-626-8574
Wholesale Sports, 12505 97 St., Edmonton, Alberta, CANADA T5G 1Z8/403-426-4417; 403-477-3737
Wichita Arms, Inc., 923 E. Gilbert, P.O. Box 11371, Wichita, KS 67211/316-265-0661; FAX: 316-265-0760
Wichita Guncraft, Inc., 4607 Barnett Rd., Wichita Falls, TX 76310/817-692-5622
Wilderness Sport & Electronics, 14430 S. Pulaski Rd., Midlothian, IL 60445/708-389-1776
Wildey, Inc., P.O. Box 475, Brookfield, CT 06804/203-355-9000; FAX: 203-354-7759
Wilkinson Arms, 26884 Pearl Rd., Parma, ID 83660/208-722-6771; FAX: 208-722-5197/602-998-3941; FAX: 602-998-3941
Will's Gun Shop, 5603 N. Hubbard Lake Rd., Spruce, MI 48762/517-727-2500
Willborn Outdoors & Feed, 505 Main Avenue N.W., Cullman, AL 35055/205-737-9595
William's Gun Shop, Ben, 1151 S. Cedar Ridge, Duncanville, TX 75137/214-780-1807
Williams Gun Shop, 7389 Lapeer Rd., Davison, MI 48423/313-653-2131
Williams Gun Sight Co., 7389 Lapeer Rd., Box 329, Davison, MI 48423/810-653-2131, 800-530-9028; FAX: 810-658-2140
Williams Gunsmithing, 4985 Cole Rd., Saginaw, MI 48601/517-777-1240
Williamson Gunsmith Service, 117 West Pipeline Rd., Hurst, TX 76053/817-285-0064
Winchester (See page 457)
Windsor Gun Shop, 8410 Southeastern Ave., Indianapolis, IN 46239/317-862-2512
Wisner's Gun Shop, Inc., 287 NW Chehalis Ave., Chehalis, WA 98532/206-748-8942; FAX: 206-748-7011
Wolf Custom Gunsmithing, Gregory, c/o Albright's Gun Shop, 36 E. Dover St., Easton, MD 21601/410-820-8811
Wolfer Brothers, Inc., 1701 Durham, Houston, TX 77007/713-869-7640
Woodman's Sporting Goods, 223 Main Street, Norway, ME 04268/207-743-6602
Wortner Gun Works, Ltd., 433 Queen St., Chatham, Ont., CANADA N7M 2J1/519-352-0924

Y

Ye Olde Blk Powder Shop, 994 W. Midland Rd., Auburn, MI 48611/517-662-2271
Ye Olde Gun Shop, 12½ Woodlawn Ave., Bradford, PA 16701/814-368-3034
Ye Olde Gun Shoppe, P.O. Box 358, Sitka, AK 99835/907-747-5720

Z

Zabala Hermanos S.A. (See U.S. importer—American Arms, Inc.)
Zanes Gun Rack, 4167 N. High St., Columbus, OH 43214/614-263-0369
Zanoletti, Pietro (See U.S. importer—Mandall Shooting Supplies, Inc.)
Zeiss Optical, Carl, 1015 Commerce St., Petersburg, VA 23803/804-861-0033; FAX: 804-733-4024

Warranty Service Centers

■BR=Browning ■CR=Crosman ■MO=Mossberg ■RE=Remington ■ST=Stoeger ■SW=Smith & Wesson ■TC=Thompson/Center ■WN=Winchester ■WE=Weatherby

SERVICE CENTER	CITY	BR	CR	MO	RE	ST	SW	TC	WN	WE
ALABAMA										
B&W Gunsmithing	Cullman	•								
Dubbs, Gunsmith, Dale R.	Seminole				•					
Fred's Gun Shop	Mobile				•					
Nusbaum Enterprises, Inc.	Mobile			•	•					
Ott's Gun Service	Atmore	•			•					
Plaza Gunworks, Inc.	Birmingham				•					
Walker Arms Co., Inc.	Selma	•		•	•	•	•	•		
Wallace Gatlin Gun	Oxford					•		•		
Willborn Outdoors & Feed	Cullman								•	•
ALASKA										
Down Under Gunsmiths	Fairbanks	•			•					
Red's Gunsmithing	Chickaloon	•	•	•	•				•	
Ye Olde Gun Shoppe	Sitka				•					
ARIZONA										
Don's Sport Shop, Inc.	Scottsdale	•		•	•				•	
Jensen's Custom Ammunition/Lathrops	Tucson	•		•	•			•	•	
Joe's Gun Shop	Phoenix		•	•	•					
Millie "D" Enterprises	Tucson		•							
Weapon Works, The	Phoenix				•					
ARKANSAS										
Broadway Arms	North Little Rock	•			•					
Gun Exchange, Inc.	Little Rock				•		•		•	
Hunters Den	North Little Rock	•		•	•					
Jim's Sporting Goods	Newport					•				
Jim's Trading Post	Pine Bluff	•		•	•					
Sipes Gun Shop	Little Rock			•	•				•	
CALIFORNIA										
Air Guns Unlimited	La Puente		•							
Air Venture Air Guns	Bellflower		•							
Andersen Gunsmithing	Petaluma			•	•					
Argonaut Gun Shop	Modesto			•	•					
Bain & Davis	San Gabriel			•	•					
Beeman Precision Arms, Inc.	Santa Rosa									•
Bolsa Gunsmithing	Westminster	•		•	•				•	
Bridge Sportsman's Ctr.	Paso Robles				•	•				
Cat's Customs	Fallbrook	•								
Duncan's Gunworks	San Marcos			•						
Grundman's	Rio Dell			•	•					
Gunshop, Inc., The	Lancaster							•	•	

SERVICE CENTER	CITY	BR	CR	MO	RE	ST	SW	TC	WN	WE
Gunsmith, The	Chico									
Huntington Sportsman's Store	Oroville				•				•	
Imbert & Smithers, Inc.	San Carlos	•			•				•	
J&G Gunsmithing	Roseville	•			•					
John Q's Quality Gunsmithing	Sacramento				•					
King's Gun Works, Inc.	Glendale				•					
Long Beach Uniform Co., Inc.	Long Beach						•			
Mac-1	Gardena		•							
Miclean, Bill	San Jose		•							
Pacific International Service Co.	Janesville	•			•	•		•		
Pachmayr Gun Works	Monrovia	•	•		•					
PHOXX Shooters Supply	N. Highlands		•		•					
Preuss Gun Shop	Clovis	•		•						
Ray's Liquor and Sporting Goods	Corning	•			•					
Rue's Gunsmithing	El Cajon				•					
Siegle's Gunshop, Inc.	Oakland	•			•			•		
Sportsman's Exchange, Inc.	Oxnard	•			•					
Traders, The	San Leandro		•					•		
COLORADO										
Foothills Shooting Ctr.	Lakewood	•		•	•					
Gart Brothers Sporting Goods	Denver	•		•	•				•	
L&M Firing Line, Inc.	Aurora									
Ray's Gunsmith Shop	Grand Junction		•							
Sievert's Guns	Pueblo									
Spradlin's	Pueblo	•		•	•			•		•
Taylor's Sporting Goods, Gene	Grand Junction			•	•			•	•	•
300 Gunsmith Service (Wichita Guncraft)	Englewood			•	•				•	
CONNECTICUT										
Gunsmithing Limited	Fairfield	•			•				•	
Hoffman's Gun Center, Inc.	Newington			•	•					
Horchler's Gun Shop	Collinsville				•					
Keller's Co. Inc.	Burlington									
Modern Guncraft	Collinsville				•					
Nicholson's Gunsmithing	Shelton									
DELAWARE										
Magnum Gun Service	Newark				•					
FLORIDA										
Air Gun Rifle Repair	Sebring		•							
Alexander, Gunsmith, W.R.	Tallahassee				•					
Firearms Unlimited, Inc.	Naples						•			
Green Acres Sporting Goods, Inc.	Jacksonville	•		•	•			•		

See page 451 for Service Center addresses.

Warranty Service Centers (cont.)

■BR=Browning ■CR=Crosman ■MO=Mossberg ■RE=Remington ■ST=Stoeger ■SW=Smith & Wesson ■TC=Thompson/Center ■WN=Winchester ■WE=Weatherby

SERVICE CENTER	CITY	BR	CR	MO	RE	ST	SW	TC	WN	WE
Gun Doc, Inc.	Miami			●	●					
Gun Shop, Inc., The	Miami Shores				●					
Jackson, Inc., Bill	Pinellas Park		●							
Lawsons Custom Firearms, Inc., Art	Ocala			●	●					
Loftin & Taylor	Jacksonville				●					●
Rice Hardware	Gainesville				●					
Sillman, Hal, Associated Services	Miami		●						●	
Ten Ring Service	Jacksonville									
GEORGIA										
Accuracy Gun Shop	Columbus	●		●	●				●	
Dorn's Outdoor Center	Macon	●	●	●	●				●	
Ed's Gun & Tackle Shop, Inc.	Marietta		●	●	●					
Franklin Sports, Inc.	Bogart				●					
Gun Corral, Inc.	Decatur				●		●		●	
Jordan Gun & Pawn Shop	Tifton	●			●					
Kick's Sport Center	Claxton				●					
Sanders Custom Gun Shop	Augusta				●				●	
HAWAII										
Chung, Gunsmith, Mel	Kaunakakai			●	●		●		●	
IDAHO										
Bob's Repair	Menan	●	●		●					
Intermountain Arms & Tackle, Inc.	Meridian	●			●				●	●
Lolo Sporting Goods	Lewiston			●	●				●	
Quality Firearms	Nampa	●		●	●				●	
Reloading Center	Burley				●					
Shapel's Gun Shop	Boise				●					
ILLINOIS										
A&M Sales	North Lake		●		●					
Bill Barton Sport Center	Niles				●				●	
Darnall's Gun Works	Bloomington			●	●					
Gat Guns	East Dundee			●	●					
Henry's Airguns	Belvidere		●		●					
Krebs Gunsmithing	Niles				●					
Midwest Sporting Goods Co., Inc.	Lyons						●			
Ott's Gunsmith Service	Decatur		●	●	●					
Outdoorsman Sporting Goods Co.	Geneva		●		●					
Pekin Gun & Sporting Goods	Pekin		●		●					
Wilderness Sport & Electronics	Midlothian		●		●					
INDIANA										
Airgun Centre, Ltd.	Lawrenceburg		●		●					
Blythe's Sport Shop, Inc.	Valparaiso		●		●					
Hodson & Son Pell Gun Repair	Anderson		●	●						
Lutter, Robert E.	Ft. Wayne		●		●					
Rajo Corporation	Evansville		●		●					
Treaster, Inc.	Indianapolis			●						
Windsor Gun Shop	Indianapolis		●				●			

SERVICE CENTER	CITY	BR	CR	MO	RE	ST	SW	TC	WN	WE
IOWA										
Daryl's Gun Shop, Inc.	State Center				●					
Glenn's Reel & Rod Repair	Des Moines		●		●					
G&S Gunsmithing	Eldridge		●		●					●
Jacobson's Gun Center	Story City				●					
Nelson's Engine Shop	Cedar Falls		●	●	●				●	
Valley Gunsmithing, John A. Foster	Webster City				●					
KANSAS										
Bullseye Gun Works	Overland Park				●					
Gordon's Wigwam	Wichita		●		●				●	
Gun & Stuff, Inc.	Wichita				●					
Northwest Arms Service	Atwood		●		●					
Ray's Rod & Reel Service	Wichita			●					●	
Simmons Gun Repair	Olathe				●					
KENTUCKY										
Danny's Gun Repair, Inc.	Louisville				●				●	
Firearms Service Center	Louisville				●					
Garrett Gunsmiths, Inc.	Newport				●					
Paducah Shooters Supply, Inc.	Paducah			●						
LOUISIANA										
Atlas Gun Repair	Violet	●			●					
Boudreaux, Gunsmith	Lake Charles	●			●					
Brazdas Top Guns	Lafayette				●					
Burton Hardware	Sulphur				●					
Caddo Arms & Cycle	Shreveport	●			●					
Chalmette Jewelry & Guns	Chalmette	●								
Cherry's Gun Shop	Ruston				●					
Clark Custom Guns, Inc.	Keithville						●			
Custom Gun Works	Lafayette				●					
Houma Gun Works	Houma	●		●	●					
Hutchinson's Gun Repair	Pineville	●		●	●					
Lafayette Shooters	Lafayette			●	●					
Martin Gun Shop	Shreveport	●			●					
N.A. Guns, Inc.	Baton Rouge				●					
Southwest Airguns	Lake Charles		●							
Sportsman's Paradise Gunsmith	Pineville				●				●	
Ted's Gun & Reel Repair	W. Monroe				●					
MAINE										
Brunswick Gun Shop	Brunswick				●				●	●
Morrison, Carl Bill	Bradford								●	
Woodman's Sporting Goods	Norway				●					
MARYLAND										
Atlantic Guns, Inc.	Silver Springs	●			●		●		●	
Baltimore Gunsmiths	Baltimore	●		●	●					
Firearms Repair & Refinish Shoppe	Woodbine									●
Gun Center, The	Frederick						●			

See page 451 for Service Center addresses.

Warranty Service Centers (cont.)

BR=Browning ■CR=Crosman ■MO=Mossberg ■RE=Remington ■ST=Stoeger ■SW=Smith & Wesson ■TC=Thompson/Center ■WN=Winchester ■WE=Weatherby

SERVICE CENTER	CITY	BR	CR	MO	RE	ST	SW	TC	WN	WE
Precision Pellet	Joppa		●							
Valley Gun Shop	Baltimore	●		●	●				●	
Wolf Custom Gunsmithing, Gregory, c/o Albright's Gun Shop	Easton	●			●					
MASSACHUSETTS										
Bellrose & Son, L.E.	Granby		●							
Four Seasons	Woburn			●						
Pete's Gun Shop	Adams			●						
MICHIGAN										
Adventure A.G.R.	Waterford	●	●		●	●				
Bachelder Custom Arms	Grand Rapids	●			●	●				
Daenzer, Charles E.	Otisville					●				
Fricano, Gunsmith, J.	Grand Haven				●	●				
Geake & Son, Inc.	Ferndale				●					
Hampel's, Inc.	Traverse City		●		●					
Joe's Gun Shop	Dorr		●		●	●				
Johnson Gunsmithing, Don	Powers				●	●				
Johnson Service, Inc., W.	Adrian				●	●				
McDaniel Co., Inc., B.	South Lyon				●	●				
Mill Creek Sport Center	Dexter				●	●				
Moreau, Gunsmith, Pete	Bay City	●	●							
Northern Precision Airguns	Tawas City	●	●							
Oakland Custom Arms	Waterford				●	●				
On Target Gunshop, Inc.	Kalamazoo	●	●		●	●				
Outpost, The	Eureka				●					
Pederson & Son, C.R.	Ludington				●					
Thompson's Gunshop, Inc.	Alto				●	●				
Wessel Gun Service	Warren	●			●	●				
Williams Gun Shop	Davison	●	●		●	●				
Williams Gunsmithing	Saginaw		●		●					
Will's Gun Shop	Spruce				●	●				
Ye Olde Blk Powder Shop	Auburn							●		●
MINNESOTA										
Ahlman's Custom Gun Shop, Inc.	Morristown	●		●	●	●			●	
Antonowicz, Frank	Minneapolis	●	●							
B&B Supply Co.	Minneapolis				●	●				
Dale's Guns & Archery Center	Rochester		●		●					
Gander Mt., Inc.	Duluth				●	●				
Gun Shop, The	Excelsior				●	●				
Frontiersman's Sports	Minneapolis	●			●	●				
Kotila Gun Shop	Cokato				●	●				
Laibs Gunsmithing	Spicer				●	●				
Matt's 10X Gunsmithing, Inc.	Duluth				●	●				
Northland Sport Center	Bagley				●	●				
Poor Borch's, Inc.	Marshall				●	●				
Stan's Gun Repair	Westbrook				●	●				

SERVICE CENTER	CITY	BR	CR	MO	RE	ST	SW	TC	WN	WE
MISSISSIPPI										
Grenada Gun Works	Grenada				●				●	
Martins Gun Shop	Natchez				●				●	
May & Company, Inc.	Jackson		●							
Millers Gun Shop	Gulfport							●		
Saffle Repair Service	Jackson		●							
Sanders Gun Shop	Meridian				●		●			●
MISSOURI										
Beard's Sport Shop	Cape Girardeau			●	●				●	
Bickford's Gun Repair	Joplin			●	●				●	●
Carl's Gun Shop	El Dorado Springs								●	
Catfish Guns	Imperial		●				●			
CR Specialty	Kansas City		●							
Dollar Drugs, Inc.	Lee's Summit			●						
F&D Guns	St. Charles				●		●			●
Kopp, Prof. Gunsmith, Terry K.	Lexington				●		●			
Marshall Gun Shop	Dellwood				●			●		
Nu-Line Guns, Inc.	Harvester	●		●	●		●		●	
Ozark Shooters, Inc.	Branson				●				●	
MONTANA										
Air Gun Shop, The	Billings	●	●							
Billings Gunsmiths	Billings		●		●					
Brady's Sportsmans Surplus	Missoula			●	●		●		●	
Capitol Sports & Western Wear	Helena			●	●				●	
Don's Sporting Goods	Lewiston				●			●		
Montana Gun Works	Great Falls				●		●			
NEBRASKA										
Bedlan's Sporting Goods, Inc.	Fairbury	●			●					
Cylinder & Slide, Inc.	Fremont		●						●	
G.H. Gun Shop	McCook			●	●					
G.I. Loan Shop	Grand Island			●	●				●	●
Gun Works, The	Omaha								●	
Gunsmithing Specialties, Co.	Papillion	●								
Labs Air Gun Shop	Omaha		●							
Moneymaker Gun Craft, Inc.	Omaha				●		●		●	
Sporting Goods, Inc.	Hastings				●					
Upper Missouri Trading Co., Inc.	Crofton			●	●					
NEVADA										
Accuracy Gun Shop, Inc.	Las Vegas			●	●				●	
Gun World	Elko			●	●					
Nevada Air Guns	N. Las Vegas		●							
NEW HAMPSHIRE										
Lewis Arms	Hooksett			●	●				●	
Stratemeyer, H.P.	Langdon	●			●					●

See page 451 for Service Center addresses.

See page 451 for Service Center addresses.

■BR=Browning ■CR=Crosman ■MO=Mossberg ■RE=Remington ■ST=Stoeger ■SW=Smith & Wesson ■TC=Thompson/Center ■WN=Winchester ■WE=Weatherby

NEW JERSEY

SERVICE CENTER	CITY	BR	CR	MO	RE	ST	SW	TC	WN	WE
Belleplain Supply, Inc.	Belleplain	•								
Brenner Sport Shop, Charlie	Rahway		•							
Efinger Sporting Goods	Bound Brook									
Garfield Gunsmithing	Garfield	•			•					
Harry's Army & Navy Store	Robbinsville	•	•		•					
Ray's Sport Shop, Inc.	Plainfield	•			•		•		•	
Sportsman's Center	Bordentown				•					
The Way It Was Sporting	Moorestown	•		•	•					
Treptow, Inc., Herman	Milltown				•					
Weinberger Gunsmithing, Herbert	Waldwick									

NEW MEXICO

SERVICE CENTER	CITY	BR	CR	MO	RE	ST	SW	TC	WN	WE
Charlie's Sporting Goods, Inc.	Albuquerque		•		•		•		•	
Chuck's Gun Shop	Ranchos De Taos				•					
Covey's Precision Gunsmith	Roswell									
D&J Coleman Service	Hobbs		•		•					
Hobb's Bicycle & Gun Sales	Hobbs		•		•					
Ross Sporting Goods	Farmington									

NEW YORK

SERVICE CENTER	CITY	BR	CR	MO	RE	ST	SW	TC	WN	WE
Alpine Arms Corp.	Brooklyn	•					•			
Apple Town Gun Shop	Williamson		•							
B&T, Inc.	Albany			•						
Benson Gun Shop	Coram L.I.		•							
Boracci, E. John, Village Sport Ctr.	Seaford L.I.			•	•					
Buffalo Gun Center, Inc.	Buffalo									
Bugins Gun Shop	Sidney Center		•	•	•					
Centre Firearms Co., Inc.	New York City									
Coliseum Gun Traders, Ltd.	Uniondale		•	•	•		•			
Creekside Gun Shop	Holcomb	•	•		•					
Damiano's Field & Stream	Ossining									
Davco Stores, 305 Broadway	Monticello		•		•					
Gemini Arms Ltd.	Hicksville			•						
Hart's Gun Supply, Ed	Bath		•							
Hill Top Gunsmithing	Canton									
Jovino Co., Inc. John	New York									
Klelon, Gunsmith, Dave	Webster		•							
LeFever & Sons, Inc., Frank	Lee Center									
Lounsbury Sporting Goods, Bob	Middletown		•		•					
Mulvey's Marine & Sport Shop	Monticello		•		•					
Rapids Gun Shop	Niagra Falls		•							
Scalzo's Sporting Goods	Endicott		•		•					
Schultheis Sporting Goods	Arkport									
Smith's Lawn & Marine Svc.	Clarence		•							
Solvay Home & Outdoor Center	Solvay		•							•
Sports Mart, The	Ogdensburg		•						•	
Taylor & Vadney, Inc.	Albany		•		•					
Van's Gunsmith Service	Parish				•					
White Dog Gunsmithing	Ilion									

NORTH CAROLINA

SERVICE CENTER	CITY	BR	CR	MO	RE	ST	SW	TC	WN	WE
Baity's Custom Gunworks	North Wilksboro				•				•	
Blue Ridge Outdoor Sports, Inc.	E. Flat Rock	•		•	•		•		•	•
Cumberland Knife & Gun Works	Fayetteville				•				•	
Don's Gun Shop	Ashville		•							
Duncan Gun Shop, Inc.	North Wilksboro	•			•					
Hill's, Inc.	Raleigh	•			•					
Marine Gun & Lock Shop	Jacksonville			•						
Mike's Crosman Service	Winston-Salem		•							
Perry's of Wendell, Inc.	Wendell				•					
Warren's Sports Hdqts.	Washington				•					

NORTH DAKOTA

SERVICE CENTER	CITY	BR	CR	MO	RE	ST	SW	TC	WN	WE
Gun City, Inc.	Bismarck	•			•					
Outdoorsman, Inc.	Fargo	•			•					•
S.K. Guns, Inc.	Fargo				•				•	

OHIO

SERVICE CENTER	CITY	BR	CR	MO	RE	ST	SW	TC	WN	WE
Airgun Centre, Ltd.	Cincinnati		•		•			•		
All Game Sport Center	Milford		•							
Central Ohio Police Supply, c/o Wammes Guns	Bellefontaine									
Cherry Corners, Inc.	Lodi		•							
Eyster Heritage Gunsmiths, Ken	Centerburg				•					
Griffiths & Sons, E.J.	Lima			•					•	
Heckman Arms Company	Richmond Heights								•	
Keller Gunsmithing	Bradford				•			•		
Log Cabin Sport Shop	Lodi	•								
Precision Airgun Sales	Maple Heights		•							
Rutko Corp. (Stonewall Range)	Broadview Heights						•			
Sportsman's Depot	Urban	•			•					
Sportsman's Haven	Cambridge	•		•	•		•		•	•
Sportsmen's Repair Ctr., Inc.	Columbus Groves		•		•					
Stocker's Shop	Warren		•		•					
Trading Post, The	Massillon		•							
Upton's Gun Shop	Fremont		•							
VanBurne's Gun Shop	Toledo		•				•		•	
Zanes Gun Rack	Columbus							•		

OKLAHOMA

SERVICE CENTER	CITY	BR	CR	MO	RE	ST	SW	TC	WN	WE
D&D Sporting Goods	Tishomingo				•					
Junior's Gun & Lock Shop	Ponca City				•					
Mashburn Arms Co., Inc.	Oklahoma City		•							
Meydag, Peter	Tulsa									
Outdoor America Store	Oklahoma City		•							
Shamburg's Wholesale Spt. Gds.	Clinton						•			
Skeet's Gun Shop	Tahlequah		•							
Southwest Shooters Supply, Inc.	Oklahoma City	•								
Sport Shop, The	Kingfisher		•							

See page 451 for Service Center addresses.

Warranty Service Centers (cont.)

■BR=Browning ■CR=Crosman ■MO=Mossberg ■RE=Remington ■ST=Stoeger ■SW=Smith & Wesson ■TC=Thompson/Center ■WN=Winchester ■WE=Weatherby

SERVICE CENTER	CITY	BR	CR	MO	RE	ST	SW	TC	WN	WE
Sports World, Inc.	Tulsa	●		●	●				●	●
OREGON										
Allison & Carey Gun Works	Portland	●		●	●					
Enstad & Douglas	Oregon City			●	●				●	
Felton, James	Eugene			●	●			●		
Lock Stock & Barrel	Grants Pass									
Metro Rod & Reel	Portland		●							
Starnes, Gunmaker, Ken	Hillsboro			●	●					
Surplus Center	Roseburg		●	●	●				●	
PENNSYLVANIA										
Auto Electric & Parts, Inc.	Media		●	●	●					
Braverman Arms Co.	Wilkinsburg			●	●					
Colabaugh Gunsmith, Inc., Craig	Stroudsburg		●	●	●					
Federal Firearms Co., Inc.	Oakdale			●	●					
Fix Gunshop, Inc., Michael D.	Reading				●					
Flaig's Inc.	Pittsburgh	●			●					
Garber & Sams Gunsmithing	Elizabethtown				●					
Gorenflo Gunsmithing	Erie				●				●	
Grice Gun Shop, Inc.	Clearfield			●	●		●			
Hart & Son, Robert W.	Nescopeck		●	●						
Hemlock Gun Shop	Lakeville		●							
Herold's Gun Shoppe	Waynesboro		●		●					
Keeley, John L.	Spring City			●	●					
Keidel's Gunsmithing Service	Washington			●	●				●	
Leo's Custom Stocks	Library	●								
Levan's Sport Goods	Lebanon			●	●					
Miller's Sport Shop	Mountaintop				●					
Phoenix Armoury, Inc.	Norristown				●					
Richland Gun Shop	Richland			●	●					
Somerset Sports Shop	Somerset			●	●					
Sportsman's Shop	New Holland	●			●					
Unique Sporting Goods	Loreto				●					
Wholesale Shooters Supplies	Lititz			●	●					
Ye Olde Gun Shop	Bradford				●					
RHODE ISLAND										
D&L Shooting Supplies	Warwick			●	●				●	
Gun Hospital, The	E. Providence									●
SOUTH CAROLINA										
Borgheresi, Enrique	Greenville			●						
Bryan & Associates	Belton									
Gun Rack, Inc., The	Aiken			●	●					
Gun Room, The	Chapin			●	●		●			
Gunsmith, Inc., The	West Columbia			●	●					
Roy's Antiques & Things	Mountain Rest		●							
S.E.M. Gun Works	Greenville		●							
Smith & Smith Gun Shop, Inc.	Charleston Hghts.	●								
Southland Gun Works, Inc.	Darlington				●					

SERVICE CENTER	CITY	BR	CR	MO	RE	ST	SW	TC	WN	WE
SOUTH DAKOTA										
Gary's Gun Shop	Sioux Falls				●					
Jim's Gun & Service Center	Aberdeen			●	●				●●	
Ron's Gun Repair	Sioux Falls	●		●	●				●	
Roy's Sport Shop	Watertown				●				●	
Sodak Sport & Bait	Aberdeen	●		●	●					
TENNESSEE										
D&L Gunsmithing/Guns & Ammo	Memphis	●		●	●					
Fox & Company	Knoxville		●		●					
Friedman's Army Surplus	Nashville		●							
Gun City USA, Inc.	Nashville	●		●	●			●	●	
Hagstrom, E.G.	Memphis				●					
Hill's Hardware & Sporting Goods	Union City	●		●	●					
McGuns, W.H.	Humboldt									●
Mines Gun Shack	Tullahoma				●					
Shaler Eagle	Jonesbrough		●							
TEXAS										
Alpine Range	Fort Worth	●								
Armadillo Air Gun Repair	Corpus Christi		●		●					
Ben's Gun Shop	Duncanville		●	●	●					
Billy Freds	Amarillo	●								
Boggus Gun Shop	San Marcos				●				●	
Carroll's Gun Shop, Inc.	Wharton			●	●					
Carter's Country	Houston	●		●	●					
Cogdell's, Inc.	Waco				●					
Coleman, Inc., Ron	Carrollton	●			●	●			●	
Custom Gun Service	McAllen				●					
Don & Tim's Gun Shop	San Antonio				●				●	
Ewell Cross Gun Shop, Inc.	Ft. Worth			●	●				●	
Freer's Gun Shop	Houston	●			●					
Gun & Tackle Store, The	Dallas				●					
Kirkpatrick, Gunsmith, Larry	Lubbock				●					
Les Gun & Pawn Shop	Texarkana			●	●					
Lone Star Guns, Inc.	Plano				●		●		●	●
Longacres, Inc.	Abilene				●					
Master Gunsmiths, Inc.	Houston	●		●	●	●			●	
McBride's Guns, Inc.	Austin	●●		●	●				●	
McClelland Gun Shop	Dallas	●			●	●			●	
Mueschke Manufacturing Co.	Houston				●					
Nagel Gun Shop. Inc.	San Antonio	●		●	●		●		●	
Oshman's Sporting Goods, Inc.	Houston				●					
Pasadena Gun Center	Pasadena							●		
Precision Gunsmithing	Amarillo									
Ray's Sporting Goods	Dallas						●			
Reynolds Gun Shop, Inc.	Tyler				●					
Texas Gun Shop, Inc.	Corpus Christi				●				●	
Wichita Guncraft, Inc.	Wichita Falls				●	●		●	●	●
Williamson Gunsmith Service	Hurst				●				●	

See page 451 for Service Center addresses.

■BR=Browning ■CR=Crosman ■MO=Mossberg ■RE=Remington ■ST=Stoeger ■SW=Smith & Wesson ■TC=Thompson/Center ■WN=Winchester ■WE=Weatherby

SERVICE CENTER	CITY	BR	CR	MO	RE	ST	SW	TC	WN	WE
Wolfer Brothers, Inc.	Houston		●							
UTAH										
Gun Ace Gunsmithing	Cedar City	●								
Gun Shop, The	Salt Lake City			●	●				●	
Gunsmith Co., The	Salt Lake City			●	●			●		
Hutch's	Lehi		●	●						
Professional Armaments, Inc.	Murray		●	●			●			
VERMONT										
Barrows Point Trading Post	Quechee			●	●					
Burby, Inc. Guns & Gunsmithing	Middlebury				●					
Carpenters Gun Works	Proctorsville									
Clapps Gun Shop	Brattleboro		●							
VIRGINIA										
Atlantic & Pacific Guns	Virginia Beach	●		●	●				●	
Bob's Gun & Tackle Shop, (Blaustein & Reich, Inc.)	Norfolk		●	●	●		●	●		
Cervera, Albert J.	Hanover	●								
King's Gun Shop, Inc.	Franklin	●								
Moates Sport Shop, Bob	Midlothian			●	●				●	
Northern Virginia Gun Works, Inc.	Springfield		●							
Old Dominion Engraver, Inc.	Lynchburg									
Princess Anne Marine & Sport Center	Virginia Beach				●					
Richmond Gun Shop	Richmond			●	●					
WASHINGTON										
Brock's Gunsmithing, Inc.	Spokane								●	
Chet Paulson Outfitters	Tacoma								●	
Greene's Gun Shop	Oak Harbor									
Karrer's Gunatorium	Spokane									
Kesselring Gun Shop	Burlington		●	●	●					
Pintos Gun Shop	Kent									
Shooters Supply	Yakima							●		
Wisner's Gun Shop, Inc.	Chehalis			●	●			●	●	
Wheeler Gun Shop, C.	Richland			●				●	●	●
WEST VIRGINIA										
Bait & Tackle Shop, The	Fairmont		●							
J.T. Gunshop, Inc., d/b/a Carolina Gun & Sports	Beckley			●	●				●	
Lew's Mountaineer Gunsmithing	Charleston									
Milliken's Gun Shop	Elm Grove		●		●				●	
Shooting Gallery, The	Weirton									
WISCONSIN										
Badgers Shooters Supply, Inc.	Owen		●							
Bob's Crosman Repair	Cudahy		●							
Custom Firearms Shop, The	Sheboygan				●					
Flintrop Arms Corp.	Milwaukee			●						

SERVICE CENTER	CITY	BR	CR	MO	RE	ST	SW	TC	WN	WE
Gander Mountain, Inc.	Wilmot			●	●		●		●	●
Jack's Lock & Gun Shop	Fond Du Lac		●							
Jay's Sports, Inc.	Menomonee Falls	●							●	
Midwestern Shooters Supply, Inc.	Lomira	●			●					
Phillips, D.J. Gunsmithing	Pewaukee				●					
Potter Gunsmithing	Muskego				●					
Precision Gun Works	Oshkosh			●	●					
River Bend Sport Shop	Waupaca			●						
R&R Shooters Supply	Mauston		●	●	●				●	●
Rusk Gun Shop, Inc.	Madison									
Sea Gull Marina	Two Rivers									
WYOMING										
Elbe Arms Co., Inc.	Cheyenne				●				●	
Jackalope Gun Shop	Douglas				●				●	
CANADA										
Armurie De L'Outaouais	Hull, PQ			●	●		●		●	
Casey's Gun Shop	Rogersville, NB	●		●	●		●		●	●
Charlton Co., Ltd.	Brentwood Bay, BC									
Custom Gun Shop	Edmonton, AB			●	●				●	
Davidson's of Canada	Peterborough, ON			●	●				●	
Delhi Small Arms	Delhi, ON				●					
Delisle Thompson Sport Goods	Saskatoon, SK									
Epps, Ellwood	Orilla, ON				●					
Ernie's Gun Shop, Ltd.	Winnipeg, MB			●	●				●	●
Gene's Gunsmithing	Selkirk, MB							●		
Girard, Florent, Gunsmith	Chicoutimi, PQ			●					●	
L'Armurier Alain Bouchard, Inc.	St. Chryostome, PQ	●							●	●
Long Gunsmithing Ltd., W.R.	Coburg, ON				●					
Lusignant Armurier, A. Richard	St. Hyacinthe, PQ			●	●				●	
Magasin Latulippe, Inc.	Quest, PQ									
Newby, Stewart, Gunsmith	New Burgh, ON			●	●				●	●
Precision Arms & Gunsmithing Ltd.	Nobleton, ON				●				●	
Ralph's Gun Shop	Niverville, MB			●						
Randy's Gun Repair	Tabustinac, NB				●				●	
Reliable Gun & Tackle, Ltd.	Vancouver, BC	●			●				●	
Robinson's Sporting Goods, Ltd.	Victoria, BC						●		●	●
Russel's Sporting Goods	Calgary, AB								●	
Saskatoon Gunsmith Shoppe, Ltd.	Saskatoon, SK			●	●				●	●
Selin Gunsmith, Ltd., Del	Vernon, BC						●			
Taylor's Technical Gunsmithing Co.	Gormely, ON			●	●				●	
West Gate Gunsports, Inc.	Edmonton, AB				●					
West Luther Gun Repair	Conn, ON									
Wholesale Sports	Edmonton, AB	●		●	●				●	●
Wortner Gun Works, Ltd.	Chatham, ON			●	●		●		●	●

See page 451 for Service Center addresses.

METALLIC SIGHTS

Sporting Leaf and Open Sights

ERA EXPRESS SIGHTS A wide variety of open sights and bases for custom installation. Partial listing shown. From New England Custom Gun Service.
Price: One-leaf express **$55.00**
Price: Two-leaf express **$65.00**
Price: Three-leaf express **$70.00**
Price: Bases for above **$25.00**
Price: Standing rear sight, straight **$10.50**
Price: Base for above **$15.00**

LYMAN No. 16 Middle sight for barrel dovetail slot mounting. Folds flat when scope or peep sight is used. Sight notch plate adjustable for elevation. White triangle for quick aiming. 3 heights: A—.400" to .500", B—.345" to .445", C—.500" to .600".
Price: **$13.50**

MARBLE FALSE BASE #76, #77, #78 New screw-on base for most rifles replaces factory base. ⅜" dovetail slot permits installation of any folding rear sight. Can be had in sweat-on models also.
Price: **$7.50**

MARBLE CONTOUR RAMP #14R For late model Rem. 725, 740, 760, 742 rear sight mounting. ⁹⁄₁₆" between mounting screws. Accepts all sporting rear sights.
Price: **$9.95**

MARBLE FOLDING LEAF Flat-top or semi-buckhorn style. Folds down when scope or peep sights are used. Reversible plate gives choice of "U" or "V" notch. Adjustable for elevation.
Price: **$13.75**
Price: Also available with both windage and elevation adjustment . . . **$15.75**

MARBLE SPORTING REAR With white enamel diamond, gives choice of two "U" and two "V" notches or different sizes. Adjustment in height by means of double step elevator and sliding notch piece. For all rifles; screw or dovetail installation.
Price: . . . . **$13.75-$15.75**

MARBLE #20 UNIVERSAL New screw or sweat-on base. Both have .100" elevation adjustment. In five base sizes. Three styles of U-notch, square notch, peep. Adjustable for windage and elevation.
Price: Screw-on **$21.25**
Price: Sweat-on **$19.50**

MILLETT RIFLE SIGHT Open, fully adjustable rear sight fits standard ⅜" dovetail cut in barrel. Choice of white outline or target rear blades, .360". Front with white or orange bar, .343", .400", .430", .460", .500", .540".
Price: Rear sight **$55.60**
Price: Front sight **$12.34**

MILLETT SCOPE-SITE Open, adjustable or fixed rear sights dovetail into a base integral with the top scope-mounting ring. Blaze orange front ramp sight is integral with the front ring half. Rear sights have white outline aperture. Provides fast, short-radius, Patridge-type open sights on the top of the scope. Can be used with all Millett rings, Weaver-style bases, Ruger 77 (also fits Redhawk), Ruger Ranch Rifle, No. 1, No. 3, Rem. 870, 1100; Burris, Leupold and Redfield bases.
Price: Scope-Site top only, windage only **$31.15**
Price: As above, fully adjustable **$66.10**
Price: Scope-Site Hi-Turret, fully adjustable, low, medium, high **$66.10**

WICHITA MULTI RANGE SIGHT SYSTEM Designed for silhouette shooting. System allows you to adjust the rear sight to four repeatable range settings, once it is pre-set. Sight clicks to any of the settings by turning a serrated wheel. Front sight is adjustable for weather and light conditions with one adjustment. Specify gun when ordering.
Price: Rear sight **$93.50**
Price: Front sight **$69.95**

WILLIAMS DOVETAIL OPEN SIGHT (WDOS) Open rear sight with windage and elevation adjustment. Furnished with "U" notch or choice of blades. Slips into dovetail and locks with gib lock. Heights from .281" to .531".
Price: With blade **$14.95**
Price: Less Blade **$9.35**

WILLIAMS GUIDE OPEN SIGHT (WGOS) Open rear sight with windage and elevation adjustment. Bases to fit most military and commercial barrels. Choice of square "U" or "V" notch blade, ³⁄₁₆", ¼", ⁵⁄₁₆", or ⅜" high.
Price: Less blade **$14.95**
Price: Extra blades, each **$5.88**

WILLIAMS WGOS OCTAGON Open rear sight for 1" octagon barrels. Installs with two 6-48 screws and uses same hole spacing as most T/C muzzleloading rifles. Four heights, choice of square, U, V, B blade.
Price: **$19.95**

WILLIAMS WSKS, WAK47 Replaces original military-type rear sight. Adjustable for windage and elevation. No drilling or tapping. Peep aperture or open. For SKS carbines, AK-47.
Price: Aperture **$22.35**
Price: Open **$19.95**

WILLIAMS WM-96 Fits Mauser 96-type military rifles, replaces original rear sight with open blade or aperture. Fully adjustable for windage and elevation. No drilling; tapping.
Price: Aperture **$22.35**
Price: Open **$19.95**

Micrometer Receiver Sights

BEEMAN/WEIHRAUCH MATCH APERTURE SIGHT Micrometer ¼-minute click adjustment knobs with settings indicated on scales.
Price: **$120.00**

BEEMAN/FEINWERKBAU 5420 MATCH APERTURE SIGHTS Locks into one of four eye-relief positions. Micrometer ¼-minute click adjustments; may be set to zero at any range. Extra windage scale visible beside eyeshade. Primarily for use at 5 to 20 meters.
Price: **$200.00**

BEEMAN/FEINWERKBAU 5454 MATCH APERTURE SIGHT Small size, new-design sight uses constant-pressure flat springs to eliminate point of impact shifts.
Price: **$290.00**

BEEMAN SPORT APERTURE SIGHT Positive click micrometer adjustments. Standard units with flush surface screwdriver adjustments. Deluxe version has target knobs. For air rifles with grooved receivers.
Price: Standard **$35.00**
Price: Deluxe **$45.00**

LYMAN NO. 2 TANG SIGHT Designed for the Winchester Model 94. Has high index marks on aperture post; comes with both .093" quick sighting aperture, .040" large disk aperture, and replacement mounting screws.
Price: **$69.00**

LYMAN No. 57 ¼-minute clicks. Stayset knobs. Quick release slide, adjustable zero scales. Made for almost all modern rifles.
Price: **$66.00**
Price: No. 57SME, 57SMET (for White Systems Model 91 and Whitetail rifles) **$66.00**

LYMAN No. 66 Fits close to the rear of flat-sided receivers, furnished with Stayset knobs. Quick release slide, ¼-min. adjustments. For most lever or slide action or flat-sided automatic rifles.
Price: **$66.00**
Price: No. 66MK (for all current versions of the Knight MK-85 in-line rifle with flat-sided receiver) **$66.00**

LYMAN No. 66U Light weight, designed for most modern shotguns with a flat-sided, round-top receiver. ¼-minute clicks. Requires drilling, tapping. Not for Browning A-5, Rem. M11.
Price: **$66.00**

LYMAN 90MJT RECEIVER SIGHT Mounts on standard Lyman and Williams FP bases. Has ¼-minute audible micrometer click adjustments, target knobs with direction indicators. Adjustable zero scales, quick release slide. Large ⅞" diameter aperture disk.
Price: **$79.95**

MILLETT RIFLE SIGHTS Fully adjustable, heat-treated nickel steel peep aperture receiver sight for the AR-15A-1 and Mini-14. Has fine windage and elevation adjustments; replaces original.
Price: Rear sight, Mini-14 . . . . **$54.00**
Price: Front sight, Mini-14 . . . . **$18.75**
Price: Rear sight, AR-15A-1 . . . . **$51.45**
Price: Serrated ramp front sight, AR-15A-1 . . . . . . **$12.25**

WILLIAMS FP Internal click adjustments. Positive locks. For virtually all rifles, T/C Contender, Heckler & Koch HK-91, Ruger Mini-14, plus Win., Rem. and Ithaca shotguns.
Price: From **$55.40**
Price: With Target Knobs **$65.80**
Price: With Square Notched Blade **$58.25**
Price: With Target Knobs & Square Notched Blade **$68.80**
Price: FP-GR (for dovetail-grooved receivers, 22s and air guns) **$55.40**
Price: FP-94BBSE (for Win. 94 Big Bore A.E.; uses top rear scope mount holes) **$55.40**

WILLIAMS TARGET FP Similar to the FP series but developed for most bolt-action rimfire rifles. Target FP High adjustable from 1.250" to 1.750" above centerline of bore; Target FP Low adjustable from .750" to 1.250". Attaching bases for Rem. 540X, 541-S, 580, 581, 582 (#540); Rem. 510, 511, 512, 513-T, 521-T (#510); Win. 75 (#75); Savage/Anschutz 64 and Mark 12 (#64). Some rifles require drilling, tapping.
Price: High or Low **$74.99**
Price: Base only **$12.60**
Price: FP-T/C Scout rifle, from **$55.40**
Price: FP-94BBSE (for Win. 94 Big Bore A.E.; uses top rear scope mount holes) **$55.40**

WILLIAMS 5-D SIGHT Low cost sight for shotguns, 22s and the more popular big game rifles. Adjustment for windage and elevation. Fits most guns without

drilling and tapping. Also for British SMLE, Winchester M94 Side Eject.
Price: From $29.95
Price: With Shotgun Aperture $29.95
WILLIAMS GUIDE (WGRS) Receiver sight for 30 M1 Carbine, M1903A3 Springfield, Savage 24s, Savage-Anschutz and Weatherby XXII. Utilizes military dovetail; no drilling. Double-dovetail windage adjustment, sliding dovetail adjustment for elevation.
Price: $29.95
Price: WGRS-CVA (for rifles with octagon barrels, receivers) $29.95

FRONT SIGHTS

ERA FRONT SIGHTS European-type front sights inserted from the front. Various heights available. From New England Custom Gun Service.
Price: 1/16" silver bead $10.50
Price: 3/32" silver bead $14.50
Price: Sourdough bead $13.00
Price: Tritium night sight $36.00
Price: Folding night sight with ivory bead $36.00
LYMAN HUNTING SIGHTS Made with gold or white beads 1/16" to 3/32" wide and in varying heights for most military and commercial rifles. Dovetail bases.
Price: $9.95
MARBLE STANDARD Ivory, red, or gold bead. For all American-made rifles, 1/16" wide bead with semi-flat face which does not reflect light. Specify type of rifle when ordering.
Price: $8.25
MARBLE CONTOURED Has 3/8" dovetail base, .090" deep, is 5/8" long. Uses standard 1/16" or 3/32" bead, ivory, red, or gold. Specify rifle type.
Price: $9.55
POLY-CHOKE Rifle front sights available in six heights and two widths. Model A designed to be inserted into the barrel dovetail; Model B is for use with standard .350" ramp; both have standard 3/8" dovetails. Gold or ivory /16" bead. From Marble Arms.
Price: $6.65
WILLIAMS RISER BLOCKS For adding .250" height to front sights when using a receiver sight. Two widths available: .250" for Williams Streamlined RAmp or .340" on all standard ramps having this base width. Uses standard 3/8" dovetail.
Price: $5.15

Globe Target Front Sights

LYMAN 20 MJT TARGET FRONT Has 7/8" diameter, one-piece steel globe with 3/8" dovetail base. Height is .700" from bottom of dovetail to center of aperture; height on 20 LJT is .750". Comes with seven Anschutz-size steel inserts—two posts and five apertures .126" through .177".
Price: 20 MJT or 20 LJT $36.00
LYMAN No. 17A TARGET Includes seven interchangeable inserts: four apertures, one transparent amber and two posts .50" and .100" in width.
Price: $29.00
Price: Insert set $10.50
LYMAN No. 93 MATCH Has 7/8" diameter, fits any rifle with a standard dovetail mounting block. Comes with seven target inserts and accepts most Anschutz accessories. Hooked locking bolt and nut allows quick removal, installation. Base available in .860" (European) and .562" (American) hole spacing.
Price: $48.00
WILLIAMS TARGET GLOBE FRONT Adapts to many rifles. Mounts to the base with a knurled locking screw. Height is .545" from center, not including base. Comes with inserts.
Price: $29.95
Price: Dovetail base (low) .220" $16.50
Price: Dovetail base (high) .465" $16.50
Price: Screw-on base, .300" height, .300" radius $15.00
Price: Screw-on base, .450" height, .350" radius $15.00
Price: Screw-on base, .215" height, .400" radius $15.00

Ramp Sights

ERA MASTERPIECE Banded ramps; 21 sizes; hand-detachable beads and hood; beads inserted from the front. Various heights available. From New England Custom Gun Service.
Price: Banded ramp $49.00
Price: Hood $9.50
Price: 1/16" silver bead $10.50
Price: 3/32" silver bead $14.50
Price: Sourdough bead $13.00
Price: Tritium night sight $36.00
Price: Folding night sight with ivory bead $36.00
LYMAN SCREW-ON RAMP Used with 8-40 screws but may also be brazed on. Heights from .10" to .350". Ramp without sight.
Price: $15.95
MARBLE FRONT RAMPS Available in either screw-on or sweat-on style, five heights: 3/16", 5/16", 3/8", 7/16", 9/16". Standard 3/8" dovetail slot.
Price: $15.85
Price: Hoods for above ramps $3.45
WILLIAMS SHORTY RAMP Companion to "Streamlined" ramp, about 1/2" shorter. Screw-on or sweat-on. It is furnished in 1/8", 3/16", 9/32", and 3/8" heights without hood only. Also for shotguns.
Price: $12.95
Price: With dovetail lock $15.45
WILLIAMS STREAMLINED RAMP Available in screw-on or sweat-on models. Furninshed in 9/16", 7/16", 3/8", 5/16", 3/16" heights.
Price: $15.55
Price: Sight hood $3.65
WILLIAMS STREAMLINED FRONT SIGHTS Narrow (.250" width) for Williams Streamlined ramps and others with 1/4" top width; medium (.340" width) for all standard factory ramps. Available with white, gold or flourescent beads, 1/16" or 3/32".
Price: . . . . . $8.25 to 9.50

Handgun Sights

BO-MAR DELUXE BMCS Gives 3/8" windage and elevation adjustment at 50 yards on Colt Gov't 45; sight radius under 7". For GM and Commander models only. Uses existing dovetail slot. Has shield-type rear blade.
Price: $65.95
Price: BMCS-2 (for GM and 9mm) $65.95
Price: Flat bottom $65.95
Price: BMGC (for Colt Gold Cup), angled serrated blade, rear $65.95
Price: BMGC front sight $12.00
Price: BMCZ-75 (for CZ-75, TZ-75, P-9 and most clones. Works with factory front $65.95
BO-MAR FRONT SIGHTS Dovetail style for S&W 4506, 4516, 1076; undercut style (.250", .280", 5/16" high); Fast Draw style (.210", .250", .230" high).
Price $12.00
BO-MAR BMU XP-100/T/C CONTENDER No gunsmithing required; has .080" notch.
Price: $77.00
BO-MAR BMML For muzzleloaders; has .062" notch, flat bottom.
Price: $65.95
Price: With 3/8" dovetail $65.95
BO-MAR RUGER "P" ADJUSTABLE SIGHT Replaces factory front and rear sights.
Price: Rear sight $65.95
Price: Front sight $12.00
BO-MAR BMR Fully adjustable rear sight for Ruger MKI, MKII Bull barrel autos.
Price: Rear $65.95
Price: Undercut front sight $12.00
BO-MAR BMSW SMITH & WESSON SIGHTS Replace the S&W Novak-style fixed sights. A .385" high front sight and minor machining required. For models 4506, 4516, 1076; all 9mms with 5 3/4" and 6 3/16" radius.
Price: $65.95
Price: .385" front sight $12.00
Price: BM-645 rear sight (for S&W 645, 745), uses factory front $65.95
Price: BMSW-52 rear sight (for Model 52), fits factory dovetail, uses factory front $65.95
BO-MAR LOW PROFILE RIB & ACCURACY TUNER Streamlined rib with front and rear sights; 7 1/8" sight radius. Brings sight line closer to the bore than standard or extended sight and ramp. Weight 5 oz. Made for Colt Gov't 45, Super 38, and Gold Cup 45 and 38.
Price: $123.00
BO-MAR COMBAT RIB For S&W Model 19 revolver with 4" barrel. Sight radius 5 3/4", weight 5 1/2 oz.
Price: $110.00
BO-MAR HUNTER REAR SIGHT Replacement rear sight in two models—S&W K and L frames use 2 3/4" Bo-Mar base with 7/16" overhang, has two screw holes; S&W N frame has 3" base, three screw holes. A .200" taller front blade is required.
Price: $79.00
BO-MAR WINGED RIB For S&W 4" and 6" length barrels—K-38, M10, HB 14 and 19. Weight for the 6" model is about 7 1/4 oz.
Price: $123.00
BO-MAR COVER-UP RIB Adjustable rear sight, winged front guards. Fits right over revolver's original front sight. For S&W 4" M-10HB, M-13, M-58, M-64 & 65, Ruger 4" models SDA-34, SDA-84, SS-34, SS-84, GF-34, GF-84.
Price: $117.00
C-MORE SIGHTS Replacement front sight blades offered in two types and five styles. Made of Du Pont Acetal, they come in a set of five high-contrast colors: blue, green, pink, red and yellow. Easy to install. Patridge style for Colt Python (all barrels), Ruger Super Blackhawk (7 1/2"), Ruger Blackhawk (4 5/8"); ramp style for Python (all barrels), Blackhawk (4 5/8"), Super Blackhawk (7 1/2" and 10 1/2"). From C-More Systems.
Price: Per set $19.95
MMC COMBAT FIXED REAR SIGHT (Colt 1911-Type Pistols) This veteran MMC sight is well known to those who prefer a true combat sight for "carry" guns. Steel construction for long service. Choose from a wide variety of front sights.
Price: Combat Fixed Rear, plain $18.45
Price: As above, white outline $23.65
Price: Combat Front Sight for above, six styles, from $5.15
MMC M/85 ADJUSTABLE REAR SIGHT Designed to be compatible with the Ruger P-85 front sight. Fully adjustable for windage and elevation.
Price: M/85 Adjustable Rear Sight, plain $52.45
Price: As above, white outline $57.70
MMC STANDARD ADJUSTABLE REAR SIGHT Available for Colt 1911 type, Ruger Standard Auto, and now for S&W 469, and 659 pistols. No front sight

CAUTION: PRICES SHOWN ARE SUPPLIED BY THE MANUFACTURER OR IMPORTER. CHECK YOUR LOCAL GUNSHOP.

change is necessary, as this sight will work with the original factory front sight.
Price: Standard Adjustable Rear Sight, plain leaf **$46.05**
Price: Standard Adjustable Rear Sight, white outline **$51.15**
MMC MINI-SIGHT Miniature size for carrying, fully adjustable, for maximum accuracy with your pocket auto. MMC's Mini-Sight will work with the factory front sight. No machining is necessary; easy installation. Available for Walther PP, PPK, and PPK/S pistols. Will also fit fixed sight Browning Hi-Power (P-35).
Price: Mini-Sight, plain **$58.45**
Price: Mini-Sight, white bar **$63.45**
MEPROLIGHT SIGHTS Replacement tritium open sights for popular handguns and AR-15/M-16 rifles. Both front and rear sights have tritium inserts for illumination in low-light conditions. Inserts give constant non-glare green light for 5 years, even in cold weather. For most popular auto pistols, revolvers, some rifles and shotguns. **Contact Hesco, Inc. for complete details.**
Price: Shotgun bead front sight **$22.95**
Price: M-16 front sight only **$32.95**
Price: H&K SR9, MP5 front sight only **$49.95**
Price: Colt Python, King Cobra, Ruger GP-100 adj. sights **$124.95**
Price: Most other front and rear fixed sights **$94.95**
Price: Adj. sights for Beretta, Browning, Colt Gov't., Glock, Ruger P-Series, SIG, Taurus PT-92 . . . . **$139.95**
MILLETT BAR-DOT-BAR TRITIUM SIGHTS Combo set uses the Series 100 fully adjustable sight system with horizontal tritium inserts on the rear, a single insert on the front. Available for: Ruger P-85, SIG Sauer P220, P225/226, Browning Hi-Power, Colt GM, CZ/TZ, TA-90, Glock 17, 19, 20, 21, 22, 23, S&W (2nd, 3rd generations), Beretta 84, 85, 92SB, Taurus PT-92.
Price: **$135.00**
Price: Beretta, Taurus **$143.50**
MILLETT 3-DOT SYSTEM SIGHTS The 3-Dot System sights use a single white dot on the front blade and two dots flanking the rear notch. Fronts available in Dual-Crimp and Wide Stake-On styles, as well as special applications. Adjustable rear sight available for most popular auto pistols and revolvers.
Price: Front, from **$16.00**
Price: Adjustable rear . . . . **$55.60 to $56.80**
MILLETT REVOLVER FRONT SIGHTS All-steel replacement front sights with either white or orange bar. Easy to install. For Ruger GP-100, Redhawk, Security-Six, Police-Six, Speed-Six, Colt Trooper, Diamondback, King Cobra, Peacemaker, Python, Dan Wesson 22 and 15-2.
Price: . . . . **$13.60 to $16.00**
MILLETT DUAL-CRIMP FRONT SIGHT Replacement front sight for automatic pistols. Dual-Crimp uses an all-steel two-point hollow rivet system. Available in eight heights and four styles. Has a skirted base that covers the front sight pad. Easily installed with the Millett Installation Tool Set. Available in Blaze Orange Bar, White Bar, Serrated Ramp, Plain Post.
Price: **$16.00**
MILLETT STAKE-ON FRONT SIGHT Replacement front sight for automatic pistols. Stake-On sights have skirted base that covers the front sight pad. Easily installed with the Millet Installation Tool Set. Available in seven heights and four styles—Blaze Orange Bar, White Bar, Serrated Ramp, Plain Post.
Price: **$16.00**
OMEGA OUTLINE SIGHT BLADES Replacement rear sight blades for Colt and Ruger single action guns and the Interarms Virginian Dragoon. Standard Outline available in gold or white notch outline on blue metal. From Omega Sales, Inc.
Price: **$8.95**
OMEGA MAVERICK SIGHT BLADES Replacement "peep-sight" blades for Colt, Ruger SAs, Virginian Dragoon. Three models available—No. 1, Plain; No. 2, Single Bar; No. 3, Double Bar Rangefinder. From Omega Sales, Inc.
Price: Each **$6.95**
P-T TRITIUM NIGHT SIGHTS Self-luminous tritium sights for most popular handguns, Colt AR-15, H&K rifles and shotguns. Replacement handgun sight sets available in 3-Dot style (green/green, green/yellow, green/orange) with bold outlines around inserts; Bar-Dot available in green/green with or without white outline rear sight. Functional life exceeds 15 years. From Innovative Weaponry, Inc.
Price: Handgun sight sets **$89.95**
Price: Rifle sight sets **$89.95**
Price: Rifle, front only **$32.95**
Price: Shotgun, front only **$18.95**
TRIJICON NIGHT SIGHTS Three-dot night sight system uses tritium inserts in the front and rear sights. Tritium "lamps" are mounted in silicone rubber inside a metal cylinder. A polished crystal sapphire provides protection and clarity. Inlaid white outlines provide 3-dot aiming in daylight also. Available for most popular handguns with fixed or adjustable sights. From Trijicon, Inc.
Price: . . . . **$19.95 to $175.00**
THOMPSON/CENTER SILHOUETTE SIGHTS Replacement front and rear sights for the T/C Contender. Front sight has three interchangeable blades. Rear sight has three notch widths. Rear sight can be used with existing soldered front sights.
Price: Front sight **$31.95**
Price: Rear sight **$85.00**
WICHITA SERIES 70/80 SIGHT Provides click windage and elevation adjustments with precise repeatability of settings. Sight blade is grooved and angled back at the top to reduce glare. Available in Low Mount Combat or Low Mount Target styles for Colt 45s and their copies, S&W 645, Hi-Power, CZ 75 and others.
Price: Rear sight, target or combat **$66.75**
Price: Front sight, Patridge or ramp **$10.45**

WICHITA GRAND MASTER DELUXE RIBS Ventilated rib has wings machined into it for better sight acquisition and is relieved for Mag-Na-Porting. Milled to accept Weaver see-thru-style rings. Made of stainless or blued steel; front and rear sights blued. Has Wichita Multi-Range rear sight system, adjustable front sight. Made for revolvers with 6" barrel.
Price: Model 301S, 301B (adj. sight K frames with custom bbl. of 1" to 1.032" dia. L and N frame with 1.062" to 1.100" dia. bbl.) **$160.00**
Price: Model 303S, 303B (adj. sight K, L, N frames with factory barrel) **$160.00**

Shotgun Sights

ACCURA-SITE For shooting shotgun slugs. Three models to fit most shotguns—"A" for vent. rib barrels, "B" for solid ribs, "C" for plain barrels. Rear sight has windage and elevation provisions. Easily removed and replaced. Includes front and rear sights. From All's, The Jim Tembeils Co.
Price: . . . . **$27.95 to $34.95**
FIRE FLY EM-109 SL SHOTGUN SIGHT Made of aircraft-grade aluminum, this ¼-oz. "channel" sight has a thick, sturdy hollowed post between the side rails to give a Patridge sight picture. All shooting is done with both eyes open, allowing the shooter to concentrate on the target, not the sights. The hole in the sight post gives reduced-light shooting capability and allows for fast, precise aiming. For sport or combat shooting. Model EM-109 fits all vent. rib and double barrel shotguns and muzzleloaders with octagon barrel. Model MOC-110 fits all plain barrel shotguns without screw-in chokes. From JAS, Inc.
Price: **$35.00**
LYMAN Three sights of over-sized ivory beads. No. 10 Front (press fit) for double barrel or ribbed single barrel guns...**$5.00**; No. 10D Front (screw fit) for non-ribbed single barrel guns (comes with wrench)...**$6.50**; No. 11 Middle (press fit) for double and ribbed single barrel guns...**$5.30**.
MMC M&P COMBAT SHOTGUN SIGHT SET A durable, protected ghost ring aperture, combat sight made of steel. Fully adjustable for windage and elevation.
Price: M&P Sight Set (front and rear) **$73.45**
Price: As above, installed **$83.95**
MARBLE SHOTGUN BEAD SIGHTS No. 214—Ivory front bead, ¹¹⁄₆₄", tapered shank...**$4.15**; No. 223—Ivory rear bead, .080", tapered shank...**$4.15**; No. 217—Ivory front bead, ¹¹⁄₆₄", threaded shank...**$4.15**; No. 223-T—Ivory rear bead, .080", threaded shank...**$5.60**. Reamers, taps and wrenches available from Marble Arms.
MILLETT SHURSHOT SHOTGUN SIGHT A sight system for shotguns with ventilated rib. Rear sight attaches to the rib, front sight replaces the front bead. Front has an orange face, rear has two orange bars. For 870, 1100 or other models.
Price: Front and rear **$13.15**
Price: Adjustable front and rear **$22.00**
POLY-CHOKE Replacement front shotgun sights in four styles—Xpert, Poly Bead, Xpert Mid Rib sights, and Bev-L-Block. Xpert Front available in 3x56, 6x48 thread, ³⁄₃₂" or ⁵⁄₃₂" shank length, gold, ivory...**$4.70**; or Sun Spot orange bead...**$5.00**; Poly Bead is standard replacement ⅛" bead, 6x48...**$2.85**; Xpert Mid Rib in tapered carrier (ivory only) **$4.15**, or 3x56 threaded shank (gold only)...**$2.85**; Hi and Lo Blok sights with 6x48 thread, gold or ivory...**$4.70** or Sun Spot Orange...**$5.00**. From Marble Arms.
SLUG SIGHTS Made of non-marring black nylon, front and rear sights stretch over and lock onto the barrel. Sights are low profile with blaze orange front blade. Adjustable for windage and elevation. For plain-barrel (non-ribbed) guns in 12-, 16- and 20-gauge, and for shotguns with ⁵⁄₁₆" and ⅜" ventilated ribs. From Innovision Ent.
Price: **$11.95**
WILLIAMS GUIDE BEAD SIGHT Fits all shotguns, ⅛" ivory, red or gold bead. Screws into existing sight hole. Various thread sizes and shank lengths.
Price: **$4.50**
WILLIAMS SLUGGER SIGHTS Removable aluminum sights attach to the shotgun rib. High profile front, fully adjustable rear. Fits ¼", ⁵⁄₁₆" or ⅜" (special) ribs.
Price: **$34.95**

Sight Attachments

MERIT IRIS SHUTTER DISC Eleven clicks give 12 different apertures. No. 3 Disc and Master, primarily target types, 0.22" to .125"; No. 4, ½" dia. hunting type, .025" to .155". Available for all popular sights. The Master Deluxe, with flexible rubber light shield, is particularly adapted to extension, scope height, and tang sights. All Merit Deluxe models have internal click springs; are hand fitted to minimum tolerance.
Price: Master Deluxe **$63.00**
Price: No. 3 Disc **$52.00**
Price: No. 4 Hunting Disc **$45.00**
MERIT LENS DISC Similar to Merit Iris Shutter (Model 3 or Master) but incorporates provision for mounting prescription lens integrally. Lens may be obtained locally from your optician. Sight disc is ⁷⁄₁₆" wide (Model 3), or ¾" wide (Master). Model 3 Target.
Price: **$65.00**
Price: Master Deluxe **$75.00**
MERIT OPTICAL ATTACHMENT For revolver and pistol shooters, instantly attached by rubber suction cup to regular or shooting glasses. Any aperture .020" to .156".
Price: Deluxe (swings aside) **$63.00**
WILLIAMS APERTURES Standard thread, fits most sights. Regular series ⅜" to ½" O.D., .050" to .125" hole. "Twilight" series has white reflector ring.
Price: Regular series **$4.68**
Price: Twilight series **$6.40**
Price: Wide open ⁵⁄₁₆" aperture for shotguns fits 5-D or Foolproof sights (specify model) **$8.27**

CAUTION: PRICES SHOWN ARE SUPPLIED BY THE MANUFACTURER OR IMPORTER. CHECK YOUR LOCAL GUNSHOP.

49th EDITION, 1995 **465**

CHOKES & BRAKES

Briley Screw-In Chokes

Installation of these choke tubes requires that all traces of the original choking be removed, the barrel threaded internally with square threads and then the tubes are custom fitted to the specific barrel diameter. The tubes are thin and, therefore, made of stainless steel. Cost of installation for single-barrel guns (pumps, autos), lead shot, 12-gauge, **$129.00**, 20-gauge **$139.00**; steel shot **$159.00** and **$169.00**, all with three chokes; un-single target guns run **$190.00**; over/unders and side-by-sides, lead shot, 12-gauge, **$349.00**, 20-gauge **$369.00**; steel shot **$449.00** and **$469.00**, all with five chokes. For 10-gauge auto or pump with two steel shot chokes, **$149.00**; over/unders, side-by-sides with three steel shot chokes, **$329.00**. For 16-gauge auto or pump, three lead shot chokes, **$239.00**; over/unders, side-by-sides with five lead shot chokes, **$429.00**. The 28 and 410-bore run **$159.00** for autos and pumps with three lead shot chokes, **$429.00** for over/unders and side-by-sides with five lead shot chokes.

Cutts Compensator

The Cutts Compensator is one of the oldest variable choke devices available. Manufactured by Lyman Gunsight Corporation, it is available with a steel body. A series of vents allows gas to escape upward and downward. For the 12-ga. Comp body, six fixed-choke tubes are available: the Spreader—popular with Skeet shooters; Improved Cylinder; Modified; Full; Superfull, and Magnum Full. Full, Modified and Spreader tubes are available for 12 or 20, and an Adjustable Tube, giving Full through Improved Cylinder chokes, is offered in 12 and 20 gauges. Cutts Compensator, complete with wrench, adaptor and any single tube **$69.80**; with adjustable tube **$91.00**. All single choke tubes **$24.00** each. No factory installation available.

Gentry Quiet Muzzle Brake

Developed by gunmaker David Gentry, the "Quiet Muzzle Brake" is said to reduce recoil by up to 85 percent with no loss of accuracy or velocity. There is no increase in noise level because the noise and gases are directed away from the shooter. The barrel is threaded for installation and the unit is blued to match the barrel finish. Price, installed, is **$150.00**. Add **$15.00** for stainless steel, **$25.00** for knurled cap to protect threads.

Intermountain Arms Recoil Brake

The Custom Compact Recoil Brake is said to reduce felt recoil by 50 percent in most calibers. Machined with an expansion chamber to maximize efficiency. There are 42 ports to direct gases away from the shooter. Individually machined, polished and blued to match each barrel. Adds 1¾" to the barrel. Blued or stainless steel, **$169.00**. From Intermountain Arms.

JP Muzzle Brake

Designed for single shot handguns, AR-15, Ruger Mini-14, Ruger Mini Thirty and other sporting rifles, the JP Muzzle Brake redirects high pressure gases against a large frontal surface which applies forward thrust to the gun. All gases are directed up, rearward and to the sides. Priced at **$49.95** (AR-15), **$59.95** (bull barrel model), **$69.95** (Ruger Minis and Dual Chamber model). From JP Enterprises, Inc.

KDF Slim Line Muzzle Brake

This threaded muzzlebrake has 30 pressure ports that direct combustion gases in all directions to reduce felt recoil up to a claimed 80 percent without affecting accuracy or ballistics. It is said to reduce felt recoil of a 30-06 to that of a 243. Price, installed, is **$179.00**. From KDF, Inc.

Mag-Na-Port

Electrical Discharge Machining works on any firearm except those having non-conductive shrouded barrels. EDM is a metal erosion technique using carbon electrodes that control the area to be processed. The Mag-Na-Port venting process utilizes small trapezoidal openings to direct powder gases upward and outward to reduce recoil.

No effect is had on bluing or nickeling outside the Mag-Na-Port area so no refinishing is needed. Cost for the Mag-Na-Port treatment is **$65.00** for revolvers, **$90.00** for auto pistols, **$115.00** for rifles, not including shipping, handling and insurance. From Mag-Na-Port International.

Mag-Na-Brake

A screw-on brake under 2" long with progressive integrated exhaust chambers to neutralize expanding gases. Gases dissipate with an opposite twist to prevent the brake from unscrewing, and with a 5-degree forward angle to minimize sound pressure level. Available in blue, satin blue, bright or satin stainless. Standard installation costs **$159.00** for bolt-action rifles, many single action and single shot handguns. Auto, pump, lever-action, rolling block rifles, add **$20.00**. Light contour model, **$20.00** extra. From Mag-Na-Port International.

Poly-Choke

Marble Arms Corp., manufacturer of the Poly-Choke adjustable shotgun choke, now offers two models in 12-, 16-, 20-, and 28-gauge—the Ventilated and Standard style chokes. Each provides nine choke settings including Xtra-Full and Slug. The Ventilated model reduces 20 percent of a shotgun's recoil, the company claims, and is priced at **$88.00**. The Standard Model is **$79.75**. Postage not included. Contact Marble Arms for more data.

Reed-Choke

Reed-Choke is a system of interchangeable choke tubes that can be installed in any single or double-barreled shotgun, including over/unders. The existing chokes are bored out, the muzzles over-bored and threaded for the tubes. A choice of three Reed-Choke tubes are supplied—Skeet, Imp. Cyl., Mod., Imp. Mod., or Full. Flush fitting, no notches exposed. Designed for thin-walled barrels. Made from 174 stainless steel. Cost of the installation is **$179.95** for single-barrel guns, **$229.95** for doubles. Extra tubes cost **$40.00** each. Postage and handling charges are **$8.50**. From Clinton River Gun Service.

Pro-port

A compound ellipsoid muzzle venting process similar to Mag-Na-Porting, only exclusively applied to shotguns. Like Mag-Na-Porting, this system reduces felt recoil, muzzle jump, and shooter fatigue. Very helpful for trap doubles shooters. Pro-Port is a patented process and installation is available in both the U.S. and Canada. Cost for the Pro-Port process is **$110.00** for over/unders (both barrels); **$80.00** for only the top or bottom barrel; and **$69.00** for single-barrel shotguns. Prices do not include shipping and handling. From Pro-port Ltd.

SSK Arrestor Brake

This is a true muzzlebrake with an expansion chamber. It takes up about 1" of barrel and reduces velocity accordingly. Some Arrestors are added to a barrel, increasing its length. Said to reduce the felt recoil of a 458 to that approaching a 30-06. Can be set up to give zero muzzle rise in any caliber, and can be added to most guns. For handgun or rifle. Prices start at **$95.00**. Contact SSK Industries for full data.

Walker Choke Tubes

This interchangeable choke tube system uses an adaptor fitted to the barrel without swaging. Therefore, it can be fitted to any single-barreled gun. The choke tubes use the conical-parallel system as used on all factory-choked barrels. These tubes can be used in Winchester, Mossberg, Smith & Wesson, Weatherby, or similar barrels made for the standard screw-in choke system. Available for 10-, 12-, 16- and 20-gauge. Factory installation (single barrel) with standard Walker choke tube is **$95.00**, **$190.00** for double barrels with two choke tubes. A full range of constriction is available. Contact Walker Arms for more data.

Walker Full Thread Choke Tubes

An interchangeable choke tube system using fully threaded inserts. No swaging, adaptor or change in barrel exterior dimensions. Available in 12- or 20-gauge. Factory installation cost: **$95.00** with one tube; extra tubes **$20.00** each. Contact Walker Arms Co. for more data.

Maker and Model	Magn.	Field at 100 Yds. (feet)	Eye Relief (in.)	Length (in.)	Tube Dia. (in.)	W&E Adjust- ments	Weight (ozs.)	Price	Other Data
ACTION ARMS									
Micro-Dot									
1.5-4.5x LER Pistol	1.5-4.5	80-26	12-24	8.8	1	Int.	9.5	$199.00	[1]56mm objective. Variable intensity LED red aiming dot. Average battery life 20 to 4500 hours. Waterproof, nitrogen-filled aluminum tube. Fits most standard 1" rings. Both Ultra Dot models avail. in black and satin chrome. Imported by Action Arms Ltd.
1.5-4.5x Rifle	1.5-4.5	80-26	3	9.8	1	Int.	10.5	275.00	
2-7x32	2-7	54-18	3	11	1	Int.	12.1	295.00	
3-9x40[1]	3-9	40-14	3	12.2	1	Int.	13.3	310.00	
4x-12x[1]	4-12	—	3	14.3	1	Int.	18.3	419.00	
Ultra-Dot 25 1x	—	—	—	5.1	1	Int.	4.0	139.00	
Ultra-Dot 30 1x	—	—	—	5.1	30mm	Int.	3.9	149.00	
ADCO									
MiRAGE Ranger 1"	0	—	—	5.2	1	Int.	4.5	139.00	[1]Multi-Color Dot system changes from red to green. [2]For airguns, paintball, rimfires. Uses common lithium wafer battery. [3]Comes with standard dovetail mount. [4]3/8" dovetail mount; poly body; adj. intensity diode. All come with extension tube for mounting. Black or matte nickel finish. Optional 2x booster available. Five year warranty. From ADCO Sales.
MiRAGE Ranger 30mm	0	—	—	5.5	30mm	Int.	5.5	149.00	
MiRAGE Sportsman[1]	0	—	—	5.2	1	Int.	4.5	219.00	
MiRAGE Competitor[1]	0	—	—	5.5	30mm	Int.	5.5	249.00	
IMP Sight[2]	0	—	—	4.5	—	Int.	2	19.95	
Square Shooter[3]	0	—	—	5.0	—	Int.	5	98.00	
MiRAGE Eclipse[1]	0	—	—	5.5	30mm	Int.	5.3	215.00	
MiRAGE Champ Red Dot	0	—	—	4.5	—	Int.	2	39.95	
AIMPOINT									
Comp	0	—	—	4.6	30mm	Int.	4.3	308.00	Illuminates red dot in field of view. Noparallax (dot does not need to be centered). Unlimited field of view and eye relief. On/off, adj. intensity. Dot covers 3" @ 100 yds. Mounts avail. for all sights and scopes. [1]Comes with 30mm rings, battery, lens cloth. [2]Requires 1" rings. Black or stainless finish. 3x scope attachment (for rifles only), $129.95. [3]Projects red dot of visible laser light onto target. Black finish (LSR-2B) or stainless (LSR-2S); or comes with rings and accessories. Optional toggle switch, $34.95. Lithium battery life up to 15 hours. [4]Black finish (AP 5000-B) or stainless (AP 5000-S); avail. with regular 3-min. or 10-min. Mag Dot as B2 or S2. [5] For Beretta, Browning, Colt Gov't., Desert Eagle, Glock, Ruger, SIG-Sauer, S&W. [6]For Colt, S&W. From Aimpoint.
Series 5000[4]	0	—	—	5.75	30mm	Int.	5.8	277.00	
Series 3000 Universal[2]	0	—	—	5.5	1	Int.	5.5	232.00	
Series 5000/2x[1]	2	—	—	7	30mm	Int.	9	367.00	
Laserdot[3]	—	—	—	3.5	1	Int.	4.0	319.95	
Autolaser[5]	—	—	—	3.75	1	Int.	4.3	351.00	
Revolver Laser[6]	—	—	—	3.5	1	Int.	3.6	339.00	
APPLIED LASER SYSTEMS									
MiniAimer MA-3[1]	—	—	—	1.36	—	Int.	.88	246.00	[1]Output power 5mW; also MA-35, power less than 3mW, $350.00. [2]for HK USP; 5mW; also HK USP 635nm (3mW), $350.00. [3]also SP 89/MP5 635nm (3mW), $350.00. [4]5mW power. Mounts avail. for Browning Hi-Power, S&W, Colt 1911, Beretta 92F, Glock, SIG-Sauer, Ruger P-85 MkII, Firestor. From Applied Laser Systems.
Custom MiniAimer[2]	—	—	—	1.74	—	Int.	1.6	298.00	
Custom MiniAimer[3]	—	—	—	2.08	—	Int.	1.2	298.00	
T2 Custom Aimer[4]	—	—	—	2.8	—	Int.	2.2	198.00	
AR-15 Custom Aimer[4]	—	—	—	2.0	—	Int.	3.0	279.00	
Custom Glock Mini Laser[4]	—	—	—	.75	—	Int.	.8	385.00	
ARMSON O.E.G.									
Standard	0	—	—	5 1/8	1	Int.	4.3	175.00	Shows red dot aiming point. No batteries needed. Standard model fits 1" ring mounts (not incl.). Other models available for many popular shotguns, para-military rifles and carbines. [1]Daylight Only Sight with 3/8" dovetail mount for 22s. Does not contain tritium. From Trijicon, Inc.
22 DOS[1]	0	—	—	3 3/4	—	Int.	3.0	104.00	
22 Day/Night	0	—	—	3 3/4	—	Int.	3.0	146.00	
M16/AR-15	0	—	—	5 1/8	—	Int.	5.5	209.00	
Colt Pistol	0	—	—	3 3/4	—	Int.	3.0	209.00	
BAUSCH & LOMB									
Elite 4000									
40-6244A[1]	6-24	18-4.5	3	16.9	1	Int.	20.2	675.00	[1]Adj. objective, sunshade. [2]Also in matte and silver finish, $625.00. [3]Also in matte finish, $575.00. [4]Also in matte finish, $367.95; silver finish, $367.95. [5]Also in matte finish, $341.95. [6]50mm objective; matte finish $424.95. [7]Also in matte finish, $413.95. [8]Also in silver finish, 303.95. [9]Also in silver finish, $411.95 Contact Bausch & Lomb Sports Optics Div. for details.
40-2104G[2]	2.5-10	41.5-10.8	3	13.5	1	Int.	16	600.00	
40-1636G[3]	1.5-6	61.8-16.1	3	12.8	1	Int.	15.4	550.00	
40-1040	10	10.5	3.6	13.8	1	Int.	22.1	1,725.00	
Elite 3000									
30-4124A[1]	4-12	26.9-9	3	13.2	1	Int.	15.0	401.95	
30-3940G[4]	3-9	33.8-11.5	3	12.6	1	Int.	13.0	346.95	
30-2732G[5]	2-7	44.6-12.7	3	11.6	1	Int.	12.0	322.95	
30-3950G[6]	3-9	31.5-10.5	3	15.7	1	Int.	19	411.95	
30-1545G[7]	1.5-4.5	73-24	3.3	9.7	1	Int.	10	394.95	
30-3955E	3-9	31.5-10.5	3	15.6	30mm	Int.	22	604.95	
Elite 3000 Handgun									
30-2028G[8]	2	23	9-26	8.4	1	Int.	6.9	284.95	
30-2632G[9]	2-6	10-4	20	9.0	1	Int.	10.0	392.95	
BEEMAN									
Blue Ring 20[1]	1.5	14	11-16	8.3	3/4	Int.	3.6	59.95	All scopes have 5-pt. reticle, all glass, fully coated lenses. [1]Pistol scope; cast mounts included. [2]Pistol scope; silhouette knobs. [3]Rubber armor coating; built-in double adj. mount, parallax-free setting. [4]Objective focus, built-in double-adj. mount; matte finish. [5]Objective focus. [6]Also available with color reticle. [7]Objective focus; silhouette knobs; matte finish. [8]Also in "L" models with reticle lighted by ambient light or tiny add-on illuminator. Lighted models slightly higher priced. Imported by Beeman.
Blue Ribbon 25[2]	2	19	10-24	9 1/16	1	Int.	7.4	154.95	
Blue Ribbon 50R[5]	2.5	33	3.5	12	1	Int.	11.8	198.95	
Blue Ribbon 66R[6,7,8]	2-7	62-16	3	11.4	1	Int.	14.9	298.50	
SS-3[3,4]	1.5-4	44.6-24.6	3	5.75	7/8	Int.	8.5	299.95	
Blue Ribbon 54R[5]	4	29	3.5	12	1	Int.	12.3	229.95	
SS-2[4,6,7]	4	24.6	5	7	1.38	Int.	13.7	299.95	

CAUTION: PRICES SHOWN ARE SUPPLIED BY THE MANUFACTURER OR IMPORTER. CHECK YOUR LOCAL GUNSHOP.

Maker and Model	Magn.	Field at 100 Yds. (feet)	Eye Relief (in.)	Length (in.)	Tube Dia. (in.)	W&E Adjust- ments	Weight (ozs.)	Price	Other Data
B-SQUARE									
BSL-1[1]	—	—	—	2.75	.75	Int.	2.25	229.95	[1]Blue finish; stainless, **$239.95**. T-slot mount; cord or integral switch. [2]Blue finish; stainless, **$309.95**. T-slot mount; cord or integral switch. Uses common A76 batteries. Dimensions 1.1"x1.1"x.6". From B-Square.
Mini-Laser[2]	—	—	—	1.1	—	Int.	2.9	299.95	
BURRIS									
Fullfield									
1½x[9]	1.6	62	3¼	10¼	1	Int.	9.0	236.95	All scopes avail. in Plex reticle. Steel-on-steel click adjustments. [1]Dot reticle on some models. [2]Post crosshair reticle $13 extra. [3]Matte satin finish. [4]Available with parallax adjustment $28 extra (standard on 10x, 12x, 4-12x, 6-12x, 6-18x, 6x HBR and 3-12x Signature). [5]Silver matte finish $30 extra. [6]Target knobs extra, standard on silhouette models, LER and XER with P.A., 6x HBR. [7]Sunshade avail. [8]Avail. with Fine Plex reticle. [9]Available with Heavy Plex reticle. [10]Available with Posi-Lock. [11]Available with Peep Plex reticle. [12]Also avail. for rimfires, airguns, **$652.95**.
2½x[9]	2.5	55	3¼	10¼	1	Int.	9.0	248.95	
4x[1,2,3]	3.75	36	3¼	11¼	1	Int.	11.5	265.95	
6x[1,3]	5.8	23	3¼	13	1	Int.	12.0	302.95	
12x[1,4,6,7,8]	11.8	10.5	3¼	15	1	Int.	15	358.95	
1¾-5x[1,2,9,10]	1.7-4.6	66-25	3¼	10⅞	1	Int.	13	312.95	
2-7x[1,2,3]	2.5-6.8	47-18	3¼	12	1	Int.	14	334.95	
3-9x[1,2,3,10]	3.3-8.7	38-15	3¼	12⅝	1	Int.	15	331.95	
3.5-10x50mm[3,5,10]	3.7-9.7	29.5-11	3-3.25	14	1	Int.	19	422.95	
4-12x[1,4,8,11]	4.4-11.8	27-10	3¼	15	1	Int.	18	419.95	
6-18x[1,3,4,6,7,8]	6.5-17.6	16-7	3¼	15.8	1	Int.	18.5	437.95	
Compact Scopes									
4x[4,5]	3.6	24	3¾-5	8¼	1	Int.	7.8	213.95	
6x[1,4]	5.5	17	3¾-5	9	1	Int.	8.2	228.95	
6x HBR[1,5,8]	6.0	13	4.5	11¼	1	Int.	13.0	294.95	
2-7x	2.5-6.9	32-14	3¾-5	12	1	Int.	10.5	292.95	
3-9x[5]	3.6-8.8	25-11	3¾-5	12⅝	1	Int.	11.5	299.95	
4-12x[1,4,6]	4.5-11.6	19-8	3¾-4	15	1	Int.	15	395.95	
Signature Series									
1.5-6x[2,3,5,9,10]	1.7-5.8	70-20	3½-4	10.8	1	Int.	13.0	395.95	LER=Long Eye Relief; IER=Intermediate Eye Relief; XER=Extra Eye Relief. Partial listing shown, contact maker for complete data. From Burris.
4x[3]	4.0	30	3	12⅛	1	Int.	14	325.95	
6x[3]	6.0	20	3	12⅛	1	Int.	14	341.95	
2-8x[3,5,11]	2.1-7.7	53-17	3-3.25	11.75	1	Int.	14	459.95	
3-9x[3,5,10]	3.3-8.8	36-14	3	12⅞	1	Int.	15.5	469.95	
2½-10x[3,5,10]	2.7-9.5	37-10.5	3-3¾	14	1	Int.	19.0	530.95	
3-12x[3,10]	3.3-11.7	34-9	3	14¼	1	Int.	21	587.95	
6-24x[1,3,5,6,8,10]	6.6-23.8	17-6	3-2½	16.0	1	Int.	22.7	611.95	
8-32x[8,10,12]	8.6-31.4	13-3.8	3-3.75	17	1	Int.	24	671.95	
Handgun									
1½-4x LER[1,5,10]	1.6-3.	16-11	11-25	10¼	1	Int.	11	328.95	
2-7x LER[3,4,5,10]	2-6.5	21-7	7-27	9.5	1	Int.	12.6	321.95	
3-9x LER[4,5,10]	3.4-8.4	12-5	22-14	11	1	Int.	14	359.95	
1x LER[1]	1.1	27	10-24	8¾	1	Int.	6.8	202.95	
2x LER[4,5,6]	1.7	21	10-24	8¾	1	Int.	6.8	209.95	
3x LER[4,6]	2.7	17	10-20	8⅞	1	Int.	6.8	226.95	
4x LER[1,4,5,6,10]	3.7	11	10-22	9⅝	1	Int.	9.0	235.95	
7x IER[1,4,5,6]	6.5	6.5	10-16	11¼	1	Int.	10	258.95	
10x IER[1,4,6]	9.5	4	8-12	13½	1	Int.	14	348.95	
Scout Scope									
1½x XER[3,9]	1.5	22	7-18	9	1	Int.	7.3	208.95	
2¾x XER[3,9]	2.7	15	7-14	9⅜	1	Int.	7.5	213.95	
BUSHNELL									
Trophy									
73-0130[1]	1	61	—	5.25	30mm	Int.	5.5	269.95	[1]45mm objective. [2]Wide angle. [3]Also silver finish, **$204.95**. [4]Also silver finish, **$248.95**. [5]56mm objective. [6]Selective red L.E.D. dot for low light hunting. [7]Rings included. **Only selected models shown.** [8]Also silver finish, **$66.95**. [9]Adj. obj. Contact Bausch & Lomb Sports Optics Div. for details.
73-0150[7]	1	26	—	4.8	50mm	Int.	8.3	403.95	
73-2545[1]	2.5-10	39-10	3	13.75	1	Int.	14	301.95	
73-1500[2]	1.75-5	68-23	3.5	10.8	1	Int.	12.3	257.95	
73-2733[2]	2-7	63-18	3	10	1	Int.	11.3	248.95	
73-4124[2]	4-12	32-11	3	12.5	1	Int.	16.1	273.95	
73-3940[2]	3-9	42-14	3	11.7	1	Int.	13.2	180.95	
73-6184	6-18	17.3-6	3	14.8	1	Int.	17.9	322.95	
Trophy Handgun									
73-0232[3]	2	20	9-26	8.7	1	Int.	7.7	189.95	
73-2632[4]	2-6	21-7	9-26	9.1	1	Int.	9.6	235.95	
Banner Standard									
71-2520	2.5	44	3.6	10	1	Int.	7.5	84.95	
71-3956[5]	3-9	37-12	3.5	13.7	1	Int.	17.3	273.95	
Lite-Site									
71-3940[6]	3-9	36-13	3.1	12.8	1	Int.	15.5	350.95	
Sportview									
74-0004	4	31	4	11.7	1	Int.	11.2	87.95	
74-0039	3-9	38-13	3.5	10.75	1	Int.	11.2	104.95	
74-0412[9]	4-12	27-9	3.2	13.1	1	Int.	14.6	125.95	
74-0640	6	20.5	3	12.25	1	Int.	10.4	86.95	
74-1393[8]	3-9	35-12	3.5	11.75	1	Int.	10	63.95	
74-1545	1.5-4.5	69-24	3	10.7	1	Int.	8.6	84.95	
74-2532	2.5	44	3.5	10.75	1	Int.	9	84.95	
74-3145	3.5-10	36-13	3	12.75	1	Int.	13.9	138.95	
74-1403	4	29	4	11.75	1	Int.	9.2	50.95	
74-3938	3-9	42-14	3	12.7	1	Int.	12.5	105.95	
74-3720	3-7	23-11	2.6	11.3	.75	Int.	5.7	40.95	

CAUTION: PRICES SHOWN ARE SUPPLIED BY THE MANUFACTURER OR IMPORTER. CHECK YOUR LOCAL GUNSHOP.

Maker and Model	Magn.	Field at 100 Yds. (feet)	Eye Relief (in.)	Length (in.)	Tube Dia. (in.)	W&E Adjust-ments	Weight (ozs.)	Price	Other Data
Bushnell (cont.)									
Turkey & Brush									
73-1420	1.75-4	73-30	3.5	10.8	32mm	Int.	10.9	263.95	
CHARLES DALY									
4x32	4	28	3.25	11.75	1	Int.	9.5	70.00	Waterproof, fog-proof. [1]Shotgun scope. From Outdoor Sports Headquarters.
4x32[1]	4	16	6	8.8	1	Int.	9.2	90.00	
4x40 WA	4	36	3.25	13	1	Int.	11.5	98.00	
2-7x32 WA	2-7	56-17	3	11.5	1	Int.	12	125.00	
3-9x40	3-9	35-14	3	12.5	1	Int.	11.25	110.00	
3-9x40 WA	3-9	36-13	3	12.75	1	Int.	12.5	125.00	
4-12x40 WA	4-12	30-11	3	13.75	1	Int.	14.5	133.00	
FROM JENA									
4x36	4	39	3.5	11.6	26mm	Int.	14	695.00	[1]Military scope with adjustable parallax. Fixed powers have 26mm tubes, variables have 30mm tubes. Some models avail. with steel tubes. All lenses multi-coated. Dust and water tight. From Jena, Europtik, Ltd.
6x36	6	21	3.5	12	26mm	Int.	14	795.00	
6x42	6	21	3.5	13	26mm	Int.	15	860.00	
8x56	8	18	3.5	14.4	26mm	Int.	20	890.00	
1.5-6x42	1.5-6	61.7-23	3.5	12.6	30mm	Int.	17	975.00	
2-8x42	2-8	52-17	3.5	13.3	30mm	Int.	17	1,050.00	
2.5-10x56	2.5-10	40-13.6	3.5	15	30mm	Int.	21	1,195.00	
3-12x56	3-12	NA	NA	NA	30mm	Int.	NA	1,195.00	
4-16x56	4-16	NA	NA	NA	30mm	Int.	NA	1,225.00	
3-9x40	3-9	NA	NA	NA	1	Int.	NA	1,120.00	
2.5-10x46	2.5-10	NA	NA	NA	30mm	Int.	NA	1,150.00	
4-16x56[1]	4-16	NA	NA	NA	30mm	Int.	NA	1,490.00	
INTERAIMS									
One V	0	—	—	4.5	1	Int.	4	145.95	Intended for handguns. Comes with rings. Dot size less than 1½" @ 100 yds. Waterproof. Battery life 50-10,000 hours. Black or nickel finish. 2x booster, 1" or 30mm, $139.00 Imported by Stoeger.
One V 30	0	—	—	4.5	30mm	Int.	4	159.95	
KAHLES									
K4x32-L	4	33	—	11.3	1	Int.	11.2	555.00	[1]Steel tube. [2]Ballistic cam system with military rangefinder. Waterproof, fogproof, nitrogen filled. Choice of reticles. Imported from Austria by Kahles USA.
K6x42-L	6	23	—	12.5	1	Int.	13	615.00	
K7x56-L	7	19.7	—	14.4	26mm	Int.	16.1	695.00	
K8x56-L	8	17.1	—	14.4	1	Int.	16.1	715.00	
K1.1-4.5x20-L	1.1-4.5	78.7-30	—	10.5	30mm	Int.	12.6	685.00	
K1.5-6x42-L	1.5-6	61-21	—	12.5	30mm	Int.	15.8	785.00	
K2.2-9x42-L	2.2-9	39.5-15	—	13.3	30mm	Int.	15.5	945.00	
K3-12x56-L	3-12	30-11	—	15.2	30mm	Int.	18	1,045.00	
K2.5x20-S[1]	2.5	54	—	9.6	1	Int.	12.6	525.00	
KZF84-6[1,2]	6	23	—	12.5	1	Int.	17.6	995.00	
KZF84-10[1,2]	10	13	—	13.25	1	Int.	18	1,045.00	
KILHAM									
Hutson Handgunner II	1.7	8	—	5½	7/8	Int.	5.1	119.95	Unlimited eye relief; internal click adjustments; crosshair reticle. Fits Thompson/Center rail mounts, for S&W K, N, Ruger Blackhawk, Super, Super Single-Six, Contender.
Hutson Handgunner	3	8	10-12	6	7/8	Int.	5.3	119.95	
LASERAIM									
LA8[1]	—	—	—	2.94	.74	Int.	NA	139.95	[1]300-yd. range; 15-hr. batt. [2]Red dot laser; fits Weaver-style mounts; also LA2XM with Hotdot, $269.95. [3]300-yd. range; 2" dot at 100 yds.; rechargeable Nicad battery; also LA5 Magnum—1000-yd. range, 1" dot at 100 yds, $209.95. [4]500-yd. range; 2" dot at 100 yds.; rechargeable Nicad battery. [5]1.5-mile range; 1" dot at 100 yds.; 20+ hrs. batt. life. [6]1.5-mile range; 1" dot at 100 yds.; rechargeable Nicad battery (comes with in-field charger); [7]Trigger guard mount for S&W 3900, 5900, 6900, Glock, Ruger P-Series, Beretta 93F, FS. All have w&e adj.; black or satin silver finish. From Emerging Technologies, Inc.
LA2X Dualdot[2]	—	—	—	NA	30mm	Int.	NA	249.95	
LA5[3]	—	—	—	2	.75	Int.	1.2	199.95	
LA9 Hotdot[4]	—	—	—	2	.75	Int.	NA	239.95	
LA10 Hotdot[5]	—	—	—	3.87	.75	Int.	NA	249.95	
LA11 Hotdot[6]	—	—	—	2.75	.75	Int.	NA	249.95	
LA14[7]	—	—	—	NA	NA	Int.	NA	283.00	
LASER DEVICES									
He Ne FA-6	—	—	—	6.2	—	Int.	11	229.50	Projects high intensity beam of laser light onto target as an aiming point. Adj. for w. & e. [1]Diode laser system. From Laser Devices, Inc.
He Ne FA-9	—	—	—	12	—	Int.	16	299.00	
He Ne FA-9P	—	—	—	9	—	Int.	14	299.00	
FA-4[1]	—	—	—	4.5	—	Int.	3.5	299.00	
LASERSIGHT									
LS45	0	—	—	7.5	—	Int.	8.5	245.00	Projects a highly visible beam of concentrated laser light onto the target. Adjustable for w.& e. Visible up to 500 yds. at night. For handguns, rifles, shotguns. Uses two standard 9V batteries. From Imatronic Lasersight.
LS25	0	—	—	6	3/4	Int.	3.5	270.00	
LS55	0	—	—	7	1	Int.	7	299.00	
LEATHERWOOD									
ART II	3.0-8.8	31-12	3.5	13.9	1	Int.	42	750.00	Compensates for bullet drop via external circular cam. Matte gray finish. Designed specifically for the M1A/M-14 rifle. Quick Detachable model for rifles with Weaver-type bases. From North American Specialties.
LEATHERWOOD-MEOPTA, INC.									
ART II	3.0-8.8	31-12	3.5	13.9	1	Int.	42	750.00	ART CZ-4 and CZ-6 have range-finding reticles with hold-over marks, multi-coated optics. Black or gray finish. From Leatherwood-Meopta, Inc.
ART CZ-4	4	32	—	11	1	Int.	13.4	257.90	
ART CZ-6	6	21	—	13.7	1	Int.	18.3	287.90	

CAUTION: PRICES SHOWN ARE SUPPLIED BY THE MANUFACTURER OR IMPORTER. CHECK YOUR LOCAL GUNSHOP.

Maker and Model	Magn.	Field at 100 Yds. (feet)	Eye Relief (in.)	Length (in.)	Tube Dia. (in.)	W&E Adjustments	Weight (ozs.)	Price	Other Data
LEUPOLD									Constantly centered reticles, choice of Duplex, tapered CPC, Leupold Dot, Crosshair and Dot. CPC and Dot reticles extra. [1]2x and 4x scopes have from 12"-24" of eye relief and are suitable for handguns, top ejection arms and muzzleloaders. [2]3x9 Compact, 6x Compact, 12x, 3x9, 3.5x10 and 6.5x20 come with adjustable objective. [3]Target scopes have 1-min. divisions with ¼-min. clicks, and adjustable objectives. 50-ft. Focus Adaptor available for indoor target ranges, **$51.80.** Sunshade available for all adjustable objective scopes, **$19.60-37.50.** [4]Also available in matte finish for about **$22.00** extra. [5]Silver finish about **$22.00** extra. [6]Matte finish. [7]Battery life 60 min.; dot size .625" @ 25 yds. Black matte finish Partial listing shown. **Contact Leupold for complete details.**
Vari-X III 3.5x10 STD Tactical	3.5-10	29.5-10.7	3.6-4.6	12.5	1	Int.	13.5	680.40	
M8-2X EER[1]	1.7	21.2	12-24	7.9	1	Int.	6.0	257.10	
M8-2X EER Silver[1]	1.7	21.2	12-24	7.9	1	Int.	6.0	278.00	
M8-4X EER[1]	3.7	9	12-24	8.4	1	Int.	7.0	346.40	
M8-4X EER Silver[1]	3.7	9	12-24	8.4	1	Int.	7.0	346.40	
Vari-X 2.5-8 EER	2.5-8.0	13-4.3	11.7-12	9.7	1	Int.	10.9	521.40	
M8-4X Compact	3.6	25.5	4.5	9.2	1	Int.	7.5	317.90	
Vari-X 2-7x Compact	2.5-6.6	41.7-16.5	5-3.7	9.9	1	Int.	8.5	405.40	
Vari-X 3-9x Compact	3.2-8.6	34-13.5	4.0-3.0	11-11.3	1	Int.	11.0	419.60	
M8-4X[4]	4.0	24	4.0	10.7	1	Int.	9.3	317.90	
M8-6X[6]	5.9	17.7	4.3	11.4	1	Int.	10.0	337.50	
M8-6x 42mm	6.0	17	4.5	12	1	Int.	11.3	419.60	
M8-12x A.O. Varmint	11.6	9.1	4.2	13.0	1	Int.	13.5	544.60	
BR-24X[3]	24.0	4.7	3.2	13.8	1	Int.	15.3	844.60	
BR-36X[3]	36.0	3.2	3.4	14.1	1	Int.	15.6	883.90	
Vari-X 3-9x Compact EFR A.O.	3.8-8.6	34.0-13.5	4.0-3.0	11.0	1	Int.	11	475.90	
Vari-X-II 1x4	1.6-4.2	70.5-28.5	4.3-3.8	9.2	1	Int.	9.0	367.90	
Vari-X-II 2x7[4]	2.5-6.6	42.5-17.8	4.9-3.8	11.0	1	Int.	10.5	408.90	
Vari-X-II 3x9[1,4,5]	3.3-8.6	32.3-14.0	4.1-3.7	12.3	1	Int.	13.5	391.10	
Vari-X-II 3-9x50mm[4]	3.3-8.6	32.3-14	4.7-3.7	12	1	Int.	13.6	458.90	
Vari-X-II 4-12 A.O. Matte	4.4-11.6	22.8-11.0	5.0-3.3	12.3	1	Int.	13.5	535.70	
Vari-X-II 1.5x5	1.5-4.5	66.0-23.0	5.3-3.7	9.4	1	Int.	9.5	516.10	
Vari-X-III 1.75-6x 32	1.9-5.6	47-18	4.8-3.7	9.8	1	Int.	11	539.30	
Vari-X-III 2.5x8[4]	2.6-7.8	37.0-13.5	4.7-3.7	11.3	1	Int.	11.5	557.10	
Vari-X-III 3.5-10x50 A.O.	3.3-9.7	29.5-10.7	4.6-3.6	12.4	1	Int.	13.0	735.70	
Vari-X-III 3.5-10x50[2,4]	3.3-9.7	29.5-10.7	4.6-3.6	12.4	1	Int.	14.4	680.40	
Vari-X-III 4.5-14	4.7-13.7	20.8-7.4	5.0-3.7	12.4	1	Int.	14.5	669.60	
Vari-X-III 4.5-14x50	4.7-13.7	20.8-7.4	5.0-3.7	12.4	1	Int.	14.5	766.10	
Vari-X-III 6.5-20 A.O. Varmint	6.5-19.2	14.2-5.5	5.3-3.6	14.2	1	Int.	17.5	755.40	
Vari-X-III 6.5-20x Target EFR A.O.	6.5-19.2	—	5.3-3.6	14.2	1	Int.	16.5	746.40	
Mark 4 M3-6x	6	17.7	4.5	13.1	30mm	Int.	21	1,505.40	
Mark 4 M1-10x[6]	10	11.1	3.6	13⅛	1	Int.	21	1,505.40	
Mark 4 M1-16x[6]	16	6.6	4.1	12⅞	1	Int.	22	1,505.40	
Mark 4 M3-10x[6]	10	11.1	3.6	13⅛	1	Int.	21	1,505.40	
Vari-X-III 6.5x20[2]	6.5-19.2	14.2-5.5	5.3-3.6	14.2	1	Int.	16.0	675.00	
Rimfire									
Vari-X-II 2-7x RF Special	3.6	25.5	4.5	9.2	1	Int.	7.5	405.40	
Shotgun									
M8 4x	3.7	9.0	12-24	8.4	1	Int.	6.0	339.30	
Vari-X-II 1x4	1.6-4.2	70.5-28.5	4.3-3.8	9.2	1	Int.	9.0	367.90	
Vari-X-II 2x7	2.5-6.6	42.5-17.8	4.9-3.8	11.0	1	Int.	9.0	408.90	
Laser									
LaserLight[7]	—	—	—	1.18	NA	Int.	.5	258.90	
LYMAN									Data listed are for 20x model. [1]Price approximate. Made in U.S. by Parsons Optical Mfg. Co.
Super TargetSpot[1]	10,12,15,20, 25,30	5.5	2	24.3	.75	Int.	27.5	600.00	
McMILLAN									42mm obj. lens; ¼-MOA clicks; nitrogen filled, fogproof, waterproof; etched duplex-type reticle. [1]Tactical Scope with external adj. knobs, military reticle; 60+ min. adj.
Vision Master 2.5-10x	2.5-10	14.2-4.4	4.3-3.3	13.3	30mm	Int.	17.0	1,250.00	
Vision Master Model I[1]	2.5-10	14.2-4.4	4.3-3.3	13.3	30mm	Int.	17.0	1,250.00	
MIRADOR									[1]Wide Angle scope. Multi-coated objective lens. Nitrogen filled; waterproof; shockproof. From Mirador Optical Corp.
RXW 4x40[1]	4	37	3.8	12.4	1	Int.	12	179.95	
RXW 1.5-5x20[1]	1.5-5	46-17.4	4.3	11.1	1	Int.	10	188.95	
RXW 3-9x40	3-9	43-14.5	3.1	12.9	1	Int.	13.4	251.95	
NICHOLS									Matte finish. Imported by G.U., Inc.
"Light" Series									
1.5-5x20 WA	1.5-5	80.8-24.2	3.2-4.5	9.5	1	Int.	10.1	264.00	
2-7x32 WA	2-7	60.4-17.5	3.3-4.2	10.0	1	Int.	11.3	280.00	
3-9x40 WA	3-9	40.2-13.3	3.2-3.9	11.7	1	Int.	12.9	290.00	
3-10x44 WA	3-10	40.2-12.1	3.1-4.0	11.9	1	Int.	14.1	310.00	
4-12x44 WA A.O.	4-12	30.1-10	3.1-3.6	12.3	1	Int.	16.7	320.00	
"Magnum Target"									
12x44	12	8.7	3.1	14.3	1	Int.	19.1	525.00	
24x44	24	4.3	2.9	14.3	1	Int.	18.4	525.00	
6-20x44	6-20	17.4-5.4	3.1-3.0	14.4	1	Int.	19.8	577.00	
NIKON									Super multi-coated lenses and blackening of all internal metal parts for maximum light gathering capability; positive ¼-MOA; fogproof; waterproof; shockproof; luster and matte finish. [1]Also available in matte silver finish, **$448.00.** [2]Available in silver matte finish, **$333.00.** From Nikon, Inc.
4x40[2]	4	26.7	3.5	11.7	1	Int.	11.7	295.00	
1.5-4.5x20	1.5-4.5	67.8-22.5	3.7-3.2	10.1	1	Int.	9.5	387.00	
1.5-4.5x24 EER	1.5-4.4	13.7-5.8	24-18	8.9	1	Int.	9.3	387.00	
2-7x32	2-7	46.7-13.7	3.9-3.3	11.3	1	Int.	11.3	426.00	
3-9x40[1]	3-9	33.8-11.3	3.6-3.2	12.5	1	Int.	12.5	433.00	
3.5-10x50	3.5-10	25.5-8.9	3.9-3.8	13.7	1	Int.	15.5	653.00	
4-12x40 A.O.	4-12	25.7-8.6	3.6-3.2	14	1	Int.	16.6	563.00	
4-12x50 A.O.	4-12	25.4-8.5	3.6-3.5	14.0	1	Int.	18.3	712.00	
6.5-20x44	6.5-19.4	16.2-5.4	3.5-3.1	14.8	1	Int.	19.6	653.00	
2x20 EER	2	22	26.4	8.1	1	Int.	6.3	234.00	

Maker and Model	Magn.	Field at 100 Yds. (feet)	Eye Relief (in.)	Length (in.)	Tube Dia. (in.)	W&E Adjustments	Weight (ozs.)	Price	Other Data
OAKSHORE ELECTRONICS									
UltraDOT[1]	0	—	—	5	1	Int.	3.9	139.00	[1]Also 30mm tube, $149.00. [2]Variable intensity red dot appears in center of the duplex crosshair. Waterproof; nitrogen filled; coated lenses; 1/2-MOA dot at 100 yds. From Oakshore Electronic Sights, Inc.
MicroDOT 1.5-4.5x LER[2]	1.5-4.5	14.9-6.9	12-24	9	1	Int.	10	199.00	
MicroDOT 1.5-4.5x[2]	1.5-4.5	73.8-24.6	3	9.8	1	Int.	10.5	275.00	
MicroDOT 2-7x[2]	2-7	48.2-13.8	3	11	1	Int.	12	295.00	
MicroDOT 3-9x[2]	3-9	37-12.5	3	12.3	1	Int.	13.4	310.00	
MicroDOT 4-12x[2]	1.5-4.5	28.1-9.2	3	14.4	1	Int.	21	419.00	
PARSONS									
Parsons Tube Sight	0	—	—	16	3/4	Int.	13	325.00	No magnification. Merit Lens Disk optionally avail. Micrometer rear mount with 1/4-min. click adjustments. Price is approximate. Made in U.S. by Parsons Optical Mfg. Co.
PENTAX									
1.5-5x	1.5-5	66-25	3-3 1/4	11	1	Int.	13	320.00	Multi-coated lenses, fogproof, waterproof, nitrogen-filled. Penta-Plex reticle. Click 1/3-1/2-MOA adjustments. Matte finish $20.00 extra. [1]Also in matte chrome $260.00. [2]Also in matte chrome $380.00. [3]Matte finish $450.00. [4]Matte finish $540.00; satin chrome $560.00. [5]Chrome-Matte finish $390.00. [6]Matte finish $560.00; satin chrome $580.00. [7]Gloss finish; matte, $300.00. Mossy Oak $320.00. [8]Gloss finish; matte, $560.00. [9]Gloss finish; matte, $700.00; satin chrome $720.00. [10]Glossy finish; matte, $780.00; gloss, dot reticle, $770.00; matte, dot reticle, $790.00. Imported by Pentax Corp.
4x	4	35	3 1/4	11.6	1	Int.	12.2	285.00	
6x	6	20	3 1/4	13.4	1	Int.	13.5	310.00	
2-7x	2-7	42.5-17	3-3 1/4	12	1	Int.	14	360.00	
3-9x	3-9	33-13.5	3-3 1/4	13	1	Int.	15	380.00	
2.5x Lightseeker[7]	2.5	55	3-3.5	10	1	Int.	9	280.00	
2-8x Lightseeker[6]	2-8	53-17	3.5	11 7/8	1	Int.	14	490.00	
3-9x Lightseeker[4]	3-9	36-14	3	12.7	1	Int.	15	520.00	
3.5-10x Lightseeker[8]	3.5-10	29.5-11	3-3.25	14	1	Int.	19.5	540.00	
3-11x Lightseeker[9]	3-11	38.5-13	3-3.25	13.3	1	Int.	19	680.00	
6-24x Lightseeker[10]	6-24	18-5.5	3.25	16	1	Int.	22.7	760.00	
3-9x Mini	3-9	26.5-10.5	3 3/4	10.4	1	Int.	13	320.00	
4-12x Mini[3]	4-12	19-8	3.75-4	11.3	1	Int.	11.3	430.00	
6-18x[3]	6-18	16-7	3-3.25	15.8	1	Int.	15.8	480.00	
Pistol									
2x LER[1]	2	21	10-24	8 3/4	1	Int.	6.8	230.00	
1.5-4x LER[2]	1.5-4	16-11	11-25	10	1	Int.	11	350.00	
2 1/2-7x[5]	2.5-7	12.0-7.5	11-28	12	1	Int.	12.5	370.00	
RWS									
300	4	—	8	12 3/4	1	Int.	11	160.00	Air gun scopes. All have Dyna-Plex reticle. Model 800 is for air pistols. [1]M450, 3-9x40mm, $200.00. Imported from Japan by Dynamit Nobel-RWS.
350	4	—	8	10	1	Int.	10	125.00	
400[1]	2-7	—	8	12 3/4	1	Int.	12	170.00	
CS-10	2.5	—	8	5 3/4	1	Int.	7	125.00	
REDFIELD									
Ultimate Illuminator 3-9x	3.4-9.1	27-9	3-3.5	15.1	30mm	Int.	20.5	683.95	*Accutrac feature avail. on these scopes at extra cost. Traditionals have round lenses. 4-Plex reticle is standard. [1]Magnum proof. Specially designed for magnum and auto pistols. Uses Double Dovetail mounts. Also in nickel-plated finish, 2x, $232.95, 4x, $232.95, 2 1/2-7x, $310.95, 2 1/2-7x matte black, $310.95. [2]With matte finish $601.95. [3]Also available with matte finish at extra cost. [4]All Golden Five Star scopes come with Butler Creek flip-up lens covers. [5]Black anodized finish, also in nickel finish, $303.95. [6]56mm adj. objective; European #4 or 4-Plex reticle; comes with 30mm steel rings with Rotary Dovetail System. 1/4-min. click adj. Also in matte finish, $789.95. [7]Also available nickel-plated $361.95. [8]With target knob, $455.95. [9]With target knob, 481.95; black matte finish, $473.95; black matte with target knob, $469.95. [10]Available with RealTree camo finish $207.95. [11]With RealTree camo finish $277.95. [12]Also with RealTree camo finish $436.95; with matte finish $426.95. [13]With RealTree camo finish $332.95. [14]With target knob, $798.95; with target knob, matte black, $808.95. [15]Black matte finish, $386.95 Selected models shown. **Contact Redfield for full data.**
Ultimate Illuminator 3-12x[6,14]	2.9-11.7	27-10.5	3-3 1/2	15.4	30mm	Int.	23	781.95	
Illuminator Trad. 3-9x	2.9-8.7	33-11	3 1/2	12 3/4	1	Int.	17	530.95	
Illuminator Widefield 4x	4.2	28	3-3.5	11.7	1	Int.	13.5	395.95	
Illuminator Widefield 2-7x	2.0-6.8	56-17	3-3.5	11.7	1	Int.	13.5	523.95	
Illuminator Widefield 3-9x[2]	2.9-8.7	38-13	3 1/2	12 3/4	1	Int.	17	591.95	
Tracker 4x[3,10]	3.9	28.9	3 1/2	11.02	1	Int.	9.8	180.95	
Tracker 6x[3]	6.2	18	3.5	12.4	1	Int.	11.1	202.95	
Tracker 2-7x[3]	2.3-6.9	36.6-12.2	3 1/2	12.20	1	Int.	11.6	229.95	
Tracker 3-9x[3,11]	3.0-9.0	34.4-11.3	3 1/2	14.96	1	Int.	13.4	259.95	
Traditional 4x 3/4"	4	24 1/2	3 1/2	9 3/8	3/4	Int.	—	172.95	
Traditional 2 1/2x	2 1/2	43	3 1/2	10 1/4	1	Int.	8 1/2	172.95	
Golden Five Star 4x[4]	4	28.5	3.75	11.3	1	Int.	9.75	247.95	
Golden Five Star 6x[4]	6	18	3.75	12.2	1	Int.	11.5	272.95	
Golden Five Star 2-7x[4]	2.4-7.4	42-14	3-3.75	11.25	1	Int.	12	319.95	
Golden Five Star 3-9x[4,7]	3.0-9.1	34-11	3-3.75	12.50	1	Int.	13	393.95	
Golden Five Star 3-9x 50mm[4,12]	3.0-9.1	36.0-11.5	3-3.5	12.8	1	Int.	16	416.95	
Golden Five Star 4-12x A.O.*[4,8]	3.9-11.4	27-9	3-3.75	13.8	1	Int.	16	486.95	
Golden Five Star 6-18x A.O.*[4,9]	6.1-18.1	18.6	3-3.75	14.3	1	Int.	18	465.95	
I.E.R. 1-4x Shotgun[13]	1.3-3.8	48-16	6	10.2	1	Int.	12	313.95	
Compact Scopes									
Golden Five Star Compact 4x	3.8	28	3.5	9.75	1	Int.	8.8	239.95	
Golden Five Star Compact 2-7x	2.4-7.1	40-16	3-3.5	9.75	1	Int.	9.8	316.95	
Golden Five Star Compact 3-9x	3.3-9.1	32-11.25	3-3.5	10.7	1	Int.	10.5	336.95	
Golden Five Star Compact 4-12x	4.1-12.4	22.4-8.3	3-3.5	12	1	Int.	13	425.95	
Handgun Scopes									
Golden Five Star 2x	2	24	9.5-20	7.88	1	Int.	6	216.95	
Golden Five Star 4x	4	75	13-19	8.63	1	Int.	6.1	216.95	
Golden Five Star 2 1/2-7x	2 1/2-7	11-3.75	11-26	9.4	1	Int.	9.3	295.95	
Widefield Low Profile Compact									
Widefield 4xLP Compact	3.7	33	3.5	9.35	1	Int.	10	295.95	
Widefield 3-9x LP Compact	3.3-9	37.0-13.7	3-3.5	10.20	1	Int.	13	375.95	
Low Profile Scopes									
Widefield 2 3/4xLP	2 3/4	55 1/2	3 1/2	10 1/2	1	Int.	8	274.95	
Widefield 4xLP	3.6	37 1/2	3 1/2	11 1/2	1	Int.	10	307.95	

CAUTION: PRICES SHOWN ARE SUPPLIED BY THE MANUFACTURER OR IMPORTER. CHECK YOUR LOCAL GUNSHOP.

49th EDITION, 1995 **471**

Maker and Model	Magn.	Field at 100 Yds. (feet)	Eye Relief (in.)	Length (in.)	Tube Dia. (in.)	W&E Adjustments	Weight (ozs.)	Price	Other Data
Redfield (cont.)									
Widefield 6xLP	5.5	23	3½	12¾	1	Int.	11	330.95	
Widefield 1¾x-5xLP[15]	1¾-5	70-27	3½	10¾	1	Int.	11½	376.95	
Widefield 2x-7xLP*	2-7	49-19	3½	11¾	1	Int.	13	387.95	
Widefield 3x-9xLP*	3-9	39-15	3½	12½	1	Int.	14	430.95	
SCHMIDT & BENDER									
Fixed									All steel. 30-yr. warranty, click
4x36	4	30	3.25	11	1	Int.	14	648.00	adjustments, centered reticles, rotation
6x42	6	21	3.25	13	1	Int.	17	707.00	indicators. [1]Glass reticle available. All
8x56	8	16.5	3.25	14	1	Int.	22	793.00	available in aluminum with mounting rail.
10x42	10	10.5	3.25	13	1	Int.	18	773.00	From Schmidt & Bender, Inc.
Variables									
1.25-4x20[1]	1.25-4	96-16	3.25	10	30mm	Int.	15.5	858.00	
1.5-6x42[1]	1.5-6	60-19.5	3.25	12	30mm	Int.	19.7	930.00	
2.5-10x56[1]	2.5-10	37.5-12	3.25	14	30mm	Int.	24.6	1,117.00	
3-12x50[1]	3-12	33.3-12.6	3.25	13.5	30mm	Int.	22.9	1,048.00	
4-12x42	4-12	34.5-11.5	3.25	13	30mm	Int.	22.5	1,024.00	
SHEPHERD									[1]Also avail. as 310-P, 310-PE, **$478.28**.
3940-E	3-9	43.5-15	3.3	13	1	Int.	17	622.00	[2]Also avail. as 310-P1, 310-P2, 310-P3,
310-2[1,2]	3-10	35.3-11.6	3-3.75	12.8	1	Int.	18	478.28	310-Pla, 310-PE1, 310-P22, 310-P22 Mag., 310-PE, **$478.28**. All have patented Dual Reticle system with rangefinder bullet drop compensation; multi-coated lenses, waterprooof, shockproof, nitrogen filled, matte finish. From Shepherd Scope, Ltd.
SIGHTRON									Red dot sights. All come with haze filter
S33-3[1]	1	40	—	5.31	33mm	Int.	5.6	259.95	caps, polarized lens, ring mounts, two sunshades, 3-volt lithium battery, Allen wrench. Matte black finish; also avail. with stainless finish. [1]3 MOA dot; also 5 MOA dot (S33-5), 12 MOA dot (S33-12). Avail. with interchangeable dot size— 3-5-12 MOA, (S33-3D) **$369.95**. From Sightron, Inc.
SIMMONS									[1]Matte; also polished finish. [2]Silver; also
44 Mag									black matte or polished. [3]Black matte
M-1043	2-7	56-16	3.3	11.8	1	Int.	13	256.95	finish. [4]Granite finish; black polish
M-1044	3-10	36.2-10.5	3.4-3.3	13.1	1	Int.	16.3	268.95	**$216.95**; silver $218.95; also with 50mm
M-1045	4-12	27-9	3	12.6	1	Int.	19.5	280.95	obj., black granite **$336.95**. [5]Camouflage.
M-1047	6.5-20	14-.5	2.6-3.4	12.8	1	Int.	19.5	284.95	[6]Black polish. [7]With ring mounts. **Only selected models shown. Contact Simmons Outdoor Corp. for complete details.**
Prohunter									
7700[1]	2-7	58-17	3.25	11.6	1	Int.	12.4	159.95	
7710[2]	3-9	40-15	3	12.6	1	Int.	13.4	169.95	
7716	4-12	29.6-10.0	3	13.6	1	Int.	20	179.95	
7720	6-18	38-13	2.5	12.5	1	Int.	13.5	209.95	
7725	4.5	26	3	9.9	1	Int.	9.9	109.95	
7740[3]	6	34.1	3	12.6	1	Int.	9.5	139.95	
Whitetail Classic									
WTC10[4]	4	36.8	4	12.3	1	Int.	9.8	139.95	
WTC11[4]	1.5-5	80-23.5	3.4-3.2	12.6	1	Int.	11.8	174.95	
WTC12[4]	2.5-8	46.5-14.5	3.2-3	12.6	1	Int.	12.8	189.95	
WTC13[4]	3.5-10	35-12	3.2-3	12.4	1	Int.	12.8	209.95	
WTC14[4]	2-10	50-11	3	12.8	1	Int.	16.9	256.95	
WTC16	4	36.8	4	9.9	1	Int.	12	149.95	
WTC17	4-12	26-7.9	3	12.8	1	Int.	19.5	329.95	
Deerfield									
21006	4	28	4	12.0	1	Int.	9.1	74.95	
21029	3-9	32-11	3.4	12.6	1	Int.	12.3	104.95	
21031	4-12	28-11	3-2.8	13.9	1	Int.	14.6	139.95	
Gold Medal Silhouette									
23000	12	8.7	3.1-3	14.5	1	Int.	18.3	449.95	
23001	24	4.3	3	14.5	1	Int.	18.3	455.95	
23002	6-20	17.4-5.4	3	14.5	1	Int.	18.3	499.95	
Gold Medal Handgun									
22002[6]	2.5-7	9.7-4.0	8.9-19.4	9.25	1	Int.	9.0	319.95	
22004[6]	2	3.9	8.6-19.5	7.3	1	Int.	7.4	219.95	
22006[6]	4	8.9	9.8-18.7	9	1	Int.	8.8	249.95	
Shotgun									
21005	2.5	29	4.6	7.1	1	Int.	7.2	85.95	
7789D	2	27	6	8.8	1	Int.	8.1	129.95	
7788	1	60	3.8	9.4	1	Int.	10.2	129.95	
7790D	4	16	5.5	8.8	1	Int.	9.2	139.95	
7791	1.5-5	75-23	3.4	9.3	1	Int.	9.7	139.95	
7790	4	16	5.5	8.8	1	Int.	9.2	139.95	
Rimfire									
1022[7]	4	36	3.5	11.5	¾	Int.	10	74.95	
21007[7]	4	29	3.5	12.0	¾	Int.	11.5	108.95	
STEINER									
Penetrator									Waterproof, fogproof, nitrogen filled,
6x42	6	20.4	3.1	14.8	26mm	Int.	14	1,099.00	accordion-type eye cup. From Pioneer
8x56	8	15	3.1	14.8	26mm	Int.	17	1,299.00	Marketing & Research, Inc.
1.5x6x42	1.5-6	64-21	3.1	12.8	30mm	Int.	17	1,389.00	
3-12x56	3-12	29-10	3.1	14.8	30mm	Int.	21	1,629.00	

Maker and Model	Magn.	Field at 100 Yds. (feet)	Eye Relief (in.)	Length (in.)	Tube Dia. (in.)	W&E Adjustments	Weight (ozs.)	Price	Other Data
SWAROVSKI HABICHT									All models offered in either steel or lightweight alloy tubes. Weights shown are for lightweight versions. Choice of nine constantly centered reticles. Eyepiece recoil mechanism and rubber ring shield to protect face. American-style plex reticle available in 2.2-9x42 and 3-12x56 traditional European scopes. [1]Alloy weighs 12.3 oz. [2]Alloy weighs 15.9 oz. [3]Alloy weighs 14.8 oz. [4]Alloy weighs 18.3 oz. [5]Alloy weighs 16.6 oz. Imported by Swarovski Optik North America Ltd.
Professional Hunter Series									
1.25-4x24[1]	1.25-4	86-27	4.5	10.6	30mm	Int.	15.9	861.00	
1.5-6x42[2]	1.5-6	65.4-21	3.75	13	30mm	Int.	20.5	972.00	
2.5-10x42[3]	2.5-10	39.6-12.3	3.75	13.2	30mm	Int.	19.4	1,105.00	
2.5-10x56[4]	2.5-10	39.6-12.3	3.75	14.7	30mm	Int.	24.3	1,216.00	
3-12x50[5]	3-12	33-10.5	3.75	14.3	30mm	Int.	22.0	1,166.00	
4x32	4	33	3¼	11.3	1	Int.	15	625.00	
6x42	6	23	3¼	12.6	1	Int.	17.9	690.00	
8x56	8	17	3¼	14.4	1	Int.	23	819.00	
AL Scopes									
4x32A	4	30	3.2	11.5	1	Int.	10.8	495.00	
6x36A	6	21	3.2	11.9	1	Int.	11.5	530.00	
1.5-4.5x20A	1.5-4.5	75-25.8	3.5	9.53	1	Int.	10.6	595.00	
3-9x36	3-9	39-13.5	3.3	11.9	1	Int.	13	640.00	
SWIFT									All Swift scopes, with the exception of the 4x15, have Quadraplex reticles and are fogproof and waterproof. The 4x15 has crosshair reticle and is non-waterproof. [1]Available in black or silver finish—same price. [2]Comes with ring mounts, wrench, lens caps, extension tubes, filter, battery. From Swift Instruments.
600 4x15	4	16.2	2.4	11	¾	Int.	4.7	24.00	
601 3-7x20	3-7	25-12	3-2.9	11	1	Int.	5.6	53.00	
649 4-12x50	4-12	30-10	3-2.8	13.2	1	Int.	14.6	215.00	
650 4x32	4	29	3.5	12	1	Int.	9	80.00	
653 4x40WA[1]	4	35.5	3.75	12.25	1	Int.	12	96.00	
654 3-9x32	3-9	35.75-12.75	3	12.75	1	Int.	13.75	95.00	
656 3-9x40WA[1]	3-9	42.5-13.5	2.75	12.75	1	Int.	14	102.00	
657 6x40	6	18	3.75	13	1	Int.	10	99.50	
660 4x20	4	25	4	11.8	1	Int.	9	89.00	
664 4-12x40[1]	4-12	27-9	3-2.8	13.3	1	Int.	14.8	143.00	
665 1.5-4.5x21	1.5-4.5	69-24.5	3.5-3	10.9	1	Int.	9.6	98.00	
666 Shotgun 1x20	1	113	3.2	7.5	1	Int.	9.6	99.50	
667 Fire-Fly[2]	1	—	—	5.3	30mm	Int.	5	212.00	
668 4x32	4	25	4	10	1	Int.	8.9	90.00	
Pistol Scopes									
661 4x32	4	90	10-22	9.2	1	Int.	9.5	115.00	
662 2.5x32	2.5	14.3	9-22	8.9	1	Int.	9.3	105.00	
663 2x20[1]	2	18.3	9-21	7.2	1	Int.	8.4	110.00	
TASCO									[1]Water, fog & shockproof; fully coated optics; ¼-min. click stops; haze filter caps; 30-day/limited lifetime warranty. [2]30/30 range finding reticle. [3]World Class Wide Angle; Supercon multi-coated optics; Opti-Centered® 30/30 range finding reticle; lifetime warranty. [4]⅓ greater zoom range. [5]Trajectory compensating scopes, Opti-Centered® stadia reticle. [6]Anodized finish. [7]True one-power scope. [8]Coated optics; crosshair reticle; ring mounts included to fit most 22, 10mm receivers. [9]Fits Remington 870, 1100, 11-87. [10]Electronic dot reticle with rheostat; coated optics; adj. for windage and elevation; waterproof, shockproof, fogproof; Lithium battery; 3x power booster avail.; matte black or matte aluminum finish; dot or T-3 reticle. [11]TV view. [12]Also matte aluminum finish. [13]Also with crosshair reticle. [14]Also 30/30 reticle. [15]Dot size 1.5" at 100 yds.; waterproof. [16]Stainless finish. [17]Black matte or stainless finish. [18]Also with stainless finish. [19]Also in matte black. [20]Available with 5-min. or 10-min. dot. [21]Available with 10, 15, 20-min. dot. **Contact Tasco for details on complete line.**
World Class									
WA4x40	4	36	3	13	1	Int.	11.5	161.00	
WA4x32ST[16]	4	34	3	—	1	Int.	10.5	218.00	
WA6x40	6	23	3	12.75	1	Int.	11.5	227.00	
WA13.5x20[1,3,10]	1-3.5	115-31	3.5	9.75	1	Int.	10.2	260.00	
WA1.75-5x20[1,3]	1.75-5	72-24	3	10⅝	1	Int.	10.0	266.00	
WA2.58x40[18]	2.5-8	44-14	3	11.75	1	Int.	14.25	191.00	
WA27x32[1,3,9]	2-7	56-17	3.25	11.5	1	Int.	12	191.00	
WA39x40[1,3,6,11,18]	3-9	43.5-15	3	12.75	1	Int.	13.0	199.00	
World Class Compact									
CW4x32LE	4	25	5	9.5	1	Int.	9.5	221.00	
CW28x32	2-8	55-16	3	11.5	1	Int.	11.5	225.00	
World Class Airgun									
AG4x40WA	4	36	3	13	1	Int.	14	306.00	
AG39x50WA	3-9	41-14	3	15	1	Int.	17.5	475.00	
World Class Electronic									
ER39x40WA	3-9	41-14	3	12.75	1	Int.	16	543.00	
World Class Mag IV-44									
WC2510x44[6,19]	2.5-10	41-11	3.5	12.5	1	Int.	14.4	290.00	
World Class TS									
TS24x44	24	4.5	3	14	1	Int.	17.9	478.00	
TS36x44	36	3	3	14	1	Int.	17.9	511.00	
TS832x44	8-24	11-3.5	3	14	1	Int.	19.5	611.00	
TS624x44	6-24	15-4.5	3	14	1	Int.	18.5	567.00	
World Class TR									
TR39x40WA	3-9	41-14	3	13.0	1	Int.	12.5	289.00	
World Class Pistol									
PWC2x22[12]	2	25	11-20	8.75	1	Int.	7.3	206.00	
PWC4x28[12]	4	8	12-19	9.45	1	Int.	7.9	252.00	
Mag IV									
W312x40[1,2,4]	3-12	35-9	3	12.25	1	Int.	12	183.00	
W416x40[1,2,4,18]	4-16	26-7	3	14.25	1	Int.	15.6	229.00	
W624x40	6-24	17-4	3	15.25	1	Int.	16.8	290.00	
Golden Antler									
GA4x32TV	4	32	3	13	1	Int.	12.7	79.00	
GA2.510x44TV	2.5-10	35-9	3.5	12.5	1	Int.	14.4	214.00	
GA39x32TV[11]	3-9	39-13	3	—	1	Int.	12.2	102.00	
GA39x40TV	3-9	39-13	3	12.5	1	Int.	13	135.00	
GA39x40WA	3-9	41-15	3	12.75	1	Int.	13	152.00	
Silver Antler									
SA2.5x32	2.5	42	3¼	11	1	Int.	10	86.00	
SA4x40	4	32	3	12	1	Int.	12.5	99.00	
SA39x32WA	3-9	40-14	3	13.25	1	Int.	12.2	129.00	
SA39x40WA	3-9	41-15	3	12.75	1	Int.	13	152.00	
SA39x40	3-9	39-13	3	12.5	1	Int.	13	135.00	
SA2.150x44	2.5-10	35-9	3.5	—	1	Int.	14.4	214.00	

CAUTION: PRICES SHOWN ARE SUPPLIED BY THE MANUFACTURER OR IMPORTER. CHECK YOUR LOCAL GUNSHOP.

49th EDITION, 1995 **473**

Maker and Model	Magn.	Field at 100 Yds. (feet)	Eye Relief (in.)	Length (in.)	Tube Dia. (in.)	W&E Adjustments	Weight (ozs.)	Price	Other Data
Tasco (cont.)									
Pronghorn									
PH2.5x20	2.5	43	3.75	10	1	Int.	7.1	76.00	
PH2.5x32	2.5	42	3.25	11	1	Int.	10	84.00	
PH4x32	4	32	3	12	1	Int.	12.5	73.00	
PH6x40	6	20	3	12.5	1	Int.	11.5	109.00	
PH39x32	3-9	39-13	3	12	1	Int.	11	91.00	
PH39x40	3-9	39-13	3	13	1	Int.	12.1	122.00	
High Country									
HC416x40	4-16	26-7	3.25	14.25	1	Int.	15.6	221.00	
HC624x10	6-24	17-4	3	15.25	1	Int.	16.8	255.00	
HC39x40	3-9	41-15	3	12.75	1	Int.	13.0	182.00	
HC3.510x40	3.5-10	30-10.5	3	11.75	1	Int.	14.25	204.00	
Rubber Armored									
RC39x40A	3-9	35-12	3.25	12.5	1	Int.	14.3	206.00	
TR Scopes									
TR39x40WA	3-9	41-14	3	13	1	Int.	12.5	289.00	
TR416x40	4-16	26-7	3	14.25	1	Int.	16.8	323.00	
TR624x40	6-24	17-4	3	15.5	1	Int.	17.5	356.00	
Shotgun Scopes									
WA1.75-5x20[9]	1.75-5	74-24	3	10.5	1	Int.	10	257.00	
WA13.5x20[9]	1-3.5	103-31	3	9	1	Int.	12	260.00	
SG2.5x20	2.5	43	3.75	10	1	Int.	7.1	113.00	
SG2.5x32	2.5	42	3.25	11	1	Int.	10	121.00	
Airgun									
AG4x20	4	20	2.5	10.75	.75	Int.	5	46.00	
AG4x32	4	28	3	12	1	Int.	12	255.00	
AG4x32N	4	30	3	—	1	Int.	12.25	255.00	
AG27x32	2-7	48-17	3	12.25	1	Int.	14	170.00	
AG39x50WA	3-9	41-14	3	15	1	Int.	17.5	475.00	
Rimfire									
RF4x15[8]	4	22.5	2.5	11	.75	Int.	4	17.00	
RF4x32	4	31	3	12.25	1	Int.	12.6	91.00	
RF37x20	3-7	24-11	2.5	11.5	.75	Int.	5.7	49.00	
P1.5x15	1.5	22.5	9.5-20.75	8.75	.75	Int.	3.25	37.00	
Propoint									
PDP2[10,12,20]	1	40	—	5	30mm	Int.	5	267.00	
PDP3[10,12,20]	1	52	—	5	30mm	Int.	5	367.00	
PDP4[17,21]	1	82	—	—	45mm	Int.	6.1	458.00	
PB1[13]	3	35	3	5.5	30mm	Int.	6.0	183.00	
PB3	2	30	—	1.25	30mm	Int.	2.6	214.00	
World Class Plus									
WCP4x44	4	32	3¼	12.75	1	Int.	13.5	260.00	
WCP3.510x50	3.5-10	30-10.5	3¾	13	1	Int.	17.1	382.00	
WCP24x50	24	4.8	3.25	13.25	1	Int.	15.9	645.00	
WCP36x50	36	3	3.5	14	1	Int.	15.9	679.00	
WCP6x44	6	21	3.25	12.75	1	Int.	13.6	260.00	
WCP39x44	3-9	39-14	3.5	12.75	1	Int.	15.8	306.00	
LaserPoint[15]	—	—	—	2	⅝	Int.	.75	435.00	
THOMPSON/CENTER RECOIL PROOF PISTOL SCOPES									[1]Also silver finish, **$325.00** (#8316); with rail mount, black, **$308.95** (#8317); with rail, lighted reticle, black, **$370.75** (#8327). [2]With lighted reticle, **$280.90** (#8322); silver, **$292.10** (#8323); with lighted reticle, rail mount, black, **$292.10** (#8320). [3]With lighted reticle, **$348.30** (#8626). From Thompson/Center.
8312 Compact Rail[2]	2.5	15	9-21	7.25	1	Int.	6.6	202.00	
8315 Compact[1]	2.5-7	15-5	8-21	9.25	1	Int.	9.2	297.75	
Rifle Scopes									
8621 Compact	1.5-5	61-20	3	10	1	Int.	8.5	235.95	
8623 Compact WA[3]	3-9	33-11	3	10.75	1	Int.	9.9	258.40	
8624 Compact	4	26	3	10	1	Int.	8.2	196.60	
TRIJICON									[1]Self-luminous low-light reticle glows in poor light; allows choice of red, amber or green via a selector ring on objective end. [2]Advanced Combat Optical Gunsight for AR-15, M-16, with integral mount. [3]Reticle glows red in low light. From Trijicon, Inc.
6x56[1]	6	24	3.0	14.1	1	Int.	20.3	579.00	
1-3x20[1]	1-3	94-33	3.7-4.9	9.6	1	Int.	13.2	594.00	
3-9x40[1]	3-9	35-14	3.3-3.0	13.1	1	Int.	16.0	569.00	
3-9x56[1]	3-9	35-14	3.3-3.0	14.2	1	Int.	21.5	649.00	
ACOG 3.5x35	3.5	29	2.4	8.0	—	Int.	14.0	995.00	
ACOG 4x32[2]	4	37	1.5	5.8	—	Int.	9.7	695.00	
UNERTL									[1]Dural ¼-MOA click mounts. Hard coated lenses. Non-rotating objective lens focusing. [2]¼-MOA click mounts. [3]With target mounts. [4]With calibrated head. [5]Same as 1" Target but without objective lens focusing. [6]With new Posa mounts. [7]Range focus unit near rear of tube. Price is with Posa or standard mounts. Magnum clamp. From Unertl.
1" Target	6,8,10	16-10	2	21½	¾	Ext.	21	307.00	
1¼" Target[1]	8,10,12,14	12-16	2	25	¾	Ext.	21	399.00	
1½" Target	10,12,14, 16,18,20	11.5-3.2	2¼	25½	¾	Ext.	31	416.00	
2" Target[2]	10,12,14, 16,18,24, 30,32,36	8	2¼	26¼	1	Ext.	44	549.00	
Varmint, 1¼"[3]	6,8,10,12	1-7	2½	19½	⅞	Ext.	26	395.00	
Ultra Varmint, 2"[4]	8,10,12,15	12.6-7	2½	24	1	Ext.	34	538.00	
Small Game[5]	3,4,6	25-17	2¼	18	¾	Ext.	16	243.00	
Programmer 200[7]	10,12,14, 16,18,20, 24,30,36	11.3-4	—	26½	1	Ext.	45	688.00	
BV-20[8]	20	8	4.4	17⅞	1	Ext.	21¼	508.00	
Tube Sight	—	—	—	17		Ext.	—	226.00	

CAUTION: PRICES SHOWN ARE SUPPLIED BY THE MANUFACTURER OR IMPORTER. CHECK YOUR LOCAL GUNSHOP.

Maker and Model	Magn.	Field at 100 Yds. (feet)	Eye Relief (in.)	Length (in.)	Tube Dia. (in.)	W&E Adjustments	Weight (ozs.)	Price	Other Data
U.S. OPTICS									
SN-1/TAR Fixed Power System									Prices shown are estimates; scopes built as ordered, to order; choice of reticles; choice of front or rear focal plane; extra-heavy MIL-SPEC construction; extra-long turrets; individual w&e rebound springs; up to 88mm dia. objectives; up to 50mm tubes; all lenses multi-coated. Made in U.S. by U. S. Optics.
9.6x	10	11.3	3.8	14.5	30mm	Int.	24	1,100.00	
16.2x	15	8.6	4.3	16.5	30mm	Int.	27	1,200.00	
22.4x	20	5.8	3.8	18.0	30mm	Int.	29	1,300.00	
26x	24	5.0	3.4	18.0	30mm	Int.	31	1,400.00	
31x	30	4.6	3.5	18.0	30mm	Int.	32	1,500.00	
37x	36	4.0	3.6	18.0	30mm	Int.	32	1,600.00	
42x	40	3.6	3.7	18.0	30mm	Int.	32	1,700.00	
48x	50	3.0	3.8	18.0	30mm	Int.	32	1,800.00	
Variables									
SN-2	4-22	26.8-5.8	5.4-3.8	18.0	30mm	Int.	24	1,256.00	
SN-3	1.6-8	—	4.4-4.8	18.4	30mm	Int.	36	1,010.00	
SN-4	1-4	116-31.2	4.6-4.9	18.0	30mm	Int.	35	680.00	
Fixed Power									
SN-6	4,6,8,10	—	4.2-4.8	9.2	30mm	Int.	18	655.00	
SN-8	4	28.8	5.2	7	30mm	Int.	18	620.00	
WEAVER									
K2.5	2.5	35	3.7	9.5	1	Int.	7.3	129.83	Micro-Trac adjustment system with ¼-minute clicks on all models. All have Dual-X reticle. One-piece aluminum tube, satin finish, nitrogen filled, multi-coated lenses, waterproof. [1]Also available in matte finish: V3, **$177.23**; K4, **$147.86**; V9, **$192.50**; V10, **$204.83**. [2]Available with Dual-X, fine crosshair or ¼-min. dot reticles. From Weaver.
K4[1]	3.7	26.5	3.3	11.3	1	Int.	10	140.76	
K6	5.7	18.5	3.3	11.4	1	Int.	10	153.39	
V3[1]	1.1-2.8	88-32	3.9-3.7	9.2	1	Int.	8.5	170.14	
V9[1]	2.8-8.7	33-11	3.5-3.4	12.1	1	Int.	11.1	183.39	
V10[1]	2.2-9.6	38.5-9.5	3.4-3.3	12.2	1	Int.	11.2	194.97	
V16[2]	3.8-15.5	26.8-6.8	3.1	13.9	1	Int.	16.5	341.79	
KT15	14.6	7.5	3.2	12.9	1	Int.	14.7	305.57	
WILLIAMS									
Twilight Crosshair TNT	1½-5	57¾-21	3½	10¾	1	Int.	10	214.92	[1]Matte or glossy black finish. TNT models. From Williams Gunsight Co.
Twilight Crosshair TNT	2½	32	3¾	11¼	1	Int.	8½	152.10	
Twilight Crosshair TNT	4	29	3½	11¾	1	Int.	9½	159.02	
Twilight Crosshair TNT	2-6	45-17	3	11½	1	Int.	11½	214.92	
Twilight Crosshair TNT	3-9	36-13	3	12¾	1	Int.	13½	225.84	
Guideline II									
4x[1]	4	29	3.6	11¾	1	Int.	9½	230.88	
1.5-5x[1]	1.5-5	57¾-21	3.5	10¾	1	Int.	10	272.68	
2-6x[1]	2-6	45½-10¾	3	11½	1	Int.	11½	272.68	
3-9x[1]	3-9	36½-12¾	3.1-2.9	12¾	1	Int.	13½	307.84	
Pistol Scopes									
Twilight 1.5x TNT	1.5	19	18-25	8.2	1	Int.	6.4	157.30	
Twilight 2x TNT	2	17.5	18-25	8.5	1	Int.	6.4	159.64	
ZEISS									
Diatal C 4x32	4	30	3.5	10.6	1	Int.	11.3	519.75	All scopes have ¼-minute click-stop adjustments. Choice of Z-Plex or fine crosshair reticles. Rubber armored objective bell, rubber eyepiece ring. Lenses have T-Star coating for highest light transmission. Z-Series scopes offered in non-rail tubes with duplex reticles only; 1" and 30mm. [1]Black matte finish. [2]Also in stainless matte finish. Imported from Germany by Carl Zeiss Optical, Inc.
Diatal C 6x32	6	20	3.5	10.6	1	Int.	11.3	539.95	
Diatal C 10x36	10	12	3.5	12.7	1	Int.	14.1	610.00	
Diatal Z 6x42	6	22.9	3.5	12.7	1.02 (26mm)	Int.	13.4	890.50	
Diatal Z 8x56	8	18	3.5	13.8	1.02 (26mm)	Int.	17.6	1,060.50	
Diavari C 1.5-4.5	1.5-4.5	72-27	3.5	11.8	1	Int.	13.4	695.00	
Diavari Z 2.5x10x48[1,2]	2.5-10	33-11.7	3.2	14.5	30mm	Int.	24	1,365.70	
Diavari Z 3-9x36	3-9	36-13	3.5	11.2	1	Int.	15.2	760.00	
Diavari Z 1.5-6x42[1,2]	1.5-6	65.5-22.9	3.5	12.4	1.18 (30mm)	Int.	18.5	1,155.60	
Diavari Z 3-12x56[1,2]	3-12	27.6-9.9	3.2	15.3	1.18 (30mm)	Int.	25.8	1,470.75	

Hunting scopes in general are furnished with a choice of reticle—crosshairs, post with crosshairs, tapered or blunt post, or dot crosshairs, etc. The great majority of target and varmint scopes have medium or fine crosshairs but post or dot reticles may be ordered. W—Windage E—Elevation MOA—Minute of angle or 1" (approx.) at 100 yards, etc.

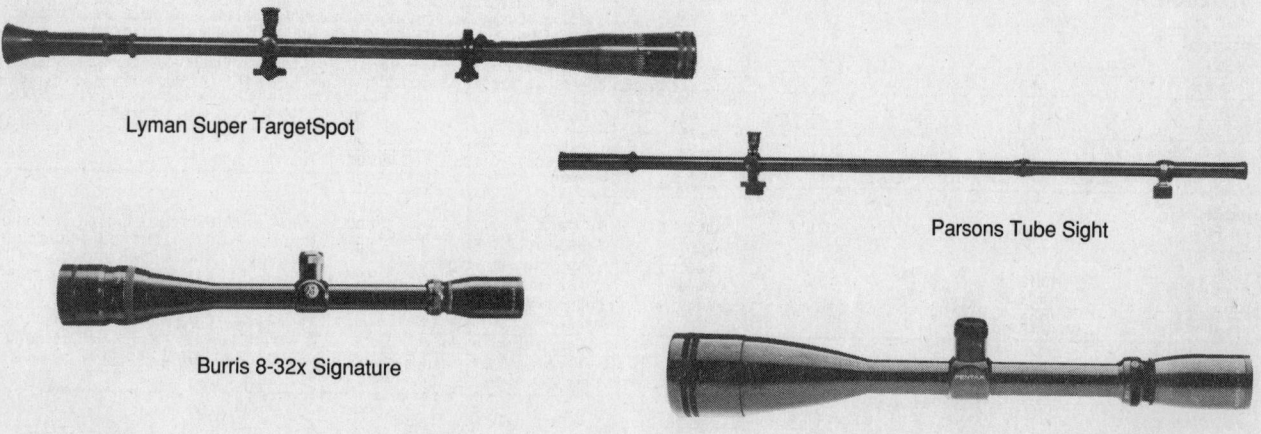

Lyman Super TargetSpot

Parsons Tube Sight

Burris 8-32x Signature

Pentax 6-24x Lightseeker

CAUTION: PRICES SHOWN ARE SUPPLIED BY THE MANUFACTURER OR IMPORTER. CHECK YOUR LOCAL GUNSHOP.

49th EDITION, 1995 **475**

SCOPE MOUNTS

Maker, Model, Type	Adjust.	Scopes	Price
ACTION ARMS	No	1" split rings	From $12.00

For UZI, Galil, Ruger Mk. II, Mini-14, Win. 94, AR-15, Rem. 870, Ithaca 37, and many other popular rifles, handguns. Accept Weaver rings. All allow use of iron sights; some include rings; many in satin stainless finish. **Partial list shown. From Action Arms.**

Maker, Model, Type	Adjust.	Scopes	Price
AIMPOINT	No	1"	49.95-89.95
Laser Mounts[1]	No	1", 30mm	51.95

Mounts/rings for all Aimpoint sights and 1" scopes. For many popular revolvers, auto pistols, shotguns, military-style rifles/carbines, sporting rifles. Most require no gunsmithing. [1]Mounts Aimpoint Laser-dot below barrel; many popular handguns, military-style rifles. Contact Aimpoint.

Maker, Model, Type	Adjust.	Scopes	Price
AIMTECH			
Handguns			
AMT Auto Mag II, III	No	1"	56.99-64.95
Auto Mag IV	No	1"	64.95
Astra revolvers	No	1"	63.25
Beretta/Taurus auto	No	1"	63.25
Browning Buck Mark/Challenger II	No	1"	56.99
Browning Hi-Power	No	1"	63.25
Glock 17, 17L, 19, 22, 23	No	1"	63.25
Govt. 45 Auto	No	1"	63.25
Rossi revolvers	No	1"	63.25
Ruger Mk I, Mk II	No	1"	49.95
S&W K,L,N frame	No	1"	63.25
S&W Model 41 Target	No	1"	63.25
S&W Model 52 Target	No	1"	63.25
S&W 45, 9mm autos	No	1"	56.99
S&W 422/622/2206	No	1"	56.99
Taurus revolvers	No	1"	63.25
TZ/CZ/P9 9mm	No	1"	63.25
Rifles			
AR-15	No	1"	21.95
Browning A-Bolt	No	1"	21.95
Knight MK85	No	1"	21.95
Remington 700	No	1"	21.95
Ruger 10/22	No	1"	21.95
Savage 110G	No	1"	21.95
Winchester 70	No	1"	21.95
Winchester 94	No	1"	21.95
Shotguns			
Benelli Super 90	No	1"	39.95
Ithaca 37	No	1"	39.95
Mossberg 500	No	1"	39.95
Mossberg 835 Ultimag	No	1"	39.95
Mossberg 5500	No	1"	39.95
Remington 870/1100	No	1"	39.95
Winchester 1300/1400	No	1"	39.95

Mount scopes, lasers, electronic sights using Weaver-style base. All mounts allow use of iron sights; no gunsmithing. Available in satin black or satin stainless finish. **Partial listing shown.** Contact maker for full details. From L&S Technologies, Inc.

Maker, Model, Type	Adjust.	Scopes	Price
A.R.M.S.			
FN FAL LAR	No	Weaver-type rail	98.00
FN FAL LAR Para.	No	—	120.00
M21/14	No	—	135.00
M16A1/A2/AR-15	No	Weaver-type rail	59.95
Multibase Weaver Rail[1]	No		59.95
Ring Inserts	No	30mm to 1"	29.00
STANAG Rings	No	30mm	65.00
Throw Lever Weaver Rings	No	1"	78.75
#19 Weaver/STANAG Throw Lever Rail	No	—	140.00

[1]For rifles with detachable carry handle, other Weaver rails. From A.R.M.S., Inc.

Maker, Model, Type	Adjust.	Scopes	Price
ARMSON			
AR-15[1]	No	1"	33.00
Mini-14[2]	No	1"	47.00
H&K[3]	No	1"	64.00
UZI[4]	No	1"	64.00

[1]Fastens with one nut. [2]Models 181, 182, 183, 184, etc. [3]Claw mount. [4]Claw mount, bolt cover still easily removable. From Trijicon, Inc.

Maker, Model, Type	Adjust.	Scopes	Price
ARMSPORT			
100 Series[1]	No	1" rings. Low, med., high	10.75
104 22-cal.	No	1"	10.75
201 See-Thru	No	1"	13.00
1-Piece Base[2]	No	—	5.50
2-Piece Base[2]	No	—	2.75

[1]Weaver-type rings. [2]Weaver-type base; most popular rifles. Made in U.S. From Armsport.

Maker, Model, Type	Adjust.	Scopes	Price
B-SQUARE			
Pistols			
Beretta/Taurus 92/99[6]	—	1"	69.95
Browning Buck Mark[6]	No	1"	49.95
Colt 45 Auto	E only	1"	69.95
Colt Python/MkIV, 4",6",8"[1,6]	E	1"	59.95
Dan Wesson Clamp-On[2,6]	E	1"	59.95
Ruger 22 Auto Mono-Mount[3]	No	1"	59.95
Ruger Single-Six[4]	No	1"	59.95
Ruger Blackhawk, Super B'hwk[8]	W&E	1"	59.95
Ruger GP-100[9]	No	1"	59.95
Ruger Redhawk[8]	W&E	1"	59.95
S&W 422/2206[9]	No	1"	59.95
Taurus 66[9]	No	1"	59.95
S&W K, L, N frame[2,6]	No	1"	59.95
T/C Contender (Dovetail Base)	W&E	1"	39.95
Rifles			
Charter AR-7	No	1"	29.95
Mini-14 (dovetail/NATO Stanag)[5,6]	W&E	1"	59.95
M-94 Side Mount	W&E	1"	49.95
RWS, Beeman/FWB Air Rifles	E only	—	49.95
SMLE Side Mount with rings	W&E	1"	69.95
Rem. Model Seven, 600, 660, etc.[6]	No	1" One-piece base	9.95
Military			
AK-47/AKS/SKS-56[10]	No	1"	59.95
AK-47, SKS-56[11]	No	1"	59.95
M1-A[7]	W&E	1"	99.95
AR-15/16[7]	W&E	1"	59.95
FN-LAR/FAL[6,7]	E only	1"	99.95
HK-91/93/94[6,7]	E only	1"	99.95
Shotguns[6]			
Ithaca 37[6]	No	1"	49.95
Mossberg 500, 712, 5500[6]	No	1"	49.95
Rem. 870/1100 (12 & 20 ga.)[6]	No	1"	49.95
Rem. 870, 1100 (and L.H.)[6]	No	1"	49.95
BSL Laser Mounts			
Scope Tube Clamp[12,13,16]	No	—	39.95
45 Auto[12,13,16]	No	—	39.95
SIG P226[12,13,16]	No	—	39.95
Beretta 92F/Taurus PT99[12,13,16]	No	—	39.95
Colt King Cobra, Python, MkV[12,13,16]	No	—	39.95
S&W L Frame[13,16]	No	—	39.95
Browning HP[12,13,16]	No	—	39.95
Glock	No	—	39.95
Star Firestar[12,13,16]	No	—	39.95
Rossi small frame revolver[12,13,16]	No	—	39.95
Taurus 85 revolver[12,13,16]	No	—	39.95

[1]Clamp-on; blue finish; stainless finish **$59.95.** [2]Blue finish; stainless finish **$59.95.** [3]Clamp-on, blue; stainless finish **$59.95.** [4]Dovetail; stainless finish **$59.95.** [5]No gunsmithing, no sight removal; blue; stainless finish **$79.95.** [6]Weaver-style rings. Rings not included with Weaver-type bases; stainless finish add $10. [7]NATO Stanag dovetail model, **$99.50.** [8]Blue; stainless **$69.95.** [9]Blue; stainless **$69.95.** [10]Handguard mounts. [11]Receiver mounts. [12]Stainless finish add $10. [13]Under-barrel mount, no gunsmithing. [14]Ejector rod mount. [15]Guide rod mount. [16]Used with B-Square BSL-1 Laser Sight only. Mounts for many shotguns, airguns, military and law enforcement guns also available. **Partial listing of mounts shown here.** Contact B-Square for more data. B-Square makes mounts for the following military rifles: AK47/AKS, Egyptian Hakim, French MAS 1936, M91 Argentine Mauser, Model 98 Brazilian and German Mausers, Model 93, Spanish Mauser (long and short), Model 1916 Mauser, Model 38 and 96 Swedish Mausers, Model 91 Russian (round and octagon receivers), Chinese SKS 56, SMLE No. 1, Mk. III, 1903 Springfield, U.S. 30-cal. Carbine, and others. Those following replace gun's rear sight: AK47/AKS, P14/1917 Enfield, FN49, M1 Garand, M1-A/M14 (no sight removal), SMLE No. 1, Mk III/No. 4 & 5, Mk. 1, 1903/1903-A3 Springfield, Beretta AR 70 (no sight removal).

Maker, Model, Type	Adjust.	Scopes	Price
BEEMAN			
Two-Piece, Med.	No	1"	28.00
Deluxe Two-Piece, High	No	1"	30.00
Deluxe Two-Piece	No	30mm	38.00
Deluxe One-Piece	No	1"	46.00
Dampamount	No	1"	90.00
Professional Mounts	W&E	1"	150.00

All grooved receivers and scope bases on all known air rifles and 22-cal. rimfire rifles (1/2" to 5/8"—6mm to 15mm).

Maker, Model, Type	Adjust.	Scopes	Price
BOCK			
Swing ALK[1]	W&E	1", 26mm, 30mm	224.00
Safari KEMEL[2]	W&E	1", 26mm, 30mm	149.00
Claw KEMKA[3]	W&E	1", 26mm, 30mm	224.00

CAUTION: PRICES SHOW ARE SUPPLIED BY THE MANUFACTURER OR IMPORTER. CHECK YOUR LOCAL GUNSHOP.

Maker, Model, Type	Adjust.	Scopes	Price
Bock (cont.)			
ProHunter Fixed[4]	No	1", 26mm, 30mm	95.00
Dovetail 22[5]	No	1", 26mm	59.00

[1]Q.D.; pivots right for removal. For Steyr-Mannlicher, Win. 70, Rem. 700, Mauser 98, Dakota, Sako, Sauer 80, 90. Magnum has extra-wide rings, same price. [2]Heavy-duty claw-type; reversible for front or rear removal. For Steyr-Mannlicher rifles. [3]True claw mount for bolt-action rifles. Also in extended model. For Steyr-Mannlicher, Win. 70, Rem. 700. Also avail. as Gunsmith Bases—bases not drilled or contoured—same price. [4]Extra-wide rings. [5]Fit most 22 rimfires with dovetail receivers. Imported from Germany by GSI, Inc.

BURRIS			
Supreme (SU) One Piece (T)[1]	W only	1" split rings, 3 heights	1 piece base—25.95
Trumount (TU) Two Piece (T)	W only	1" split rings, 3 heights	2 piece base—23.95
Trumount (TU) Two Piece Ext.	W only	1" split rings	29.95
Browning Auto Mount[2]	No	1" split rings	19.95
Ring Mounts[3]	No	1" split rings	1" rings—21.95
L.E.R. (LU) Mount Bases[4]	W only	1" split rings	23.95
L.E.R. No Drill-No Tap Bases[4,7,8]	W only	1" split rings	23.95-50.95
Extension Rings[5]	No	1" scopes	24.95-48.95
Ruger Ring Mount[6]	W only	1" split rings	37.95-56.95
Std. 1" Rings	—	Low, medium, high heights	33.95-42.95
Zee Rings	—	Fit Weaver bases; medium and high heights	30.95-38.95

[1]Most popular rifles. Universal rings, mounts fit Burris, Universal, Redfield, Leupold and Browning bases. Comparable prices. [2]Browning Standard 22 Auto rifle. [3]Grooved receivers. [4]Universal dovetail; accept Burris, Universal, Redfield, Leupold rings. For Dan Wesson, S&W, Virginian, Ruger Blackhawk, Win. 94. [5]Medium standard front, extension rear, per pair. Low standard front, extension rear, per pair. [6]Compact scopes, scopes with 2" bell, for M77R. [7]Selected rings and bases available with matte Safari or silver finish. [8]For S&W K,L,N frames, Colt Python, Dan Wesson with 6" or longer barrels.

CAPE OUTFITTERS			
Quick Detachable	No	1" split rings, lever quick detachable	99.95

Double rifles; Rem. 700-721, Colt Sauer, Sauer 200, Kimber, Win. 61-63-07-100-70, Browning High Power, 22, BLR, BAR, BBR, A-Bolt; Wea. Mark V, Vanguard; Modern Muzzle Loading, Knight, Thompson/Center, CVA rifles, Dixie rifles. All steel; returns to zero. From Cape Outfitters.

CLEAR VIEW			
Universal Rings, Mod. 101[1]	No	1" split rings	21.95
Standard Model[2]	No	1" split rings	21.95
Broad View[3]	No	1"	21.95
22 Model[4]	No	¾", ⅞", 1"	13.95
SM-94 Winchester[5]	No	1" split rings	23.95
94 EJ[6]	No	1" split rings	21.95

[1]Most rifles by using Weaver-type base; allows use of iron sights. [2]Most popular rifles; allows use of iron sights. [3]Most popular rifles; low profile, wide field of view. [4]22 rifles with grooved receiver. [5]Side mount. [6]For Win. A.E. From Clear View Mfg.

CONETROL			
Huntur[1]	W only	1", 26mm, 26.5mm solid or split rings, 3 heights	59.88
Gunnur[2]	W only	1", 26mm, 26.5mm solid or split rings, 3 heights	74.92
Custum[3]	W only	1", 26mm, 26.5mm solid or split rings, 3 heights	99.96
One Piece Side Mount Base[4]	W only	1", 26mm, 26.5mm solid or split rings, 3 heights	—
DapTar Bases[5]	W only	1", 26mm, 26.5mm solid or split rings, 3 heights	—
Pistol Bases, 2 or 3-ring[6]	W only	1" scopes	—
Fluted Bases[7]	W only	Standard Conetrol rings	99.99
30mm Rings[8]	W only	30mm	49.98-69.96

[1]All popular rifles, including metric-drilled foreign guns. Price shown for base, two rings. Matte finish. [2]Gunnur grade has mirror-finished rings, satin-finish base. Price shown for base, two rings. [3]Custum grade has mirror-finished rings and mirror-finished, streamlined base. Price shown for base, two rings. [4]Win. 94, Krag, older split-bridge Mannlicher-Schoenauer, Mini-14, etc. Prices same as above. [5]For all popular guns with integral mounting provision, including Sako, BSA, Ithacagun, Ruger, Tikka, H&K, BRNO—$29.94-$49.98—and many others. Also for grooved-receiver rimfires and air rifles. Prices same as above. [6]For XP-100, T/C Contender, Colt SAA, Ruger Blackhawk, S&W. [7]Sculptured two-piece bases as found on fine custom rifles. Price shown is for base alone. Also available unfinished—$74.91, or finished but unblued—$87.45. [8]30mm rings made in projectionless style, medium height only. Three-ring mount available for T/C Contender and other pistols in Conetrol's three grades.

Maker, Model, Type	Adjust.	Scopes	Price
EAW			
Quick Detachable Top Mount[1]	W&E	1",26mm	248.00
	W&E	30mm	265.00

[1]Also avail. as Magnum fixed mount, from $175.00. Also 30mm rings to fit Burris, Redfield or Leupold-type bases, low and high, $145.00; 1" or 26mm rings only, $135.00. Most popular rifles. Elevation adjusted with variable-height sub-bases for rear ring. Imported by New England Custom Gun Svc.

GENTRY			
Feather-Light Rings	No	1", 30mm	75.00

One-piece of stainless or chrome moly; matte blue or gray. From David Gentry.

GRACE			
Swan G-3	No	Weaver-type	259.95

For HK G-3 guns. All-steel; provides iron sight see-through. From Grace Tool, Inc.

GRIFFIN & HOWE			
Standard Double Lever (S)	No	1" or 26mm split rings.	305.00

All popular models (Garand $215). All rings $75. Top ejection rings available. Price installed for side mount.

GUNS, GEAR & GADGETS, L.L.C.			
NATO Weaver Rail Rings[1]	No	1", 30mm	65.00
M-14/M1A Mount[2]	No	—	195.00
Mauser/Weaver Rail Base[3]	No	—	75.00

[1]Aluminum, 1"; steel, $80.00; titanium, $195.00; aluminum, 30mm, $75.00; steel, 30mm, $89.00; titanium, 30mm, $215.00. [2]Steel; slim-line profile. [3]Mount replaces 38, 96, 98k, etc., Mauser Rear sight; no gunsmithing; uses Weaver rail; for I.E.R. scopes. From Guns, Gear & Gadgets.

HOLDEN			
Wide Ironsighter™	No	1" split rings	28.95
Ironsighter Center Fire[1]	No	1" split rings	28.95
Ironsighter S-94	No	1" split rings	33.95
Ironsighter 22-Cal. Rimfire			
Model #500[2]	No	1" split rings	20.95
Model #600[3]	No	⅞" split rings also fits ¾"	16.95
Series #700[5]	No	1" split rings	28.95
Ruger Base Mounts[6]	No	1" split rings	53.95
Ironsighter Handguns[4]	No	1" split rings	33.95-58.95
Blackpowder Mount[7]	No	1"	28.95-59.95

[1]Most popular rifles, including Ruger Mini-14, H&R M700, and muzzleloaders. Rings have oval holes to permit use of iron sights. [2]For 1" dia. scopes. [3]For ¾" or ⅞" dia. scopes. [4]For 1" dia. extended eye relief scopes. [5]702—Browning A-Bolt; 709—Marlin 39A. [6]732—Ruger 77/22 R&RS; No. 1, Ranch Rifle; 777 fits Ruger 77R, RS. Both 732, 777 fit Ruger integral bases. [7]Fits most popular blackpowder rifles; one model for Holden Ironsighter mounts, one for Weaver rings. Adj. rear sight is integral. Some models in stainless finish. From J.B. Holden Co.

KENPATABLE MOUNT			
Shotgun Mount	No	1", laser or red dot device	49.95

Wrap-around design; no gunsmithing required. Models for Browning BPS, A-5 12-ga., Sweet 16, 20, Rem. 870/1100 (LTW and L.H.), S&W 916, Mossberg 500, Ithaca 37 & 51 12-ga., S&W 1000/3000, Win. 1400. From KenPatable Ent.

KRIS MOUNTS			
Side-Saddle[1]	No	1", 26mm split rings	12.98
Two Piece (T)[2]	No	1", 26mm split rings	8.98
One Piece (T)[3]	No	1", 26mm split rings	12.98

[1]One-piece mount for Win. 94. [2]Most popular rifles and Ruger. [3]Blackhawk revolver. Mounts have oval hole to permit use of iron sights.

KWIK-SITE			
KS-See-Thru[1]	No	1"	25.95
KS-22 See-Thru[2]	No	1"	22.95
KS-W94[3]	No	1"	30.95
Imperial Bench Rest	No	1"	30.95
KS-WEV	No	1"	21.95
KS-WEV-HIGH	No	1"	21.95
KS-T22 1"[4]	No	1"	22.95
KS-FL Flashlite[5]	No	Mini or C cell flashlight	49.95
KS-T88[6]	No	1"	10.95
KS-T89	No	30mm	14.95
KSN 22 See-Thru	No	1", ⅞"	19.95
KSN-T22	No	1", ⅞"	19.95
KSN-M16 See-Thru	No	1"	99.95
KSB Base Set	—		5.65
Combo Bases & Rings	No	1"	26.75

Bases interchangeable with Weaver bases. [1]Most rifles. Allows use of iron sights. [2]22-cal. rifles with grooved receivers. Allows use of iron sights. [3]Model 94, 94 Big Bore. No drilling or tapping. Also in adjustable model $49.95. [4]Non-see-through model for grooved receivers. [5]Allows Mag Lite or C or D, Mini Mag Lites to be mounted atop See-Thru mounts. [6]Fits any Redfield, Tasco, Weaver or universal-style Kwik-Site dovetail base. Bright blue, black matte or satin finish. Standard, high heights.

Maker, Model, Type	Adjust.	Scopes	Price
LASER AIM	No	Laser Aim	35.00-59.00
Mounts Laser Aim above or below barrel. Avail. for most popular handguns, rifles, shotguns, including militaries. From Emerging Technologies, Inc.			
LASERSIGHT	No	LS45 only	29.95-149.00
For the LS45 Lasersight. Allows LS45 to be mounted alongside any 1" scope. Universal adapter attaches to any full-length Weaver-type base. For most popular military-type rifles, Mossberg, Rem. shotguns, Python, Desert Eagle, S&W N frame, Colt 45ACP. From Imatronic Lasersight.			
LEUPOLD			
STD Bases[1]	W only	One- or two-piece bases	22.90
STD Rings[2]	—	1" super low, low, medium, high	32.00
STD Handgun mounts[3]	No	—	57.90
Dual Dovetail Bases[1,4]	No	—	22.90
Dual Dovetail Rings[10]	—	1", super low, low	32.00
Ring Mounts[5,6,7]	No	7/8", 1"	81.10
22 Rimfire[10]	No	7/8", 1"	60.00
Gunmaker Base[8]	W only	1"	16.00
Gunmaker Ring Blanks[9]	—	1"	22.00
Quick Release Rings	—	1", low, med., high	32.00
Quick Release Bases[11]	No	1", one- or two-piece	66.00
Airgun Ringmount[12]	No	1"	92.00

[1]Rev. front and rear combinations; matte finish **$22.90**. [2]Avail. polished, matte or silver (low, med. only) finish. [3]Base and two rings; Casull, Ruger, S&W, T/C; add $5.00 for silver finish. [4]Rem. 700, Win. 70-type actions. [5]For Ruger No. 1, 77, 77/22; interchangeable with Ruger units. [6]For dovetailed rimfire rifles. [7]Sako; high, medium, low. [8]Must be drilled, tapped for each action. [9]Unfinished bottom, top completed; sold singly. [10]Most dovetail-receiver 22s. [11]BSA Monarch, Rem. 40X, 700, 721, 725, Ruger M77, S&W 1500, Weatherby Mark V, Vanguard, Win M70. [12]Receiver grooves 9.5mm to 11.0mm; matte finish.

Maker, Model, Type	Adjust.	Scopes	Price
LEATHERWOOD			
Bridge Bases[1]	No	ART II or all dovetail rings	15.00
M1A/M-14 Q.D.	No	ART II or all dovetail rings	105.00
AR-15/M-16 Base	No	ART II or all dovetail rings	25.00
FN-FAL Base	No	ART II or all dovetail rings	100.00
FN Para. Base	No	ART II or all dovetail rings	110.00
Steyr SSG Base	No	ART II or all dovetail rings	55.00

[1]Many popular bolt actions. Mounts accept Weaver or dovetail-type rings. From North American Specialties.

Maker, Model, Type	Adjust.	Scopes	Price
MARLIN			
One Piece QD (T)	No	1" split rings	14.95
Most Marlin lever actions.			

Maker, Model, Type	Adjust.	Scopes	Price
MILLETT			
Black Onyx Smooth	—	1", low, medium, high	31.15
Chaparral Engraved	—	engraved	46.15
One-Piece Bases[6]	Yes	1"	23.95
Universal Two-Piece Bases			
700 Series	W only	Two-piece bases	25.15
FN Series	W only	Two-piece bases	25.15
70 Series[1]	W only	1", two-piece bases	25.15
Angle-Loc Rings[2]	W only	1", low, medium, high	32.20-47.20
Ruger 77 Rings[3]	—	1"	47.20
Shotgun Rings[4]	—	1"	28.29
Handgun Bases, Rings[5]	—	1"	34.60-69.15
30mm Rings[7]	—	30mm	37.75-42.95
Extension Rings[8]	—	1"	35.65
See-Thru Mounts[9]	No	1"	27.95-32.95
Shotgun Mounts[10]	No	1"	49.95

[1]Rem. 40X, 700, 722, 725, Ruger 77 (round top), Weatherby, FN Mauser, FN Brownings, Colt 57, Interarms Mark X, Parker-Hale, Sako (round receiver), many others. [2]Fits Win. M70, 70XTR, 670, Browning BBR, BAR, BLR, A-Bolt, Rem. 7400/7600, Four, Six, Marlin 336, Win. 94 A.E., Sav. 110. [3]To fit Weaver-type bases. [4]For Rem. 870, 1100; smooth. [5]Two and three-ring sets for Colt Python, Trooper, Diamondback, Peacekeeper, Dan Wesson, Ruger Redhawk, Super Redhawk. [6]Turn-in bases and Weaver-style for most popular rifles and T/C Contender, XP-100 pistols. [7]Both Weaver and turn-in styles; three heights. [8]Med. or high; ext. front—std. rear, ext. front—ext. rear; **$40.90** for double extension. [9]Many popular rifles, Knight MK-85, T/C Hawken, Renegade, Mossberg 500 Slugster, 835 Slug. [10]For Rem. 870/1100, Win. 1200, 1300/1400, 1500, Mossberg 500. Some models available in nickel at extra cost. From Millett Sights.

Maker, Model, Type	Adjust.	Scopes	Price
OAKSHORE			
Handguns			
Browning Buck Mark	No	1"	29.00
Colt Cobra, Diamondback, Python, 1911	No	1"	38.00-52.00
Ruger 22 Auto, GP100	No	1"	33.00-49.00
S&W N Frame	No	1"	45.00-60.00
S&W 422	No	1"	35.00-38.00
Rifles			
Colt AR-15	No	1"	26.00-34.00
H&K 91, 93, 94, MP-5, G-3	No	1"	56.00
Galil	No	1"	75.00
Marlin 336 & 1800 Series	No	1"	21.00
Win. 94	No	1"	39.00
Shotguns			
Mossberg 500	No	1"	40.00
Rem. 870, 1100	No	1"	33.00-52.00
Rings	—	1", med., high	5.20-9.80

See Through offered in some models. Black or silver finish; 1" rings also avail. for 3/8" grooved receivers (See Through). From Oakshore Electronic Sights, Inc.

Maker, Model, Type	Adjust.	Scopes	Price
PEM'S			
22T Mount[1]	No	1"	17.95
The Mount[2]	Yes	1"	27.50

[1]Fit all 3/8" dovetail on rimfire rifles. [2]Base and ring set; for over 100 popular rifles; low, medium rings. From Pem's.

Maker, Model, Type	Adjust.	Scopes	Price
RAM-LINE			
Mini-14 Mount	Yes	1"	24.97

No drilling or tapping. Use std. dovetail rings. Has built-in shell deflector. Made of solid black polymer. From Ram-Line, Inc.

Maker, Model, Type	Adjust.	Scopes	Price
REDFIELD			
American Rings[6]	No	1", low, med., high	16.95
American Bases[6]	No	—	2.65-10.15
American Widefield See-Thru[7]	No	1"	16.95
JR-SR (T)[1]	W only	3/4", 1", 26mm, 30mm	JR—20.95-52.95 SR—22.95-39.95
Ring (T)[2]	No	3/4" and 1"	29.95-45.95
Three-Ring Pistol System SMP[3]	No	1" split rings (three)	56.95-62.95
Widefield See-Thru Mounts	No	1"	16.95
Ruger Rings[4]	No	1", med., high	35.95
Ruger 30mm[5]	No	1"	46.95
Midline Ext. Rings	No	1"	22.95

[1]Low, med. & high, split rings. Reversible extension front rings for 1". 2-piece bases for Sako. Colt Sauer bases **$39.95**. Med. Top Access JR rings nickel-plated, **$29.95**. SR two-piece ABN mount nickel-plated. **$22.95**; RealTree Camo rings, med., high **$31.95**; RealTree Camo JR bases **$25.95**; RealTree bases **$25.95**. [2]Split rings for grooved 22s; 30mm, black matte **$42.95**.; 30mm nickel matte, **45.95**. [3]Used with MP scopes for: S&W K, L or N frame, XP-100, T/C Contender, Ruger receivers. [4]For Ruger Model 77 rifles, medium and high; medium only for M77/22. [5]For Model 77. Also in matte finish, **$44.95**. [6]Aluminum 22 groove mount **$14.95**; base and medium rings **$17.95**. [7]Fits American or Weaver-style base.

Maker, Model, Type	Adjust.	Scopes	Price
S&K			
Insta-Mount (T) bases and rings[1]	W only	Use S&K rings only	47.00-117.00
Conventional rings and bases[2]	W only	1" split rings	From 65.00
Skulptured Bases, Rings[2]	W only	1", 26mm, 30mm	From 65.00
Smooth Kontoured Rings[3]	No	1", 26mm, 30mm	50.00-74.00

[1]1903, A3, M1 Carbine, Lee Enfield #1, Mk. III, #4, #5, M1917, M98 Mauser, AR-15, AR-180, M-14, M-1, Ger. K-43, Mini-14, M1-A, Krag, AKM, Win. 94, SKS Type 56, Daewoo, H&K. [2]Most popular rifles already drilled and tapped. [3]No projections; weigh 1/2-oz. each; matte or gloss finish. Horizontally and vertically split rings, matte or high gloss.

Maker, Model, Type	Adjust.	Scopes	Price
SSK INDUSTRIES			
T'SOB	No	1"	65.00-145.00
Quick Detachable	No	1"	From 160.00

Custom installation using from two to four rings (included). For T/C Contender, most 22 auto pistols, Ruger and other S.A. revolvers, Ruger, Dan Wesson, S&W, Colt DA revolvers. Black or white finish. Uses Kimber rings in two- or three-ring sets. In blue or SSK Khrome. For T/C Contender or most popular revolvers. Standard, non-detachable model also available, from **$65.00**.

Maker, Model, Type	Adjust.	Scopes	Price
SAKO			
QD Dovetail	W only	1" only	70.00-145.00

Sako, or any rifle using Sako action, 3 heights available. Stoeger, importer.

Maker, Model, Type	Adjust.	Scopes	Price
SPRINGFIELD, INC.			
Competition—Rings[1]	No	30mm	129.95
Competition—Ringless[2]	No	—	129.95

[1]For red dot sights; 3.0 oz. [2]Weaver-style base; 2.16 oz. Drilling, tapping required. From Springfield, Inc.

Maker, Model, Type	Adjust.	Scopes	Price
TASCO			
World Class			
Universal "W" Ringmount[1]	No	1", 30mm	25.00-31.00
Ruger[2]	No	1", 30mm	31.00-73.00

Maker, Model, Type	Adjust.	Scopes	Price
Tasco (cont.)			
22, Air Rifle[3]	No	1", 30mm	18.00-82.00
Center-Fire Ringmount[4]	No	1", 26mm, 30mm	58.00-82.00
Desert Eagle Ringmount[5]	No	1", 30mm	64.00-90.00
Ringsets[6]	No	1", 26mm, 30mm	39.00-66.00
Bases[7]	Yes	—	24.00-61.00

[1]Steel; low, high only; also high-profile see-through; fit Tasco, Weaver, other universal bases; black gloss or satin chrome. [2]Low, high only; for Redhawk and Super, No.1, Mini-14 & Thirty, 77, 77/22; blue or stainless. [3]Low, med., high; 3/8" grooved receivers; black or satin chrome. [4]Low, med., high; for Tasco W.C. bases, some dovetail; black gloss only. [5]For Desert Eagle pistols, 22s, air rifles with deep dovetails. [6]Low, med., high; black gloss, matte satin chrome; also Traditional Ringsets **$31.00** (1"), **$42.00** (26mm), **$53.00** (30mm). [7]For popular rifles and shotguns; one-piece, two-piece, Q.D., long and short action, extension. Handgun bases have w&e adj. From Tasco.

Maker, Model, Type	Adjust.	Scopes	Price
THOMPSON/CENTER			
Contender 9741[1]	No	2½, 4 RP	17.00
S&W 9747[2]	No	Lobo or RP	17.00
Ruger 9748[3]	No	Lobo or RP	17.00
Hawken 9749[4]	No	Lobo or RP	17.00
Hawken/Renegade 9754[5]	No	Lobo or RP	17.00
New Englander 9757	No	Lobo or RP	17.00
Quick Release System[6]	No	1"	Rings 48.00 Base 24.50

[1]T/C rail mount scopes; all Contenders except vent. rib. [2]All S&W K and Combat Masterpiece, Hi-Way Patrolman, Outdoorsman, 22 Jet, 45 Target 1955. Requires drilling, tapping. [3]Blackhawk, Super Blackhawk, Super Single-Six. Requires drilling, tapping. [4]45 or 50 cal.; replaces rear sight. [5]Rail mount scopes; 54-cal. Hawken, 50, 54, 56-cal. Renegade. Replaces rear sight. [6]For Contender pistol, Carbine, Scout, all M/L long guns. From Thompson/Center.

Maker, Model, Type	Adjust.	Scopes	Price
UNERTL			
¼ Click[1]	Yes	¾", 1" target scopes	Per set 165.00

[1]Unertl target or varmint scopes. Posa or standard mounts, less bases. From Unertl

Maker, Model, Type	Adjust.	Scopes	Price
WARNE			
Deluxe Series[1]	No	1", 3 heights	76.50
		30mm, 2 heights	88.50
Premier Series			
Adjustable Double Lever	No	1", 4 heights	99.50
		26mm, 2 heights	111.50
		30mm, 3 heights	111.50
Thumb Knob[2]	No	1", 4 heights	79.50
		26mm, 2 heights	91.50
		30mm, 3 heights	91.50
Brno 19mm[3,4]	No	1", 3 heights	99.50
		30mm, 2 heights	111.50
Brno 16mm[3,4]		1" 2 heights	99.50
Ruger[3,4]	No	1", 4 heights	99.50
		30mm, 3 heights	111.50
Ruger M77[3,4]	No	1", 3 heights	99.50
		30mm, 2 heights	111.50
Sako[3,4]	No	1", 4 heights	99.50
		30mm, 3 heights	111.50
Sako Non-Quick Detachable[1,4]	No	1", 4 heights	76.50
		30mm, 3 heights	88.50
Steyer SSG[3,4]	No	1", 1 height	99.50
		30mm, 1 height	111.50
Supra Series			
Adjustable Double Lever[5]	No	1", 3 heights	54.50
Thumb Knob[2,5]	No	1", 3 heights	49.50
Ruger[3,4]	No	1", 3 heights	54.50
Ruger M77[3,4]	No	1", 2 heights	54.50
Ruger Pistol Kit[3,4]	No	1", 3 heights	94.50
Premier One-Piece Base	—	—	32.00
Premier Two-Piece Bases (pr.)	—	—	25.00
Supra One-Piece Base	—	—	24.00
Supra Two-Piece Bases (pr.)	—	—	17.00

Vertically split rings with dovetail clamp, precise return to zero. Fit most popular rifles, handguns. Regular blue, matte blue, silver finish. [1]Non-quick detachable. [2]Available with coin-slotted machine screws. [3]Adjustable Double Lever only. [4]Fit directly onto integral dovetail. [5]Available for grooved (3/8") receivers. From Warne Mfg. Co.

Maker, Model, Type	Adjust.	Scopes	Price
WEAVER			
Detachable Mounts			
Top Mount[1]	No	7/8", 1"	22.71-36.12
Side Mount[2]	No	1", 1" Long	27.79-32.85

Maker, Model, Type	Adjust.	Scopes	Price
Weaver (cont.)			
Pivot Mount[3]	No	1"	36.32
Tip-Off Mount[4]	No	7/8", 1"	20.21-25.79
See-Thru Mount			
Traditional[5]	No	1"	16.06
Tip-Off[4]	No	1", 7/8"	18.38
Pro View[5]	No	1"	15.74-18.04
Mount Base System[6]			
Blue Finish	No	1"	68.37
Stainless Finish	No	1"	95.63
Shotgun Converta-Mount System[7]	No	1"	68.37
Rifle Mount System[8]	No	1"	30.33
Paramount Mount Systems[9]			
Bases, pair	Yes	1"	24.19
Rings, pair	No	1"	32.01

[1]Nearly all modern rifles. Low, med., high. 1" extension **$28.14**. 1" low, med., high stainless steel **$40.53**. [2]Nearly all modern rifles, shotguns. [3]Most modern big bore rifles; std., high. [4]22s with 3/8" grooved receivers. [5]Most modern big bore rifles. Some in stainless finish, **$20.22-21.44**. [6]No drilling, tapping. For Colt Python, Trooper, 357, Officer's Model, Ruger Blackhawk & Super, Mini-14, Security-Six, 22 auto pistols, Single-Six 22, Redhawk, Blackhawk SRM 357, S&W current K, L with adj. sights. [7]For Rem. 870, 1100, 11-87, Browning A-5, BPS, Ithaca 37, 87, Beretta A303, Beretta A-390, Winchester 1200-1500, Mossberg 500. [8]For some popular sporting rifles. [9]Dovetail design mount for Rem. 700, Win. 70, FN Mauser, low, med., high rings; std., extension bases. From Weaver.

Maker, Model, Type	Adjust.	Scopes	Price
WEIGAND			
1911 PDP4[1]	No	40mm, PDP4	69.95
1911 General Purpose[2]	No	—	59.95
Ruger Mark II[3]	No	—	49.95
3rd Generation[4]	No	—	99.95
Pro Ringless[5]	No	30mm	99.95
Stabilizer I Ringless[6,7]	No	30mm	99.95
Revolver Mount[8]	No	—	35.50
Ruger 10/22[9]	No	—	39.95

[1]For Tasco PDP4 and similar 40mm sights. [2]Weaver rail; takes any standard rings. [3]No drilling, tapping. [4]For M1911; grooved top for Weaver-style rings; requires drilling, tapping. [5]Two-piece design; for M1911, P9/EA-9, CZ-75 copies; integral rings; silver alum. finish. [6]Three-piece design; fits M1911, P9/EA-9, TZ, CZ-75 copies; silver alum. finish. [7]Stabilizer II — more forward position; for M1911, McCormick frames. [8]Frame mount. [9]Barrel mount. From Weigand Combat Handguns, Inc.

Maker, Model, Type	Adjust.	Scopes	Price
WIDEVIEW			
Premium 94 Angle Eject	No	1"	24.00
Premium See-Thru	No	1"	22.00
22 Premium See-Thru	No	¾", 1"	16.00
Universal Ring Angle Cut	No	1"	24.00
Universal Ring Straight Cut	No	1"	22.00
Solid Mounts			
Lo Ring Solid[1]	No	1"	16.00
Hi Ring Solid[1]	No	1"	16.00
SR Rings	—	1", 30mm	16.00
22 Grooved Receiver	No	1"	16.00
94 Side Mount	No	1"	26.00
Blackpowder Mounts[2]	No	1"	30.00

[1]For Weaver-type bases. Models for many popular rifles. Low ring, high ring and grooved receiver types. [2]No drilling, tapping; for T/C Renegade, Hawken, CVA guns; for guns drilled and tapped, **$16.00**. From Wideview Scope Mount Corp.

Maker, Model, Type	Adjust.	Scopes	Price
WILLIAMS			
Sidemount with HCO Rings[1]	No	1", split or extension rings	72.05
Sidemount, offset rings[2]	No	Same	59.30
Sight-Thru Mounts[3]	No	1", 7/8" sleeves	23.95
Streamline Mounts	No	1" (bases form rings)	24.95
Guideline Handgun[4]	No	1" split rings.	79.95

[1]Most rifles, Br. S.M.L.E. (round rec.) **$13.99** extra. [2]Most rifles including Win. 94 Big Bore. [3]Many modern rifles, including CVA Apollo, others with 1" octagon barrels. [4]No drilling, tapping required; heat treated alloy. For Ruger Blackhawk, Super Blackhawk, Redhawk; S&W N frame, M29 with 10⅝" barrel (**$79.95**); S&W K, L frames; Colt Python, King Cobra; Ruger MkII Bull Barrel; Streamline Top Mount for T/C Contender, Scout Rifle, CVA Apollo (**$39.95**), High Top Mount with sub-base (**$49.95**). From Williams Gunsight Co.

Maker, Model, Type	Adjust.	Scopes	Price
YORK			
M-1 Garand	Yes	1"	39.95

Centers scope over the action. No drilling, tapping or gunsmithing. Uses standard dovetail rings. From York M-1 Conversions.

NOTES

(S)—Side Mount (T)—Top Mount; 22mm=.866"; 25.4mm=1.024"; 26.5mm=1.045"; 30mm=1.81"

CAUTION: PRICES SHOWN ARE SUPPLIED BY THE MANUFACTURER OR IMPORTER. CHECK YOU LOCAL GUNSHOP.

49th EDITION, 1995 **479**

Simmons 1208 Compact

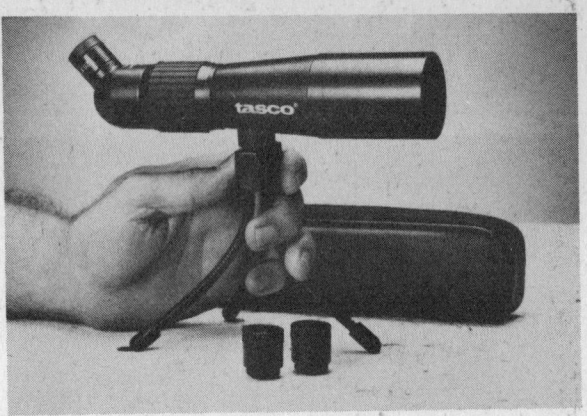

Tasco MS2040 Mini

BAUSCH & LOMB DISCOVERER—15x to 60x zoom, 60mm objective. Constant focus throughout range. Field at 1000 yds. 38 ft (60x), 150 ft. (15x). Comes with lens caps. Length 17½"; weight 48.5 oz.
Price: **$364.95**
BAUSCH & LOMB ELITE—15x to 45x zoom, 60mm objective. Field at 1000 yds., 119-62 ft. Length is 12.2"; weight, 26.5 oz. Waterproof, armored. Tripod mount. Comes with black case.
Price: **$713.95**
BAUSCH & LOMB 77MM ELITE—20x, 30x or 20-60x zoom, 77mm objective. Field of view at 1000 yds. 175 ft. (20x), 78 ft. (30x), 108-62 ft. (zoom). Weight 51 oz. (20x, 30x), 54 oz. (zoom); length 16.8". Interchangeable bayonet-style eyepieces. Built-in peep sight.
Price: **$750.00**
Price: With EDPrime Glass **$1,550.00**
Price: 20-60x zoom eyepiece **$386.95**
Price: 20x wide angle eyepiece **$276.95**
Price: 30x eyepiece **$275.95**
BURRIS 20x SPOTTER—20x, 50mm objective. Straight type. Field at 100 yds. 15 ft. Length 10"; weight 21 oz. Rubber armor coating, multi-coated lenses, 22mm eye relief. Recessed focus adjustment. Nitrogen filled. Retractable sunshade.
Price: 20x 50mm **$471.95**
Price: 24x 60mm **$499.95**
Price: 30x 60mm **$560.95**
BUSHNELL BANNER SENTRY—18-36x zoom, 50mm objective. Field at 1000 yds. 115-78 ft. Length 14.5", weight 27 oz. Black rubber armored. Built-in peep sight. Comes with tripod.
Price: **$189.95**
Price: With 45° field eyepiece, includes tripod . . . **$210.00**
BUSHNELL COMPACT COMPETITOR—20x, 40mm objective. Field at 1000 yds. 141 ft. Focuses down to 40 ft. for indoor use. Tripod mount. Length 10.5"; weight 14.5 oz. Comes with tripod.
Price: **$143.95**
BUSHNELL SPACEMASTER—15x-45x zoom. Rubber armored, prismatic. 60mm objective. Field at 1000 yds. 125-65 ft. Minimum focus 20 ft. Length with caps 11.6"; weight 38.4 oz.
Price: With tripod and carrying case **$496.95**
Price: Interchangeable eyepieces—15x, 20x, 25x, 60x, each **$55.95**
Price: 22x Wide Angle **$87.95**
Price: 15-45x zoom eyepiece **$159.95**
BUSHNELL STALKER—10x to 30x zoom, 50mm objective. Field at 1000 yds. 142 ft. (10x) to 86 ft. (30x). Length 10.5"; weight 16 oz. Camo armored. Comes with tripod.
Price: **$412.95**
KOWA TSN-1-45°—Offset-type. 77mm objective, 25x, fixed and zoom eyepieces; field at 1000 yds. 94 ft.; relative brightness 9.6; length 15.4"; weight 48.8 oz. Lens shade and caps. Straight-type (TSN-2) also available with similar specs and prices.
Price: Without eyepiece **$575.00**
Price: 20x-60x zoom eyepiece **$250.00**
Price: 20x eyepiece (wide angle) **$190.00**
Price: 25x, 40x eyepiece **$119.00, $132.00**
Price: 25x LER eyepiece **$178.00**
Price: 30x eyepiece (wide angle) **$220.00**
Price: 60x eyepiece **$190.00**
Price: 77x eyepiece **$195.00**
Price: TSN-2 (straight), no eyepiece **$545.00**

KOWA TS-601—45° off-set type. 60mm multi-coated objective, 25x fixed and zoom eyepieces; field at 1000 yds. 93 ft.; relative brightness 5.8; length 14.8"; weight 37 oz. Comes with lens shade and caps. Straight-type also available (TS-602).
Price: Without eyepiece **$425.00**
Price: 25x eyepiece **$95.00**
Price: 20x eyepiece (wide angle) **$114.00**
Price: 40x eyepiece **$99.00**
Price: 20-60x zoom eyepiece **$205.00**
Price: 25x LER eyepiece **$175.00**
KOWA TS-610 SERIES SPOTTING SCOPES—60mm objective lens. Straight or angled, fixed (20x WA, 25x LER, 25x, 27x WA, 40x) or zoom (20x-60x) eyepieces. Partly rubber armored composite body. Field at 1000 yds. 102 ft. (25x), 162-56 ft. (20x-60x). Length 11.7"; weight 27.5 oz. Partial listing shown.
Price: TS-611, 45°, 20x-60x zoom **$725.00**
Price: TS-611, 40x, fixed **$619.00**
Price: TS-612, straight, 20x-60x zoom **$670.00**
Price: TS-612, 25x LER **$640.00**
Price: TS-613 ED, 45°, 20x-60x zoom **$1,215.00**
Price: TS-613 ED, 27x, Wide Angle **$1,180.00**
Price: TS-614 ED, straight, 20x-60x zoom **$1,140.00**
Price: TS-614 ED, 20x Wide Angle **$1,049.00**
KOWA TS-9C—Straight-type. 50mm objective, 20x compact model; fixed power eyepieces; objective focusing down to 17 ft.; field at 1000 yds. 157 ft.; relative brightness 6.3; length 9.65"; weight 22.9 oz. Lens caps.
Price: With 20x eyepiece **$193.00**
Price: 15x, 20x eyepieces, each **$35.00, $33.00**
Price: 11x-33x zoom eyepiece **$111.00**
Price: As above, rubber armored, 20x (TS-9R) . . . **$212.00**
Price: TS-9B (45° offset), 20x **$236.00**
LEUPOLD 12-40x60 VARIABLE—60mm objective, 12-40x. Field at 100 yds. 17.5-5.3 ft.; eye relief 1.2" (20x). Overall length 11.5", weight 32 oz. Rubber armored.
Price: **$1,026.80**
LEUPOLD 20x50 COMPACT—50mm objective, 20x. Field at 100 yards 11.5 ft.; eye relief 1"; length 9.4"; weight 20.5 oz.
Price: Armored model **$646.40**
Price: Packer Tripod **$87.50**
LEUPOLD 25x50 COMPACT—50mm objective, 25x. Field at 100 yds. 8.3 ft.; eye relief 1"; length overall 9.4"; weight 20.5 oz.
Price: Armored model **$646.40**
Price: Armored, with reticle **$689.30**
Price: Packer Tripod **$87.50**
LEUPOLD 30x60 COMPACT—60mm objective, 30x. Field at 100 yds. 6.4 ft.; eye relief 1"; length overall 12.9"; weight 26 oz.
Price: Armored model **$710.70**
Price: Packer Tripod **$87.50**
MIRADOR TTB SERIES—Draw tube armored spotting scopes. Available with 75mm or 80mm objective. Zoom model (28x-62x, 80mm) is 11⅞" (closed), weighs 50 oz. Field at 1000 yds. 70-42 ft. Comes with lens covers.
Price: 28-62x80mm **$1,133.95**
Price: 32x80mm **$971.95**
Price: 26-58x75mm **$989.95**
Price: 30x75mm **$827.95**
MIRADOR SSD SPOTTING SCOPES—60mm objective, 15x, 20x, 22x, 25x, 40x, 60x, 20-60x; field at 1000 yds. 37 ft.; length 10¼"; weight 33 oz.
Price: 25x **$575.95**
Price: 22x Wide Angle **$593.95**
Price: 20-60x Zoom **$746.95**
Price: As above, with tripod, case **$944.95**

CAUTION: PRICES SHOWN ARE SUPPLIED BY THE MANUFACTURER OR IMPORTER. CHECK YOUR LOCAL GUNSHOP.

MIRADOR SIA SPOTTING SCOPES—Similar to the SSD scopes except with 45° eyepiece. Length 12¼"; weight 39 oz.
Price: 25x $809.95
Price: 22x Wide Angle $827.95
Price: 20-60x Zoom $980.95
MIRADOR SSR SPOTTING SCOPES—50mm or 60mm objective. Similar to SSD except rubber armored in black or camouflage. Length 11⅛"; weight 31 oz.
Price: Black, 20x $521.95
Price: Black, 18x Wide Angle $539.95
Price: Black, 16-48x Zoom $692.95
Price: Black, 20x, 60mm, EER $692.95
Price: Black, 22x Wide Angle, 60mm $701.95
Price: Black, 20-60x Zoom $854.95
MIRADOR SSF FIELD SCOPES—Fixed or variable power, choice of 50mm, 60mm, 75mm objective lens. Length 9¾"; weight 20 oz. (15-32x50).
Price: 20x50mm $359.95
Price: 25x60mm $440.95
Price: 30x75mm $584.95
Price: 15-32x50mm Zoom $548.95
Price: 18-40x60mm Zoom $629.95
Price: 22-47x75mm Zoom $773.95
MIRADOR SRA MULTI ANGLE SCOPES—Similar to SSF Series except eyepiece head rotates for viewing from any angle.
Price: 20x50mm $503.95
Price: 25x60mm $647.95
Price: 30x75mm $764.95
Price: 15-32x50mm Zoom $692.95
Price: 18-40x60mm Zoom $836.95
Price: 22-47x75mm Zoom $953.95
MIRADOR SIB FIELD SCOPES—Short-tube, 45° scopes with porro prism design. 50mm and 60mm objective. Length 10¼"; weight 18.5 oz. (15-32x50mm); field at 1000 yds. 129-81 ft.
Price: 20x50mm $386.95
Price: 25x60mm $449.95
Price: 15-32x50mm Zoom $575.95
Price: 18-40x60mm Zoom $638.95
NIKON FIELDSCOPES—60mm and 78mm lens. Field at 1000 yds. 105 ft. (60mm, 20x), 126 ft. (78mm, 25x). Length 12.8" (straight 60mm), 12.6" (straight 78mm); weight 34.5-47.5 oz. Eyepieces available separately.
Price: 60mm straight body $610.00
Price: 60mm angled body $740.00
Price: 60mm straight ED body $1,090.00
Price: 60mm angled ED body $1,190.00
Price: 78mm straight body $1,860.00
Price: 78mm angled body $1,980.00
Price: Eyepieces (15x to 60x) . . . . $134.00 to $242.00
Price: 20-45x eyepiece (25-56x for 78mm) $290.00
NIKON SPOTTING SCOPE—60mm objective, 20x fixed power or 15-45x zoom. Field at 1000 yds. 145 ft. (20x). Gray rubber armored. Straight or angled eyepiece. Weighs 44.2 oz., length 12.1" (20x).
Price: 20x60 fixed $384.00
Price: 15-45x zoom $570.00
PENTAX 30x60 HG—60mm objective lens, 30x. Field of view 86 ft. at 1000 yds. Length 12.1"; weight 35 oz. Waterproof, rubber armor, multi-coated lenses. Comes with lens cap, case, neck strap.
Price: $600.00
REDFIELD WATERPROOF 20-45x SPOTTER—60mm objective, 20-45x. Field at 1000 yds. 45-63 ft. Length 12.5"; weight 23 oz. Black rubber armor coat. With vinyl carrying case.
Price: $529.95
Price: As above, with adjustable tripod, aluminum carrying case with shoulder strap $699.95
REDFIELD REGAL II—Regal II has 60mm objective, interchangeable 25x and 18x-40x zoom eyepieces. Field at 1000 yds.—125 ft. (25x). Dual rotation of eyepiece and scope body. With aluminum carrying case, tripod.
Price: $755.95
REDFIELD REGAL IV—Conventional straight through viewing. Regal IV has 60mm objective and interchangeable 25x and 20x-60x zoom eyepieces. Field at 1000 yds. 94 ft. (25x). With tripod and aluminum carrying case.
Price: Regal IV with black rubber Armorcoat $887.95
REDFIELD REGAL VI—60mm objective, 25x fixed and 20x-60x interchangeable eyepieces. Has 45° angled eyepiece, front-mounted focus ring, 180° tube rotation. Field at 1000 yds. 94 ft. (25x); length 12¼"; weight 40 oz. Comes with tripod, aluminum carrying case.
Price: Regal VI $944.95
SCHMIDT & BENDER TRADITIONAL—Draw tube design. 25x, 50mm objective. Field at 1000 yds. 92 ft. Shortest focusing distance 32 ft. Length open 31"; length closed 10.5"; weighs 28 oz. Leather covered anodized aluminum.
Price: $595.00
SIMMONS 1204 COMPACT—50mm objective, 12-36x zoom. Camouflage rubber armored finish. Ocular focus and variable power magnification.
Price: With tripod $243.95
Price: Model 1205 (black non-armored finish) $206.95

SIMMONS 1207 COMPACT—50mm objective, 25x fixed power. Ocular focus. Green rubber-armored finish.
Price: With tripod $199.95
Price: Model 1206 (black rubber-armored finish) $199.95
SIMMONS 1208 COMPACT—50mm objective, 25x fixed power. Ocular focus. Non-reflective finish.
Price: With tripod $169.95
SWAROVSKI HABICHT HAWK 30x75S TELESCOPE—75mm objective, 30x. Field at 1000 yds. 90 ft. Minimum focusing distance 65 ft. Length: closed 13", extended 20.9"; weight 47 oz. Precise recognition of smallest details even at dusk. Rubber covered, with caps and carrying case.
Price: $865.00
SWAROVSKI 25-40x75 TELESCOPE—75mm objective, variable power from 25x to 40x with a field of 90 ft. (25x) and 66 ft. (40x). Minimum focusing distance 66 ft. Length: closed 14.2", extended 21.7"; weight 50 oz. Rubber covered.
Price: Standard $1,075.00
SWIFT LEOPARD M837—50mm objective, 25x. Length 9¹¹⁄₁₆" to 10½". Weight with tripod 28 oz. Rubber armored. Comes with tripod.
Price: $150.00
SWIFT TELEMASTER M841—60mm objective. 15x to 60x variable power. Field at 1000 yds. 160 feet (15x) to 40 feet (60x). Weight 3.4 lbs.; length 18" overall.
Price: $399.50
SWIFT M700R—10x-40x, 40mm objective. Field of 210 feet at 10x, 70 feet at 40x. Length 16.3", weight 21.4 oz. Has 45° eyepiece.
Price: $198.00
SWIFT SEARCHER M839—60mm objective, 20x, 40x. Field at 1000 yds. 118 ft. (30x), 59 ft. (40x). Length 12.6"; weight 3 lbs. Rotating eyepiece head for straight or 45° viewing.
Price: $460.00
Price: 30x, 50x eyepieces, each $59.00
Price: Tripod, from $68.00
TASCO CW50TZB, CW50TZBC ZOOM SPOTTING SCOPES—50mm objective lens, 12-36x zoom. Field at 100 yds. 16-9 ft. Available in black or brown camo rubber armor. With panhead lever tripod.
Price: CW50TZB (brown) $289.00
Price: CW50TZBC (camo) $289.00
TASCO CW50TR COMPACT SPOTTING SCOPE—50mm objective lens, 25x fixed power. Field at 100 yds. 11 ft. Comes with panhead lever tripod.
Price: $226.00
TASCO 17EB SPOTTING SCOPE—60mm objective lens, 20-60x zoom with black metal tripod, micro-adjustable elevation control. Built-in sights.
Price: $214.00
TASCO 20EB SPOTTING SCOPE—50mm objective lens, 15-45x zoom. Field at 100 yds. 8-3.7 ft.; includes tripod with pan-head lever. Built-in sights.
Price: $115.00
TASCO 21EB ZOOM—50mm objective lens, 15-45x zoom. Field at 100 yds. 11 ft. (15x). Weight 22 oz.; length 18.3" overall. Comes with panhead lever tripod.
Price: $115.00
TASCO 22EB ZOOM—60mm objective lens, 20-60x zoom. Field at 100 yds. 7 ft., 2 in. (20x). Weight 28 oz.; length 21.5" overall. Comes with micro-adjustable tripod.
Price: $214.00
TASCO 35TZB COMPACT ZOOM—50mm objective lens, 10-25x zoom. Field at 100 yds. 22 ft. (10x) Weight 23.3 oz.; length 11" overall. Comes with panhead lever tripod.
Price: $238.00
TASCO MS2040 MINI SPOTTING SCOPE—40mm objective lens, 20x fixed power. Field at 100 yds. 7 ft., 8 in. Weight 12.4 oz.; length 8.5" overall. Comes with tripod with bendable legs.
Price: $122.00
TASCO 9002T WORLD CLASS SPOTTING SCOPE—60mm objective lens, 15-60x zoom. Field at 100 yds. 14.6 ft. (15x). Fully multi-coated optics, includes camera adaptor, camera case, tripod with pan-head lever.
Price: $682.00
UNERTL "FORTY-FIVE"—54mm objective. 20x (single fixed power). Field at 100 yds. 10',10"; eye relief 1"; focusing range infinity to 33 ft. Weight about 32 oz.; overall length 15¾". With lens covers.
Price: With multi-layer lens coating $496.00
Price: With mono-layer magnesium coating $414.00
UNERTL STRAIGHT PRISMATIC—63.5mm objective, 24x. Field at 100 yds., 7 ft. Relative brightness, 6.96. Eye relief ½". Weight 40 oz.; length closed 19". Push-pull and screw-focus eyepiece. 16x and 32x eyepieces $100.00 each.
Price: $369.00
UNERTL 20x STRAIGHT PRISMATIC—54mm objective, 20x. Field at 100 yds. 8.5 ft. Relative brightness 6.1. Eye relief ½". Weight 36 oz.; length closed 13½". Complete with lens covers.
Price: $343.00
UNERTL TEAM SCOPE—100mm objective. 15x, 24x, 32x eyepieces. Field at 100 yds. 13 to 7.5 ft. Relative brightness, 39.06 to 9.79. Eye relief 2" to 1½". Weight 13 lbs.; length 29⅞" overall. Metal tripod, yoke and wood carrying case furnished (total weight 80 lbs.).
Price: $2,200.00

PERIODICAL PUBLICATIONS

Action Pursuit Games Magazine (M)
CFW Enterprises, Inc., 4201 W. Vanowen Pl., Burbank, CA 91505. $2.95 single copy U.S., $3.50 Canada. Editor: Randy Kamiya, 818-845-2656. World's leading magazine of paintball sports.

Airgun World
10 Sheet St., Windsor, Berks., SL4 1BG, England. £19.20 (£26.00 overseas) for 12 issues. Monthly magazine catering exclusively to the airgun enthusiast.

Alaska Magazine
Alaska Publishing Properties Inc., 808 E St., Suite 200, Anchorage, AK 99501. $24.00 yr. Hunting, Fishing and Life on the Last Frontier articles of Alaska and western Canada. Outdoors Editor, Ken Marsh.

American Firearms Industry
Nat'l. Assn. of Federally Licensed Firearms Dealers, 2455 E. Sunrise Blvd., Suite 916, Ft. Lauderdale, FL 33304. $25.00 yr. For firearms retailers, distributors and manufacturers.

American Handgunner*
591 Camino de la Reina, Suite 200, San Diego, CA 92108. $16.75 yr. Articles for handgun enthusiasts, competitors, police and hunters.

American Hunter (M)
National Rifle Assn., 11250 Waples Mill Rd., Fairfax, VA 22030 (Same address for both.) Publications Div. $25.00 yr. Wide scope of hunting articles.

American Rifleman (M)
National Rifle Assn., 11250 Waples Mill Rd., Fairfax, VA 22030 (Same address for both). Publications Div. $25.00 yr. Firearms articles of all kinds.

American Survival Guide
McMullen and Yee Publishing, Inc., 774 S. Placentia Ave., Placentia, CA 92670-6846. 12 issues $26.95/714-572-2255; FAX: 714-572-1864.

American West*
American West Management Corp., 7000 E. Tanque Verde Rd., Suite #30, Tucson, AZ 85715. $15.00 yr.

Arms Collecting (Q)
Museum Restoration Service, P.O. Box 70, Alexandria Bay, NY 13607-0070. $20.00 yr.; $54.00 3 yrs.; $100.00 5 yrs.

Australian Shooters Journal
Sporting Shooters' Assn. of Australia, Inc., P.O. Box 2066, Kent Town SA 5071, Australia. $45.00 yr. locally; $55.00 yr. overseas surface mail only. Hunting and shooting articles.

The Backwoodsman Magazine
P.O. Box 627, Westcliffe, CO 81252. $15.00 for 6 issues per yr.; $28.00 for 2 yrs.; sample copy $2.50. Subjects include muzzle-loading, woodslore, primitive survival, trapping, homesteading, blackpowder cartridge guns, 19th century how-to.

Black Powder Times
P.O. Box 1131, Stanwood, WA 98292. $15.00 yr.; add $2 per year for Canada, $5 per year other foreign. Tabloid newspaper for blackpowder activities; test reports.

The Blade Magazine*
P.O. Box 22007, Chattanooga, TN 37422. $17.99 for 8 issues. Foreign price $35.00. A magazine for all enthusiasts of the edged blade.

Caliber
GFI-Verlag, Theodor-Heuss Ring 62, 50668 Köln, Germany. For hunters, target shooters and reloaders.

The Caller (Q) (M)
National Wild Turkey Federation, P.O. Box 530, Edgefield, SC 29824. Tabloid newspaper for members; 4 issues per yr.

The Cast Bullet*(M)
Official journal of The Cast Bullet Assn. Director of Membership, 4103 Foxcraft Dr., Traverse City, MI 49684. Annual membership dues $14, includes 6 issues.

Combat Handguns*
Harris Publications, Inc., 1115 Broadway, New York, NY 10010. Single copy $2.95 U.S.A.; $3.25 Canada.

The Derringer Peanut (M)
The National Association of Derringer Collectors, P.O. Box 20572, San Jose, CA 95160. A newsletter dedicated to developing the best derringer information. Write for details.

Deutsches Waffen Journal
Journal-Verlag Schwend GmbH, Postfach 100340, D-74523 Schwäbisch Hall, Germany/0791-404-500; FAX:0791-404-505. DM97.10 yr. (interior); DM114.60 (abroad), postage included. Antique and modern arms and equipment. German text.

Ducks Unlimited, Inc. (M)
1 Waterfowl Way, Memphis, TN 38120

The Engraver (M) (Q)
P.O. Box 4365, Estes Park, CO 80517. Mike Dubber, editor. The journal of firearms engraving.

The Field
Astley House, 33 Notting Hill Gate, Notting Hill, London W11 3JQ, England. £35.00 sterling U.S. (approx. $70.00) yr. Hunting and shooting articles, and all country sports.

Field & Stream
Times Mirror Magazines, Two Park Ave., New York, NY 10016. $11.94 yr. Monthly shooting column. Articles on hunting and fishing.

FIRE
Euro-Editions, Boulevard Lambermont 140, B1030 Brussels, Belgium. Belg. Franc 1500 for 6 issues. Arms, shooting, ammunition. French text.

Fur-Fish-Game
A.R. Harding Pub. Co., 2878 E. Main St., Columbus, OH 43209. $15.95 yr. "Gun Rack" column by Don Zutz.

Gray's Sporting Journal
Gray's Sporting Journal, Inc., P.O. Box 1207, Augusta, GA 30903. $35.95 per yr. for 6 consecutive issues. Hunting and fishing journals. Expeditions and Guide Book (Annual Grouse Guide).

Gun List
700 E. State St., Iola, WI 54990. $27.95 yr. (26 issues); $52.00 2 yrs. (52 issues). Indexed market publication for firearms collectors and active shooters; guns, supplies and services.

The Gun Report
World Wide Gun Report, Inc., Box 38, Aledo, IL 61231-0038. $29.95 yr. For the antique and collectable gun dealer and collector.

Gunmaker (M)†
ACGG, P.O. Box 812, Burlington, IA 52601-0812. The journal of custom gunmaking.

The Gunrunner
Div. of Kexco Publ. Co. Ltd., Box 565G, Lethbridge, Alb., Canada T1J 3Z4. $23.00 yr. Monthly newspaper, listing everything from antiques to artillery.

Gun Show Calendar (Q)
700 E. State St., Iola, WI 54990. $12.95 yr. (4 issues). Gun shows listed chronologically by date, and alphabetically by state.

Gun Tests
11 Commerce Blvd., Palm Coast, FL 32142. The consumer resource for the serious shooter. Write for information.

Gun Week†
Second Amendment Foundation, P.O. Box 488, Station C, Buffalo, NY 14209. $32.00 yr. U.S. and possessions; $40.00 yr. other countries. Tabloid paper on guns, hunting, shooting and collecting.

Gun World
Gallant/Charger Publications, Inc., 34249 Camino Capistrano, Capistrano Beach, CA 92624. $20.00 yr. For the hunting, reloading and shooting enthusiast.

Guns & Ammo
Petersen Publishing Co., 6420 Wilshire Blvd., Los Angeles, CA 90048. $21.94 yr. Guns, shooting, and technical articles.

Guns
Guns Magazine, P.O. Box 85201, San Diego, CA 92138. $19.95 yr.; $34.95 2 yrs.; $46.95 3 yrs. In-depth articles on a wide range of guns, shooting equipment and related accessories for gun collectors, hunters and shooters.

Guns and Gear
Creative Arts, Inc., 4901 Northwest 17th Way, Fort Lauderdale, FL 33309/305-772-2788; FAX: 305-351-0484. Single copy $4.95. Covering all aspects of the shooting sports.

Guns Review
Ravenhill Publishing Co. Ltd., Box 35, Standard House, Bonhill St., London EC 2A 4DA, England. £20.00 sterling (approx. U.S. $38 USA & Canada) yr. For collectors and shooters.

Handgunning (Q)
PJS Publications, News Plaza, P.O. Box 1790, Peoria, IL 61656. Cover price $3.95; subscriptions $19.98 for 6 issues. Premier journal for multi-sport handgunners: hunting, reloading, law enforcement, practical pistol and target shooting, and home defense.

Handgun Times
Creative Arts, Inc., 4901 NW 17th Way, Fort Lauderdale, FL 33309/305-772-2788; FAX: 305-351-0484. Single copy $4.95. Technical evaluations, detailed information and testing by handgun experts.

Handloader*
Wolfe Publishing Co., 6471 Airpark Dr., Prescott, AZ 86301. $29.00 yr. The journal of ammunition reloading.

Hunting Horizons
Wolfe Publishing Co., 6471 Airpark Dr., Prescott, AZ 86301. $34.00 yr. Dedicated to the finest pursuit of the hunt.

The Insider Gun News
The Gunpress Publishing Co., 1347 Webster St. NE, Washington, DC 20017. Editor, John D. Aquilino. $50.00 yr. (12 issues). Newsletter by former NRA communications director.

INSIGHTS*
NRA, 11250 Waples Mill Rd., Fairfax, VA 22030. Editor, John E. Robbins. $15.00 yr., which includes NRA junior membership; $10.00 for adult subscriptions (6 issues). Plenty of details for the young hunter and target shooter; emphasizes gun safety, marksmanship training, hunting skills.

International Shooting Sport*/UIT Journal
International Shooting Union (UIT), Bavariaring 21, D-80336 Munich, Germany. Europe: (Deutsche Mark) DM44.00 yr.; outside Europe: DM50.00 yr. (air mail postage included.) For international sport shooting.

Internationales Waffen-Magazin
Habegger-Verlag Zürich, Postfach 9230, CH-8036 Zürich, Switzerland. SF 91.00 (approx. U.S. $61.00) surface mail for 10 issues. Modern and antique arms, self-defense. German text; English summary of contents.

The Journal of the Arms & Armour Society (M)
E.J.B. Greenwood (Hon. Sec.), Field House, Upper Dicker, Hailsham, East Sussex, BN27 3PY, England. £15.00 surface mail; £20.00 airmail sterling only yr. Articles for the historian and collector.

Journal of the Historical Breechloading Smallarms Assn.
Published annually. Imperial War Museum, Lambeth Road, London SE1 6HZ, England. $13.00 yr. Articles for the collector plus mailings of short articles on specific arms, reprints, newsletters, etc.; a surcharge is made for airmail.

Knife World
Knife World Publications, P.O. Box 3395, Knoxville, TN 37927. $15.00 yr.; $25.00 2 yrs. Published monthly for knife enthusiasts and collectors. Articles on custom and factory knives; other knife-related interests.

Law and Order
Law and Order Magazine, 1000 Skokie Blvd., Wilmette, IL 60091. $20.00 yr. Articles for law enforcement professionals.

Machine Gun News
Lane Publishing, P.O. Box 759, Dept. GD, Hot Springs, AR 71902/501-525-7541. $29.95 yr. (12 issues); $4.00 sample copy. The magazine for full-auto enthusiasts, full-auto news, how to solve functioning problems, machinegun shoots from around the country and free classifieds for subscribers.

Man At Arms*
P.O. Box 460, Lincoln, RI 02865. $24.00 yr., $46.00 2 yrs. plus $8.00 for foreign subscribers. The N.R.A. magazine of arms collecting-investing, with excellent articles for the collector of antique arms and militaria.

MAN/MAGNUM
S.A. Man (Pty) Ltd., P.O. Box 35204, Northway, Durban 4065, Republic of South Africa. SA Rand 100.00 for 12 issues. Africa's only publication on hunting, shooting, firearms, bushcraft, knives, etc.

The Marlin Collector (M)
R.W. Paterson, 407 Lincoln Bldg., 44 Main St., Champaign, IL 61820.

Muzzle Blasts (M)
National Muzzle Loading Rifle Assn., P.O. Box 67, Friendship, IN 47021. $30.00 yr. annual membership. For the blackpowder shooter.

Muzzleloader Magazine*
Rebel Publishing Co., Inc., Dept. Gun, Route 5, Box 347-M, Texarkana, TX 75501. $16.00 U.S.; $19.00 U.S. for foreign subscribers a yr. The publication for blackpowder shooters.

National Defense (M)*
American Defense Preparedness Assn., Two Colonial Place, Suite 400, 2101 Wilson Blvd., Arlington, VA 22201-3061/703-522-1820; FAX: 703-522-1885. $35.00 yr. Articles on both military and civil defense field, including weapons, materials technology, management.

National Knife Magazine (M)
Natl. Knife Coll. Assn., 7201 Shallowford Rd., P.O. Box 21070, Chattanooga, TN 37424-0070. Membership $35 yr.; $64.00 International yr.

National Rifle Assn. Journal (British) (Q)
Natl. Rifle Assn. (BR.), Bisley Camp, Brookwood, Woking, Surrey, England. GU24, OPB. £19.00 Sterling including postage.

National Wildlife*
Natl. Wildlife Fed., 1400 16th St. NW, Washington, DC 20036, $16.00 yr. (6 issues); *International Wildlife*, 6 issues, $16.00 yr. Both, $22.00 yr., includes all membership benefits. Write attn.: Membership Services Dept., for more information.

New Zealand GUNS*
Waitekauri Publishing, P.O. 45, Waikino 3060, New Zealand. $NZ90.00 (6 issues) yr. Covers the hunting and firearms scene in New Zealand.

New Zealand Wildlife (Q)
New Zealand Deerstalkers Assoc., Inc., P.O. Box 6514, Wellington, N.Z. $30.00 (N.Z.). Hunting, shooting and firearms/game research articles.

North American Hunter* (M)
P.O. Box 3401, Minnetonka, MN 55343. $18.00 yr. (7 issues). Articles on all types of North American hunting.

Outdoor Life
Times Mirror Magazines, Two Park Ave., New York, NY 10016. Special 1-yr. subscription, $11.97. Extensive coverage of hunting and shooting. Shooting column by Jim Carmichel.

La Passion des Courteaux (Q)
Phenix Editions, 25 rue Mademoiselle, 75015 Paris, France. French text.

Petersen's HUNTING Magazine
Petersen Publishing Co., 6420 Wilshire Blvd., Los Angeles, CA 90048. $19.94 yr.; Canada $29.34 yr.; foreign countries $29.94 yr. Hunting articles for all game; test reports.

P.I. Magazine
America's Private Investigation Journal, 755 Bronx Dr., Toledo, OH 43609. Chuck Klein, firearms editor with column about handguns.

Point Blank
Citizens Committee for the Right to Keep and Bear Arms (sent to contributors), Liberty Park, 12500 NE 10th Pl., Bellevue, WA 98005

POINTBLANK (M)
Natl. Firearms Assn., Box 4384 Stn. C, Calgary, AB T2T 5N2, Canada. Official publication of the NFA.

The Police Marksman*
6000 E. Shirley Lane, Montgomery, AL 36117. $17.95 yr. For law enforcement personnel.

Police Times (M)
Membership Records, 3801 Biscayne Blvd., Miami, FL 33137.

Popular Mechanics
Hearst Corp., 224 W. 57th St., New York, NY 10019. $15.94 yr. Firearms, camping, outdoor oriented articles.

Precision Shooting
Precision Shooting, Inc., 37 Burnham St., East Hartford, CT 06108. $25.00 yr. Journal of the International Benchrest Shooters, and target shooting in general. Also considerable coverage of varmint shooting, as well as big bore, small bore, schuetzen, lead bullet and wildcats.

Rifle*
Wolfe Publishing Co., 6471 Airpark Dr., Prescott, AZ 86301. $19.00 yr. The sporting firearms journal.

Rod & Rifle Magazine
Lithographic Serv. Ltd., P.O. Box 38-138, Wellington, New Zealand. $50.00 yr. (6 issues). Hunting, shooting and fishing articles.

Safari* (M)
Safari Magazine, 4800 W. Gates Pass Rd., Tucson, AZ 85745/602-620-1220. $30.00 (6 times). The journal of big game hunting, published by Safari Club International. Also publish *Safari Times*, a monthly newspaper, included in price of $30.00 field membership.

Second Amendment Reporter
Second Amendment Foundation, James Madison Bldg., 12500 NE 10th Pl., Bellevue, WA 98005. $15.00 yr. (non-contributors).

Shooting Industry
Publisher's Dev. Corp., 591 Camino de la Reina, Suite 200, San Diego, CA 92108. $50.00 yr. To the trade $25.00.

Shooting Sports Retailer*
SSR Publishing, Inc., P.O. Box 25, Cuba, NY 14727-0025/716-968-3858. 6 issues yr. Free to

qualifying retailers, wholesalers, manufacturers, distributors; $30 annually for all other subscribers; $35 for foreign subscriptions; single copy $5.

Shooting Sports USA
National Rifle Assn. of America, 11250 Waples Mill Road, Fairfax, VA 22030. Annual subscriptions for NRA members are $5 for classified shooters and $10 for non-classified shooters. Non-NRA member subscriptions are $15. Covering events, techniques and personalities in competitive shooting.

The Shooting Times & Country Magazine (England)†
Astley House, 33 Notting Hill Gate, Notting Hill, London W11 3JQ, England. £65 (approx. $98.00) yr.; £79 yr. overseas (52 issues). Game shooting, wild fowling, hunting, game fishing and firearms articles. Britain's best selling field sports magazine.

Shooting Times
PJS Publications, News Plaza, P.O. Box 1790, Peoria, IL 61656. $21.98 yr. Guns, shooting, reloading; articles on every gun activity.

The Shotgun News‡
Snell Publishing Co., Box 669, Hastings, NE 68902. $20.00 yr.; all other countries $100.00 yr. Sample copy $3.00. Gun ads of all kinds.

SHOT Business
Flintlock Ridge Office Center, 11 Mile Hill Rd., Newtown, CT 06470-2359/203-426-1320; FAX: 203-426-1087. For the shooting, hunting and outdoor trade retailer.

Shotgun Sports
P.O. Box 6810, Auburn, CA 95604/916-889-2220; FAX:916-889-9106. $28.00 yr. Trapshooting how-to's, shotshell reloading, shotgun patterning, shotgun tests and evaluations, Sporting Clays action, waterfowl/upland hunting.

The Sixgunner (M)
Handgun Hunters International, P.O. Box 357, MAG, Bloomingdale, OH 43910

The Skeet Shooting Review
National Skeet Shooting Assn., P.O. Box 680007, San Antonio, TX 78268. $15.00 yr. (Assn. membership of $20.00 includes mag.) Competition results, personality profiles of top Skeet shooters, how-to articles, technical, reloading information.

Soldier of Fortune
Subscription Dept., P.O. Box 348, Mt. Morris, IL 61054. $24.95 yr.; $34.95 Canada; $45.95 foreign.

SPG Lubricants/BP Cartridge (Q)
SPG Lubricant, P.O. Box 761, Livingston, MT 59047. $13 yr. For the blackpowder cartridge enthusiast.

Sporting Clays Magazine*
5211 South Washington Ave., Titusville, FL 32780/407-268-5010; FAX: 407-267-7216. $29.95 yr. (9 issues).

Sporting Goods Business
Miller Freeman, Inc., 1515 Broadway, New York, NY 10036. Trade journal.

Sporting Goods Dealer
Two Park Ave., New York, NY 10016. $100.00 yr. Sporting goods trade journal.

Sporting Gun
Bretton Court, Bretton, Peterborough PE3 8DZ, England. £27.00 (approx. U.S. $36.00), airmail £35.50 yr. For the game and clay enthusiasts.

Sports Afield
The Hearst Corp., 250 W. 55th St., New York, NY 10019. $13.97 yr. Tom Gresham on firearms, ammunition; Grits Gresham on shooting and Thomas McIntyre on hunting.

The Squirrel Hunter
P.O. Box 368, Chireno, TX 75937. $14.00 yr. Articles about squirrel hunting.

TACARMI
Via E. De Amicis, 25; 20123 Milano, Italy. $120.00 yr. approx. Antique and modern guns. (Italian text.)

Trap & Field
1200 Waterway Blvd., Indianapolis, IN 46202. $22.00 yr. Official publ. Amateur Trapshooting Assn. Scores, averages, trapshooting articles.

Turkey Call* (M)
Natl. Wild Turkey Federation, Inc., P.O. Box 530, Edgefield, SC 29824. $20.00 with membership (6 issues per yr.)

The U.S. Handgunner* (M)
U.S. Revolver Assn., 40 Larchmont Ave., Taunton, MA 02780. $10.00 yr. General handgun and competition articles. Bi-monthly sent to members.

U.S. Airgun Magazine
2603 Rollingbrook, Benton, AR 72015. Cover the sport from hunting, 10-meter, field target and collecting. Write for details.

The Varmint Hunter Magazine (Q)
The Varmint Hunters Assn., Box 759, Pierre, SD 57501/800-528-4868. $24.00 yr.

Waffenmarkt-Intern
GFI-Verlag, Theodor-Heuss Ring 62, 50668 Köln, Germany. Only for gunsmiths, licensed firearms dealers and their suppliers in Germany, Austria and Switzerland.

Wild Sheep (M) (Q)
Foundation for North American Wild Sheep, 720 Allen Ave., Cody, WY 82414. Official journal of the foundation.

Women & Guns
P.O. Box 488, Sta. C, Buffalo, NY 14209. $24.00 yr. U.S.; (12 issues). Only magazine edited by and for women gun owners.

---

*Published bi-monthly †Published weekly ‡Published three times per month. All others are published monthly.
M=Membership requirements; write for details. Q=Published Quarterly.

The ARMS LIBRARY

FOR COLLECTOR • HUNTER • SHOOTER • OUTDOORSMAN

IMPORTANT NOTICE TO BOOK BUYERS

Books listed here may be bought from Ray Riling Arms Books Co., 6844 Gorsten St., P.O. Box 18925, Philadelphia, PA 19119, phone 215/438-2456. Joe Riling is the researcher and compiler of "The Arms Library" and a seller of gun books for over 30 years.

The Riling stock includes books classic and modern, many hard-to-find items, and many not obtainable elsewhere. These pages list a portion of the current stock. They offer prompt, complete service, with delayed shipments occurring only on out-of-print or out-of-stock books.

NOTICE FOR ALL CUSTOMERS: Remittance in U.S. funds must accompany all orders. For U.S. add $2.00 per book for postage and insurance. Minimum order $10.00. For UPS add 50% to mailing costs.

All foreign countries add $5.00 per book. All foreign orders are shipped at the buyer's risk unless an additional $5 for insurance is included.

Payments in excess of order or for "Backorders" are credited or fully refunded at request. Books "As-Ordered" are not returnable except by permission and a handling charge on these of $2.00 per book is deducted from refund or credit. Only Pennsylvania customers must include current sales tax.

A full variety of arms books also available from Rutgers Book Center, 127 Raritan Ave., Highland Park, NJ 08904.

*New Book

BALLISTICS and HANDLOADING

ABC's of Reloading, 5th Edition, by Dean A. Grennell, DBI Books, Inc., Northbrook, IL, 1993. 288 pp., illus. Paper covers. $18.95.
The definitive guide to every facet of cartridge and shotshell reloading.

*African Cartridge Reloading Data, Thunderbird Cartridge Co. Inc., Phoenix, AZ, 1994. 32 pp. Paper covers.
Loading techniques and recipes for the .8577 Nitro Express 3" using common American extruded powders with ballistics and cartridge specifications.

Ammunition Making, by George E. Frost, National Rifle Association of America, Washington, D.C., 1990. 160 pp., illus. Paper covers. $17.95.
Reflects the perspective of "an insider" with half a century's experience in successful management of ammunition manufacturing operations.

Basic Handloading, by George C. Nonte, Jr., Outdoor Life Books, New York, NY, 1982. 192 pp., illus. Paper covers. $6.95.
How to produce high-quality ammunition using the safest, most efficient methods known.

Black Powder Guide, 2nd Edition, by George C. Nonte, Jr., Stoeger Publishing Co., So. Hackensack, NJ, 1991. 288 pp., illus. Paper covers. $12.95.
How-to instructions for selection, repair and maintenance of muzzleloaders, making your own bullets, restoring and refinishing, shooting techniques.

Big Bore Rifles And Cartridges, Wolfe Publishing Co., Prescott, AZ, 1991. Paper cover. $26.00.
This book covers cartridges from 8mm to .600 Nitro with loading tables and commentary.

Black Powder Loading Manual, Revised Edition, The Gun Digest, by Sam Fadala, DBI Books, Inc., Northbrook, IL, 1991. 320 pp., illus. Paper covers. $16.95.
Revised and expanded edition of this landmark loading book first published in 1982. Covers 600 loads for 120 of the most popular blackpowder rifles, handguns and shotguns.

The Bullet Swage Manual. MDSU/I, by Ted Smith, Corbin Manufacturing and Supply Co., White City, OR, 1988. 45 pp., illus. Paper covers. $10.00.
A book that fills the need for information on bullet swaging.

Cartridge Case Measurements, by Dr. Arthur J. Mack, Amrex Enterprises, Vienna, VA, 1990. 300 pp., illus. Paper covers. $49.95.
Lists over 5000 cartridges of all kinds. Gives basic measurements (rim, head, shoulder, neck, length, plus bullet diameter) in both English and Metric. Hundreds of experimental and wildcats.

Cartridges of the World, 7th Edition, by Frank Barnes, edited by Mike Bussard, DBI Books, Inc., Northbrook, IL, 1993. 464 pp., illus. Paper covers. $21.95.
Completely revised edition of the general purpose reference work for which collectors, police, scientists and laymen reach first for answers to cartridge identification questions.

Cast Bullets, by Col. E. H. Harrison, A publication of the National Rifle Association of America, Washington, DC, 1979. 144 pp., illus. Paper covers. $12.95.
An authoritative guide to bullet casting techniques and ballistics.

The Complete Handloader, by John Wootters, Stackpole Books, Harrisburg, PA, 1989. 224 pp., illus. $29.95.
One of the deans of gun writers shares a lifetime of experience and recommended procedures on handloading for rifles, handguns, and shotguns.

The Complete Handloader for Rifles, Handguns and Shotguns, by John Wootters, Stackpole Books, Harrisburg, PA, 1988. 214 pp., $29.95.
Loading-bench know-how.

Extended Ballistics for the Advanced Rifleman, by Art Blatt, Pachmayr, Inc., Los Angeles, CA, 1986. 379 pp. Spiral bound. $15.95.
Enhanced data on all factory centerfire rifle loads from Federal, Hornady, Norma, Remington, Weatherby, and Winchester.

Firearms Pressure Factors, by Dr. Lloyd Brownell, Wolfe Publishing Co., Prescott, AZ, 1990. 200 pp., illus. $14.00.
The only book available devoted entirely to firearms and pressure. Contains chapters on secondary explosion effect, modern pressure measuring techniques in revolvers and rifles, and Dr. Brownell's series on pressure factors.

Game Loads and Practical Ballistics for the American Hunter, by Bob Hagel, Wolfe Publishing Co., Prescott, AZ, 1992. 310 pp., illus. $27.90.
Hagel's knowledge gained as a hunter, guide and gun enthusiast is gathered in this informative text.

Gibbs' Cartridges and Front Ignition Loading Technique, by Roger Stowers, Wolfe Publishing Co., Prescott, AZ, 1991. 64 pp., illus. Paper covers. $14.95.
The story of this innovative gunsmith who designed his own wildcat cartridges known for their flat trajectories, high velocity and accuracy.

Handbook of Bullet Swaging No. 7, by David R. Corbin, Corbin Manufacturing and Supply Co., White City, OR, 1986. 199 pp., illus. Paper covers. $10.00.
This handbook explains the most precise method of making quality bullets.

Handbook for Shooters and Reloaders, by P.O. Ackley, Salt Lake City, UT, 1970, (Vol. I), 567 pp., illus. (Vol. II), a new printing with specific new material. 495 pp., illus. $17.00 each.

Handbook of Metallic Cartridge Reloading, by Edward Matunas, Winchester Press, Piscataway, NJ, 1981. 272 pp., illus. $19.95.
Up-to-date, comprehensive loading tables prepared by four major powder manufacturers.

Handgun Reloading, The Gun Digest Book of by Dean A. Grennell and Wiley M. Clapp, DBI Books, Inc., Northbrook, IL, 1987. 256 pp., illus. Paper covers. $15.95.
Detailed discussions of all aspects of reloading for handguns, from basic to complex. New loading data.

*Handloader's Digest 1995, 14th Edition, edited by Bob Bell, DBI Books, Inc., Northbrook, IL, 1994. 480 pp., illus. Paper covers. $21.95
Top writers in the field contribute helpful information on techniques and components. Greatly expanded and fully indexed catalog of all currently available tools, accessories and components for metallic, blackpowder cartridge, shotshell reloading and swaging.

Handloader's Guide, by Stanley W. Trzoniec, Stoeger Publishing Co., So. Hackensack, NJ, 1985. 256 pp., illus. Paper covers. $14.95.
The complete step-by-step fully illustrated guide to handloading ammunition.

Handloader's Manual of Cartridge Conversions, by John J. Donnelly, Stoeger Publishing Co., So. Hackensack, NJ, 1986. Unpaginated. $34.95.
From 14 Jones to 70-150 Winchester in English and American cartridges, and from 4.85 U.K. to 15.2x28R Gevelot in metric cartridges. Over 900 cartridges described in detail.

Handloading, by Bill Davis, Jr., NRA Books, Wash., D.C., 1980. 400 pp., illus. Paper covers. $15.95.
A complete update and expansion of the NRA Handloader's Guide.

Handloading for Hunters, by Don Zutz, Winchester Press, Piscataway, NJ, 1977. 288 pp., illus. $30.00.
Precise mixes and loads for different types of game and for various hunting situations with rifle and shotgun.

Hatcher's Notebook, by S. Julian Hatcher, Stackpole Books, Harrisburg, PA, 1992. 488 pp., illus. $29.95.
A reference work for shooters, gunsmiths, ballisticians, historians, hunters and collectors.

The Home Guide to Cartridge Conversions, by Maj. George C. Nonte Jr., The Gun Room Press, Highland Park, NJ, 1976. 404 pp., illus. $24.95.
Revised and updated version of Nonte's definitive work on the alteration of cartridge cases for use in guns for which they were not intended.

Hornady Handbook of Cartridge Reloading, 4th Edition Hornady Mfg. Co., Grand Island, NE, 1991. 1200 pp., illus. $28.50.

New edition of this famous reloading handbook. Latest loads, ballistic information, etc.

Hornady Handbook of Cartridge Reloading, Abridged Edition Hornady Mfg. Co., Grand Island, NE, 1991. $19.95.

Ballistic data for 25 of the most popular cartridges.

Hornady Load Notes Hornady Mfg. Co., Grand Island, NE, 1991. $4.95.

Complete load data and ballistics for a single caliber. Eight pistol 9mm-45ACP; 16 rifle, 222-45-70.

The Ideal Handbook of Useful Information for Shooters, No. 15, originally published by Ideal Manufacturing Co., reprinted by Wolfe Publishing Co., Prescott, AZ, 1991. 142 pp., illus. Paper covers. $10.95.

A facsimile reprint of one of the early Ideal Handbooks.

The Ideal Handbook, No. 5, Facsimile reprint by Armory Publications, Oceanside, CA, 1993. 80 pp., illus. Paper covers. $12.95.

A limited reprinting of the rare 1893 edition of the handbook issued by the Ideal manufacturing Co., of New Haven, CT.

Loading the Black Powder Rifle Cartridge, by Paul A Matthews, Wolfe Publishing Co., Prescott, AZ, 1993. 121 pp., illus. Paper covers. $22.50.

Author Matthews brings the black powder cartridge shooter valuable information on the basics, including cartridge care, lubes and moulds, powder charges and developing and testing loads in his usual authoritative style.

*Loading Cartridges for the Original .45-70 Springfield Rifle and Carbine, by J.S. and Pat Wolf, Wolf's Western Traders, Hill City, SD, 1991. 169 pp., illus. Paper covers. $16.95.

From sighting-in to reloading, this book tells you everything you need to know about the .45-70 Springfield rifle and carbine.

Lyman Cast Bullet Handbook, 3rd Edition, edited by C. Kenneth Ramage, Lyman Publications, Middlefield, CT, 1980. 416 pp., illus. Paper covers. $18.95.

Information on more than 5000 tested cast bullet loads and 19 pages of trajectory and wind drift tables for cast bullets.

Lyman Black Powder Handbook, ed. by C. Kenneth Ramage, Lyman Products for Shooters, Middlefield, CT, 1975. 239 pp., illus. Paper covers. $14.95.

Comprehensive load information for the modern blackpowder shooter.

Lyman Pistol & Revolver Handbook, edited by C. Kenneth Ramage, Lyman Publications, Middlefield, CT, 1978. 280 pp., illus. Paper covers. $14.95.

An extensive reference of load and trajectory data for the handgun.

Lyman Reloading Handbook No. 47, edited by Edward A. Matunas, Lyman Publications, Middlefield, CT, 1992. 480 pp., illus. Paper covers. $21.95.

"The world's most comprehensive reloading manual." Complete "How to Reload" information. Expanded data section with all the newest rifle and pistol calibers.

Lyman Shotshell Handbook, 3rd Edition, edited by C. Kenneth Ramage, Lyman Publications, Middlefield, CT, 1984. 312 pp., illus. Paper covers. $19.95.

Has 2000 loads, including slugs and buckshot, plus feature articles and a full color I.D. section.

*Making Loading Dies and Bullet Molds, by Harold Hoffman, H&P Publishing, San Angelo, TX, 1993. 230 pp., illus. Paper covers. $22.95.

A good book for learning tool and die making.

Manual of Pistol and Revolver Cartridges, Volume 2, Centerfire U.S. and British Calibers, by Hans A. Erlmeier and Jakob H. Brandt, Journal-Verlag, Wiesbaden, Germany, 1981. 270 pp., illus. $34.95.

Catalog system allows cartridges to be traced by caliber or alphabetically.

Metallic Cartridge Reloading, 2nd Edition, by Edward A. Matunas, DBI Books, Inc., Northbrook, IL., 1988. 320 pp., illus. Paper covers. $17.95.

A true reloading manual with a wealth of invaluable technical data provided by a recognized expert.

Modern Handloading, by Maj. Geo. C. Nonte, Winchester Press, Piscataway, NJ, 1972. 416 pp., illus. $15.00.

Covers all aspects of metallic and shotshell ammunition loading, plus more loads than any book in print.

Modern Practical Ballistics, by Art Pejsa, Pejsa Ballistics, Minneapolis, MN, 1990. 150 pp., illus. $24.95.

Covers all aspects of ballistics and new, simplified methods. Clear examples illustrate new, easy but very accurate formulas.

Nosler Reloading Manual No. 3, edited by Gail Root, Nosler Bullets, Inc., Bend, OR, 1989. 516 pp., illus. $21.95.

All-new book. New format including featured articles and cartridge introductions by well-known shooters, gun writers and editors.

The Paper Jacket, by Paul Matthews, Wolfe Publishing Co., Prescott, AZ, 1991. Paper covers. $13.50.

Up-to-date and accurate information about paper-patched bullets.

Precision Handloading, by John Withers, Stoeger Publishing Co., So. Hackensack, NJ, 1985. 224 pp., illus. Paper covers. $12.95.

An entirely new approach to handloading ammunition.

Propellant Profiles New and Expanded, 3rd Edition, Wolfe Publishing Co., Prescott, AZ, 1991. Paper covers. $16.95.

Reloader's Guide, 3rd Edition, by R.A. Steindler, Stoeger Publishing Co., So. Hackensack, NJ, 1984. 224 pp., illus. Paper covers. $11.95.

Complete, fully illustrated step-by-step guide to handloading ammunition.

The very latest in reloading information for the shotgunner.

Reloading for Shotgunners, 3rd Edition, by Edward A. Matunas, DBI Books, Inc., Northbrook, IL, 1993. 288 pp., illus. Paper covers. $16.95.

Expanded reloading tables with over 2,000 loads. Bushing charts for every major press and component maker. All new presentation on all aspects of shotshell reloading by one of the top experts in the field.

Sierra Handgun Manual, 3rd Edition, edited by Kenneth Ramage, Sierra Bullets, Santa Fe Springs, CA, 1990. 704 pp., illus. 3-ring binder. $19.95.

New listings for XP-100 and Contender pistols and TCU cartridges...part of a new single shot section. Covers the latest loads for 10mm Auto, 455 Super Mag, and Accurate powders.

Sierra Rifle Manual, 3rd Edition, edited by Kenneth Ramage, Sierra Bullets, Santa Fe Springs, CA, 1990. 856 pp., illus. 3-ring binder. $24.95.

Updated load information with new powder listings and a wealth of inside tips.

Sixgun Cartridges and Loads, by Elmer Keith, The Gun Room Press, Highland Park, NJ, 1986. 151 pp., illus. $24.95.

A manual covering the selection, uses and loading of the most suitable and popular revolver cartridges. Originally published in 1936. Reprint.

*Speer Reloading Manual Number 12, edited by members of the Speer research staff, Omark Industries, Lewiston, ID, 1987. 621 pp., illus.

Reloading manual for rifles and pistols.

The Sporting Ballistics Book, by Charles W. Matthews, Bill Matthews, Inc., Lakewood, CO, 1992. 182 pp. Wirebound. $19.95.

A useful book for those interested in doing their own exterior-ballistic calculations without the aid of a computer.

Why Not Load Your Own? by Col. T. Whelen, A. S. Barnes, New York, 1957, 4th ed., rev. 237 pp., illus. $10.95.

A basic reference on handloading, describing each step, materials and equipment. Loads for popular cartridges are given.

Wildcat Cartridges, Volume I, Wolfe Publishing Company, Prescott, AZ, 1992. 125 pp. Soft cover. $16.95.

From *Handloader* magazine, the more popular and famous wildcats are profiled.

Wildcat Cartridges, Volume II, compiled from *Handloader* and *Rifle* magazine articles written by featured authors, Wolfe Publishing Co., Prescott, AZ, 1992. 971 pp., illus. Paper covers. $34.95.

This volume details rifle and handtgun cartridges from the 14-221 to the 460 Van Horn. A comprehensive work containing loading tables and commentary.

Yours Truly, Harvey Donaldson, by Harvey Donaldson, Wolfe Publ. Co., Inc., Prescott, AZ, 1980. 288 pp., illus. $19.50.

Reprint of the famous columns by Harvey Donaldson which appeared in "Handloader" from May 1966 through December 1972.

COLLECTORS

The American Cartridge, by Charles R. Suydam, Borden Publishing Co., Alhambra, CA, 1986. 184 pp., illus. $12.50.

An illustrated study of the rimfire cartridge in the United States.

*American Military Shoulder Arms: Volume 1, Colonial and Revolutionary War Arms, by George D. Moller, University Press of Colorado, Niwot, CO, 1993. 538 pp., illus. $65.00.

A superb in-depth study of the shoulder arms of the United States. This volume covers the pre-colonial period to the end of the American Revolution.

*American Military Shoulder Arms: Volume 2, From the 1790's to the End of the Flintlock Period, by George D. Moller, University Press of Colorado, Niwot, CO, 1994. 496 pp., illus. $75.00.

Describes the rifles, muskets, carbines and other shoulder arms used by the armed forces of the United States from the 1790s to the end of the flintlock period in the 1840s.

Antique Guns: The Collector's Guide, by John E. Traister, Stoeger Publishing Co., So. Hackensack, NJ, 1988. 320 pp., illus. Paper covers. $16.95.

Covers all categories, history, craftsmanship, firearms components, gunmakers and values on the gun-trading market.

Arms & Accoutrements of the Mounted Police 1873-1973, by Roger F. Phillips and Donald J. Klancher, Museum Restoration Service, Ont., Canada, 1982. 224 pp., illus. $49.95.

A definitive history of the revolvers, rifles, machine guns, cannons, ammunition, swords, etc. used by the NWMP, the RNWMP and the RCMP during the first 100 years of the Force.

Arms Makers of Maryland, by Daniel D. Hartzler, George Shumway, York, PA, 1975. 200 pp., illus. $45.00.

A thorough study of the gunsmiths of Maryland who worked during the late 18th and early 19th centuries.

*Artistry in Arms: The Guns of Smith & Wesson, by Roy G. Jinks, Smith & Wesson, Springfield, MA, 1991. 85 pp., illus. Paper covers. $19.95.

Catalog of the Smith & Wesson International Museum Tour 1991-1995 organized by the Connecticut Valley Historical Museum and Springfield Library and Museum Association.

Astra Automatic Pistols, by Leonardo M. Antaris, FIRAC Publishing Co., Sterling, CO, 1989. 248 pp., illus. $45.00.

Charts, tables, serial ranges, etc. The definitive work on Astra pistols.

Basic Documents on U.S. Marital Arms, commentary by Col. B. R. Lewis, reissue by Ray Riling, Phila., PA, 1956 and 1960. *Rifle Musket Model 1855.* The first issue rifle of musket caliber, a muzzle loader equipped with the Maynard Primer, 32 pp. $2.50. *Rifle Musket Model 1863.* The typical Union muzzle-loader of the Civil War, 26 pp. $1.75. *Breech-Loading Rifle Musket Model 1866.* The first of our 50-caliber breechloading rifles, 12 pp. $1.75. *Remington Navy Rifle Model 1870.* A commercial type breech-loader made at Springfield, 16 pp. $1.75. *Lee Straight Pull Navy Rifle Model 1895.* A magazine cartridge arm of 6mm caliber. 23 pp. $3.00. *Breech-Loading Arms* (five models) 27 pp. $2.75. *Ward-Burton Rifle Musket 1871-16* pp. $2.50. *U.S. Magazine Rifle and Carbine (cal. 30) Model 1892* (the Krag rifle) 36 pp. $3.00.

*Behold, the Longrifle, by Roy F. Chandler and James B. Whisker, Old Bedford Village Press, Bedford, PA, 1993. 241 pp., illus. $45.00.

Arranged as a fine art "coffee table" book; many unsigned and unviewed rifles in private collections are presented.

Beretta Automatic Pistols, by J.B. Wood, Stackpole Books, Harrisburg, PA, 1985. 192 pp., illus. $24.95.

Only English-language book devoted entirely to the Beretta line. Includes all important models.

Blacksmith Guide to Ruger Flat-top & Super Blackhawks, by H.W. Ross, Jr., Blacksmith Corp., Chino Valley, AZ, 1990. 96 pp., illus. Paper covers. $9.95.

A key source on the extensively collected Ruger Blackhawk revolvers.

Blue Book of Gun Values, 14th edition, compiled by S.P. Fjestad, Investment Rarities, Inc., Minneapolis, MN, 1993. 621 pp., illus. Soft covers. $24.95.

Uses percentage grading system to determine each gun's value based on its unique condition.

*Boarders Away, Volume II: Firearms of the Age of Fighting Sail, by William Gilkerson, Andrew Mowbray, Inc. Publishers, Lincoln, RI, 1993. 331 pp., illus. $65.00.

Covers the pistols, muskets, combustibles and small cannon used aboard American and European fighting ships, 1626-1826.

The Book of the Springfield, by Edward C. Crossman and Roy F. Dunlap, Wolfe Publishing Co., Prescott, AZ, 1990. 567 pp., illus. $49.00.

A textbook covering the military, sporting and target rifles chambered for the caliber 30 Model 1906 cartridge; their metallic and telescopic sights and ammunition used in them.

Breech-Loading Carbines of the United States Civil War Period, by Brig. Gen. John Pitman, Armory Publications, Tacoma, WA, 1987. 94 pp., illus. $29.95.

The first in a series of previously unpublished manuscripts originated by the late Brigadier General John Putnam. Exploded drawings showing parts actual size follow each sectioned illustration.

The Bren Gun Saga, by Thomas B. Dugelby, Collector Grade Publications, Toronto, Canada, 1986. 300 pp., illus. $50.00.
Contains information on all models of Bren guns used by all nations.

***British Service Rifles and Carbines 1888-1900,** by Alan M. Petrillo, Excaliber Publications, Latham, NY, 1994. 72 pp., illus, Paper covers. $11.95.
A complete review of the Lee-Metford and Lee-Enfield rifles and carbines.

***British Small Arms Ammunition, 1864-1938,** by Peter Labett, Armory Publications, Oceanside, CA, 1994. 352 pp., illus. $75.00.
The military side of the story illustrating the rifles, carbines, machine guns, revolvers and automatic pistols and their ammunition, experimental and adopted, from 577 Snider to modern times.

***British Sporting Rifle Cartridges,** by Bill Fleming, Armory Publications, Oceanside, CA, 1994. 302 pp., illus. $60.00.
An expanded study of volume three of *The History & Development of Small Arms Ammunition.* Includes pertinent trade catalog pages, etc.

Browning Dates of Manufacture, compiled by George Madis, Art and Reference House, Brownsboro, TX, 1989. 48 pp. $5.00.
Gives the date codes and product codes for all models from 1824 to the present.

Bullard Arms, by G. Scott Jamieson, The Boston Mills Press, Ontario, Canada, 1989. 244 pp., illus. $35.00.
The story of a mechanical genius whose rifles and cartridges were the equal to any made in America in the 1880s.

Burning Powder, compiled by Major D.B. Wesson, Wolfe Publishing Company, Prescott, AZ, 1992. 110 pp. Soft cover. $10.95.
A rare booklet from 1932 for Smith & Wesson collectors.

The Burnside Breech Loading Carbines, by Edward A. Hull, Andrew Mowbray, Inc., Lincoln, RI, 1986. 95 pp., illus. $16.00.
No. 1 in the "Man at Arms Monograph Series." A model-by-model historical/technical examination of one of the most widely used cavalry weapons of the American Civil War based upon important and previously unpublished research.

California Gunsmiths 1846-1900, by Lawrence P. Sheldon, Far Far West Publ., Fair Oaks, CA, 1977. 289 pp., illus. $29.65.
A study of early California gunsmiths and the firearms they made.

Carbines of the Civil War, by John D. McAulay, Pioneer Press, Union City, TN, 1981. 123 pp., illus. Paper covers. $7.95.
A guide for the student and collector of the colorful arms used by the Federal cavalry.

Cartridges for Breechloading Rifles, by A. Mattenheimer, Armory Publications, Oceanside, CA, 1989. 90 pp. with two 15"x19" color lithos containing 163 drawings of cartridges and firearms mechanisms. $29.95.
Reprinting of this German work on cartridges. Text in German and English.

Cartridges of the World, 7th Edition, by Frank Barnes, edited by Mike Bussard, DBI Books, Inc., Northbrook, IL, 1993. 464 pp., illus. Paper covers. $21.95
Completely revised edition of the general purpose reference work for which collectors, police, scientists and laymen reach first for answers to cartridge identification questions.

Cast Iron Toy Guns and Capshooters, by Samuel H. Logan, and Charles W. Best, Samuel Logan, Davis, CA, 1991. 251 pp., illus. $55.00.
Covers 1860s to 1950 with some 1,250 toys shown with brief descriptions, estimated dates of production and indication of rarity.

A Catalog Collection of 20th Century Winchester Repeating Arms Co., compiled by Roger Rule, Alliance Books, Inc., Northridge, CA, 1985. 396 pp., illus. $29.95.
Reflects the full line of Winchester products from 1901-1931 with emphasis on Winchester firearms.

Civil War Breech Loading Rifles, by John D. McAulay, Andrew Mowbray, Inc., Lincoln, RI, 1991. 144 pp., illus. Paper covers. $15.00.
All the major breech-loading rifles of the Civil War and most, if not all, of the obscure types are detailed, illustrated and set in their historical context.

Civil War Carbines, by A.F. Lustyik, World Wide Gun Report, Inc., Aledo, IL, 1962. 63 pp., illus. Paper covers. $3.50.
Accurate, interesting summary of most carbines of the Civil War period, in booklet form, with numerous good illus.

Civil War Carbines Volume 2: The Early Years, by John D. McAulay, Andrew Mowbray, Inc., Lincoln, RI, 1991. 144 pp., illus. Paper covers. $15.00.
Covers the carbines made during the exciting years leading up to the outbreak of war and used by the North and South in the conflict.

Civil War Pistols, by John D. McAulay, Andrew Mowbray Inc., Lincoln, RI, 1992. 166 pp., illus. $38.50.
A survey of the handguns used during the American Civil War.

A Collector's Guide to United States Combat Shotguns, by Bruce N. Canfield, Andrew Mowbray Inc., Lincoln, RI, 1992. 184 pp., illus. Paper covers. $24.00
This book provides full coverage of combat shotguns, from the earliest examples right up to the Gulf War and beyond.

A Collector's Guide to Winchester in the Service, by Bruce N. Canfield, Andrew Mowbray, Inc., Lincoln, RI, 1991. 192 pp., illus. $38.00.
The firearms produced by Winchester for the national defense. From Hotchkiss to the M14, each firearm is examined and illustrated.

A Collector's Guide to the M1 Garand and the M1 Carbine, by Bruce N. Canfield, Andrew Mowbray, Inc., Publisher, Lincoln, RI, 1988. 144 pp., illus., paper covers. $22.98.
A comprehensive guide to the most important and ubiquitous American arms of WWII and Korea.

A Collector's Guide to the '03 Springfield, by Bruce N. Canfield, Andrew Mowbray Inc, Lincoln, RI, 1989. 160 pp., illus. $35.00.
A comprehensive guide follows the '03 through its unparalleled tenure of service. Covers all of the interesting variations, modifications and accessories of this highly collectible military rifle.

Collector's Illustrated Encyclopedia of the American Revolution, by George C. Neumann and Frank J. Kravic, Rebel Publishing Co., Inc., Texarkana, TX, 1989. 286 pp., illus. $29.95.
A showcase of more than 2,300 artifacts made, worn, and used by those who fought in the War for Independence.

Colonial Frontier Guns, by T.M. Hamilton, Pioneer Press, Union City, TN, 1988. 176 pp., illus. Paper covers. $13.95.
A complete study of early flint muskets of this country.

Colt 45 Service Pistol Models of 1911 and 1911A1, by Charles W. Clawson, Charles W. Clawson, Fort Wayne, IN, 1991. 429 pp., illus. $65.00.
Complete military history, development and production 1900 through 1945 plus foreign pistols, gallery pistols, revolvers, cartridge development, and much more.

Colt Heritage, by R.L. Wilson, Simon & Schuster, 1979. 358 pp., illus. $75.00.
The official history of Colt firearms 1836 to the present.

Colt Peacemaker British Model, by Keith Cochran, Cochran Publishing Co., Rapid City, SD, 1989. 160 pp., illus. $35.00.
Covers those revolvers Colt squeezed in while completing a large order of revolvers for the U.S. Cavalry in early 1874, to those magnificent cased target revolvers used in the pistol competitions at Bisley Commons in the 1890s.

Colt Peacemaker Encyclopedia, by Keith Cochran, Keith Cochran, Rapid City, SD, 1986. 434 pp., illus. $59.95.
A must book for the Peacemaker collector.

Colt Peacemaker Encyclopedia, Volume 2, by Keith Cochran, Cochran Publishing Co., SD, 1992. 416 pp., illus. $60.00.
Included in this volume are extensive notes on engraved, inscribed, historical and noted revolvers, as well as those revolvers used by outlaws, lawmen, movie and television stars.

Colt Peacemaker Yearly Variations, by Keith Cochran, Keith Cochran, Rapid City, SD, 1987. 96 pp., illus. $17.95.
A definitive, precise listing for each year the Peacemaker was manufactured from 1873-1940.

Colt Pistols 1836-1976, by R.L. Wilson in association with R.E. Hable, Jackson Arms, Dallas, TX, 1976. 380 pp., illus. $125.00.
A magnificently illustrated book in full color featuring Colt firearms from the famous Hable collection.

Colt Revolvers and the Tower of London, by Joseph G. Rosa, Royal Armouries of the Tower of London, London, England, 1988. 72 pp., illus. Soft covers. $15.00.
Details the story of Colt in London through the early cartridge period.

Colt Revolvers and the U.S. Navy 1865-1889, by C. Kenneth Moore, Dorrance and Co., Bryn Mawr, PA, 1987. 140 pp., illus. $29.95.
The Navy's use of all Colt handguns and other revolvers during this era of change.

Colt Single Action Army Revolvers and the London Agency, by C. Kenneth Moore, Andrew Mowbray Publishers, Lincoln, RI, 1990. 144 pp., illus. $35.00.
Drawing on vast documentary sources, this work chronicles the relationship between the London Agency and the Hartford home office.

The Colt U.S. General Officers' Pistols, by Horace Greeley IV, Andrew Mowbray Inc., Lincoln, RI, 1990. 199 pp., illus. $38.00.
These unique weapons, issued as a badge of rank to General Officers in the U.S. Army from WWII onward, remain highly personal artifacts of the military leaders who carried them. Includes serial numbers and dates of issue.

Colt's Dates of Manufacture 1837-1978, by R.L. Wilson, published by Maurie Albert, Coburg, Australia; N.A. distributor I.D.S.A. Books, Hamilton, OH, 1983. 61 pp. $10.00.
An invaluable pocket guide to the dates of manufacture of Colt firearms up to 1978.

Colt's 100th Anniversary Firearms Manual 1836-1936: A Century of Achievement, Wolfe Publishing Co., Prescott, AZ, 1992. 100 pp., illus. Paper covers. $12.95.
Originally published by the Colt Patent Firearms Co., this booklet covers the history, manufacturing procedures and the guns of the first 100 years of the genius of Samuel Colt.

Colt's SAA Post War Models, George Garton, revised edition, Gun Room Press, Highland Park, NJ, 1987. 166 pp., illus. $29.95.
The complete facts on Colt's famous post war single action army revolver using factory records to cover types, calibers, production numbers and many variations of this popular firearm.

The Colt Whitneyville-Walker Pistol, by Lt. Col. Robert D. Whittington, Brownlee Books, Hooks, TX, 1984. 96 pp., illus. Limited edition. $20.00.
A study of the pistol and associated characters 1846-1851.

Compliments of Col. Ruger: A Study of Factory Engraved Single Action Revolvers, by John C. Dougan, Taylor Publishing Co., El Paso, TX, 1992. 238 pp., illus. $46.50.
Clearly detailed black and white photographs and a precise text present an accurate istory of the Sturm, Ruger & Co. single-action revolver engraving project.

Confederate Revolvers, by William A. Gary, Taylor Publishing Co., Dallas, TX, 1987. 174 pp., illus. $45.00.
Comprehensive work on the rarest of Confederate weapons.

Coykendall's 2nd Sporting Collectible Price Guide, by Ralf Coykendall, Jr., Lyons & Burford Publlishers, New York, NY, 1992. 223 pp., illus. Paper covers. $16.95.
The all-new second volume with new sections on knives and sporting magazines.

Cowboy Collectibles and Western Memorabilia, by Bob Bell and Edward Vebell, Schiffer Publishing, Atglen, PA, 1992. 160 pp., illus. Paper covers. $29.95.
The exciting era of the cowboy and the wild west collectibles including rifles, pistols, gun rigs, etc.

Dance & Brothers; Texas Gunmakers of the Confederacy, by Gary Wiggins, Moss Publications, Orange, VA, 1986. 151 pp., illus. $29.95.
Presents a thorough and detailed study of the legendary Texas gunmakers, Dance & Brothers.

The Deringer in America, Volume 1, The Percussion Period, by R.L. Wilson and L.D. Eberhart, Andrew Mowbray Inc., Lincoln, RI, 1985. 271 pp., illus. $48.00.
A long awaited book on the American percussion deringer.

***The Deringer in America, Volume 2, The Cartridge Period,** by L.D. Eberhart and R.L. Wilson, Andrew Mowbray Inc., Publishers, Lincoln, RI, 1993. 284 pp., illus. $65.00.
Comprehensive coverage of cartridge deringers organized alphabetically by maker. Includes all types of deringers known by the authors to have been offered to the American market.

Development of the Henry Cartridge and Self-Contained Cartridges for the Toggle-Link Winchesters, by R. Bruce McDowell, A.M.B., Metuchen, NJ, 1984. 69 pp., illus. Paper covers. $10.00.
From powder and ball to the self-contained metallic cartridge.

The Devil's Paintbrush: Sir Hiram Maxim's Gun, by Dolf Goldsmith, 2nd Edition, expanded and revised, Collector Grade Publications, Toronto, Canada, 1993. 384 pp., illus. $69.95
The classic work on the world's first true automatic machine gun.

***Drums A'beating Trumpets Sounding,** by William H. Guthman, The Connecticut Historical Society, Westport, CT, 1993. 232 pp., illus. $75.00.
Artistically carved powder horns in the provincial manner, 1746-1781.

***The Eagle on U.S. Firearms,** by John W. Jordan, Pioneer Press, Union City, TN, 1992. 140 pp., illus. Paper covers. $14.95.
Stylized eagles have been stamped on government owned or manufactured firearms in the U.S. since the beginning of our country. This book lists and illustrates these various eagles in an informative and refreshing manner.

Early Indian Trade Guns: 1625-1775, by T.M. Hamilton, Museum of the Great Plains, Lawton, OK, 1968. 34 pp., illus. Paper covers. $7.95.
Detailed descriptions of subject arms, compiled from early records and from the study of remnants found in Indian country.

Encyclopedia and Price Guide of American Paper Shotshells, compiled by Dick Iverson, prices by Bob Strauss, Circus Promotions Corp., Spring, TX, 1991. 436 pp., illus. Paper covers. $25.00.
Pages of headstamps, head types, dimensions, color listed, and 3,100 individual prices.

Encyclopedia of Ruger Rimfire Semi-Automatic Pistols: 1949-1992, by Chad Hiddleson, Krause Publications, Iola, WI, 1993. 250 pp., illus. $29.95.

Covers all physical aspects of Ruger 22-caliber pistols including important features such as boxes, grips, muzzlebrakes, instruction manuals, serial numbers, etc.

English Pistols: The Armories of H.M. Tower of London Collection, by Howard L. Blackmore, Arms and Armour Press, London, England, 1985. 64 pp., illus. Soft covers. $14.95.

All the pistols described and pictured are from this famed collection.

European Firearms in Swedish Castles, by Kaa Wennberg, Bohuslaningens Boktryckeri AB, Uddevalla, Sweden, 1986. 156 pp., illus. $45.00.

The famous collection of Count Keller, the Ettersburg Castle collection, and others. English text.

Evolution of the Winchester, by R. Bruce McDowell, Armory Publications, Tacoma, WA, 1986. 200 pp., illus. $37.50.

Historic lever-action, tubular-magazine firearms.

Fifteen Years in the Hawken Lode, by John D. Baird, The Gun Room Press, Highland Park, NJ, 1976. 120 pp., illus. $24.95.

A collection of thoughts and observations gained from many years of intensive study of the guns from the shop of the Hawken brothers.

'51 Colt Navies, by Nathan L. Swayze, The Gun Room Press, Highland Park, NJ, 1993. 243 pp., illus. $59.95.

The Model 1851 Colt Navy, its variations and markings.

Firearms and Tackle Memorabilia, by John Delph, Schiffer Publishing, Ltd., West Chester, PA, 1991. 124 pp., illus. $39.95.

A collector's guide to signs and posters, calendars, trade cards, boxes, envelopes, and other highly sought after memorabilia. With a value guide.

The Firearms of Tipu Sultan 1785-1799, by Robin Wigington, Robin Wigington, Warwichshire, England, 1993. 148 pp., illus. Limited edition. $95.00.

A general survey of the characteristics of the arms with references to the man they were made for, Tipu Sultan himself, and the craftsmen who made them.

*Flayderman's Guide to Antique American Firearms...and Their Values, 6th Edition, by Norm Flayderman, DBI Books, Inc., Northbrook, IL, 1994. 624 pp., illus. Paper covers. $29.95.

Updated edition of this bible of the antique gun field. (September, 1994)

The .45-70 Springfield, by Joe Poyer and Craig Riesch, North Cape Publications, Tustin, CA, 1991. 112 pp., illus. Soft covers. $14.95.

A definitive work on the 45-70 Springfield. Organized by serial number and date of production to aid the collector in identifying models and rifle parts.

Frank and George Freund and the Sharps Rifle, by Gerald O. Kelver, Gerald O. Kelver, Brighton, CO, 1986. 60 pp., illus. Paper covers. $12.00.

Pioneer gunmakers of Wyoming Territory and Colorado.

French Military Weapons, 1717-1938, Major James E. Hicks, N. Flayderman & Co., Publishers, New Milford, CT, 1973. 281 pp., illus. $24.95.

Firearms, swords, bayonets, ammunition, artillery, ordnance equipment of the French army.

*From the Kingdom of Lilliput: The Miniature Firearms of David Kucer, by K. Corey Keeble and **The Making of Miniatures,** by David Kucer, Museum Restoration Service, Ontario, Canada, 1994. 51 pp., illus. $25.00.

An overview of the subject of miniatures in general combined with an outline by the artist himself on the way he makes a miniature firearm.

*Game Guns & Rifles: Percussion to Hammerless Ejector in Britain, by Richard Akehurst, Trafalgar Square, N. Pomfret, VT, 1993. 192 pp., illus. $34.95.

Long considered a classic this important reprint covers the period of British gunmaking between 1830-1900.

George Schreyer, Sr. and Jr., Gunmakers of Hanover, Pennsylvania, by George Shumway, George Shumway Publishers, York, PA, 1990. 160pp., illus. $45.00.

This monograph is a detailed photographic study of almost all known surviving long rifles and smoothbore guns made by highly regarded gunsmiths George Schreyer, Sr. and Jr.

The German Assault Rifle 1935-1945, by Peter R. Senich, Paladin Press, Boulder, CO, 1987. 328 pp., illus. $49.95.

A complete review of machine carbines, machine pistols and assault rifles employed by Hitler's Wehrmacht during WWII.

*The German K98k Rifle, 1934-1945: The Backbone of the Wehrmacht, by Richard D. Law, Collector Grade Publications, Inc., Toronto, Canada, 1993. 336 pp., illus. $69.95.

The most comprehensive study ever published on the 14,000,000 bolt-action K98k rifles produced in Germany between 1934 and 1945.

German Machineguns, by Daniel D. Musgrave, Revised edition, Ironside International Publishers, Inc. Alexandria, VA, 1992. 586 pp., 650 illus. $49.95.

The most definitive book ever written on German machineguns. Covers the introduction and development of machineguns in Germany from 1899 to the rearmament period after World War II.

German Military Pistols 1904-1930, by Fred A. Datig, Michael Zomber Co., Culver City, CA, 1990. 88 pp., illus. Paper covers. $14.95.

Monograph #2 in the series "The Luger Pistol Its History & Development from 1893-1945."

German Military Rifles and Machine Pistols, 1871-1945, by Hans Dieter Gotz, Schiffer Publishing Co., West Chester, PA, 1990. 245 pp., illus. $35.00.

This book portrays in words and pictures the development of the modern German weapons and their ammunition including the scarcely known experimental types.

German Pistols and Holsters 1934-1945, Vol. 2, by Robert Whittington, Brownlee Books, Hooks, TX, 1990. 312 pp., illus. $55.00.

This volume addresses pistols only: military (Heer, Luftwaffe, Kriegsmarine & Waffen-SS), captured, commercial, police, NSDAP and government.

German 7.9mm Military Ammunition, by Daniel W. Kent, Daniel W. Kent, Ann Arbor, MI, 1991. 244 pp., illus. $35.00.

The long-awaited revised edition of a classic among books devoted to ammunition.

German Pistols and Holsters, 1934-1945, Volume 4, by Lt. Col. Robert D. Whittington, 3rd, U.S.A.R., Brownlee Books, Hooks, TX, 1991. 208 pp. $30.00.

Pistols and holsters issued in 412 selected armed forces, army and Waffen-SS units including information on personnel, other weapons and transportation.

*Great British Gunmakers: The Mantons 1782-1878, by D.H.L. Back, Historical Firearms, Norwich, England, 1994. 218 pp., illus. Limited edition of 500 copies. $175.00.

Contains detailed descriptions of all the firearms made by members of this famous family.

Great Irish Gunmakers: Messrs. Rigby 1760-1869, by D.H.L. Back, Historical Firearms, Norwich, England, 1993. 196 pp., illus. $150.00.

The history of this famous firm of Irish gunmakers illustrated with a wide selection of Rigby arms.

*A Guide to the Maynard Breechloader, by George J. Layman, George J. Layman, Ayer, MA, 1993. 125 pp., illus. Paper covers. $17.95.

The first book dedicated entirely to the Maynard family of breech-loading firearms. Coverage of the arms is given from the 1850s through the 1880s.

Guide to Ruger Single Action Revolvers Production Dates, 1953-73, by John C. Dougan, Blacksmith Corp., Chino Valley, AZ, 1991. 22 pp., illus. Paper covers. $9.95.

A unique pocket-sized handbook providing production information for the popular Ruger single-action revolvers manufactured during the first 20 years.

Gun Collecting, by Geoffrey Boothroyd, Sportsman's Press, London, 1989. 208 pp., illus. $29.95.

The most comprehensive list of 19th century British gunmakers and gunsmiths ever published.

Gun Collector's Digest, 5th Edition, edited by Joseph J. Schroeder, DBI Books, Inc., Northbrook, IL, 1989. 224 pp., illus. Paper covers. $16.95.

The latest edition of this sought-after series.

Gunmakers of London 1350-1850, by Howard L. Blackmore, George Shumway Publisher, York, PA, 1986. 222 pp., illus. $35.00.

A listing of all the known workmen of gun making in the first 500 years, plus a history of the guilds, cutlers, armourers, founders, blacksmiths, etc. 260 gunmarks are illustrated.

The Gunsmiths of Manhattan, 1625-1900: A Checklist of Tradesmen, by Michael H. Lewis, Museum Restoration Service, Bloomfield, Ont., Canada, 1991. 40 pp., illus. Paper covers. $4.95.

This listing of more than 700 men in the arms trade in New York City prior to about the end of the 19th century will provide a guide for identification and further research.

Gunsmiths of Ohio—18th & 19th Centuries: Vol. I, Biographical Data, by Donald A. Hutslar, George Shumway, York, PA, 1973. 444 pp., illus. $45.00.

An important source book, full of information about the old-time gunsmiths of Ohio.

Gun Tools, Their History and Identification, by James B. Shaffer, Lee A. Rutledge and R. Stephen Dorsey, Collector's Library, Eugene, OR, 1992. 375 pp., illus. $32.00.

Written history of foreign and domestic gun tools from the flintlock period to World War II.

The Handgun, by Geoffrey Boothroyd, David and Charles, North Pomfret, VT, 1989. 566 pp., illus. $60.00.

Every chapter deals with an important period in handgun history from the 14th century to the present.

The Hawken Rifle: Its Place in History, by Charles E. Hanson, Jr., The Fur Press, Chadron, NE, 1979. 104 pp., illus. Paper covers. $8.00.

A definitive work on this famous rifle.

Hawken Rifles, The Mountain Man's Choice, by John D. Baird, The Gun Room Press, Highland Park, NJ, 1976. 95 pp., illus. $24.95.

Covers the rifles developed for the Western fur trade. Numerous specimens are described and shown in photographs.

High Standard: A Collector's Guide to the Hamden & Hartford Target Pistols, by Tom Dance, Andrew Mowbray, Inc., Lincoln, RI, 1991. 192 pp., illus. Paper covers. $24.00.

From Citation to Supermatic, all of the production models and specials made from 1951 to 1984 are covered according to model number or series.

Hi-Standard Autoloading Pistols 1951-1984, by James V. Spacek, Jr., James V. Spacek, Jr., Berlin, CT, 1993. 60 pp., illus. Paper covers. $10.00.

Information on takedown styles, serial numbers, production numbers, model charts and magazine references. Includes a price guide.

Historic Pistols: The American Martial Flintlock 1760-1845, by Samuel E. Smith and Edwin W. Bitter, The Gun Room Press, Highland Park, NJ, 1986. 353 pp., illus. $45.00.

Covers over 70 makers and 163 models of American martial arms.

Historical Hartford Hardware, by William W. Dalrymple, Colt Collector Press, Rapid City, SD, 1976. 42 pp., illus. Paper covers. $5.50.

Historically associated Colt revolvers.

The History and Development of Small Arms Ammunition, Volume 1, by George A. Hoyem, Armory Publications, Oceanside, CA, 1991. 230 pp., illus. $75.00.

Military musket, rifle, carbine and primitive machine gun cartridges of the 18th and 19th centuries, together with the firearms that chambered them.

The History and Development of Small Arms Ammunition, Volume 2, by George A. Hoyem, Armory Publications, Oceanside, CA, 1991. 303 pp., illus. $65.00.

Covers the blackpowder military centerfire rifle, carbine, machine gun and volley gun ammunition used in 28 nations and dominions, together with the firearms that chambered them.

The History and Development of Small Arms Ammunition (British Sporting Rifle) Volume 3, by George A. Hoyem, Armory Publications, Oceanside, CA, 1991. 300 pp., illus. $60.00.

Concentrates on British sporting rifle cartridges that run from the 4-bore through the .600 Nitro to the .297/.230 Morris.

The History of Smith and Wesson, by Roy G. Jinks, Willowbrook Enterprises, Springfield, MA, 1988. 290 pp., illus. $27.95.

Revised 10th Anniversary edition of the definite book on S&W firearms.

The History of Winchester Firearms 1866-1992, sixth edition, updated, expanded, and revised by Thomas Henshaw, New Win Publishing, Clinton, NJ, 1993. 280 pp., illus. $24.95.

This classic is the standard reference for all collectors and others seeking the facts about any Winchester firearm, old or new.

*History of Winchester Repeating Arms Company, by Herbert G. House, Krause Publications, Iola, WI, 1994. 800 pp., illus. $55.00.

The complete Winchester history from 1856-1981.

How to Buy and Sell Used Guns, by John Traister, Stoeger Publishing Co., So. Hackensack, NJ, 1984. 192 pp., illus. Paper covers. $10.95.

A new guide to buying and selling guns.

Illustrations of United States Military Arms 1776-1903 and Their Inspector's Marks, compiled by Turner Kirkland, Pioneer Press, Union City, TN, 1988. 37 pp., illus. Paper covers. $4.95.

Reprinted from the 1949 Bannerman catalog. Valuable information for both the advanced and beginning collector.

*Indian War Cartridge Pouches, Boxes and Carbine Boots, by R. Stephen Dorsey, Collector's Library, Eugene, OR, 1993. 156 pp., illus. Paper Covers. $25.00.

The key reference work to the cartridge pouches, boxes, carbine sockets and boots of the Indian War period 1865-1890.

An Introduction the Civil War Small Arms, by Earl J. Coates and Dean S. Thomas, Thomas Publishing Co., Gettysburg, PA, 1990. 96 pp., illus. Paper covers. $6.95.

The small arms carried by the individual soldier during the Civil War.

Iver Johnson's Arms & Cycle Works Handguns, 1871-1964, by W.E. "Bill" Goforth, Blacksmith Corp., Chino Valley, AZ, 1991. 160 pp., illus. Paper covers. $14.95.

Covers all of the famous Iver Johnson handguns from the early solid-frame pistols and revolvers to optional accessories, special orders and patents.

James Reid and His Catskill Knuckledusters, by Taylor Brown, Andrew Mowbray Publishers, Lincoln, RI, 1990. 288 pp., illus. $24.95.

A detailed history of James Reid, his factory in the picturesque Catskill Mountains, and the pistols which he manufactured there.

Japanese Handguns, by Frederick E. Leithe, Borden Publishing Co., Alhambra, CA, 1985. 160 pp., illus. $19.95.
This book is an identification guide to all models and variations of Japanese handguns.

***The Kentucky Rifle,** by Captain John G.W. Dillin, George Shumway Publisher, York, PA, 1993. 221 pp., illus. $45.00.
This well-known book was the first attempt to tell the story of the American longrifle. This edition retains the original text and illustrations with supplemental footnotes provided by Dr. George Shumway.

Kentucky Rifles and Pistols 1756-1850, compiled by members of the Kentucky Rifle Association, Wash., DC, Golden Age Arms Co., Delaware, OH, 1976. 275 pp., illus. $45.00.
Profusely illustrated with more than 300 examples of rifles and pistols never before published.

Know Your Broomhandle Mausers, by R.J. Berger, Blacksmith Corp., Southport, CT, 1985. 96 pp., illus. Paper covers. $9.95.
An interesting story on the big Mauser pistol and its variations.

Krag Rifles, by William S. Brophy, The Gun Room Press, Highland Park, NJ, 1980. 200 pp., illus. $35.00.
The first comprehensive work detailing the evolution and various models, both military and civilian.

The Krieghoff Parabellum, by Randall Gibson, Midland, TX, 1988. 279 pp., illus. $40.00.
A comprehensive text pertaining to the Lugers manufactured by H. Krieghoff Waffenfabrik.

Levine's Guide to Knives And Their Values, 3rd Edition, by Bernard Levine, DBI Books, Inc., Northbrook, IL, 1993. 480 pp., illus. Paper covers. $24.95
All the basic tools for identifying, valuing and collecting folding and fixed blade knives.

Longrifles of North Carolina, by John Bivens, George Shumway Publisher, York, PA, 1988. 256 pp., illus. $45.00.
Covers art and evolution of the rifle, immigration and trade movements. Committee of Safety gunsmiths, characteristics of the North Carolina rifle.

Longrifles of Pennsylvania, Volume 1, Jefferson, Clarion & Elk Counties, by Russel H. Harringer, George Shumway Publisher, York, PA, 1984. 200 pp., illus. $45.00.
First in series that will treat in great detail the longrifles and gunsmiths of Pennsylvania.

Luger Holsters and Accessories of the 20th Century, by Eugene J. Bender, Eugene J. Bender, Margate, FL, 1993. 640 pp., illus. $65.00.
A major new book for collectors, dealers, and historians, with over 1,000 photographs.

Lugers at Random, by Charles Kenyon, Jr., Handgun Press, Glenview, IL, 1990. 420 pp., illus. $39.95.
A new printing of this classic and sought-after work on the Luger pistol. A boon to the Luger collector/shooter.

The Luger Pistol Its History & Development From 1893 to 1947; Monograph IV: The Swiss Variations 1897-1947, by Fred A. Datig, Fred A. Datig, Los Angeles, CA, 1992. 88 pp., illus. Paper covers. $14.95.
A definitive work on the Swiss variations of this most collectible pistol.

Luger: The Multi-National Pistol, by Charles Kenyon, Jr., Richard Ellis Publications, Moline, IL, 1991. 192 pp., illus. $69.95 (hardcover); $150.00 (leather bound).
A fresh approach to this historical handgun. A must for the serious collector.

Marlin Firearms: A History of the Guns and the Company That Made Them, by Lt. Col. William S. Brophy, USAR, Ret., Stackpole Books, Harrisburg, PA, 1989. 672 pp., illus. $59.95.
The definitive book on the Marlin Firearms Co. and their products.

Massachusetts Military Shoulder Arms 1784-1877, by George D. Moller, Andrew Mowbray Publisher, Lincoln, RI, 1989. 250 pp., illus. $24.00.
A scholarly and heavily researched study of the military shoulder arms used by Massachusetts during the 90-year period following the Revolutionary War.

Mauser Bolt Rifles, by Ludwig Olson, F. Brownell & Son, Inc., Montezuma, IA, 1976. 364 pp., illus. $47.50.
The most complete, detailed, authoritative and comprehensive work ever done on Mauser bolt rifles.

Mauser Rifles and Pistols, by Walter H.B. Smith, Wolfe Publishing Co., Prescott, AZ, 1990. 234 pp., illus. $30.00.
A handbook covering Mauser history and the amrs Mauser manufactured.

***Military Handguns of France 1858-1958,** by Eugene Medlin and Jean Huon, Excaliber Publications, Latham, NY, 1993. 128 pp., illus. Paper covers. $24.95.
The first book in English on the subject, providing students of arms with a thorough history of French service handguns.

Military Pistols of Japan, by Fred L. Honeycutt, Jr., Julin Books, Palm Beach Gardens, FL, 1991. 168 pp., illus. $34.00.
Covers every aspect of military pistol production in Japan through WWII.

The Military Remington Rolling Block Rifle, by George Layman, Wolfe Publishing Company, Prescott, AZ, 1992. 250 pp., illus. Soft cover. $21.00.
A reference work for the collector, tracing the history of this military rifle and disclosing previously unpublished data.

Military Rifles of Japan, 4th Edition, by F.L. Honeycutt, Julin Books, Lake Park, FL, 1989. 208 pp., illus. $42.00.
A new revised and updated edition. Includes the early Murata-period markings, etc.

Military Small Arms of the 20th Century, 6th Edition, by Ian V. Hogg, DBI Books, Inc., Northbrook, IL, 1991. 352 pp., illus. Paper covers. $19.95.
Fully revised and updated edition of the standard reference in its field.

M1 Carbine, by Larry Ruth, Gunroom Press, Highland Park, NJ, 1987. 291 pp., illus. Cloth $24.95; Paper $19.95.
The origin, development, manufacture and use of this famous carbine of World War II.

The M1 Garand: Post World War, by Scott A. Duff, Scott A. Duff, Export, PA, 1990. 139 pp., illus. Soft covers. $19.95.
A detailed account of the activities at Springfield Armory through this period. International Harvester, H&R, Korean War production and quantities delivered. Serial numbers.

***The M1 Garand: World War 2,** by Scott A. Duff, Scott A. Duff, Export, PA, 1993. 210 pp., illus. Paper covers. $39.95.
The most comprehensive study available to the collector and historian on the M1 Garand of World War II.

Modern Guns Identification & Values, 9th Edition, by Russell & Steve Quertermous, Collector Books, Paducah, KY, 1992. 480 pp., illus. Paper covers, $12.95.
Over 2,250 models of rifles, handguns and shotguns from 1900 to the present are described and priced in excellent and very good condition with suggested retail prices for those models still in production.

Modern Gun Values, The Gun Digest Book of 9th Edition, Edited by Jack Lewis, DBI Books, Inc., Northbrook, IL, illus. Paper covers. $20.95
Updated and expanded edition of the book that has become the standard for valuing modern firearms.

***Modern Gun Values, The Gun Digest Book of** 10th Edition, Edited by Joe Schroeder, DBI Books, Inc., Northbrook, IL., illus. Paper covers.
Updated and expanded edition of the book that has become the standard for valuing modern firearms. (February '95)

More Single Shot Rifles, by James C. Grant, The Gun Room Press, Highland Park, NJ, 1976. 324 pp., illus. $29.95.
Details the guns made by Frank Wesson, Milt Farrow, Holden, Borchardt, Stevens, Remington, Winchester, Ballard and Peabody-Martini.

Mortimer, the Gunmakers, 1753-1923, by H. Lee Munson, Andrew Mowbray Inc., Lincoln, RI, 1992. 320 pp., illus. $65.00.
Seen through a single, dominant, English gunmaking dynasty this fascinating study provides a window into the classical era of firearms artistry.

The Muzzle-Loading Cap Lock Rifle, by Ned H. Roberts, reprinted by Wolfe Publishing Co., Prescott, AZ, 1991. 432 pp., illus. $30.00.
Originally published in 1940, this fascinating study of the muzzle-loading cap lock rifle covers rifles on the frontier to hunting rifles, including the famous Hawken.

The Navy Luger, by Joachim Gortz and John Walter, Handgun Press, Glenview, IL, 1988. 128 pp., illus. $24.95.
The 9mm Pistole 1904 and the Imperial German Navy. A concise illustrated history.

The Northwest Gun, by Charles E. Hanson, Jr., Nebraska State Historical Society, Lincoln, NE, 1976. 85 pp., illus., paper covers. $6.00.
Number 2 in the Society's "Publications in Anthropology." Historical survey of rifles which figured in the fur trade and settlement of the Northwest.

The P-08 Parabellum Luger Automatic Pistol, edited by J. David McFarland, Desert Publications, Cornville, AZ, 1982. 20 pp., illus. Paper covers. $8.00.
Covers every facet of the Luger, plus a listing of all known Luger models.

***Packing Iron,** by Richard C. Rattenbury, Zon International Publishing, Millwood, NY, 1993. 216 pp., illus. $45.00.
The best book yet produced on pistol holsters and rifle scabbards. Over 300 variations of holster and scabbards are illustrated in large, clear plates.

***Patents for Inventions, Class 119 (Small Arms), 1855-1930.** British Patent Office, Armory Publications, Oceanside, CA, 1993. 7 volume set. $350.00.
Contains 7980 abridged patent descriptions and their sectioned line drawings, plus a 37-page alphabetical index of the patentees.

Paterson Colt Pistol Variations, by R.L. Wilson and R. Phillips, Jackson Arms Co., Dallas, TX, 1979. 250 pp., illus. $35.00.
A book about the different models and barrel lengths in the Paterson Colt story.

Pennsylvania Longrifles of Note, by George Shumway, George Shumway, Publisher, York, PA, 1977. 63 pp., illus. Paper covers. $10.00.
Illustrates and describes rifles from a number of Pennsylvania rifle-making schools.

Pistols of the World, 3rd Edition, by Ian Hogg and John Weeks, DBI Books, Inc., Northbrook, IL, 1992. 320 pp., illus. Paper covers. $19.95.
A totally revised edition of one of the leading studies of small arms.

The Pitman Notes on U.S. Martial Small Arms and Ammunition, 1776-1933, Volume 2, Revolvers and Automatic Pistols, by Brig. Gen. John Pitman, Thomas Publications, Gettysburg, PA, 1990. 192 pp., illus. $29.95.
A most important primary source of information on United States military small arms and ammunition.

The Plains Rifle, by Charles Hanson, Gun Room Press, Highland Park, NJ, 1989. 169 pp., illus. $29.95.
All rifles that were made with the plainsman in mind, including pistols.

The Powder Flask Book, by Ray Riling, R&R Books, Livonia, NY, 1993. 514 pp., illus. $70.00.
The complete book on flasks of the 19th century. Exactly scaled pictures of 1,600 flasks are illustrated.

Prices Paid for British Sporting Rifle Cartridges, by Bill Fleming, Armory Publications, Oceanside, CA, 1992. 31 pp. Paper covers. $15.00.
A list reflecting the relative scarcity of case types, particular load variations, and unusual headstamps of cartridges for British sporting rifles.

Proving Ground History of the Carbine Caliber .30, M1, by G.P. Grant, Desert Publications, Cornville, AZ, 1990. 21 pp., illus. Paper covers. $5.49
Reprint of the Addenda to Volume 2, Historical Data, Aberdeen Proving Ground, MD. Added to this is "Weapons Usage in Korea" by S.L.A. Marshall.

The Rare and Valuable Antique Arms, by James E. Serven, Pioneer Press, Union City, TN, 1976. 106 pp., illus. Paper covers. $4.95.
A guide to the collector in deciding which direction his collecting should go, investment value, historic interest, mechanical ingenuity, high art or personal preference.

Reloading Tools, Sights and Telescopes for Single Shot Rifles, by Gerald O. Kelver, Brighton, CO, 1982. 163 pp., illus. Paper covers. $15.00.
A listing of most of the famous makers of reloading tools, sights and telescopes with a brief description of the products they manufactured.

Revolvers of the British Services 1854-1954, by W.H.J. Chamberlain and A.W.F. Taylerson, Museum Restoration Service, Ottawa, Canada, 1989. 80 pp., illus. $27.50.
Covers the types issued among many of the United Kingdom's naval, land or air services.

Rhode Island Arms Makers & Gunsmiths, by William O. Archibald, Andrew Mowbray, Inc., Lincoln, RI, 1990. 108 pp., illus. $16.50.
A serious and informative study of an important area of American arms making.

Rifles of the World, by John Walter, DBI Books, Inc., Northbrook, IL, 1993. 320 pp., illus. Paper covers. $19.95.
Compiled as a companion valume to *Pistols of the World*, this brand new reference work covers all centerfire military and commercial rifles produced from the perfection of the metal-case cartridge in the 1870's to the present time.

The Rock Island '03, by C.S. Ferris, C.S. Ferris, Arvada, CO, 1993. 58 pp., illus. Paper covers. $12.50.
A monograph of interenst to the collector or historian concentrating on the U.S. M1903 rifle made by the less publicized of our two producing facilities.

Ruger, edited by Joseph Roberts, Jr., the National Rifle Association of America, Washington, D.C., 1991. 109 pp. illus. Paper covers. $14.95.
The story of Bill Ruger's indelible imprint in the history of sporting firearms.

Sam Colt's Own Record 1847, by John Parsons, Wolfe Publishing Co., Prescott, AZ, 1992. 167 pp., illus. $24.50.
Chronologically presented, the correspondence published here completes the account of the manufacture, in 1847, of the Walker Model Colt revolver.

Sharps Firearms, by Frank Seller, Frank M. Seller, Denver, CO, 1982. 358 pp., illus. $45.00.
Traces the development of Sharps firearms with full range of guns made including all martial variations.

The Shotshell in the United States, by Richard J. Iverson, Circus Promotions Corp., Jefferson, ME, 1988. 193 pp., illus. Paper covers. $35.00.
Lists manufacturers, distributors, trade brands, headstamps, gauges, shot sizes, colors and configurations.

Simeon North: First Official Pistol Maker of the United States, by S. North and R. North, The Gun Room Press, Highland Park, NJ, 1972. 207 pp., illus. $15.95.
Reprint of the rare first edition.

The SKS Type 45 Carbines, by Duncan Long, Desert Publications, El Dorado, AZ, 1992. 110 pp., illus. Paper covers.
Covers the history and practical aspects of operating, maintaining and modifying this abundantly available rifle.

***Small Arms: Pistols & Rifles,** by Ian V. Hogg, Greenhill Books, London, England, 1994. 160 pp., illus. $19.95.
An in-depth description of small arms, focusing on pistols and rifles, with detailed information about all small arms used by the world's armed forces.

***Smith & Wesson Hand Guns,** by Roy C. McHenry and Walter F. Roper, Wolfe Publishing Co., Prescott, AZ, 1994. 244 pp., illus. $32.00.
Originally published in 1945, this is simply the bible on the subject.

Southern Derringers of the Mississippi Valley, by Turner Kirkland, Pioneer Press, Tenn., 1971. 80 pp., illus., paper covers. $5.00.
A guide for the collector, and a much-needed study.

Soviet Russian Postwar Military Pistols and Cartridges, by Fred A. Datig, Handgun Press, Glenview, IL, 1988. 152 pp., illus. $29.95.
Thoroughly researched, this definitive sourcebook covers the development and adoption of the Makarov, Stechkin and the new PSM pistols. Also included in this source book is coverage on Russian clandestine weapons and pistol cartridges.

***Soviet Russian Tokarev "TT" Pistols and Cartridges 1929-1953,** by Fred Datig, Graphic Publishers, Santa Ana, CA, 1993. 168 pp., illus. $39.95.
Details of rare arms and their accessories are shown in hundreds of photos. It also contains a complete bibliography and index.

Sporting Collectibles, by Jim and Vivian Karsnitz, Schiffer Publishing Ltd., West Chester, PA, 1992. 160 pp., illus. Paper covers. $29.95.
The fascinating world of hunting related collectibles presented in an informative text.

The Springfield 1903 Rifles, by Lt. Col. William S. Brophy, USAR, Ret., Stackpole Books Inc., Harrisburg, PA, 1985. 608 pp., illus. $49.95.
The illustrated, documented story of the design, development, and production of all the models, appendages, and accessories.

Springfield Shoulder Arms 1795-1865, by Claud E. Fuller, S. & S. Firearms, Glendale, NY, 1986. 76 pp., illus. Paper covers. $15.00.
Exact reprint of the scarce 1930 edition of one of the most definitive works on Springfield flintlock and percussion muskets ever published.

***Standard Catalog of Firearms, 4th Edition,** by Ned Schwing and Herbert Houze, Krause Publications, Iola, WI, 1994. 720 pp., illus. Paper covers. $24.95.
This updated and expanded edition includes proper physical descriptions for over 11,000 guns from more than 1000 manufacturers with accurate prices.

Stevens Pistols & Pocket Rifles, by K.L. Cope, Museum Restoration Service, Alexandria Bay, NY, 1992. 114 pp., illus. $24.50.
This is the story of the guns and the man who designed them and the company which he founded to make them.

The Sumptuous Flaske, by Herbert G. Houze, Andrew Mowbray, Inc., Lincoln, RI, 1989. 158 pp., illus. Soft covers. $35.00.
Catalog of a recent show at the Buffalo Bill Historical Center bringing together some of the finest European and American powder flasks of the 16th to 19th centuries.

Textbook of Automatic Pistols, by R.K. Wilson, Wolfe Publishing Co., Prescott, AZ, 1990. 349 pp., illus. $54.00.
Reprint of the 1943 classic being a treatise on the history, development and functioning of modern military self-loading pistols.

Thoughts on the Kentucky Rifle in its Golden Age, by Joe Kindig, George Shumway, Publisher, York, PA, 1984. 561 pp., illus. $85.00.
A new printing of the classic work on Kentucky rifles.

The Trapdoor Springfield, by M.D. Waite and B.D. Ernst, The Gun Room Press, Highland Park, NJ, 1983. 250 pp., illus. $39.95.
The first comprehensive book on the famous standard military rifle of the 1873-92 period.

UK and Commonwealth FALS, by R. Blake Stevens, Collector Grade Publications, Toronto, Canada, 1987. 260 pp., illus. $36.00.
The complete story of the L1A1 in the UK, Australia and India.

Underhammer Guns, by H.C. Logan, Stackpole Books, Harrisburg, PA, 1965. 250 pp., illus. $20.00.
A full account of an unusual form of firearm dating back to flintlock days. Both American and foreign specimens are included.

United States Martial Flintlocks, by Robert M. Reilly, Andrew Mowbray, Inc., Lincoln, RI, 1986. 263 pp., illus. $39.50.
A comprehensive illustrated history of the flintlock in America from the Revolution to the demise of the system.

U.S. Breech-Loading Rifles and Carbines, Cal. 45, by Gen. John Pitman, Thomas Publications, Gettysburg, PA, 1992. 192 pp., illus. $29.95.
The third volume in the Pitman Notes on U.S. Martial Small Arms and Ammunition, 1776-1933. This book centers on the "Trapdoor Springfield" models.

U.S. Military Arms Dates of Manufacture from 1795, by George Madis, David Madis, Dallas, TX, 1989. 64 pp. Soft covers. $5.00.
Lists all U.S. military arms of collector interest alphabetically, covering about 250 models.

U.S. Military Small Arms 1816-1865, by Robert M. Reilly, The Gun Room Press, Highland Park, NJ, 1983. 270 pp., illus. $39.95.
Covers every known type of primary and secondary martial firearms used by Federal forces.

U.S. Naval Handguns, 1808-1911, by Fredrick R. Winter, Andrew Mowbray Publishers, Lincoln, RI, 1990. 128 pp., illus. $26.00.
The story of U.S. Naval Handguns spans an entire century—included are sections on each of the important naval handguns within the period.

***Variations of the Smooth Bore H&R Handy Gun,** by Eric M. Larson, Eric M. Larson, Takoma Park, MD, 1993. 63 pp., illus. Paper covers. $10.00.
A pocket guide to the identification of the variations of the H&R Handy Gun.

Walther Models PP and PPK, 1929-1945, by James L. Rankin, assisted by Gary Green, James L. Rankin, Coral Gables, FL, 1974. 142 pp., illus. $35.00.
Complete coverage on the subject as to finish, proofmarks and Nazi Party inscriptions.

Walther P-38 Pistol, by Maj. George Nonte, Desert Publications, Cornville, AZ, 1982. 100 pp., illus. Paper covers. $9.95.
Complete volume on one of the most famous handguns to come out of WWII. All models covered.

Walther Volume II, Engraved, Presentation and Standard Models, by James L. Rankin, J.L. Rankin, Coral Gables, FL, 1977. 112 pp., illus. $35.00.
The new Walther book on embellished versions and standard models. Has 88 photographs, including many color plates.

Walther, Volume III, 1908-1980, by James L. Rankin, Coral Gables, FL, 1981. 226 pp., illus. $35.00.
Covers all models of Walther handguns from 1908 to date, includes holsters, grips and magazines.

Webley Revolvers, by Gordon Bruce and Christien Reinhart, Stocker-Schmid, Zurich, Switzerland, 1988. 256 pp., illus. $69.50.
A revised edition of Dowell's "Webley Story."

Westley Richards Guns and Rifles, a reprint of the Westley Richards firm's centennial catalog of 1912, by Armory Publications, Oceanside, CA, 1988. 211 pp., illus. Paper covers. $27.95.
A century of gun and rifle manufacture, 1812-1912.

The Whitney Firearms, by Claud Fuller, Standard Publications, Huntington, WV, 1946, 334 pp., many plates and drawings, $50.00.
An authoritative history of all Whitney arms and their maker. Highly recommended. An exclusive with Ray Riling Arms Books Co.

Winchester: An American Legend, by R.L. Wilson, Random House, New York, NY, 1991. 403 pp., illus. $65.00.
The official history of Winchester firearms from 1849 to the present.

The Winchester Book, by George Madis, David Madis Gun Book Distributor, Dallas, TX, 1986. 650 pp., illus. $45.50.
A new, revised 25th anniversary edition of this classic book on Winchester firearms. Complete serial ranges have been added.

Winchester Dates of Manufacture 1849-1984, by George Madis, Art & Reference House, Brownsboro, TX, 1984. 59 pp. $5.95.
A most useful work, compiled from records of the Winchester factory.

Winchester Engraving, by R.L. Wilson, Beinfeld Books, Springs, CA, 1989. 500 pp., illus. $115.00.
A classic reference work, of value to all arms collectors.

The Winchester Handbook, by George Madis, Art & Reference House, Lancaster, TX, 1982. 287 pp., illus. $19.95.
The complete line of Winchester guns, with dates of manufacture, serial numbers, etc.

The Winchester Model 94: The First 100 Years, by Robert C. Renneberg, Krause Publications, Iola, WI, 1991. 208 pp., illus. $34.95.
Covers the design and evolution from the early years up to the many different editions that exist today.

Winchester Slide-Action Rifles, Volume 1: Model 1890 & 1906, by Ned Schwing, Krause Publications, Iola, WI, 1992. 352 pp., illus. $39.95.
First book length treatment of models 1890 & 1906 with over 50 charts and tables showing significant new information about caliber style and rarity.

***Winchester Slide-Action Rifles, Volume 2: Model 61 & Model 62,** by Ned Schwing, Krause Publications, Iola, WI, 1993. 256 pp., illus. $34.95.
A complete historic look into the Model 61 and the Model 62. These favorite slide-action guns receive a thorough presentation which takes you to the factory to explore receivers, barrels, markings, stocks, stampings and engraving in complete detail.

Winchester's 30-30, Model 94, by Sam Fadala, Stackpole Books, Inc., Harrisburg, PA, 1986. 223 pp., illus. $24.95.
The story of the rifle America loves.

World War 2 Small Arms, by John Weeks, Chartwell Books, Inc., Secaucus, NJ, 1989. 144 pp., illus. $10.95.
Assesses the weapons of each of the major combatant nations, their production, history, design and features.

EDGED WEAPONS

A.G. Russell's Knife Trader's Guide, by A.G. Russell, Paul Wahl Corp., Bogata, NJ, 1991. 160 pp., illus. Paper covers. $10.00.
Recent sales prices of many popular collectible knives.

The American Eagle Pommel Sword: The Early Years 1793-1830, by Andrew Mowbray, Publisher, Lincoln, RI, 1988. 224 pp., illus. $45.00.
Provides an historical outline, a collecting structure and a vast new source of information for this rapidly growing field.

***American Indian Tomahawks,** by Harold L. Peterson, The Gun Room Press, Highland Park, NJ, 1993. 142 pp., illus. $49.95.
The tomahawk of the American Indian, in all its forms, as a weapon and as a tool.

American Knives; The First History and Collector's Guide, by Harold L. Peterson, The Gun Room Press, Highland Park, NJ, 1980. 178 pp., illus. $24.95.
A reprint of this 1958 classic. Covers all types of American knives.

American Primitive Knives 1770-1870, by G.B. Minnes, Museum Restoration Service, Ottawa, Canada, 1983. 112 pp., illus. $24.95.
Origins of the knives, outstanding specimens, structural details, etc.

American Socket Bayonets and Scabbards, by Robert M. Reilly, Andrew Mowbray, Inc., Lincoln, RI, 1990. 209 pp., illus. $40.00.
A comprehensive illustrated history of socket bayonets, scabbards and frogs in America from the Colonial period through the Civil War period.

The American Sword, 1775-1945, by Harold L. Peterson, Ray Riling Arms Books, Co., Phila., PA, 1980. 286 pp. plus 60 pp. of illus. $45.00.
1977 reprint of a survey of swords worn by U.S. uniformed forces, plus the rare "American Silver Mounted Swords, (1700-1815)."

***American Swords and Sword Makers,** by Richard H. Bezdek, Paladin Press, Boulder, CO, 1994. 648 pp., illus. $79.95.
The long-awaited definitive reference volume to American swords, sword makers and sword dealers from Colonial times to the present.

***The Arms and Armour of Arabia in the 18th-19th and 20th Centuries,** by Robert Elgood, Scolar Press, Brookfield, VT, 1994. 190 pp., illus. $99.50.
An outstanding documentary on this aspect of Arab culture. Examines surviving weapons, identifies new centers of manufacture and questions the origin of "Damascus" swords.

***Battle Blades: A Professional's Guide to Combat/Fighting Knives,** by Greg Walker; Foreword by Al Mar, Paladin Press, Boulder, CO, 1993. 168 pp., illus. $30.00.
The author evaluates daggers, Bowies, switchblades and utility blades according to their design, performance, reliability and cost.

The Book of the Sword, by Richard F. Burton, Dover Publications, New York, NY, 1987. 199 pp., illus. Paper covers.
Traces the swords origin from its birth as a charged and sharpened stick through diverse stages of development.

Borders Away, Volume 1: With Steel, by William Gilkerson, Andrew Mowbray, Inc., Lincoln, RI, 1991. 184 pp., illus. $48.00.

A comprehensive study of naval armament under fighting sail. This first voume covers axes, pikes and fighting blades in use between 1626-1826.

The Bowie Knife, by Raymond Thorp, Phillips Publications, Wiliamstown, NJ, 1992. 167 pp., illus. $9.95.

After forty-five years, the classic work on the Bowie knife is once again available.

Bowie Knives, by Robert Abels, Sherwood International Corp., Northridge, CA, 1988. 30 pp., illus. Paper covers. $14.95.

Reprint of the classic work on Bowie knives.

Collecting the Edged Weapons of Imperial Germany, by Thomas M. Johnson and Thomas T. Wittmann, Johnson Reference Books, Fredricksburg, VA, 1989. 363 pp., illus. $39.50.

An in-depth study of the many ornate military, civilian, and government daggers and swords of the Imperial era.

Collector's Guide to Ames U.S. Contract Military Edged Weapons: 1832-1906, by Ron G. Hickox, Pioneer Press, Union City, IN, 1993. 70 pp., illus. Paper covers. $14.95.

While this book deals primarily with edged weapons made by the Ames Manufacturing Company, this guide refers to other manufactureres of United States swords.

Collector's Handbook of World War 2 German Daggers, by LtC. Thomas M. Johnson, Johnson Reference Books, Fredericksburg, VA, 2nd edition, 1991. 252 pp., illus. Paper covers. $25.00.

Concise pocket reference guide to Third Reich daggers and accoutrements in a convenient format. With value guide.

The Complete Bladesmith: Forging Your Way to Perfection, by Jim Hrisoulas, Paladin Press, Boulder, CO, 1987. 192 pp., illus. $25.00.

Novice as well as experienced bladesmith will benefit from this definitive guide to smithing world-class blades.

The Craft of the Japanese Sword, by Leon & Hiroko Kapp, Yoshindo Yoshihara, Kodanska Interantional, Tokyo, Japan, 1990. 167 pp., illus. $34.95.

The first book in English devoted entirely to contemporary sword manufacturing in Japan.

Custom Knifemaking,55D by Tim McCreight, Stackpole Books, Inc., Harrisburg, PA, 1985. 224 pp., illus. $14.95.

Ten projects from a master craftsman.

*__German Clamshells and Other Bayonets,__ by G. Walker and R.J. Weinard, Johnson Reference Books, Fredericksburg, VA, 1994. 157 pp., illus. $22.50.

Includes unusual bayonets, many of which are shown for the first time. Current market values are listed.

*__German Military Fighting Knives 1914-1945,__ by Gordon A. Hughes, Johnson Reference Books, Fredericksburg, VA, 1992. 64 pp., illus. $24.50.

Documents the different types of German military fighting knives used during WWI and WWII, as well as examining examples produced during the inter-war years.

How to Make Knives, by Richard W. Barney & Robert W. Loveless, Beinfeld Publ., Inc., No. Hollywood, CA, 1977. 178 pp., illus. $17.95.

A book filled with drawings, illustrations, diagrams, and 500 how-to-do-it photos.

The Japanese Sword, by Kanzan Sato, Kodansha International Ltd. and Shibundo, Tokyo, Japan, 1983. 210 pp., illus. $29.95.

The history and appreciation of the Japanese sword, with a detailed examination of over a dozen of Japan's most revered blades.

Kentucky Knife Traders Manual No. 6, by R.B. Ritchie, Hindman, KY, 1980. 217 pp., illus. Paper covers. $10.00.

Guide for dealers, collectors and traders listing pocket knives and razor values.

Knife and Tomakawk Throwing: The Art of the Experts, by Harry K. McEvoy, Charles E. Tuttle, Rutland, VT, 1989. 150 pp., illus. Soft covers. $8.95.

The first book to employ side-by-side the fascinating art and science of knives and tomahawks.

Knifemaking, The Gun Digest Book of by Jack Lewis and Roger Combs, DBI Books, Inc., Northbrook, IL, 1989. 256 pp., illus. Paper covers. $15.95.

All the ins and outs from the world of knifemaking in a brand new book.

Knife Throwing a Practical Guide, by Harry K. McEvoy, Charles E. Tuttle Co., Rutland, VT, 1973. 108 pp., illus. Paper covers. $8.95.

If you want to learn to throw a knife this is the "bible."

Knives, 4th Edition, The Gun Digest Book of by Jack Lewis and Roger Combs, DBI Books, Inc., Northbook, IL, 1992. 256 pp., illus. Paper covers. $16.95.

All new edition covers practically every aspect of the knife world.

*__Knives '95, 15th Edition,__ by Ken Warner, DBI Books, Inc., Northbrook, IL, 1993. 304 pp., illus. Paper covers. $18.95.

Visual presentation of current factory and custom designs in straight and folding patterns, in swords, miniatures and commercial cutlery. (September, 1994)

Levine's Guide to Knives And Their Values, 3rd Edition, by Bernard Levine, DBI Books, Inc., Northbrook, IL, 1989. 512 pp., illus. Paper covers. $24.95.

All the basic tools for identifying, valuing and collecting folding and fixed blade knives.

The Master Bladesmith: Advanced Studies in Steel, by Jim Hrisoulas, Paladin Press, Boulder, CO, 1990. 296 pp., illus. $45.00.

The author reveals the forging secrets that for centuries have been protected by guilds.

Military Swords of Japan 1868-1945, by Richard Fuller and Ron Gregory, Arms and Armour Press, London, England, 1986. 127 pp., illus. Paper covers. $18.95.

A wide-ranging survey of the swords and dirks worn by the armed forces of Japan until the end of World War II.

*__Modern Combat Blades,__ by Duncan Long, Paladin Press, Boulder, CO, 1993. 128 pp., illus. $25.00.

Long discusses the pros and cons of bowies, bayonets, commando daggers, kukris, switchblades, butterfly knives, belt-buckle blades and many more.

On Damascus Steel, by Dr. Leo S. Figiel,Atlantis Arts Press, Atlantis, FL, 1991. 145 pp., illus. $65.00.

The historic, technical and artistic aspects of Oriental and mechanical Damascus. Persian and Indian sword blades, from 1600-1800, which have never been published, are illustrated.

Randall Made Knives: The History of the Man and the Blades, by Robert L. Gaddis, Paladin Press, Boulder, CO, 1993. 304 pp., illus. $50.00.

The authorized history of Bo Randall and his blades, told in his own words and those of the people who knew him best.

*__A Rebounding Lock for the Side-Hammer Gun,__ by Louis S. Cherepy Sr., Museum Restoration Service, Ontario, Canada, 1994. 116 pp., illus. $35.00.

The author traces the rebounding lock through its development from the percussion lock by illustrating all of the American and English patents for this type.

Rice's Trowel Bayonet, reprinted by Ray Riling Arms Books, Co., Phila., PA, 1968. 8 pp., illus. Paper covers. $3.00.

A facsimile reprint of a rare circular originally published by the U.S. government in 1875 for the information of U.S. troops.

The Samurai Sword, by John M. Yumoto, Charles E. Tuttle Co., Rutland, VT, 1958. 191 pp., illus. $21.95.

A must for anyone interested in Japanese blades, and the first book on this subject written in English.

Scottish Swords from the Battlefield at Culloden, by Lord Archibald Campbell, The Mowbray Co., Providence, RI, 1973. 63 pp., illus. $15.00.

A modern reprint of an exceedingly rare 1894 privately printed edition.

Secrets of the Samurai, by Oscar Ratti and Adele Westbrook, Charles E. Tuttle Co., Rutland, VT, 1983. 483 pp., illus. $35.00.

A survey of the martial arts of feudal Japan.

Sword of the Samurai, by George R. Parulski, Jr., Paladin Press, Boulder, CO, 1985. 144 pp., illus. $34.95.

The classical art of Japanese swordsmanship.

Swords for the Highland Regiments 1757-1784, by Anthony D. Darling, Andrew Mowbray, Inc., Publisher, Lincoln, RI, 1988. 62 pp., illus. $18.00.

The basket-hilted swords used by private highland regiments in the 18th century British army.

Swords from Public Collections in the Commonwealth of Pennsylvania, edited by Bruce S. Bazelon, Andrew Mowbray Inc., Lincoln, RI, 1987. 127 pp., illus. Paper covers. $12.00.

Contains new information regarding swordmakers of the Philadelphia area.

Swords of Germany 1900/1945, by John R. Angolia, Johnson Reference Books, Fredericksburg, VA, 1990. 460 pp., illus. $37.95.

If you have an interest in edged weapons of Imperial and Nazi Germany, this is a highly recommended book.

The Scottish Dirk, by James D. Forman, Museum Restoration Service, Bloomfield, Ont., Canada, 1991. 60 pp., illus. Paper covers. $4.95.

More than 100 dirks are illustrated with a text that sets the dirk and Sgian Dubh in their socio-historic content following design changes through more than 300 years of evolution.

Swords and Blades of the American Revolution, by George C. Neumann, Rebel Publishing Co., Inc., Texarkana, TX, 1991. 288 pp., illus. $35.95.

The encyclopedia of bladed weapons–swords, bayonets, spontoons, halberds, pikes, knives, daggers, axes–used by both sides, on land and sea, in America's struggle for independence.

Tomahawks Illustrated, by Robert Kuck, Robert Kuck, New Knoxville, OH, 1977. 112 pp., illus. Paper covers. $15.00.

A pictorial record to provide a reference in selecting and evaluating tomahawks.

World Bayonets, 1800 to the Present, by Anthony Carter, Sterling Publishing Co., New York, NY, 1990. 72 pp., illus. $24.95.

An incredible bayonet-fancier's buying encyclopedia. Includes buying and selling prices, plus over 250 closeup photos.

GENERAL

Advanced Muzzleloader's Guide, by Toby Bridges, Stoeger Publishing Co., So. Hackensack, NJ, 1985. 256 pp., illus. Paper covers. $14.95.

The complete guide to muzzle-loading rifles, pistols and shotguns—flintlock and percussion.

*__Air Gun Digest, 3nd Edition,__ by J.I. Galan, DBI Books, Inc., Northbrook, IL, 1995. 256 pp., illus. Paper covers. $16.95

Everything from A to Z on air gun history, trends and technology.

The AK47 Story, by Edward Ezell, Stackpole Books, Harrisburg, PA, 1988. 256 pp., illus. $16.95.

Evolution of the Kalashnikov weapons.

American Gunsmiths, by Frank M. Sellers, The Gun Room Press, Highland Park, NJ, 1983. 349 pp. $39.95.

A comprehensive listing of the American gun maker, patentee, gunsmith and entrepreneur.

American and Imported Arms, Ammunition and Shooting Accessories, Catalog No. 18 of the Shooter's Bible, Stoeger, Inc., reprinted by Fayette Arsenal, Fayetteville, NC, 1988. 142 pp., illus. Paper covers. $10.95.

A facsimile reprint of the 1932 Stoeger's Shooter's Bible.

America's Great Gunmakers, by Wayne van Zwoll, Stoeger Publishing Co., So. Hackensack, NJ, 1992. 288 pp., illus. Paper covers. $16.95.

This book traces in great detail the evolution of guns and ammunition in America and the men who formed the companies that produced them.

Archer's Digest, 5th Edition, edited by Roger Combs, DBI Books, Inc., Northbrook, IL, 1990. 256 pp., illus. Paper covers. $16.95.

Authoritative information on all facets of the archer's sport.

Armed and Female, by Paxton Quigley, E.P. Dutton, New York, NY, 1989. 237 pp., illus. $16.95.

The first complete book on one of the hottest subjects in the media today, the arming of the American woman.

Arms and Equipment of the British Army, 1886, edited by John Walter, Presidio Press, Novato, CA, 1991. $30.00.

Victorian military equipment from the Enfield to the Snider.

Arsenal of Freedom, The Springfield Armory, 1890-1948: A Year-by-Year Account Drawn from Official Records, compiled and edited by Lt. Col, William S. Brophy, USAR Ret., Andrew Mowbray, Inc., Lincoln, RI, 1991. 400 pp., illus. Soft covers. $29.95.

A "must buy" for all students of American military weapolns, equipment and accoutrements.

Assault Weapons, 3rd Edition, The Gun Digest Book of edited by Jack Lewis, DBI Books, Inc., Northbrook, IL, 1993. 256 pp., illus. Paper covers. $17.95.

An in-depth look at the history and uses of these arms.

Beginner's Guide to Guns and Shooting, Revised Edition, by Clair F. Rees, DBI Books, Inc., Northbrook, IL, 1988. 224 pp., illus. Paper covers. $15.95.

The "how to" book for beginning shooters. The perfect teaching tool for America's youth, the future of our sport, for novices of any age.

A Bibliography of American Sporting Books, compiled by John C. Phillips, James Cummins, Bookseller, New York, NY, 1991. 650 pp. Edition limited to 250 numbered copies. $75.00.

A reprinting of the very scarce 1930 edition originally published by the Boone & Crockett Club.

Black Powder Loading Manual, Revised Edition, The Gun Digest, by Sam Fadala, DBI Books, Inc., Northbrook, IL, 1991. 320 pp., illus. Paper covers. $16.95.

Revised and expanded edition of this landmark loading book first published in 1982. Covers 600 loads for 120 of the most popular blackpowder rifles, handguns and shotguns.

***The Blackpowder Notebook,** by Sam Fadala, Wolfe Publishing Co., Prescott, AZ, 1994. 212 pp., illus. $22.50.

For anyone interested in shooting muzzleloaders, this book will help improve scores and obtain accuracy and reliability.

Bows and Arrows of the Native Americans, by Jim Hamm, Lyons & Burford Publishers, New York, NY, 1991. 156 pp., illus. $19.95.

A complete step-by-step guide to wooden bows, sinew-backed bows, composite bows, strings, arrows and quivers.

Bowhunter's Digest, 3rd Edition, by Chuck Adams, DBI Books, Inc., Northbrook, IL, 1990. 288 pp., illus. Soft covers. $16.95.

All-new edition covers all the necessary equipment and how to use it, plus the fine points on how to improve your skill.

Cartridges of the World, 7th Edition, by Frank Barnes, edited by Mike Bussard, DBI Books, Inc., Northbrook, IL, 1993. 464 pp., illus. Paper covers. $21.95

Completely revised edition of the general purpose reference work for which collectors, police, scientists and laymen reach first for answers to cartridge identification questions.

Civil War Chief of Sharpshooters Hiram Berdan, Military Commander and Firearms Inventor, by Roy M. Marcot, Northwood Heritage Press, Irvine, CA, 1990. 400 pp., illus. $59.95.

Details the life and career of Col. Hiram Berdan and his U.S. Sharpshooters.

Combat Handgunnery, 3rd Edition, The Gun Digest Book of by Chuck Karwan, DBI Books, Inc., Northbrook, IL, 1992. 256 pp., illus. Paper covers. $16.95.

This all-new edition looks at real world combat handgunnery from three different perspectives–military, police and civilian.

Competitive Shooting, by A.A. Yuryev, introduction by Gary L. Anderson, NRA Books, The National Rifle Assoc. of America, Wash., DC, 1985. 399 pp., illus. $29.95.

A unique encyclopedia of competitive rifle and pistol shooting.

The Complete Black Powder Handbook, Revised Edition, by Sam Fadala, DBI Books, Inc., Northbrook, IL, 1990. 320 pp., illus. Soft covers. $17.95.

Expanded and refreshed edition of the definitive book on the subject of blackpowder.

Complete Book of Shooting: Rifles, Shotguns, Handguns, by Jack O'Connor, Stackpole Books, Harrisburg, PA, 1983. 392 pp., illus. $24.95.

A thorough guide to each area of the sport, appealing to those with a new or ongoing interest in shooting.

***The Complete Guide to Game Care and Cookery, 3rd Edition,** by Sam Fadala, DBI Books, Inc., Northbrook, IL, 1994. 320 pp., illus. Paper covers. $18.95.

Over 500 photos illustrating the care of wild game in the field and at home with a separate recipe section providing over 400 tested recipes. (September, 1994)

Corn-Fed Giants by Tom Miranda and Bernie Barringer, Moving Mountain Publishing, Crystal Lake, IA, 1993. 190 pp., illus.

A step-by-step guide to locating and harvesting whitetails in farmland.

Crossbows, Edited by Roger Combs, DBI Books, Inc., Northbrook, IL, 1986. 192 pp., illus. Paper covers. $14.95.

Complete, up-to-date coverage of the hottest bow going—and the most controversial.

Death from Above: The German FG42 Paratrooper Rifle, by Thomas B. Dugelby and R. Blake Stevens, Collector Grade Publications, Toronto, Canada, 1990. 147 pp., illus. $39.95.

The first comprehensive study of all seven models of the FG42.

The Emma Gees, by Herbert W. McBride, Lancer Publications, Mt. Ida, AR, 1988. 218 pp., illus. $18.95.

The author's service with the Machine Gun Section of the 21st Battalion Canadian Expeditionary Force in World War I.

Encyclopedia of Modern Firearms, Vol. 1, compiled and publ. by Bob Brownell, Montezuma, IA, 1959. 1057 pp. plus index, illus. $60.00. Dist. By Bob Brownell, Montezuma, IA 50171.

Massive accumulation of basic information of nearly all modern arms pertaining to "parts and assembly." Replete with arms photographs, exploded drawings, manufacturers' lists of parts, etc.

The Encyclopedia of Sporting Firearms, by David E. Petzal, Facts on File, New York, NY, 1992. 237 pp., illus. $50.00.

The best and most authoritative single-volume reference to handguns, rifles and shotguns now available.

Firearms Engraving as Decorative Art, by Dr. Fredric A. Harris, Barbara R. Harris, Seattle, WA, 1989. 172 pp., illus. $110.00.

The origin of American firearms engraving motifs in the decorative art of the Middle East. Illustrated with magnificent color photographs.

***Flayderman's Guide to Antique American Firearms...and Their Values, 6th Edition,** by Norm Flayderman, DBI Books, Inc., Northbrook, IL, 1994. 624 pp., illus. Paper covers. $29.95.

Updated edition of this bible of the antique gun field. (September, 1994)

The Frontier Rifleman, by H.B. LaCrosse Jr., Pioneer Press, Union City, TN, 1989. 183 pp., illus. Soft covers. $14.95.

The Frontier rifleman's clothing and equipment during the era of the American Revolution, 1760-1800.

***Gatling: A Photographic Remembrance,** by E. Frank Stephenson, Jr., Meherrin River Press, Murfreesboro, NC, 1994. 140 pp., illus. $25.00.

A new book on Richard Gatling and the Gatling Gun featuring 145 photographs, many rare and never before published.

The Gatling Gun: 19th Century Machine Gun to 21st Century Vulcan, by Joseph Berk, Paladin Press, Boulder, CO, 1991. 136 pp., illus. $29.95.

Here is the fascinating on-going story of a truly timeless weapon, from its beginnings during the Civil War to its current role as a state-of-the-art modern combat system.

Good Friends, Good Guns, Good Whiskey: The Selected Works of Skeeter Skelton, by Skeeter Skelton, PJS Publications, Peoria, IL, 1989. 347 pp. $21.95.

A guidebook to the world of Skeeter Skelton.

Great Shooters of the World, by Sam Fadala, Stoeger Publishing Co., So. Hackensack, NJ, 1991. 288 pp., illus. Paper covers. $18.95.

This book offers gun enthusiasts an overview of the men and women who have forged the history of firearms over the past 150 years.

Guerrilla Warfare Weapons, by Terry Gander, Sterling Publishing Co., Inc., 1990. 128 pp., illus. Paper covers. $9.95.

The latest and most sophisticated armaments of the modern underground fighter's armory.

***Gun Digest, 1995, 49th Edition,** edited by Ken Warner, DBI Books, Inc., Northbrook, IL, 1994. 544 pp., illus. Paper Covers. $21.95.

All-new edition of the world's best selling gun book; the only one to make the *USA Today* list of best-selling sports books.

***Gun Digest Treasury, 7th Edition,** edited by Harold A. Murtz, DBI Books, Inc., Northbrook, IL, 1994. 320 pp., illus. Paper covers. $16.95.

A collection of some of the most interesting articles which have appeared in Gun Digest over its first 45 years.

Gunshot Injuries: How They Are Inflicted, Their Complications and Treatment, by Col. Louis A. La Garde, 2nd revised edition, Lancer Militaria, Mt. Ida, AR, 1991. 480 pp., illus. $34.95.

A classic work which was the standard textbook on the subject at the time of World War I.

***Guns Illustrated, 1995, 27th Edition,** edited by Harold A. Murtz, DBI Books, Inc., Northbrook, IL, 1994. 336 pp., illus. Paper covers. $19.95.

Truly the Journal of Gun Buffs, this all-new edition consists of articles of interest to every shooter as well as a complete catalog of all U.S. and imported firearms with latest specs and prices.

Guns of the Empire, by George Markham, Arms & Armour Press, London, England, 1991. 160 pp., illus. $29.95

The firearms that carved out the worldwide British Empire come together in a riveting display of handguns, rifles, and automatics.

Guns of the Wild West, by George Markham, Arms & Armour Press, London, England, 1991. 160 pp., illus. $19.95.

The handguns, longarms and shotguns of the Gold Rush, the American Civil War, and the Armed Forces.

***Guns of the Wild West,** by George Markham, Sterling Publishing Co., New York, NY, 1993. 160 pp., illus. Paper covers. $19.95.

Firearms of the American Frontier, 1849-1917.

Gun Talk, edited by Dave Moreton, Winchester Press, Piscataway, NJ, 1973. 256 pp., illus. $9.95.

A treasury of original writing by the top gun writers and editors in America. Practical advice about every aspect of the shooting sports.

The Gun That Made the Twenties Roar, by Wm. J. Helmer, rev. and enlarged by George C. Nonte, Jr., The Gun Room Press, Highland Park, NJ, 1977. Over 300 pp., illus. $24.95.

Historical account of John T. Thompson and his invention, the infamous "Tommy Gun."

The Gunfighter, Man or Myth? by Joseph G. Rosa, Oklahoma Press, Norman, OK, 1969. 229 pp., illus. (including weapons). Paper covers. $12.95.

A well-documented work on gunfights and gunfighters of the West and elsewhere. Great treat for all gunfighter buffs.

Gunproof Your Children/Handgun Primer, by Massad Ayoob, Police Bookshelf, Concord, NH, 1989. Paper covers. $4.95.

Two books in one. The first, keeping children safe from unauthorized guns in their hands; the second, a compact introduction to handgun safety.

Guns & Shooting: A Selected Bibliography, by Ray Riling, Ray Riling Arms Books Co., Phila., PA, 1982. 434 pp., illus. Limited, numbered edition. $75.

A limited edition of this superb bibliographical work, the only modern listing of books devoted to guns and shooting.

Guns, Loads, and Hunting Tips, by Bob Hagel, Wolfe Publishing Co., Prescott, AZ, 1986. 509 pp., illus. $19.95.

A large hardcover book packed with shooting, hunting and handloading wisdom.

Guns of the Elite, by George Markham, Arms and Armour Press, Poole, England, 1987. 184 pp., illus. $24.95.

Special Forces firearms, 1940 to the present.

Guns of the First World War, Rifle, Handguns and Ammunition from the Text Book of Small Arms, 1909, edited by John Walter, Presidio Press, Novato, CA, 1991. $30.00.

Details of the Austro-Hung. Mann., French Lebels, German Mausers, U.S. Springfields, etc.

Guns of the Reich, by George Markham, Arms & Armour Press, London, England, 1989. 175 pp., illus. $24.95.

The pistols, rifles, submachine guns, machineguns and support weapons of the German armed forces, 1939-1945.

Gunshot Wounds, by Vincent J.M. DiMaio, M.D., Elsevier Science Publishing Co., New York, NY, 1985. 331 pp., illus. $70.00.

Practical aspects of firearms, ballistics, and forensic techniques.

Gun Trader's Guide, 16th Edition, published by Stoeger Publishing Co., S. Hackensack, NJ, 1993. 528 pp., illus. Paper covers. $18.95.

Complete guide to identification of modern firearms with current values.

***Gun Writers of Yesteryear,** compiled by James Foral, Wolfe Publishing Co., Prescott, AZ, 1993. 449 pp. $35.00.

Here, from the pre-American rifleman days of 1898-1920, are collected some 80 articles by 34 writers from eight magazines.

***Handguns '95, 7th Edition,** Edited by Hal Swiggett, DBI Books, Inc., Northbrook, IL, 1994. 352 pp., illus. Paper covers. $19.95

What's new in handguns plus informative and interesting articles on all aspects of handguns plus a complete catalog on all handguns currently on the market with prices.

***Handloader's Digest 1995, 14th Edition,** edited by Bob Bell, DBI Books, Inc., Northbrook, IL, 1994. 480 pp., illus. Paper covers. $21.95

Top writers in the field contribute helpful information on techniques and components. Greatly expanded and fully indexed catalog of all currently available tools, accessories and components for metallic, blackpowder cartridge, reloading and swaging.

"Hell, I Was There!," by Elmer Keith, Petersen Publishing Co., Los Angeles, CA, 1979. 308 pp., illus. $24.95.

Adventures of a Montana cowboy who gained world fame as a big game hunter.

***Il Grande Libro Delle Incision (Modern Engravings Real Book),** by Marco E. Nobili, Editrice Il Volo, Milano, Italy, 1992. 399 pp., illus. $95.00.

The best existing expressions of engravings on guns, knives and other items. Text in English and Italian.

Jim Dougherty's Guide to Bowhunting Deer, by Jim Dougherty, DBI Books, Inc., Northbrook, IL, 1992. 256 pp., illus. Paper covers. $16.95.

Dougherty sets down some important guidelines for bowhunting and bowhunting equipment.

***Knives '95, 15th Edition,** by Ken Warner, DBI Books, Inc., Northbrook, IL, 1993. 304 pp., illus. Paper covers. $18.95.

Visual presentation of current factory and custom designs in straight and folding patterns, in swords, miniatures and commercial cutlery. (September, 1994)

Lasers and Night Vision Devices, by Duncan Long, Desert Publications, El Dorado, AZ, 1993. 150 pp., illus. Paper covers. $29.95.

A comprehensive look at the evolution of devices that allow firearms to be operated in low light conditions and at night.

The Last Book: Confessions of a Gun Editor, by Jack O'Connor, Amwell Press, Clinton, NJ, 1984. 247 pp., illus. $30.00.

Jack's last book. Semi-autobiographical.

The Lewis Gun, by J. David Truby, Paladin Press, Boulder, CO, 1988. 206 pp., illus. $39.95.

The development and employment of this weapon throughout early decades of this century.

The Manufacture of Gunflints, by Sydney B.J. Skertchly, facsimile reprint with new introduction by Seymour de Lotbiniere, Museum Restoration Service, Ontario, Canada, 1984. 90 pp., illus. $24.50.

Limited edition reprinting of the very scarce London edition of 1879.

Master Tips, by J. Winokur, Potshot Press, Pacific Palisades, CA, 1985. 96 pp., illus. Paper covers. $11.95.

Basics of practical shooting.

Meditations on Hunting, by Jose Ortega y Gasset, Charles Scribner's Sons, New York, NY, 1985. 132 pp. Paper covers. $9.95.

Anticipates with profound accuracy the direction and basic formations of discipline which does not yet exist, a true ecology of men. A new printing of this 1942 classic.

Metallic Silhouette Shooting, 2nd Edition, The Gun Digest Book of by Elgin Gates, DBI Books, Inc., Northbrook, IL, 1988. 256 pp., illus. Paper covers. $16.95.

Examines all aspects of this fast growing sport including history, rules and meets.

Military Rifle & Machine Gun Cartridges, by Jean Huon, Paladin Press, Boulder, CO, 1990. 392 pp., illus. $34.95.

Describes the primary types of military cartridges and their principal loadings, as well as their characteristics, origin and use.

Military Small Arms of the 20th Century, 6th Edition, by Ian V. Hogg, DBI Books, Inc., Northbrook, IL, 1991. 352 pp., illus. Paper covers. $19.95.

Fully revised and updated edition of the standard reference in its field.

Modern Gun Values, The Gun Digest Book of 9th Edition, Edited by Jack Lewis, DBI Books, Inc., Northbrook, IL, illus. Paper covers. $20.95.

Updated and expanded edition of the book that has become the standard for valuing modern firearms.

***Modern Gun Values, The Gun Digest Book of** 10th Edition, Edited by Joe Schroeder, DBI Books, Inc., Northbrook, IL., illus. Paper covers.

Updated and expanded edition of the book that has become the standard for valuing modern firearms. (February '95)

Modern Law Enforcement Weapons & Tactics, 2nd Edition, by Tom Ferguson, DBI Books, Inc., Northbrook, IL, 1991. 256 pp., illus. Paper covers. $17.95.

An in-depth look at the weapons and equipment used by law enforcement agencies of today.

The More Complete Cannoneer, by M.C. Switlik, Museum & Collectors Specialties Co., Monroe, MI, 1990. 199 pp., illus. $19.95.

Compiled agreeably to the regulations for the U.S. War Department, 1861, and containing current observations on the use of antique cannon.

L.D. Nimschke Firearms Engraver, by R.L. Wilson, R&R Books, Livonia, NY, 1992. 108 pp., illus. $100.00.

The personal work record of one of the 19th century America's foremost engravers. Augmented by a comprehensive text, photographs of deluxe-engraved firearms, and detailed indexes.

No Second Place Winner, by Wm. H. Jordan, publ. by the author, Shreveport, LA (Box 4072), 1962. 114 pp., illus. $15.95.

Guns and gear of the peace officer, ably discussed by a U.S. Border Patrolman for over 30 years, and a first-class shooter with handgun, rifle, etc.

Outdoor Life Gun Data Book, by F. Philip Rice, Outdoor Life Books, New York, NY, 1987. 412 pp., illus. $27.95.

All the facts and figures that hunters, marksmen, handloaders and other gun enthusiasts need to know.

***The Owen Gun,** by Wayne Wardman, Wayne Wardman, Curtain, Australia, 1991. 209 pp., illus. $42.50.

The story of the Owen gun and its rise to the pinnacle of success to be recognized as the world's best submachine gun of its time.

Pin Shooting: A Complete Guide, by Mitchell A. Ota, Wolfe Publishing Co., Prescott, AZ, 1992. 145 pp., illus. Paper covers. $14.95.

Traces the sport from its humble origins to today's thoroughly enjoyable social event, including the mammoth eight-day Second Chance Pin Shoot in Michigan.

E.C. Prudhomme, Master Gun Engraver, A Retrospective Exhibition: 1946-1973, intro. by John T. Amber, The R. W. Norton Art Gallery, Shreveport, LA, 1973. 32 pp., illus. Paper covers. $9.95.

Examples of master gun engravings by Jack Prudhomme.

A Rifleman Went to War, by H. W. McBride, Lancer Militaria, Mt. Ida, AR, 1987. 398 pp., illus. $24.95.

The classic account of practical marksmanship on the battlefields of World War I.

Second to None, edited by John Culler and Chuck Wechsler, Live Oak Press, Inc., Camden, SC, 1988. 227 pp., illus. $39.95.

The most popular articles from *Sporting Classics* magazine on great sporting firearms.

Shooter's Bible, 1940, Stoeger Arms Corp., Stoeger, Inc., So. Hackensack, NJ, 1990. 512 pp., illus. Soft covers. $16.95.

Reprint of the Stoeger Arms Corp. catalog No. 33 of 1940.

***Shooter's Bible 1995, No. 86,** edited by William S. Jarrett, Stoeger Publishing Co., So. Hackensack, NJ, 1993. 576 pp., illus. Paper covers. $19.95.

"The world's standard firearms reference book."

***Shooting,** by J.H. FitzGerald, Wolfe Publishing Co., Prescott, AZ, 1993. 421 pp., illus. $29.00.

This is a classic book and reference for anyone interested in pistol and revolver shooting.

Shooting, by Edward A. Matunas, Stackpole Books, Harrisburg, PA, 1986. 416 pp., illus. $31.95.

How to become an expert marksman with rifle, shotgun, handgun, muzzle loader and bow.

Shots Fired in Anger, by Lt. Col. John George, The National Rifle Association of America, Washington, D.C., 2nd printing, 1991. 535 pp., illus. $19.95.

A rifleman's view of the war in the Pacific, 1942-45.

Sniping in France, by Major H. Hesketh-Prichard, Lancer Militaria, Mt. Ida, AR, 1993. 224 pp., illus. $24.95.

The author was a well-known British adventurer and big game hunter. He was called upon in the early days of "The Great War" to develop a program to offset an initial German advantage in sniping. How the British forces came to overcome this advantage.

The SPIW: Deadliest Weapon that Never Was, by R. Blake Stevens, and Edward C. Ezell, Collector Grade Publications, Inc., Toronto, Canada, 1985. 138 pp., illus. $29.95.

The complete saga of the fantastic flechette-firing Special Purpose Individual Weapon.

Steindler's New Firearms Dictionary, by R.A. Steindler, Stackpole Books, Inc., Harrisburg, PA, 1985. 320 pp., illus. $24.95.

Completely revised and updated edition of this standard work.

The Street Smart Gun Book, by John Farnam, Police Bookshelf, Concord, NH, 1986. 45 pp., illus. Paper covers. $11.95.

Weapon selection, defensive shooting techniques, and gunfight-winning tactics from one of the world's leading authorities.

Stress Fire, Vol. 1: Stress Fighting for Police, by Massad Ayoob, Police Bookshelf, Concord, NH, 1984. 149 pp., illus. Paper covers. $9.95.

Gunfighting for police, advanced tactics and techniques.

Survival Guns, by Mel Tappan, Desert Publications, El Dorado, AZ, 1993. 456 pp., illus. Paper covers. $21.95.

Discusses in a frank and forthright manner which handguns, rifles and shotguns to buy for personal defense and securing food, and the ones to avoid.

Thompson Guns 1921-1945, Anubis Press, Houston, TX, 1980. 215 pp., illus. Paper covers. $11.95.

Facsimile reprinting of five complete manuals on the Thompson submachine gun.

Triggernometry, by Eugene Cunningham, Caxton Printers Ltd., Caldwell, ID, 1970. 441 pp., illus. $17.95.

A classic study of famous outlaws and lawmen of the West—their stature as human beings, their exploits and skills in handling firearms. A reprint.

U.S. Marine Corp Rifle and Pistol Marksmanship, 1935, reprinting of a government publication, Lancer Militaria, Mt. Ida, AR, 1991. 99 pp., illus. Paper covers. $11.95.

The old corps method of precision shooting.

U.S. Marine Corps Scout/Sniper Training Manual, Lancer Militaria, Mt. Ida, AR, 1989. Soft covers. $14.95.

Reprint of the original sniper training manual used by the Marksmanship Training Unit of the Marine Corps Development and Education Command in Quantico, Virginia.

U.S. Marine Corps Sniping, Lancer Militaria, Mt. Ida, AR, 1989. Irregular pagination. Soft covers. $14.95.

A reprint of the official Marine Corps FMFM1-3B.

Unrepentant Sinner, by Charles Askins, Tejano Publications, San Antonio, TX, 1985. 322 pp., illus. Soft covers. $17.95.

The autobiography of Colonel Charles Askins.

Weapons of the Waffen-SS, by Bruce Quarrie, Sterling Publishing Co., Inc., 1991. 168 pp., illus. $24.95.

An in-depth look at the weapons that made Hitler's Waffen-SS the fearsome fighting machine it was.

Weatherby: The Man, The Gun, The Legend, by Grits and Tom Gresham, Cane River Publishing Co., Natchitoches, LA, 1992. 290 pp., illus. $24.95.

A fascinating look at the life of the man who changed the course of firearms development in America.

The Winchester Era, by David Madis, Art & Reference House, Brownsville, TX, 1984. 100 pp., illus. $14.95.

Story of the Winchester company, management, employees, etc.

With British Snipers to the Reich, by Capt. C. Shore, Lander Militaria, Mt. Ida, AR, 1988. 420 pp., illus. $24.95.

One of the greatest books ever written on the art of combat sniping.

You Can't Miss, by John Shaw and Michael Bane, John Shaw, Memphis, TN, 1983. 152 pp., illus. Paper covers. $12.95.

The secrets of a successful combat shooter; how to better defensive shooting skills.

GUNSMITHING

The Art of Engraving, by James B. Meek, F. Brownell & Son, Montezuma, IA, 1973. 196 pp., illus. $33.95.

A complete, authoritative, imaginative and detailed study in training for gun engraving. The first book of its kind—and a great one.

Artistry in Arms, The R. W. Norton Gallery, Shreveport, LA, 1970. 42 pp., illus. Paper covers. $9.95.

The art of gunsmithing and engraving.

Barrels & Actions, by Harold Hoffman, H&P Publishers, San Angelo, TX, 1990. 309 pp., illus. Sprial bound. $25.95.

A manual on barrel making.

Black Powder Hobby Gunsmithing, by Sam Fadala and Dale Storey, DBI Books, Inc., Northbrook, IL., 1994. 256 pp., illus. Paper covers. $17.95.

A how-to guide for gunsmithing blackpowder pistols, rifles and shotguns from two men at the top of their respective fields.

Checkering and Carving of Gun Stocks, by Monte Kennedy, Stackpole Books, Harrisburg, PA, 1962. 175 pp., illus. $34.95.

Revised, enlarged cloth-bound edition of a much sought-after, dependable work.

The Colt .45 Automatic Shop Manual, by Jerry Kuhnhausen, VSP Publishers, McCall, ID, 1987. 200 pp., illus. Paper covers. $19.95.

Covers repairing, accurizing, trigger/sear work, action tuning, springs, bushings, rebarreling, and custom .45 modification.

The Colt Double Action Revolvers: A Shop Manual, Volume 1, by Jerry Kuhnhausen, VSP Publishers, McCall, ID, 1988. 224 pp., illus. Paper covers. $22.95.

Covers D, E, and I frames.

The Colt Double Action Revolvers: A Shop Manual, Volume 2, by Jerry Kuhnhausen, VSP Publishers, McCall, ID, 1988. 156 pp., illus. Paper covers. $17.95.

Covers J, V, and AA models.

The Complete Metal Finishing Book, by Harold Hoffman, H&P Publishers, San Angelo, TX, 1992. 364 pp., illus. Paper covers. $28.95.

Instructions for the different metal finishing operations that the normal craftsman or shop will use. Primarily firearm related.

Exploded Handgun Drawings, The Gun Digest Book of edited by Harold A. Murtz, DBI Books, Inc., Northbrook, IL. 1992. 512 pp., illus. Paper covers. $19.95.

Exploded or isometric drawings for 494 of the most popular handguns.

Exploded Long Gun Drawings, The Gun Digest Book of edited by Harold A. Murtz, DBI Books, Inc., Northbrook, IL. 512 pp., illus. Paper covers. $19.95.

Containing almost 500 rifle and shotgun exploded drawings. An invaluable aid to both professionals and hobbyists.

***The Finishing of Gun Stocks,** by Harold Hoffman, H&P Publishing, San Angelo, TX, 1993. 98 pp. Paper covers. $15.95.

This book explains all the processes of finish and finishing.

Firearms Assembly/Disassembly, Part I: Automatic Pistols, Revised Edition, The Gun Digest Book of by J.B. Wood, DBI Books, Inc., Northbrook, IL, 1990. 480 pp., illus. Soft covers. $18.95.

Covers 58 popular autoloading pistols plus nearly 200 variants of those models integrated into the text and completely cross-referenced in the index.

Firearms Assembly/Disassembly Part II: Revolvers, Revised Edition, The Gun Digest Book of by J.B. Wood, DBI Books, Inc., Northbrook, IL, 1990. 480 pp., illus. Soft covers. $18.95.

Covers 49 popular revolvers plus 130 variants. The most comprehensive and professional presentation available to either hobbyist or gunsmith.

Firearms Assembly/Disassembly Part III: Rimfire Rifles, Revised Edition, The Gun Digest Book of by J. B. Wood, DBI Books, Inc., Northbrook, IL., 1994. 480 pp., illus. Paper covers. $18.95.

Greatly expanded edition covering 65 popular rimfire rifles plus over 100 variants all completely cross-referenced in the index.

Firearms Assembly/Disassembly Part IV: Centerfire Rifles, Revised Edition, The Gun Digest Book of by J.B. Wood, DBI Books, Inc., Northbrook, IL, 1991. 480 pp., illus. Paper covers. $18.95.

Covers 54 popular centerfire rifles plus 300 variants. The most comprehensive and professional presentation available to either hobbyist or gunsmith.

Firearms Assembly/Disassembly, Part V: Shotguns, Revised Edition, The Gun Digest Book of by J.B. Wood, DBI Books, Inc., Northbrook, IL, 1992. 480 pp., illus. Paper covers. $18.95.

Covers 46 popular shotguns plus over 250 variants with step-by-step instructions on how to dismantle and reassemble each. The most comprehensive and professional presentation available to either hobbyist or gunsmith.

Firearms Assembly/Disassembly Part VI: Law Enforcement Weapons, The Gun Digest Book of by J.B. Wood, DBI Books, Inc., Northbrook, IL, 1981. 288 pp., illus. Paper covers. $15.95.

Step-by-step instructions on how to completely dismantle and reassemble the most commonly used firearms found in law enforcement arsenals.

Firearms Assembly 3: The NRA Guide to Rifle and Shotguns, NRA Books, Wash., DC, 1980. 264 pp., illus. Paper covers. $13.95.

Text and illustrations explaining the takedown of 125 rifles and shotguns, domestic and foreign.

Firearms Assembly 4: The NRA Guide to Pistols and Revolvers, NRA Books, Wash., DC, 1980. 253 pp., illus. Paper covers. $13.95.

Text and illustrations explaining the takedown of 124 pistol and revolver models, domestic and foreign.

Firearms Bluing and Browning, By R.H. Angier, Stackpole Books, Harrisburg, PA. 151 pp., illus. $16.95.

A world master gunsmith reveals his secrets of building, repairing and renewing a gun, quite literally, lock, stock and barrel. A useful, concise text on chemical coloring methods for the gunsmith and mechanic.

First Book of Gunsmithing, by John E. Traister, Stackpole Books, Harrisburg, PA, 1981. 192 pp., illus. $18.95.

Beginner's guide to gun care, repair and modification.

Guns and Gunmaking Tools of Southern Appalachia, by John Rice Irwin, Schiffer Publishing Ltd., 1983. 118 pp., illus. Paper covers. $9.95.

The story of the Kentucky rifle.

Gunsmithing Tips and Projects, a collection of the best articles from the *Handloader* and *Rifle* magazines, by various authors, Wolfe Publishing Co., Prescott, AZ, 1992. 443 pp., illus. Paper covers. $25.00.

Includes such subjects as shop, stocks, actions, tuning, triggers, barrels, customizing, etc.

Gunsmith Kinks, by F.R. (Bob) Brownell, F. Brownell & Son, Montezuma, IA, 1st ed., 1969. 496 pp., well illus. $18.95.

A widely useful accumulation of shop kinks, short cuts, techniques and pertinent comments by practicing gunsmiths from all over the world.

Gunsmith Kinks 2, by Bob Brownell, F. Brownell & Son, Publishers, Montezuma, IA, 1983. 496 pp., illus. $18.95.

A collection of gunsmithing knowledge, shop kinks, new and old techniques, shortcuts and general know-how straight from those who do them best—the gunsmiths.

*****Gunsmith Kinks 3**, edited by Frank Brownell, Brownells Inc., Montezuma, IA, 1993. 504 pp., illus. $19.95.

Tricks, knacks and "kinks" by professional gunsmiths and gun tinkerers. Hundreds of valuable ideas are given in this volume.

Gunsmithing, by Roy F. Dunlap, Stackpole Books, Harrisburg, PA, 1990. 742 pp., illus. $29.95.

A manual of firearm design, construction, alteration and remodeling. For amateur and professional gunsmiths and users of modern firearms.

Gunsmithing at Home, by John E. Traister, Stoeger Publishing Co., So. Hackensack, NJ, 1985. 256 pp., illus. Paper covers. $14.95.

Over 25 chapters of explicit information on every aspect of gunsmithing.

The Gunsmith's Manual, by J.P. Stelle and Wm. B. Harrison, The Gun Room Press, Highland Park, NJ, 1982. 376 pp., illus. $19.95.

For the gunsmith in all branches of the trade.

The Mauser M91 Through M98 Bolt Actions: A Shop Manual, by Jerry Kuhnhausen, VSP Books, McCall, ID, 1991. 224 pp., illus. Paper covers. $22.95.

An essential book if you work on or plan to work on a Mauser action.

The NRA Gunsmithing Guide—Updated, by Ken Raynor and Brad Fenton, National Rifle Association, Wash., DC, 1984. 336 pp., illus. Paper covers. $15.95.

Material includes chapters and articles on all facets of the gunsmithing art.

Pistolsmithing, The Gun Digest Book of, by Jack Mitchell, DBI Books, Inc., Northbrook, IL, 1980. 256 pp., illus. Paper covers. $15.95.

An expert's guide to the operation of each of the handgun actions with all the major functions of pistolsmithing explained.

Pistolsmithing, by George C. Nonte, Jr., Stackpole Books, Harrisburg, PA, 1974. 560 pp., illus. $29.95.

A single source reference to handgun maintenance, repair, and modification at home, unequaled in value.

Practical Gunsmithing, by Edward A. Matunas, Stackpole Books, Harrisburg, PA, 1989. 352 pp., illus. $31.95.

A complete guide to maintaining, repairing, and improving firearms.

Recreating the American Longrifle, by William Buchele, et al., George Shumway, Publisher, York, PA, 1983. 175 pp., illus. Paper covers. $20.00.

Includes full-scale plans for building a Kentucky rifle.

The Remington M870 and M1100/M11-87 Shotguns: A Shop Manual, by Jerry Kuhnhausen, VSP Publishers, McCall, ID, 1992. 226 pp., illus. Paper covers. $26.95.

Covers everything about gunsmithing the most popular Remington shotguns from fitting a recoil pad to installing choke tubes, and everything in between.

Riflesmithing, The Gun Digest Book of, by Jack Mitchell, DBI Books, Inc., Northbrook, IL, 1982. 256 pp., illus. Paper covers. $15.95.

The art and science of rifle gunsmithing. Covers tools, techniques, designs, finishing wood and metal, custom alterations.

Ruger Double Action Revolvers, Vol. 1, Shop Manual, by Jerry Kuhnhausen, VSP Publishers, McCall, ID, 1989. 176 pp., illus. Soft covers. $18.95.

Covers the Ruger Six series of revolvers: Security-Six, Service-Six, and Speed-Six. Includes step-by-step function checks, disassembly, inspection, repairs, rebuilding, reassembly, and custom work.

The S&W Revolver: A Shop Manual, by Jerry Kuhnhausen, VSP Publishers, McCall, ID, 1987. 152 pp., illus. Paper covers. $17.95.

Covers accurizing, trigger jobs, action tuning, rebarreling, barrel setback, forcing cone angles, polishing and rebluing.

Shotgun Gunsmithing, The Gun Digest Book of, by Ralph Walker, DBI Books, Inc., Northbrook, IL, 1983. 256 pp., illus. Paper covers. $15.95.

The principles and practices of repairing, individualizing and accurizing modern shotguns by one of the world's premier shotgun gunsmiths.

*****The Story of Pope's Barrels**, by Ray M. Smith, R&R Books, Livonia, NY, 1993. 203 pp., illus. $39.00.

A reissue of a 1960 book whose author knew Pope personally. It will be of special interest to Schuetzen rifle fans, since Pope's greatest days were at the height of the Schuetzen-era before WWI.

Survival Gunsmithing, by J.B. Wood, Desert Publications, Cornville, AZ, 1986. 92 pp., illus. Paper covers. $9.95.

A guide to repair and maintenance of the most popular rifles, shotguns and handguns.

The Trade Gun Sketchbook, by Charles E. Hanson, The Fur Press, Chadron, NE, 1979. 48 pp., illus. Paper covers. $9.95.

Complete full-size plans to build seven different trade guns from the Revolution to the Indian Wars and a two-thirds size for your son.

The Trade Rifle Sketchbook, by Charles E. Hanson, The Fur Press, Chadron, NE, 1979. 48 pp., illus. Paper covers. $9.95.

Includes full-scale plans for 10 rifles made for Indian and mountain men; from 1790 to 1860, plus plans for building three pistols.

HANDGUNS

Black Powder Hobby Gunsmithing, by Sam Fadala and Dale Storey, DBI Books, Inc., Northbrook, IL., 1994. 256 pp., illus. Paper covers. $17.95.

A how-to guide for gunsmithing blackpowder pistols, rifles and shotguns from two men at the top of their respective fields.

Blue Steel and Gun Leather, by John Bianchi, Beinfeld Publishing, Inc., No. Hollywood, CA, 1978. 200 pp., illus. $19.95.

A complete and comprehensive review of holster uses plus an examination of available products on today's market.

Browning Hi-Power Pistols, Desert Publications, Cornville, AZ, 1982. 20 pp., illus. Paper covers. $9.00.

Covers all facets of the various military and civilian models of the Browning Hi-Power pistol.

Colt Automatic Pistols, by Donald B. Bady, Borden Publ. Co., Alhambra, CA, 1974, 368 pp., illus. $19.95.

The rev. and enlarged ed. of a key work on a fascinating subject. Complete information on every automatic marked with Colt's name.

The Colt .45 Auto Pistol, compiled from U.S. War Dept. Technical Manuals, and reprinted by Desert Publications, Cornville, AZ, 1978. 80 pp., illus. Paper covers. $9.95.

Covers every facet of this famous pistol from mechanical training, manual of arms, disassembly, repair and replacement of parts.

Combat Handgunnery, 3rd Edition, The Gun Digest Book of by Chuck Karwan, DBI Books, Inc., Northbrook, IL, 1992. 256 pp., illus. Paper covers. $16.95.

This all-new edition looks at real world combat handgunnery from three different perspectives—military, police and civilian.

Combat Pistols, by Terry Gander, Sterling Publishing Co., Inc., 1991. Paper covers. $9.95.

The world's finest and deadliest pistols are shown close-up, with detailed specifications, muzzle velocity, rate of fire, ammunition, etc.

*****Combat Raceguns: The World's Best Custom Pistols**, by J.M. Ramos, Paladin Press, Boulder, CO, 1994. 168 pp., illus. Paper covers. $25.00.

Learn how to put together your own precision combat racegun with the best compensators, frames, controls, sights and custom accessories.

The Complete Book of Combat Handgunning, by Chuck Taylor, Desert Publications, Cornville, AZ, 1982. 168 pp., illus. Paper covers. $16.95.

Covers virtually every aspect of combat handgunning.

Competitive Pistol Shooting, by Laslo Antal, A&C Black, Cambs, England, 1989. 176 pp., illus. Soft covers. $24.00.

Covers free pistol, air pistol, rapid fire, etc.

The Custom Government Model Pistol, by Layne Simpson, Wolfe Publishing Co., Prescott, AZ, 1992. 639 pp., illus. $24.50.

This book is about one of the world's greatest firearms and the things pistolsmiths do to make it even better.

The CZ-75 Family: The Ultimate Combat Handgun, by J.M. Ramos, Paladin Press, Boulder, CO, 1990. 100 pp., illus. Soft covers. $16.00.

And in-depth discussion of the early-and-late model CZ-75s, as well as the many newest additions to the Czech pistol family.

Experiments of a Handgunner, by Walter Roper, Wolfe Publishing Co., Prescott, AZ, 1989. 202 pp., illus. $37.00.

A limited edition reprint. A listing of experiments with functioning parts of handguns, with targets, stocks, rests, handloading, etc.

Exploded Handgun Drawings, The Gun Digest Book of, edited by Harold A. Murtz, DBI Books, Inc., Northbrook, IL. 1992. 512 pp., illus. Paper covers. $19.95.

Exploded or isometric drawings for 494 of the most popular handguns.

Fast and Fancy Revolver Shooting, by Ed. McGivern, Anniversary Edition, Winchester Press, Piscataway, NJ, 1984. 484 pp., illus. $18.95.

A fascinating volume, packed with handgun lore and solid information by the acknowledged dean of revolver shooters.

Firearms Assembly/Disassembly, Part I: Automatic Pistols, Revised Edition, The Gun Digest Book of, by J.B. Wood, DBI Books, Inc., Northbrook, IL, 1990. 480 pp., illus. Soft covers. $18.95.

Covers 58 popular autoloading pistols plus nearly 200 variants of those models integrated into the text and completely cross-referenced in the index.

Firearms Assembly/Disassembly, Part II: Revolvers, Revised Edition, The Gun Digest Book of, by J.B. Wood, DBI Books, Inc., Northbrook, IL, 1990. 480 pp., illus. Soft covers. $18.95.

Covers 49 popular revolvers plus 130 variants. The most comprehensive and professional presentation available to either hobbyist or gunsmith.

.45 ACP Super Guns, by J.M. Ramos, Paladin Press, Boulder, CO, 1991. 144 pp., illus. Paper covers. $20.00.

Modified .45 automatic pistols for competition, hunting and personal defense.

The .45, The Gun Digest Book of by Dean A. Grennell, DBI Books, Inc., Northbrook, IL, 1989. 256 pp., illus. Paper covers. $16.95.

Definitive work on one of America's favorite calibers.

*****Glock: The New Wave in Combat Handguns**, by Peter Alan Kasler, Paladin Press, Boulder, CO, 1993. 304 pp., illus. $25.00.

In this book the author debunks the myths that surround what is the most innovative handgun to be introduced in some time.

***Great Combat Handguns,** by Leroy Thompson and Rene Smeets, Sterling Publishing Co., New York, NY, 1993. 256 pp., illus. $29.95.

Fully revised, updated and newly designed edition of the successful classic in handgun use and reference.

Handgun Digest, 2nd Edition, by Dean A. Grennell, DBI Books, Inc., Northbrook, IL, 1991. 256 pp., illus. Paper covers. $16.95.

Full coverage of all aspects of handguns and handgunning from a highly readable, knowledgeable author.

Handgun Reloading, The Gun Digest Book of, by Dean A. Grennell and Wiley M. Clapp, DBI Books, Inc., Northbrook, IL, 1987. 256 pp., illus. Paper covers. $15.95.

Detailed discussions of all aspects of reloading for handguns, from basic to complex. New loading data.

***Handguns '95, 7th Edition,** Edited by Hal Swiggett, DBI Books, Inc., Northbrook, IL, 1994. 352 pp., illus. Paper covers. $19.95

What's new in handguns plus informative and interesting articles on all aspects of handguns plus a complete catalog on all handguns currently on the market with prices.

High Standard Automatic Pistols 1932-1950, by Charles E. Petty, The Gunroom Press, Highland Park, NJ, 1989. 124 pp., illus. $19.95.

A definitive source of information for the collector of High Standard arms.

How to Become a Master Handgunner: The Mechanics of X-Count Shooting, by Charles Stephens, Paladin Press, Boulder, CO, 1993. 64 pp., illus. Paper covers. $10.00.

Offers a simple formula for success to the handgunner who strives to master the technique of shooting accurately.

Hunting for Handgunners, by Larry Kelly and J.D. Jones, DBI Books, Inc., Northbrook, IL, 1990. 256 pp., illus. Paper covers. $16.95.

Covers the entire spectrum of hunting with handguns in an amusing, easy-flowing manner that combines entertainment with solid information.

Instinct Combat Shooting, by Chuck Klein, Chuck Klein, The Goose Creek, IN, 1989. 49 pp., illus. Paper covers. $12.00.

Defensive handgunning for police.

Know Your Czechoslovakian Pistols, by R.J. Berger, Blacksmith Corp., Chino Valley, AZ, 1989. 96 pp., illus. Soft covers. $9.95.

A comprehensive reference which presents the fascinating story of Czech pistols.

Know Your 45 Auto Pistols—Models 1911 & A1, by E.J. Hoffschmidt, Blacksmith Corp., Southport, CT, 1974. 58 pp., illus. Paper covers. $9.95.

A concise history of the gun with a wide variety of types and copies.

Know Your Walther P.38 Pistols, by E.J. Hoffschmidt, Blacksmith Corp., Southport, CT, 1974. 77 pp., illus. Paper covers. $9.95.

Covers the Walther models Armee, M.P., H.P., P.38—history and variations.

Know Your Walther PP & PPK Pistols, by E.J. Hoffschmidt, Blacksmith Corp., Southport, CT, 1975. 87 pp., illus. Paper covers. $9.95.

A concise history of the guns with a guide to the variety and types.

Luger Variations, by Harry E. Jones, Harry E. Jones, Torrance, CA, 1975. 328 pp., 160 full page illus., many in color. $45.00.

A rev. ed. of the book known as "The Luger Collector's Bible."

The Mauser Self-Loading Pistol, by Belford & Dunlap, Borden Publ. Co., Alhambra, CA. Over 200 pp., 300 illus., large format. $24.95.

The long-awaited book on the "Broom Handles," covering their inception in 1894 to the end of production. Complete and in detail: pocket pistols, Chinese and Spanish copies, etc.

Metallic Silhouette Shooting, 2nd Edition, The Gun Digest Book of, by Elgin Gates, DBI Books, Inc., Northbrook, IL, 1988. 256 pp., illus. Paper covers. $16.95.

All about the rapidly growing sport. With a history and rules of the International Handgun Metallic Silhouette Association.

Modern American Pistols and Revolvers, by A.C. Gould, Wolfe Publishing Co., Prescott, AZ, 1988. 222 pp., illus. $37.00.

A limited edition reprint. An account of the development of those arms as well as the manner of shooting them.

The Modern Technique of the Pistol, by Gregory Boyce Morrison, Gunsite Press, Paulden, AZ, 1991. 153 pp., illus. $45.00.

The theory of effective defensive use of modern handguns.

9mm Handguns, 2nd Edition, The Gun Digest Book of, edited by Steve Comus, DBI Books, Inc., Northbrook, IL, 1993. 256 pp., illus. Paper covers. $17.95.

Covers the 9mmP cartridge and the guns that have been made for it in greater depth than any other work available.

9mm Parabellus; The History & Developement of the World's 9mm Pistols & Ammunition, by Klaus-Peter Konig and Martin Hugo, Schiffer Publishing Ltd., Atglen, PA, 1993. 304 pp., illus. $39.95.

Detailed history of 9mm weapons from Belguim, Italy, Germany, Israel, France, USA, Czechoslovakia, Hungary, Poland, Brazil, Finland and Spain.

P-38 Automatic Pistol, by Gene Gangarosa, Jr., Stoeger Publishing Co., S. Hackensack, NJ, 1993. 272 pp., illus. Paper covers. $16.95

This book traces the origins and development of the P-38, including the momentous political forces of the World War II era that caused its near demise and, later, its rebirth.

Pistol & Revolver Guide, 3rd Ed., by George C. Nonte, Stoeger Publ. Co., So. Hackensack, NJ, 1975. 224 pp., illus. Paper covers. $11.95.

The standard reference work on military and sporting handguns.

Pistol Guide, by George C. Nonte, Jr., Stoeger Publishing Co., So. Hackensack, NJ, 1991. 280 pp., illus. Paper covers. $13.95.

Covers handling and marksmanship, care and maintenance, pistol ammunition, how to buy a used gun, military pistols, air pistols and repairs.

Pistols of the World, 3rd Edition, by Ian Hogg and John Weeks, DBI Books, Inc., Northbrook, IL, 1992. 320 pp., illus. Paper covers. $19.95.

A totally revised edtion of one of the leading studies of small arms.

Pistolsmithing, The Gun Digest Book of, by Jack Mitchell, DBI Books, Inc., Northbrook, IL, 1980, 288 pp., illus. Paper covers. $15.95.

An expert's guide to the operation of each of the handgun actions with all the major functions of pistolsmithing explained.

Police Handgun Manual, by Bill Clede, Stackpole Books, Inc., Harrisburg, PA, 1985. 128 pp., illus. $18.95.

How to get street-smart survival habits.

Powerhouse Pistols—The Colt 1911 and Browning Hi-Power Source book, by Duncan Long, Paladin Press, Boulder, CO, 1989. 152 pp., illus. Soft covers. $19.95.

The author discusses internal mechanisms, outward design, test-firing results, maintenance and accessories.

Report of Board on Tests of Revolvers and Automatic Pistols. From the Annual Report of the Chief of Ordnance, 1907. Reprinted by J.C. Tillinghast, Marlow, NH, 1969. 34 pp., 7 plates, paper covers. $9.95.

A comparison of handguns, including Luger, Savage, Colt, Webley-Fosbery and other makes.

Revolver Guide, by George C. Nonte, Jr., Stoeger Publishing Co., So. Hackensack, NJ, 1991. 288 pp., illus. Paper covers. $10.95.

A detailed and practical encyclopedia of the revolver, the most common handgun to be found.

***Ruger Automatic Pistols and Single Action Revolvers,** by Hugo A. Lueders, edited by Don Findley, Blacksmith Corp., Chino Valley, AZ, 1993. 79 pp., illus. Paper covers. $14.95.

The definitive work on Ruger automatic pistols and single action revolvers.

***The Ruger "P" Family of Handguns,** by Duncan Long, Desert Publications, El Dorado, AZ, 1993. 128 pp., illus. Paper covers. $14.95.

A full-fledged documentary on a remarkable series of Sturm Ruger handguns.

The Ruger .22 Automatic Pistol, Standard/Mark I/Mark II Series, by Duncan Long, Paladin Press, Boulder, CO, 1989. 168 pp., illus. Paper covers. $12.00.

The definitive book about the pistol that has served more than 1 million owners so well.

The Semiautomatic Pistols in Police Service and Self Defense, by Massad Ayoob, Police Bookshelf, Concord, NH, 1990. 25 pp., illus. Soft covers. $9.95.

First quantitative, documented look at actual police experience with 9mm and 45 police service automatics.

The Sharpshooter—How to Stand and Shoot Handgun Metallic Silhouettes, by Charles Stephens, Yucca Tree Press, Las Cruces, NM, 1993. 86 pp., illus. Paper covers. $10.00.

A narration of some of the author's early experiences in silhouette shooting, plus how-to information.

Shoot a Handgun, by Dave Arnold, PVA Books, Canyon County, CA, 1983. 144 pp., illus. Paper covers. $11.95.

A complete manual of simplified handgun instruction.

Shoot to Win, by John Shaw, Blacksmith Corp., Southport, CT, 1985. 160 pp., illus. Paper covers. $11.95.

The lessons taught here are of interest and value to all handgun shooters.

Shooting, by J.H. FitzGerald, Wolfe Publishing Co., Prescott, AZ, 1993. 421 pp., illus. $29.00

Exhaustive coverage of handguns and their use for target shooting, defense, trick shooting, and in police work by an noted firearms expert.

Sixgun Cartridges and Loads, by Elmer Keith, reprint edition by The Gun Room Press, Highland Park, NJ, 1984. 151 pp., illus. $24.95.

A manual covering the selection, use and loading of the most suitable and popular revolver cartridges.

Sixguns, by Elmer Keith, Wolfe Publishing Company, Prescott, AZ, 1992. 336 pp. Hardcover. $34.95.

The history, selection, repair, care, loading, and use of this historic frontiersman's friend–the one-hand firearm.

Skeeter Skelton on Handguns, by Skeeter Skelton, PJS Publications, Peoria, IL, 1980. 122 pp., illus. Soft covers. $5.00.

A treasury of facts, fiction and fables.

Successful Pistol Shooting, by Frank and Paul Leatherdale, The Crowood Press, Ramsbury, England, 1988. 144 pp., illus. $34.95.

Easy-to-follow instructions to help you achieve better results and gain more enjoyment from both leisure and competitive shooting.

Webley & Scott Automatic Pistols, by Gordon Bruch, Stocker-Schmid Publishing Co., Dietikon, Switzerland, 1992. 256 pp., illus. $69.50.

The fundamental representation of the history and development of all Webley & Scott automatic pistols.

World's Deadliest Rimfire Battleguns, by J.M. Ramos, Paladin Press, Boulder, CO, 1990. 184 pp., illus. Paper covers. $14.00.

This heavily illustrated book shows international rimfire assault weapon innovations from World War II to the present.

HUNTING

NORTH AMERICA

Advanced Deer Hunting, by John Weiss, Stackpole Books, Harrisburg, PA, 1988. 352 pp., illus. $28.95.

New strategies based on the latest studies of whitetail behavior.

Advanced Wild Turkey Hunting & World Records, by Dave Harbour, Winchester Press, Piscataway, NJ, 1983. 264 pp., illus. $19.95.

The definitive book, written by an authority who has studied turkeys and turkey calling for over 40 years.

Alaska Safari, by Harold Schetzle, Great Northwest Publishing and Distributing Co., Inc., Anchorage, AK, 1990. 366 pp., illus. $35.00.

The most comprehensive and up-to-date guide to Alaska big game hunting currently available.

Alaska Wilderness Hunter, by Harold Schetzle, Great Northwest Publishing and Distributing Co., Anchorage, AK, 1987. 224 pp., illus. $35.00.

A superb collection of Alaska hunting adventures by master guide Harold Schetzle.

All About Bears, by Duncan Gilchrist, Stoneydale Press Publishing Co., Stevensville, MT, 1989. 176 pp., illus. $19.95.

Covers all kinds of bears—black, grizzly, Alaskan brown, polar and leans on a lifetime of hunting and guiding experiences to explore proper hunting techniques.

All About Deer in America, edited by Robert Elman, Winchester Press, Piscataway, NJ, 1976. 256 pp., illus. $15.95.

Twenty of America's great hunters share the secrets of their hunting success.

All-American Deer Hunter's Guide, edited by Jim Zumbo and Robert Elman, Winchester Press, Piscataway, NJ, 1983. 320 pp., illus. $29.95.

The most comprehensive, thorough book yet published on American deer hunting.

All Season Hunting, by Bob Gilsvik, Winchester Press, Piscataway, NJ, 1976. 256 pp., illus. $14.95.

A guide to early-season, late-season and winter hunting in America.

American Duck Shooting, by George Bird Grinnell, Stackpole Books, Harrisburg, PA, 1991. 640 pp., illus. Paper covers. $17.95.

First published in 1901 at the height of the author's career. Describes 50 species of waterfowl, and discusses hunting methods common at the turn of the century.

Awesome Antlers of North America, by Odie Sudbeck, HTW Publications, Seneca, KS, 1993. 150 pp., illus. $35.00.

500 world-class bucks in color and black and white. This book starts up where the Boone & Crockett recordbook leaves off.

Bare November Days, by George Bird Evans et al, Countrysport Press, Traverse City, MI, 1992. 136 pp., illus. $39.50.

A new, original anthology, a tribute to ruffed grouse, king of upland birds.

The Bear Hunter's Century, by Paul Schullery, Stackpole Books, Harrisburg, PA, 1989. 240 pp., illus. $19.95.

Thrilling tales of the bygone days of wilderness hunting.

Bear in Their World, by Erwin Bauer, an Outdoor Life Book, New York, NY, 1985. 254 pp., illus. $32.95.

Covers all North American bears; including grizzlies, browns, blacks, and polars.

The Best of Babcock, by Havilah Babcock, selected and with an introduction by Hugh Grey, The Gunnerman Press, Auburn Hills, MI, 1985. 262 pp., illus. $19.95.

A treasury of memorable pieces, 21of which have never before appeared in book form.

The Best of Nash Buckingham, by Nash Buckingham, selected, edited and annotated by George Bird Evans, Winchester Press, Piscataway, NJ, 1973. 320 pp., illus. $17.95.

Thirty pieces that represent the very cream of Nash's output on his whole range of outdoor interests—upland shooting, duck hunting, even fishing.

The Best of Sheep Hunting, by John Batten, Amwell Press, Clinton, NJ, 1992. 616 pp., illus. $47.50.

This "Memorial Edition" is a collection of 40 articles and appendices covering sheep hunting in the North American area of Canada, Alaska, the West and Midwest as well as Africa and Europe.

Big Game, Big Country, by Dr. Chauncey Guy Suits, Great Northwest Publishing and Distributing Co., Anchorage, AK, 1987. 224 pp., illus. $29.50.

Chronicles more than a decade of high-quality wilderness hunting by one of this country's more distinguished big game hunters.

Big Game of North America, Ecology and Management, by Wildlife Management Institute, Stackpole Books, Harrisburg, PA, 1983. 512 pp., illus. $34.95.

An outstanding reference for professionals and students of wildlife management.

Big Game Trails in the Far North, by Col. Philip Neuweiler, Great Northwest Publishing and Distributing Co., Inc., Anchorage, AK, 1990. 320 pp., illus. $35.00.

This book is the result of 50 years hunting big game in the Far North.

Bird Hunting with Dalrymple, by Byron W. Dalrymple, Stackpole Books, Harrisburg, PA, 1987. 256 pp., illus. $24.95.

The rewards of shotgunning across North America.

Birds on the Horizon, by Stuart Williams, Countrysport Press, Traverse City, MI, 1993. 288 pp., illus. $49.50.

Wingshooting adventures around the world.

Blacktail Trophy Tactics, by Boyd Iverson, Stoneydale Press, Stevensville, MI, 1992. 166 pp., illus. Paper covers. $14.95.

A comprehensive analysis of blacktail deer habits, describing a deer's and man's use of scents, still hunting, tree techniques, etc.

Boone & Crockett Club's 21st Big Game Awards, edited by Gary Sitton & Jack Reneau, Missoula, MT, 1992. 537 pp., illus. $39.95.

A book of the Boone & Crockett Club containing tabulations of outstanding North American big game trophies accepted during the 21st awards entry period of 1989-1991.

Bowhunter's Digest, 3rd Edition, by Chuck Adams, DBI Books, Inc., Northbrook, IL, 1990. 288 pp., illus. Soft covers. $16.95.

All-new edition covers all the necessary equipment and how to use it, plus the fine points on how to improve your skill.

Brown Feathers, by Steven J. Julak, Stackpole Books, Harrisburg, PA, 1988. 224 pp., illus. $16.95.

Waterfowling tales and upland dreams.

Bugling for Elk, by Dwight Schuh, Stoneydale Press Publishing Co., Stevensville, MT, 1983. 162 pp., illus. $18.95.

A complete guide to early season elk hunting.

Call of the Quail: A Tribute to the Gentleman Game Bird, by Michael McIntosh, et al., Countrysport Press, Traverse City, MI, 1990. 175 pp., illus. $39.50.

A new anthology on quail hunting.

Calling All Elk, by Jim Zumbo, Jim Zumbo, Cody, WY, 1989. 169 pp., illus. Paper covers. $14.95.

The only book on the subject of elk hunting that covers every aspect of elk vocalization.

Campfires and Game Trails: Hunting North American Big Game, by Craig Boddington, Winchester Press, Piscataway, NJ, 1985. 295 pp., illus. $23.95.

How to hunt North America's big game species.

Come October, by Gene Hill et al, Countrysport Press, Inc., Traverse City, MI, 1991. 176 pp., illus. $39.50.

A new and all-original anthology on the woodcock and woodcock hunting.

The Complete Book of the Wild Turkey, by Roger M. Latham, Stackpole Books, Harrisburg, PA, 1978. 228 pp., illus. $14.95.

A new revised edition of the classic on American wild turkey hunting.

The Complete Guide to Bowhunting Deer, by Chuck Adams, DBI Books, Inc., Northbrook, IL, 1984. 256 pp., illus. Paper covers. $15.95.

Plenty on equipment, bows, sights, quivers, arrows, clothes, lures and scents, stands and blinds, etc.

***The Complete Guide to Game Care and Cookery, 3rd Edition,** by Sam Fadala, DBI Books, Inc., Northbrook, IL, 1994. 320 pp., illus. Paper covers. $18.95.

Over 500 photos illustrating the care of wild game in the field and at home with a separate recipe section providing over 400 tested recipes. (September, 1994)

The Complete Smoothbore Hunter, by Brook Elliot, Winchester Press, Piscataway, NJ, 1986. 240 pp., illus. $16.95.

Advice and information on guns and gunning for all varieties of game.

The Complete Turkey Hunt, by William Morris Daskal, El-Bar Enterprises Publishers, New York, NY, 1982. 129 pp., illus. Paper covers. $10.00.

Covers every aspect of turkeys and turkey hunting, by an expert.

Complete Turkey Hunting, by John Phillips, Stackpole Books, Harrisburg, PA, 1988. 320 pp., illus. $24.95.

The definitive work on hunting America's largest game bird.

Confessions of an Outdoor Maladroit, by Joel M. Vance, Amwell Press, Clinton, NJ, 1983. $20.00.

Anthology of some of the wildest, irreverent, and zany hunting tales ever.

Covey Rises and Other Pleasures, by David H. Henderson, Amwell Press, Clinton, NJ, 1983. 155 pp., illus. $17.50.

A collection of essays and stories concerned with field sports.

Coveys and Singles: The Handbook of Quail Hunting, by Robert Gooch, A.S. Barnes, San Diego, CA, 1981. 196 pp., illus. $11.95.

The story of the quail in North America.

***Deer & Deer Hunting,** by Al Hofacker, Krause Publications, Iola, WI, 1993. 208 pp., illus. $34.95.

Coffee-table volume packed full of how-to-information that will guide hunts for years to come.

Deer and Deer Hunting: The Serious Hunter's Guide, by Dr. Robert Wegner, Stackpole Books, Harrisburg, PA, 1984. 384 pp., illus. $24.95.

In-depth information from the editor of "Deer & Deer Hunting" magazine. Major bibliography of English language books on deer and deer hunting from 1838-1984.

Deer and Deer Hunting Book 2, by Dr. Robert Wegner, Stackpole Books, Harrisburg, PA, 1987. 400 pp., illus. $29.95.

Strategies and tactics for the advanced hunter.

Deer and Deer Hunting, Book 3, by Dr. Robert Wegner, Stackpole Books, Harrisburg, PA, 1990. 368 pp., ilus. $29.95.

This comprehensive volume covers natural history, deer hunting lore, profiles of deer hunters, and discussion of important issues facing deer hunters today.

The Deer Book, edited by Lamar Underwood, Amwell Press, Clinton, NJ, 1982. 480 pp., illus. $25.00.

An anthology of the finest stories on North American deer ever assembled under one cover.

Deer Hunter's Guide to Guns, Ammunition, and Equipment, by Edward A. Matunas, an Outdoor Life Book, distributed by Stackpole Books, Harrisburg, PA, 1983. 352 pp., illus. $24.95.

Where to hunt for North American deer. An authoritative guide that will help every deer hunter get maximum enjoyment and satisfaction from his sport.

Deer Hunting, by R. Smith, Stackpole Books, Harrisburg, PA, 1978. 224 pp., illus. Paper covers. $14.95.

A professional guide leads the hunt for North America's most popular big game animal.

Deer Hunting Coast to Coast, by C. Boddington and R. Robb, Safari Press, Long Beach, CA, 1989. 248 pp., illus. $24.95.

Join the authors as they hunt whitetail deer in eastern woodlot, southern swamps, midwestern prairies, and western river bottom; mule deer in badland, deserts, and high alpine basins; blacktails in oak grasslands and coastal jungles.

Deer in Their World, by Erwin Bauer, Stackpole Books, Harrisburg, PA, 1984. 256 pp., illus. $29.95.

More than 250 natural habitat deer photos. Substantial natural history of North American deer.

The Deer of North America, edited by Leonard Lee Rue, Stackpole Books, Harrisburg, PA, 1989. 544 pp., illus. $32.95.

Updated and expanded edition of this definitive work on North American deer.

Doves and Dove Shooting, by Byron W. Dalrymple, New Win Publishing, Inc., Hampton, NJ, 1992. 256 pp., illus. $17.95.

The author reveals in this classic book his penchant for observing, hunting, and photographing this elegantly fashioned bird.

Dove Hunting, by Charley Dickey, Galahad Books, NY, 1976. 112 pp., illus. $10.00.

This indispensable guide for hunters deals with equipment, techniques, types of dove shooting, hunting dogs, etc.

Drummer in the Woods, by Burton L. Spiller, Stackpole Books, Harrisburg, PA, 1990. 240 pp., illus. Soft covers. $16.95.

Twenty-one wonderful stories on grouse shooting by "the Poet Laureate of Grouse."

Duck Decoys and How to Rig Them, by Ralf Coykendall, revised by Ralf Coykendall, Jr., Nick Lyons Books, New York, NY, 1990. 137 pp., illus. Paper covers. $14.95.

Sage and practical advice on the art of decoying ducks and geese.

The Duck Hunter's Handbook, by Bob Hinman, revised, expanded, updated edition, Winchester Press, Piscataway, NJ, 1985. 288 pp., illus. $15.95.

The duck hunting book that has it all.

Ducks of the Mississippi Flyway, ed. by John McKane, North Star Press, St. Cloud, MN, 1969. 54 pp., illus. Paper covers. $10.00.

A duck hunter's reference. Full color paintings of some 30 species, plus descriptive text.

Early American Waterfowling, 1700's-1930, by Stephen Miller, Winchester Press, Piscataway, NJ, 1986. 256 pp., illus. $27.95.

Two centuries of literature and art devoted to the nation's favorite hunting sport—water-fowling.

Eastern Upland Shooting, by Dr. Charles C. Norris, Countrysport Press, Traverse City, MI, 1990. 424 pp., illus. $29.50.

A new printing of this 1946 classic with a new, original Foreword by the author's friend and hunting companion, renowned author George Bird Evans.

The Education of Pretty Boy, by Havilah Babcock, The Gunnerman Press, Auburn Hills, MI, 1985. 160 pp., illus. $19.95.

Babcock's only novel, a heartwarming story of an orphan boy and a gun-shy setter.

Elk and Elk Hunting, by Hart Wixom, Stackpole Books, Harrisburg, PA, 1986. 288 pp., illus. $29.95.

Your practical guide to fundamentals and fine points of elk hunting.

Elk Hunting in the Northern Rockies, by Ed. Wolff, Stoneydale Press, Stevensville, MT, 1984. 162 pp., illus. $18.95.

Helpful information about hunting the premier elk country of the northern Rocky Mountain states—Wyoming, Montana and Idaho.

Elk Hunting with the Experts, by Bob Robb, Stoneydale Press, Stevensville, MT, 1992. 176 pp., illus. Paper covers. $15.95.

A complete guide to elk hunting in North America by America's top elk hunting expert.

Elk Rifles, Cartridges and Hunting Tactics, by Wayne van Zwoll, Larsen's Outdoor Publishing, Lakeland, FL, 1992. 414 pp., illus. $24.95.

The definitive work on which rifles and cartridges are proper for hunting elk plus the tactics for hunting them.

Encyclopedia of Deer, by G. Kenneth Whitehead, Safari Press, Huntington, CA, 1993. 704 pp., illus. $130.00.

This massive tome will be the reference work on deer for well into the next century.

Fair Chase, by Jim Rikhoff, Amwell Press, Clinton, NJ, 1984. 323 pp., illus. $25.00.

A collection of hunting experiences from the Arctic to Africa, Mongolia to Montana, taken from over 25 years of writing.

Field Dressing Big Game, by James Churchill, Stackpole Books, Harrisburg, PA, 1989. 88 pp., illus. Soft covers. $10.95.

Dressing, caping, skinning and butchering instructions.

Field Dressing Small Game and Fowl, by James Churchill, Stackpole Books, Harrisburg, PA, 1987. 112 pp., illus. Paper covers. $10.95.

The illustrated guide to dressing 20 birds and animals.

Field Judging Trophy Animals, by William Shuster, Stackpole Books, Harrisburg, PA, 1987. 132 pp., illus. Paper covers. $8.95.

Expert advice and practical suggestions.

Firelight, by Burton L. Spiller, Gunnerman Press, Auburn Hills, MI, 1990. 196 pp., illus. $19.95.

Enjoyable tales of the outdoors and stalwart companions.

Fireside Waterfowler, edited by David E. Wesley and William G. Leitch, A Ducks Unlimited Book, Stackpole Books, Harrisburg, PA, 1987. 357 pp., illus. $29.95.

Fundamentals of duck and goose hunting.

The Formidable Game, by John H. Batten, Amwell Press, Clinton, NJ. 1983. 264 pp., illus. $175.00.

Deluxe, limited, signed and numbered edition. Big game hunting in India, Africa and North America by a world famous hunter.

Fresh Looks at Deer Hunting, by Byron W. Dalrymple, New Win Publishing, Inc., Hampton, NJ, 1993. 288 pp., illus. $24.95.

Tips and techniques abound throughout the pages of this latest work by Mr. Dalrymple whose name is synonymous with hunting proficiency.

Fur Trapping In North America, by Steven Geary, Winchester Press, Piscataway, NJ, 1985. 160 pp., illus. Paper covers. $19.95.

A comprehensive guide to techniques and equipment, together with fascinating facts about fur bearers.

A Gallery of Waterfowl and Upland Birds, by Gene Hill, with illustrations by David Maass, Petersen Prints, Los Angeles, CA, 1978. 132 pp., illus. $44.95.

Gene Hill at his best. Liberally illustrated with 51 full-color reproductions of David Maass' finest paintings.

Game in the Desert Revisited, by Jack O'Connor, Amwell Press, Clinton, NJ, 1984. 306 pp., illus. $27.50.

Reprint of a Derrydale Press classic on hunting in the Southwest

Getting the Most Out of Modern Waterfowling, by John O. Cartier, St. Martin's Press, NY, 1974. 396 pp., illus. $22.50.

The most comprehensive, up-to-date book on waterfowling imaginable.

*Getting a Stand, by Miles Gilbert, Pioneer Press, Union City, TN, 1993. 204 pp., illus. Paper covers. $10.95.

An anthology of 18 short personal experiences by buffalo hunters of the late 1800s, specifically from 1870-1882.

The Grand Passage: A Chronicle of North American Waterfowling, by Gene Hill, et al., Countrysport Press, Traverse City, MI, 1990. 175 pp., illus. $39.50.

A new original anthology by renowned sporting authors on our world of waterfowling.

The Grand Spring Hunt for America's Wild Turkey Gobbler, by Bart Jacob with Ben Conger, Winchester Press, Piscataway, NJ, 1985. 176 pp., illus. $15.95.

The turkey book for novice and expert alike.

Grizzlies Don't Come Easy, by Ralph Young, Winchester Press, Piscataway, NJ, 1981. 200 pp., illus. $15.95.

The life story of a great woodsman who guided famous hunters such as O'Connor, Keith, Fitz, Page and others.

Grizzly Country, by Andy Russell, A.A. Knopf, NYC, 1973, 302 pp., illus. $15.95.

Many-sided view of the grizzly bear by a noted guide, hunter and naturalist.

Grouse and Grouse Hunting, by Frank Woolner, Nick Lyons Books, N.Y., NY, 1987. 192 pp., illus. $18.95.

An authoritative and affectionate portrait of one of America's greatest game birds.

Grouse of North America, by Tom Huggler, NorthWord Press, Inc., Minocqua, WI, 1990. 160 pp., illus. $29.95.

A cross-continental hunting guide.

Grouse Hunter's Guide, by Dennis Walrod, Stackpole Books, Harrisburg, PA, 1985. 192 pp., illus. $16.95.

Solid facts, observations, and insights on how to hunt the ruffed grouse.

Gun Clubs & Decoys of Back Bay & Currituck Sound, by Archie Johnson and Bud Coppedge, CurBac Press, Virginia Beach, VA, 1991. 224 pp., illus. $40.00.

This book identifies and presents a photographic history of over 100 hunting clubs and lodges on Back Bay, VA and Currituck Sound, NC.

Gunning for Sea Ducks, by George Howard Gillelan, Tidewater Publishers, Centreville, MD, 1988. 144 pp., illus. $14.95.

A book that introduces you to a practically untouched arena of waterfowling.

Heartland Trophy Whitetails, by Odie Sudbeck, HTW Publications, Seneca, KS, 1992. 130 pp., illus. $35.00.

A completely revised and expanded edition which includes over 500 photos of Boone & Crockett class whitetail, major mulies and unusual racks.

Horned and Antlered Game, by Erwin Bauer, Stackpole Books, Harrisburg, PA, 1987. 256 pp., illus. $32.95.

This book features spectacular color photographs and text brimming with animal lore.

Horns in the High Country, by Andy Russell, Alfred A. Knopf, NY, 1973. 259 pp., illus. Paper covers. $12.95.

A many-sided view of wild sheep and their natural world.

How to Get Your Deer, by John O. Cartier, Stackpole Books, Harrisburg, PA, 1986. 320 pp., illus. $24.95.

An authoritative guide to deer hunting that shows you how to match wits with your quarry and win.

How to Hunt, by Dave Bowring, Winchester Press, Piscataway, NJ, 1982. 208 pp., illus. Paper covers. $10.95; cloth, $15.00.

A basic guide to hunting big game, small game, upland birds, and waterfowl.

Hunt High, by Duncan Gilchrist, Outdoor Expeditions & Books, Cowallis, MT, 1992. 192 pp., illus. Limited, signed edition. $34.95.

High country lore and how-to information on hunting Rocky Mountain Goats, Bighorn Sheep, Chamois, and Tahr.

The Hunters and the Hunted, by George Laycock, Outdoor Life Books, New York, NY, 1990. 280 pp., illus. $34.95.

The pursuit of game in America from Indian times to the present.

A Hunter's Fireside Book, by Gene Hill, Winchester Press, Piscataway, NJ, 1972. 192 pp., illus. $16.95.

An outdoor book that will appeal to every person who spends time in the field—or who wishes he could.

A Hunter's Road, by Jim Fergus, Henry Holt & Co., NY, 1992. 290 pp. $22.50

A journey with gun and dog across the American uplands.

Hunt High for Rocky Mountain Goats, Bighorn Sheep, Chamois & Tahr, by Duncan Gilchrist, Stoneydale Press, Stevensville, MT, 1992. 192 pp., illus. Paper covers. $19.95.

The source book for hunting mountain goats.

The Hunter's Shooting Guide, by Jack O'Connor, Outdoor Life Books, New York, NY, 1982. 176 pp., illus. Paper covers. $5.95.

A classic covering rifles, cartridges, shooting techniques for shotguns/rifles/handguns.

The Hunter's World, by Charles F. Waterman, Winchester Press, Piscataway, NJ, 1983. 250 pp., illus. $29.95.

A classic. One of the most beautiful hunting books that has ever been produced.

Hunting America's Game Animals and Birds, by Robert Elman and George Peper, Winchester Press, Piscataway, NJ, 1975. 368 pp., illus. $16.95.

A how-to, where-to, when-to guide—by 40 top experts—covering the continent's big, small, upland game and waterfowl.

Hunting Boar, Hogs & Javelinas, by Bob Gooch, Atlantic Publishing Co., Tabor City, NC, 1989. 204 pp., illus. Paper covers. $9.95.

Thorough in explaining where, when and how to hunt these elusive creatures, along with a state-by-state hunting guide and a list of recipes.

Hunting Ducks and Geese, by Steven Smith, Stackpole Books, Harrisburg, PA, 1984. 160 pp., illus. $15.95.

Hard facts, good bets, and serious advice from a duck hunter you can trust.

Hunting for Handgunners, by Larry Kelly and J.D. Jones, DBI Books, Inc., Northbrook, IL, 1990. 256 pp., illus. Soft covers. $16.95.

A definitive work on an increasingly popular sport.

Hunting Fringeland Deer, by David Richey, Stackpole Books, Harrisburg, PA, 1987. 208 pp., illus. $24.95.

Tactics for trail watching, stillhunting and driving whitetails in farmlands, edge country and populated areas.

Hunting in Many Lands, edited by Theodore Roosevelt and George Bird Grinnell, et al., Boone & Crockett Club, Dumphries, VA, 1990. 447 pp., illus. $40.00.

A limited edition reprinting of the original Boone & Crockett Club 1895 printing.

Hunting North America's Big Game, by Bob Hagel, Stackpole Books, Harrisburg, PA, 1987. 220 pp., illus. $27.95.

Complete coverage on how to approach, track, and shoot game in different terrains.

Hunting Open-Country Mule Deer, by Dwight Schuh, Sage Press, Nampa, ID, 1989. 180 pp., illus. $18.95.

A guide taking Western bucks with rifle and bow.

Hunting Predators for Hides and Profits, by Wilf E. Pyle, Stoeger Publishing Co., So. Hackensack, NJ, 1985. 224 pp., illus. Paper covers. $11.95.

The author takes the hunter through every step of the hunting/marketing process.

Hunting the Alaskan Brown Bear, by John Eddy, Wolfe Publishing Co., Prescott, AZ, 1988. 253 pp., illus. $47.00.

A limited edition reprint of the best book on the big brown bear of the North.

Hunting the American Wild Turkey, by Dave Harbour, Stackpole Books, Harrisburg, PA, 1975. 256 pp., illus. $14.95.

The techniques and tactics of hunting North America's largest, and most popular, woodland game bird.

Hunting Superbucks, by Kathy Etling, Grolier Book Clubs, Danbury, CT, 1989. 444 pp., illus. $32.95.

How to find and hunt today's trophy mule and whitetail deer.

Hunting Trips in North America, by F.C. Selous, Wolfe Publishing Co., Prescott, AZ, 1988. 395 pp., illus. $52.00.

A limited edition reprint. Coverage of caribou, moose and other big game hunting in virgin wilds.

Hunting Trophy Deer, by John Wootters, Winchester Press, Piscataway, NJ, 1983. 265 pp., illus. $15.95.

All the advice you need to succeed at bagging trophy deer.

*Hunting Trophy Whitetails, by David Morris, Stoneydale Press, Stevensville, MT, 1993. 483 pp., illus. $29.95.

This is one of the best whitetail books published in the last two decades. The author is the former editor of *North American Whitetail* magazine.

Hunting Upland Gamebirds, by Steve Smith, Stackpole Books, Harrisburg, PA, 1987. 176 pp., illus. $16.95.

What the wingshooter needs to know about the birds, the game, and the new clay games.

Hunting Wild Turkeys in the Everglades, by Frank P. Harben, Harben Publishing Co., Safety Harbor, FL, 1983. 341 pp., illus. Paper covers. $8.95.

Describes techniques, ways and means of hunting this wary bird.

Hunting Wild Turkeys in the West, by John Higley, Stoneydale Press, Stevensville, MT, 1992. 154 pp., illus. Paper covers. $12.95.

Covers the basics of calling, locating and hunting turkeys in the western states.

Hunting Wild Turkeys with Ray Eye, by Michael Pearce and Ray Eye, Stackpole Books, Harrisburg, PA, 1990. 208 pp., illus. $22.95.

Whether you hunt in spring or fall, with a gun or bow and arrow, alone or with a partner, you will find in this book a wealth of practical information.

*Hunting with the Twenty-two, by Charles Singer Landis, R&R Books, Livonia, NY, 1994. 429 pp., illus. $45.00.

A miscellany of articles touching on the hunting and shooting of small game.

I Don't Want to Shoot an Elephant, by Havilah Babcock, The Gunnerman Press, Auburn Hills, MI, 1985. 184 pp., illus. $19.95.

Eighteen delightful stories that will enthrall the upland gunner for many pleasurable hours.

In Search of the Wild Turkey, by Bob Gooch, Greatlakes Living Press, Ltd., Waukegan, IL, 1978. 182 pp., illus. $9.95.

A state-by-state guide to wild turkey hot spots, with tips on gear and methods for bagging your bird.

Indian Hunts and Indian Hunters of the Old West, by Dr. Frank C. Hibben, Safari Press, Long Beach, CA, 1989. 228 pp., illus. $24.95.

Tales of some of the most famous American Indian hunters of the Old West as told to the author by an old Navajo hunter.

Instinctive Shooting, by G. Fred Asbell, Stackpole Books, Harrisburg, PA, 1988. 132 pp., illus. Paper covers. $13.95.

Expert advice on applying instinctive shooting to bowhunting. Written by the president of the Pope & Young Club.

Jack O'Connor's Gun Book, by Jack O'Connor, Wolfe Publishing Company, Prescott, AZ, 1992. 208 pp. Hardcover. $26.00.

Jack O'Connor imparts a cross-section of his knowledge on guns and hunting. Brings back some of his writings that have here-to-fore been lost.

Jaybirds Go to Hell on Friday, by Havilah Babcock, The Gunnerman Press, Auburn Hills, MI, 1985. 149 pp., illus. $19.95.

Sixteen jewels that reestablish the lost art of good old-fashioned yarn telling.

Jim Dougherty's Guide to Bowhunting Deer, by Jim Dougherty, DBI Books, Inc., Northbrook, IL, 1992. 256 pp., illus. Paper covers. $16.95.

Dougherty sets down some important guidelines for bowhunting and bowhunting equipment.

A Listening Walk...and Other Stories, by Gene Hill, Winchester Press, Piscataway, NJ, 1985. 208 pp., illus. $15.95.

Vintage Hill. Over 60 stories.

*Longbows in the Far North, by E. Donnall Thomas, Jr. Stackpole Books, Mechanicsburg, PA, 1994. 200 pp., illus. $16.95.

An archer's adventures in Alaska and Siberia.

Making Game: An Essay on Woodcock, by Guy De La Valdene, Willow Creek Press, Oshkosh, WI, 1985. 202 pp., illus. $35.00.

The most delightful book on woodcock yet published.

Matching the Gun to the Game, by Clair Rees, Winchester Press, Piscataway, NJ, 1982. 272 pp., illus. $17.95.

Covers selection and use of handguns, blackpowder firearms for hunting, matching rifle type to the hunter, calibers for multiple use, tailoring factory loads to the game.

Measuring and Scoring North American Big Game Trophies, by Wm. H. Nesbitt and Philip L. Wright, The Boone and Crockett Club, Alexandria, VA, 1986. 176 pp., illus. $15.00.

The Boone and Crockett Club official scoring system, with tips for trophy evaluation.

Meat on the Table: Modern Small-Game Hunting, by Galen Geer, Paladin Press, Boulder, CO, 1985. 216 pp., illus. $16.95.

All you need to know to put meat on your table from this comprehensive course in modern small-game hunting.

Mixed Bag, by Jim Rikhoff, National Rifle Association of America, Wash., DC, 1981. 284 pp., illus. Paper covers. $9.95.

Reminiscences of a master raconteur.

Modern Pheasant Hunting, by Steve Grooms, Stackpole Books, Harrisburg, PA, 1982. 224 pp., illus. Paper covers. $10.95.

New look at pheasants and hunters from an experienced hunter who respects this splendid gamebird.

Modern Waterfowl Guns and Gunning, by Don Zutz, Stoeger Publishing Co., So. Hackensack, NJ, 1985. 224 pp., illus. Paper covers. $11.95.

Up-to-date information on the fast-changing world of waterfowl guns and loads.

Montana—Land of Giant Rams, by Duncan Gilchrist, Stoneydale Press Publishing Co., Stevensville, MT, 1990. 208 pp., illus. $19.95.

Latest information on Montana bighorn sheep and why so many Montana bighorn rams are growing to trophy size.

Montana—Land of Giant Rams, Volume 2, by Duncan Gilchrist, Outdoor Expeditions and Books, Corvallis, MT, 1992. 208 pp., illus. $34.95.

The reader will find stories of how many of the top-scoring trophies were taken.

More and Better Pheasant Hunting, by Steve Smith, Winchester Press, Piscataway, NJ, 1986. 192 pp., illus. $15.95.

Complete, fully illustrated, expert coverage of the bird itself, the dogs, the hunt, the guns, and the best places to hunt.

More Grouse Feathers, by Burton L. Spiller, Crown Publ., NY, 1972. 238 pp., illus. $25.00.

Facsimile of the original Derrydale Press issue of 1938. Guns and dogs, the habits and shooting of grouse, woodcock, ducks, etc. Illus. by Lynn Bogue Hunt.

More Than a Trophy, by Dennis Walrod, Stackpole Books, Harrisburg, PA, 1983. 256 pp., illus. Paper covers. $12.95.

Field dressing, skinning, quartering, and butchering to make the most of your valuable whitetail, blacktail or mule deer.

More Tracks: 78 Years of Mountains, People & Happinesss by Howard Copenhaver, Stoney dale Press, Stevensville, MT, 1992. 150 pp., illus. $18.95.

A collection of stories by one of the back country's best storytellers about the people who shared with Howard his great adventure in the high places and wild Montana country.

Mostly Huntin', by Bill Jordan, Everett Publishing Co., Bossier City, LA, 1987. 254 pp., illus. $21.95.

Jordan's hunting adventures in North America, Africa, Australia, South America and Mexico.

Mostly Tailfeathers, by Gene Hill, Winchester Press, Piscataway, NJ, 1975. 192 pp., illus. $15.95.

An interesting, general book about bird hunting.

Movin' Along with Charley Dickey, by Charlie Dickey, Winchester Press, Piscataway, NJ, 1985. 224 pp., illus. $14.95.

More wisdom, wild tales, and wacky wit from the Sage of Tallahassee.

"Mr. Buck": The Autobiography of Nash Buckingham, by Nash Buckingham, Countrysport Press, Traverse City, MI, 1990. 288 pp., illus. $39.50.

A lifetime of shooting, hunting, dogs, guns, and Nash's reflections on the sporting life, along with previously unknown pictures and stories written especially for this book.

Murry Burnham's Hunting Secrets, by Murry Burnham with Russell Tinsley, Winchester Press, Piscataway, NJ, 1984. 244 pp., illus. $17.95.

One of the great hunters of our time gives the reasons for his success in the field.

My Health is Better in November, by Havilah Babcock, University of S. Carolina Press, Columbia, SC, 1985. 284 pp., illus. $19.95.

Adventures in the field set in the plantation country and backwater streams of SC.

My Lost Wilderness: Tales of an Alaskan Woodsman, by Ralph Young, Winchester Press, Piscataway, NJ, 1983. 193 pp., illus. $22.50.

True tales of an Alaskan hunter, guide, fisherman, prospector, and backwoodsman.

New England Grouse Shooting, by William Harnden Foster, Willow Creek Press, Oshkosh, WI, 1983. 213 pp., illus. $45.00.

A new release of a classic book on grouse shooting.

North American Big Game Animals, by Byron W. Dalrymple and Erwin Bauer, Outdoor Life Books/Stackpole Books, Harrisburg, PA, 1985. 258 pp., illus. $29.95.

Complete illustrated natural histories. Habitat, movements, breeding, birth and development, signs, and hunting.

*****The North American Big Game Muzzleloading Record Book,** published by the Longhunter Society of the National Muzzle Loading Rifle Association, Friendship, IN, 1992. 180 pp., illus. $35.00.

Over 400 entries in 27 categories, personal hunting stories and over 100 photos of trophy animals.

North American Elk: Ecology and Management, edited by Jack Ward Thomas and Dale E. Toweill, Stackpole Books, Harrisburg, PA, 1982. 576 pp., illus. $39.95.

The definitive, exhaustive, classic work on the North American elk.

The North American Waterfowler, by Paul S. Bernsen, Superior Publ. Co., Seattle, WA, 1972. 206 pp. Paper covers. $9.95.

The complete inside and outside story of duck and goose shooting. Big and colorful, illus. by Les Kouba.

Northeast Upland Hunting Guide, by Jim Capossela, Stackpole Books, Harrisburg, PA, 1991. 120 pp., illus. Paper covers. $12.95.

Useful strategies and techniques for bagging all the region's most popular upland game.

Of Bears and Man, by Mike Cramond, University of Oklahoma Press, Norman, OK, 1986. 433 pp., illus. $29.95.

The author's lifetime association with bears of North America. Interviews with survivors of bear attacks.

The Old Man and the Boy and The Old Man Grows Older, by Robert Ruark, Stackpole Books, Harrisburg, PA, 1989. 620 pp., illus. Soft covers. $17.95.

Two novels in one volume. Classic tales of the coming of age of a boy and young man as he is nurtured and educated by his remarkable sportsman grandfather.

*****The Old Man's Boy Grows Older,** by Robert Ruark, Henry Holt & Co., Inc., New York, NY, 1993. 300 pp., illus. Paper covers. $12.95.

The heartwarming sequel to the best-selling *The Old Man and the Boy*. A warm and rewarding book.

The Old Pro Turkey Hunter, by Gene Nunnery, Gene Nunnery, Meridian, MS, 1980. 144 pp., illus. $12.95.

True facts and old tales of turkey hunters.

1001 Hunting Tips, by Robert Elman, Winchester Press, Piscataway, NJ, 1983. 544 pp., illus. $22.95.

New edition, updated and expanded. A complete course in all types of hunting.

The Only Good Bear is a Dead Bear, by Jeanette Hortick Prodgers, Falcon Press, Helena, MT, 1986. 204 pp. Paper covers. $12.50.

A collection of the West's best bear stories.

Opening Shots and Parting Lines: The Best of Dickey's Wit, Wisdom, and Wild Tales for Sportsmen, by Charley Dickey, Winchester Press, Piscataway, NJ, 1983. 208 pp., illus. $14.95.

Selected by the writer who has entertained millions of readers in America's top sporting publications—49 of his best pieces.

The Outdoor Life Bear Book, edited by Chet Fish, an Outdoor Life book, distributed by Stackpole Books, Harrisburg, PA, 1983. 352 pp., illus. $26.95.

All-time best personal accounts of terrifying attacks, exciting hunts, and intriguing natural history.

The Outdoor Life Deer Hunter's Encyclopedia, by John Madson, et al., Stackpole Books, Harrisburg, PA, 1985. 800 pp., illus. $49.95.

The largest, most comprehensive volume of its kind ever published.

Outdoor Yarns & Outright Lies, by Gene Hill and Steve Smith, Stackpole Books, Harrisburg, PA, 1984. 168 pp., illus. $16.95.

Fifty or so stories by two good sports.

The Outlaw Gunner, by Harry M. Walsh, Tidewater Publishers, Cambridge, MD, 1973. 178 pp., illus. $15.95.

A colorful story of market gunning in both its legal and illegal phases.

Pheasant Hunter's Harvest, by Steve Grooms, Lyons & Burford Publishers, New York, NY, 1990. 180 pp. $18.95.

A celebration of pheasant, pheasant dogs and pheasant hunting. Practical advice from a passionate hunter.

Picking Your Shots, by Steve Smith, Stackpole Books, Harrisburg, PA, 1986. 160 pp., illus. $16.95.

Stories of dogs and birds, and guns and days afield.

Pinnell and Talifson: Last of the Great Brown Bear Men, by Marvin H. Clark, Jr., Great Northwest Publishing and Distributing Co., Spokane, WA, 19880. 224 pp., Illus. $39.95

The story of these famous Alaskan guides and some of the record bears taken by both of them.

Predator Caller's Companion, by Gerry Blair, Winchester Press, Piscataway, NJ, 1981. 280 pp., illus. $18.95.

Predator calling techniques and equipment for the hunter and trapper.

Predators of North America, by Erwin Bauer, Stackpole Books, Harrisburg, PA, 1988. 256 pp., illus. $34.95.

Pronghorn, North America's Unique Antelope, by Charles L. Cadieux, Stackpole Books, Harrisburg, PA, 1986. 256 pp., illus. $24.95.

The practical guide for hunters.

Quail Hunting in America, by Tom Huggler, Stackpole Books, Harrisburg, PA, 1987. 288 pp., illus. $19.95.

Tactics for finding and taking bobwhite, valleys, Gambel's Mountain, scaled-blue, and Mearn's quail by season and habitat.

Radical Elk Hunting Strategies, by Mike Lapinski, Stoneydale Press Publishing Co., Stevensville, MT, 1988. 161 pp., illus. $18.95.

Secrets of calling elk in close.

Ranch Life and the Hunting Trail, by Theodore Roosevelt, Readex Microprint Corp., Dearborn, MI, 1966. 186 pp. With drawings by Frederic Remington. $22.50.

A facsimile reprint of the original 1899 Century Co. edition. One of the most fascinating books of the West of that day.

*****Records of Hunting North American Big Game, 10th Edition, 1993,** Edited by the Boone & Crockett Club, Missoula, MT, 1993. 624 pp., illus. $49.95.

The largest B&C record book, includes 84 new trophies which rank in the top ten, 8 new world records and 439 pages of trophy listings.

Records of North American Big Game 1932, by Prentis N. Grey, Boone and Crockett Club, Dumfries, VA, 1988. 178 pp., illus. $79.95.

A reprint of the book that started the Club's record keeping for native North American big game.

Records of North American Whitetailed Deer, by the editors of the Boone and Crockett Club, Dumfries, VA, 1987. 256 pp., illus. Flexible covers. $15.00.

Contains data on 1293 whitetail trophies over the all-time record book minimum, listed and ranked by state or province and divided into typical and non-typical categories.

Ridge Runners & Swamp Rats, by Charles F. Waterman, Amwell Press, Clinton, NJ, 1983. 347 pp., illus. $25.00.

Tales of hunting and fishing.

The Rifles, the Cartridges, and the Game, by Clay Harvey, Stackpole Books, Harrisburg, PA, 1991. 254 pp., illus. $32.95.

Engaging reading combines with exciting photos to present the hunt with an intense level of awareness and respect.

Ringneck! Pheasants & Pheasant Hunting, by Ted Janes, Crown Publ., NY, 1975. 120 pp., illus. $15.95.

A thorough study of one of our more popular game birds.

Ruffed Grouse, edited by Sally Atwater and Judith Schnell, Stackpole Books, Harrisburg, PA, 1989. 370 pp., illus. $59.95.

Everything you ever wanted to know about the ruffed grouse. More than 25 wildlife professionals provided in-depth information on every aspect of this popular game bird's life. Lavishly illustrated with over 300 full-color photos.

Shadows of the Tundra, by Tom Walker, Stackpole Books, Harrisburg, PA, 1990. 192 pp., illus. $19.95.

Alaskan tales of predator, prey, and man.

Sheep & Sheep Hunting, by Jack O'Connor, Safari Press, Huntington Beach, CA, 1992. 308 pp., illus. $35.00.

A new printing of the definitive book on wild sheep.

Shorebirds: The Birds, The Hunters, The Decoys, by John M. Levinson & Somers G. Headley, Tidewater Publishers, Centreville, MD, 1991. 160 pp., illus. $49.95.

A thorough study of shorebirds and the decoys used to hunt them. Photographs of more than 200 of the decoys created by prominent carvers are shown.

Shots at Big Game, by Craig Boddington, Stackpole Books, Harrisburg, PA, 1989. 198 pp., illus. $24.95.

How to shoot a rifle accurately under hunting conditions.

Small Game & Varmint Hunting, by Wilf E. Pyle, Stoeger Publishing Co., So. Hackensack, NJ, 1989. 288 pp., illus. Soft covers. $16.95.

Provides information on modern techniques and methods needed for successful hunting of small game.

Sport and Travel; East and West, by Frederick Courteney Selous, Wolfe Publishing Co., Prescott, AZ, 1988. 311 pp., illus. $29.00.

A limited edition reprint. One of the few books Selous wrote covering North American hunting. His daring in Africa is equalled here as he treks after unknown trails and wild game.

Spring Turkey Hunting, by John M. McDaniel, Stackpole Books, Harrisburg, PA, 1986. 224 pp., illus. $21.95.

The serious hunter's guide.

Sunlight and Shadows, by Gene Hill, Petersen Publishing Co., Los Angeles, CA, 1990. 173 pp., illus. $24.50.

Essays and stories on the out-of-doors.

Squirrels and Squirrel Hunting, by Bob Gooch. Tidewater Publ., Cambridge, MD, 1973. 148 pp., illus. $10.95.

A complete book for the squirrel hunter, beginner or old hand. Details methods of hunting, squirrel habitat, management, proper clothing, care of the kill, cleaning and cooking.

Strayed Shots and Frayed Lines, edited by John E. Howard, Amwell Press, Clinton, NJ, 1982. 425 pp., illus. $25.00.

Anthology of some of the finest, funniest stories on hunting and fishing ever assembled.

Successful Goose Hunting, by Charles L. Cadieux, Stone Wall Press, Inc., Washington, DC, 1986. 223 pp., illus. $24.95.

Here is a complete book on modern goose hunting by a lifetime waterfowler and professional wildlifer.

Supreme Duck Shooting Stories, by William Hazelton, The Gunnerman Press, Auburn Hills, MI, 1989. 160 pp. $19.95.

Originally published in 1931, this is about duck hunting as it was.

Taking Big Bucks, by Ed Wolff, Stoneydale Press, Stevensville, MT, 1987. 169 pp., illus. $18.95.

Solving the whitetail riddle.

***Taking More Birds,** by Dan Carlisle and Dolph Adams, Lyons & Burford Publishers, New York, NY, 1993. 160 pp., illus. $19.95.

A practical handbook for success at Sporting Clays and wing shooting.

Tales of Alaska's Big Bears, by Jim Rearden, Wolfe Publishing Co., Prescott, AZ, 1989. 125 pp., illus. Soft covers. $12.95.

A collection of bear yarns covering nearly three-quarters of a century.

Tales of Quails 'n Such, by Havilah Babcock, University of S. Carolina Press, Columbia, SC, 1985. 237 pp. $19.95.

A group of hunting stories, told in informal style, on field experiences in the South in quest of small game.

They Left Their Tracks, by Howard Coperhaver, Stoneydale Press Publishing Co., Stevensville, MT, 1990. 190 pp., illus. $18.95.

Recollections of 60 years as an outfitter in the Bob Marshall Wilderness.

Timberdoodle, by Frank Woolner, Nick Lyons Books, N. Y., NY, 1987. 168 pp., illus. $18.95.

The classic guide to woodcock and woodcock hunting.

Track of the Kodiak, by Marvin H. Clark, Great Northwest Publishing and Distributing Co., Anchorage, AK, 1984. 224 pp., illus. $39.95.

A full perspective on Kodiak Island bear hunting.

Tracking Wounded Deer, by Richard P. Smith, Stackpole Books, Harrisburg, PA, 1988. 159 pp., illus. Paper covers. $15.95.

How to find and tag deer shot with bow or gun.

Trail and Campfire, edited by George Bird Grinnel and Theodore Roosevelt, The Boone and Crockett Club, Dumfries, VA, 1989. 357 pp., illus. $39.50.

Reprint of the Boone and Crockett Club's 3rd book published in 1897.

Trail of the Eagle, by Bud Conkle, as told to Jim Rearden, Great Northwest Publishing & Distributing Co., Anchorage, AK, 1991. 280 pp., illus. $29.50.

Hunting Alaska with master guide Bud Conkle.

Trophy Hunter in Asia, by Elgin T. Gates, Charger Productions Inc., Capistrano Beach, CA, 1982. 272 pp., illus. $19.95.

Fascinating high adventure with Elgin Gates, one of America's top trophy hunters.

Trophy Rams of the Brooks Range Plus Secrets of a Sheep and Mountain Goat Guide, by Duncan Gilchrist, Pictorial Histories Publishing Co., Missoula, MT, 1984. 176 pp., illus. $19.95.

Covers hunting a remote corner of the Brooks Range for virgin herds of dall rams.

The Turkey Hunter's Book, by John M. McDaniel, Amwell Press, Clinton, NJ, 1980. 147 pp., illus. Paper covers. $9.95.

One of the most original turkey hunting books to be published in many years.

***Turkey Hunter's Digest, Revised Edition** by Dwain Bland, DBI Books, Inc., Northbrook, IL, 1986. 256 pp., illus. Paper covers. $17.95. (October 1994)

Presents no-nonsense approach to hunting all five sub-species of the North American wild turkey.

Turkey Hunting, Spring and Fall, by Doug Camp, Outdoor Skills Bookshelf, Nashville, TN, 1983. 165 pp., illus. Paper covers. $12.95.

Practical turkey hunting, calling, dressing and cooking, by a professional turkey hunting guide.

***Turkey Hunting with Gerry Blair,** by Gerry Blair, Krause Publications, Iola, WI, 1993. 280 pp., illus. $19.95.

Novice and veteran turkey hunters alike will enjoy this complete examination of the varied wild turkey subspecies, their environments, equipment needed to pursue them and the tactics to outwit them.

The Upland Gunner's Book, edited by George Bird Evans, The Amwell Press, Clinton, NJ, 1985. 263 pp., illus. In slipcase. $27.50.

An anthology of the finest stories ever written on the sport of upland game hunting.

***Varmint and Small Game Rifles and Cartridges,** by various authors, Wolfe Publishing Co., Prescott, AZ, 1993. 228 pp., illus. Paper covers. $26.00.

This is a collection of reprints of articles originally appearing in Wolfe's *Rifle* and *Handloader* magazines from 1966 through 1990.

Wegner's Bibliography on Dear and Deer Hunting, by Robert Wegner, St. Hubert's Press, Deforest, WI, 1993. 333 pp., 16 full-page illustrations. $45.00.

A comprehensive annotated compilation of books in English pertaining to deer and their hunting 1413-1991.

Western Hunting Guide, by Mike Lapinski, Stoneydale Press Publishing Co., Stevensville, MT, 1989. 168 pp., illus. $18.95.

A complete where-to-go and how-to-do-it guide to Western hunting.

White-Tailed Deer: Ecology and Management, by Lowell K. Halls, Stackpole Books, Harrisburg, PA, 1984. 864 pp., illus. $59.95.

The definitive work on the world's most popular big game animal.

Whitetails, by Leonard Lee Rue III, Stackpole Books, Harrisburg, PA, 1991. 320 pp., illus. $32.95.

Answers to all your questions on life cycle, feeding patterns, antlers, scrapes and rubs, behavior during the rut, and habitat.

The Wild Bears, by George Laycock, Outdoor Life Books, N. Y., NY, 1987. 272 pp., illus. Soft covers. $19.95.

The story of the grizzly, brown and black bears, their conflicts with man, and their chances of survival in the future.

The Wild Turkey Book, edited and with special commentary by J. Wayne Fears, Amwell Press, Clinton, NJ, 1982. 303 pp., illus. $22.50.

An anthology of the finest stories on wild turkey ever assembled under one cover.

Wilderness Hunting and Wildcraft, by Townsend Whelen, Wolfe Publishing Co., Prescott, AZ, 1988. 338 pp., illus. $39.00.

A limited edition reprint. Plentiful information on sheep and mountain hunting with horses and on life histories of big game animals.

The Wildfowler's Quest, by George Reiger, Lyons & Burford, Publishers, New York, NY, 1989. 320 pp., illus. $24.95.

A richly evocative look into one man's passionate pursuit of ducks, geese, turkey, woodcock, and other wildfowl all over the world.

Wind on the Water, as told to Jim Rearden, Great Northwest Publishing & Distributing Co., Anchorage, AK, 1991. 280 pp., illus. $19.95.

The true-life account of a pioneering couple, Bud and Lenora Conkle, in the wilds. Hunting stories as well as takes of the trapline, winter hardship and wilderness life in the far North.

Wings for the Heart, by Jerry A. Lewis, West River Press, Corvallis, MT, 1991. 324 pp., illus. Paper covers. $14.95.

A delightful book on hunting Montan's upland birds and waterfowl.

The Wings of Dawn, by George Reiger, Lyons & Burford, Publishers, New York, NY, 1989. 320 pp., illus. Soft covers. $15.95.

This memorable and rich portrait of the waterfowler's world includes the history of the sport, natural history of all types of ducks and geese, useful hunting advice, and more.

***The Woodchuck Hunter,** by Paul C. Estey, R&R Books, Livonia, NY, 1994. 135 pp., illus. $25.00.

This book contains information on woodchuck equipment, the rifle, telescopic sights and includes interesting stories.

Woodcock, by John Alden Knight, Gunnerman Press, Auburn Hills, MI, 1989. 160 pp., illus. $21.95.

A new printing of one of the finest books ever written on the subject.

Woodcock Shooting, by Steve Smith, Stackpole Books, Inc., Harrisburg, PA, 1988. 142 pp., illus. $16.95.

A definitive book on woodcock hunting and the characteristics of a good woodcock dog.

AFRICA/ASIA

Aagaard's Africa: A Hunter Remembers, by Finn Aagaard, National Rifle Association, Washington, DC, 1991. 196 pp., illus. $16.95.

Tales of life and livelihood in Kenya in the twilight of its glory days is told by native Kenyan Finn Aagaard.

***African Adventures,** by J.F. Burger, Safari Press, Huntington Beach, CA, 1993. 222 pp., illus. $35.00.

The reader shares adventures on the trail of the lion, the elephant and buffalo.

The African Adventures: A Return to the Silent Places, by Peter Hathaway Capstick, St. Martin's Press, New York, NY, 1992. 220 pp., illus. $22.95.

This book brings to life four turn-of-the-century adventurers and the savage frontier they braved. Frederick Selous, Constatine "Iodine" Ionides, Johnny Boyes and Jim Sutherland.

***African Camp-fire Nights,** by J.E. Burger, Safari Press, Huntington Beach, CA, 1993. 192 pp., illus. $32.50.

In this book the author writes of the men who made hunting their life's profession.

African Hunter, by James Mellon, Safari Press, Long Beach, CA, 1988. 522 pp., illus. $100.00.

The most ardent and intricately detailed book on African game hunting to appear in 50 years.

African Hunter, by Baron Bror von Blixen-Finecke, St. Martin's Press, New York, NY, 1986. 284 pp., illus. $14.95.

Reprint of the scarce 1938 edition. An African hunting classic.

African Hunting and Adventure, by William Charles Baldwin, Books of Zimbabwe, Bulawayo, 1981. 451 pp., illus. $75.00.

Facsimile reprint of the scarce 1863 London edition. African hunting and adventure from Natal to the Zambezi.

***African Jungle Memories,** by J.F. Burger, Safari Press, Huntington Beach, CA, 1993. 192 pp., illus. $32.50.

A book of reminiscences in which the reader is taken on many exciting adventures on the trail of the buffalo, lion, elephant and leopard.

***African Nature Notes and Reminiscences,** by Frederick Courteney Selous, St. Martin's Press, New York, NY, 1993. 356 pp., illus. $22.95.

This classic reprint shows both sides of Selous, the fearless tracker of game who became a legend in his hunting prowess, and the avowed conservationist who recorded his vast personal reserves of Africa lore.

African Rifles & Cartridges, by John Taylor, The Gun Room Press, Highland Park, NJ, 1977. 431 pp., illus. $35.00.

Experiences and opinions of a professional ivory hunter in Africa describing his knowledge of numerous arms and cartridges for big game. A reprint.

The African Safari, by P. Jay Fetner, St. Martin's Press, Inc., N. Y., NY, 1987. 700 pp., illus. $70.00.

A lavish, superbly illustrated, definitive work that brings together the practical elements of planning a safari with a proper appreciation for the animals and their environment.

After Big Game in Central Africa, by Edouard Foa, St. Martin's Press, New York, NY, 1989. 400 pp., illus. $16.95.

Reprint of the scarce 1899 edition. This sportsman covered 7200 miles, mostly on foot—from Zambezi delta on the east coast to the mouth of the Congo on the west.

Bell of Africa, compiled and edited by Townsend Whelen, Safari Press, Huntington Beach, CA, 1990. 236 pp., illus. $24.95.

The autobiography of W.D.M. Bell compiled and edited by his lifetime friend from Bell's own papers.

***Big Game and Big Game Rifles,** by John Taylor, Safari Press, Huntington Beach, CA, 1993. 215 pp., illus. $24.95.

A classic by the man who probably knew more about ammunition and rifles for African game than any other hunter.

The Big Game Hunters, by Michael Brander, St. Martin's Press, New York, NY, 1989. 192 pp., illus. $24.95.

The adventures of 19 sportsmen of yore in Asia, Africa, and America.

Big Game Hunting and Collecting in East Africa 1903-1926, by Kalman Kittenberger, St. Martin's Press, New York, NY, 1989. 496 pp., illus. $16.95.

One of the most heart stopping, charming and funny accounts of adventure in the Kenya Colony ever penned.

Big Game Hunting Around the World, by Bert Klineburger and Vernon W. Hurst, Exposition Press, Jericho, NY, 1969. 376 pp., illus. $30.00.
The first book that takes you on a safari all over the world.
***Big Game Hunting in Asia, Africa, and Elsewhere,** by Jacques Vettier, Trophy Room Books, Agoura, CA, 1993. 400 pp., illus. Limited, numbered edition. $150.00.
The first English language edition of the book that set a new standard in big game hunting book literature.
Big Game Hunting in North-Eastern Rhodesia, by Owen Letcher, St. Martin's Press, New York, NY, 1986. 272 pp., illus. $15.95.
A classic reprint and one of the very few books to concentrate on this fascinating area, a region that today is still very much safari country.
Big Game Shooting in Cooch Behar, the Duars and Assam, by The Maharajah of Cooch Behar, Wolfe Publishing Co., Prescott, AZ, 1993. 461 pp., illus. $118.00.
A reprinting of the book that has become legendary. This is the Maharajah's personal diary of killing 365 tigers.
The Book of the Lion, by Sir Alfred E. Pease, St. Martin's Press, New York, NY, 1986. 305 pp., illus. $15.95.
Reprint of the finest book ever published on the subject. The author describes all aspects of lion history and lion hunting, drawing heavily on his own experiences in British East Africa.
Death in a Lonely Land, by Peter Capstick, St. Martin's Press, New York, NY, 1990. 284 pp., illus. $19.95.
Twenty-three stories of hunting as only the master can tell them.
Death in the Dark Continent, by Peter Capstick, St. Martin's Press, New York, NY, 1983. 238 pp., illus. $15.95.
A book that brings to life the suspense, fear and exhilaration of stalking ferocious killers under primitive, savage conditions, with the ever present threat of death.
Death in the Long Grass, by Peter Hathaway Capstick, St. Martin's Press, New York, NY, 1977. 297 pp., illus. $17.95.
A big game hunter's adventures in the African bush.
Death in the Silent Places, by Peter Capstick, St. Martin's Press, New York, NY, 1981. 243 pp., illus. $15.95.
The author recalls the extraordinary careers of legendary hunters such as Corbett, Karamojo Bell, Stigand and others.
East Africa and its Big Game, by Captain Sir John C. Willowghby, Wolfe Publishing Co., Prescott, AZ, 1990. 312 pp., illus. $52.00.
A deluxe limited edition reprint of the very scarce 1889 edition of a narrative of a sporting trip from Zanzibar to the borders of the Masai.
East of the Sun and West of the Moon, by Theodore and Kermit Roosevelt, Wolfe Publishing Co., Prescott, AZ, 1988. 284 pp., illus. $25.00.
A limited edition reprint. A classic on Marco Polo sheep hunting. A life experience unique to hunters of big game.
Elephant, by Commander David Enderby Blunt, The Holland Press, London, England, 1985. 260 pp., illus. $35.00.
A study of this phenomenal beast by a world-leading authority.
Elephant Hunting in East Equatorial Africa, by Arthur H. Neumann, Books of Zimbabwe, Bulawayo, 1982. 455 pp., illus. $85.00.
Facsimile reprint of the scarce 1898 London edition. An account of three years ivory hunting under Mount Kenya.
***Elephant Hunting in East Equatorial Africa,** by A. Neumann, St. Martin's Press, New York, NY, 1994. 455 pp., illus. $26.95.
This is a reprint of one of the rarest elephant hunting titles ever.
Elephant Hunting in Portuguese East Africa, by Jose Pardal, Safari Press, Huntington Beach, CA, 1990. 256 pp., illus. $60.00.
This book chronicles the hunting-life story of a nearly vanished breed of man—those who single-handedly hunted elephants for prolonged periods of time.
Elephants of Africa, by Dr. Anthony Hall-Martin, New Holland Publishers, London, England, 1987. 120 pp., illus. $75.00.
A superbly illustrated overview of the African elephant with reproductions of paintings by the internationally acclaimed wildlife artist Paul Bosman.
Ends of the Earth, by Roy Chapman Andrews, Wolfe Publishing Co., Prescott, AZ, 1988. 230 pp., illus. $27.00.
A limited edition reprint. Includes adventures in China and hunting in Mongolia. Andrews was a distinguished hunter and scout.
First Wheel, by Bunny Allen, Amwell Press, Clinton, NJ, 1984. Limited, signed and numbered edition in the NSFL "African Hunting Heritage Series." 292 pp., illus. $100.00.
A white hunter's diary, 1927-47.
Green Hills of Africa, by Ernest Hemingway. Charles Scribner's Sons, NY, 1963. 285 pp., illus. Paper covers. $11.95.
A famous narrative of African big game hunting, that was first published in 1935.
Gun and Camera in Southern Africa, by H. Anderson Bryden, Wolfe Publishing Co., Prescott, AZ, 1989. 201 pp., illus. $37.00.
A limited edition reprint. The year was 1893 and author Bryden wandered for a year in Bechuanaland and the Kalahari Desert hunting the white rhino, lechwe, eland, and more.
Horned Death, by John F. Burger, Safari Press, Huntington Beach, CA, 1992. 343 pp., illus. $35.00.
The classic work on hunting the African buffalo.
Horn of the Hunter, by Robert Ruark, Safari Press, Long Beach, CA, 1987. 315 pp., illus. $35.00.
Ruark's most sought-after title on African hunting, here in reprint.
Hunting Big Game, 2 volumes, by Townsend Whelen, Wolfe Publishing Co., Prescott, AZ, 1989. Volume I, Africa and Asia, 339 pp., illus.; Volume 2, The America's, 282 pp., illus. $90.00.
A limited edition reprint. Articles and stories by F.C. Selous, Sir Samuel Baker, Arthur H. Neumann, Theodore Roosevelt and others.
***Hunting in Botswana, An Anthology,** by Tony Sanchez-Arino, Safari Press, Huntington Beach, CA, 1994. 416 pp., illus. Limited, signed and numbered edition, in a slipcase. $135.00.
The finest selection of stories compiled on hunting in Botswana.
Hunting in Many Lands, by Theodore Roosevelt and George Bird Grinnel, The Boone and Crockett Club, Dumfries, VA, 1987. 447 pp., illus. $40.00.
Limited edition reprint of this 1895 classic work on hunting in Africa, India, Mongolia, etc.
Hunting in the Sudan, An Anthology, compiled by Tony Sanchez-Arino, Safari Press, Huntington Beach, CA, 1992. 350 pp., illus. Limited, signed and numbered edition in a slipcase. $125.00.
The finest selection of junting stories ever compiled on hunting in this great game country.
Hunting in Tanzania, An Anthology, by Tony Sanchez-Arino, Safari Press, Huntington Beach, CA, 1991. 416 pp., illus. Limited, signed and numbered edition, in a slipcase. $125.00.
The finest selection of hunting stories ever compiled on that great East African game country, Tanzania.
Hunting in Zimbabwe, An Anthology, by Tony Sanchez-Arino, Safari Press, Huntington Beach, CA, 1992. 350 pp., illus. Limited, signed and numbered edition, in a slipcase. $125.00.
The finest selection of hunting stories ever compiled on hunting in this gread game country.
Hunting the Elephant in Africa, by Captain C.H. Stigand, St. Martin's Press, New York, NY, 1986. 379 pp., illus. $14.95.
A reprint of the scarce 1913 edition; vintage Africana at its best.
Jaguar Hunting in the Mato Grosso and Bolivia, by T. Almedia, Safari Press, Long Beach, CA, 1989. 256 pp., illus. $35.00.
Not since Sacha Siemel has there been a book on jaguar hunting like this one.
The Jim Corbett Collection, by Jim Corbett. Safari Press, Huntington, CA, 1991. 1124 pp., illus., five volumes in slipcase. $105.00.
This slip-cased set of Jim Corbett's works includes: *Jungle Lore, The Man-Eating Leopard of Rudraprayag, My India, Man-Eaters of Kumaon, Tree Tops,* and *Temple Tiger.*
Jim Corbett's India, stories selected by R.E. Hawkins, Oxford University Press, New York, NY, 1993. 250 pp., $24.95.
Stories and extracts from Jim Corbett's writings on tiger hunting by his publisher and editor.
Karamojo Safari, by W.D.M. Ball, Safari Press, Huntington Beach, CA, 1990. 288 pp., illus. $24.95.
The story of Bell's caravan travels through Karamojo, his exciting elephant hunts, and his life among the uncivilized and uncorrupted natives.
***King of the Wa-Kikuyu,** by John Boyes, St. Martin Press, New York, NY, 1993. 240 pp., illus. $19.95.
In the 19th and 20th centuries, Africa drew to it a large number of great hunters, explorers, adventurers and rogues. Many have become legendary, but John Boyes (1874-1951) was the most legendary of them all.
Lake Ngami, by Charles Anderson, New Holland Press, London, England, 1987. 576 pp., illus. $35.00.
Originally published in 1856. Describes two expeditions into what is now Botswana, depicting every detail of landscape and wildlife.
Last Horizons: Hunting, Fishing and Shooting on Five Continents, by Peter Capstick, St. Martin's Press, New York, NY, 1989. 288 pp., illus. $19.95.
The first in a two volume collection of hunting, fishing and shooting tales from the selected pages of The American Hunter, Guns & Ammo and Outdoor Life.
The Last Ivory Hunter: The Saga of Wally Johnson, by Peter Capstick, St. Martin's Press, New York, NY, 1988. 220 pp., illus. $18.95.
A grand tale of African adventure by the foremost hunting author of our time. Wally Johnson spent half a century in Mozambique hunting white gold—ivory.
Last of the Ivory Hunters, by John Taylor, Safari Press, Long Beach, CA, 1990. 354 pp., illus. $29.95.
Reprint of the classic book "Pondoro" by one of the most famous elephant hunters of all time.
The Man-Eaters of Tsavo, by Lt. Col. J.H. Patterson, St. Martin's Press, New York, NY, 1986. 346 pp., illus. $14.95.
A reprint of the scarce original book on the man-eating lions of Tsavo.
Memories of an African Hunter, by Denis D. Lyell, St. Martin's Press, New York, NY, 1986. 288 pp., illus. $15.95.
A reprint of one of the truly great writers on African hunting. A gripping and highly readable account of Lyell's many years in the African bush.
***One Happy Hunter,** by George Barrington, Safari Press, Huntington Beach, CA, 1994. 240 pp., illus. $40.00.
A candid, straightforward look at safari hunting.
Peter Capstick's Africa: A Return to the Long Grass, by Peter Hathaway Capstick, St. Martin's Press, N. Y., NY, 1987. 213 pp., illus. $29.95.
A first-person adventure in which the author returns to the long grass for his own dangerous and very personal excursion.
The Recollections of an Elephant Hunter 1864-1875, by William Finaughty, Books of Zimbabwe, Bulawayo, Zimbabwe, 1980. 244 pp., illus. $85.00.
Reprint of the scarce 1916 privately published edition. The early game hunting exploits of William Finaughty in Matabeleland and Nashonaland.
Robert Ruark's Africa, by Robert Ruark, Countrysport Press, Inc., Traverse City, MI, 1991. 256 pp., illus. $29.50.
A new release of previously uncollected stories of the wanderings through Africa of this giant in American sporting literature.
Safari: A Chronicle of Adventure, by Bartle Bull, Viking/Penguin, London, England, 1989. 383 pp., illus. $40.00.
The thrilling history of the African safari, highlighting some of Africa's best-known personalities.
Safari Rifles: Double, Magazine Rifles and Cartridges for African Hunting, by Craig Boddington, Safari Press, Huntington Beach, CA, 1990. 416 pp., illus. $37.50.
A wealth of knowledge on the safari rifle. Historical and present double-rifle makers, ballistics for the large bores, and much, much more.
Safari: The Last Adventure, by Peter Capstick, St. Martin's Press, New York, NY, 1984. 291 pp., illus. $15.95.
A modern comprehensive guide to the African Safari.
Sands of Silence, by Peter H. Capstick, Saint Martin's Press, New York, NY, 1991. 224 pp., illus. $35.00.
Join the author on safari in Nambia for his latest big-game hunting adventures.
The Shamba Raiders: Memories of a Game Warden, by Bruce Kinlock, Safari Press, Long Beach, CA, 1988. 405 pp., illus. $35.00.
Thrilling stories of encounters with rogue elephants, buffalo and other dangerous animals.
South Pacific Trophy Hunter, by Murray Thomas, Safari Press, Long Beach, CA, 1988. 181 pp., illus. $37.50.
A record of a hunter's search for a trophy of each of the 15 major game species in the South Pacific region.
Sport on the Pamirs and Turkestan Steppes, by Major C.S. Cumberland, Moncrieff & Smith, Victoria, Autralia, 1992. 278 pp., illus. $45.00.
The first in a series of facsimile reprints of great trophy hunting books by Moncrieff & Smith.
Tales of the Big Game Hunters, selected and introduced by Kenneth Kemp, The Sportsman's Press, London, 1986. 209 pp., illus. $15.00.
Writings by some of the best known hunters and explorers, among them: Frederick Courteney Selous, R.G. Gordon Cumming, Sir Samuel Baker, and elephant hunters Neumann and Sutherland.
Those Were the Days, by Rudolf Sand, Safari Press, Huntington Beach, CA, 1993. 300 pp., illus. $100.00.

Travel with Rudolf Sand to the pinnacles of the world in his pursuit of wild sheep and goats.

Uganda Safaris, by Brian Herne, Winchester Press, Piscataway, NJ, 1979. 236 pp., illus. $12.95.

The chronicle of a professional hunter's adventures in Africa.

Use Enough Gun, by Robert Ruark, Safari Press, Huntington Beach, CA, 1992. 333 pp., illus. $30.00.

A record of a lifetime's bag hunting big game.

The Wanderings of an Elephant Hunter, by W.D.M. Bell, Safari Press, Huntington Beach, CA, 1990. 187 pp., illus. $24.95.

The greatest of elephant books by the greatest-of-all elephant hunter.

A White Hunters Life, by Angus MacLagan, an African Heritage Book, published by Amwell Press, Clinton, NJ, 1983. 283 pp., illus. Limited, signed, and numbered deluxe edition, in slipcase. $100.00.

True to life, a sometimes harsh yet intriguing story.

Wild Sports of Southern Africa, by William Cornwallis Harris, New Holland Press, London, England, 1987. 376 pp., illus. $35.00.

Originally published in 1863, describes the author's travels in Southern Africa.

RIFLES

The Accurate Varmint Rifle, by Boyd Mace, Precision Shooting, Inc., Whitehall, NY, 1991. 184 pp., illus. $24.95.

A long overdue and long needed work on what factors go into the selection of components for and the susequent assembly of...the accurate varmint rifle.

The AK-47 Assault Rifle, Desert Publications, Cornville, AZ, 1981. 150 pp., illus. Paper covers. $10.00.

Complete and practical technical information on the only weapon in history to be produced in an estimated 30,000,000 units.

The AR-15/M16, A Practical Guide, by Duncan Long. Paladin Press, Boulder, CO, 1985. 168 pp., illus. Paper covers. $16.95.

The definitive book on the rifle that has been the inspiration for so many modern assault rifles.

Assault Weapons, 3rd Edition, The Gun Digest Book of, edited by Jack Lewis, DBI Books, Inc., Northbrook, IL, 1993. 256 pp., illus. Paper covers. $17.95

An in-depth look into the history and uses of these arms.

The Big-Bore Rifle, by Michael McIntosh, Countrysport Press, Traverse City, MI, 1990. 224 pp., illus. $39.50.

The book of fine magazine and double rifles 375 to 700 calibers.

***The Big Game Rifle,** by Jack O'Connor, Safari Press, Huntington Beach, CA, 1994. 370 pp., illus. $37.50.

An outstanding description of every detail of construction, purpose and use of the big game rifle.

Big Game Rifles and Cartridges, by Elmer Keith, reprint edition by The Gun Room Press, Highland Park, NJ, 1984. 161 pp., illus. $29.95.

Reprint of Elmer Keith's first book, a most original and accurate work on big game rifles and cartridges.

Black Powder Hobby Gunsmithing, by Sam Fadala and Dale Storey, DBI Books, Inc., Northbrook, IL., 1994. 256 pp., illus. Paper covers. $17.95.

A how-to guide for gunsmithing blackpowder pistols, rifles and shotguns from two men at the top of their respective fields.

The Black Rifle, M16 Retrospective, R. Blake Stevens and Edward C. Ezell, Collector Grade Publications, Toronto, Canada, 1987. 400 pp., illus. $59.95

The complete story of the M16 rifle and its development.

Bolt Action Rifles, revised edition, by Frank de Haas, DBI Books, Inc., Northbrook, IL, 1984. 448 pp., illus. Paper covers. $18.95.

A revised edition of the most definitive work on all major bolt-action rifle designs. Detailed coverage of over 110 turnbolt actions, including how they function, takedown and assembly, strengths and weaknesses, dimensional specifications.

The Book of the Garand, by Maj.-Gen. J.S. Hatcher, The Gun Room Press, Highland Park, NJ, 1977. 292 pp., illus. $26.95.

A new printing of the standard reference work on the U.S. Army M1 rifle.

The Book of the Rifle, by T.F. Fremantle, Wolfe Publishing Co., Prescott, AZ, 1988. 558 pp., illus. $54.00.

A limited edition reprint. This book records the point of the rifle's evolution at the opening of the 19th century.

The Book of the Twenty-Two: The All American Caliber, by Sam Fadala, Stoeger Publishing Co., So. Hackensack, NJ, 1989. 288 pp., illus. Soft covers. $16.95.

The All American Caliber from BB caps up to the powerful 226 Barnes. It's about ammo history, plinking, target shooting, and the quest for the one-hole group.

***British .22RF Training Rifles,** by Dennis Lewis and Robert Washburn, Excaliber Publications, Latham, NY, 1993. 64 pp., illus. Paper covers. $10.95.

The story of Britain's training rifles from the early Aiming Tube models to the post-WWII trainers.

Combat Rifles of the 21st Century, by Duncan Long, Paladin Press, Boulder, CO, 1991. 115 pp., illus. Paper covers. $15.00.

An inside look at the U.S. Army's program to develop a super advanced combat rifle to replace the M16.

***The Complete AR15/M16 Sourcebook,** by Duncan Long, Paladin Press, Boulder, CO, 1993. 232 pp., illus. Paper covers. $35.00.

The latest development of the AR15/M16 and the many spin-offs now available, selective-fire conversion systems for the 1990s, the vast selection of new accessories.

Exploded Long Gun Drawings, The Gun Digest Book of edited by Harold A. Murtz, DBI Books, Inc., Northbrook, IL. 512 pp., illus. Paper covers. $19.95.

Containing almost 500 rifle and shotgun exploded drawings. An invaluable aid to both professionals and hobbyists.

The Fighting Rifle, by Chuck Taylor, Paladin Press, Boulder, CO, 1983. 184 pp., illus. Paper covers. $16.95.

The difference between assault and battle rifles and auto and light machine guns.

Firearms Assembly/Disassembly Part III: Rimfire Rifles, Revised Edition, The Gun Digest Book of by J. B. Wood, DBI Books, Inc., Northbrook, IL., 1994. 480 pp., illus. Paper covers. $18.95.

Covers 65 popular rimfires plus over 100 variants, all cross-referenced in the index.

Firearms Assembly/Disassembly Part IV: Centerfire Rifles, Revised Edition, The Gun Digest Book of, by J.B. Wood, DBI Books, Inc., Northbrook, IL, 1991. 480 pp., illus. Paper covers. $18.95.

Covers 54 popular centerfire rifles plus 300 variants. The most comprehensive and professional presentation available to either hobbyist or gunsmith.

F.N.-F.A.L. Auto Rifles, Desert Publications, Cornville, AZ, 1981. 130 pp., illus. Paper covers. $13.95.

A definitive study of one of the free world's finest combat rifles.

***Highpower Rifle,** by G. David Tubb, Sports Enhancement Associates, Sedona, AZ, 1993. 205 pp., illus. Paper covers. $19.95.

The secrets of the success of G. David Tubb as the most successful U.S. high-power rifle and silhouette shooter of recent years.

The History and Development of the M16 Rifle and Its Cartridge, by David R. Hughes, Armory Publications, Oceanside, CA, 1990. 294 pp., illus. $49.95.

Study of small caliber rifle development culminating in the M16 with encyclopedic coverage of the .223/5.56mm cartridge.

Illustrated Handbook of Rifle Shooting, by A.L. Russell, Museum Restoration Service, Alexandria Bay, NY, 1992. 194 pp., illus. $24.50.

A new printing of the 1869 edition by one of the leading military marksman of the day.

Keith's Rifles for Large Game, by Elmer Keith, The Gun Room Press, Highland Park, NJ, 1986. 406 pp., illus. $39.95.

Covers all aspects of selecting, equipping, use and care of high power rifles for hunting big game, especially African.

Know Your M1 Garand, by E. J. Hoffschmidt, Blacksmith Corp., Southport, CT, 1975, 84 pp., illus. Paper covers. $9.95.

Facts about America's most famous infantry weapon. Covers test and experimental models, Japanese and Italian copies, National Match models.

Know Your Ruger 10/22 Carbine, by William E. Workman, Blacksmith Corp., Chino Valley, AZ, 1991. 96 pp., illus. Paper covers. $9.95.

The story and facts about the most popular 22 autoloader ever made.

The Lee Enfield No. 1 Rifles, by Alan M. Petrillo, Excaliber Publications, Latham, NY, 1992. 64 pp., illus. Paper covers. $10.95.

Highlights the SMLE rifles from the Mark 1-VI.

The Lee Enfield Number 4 Rifles, by Alan M. Petrillo, Excalibur Publications, Latham, NY, 1992. 64 pp., illus. Paper covers. $10.95.

A pocket-sized, bare-bones reference devoted entirely to the .303 World War II and Korean War vintage service rifle.

Legendary Sporting Rifles, by Sam Fadala, Stoeger Publishing Co., So. Hackensack, NJ, 1992. 288 pp., illus. Paper covers. $16.95.

Covers a vast span of time and technology beginning with the Kentucky Long-rifle.

The M-14 Rifle, facsimile reprint of FM 23-8, Desert Publications, Cornville, AZ, 50 pp., illus. Paper $7.95.

Well illustrated and informative reprint covering the M-14 and M-14E2.

Military Bolt Action Rifles, 1841-1918, by Donald B. Webster, Museum Restoration Service, Alexander Bay, NY, 1993. 150 pp., illus. $34.50.

A photographic survey of the principal rifles and carbines of the European and Asiatic powers of the last half of the 19th century and the first years of the 20th century.

Military and Sporting Rifle Shooting, by Captain E.C. Crossman, Wolfe Publishing Co., Prescott, AZ, 1988. 449 pp., illus. $45.00.

A limited edition reprint. A complete and practical treatise covering the use of rifles.

The Mini-14, by Duncan Long, Paladin Press, Boulder, CO, 1987. 120 pp., illus. Paper covers. $10.00.

History of the Mini-14, the factory-produced models, specifications, accessories, suppliers, and much more.

Modern Sportsman's Gun and Rifle, by J.H. Walsh ("Stonehenge"), Wolfe Publishing Co., Prescott, AZ, 1988. In two volumes, Vol. 1, 459 pp., Vol. 2, 546 pp., illus. $110.00.

A limited edition reprint. An extremely rare set of books first published in 1880s. Covers game, sporting and match rifles, and revolvers.

M1 Carbine Owner's Manual, M1, M2 & M3 .30 Caliber Carbines, Firepower Publications, Cornville, AZ, 1984. 102 pp., illus. Paper covers. $9.95.

The complete book for the owner of an M1 Carbine.

More Single Shot Rifles and Actions, by Frank de Haas, Frank de Haas, Orange City, IA, 1989. 146 pp., illus. Soft covers. $29.95.

A definitive book with in-depth studies, illustrations, drawings and descriptions of over 45 obsolete single shot rifles and actions.

***The Muzzle-Loading Rifle...Then and Now,** by Walter M. Cline, National Muzzle Loading Rifle Association, Friendship, IN, 1991. 161 pp., illus. $32.00.

This extensive compilation of the muzzleloading rifle exhibits accumulative preserved data concerning the development of the "hallowed old arms of the Southern highlands."

The Pennsylvania Rifle, by Samuel E. Dyke, Sutter House, Lititz, PA, 1975. 61 pp., illus. Paper covers. $5.00.

History and development, from the hunting rifle of the Germans who settled the area. Contains a full listing of all known Lancaster, PA, gunsmiths from 1729 through 1815.

***A Potpourri of Single Shot Rifles and Actions,** by Frank de Haas, Mark de Haas, Ridgeway, MO, 1993. 153 pp., illus. Paper covers. $22.50.

The author's 6th book on non-bolt-action single shots. Covers more than 40 single-shot rifles in historical and technical detail.

The Remington 700, by John F. Lacy, Taylor Publishing Co., Dallas, TX, 1990. 208 pp., illus. $44.95.

Covers the different models, limited editions, chamberings, proofmarks, serial numbers, military models, and much more.

The Revolving Rifles, by Edsall James, Pioneer Press, Union City, TN, 1975. 23 pp., illus. Paper covers. $2.50.

Valuable information on revolving cylinder rifles, from the earliest matchlock forms to the latest models of Colt and Remington.

Rifle and Marksmanship, by Judge H.A. Gildersleeve, reprinted by W.S. Curtis, Buckinghamshire, England, 1986. 131 pp., illus. $25.00.

Reprint of a book first published in 1878 in New York, catering to the shooter of early breechloaders and late muzzleloaders.

Rifle Guide, by Sam Fadala, Stoeger Publishing Co., S. Hackensack, NJ, 1993. 288 pp., illus. Paper covers. $16.95.

This comprehensive, fact-filled book beckons to both the seasoned rifleman as well as the novice shooter.

The Rifle in America, by Philip B. Sharpe, Wolfe Publishing Co., Prescott, AZ, 1988. 641 pp., illus. $59.00.

A limited edition reprint. A marvelous volume packed with information for the man who is interested in rifles, from the man whose life was guns.

The Rifle: Its Development for Big-Game Hunting, by S.R. Truesdell, Safari Press, Huntington Beach, CA, 1992. 274 pp., illus. $35.00.

The full story of the development of the big-game rifle from 1834-1946.

Rifle Shooting as a Sport, by Bernd Klingner, A.S. Barnes and Co., Inc., San Diego, CA, 1980. 186 pp., illus. Paper covers. $15.00.

Basic principles, positions and techniques by an international expert.

Rifleman's Handbook: A Shooter's Guide to Rifles, Reloading & Results, by Rick Jamison, NRA Publications, Washington, DC, 1990. 303 pp., illus. $21.95.
Helpful tips on precision reloading, how to squeeze incredible accuracy out of an "everyday" rifle, etc.

Riflesmithing, The Gun Digest Book of, by Jack Mitchell, DBI Books, Inc., Northbrook, IL, 1982. 256 pp., illus. Paper covers. $15.95.
Covers tools, techniques, designs, finishing wood and metal, custom alterations.

Rifles of the World, by John Walter, DBI Books, Inc., Northbrook, IL, 1993. 320 pp., illus. Paper covers. $19.95.
Compiled as a companion volume to *Pistols of the World*, this brand new reference work covers all centerfire military and commercial rifles produced from the perfection of the metal-case cartridge in the 1870's to the present time.

Ned H. Roberts and the Schuetzen Rifle, edited by Gerald O. Kelver, Brighton, CO, 1982. 99 pp., illus. $15.00.
A compilation of the writings of Major Ned H. Roberts which appeared in various gun magazines.

***The Ruger 10/22,** by William E. Workman, Krause Publications, Iola, WI, 1994. 304 pp., illus. Paper covers. $19.95.
A definitive work on one of the most popular, best-selling and perhaps best-built 22 caliber semi-automatic rifles of all time.

Schuetzen Rifles, History and Loading, by Gerald O. Kelver, Gerald O. Kelver, Publisher, Brighton, CO, 1972. Illus. $15.00.
Reference work on these rifles, their bullets, loading, telescopic sights, accuracy, etc. A limited, numbered ed.

Semi-Auto Rifles: Data and Comment, edited by Robert W. Hunnicutt, The National Rifle Association, Washington, DC, 1988. 156 pp., illus. Paper covers. $15.95.
A book for those who find military-style self-loading rifles interesting for their history, intriguing for the engineering that goes into their design, and a pleasure to shoot.

Single-Shot Actions, Their Design and Construction, by Frank and Mark Delisse, de Haas Books, Orange City, IA 1991. 247 pp., illus. $35.00.
Covers the best single shot rifles of the past plus a potpourri of modern single shot rifle actions.

Single-Shot Rifle Finale, by James Grant, Wolfe Publishing Co., Prescott, AZ, 1992. 556 pp., illus. $36.00.
The master's 5th book on the subject and his best.

Single Shot Rifles and Actions, by Frank de Haas, Orange City, IA, 1990. 352 pp., illus. Soft covers. $25.00.
The definitive book on over 60 single shot rifles and actions.

The Springfield Rifle M1903, M1903A1, M1903A3, M1903A4, Desert Publications, Cornville, AZ, 1982. 100 pp., illus. Paper covers. $10.00.
Covers every aspect of disassembly and assembly, inspection, repair and maintenance.

Sixty Years of Rifles, by Paul A. Matthews, Wolfe Publishing Co., Prescott, AZ, 1991. 224 pp., illus. $19.50.
About rifles and the author's experience and love affair with shooting and hunting.

The Sturm, Ruger 10/22 Rifle and .44 Magnum Carbine, by Duncan Long, Paladin Press, Boulder, CO, 1988. 108 pp., illus. Paper covers. $12.00.
An in-depth look at both weapons detailing the elegant simplicity of the Ruger design. Offers specifications, troubleshooting procedures and ammunition recommendations.

***Successful Rifle Shooting,** by David Parish, Trafalgar Square, N. Pomfret, VT, 1993. 250 pp., illus. $39.95.
For the beginner and advanced shooter as well. Each position and firing the shot are closely examined as is each stage of entry and participation in competition.

***To the Dreams of Youth: The .22 Caliber Single Shot Winchester Rifle,** by Herbert Houze, Krause Publications, Iola, WI, 1993. 208 pp., illus. $34.95.
A thoroughly researched history of the 22-caliber Winchester single shot rifle, including interesting photographs.

***U.S. Marine Corps AR15/M16 A2 Manual,** reprinted by Desert Publications, El Dorado, AZ, 1993. 262 pp., illus. Paper covers. $16.95.
A reprint of TM05538C-23&P/2, August, 1987. The A-2 manual for the Colt AR15/M16.

U.S. Rifle M14—From John Garand to the M21, by R. Blake Stevens, Collector Grade Publications, Inc., Toronto, Canada, revised second edition, 1991. 350 pp., illus. $47.50.
A classic, in-depth examination of the development, manufacture and fielding of the last wood-and-metal ("lock, stock, and barrel") battle rifle to be issued to U.S. troops.

War Baby!: The U.S. Caliber 30 Carbine, Volume I, by Larry Ruth, Collector Grade Publications, Toronto, Canada, 1992. 512 pp., illus. $69.95.
Volume 1 of the in-depth story of the phenomenally popular U.S. caliber 30 carbine. Concentrates on design and production of the military 30 carbine during World War II.

War Baby Comes Home: The U.S. Caliber 30 Carbine, Volume 2, by Larry Ruth, Collector Grade Pulications, Toronto, Canada, 1993. 386 pp., illus. $49.95.
The triumphant competion of Larry Ruth's two-volume in-depth series on the most popular U.S. military small arm in history.

The Winchester Model 94: The First 100 Years, by Robert C. Renneberg, Krause Publications, Iola, WI, 1991. 207 pp., illus. $34.95.
Covers the design and evolution from the early years up to today.

SHOTGUNS

***Advanced Combat Shotgun: The Stress Fire Concept,** by Massad Ayoob, Police Bookshelf, Concord, NH, 1993. 197 pp., illus. Paper covers. $9.95.
Advanced combat shotgun fighting for police.

The American Shotgun, by Charles Askins, Wolfe Publishing Co., Prescott, AZ, 1988. 321 pp., illus. $39.00.
A limited edition reprint. Askins covers shotguns and patterning extremely well.

The American Shotgun, by David F. Butler, edited by C. Kenneth Ramage, Lyman Publications, Middlefield, CT, 1973. 243 pp., illus. Paper covers. $14.95.
A comprehensive history of the American smoothbore's evolution from Colonial times to the present day.

American Shotgun Design and Performance, by L.R. Wallack, Winchester Press, Piscataway, NJ, 1977. 184 pp., illus. $16.95.
An expert lucidly recounts the history and development of American shotguns.

The American Single Barrel Trap Gun, by Frank F. Conley, Frank F. Conley, Carmel Valley, CA, 1989. 241 pp., illus. $39.95.
History, serial numbers, collecting and how they were made. Covers Baker, Fox, Ithaca, Levefer, Meriden, Parker, L.C. Smith, etc.

Best Guns, by Michael McIntosh, Countrysport, Inc., Traverse City, MI, 1989. 288 pp., illus. $39.50.
Devoted to the best shotguns ever made in the United States and the best presently being made in the world.

***The Better Shot,** by Ken Davies, Quiller Press, London, England, 1992. 136 pp., illus. $39.95.
Step-by-step shotgun technique with Holland and Holland.

Black Powder Hobby Gunsmithing, by Sam Fadala and Dale Storey, DBI Books, Inc., Northbrook, IL., 1994. 256 pp., illus. Paper covers. $17.95.
A how-to guide for gunsmithing blackpowder pistols, rifles and shotguns from two men at the top of their respective fields.

***Black's Wing & Clay, 1994 Annual Edition,** JFB, Inc., Red Bank, NJ, 1994. 177 pp., illus. Paper covers. $10.00.
The sportsman's annual guide to wing and clay shooting locations.

The British Shotgun, Volume 1, 1850-1870, by I.M. Crudington and D.J. Baker, Barrie & Jenkins, London, England, 1979. 256 pp., illus. $59.95.
An attempt to trace, as accurately as is now possible, the evolution of the shotgun during its formative years in Great Britain.

The British Shotgun, Volume 2, 1871-1890, by I.M. Crudginton and D.J. Baker, Ashford Press, Southampton, England, 1989. 250 pp., illus. $59.95.
The second volume of a definitive work on the evolution and manufacture of the British shotgun.

Clay Pigeon Shooting for Beginners and Enthusiasts, by John King, The Sportsman's Press, London, England, 1991. 94 pp., illus. $24.95.
John King has devised this splendid guide to clay pigeon shooting in the same direct style in which he teaches at his popular Barbury Shooting School near Swindon.

Clay Shooting, by Peter Croft, Ward Lock, London, England, 1990. 160 pp., illus. $29.95.
A complete guide to Skeet, trap and sporting shooting.

Clay Target Handbook by Jerry Meyer, Lyons & Buford, Publisher, New York, NY, 1993. 182 pp., illus. $22.95.
Contains in-depth, how-to-do-it information on trap, Skeet, sporting clays, international trap, international Skeet and clay target games played around the country.

Clay Target Shooting, by Paul Bentley, A&C Black, London, England, 1987. 144 pp., illus. $25.00.
Practical book on clay target shooting written by a very successful international competitor, providing valuable professional advice and instruction for shooters of all disciplines.

***A Collector's Guide to United States Combat Shotguns,** by Bruce N. Canfield, Andrew Mowbray Inc., Publishers, Lincoln, RI, 1993. 184 pp., illus. Paper covers. $24.00.
Full coverage of the combat shotgun, from the earliest examples to the Gulf War and beyond.

***The Complete Clay Shot,** by Mike Barnes, Trafalgar Square, N. Pomfret, VT, 1993. 192 pp., illus. $39.95.
The latest compendium on the clay sports by Mike Barnes, a well-known figure in shotgunning in the U.S. and England.

Cradock on Shotguns, by Chris Cradock, Banford Press, London, England, 1989. 200 pp., illus. $45.00.
A definitive work on the shotgun by a British expert on shotguns.

The Defensive Shotgun, by Louis Awerbuck, S.W.A.T. Publications, Cornville, AZ, 1989. 77 pp., illus. Soft covers. $12.95.
Cuts through the myths concerning the shotgun and its attendant ballistic effects.

The Double Shotgun, by Don Zutz, Winchester Press, Piscataway, NJ, 1985. 304 pp., illus. $19.95.
Revised, updated, expanded edition of the history and development of the world's classic sporting firearms.

Ed Scherer on Sporting Clays, by Ed Scherer, Ed Scherer, Elk Grove, WI, 1993. 200 pp., illus. Paper covers. $29.95.
Covers footwork, gun fit, master eye checks, recoil reduction, noise abatement, eye and ear protection, league shooting, shot sizes and chokes.

Exploded Long Gun Drawings, The Gun Digest Book of edited by Harold A. Murtz, DBI Books, Inc., Northbrook, IL. 512 pp., illus. Paper covers. $19.95.
Containing almost 500 rifle and shotgun exploded drawings. An invaluable aid to both professionals and hobbyists.

Field, Cover and Trap Shooting, by Adam H. Bogardus, Wolfe Publishing Co., Prescott, AZ, 1988. 446 pp., illus. $43.00.
A limited edition reprint. Hints for skilled marksmen as well as young sportsmen. Includes haunts and habits of game birds and waterfowl.

Finding the Extra Target, by Coach John R. Linn & Stephen A. Blumenthal, Shotgun Sports, Inc., Auburn, CA, 1989. 126 pp., illus. Paper covers. $14.95.
The ultimate training guide for all the clay target sports.

Firearms Assembly/Disassembly, Part V: Shotguns, Revised Edition, The Gun Digest Book of, by J.B. Wood, DBI Books, Inc., Northbrook, IL, 1992. 480 pp., illus. Paper covers. $18.95.
Covers 46 popular shotguns plus over 250 variants. The most comprehensive and professional presentation available to either hobbyist or gunsmith.

A.H. Fox "The Finest Gun in the World", by Michael McIntosh, Countrysport Press, Traverse City, MI, 1993. 392 pp., illus. $49.95.
The first full-length biography of famed American gunmaker Ansley H. Fox and the detailed history of one of America's finest shotguns.

Fucili D'Autore (The Best Guns), by Marco E. Nobili, London Guns, Ltd., Santa Barbara, CA, 1992. 845 pp., illus. $125.00.
An exhaustive study on Italian luxury-grade shotguns and their makers, with information on European makers as well. Text in English and Italian.

The Golden Age of Shotgunning, by Bob Hinman, Wolfe Publishing Co., Inc., Prescott, AZ, 1982. $17.95.
A valuable history of the late 1800s detailing that fabulous period of development in shotguns, shotshells and shotgunning.

***Gunfitting: The Quest for Perfection,** by Michael Yardley, The Sportsman's Press, London, England, 1993. 103 pp., illus. $24.95.
Apart from providing a practical and historical guide to this fascinating subject, the aim of this book is to establish gunfitting as more of a science than an art.

Hartman on Skeet, By Barney Hartman, Stackpole Books, Harrisburg, PA, 1973. 143 pp., illus. $14.95.
A definitive book on Skeet shooting by a pro.

The Ithaca Gun Company From the Beginning, by Walter Claude Snyder, Cook & Uline Publishing Co., Spencerport, NY, 1991. 256 pp., illus. $59.95.
The entire "familyk of Ithaca Gun Company products is described together with a photo gallery section containing many previously unpublished photographs of the gun makers.

L.C. Smith Shotguns, by Lt. Col. William S. Brophy, The Gun Room Press, Highland Park, NJ, 1979. 244 pp., illus. $35.00.
The first work on this very important American gun and manufacturing company.

Lefever: Guns of Lasting Fame, by Robert W. (Bob) Elliot and Jim Cobb, Robert W. (Bob) Elliot, Lindale, TX, 1986. 174 pp., illus. $35.00.
Hundreds of photographs, patent drawings and production figures are given on this famous maker's shotguns.

A Manual of Clayshooting, by Chris Cradock, Hippocrene Books, Inc., New York, NY, 1983. 192 pp., illus. $39.95.

Covers everything from building a range to buying a shotgun, with lots of illus. & dia.

The Mysteries of Shotgun Patterns, by George G. Oberfell and Charles E. Thompson, Oklahoma State University Press, Stillwater, OK, 1982. 164 pp., illus. Paper covers. $25.00.

Shotgun ballistics for the hunter in non-technical language.

The Orvis Wing-Shooting Handbook, by Bruce Bowlen, Nick Lyons Books, New York, NY, 1985. 83 pp., illus. Paper covers. $10.95.

Proven techniques for better shotgunning.

Police Shotgun Manual, by Bill Clede, Stackpole Books, Harrisburg, PA, 1986. 128 pp., illus. $18.95.

Latest shotgun techniques for tough situations.

Purdey's, the Guns and the Family, by Richard Beaumont, David and Charles, Pomfret, VT, 1984. 248 pp., illus. $39.95.

Records the history of the Purdey family from 1814 to today, how the guns were and are built and daily functioning of the factory.

Recreating the Double Barrel Muzzle-Loading Shotgun, by William R. Brockway, George Shumway Publisher, York, PA, 1985. 198 pp., illus. Paper covers. $20.00.

Treats the making of double guns of classic type.

Reloading for Shotgunners, 3rd Edition, by Edward A. Matunas, DBI Books, Inc., Northbrook, IL, 1993. 288 pp., illus. Paper covers. $16.95.

Expanded reloading tables with over 2,000 loads. Bushing charts for every major press and component maker. All new presentation on all aspects of shotshell reloading by one of the top experts in the field.

Robert Churchill's Game Shooting, edited by MacDonald Hastings, Countrysport Press, Traverse City, MI, 1990. 252 pp., illus. $29.50.

A new revised edition of the definitive book on the Churchill method of instinctive wingshooting for game and Sporting Clays.

75 Years with the Shotgun, by C.T. (Buck) Buckman, Valley, Publ., Fresno, CA, 1974. 141 pp., illus. $10.00.

An expert hunter and trapshooter shares experiences of a lifetime.

Scherer on Skeet 2, by Ed Scherer, Ed. Scherer, Waukesha, WI, 1993. 121 pp., illus. Paper covers. $19.95.

A "teaching" book, featuring the eight Skeet stations plus shootoff doubles.

Shooting at Clays, by Alan Jarrett, Stanley Paul, London, England, 1991. 176 pp., illus. $34.95.

This book unravels the complexities of clay pigeon shooting.

The Shooting Field with Holland & Holland, by Peter King, Quiller Press, London, England, new & enlarged edition, 1990. 184 pp., illus. $49.95.

The story of a company which has produced excellence in all aspects of gunmaking.

The Shotgun in Combat, by Tony Lesce, Desert Publications, Cornville, AZ, 1979. 148 pp., illus. Paper covers. $10.00.

A history of the shotgun and its use in combat.

Shotgun Digest, 4th Edition, edited by Jack Lewis, DBI Books, Inc., Northbrook, IL, 1993. 256 pp., illus. Paper covers. $16.95.

The all-new edition looking at what's happening with shotguns and shotgunning today.

Shotgun Gunsmithing, The Gun Digest Book of, by Ralph Walker, DBI Books, Inc., Northbrook, IL, 1983. 256 pp., illus. Paper covers. $15.95.

The principles and practices of repairing, individualizing and accurizing modern shotguns by one of the world's premier shotgun gunsmiths.

Shotgun Stuff, by Don Zutz, Shotgun Sports, Inc., Auburn, CA, 1991. 172 pp., illus. Paper covers. $19.95.

This book gives shotgunners all the "stuff" they need to achieve better performance and get more enjoyment from their favorite smoothbore.

Shotgunner's Notebook: The Advice and Reflections of a Wingshooter, by Gene Hill, Countrysport Press, Traverse City, MI, 1990. 192 pp., illus. $24.50.

Covers the shooting, the guns and the miscellany of the sport.

Shotgunning: The Art and the Science, by Bob Brister, Winchester Press, Piscataway, NJ, 1976. 321 pp., illus. $18.95.

Hundreds of specific tips and truly novel techniques to improve the field and target shooting of every shotgunner.

Shotgunning Trends in Transition, by Don Zutz, Wolfe Publishing Co., Prescott, AZ, 1990. 314 pp., illus. $29.95.

This book updates American shotgunning from post WWII to present.

Shotguns and Cartridges for Game and Clays, by Gough Thomas, edited by Nigel Brown, A & C Black, Ltd., Cambs, England, 1989. 256 pp., illus. Soft covers. $24.95.

Gough Thomas' well-known and respected book for game and clay pigeon shooters in a thoroughly up-dated edition.

Sidelocks & Boxlocks, by Geoffrey Boothroyd, Sand Lake Press, Amity, OR, 1991. 271 pp., illus. $29.95.

The story of the classic British shotgun.

The Sporting Clay Handbook, by Jerry Meyer, Lyons and Burford Publishers, New York, NY, 1990. 140 pp., illus. Soft covers. $15.95.

Introduction to the fastest growing, and most exciting, gun game in America.

Sporting Clays, The Gun Digest Book of, by Jack Lewis, DBI Books, Inc., Northbrook, IL, 1991. 224 pp., illus. Paper covers. $16.95.

A superb introduction to the fastest growing gun game in America.

Sporting Clays, by Michael Pearce, Stackpole Books, Harrisburg, PA, 1991. 192 pp., illus. $16.95.

Expert techniques for every kind of clays course.

The Story of the Sporting Gun, by Ranulf Rayner, Trafalgar Square, North Pomfret, VT, 1991. 96 pp., illustrated. $75.00.

This magnificent volume traces the story of game shooting from the early development of the shotgun to the present day.

*Successful Clay Pigeon Shooting, compiled by T. Hoare, Trafalgar Square, N. Pomfret, VT, 1993. 176 pp., illus. $39.95.

This comprehensive guide has been written by ten leading personalities for all aspiring clay pigeon shooters.

*Trap & Skeet Shooting, 3rd Edition, The Gun Digest Book of, by Chris Christian, DBI Books, Inc., Northbrook, IL, 1994. 288 pp., illus. Paper covers. $17.95.

This new edition gives a detailed look at the contemporary world of trap, skeet and Sporting Clays. (October 1994)

*Turkey Hunter's Digest, Revised Edition by Dwain Bland, DBI Books, Inc., Northbrook, IL, 1994. 256 pp., illus. Paper covers. $17.95.

Presents no-nonsense approach to hunting all five sub-species of the North American wild turkey. (October 1994)

U.S. Shotguns, All Types, reprint of TM9-285, Desert Publications, Cornville, AZ, 1987. 257 pp., illus. Paper covers. $9.95.

Covers operation, assembly and disassembly of nine shotguns used by the U.S. armed forces.

U.S. Winchester Trench and Riot Guns and Other U.S. Military Combat Shotguns, by Joe Poyer, North Cape Publications, Tustin, CA, 1992. 124 pp., illus. Paper covers. $15.95.

A detailed history of the use of military shotguns, and the acquisition procedures used by the U.S. Army's Ordnance Department in both World Wars.

The Winchester Model Twelve, by George Madis, David Madis, Dallas, TX, 1984. 176 pp., illus. $19.95.

A definitive work on this famous American shotgun.

The Winchester Model 42, by Ned Schwing, Krause Pub., Iola, WI, 1990. 159 pp., illus. $39.95.

Behind-the-scenes story of the model 42's invention and its early development. Production totals and manufacturing dates; reference work.

Winchester Shotguns and Shotshells, by Ronald W. Stadt, Armory Publications, Tacoma, WA, 1984. 184 pp., illus. $34.95.

From the hammer and double guns to the Model 59.

Winchester's Finest, the Model 21, by Ned Schwing, Krause Publicatons, Inc., Iola, WI, 1990. 360 pp., illus. $49.95.

The classic beauty and the interesting history of the Model 21 Winchester shotgun.

The World's Fighting Shotguns, by Thomas F. Swearengen, T. B. N. Enterprises, Alexandria, VA, 1979. 500 pp., illus. $34.95.

The complete military and police reference work from the shotgun's inception to date, with up-to-date developments.

ARMS ASSOCIATIONS

UNITED STATES

ALABAMA
Alabama Gun Collectors Assn.
Secretary, P.O. Box 70965, Tuscaloosa, AL 35407

ALASKA
Alaska Gun Collectors Assn., Inc.
C.W. Floyd, Pres., 5240 Little Tree, Anchorage, AK 99507

ARIZONA
Arizona Arms Assn.
Don DeBusk, President, 4837 Bryce Ave., Glendale, AZ 85301

CALIFORNIA
California Waterfowl Assn.
4630 Northgate Blvd., #150, Sacramento, CA 95834
Greater Calif. Arms & Collectors Assn.
Donald L. Bullock, 8291 Carburton St., Long Beach, CA 90808-3302
Los Angeles Gun Ctg. Collectors Assn.
F.H. Ruffra, 20810 Amie Ave., Apt. #9, Torrance, CA 90503

COLORADO
Colorado Gun Collectors Assn.
L.E.(Bud) Greenwald, 2553 S. Quitman St., Denver, CO 80219/303-935-3850

CONNECTICUT
Ye Connecticut Gun Guild, Inc.
Dick Fraser, P.O. Box 425, Windsor, CT 06095

FLORIDA
Unified Sportsmen of Florida
P.O. Box 6565, Tallahassee, FL 32314

GEORGIA
Georgia Arms Collectors Assn., Inc.
Michael Kindberg, President, P.O. Box 277, Alpharetta, GA 30239-0277

ILLINOIS
Illinois State Rifle Assn.
P.O. Box 637, Chatsworth, IL 60921
Illinois Gun Collectors Assn.
T.J. Curl, Jr., P.O. Box 971, Kankakee, IL 60901
Mississippi Valley Gun & Cartridge Coll. Assn.
Bob Filbert, P.O. Box 61, Port Byron, IL 61275/309-523-2593
Sauk Trail Gun Collectors
Gordell M. Matson, P.O. Box 1113, Milan, IL 61264
Wabash Valley Gun Collectors Assn., Inc.
Roger L. Dorsett, 2601 Willow Rd., Urbana, IL 61801/217-284-7302

INDIANA
Indiana State Rifle & Pistol Assn.
Thos. Glancy, P.O. Box 552, Chesterton, IN 46304
Southern Indiana Gun Collectors Assn., Inc.
Sheila McClary, 309 W. Monroe St., Boonville, IN 47601/812-897-3742

IOWA
Beaver Creek Plainsmen Inc.
Steve Murphy, Secy., P.O. Box 298, Bondurant, IA 50035
Central States Gun Collectors Assn.
Avery Giles, 1104 S. 1st Ave., Marshtown, IA 50158

KANSAS

Kansas Cartridge Collectors Assn.
Bob Linder, Box 84, Plainville, KS 67663

KENTUCKY
Kentuckiana Arms Collectors Assn.
Charles Billips, President, Box 1776, Louisville, KY 40201
Kentucky Gun Collectors Assn., Inc.
Ruth Johnson, Box 64, Owensboro, KY 42302/502-729-4197

LOUISIANA
Washitaw River Renegades
Sandra Rushing, P.O. Box 256, Main St., Grayson, LA 71435

MARYLAND
Baltimore Antique Arms Assn.
Mr. Cillo, 1034 Main St., Darlington, MD 21304

MASSACHUSETTS
Bay Colony Weapons Collectors, Inc.
John Brandt, Box 111, Hingham, MA 02043
Massachusetts Arms Collectors
Bruce E. Skinner, P.O. Box 31, No. Carver, MA 02355/508-866-5259

MISSISSIPPI
Mississippi Gun Collectors Assn.
Jack E. Swinney, P.O. Box 16323, Hattiesburg, MS 39402

MISSOURI
Mineral Belt Gun Collectors Assn.
D.F. Saunders, 1110 Cleveland Ave., Monett, MO 65708
Missouri Valley Arms Collectors Assn., Inc.
L.P Brammer II, Membership Secy., P.O. Box 33033, Kansas City, MO 64114

MONTANA
Montana Arms Collectors Assn.
Lewis E. Yearout, 308 Riverview Dr. East, Great Falls, MT 59404
The Winchester Arms Collectors Assn.
Richard Berg, P.O. Box 6754, Great Falls, MT 59406

NEW HAMPSHIRE
New Hampshire Arms Collectors, Inc.
Frank H. Galeucia, Rt. 28, Box 44, Windham, NH 03087

NEW JERSEY
Englishtown Benchrest Shooters Assn.
Michael Toth, 64 Cooke Ave., Carteret, NJ 07008
Jersey Shore Antique Arms Collectors
Joe Sisia, P.O. Box 100, Bayville, NJ 08721-1950
New Jersey Arms Collectors Club, Inc.
Angus Laidlaw, President, 230 Valley Rd., Montclair, NJ 07042/201-746-0939

NEW YORK
Iroquois Arms Collectors Assn.
Bonnie Robinson, Show Secy., P.O. Box 142, Ransomville, NY 14131/716-791-4096
Mid-State Arms Coll. & Shooters Club
Jack Ackerman, 24 S. Mountain Terr., Binghamton, NY 13903

NORTH CAROLINA
North Carolina Gun Collectors Assn.
Jerry Ledford, 3231-7th St. Dr. NE, Hickory, NC 28601

OHIO
Ohio Gun Collectors Assn.

P.O. Box 24170, Cincinnati, OH 45224-0170
The Stark Gun Collectors, Inc.
William I. Gann, 5666 Waynesburg Dr., Waynesburg, OH 44688

OKLAHOMA
Indian Territory Gun Collector's Assn.
P.O. Box 4491, Tulsa, OK 74159/918-745-9141

OREGON
Oregon Arms Collectors Assn., Inc.
Phil Bailey, P.O. Box 13000-A, Portland, OR 97213
Oregon Cartridge Collectors Assn.
Gale Stockton, 52 N.W. 2nd, Gresham, OR 97030

PENNSYLVANIA
Presque Isle Gun Collectors Assn.
James Welch, 156 E. 37 St., Erie, PA 16504

SOUTH CAROLINA
Belton Gun Club, Inc.
J.K. Phillips, 195 Phillips Dr., Belton, SC 29627
South Carolina Shooting Assn.
P.O. Box 12658, Columbia, SC 29211-2658
Membership Div.: William Strozier, Secretary, P.O. Box 70, Johns Island, SC 29457-0070

SOUTH DAKOTA
Dakota Territory Gun Coll. Assn., Inc.
Curt Carter, Castlewood, SD 57223

TENNESSEE
Smoky Mountain Gun Coll. Assn., Inc.
Hugh W. Yabro, President, P.O. Box 23225, Knoxville, TN 37933
Tennessee Gun Collectors Assn., Inc.
M.H. Parks, 3556 Pleasant Valley Rd., Nashville, TN 37204

TEXAS
Houston Gun Collectors Assn., Inc.
P.O. Box 741429, Houston, TX 77274-1429
Texas Cartridge Collectors Assn., Inc.
Peter E. Davis, Memb. Contact, 14738 C Perthshire Rd., Houston, TX 77079
Texas Gun Collectors Assn.
13201 Wells Fargo Trail, Austin, TX 78737
Texas State Rifle Assn.
P.O. Drawer 710549, Dallas, TX 75371

WASHINGTON
Washington Arms Collectors, Inc.
J. Dennis Cook, P.O. Box 7335, Tacoma, WA 98407/206-752-2268

WISCONSIN
Great Lakes Arms Collectors Assn., Inc.
Edward C. Warnke, 2913 Woodridge Lane, Waukesha, WI 53188
Wisconsin Gun Collectors Assn., Inc.
Lulita Zellmer, P.O. Box 181, Sussex, WI 53089

WYOMING
Wyoming Weapons Collectors
P.O. Box 284, Laramie, WY 82070/307-745-4652 or 745-9530

NATIONAL ORGANIZATIONS
Amateur Trapshooting Assn.
601 W. National Rd., Vandalia, OH 45377
American Coon Hunters Assn.
Opal Johnston, P.O. Cadet, Route 1, Box 492, Old Mines, MO 63630
American Custom Gunmakers Guild
Jan Billeb, Exec. Director, P.O. Box 812,

Burlington, IA 52601-0812/319-752-6114 (Phone or Fax)

American Defense Preparedness Assn.
Two Colonial Place, 2101 Wilson Blvd., Suite 400, Arlington, VA 22201-3061

American Pistolsmiths Guild
Hamilton S. Bowen, President, P.O. Box 67, Louisville, TN 37777

American Police Pistol & Rifle Assn.
3801 Biscayne Blvd., Miami, FL 33137

American Single Shot Rifle Assn.
Gary Staup, Secy., 709 Carolyn Dr., Delphos, OH 45833/419-692-3866

American Society of Arms Collectors
George E. Weatherly, P.O. Box 2567, Waxahachie, TX 75165

Association of Firearm and Toolmark Examiners
Eugenia A. Bell, Secy., 7857 Esterel Dr., LaJolla, CA 92037; Membership Secy., Andrew B. Hart, 80 Mountain View Ave., Rensselaer, NY 12144

Boone & Crockett Club
250 Station Dr., Missoula, MT 59801-2753

Browning Collectors Assn.
Bobbie Hamit, P.O. Box 526, Aurora, NE 68818/402-694-6602

The Cast Bullet Assn., Inc.
Ralland J. Fortier, Membership Director, 4103 Foxcraft Dr., Traverse City, MI 49684

Citizens Committee for the Right to Keep and Bear Arms
Natl. Hq., Liberty Park, 12500 NE Tenth Pl., Bellevue, WA 98005

Colt Collectors Assn.
3200 Westminster, Dallas, TX 75205

Ducks Unlimited, Inc.
One Waterfowl Way, Memphis, TN 38120

Fifty Caliber Shooters Assn.
11469 Olive St. Rd., Suite 50, St. Louis, MO 63141

Firearms Coalition
Box 6537, Silver Spring, MD 20906/301-871-3006

Firearms Engravers Guild of America
Robert Evans, Secy., 332 Vine St., Oregon City, OR 97045

Foundation for North American Wild Sheep
720 Allen Ave., Cody, WY 82414

Garand Collectors Assn.
P.O. Box 181, Richmond, KY 40475

Golden Eagle Collectors Assn.
Chris Showler, 11144 Slate Creek Rd., Grass Valley, CA 95945

Gun Owners of America
8001 Forbes Place, Suite 102, Springfield, VA 22151/703-321-8585

Handgun Hunters International
J.D. Jones, Director, P.O. Box 357 MAG, Bloomingdale, OH 43910

Harrington & Richardson Gun Coll. Assn.
George L. Cardet, 330 S.W. 27th Ave., Suite 603, Miami, FL 33135

Hopkins & Allen Arms & Memorabilia Society (HAAMS)
1309 Pamela Circle, Delphos, OH 45833

International Benchrest Shooters
Joan Borden, RD 1, Box 244A, Tunkhannock, PA 18657

International Blackpowder Hunting Assn.
P.O. Box 1180, Glenrock, WY 82637/307-436-9817

International Cartridge Coll. Assn., Inc.
Charles Spano, P.O. Box 5297, Ormond Beach, FL 32174-5297

IHMSA (Intl. Handgun Metallic Silhouette Assn.)
Frank Scotto, P.O. Box 5038, Meriden, CT 06450

International Handloading Assn.
6471 Airpark Dr., Prescott, AZ 86301

IPPA (International Paintball Players Assn.)
P.O. Box 26669, San Diego, CA 92196-0669/619-695-8882

Jews for the Preservation of Firearms Ownership (JPFO)
2872 S. Wentworth Ave., Milwaukee, WI 53207/414-769-0760

The Mannlicher Collectors Assn.
Rev. Don L. Henry, Secy., P.O. Box 7144, Salem, OR 97303

Marlin Firearms Collectors Assn., Ltd.
Dick Paterson, Secy., 407 Lincoln Bldg., 44 Main St., Champaign, IL 61820

Miniature Arms Collectors/Makers Society, Ltd.
Ralph Koebbeman, Pres., 4910 Kilburn Ave., Rockford, IL 61101/815-963-1466

M1 Carbine Collectors Assn. (M1-CCA)
P.O. Box 4895, Stateline, NV 89449

National Association of Buckskinners
Tim Pray, 1981 E. 94th Ave., Thornton, CO 80229

The National Association of Derringer Collectors
P.O. Box 20572, San Jose, CA 95160

National Assn. of Federally Licensed Firearms Dealers
Andrew Molchan, 2455 E. Sunrise, Ft. Lauderdale, FL 33304

National Association to Keep and Bear Arms
P.O. Box 78336, Seattle, WA 98178

National Automatic Pistol Collectors Assn.
Tom Knox, P.O. Box 15738, Tower Grove Station, St. Louis, MO 63163

National Bench Rest Shooters Assn., Inc.
Pat Baggett, 2027 Buffalo, Levelland, TX 79336

National Firearms Assn.
P.O. Box 160038, Austin, TX 78716/403-439-1094; FAX: 403-439-4091

National Muzzle Loading Rifle Assn.
Box 67, Friendship, IN 47021

National Reloading Manufacturers Assn.
One Centerpointe Dr., Suite 300, Lake Oswego, OR 97035

National Rifle Assn. of America
11250 Waples Mill Rd., Fairfax, VA 22030

National Shooting Sports Foundation, Inc.
Robert T. Delfay, President, Flintlock Ridge Office Center, 11 Mile Hill Rd., Newtown, CT 06470-2359/203-426-1320; FAX: 203-426-1087

National Skeet Shooting Assn.
Mike Hampton, Exec. Director, P.O. Box 680007, San Antonio, TX 78268-0007

National Sporting Clays Association
P.O. Box 680007, San Antonio, TX 78268/800-877-5338

National Wild Turkey Federation, Inc.
P.O. Box 530, Edgefield, SC 29824

North American Hunting Club
P.O. Box 3401, Minnetonka, MN 55343

North-South Skirmish Assn., Inc.
Stevan F. Meserve, Exec. Secretary, 204 W. Holly Ave., Sterling, VA 20164-4006

Remington Society of America
Leon W. Wier Jr., President, 8268 Lone Feather Ln., Las Vegas, NV 89123

Rocky Mountain Elk Foundation
P.O. Box 8249, Missoula, MT 59807-8249

Ruger Collector's Assn., Inc.
P.O. Box 1441, Yazoo City, MS 39194

Safari Club International
Philip DeLone, Executive Dir., 4800 W. Gates Pass Rd., Tucson, AZ 85745/602-620-1220

Sako Collectors Assn., Inc.
Karen Reed, 1725 Woodhill Ln., Bedford, TX 76021

Second Amendment Foundation
James Madison Building, 12500 NE 10th Pl., Bellevue, WA 98005

Smith & Wesson Collectors Assn.
George Linne, 2711 Miami St., St. Louis, MO 63118

The Society of American Bayonet Collectors
P.O. Box 234, East Islip, NY 11730-0234

Southern California Schuetzen Society
Dean Lillard, 34657 Ave. E., Yucaipa, CA 92399

Sporting Arms & Ammunition Manufacturers Institute (SAAMI)
Flintlock Ridge Office Center, 11 Mile Hill Rd., Newtown, CT 06470-2359/203-426-1320; FAX: 203-426-1087

Sporting Clays of America (SCA)
Ellen McCormick, Director of Membership Services, 9 Mott Ave., Suite 103, Norwalk, CT 06850/203-831-8483; FAX: 203-831-8497

The Thompson/Center Assn.
Joe Wright, President, Box 792, Northboro, MA

01532/508-393-3834

U.S. Practical Shooting Assn./IPSC
Marilyn Stanford, P.O. Box 811, Sedro Woolley, WA 98284/206-855-2245

U.S. Revolver Assn.
Brian J. Barer, 40 Larchmont Ave., Taunton, MA 02780

The Varmint Hunters Assn., Inc.
Box 759, Pierre, SD 57501/Member Services 800-528-4868

Weatherby Collectors Assn., Inc.
P.O. Box 128, Moira, NY 12957

The Wildcatters
P.O. Box 170, Greenville, WI 54942

Winchester Arms Collectors Assn.
Richard Berg, Executive Secy., P.O. Box 6754, Great Falls, MT 59406

The Women's Shooting Sports Foundation (WSSF)
1505 Highway 6 South, Suite 101, Houston, TX 77077

AUSTRALIA

Sporting Shooters Assn. of Australia, Inc.
P.O. Box 2066, Kent Town, SA 5071, Australia

CANADA

ALBERTA

Canadian Historical Arms Society
P.O. Box 901, Edmonton, Alb., Canada T5J 2L8

National Firearms Assn.
Natl. Hq: P.O. Box 1779, Edmonton, Alb., Canada T5J 2P1

ONTARIO

Tri-County Antique Arms Fair
P.O. Box 122, RR #1, North Lancaster Ont., Canada K0C 1Z0

EUROPE

ENGLAND

Arms and Armour Society
E.J.B. Greenwood, Field House, Upper Dicker, Hailsham, East Sussex, BN27 3PY, England

Historical Breechloading Smallarms Assn.
D.J. Penn M.A., Imperial War Museum, Lambeth Rd., London SE 1 6HZ, England. Journal and newsletter are $13 a yr., plus surcharge for airmail.

National Rifle Assn.
(Great Britain) Bisley Camp, Brookwood, Woking Surrey GU24 OPB, England/0483.797777

FRANCE

Syndicat National de l'Arquebuserie du Commerce de l'Arme Historique
B.P. No. 3, 78110 Le Vesinet, France

GERMANY

Bund Deutscher Sportschützen e.v. (BDS)
Borsigallee 10, 53125 Bonn 1, Germany

NEW ZEALAND

New Zealand Deerstalkers Assn.
Michael Watt, P.O. Box 6514, Wellington, New Zealand

SOUTH AFRICA

Historical Firearms Soc. of South Africa
P.O. Box 145, 7725 Newlands, Republic of South Africa

SAGA (S.A. Gunowners' Assn.)
P.O. Box 35204, Northway 4065, Republic of South Africa

DIRECTORY
OF THE
ARMS TRADE

The **Product Directory** contains 53 product categories. Note that in the Product Directory, a black bullet preceeding a manufacturer's name indicates the availability of a Warranty Service Center address, which can be found on page 451.

The **Manufacturers' Directory** alphabetically lists the manufacturers with their addresses, phone numbers and FAX numbers, if available.

DIRECTORY OF THE ARMS TRADE INDEX

PRODUCT DIRECTORY

AMMUNITION, COMMERCIAL

Action Arms Ltd.
ACTIV Industries, Inc.
American Ammunition
Amtech International, Inc.
Amtech-Overseas, Inc.
A-Square Co., Inc.
Ballistic Products, Inc.
Black Hills Ammunition
Blammo Ammo
Blount, Inc.
Brenneke KG, Wilhelm
Buck-X, Inc.
California Magnum
CBC
Cherokee Gun Accessories
ChinaSports, Inc.
Cor-Bon Bullet & Ammo Co.
C.W. Cartridge Co.
Daisy Mfg. Co.
Denver Bullets, Inc.
Diana
DKT, Inc.
Dynamit Nobel-RWS, Inc.
Eley Ltd.
Elite Ammunition
Estate Cartridge, Inc.
Federal Cartridge Co.
Fiocchi of America, Inc.
FN Herstal
Gamo
Garrett Cartridges, Inc.
GDL Enterprises
Glaser Safety Slug, Inc.
"Gramps" Antique Cartridges
Hansen & Co.
Hansen Cartridge Co.
Hirtenberger Aktiengesellschaft
Hornady Mfg. Co.
ICI-America
IMI
IMI Services USA, Inc.
Jones, J.D.
Keng's Firearms Specialty, Inc.
Kent Cartridge Mfg. Co. Ltd.
Lapua Ltd.
Lethal Force Institute

Lomont Precision Bullets
M&D Munitions Ltd.
Magnum Research, Inc.
MagSafe Ammo Co.
MAGTECH Recreational
    Products, Inc.
Maionchi-L.M.I.
Markell, Inc.
Master Class Bullets
Men-Metallwerk
    Elisenhuette, GmbH
Mullins Ammo
NECO
Neutralizer Police Munitions
New England Ammunition Co.
Oklahoma Ammunition Co.
Old Western Scrounger, Inc.
Omark Industries
Patriot Manufacturing
PMC/Eldorado Cartridge Corp.
Police Bookshelf
Polywad, Inc.
Pony Express Reloaders
Precision Delta Corp.
Pro Load Ammunition, Inc.
Ravell Ltd.
Remington Arms Co., Inc.
Rocky Fork Enterprises
Royal Arm International Products
Rucker Ammunition Co.
RWS
Sherwood Intl. Export Corp.
Speer Products
SSK Industries
Star Reloading Co., Inc.
The BulletMakers Workshop
3-D Ammunition & Bullets
3-Ten Corp.
True Flight Bullet Co.
USAC
Valor Corp.
Victory USA
Vom Hofe
Weatherby, Inc.
Winchester Div., Olin Corp.
Zero Ammunition Co., Inc.

AMMUNITION, CUSTOM

Accuracy Unlimited (Littleton, CO)
AFSCO Ammunition
All American Bullets
American Derringer Corp.
A-Square Co., Inc.
Ballard Built
Ballistic Products, Inc.
Ballistica Maximus North
Bear Arms
Beeline Custom Bullets
Berger Bullets
Bertram Bullet Co.
Black Hills Ammunition
Brynin, Milton
BulletMakers Workshop, The
Champlin Firearms, Inc.
Christman Jr., David
Country Armourer, The
Cubic Shot Shell Co., Inc.
Custom Hunting Ammo & Arms
Custom Tackle & Ammo
C.W. Cartridge Co.
Dakota Arms
Deadeye Sport Center
DKT, Inc.
Eagle Flight Bullet Co.
Eley Ltd.
Elite Ammunition
Elko Arms
Ellis Sport Shop, E.W.
Epps "Orillia" Ltd., Ellwood
Estate Cartridge, Inc.
Fitz Pistol Grip Co.
Fox Cartridge Division

Freedom Arms, Inc.
Gammog, Gregory B. Gally
Gonzalez Guns, Ramon B.
"Gramps" Antique Cartridges
Granite Custom Bullets
Green Bay Bullets
Heidenstrom Bullets
Hindman, Ace
Hirtenberger Aktiengesellschaft
Hoelscher, Virgil
Horizons Unlimited
Hornady Mfg. Co.
Jackalope Gun Shop
JägerSport, Ltd.
Jaro Manufacturing
Jensen Bullets
Jensen's Custom Ammunition
Jensen's Firearm Academy
Jett & Co., Inc.
Jones, J.D.
Kaswer Custom, Inc.
Keeler, R.H.
Kent Cartridge Mfg. Co. Ltd.
KJM Fabritek, Inc.
Kortz, Dr. L.
Lindsley Arms Cartridge Co.
Lomont Precision Bullets
M&D Munitions Ltd.
Marple & Associates, Dick
Master Class Bullets
McMurdo, Lynn
Men-Metallwerk
    Elisenhuette, GmbH
Mullins Ammo

NECO
Old Western Scrounger, Inc.
Parts & Surplus
Pasadena Gun Center
Personal Protection Systems Ltd.
Precision Delta Corp.
Precision Munitions, Inc.
Professional Hunter Supplies
Sanders Custom Gun Service
Sandia Die & Cartridge Co.
Slings & Arrows
Specialty Gunsmithing
Spence, George W.
SSK Industries
Star Custom Bullets

State Arms Gun Co.
Stewart's Gunsmithing
Three-Ten Corp.
True Flight Bullet Co.
Vitt/Boos
Vom Hofe
Vulpes Ventures, Inc.
Warren Muzzleloading Co., Inc.
Weaver Arms Corp.
Westley Richards & Co.
Worthy Products, Inc.
Wosenitz VHP, Inc.
Wyoming Armory, Inc.
Wyoming Bonded Bullets
Zero Ammunition Co., Inc.

AMMUNITION, FOREIGN

Action Arms Ltd.
AFSCO Ammunition
Allred Bullet Co.
Ammunition Consulting
    Services, Inc.
Armscorp USA, Inc.
A-Square Co., Inc.
Ballistic Products, Inc.
Bertram Bullet Co.
BulletMakers Workshop, The
B-West Imports, Inc.
Century International Arms, Inc.
Cubic Shot Shell Co., Inc.
Deadeye Sport Center
Diana
DKT, Inc.
Dynamit Nobel-RWS, Inc.
Estate Cartridge, Inc.
Fiocchi of America, Inc.
FN Herstal
Gamo
Gonzalez Guns, Ramon B.
"Gramps" Antique Cartridges

Hirtenberger Aktiengesellschaft
Hornady Mfg. Co.
IMI
Jackalope Gun Shop
Kassnar
K.B.I., Inc.
Maionchi-L.M.I.
Merkuria Ltd.
New England Arms Co.
Oklahoma Ammunition Co.
Old Western Scrounger, Inc.
Paragon Sales & Services, Inc.
Precision Delta Corp.
R.E.T. Enterprises
RWS
Samco Global Arms, Inc.
Sherwood Intl. Export Corp.
Southern Ammunition Co., Inc.
Spence, George W.
Talon Mfg. Co., Inc.
T.F.C. S.p.A.
Vom Hofe

AMMUNITION COMPONENTS—BULLETS, POWDER, PRIMERS, CASES

Acadian Ballistic Specialties
Accuracy Unlimited (Littleton, CO)
Accurate Arms Co., Inc.
Action Bullets, Inc.
ACTIV Industries, Inc.
Advance Car Mover Co.,
    Rowell Div.
Alaska Bullet Works
Allred Bullet Co.
Alpha LaFranck
American Bullets
American Products Co.
Ames Metal Products Co.
Armfield Custom Bullets
A-Square Co., Inc.
Badger Shooters Supply, Inc.
Ballard Built
Ballistic Products, Inc.
Banaczkowski Bullets
Barnes Bullets, Inc.
Beartooth Bullets
Bell Reloading, Inc.
Berger Bullets
Bergman & Williams
Berry's Bullets
Bertram Bullet Co.
Bitterroot Bullet Co.
Black Hills Shooters Supply
Black Mountain Bullets
Blount, Inc.
Blue Mountain Bullets
Brenneke KG, Wilhelm
Briese Bullet Co., Inc.
Brown Co., E. Arthur
Brownells, Inc.
BRP, Inc.
Bruno Shooters Supply
Buck Stix
Buckeye Custom Bullets
Buffalo Arms

Buffalo Bullet Co., Inc.
Buffalo Rock Shooters Supply
Bullet, Inc.
Bullet Mills
Bullseye Bullets
Bull-X, Inc.
Butler Enterprises
Buzztail Brass
Calhoon Varmint Bullets, James
Canadian Custom Bullets
Canyon Cartridge Corp.
Carnahan Bullets
Carroll Bullets
Cascade Bullet Co., Inc.
CBC
CCI
CFVentures
Champion's Choice, Inc.
Cheddite France S.A.
CheVron Bullets
Circle M Custom Bullets
Classic Brass
Competitor Corp., Inc.
Complete Handloader, The
Cook Bullets
Cook Engineering Service
Cor-Bon Bullet & Ammo Co.
Crawford Co., Inc., R.M.
Creative Cartridge Co.
Cummings Bullets
Curtis Gun Shop
Custom Bullets by Hoffman
Cutsinger Benchrest Bullets
D&J Bullet Co. & Custom Gun
    Shop, Inc.
Dakota Arms
Deadeye Sport Center
DKT, Inc.
Dohring Bullets
DuPont

Eichelberger Bullets, Wm.
Eiland Custom Bullets
Elkhorn Bullets
Enguix Import-Export
Federal Cartridge Co.
Finch Custom Bullets
Fiocchi of America, Inc.
Fitz Pistol Grip Co.
Fowler Bullets
Foy Custom Bullets
Freedom Arms, Inc.
Fusilier Bullets
G&C Bullet Co., Inc.
Gehmann, Walter
GOEX, Inc.
Gotz Bullets
"Gramps" Antique Cartridges
Grand Falls Bullets
Granite Custom Bullets
Green Bay Bullets
Grizzly Bullets
Group Tight Bullets
Gun City
Hammets VLD Bullets
Hardin Specialty Dist.
Harris Enterprises
Hart & Son, Inc., Robert W.
Haselbauer Products, Jerry
Hawk Co.
Heidenstrom Bullets
Hercules, Inc.
HH Engineering
Hirtenberger Aktiengesellschaft
Hobson Precision Manufacturing Co.
Hodgdon Powder Co., Inc.
Hornady Mfg. Co.
HT Bullets
Huntington Die Specialties
Idaho Bullets
IMI
IMI Services USA, Inc.
Imperial Magnum Corp.
IMR Powder Co.
J-4, Inc.
J&D Components
J&L Superior Bullets
Jaro Manufacturing
Jensen Bullets
Jensen's Firearms Academy
Jester Bullets
JLK Bullets
Jones, J.D.
Ka Pu Kapili
Kasmarsnik Bullets
Kaswer Custom, Inc.
Keith's Bullets
Ken's Kustom Kartridge
Kent Cartridge Mfg. Co. Ltd.
KJM Fabritek, Inc.
Kodiak Custom Bullets
Lachaussee, S.A.
Lage Uniwad, Inc.
Lane Bullets, Inc.
Lapua Ltd.
Lathrop's, Inc.
Lawrence Brand Shot
Liberty Shooting Supplies
Lightfield Ammunition Corp., The
  Slug Group
Lindsley Arms Cartridge Co.
Lomont Precision Bullets
M&D Munitions Ltd.
Magnus Bullets
Maine Custom Bullets
Maionchi-L.M.I.
Marchmon Bullets
Master Class Bullets
McKenzie Bullet Co.
McMurdo, Lynn
MCRW Associates Shooting Supplies
MEC, Inc.
Men-Metallwerk Elisenhuette, GmbH
Merkuria Ltd.
Michael's Antiques
Miller Enterprises, Inc.
Miller Enterprises, Inc., R.P.
Mitchell Bullets, R.F.
Mi-Te Bullets
MoLoc Bullets
Montana Precision Swaging
Mt. Baldy Bullet Co.
Mulhern, Rick
Murmur Corp.
Mushroom Express Bullet Co.
Nagel's Bullets
National Bullet Co.
Naval Ordnance Works

Necromancer Industries, Inc.
Norma
Northern Prec. Swaged Bullets
Nosler, Inc.
O'Connor Rifle Products Co., Ltd.
Oklahoma Ammunition Co.
Old Wagon Bullets
Old Western Scrounger, Inc.
Omark Industries
Ordnance Works, The
Pace Marketing, Inc.
Page Custom Bullets
Paragon Sales & Services, Inc.
Pasadena Gun Center
Patrick Bullets
Pattern Control
Peerless Alloy, Inc.
Petro-Explo, Inc.
Phillippi Custom Bullets, Justin
Polywad, Inc.
Pomeroy, Robert
Precision Ballistics Co.
Precision Components
Precision Components & Guns
Precision Delta Corp.
Precision Munitions, Inc.
Precision Reloading, Inc.
Prescott Projectile Co.
Price Bullets, Patrick W.
Professional Hunter Supplies
Rainier Ballistic Corp.
Ranch Products
Ravell Ltd.
Redwood Bullet Works
Reloading Specialties, Inc.
Remington Arms Co., Inc.
Rencher Bullets
Renner Co., R.J./Radical Concepts
Rifle Works & Armory
R.I.S. Co., Inc.
Robinson H.V. Bullets
Rolston, Jr., Fred W.
Rubright Bullets
Rucker Ammunition Co.
Sabertooth Industries
Scharch Mfg., Inc.
Schmidtman Custom Ammunition
Schneider Bullets
Scot Powder Co. of Ohio, Inc.
Shappy Bullets
Sheridan USA, Inc., Austin
Shotgun Bullets Mfg.
Sinclair International, Inc.
Sioux Bullets
Small Group Bullets
SOS Products Co.
Southern Ammunition Co., Inc.
Specialty Gunsmithing
Speer Products
SSK Industries
Stanley Bullets
Star Custom Bullets
Stark's Bullets Manufacturing
Stewart's Gunsmithing
Swift Bullet Co.
Talon Mfg. Co., Inc.
Taracorp Industries
TCCI
TCSR
T.F.C. S.p.A.
Thompson Precision
3-D Ammunition & Bullets
TMI Products
Trico Plastics
Trophy Bonded Bullets, Inc.
True Flight Bullet Co.
USAC
Vann Custom Bullets
Vihtavuori Oy
Vihtavuori Oy/Kaltron-Pettibone
Vincent's Shop
Vitt/Boos
Vom Hofe
Watson Trophy Match Bullets
Widener's Reload. & Shoot. Supply
Williams Bullet Co., J.R.
Winchester Div., Olin Corp.
Windjammer Tournament Wads, Inc.
Winkle Bullets
Woodleigh
Worthy Products, Inc.
Wosenitz VHP, Inc.
Wyant Bullets
Wyoming Armory, Inc.
Wyoming Bonded Bullets
Wyoming Custom Bullets
Zero Ammunition Co., Inc.

ANTIQUE ARMS DEALERS

Ad Hominem
Antique American Firearms
Antique Arms Co.
Aplan Antiques & Art, James O.
Armoury, Inc., The
Arms, Jackson
Bear Mountain Gun & Tool
Beeman Precision Airguns, Inc.
Big 45 Frontier Gun Shop
Boggs, Wm.
British Arms Co. Ltd.
Buckskin Machine Works
Bustani Appraisers, Leo
Cannons Guns
Cape Outfitters
Carlson, Douglas R.
Chadick's Ltd.
Champlin Firearms, Inc.
Chuck's Gun Shop
Classic Guns, Inc.
Cole's Gun Works
Colonial Repair
Condon, Inc., David
Corry, John
Cullity Restoration, Daniel
D&D Gunsmiths, Ltd.
Dyson & Son Ltd., Peter
Ed's Gun House
Epps "Orillia" Ltd., Ellwood
Fagan & Co., William
Fish, Marshall F.
Flayderman & Co., N.
Flintlock Muzzle Loading Gun
  Shop, The
Forty Five Ranch Enterprises
Frielich Police Equipment
Fulmer's Antique Firearms, Chet
Galazan Shotgun Mfg. Co.
Glass, Herb

Goergen's Gun Shop, Inc.
Golden Age Arms Co.
Gun Works, The
Guncraft Sports, Inc.
Hallowell & Co.
Hansen & Co.
Hunkeler, A.
Johns, Bill
Kelley's
Ledbetter Airguns, Riley
LeFever Arms Co., Inc.
Lever Arms Service Ltd.
Lock's Philadelphia Gun Exchange
Log Cabin Sport Shop
McCann's Muzzle-Gun Works
Mendez, John A.
Montana Outfitters
Museum of Historical Arms, Inc.
Muzzleloaders Etcetera, Inc.
Navy Arms Co.
New England Arms Co.
New Orleans Arms Co.
Parker-Hale
Pioneer Guns
Pony Express Sport Shop, Inc.
Pre-Winchester 92-90-62 Parts Co.
P.S.M.G. Gun Co.
Ravell Ltd.
Retting, Inc., Martin B.
Rutgers Gun & Boat Center
Scott Fine Guns, Inc., Thad
Semmer, Charles
Sherwood Intl. Export Corp.
Steves House of Guns
Stott's Creek Armory, Inc.
Vintage Arms, Inc.
Wood, Frank S.
Yearout, Lewis E.

APPRAISERS—GUNS, ETC.

Ahlman Guns
Ammunition Consulting
  Services, Inc.
Amodei, Jim
Antique Arms Co.
Armoury, Inc., The
Beeman Precision Airguns, Inc.
Behlert Precision
Blue Book Publications, Inc.
Bustani Appraisers, Leo
Butterfield & Butterfield
Camilli, Lou
Cannons Guns
Cape Outfitters
Chadick's Ltd.
Champlin Firearms, Inc.
Christie's East
Clark Firearms Engraving
Classic Guns, Inc.
Clements' Custom Leathercraft,
  Chas
Condon, Inc., David
Cullity Restoration, Daniel
Custom Tackle & Ammo
D&D Gunsmiths, Ltd.
Dixon Muzzleloading Shop, Inc.
D.O.C. Specialists, Inc.
Ed's Gun House
Ellis Sport Shop, E.W.
Epps "Orillia" Ltd., Ellwood
Fagan & Co., William
Fish, Marshall F.
Flayderman & Co., Inc., N.
Forgett Jr., Valmore J.
Fredrick Gun Shop
Frontier Arms Co., Inc.
Goergen's Gun Shop, Inc.
Golden Age Arms Co.
Gonzalez Guns, Ramon B.
Goodwin, Fred
Greenwald, Leon E. "Bud"
Griffin & Howe, Inc.
Gun City
Gun Shop, The
Gun Works, The
Guncraft Sports, Inc.
Hallowell & Co.
Hank's Gun Shop
Hansen & Co.
Hughes, Steven Dodd
Irwin, Campbell H.
Jaeger, Inc., Paul/Dunn's

Jonas Appraisers & Taxidermy, Jack
Kelley's
Ledbetter Airguns, Riley
LeFever Arms Co., Inc.
Lock's Philadelphia Gun Exchange
Lynx-Line, The
Mac's .45 Shop
Mack's Sport Shop
Madis, George
Marple & Associates, Dick
Martin's Gun Shop
McGowan Rifle Barrels
Montana Outfitters
Moreton/Fordyce Enterprises
Mowreys Guns & Gunsmithing
Muzzleloaders Etcetera, Inc.
Oakland Custom Arms, Inc.
Orvis Co., The
Parke-Bernet
Pentheny de Pentheny
Perazzi U.S.A., Inc.
Pettinger Books, Gerald
Pioneer Guns
Pony Express Sport Shop, Inc.
Precision Arms International, Inc.
Pre-Winchester 92-90-62 Parts Co.
P.S.M.G. Gun Co.
R.E.T. Enterprises
Richards, John
Rutgers Gun & Boat Center
Safari Outfitters Ltd.
Scott Fine Guns, Inc., Thad
Shell Shack
Silver Ridge Gun Shop
S.K. Guns, Inc.
Sotheby's
Stratco, Inc.
300 Gunsmith Service, Inc.
Thurston Sports, Inc.
Tillinghast, James C.
Ulrich, Doc & Bud
Unick's Gunsmithing
Vic's Gun Refinishing
Wayne Firearms for Collectors and
  Investors, James
Wells Custom Gunsmith, R.A.
Whildin & Sons Ltd., E.H.
Whitestone Lumber Corp.
Wiest, M.C.
Williams Shootin' Iron Service
Wood, Frank S.
Yearout, Lewis E.

AUCTIONEERS—GUNS, ETC.

Ammunition Consulting
  Services, Inc.
Bourne Co., Inc., Richard A.
Butterfield & Butterfield
Christie's East
Fagan & Co., William
Goodwin, Fred

Kelley's
"Little John's" Antique Arms
Parke-Bernet
Silver Ridge Gun Shop
Sotheby's
Tillinghast, James C.

BOOKS (Publishers and Dealers)

American Handgunner Magazine
Armory Publications
Arms & Armour Press
Ballistic Products, Inc.
Barnes Bullets, Inc.
Beeman Precision Airguns, Inc.
Bellm Contenders
Blackhawk East
Blackhawk Mountain
Blackhawk West
Blacksmith Corp.
Blacktail Mountain Books
Blue Book Publications, Inc.
Brown Co., E. Arthur
Brownell's, Inc.
Calibre Press, Inc.
Colorado Sutlers Arsenal
Corbin, Inc.
DBI Books, Inc.
Flores Publications, Inc., J.
Golden Age Arms Co.
"Gramps" Antique Cartridges
Gun City
Gun Hunter Books
Gun List
Gun Room Press, The
Gunnerman Books
GUNS Magazine
H&P Publishing
Handgun Press
Haydon Shooters' Supply, Russ
Hodgdon Powder Co., Inc.
Home Shop Machinist, The
Hornady Mfg. Co.
Hungry Horse Books
Ironside International
  Publishers, Inc.
King & Co.

Krause Publications
Lane Publishing
Lapua Ltd.
Lyman Instant Targets, Inc.
Lyman Products Corp.
Madis, David
Magma Engineering Co.
Martin Bookseller, J.
McKee Publications
Mountain South
New Win Publishing, Inc.
Old Western Scrounger, Inc.
Outdoorsman's Bookstore, The
Pejsa Ballistics
Petersen Publishing Co.
Pettinger Books, Gerald
Pointing Dog Journal
Precision Shooting, Inc.
Ravell Ltd.
Reloading Specialties, Inc.
Riling Arms Books Co., Ray
Rutgers Book Center
Rutgers Gun & Boat Center
Safari Press, Inc.
Shootin' Accessories, Ltd.
Stackpole Books
Stoeger Publishing Co.
Survival Books/The Larder
Thomas, Charles C.
Trafalgar Square
Trotman, Ken
Vom Hofe
VSP Publishers
WAMCO—New Mexico
Weisz Antique Gun Parts
Wilderness Sound Products Ltd.
Wolfe Publishing Co.

BULLET AND CASE LUBRICANTS

Blackhawk East
Blackhawk Mountain
Blackhawk West
Blount, Inc.
Brown Co., E. Arthur
Camp-Cap Products
CFVentures
C-H Tool & Die Corp.
Chem-Pak, Inc.
Cooper-Woodward
Corbin, Inc.
Cunard & Co., J.
Dillon Precision Prods., Inc.
Eezox, Inc.
Elkhorn Bullets
E-Z-Way Systems
Fitz Pistol Grip Co.
Forster Products
4-D Custom Die Co.
GAR
Guardsman Products
HEBB Resources
Hollywood Engineering
Hornady Mfg. Co.
INTEC International, Inc.

Javelina Products
Jonad Corp.
Lee Precision, Inc.
Lithi Bee Bullet Lube
M&N Bullet Lube
Magma Engineering Co.
Micro-Lube
NECO
Old Western Scrounger, Inc.
Ravell Ltd.
RCBS
Reardon Products
Redding Reloading, Inc.
Rooster Laboratories
SAECO
Shay's Gunsmithing
Slipshot MTS Group
Small Custom Mould & Bullet Co.
SPG Lubricants
Tamarack Products, Inc.
Thompson Bullet Lube Co.
Vom Hofe
Warren Muzzleloading Co., Inc.
Young Country Arms

BULLET SWAGE DIES AND TOOLS

Berger Bullets
Blount, Inc.
Bruno Shooters Supply
Brynin, Milton
Bullet Swaging Supply, Inc.
C-H Tool & Die Corp.
Corbin, Inc.
Fitz Pistol Grip Co.
4-D Custom Die Co.
"Gramps" Antique Cartridges

Hollands
Hollywood Engineering
King & Co.
Lachaussee, S.A.
Necromancer Industries, Inc.
Niemi Enterprises, W.B.
Rorschach Precision Products
Speer Products
Sport Flite Manufacturing Co.
Vega Tool Co.

CARTRIDGES FOR COLLECTORS

Ad Hominem
Ammunition Consulting Services, Inc.
Baekgaard Ltd.

Big 45 Frontier Gun Shop
Cameron's
Campbell, Dick

Duffy, Chas. E.
Ed's Gun House
Eichelberger Bullets, Wm.
Enguix Import-Export
Epps "Orillia" Ltd., Ellwood
First Distributors, Inc., Jack
Forty Five Ranch Enterprises
"Gramps" Antique Cartridges
Idaho Ammunition Service
Kelley's
Michael's Antiques
Montana Outfitters

Mountain Bear Rifle Works, Inc.
Muzzleloaders Etcetera, Inc.
Naval Ordnance Works
Old Western Scrounger, Inc.
Ravell Ltd.
Rifle Works & Armory
San Francisco Gun Exchange
Tillinghast, James C.
Vom Hofe
Ward & Van Valkenburg
Weatherby, Inc.
Yearout, Lewis E.

CASES, CABINETS, RACKS AND SAFES—GUN

Abel Safe & File, Inc.
Alco Carrying Cases
All Rite Products, Inc.
Allen Co., Bob
Allen Co., Inc.
Allen Sportswear, Bob
Aluma Sport by Dee Zee
American Display Co.
American Security Products Co.
Americase
Ansen Enterprises
Arizona Custom Case
Arkfeld Mfg. & Dist. Co., Inc.
Art Jewel Enterprises Ltd.
Ashby Turkey Calls
Bandera Gun Locker
Barramundi Corp.
Berry's Mfg. Inc.
Big Sky Racks, Inc.
Big Spring Enterprises "Bore Stores"
Bill's Custom Cases
Black Sheep Brand
Boyt
Brauer Bros. Mfg. Co.
Browning
Brunsport, Inc.
Bucheimer, J.M.
Bushmaster Hunting & Fishing
Cannon Safe, Inc.
Cascade Fabrication
Catoctin Cutlery
Chipmunk
CoBalt Mfg., Inc.
D&L Industries
Dara-Nes, Inc.
Doskocil Mfg. Co., Inc.
DTM International, Inc.
Elk River, Inc.
EMF Co., Inc.
English Inc., A.G.
Enhanced Presentations, Inc.
Epps "Orillia" Ltd., Ellwood
Eversull Co., Inc., K.
Fort Knox Security Products
Frontier Safe Co.
Galati Internationl
Galaxy Imports Ltd., Inc.
GAR
Granite Custom Bullets
Gun Locker
Gun-Alert
Gun-Ho Sports Cases
Gusdorf Corp.
Hafner Creation, Inc.
Hall Plastics, Inc., John
Harrison-Hurtz Enterprises, Inc.
Hastings Barrels
Homak Mfg. Co., Inc.
Huey Gun Cases, Marvin
Hugger Hooks Co.

Hunter Co., Inc.
Impact Case Co.
Johanssons Vapentillbehor, Bert
Johnston Bros.
Jumbo Sports Products
Kalispel Case Line
Kane Products, Inc.
KK Air International
Knock on Wood Antiques
Kodiak Safe
Kolpin Mfg., Inc.
Lakewood Products, Inc.
Liberty Safe
Maloni, Russ
Marsh, Mike
Master Products, Inc.
Maximum Security Corp.
McWelco Products
Morton Booth Co.
Mountain States Engraving
MPC (McMinnville, TN)
M/S Deepeeka Exports Pvt. Ltd.
MTM Molded Products Co., Inc.
National Security Safe Co., Inc.
Nesci Enterprises, Inc.
Nielsen Custom Cases
Oregon Arms, Inc.
Outa-Site Gun Carriers
Outdoor Connection, Inc., The
Pachmayr Ltd.
Palmer Metal Products
Palmer Security Products
Penguin Industries, Inc.
Perazzi U.S.A., Inc.
Pflumm Mfg. Co.
Protecto Plastics
Prototech Industries, Inc.
Quality Arms, Inc.
San Angelo Sports Products, Inc.
Savana Sports, Inc.
Schulz Industries
Shiloh Creek
Sonderman, Robert
Sportsman's Communicators
Sun Welding Safe Co.
Surecase Co., The
Sweet Home, Inc.
Tinks & Ben Lee Hunting Products
Tread Corp.
Verdemont Fieldsports
Waller & Son, Inc., W.
WAMCO, Inc.
WAMCO—New Mexico
Warren, Kenneth W.
Weather Shield Sports Equipment, Inc.
Weatherby, Inc.
Wilson Case, Inc.
Woodstream
Zanotti Armor
Ziegel Engineering

CHOKE DEVICES, RECOIL ABSORBERS AND RECOIL PADS

Action Products, Inc.
Allen Sportswear, Bob
American Import Co., The
Answer Products Co.
Arms Ingenuity Co.
Baker, Stan
Boyd's Inc.
Briley Mfg., Inc.
Butler Creek Corp.
C&H Research
Cation
Cellini, Inc., Vito Francesca
Colonial Arms, Inc.
Danuser Machine Co.
Dayson Arms Ltd.
Delta Vectors, Inc.
Dragun Enterprises
Fabian Bros. Sporting Goods, Inc.
FAPA Corp.

Franchi S.p.A., Luigi
Frontier Arms Co., Inc.
Galazan Shotgun Mfg. Co.
Gentry Custom Gunmaker, David
Graybill's Gun Shop
Great 870 Co., The
Harper, William E.
Hastings Barrels
Hollands
I.N.C., Inc.
Intermountain Arms & Tackle, Inc.
Jaeger, Inc., Paul/Dunn's
Jenkins Recoil Pads, Inc.
KDF, Inc.
Kick Eez
Kleen-Bore, Inc.
LaRocca Gun Works, Inc.
Mag-Na-Port Int'l, Inc.
Marble Arms Corp.

Meadow Industries
Menck, Thomas W.
Middlebrooks Custom Shop
Morrow, Bud
Nelson/Weather-Rite
North Fork Custom Gunsmithing
One Of A Kind
Pachmayr Ltd.
Palsa Outdoor Products
PAST Sporting Goods, Inc.

Pro-Port Ltd.
Protektor Model
Ravell Ltd.
Shooter Shop, The
Shotguns Unlimited
S.K. Guns, Inc.
Stone Enterprises Ltd.
Trulock Tool
Upper Missouri Trading Co.

CHRONOGRAPHS AND PRESSURE TOOLS

Brown Co., E. Arthur
Canons Delcour
Chronotech
Competition Electronics, Inc.
Custom Chronograph, Inc.
D&H Precision Tooling
Dedicated Systems
Hornady Mfg. Co.

Lachaussee, S.A.
Oehler Research, Inc.
Old Western Scrounger, Inc.
P.A.C.T., Inc.
Shooting Chrony, Inc.
Stratco, Inc.
Tepeco
Vom Hofe

CLEANING AND REFINISHING SUPPLIES

Acculube II, Inc.
Accupro Gun Care
Accuracy Products, S.A.
ADCO International
American Gas & Chemical Co., Ltd.
American Import Co., The
Armoloy Co. of Ft. Worth
Ballistic Products, Inc.
Barnes Bullets, Inc.
Belltown, Ltd.
Beretta, Dr. Franco
Big 45 Frontier Gun Shop
Bill's Gun Repair
Birchwood Laboratories, Inc.
Blount, Inc.
Blue and Gray Products, Inc.
Break-Free Inc.
Bridgers Best
Brobst, Jim
Brown Co., E. Arthur
Brown Precision, Inc.
Bruno Shooters Supply
Camp-Cap Products
Chem-Pak, Inc.
Chopie Mfg., Inc.
Clenzoil Corp.
Clymer Manufacturing Co., Inc.
Corbin, Inc.
Crane & Crane Ltd.
Creedmoor Sports, Inc.
Crouse's Country Cover
Decker Shooting Products
Dewey Mfg. Co., Inc., J.
Du-Lite Corp.
Dutchman's Firearms, Inc., The
Dykstra, Doug
E&L Mfg., Inc.
E.A.A. Corp.
Eezox, Inc.
Ekol Leather Care
Faith Associates, Inc.
Flaig's
Flitz International Ltd.
Flouramics, Inc.
Forster Products
Forty-Five Ranch
Frontier Products Co.
G96 Products Co., Inc.
G.B.C. Industries, Inc.
Goddard, Allen
Golden Age Arms Co.
Gozon Corp.
Graves Co.
Guardsman Products
Half Moon Rifle Shop
Hart & Son, Inc., Robert W.
Heatbath Corp.
Hoppe's Div.
Hornady Mfg. Co.
Hydrosorbent Products
INTEC International, Inc.
Iosso Marine Products
Jackalope Gun Shop
Jantz Supply
J-B Bore Cleaner
Johnston Bros.
Jonad Corp.
Jones Custom Products, Neil
Kesselring Gun Shop
Koppco Industries
Lee Supplies, Mark

LEM Gun Specialties, Inc.
LPS Laboratories, Inc.
Lynx-Line, The
Marble Arms Corp.
MCRW Associates Shooting
  Supplies
Micro Sight Co.
Minute Man High Tech. Ind.
Mountain View Sports, Inc.
M/S Deepeeka Exports Pvt. Ltd.
MTM Molded Products Co., Inc.
Muscle Products Corp.
Nesci Enterprises, Inc.
Northern Precision Custom
  Swaged Bullets
Nygord Precision Products
Old World Oil Products
Omark Industries
Original Mink Oil, Inc.
Outers Laboratories, Div. of Blount
Ox-Yoke Originals, Inc.
P&M Sales and Service
Pachmayr Ltd.
Parker Gun Finishes
Pendleton Royal
Penguin Industries, Inc.
Precision Reloading, Inc.
Prolix
Pro-Shot Products, Inc.
R&S Industries Corp.
Radiator Specialty Co.
Ravell Ltd.
Raytech
Richards Classic Oil Finish, John
Rickard, Inc., Pete
RIG Products Co.
Rod Guide
Rooster Laboratories
Rusteprufe Laboratories
Rusty Duck Premium Gun Care
  Products
San Angelo Sports Products, Inc.
Sharp Shooter, Inc.
Sheridan USA, Inc., Austin
Shiloh Creek
Shooter's Choice
Shootin' Accessories, Ltd.
Slipshot MTS Group
Speer Products
Stock Shop, The
Stoney Point Products, Inc.
Svon Corp.
TDP Industries, Inc.
Tetra Gun Lubricants
Texas Platers Supply Co.
T.F.C. S.p.A.
Treso, Inc.
Tyler Scott, Inc.
United States Products Co.
Valor Corp.
Van Gorden & Son, Inc., C.S.
Venco Industries, Inc.
Verdemont Fieldsports
Warren Muzzleloading Co., Inc.
WD-40 Co.
Whitestone Lumber Corp.
Williams Shootin' Iron Service
Willow Bend
World of Targets
Young Country Arms
Z-Coat Industrial Coatings, Inc.

COMPUTER SOFTWARE—BALLISTICS

Action Target, Inc.
ADC, Inc./PC Bullet
AmBr Software Group Ltd.
Arms, Peripheral Data Systems
Ballistic Products, Inc.
Ballistic Program Co., Inc., The
Barnes Bullets, Inc.
Beartooth Bullets
BestLoad, Inc.
Blackwell, W.
Blount, Inc.
Canons Delcour
Corbin, Inc.
Corbin Applied Technology
Country Armourer, The
Data Tech Software Systems
Exe, Inc.

Ford, Jack
JBM Software
Jensen Bullets
J.I.T. Ltd.
Lachaussee, S.A.
Lee Precision, Inc.
Load From A Disk
Magma Engineering Co.
Maionchi-L.M.I.
Oehler Research, Inc.
P.A.C.T., Inc.
Pejsa Ballistics
Precision Ballistics Co.
Ravell Ltd.
Regional Associates
Sierra Bullets
Tioga Engineering Co., Inc.

CUSTOM GUNSMITHS

A&W Repair
Accuracy Gun Shop
Accuracy Unlimited (Glendale, AZ)
Accurate Plating & Weaponry, Inc.
Ackley Rifle Barrels, P.O.
Adair Custom Shop, Bill
Ahlman Guns
Aldis Gunsmithing & Shooting
  Supply
Alpine's Precision Gunsmithing &
  Indoor Shooting Range
American Custom Gunmakers Guild
Amrine's Gun Shop
Answer Products Co.
Antique Arms Co.
Armament Gunsmithing Co., Inc.
Arms Craft Gunsmithing
Arms Ingenuity Co.
Armurier Hiptmayer
Arrieta, S.L.
Art's Gun & Sport Shop, Inc.
Artistry In Wood
AWC Systems Technology
Baer Custom, Inc., Les
Bain & Davis, Inc.
Baity's Custom Gunworks
Barnes Bullets, Inc.
Barta's Gunsmithing
Barton Technology
Baumannize Custom
Bear Arms
Bear Mountain Gun & Tool
Beaver Lodge
Beeman Precision Airguns, Inc.
Behlert Precision
Beitzinger, George
Belding's Custom Gun Shop
Bellm Contenders
Benchmark Guns
Bengtson Arms Co., L.
Biesen, Al
Biesen, Roger
Billeb, Stephen L.
Billings Gunsmiths, Inc.
Blackstar Barrel Accurizing
Bolden's
Bone Engraving, Ralph
Borden Accuracy
Borovnik KG, Ludwig
Bowerly, Kent
Brace, Larry D.
Brgoch, Frank
Brian, C.T.
Briese Bullet Co., Inc.
Briganti & Co., A.
Briley Mfg., Inc.
Broad Creek Rifle Works
Broken Gun Ranch
Brown Precision, Inc.
Bruno Shooters Supply
Buck Stix
Buckhorn Gun Works
Buckskin Machine Works
Budin, Dave
Bullet Meister Bullets
Burgess and Son Gunsmiths, R.W.
Burkhart Gunsmithing, Don
Burres, Jack
Cache La Poudre Rifleworks
CAM Enterprises
Camilli, Lou
Campbell, Dick
Cannons Guns
Carter's Gun Shop
Caywood, Shane J.

Champlin Firearms, Inc.
Chicasaw Gun Works
Christman Jr., David
Chuck's Gun Shop
Clark Custom Guns, Inc.
Clark Firearms Engraving
Classic Arms Corp.
Classic Guns, Inc.
Cloward's Gun Shop
Cochran, Oliver
Cogar's Gunsmithing
Cole's Gun Works
Colt's Mfg. Co., Inc.
Competitive Pistol Shop, The
Conrad, C.A.
Cook, John
Corkys Gun Clinic
Costa, David
Cox, C. Ed
Creekside Gun Shop, Inc.
Cumberland Knife & Gun Works
Curtis Custom Shop
Custom Gun Products
Custom Gun Stocks
Custom Gunsmiths
Custom Shop, The
Cylinder & Slide, Inc.
D&D Gunsmiths, Ltd.
D&J Bullet Co. & Custom Gun
  Shop, Inc.
Dangler, Homer L.
Darlington Gun Works, Inc.
Davis Service Center, Bill
Dever Co., Jack
Devereaux, R.H. "Dick"
DGS, Inc.
Dietz Gun Shop & Range Inc.
Dilliott Gunsmithing, Inc.
Donnelly, C.P.
Dowtin Gunworks
Duffy, Charles E.
Duncan's Gun Works, Inc.
Dyson & Son Ltd., Peter
Eagle Flight Bullet Co.
Echols & Co., D'Arcy
Eckelman Gunsmithing
Eggleston, Jere D.
EGW Evolution Gun Works
Ellicott Arms Inc./Woods
  Pistolsmithing
EMF Co., Inc.
Erhardt, Dennis
Eyster Heritage Gunsmiths, Inc.,
  Ken
Fanzoj GmbH
Fautheree, Andy
Ferris Firearms
First Distributors, Inc., Jack
Fish, Marshall F.
Fisher, Jerry A.
Fisher Custom Firearms
Flaig's
Fleming Firearms
Flynn's Custom Guns
Fogle, James W.
Forster, Kathy
Forster, Larry L.
Forthofer's Gunsmithing &
  Knifemaking
Francesca, Inc.
Francotte & Cie S.A., Auguste
Frank Custom Gun Service, Ron
Frazier Brothers Enterprises
Fredrick Gun Shop
Frontier Arms Co., Inc.

Fullmer, Geo. M.
Gaillard Barrels
Gander Mountain, Inc.
Gator Guns & Repair
Genecco Gun Works, K.
Gillmann, Edwin
Gilman-Mayfield, Inc.
Giron, Robert E.
Goens, Dale W.
Goodling's Gunsmithing
Goodwin, Fred
Gordie's Gun Shop
Grace, Charles E.
Graybill's Gun Shop
Green, Roger M.
Greg Gunsmithing Repair
Griffin & Howe, Inc.
Gun Shop, The
Gun Works, The
Guns
Gunsite Gunsmithy
Gunsmithing Ltd.
H&L Gun Works
Hagn Rifles & Actions, Martin
Hallberg Gunsmith, Fritz
Hamilton, Alex B.
Hammans, Charles E.
Hammond Custom Guns Ltd., Guy
Hank's Gun Shop
Hanson's Gun Center, Dick
Hardison, Charles
Hart & Son, Inc., Robert W.
Hecht, Hubert J.
Heilmann, Stephen
Heinie Specialty Products
Hensler, Jerry
Hensley, Darwin
Heppler, Keith
High Bridge Arms, Inc.
High Performance International
Hill, Loring F.
Hiptmayer, Klaus
Hoag, James W.
Hobaugh, Wm.
Hobbie Gunsmithing, Duane A.
Hodgson, Richard
Hoelscher, Virgil
Hoenig & Rodman
Hofer Jagdwaffen, P.
Holland, Dick
Hollands
Hollis Gun Shop
Home Shop Machinist, The
Horst, Alan K.
Huebner, Corey O.
Hughes, Steven Dodd
Hunkeler, Al
Hyper-Single, Inc.
Imperial Magnum Corp.
Intermountain Arms & Tackle, Inc.
Irwin, Campbell H.
Island Pond Gun Shop
Ivanoff, Thomas G.
J&S Heat Treat
Jackalope Gun Shop
Jaeger, Inc., Paul/Dunn's
Jarrett Rifles, Inc.
Jim's Gun Shop
Johnston, James
Jones, J.D.
Juenke, Vern
Jurras, L.E.
K-D, Inc.
KDF, Inc.
Keith's Custom Gunstocks
Ken's Gun Specialties
Kimball, Gary
King's Gun Works
Klein Custom Guns, Don
Kleinendorst, K.W.
Kneiper Custom Rifles, Jim
Knippel, Richard
KOGOT
Kopp, Terry K.
Korzinek Riflesmith, J.
LaFrance Specialties
Lair, Sam
Lampert, Ron
LaRocca Gun Works, Inc.
Laughridge, William R.
Lawson Co., Harry
Lebeau-Courally
Lee's Red Ramps
LeFever Arms Co., Inc.
Liberty Antique Gunworks
Lilja Precision Rifle Barrels
Lind Custom Guns, Al

Linebaugh Custom Sixguns & Rifle
  Works
Lock's Philadelphia Gun Exchange
Long, George F.
Lynx-Line, The
Mac's .45 Shop
Mag-Na-Port Int'l, Inc.
Makinson, Nicholas
Mandarino, Monte
Manley Shooting Supplies, Lowell
Marent, Rudolf
Martin's Gun Shop
Martz, John V.
Masker, Seely
Mathews & Son, Inc., George E.
Maxi-Mount
Mazur Restoration, Pete
McCament, Jay
McCluskey Precision Rifles
McMillan Gunworks, Inc.
MCRW Associates Shooting
  Supplies
MCS, Inc.
Mercer Custom Stocks, R.M.
Michael's Antiques
Mid-America Recreation, Inc.
Middlebrooks Custom Shop
Miller Co., David
Miller Custom
Mills Jr., Hugh B.
Moeller, Steve
Morrison Custom Rifles, J.W.
Morrow, Bud
Mountain Bear Rifle Works, Inc.
Mowreys Guns & Gunsmithing
Mullis Guncraft
Mustra's Custom Guns, Inc., Carl
Nastoff's 45 Shop Inc., Steve
Nelson, Stephen
Nettestad Gun Works
New England Custom Gun Service
Newman Gun Shop
Nicholson Custom
Nickels, Paul R.
Nicklas, Ted
Nolan, Dave
North American Shooting Systems
North Fork Custom Gunsmithing
Nu-Line Guns, Inc.
Oakland Custom Arms, Inc.
Old World Gunsmithing
Olson, Vic
Orvis Co., The
Ottmar, Maurice
Ozark Gun Works
P&S Gun Service
Pace Marketing, Inc.
Pagel Gun Works, Inc.
Pasadena Gun Center
Paterson Gunsmithing
Pell, John T.
PEM's Mfg. Co.
Pence Precision Barrels
Penrod Precision
Pentheny de Pentheny
Peters & Hosea Gunmakers
Powell & Son (Gunmakers) Ltd.,
  William
Power Custom, Inc.
Precision Arms International, Inc.
Pro-Port Ltd.
Quality Firearms of Idaho, Inc.
Ray's Gunsmith Shop
Renfrew Guns & Supplies
Ridgetop Sporting Goods
Ries, Chuck
Rifle Shop, The
Rigby & Co., John
Rizzini Battista
RMS Custom Gunsmithing
Robar Co.'s, Inc., The
Roberts, J.J.
Robinson, Don
Rocky Mountain Rifle Works Ltd.
Rogers Gunsmithing, Bob
Romain's Custom Guns
Ryan, Chad L.
Sanders Custom Gun Service
Sandy's Custom Gunshop
Schiffman, Curt
Schiffman, Mike
Schiffman, Norman
Schumakers Gun Shop, William
Schwartz Custom Guns, Wayne E.
Scott Fine Guns, Inc., Thad
Scott, Dwight
Scott, McDougall & Associates

Shaw, Inc., E.R.
Shay's Gunsmithing
Shell Shack
Shockley, Harold H.
Shooter Shop, The
Shooters Supply
Shootin' Shack, Inc.
Shooting Specialties
Shotgun Shop, The
Shotguns Unlimited
Silver Ridge Gun Shop
Singletary, Kent
Sipes Gun Shop
Siskiyou Gun Works
S.K. Guns, Inc.
Skeoch, Brian R.
Sklany, Steve
Slezak, Jerome F.
Small Arms Mfg. Co.
Smith, Art
Smith, Sharmon
Snapp's Gunshop
SOS Products Co.
Spencer Reblue Service
Sportsmen's Exchange & Western
  Gun Traders, Inc.
Spradlin's
Springfield, Inc.
SSK Industries
Starnes, Ken
Steelman's Gun Shop
Steffens, Ron
Stiles Custom Guns
Storey, Dale A.
Stott's Creek Armory, Inc.
Sullivan, David S.
Swann, D.J.
Swenson's 45 Shop, A.D.
S.W.I.F.T.
Swift River Gunworks, Inc.
Szweda, Robert
Talmage, William G.
Tank's Rifle Shop
Taylor & Robbins
Tennessee Valley Mfg.
Ten-Ring Precision, Inc.
Tertin, James A.

CUSTOM METALSMITHS

Ackley Rifle Barrels, P.O.
Ahlman Guns
Aldis Gunsmithing & Shooting
  Supply
Amrine's Gun Shop
Armurier Hiptmayer
Artistry In Wood
Baron Technology, Inc.
Bear Mountain Gun & Tool
Beitzinger, George
Bellm Contenders
Benchmark Guns
Biesen, Al
Billingsley & Brownell
Brace, Larry D.
Briganti & Co., A.
Broad Creek Rifle Works
Brown Precision, Inc.
Campbell, Dick
Carter's Gun Shop
Checkmate Refinishing
Classic Guns, Inc.
Craftguard
Crandall Tool & Machine Co.
Cullity Restoration, Daniel
Custom Gun Products
Custom Gunsmiths
D&D Gunsmiths, Ltd.
D&H Precision Tooling
Duncan's Gunworks, Inc.
Dyson & Son Ltd., Peter
Eyster Heritage Gunsmiths, Inc.,
  Ken
First Distributors, Inc., Jack
Forster, Larry L.
Francesca, Inc.
Fullmer, Geo. M.
Gentry Custom Gunmaker, David
Gilman-Mayfield, Inc.
Goodwin, Fred
Graybill's Gun Shop
Green, Roger M.
Griffin & Howe, Inc.
Gun Shop, The
Guns
Gunsmithing Ltd.
Hagn Rifles & Actions, Martin

300 Gunsmith Service, Inc.
Thurston Sports, Inc.
Titus, Daniel
Tom's Gun Repair
Tooley Custom Rifles
Trevallion Gunstocks
T.S.W. Conversions, Inc.
Upper Missouri Trading Co.
Van Epps, Milton
Van Horn, Gil
Van Patten, J.W.
Varmintmasters
Vest, John
Vic's Gun Refinishing
Vintage Arms, Inc.
Volquartsen Custom Ltd.
Waffen-Weber Custom Gunsmithing
Walker Arms Co., Inc.
Wardell Precision Handguns Ltd.
Weaver Arms Corp.
Weaver's Gun Shop
Weems, Cecil
Weigand Combat Handguns, Inc.
Wells, Fred F.
Wells Custom Gunsmith, R.A.
Welsh, Bud
Werth, T.W.
Wessinger Custom Guns &
  Engraving
West, Robert G.
Westchester Carbide
Westley Richards & Co.
Westwind Rifles, Inc.
Wichita Arms, Inc.
Wiebe, Duane
Williams Gun Sight Co.
Williams Shootin' Iron Service
Williamson Precision Gunsmithing
Wilson's Gun Shop
Winter, Robert M.
Wise Guns, Dale
Wisner's Gun Shop, Inc.
Wood, Frank S.
Yankee Gunsmith
Yavapai College
Zeeryp, Russ

Hallberg Gunsmith, Fritz
Hamilton, Alex B.
Hart & Son, Inc., Robert W.
Hecht, Hubert J.
Heilmann, Stephen
Heppler's Machining
Highline Machine Co.
Hiptmayer, Klaus
Hoag, James W.
Hobaugh, Wm. H.
Hoelscher, Virgil
Hollands
Hollis Gun Shop
Home Shop Machinist, The
Hyper-Single, Inc.
Intermountain Arms & Tackle
Ivanoff, Thomas G.
J&S Heat Treat
Jaeger, Inc., Paul/Dunn's
Jamison's Forge Works
Jeffredo Gunsight
Johnston, James
Jones Custom Products, Neil
Kilham & Co.
Klein Custom Guns, Don
Kleinendorst, K.W.
Lampert, Ron
Lawson Co., Harry
Long, George F.
Mac's .45 Shop
Mains Enterprises, Inc.
Makinson, Nicholas
Marek, George
McCament, Jay
McCormick's Custom Gun Bluing
McFarland, Stan
Mid-America Recreation, Inc.
Morrison Custom Rifles, J.W.
Morrow, Bud
Mullis Guncraft
Nastoff's 45 Shop, Inc., Steve
Nettestad Gun Works
New England Custom Gun Service
Nicholson Custom
Noreen, Peter H.
North Fork Custom Gunsmithing
Olson, Vic

Ozark Gun Works
Pagel Gun Works, Inc.
Parker Gun Finishes
Pasadena Gun Center
Penrod Precision
Precise Metal Finishing
Precise Metalsmithing Enterprises
Precision Metal Finishing
Precision Specialties
Pre-Winchester 92-90-62 Parts Co.
Rice, Keith
Rifle Shop, The
RMS Custom Gunsmithing
Robar Co.'s, Inc., The
Roberts, J.J.
Robinson, Don
Shell Shack
Shirley Co. Gun &
   Riflemakers Ltd., J.A.
Silver Ridge Gun Shop
S.K. Guns, Inc.
Skeoch, Brian R.
Smith, Art
Snapp's Gunshop
Societa Armi Bresciane Srl.
Sportsmatch Ltd.
Sportsmen's Exchange & Western
   Gun Traders, Inc.

Stalwart Corp.
Steffens, Ron
Stiles Custom Guns
Szweda, Robert
Talley, Dave
Ten-Ring Precision, Inc.
Thompson, Randall
Tom's Gun Repair
T.S.W. Conversions, Inc.
Unick's Gunsmithing
Van Horn, Gil
Vic's Gun Refinishing
Waffen-Weber Custom Gunsmithing
Waldron, Herman
Wells, Fred F.
Welsh, Bud
Werth, T.W.
Wessinger Custom Guns &
   Engraving
West, Robert G.
Westchester Carbide
Western Design
Westrom, John
White Rock Tool & Die
Wiebe, Duane
Wilson's Gun Shop
Wisner's Gun Shop, Inc.
Wood, Frank S.

DECOYS

A&M Waterfowl, Inc.
Baekgaard Ltd.
Belding's Custom Gun Shop
Carry-Lite, Inc.
Deer Me Products Co.
Fair Game International
Farm Form, Inc.
Feather Flex Decoys
Flambeau Products Corp.
G&H Decoys, Inc.
Herter's Manufacturing, Inc.
Hiti-Schuch, Atelier Wilma

Klingler Woodcarving
Molin Industries
North Wind Decoys Co.
Penn's Woods Products, Inc.
Quack Decoy & Sporting Clays
Ravell Ltd.
Royal Arms
Sports Innovations, Inc.
Tanglefree Industries
Waterfield Sports, Inc.
Woods Wise Products

ENGRAVERS, ENGRAVING TOOLS

Adair Custom Shop, Bill
Adams, John J.
Ahlman Guns
Alfano, Sam
Allard, Gary
Allen, Richard L.
Altamont Co.
Anthony and George Ltd.
Armurier Hiptmayer
Artistic Engraving
Baron Technology, Inc.
Bates Engraving, Billy
Bledsoe, Weldon
Bleile, C. Roger
Boessler, Erich
Bone Engraving, Ralph
Bratcher, Dan
Brgoch, Frank
Brooker, Dennis
Brownell Checkering Tools, W.E.
CAM Enterprises
Churchill, Winston
Clark, Frank
Clark Firearms Engraving
Collings, Ronald
Creek Side Metal & Woodcrafters
Davidson, Jere
Delorge, Ed
Dolbare, Elizabeth
Drain, Mark
Dubber, Michael W.
Dyson & Son Ltd., Peter
EMF Co., Inc.
Engraving Artistry
Evans Engraving, Robert
Eyster Heritage Gunsmiths, Inc.,
   Ken
Fanzoj GesmbH
Firearms Engraver's Guild of
   America
Flannery Engraving Co., Jeff W.
Floatstone Mfg. Co.
Fogle, James W.
Fountain Products
Francolini, Leonard
Frank Knives
French, J.R.
Gene's Custom Guns
George, Tim and Christy
Glimm, Jerome C.
Golden Age Arms Co.

Gournet, Geoffroy
Grant, Howard V.
Griffin & Howe, Inc.
GRS Corp.
Gun Room, The
Gurney, F.R.
Gwinnell, Bryson J.
Hale, Peter
Hand Engravers Supply Co.
Hands, Barry Lee
Harris Hand Engraving, Paul A.
Harwood, Jack O.
Hendricks, Frank E.
Herrett's Stocks, Inc.
Hiptmayer, Heidemarie
Horst, Alan K.
Ingle, Ralph W.
Jaeger, Inc., Paul/Dunn's
Johns, Bill
Kamyk Engraving Co., Steve
Kehr, Roger L.
Kelly, Lance
Klingler Woodcarving
Koevenig's Engraving Service
Kudlas, John M.
Lebeau-Courally
LeFever Arms Co., Inc.
Leibowitz, Leonard
Letschnig, Franz
Lindsay, Steve
Little Trees Ramble
Lutz Engraving, Ron
Mains Enterprises, Inc.
Maki School of Engraving, Robert E.
Marek, George
Master Engravers, Inc.
McCombs, Leo
McDonald, Dennis
McKenzie, Lynton
Mele, Frank
Mid-America Recreation, Inc.
Mittermeier, Inc., Frank
Montgomery Community College
Moschetti, Mitchell R.
Mountain States Engraving
Nelson, Gary K.
New Orleans Arms Co.
New Orleans Jewelers Supply Co.
NgraveR Co., The
Oker's Engraving
Old Dominion Engravers

P&S Gun Service
Palmgren Steel Products
Pedersen, C.R.
Pedersen, Rex C.
Pilkington, Scott
Piquette, Paul R.
Potts, Wayne E.
Rabeno, Martin
Ravell Ltd.
Reed, Dave
Reno, Wayne
Riggs, Jim
Roberts, J.J.
Rohner, Hans
Rohner, John
Rosser, Bob
Rundell's Gun Shop
Runge, Robert P.
Sampson, Roger
Schiffman, Mike
Sheffield Knifemakers Supply
Sherwood, George
Sinclair, W.P.
Singletary, Kent

Skaggs, R.E.
Smith, Mark A.
Smith, Ron
Smokey Valley Rifles
Theis, Terry
Thiewes, George W.
Thirion Hand Engraving, Denise
Tuscano, Tony
Valade, Robert B.
Vest, John
Viramontez, Ray
Vorhes, David
Waffen-Weber Custom Gunsmithing
Wagoner, Vernon G.
Wallace, Terry
Warenski, Julie
Warren, Kenneth W.
Welch, Sam
Wells, Rachel
Wessinger Custom Guns &
   Engraving
Willig Custom Engraving, Claus
Wood, Mel

GAME CALLS

Adventure Game Calls
Arkansas Mallard Duck Calls
Ashby Turkey Calls
Baekgaard Ltd.
Blakemore Game Calls, Jim
Bostick Wildlife Calls, Inc.
Buck Stix
Carter's Wildlife Calls, Inc., Garth
Cedar Hill Game Calls, Inc.
Crawford Co., Inc., R.M.
D-Boone Ent., Inc.
Dr. O's Products Ltd.
Duck Call Specialists
Faulhaber Wildlocker
Faulk's Game Call Co., Inc.
Flow-Rite of Tennessee, Inc.
Green Head Game Call Co.
Hally Caller
Hastings Barrels
Haydel's Game Calls, Inc.
Herter's Manufacturing, Inc.
Hunter's Specialties, Inc.
Keowee Game Calls
Kingyon, Paul L.
Knight & Hale Game Calls
Lohman Mfg. Co., Inc.
Mallardtone Game Calls
Marsh, Johnny
Moss Double Tone, Inc.

Mountain Hollow Game Calls
M/S Deepeeka Exports Pvt. Ltd.
Oakman Turkey Calls
Olt Co., Philip S.
Penn's Woods Products, Inc.
Primos Wild Game Calls, Inc.
Quaker Boy, Inc.
Rickard, Inc., Pete
Robbins Scent, Inc.
Rocky Mountain Wildlife Products
Salter Calls, Inc., Eddie
San Angelo Sports Products, Inc.
Savana Sports, Inc.
Sceery Co., E.J.
Scobey Duck & Goose Calls, Glynn
Scotch Hunting Products Co., Inc.
Scruggs' Game Calls, Stanley
SOS Products Co.
Sports Innovations, Inc.
Stewart Game Calls, Inc., Johnny
Sure-Shot Game Calls, Inc.
Tanglefree Industries
Tink's & Ben Lee Hunting Products
Tink's Safariland Hunting Corp.
Wellington Outdoors
Wilderness Sound Products Ltd.
Woods Wise Products
Wyant's Outdoor Products, Inc.

GUN PARTS, U.S. AND FOREIGN

Ad Hominem
Ahlman Guns
Amherst Arms
Armscorp USA, Inc.
Bear Mountain Gun & Tool
Bob's Gun Shop
Briese Bullet Co., Inc.
British Arms Co. Ltd.
Bushmaster Firearms
Can Am Enterprises
Cape Outfitters
Caspian Arms
Century International Arms, Inc.
Chuck's Gun Shop
Colonial Repair
Costa, David
Cylinder & Slide, Inc.
Defense Moulding Enterprises
Delta Arms Ltd.
Dibble, Derek A.
Dragun Enterprises
Duffy, Charles E.
E&L Mfg., Inc.
Eagle International, Inc.
EMF Co., Inc.
Fabian Bros. Sporting Goods, Inc.
FAPA Corp.
First Distributors, Inc., Jack
Fleming Firearms
Forrest, Inc., Tom
Greider Precision
Gun Parts Corp., The
Gun Shop, The
Gun-Tec
Hastings Barrels
High Performance International
Irwin, Campbell H.
Island Pond Gun Shop

Jaeger, Inc., Paul/Dunn's
J.O. Arms & Ammunition Co.
Johnson Gunsmithing, Inc., Neal G.
K&T Co.
Kimber, Inc.
K.K. Arms Co.
Krico/Kriegeskorte GmbH, A.
Laughridge, William R.
Liberty Antique Gunworks
Lodewick, Walter H.
Mac's .45 Shop
Markell, Inc.
McCormick Corp., Chip
Merkuria Ltd.
Moreton/Fordyce Enterprises
Morrow, Bud
Mountain Bear Rifle Works, Inc.
MPI Stocks
North American Specialties
Nu-Line Guns, Inc.
Oakland Custom Arms, Inc.
Old Western Scrounger, Inc.
Pace Marketing, Inc.
Pachmayr Ltd.
Parts & Surplus
Peacemaker Specialists
Pennsylvania Gun Parts
Perazzi U.S.A., Inc.
Pre-Winchester 92-90-62 Parts Co.
Quality Firearms of Idaho, Inc.
Quality Parts Co.
Ranch Products
Randco UK
Ravell Ltd.
Retting, Inc., Martin B.
Rizzini Battista
Rutgers Gun & Boat Center
Safari Arms, Inc./SGW

Sarco, Inc.
Scherer
Shell Shack
Sheridan USA, Inc., Austin
Sherwood Intl. Export Corp.
Smires, C.
Southern Ammunition Co., Inc.
Southern Armory, The
Sportsmen's Exchange & Western
 Gun Traders, Inc.
Springfield, Inc.
Springfield Sporters, Inc.
"Su-Press-On," Inc.
Tank's Rifle Shop
Tapco, Inc.
Tradewinds, Inc.

T.S.W. Conversions, Inc.
Twin Pine Armory
Uberti USA, Inc.
Vintage Arms, Inc.
Vintage Industries, Inc.
Vom Hofe
Walker Arms Co., Inc.
Wardell Precision Handguns Ltd.
Weaver's Gun Shop
Weigand Combat Handguns, Inc.
Weisz Antique Gun Parts
Westfield Engineering
Wilson's Gun Shop
Wisner's Gun Shop, Inc.
Wolff Co., W.C.

GUNS, AIR

• Action Arms Ltd.
• Air Rifle Specialists
• Air Venture
• Airgun Repair Centre
• Anschutz GmbH
• Beeman Precision Airguns, Inc.
• Benjamin/Sheridan Co.
 Brass Eagle, Inc.
• BSA Guns Ltd.
 Champion's Choice, Inc.
 Component Concepts, Inc.
 Crawford Co., Inc., R.M.
 Creedmoor Sports, Inc.
• Crosman Airguns
 Crosman Products of Canada Ltd.
• Daisy Mfg. Co.
• Diana
• Dynamit Nobel-RWS, Inc.
• FAS
 Frankonia Jagd
• FWB
• Gamo
• GFR Corp.
• Great Lakes Airguns
 GZ Paintball Sports Products
 Hartmann & Weiss GMBH
 Hebard Guns, Gil
 Hofmann & Co.
 Hy-Score Arms Co. Ltd.
• Interarms

I.S.S.
• Mac-1 Distributors
• Marksman Products
 Merkuria Ltd.
 National Survival Game, Inc.
 Nationwide Airgun Repairs
 P&S Gun Service
• Pardini Armi Commerciale Srl
 Penguin Industries, Inc.
• Precision Airgun Sales, Inc.
• Precision Sales Int'l, Inc.
 Ravell Ltd.
• Rossi S.A., Amadeo
• RWS
 Savana Sports, Inc.
 S.G.S. Sporting Guns Srl
• Sheridan USA, Inc., Austin
 Sportsmatch Ltd.
• Steyr-Mannlicher AG
 Stone Enterprises Ltd.
• Swivel Machine Works, Inc.
 Taurus, S.A., Forjas
 Tippman Pneumatics, Inc.
• Uberti, Aldo
 UltraSport Arms, Inc.
 Valor Corp.
• Walther GmbH, Carl
• Webley and Scott Ltd.
• Weihrauch KG, Hermann

GUNS, FOREIGN—IMPORTERS (Manufacturers)

• Action Arms Ltd. (BRNO; CZ)
• Air Rifle Specialists (Air Arms; BSA
 Guns Ltd.; Theoben Engineering)
• Air Venture (airguns)
• Alessandri & Son, Lou (Rizzini,
 Battista)
• American Arms, Inc. (Fausti &
 Figlie s.n.c., Stefano; Franchi
 S.p.A., Luigi; Grulla Armes;
 INDESAL; Norica, Avnda Otaloa;
 Uberti, Aldo; Zabala Hermanos
 S.A.; blackpowder arms)
 Armas Kemen S.A. (USA Sporting)
• Armes de Chasse (AYA; Francotte
 & Cie S.A., Auguste)
 Armoury, Inc., The (blackpowder)
• Armscorp USA, Inc.
 Armsport, Inc. (airguns;
 blackpowder arms)
• Autumn Sales, Inc. (Blaser
 Jagdwaffen GmbH)
• Beauchamp & Son, Inc. (Pedersoli,
 Davide & C.)
• Beeman Precision Airguns, Inc.
 (Beeman Precision Airguns, Inc.;
 FWB; Hammerli Ltd.; Webley &
 Scott Ltd.; Weihrauch KG,
 Hermann)
• Bell's Legendary Country Wear
 (Miroku, B.C./Daly, Charles;
 Powell & Son, Ltd.; William)
• Beretta U.S.A. Corp. (Beretta
 Firearms, Pietro)
• Bohemia Arms Co. (BRNO)
 British Arms Co. Ltd.
• British Sporting Arms (Miroku,
 B.C./Daly, Charles)
• Browning Arms Co. (Browning
 Arms Co.)
 B-West Imports, Inc.
• Cabela's (Pedersoli, Davide & C.;
 blackpowder arms)
 California Armory, Inc.
• Cape Outfitters (San Marco;
 Societa Armi Bresciane Srl.;

Westley Richards & Co.;
 blackpowder arms)
• Century International Arms, Inc.
 (Famas; FEG; Norinco)
• Chapuis USA (Chapuis Armes)
• ChinaSports, Inc. (Norinco)
• Christopher Firearms Co., Inc., E.
 (Uberti, Aldo)
• Cimarron Arms (Uberti, Aldo;
 blackpowder arms)
• CVA (blackpowder arms)
• Daisy Mfg. Co. (Daisy Mfg. Co.;
 Gamo)
• Dixie Gun Works (Pedersoli,
 Davide & C.; Uberti, Aldo;
 blackpowder arms)
• Dynamit Nobel-RWS, Inc.
 (Brenneke KG, Wilhelm; Diana;
 Gamo; RWS)
• E.A.A. Corp. (Astra-Unceta Y Cia,
 S.A.; Benelli Armi S.p.A.; Fabrica
 D'Armi Sabatti S.r.l.; Tanfoglio
 S.r.l., Fratelli/Witness; Weihrauch
 KG, Hermann)
• Eagle Imports, Inc. (Bersa S.A.)
• Ellett Bros. (Churchill)
• EMF Co., Inc. (Dakota; Pedersoli,
 Davide & C.; San Marco; Uberti,
 Aldo; blackpowder arms)
• Euroarms of America, Inc.
 (blackpowder arms)
• Galaxy Imports Ltd., Inc. (Laurona
 Armas S.A.)
• Giacomo Sporting, Inc. (Gamba
 S.p.A., Renato)
• Glock, Inc. (Glock GmbH)
• Great Lakes Airguns
• Griffin & Howe, Inc. (Rigby & Co.,
 John)
• GSI, Inc. (Merkel Freres; Steyr;
 Steyr-Daimler-Puch;
 Steyr-Mannlicher AG)
• G.U., Inc. (SKB Arms Co.)
• Hammerli USA (Hammerli Ltd.)
• Heckler & Koch, Inc. (Benelli Armi

S.p.A.; Heckler & Koch, GmbH)
• Hi-Grade Imports (Arrieta, S.L.)
• Interarms (Helwan; Howa
 Machinery Ltd.; Interarms;
 Norinco; Rossi, Amadeo; Star
 Bonifacio Echeverria S.A.; Walther
 GmbH, Carl)
• Ithaca Acquisition Corp. (Fabarm
 S.p.A.)
• JägerSport, Ltd. (Heym GmbH &
 Co., Friedrich Wilh.; Voere-KGH
 m.b.H.)
• Jansma, Jack J. (Arrieta, S.L.)
• J.O. Arms & Ammunition Co. (J.O.
 Arms & Ammunition Co.)
• K.B.I., Inc. (Baikal; FEG; Kassnar;
 K.B.I., Inc.)
• Keng's Firearms Specialty, Inc.
 (Poly Technologies, Inc.)
• Krieghoff International, Inc.
 (Krieghoff Gun Co., H.)
 K-Sports Imports, Inc.
 London Guns Ltd.
• Magnum Research, Inc. (IMI)
 MAGTECH Recreational Products,
 Inc. (CBC)
• Mandall Shooting Supplies, Inc.
 (Arizaga; Bretton; Cabanas;
 Crucelegoi, Hermanos; Erma
 Werke GmbH; Firearms Co.
 Ltd./Alpine; Gaucher Armes S.A.;
 Hammerli Ltd.; Korth;
 Krico/Kriegeskorte GmbH, A.;
 Morini; SIG; Tanner; Techni-Mec;
 Ugartechea S.A., Ignacio;
 Zanoletti, Pietro; blackpowder
 arms)
• Marksman Products (Marksman
 Products)
• McMillan Gunworks, Inc. (Peters
 Stahl GmbH)
• MCS, Inc. (Pardini Armi
 Commerciale Srl)
• MEC-Gar U.S.A., Inc.
 (MEC-Gar s.r.l.)
• Mitchell Arms, Inc. (Mitchell Arms,
 Inc.; Uberti, Aldo;
 blackpowder arms)
• Moore & Co., Wm. Larkin (Bertuzzi;
 FERLIB; Garbi, Armas Urki; Piotti;
 Rizzini, F.LLI)
• Nationwide Sports Distributors
 (Daewoo Precision Industries Ltd.)

• Navy Arms Co. (Navy Arms Co;
 Pedersoli, Davide & C.; Uberti,
 Aldo; blackpowder arms)
• Nevada Cartridge Co. (Beretta, Dr.
 Franco)
• New England Arms Co. (Arrieta,
 S.L.; Bertuzzi; Cosmi Americo &
 Figlio s.n.c.; FERLIB; Gamba
 S.p.A., Renato; Lebeau-Courally;
 Rizzini, F.LLI)
• Nygord Precision Products (FAS;
 Pardini Armi Commerciale Srl;
 Steyr; Unique/M.A.P.F.)
• Olympic Arms (Peters Stahl GmbH)
• Orvis Co., Inc., The (Arrieta, S.L.)
• Pachmayr Co. (FERLIB)
• Para-Ordnance, Inc.
 (Para-Ordnance Mfg., Inc.)
• Paul Co., The (Sauer)
• Perazzi U.S.A., Inc. (Perazzi m.a.p.
 S.p.A.)
• Precision Sales International, Inc.
 (Anschutz GmbH; Erma Werke
 GmbH; Marocchi F.lli S.p.A.)
• Quality Arms, Inc. (Arrieta, S.L.;
 FERLIB)
• Ruko Products (Armscor)
• SGS Importers International, Inc.
 (Llama Gabilondo Y Cia)
• Sigarms, Inc. (SIG-Sauer)
• Sile Distributors (Benelli Armi
 S.p.A.; Marocchi F.lli S.p.A.;
 Solothurn)
• Specialty Shooters Supply, Inc.
 (JSL Ltd.)
• Sportarms of Florida (Schmidt,
 Herbert)
• Springfield, Inc. (Springfield, Inc.)
• Stoeger Industries (IGA; Sako Ltd.;
 Tikka
 Stone Enterprises Ltd. (airguns)
• Swarovski Optik North America Ltd.
 (Heym GmbH & Co., Friedrich
 Wilh.; Voere-KGH m.b.H.)
• Taurus Firearms, Inc. (Taurus
 International Firearms)
 Tradewinds, Inc. (blackpowder
 arms)
 Turkish Firearms Corp.
• Uberti USA, Inc. (Uberti, Aldo;
 blackpowder arms)
 Vintage Arms, Inc.
• Weatherby, Inc. (Weatherby, Inc.)

GUNS, FOREIGN—MANUFACTURERS (Importers)

• Air Arms (Air Rifle Specialists)
• Anschutz GmbH (Precision Sales
 International, Inc.)
• Arizaga (Mandall Shooting
 Supplies, Inc.)
• Armscor (Ruko Products)
• Arrieta, S.L. (Hi-Grade Imports;
 Jansma, Jack J.; New England
 Arms Co.; The Orvis Co., Inc.;
 Quality Arms, Inc.)
• Astra-Unceta Y Cia, S.A. (E.A.A.
 Corp.)
• ATIS Armi S.A.S.
• AYA (Armes de Chasse)
• Baikal (K.B.I., Inc.)
• Beeman Precision Airguns, Inc.
 (Beeman Precision Airguns, Inc.)
• Benelli Armi S.p.A. (E.A.A. Corp.;
 Heckler & Koch, Inc.; Sile
 Distributors)
• Beretta, Dr. Franco (Nevada
 Cartridge Co.)
• Beretta Firearms, Pietro (Beretta
 U.S.A. Corp.)
• Bernardelli S.p.A., Vincenzo
• Bersa S.A. (Eagle Imports, Inc.)
• Bertuzzi (Moore & Co., Wm. Larkin;
 New England Arms Co.)
• Blaser Jagdwaffen GmbH (Autumn
 Sales, Inc.)
 Bondini Paolo (blackpowder arms)
 Borovnik KG, Ludwig
 Brenneke KG, Wilhelm (Dynamit
 Nobel-RWS, Inc.)
• Bretton (Mandall Shooting Supplies,
 Inc.)
• BRNO (Action Arms Ltd.; Bohemia
 Arms Co.)
• Browning Arms Co. (Browning
 Arms Co.)
• BSA Guns Ltd. (Air Rifle Specialists)

• Cabanas (Mandall Shooting
 Supplies, Inc.)
• CBC (MAGTECH Recreational
 Products, Inc.)
• Chapuis Armes (Chapuis USA)
• Churchill (Ellett Bros.)
• Cosmi Americo & Figlio s.n.c. (New
 England Arms Co.)
• Crucelegui, Hermanos (Mandall
 Shooting Supplies, Inc.)
• CVA (blackpowder arms)
• CZ (Action Arms Ltd.)
• Daewoo Precision Industries Ltd.
 (Nationwide Sports Distributors)
• Dakota (EMF Co., Inc.)
• Daisy Mfg. Co. (Daisy Mfg. Co.)
• Diana (Dynamit Nobel-RWS, Inc.)
 Dumoulin, Ernest
• Erma Werke GmbH (Mandall
 Shooting Supplies, Inc.; Precision
 Sales International, Inc.)
• Fabarm S.p.A. (Ithaca Acquisition
 Corp.)
• Fabrica D'Armi Sabatti S.R.L.
 (E.A.A. Corp.)
• Famas (Century International Arms,
 Inc.)
• FAS (Nygord Precision Products)
• Fausti & Figlie s.n.c., Stefano
 (American Arms, Inc.)
• FEG (Century International Arms,
 Inc.; K.B.I., Inc.)
• FERLIB (Moore & Co., Wm. Larkin;
 New England Arms Co.;
 Pachmayr Co.; Quality Arms, Inc.)
• Firearms Co. Ltd./Alpine (Mandall
 Shooting Supplies, Inc.)
 FN Herstal
• Franchi S.p.A, Luigi (American
 Arms, Inc.)
• Francotte & Cie S.A., Auguste

•See page 451 for Warranty Service Center Addresses

(Armes de Chasse)
- FWB (Beeman Precision Airguns, Inc.)
- Gamba S.p.A., Renato (Giacomo Sporting, Inc.; New England Arms Co.)
- Gamo (Daisy Mfg. Co.; Dynamit Nobel-RWS, Inc.)
- Garbi, Armas Urki (Moore & Co., Wm. Larkin)
- Gaucher Armes S.A. (Mandall Shooting Supplies, Inc.)
- Glock GmbH (Glock, Inc.)
- Grulla Armes (American Arms, Inc.)
- Hammerli Ltd. (Beeman Precision Airguns, Inc.; Hammerli USA; Mandall Shooting Supplies, Inc.)
- Heckler & Koch, GmbH (Heckler & Koch, Inc.)
- Helwan (Interarms)
- Heym GmbH & Co., Friedrich Wilh. (JägerSport, Ltd.; Swarovski Optik North America Ltd.)
  Holland & Holland Ltd.
- Howa Machinery Ltd. (Interarms)
- IGA (Stoeger Industries)
- IMI (Magnum Research, Inc.)
- INDESAL (American Arms, Inc.)
- Interarms (Interarms)
- J.O. Arms & Ammunition Co. (J.O. Arms & Ammunition Co.)
- JSL Ltd. (Specialty Shooters Supply, Inc.)
- Kassnar (K.B.I., Inc.)
- K.B.I., Inc. (K.B.I., Inc.)
- Korth (Mandall Shooting Supplies, Inc.)
- Krico/Kriegeskorte GmbH, A. (Mandall Shooting Supplies, Inc.)
- Krieghoff Gun Co., H. (Krieghoff International, Inc.)
- Lakefield Arms Ltd.
  Lanber Armes S.A.
- Laurona Armes S.A. (Galaxy Imports Ltd., Inc.)
- Lebeau-Courally (New England Arms Co.)
- Llama Gabilondo Y Cia (SGS Importers International, Inc.)
- Marksman Products (Marksman Products)
- Marocchi F.lli S.p.A. (Precision Sales International, Inc.; Sile Distributors)
  Mauser-Werke
- MEC-Gar s.r.l. (MEC-Gar U.S.A., Inc.)
- Merkel Freres (GSI, Inc.)
- Miroku, B.C./Daly, Charles (Bell's Legendary Country Wear; British Sporting Arms)
- Mitchell Arms, Inc. (Mitchell Arms, Inc.)
- Morini (Mandall Shooting Supplies)
- Navy Arms Co. (Navy Arms Co.)
- Norica, Avnda Otaola (American Arms, Inc.)
- Norinco (Century International Arms, Inc.; ChinaSports, Inc.; Interarms)
- Para-Ordnance Mfg., Inc. (Para-Ordnance, Inc.)
- Pardini Armi Commerciale Srl (MCS, Inc.; Nygord Precision Products)
- Pedersoli, Davide & C. (Beauchamp & Son, Inc.; Cabela's; Dixie Gun Works; EMF Co., Inc.; Navy Arms Co.)

- Perazzi m.a.p. S.p.A. (Perazzi U.S.A., Inc.)
  Perugini-Visini & Co. s.r.l.
- Peters Stahl GmbH (McMillan Gunworks, Inc.; Olympic Arms)
- Piotti (Moore & Co., Wm. Larkin)
- Poly Technologies, Inc. (Keng's Firearms Specialty, Inc.)
- Powell & Son Ltd., William (Bell's Legendary Country Wear)
- Rigby & Co., John (Griffin & Howe, Inc.)
- Rizzini, Battista (Alessandri & Son, Lou)
- Rizzini, F.LLI (Moore & Co., Wm. Larkin; New England Arms Co.)
- Rossi, Amadeo (Interarms)
- RWS (Dynamit Nobel-RWS, Inc.)
- Sako Ltd. (Stoeger Industries)
- San Marco (Cape Outfitters; EMF Co., Inc.)
  Sardius Industries Ltd.
- Sauer (Paul Co., The)
- Schmidt, Herbert (Sportarms of Florida)
- SIG (Mandall Shooting Supplies, Inc.)
- SIG-Sauer (Sigarms, Inc.)
- SKB Arms Co. (G.U., Inc.)
- Societa Armi Bresciane Srl. (Cape Outfitters)
- Solothurn (Sile Distributors)
- Springfield, Inc. (Springfield, Inc.)
- Star Bonifacio Echeverria S.A. (Interarms)
- Steyr (GSI, Inc.; Nygord Precision Products)
- Steyr-Daimler-Puch (GSI, Inc.)
- Steyr-Mannlicher AG (GSI, Inc.)
- Tanfoglio S.r.l., Fratelli/Witness (E.A.A. Corp.)
- Tanner (Mandall Shooting Supplies, Inc.)
- Taurus International Firearms (Taurus Firearms, Inc.)
- Techni-Mec (Mandall Shooting Supplies, Inc.)
  T.F.C. S.p.A.
- Theoben Engineering (Air Rifle Specialists)
- Tikka (Stoeger Industries)
- Uberti, Aldo (American Arms, Inc.; Christopher Firearms Co., Inc., E.; Cimarron Arms; Dixie Gun Works; EMF Co., Inc.; Mitchell Arms, Inc.; Navy Arms Co.; Uberti USA, Inc.)
- Ugartechea S.A., Ignacio (Mandall Shooting Supplies, Inc.)
- Unique/M.A.P.F. (Nygord Precision Products)
  USA Sporting (Armas Kemen)
- Voere-KGH m.b.H. (JägerSport, Ltd.; Swarovski Optik North America Ltd.)
- Walther GmbH, Carl (Interarms)
- Weatherby, Inc. (Weatherby, Inc.)
- Webley & Scott Ltd. (Beeman Precision Airguns, Inc.)
- Weihrauch KG, Hermann (Beeman Precision Airguns, Inc.; E.A.A. Corp.)
- Westley Richards & Co. (Cape Outfitters)
- Zabala, Hermanos S.A. (American Arms, Inc.)
- Zanoletti, Pietro (Mandall Shooting Supplies, Inc.)
  Zoli, Antonio

GUNS, U.S.-MADE
- Accu-Tek
- American Arms & Ordnance, Inc.
- American Arms, Inc.
- American Derringer Corp.
- AMT
- Armscorp USA, Inc.
- A-Square Co., Inc.
- Auto-Ordnance Corp.
- Barrett Firearms Mfg., Inc.
- Beretta U.S.A. Corp.
- Brown Co., E. Arthur
- Browning (Parts & Service)
- Bryco Arms
- Bushmaster Firearms
- Calico Light Weapon Systems
- Cape Outfitters
- Century Gun Dist., Inc.
- Century International Arms, Inc.
- CHARCO
- Charter Arms
- Claridge Hi-Tec, Inc.
- Clifton Arms, Inc.
- Colt Blackpowder Arms Co.
- Colt's Mfg. Co., Inc.
- Competitor Corp., Inc.
- Connecticut Valley Classics
- Coonan Arms, Inc.
- Cooper Arms
  Cumberland Arms
- CVA

- Dakota Arms, Inc.
- Davis Industries
- Desert Industries, Inc.
- Dixie Gun Works
- Dragun Enterprises
  E&L Mfg., Inc.
- Eagle Arms, Inc.
- EMF Co., Inc.
- Essex Arms
- Feather Industries, Inc.
- Federal Engineering Corp.
- Freedom Arms, Inc.
- Galazan Shotgun Mfg. Co.
- Gibbs Rifle Co., Inc.
- Gilbert Equipment Co., Inc.
- Gonic Arms, Inc.
- Grendel, Inc.
- H&R 1871, Inc.
- Hatfield Gun Co., Inc.
- Hawken Shop, The
  Hi-Point Firearms
- HJS Arms, Inc.
  Holston Ent. Inc.
  H-S Precision, Inc.
- IAI
  Imperial Magnum Corp.
- Intratec
- Ithaca Aquisition Corp./Ithaca Gun Co.
- Jennings Firearms, Inc.
- J.O. Arms & Ammunition Co.
- Jones, J.D.
- Kahr Arms
- Kimber of America, Inc.
- Kimel Industries
- Knight's Mfg. Co.
- L.A.R. Manufacturing, Inc.
- Laseraim Arms
- Ljutic Industries, Inc.
- Lorcin Engineering Co., Inc.
- Magnum Research, Inc.
- Marlin Firearms Co.
- Maverick Arms, Inc.
- McMillan Bros. Rifle Co., Inc.
- McMillan Gunworks, Inc.
- Miller Arms, Inc.
- Mitchell Arms, Inc.
- MKS Supply, Inc.
- M.O.A. Corp.

- Montana Armory, Inc.
- Mossberg & Sons, Inc., O.F.
- Mowrey Gun Works
- Nesika Bay Precision
- New Advantage Arms Corp.
- New England Firearms
- North American Arms
- Olympic Arms, Inc.
- Oregon Arms, Inc.
- Phelps Mfg. Co.
- Phoenix Arms
  Precision Arms International, Inc.
- Quality Parts Co.
- Ram-Line, Inc.
  Ravell Ltd.
- Remington Arms Co., Inc.
  Rocky Mountain Arms, Inc.
- RPM
- Safari Arms/SGW
- Savage Arms, Inc.
- Scattergun Technologies, Inc.
- Seecamp Co., Inc., L.W.
- Sharps Arms Co., Inc., C.
- Shiloh Rifle Mfg.
- Smith & Wesson
- Sporting Arms Mfg., Inc.
- Springfield, Inc.
  SSK Industries
- Sturm, Ruger & Co., Inc.
- Sundance Industries, Inc.
- Survival Arms, Inc.
- Swivel Machine Works, Inc.
- Tar-Hunt Custom Rifles, Inc.
- Taurus Firearms, Inc.
- Texas Arms
- Texas Longhorn Arms, Inc.
- Thompson/Center Arms
- U.F.A. Inc.
  Ultimate Accuracy
- Ultra Light Arms, Inc.
- U.S. General Technologies, Inc.
- U.S. Repeating Arms Co.
  Valor Corp.
- Wesson Firearms Co., Inc.
- White Shooting Systems, Inc.
  Wichita Arms, Inc.
- Wildey, Inc.
- Wilkinson Arms
  Wyoming Armory, Inc.

GUNS AND GUN PARTS, REPLICA AND ANTIQUE
Ahlman Guns
Armi San Paolo
Armsport, Inc.
Bear Mountain Gun & Tool
Beauchamp & Son, Inc.
Bill's Gun Repair
British Arms Co. Ltd.
Buckskin Machine Works
Burgess & Son Gunsmiths, R.W.
Cache La Poudre Rifleworks
Cape Outfitters
Century International Arms, Inc.
Champlin, R. MacDonald
Cogar's Gunsmithing
Cole's Gun Works
Colonial Repair
Dangler, Homer L.
Day & Sons, Inc., Leonard
Delhi Gun House
Delta Arms Ltd.
Dixon Muzzleloading Shop, Inc.
Dragun Enterprises
Dyson & Son Ltd., Peter
Ed's Gun House
EMF Co., Inc.
First Distributors, Inc., Jack
Flintlocks, Etc.
Forgett, Jr., Valmore J.
Franchi S.p.A., Luigi
Golden Age Arms Co.
Goodwin, Fred
Gun Parts Corp., The
Gun Works, The
Gun-Tec
House of Muskets, Inc., The
Hunkeler, A.
Ken's Gun Specialties

Liberty Antique Gunworks
Lodewick, Walter H.
Log Cabin Sport Shop
Lucas, Edw. E.
Mountain Bear Rifle Works, Inc.
Mountain State Muzzleloading Supplies
Mowrey Gun Works
Munsch Gunsmithing, Tommy
Muzzleloaders Etcetera, Inc.
Navy Arms Co.
Neumann GmbH
OMR Feinmechanik, Jagd-und Sportwaffen, GmbH
Parker Gun Finishes
Parker-Hale
PEM's Mfg. Co.
P.M. Enterprises, Inc.
Pony Express Sport Shop, Inc.
Precise Metalsmithing Enterprises
Quality Firearms of Idaho, Inc.
Randco UK
Ravell Ltd.
Rutgers Gun & Boat Center
S&S Firearms
Sarco, Inc.
Silver Ridge Gun Shop
Sklany, Steve
Stott's Creek Armory, Inc.
Taylor's & Co., Inc.
Track of the Wolf, Inc.
Upper Missouri Trading Co.
Vintage Industries, Inc.
Weihrauch KG, Hermann
Wescombe
Winchester Sutler, Inc., The

GUNS, SURPLUS—PARTS AND AMMUNITION
Armscorp USA, Inc.
Aztec International Ltd.
Ballistica Maximus North
Bohemia Arms Co.
Bondini Paolo

Braun, M.
Century International Arms, Inc.
ChinaSports, Inc.
Colonial Repair
Combat Military Ordnance Ltd.

- See page 451 for Warranty Service Center Addresses

Delta Arms Ltd.
Ed's Gun House
First Distributors, Inc., Jack
Fleming Firearms
Forgett, Jr., Valmore J.
Forrest, Inc., Tom
Fulton Armory
Garcia National Gun Traders, Inc.
Gibbs Rifle Co., Inc.
Gun Parts Corp., The
Interarms
Lever Arms Service Ltd.
Moreton/Fordyce Enterprises
Mountain Bear Rifle Works, Inc.
Navy Arms Co.
Nu-Line Guns, Inc.
Oil Rod and Gun Shop
Old Western Scrounger, Inc.

Paragon Sales & Services, Inc.
Parker-Hale
Parts & Surplus
Quality Firearms of Idaho, Inc.
Randall Firearms Research
Ravell Ltd.
Rutgers Gun & Boat Center
Sarco, Inc.
Shell Shack
Sherwood Intl. Export Corp.
Southern Ammunition Co., Inc.
Springfield Sporters, Inc.
T.F.C. S.p.A.
Thurston Sports, Inc.
Vom Hofe
Westfield Engineering
Whitestone Lumber Corp.

GUNSMITHS, CUSTOM (see Custom Gunsmiths)

GUNSMITHS, HANDGUN (see Pistolsmiths)

GUNSMITH SCHOOLS

Brooker, Dennis
Colorado School of Trades
Cylinder & Slide, Inc.
Lassen Community College,
 Gunsmithing Dept.
Laughridge, William R.
Modern Gun Repair School
Montgomery Community College
Murray State College
North American Correspondence
 Schools

Pennsylvania Gunsmith School
Piedmont Community College
Pine Technical College
Professional Gunsmiths of
 America, Inc.
Ravell Ltd.
Southeastern Community College
Trinidad State Junior College
 Gunsmithing Dept.
Yavapai College

GUNSMITH SUPPLIES, TOOLS, SERVICES

Ackley Rifle Barrels
Advance Car Mover Co.,
 Rowell Div.
Aldis Gunsmithing & Shooting
 Supply
Alley Supply Co.
Atlantic Mills, Inc.
Badger Shooters Supply, Inc.
Bald Eagle Precision Machine Co.
Bear Mountain Gun & Tool
Behlert Precision
Bellm Contenders
Bengtson Arms Co., L.
Biesen, Al
Biesen, Roger
Birchwood Laboratories, Inc.
Blue Ridge Machinery & Tools, Inc.
Briley Mfg., Inc.
Brown Products, Inc., Ed
Brownells, Inc.
B-Square Co.
Buehler Scope Mounts
Can Am Enterprises
Carbide Checkering Tools
C-H Tool & Die Corp.
Chapman Manufacturing Co., The
Chem-Pak, Inc.
Choate Machine & Tool Co., Inc.
Chopie Mfg., Inc.
Clymer Manufacturing Co., Inc.
Colonial Arms, Inc.
Conetrol Scope Mounts
Crouse's Country Cover
Cumberland Arms
Custom Checkering Service
Custom Gun Products
D&J Bullet Co. & Custom Gun
 Shop, Inc.
Dakota Arms
Davidson Products, Inc.
Dayton Traister
Decker Shooting Products
Dem-Bart Hand Checkering
 Tools, Inc.
Dremel Mfg. Co.
Duffy, Charles E.
Du-Lite Corp.
Dutchman's Firearms, Inc., The
Echols & Co., D'Arcy
Ed's Gun House
EGW Evolution Gun Works
Eilan S.A.L.
Faith Associates, Inc.
Ferris Firearms
First Distributors, Inc., Jack
Fisher, Jerry A.
Forgreens Tool Mfg., Inc.

Forster, Kathy
Forster Products
4-D Custom Die Co.
Frazier Brothers Enterprises
G.B.C. Industries, Inc.
Grace Metal Products, Inc.
GRS Corp.
Gunline Tools
Gun-Tec
Half Moon Rifle Shop
Hastings Barrels
Henriksen Tool Co., Inc.
Hoehn Sales, Inc.
Hoelscher, Virgil
Hollands
Hoppe's Div.
Huey Gun Cases, Marvin
Iosso Marine Products
Ivanoff, Thomas G.
Jantz Supply
JGS Precision Tool Mfg.
K&M Services
Kasenit Co., Inc.
KenPatable Ent., Inc.
Kimball, Gary
Kleinendorst, K.W.
Kmount
Koppco Industries
Korzinek Riflesmith, J.
Kwik Mount Corp.
LaRocca Gun Works, Inc.
Lea Mfg. Co.
Lee Supplies, Mark
Lock's Philadelphia Gun Exchange
London Guns Ltd.
Lortone, Inc.
Mag-Na-Port Int'l, Inc.
Marsh, Mike
MCRW Associates Shooting
 Supplies
Menck, Thomas W.
Metalife Industries
Michael's Antiques
Millett Sights
Milliron Custom Mittermeier, Inc.
MMC
Morrow, Bud
Mowreys Guns & Supplies
N&J Sales
Nitex, Inc.
Ole Frontier Gunsmith Shop
Palmgren Steel Products
PanaVise Products, Inc.
PEM's Mfg. Co.
Penguin Industries, Inc.
Power Custom, Inc.
Practical Tools, Inc.

Precise Metal Finishing
Precision Arms International, Inc.
Precision Specialties
Pre-Winchester 92-90-62 Parts Co.
Pro-Port Ltd.
Ravell Ltd.
Reardon Products
Rice, Keith
Riggs, Jim
Roto/Carve
Ruvel & Co., Inc.
Scott, McDougall & Associates
Sharp Shooter, Inc.
Sheridan USA, Inc., Austin
Shirley Co. Gun & Riflemakers Ltd.
Shooter's Choice
S.K. Guns, Inc.
Smith Whetstone Co., Inc.
Stalwart Corp.
Starrett Co., L.S.
Stoney Point Products, Inc.
Stuart Products, Inc.
Sullivan, David S.

Sure Shot of LA, Inc.
TDP Industries, Inc.
Texas Platers Supply
Tom's Gun Repair
Trulock Tool
Turnbull Restoration, Doug
Venco Industries, Inc.
Washita Mountain Whetstone Co.
Weaver's Gun Shop
Weigand Combat Handguns, Inc.
Welsh, Bud
Wessinger Custom Guns &
 Engraving
Westfield Engineering
Westrom, John
Westwind Rifles, Inc.
White Rock Tool & Die
Wilcox All-Pro Tools & Supply
Will-Burt Co.
Williams Gun Sight Co.
Wilson's Gun Shop
World of Targets

HANDGUN ACCESSORIES

Action Arms Ltd.
ADCO International
Adventurer's Outpost
Aimtech Mount Systems
Ajax Custom Grips, Inc.
American Bullets
American Derringer Corp.
Armite Laboratories
Auto-Ordnance Corp.
Baer Custom, Inc., Les
Bar-Sto Precision Machine
Baumannize Custom
Behlert Precision
Black Sheep Brand
Blue and Gray Products, Inc.
Boonie Packer Products
Boyd's, Inc.
Broken Gun Ranch
Brown Products, Inc., Ed
Brownells, Inc.
Bucheimer, J.M.
Bullberry Barrel Works, Ltd.
Bushmaster Firearms
C3 Systems
Centaur Systems, Inc.
Central Specialties Ltd.
Clymer Manufacturing Co., Inc.
Cobra Gunskin
Dade Screw Machine Products
Desert Industries, Inc.
Doskocil Mfg. Co., Inc
E.A.A. Corp.
Eagle International, Inc.
EGW Evolution Gun Works
Faith Associates, Inc.
Feather Industries, Inc.
Feminine Protection, Inc.
Fleming Firearms
Frielich Police Equipment
Glock, Inc.
Greider Precision
Gremmel Enterprises
Gunfitters, The
Gun-Ho Sports Cases
Haselbauer Products, Jerry
Hebard Guns, Gil
Heinie Specialty Products
Hill Speed Leather, Ernie
H.K.S. Products
Hunter Co., Inc.
Jeffredo Gunsight
Jett & Co., Inc.
J.O. Arms & Ammunition Co.
Jones, J.D.
J.P. Enterprises, Inc.
Jumbo Sports Products
K&K Ammo Wrist Band
KeeCo Impressions
Keller Co., The
King's Gun Works
L&S Technologies Inc.
Lakewood Products, Inc.
LaRocca Gun Works, Inc.

Laseraim
Lee's Red Ramps
Leupold
Loch Leven Industries
Lock's Philadelphia Gun Exchange
Lohman Mfg. Co., Inc.
Mac's .45 Shop
Magnolia Sports, Inc.
Mag-Pack Corp.
Markell Inc.
Masen Co., John
Master Products, Inc.
McCormick Corp., Chip
MEC-Gar S.R.L.
Merkuria Ltd.
Michaels of Oregon Co.
Monte Kristo Pistol Grip Co.
MPC (McMinnville, TN)
MTM Molded Products Co., Inc.
Mustra's Custom Guns, Inc., Carl
N.C. Ordnance Co.
North American Specialties
No-Sho Mfg. Co.
Outa-Site Gun Carriers
Owen, Harry
Ox-Yoke Originals, Inc.
Pace Marketing, Inc.
Pardini Armi Commerciale Srl
PAST Sporting Goods, Inc.
Power Custom, Inc.
Practical Tools, Inc.
Precision Arms International, Inc.
Protector Mfg. Co., Inc., The
Quality Parts Co.
Ram-Line, Inc.
Ranch Products
Ravell Ltd.
Round Edge, Inc.
RPM
Rutgers Gun & Boat Center
Sheridan USA, Inc., Austin
Sile Distributors, Inc.
Sling 'N Things, Inc.
Sonderman, Robert
Southwind Sanctions
Sport Specialties
SSK Industries
"Su-Press-On," Inc.
TacTell, Inc.
Tapco, Inc.
Taurus, S.A., Forjas
T.F.C. S.p.A.
Trijicon, Inc.
Triple-K Mfg. Co.
Tyler Mfg.-Dist., Melvin
Valor Corp.
Volquartsen Custom Ltd.
Weigand Combat Handguns, Inc.
Wessinger Custom Guns &
 Engraving
Western Design
Whitestone Lumber Corp.
Wichita Arms, Inc.

HANDGUN GRIPS

African Import Co.
Ahrends, Kim
Ajax Custom Grips, Inc.
Altamont Co.
American Derringer Corp.

American Gripcraft
Art Jewel Enterprises Ltd.
Artistry In Wood
Barami Corporation
Bear Hug Grips, Inc.

Behlert Precision
Bob's Gun Shop
Boone's Custom Ivory Grips, Inc.
CAM Enterprises
Cobra Gunskin
Cole-Grip
Custom Firearms
Desert Industries, Inc.
Eagle Mfg. & Engineering
EMF Co., Inc.
Eyears
Fisher Custom Firearms
Fitz Pistol Grip Co.
Forrest, Inc., Tom
Greene, M.L.
Herrett's Stocks, Inc.
Hogue Grips
IMI Services USA, Inc.
KeeCo Impressions
Linebaugh Custom Sixguns & Rifle
 Works
Logan Security Products Co.
Mac's .45 Shop
Masen Co., John
N.C. Ordnance Co.

Newell, Robert H.
North American Specialties
Old Western Scrounger, Inc.
Pardini Armi Commerciale Srl
Peacemaker Specialists
Pilgrim Pewter, Inc.
Ravell Ltd.
Renner Co., R.J./Radical Concepts
Rosenberg & Sons, Jack A.
Roy's Custom Grips
Rutgers Gun & Boat Center
Safariland Ltd., Inc.
Savana Sports, Inc.
Sheridan USA, Inc., Austin
Sile Distributors, Inc.
Spegel, Craig
Taurus, S.A., Forjas
Taurus Firearms, Inc.
Tirelli
Tyler Mfg.-Dist., Melvin
Valor Corp.
Vintage Industries, Inc.
Volquartsen Custom Ltd.
Vom Hofe
Wayland Precision Wood Products

HEARING PROTECTORS

Behlert Precision
Bilsom Intl., Inc.
Blount, Inc.
Brown Co., E. Arthur
Browning
Clark Co., Inc., David
Cobra Gunskin
Dragun Enterprises
E-A-R, Inc.
Fitz Pistol Grip Co.
Flents Products Co., Inc.
Hoppe's Div.
Kesselring Gun Shop
Marble Arms Corp.
North American Specialties

North Specialty Products
Paterson Gunsmithing
Peltor, Inc.
Penguin Industries, Inc.
R.E.T. Enterprises
Rutgers Gun & Boat Center
Safariland Ltd., Inc.
Safesport Manufacturing Co.
Silencio/Safety Direct
Smith & Wesson
Stock Shop, The
Tyler Mfg.-Dist., Melvin
Valor Corp.
Willson Safety Prods. Div.

HOLSTERS AND LEATHER GOODS

Action Products, Inc.
Aker Leather Products
Alessi Holsters, Inc.
American Import Co., The
American Sales & Mfg. Co.
Arratoonian, Andy
Artistry in Leather
Baker's Leather Goods, Roy
Bandcor Industries
Bang-Bang Boutique
Barami Corp.
Bear Hug Grips, Inc.
Beeman Precision Airguns, Inc.
Behlert Precision
Bianchi International, Inc.
Black Sheep Brand
Blocker's Custom Holsters, Ted
Brauer Bros. Mfg. Co.
Brown, H.R.
Browning Arms Co.
Bucheimer, J.M.
Bushmaster Hunting & Fishing
Bushwacker Backpack &
 Supply Co.
Carvajal Belts & Holsters
Cathey Enterprises, Inc.
Chace Leather Products
Cimarron Arms
Clements' Custom Leathercraft,
 Chas
Cobra Gunskin
Cobra Line SRL
Cobra Sport
Counter Assault
Crawford Co., Inc., R.M.
Creedmoor Sports, Inc.
Davis Leather Co., G. Wm.
Delhi Gun House
DeSantis Holster & Leather Goods
Dragun Enterprises
Easy Pull/Outlaw Products
Ekol Leather Care
El Dorado Leather
El Paso Saddlery Co.
EMF Co., Inc.
Epps "Orillia" Ltd., Ellwood
Eutaw Co., Inc., The
Faust, Inc., T.G.
Flores Publications, Inc., J.
Fobus International Ltd.
Fury Cutlery

Galati International
GALCO International Ltd.
Glock, Inc.
GML Products, Ino.
Gould & Goodrich
Gun Leather Limited
Gunfitters, The
Gusty Winds Corp.
Gutmann Cutlery Co., Inc.
Hafner Creations, Inc.
Hebard Guns, Gil
Hellweg Ltd.
Henigson & Associates, Steve
Hill Speed Leather, Ernie
Holster Outpost
Holster Shop, The
Horseshoe Leather Products
Hoyt Holster Co., Inc.
Hume, Don
Hunter Co., Inc.
J.O. Arms & Ammunition Co.
John's Custom Leather
Joy Enterprises
Jumbo Sports Products
Kane Products, Inc.
Keller Co., The
Kirkpatrick Leather Co.
Kolpin Mfg., Inc.
Kramer Handgun Leather, Inc.
L.A.R. Manufacturing, Inc.
Law Concealment Systems, Inc.
Lawrence Leather Co.
Leather Arsenal
Lethal Force Institute
Lone Star Gunleather
Magnolia Sports, Inc.
Markell, Inc.
Michaels of Oregon Co.
Minute Man High Tech. Ind.
Mixson Leathercraft, Inc.
Nelson Combat Leather, Bruce
Noble Co., Jim
North American Arms
No-Sho Mfg. Co.
Null Holsters Ltd., K.L.
Ojala Holsters, Arvo
Oklahoma Leather Products, Inc.
Old West Reproductions, Inc.
Pathfinder Sports Leather
Police Bookshelf
PWL Gunleather

Red River Frontier Outfitters
Renegade
Ringler Custom Leather Co.
Rutgers Gun & Boat Center
Rybka Custom Leather Equipment,
 Thad
Safariland Ltd., Inc.
Safety Speed Holster, Inc.
Savana Sports, Inc.
Schulz Industries
Shadow Concealment Systems
Sheridan USA, Inc., Austin
Shoemaker & Sons, Inc., Tex
Shurkatch Corp.
Silhouette Leathers
Smith Saddlery, Jesse W.
Southwind Sanctions
Sparks, Milt

Stalker, Inc.
Strong Holster Co.
Stuart, V. Pat
Tabler Marketing
Texas Longhorn Arms, Inc.
Top-Line USA Inc.
Torel, Inc.
Triple-K Mfg. Co., Inc.
Tyler Mfg.-Dist., Melvin
Valor Corp.
Venus Industries
Viking Leathercraft, Inc.
Walt's Custom Leather
Whinnery, Walt
Whitestone Lumber Corp.
Wild Bill's Originals
Winchester Sutler, Inc., The

HUNTING AND CAMP GEAR, CLOTHING, ETC.

Ace Sportswear, Inc.
Action Products, Inc.
Adventure 16, Inc.
All Weather Outerwear
Allen Co., Bob
American Import Co., The
Aristocrat Knives
Armor
Atlanta Cutlery Corp.
Atsko/Sno-Seal, Inc.
Bagmaster Mfg. Inc.
Barbour, Inc.
Barteaux Machetes, Inc.
Bauer, Eddie
Bausch & Lomb, Inc.
Bear Archery
Beaver Park Products, Inc
Better Concepts Co.
Bilsom Intl., Inc.
Boss Manufacturing Co.
Brell Mar Products
Brown Manufacturing
Browning Arms Co.
Brunton U.S.A.
Buck Stop Lure Co., Inc.
Bullet Meister Bullets
Bushmaster Hunting & Fishing
Cabela's
Camofare Co.
Camp-Cap Products
Carhartt, Inc.
Chameleon Camouflage Systems
Chippewa Shoe Co.
Churchill Glove Co., James
Clarkfield Enterprises, Inc.
Cobra Gunskin
Coghlan's Ltd.
Coleman Co., Inc.
Coulston Products, Inc.
Crane & Crane Ltd.
Crawford Co., Inc., R.M.
Creedmoor Sports, Inc.
Dakota Corp.
Danner Shoe Mfg. Co.
DeckSlider of Florida
Deer Me Products
Degen Knives
Dr. O's Products Ltd.
Dunham Co.
Duofold, Inc.
Duxbak, Inc.
Dynalite Products, Inc.
E-A-R, Inc.
Ekol Leather Care
Erickson's Mfg., Inc., C.W.
Fish-N-Hunt, Inc.
Flow-Rite of Tennessee, Inc.
Forrest Tool Co.
Fox River Mills, Inc.
Frankonia Jagd
Fury Cutlery
G&H Decoys, Inc.
Game Winner, Inc.
Gander Mountain, Inc.
Gerber Legendary Blades
Glacier Glove
Hawken Shop, The
Hinman Outfitters, Bob
Hodgman, Inc.
Hofmann & Co.
Houtz & Barwick
Hunter's Specialties, Inc.
Innovision Enterprises
Joy Enterprises

Just Brass, Inc.
K&M Industries, Inc.
Kamik Outdoor Footwear
LaCrosse Footwear, Inc.
Langenberg Hat Co.
Leatherman Tool Group, Inc.
Liberty Trouser Co.
L.L. Bean
Mack's Sport Shop
MAG Instrument, Inc.
Marathon Rubber Prods. Co., Inc.
Melton Shirt Co., Inc.
Millenium Safety Products
Molin Industries
Nelson/Weather-Rite
Noble Co., Jim
North Specialty Products
Northlake Outdoor Footwear
Olt Co., Philip S.
Original Mink Oil, Inc.
Orvis Co., The
Palsa Outdoor Products
Partridge Sales Ltd., John
PAST Sporting Goods, Inc
Pendleton Woolen Mills
Pointing Dog Journal
Porta Blind, Inc.
Pro-Mark
Pyromid, Inc.
Randolph Engineering, Inc.
Ranger Mfg. Co., Inc.
Ranging, Inc.
Rattlers Brand
Red Ball
Red River Frontier Outfitters
Refrigiwear, Inc.
Re-Heater, Inc.
Rocky, Shoes & Boots
Rocky Mountain High Sports
 Glasses
Ruko Products, Inc.
Rutgers Gun & Boat Center
Ruvel & Co., Inc.
Safesport Manufacturing Co.
San Angelo Sports Products, Inc.
Savana Sports, Inc.
Scansport, Inc.
Scotch Hunting Products Co., Inc.
Servus Footwear Co.
Silencio/Safety Direct
Slings 'N Things, Inc.
Smith Whetstone Co., Inc.
Sno-Seal, Inc.
Streamlight, Inc.
Swanndri New Zealand
Teledyne Inc.
10-X Products Group
Thompson, Norm
T.H.U. Enterprises, Inc.
Tink's Safariland Hunting Corp.
Torel, Inc.
TrailTimer Co.
Venus Industries
Wakina by Pic
Walker Shoe Co.
Walls Industries
Wideview Scope Mount Corp.
Willson Safety Prods. Div.
Wolverine Boots & Outdoor
 Footwear Division
Woolrich Woolen Mills
Wyoming Knife Corp.
Yellowstone Wilderness Supply

KNIVES AND KNIFEMAKER'S SUPPLIES—
FACTORY AND MAIL ORDER

Adventure 16, Inc.
African Import Co.
Aitor-Cuchilleria Del Norte, S.A.
American Import Co., The
American Target Knives
Aristocrat Knives
Art Jewel Enterprises Ltd.
Atlanta Cutlery Corp.
B&D Trading Co., Inc.
Barteaux Machetes, Inc.
Benchmark Knives
Beretta U.S.A. Corp.
Blackjack Knives
Blue Ridge Knives
Boker USA, Inc.
Bowen Knife Co. Inc.
Browning Arms Co.
Brunton U.S.A.
Buck Knives, Inc.
Buster's Custom Knives
CAM Enterprises
Camillus Cutlery Co.
Case & Sons Cutlery Co., W.R.
Catoctin Cutlery
Chicago Cutlery Co.
Christopher Firearms Co., Inc., E.
Clements' Custom Leathercraft,
   Chas
Coast Cutlery Co.
Cold Steel, Inc.
Coleman Co., Inc.
Colonial Knife Co.
Compass Industries, Inc.
Crawford Co., Inc., R.M.
Creative Craftsman, Inc., The
Crosman Blades
Cutco Cutlery
Cutlery Shoppe
Damascus-U.S.A.
Dan's Whetstone Co., Inc.
Degen Knives
Delhi Gun House
Diamond Machining
   Technology, Inc.
EdgeCraft Corp.
EK Knife Co.
Empire Cutlery Corp.
Eze-Lap Diamond Prods.
Fitz Pistol Grip Co.
Flintlock Muzzle Loading Gun
   Shop, The
Forrest Tool Co.
Forthofer's Gunsmithing &
   Knifemaking
Fortune Products, Inc.
Frank Knives
Frost Cutlery Co.
Fury Cutlery
Gerber Legendary Blades
Golden Age Arms Co.
Gutmann Cutlery Co., Inc.
H&B Forge Co.
Harrington Cutlery, Inc., Russell
Hawken Shop, The
Henckels Zwillingswerk, Inc., J.A.
Hubertus Schneidwarenfabrik
Hunting Classics
Hy-Score Arms Co. Ltd.
Ibberson (Sheffield) Ltd., George

Imperial Schrade Corp.
Iron Mountain Knife Co.
J.A. Blades, Inc.
Jantz Supply
Jenco Sales, Inc.
Johnson Wood Products
Joy Enterprises
KA-BAR Knives
Kasenit Co., Inc.
Kellogg's Professional Products
Ken's Finn Knives
Kershaw Knives
Knife Importers, Inc.
Koppco Industries
Koval Knives
Lamson & Goodnow Mfg. Co.
Lansky Sharpeners & Crock Stick
Leatherman Tool Group, Inc.
Linder Solingen Knives
L.L. Bean
Mar Knives, Inc., Al
Matthews Cutlery
Molin Industries
Mountain State Muzzleloading
   Supplies
Murphy Co., Inc., R.
Normark Corp.
North American Specialties
Outdoor Edge Cutlery Corp.
Plaza Cutlery, Inc.
Precise International
Queen Cutlery Co.
R&C Knives & Such
Randall-Made Knives
Ravell Ltd.
Reno, Wayne
Ruko Products, Inc.
Russell Knives, Inc., A.G.
Safesport Manufacturing Co.
Scansport, Inc.
Schiffman, Mike
Schrimsher's Custom Knifemaker's
   Supply, Bob
Sheffield Knifemakers Supply
Sheridan USA, Inc., Austin
Smith & Wesson
Smith Saddlery, Jesse W.
Smith Whetstone Co., Inc.
Soque River Knives
Spyderco, Inc.
Stone Enterprises Ltd.
Swiss Army Knives, Inc.
T.F.C. S.p.A.
Traditions
Tru-Balance Knife Co.
United Cutlery Corp.
Utica Cutlery Co.
Valor Corp.
Venus Industries
Walt's Custom Leather
Washita Mountain Whetstone Co.
Weber Jr., Rudolf
Wenoka/Seastyle
Western Cutlery Co.
Whinnery, Walt
Wostenholm
Wyoming Knife Corp.

LABELS, BOXES, CARTRIDGE HOLDERS

Accuracy Products, S.A.
Advance Car Mover Co.,
   Rowell Div.
Anderson Manufacturing Co., Inc.
Ballistic Products, Inc.
Berry's Mfg. Inc.
Brown Co., E. Arthur
Cabinet Mountain Outfitters Scents
   & Lures
Del Rey Products
Fitz Pistol Grip Co.
Flambeau Products Corp.
Flintlock Muzzle Loading Gun
   Shop, The

Hornady Mfg. Co.
J&J Products Co.
King & Co.
Lakewood Products, Inc.
Loadmaster
Lyman Instant Targets, Inc.
Lyman Products Corp.
Midway Arms, Inc.
MTM Molded Products Co., Inc.
Precision Reloading, Inc.
Ravell Ltd.
Scharch Mfg., Inc.
Zero Ammunition Co., Inc.

LOAD TESTING AND PRODUCT TESTING,
(Chronographing, Ballistic Studies)

Ammunition Consulting
   Services, Inc.
Arms, Peripheral Data Systems
A-Square Co., Inc.

Ballistic Research
BestLoad, Inc.
Briese Bullet Co., Inc.
Buck Stix

Bustani Appraisers, Leo
Clerke Co., J.A.
D&H Precision Tooling
Dever Co., Jack
Farr Studio, Inc.
Fusilier Bullets
Hank's Gun Shop
Hensler, Jerry
High Performance International
Hoelscher, Virgil
Jackalope Gun Shop
Jensen Bullets
Jones, J.D.
Jurras, L.E.
Lachaussee, S.A.
Lomont Precision Bullets
Maionchi-L.M.I.
McMurdo, Lynn

Multiplex International
Neutralizer Police Munitions
Oil Rod and Gun Shop
Pace Marketing, Inc.
Pejsa Ballistics
Ransom International Corp.
R.I.S. Co., Inc.
Romain's Custom Guns
RPM
Rupert's Gun Shop
SOS Products Co.
SSK Industries
Stock Shop, The
Tioga Engineering Co., Inc.
Vulpes Ventures, Inc.
White Laboratory, Inc., H.P.
Whitestone Lumber Corp.
X-Spand Target Systems

MISCELLANEOUS

Actions, Rifle
   Hall Manufacturing
Accurizing, Rifle
   Stoney Baroque Shooters Supply
Adapters, Cartridge
   Alex, Inc.
   Owen, Harry
Adapters, Shotshell
   PC Co.
Airgun Accessories
   Beeman Precision Airguns, Inc.
   BSA Guns Ltd.
Assault Rifle Accessories
   Feather Industries, Inc.
   Ram-Line, Inc.
Body Armor
   Faust, Inc., T.G.
   Second Chance Body Armor
   Top-Line USA Inc.
Bore Illuminator
   Flashette Co.
Bore Lights
   MDS, Inc.
   N.C. Ordnance Co.
Brass Catcher
   M.A.M. Products, Inc.
Bullets, Rubber
   CIDCO
Calendar, Gun Shows
   Stott's Creek Printers
Cannons, Miniature Replicas
   Furr Arms
   R.G.-G., Inc.
Convert-A-Pell
   Jett & Co., Inc.
Dehumidifiers
   Buenger Enterprises
   Hydrosorbent Products
Deer Drag
   D&H Prods. Co., Inc.
Dryers
   Buenger Enterprises
   Peet Shoe Dryer, Inc.
E-Z Loader
   Del Rey Products
Firearm Historian
   Kennerknecht, Rick "KK"
Firearm Restoration
   Adair Custom Shop, Bill
   Johns, Bill
   Liberty Antique Gunworks
   Mazur Restoration, Pete
   Moeller, Steve
FFL Record Keeping
   Basics Information Systems, Inc.
   PFRB Co.
   R.E.T. Enterprises
Hunting Trips
   J/B Adventures & Safaris, Inc.
   Professional Hunter Specialties
   Safaris Plus
Hypodermic Rifles/Pistols
   Multipropulseurs
Industrial Dessicants
   WAMCO—New Mexico
Insert Barrels
   Owen, Harry/Sport Specialties
Lettering Restoration System
   Pranger, Ed G.
Locks, Gun
   Brown Manufacturing
   Master Lock Co.
Military Equipment/Accessories
   Alpha 1 Drop Zone
Photographers, Gun
   Bilal, Mustafa

Hanusin, John
Macbean, Stan
Payne Photography, Robert
Semmer, Charles
Smith, Michael
Weyer International
White Pine Photographic Services
Power Tools, Rotary Flexible Shaft
   Foredom Electric Co.
Saddle Rings, Studs
   Silver Ridge Gun Shop
Safety Devices
   Gun-Alert
   Master Products, Inc.
   P&M Sales and Service
Safeties
   Harper, Wm. E./The Great 870 Co.
   Necessary Concepts, Inc.
   P.M. Enterprises, Inc.
   Taylor & Robbins
Scents and Lures
   Buck Stop Lure Co., Inc.
   Cabinet Mountain Outfitters
      Scents & Lures
   Dr. O's Products Ltd.
   Flow-Rite of Tennessee, Inc.
   Mountain Hollow Game Calls
   Rickard, Inc., Pete
   Robbins Scent, Inc.
   Tink's Safariland Hunting Corp.
   Tinks & Ben Lee Hunting Products
   Wellington Outdoors
   Wildlife Research Center, Inc.
Scoring Plug
   RIG Products
Scrimshaw
   Boone's Custom Ivory Grips, Inc.
   Dolbare, Elizabeth
   Gun Room, The
   Marek, George
   Reno, Wayne
   Sherwood, George
Self-Defense Sprays
   Bushwacker Backpack &
      Supply Co.
   Counter Assault
Shell Dispenser
   Loadmaster
Shooting Range Equipment
   Caswell International Corp.
Silencers
   AWC Systems Technology
   Ciener, Jonathan Arthur
   DLO Mfg.
   Fleming Firearms
   Norrell Arms, John
   Precision Arms International, Inc.
   S&H Arms Mfg. Co.
   S.C.R.C.
   Sound Technology
   Ward Machine
Slings and Swivels
   Boonie Packer Products
   Butler Creek Corp.
   DTM International, Inc.
   High North Products, Inc.
   Leather Arsenal
   Michaels of Oregon Co.
   Outdoor Connection, Inc., The
   Palsa Outoor Products
   Pathfinder Sports Leather
   Schulz Industries
   Sile Distributors, Inc.
   Torel, Inc.
Treestands and Steps
   A&J Products

Amacker International, Inc.
Apache Products, Inc.
Dr. O's Products Ltd.
Silent Hunter
Summit Specialties, Inc.
Trax America, Inc.
Treemaster
Warren & Sweat Mfg. Co.
Trophies
Blackinton & Co., Inc., V.H.
Ventilation
ScanCo Environmental Systems

Video Tapes
Calibre Press, Inc.
Dangler, Homer L.
Eastman Products, R.T.
Foothills Video Productions, Inc.
MagSafe Ammo Co.
New Historians Productions, The
Rocky Mountain Wildlife Products
Trail Visions
Wilderness Sound Products Ltd.
Xythos-Miniature Revolver
Andres & Dworsky

MUZZLE-LOADING GUNS, BARRELS AND EQUIPMENT

Accuracy Unlimited (Littleton, CO)
Ackermann & Co.
Adkins, Luther
All American Bullets
Allen Manufacturing
American Pioneer Video
•Anderson Manufacturing Co., Inc.
Armi San Paolo
•Armoury, Inc., The
•Armsport, Inc.
Barton, Michael D.
Bauska Barrels
•Beauchamp & Son, Inc.
Beaver Lodge
Bentley, John
Birdsong & Associates, W.E.
Blackhawk East
Blackhawk Mountain
Blackhawk West
Blake Affiliates
•Blount, Inc.
Blue and Gray Products, Inc.
Bridgers Best
Buckskin Machine Works
Buffalo Bullet Co., Inc.
Burgess and Son Gunsmiths, R.W.
Butler Creek Corp.
Cache La Poudre Rifleworks
Camas Hot Springs Mfg.
•Cape Outfitters
Cash Manufacturing Co., Inc.
CenterMark
Chambers Flintlocks, Ltd., Jim
Chopie Mfg., Inc.
•Cimarron Arms
Cogar's Gunsmithing
•Colt Blackpowder Arms Co.
Cousin Bob's Mountain Products
•Cumberland Arms
•Cumberland Knife & Gun Works
•CVA
Dangler, Homer L.
Day & Sons, Inc., Leonard
•Dayton Traister
deHaas Barrels
Delhi Gun House
•Denver Arms, Ltd.
•Dixie Gun Works
Dixon Muzzleloading Shop, Inc.
Eades' Muzzleloader Builders'
  Supply, Don
Ed's Gun House
•EMF Co., Inc.
•Euroarms of America, Inc.
Eutaw Co., Inc., The
Fautheree, Andy
Feken, Dennis
Fellowes, Ted
Fish, Marshall F.
Flintlock Muzzle Loading Gun
  Shop, The
Flintlocks, Etc.
•Forster Products
Fort Hill Gunstocks
Frontier
•Gibbs Rifle Co., Inc.
Golden Age Arms Co.
•Gonic Arms, Inc.
Hastings Barrels
•Hatfield Gun Co., Inc.
•Hawken Shop, The
Hege Jagd-u. Sporthandels, GmbH
•Hornady Mfg. Co.
House of Muskets, Inc., The
Hunkeler, A.
Jamison's Forge Works
Jones Co., Dale

•JSL (Hereford) Ltd.
K&M Industries, Inc.
Kennedy Firearms
Kolpin Mfg., Inc.
Kwik-Site Co.
Laurel Mountain Forge
Lite Tek International
•Log Cabin Sport Shop
Lutz Engraving, Ron
Lyman Instant Targets, Inc.
•Lyman Products Corp.
McCann's Muzzle-Gun Works
MMP
•Modern MuzzleLoading, Inc.
•Montana Armory, Inc.
Montana Precision Swaging
•Mossberg & Sons, Inc., O.F.
Mountain State Muzzleloading
  Supplies
•Mowrey Gun Works
MSC Industrial Supply Co.
Mt. Alto Outdoor Products
Mushroom Express Bullet Co.
Muzzleloaders Etcetera, Inc.
Newman Gun Shop
North Star West
October Country
Oklahoma Leather Products, Inc.
Olde Pennsylvania
Olson, Myron
Orion Rifle Barrel Co.
Ox-Yoke Originals, Inc.
Parker Gun Finishes
Pecatonica River Longrifle
•Pedersoli, Davide & C.
Phyl-Mac
•Pioneer Arms Co.
Rapine Bullet Mould Mfg. Co.
R.E. Davis
Rusty Duck Premium Gun Care
  Products
R.V.I.
S&B Industries
S&S Firearms
Selsi Co., Inc.
•Sharps Arms Co., Inc., C.
Shooter's Choice
•Sile Distributors, Inc.
Single Shot, Inc.
Slings 'N Things, Inc.
Smokey Valley Rifles
South Bend Replicas, Inc.
Southern Bloomer Mfg. Co.
SPG Bullet Lubricant
•Sturm, Ruger & Co., Inc.
TDP Industries, Inc.
Tennessee Valley Mfg.
Thompson Bullet Lube Co.
Thompson/Center Arms
•Thunder Mountain Arms
Tiger-Hunt
Track of the Wolf, Inc.
•Traditions
Tyler Scott, Inc.
•Uberti, Aldo
•Uberti USA, Inc.
Upper Missouri Trading Co.
Venco Industries, Inc.
Warren Muzzleloading Co., Inc.
Wescombe
White Owl Enterprises
•White Shooting Systems, Inc.
Wideview Scope Mount Corp.
Winchester Sutler, Inc., The
Woodworker's Supply
Young Country Arms

PISTOLSMITHS

Accuracy Gun Shop
Accuracy Unlimited (Glendale, AZ)
Accurate Plating & Weaponry, Inc.
Ahlman Guns
Ahrends, Kim
Aldis Gunsmithing & Shooting Supply
Alpha Precision, Inc.
Alpine's Precision Gunsmithing &
  Indoor Shooting Range
American Pistolsmiths Guild
Amodei, Jim
Armament Gunsmithing Co., Inc.
Bain & Davis, Inc.
Baity's Custom Gunworks
Banks, Ed
Bar-Sto Precision Machine
Bengtson Arms Co., L.
Bowen Classic Arms Corp.
Boyd's Inc.
Brian, C.T.
Broken Gun Ranch
Brown Products, Inc., Ed
Cannons Guns
Caraville Manufacturing
Cellini, Inc., Vito Francesca
Clark Custom Guns, Inc.
Corkys Gun Clinic
Curtis Custom Shop
Custom Firearms
Custom Gunsmiths
D&D Gunsmiths, Ltd.
D&L Sports
Davis Service Center, Bill
D.O.C. Specialists, Inc.
Ellicott Arms Inc./Woods Pistolsmithing
EMF Co., Inc.
Ferris Firearms
First Distributors, Inc., Jack
Fisher Custom Firearms
Francesca, Inc.
Frielich Police Equipment
Frontier Arms Co., Inc.
Garthwaite, Jim
Giron, Robert E.
Greider Precision
Guncraft Sports, Inc.
Gunsite Gunsmithy
Gunsmithing Ltd.
Hamilton, Alex B.
Hamilton, Keith
Hank's Gun Shop
Hanson's Gun Center, Dick
Hardison, Charles
Hebard Guns, Gil
Heinie Specialty Products
High Bridge Arms, Inc.
Highline Machine Co.
Hindman, Ace
Hoag, James W.
Intermountain Arms & Tackle, Inc.
Irwin, Campbell H.
Ivanoff, Thomas G.
Jarvis Gunsmithing, Inc.
Johnston, James
Jones, J.D.
J.P. Enterprises, Inc.
Jungkind, Reeves C.
K-D, Inc.
Ken's Gun Specialties
Kilham & Co.
Kimball, Gary
Kopec Enterprises, John
Kopp, Terry K.
La Clinique du .45
LaFrance Specialties
LaRocca Gun Works, Inc.

Lawson, John G.
Lee's Red Ramps
Linebaugh Custom Sixguns & Rifle
  Works
Long, George F.
Mac's .45 Shop
Mahony, Philip Bruce
Martin's Gun Shop
Marvel, Alan
Mathews & Son, Inc., George E.
McMillan Gunworks, Inc.
Mid-America Recreation, Inc.
Middlebrooks Custom Shop
Miller Custom
Mitchell's Accuracy Shop
MJK Gunsmithing, Inc.
Moran, Jerry
Mountain Bear Rifle Works, Inc.
Mullis Guncraft
Mustra's Custom Guns, Inc., Carl
Nicholson Custom
North Fork Custom Gunsmithing
Novak's Inc.
Nowlin Custom Barrels Mfg.
Oglesby & Oglesby Gunmakers, Inc.
Pace Marketing, Inc.
Pardini Armi Commerciale Srl
Paris, Frank J.
Peacemaker Specialists
PEM's Mfg. Co.
Performance Specialists
Peterson Gun Shop, Inc., A.W.
Pierce Pistols
Plaxco, J. Michael
Practical Tools, Inc.
Precision Arms International, Inc.
Precision Specialties
Randco UK
Ravell Ltd.
Ries, Chuck
Rim Pac Sports, Inc.
Roberts, J.J.
Rogers Gunsmithing, Bob
Rutgers Gun & Boat Center
Scott, McDougall & Associates
Seecamp Co., Inc., L.W.
Shell Shack
Shooters Supply
Sight Shop, The
Sipes Gun Shop
S.K. Guns, Inc.
Spokhandguns, Inc.
Springfield, Inc.
SSK Industries
Steger, James R.
Swampfire Shop, The
Swenson's 45 Shop, A.D.
Ten-Ring Precision, Inc.
Thompson, Randall
300 Gunsmith Service, Inc.
Thurston Sports, Inc.
Tom's Gun Repair
T.S.W. Conversions, Inc.
Ulrich, Doc & Bud
Unick's Gunsmithing
Vic's Gun Refinishing
Volquartsen Custom Ltd.
Walker Arms Co., Inc.
Walters Industries
Wardell Precision Handguns Ltd.
Weigand Combat Handguns, Inc.
Wessinger Custom Guns &
  Engraving
Wichita Arms, Inc.
Williamson Precision Gunsmithing
Wilson's Gun Shop

REBORING AND RERIFLING

Ackley Rifle Barrels, P.O.
Bellm Contenders
Blackstar Barrel Accurizing
Colonial Repair
D&D Gunsmiths, Ltd.
Flaig's
H&S Liner Service
Hart & Son, Inc., Robert W.
Home Shop Machinist, The
Ivanoff, Thomas G.
Jackalope Gun Shop
K-D, Inc.
LaBounty Precision Reboring
Matco, Inc.
Mid-America Recreation, Inc.
Nicholson Custom

Pac-Nor Barreling
Pence Precision Barrels
Redman's Rifling & Reboring
Rice, Keith
Ridgetop Sporting Goods
Schumakers Gun Shop, William
Sharon Rifle Barrel Co.
Shaw, Inc., E.R.
Siegrist Gun Shop
300 Gunsmith Service, Inc.
Tom's Gun Repair
Van Patten, J.W.
Wells, Fred F.
West, Robert G.
White Rock Tool & Die

RELOADING TOOLS AND ACCESSORIES

Accuracy Components Co.
American Products Co.
• Ammo Load, Inc.
• AMT
Andela Tool & Machinery, Inc.
• ASI
Ballistic Products, Inc.
Ballisti-Cast, Inc.
Barlett, J.
Bear Reloaders
Ben's Machines
Berry's Mfg. Inc.
• Blount, Inc.
• Brown Co., E. Arthur
Brynin, Milton
Buck Stix
Bullet Swaging Supply, Inc.
C&D Special Products
• Camdex, Inc.
Carbide Die & Mfg. Co., Inc.
Case Sorting System
CCI
• C-H Tool & Die Corp.
Chem-Pak, Inc.
CheVron Case Master
Claybuster
Coats, Mrs. Lester
Colorado Shooter's Supply
• Competitor Corp., Inc.
CONKKO
• Corbin, Inc.
D.C.C. Enterprises
• Denver Instrument Co.
Dever Co., Jack
Dewey Mfg. Co., Inc., J.
• Dillon Precision Prods., Inc.
E&L Mfg., Inc.
Eagan, Donald V.
Efemes Enterprises
Engineered Accessories
Enguix Import-Export
Feken, Dennis
Fisher Enterprises
Fitz Pistol Grip Co.
Flambeau Products Corp.
• Forster Products
• 4-D Custom Die Co.
• Fremont Tool Works
G&C Bullet Co., Inc.
Gehmann, Walter
Goddard, Allen
"Gramps" Antique Cartridges
Graphics Direct
Green, Arthur S.
Hanned Line, The
Hanned Precision
Harrell's Precision
• Hart & Son, Inc., Robert W.
Haydon Shooters' Supply, Russ
Heidenstrom Bullets
Hensley & Gibbs
Hindman, Ace
Hoch Custom Bullet Moulds
Hoehn Sales, Inc.
Hoelscher, Virgil
• Hollywood Engineering
Hondo Industries
• Hornady Mfg. Co.
• Huntington Die Specialties
INTEC International, Inc.
Iosso Marine Products
J&L Superior Bullets
JGS Precision Tool Mfg.
Jones Custom Products, Neil
Jones Moulds, Paul
• K&M Services
King & Co.
Lachaussee, S.A.
LAP Systems Group, N.A.
LBT
• Lee Precision, Inc.
Liberty Metals
Liberty Shooting Supplies
Lortone, Inc.
Loweth Firearms, Richard
Lyman Instant Targets, Inc.
• Lyman Products Corp.
MA Systems
• Magma Engineering Co.
Marquart Precision Co., Inc.
Match Prep
McKillen & Heyer, Inc.
MCRW Assoc. Shooting Supplies

• MCS, Inc.
• MEC, Inc.
Midway Arms, Inc.
Miller Engineering
MMP
Mountain South
Mt. Baldy Bullet Co.
MTM Molded Products Co., Inc.
Multi-Scale Charge Ltd.
Necromancer Industries, Inc.
NEI Handtools, Inc.
Niemi Enterprises, W.B.
OK Weber, Inc.
Old West Bullet Moulds
• Old Western Scrounger, Inc.
Omark Industries
Pace Marketing, Inc.
Pattern Control
Pend Oreille Sport Shop
Plum City Ballistic Range
Policlips North America
• Ponsness/Warren
Precision Castings & Equip.
• Precision Reloading, Inc.
Protector Mfg. Co., Inc., The
Quinetics Corp.
R&D Engineering & Manufacturing
Ransom International Corp.
Rapine Bullet Mould Mfg. Co.
Ravell Ltd.
Raytech
• RCBS
• R.D.P. Tool Co., Inc.
• Redding Reloading, Inc.
R.E.I.
Rice, Keith
Riebe Co., W.J.
Roberts Products
Rochester Lead Works, Inc.
Rooster Laboratories
Rorschach Precision Products
Rosenthal, Brad and Sallie
Rucker Ammunition Co.
SAECO
Sandia Die & Cartridge Co.
• Scharch Mfg., Inc.
Scot Powder Co. of Ohio, Inc.
Scott, Dwight
Sierra Bullets
Sierra Specialty Prod. Co.
Silver Eagle Machining
Simmons, Jerry
Sinclair International, Inc.
Skip's Machine
S.L.A.P. Industries
Slipshot MTS Group
Small Custom Mould & Bullet Co.
SOS Products Co.
Speer Products
Sportsman Supply Co.
• Stalwart Corp.
• Star Machine Works
Stoney Point Products, Inc.
Taracorp Industries
TCSR
Tetra Gun Lubricants
Thompson Bullet Lube Co.
• Thompson/Center Arms
Timber Heirloom Products
Trammco, Inc.
Tru-Square Metal Prods., Inc.
Varner's Service
Vega Tool Co.
VibraShine, Inc.
Vibra-Tek Co.
Vom Hofe
Walters, John
Webster Scale Mfg. Co.
Welsh, Bud
Werner, Carl
Westfield Engineering
Wheel Weights Corp.
White Rock Tool & Die
Whitestone Lumber Corp.
Whitetail Design & Engineering Ltd.
Widener's Reloading & Shooting
Supply
Wilcox All-Pro Tools & Supply
• William's Gun Shop, Ben
Wilson, Inc., L.E.
Wolf's Western Traders
Woodleigh
Yesteryear Armory & Supply
Young Country Arms

RESTS—BENCH, PORTABLE—AND ACCESSORIES

Accuright
Adaptive Technology
Adventure 16, Inc.
Armor Metal Products
Aspen Outdoors Inc.
Bald Eagle Precision Machine Co.
Blount, Inc.
Boyd's Inc.
Browning
Chem-Pak, Inc.
Clift Mfg., L.R.
Clift Welding Supply
Clifton Arms, Inc.
Cravener's Gun Shop
Davidson Products, Inc.
Decker Shooting Products
Desert Mountain Mfg.
Forster Products
Greenwood Precision
Harris Engineering, Inc.
Hart & Son, Inc., Robert W.
Hidalgo, Tony
Hoelscher, Virgil
Holden Co., J.B.

Home Shop Machinist, The
Hoppe's Div.
Hornady Mfg. Co.
Kramer Designs
Midway Arms, Inc.
Millett Sights
MJM Manufacturing
Pease Accuracy, Bob
Penguin Industries, Inc.
Portus, Robert
Protektor Model
Ransom International Corp
Saville Iron Co.
Sinclair International, Inc.
Sports Support Systems, Inc.
Sportsman Supply Co.
Stoney Point Products, Inc.
Sure Shot of LA, Inc.
Thompson Target Technology
T.H.U. Enterprises, Inc.
Tonoloway Tack Drivers
Varner's Service
Verdemont Fieldsports
Wichita Arms, Inc.

RIFLE BARREL MAKERS
(See also Muzzle-Loading Guns, Barrels and Equipment)

Ackley Rifle Barrels, P.O.
American Bullets
Bellm Contenders
BlackStar Barrel Accurizing
Border Barrels Ltd.
Broad Creek Rifle Works
Brown Co., E. Arthur
Bullberry Barrel Works, Ltd.
Bustani Appraisers, Leo
Camas Hot Springs Mfg.
Carter's Gun Shop
Cincinnati Swaging
Clark Custom Guns, Inc.
Clerke Co., J.A.
Competition Limited
D&D Gunsmiths, Ltd.
D&J Bullet Co. & Custom Gun
  Shop, Inc.
DKT, Inc.
Donnelly, C.P.
Douglas Barrels, Inc.
Enguix Import-Export
Fabrica D'Armi Sabatti S.R.L.
Gaillard Barrels
Getz Barrel Co.
Green Mountain Rifle Barrel
  Co., Inc.
Half Moon Rifle Shop
Hart Rifle Barrels, Inc.
Hastings Barrels
Hoelscher, Virgil
Home Shop Machinist, The
H-S Precision, Inc.
Jackalope Gun Shop
K-D, Inc.
KOGOT

Kopp, Terry K.
Krieger Barrels, Inc.
Lilja Precision Rifle Barrels
Mac's .45 Shop
Marquart Precision Co., Inc.
Matco, Inc.
McGowen Rifle Barrels
McMillan Gunworks, Inc.
McMillan Rifle Barrels
Mid-America Recreation, Inc.
Obermeyer Rifled Barrels
Olympic Arms, Inc.
Pell, John T.
Pence Precision Barrels
Pre-Winchester 92-90-62 Parts Co.
Ravell Ltd.
Rocky Mountain Rifle Works Ltd.
Rosenthal, Brad and Sallie
Safari Arms, Inc./SGW
Sanders Custom Gun Service
Schneider Rifle Barrels, Inc., Gary
Schumakers Gun Shop, William
Sharon Rifle Barrel Co.
Shaw, Inc., E.R.
Shilen Rifles, Inc.
Siskiyou Gun Works
Small Arms Mfg. Co.
Specialty Shooters Supply, Inc.
Springfield, Inc.
Stock Shop, The
Strutz Rifle Barrels, Inc., W.C.
Swivel Machine Works, Inc.
Unique/M.A.P.F.
Verney-Carron
Welsh, Bud
Wilson Arms Co., The

SCOPES, MOUNTS, ACCESSORIES, OPTICAL EQUIPMENT

Accuracy Innovations, Inc.
Ackley Rifle Barrels
• Action Arms Ltd.
ADCO International
Adventurer's Outpost
• Aimpoint, Inc.
• Aimtech Mount Systems
Air Venture
Ajax Custom Grips, Inc.
All's, The Jim J. Tembelis Co., Inc.
Alley Supply Co.
American Import Co. The
Andela Tool & Machine, Inc.
• Anderson Manufacturing Co., Inc.
Applied Laser Systems, Inc.
A.R.M.S., Inc.
• Armscorp. USA, Inc.
Armurier Hiptmayer
Ballentine's Scopes Unl.
• Barrett Firearms Mfg., Inc.
• Bausch & Lomb, Inc.
Beaver Park Products, Inc.
• Beeman Precision Airguns, Inc.
Bellm Contenders
• Blount, Inc.
B.M.F. Activator, Inc.
• Bohemia Arms Co.

• Brown Co., E. Arthur
Brownells, Inc.
• Browning
Brunton U.S.A.
• B-Square Co.
Buehler Scope Mounts
• Burris
• Bushnell
Butler Creek Corp.
California Grip
• Cape Outfitters
Celestron International
Center Lock Scope Rings
Champion's Choice, Inc.
Clearview Mfg. Co., Inc.
Combat Military Ordnance Ltd.
Compass Industries, Inc.
Conetrol Scope Mounts
Creedmoor Sports, Inc.
D&H Prods. Co., Inc.
D.C.C. Enterprises
Del-Sports, Inc.
DHB Products
Eagle Mfg. & Engineering
E.A.W. GmbH
Edmund Scientific Co.
Ednar, Inc.

•See page 451 for Warranty Service Center Addresses

Eggleston, Jere D.
• Europtik Ltd.
  Excaliber Enterprises
  Farr Studio, Inc.
• Feather Industries, Inc.
• Forster Products
  From Jena
  Fujinon, Inc.
  Galati International
  Gentry Custom Gunmaker, David
  Gonzalez Guns, Ramon B.
  Grace Tool, Inc.
• GSI, Inc.
• G.U., Inc.
  Guns, Gear & Gadgets, L.L.C.
  Hakko Co. Ltd.
• Hammerli USA
• Hart & Son, Inc., Robert W.
  Hastings Barrels
  Hermann Leather Co., H.J.
  Hertel & Reuss
  Hiptmayer, Klaus
  Holden Co., J.B.
  Hollands
• Jackalope Gun Shop
• Jaeger, Inc., Paul/Dunn's
• Jason Empire, Inc.
  Jeffredo Gunsight
  Jewell, Arnold W.
  Jones, J.D.
  J.P. Enterprises, Inc.
• JSL (Hereford) Ltd.
• Kahles USA
  KDF, Inc.
  Kelbly, Inc.
• Keng's Firearms Specialty, Inc.
  KenPatable Ent., Inc.
• Kesselring Gun Shop
  Kimber of America, Inc.
  Kmount
• Kowa Optimed, Inc.
  Kris Mounts
  KVH Industries, Inc.
  Kwik Mount Corp.
  Kwik-Site Co.
• L&S Technologies, Inc.
• Laser Devices, Inc.
• Laseraim
  Leatherwood-Meopta, Inc.
  Lectro Science, Inc.
  Lee Co., T.K.
  Lee Supplies, Mark
• Leica USA, Inc.
• Leupold
  Lightforce USA
  Lite Tek International
  Lohman Mfg. Co., Inc.
  Mac's .45 Shop
  Maxi-Mount
  McMillan Optical Gunsight Co.
  MDS
  Meier Works
  Merit Corp.
  Military Armament Corp.
  Millett Sights
• Mirador Optical Corp.
  Morrow, Bud
  Muzzle-Nuzzle Co.
  New Democracy, Inc.
  New England Custom Gun Svc.
• Nichols Sports Optics
• Nikon, Inc.
  North American Specialties
  Nygord Precision Products
  Oakshore Electronic Sights, Inc.
• Old Western Scrounger, Inc.

Olympic Optical Co.
OMR Feinmechanik, Jagd-und
  Sportwaffen, GmbH
Optolyth-USA, Inc.
Orchard Park Enterprise
Outdoor Connection, Inc., The
Pace Marketing, Inc.
Parsons Optical Mfg. Co.
PECAR Herbert Schwarz, GmbH
PEM's Mfg. Co.
• Pentax Corp.
  Pilkington Gun Co.
  Precise Metalsmithing Enterprises
• Precision Sport Optics
  Premier Reticles
  Protektor Model
• Ram-Line, Inc.
  Ranch Products
  Randolph Engineering, Inc.
• Ranging, Inc.
  Ravell Ltd.
• Redfield, Inc.
  Rice, Keith
  Rockwood Corp., Speedwell Div.
  Rocky Mountain High Sports
    Glasses
  Royal Arm International Products
• RPM
  Rutgers Gun & Boat Center
  S&K Mfg. Co.
• Sanders Custom Gun Service
• Schmidt & Bender, Inc.
  Scope Control Inc.
  ScopLevel
  Seattle Binocular & Scope
    Repair Co.
  Selsi Co., Inc.
• Shepherd Scope Ltd.
• Sheridan USA, Inc., Austin
  Sightron, Inc.
  Silencio/Safety Direct
• Simmons Enterprises, Ernie
• Simmons Outdoor Corp.
• Speer Products
  Sportsmatch Ltd.
• Springfield, Inc.
  SSK Industries
  Stock Shop, The
  Sure Shot of LA, Inc.
• Swift Instruments, Inc.
• Tapco, Inc.
• Tasco Sales, Inc.
  Tele-Optics
• Thompson/Center Arms
• Trijicon, Inc.
• Unertl Optical Co., Inc., John
  United Binocular Co.
  United States Optics
    Technologies, Inc.
  Valor Corp.
• Voere-KGM m.b.H.
  Vom Hofe
  Warne Manufacturing Co.
  Warren Muzzleloading Co., Inc.
  WASP Shooting Systems
  Weaver Products
• Weaver Scope Repair Service
  Weigand Combat Handguns, Inc.
  Western Design
  Westfield Engineering
  White Rock Tool & Die
• White Shooting Systems, Inc.
  Wideview Scope Mount Corp.
• Williams Gun Sight Co.
  York M-1 Conversions
• Zeiss Optical, Carl

SHOOTING/TRAINING SCHOOLS

Alpine Precision Gunsmithing &
  Indoor Shooting Range
American Small Arms Academy
Auto Arms
Bob's Tactical Indoor Shooting
  Range & Gun Shop
Chapman Academy of Practical
  Shooting
Chelsea Gun Club of New York
  City, Inc.
CQB Training
Daisy Mfg. Co.
Defense Training International, Inc.
Dowtin Gunworks
Executive Protection Institute
Firearm Training Center, The
Firearms Academy of Seattle
G.H. Enterprises Ltd.

Gunfitters, The
Gunsite Training Center
InSights Training Center, Inc.
International Shootists, Inc.
Jensen's Firearms Acadamy
Lethal Force Institute
McMurdo, Lynn
Mendez, John A.
North Mountain Pines Training
  Center
Pacific Pistolcraft
Police Bookshelf
Quack Decoy & Sporting Clays
Quigley's Personal Protection
  Strategies, Paxton
River Road Sporting Clays
SAFE
Scott, McDougall & Associates

Shooter's World
Shooting Gallery, The
Shotgun Shop, The
Sipes Gun Shop
Specialty Gunsmithing

Starlight Training Center, Inc.
S.W.I.F.T.
Tactical Training Center
Western Missouri Shooters Alliance
Yavapai Firearms Academy Ltd.

SIGHTS, METALLIC

All's, The Jim J. Tembelis Co., Inc.
Alley Supply Co.
Alpec Team, Inc.
Andela Tool & Machine, Inc.
Armurier Hiptmayer
Bo-Mar Tool & Mfg. Co.
Bradley Gunsight Co.
Brown Co., E. Arthur
Cape Outfitters
Carter's Gun Shop
Champion's Choice, Inc.
C-More Systems
Colonial Repair
DGS, Inc.
DHB Products
Engineered Accessories
Evans Gunsmithing
Fautheree, Andy
Gun Doctor, The
Hart & Son, Inc., Robert W.
Heinie Specialty Products
Hesco-Meprolight
Hiptmayer, Klaus
IMI Services USA, Inc.
Innovative Weaponry, Inc.
Innovision Enterprises
Jackalope Gun Shop
Jaeger, Inc., Paul/Dunn's
J.O. Arms & Ammunition Co.
Lee's Red Ramps
Lofland, James W.
L.P.A. Snc
Lyman Instant Targets, Inc.

Lyman Products Corp.
Mac's .45 Shop
Marble Arms Corp.
MCS, Inc.
Meadow Industries
MEC-Gar S.R.L.
Meier Works
Meprolight
Merit Corp.
Mid-America Recreation, Inc.
Millett Sights
MMC
Montana Vintage Arms
North American Specialties
Novak's, Inc.
Oakshore Electronic Sights, Inc.
OMR Feinmechanik, Jagd-und
  Sportwaffen, GmbH
Pachmayr Ltd.
PEM's Mfg. Co.
P.M. Enterprises, Inc.
Ravell Ltd.
RPM
Sheridan USA, Inc., Austin
Slug Site Co.
Stoeger Industries
Storey, Dale A.
Tanfoglio S.r.l., Fratelli
T.F.C. S.p.A
Trijicon, Inc.
Wichita Arms, Inc.
Williams Gun Sight Co.

STOCKS (Commercial and Custom)

Accuracy Unlimited (Glendale, AZ)
Ajax Custom Grips, Inc.
Amrine's Gun Shop
Angelo & Little Custom Gun Stock
  Blanks
Arms Ingenuity Co.
Armurier Hiptmayer
Artistry In Wood
Bain & Davis, Inc.
Balickie, Joe
Barnes Bullets, Inc.
Barta's Gunsmithing
Bartlett, Don
Barton, Michael D.
Bear Arms
Beeman Precision Airguns, Inc.
Beitzinger, George
Belding's Custom Gun Shop
Bell & Carlson, Inc.
Benchmark Guns
Biesen, Al
Biesen, Roger
Billeb, Stephen L.
B.M.F. Activator, Inc.
Bob's Gun Shop
Boltin, John M.
Bowerly, Kent
Boyd's Inc.
Brace, Larry D.
Brgoch, Frank
Brown Co., E. Arthur
Brown Precision, Inc.
Buckhorn Gun Works
Bullberry Barrel Works, Ltd.
Burkhart Gunsmithing, Don
Burres, Jack
Butler Creek Corp.
Cali'co Hardwoods, Inc.
Camilli, Lou
Campbell, Dick
Cape Outfitters
Caywood, Shane J.
Cherokee Gun Accessories
Chicasaw Gun Works
Christman Jr., David
Chuck's Gun Shop
Churchill, Winston
Clifton Arms, Inc.
Cloward's Gun Shop
Cochran, Oliver
Coffin, Charles H.
Coffin, Jim
Colonial Repair

Conrad, C.A.
Costa, David
Crane Sales Co., George S.
Creedmoor Sports, Inc.
Custom Checkering Service
Custom Gun Products
Custom Gun Stocks
D&D Gunsmiths, Ltd.
D&J Bullet Co. & Custom Gun
  Shop, Inc.
Dahl's Custom Stocks
Dakota Arms
Dangler, Homer L.
D.D. Custom Stocks
de Treville & Co., Stan
Dever Co., Jack
Devereaux, R.H. "Dick"
DGS, Inc.
Dillon, Ed
Dowtin Gunworks
Dragun Enterprises
Dressel Jr., Paul G.
Duane Custom Stocks, Randy
Duncan's Gunworks, Inc.
Dutchman's Firearms, Inc., The
Echols & Co., D'Arcy
Eggleston, Jere D.
Erhardt, Dennis
Eversull Co., Inc., K.
Fajen, Inc., Reinhart
Farmer-Dressel, Sharon
Fibron Products, Inc.
Fisher, Jerry A.
Flaig's
Folks, Donald E.
Forster, Kathy
Forster, Larry L.
Frank Custom Gun Service, Ron
Gaillard Barrels
Game Haven Gunstocks
Gene's Custom Guns
Gervais, Mike
Gilman-Mayfield, Inc.
Giron, Robert E.
Glaser Safety Slug, Inc.
Goens, Dale W.
Golden Age Arms Co.
Gordie's Gun Shop
Goudy Classic Stocks, Gary
Grace, Charles E.
Grace Tool, Inc.
Green, Roger M.
Greene, M.L.

•See page 451 for Warranty Service Center Addresses

Greenwood Precision
Griffin & Howe, Inc.
Gun Shop, The
Guns
Gunsmithing Ltd.
Hallberg Gunsmith, Fritz
Halstead, Rick
Hank's Gun Shop
Hanson's Gun Center, Dick
Harper's Custom Stocks
Hart & Son, Inc., Robert W.
Hastings Barrels
Hecht, Hubert J.
Heilmann, Stephen
Hensley, Darwin
Heppler, Keith M.
Herrett's Stocks, Inc.
Heydenberk, Warren R.
Hillmer Custom Gunstocks, Paul D.
Hiptmayer, Klaus
Hoelscher, Virgil
Hoenig & Rodman
H-S Precision, Inc.
Huebner, Corey O.
Hughes, Steven Dodd
Intermountain Arms & Tackle, Inc.
Island Pond Gun Shop
Ivanoff, Thomas G.
Jackalope Gun Shop
Jaeger, Inc., Paul/Dunn's
Jamison's Forge Works
Jarrett Rifles, Inc.
Johnson Gunsmithing, Inc., Neal G.
Johnson Wood Products
KDF, Inc.
Keith's Custom Gunstocks
Ken's Rifle Blanks
Kilham & Co.
Klein Custom Guns, Don
Klingler Woodcarving
Knippel, Richard
Laseraim
Lawson Co., Harry
Lind Custom Guns, Al
Lynn's Custom Gunstocks
Mac's .45 Shop
Mandarino, Monte
Masen Co., John
Mathews & Son, Inc., George E.
McCament, Jay
McCullough, Ken
McDonald, Dennis
McFarland, Stan
McGowen Rifle Barrels
McGuire, Bill
McMillan Fiberglass Stocks, Inc.
McMillan Gunworks, Inc.
McMillan Rifle Barrels
Meadow Industries
Mercer Custom Stocks, R.M.
Mid-America Recreation, Inc.
Miller Co., David
Miller Gun Woods
Monell Custom Guns
Morrison Custom Rifles, J.W.
Morrow, Bud
Mountain Bear Rifle Works, Inc.
MPI Stocks
Muzzelite Corp.
Nettestad Gun Works
New England Arms Co.
New England Custom Gun Service
Nickels, Paul R.

Norman Custom Gunstocks, Jim
North American Shooting Systems
Oakland Custom Arms, Inc.
Oil Rod and Gun Shop
Old World Gunsmithing
One Of A Kind
Or-Ün
Orvis Co., The
Pagel Gun Works, Inc.
Paulsen Gunstocks
PEM's Mfg. Co.
Pentheny de Pentheny
Perazzi U.S.A., Inc.
R&J Gun Shop
Ram-Line, Inc.
Reiswig, Wallace E.
Richards Micro-Fit Stocks
Rimrock Rifle Stocks
RMS Custom Gunsmithing
Robinson, Don
Robinson Firearms Mfg. Ltd.
Romain's Custom Guns
Roto Carve
Royal Arms
Ryan, Chad L.
Sanders Custom Gun Service
Saville Iron Co.
Schiffman, Curt
Schiffman, Mike
Schwartz Custom Guns, David W.
Sherk, Dan A.
Sile Distributors, Inc.
Six Enterprises
Skeoch, Brian R.
Smith, Art
Smith, Sharmon
Snider Stocks, Walter S.
Speedfeed, Inc.
Speiser, Fred D.
Stiles Custom Guns
Stock Shop, The
Storey, Dale A.
Strawbridge, Victor W.
Swan, D.J.
Szweda, Robert
Talmage, William G.
Tecnolegno S.p.A.
T.F.C. S.p.A.
Tiger-Hunt
Tirelli
Tom's Gun Repair
Tom's Gun Shop
Trevallion Gunstocks
Tucker, James C.
Vest, John
Vic's Gun Refinishing
Vintage Industries, Inc.
Waffen-Weber Custom Gunsmithing
Walnut Factory, The
Weatherby, Inc.
Weems, Cecil
Wells Custom Gunsmith, R.A.
Wenig Custom Gunstocks, Inc.
Werth, T.W.
West, Robert G.
Western Gunstock Mfg. Co.
Williamson Precision Gunsmithing
Windish, Jim
Winter, Robert M.
Wright's Hardwood Sawmill
Yee, Mike
York M-1 Conversions
Zeeryp, Russ

TARGETS, BULLET AND CLAYBIRD TRAPS

Action Target, Inc.
American Target
American Whitetail Target Systems
Armor Metal Products
A-Tech Corp.
Ballistic Products, Inc.

Barsotti, Bruce
Birchwood Laboratories, Inc.
Blount, Inc.
Blue and Gray Products, Inc.
Caswell International Corp.
Champion Target Co.

Champion's Choice, Inc.
Clay Target Enterprises
Cunningham Co., Eaton
Dapkus Co., J.G.
Datumtech Corp.
D.C.C. Enterprises
Detroit-Armor Corp.
Diamond Mfg. Co.
Dutchman's Firearms, Inc., The
Epps "Orillia" Ltd., Ellwood
Federal Champion Target Co.
Freeman Animal Targets
G.H. Enterprises Ltd.
Gozon Corp.
Hart & Son, Inc., Robert W.
Hiti-Schuch, Atelier Wilma
Hoppe's Div.
Hornady Mfg. Co.
Hunterjohn
Imperial Magnum Corp.
Innovision Enterprises
Jackalope Gun Shop
Kennebec Journal
Littler Sales Co.
Lyman Instant Targets, Inc.
M&D Munitions Ltd.
Marksman Products
National Target Co.
North American Shooting Systems
Nu-Teck

Old Western Scrounger, Inc.
Outers Laboratories
Ox-Yoke Originals, Inc.
Parker Reproductions
Pease Accuracy, Bob
Penguin Industries, Inc.
Primos Wild Game Calls, Inc.
Protektor Model
Quack Decoy & Sporting Clays
Red Star Target Co.
Remington Arms Co., Inc.
Richards, John
River Road Sporting Clays
Rockwood Corp., Speedwell Div.
Rocky Mountain Target Co.
Schaefer Shooting Sports
Seligman Shooting Products
Shooters Supply
Shooting Arts Ltd
Shotgun Shop, The
Stoney Baroque Shooters Supply
Stoney Point Products, Inc.
Thompson Target Technology
Trius Traps
Verdemont Fieldsports
Vom Hofe
White Flyer
White Flyer Targets
World of Targets
X-Spand Target Systems

TAXIDERMY

Jonas Appraisers & Taxidermy,
  Jack
Kulis Freeze Dry Taxidermy
Parker, Mark D.

Piedmont Community College
Shell Shack
World Trek, Inc.

TRAP AND SKEET SHOOTER'S EQUIPMENT

Allen Sportswear, Bob
Baker, Stan
Ballistic Products, Inc.
Blount, Inc.
C&H Research
Clymer Manufacturing Co., Inc.
Crane & Crane Ltd.
D&H Prods. Co., Inc.
Ganton Manufacturing Ltd.
G.H. Enterprises Ltd.
Great 870 Co., The
Hafner Creations, Inc.
Harper, William E.
Hastings Barrels
K&T Co.
Lynn's Custom Gunstocks
Mag-Na-Port Int'l., Inc.
Maionchi-L.M.I.
Meadow Industries
Moneymaker Guncraft Corp.

MTM Molded Products Co., Inc.
Nielsen Custom Cases
Noble Co., Jim
Outers Laboratories
PAST Sporting Goods, Inc.
Perazzi U.S.A., Inc.
Pro-Port Ltd.
Protektor Model
Ravell Ltd.
Remington Arms Co., Inc.
Rhodeside, Inc.
Shootin' Accessories, Ltd.
Shooting Specialties
Shotgun Shop, The
Speer Products
10-X Products Group
Titus, Daniel
Trius Traps
Universal Clay Pigeon Traps
X-Spand Target Systems

TRIGGERS, RELATED EQUIPMENT

B&D Trading Co., Inc.
Canjar Co., M.H.
Central Specialties Ltd.
Costa, David
Cycle Dynamics, Inc.
Dayton Traister
E.A.A. Corp.
Electronic Trigger Systems, Inc.
Eversull Co., Inc., K.
Forster Products
Grace Tool, Inc.
Hart & Son, Inc., Robert W.
Hoelscher, Virgil
Hollands
Home Shop Machinist, The
Island Pond Gun Shop
Jackalope Gun Shop
Jaeger, Inc., Paul/Dunn's
Jewell, Arnold W.

Jones Custom Products, Neil
Krieger Barrels, Inc.
Mahony, Philip Bruce
Master Lock Co.
Mid-America Recreation, Inc.
Miller Single Trigger Mfg. Co.
Morrow, Bud
Pace Marketing, Inc.
Pease Accuracy, Bob
PEM's Mfg. Co.
Penrod Precision
Perazzi U.S.A., Inc.
S&B Industries
Sheridan USA, Inc., Austin
Shilen Rifles, Inc.
Stock Shop, The
Timney Mfg., Inc.
Tyler Mfg.-Dist., Melvin
Voere-KGH m.b.H.

MANUFACTURERS' DIRECTORY

A

A&B Industries, Inc. (See Top-Line USA, Inc.)
A&J Products, Inc., 5791 Hall Rd., Muskegon, MI 49442-1964
A&M Waterfowl, Inc., P.O. Box 102, Ripley, TN 38063/901-635-4003; FAX: 901-635-2320
A&W Repair, 2930 Schneider Dr., Arnold, MO 63010/314-287-3725
A.A. Arms, Inc., 4811 Persimmont Ct., Monroe, NC 28110/704-289-5356; FAX: 704-289-5859
AAL Optics, Inc., 2316 NE 8th Rd., Ocala, FL 34470/904-629-3211
Abel Safe & File, Inc., 124 West Locust St., Fairbury, IL 61739/800-346-9280, 815-692-2131; FAX: 815-692-3350
A.B.S. III, 9238 St. Morritz Dr., Fern Creek, KY 40291
Acadian Ballistic Specialties, P.O. Box 61, Covington, LA 70434
Acculube II, Inc., 4366 Shackleford Rd., Norcross, GA 30093-2912
Accupro Gun Care, 15512-109 Ave., Surrey, BC U3R 7E8, CANADA/604-583-7807
Accuracy Components Co., P.O. Box 60034, Renton, WA 98058/206-255-4577
Accuracy Den, The, 25 Bitterbrush Rd., Reno, NV 89523/702-345-0225
Accuracy Gun Shop, 3651 University Ave., San Diego, CA 92104/619-283-8500
Accuracy Innovations, Inc., P.O. Box 376, New Paris, PA 15554/814-839-4517; FAX: 814-839-2601
Accuracy Products, S.A., 14 rue de Lawsanne, Brussels, 1060 BELGIUM/32-2-539-34-42; FAX: 32-2-539-39-60
Accuracy Unlimited, 7479 S. DePew St., Littleton, CO 80123
Accuracy Unlimited, 16036 N. 49 Ave., Glendale, AZ 85306/602-978-9089
Accura-Site (See All's, The Jim Tembellis Co., Inc.)
Accurate Arms Co., Inc., Rt. 1, Box 167, McEwen, TN 37101/615-729-4207; FAX 615-729-4217
Accurate Plating & Weaponry, Inc., 1937 Calumet St., Clearwater, FL 34625/813-449-9112
Accuright, 119 E. Main, Belgrade, MT 59714/406-388-7234; FAX: 406-388-7234
Accu-Tek, 4525 Carter Ct., Chino, CA 91710/909-627-2404; FAX: 909-627-7817
Ace Sportswear, Inc., 700 Quality Rd., Fayetteville, NC 28306/919-323-1223
Ackerman & Co., 16 Cortez St., Westfield, MA 01085/413-568-8008
Ackerman, Bill, 10236 Woodway, El Paso, TX 79925/915-592-5338
Ackley Rifle Barrels, P.O. (See Bellm Contenders)
Action Ammo Ltd. (See Action Arms Ltd.)
Action Arms Ltd., P.O. Box 9573, Philadelphia, PA 19124/215-744-0100; FAX: 215-533-2188
Action Bullets, Inc., 1811 W. 13th Ave., Denver, CO 80204/303-595-9636; FAX: 303-893-9161
Action Products, Inc., 22 N. Mulberry St., Hagerstown, MD 21740/301-797-1414
Action Target, Inc., P.O. Box 636, Provo, UT 84603/801-377-8033; FAX: 801-377-8096
Actions by "T", Teddy Jacobson, 16315 Redwood Forest Ct., Sugarland, TX 77478/713-277-4008
ACTIV Industries, Inc., 1000 Zigor Rd., P.O. Box 339, Kearneysville, WV 25430/304-725-0451; FAX: 304-725-2080
Ad Hominem, RR 3, Orillia, Ont. L3V 6H3, CANADA/705-689-5303
Adair Custom Shop, Bill, 2886 Westridge, Carrollton, TX 75006
Adams, John J., P.O. Box 467, Corinth, VT 05039-0467/802-439-5904
Adaptive Technology, 939 Barnum Ave, Bridgeport, CT 06609/800-643-6735; FAX: 800-643-6735
ADC, Inc./PC Bullet, 32654 Coal Creek Rd., Scappoose, OR 97056-2601/503-543-5088; FAX: 503-543-5990
ADCO International, 10 Cedar St., Woburn, MA 01801-2341/617-935-1799; FAX: 617-932-4807
Adkins, Luther, 1292 E. McKay Rd., Shelbyville, IN 46176-9353/317-392-3795
Advance Car Mover Co., Rowell Div., P.O. Box 1, 240 N. Depot St., Juneau, WI 53039/414-386-4464; FAX: 414-386-4416
Adventure 16, Inc., 4620 Alvarado Canyon Rd., San Diego, CA 92120/619-283-6314
Adventure Game Calls, R.D. 1, Leonard Rd., Spencer, NY 14883/607-589-4611
Adventurer's Outpost, P.O. Box 70, Cottonwood, AZ 86326/800-762-7471; FAX: 602-634-8781
African Import Co., 20 Braunecker Rd., Plymouth, MA 02360/508-746-8552
AFSCO Ammunition, 731 W. Third St., P.O. Box L, Owen, WI 54460/715-229-2516
Ahlman Guns, Rt. 1, Box 20, Morristown, MN 55052/507-685-4243; FAX: 507-685-4247
Ahrends, Kim, Custom Firearms, Box 203, Clarion, IA 50525/515-532-3449
Aimpoint, Inc., 580 Herndon Parkway, Suite 500, Herndon, VA 22070/703-471-6828; FAX: 703-689-0575
Aimtech Mount Systems, P.O. Box 223, Thomasville, GA 31799/912-226-4313; FAX: 912-227-0222
Air Arms (See U.S. importer—Air Rifle Specialists)
Air Rifle Specialists, 311 East Water St., Elmira, NY 14901/607-734-7340; FAX: 607-733-3261
Air Venture, 9752 E. Flower St., Bellflower, CA 90706/310-867-6355
Airgun Repair Centre, 3227 Garden Meadows, Lawrenceburg, IN 47025/812-637-1463

Airrow (See Swivel Machine Works, Inc.)
Aitor-Cuchilleria Del Norte, S.A., Izelaieta, 17, 48260 Ermua (Vizcaya), SPAIN/43-17-08-50; FAX: 43-17-00-01
Ajax Custom Grips, Inc., Div. of A. Jack Rosenberg & Sons, 9130 Viscount Row, Dallas, TX 75247/214-630-8893; FAX: 214-630-4942
Aker Leather Products, 2248 Main St., Suite 6, Chula Vista, CA 91911/619-423-5182
Alaska Bullet Works, P.O. Box 54, Douglas, AK 99824/907-789-3834
Alcas Cutlery Corp. (See Cutco Cutlery)
Alco Carrying Cases, 601 W. 26th St., New York, NY 10001/212-675-5820; FAX: 212-691-5935
Aldis Gunsmithing & Shooting Supply, 502 S. Montezuma St., Prescott, AZ 86303/602-445-6723; FAX: 602-445-6763
Alessandri & Son, Lou, 24 French St., Rehoboth, MA 02769/508-252-5590, 800-248-5652; FAX: 508-252-3436
Alessi Holsters, Inc., 2465 Niagara Falls Blvd., Amherst, NY 14228-3527/716-691-5615
Alex, Inc., Box 3034, Bozeman, MT 59772/406-282-7396; FAX: 406-282-7396
Alfano, Sam, 36180 Henry Gaines Rd., Pearl River, LA 70452/504-863-3364; FAX: 504-863-7715
All American Bullets, 889 Beatty St., Medford, OR 97501/503-770-5649
All American Lead Shot Corp., P.O. Box 224566, Dallas, TX 75062
All Rite Products, Inc., 5752 N. Silver Stone Circle, Mountain Green, UT 84050/801-876-3330; 801-876-2216
All Weather Outerwear, 1270 Broadway, Rm 1005, New York, NY 10001/212-244-2690
All's, The Jim J. Tembelis Co., Inc., 280 E. Fernau Ave., Oshkosh, WI 54901/414-426-1080; FAX: 414-426-1080
Allard, Gary, Creek Side Metal & Woodcrafters, Fishers Hill, VA 22626/703-465-3903
Allen, Richard L., 339 Grove Ave., Prescott, AZ 86301/602-778-1237
Allen Co., Bob, 214 SW Jackson, Des Moines, IA 50315/515-283-2191; 800-685-7020
Allen Co., Inc., 525 Burbank St., Broomfield, CO 80020/303-469-1857
Allen Mfg., 6449 Hodgson Rd., Circle Pines, MN 55014/612-429-8231
Allen Sportswear, Bob, P.O. Box 477, Des Moines, IA 50302/515-283-2191; FAX: 515-283-0779
Alley Supply Co., P.O. Box 848, Gardnerville, NV 89410/702-782-3800
Allred Bullet Co., 932 Evergreen Drive, Logan, UT 84321/801-752-6983
Alpec Team, Inc., 55 Oak Ct., Danville, CA 94526/510-820-1763; FAX: 510-820-8738
Alpha 1 Drop Zone, 2121 N. Tyler, Wichita, KS 67212/316-729-0800
Alpha LaFranck Enterprises, P.O. Box 81072, Lincoln, NE 68501/402-466-3193
Alpha Precision, Inc., 2765-B Preston Rd. NE, Good Hope, GA 30641/404-267-6163
Alpine's Precision Gunsmithing & Indoor Shooting Range, 2401 Government Way, Coeur d'Alene, ID 83814/208-765-3559; FAX: 208-765-3559
Altamont Co., 901 N. Church St., P.O. Box 309, Thomasboro, IL 61878/217-643-3125; FAX: 217-643-7973
Alumna Sport by Dee Zee, 1572 NE 58th Ave., P.O. Box 3090, Des Moines, IA 50316/800-798-9899
Amacker International, Inc., 1212 Main St., Amacker Park, Delhi, LA 71232/318-878-9061; FAX: 318-878-5532
AmBr Software Group Ltd., The, 2205 Maryland Ave., Baltimore, MD 21218/410-243-7717; FAX: 410-368-8742
American Ammunition, 3545 NW 71st St., Miami, FL 33147/FAX: 305-638-1014
American Arms & Ordnance, Inc., P.O. Box 2691, 1303 S. College Ave., Bryan, TX 77805/409-822-4983
American Arms, Inc., 715 E. Armour Rd., N. Kansas City, MO 64116/816-474-3161; FAX: 816-474-1225
American Bullets, 2190 C. Coffee Rd., Lithonia, GA 30058/404-482-4253
American Custom Gunmakers Guild, P.O. Box 812, Burlington, IA 52601/319-752-6114
American Derringer Corp., 127 N. Lacy Dr., Waco, TX 76705/800-642-7817, 817-799-9111; FAX: 817-799-7935
American Display Co., 55 Cromwell St., Providence, RI 02907/401-331-2464; FAX: 401-421-1264
American Gas & Chemical Co., Ltd., 220 Pegasus Ave., Northvale, NJ 07647/201-767-7300
American Gripcraft, 3230 S. Dodge 2, Tucson, AZ 85713/602-790-1222
American Handgunner Magazine, 591 Camino de la Reina, Suite 200, San Diego, CA 92108/619-297-5350; FAX: 619-297-5353
American Import Co., The, 1453 Mission St., San Francisco, CA 94103/415-863-1506; FAX: 415-863-0939
American Pioneer Video, P.O. Box 50049, Bowling Green, KY 42102-2649/800-743-4675
American Pistol Institute (See Gunsite Training Center)
American Pistolsmiths Guild, P.O. Box 67, Louisville, TN 37777/615-984-3583
American Products Co., 14729 Spring Valley Road, Morrison, IL 61270/815-772-3336; FAX: 815-772-7921
American Sales & Mfg. Co., P.O. Box 677, Laredo, TX 78042/210-723-6893; FAX: 210-725-0672
American Security Products Co., 11925 Pacific Ave., Fontana, CA 92335/909-685-9680, 800-421-6142; FAX: 909-685-9685
American Small Arms Academy, P.O. Box 12111, Prescott, AZ 86304/602-778-5623

American Target Knives, 1030 Brownwood NW, Grand Rapids, MI 49504/616-453-1998
American Target, 1328 S. Jason St., Denver, CO 80223/303-733-0433; FAX: 303-777-0311
American Whitetail Target Systems, P.O. Box 41, 106 S. Church St., Tennyson, IN 47637/812-567-4527
Americase, P.O. Box 271, Waxahachie, TX 75165/800-972-2737
Ames Metal Products Co., 4324 S. Western Blvd., Chicago, IL/312-523-3230; FAX: 312-523-3854
Amherst Arms, P.O. Box 1457, Englewood, FL 34295/813-475-2020
Ammo Load, Inc., 1560 East Edinger, Suite G., Santa Ana, CA 92705/714-558-8858; FAX: 714-569-0319
Amm-O-Mart, Ltd., P.O. Box 125, Hawkesbury, Ont., K6A 2R8 CANADA/613-632-9300
Ammunition Consulting Services, Inc., P.O. Box 701084, San Antonio, TX 78270-1084/201-646-9624; FAX: 210-646-0141
Amodei, Jim (See D.O.C. Specialists, Inc.)
Amrine's Gun Shop, 937 La Luna, Ojai, CA 93023/805-646-2376
Amsec, 11925 Pacific Ave., Fontana, CA 92337
AMT, 6226 Santos Diaz St., Irwindale, CA 91702/818-334-6629; FAX: 818-969-5247
Amtech International, Inc., 4942 Industrial Ave. E., Coeur D'Alene, ID 83814
Amtech-Overseas, Inc., 1015 15th St. NW, Suite 402, Washington, D.C. 20005/202-408-4760; FAX: 202-408-4746
Analog Devices, Box 9106, Norwood, MA 02062
Andela Tool & Machine, Inc., RD3, Box 246, Richfield Springs, NY 13439
Anderson Manufacturing Co., Inc., P.O. Box 2640, 2741 N. Crosby Rd., Oak Harbor, WA 98277/206-675-7300; FAX: 206-675-3939
Andres & Dworsky, Bergstrasse 18, A-3822 Karlstein, Thaya, Austria, EUROPE, 0 28 44-285
Angelo & Little Custom Gun Stock Blanks, Chaffin Creek Rd., Darby, MT 59829/406-821-4530
Anschutz GmbH, Postfach 1128, D-89001 Ulm, Donau, GERMANY (U.S. importer—PSI, Inc.)
Ansen Enterprises, Inc., 1506 W. 228th St., Torrance, CA 90501-5105/310-534-3162
Answer Products Co., 1519 Westbury Drive, Davison, MI 48423/313-653-2911
Anthony and George Ltd., Rt. 1, P.O. Box 45, Evington, VA 24550/804-821-8117
Antique American Firearms (See Carlson, Douglas R.)
Antique Arms Co., 1110 Cleveland Ave., Monett, MO 65708/417-235-6501
AO Safety Products, Div. of American Optical Corp. (See E-A-R, Inc.)
Apache Products, Inc., 4224 Old Sterington Rd., Monroe, LA 71203/318-325-1761; FAX: 318-325-4873
Aplan Antiques & Art, James O., HC 80, Box 793-25, Piedmont, SD 57769/605-347-5016
Applied Laser Systems, 2160 NW Vine St., Grants Pass, OR 97526/503-479-0484; FAX: 503-476-5105
Applied Laser Systems, Inc., 2160 NW Vine St., Grants Pass, OR 97526/503-479-0484; FAX: 503-476-5105
Arcadia Machine & Tool, Inc. (See AMT)
Aristocrat Knives, 1800 N. Highland Ave. No. 600, Los Angeles, CA 90028/213-461-1065; FAX: 213-461-3598
Arizaga (See U.S. importer—Mandall Shooting Supplies, Inc.)
Arizona Custom Case, 1015 S. 23rd St., Phoenix, AZ 85034/602-273-0220
Arkansas Mallard Duck Calls, Rt. Box 182, England, AR 72046/501-842-3597
Arkfeld Mfg. & Dist. Co., Inc., P.O. Box 54, Norfolk, NE 68702-0054/402-371-9430; 800-533-0676
Armament Gunsmithing Co., Inc., 525 Rt. 22, Hillside, NJ 07205/908-686-0960
Armas Kemen (See U.S. importer—USA Sporting)
Armes de Chasse, P.O. Box 827, Chadds Ford, PA 19317/215-388-1146; FAX: 215-388-1147
Armfield Custom Bullets, 4775 Caroline Drive, San Diego, CA 92115/619-582-7188; FAX: 619-287-3238
Armi San Paolo, via Europa 172-A, I-25062 Concesio, 030-2751725 (BS) ITALY
Armite Laboratories, 1845 Randolph St., Los Angeles, CA 90001/213-587-7768; FAX: 213-587-5075
Armoloy Co. of Ft. Worth, 204 E. Daggett St., Fort Worth, TX 76104/817-332-5604; FAX: 817-335-6517
Armor (See Buck Stop Lure Co., Inc.)
Armor Metal Products, P.O. Box 4609, Helena, MT 59604/406-442-5560
Armory Publications, P.O. Box 4206, Oceanside, CA 92052-4206/619-757-3930; FAX: 619-722-4108
Armoury, Inc., The, Rt. 202, Box 2340, New Preston, CT 06777/203-868-0001
Arms & Armour Press, Villiers House, 41-47 Strand, London WC2N 5JE ENGLAND/071-839-4900; FAX: 071-839-1804
A.R.M.S., Inc., 375 West St., West Bridgewater, MA 02379/508-584-7816; FAX: 508-588-8045
Arms Corp. of the Phillipines, 550E Delos Santos Ave., Cubau, Quezon City, PHILLIPINES
Arms Craft Gunsmithing, 1106 Linda Dr., Arroyo Grande, CA 93420/805-481-2830
Arms Ingenuity Co., P.O. Box 1, 51 Canal St., Weatogue, CT 06089/203-658-5624
Arms, Peripheral Data Systems, P.O. Box 1526, Lake Oswego, OR 97035/800-366-5559, 503-697-0533; FAX: 503-697-3337
Armscor (See U.S. importer—Ruko Products)
Armscor Precision, 225 Lindbergh St., San Mateo, CA 94401/415-347-9556; FAX: 415-347-7634
Armscorp USA, Inc., 4424 John Ave., Baltimore, MD 21227/410-247-6200
Armsport, Inc., 3950 NW 49th St., Miami, FL 33142/305-635-7850; FAX: 305-633-2877
Armurier Hiptmayer, RR 112 750, P.O. Box 136, Eastman, Quebec JOE 1P0, CANADA/514-297-2492
Aro-Tek, Ltd., 201 Frontage Rd. North, Suite C, Pacific, WA 98047/206-351-2984
Arratoonian, Andy (See Horseshoe Leather Products)

Arrieta, S.L., Morkaiko, 5, Elgoibar, E-20870, SPAIN/(43) 74 31 50; FAX: (43) 74 31 54 (U.S. importers—Hi-Grade Imports; Jansma, Jack J.; New England Arms Co.; The Orvis Co., Inc.; Quality Arms, Inc.)
Art Jewel Enterprises Ltd., Eagle Business Ctr., 460 Randy Rd., Carol Stream, IL 60188/708-260-0400
Art's Gun & Sport Shop, Inc., 6008 Hwy. Y, Hillsboro, MO 63050
Artistry in Leather (See Stuart, V. Pat)
Artistry in Wood, 134 Zimmerman Rd., Kalispell, MT 59901/406-257-9003
Ashby Turkey Calls, HCR 5, Box 345, Houston, MO 65483/417-967-3787
ASI, 6226 Santos Dias St., Irwindale, CA 91706/818-334-6629
Aspen Outdoors, 1059 W. Market St., York, PA 17404/717-846-0255; FAX: 717-845-7747
A-Square Co., Inc., One Industrial Park, Bedford, KY 40006-9667/502-255-7456; FAX: 502-255-7657
Astra-Unceta Y Cia, S.A., Apartado 3, 48300 Guernica, Espagne, SPAIN/34-4-6250100; FAX: 34-4-6255186 (U.S. importer—E.A.A. Corp.)
A-Tech Corp., P.O. Box 1281, Cottage Grove, OR 97424
ATIS Armi S.A.S., via Gussalli 24, Zona Industriale-Loc. Fornaci, 25020 Brescia, ITALY
Atlanta Cutlery Corp., 2143 Gees Mill Rd., Box 839 CIS, Conyers, GA 30207/800-883-0300; FAX: 404-388-0246
Atlantic Mills, Inc., 1325 Washington Ave., Asbury Park, NJ 07712/201-774-4882
Atlantic Research Marketing Systems (See A.R.M.S., Inc.)
Atsko/Sno-Seal, Inc., 2530 Russell SE, Orangeburg, SC 29115/803-531-1820; FAX: 803-531-2139
Audette, Creighton, 19 Highland Circle, Springfield, VT 05156/802-885-2331
Austin's Calls, Bill, Box 284, Kaycee, WY 82639/307-738-2552
Auto Arms, 738 Clearview, San Antonio, TX 78228/512-434-5450
Automatic Equipment Sales, 627 E. Railroad Ave., Salesburg, MD 21801
Automatic Weaponry (See Scattergun Technologies, Inc.)
Auto-Ordnance Corp., Williams Lane, West Hurley, NY 12491/914-679-7225; FAX: 914-679-2698
Autumn Sales, Inc. (Blaser), 1320 Lake St., Fort Worth, TX 76102/817-335-1634; FAX: 817-338-0119
Avtac, 489 Rt. 32, Highland Mills, NY 10930-0522/800-348-9127
AWC Systems Technology, P.O. Box 41938, Phoenix, AZ 85080-1938/602-780-1050
AYA (See U.S. importer—Armes de Chasse)
A Zone Bullets, 2039 Walter Rd., Billings, MT 59105/800-252-3111
Aztec International Ltd., P.O. Box 1384, Clarkesville, GA 30523/706-754-7263

B

B&D Trading Co., Inc., 3935 Fair Hill Rd., Fair Oaks, CA 95628/916-967-9366
B&G Bullets, P.O. Box 14313, Oklahoma City, OK 73114/405-840-2353
Badger Shooters Supply, Inc., 202 N. Harding, Owen, WI 54460/715-229-2101; FAX: 715-229-2332
Baekgaard Ltd., 1855 Janke Dr., Northbrook, IL 60062/708-498-3040; FAX: 708-493-3106
Baer Custom, Inc., Les, 29601 34th Ave., Hillsdale, IL 61257/309-794-1166; FAX: 309-794-9882
Bagmaster Mfg., Inc., 2731 Sutton Ave., St. Louis, MO 63143/314-781-8002
Baikal (See U.S. importer—K.B.I., Inc.)
Bain & Davis, Inc., 307 E. Valley Blvd., San Gabriel, CA 91776-3522/818-573-4241, 213-283-7449
Baity's Custom Gunworks, 414 2nd St., N. Wilkesboro, NC 28659/919-667-8785
Baker, Stan, 10,000 Lake City Way, Seattle, WA 98125/206-522-4575
Baker's Leather Goods, Roy, P.O. Box 893, Magnolia, AR 71753/501-234-0344
Balaance Co., 340-39 Ave. S.E. Box 505, Calgary, AB, T2G 1X6 CANADA
Bald Eagle Precision Machine Co., 101 Allison St., Lock Haven, PA 17745/717-748-6772; FAX: 717-748-4443
Balickie, Joe, 408 Trelawney Lane, Apex, NC 27502/919-362-5185
Ballard Built, P.O. Box 1443, Kingsville, TX 78364/512-592-0853
Ballentine's Scopes Unlimited, 22525 Ballentine Lane, Onaga, KS 66521/913-889-4859
Ballistic Engineering & Software, Inc., 2440 Freeman Dr., Lake Orion, MI 48360/313-391-1074
Ballistic Products, Inc., 20015 75th Ave. North, Corcoran, MN 55340-9456/612-494-9237; FAX: 612-494-9236
Ballistic Program Co., Inc., The, 2417 N. Patterson St., Thomasville, GA 31792/912-228-5739, 800-368-0835
Ballistic Research, 1108 W. May Ave., McHenry, IL 60050/815-385-0037
Ballistica Maximus North, 107 College Park Plaza, Johnstown, PA 15904/814-266-8380
Ballisti-Cast, Inc., Box 383, Parshall, ND 58770/701-862-3324; FAX: 701-862-3331
Banaczkowski Bullets, 56 Victoria Dr., Mount Barker, S.A. 5251 AUSTRALIA
Bandcor Industries, Div. of Man-Sew Corp., 6108 Sherwin Dr., Port Richey, FL 34668/813-848-0432
Bandera Gun Locker, 2146 NE 4th St., Bend, OR 97701/800-441-6773
Bang-Bang Boutique (See Holster Shop, The)
Banks, Ed, 2762 Hwy. 41 N., Ft. Valley, GA 31030/912-987-4665
Barami Corp., 6689 Orchard Lake Rd. No. 148, West Bloomfield, MI 48322/810-738-0462; FAX: 810-855-4084
Barbour, Inc., 55 Meadowbrook Dr., Milford, NH 03055/603-673-1313; FAX: 603-673-6510
Barlett, J., 6641 Kaiser Ave., Fontana, CA 92336-3265
Barnes Bullets, Inc., P.O. Box 215, American Fork, UT 84003/801-756-4222; FAX: 801-756-2465
Baron Technology, 62 Spring Hill Rd., Trumbull, CT 06611/203-452-0515; FAX: 203-452-0663
Barramundi Corp., P.O. Drawer 4259, Homosassa Springs, FL 32687/904-628-0200
Barrett Firearms Mfg., Inc., P.O. Box 1077, Murfreesboro, TN 37133/615-896-2938; FAX: 615-896-7313
Barsotti, Bruce (See River Road Sporting Clays)

Bar-Sto Precision Machine, 73377 Sullivan Rd., P.O. Box 1838, Twentynine Palms, CA 92277/619-367-2747; FAX: 619-367-2407
Barta's Gunsmithing, 10231 US Hwy. 10, Cato, WI 54206/414-732-4472
Barteaux Machete, 1916 SE 50th Ave., Portland, OR 97215-3238/503-233-5880
Bartlett, Don, 3704 E. Pine Needle Ave., Colbert, WA 99005/509-467-5009
Barton, Michael D. (See Tiger-Hunt)
Basics Information Systems, Inc., 1141 Georgia Ave., Suite 515, Wheaton, MD 20902/301-949-1070; FAX: 301-949-5326
Bates Engraving, Billy, 2302 Winthrop Dr., Decatur, AL 35603/205-355-3690
Bauer, Eddie, 15010 NE 36th St., Redmond, WA 98052
Baumannize Custom, 4784 Sunrise Hwy., Bohemia, NY 11716/800-472-4387; FAX: 516-567-0001
Baumgartner Bullets, 3011 S. Alane St., W. Valley City, UT 84120
Bausch & Lomb, Inc., 42 East Ave., Rochester, NY 14603/800-828-5423
Bausch & Lomb Sports Optics Div., 9200 Cody, Overland Park, KS 66214/913-752-3400, 800-423-3537; FAX: 913-752-3550
Bauska Barrels, 105 9th Ave. W., Kalispell, MT 59901/406-752-7706
Bear Archery, RR 4, 4600 Southwest 41st Blvd., Gainesville, FL 32601/904-376-2327
Bear Arms, 121 Rhodes St., Jackson, SC 29831/803-471-9859
Bear Hug Grips, Inc., 17230 County Rd. 338, Buena Vista, CO 81211/800-232-7710
Bear Mountain Gun & Tool, 120 N. Plymouth, New Plymouth, ID 83655/208-278-5221; FAX: 208-278-5221
Bear Reloaders, P.O. Box 1613, Akron, OH 44309-1613/216-920-1811
Beartooth Bullets, P.O. Box 491, Dept. HLD, Dover, ID 83825-0491/208-448-1865
Beauchamp & Son, Inc., 160 Rossiter Rd., Richmond, MA 01254/413-698-3822; FAX: 413-698-3866
Beaver Lodge (See Fellowes, Ted)
Beaver Park Products, Inc., 840 J St., Penrose, CO 81240/719-372-6744
Bedford Technologies, Inc., P.O. Box 820, Fairland, OK 74343/800-467-7233
Beeline Custom Bullets, P.O. Box 85, Yarmouth, Nova Scotia CANADA B5A 4B1/902-648-3494; FAX: 902-648-0253
Beeman Precision Airguns, 5454 Argosy Dr., Huntington Beach, CA 92649/714-890-4800; FAX: 714-890-4808
Behlert Precision, P.O. Box 288, 7067 Easton Rd., Pipersville, PA 18947/215-766-8681; FAX: 215-766-8681
Beitzinger, George, 116-20 Atlantic Ave., Richmond Hill, NY 11419/718-847-7661
Belding's Custom Gun Shop, 10691 Sayers Rd., Munith, MI 49259/517-596-2388
Bell & Carlson, Inc., 509 N. 5th St., Atwood, KS 67730/800-634-8586, 913-626-3204; FAX: 913-626-9602
Bell Originals, Sid, Inc., 7776 Shackham Rd., Tully, NY 13159-9333/607-842-6431
Bell Reloading, Inc., 1725 Harlin Lane Rd., Villa Rica, GA 30180
Bell's Gun & Sport Shop, 3309-19 Mannheim Rd, Franklin Park, IL 60131
Bell's Legendary Country Wear, 22 Circle Dr., Bellmore, NY 11710/516-679-1158
Bellm Contenders, P.O. Ackley Rifle Barrels, P.O. Box 459, Cleveland, UT 84518/801-653-2530
Belltown, Ltd., 11 Camps Rd., Kent, CT 06757/203-354-5750
Ben's Machines, 1151 S. Cedar Ridge, Duncanville, TX 75137/214-780-1807
Benchmark Guns, 12593 S. Ave. 5 East, Yuma, AZ 85365
Benchmark Knives (See Gerber Legendary Blades)
Benelli Armi, S.p.A., Via della Stazione, 61029 Urbino, ITALY/39-722-328633; FAX: 39-722-327427 (U.S. importers—E.A.A. Corp.; Heckler & Koch, Inc.; Sile Distributors)
Bengtson Arms Co., L., 6345-B E. Akron St., Mesa, AZ 85205/602-981-6375
Benjamin/Sheridan Co., Crossman, Rts. 5 and 20, E. Bloomfield, NY 14443/716-657-6161; FAX: 716-657-5405
Bentley, John, 128-D Watson Dr., Turtle Creek, PA 15145
Beretta, Dr. Franco, via Rossa, 4, Concesio (BC), Italy I-25062/030-2751955; FAX: 030-218-0414 (U.S. importer—Nevada Cartridge Co.)
Beretta Firearms, Pietro, 25063 Gardone V.T., ITALY (U.S. importer—Beretta U.S.A. Corp.)
Beretta U.S.A. Corp., 17601 Beretta Drive, Accokeek, MD 20607/301-283-2191
Berger Bullets, Ltd., 5342 W. Camelback Rd., Suite 500, Glendale, AZ 85301/602-842-4001; FAX: 602-934-9083
Bergman & Williams, 2450 Losee Rd., Suite F, Las Vegas, NV 89030/702-642-1901; FAX: 702-642-1540
Bernardelli Vincenzo S.p.A., Via Matteotti 125, Gardone V.T., ITALY I-25063/30-8912851-2-3
Berry's Bullets, Div. of Berry's Mfg., Inc., Box 100, Bloomington, CA 92316/801-634-1682
Berry's Mfg., Inc., 401 North 3050 East, St. George, UT 84770
Bersa S.A., Gonzales Castillo 312, 1704 Ramos Mejia, ARGENTINA/541-656-2377; FAX: 541-656-2093 (U.S. importer—Eagle Imports, Inc.)
Bertram Bullet Co., P.O. Box 313, Seymour, Victoria 3660, AUSTRALIA/61-57-922912; FAX: 61-57-991650
Bertuzzi (See U.S. importers—Moore & Co., Wm. Larkin; New England Arms Co.)
Bestload, Inc., P.O. Box 4354, Stamford, CT 06907/FAX: 203-978-0796
Better Concepts Co., 663 New Castle Rd., Butler, PA 16001/412-285-9000
Bianchi International, Inc., 100 Calle Cortez, Temecula, CA 92590/909-676-5621
Biesen, Al, 5021 Rosewood, Spokane, WA 99208/509-328-9340
Biesen, Roger, 5021 W. Rosewood, Spokane, WA 99208/509-328-9340
Big 45 Frontier Gun Shop, P.O. Box 70, Hill City, SD 57745/800-342-1548; FAX: 800-342-1548
Big Bear Arms & Sporting Goods, 2714 Fairmount St., Dallas, TX 75201/214-871-7061; FAX: 214-754-0449
Big Sky Racks, Inc., P.O. Box 729, Bozeman, MT 59771-0729/406-586-9393

Big Spring Enterprises "Bore Stores", P.O. Box 1115, Big Spring Rd., Yellville, AR 72687/501-449-5297; FAX: 501-449-4446
Bilal, Mustafa, 5429 Russell Ave. NW, Suite 202, Seattle, WA 98107/206-782-4164
Bill's Custom Cases, P.O. Box 2, Dunsmuir, CA 96025/916-235-0177
Bill's Gun Repair, 1007 Burlington St., Mendota, IL 61342/815-539-5786
Billeb, Stephen L., 1101 N. 7th St., Burlington, IA 52601/319-753-2110
Billings Gunsmiths, Inc., 1940 Grand Ave., Billings, MT 59102/406-652-3104
Billingsley & Brownell, P.O. Box 25, Dayton, WY 82836/307-655-9344
Bilsom Intl., Inc., 109 Carpenter Dr., Sterling, VA 20164/703-834-1070
Birchwood Casey, 7900 Fuller Rd., Eden Prairie, MN 55344/800-328-6156; FAX: 612-937-7979
Birdsong & Assoc., W.E., 4832 Windermere, Jackson, MS 39206/601-366-8270
Bismuth Cartridge Co., 3500 Maple Ave., Suite 1650, Dallas, TX 75129/800-759-3333; 214-521-5882
Bitterroot Bullet Co., Box 412, Lewiston, ID 83501-0412/208-743-5635
Black Hills Ammunition, P.O. Box 3090, Rapid City, SD 57709-3090/605-348-5150; FAX: 605-348-9827
Black Hills Shooters Supply, P.O. Box 4220, Rapid City, SD 57709
Black Mountain Bullets, Rt. 7, Box 297, Warrenton, VA 22186/703-347-1199
Black Sheep Brand, 3220 W. Gentry Parkway, Tyler, TX 75702/903-592-3853
Blackhawk East, Box 2274, Loves Park, IL 61131
Blackhawk Mountain, Box 210, Conifer, CO 80433
Blackhawk West, Box 285, Hiawatha, KS 66434
Blackinton & Co., Inc., V.H., 221 John L. Dietsch, Attleboro Falls, MA 02763-0300/508-699-4436; FAX: 508-695-5349
Blackjack Knives, 1307 W. Wabash, Effingham, IL 62401/217-347-7700; FAX: 217-347-7737
Blacksmith Corp., 830 N. Road 1 E.,Box 1752, Chino Valley, AZ 86323/602-636-4456; FAX: 602-636-4457
BlackStar Barrel Accurizing, 11609 Galayda St., Houston, TX 77086/713-448-5300; FAX: 713-448-7298
Blacktail Mountain Books, 42 First Ave. West, Kalispell, MT 59901/406-257-5573
Blackwell, W., Load From A Disk, Dept. GD, 9826 Sagedale, Houston, TX 77089/713-484-0935
Blake Affiliates, Box 133, Roscoe, IL 61073
Blakemore Game Calls, Jim, Rt. 2, Box 544, Cape Girardeau, MO 63701
Blammo Ammo, P.O. Box 1677, Seneca, SC 29679/803-882-1768
Blaser Jagdwaffen GmbH, D-88316 Isny Im Allgau, GERMANY (U.S. importer—Autumn Sales, Inc.)
Bledsoe, Weldon, 6812 Park Place Dr., Fort Worth, TX 76118/817-589-1704
Bleile, C. Roger, 5040 Ralph Ave., Cincinnati, OH 45238/513-251-0249
Blocker's Holsters, Inc., Ted, 5360 NE 112, Portland, OR 97220/503-254-9950
Blount, Inc., Sporting Equipment Div., 2299 Snake River Ave., P.O. Box 856, Lewiston, ID 83501/800-627-3640, 208-746-2351
Blue and Gray Products, Inc. (See Ox-Yoke Originals, Inc.)
Blue Book Publications, Inc., One Appletree Square, Minneapolis, MN 55425/800-877-4867; FAX: 612-853-1486
Blue Mountain Bullets, HCR 77, P.O. Box 231, John Day, OR 97845/503-820-4594
Blue Point Mfg. Co., P.O. Box 722, Massena, NY 13662
Blue Ridge Knives, Rt. 6, Box 185, Marion, VA 24354/703-783-6143; FAX: 703-783-9298
Blue Ridge Machinery & Tools, Inc., P.O. Box 536-GD, Hurricane, WV 25526/800-872-6500; FAX: 304-562-5311
Bluebonnet Specialty, P.O. Box 737, Palestine, TX 75802/214-723-2075
BMC Supply, Inc., 26051 - 179th Ave. S.E., Kent, WA 98042
B.M.F. Activator, Inc., 803 Mill Creek Run, Plantersville, TX 77363/409-894-2005, 800-527-2881
Bob's Coins & Guns, Inc., 24 Defense St., Annapolis, MD 21401/301-224-8683
Bob's Gun Shop, P.O. Box 200, Royal, AR 71968/501-767-1970
Bob's Tactical Indoor Shooting Range & Gun Shop, 122 Lafayette Rd., Salisbury, MA 01952/508-465-5561
Boessler, Erich, Am Vogeltal 3, 8732 Munnerstadt, GERMANY/9733-9443
Boggs, Wm., 1816 Riverside Dr. C, Columbus, OH 43212/614-486-6965
Bohemia Arms Co., 17101 Los Modelos, Fountain Valley, CA 92708/714-963-0809; FAX: 714-963-0809
Boker USA, Inc., 14818 West 6th Ave., Suite 10A, Golden, CO 80401-5045/303-279-5997; FAX: 303-279-5919
Bolden's, P.O. Box 33178, Kerrville, TX 78029/210-634-2703
Boltin, John M., P.O. Box 644, Estill, SC 29918/803-625-2185
Bo-Mar Tool & Mfg. Co., Rt. 12, Box 405, Longview, TX 75605/903-759-4784; FAX: 903-759-9141
Bondini Paolo, Via Sorrento, 345, San Carlo di Cesena, ITALY I-47020/0547 663 240; FAX: 0547 663 780
Bone Engraving, Ralph, 718 N. Atlanta, Owasso, OK 74055/918-272-9745
Boone's Custom Ivory Grips, Inc., 562 Coyote Rd., Brinnon, WA 98320/206-796-4330
Boonie Packer Products, P.O. Box 12204, Salem, OR 97309/800-477-3244; FAX: 503-581-3191
Borden Accuracy, RD 1, Box 244A, Tunkhannock, PA 18657/717-833-2234; FAX: 717-833-2382
Border Barrels Ltd., Riccarton Farm, Newcastleton SCOTLAND U.K. TD9 0SN
Borovnik KG, Ludwig, 9170 Ferlach, Bahnhofstrasse 7, AUSTRIA/042 27 24 42; FAX: 042 26 43 49
Boss Manufacturing Co., 221 W. First St., Kewanee, IL 61443/309-852-2131
Bostick Wildlife Calls, Inc., P.O. Box 728, Estill, SC 29918/803-625-2210, 803-625-4512
Bourne Co., Inc., Richard A., P.O. Box 141, Hyannis Port, MA 02647/508-775-0797
Bowen Classic Arms Corp., P.O. Box 67, Louisville, TN 37777/615-984-3583
Bowen Knife Co., Inc., P.O. Box 590, Blackshear, GA 31516/912-449-4794
Bowerly, Kent, HCR Box 1903, Camp Sherman, OR 97730/503-595-6028

Bowlin, Gene, Rt. 1, Box 890, Snyder, TX 79549
Boyds', Inc., 3rd & Main, Geddes, SD 57342/605-337-2125; FAX: 605-337-3363
Boyt, 509 Hamilton, Iowa Falls, IA 50126/515-648-4626
Brace, Larry D., 771 Blackfoot Ave., Eugene, OR 97404/503-688-1278
Bradley Gunsight Co., P.O. Box 140, Plymouth, VT 05056/203-589-0531; FAX: 203-582-6294
Brass and Bullet Alloys, P.O. Box 1238, Sierra Vista, AZ 85636/602-458-5321; FAX: 602-458-9125
Brass Eagle, Inc., 7050A Bramalea Rd., Unit 19, Mississauga, Ont. L4Z 1C7, CANADA/416-848-4844
Bratcher, Dan, 311 Belle Air Pl., Carthage, MO 64836/417-358-1518
Brauer Bros. Mfg. Co., 2020 Delmar Blvd., St. Louis, MO 63103/314-231-2864; FAX: 314-249-4952
Braun, M., 32, rue Notre-Dame, 2440 LUXEMBURG
Break-Free, Inc., P.O. Box 25020, Santa Ana, CA 92799/714-953-1900; FAX: 714-953-0402
Brell Mar Products, Inc., 5701 Hwy. 80 West, Jackson, MS 39209
Brenneke KG, Wilhelm, Ilmenauweg 2, D-30551 Langenhagen, GERMANY/0511/97262-0; FAX: 0511/9726262 (U.S. importer—Dynamit Nobel-RWS, Inc.)
Bretton, 19, rue Victor Grignard, F-42026 St.-Etienne (Cedex 1) FRANCE/77-93-54-69; FAX: 77-93-57-98 (U.S. importer—Mandall Shooting Supplies, Inc.)
Brgoch, Frank, 1580 S. 1500 East, Bountiful, UT 84010/801-295-1885
Brian, C.T., 1101 Indiana Ct., Decatur, IL 62521/217-429-2290
Bridgers Best, P.O. Box 1410, Berthoud, CO 80513
Briese Bullet Co., Inc., RR1, Box 108, Tappen, ND 58487/701-327-4578; FAX: 701-327-4579
Briganti & Co., A., 475 Rt. 32, Highland Mills, NY 10930/914-928-9573
Briley Mfg., Inc., 1230 Lumpkin, Houston, TX 77043/713-932-6995, 800-331-5718; FAX: 713-932-1043
British Arms Co. Ltd., P.O. Box 7, Latham, NY 12110/518-783-0773
British Sporting Arms, RR1, Box 130, Millbrook, NY 12545/914-677-8303
BRNO (See U.S. importers—Action Arms Ltd.; Bohemia Arms Co.)
Broad Creek Rifle Works, 120 Horsey Ave., Laurel, DE 19956/302-875-5446
Brobst, Jim, 299 Poplar St., Hamburg, PA 19526/215-562-2103
Broken Gun Ranch, RR2, Box 92, Spearville, KS 67876/316-385-2587
Brooker, Dennis, Rt. 1, Box 12A, Derby, IA 50068/515-533-2103
Brown, H.R. (See Silhouette Leathers)
Brown Co., E. Arthur, 3404 Pawnee Dr., Alexandria, MN 56308/612-762-8847
Brown Manufacturing, P.O. Box 9219, Akron, OH 44305/800-837-GUNS
Brown Precision, Inc., 7786 Molinos Ave., Los Molinos, CA 96055/916-384-2506; FAX: 916-384-1638
Brown Products, Inc., Ed, Rt. 2, Box 2922, Perry, MO 63462/314-565-3261; FAX: 565-2791
Brownell Checkering Tools, W.E., 9390 Twin Mountain Circle, San Diego, CA 92126/619-695-2479; FAX: 619-695-2479
Brownells, Inc., 200 S. Front St., Montezuma, IA 50171/515-623-5401; FAX: 515-623-3896
Browning Arms Co. (Gen. Offices), One Browning Place, Morgan, UT 84050/801-876-2711; FAX: 801-876-3331
Browning Arms Co. (Parts & Service), 3005 Arnold Tenbrook Rd., Arnold, MO 63010-9406/314-287-6800; FAX: 314-287-9751
BRP, Inc. High Performance Cast Bullets, 1210 Alexander Rd., Colorado Springs, CO 80909/719-633-0658
Bruno Shooters Supply, 106 N. Wyoming St., Hazleton, PA 18201/717-455-2211; FAX: 717-455-2211
Brunsport, Inc., 1131 Bayview Dr., Quincy, IL 62301/217-223-8844
Brunton U.S.A., 620 E. Monroe Ave., Riverton, WY 82501/307-856-6559; FAX: 307-856-1840
Bryco Arms (See U.S. distributor—Jennings Firearms, Inc.)
Brynin, Milton, P.O. Box 383, Yonkers, NY 10710/914-779-4333
BSA Guns Ltd., Armoury Rd. Small Heath, Birmingham, ENGLAND B11 2PX/(011)21 772 8543; FAX: (011)21 773-0845 (U.S. importer—Air Rifle Specialists)
B-Square Company, Inc., P.O. Box 11281, 2708 St. Louis Ave., Ft. Worth, TX 76110/817-923-0964, 800-433-2909; FAX: 817-926-7012
Bucheimer, J.M., Jumbo Sports Products, 721 N. 20th St., St. Louis, MO 63103/314-241-1020
Buck Knives, Inc., 1900 Weld Blvd., El Cajon, CA 92022/619-449-1100; FAX: 619-562-5774
Buck Stix—SOS Products Co., Box 3, Neenah, WI 54956
Buck Stop Lure Co., Inc., 3600 Grow Rd. NW, P.O. Box 636, Stanton, MI 48888/517-762-5091; FAX: 517-762-5124
Buckeye Custom Bullets, 6490 Stewart Rd., Elida, OH 45807/419-641-4463
Buckhorn Gun Works, 115 E. North St., Rapid City, SD 57701/605-787-6289
Buckskin Machine Works, A. Hunkeler, 3235 S. 358th St., Auburn, WA 98001/206-927-5412
Budin, Dave, Main St., Margaretville, NY 12455/914-568-4103; FAX: 914-586-4105
Buehler Scope Mounts, 17 Orinda Way, Orinda, CA 94563/510-254-3201; FAX: 510-254-9720
Buenger Enterprises, 3600 S. Harbor Blvd., Oxnard, CA 93035/800-451-6797; FAX: 805-985-1534
Buffalo Arms, 123 S. Third, Suite 6, Sandpoint, ID 83864/208-263-6953; FAX: 208-265-2096
Buffalo Bullet Co., Inc., 12637 Los Nietos Rd. Unit A, Santa Fe Springs, CA 90670/310-944-0322; FAX: 310-944-5054
Buffalo Rock Shooters Supply, R.R. 1, Ottawa, IL 61350/815-433-2471
Bullberry Barrel Works, Ltd., 2430 W. Bullberry Ln. 67-5, Hurricane, UT 84737/801-635-9866
Bullet, Inc., 3745 Hiram Alworth Rd., Dallas, GA 30132
Bullet Meister Bullets (See Gander Mountain)
Bullet Mills, P.O. Box 102, Port Carbon, PA 17965/717-622-0657
Bullet Swaging Supply, Inc., P.O. Box 1056, 303 McMillan Rd, West Monroe, LA 71291/318-387-7257; FAX: 318-387-7779

Bullet Traps, Springdale RD., Westfield, MA 01085/413-568-7001
BulletMakers Workshop, The, RFD 1 Box 1755, Brooks, ME 04921
Bullseye Bullets, 1610 State Road 60, No. 12, Valrico, FL 33594/813-654-6563
Bull-X, Inc., P.O. Box 182, Farmer City, IL 61842/309-928-2574, 800-248-3845 orders only
Burgess & Son Gunsmiths, R.W., P.O. Box 3364, Warner Robins, GA 31099/912-328-7487
Burkhart Gunsmithing, Don, P.O. Box 852, Rawlins, WY 82301/307-324-6007
Burnham Bros., P.O. Box 1148, Menard, TX 78659/915-396-4572; FAX: 915-396-4574
Burres, Jack, 10333 San Fernando Rd., Pacoima, CA 91331/818-899-8000
Burris, P.O. Box 1747, Greeley, CO 80631/303-356-1670; FAX: 303-356-8702
Busch Metal Merchants, Roger, 48861 West Rd., Wixon, MI 48393/800-876-5337
Bushman Hunters & Safaris, P.O. Box 293088, Lewisville, TX 75029/214-317-0768
Bushmaster Hunting & Fishing, 451 Alliance Ave., Toronto, Ont. M6N 2J1 CANADA/416-763-4040; FAX: 416-763-0623
Bushnell (See Bausch & Lomb)
Bushwacker Backpack & Supply Co. (See Counter Assault)
Bustani Appraisers, Leo, P.O. Box 8125, W. Palm Beach, FL 33407/305-622-2710
Buster's Custom Knives, P.O. Box 214, Richfield, UT 84701/801-896-5319
Butler Creek Corp., 290 Arden Dr., Belgrade, MT 59714/800-423-8327, 406-388-1356; FAX: 406-388-7204
Butler Enterprises, 834 Oberting Rd., Lawrenceburg, IN 47025/812-537-3584
Butterfield & Butterfield, 220 San Bruno Ave., San Francisco, CA 94103/415-861-7500
Buzztail Brass, 5306 Bryant Ave., Klamath Falls, OR 97603/503-884-1072
B-West Imports, Inc., 2425 N. Huachuca Dr., Tucson, AZ 85745-1201/602-628-1990; FAX: 602-628-3602

C

C3 Systems, 678 Killingly St., Johnston, RI 02919
C&D Special Products (Claybuster), 309 Sequoya Dr., Hopkinsville, KY 42240/800-922-6287, 800-284-1746
C&H Research, 115 Sunnyside Dr., Box 351, Lewis, KS 67552/316-324-5445
Cabanas (See U.S. importer—Mandall Shooting Supplies, Inc.)
Cabela's, 812-13th Ave., Sidney, NE 69160/308-254-5505; FAX: 308-254-7809
Cabinet Mtn. Outfitters Scents & Lures, P.O. Box 766, Plains, MT 59859/406-826-3970
Cache La Poudre Rifleworks, 140 N. College, Ft. Collins, CO 80524/303-482-6913
Cadre Supply (See Parts & Surplus)
Calhoon Varmint Bullets, James, Shambo Rt., Box 304, Havre, MT 59501
Calibre Press, Inc., 666 Dundee Rd., Suite 1607, Northbrook, IL 60062-2760/800-323-0037; FAX: 708-498-6869
Cali'co Hardwoods, Inc., 1648 Airport Blvd., Windsor, CA 95492/707-546-4045; FAX: 707-546-4027
Calico Light Weapon Systems, 405 E. 19th St., Bakersfield, CA 93305/805-323-1327; FAX: 805-323-7844
California Grip, 1323 Miami Ave., Clovis, CA 93612/209-299-1316
California Magnum, 20746 Dearborn St., Chatsworth, CA 91313/818-341-7302; FAX: 818-341-7304
California Sight, P.O. Box 4607, Pagosa Springs, CO 81157/303-731-5003
CAM Enterprises, 5090 Iron Springs Rd., Box 2, Prescott, AZ 86301/602-776-9640
Camas Hot Springs Mfg., P.O. Box 639, Hot Springs, MT 59845/406-741-3756
Camdex, Inc., 2330 Alger, Troy, MI 48083/313-528-2300
Cameron's, 16690 W. 11th Ave., Golden, CO 80401/303-279-7365; FAX: 303-628-5413
Camilli, Lou, 4700 Oahu Dr. NE, Albuquerque, NM 87111/505-293-5259
Camillus Cutlery Co./Western Cutlery Co., 54 Main St., Camillus, NY 13031/315-672-8111; FAX: 315-672-8832
Camofare Co., 712 Main St. 2800, Houston, TX 77002/713-229-9253
Campbell, Dick, 20,000 Silver Ranch Rd., Conifer, CO 80433/303-697-0150
Camp-Cap Products, P.O. Box 173, Chesterfield, MO 63006/314-532-4340
Can Am Enterprises, 350 Jones Rd., Fruitland, Ont. LOR ILO, CANADA/416-643-4357
Canadian Custom Bullets, Box 52, Anola Man. R0E 0A0 CANADA
Canjar Co., M.H., 500 E. 45th Ave., Denver, CO 80216/303-295-2638
Cannon Safe, Inc., 9358 Stephens St., Pico Rivera, CA 90660/310-692-0636, 800-242-1055; FAX: 310-692-7252
Cannon's Guns, Box 1036, 320 Main St., Polson, MT 59860/406-887-2048
Canons Delcour, Rue J.B. Cools, B-4040 Herstal, BELGIUM 32.(0)41.40.13.40; FAX: 32(0)412.40.22.88
Canyon Cartridge Corp., P.O. Box 152, Albertson, NY 11507/FAX: 516-294-8946
Cape Outfitters, Rt. 2, Box 437C, Cape Girardeau, MO 63701/314-335-4103; FAX: 314-335-1555
Caraville Manufacturing, P.O. Box 4545, Thousand Oaks, CA 91359/805-499-1234
Carbide Checkering Tools, P.O. Box 77, 200 Lyons Hill Rd., Athol, MA 01331/508-249-9241
Carbide Die & Mfg. Co., Inc., 15615 E. Arrow Hwy., Irwindale, CA 91706/818-337-2518
Carhartt, Inc., P.O. Box 600, Dearborn, MI 48121/800-358-3825; FAX: 313-271-3455
Carlson, Douglas R., Antique American Firearms, P.O. Box 71035, Dept. GD, Des Moines, IA 50325/515-224-6552
Carnahan Bullets, 17645 110th Ave. SE, Renton, WA 98055
Carolina Precision Rifles, 1200 Old Jackson Hwy., Jackson, SC 29831/803-827-2069
Carrell's Precision Firearms, P.O. Box 232, 201 S. Park, Joliet, MT 59041/406-962-3593

Carroll Bullets (See Precision Reloading, Inc.)
Carry-Lite, Inc., 5203 W. Clinton Ave., Milwaukee, WI 53223/414-355-3520
Carter's Gun Shop, 225 G St., Penrose, CO 81240/719-372-6240
Carter's Wildlife Calls, Garth, Inc., P.O. Box 821, Cedar City, UT 84720/801-586-7639
Carvajal Belts & Holsters, 422 Chestnut, San Antonio, TX 78202/210-222-1634
Cascade Bullet Co., Inc., 312 Main St., Klamath Falls, OR 97601/503-884-9316
Cascade Fabrication, 1090 Bailey Hill Rd. Unit A, Eugene, OR 97402/503-485-3433; FAX: 503-485-3543
Cascade Shooters, 2155 N.W. 12th St., Redwood, OR 97756
Case & Sons Cutlery Co., W.R., Owens Way, Bradford, PA 16701/814-368-4123; FAX: 814-362-4877
Case Sorting System, 12695 Cobblestone Creek Rd., Poway, CA 92064/619-486-9340
Cash Mfg. Co., Inc., P.O. Box 130, 201 S. Klein Dr., Waunakee, WI 53597-0130/608-849-5664
Caspian Arms, 14 North Main St., Hardwick, VT 05843/802-472-6454
Caswell International Corp., 1221 Marshall St. NE, Minneapolis, MN 55413/612-379-2000; FAX: 612-379-2367
Catco-Ambush, Inc., P.O.Box 300, Corte Madera, CA 94926
Cathey Enterprises, Inc., P.O. Box 2202, Brownwood, TX 76804/915-643-2553; FAX: 915-643-3653
Cation, 32360 Edward, Madison Heights, MI 48071/313-588-0160
Catoctin Cutlery, P.O. Box 188, Smithsburg, MD 21783/301-824-7416; FAX: 301-824-6138
Caywood, Shane J., P.O. Box 321, Minocqua, WI 54548/715-277-3866 evenings
CBC, Avenida Humberto de Campos, 3220, 09400-000 Ribeirao Pires-SP-BRAZIL/55-11-742-7500; FAX: 55-11-459-7385 (U.S. importer—MAGTECH Recreational Products, Inc.)
C.C.G. Enterprises, 5217 E. Belknap St., Halton City, TX 76117/817-834-9554
CCI, Div. of Blount, Inc., 2299 Snake River Ave., P.O. Box 856, Lewiston, ID 83501/800-627-3640, 208-746-2351
Cedar Hill Game Calls, Inc., P.O. Box 550, Farmerville, LA 71241/318-368-9004
Celestron International, P.O. Box 3578, Torrance, CA 90503/310-328-9560; FAX: 310-212-5835
Centaur Systems, Inc., 1602 Foothill Rd., Kalispell, MT 59901/406-755-8609; FAX: 406-755-8609
Center Lock Scope Rings, 9901 France Ct., Lakeville, MN 55044/612-461-2114
CenterMark, P.O. Box 4066, Parnassus Station, New Kensington, PA 15068/412-335-1319
Central Specialties Ltd., 1122 Silver Lake Road, Cary, IL 60013/708-537-3300; FAX: 708-537-3615
Century Gun Dist., Inc., 1467 Jason Rd., Greenfield, IN 46140/317-462-4524
Century International Arms, Inc., 48 Lower Newton St., St. Albans, VT 05478/802-527-1252; FAX: 802-527-0470
C-H Tool & Die Corp. (See 4-D Custom Die Co.)
Chace Leather Products, 507 Alden St., Fall River, MA 02722/508-678-7556; FAX: 508-675-9666
Chadick's Ltd., P.O. Box 100, Terrell, TX 75160/214-563-7577
Chambers Flintlocks Ltd., Jim, Rt. 1, Box 513-A, Candler, NC 28715/704-667-8361
Chameleon Camouflage Systems, 15199 S. Maplelane Rd., Oregon City, OR 97045/503-657-2266
Champion Target Co., 232 Industrial Parkway, Richmond, IN 47374/800-441-4971
Champion's Choice, Inc., 201 International Blvd., LaVergne, TN 37086/615-793-4066; FAX: 615-793-4070
Champlin, R. MacDonald, P.O. Box 132, Candia, NH 03034
Champlin Firearms, Inc., P.O. Box 3191, Woodring Airport, Enid, OK 73701/405-237-7388; FAX: 405-242-6922
Chapman Academy of Practical Shooting, 4350 Academy Rd., Hallsville, MO 65255/314-696-5544; FAX: 314-696-2266
Chapman Manufacturing Co., 471 New Haven Rd., P.O. Box 250, Durham, CT 06422/203-349-9228; FAX: 203-349-0084
Chapuis Armes, 21 La Gravoux, BP15, 42380 St. Bonnet-le-Chateau, FRANCE/(33)77.50.06.96 (U.S. importer—Chapuis USA)
Chapuis USA, 416 Business Park, Bedford, KY 40006
CHARCO, 26 Beaver St., Ansonia, CT 06401/203-735-4686; 203-735-6569
Charter Arms (See CHARCO)
Checkmate Refinishing, 8232 Shaw Rd., Brooksville, FL 34602/904-799-5774
Cheddite France, S.A., 99 Route de Lyon, F-26500 Bourg Les Valence, FRANCE/75 56 45 45; FAX: 75 56 98 89
Chelsea Gun Club of New York City, Inc., 237 Ovington Ave., Apt. D53, Brooklyn, NY 11209/718-836-9422, 718-833-2704
Chem-Pak, Inc., 11 Oates Ave., P.O. Box 1685, Winchester, VA 22601/800-336-9828; FAX: 703-722-3993
Cherokee Gun Accessories (See Glaser Safety Slug, Inc.)
Cherry's Fine Guns, P.O. Box 5307, Greensboro, NC 27435-0307/919-854-4182
Chesapeake Importing & Distributing Co. (See CIDCO)
CheVron Bullets, RR1, Ottawa, IL 61350/815-433-2471
CheVron Case Master (See CheVron Bullets)
Chicago Cutlery Co., 1536 Beech St., Terre Haute, IN 47804/800-457-2665
Chicasaw Gun Works (See Cochran, Oliver)
ChinaSports, Inc., 2010 S. Lynx Place, Ontario, CA 91761/714-923-1411; FAX: 714-923-0775
Chipmunk (See Oregon Arms, Inc.)
Chippewa Shoe Co., P.O. Box 2521, Ft. Worth, TX 76113/817-332-4385
Choate Machine & Tool Co., Inc., P.O. Box 218, Bald Knob, AR 72010/501-724-6193, 800-972-6390; FAX: 501-724-5873
Chopie Mfg., Inc., 700 Copeland Ave., LaCrosse, WI 54603/608-784-0926
Christie's East, 219 E. 67th St., New York, NY 10021/212-606-0400
Christman Jr., David, 937 Lee Hedrick Rd., Colville, WA 99114/509-684-5686 days; 509-684-3314 evenings

Christopher Firearms Co., E., Inc., Route 128 & Ferry St., Miamitown, OH 45041/513-353-1321
Chronotech, 1655 Siamet Rd. Unit 6, Mississauga, Ont. L4W 1Z4 CANADA/416-625-5200; FAX: 416-625-5190
Chu Tani Ind., Inc., Box 3782, Chula Vista, CA 92011
Chuck's Gun Shop, P.O. Box 597, Waldo, FL 32694/904-468-2264
Churchill (See U.S. importer—Ellett Bros.)
Churchill, Winston, Twenty Mile Stream Rd., RFD P.O. Box 29B, Proctorsville, VT 05153/802-226-7772
Churchill Glove Co., James, P.O. Box 298, Centralia, WA 98531
CIDCO, 21480 Pacific Blvd., Sterling, VA 22170/703-444-5353
Ciener, Inc., Jonathan Arthur, 8700 Commerce St., Cape Canaveral, FL 32920/407-868-2200; FAX: 407-868-2201
Cimarron Arms, P.O. Box 906, Fredericksburg, TX 78624-0906/210-997-9090; FAX: 210-997-0802
Cincinnati Swaging, 2605 Marlington Ave., Cincinnati, OH 45208
Circle M Custom Bullets, 29 Avenida de Silva, Abilene, TX 79602-7509/915-698-3106
Claridge Hi-Tec, Inc., 19350 Business Center Dr., Northridge, CA 91324/818-700-9093; FAX: 818-700-0026
Clark, Frank, 3714-27th St., Lubbock, TX 79410/806-799-1187
Clark Co., Inc., David, P.O. Box 15054, Worcester, MA 01615-0054/508-756-6216; FAX: 508-753-5827
Clark Custom Guns, Inc., P.O. Box 530, 11462 Keatchie Rd., Keithville, LA 71047/318-925-0836; FAX: 318-925-9425
Clark Firearms Engraving, P.O. Box 80746, San Marino, CA 91118/818-287-1652
Clarkfield Enterprises, Inc., 1032 10th Ave., Clarkfield, MN 56223/612-669-7140
Classic Arms Corp., P.O. Box 106, Dunsmuir, CA 96025-0106/916-235-2000
Classic Brass, 14 Grove St., Plympton, MA 02367/FAX: 617-585-5673
Classic Guns, Inc., Frank S. Wood, 3230 Medlock Bridge Rd., Suite 110, Norcross, GA 30092/404-242-7944
Clay Target Enterprises, 300 Railway Ave., Campbell, CA 95008/408-379-4829
Clearview Mfg. Co., Inc., 413 S. Oakley St., Fordyce, AR 71742/501-352-8557; FAX: 501-352-8557
Cleland's Gun Shop, Inc., 10306 Airport Hwy., Swanton, OH 43558/419-865-4713
Clements' Custom Leathercraft, Chas, 1741 Dallas St., Aurora, CO 80010-2018/303-364-0403
Clenzoil Corp., P.O. Box 80226, Sta. C, Canton, OH 44708-9998/216-833-9758
Clerke Co., J.A., P.O. Box 627, Pearblossom, CA 93553-0627/805-945-0713
Clift Mfg., L.R., 3821 Hammonton Rd., Marysville, CA 95901/916-755-3390; FAX: 916-755-3393
Clift Welding Supply & Cases, 1332-A Colusa Hwy., Yuba City, CA 95993/916-755-3390; FAX: 916-755-3393
Clifton Arms, Inc., P.O. Box 1471, Medina, TX 78055/210-589-2666; FAX: 210-589-2661
Cloward's Gun Shop, 4023 Aurora Ave. N, Seattle, WA 98103/206-632-2072
Clymer Manufacturing Co., Inc., 1645 W. Hamlin Rd., Rochester Hills, MI 48309-3312/810-853-5555; FAX: 810-853-1530
C-More Systems, 7806 Sudley Rd., Suite 200, Manassas, VA 22110/703-361-2663; FAX: 703-361-5881
Coast Cutlery Co., 609 SE Ankeny, Portland, OR 97214/503-234-4545
Coats, Mrs. Lester, 300 Luman Rd., Space 125, Phoenix, OR 97535/503-535-1611
CoBalt Mfg., Inc., 1020 Shady Oaks Dr., Denton, TX 76205/817-382-8986
Cobra Gunskin, 133-30 32nd Ave., Flushing, NY 11354/718-762-8181; FAX: 718-762-0890
Cobra Sport s.r.l., Via Caduti Nei Lager No. 1, 56020 San Romano, Montopoli v/Arno (Pi), ITALY/0039-571-450490; FAX: 0039-571-450492
Cochran, Oliver, Box 868, Shady Spring, WV 25918/304-763-3838
Coffin, Charles H., 3719 Scarlet Ave., Odessa, TX 79762/915-366-4729
Coffin, Jim, 250 Country Club Lane, Albany, OR 97321/503-928-4391
Cogar's Gunsmithing, P.O. Box 755, Houghton Lake, MI 48629/517-422-4591
Coghlan's Ltd., 121 Irene St., Winnipeg, Man., CANADA R3T 4C7/204-284-9550
Cold Steel, Inc., 2128 Knoll Dr., Unit D, Ventura, CA 93003/800-255-4716
Cole's Gun Works, Rt. 3, Box 159-A, Moyock, NC 27958/919-435-2345
Cole-Grip, 16135 Cohasset St., Van Nuys, CA 91406/818-782-4424
Coleman Co., Inc., 250 N. St. Francis, Wichita, KS 67201
Coleman's Custom Repair, 4035 N. 20th Rd., Arlington, VA 22207/703-528-4486
Collings, Ronald, 1006 Cielta Linda, Vista, CA 92083
Colonial Arms, Inc., P.O. Box 636, Selma, AL 36702-0636/205-872-9455; FAX: 205-872-9540
Colonial Knife Co., P.O. Box 3327, Providence, RI 02909/401-421-1600; FAX: 401-421-2047
Colonial Repair, P.O. Box 372, Hyde Park, MA 02136-9998/617-469-4951
Colorado School of Trades, 1575 Hoyt St., Lakewood, CO 80215/800-234-4594; FAX: 303-233-4723
Colorado Shooter's Supply, 138 S. Plum, P.O. Box 132, Fruita, CO 81521/303-858-9191
Colorado Sutlers Arsenal, Box 991, Granby, CO 80446-9998/303-887-3813
Colt Blackpowder Arms Co., 5 Centre Market Place, New York, NY 10013/212-925-2159; FAX: 212-966-4986
Colt's Mfg. Co., Inc., P.O. Box 1868, Hartford, CT 06144-1868/800-962-COLT, 203-236-6311; FAX: 203-244-1449
Combat Military Ordnance Ltd., 3900 Hopkins St., Savannah, GA 31405/912-238-1900; FAX: 912-236-7570
Companhia Brasileira de Cartuchos (See CBC)
Compass Industries, Inc., 104 East 25th St., New York, NY 10010/212-473-2614
Competition Electronics, Inc., 3469 Precision Dr., Rockford, IL 61109/815-874-8001; FAX: 815-874-8181
Competition Limited, 1664 S. Research Loop Rd., Tucson, AZ 85710/602-722-6455
Competitive Edge Dynamics Ltd., P.O. Box 1123, 85 Bliss Rd., White River Junction, VT 05001/802-295-1334; FAX: 802-295-1965

Competitive Pistol Shop, The, 5233 Palmer Dr., Ft. Worth, TX 76117-2433/817-834-8479

Competitor Corp., Inc., P.O. Box 244, 293 Townsend Rd., West Groton, MA 01472/508-448-3521; FAX: 603-673-4540

Complete Handloader, The, P.O. Box 5264, Arvada, CO 80005/303-460-9489

Component Concepts, Inc., 10240 SW Nimbus Ave., Suite L-8, Portland, OR 97223/503-684-9262; FAX: 503-620-4285

Condon, Inc., David, 109 E. Washington St., Middleburg, VA 22117/703-687-5642

Condon, Inc., David, P.O. Box 312, 14502-G Lee Rd., Chatilly, VA 22021/703-631-7748

Conetrol Scope Mounts, 10225 Hwy. 123 south, Seguin, TX 78155/210-379-3030, 800-CONETROL

CONKKO, P.O. Box 40, Broomall, PA 19008/215-356-0711

Connecticut Valley Arms Co. (See CVA)

Connecticut Valley Classics, P.O. Box 2068, 12 Taylor Lane, Westport, CT 06880/203-435-4600

Conrad, C.A., 3964 Ebert St., Winston-Salem, NC 27127/919-788-5469

Continental Kite & Key (See CONKKO)

Cook Bullets, 1846 Rosemeade Parkway 188, Carrollton, TX 75007/214-394-8725

Cook Engineering Service, 891 Highbury Rd., Vermont VICT 3133 AUSTRALIA

Coonan Arms, Inc., 1465 Selby Ave., St. Paul, MN 55104/612-646-6672; FAX: 612-646-0902

Cooper Arms, P.O. Box 114, Stevensville, MT 59870/406-777-5534

Cooper-Woodward, 3800 Pelican Rd., Helena, MT 59601/406-458-3800

Corbin, Inc., 600 Industrial Circle, P.O. Box 2659, White City, OR 97503/503-826-5211; FAX: 503-826-8669

Corbin Applied Technology, P.O. Box 2171, White City, OR 97503/503-826-5211

Cor-Bon, Inc., 4828 Michigan Ave., P.O. Box 10126, Detroit, MI 48210/313-894-2373

Corkys Gun Clinic, 111 North 11th Ave., Greeley, CO 80631/303-330-0516

Corry, John, 861 Princeton Ct., Neshanic Station, NJ 08853/308-369-8019

Cosmi Americo & Figlio s.n.c., Via Flaminia 307, Ancona, ITALY I-60020/071-888208; FAX: 071-887008 (U.S. importer—New England Arms Co.)

Costa, David, Island Pond Gun Shop, P.O. Box 428, Cross St., Island Pond, VT 05846/802-723-4546

Coulston Products, Inc., P.O. Box 30, Easton, PA 18044-0030/215-253-0167; FAX: 215-252-1511

Counter Assault, Box 4721, Missoula, MT 59806/406-728-6241; FAX: 406-728-8800

Country Armourer, The, P.O. Box 308, Ashby, MA 01431-0308/508-386-7590; FAX: 508-386-7789

Cousin Bob's Mountain Products, 7119 Ohio River Blvd., Ben Avon, PA 15202/412-766-5114; FAX: 412-766-5114

Cox, C. Ed, RD 2, Box 192, Prosperity, PA 15329/412-228-4984

CP Specialties, 1814 Mearns Rd., Warminster, PA 18974

CQB Training, P.O. Box 1739, Manchester, MO 63011

Craftguard, 3624 Logan Ave., Waterloo, IA 50703/319-232-2959

Craig Custom Guns, 629 E. 10th, Hutchinson, KS 67501/316-669-0601

Crandall Tool & Machine Co., 1545 N. Mitchell St., P.O. Box 569, Cadillac, MI 49601/616-775-5562

Crane & Crane Ltd., 105 N. Edison Way 6, Reno, NV 89502-2355/702-856-1516; FAX: 702-856-1616

Crane Sales Co., George S., P.O. Box 385, Van Nuys, CA 91409/818-505-8337

Cravener's Gun Shop, 1627-5th Ave., Ford City, PA 16226/412-763-8312

Crawford Co., Inc., R.M., P.O. Box 277, Everett, PA 15537/814-652-6536; FAX: 814-652-9526

CRDC Technologies, 3972 Barranca Parkway, Ste. J-484, Irvine, CA 92714/714-730-8835

Creative Cartridge Co., 56 Morgan Rd., Canton, CT 06019/203-693-2529

Creative Craftsman, Inc., The, 95 Highway 29 North, P.O. Box 331, Lawrenceville, GA 30246/404-963-2112

Creedmoor Sports, Inc., P.O. Box 1040, Oceanside, CA 92051/619-757-5529

Creek Side Metal & Woodcrafters (See Allard, Gary)

Creekside Gun Shop, Inc., Main St., Holcomb, NY 14469/716-657-6338; FAX: 716-657-7900

Crit'R Call, Box 999V, La Porte, CO 80535/303-484-2768

Crosman Airguns, Rt. 5 and 20, E. Bloomfield, NY 14443/716-657-6161; FAX: 716-657-5405

Crosman Blades (See Coleman Co., Inc.)

Crosman Products of Canada Ltd., 1173 N. Service Rd. West, Oakville, Ontario, L6M 2V9 CANADA/905-827-1822

Crouse's Country Cover, P.O. Box 160, Storrs, CT 06268/203-429-4715

Crucelegui Hermanos (See U.S. importer—Mandall Shooting Supplies, Inc.)

CRW Products, Inc., Box 2123, Des Moines, IA 50310

Cubic Shot Shell Co., Inc., 98 Fatima Dr., Campbell, OH 44405/216-755-0349; FAX: 216-755-0349

Cullity Restoration, Daniel, 209 Old County Rd., East Sandwich, MA 02537/508-888-1147

Cumberland, Dave, Dept. MCA, 12924 Highway A-12, Montague, CA 96064/916-459-5445

Cumberland Arms, Rt. l, Box 1150 Shafer Rd., Blantons Chapel, Manchester, TN 37355

Cumberland Knife & Gun Works, 5661 Bragg Blvd., Fayetteville, NC 28303/919-867-0009

Cummings Bullets, 1417 Esperanza Way, Escondido, CA 92027

Cunard & Co., J., P.O. Box 755, Newark, OH 43058-0755/614-345-6646

Cunningham Co., Eaton, 607 Superior St., Kansas City, MO 64106/816-842-2600

Curtis Custom Shop, RR1, Box 193A, Wallingford, KY 41093/703-659-4265

Curtis Gun Shop, Dept. ST, 119 W. College, Bozeman, MT 59715

Custom Barreling & Stocks, 937 Lee Hedrick Rd., Colville, WA 99114/509-684-5686 (days), 509-684-3314 (evenings)

Custom Bullets by Hoffman, 2604 Peconic Ave., Seaford, NY 11783

Custom Checkering Service, Kathy Forster, 2124 SE Yamhill St., Portland, OR 97214/503-236-5874

Custom Chronograph, Inc., 5305 Reese Hill Rd., Sumas, WA 98295/206-988-7801

Custom Firearms (See Ahrends, Kim)

Custom Gun Products, 5021 W. Rosewood, Spokane, WA 99208/509-328-9340

Custom Gun Stocks, Rt. 6, P.O. Box 177, McMinnville, TN 37110/615-668-3912

Custom Gunsmiths, 4303 Friar Lane, Colorado Springs, CO 80907/719-599-3366

Custom Hunting Ammo & Arms, 2900 Fisk Rd., Howell, MI 48843/517-546-9498

Custom Products (See Jones Custom Products, Neil)

Custom Shop, The, 890 Cochrane Crescent, Peterborough, Ont. K9H 5N3 CANADA/705-742-6693

Custom Tackle and Ammo, P.O. Box 1886, Farmington, NM 87499/505-632-3539

Cutco Cutlery, P.O. Box 810, Olean, NY 14760/716-372-3111

Cutlery Shoppe, 5461 Kendall St., Boise, ID 83706-1248/800-231-1272

Cutsinger Bench Rest Bullets, RR 8, Box 161-A, Shelbyville, IN 46176/317-729-5360

CVA, 5988 Peachtree Corners East, Norcross, GA 30071/404-449-4687; FAX: 404-242-8546

C.W. Cartridge Co., 71 Hackensack St., Wood Ridge, NJ 07075

C.W. Cartridge Co., 242 Highland Ave., Kearney, NJ 07032/201-998-1030

Cycle Dynamics, Inc., 74 Garden St., Feeding Hills, MA 01030/413-786-0141

Cylinder & Slide, Inc., William R. Laughridge, 245 E. 4th St., Fremont, NE 68025/402-721-4277; FAX: 402-721-0263

CZ (See U.S. importer—Action Arms Ltd.)

D

D&D Gunsmiths, Ltd., 363 E. Elmwood, Troy, MI 48083/313-583-1512

D&H Precision Tooling, 7522 Barnard Mill Rd., Ringwood, IL 60072/815-653-4011

D&H Prods. Co., Inc., 465 Denny Rd., Valencia, PA 16059/412-898-2840

D&J Bullet Co. & Custom Gun Shop, Inc., 426 Ferry St., Russell, KY 41169/606-836-2663; FAX: 606-836-2663

D&L Industries, 10602 Horton Ave., Downey, CA 90241/310-806-0891

D&L Sports, P.O. Box 651, Gillette, WY 82717/307-686-4008

D&R Distributing, 308 S.E. Valley St., Myrtle Creek, OR 97457/503-863-6850

Dade Screw Machine Products, 2319 NW 7th Ave., Miami, FL 33127/305-573-5050

Daewoo Precision Industries Ltd., 34-3 Yeoeuido-Dong, Yeongdeungoo-GU, 15th, Fl./Seoul, KOREA (U.S. importer—Nationwide Sports Distributors)

Dahl's Custom Stocks, N2863 Schofield Rd., Lake Geneva, WI 53147/414-248-2464

Daisy Mfg. Co., P.O. Box 220, Rogers, AR 72756/501-636-1200; FAX: 501-636-1601

Dakota (See U.S. importer—EMF Co., Inc.)

Dakota Arms, HC55, Box 326, Sturgis, SD 57785/605-347-4686; FAX: 605-347-4459

Dakota Corp., P.O. Box 543, Rutland, VT 05702/800-451-4167; FAX: 802-773-3919

Daly, Charles (See B.C. Miroku/Charles Daly)

Damascus-U.S.A., RR 1, Box 206-A, Tyner, NC 27980/919-221-2010; FAX: 919-221-2009

Dan's Whetstone Co., Inc., 130 Timbs Place, Hot Springs, AR 71913/501-767-1616; FAX: 501-767-9598

Dangler, Homer L., Box 254, Addison, MI 49220/517-547-6745

Danner Shoe Mfg. Co., 12722 NE Airport Way, Portland, OR 97230/503-251-1100; FAX: 503-251-1119

Danuser Machine Co., 550 E. Third St., P.O. Box 368, Fulton, MO 65251/314-642-2246; FAX: 314-642-2240

Dapkus Co., J.G., P.O. Box 293, Durham, CT 06422

Dara-Nes, Inc. (See Nesci Enterprises, Inc.)

Darlington Gun Works, Inc., P.O. Box 698, 516 S. 52 Bypass, Darlington, SC 29532/803-393-3931

Data Tech Software Systems, 19312 East Eldorado Drive, Aurora, CO 80013

Datumtech Corp., 2275 Wehrle Dr., Buffalo, NY 14221

Davidson, Jere, Rt. 1, Box 132, Rustburg, VA 24588/804-821-3637

Davidson Products, 2020 Huntington Dr., Las Cruces, NM 88801/505-522-5612

Davidson's, 2703 High Point Rd., Greensboro, NC 27403/800-367-4867, 919-292-5161; FAX: 919-252-2552

Davis Co., R.E., 3450 Pleasantvale NE, Pleasantville, OH 43148/614-654-9990

Davis Industries, 11186 Venture Dr., Mira Loma, CA 91752/909-360-5598

Davis Leather Co., G. Wm., 3990 Valley Blvd., Unit D, Walnut, CA 91789/714-598-5620

Davis Products, Mike, 643 Loop Dr., Moses Lake, WA 98837/509-765-6178, 800-765-6178 orders only

Davis Service Center, Bill, 10173 Croydon Way 9, Sacramento, CA 95827/916-369-6789

Day & Sons, Inc., Leonard, P.O. Box 122, Flagg Hill Rd., Heath, MA 01346/413-337-8369

Dayson Arms Ltd., P.O. Box 217, Nashville, IN 47448-0217/812-988-0082; FAX: 812-988-0431

Dayton Traister, P.O. Box 593, Oak Harbor, WA 98277/206-679-4657; FAX:206-675-1114

DBASE Consultants (See Peripheral Data Systems)

DBI Books, Inc., 4092 Commercial Ave., Northbrook, IL 60062/708-272-6310; FAX: 708-272-2051

D-Boone Ent., Inc., 5900 Colwyn Dr., Harrisburg, PA 17109

D.C.C. Enterprises, 259 Wynburn Ave., Athens, GA 30601

D.D. Custom Stocks, R.H. "Dick" Devereaux, 5240 Mule Deer Dr., Colorado Springs, CO 80919/719-548-8468

de Treville & Co., Stan, 4129 Normal St., San Diego, CA 92103/619-298-3393

Deadeye Sport Center, RD 1, Box 147B, Shickshinny, PA 18655/717-256-7432
Decker Shooting Products, 1729 Laguna Ave., Schofield, WI 54476/715-359-5873
DeckSlider of Florida, 27641-2 Reahard Ct., Bonita Springs, FL 33923/800-782-1474
Dedicated Systems, 105-B Cochrane Circle, Morgan Hill, CA 95037/408-629-1796; FAX: 408-779-2673
Deepeeka Exports Pvt. Ltd., D-78, Saket, Meerut-250-006, INDIA/0121-74483; FAX: 0121-74483
Deer Me Products Co., Box 34, 1208 Park St., Anoka, MN 55303/612-421-8971; FAX: 612-422-0536
Defense Moulding Enterprises, 16781 Daisey Ave., Fountain Valley, CA 92708/714-842-5062
Defense Training International, Inc., 749 S. Lemay, Ste. A3-337, Ft. Collins, CO 80524/303-482-2520; FAX: 303-482-0548
Degen Knives, 1800 N. Highland Ave. No. 600, Los Angeles, CA 90028/213-461-1065; FAX: 213-461-3598
deHaas Barrels, RR 3, Box 77, Ridgeway, MO 64481/816-872-6308
Del Rey Products, P.O. Box 91561, Los Angeles, CA 90009/213-823-0494
Del-Sports, Inc., Box 685, Main St., Margaretville, NY 12455/914-586-4103; FAX: 914-586-4105
Delhi Gun House, 1374 Kashmere Gate, Delhi, INDIA 110 006/(011)237375 239116; FAX: 91-11-2917344
Delorge, Ed, 2231 Hwy. 308, Thibodaux, LA 70301/504-447-1633
Delta Arms Ltd., P.O. Box 68, Sellers, SC 29592-0068/803-752-7426, 800-677-0641; 800-274-1611
Delta Co. Ammo Bunker, 1209 16th Place, Yuma, AZ 85364/602-783-4563
Delta Enterprises, 284 Hagemann Drive, Livermore, CA 94550
Delta Vectors, Inc., 7119 W. 79th St., Overland Park, KS 66204/913-642-0307
Dem-Bart Checkering Tools, Inc., 6807 Hwy. 2, Bickford Ave., Snohomish, WA 98290/206-568-7356; FAX: 206-568-3134
Denver Arms, Ltd., P.O. Box 4640, Pagosa Springs, CO 81157/303-731-2295
Denver Bullets, Inc., 1811 W. 13th Ave., Denver, CO 80204/303-893-3146; FAX: 303-893-9161
Denver Instrument Co., 6542 Fig St., Arvada, CO 80004/800-321-1135, 303-431-7255; FAX: 303-423-4831
DeSantis Holster & Leather Goods, P.O. Box 2039, New Hyde Park, NY 11040-0701/516-354-8000; FAX: 516-354-7501
Desert Industries, Inc., 3245 E. Patrick Ln., Suite H, Las Vegas, NV 89120/702-597-1066; FAX: 702-434-9495
Desert Mountain Mfg., Box 184, Coram, MT 59913/800-477-0762, 406-387-5361
Detroit-Armor Corp., 720 Industrial Dr. No. 112, Cary, IL 60013/708-639-7666; FAX: 708-639-7694
Dever Co., Jack, 8590 NW 90, Oklahoma City, OK 73132/405-721-6393
Devereaux, R.H. "Dick" (See D.D. Custom Rifles)
Dewey Mfg. Co., Inc., J., P.O. Box 2014, Southbury, CT 06488/203-598-7912; FAX: 203-598-3119
DGS, Inc., Dale A. Storey, 1117 E. 12th, Casper, WY 82601/307-237-2414
DHB Products, P.O. Box 3092, Alexandria, VA 22302/703-836-2648
Diamond Machining Technology, Inc., 85 Hayes Memorial Dr., Marlborough, MA 01752-1892/508-481-5944; FAX: 508-485-3924
Diamond Mfg. Co., P.O. Box 174, Wyoming, PA 18644/800-233-9601
Diana (See U.S. importer—Dynamit Nobel-RWS, Inc.)
Dibble, Derek A., 555 John Downey Dr., New Britain, CT 06051/203-224-2630
Dietz Gun Shop & Range, Inc., 421 Range Rd., New Braunfels, TX 78132/210-885-4662
Dilliott Gunsmithing, Inc., 657 Scarlett Rd., Dandridge, TN 37725/615-397-9204
Dillon, Ed, 1035 War Eagle Dr. N., Colorado Springs, CO 80919/719-598-4929; FAX: 719-598-4929
Dillon Precision Products, Inc., 7442 E. Butherus Dr., Scottsdale, AZ 85260/602-948-8009, 800-762-3845; FAX: 602-998-2786
Dina Arms Corp., P.O. Box 46, Royersford, PA 19468/215-287-0266
Division Lead Co., 7742 W. 61st Pl., Summit, IL 60502
Dixie Gun Works, Hwy. 51 South, Union City, TN 38261/901-885-0700, order 800-238-6785; FAX: 901-885-0440
Dixon Muzzleloading Shop, Inc., RD 1, Box 175, Kempton, PA 19529/215-756-6271
DKT, Inc., 14623 Vera Drive, Union, MI 49130-9744/616-641-7120; FAX: 616-641-2015
DLO Mfg., 415 Howe Ave., Shelton, CT 06484/203-924-2952
D-Max, Inc., Rt. 1, Box 473, Bagley, MN 56621
DMT—Diamond Machining Technology, Inc., 85 Hayes Memorial Dr., Marlborough, MA 01752/508-481-5944; FAX: 508-485-3924
D.O.C. Specialists, Inc.; Doc & Bud Ulrich, Jim Amodei, 2209 S. Central Ave., Cicero, IL 60650/708-652-3606; FAX: 708-652-2516
Dohring Bullets, 100 W. 8 Mile Rd., Ferndale, MI 48220
Dolbare, Elizabeth, 39 Dahlia, Casper, WY 82604/307-266-5924
Donnelly, C.P., 405 Kubli Rd., Grants Pass, OR 97527/503-846-6604
Doskocil Mfg. Co., Inc., P.O. Box 1246, Arlington, TX 76004/817-467-5116
Double A Ltd., Dept. ST, Box 1108, Minneapolis, MN 55411
Douglas Barrels, Inc., 5504 Big Tyler Rd., Charleston, WV 25313-1398/304-776-1341; FAX: 304-776-8560
Dowtin Gunworks, Rt. 4, Box 930A, Flagstaff, AZ 86001/602-779-1898
Dr. O's Products Ltd., P.O. Box 111, Niverville, NY 12130/518-784-3333; FAX: 518-784-2800
Dragun Enterprises, P.O. Box 222, Murfreesboro, TN 37133-2222/615-895-7373, 800-467-7375; FAX: 800-829-7536
Drain, Mark, SE 3211 Kamilche Point Rd., Shelton, WA 98584/206-426-5452
Dremel Mfg. Co., 4915-21st St., Racine, WI 53406
Dressel Jr., Paul G., 209 N. 92nd Ave., Yakima, WA 98908/509-966-9233; FAX: 509-966-3365
Dri-Slide, Inc., 411 N. Darling, Fremont, MI 49412/616-924-3950
DTM International, Inc., 40 Joslyn Rd., P.O. Box 5, Lake Orion, MI 48035/313-693-6670
Duane Custom Stocks, Randy, 110 W. North Ave., Winchester, VA 22601/703-667-9461; FAX: 703-722-3993

Dubber, Michael W., P.O. Box 312, Evansville, IN 47702/812-424-9000; FAX: 812-424-6551
Duck Call Specialists, P.O. Box 124, Jerseyville, IL 62052/618-498-9855
Duffy, Charles E., Williams Lane, West Hurley, NY 12491/914-679-2997
Du-Lite Corp., 171 River Rd., Middletown, CT 06457/203-347-2505
Dumoulin, Ernest, Rue Florent Boclinville 8-10, 13-4041 Votten, BELGIUM/41 27 78 92
Duncan's Gun Works, Inc., 1619 Grand Ave., San Marcos, CA 92069/619-727-0515
Dunham Co., P.O. Box 813, Brattleboro, VT 05301/802-254-2316
Dunphy, Ted, W. 5100 Winch Rd., Rathdrum, ID 83858/208-687-1399; FAX: 208-687-1399
Duofold, Inc., 120 W. 45th St., 15th Floor, New York, NY 10036
DuPont (See IMR Powder Co.)
Durward, John, 448 Belgreen Way, Waterloo, Ontario N2L 5X5 CANADA
Dutchman's Firearms, Inc., The, 4143 Taylor Blvd., Louisville, KY 40215/502-366-0555
Duxbak, Inc., 903 Woods Rd., Cambridge, MD 21613/301-228-2990, 800-334-1845
Dybala Gun Shop, P.O. Box 1024, FM 3156, Bay City, TX 77414/409-245-0866
Dykstra, Doug, 411 N. Darling, Fremont, MI 49412/616-924-3950
Dynalite Products, Inc., 215 S. Washington St., Greenfield, OH 45123/513-981-2124
Dynamit Nobel-RWS, Inc., 81 Ruckman Rd., Closter, NJ 07624/201-767-1995; FAX: 201-767-1589
Dyson & Son Ltd., Peter, 29-31 Church St., Honley, Huddersfield, W. Yorkshire HDL7 2AH, ENGLAND/0484-661062; FAX: 0484 663709

E

E&L Mfg., Inc., 39042 N. School House Rd., Cave Creek, AZ 85331/602-488-2598; FAX: 602-488-0813
E.A.A. Corp., P.O. Box 1299, Sharpes, FL 32959/407-639-7006
Eades' Muzzleloader Builders' Supply, Don, 201-J Beasley Dr., Franklin, TN 37064/615-791-1731
Eagan, Donald V., P.O. Box 196, Benton, PA 17814/717-925-6134
Eagle Arms, Inc., 128 E. 23rd Ave., Coal Valley, IL 61240/309-799-5619; FAX: 309-799-5150
Eagle Flight Bullet Co., 925 Lakeville St., Suite 123, Petaluma, CA 94954/707-762-6955
Eagle Grips, Eagle Business Center, 460 Randy Rd., Carol Stream, IL 60188/800-323-6144
Eagle Imports, Inc., 1750 Brielle Ave., Unit B1, Wanamassa, NJ 07712/908-493-0333; FAX: 908-493-0301
Eagle International, Inc., 5195 W. 58th Ave., Suite 300, Arvada, CO 80002/303-426-8100
Eagle Mfg. & Engineering, 2648 Keen Dr., San Diego, CA 92139/619-479-4402; FAX: 619-472-5585
Eagle Products Co., 1520 Adelia Ave., S. El Monte, CA 91733
E-A-R, Inc., Div. of Cabot Safety Corp., 5457 W. 79th St., Indianapolis, IN 46268/800-327-3431; FAX: 800-488-8007
Eastman Products, R.T., P.O. Box 1531, Jackson, WY 83001/307-733-3217, 800-624-4311
Easy Pull Outlaw Products, 316 1st St. East, Polson, MT 59860/406-883-6822
E.A.W. GmbH, Am Kirschberg 3, D-97218 Gerbrunn, GERMANY/0(931)70 71 92
Echols & Co., D'Arcy, 164 W. 580 S., Providence, UT 84332/801-753-2367
Eckelman Gunsmithing, 3125 133rd St. SW, Fort Ripley, MN 56449/218-829-3176
Ed's Gun House, Rt. 1, Box 62, Minnesota City, MN 55959/507-689-2925
Edenpine, Inc. c/o Six Enterprises, Inc., 320 D Turtle Creek Ct., San Jose, CA 95125/408-999-0201; FAX: 408-999-0216
EdgeCraft Corp., P.O. Box 3000, Avondale, PA 19311/215-268-0500, 800-342-3255; FAX: 215-268-3545
Edmisten Co., P.O. Box 1293, Boone, NC 28607
Edmund Scientific Co., 101 E. Gloucester Pike, Barrington, NJ 08033/609-543-6250
Ednar, Inc., 2-4-8 Kayabacho, Nihonbashi, Chuo-ku, Tokyo, JAPAN/81(Japan)-3-3667-1651
Eezox, Inc., P.O. Box 772, Waterford, CT 06385-0772/203-447-8282; FAX: 203-447-3484
Efemes Enterprises, P.O. Box 691, Colchester, VT 05446
Eggleston, Jere D., 400 Saluda Ave., Columbia, SC 29205/803-799-3402
EGW Evolution Gun Works, 4050 B-8 Skyron Dr., Doylestown, PA 18901/215-348-9892; FAX: 215-348-1056
Eichelberger Bullets, Wm., 158 Crossfield Rd., King of Prussia, PA 19406
Eilan S.A.L., Paseo San Andres N8, Eibar, SPAIN 20600/(34)43118916; FAX: (34)43 114038
Eiland Custom Bullets, P.O. Box 688, Buena Vista, CO 81211/719-395-2952
EK Knife Co., 601 N. Lombardy St., Richmond, VA 23220/804-257-7272
Ekol Leather Care, P.O. Box 2652, West Lafayette, IN 47906/317-463-2250; FAX: 317-463-7004
El Dorado Leather, P.O. Box 2603, Tucson, AZ 85702/602-623-0606; FAX: 602-623-0606
El Paso Saddlery Co., P.O. Box 27194, El Paso, TX 79926/915-544-2233; FAX: 915-544-2535
Eldorado Cartridge Corp. (See PMC/Eldorado Cartridge Corp.)
Electro Prismatic Collimators, Inc., 1441 Manatt St., Lincoln, NE 68521
Electronic Trigger Systems, Inc., P.O. Box 13, Hector, MN 55342/612-848-2760
Eley Ltd., P.O. Box 705, Witton, Birmingham, B6 7UT, ENGLAND/21-356-8899; FAX: 21-331-4173
Elite Ammunition, P.O. Box 3251, Oakbrook, IL 60522/708-366-9006
Elk River, Inc., 1225 Paonia St., Colorado Springs, CO 80915/719-574-4407
Elkhorn Bullets, P.O. Box 5293, Central Point, OR 97502/503-826-7440
Elko Arms, Dr. L. Kortz, 28 rue Ecole Moderne, B-7060 Soignies, BELGIUM/(32)67-33-29-34

Ellett Bros., P.O. Box 128, Columbia, SC 29036/803-345-3751, 800-845-3711; FAX: 803-345-1820

Ellicott Arms, Inc./Woods Pistolsmithing, 3840 Dahlgren Ct., Ellicott City, MD 21042/410-465-7979

Ellis Sport Shop, E.W., RD 1, Route 9N, P.O. Box 315, Corinth, NY 12822/518-654-6444

Emerging Technologies, Inc., P.O. Box 3548, Little Rock, AR 72203/501-375-2227; FAX: 501-372-1445

EMF Co., Inc., 1900 E. Warner Ave. Suite 1-D, Santa Ana, CA 92705/714-261-6611; FAX: 714-956-0133

Empire Cutlery Corp., 12 Kruger Ct., Clifton, NJ 07013/201-472-5155; FAX: 201-779-0759

Engineered Accessories, 1307 W. Wabash Ave., Effingham, IL 62401/217-347-7700; FAX: 217-347-7737

English, A.G., 708 S. 12th St., Broken Arrow, OK 74012/918-251-3399

Englishtown Sporting Goods Co., Inc., David J. Maxham, 38 Main St., Englishtown, NJ 07726/201-446-7717

Engraving Artistry, 36 Alto Rd., RFD 2, Burlington, CT 06013/203-673-6837

Enguix Import-Export, Alpujarras 58, Alzira, Valencia, SPAIN 46600/(96) 241 43 95; FAX: (96) 241 43 95

Enhanced Presentations, Inc., 5929 Market St., Wilmington, NC 28405/910-799-1622; FAX: 910-799-5004

Enlow, Charles, 895 Box, Beaver, OK 73932/405-625-4487

Ensign-Bickford Co., The, 660 Hopmeadow St., Simsbury, CT 06070

EPC, 1441 Manatt St., Lincoln, NE 68521/402-476-3946

Epps "Orillia" Ltd., Ellwood, RR 3, Hwy. 11 North, Orillia, Ont. L3V 6H3, CANADA/705-689-5333

Erhardt, Dennis, 3280 Green Meadow Dr., Helena, MT 59601/406-442-4533

Erickson's Mfg., Inc., C.W., 530 Garrison Ave. N.E., Buffalo, MN 55313/612-682-3665; FAX: 612-682-4328

Erma Werke GmbH, Johan Ziegler St., 13/15/FeldiglSt., D-8060 Dachau, GERMANY (U.S. importers—Mandall Shooting Supplies, Inc.; PSI, Inc.)

Essex Arms, P.O. Box 345, Island Pond, VT 05846/802-723-4313

Essex Metals, 1000 Brighton St., Union, NJ 07083/800-282-8369

Estate Cartridge, Inc., 2778 FM 830, Willis, TX 77378/409-856-7277; FAX: 409-856-5486

Euroarms of America, Inc., 208 E. Piccadilly St., Winchester, VA 22601/703-662-1863; FAX: 703-662-4464

European American Armory Corp. (See E.A.A. Corp.)

Europtik Ltd., P.O. Box 319, Dunmore, PA 18512/717-347-6049, 800-873-5362; FAX: 717-969-4330

Eutaw Co., Inc., The, P.O. Box 608, U.S. Hwy. 176 West, Holly Hill, SC 29059/803-496-3341

Evans Engraving, Robert, 332 Vine St., Oregon City, OR 97045/503-656-5693

Evans Gunsmithing, 47532 School St., Oakridge, OR 97463/503-782-4432

Eversull Co., Inc., K., 1 Tracemont, Boyce, LA 71409/318-793-8728; FAX: 318-793-5483

Excaliber Enterprises, P.O. Box 400, Fogelsville, OA 18051-0400/610-391-9106; FAX: 610-391-9223

Exe, Inc., 18830 Partridge Circle, Eden Prairie, MN 55346/612-944-7662

Executive Protection Institute, Rt. 2, Box 3645, Berryville, VA 22611/703-955-1128

Eyears Insurance, 4926 Annhurst Rd., Columbus, OH 43228-1341

Eyster Heritage Gunsmiths, Inc., Ken, 6441 Bishop Rd., Centerburg, OH 43011/614-625-6131

Eze-Lap Diamond Prods., P.O. Box 2229, 15164 Weststate St., Westminster, CA 92683/714-847-1555

E-Z-Way Systems, Box 700, Newark, OH 43058-0700/614-345-6645, 800-848-2072; FAX: 614-345-6600

F

Fabarm S.p.A., Via Averolda 31, 25039 Travagliato (Brescia) ITALY//(030)6863631; FAX: (030)6863684 (U.S. importer—Ithaca Acquisition Corp.)

Fabian Bros. Sporting Goods, Inc., 1510 Morena Blvd., Suite "G", San Diego, CA 92110/619-275-0816; FAX: 619-276-8733

Fabrica D'Armi Sabatti S.R.L., via Dante 179, 25068 Sarezzo, Brescia, ITALY/030-8900590; FAX: 030-8900598 (U.S. importer—E.A.A. Corp.)

Fagan & Co., William, 22952 15 Mile Rd., Mt. Clemens, MI 48043/313-465-4637; FAX: 313-792-6996

Fair Game International, P.O. Box 77234-34053, Houston, TX 77234/713-941-6269

F.A.I.R. Techni-Mec s.n.c. Di Isidoro Rizzini & C., Via Gitti 41, 25060 Marcheno (BS), ITALY

Faith Associates, Inc., 1139 S. Greenville Hwy., Hendersonville, NC 28739/704-692-1916; FAX: 704-697-6827

Fajen, Reinhart, 1000 Red Bud Dr., P.O. Box 338, Warsaw, MO 65355/816-438-5111; FAX: 816-438-5175

Famas (See U.S. importer—Century International Arms, Inc.)

Fanzoj GmbH, Griesgasse 1, 9170 Ferlach, AUSTRIA 9170/(43) 04227-2283; FAX: (43) 04227-2867

FAPA Corp., P.O. Box 1439, New London, NH 03257/603-735-5652; FAX: 603-735-5154

Far North Outfitters, Box 1252, Bethel, AK 99559

Farm Form Decoys, Inc., 1602 Biovu, Galveston, TX 77551/409-744-0762, 409-765-6361; FAX: 409-765-8513

Farmer-Dressel, Sharon, 209 N. 92nd Ave., Yakima, WA 98908/509-966-9233; FAX: 509-966-3365

Farr Studio, Inc., 1231 Robinhood Rd., Greeneville, TN 37743/615-638-8825

Farrar Tool Co., Inc., 12150 Bloomfield Ave., Suite E, Santa Fe Springs, CA 90670/310-863-4367; FAX: 310-863-5123

FAS, Via E. Fermi, 8, 20019 Settimo Milanese, Milano, ITALY/02-3285846; FAX: 02-33500196 (U.S. importer—Nygord Precision Products)

Faulhaber Wildlocker, Dipl.-Ing. Norbert Wittasek, Seilergasse 2, A-1010 Wien, EUROPE

Faulk's Game Call Co., Inc., 616 18th St., Lake Charles, LA 70601/318-436-9726

Faust, Inc., T.G., 544 Minor St., Reading, PA 19602/215-375-8549; FAX: 215-375-4488

Fausti & Figlie s.n.c., Stefano, Via Martiri Dell Indipendenza, 70, Marcheno, ITALY 25060 (U.S. importer—American Arms, Inc.)

Fautheree, Andy, P.O. Box 4607, Pagosa Springs, CO 81157/303-731-5003

Feather Flex Decoys, 1655 Swan Lake Rd., Bossier City, LA 71111/318-746-8596; FAX: 318-742-4815

Feather Industries, Inc., 2300 Central Ave. K, Boulder, CO 80301/303-442-7021; FAX: 303-447-0944

Federal Cartridge Co., 900 Ehlen Dr., Anoka, MN 55303/612-422-2840

Federal Champion Target Co., 232 Industrial Parkway, Richmond, IN 47374/800-441-4971; FAX: 317-966-7747

Federal Engineering Corp., 1090 Bryn Mawr, Bensenville, IL 60106/708-860-1938

Federated-Fry, 6th Ave., 41st St., Altuna, PA 16602/814-946-1611

FEG, Budapest, Soroksariut 158, H-1095 HUNGARY (U.S. importers—Century International Arms, Inc.; K.B.I., Inc.)

Feinwerkbau Westinger & Altenburger GmbH & Co. KG (See FWB)

Feken, Dennis, Rt. 2 Box 124, Perry, OK 73077/405-336-5611

Fellowes, Ted, Beaver Lodge, 9245 16th Ave. SW, Seattle, WA 98106/206-763-1698

Feminine Protection, Inc., 10514 Shady Trail, Dallas, TX 75220/214-351-4500

Ferdinand, Inc., P.O. Box 5, 201 Main St., Harrison, ID 83833/208-689-3012; FAX: 208-689-3142

Ferguson, Bill, P.O. Box 1238, Sierra Vista, AZ 85636

FERLIB, Via Costa 46, 25063 Gardone V.T. (Brescia) ITALY/30 89 12 586; FAX: 30 89 12 586 (U.S. importers—Wm. Larkin Moore & Co.; New England Arms Co.; Pachmayr Co.; Quality Arms, Inc.)

Ferris Firearms, HC 51, Box 1255, Suite 158, Bulverde, TX 78163/210-980-4811

Fibron Products, Inc., 170 Florida St., Buffalo, NY 14208/716-886-2378; FAX: 716-886-2394

Final Option Enterprises, P.O. Box 1128, Easthampton, MA 01027/413-548-8119

Finch Custom Bullets, 40204 La Rochelle, Prairieville, LA 70769

Fiocchi of America, Inc., 5030 Fremont Rd., Ozark, MO 65721/417-725-4118; FAX: 417-725-1039

Firearm Training Center, The, 9555 Blandville Rd., West Paducah, KY 42086/502-554-5886

Firearms Academy of Seattle, P.O. Box 2814, Kirkland, WA 98083/206-820-4853

Firearms Co. Ltd./Alpine (See U.S. importer—Mandall Shooting Supplies, Inc.)

Firearms Engraver's Guild of America, 332 Vine St., Oregon City, OR 97045/503-656-5693

Firearms Safety Products, Inc. (See FSPI)

First Distributors, Inc., Jack, 1201 Turbine, Rapid City, SD 57701/605-343-8481

Fish, Marshall F., Rt. 22 N., P.O. Box 2439, Westport, NY 12993/518-962-4897

Fish-N-Hunt, Inc., 5651 Beechnut St., Houston, TX 77096/713-777-3285; FAX: 713-777-9884

Fisher, Jerry A., 535 Crane Mt. Rd., Big Fork, MT 59911/406-837-2722

Fisher Custom Firearms, 2199 S. Kittredge Way, Aurora, CO 80013/303-755-3710

Fisher Enterprises, 655 Main St. 305, Edmonds, WA 98020/206-776-4365

Fitz Pistol Grip Co., P.O. Box 610, Douglas City, CA 96024/916-623-4019

Flaig's, 2200 Evergreen Rd., Millvale, PA 15209/412-821-1717

Flambeau Products Corp., 15981 Valplast Rd., Middlefield, OH 44062/216-632-1631; FAX: 216-632-1581

Flannery Engraving Co., Jeff W., 11034 Riddles Run Rd., Union, KY 41091/606-384-3127

Flashette Co., 4725 S. Kolin Ave., Chicago, IL 60632/312-927-1302; FAX: 312-927-3083

Flayderman & Co., Inc., N., P.O. Box 2446, Ft. Lauderdale, FL 33303/305-761-8855

Fleming Firearms, 9525-J East 51st St., Tulsa, OK 74145/918-665-3624

Flents Products Co., Inc., P.O. Box 2109, Norwalk, CT 06852/203-866-2581; FAX: 203-854-9322

Flintlock Muzzle Loading Gun Shop, The, 1238 "G" S. Beach Blvd., Anaheim, CA 92804/714-821-6655

Flintlocks, Etc. (See Beauchamp & Son, Inc.)

Flitz International Ltd., 821 Mohr Ave., Waterford, WI 53185/414-534-5898; FAX: 414-534-2991

Floatstone Mfg. Co., 106 Powder Mill Rd., P.O. Box 765, Canton, CT 06019/203-693-1977

Flores Publications, Inc., J., P.O. Box 830131, Miami, FL 33283/305-559-4652

Flouramics, Inc., 18 Industrial Ave., Mahwah, NJ 07430/800-922-0075; FAX: 201-825-7035

Flow-Rite of Tennessee, Inc., 107 Allen St., Bruceton, TN 38317/901-586-2271; FAX: 901-586-2300

Flynn's Custom Guns, P.O. Box 7461, Alexandria, LA 71306/318-455-7130

FN Herstal, Voie de Liege 33, Herstal 4040, BELGIUM/(32)41.40.82.83; FAX: (32)40.86.79

Fobus International Ltd., Kfar Hess, ISRAEL 40692/972-9-911716; FAX: 972-9-911716

Fogle, James W., RR 2, P.O. Box 258, Herrin, IL 62948/618-988-1795

Folks, Donald E., 205 W. Lincoln St., Pontiac, IL 61764/815-844-7901

Foothills Video Productions, Inc., P.O. Box 651, Spartanburg, SC 29304/803-573-7023, 800-782-5358

Ford, Jack, 1430 Elkwood, Missouri City, TX 77489/713-499-9984

Foredom Electric Co., Rt. 6, 16 Stony Hill Rd., Bethel, CT 06801/203-792-8622

Forgett Jr., Valmore J., 689 Bergen Blvd., Ridgefield, NJ 07657/201-945-2500; FAX: 201-945-6859

Forgreens Tool Mfg., Inc., P.O. Box 990, Robert Lee, TX 76945/915-453-2800

Forrest, Inc., Tom, P.O. Box 326, Lakeside, CA 92040/619-561-5800; FAX: 619-561-0227

Forrest Tool Co., P.O. Box 768, 44380 Gordon Lane, Mendocino, CA 95460/707-937-2141; FAX: 717-937-1817

Forster, Kathy (See Custom Checkering Service)

Forster, Larry L., P.O. Box 212, 220 First St. NE, Gwinner, ND 58040-0212/701-678-2475

Forster Products, 82 E. Lanark Ave., Lanark, IL 61046/815-493-6360; FAX: 815-493-2371

Fort Hill Gunstocks, 12807 Fort Hill Rd., Hillsboro, OH 45133/513-466-2763

Fort Knox Security Products, 1051 N. Industrial Park Rd., Orem, UT 84057/801-224-7233

Forthofer's Gunsmithing & Knifemaking, 5535 U.S. Hwy 93S, Whitefish, MT 59937-8411/406-862-2674

Fortune Products, Inc., HC04, Box 303, Marble Falls, TX 78654/210-693-6111; FAX: 210-693-6394

Forty Five Ranch Enterprises, Box 1080, Miami, OK 74355-1080/918-542-5875

Fouling Shot, The, 6465 Parfet St., Arvada, CO 80004

Fountain Products, 492 Prospect Ave., West Springfield, MA 01089/413-781-4651; FAX: 413-733-8217

4-D Custom Die Co., 711 N. Sandusky St., P.O. Box 889, Mt. Vernon, OH 43050-0889/614-397-7214; FAX: 614-397-6600

4W Ammunition, Rt. 1, P.O. Box 313, Tioga, TX 76271/817-437-2458; FAX: 817-437-2228

Fowler Bullets, 806 Dogwood Dr., Gastonia, NC 28054/704-867-3259

Fox River Mills, Inc., P.O. Box 298, 227 Poplar St., Osage, IA 50461/515-732-3798; FAX: 515-732-5128

Foy Custom Bullets, 104 Wells Ave., Daleville, AL 36322

Francesca, Inc., 3115 Old Ranch Rd., San Antonio, TX 78217/512-826-2584; FAX: 512-826-8211

Franchi S.p.A., Luigi, Via del Serpente, 12, 25020 Fornaci, ITALY (U.S. importer—American Arms, Inc.)

Francolini, Leonard, 106 Powder Mill Rd., P.O. Box 765, Canton, CT 06019/203-693-1977

Francotte & Cie S.A., Auguste, rue du Trois Juin 109, 4400 Herstal-Liege, BELGIUM/41-48.13.18; FAX: 41-48.11.79 (U.S. importer—Armes de Chasse)

Frank Custom Gun Service, Ron, 7131 Richland Rd., Ft. Worth, TX 76118/817-284-4426; FAX: 817-284-9300

Frank Knives, Box 984, Whitefish, MT 59937/406-862-2681; FAX: 406-862-2681

Frankonia Jagd, Hofmann & Co., D-97064 Wurzburg, GERMANY/09302-200; FAX: 09302-20200

Frazier Brothers Enterprises, 1118 N. Main St., Franklin, IN 46131/317-736-4000; FAX: 317-736-4000

Fredrick Gun Shop, 10 Elson Dr., Riverside, RI 02915/401-433-2805

Freedom Arms, Inc., P.O. Box 1776, Freedom, WY 83120/307-883-2468; FAX: 307-883-2005

Freeman Animal Targets, 2559 W. Morris St., Plainsfield, IN 46168/317-271-5314; FAX: 317-271-9106

Fremont Tool Works, 1214 Prairie, Ford, KS 67842/316-369-2338

French, J.R., 1712 Creek Ridge Ct., Irving, TX 75060/214-254-2654

Frielich Police Equipment, 211 East 21st St., New York, NY 10010/212-254-3045

From Jena, Europtik Ltd., P.O. Box 319, Dunmore, PA 18512/717-347-6049, 800-873-5362; FAX: 717-969-4330

Frontier, 2910 San Bernardo, Laredo, TX 78040/512-723-5409

Frontier Arms Co., Inc., 401 W. Rio Santa Cruz, Green Valley, AZ 85614-3932

Frontier Products Co., 164 E. Longview Ave., Columbus, OH 43202/614-262-9357

Frontier Safe Co., 1317 Chute St., Fort Wayne, IN 46803/219-422-4801

Frost Cutlery Co., P.O. Box 22636, Chattanooga, TN 37422/615-894-6079; FAX: 615-894-9576

FSPI, 5885 Glenridge Dr. Suite 220A, Atlanta, GA 30328/404-843-2881; FAX: 404-843-0271

Fujinon, Inc., 10 High Point Dr., Wayne, NJ 07470/201-633-5600

Fullmer, Geo M., 2499 Mavis St., Oakland, CA 94601/510-533-4193

Fulmer's Antique Firearms, Chet, P.O. Box 792, Rt. 2 Buffalo Lake, Detroit Lakes, MN 56501/218-847-7712

Fulton Armory, 8725 Bollman Place No. 1, Savage, MD 20763/301-490-9485; FAX: 301-490-9547

Furr Arms, 91 N. 970 W., Orem, UT 84057/801-226-3877; FAX: 801-226-0085

Fury Cutlery, 801 Broad Ave., Ridgefield, NJ 07657/201-943-5920; FAX: 201-943-1579

Fusilier Bullets, 10010 N. 6000 W., Highland, UT 84003/801-756-6813

FWB, Neckarstrasse 43, 78727 Oberndorf a. N., GERMANY/07423-814-0; FAX: 07423-814-89 (U.S. importer—Beeman Precision Airguns, Inc.)

G

G3 & Co., 18 Old Northville Rd., New Milford, CT 06776/203-354-7500

G96 Products Co., Inc., 237 River St., Paterson, NJ 07524/201-684-4050; FAX: 201-684-3848

G&C Bullet Co., Inc., 8835 Thornton Rd., Stockton, CA 95209

G&H Decoys, Inc., P.O. Box 1208, Hwy. 75 North, Henryetta, OK 74437/918-652-3314

Gage Manufacturing, 663 W. 7th St., San Pedro, CA 90731

Gaillard Barrels, P.O. Box 21, Pathlow, Sask., S0K 3B0 CANADA/306-752-3769; FAX: 306-752-5969

Galati International, P.O. Box 326, Catawissa, MO 63015/314-257-4837; FAX: 314-257-2268

Galaxy Imports Ltd., Inc., P.O. Box 3361, Victoria, TX 77903/512-573-4867; FAX: 512-576-9622

Galazan, Div. of Connecticut Shotgun Mfg. Co., P.O. Box 622, 35 Woodland St., New Britain, CT 06051-0622/203-225-6581; FAX: 203-832-8707

GALCO International Ltd., 2019 W. Quail Ave., Phoenix, AZ 85027/602-258-8295; FAX: 602-582-6854

Gamba S.p.A., Renato, Via Artigiani, 93, 25063 Gardone V.T. (Brescia), ITALY (U.S. importers—Giacomo Sporting, Inc.; New England Arms Co.)

Game Haven Gunstocks, 13750 Shire Rd., Wolverine, MI 49799/616-525-8257

Game Winner, Inc., 2625 Cumberland Parkway, Suite 220, Atlanta, GA 30339/404-434-9210; FAX: 404-434-9215

Gammog, Gregory B. Gally, 16009 Kenny Rd., Laurel, MD 20707/301-725-3838

Gamo (See U.S. importers—Daisy Mfg. Co.; Dynamit Nobel-RWS, Inc.)

Gander Mountain, Inc., P.O. Box 128, Hwy. "W,", Wilmot, WI 53192/414-862-2331,Ext. 6425

Ganton Manufacturing Ltd., Depot Lane, Seamer Rd., Scarborough, North Yorkshire, Y012 4EB ENGLAND/0723-371910; FAX: 0723-501671

GAR, 139 Park Lane, Wayne, NJ 07470/201-256-7641

Garbi, Armas Urki, 12-14, 20.600 Eibar (Guipuzcoa) SPAIN/43-11 38 73 (U.S. importer—Moore & Co., Wm. Larkin)

Garcia National Gun Traders, Inc., 225 SW 22nd Ave., Miami, FL 33135/305-642-2355

Garrett Cartridges, Inc., P.O. Box 178, Chehalis, WA 98532/206-736-0702

Garthwaite, Jim, Rt. 2, Box 310, Watsontown, PA 17777/717-538-1566

Gator Guns & Repair, 6255 Spur Hwy., Kenai, AK 99611/907-283-7947

Gaucher Armes, S.A., 46, rue Desjoyaux, 42000 Saint-Etienne, FRANCE/77 33 38 92; FAX: 767 41 95 72 (U.S. importer—Mandall Shooting Supplies, Inc.)

G.B.C. Industries, Inc., P.O. Box 1602, Spring, TX 77373/713-350-9690; FAX: 713-350-0601

G.C.C.T., 4455 Torrance Blvd., Ste. 453, Torrance, CA 90509-2806

GDL Enterprises, 409 Le Gardeur, Slidell, LA 70460/504-649-0693

Gehmann, Walter (See Huntington Die Specialties)

Genco, P.O. Box 5704, Asheville, NC 28803

Gene's Custom Guns, P.O. Box 10534, White Bear Lake, MN 55110/612-429-5105

Gene's Gun Shop, Rt. 1 Box 890, Snyder, TX 79549/915-573-2323

Genecco Gun Works, K., 10512 Lower Sacramento Rd., Stockton, CA 95210/209-951-0706

General Lead, Inc., 1022 Grand Ave., Phoenix, AZ 85007

Gentry Custom Gunmaker, David, 314 N. Hoffman, Belgrade, MT 59714/406-388-4867

George & Roy's, 2950 NW 29th, Portland, OR 97210/800-553-3022; FAX: 503-225-9409

George, Tim, Rt. 1, P.O. Box 45, Evington, VA 24550/804-821-8117

Gerber Legendary Blades, 14200 SW 72nd Ave., Portland, OR 97223/503-639-6161; FAX: 503-684-7008

Gervais, Mike, 3804 S. Cruise Dr., Salt Lake City, UT 84109/801-277-7729

Getz Barrel Co., P.O. Box 88, Beavertown, PA 17813/717-658-7263

GFR Corp., P.O. Box 430, Andover, NH 03216/603-735-5300

G.H. Enterprises Ltd., Bag 10, Okotoks, Alberta T0L 1T0 CANADA/403-938-6070

Giacomo Sporting, Inc., Delta Plaza, Rt. 26N, Rome, NY 13440

Gibbs Rifle Co., Inc., Cannon Hill Industrial Park, Rt. 2, Box 214 Hoffman, Rd./Martinsburg, WV 25401/304-274-0458; FAX: 304-274-0078

Gilbert Equipment Co., Inc., 960 Downtowner Rd., Mobile, AL 36609/205-344-3322

Gillmann, Edwin, 33 Valley View Dr., Hanover, PA 17331/717-632-1662

Gilman-Mayfield, Inc., 3279 E. Shields, Fresno, CA 93703/209-221-9415; FAX: 209-221-9419

Gilmore, 5949 S. Garnett, Tulsa, OK 74146/918-250-4867; FAX: 918-250-3845

Giron, Robert E., 1328 Pocono St., Pittsburgh, PA 15218/412-731-6041

Glacier Glove, 4890 Aircenter Circle 206, Reno, NV 89502/702-825-8225; FAX: 702-825-6544

Glaser Safety Slug, Inc., P.O. Box 8223, Foster City, CA 94404/800-221-3489, 415-345-7677; FAX: 415-345-8217

Glass, Herb, P.O. Box 25, Bullville, NY 10915/914-361-3021

Glimm, Jerome C., 19 S. Maryland, Conrad, MT 59425/406-278-3574

Glock, Inc., 6000 Highlands Parkway, Smyrna, GA 30082/404-433-8719

Glock GmbH, P.O. Box 50, A-2232 Deutsch Wagram, AUSTRIA (U.S. importer—Glock, Inc.)

GML Products, Inc., 394 Laredo Dr., Birmingham, AL 35226/205-979-4867

Goddard, Allen, 716 Medford Ave., Hayward, CA 94541/510-276-6830

Goens, Dale W., P.O. Box 224, Cedar Crest, NM 87008/505-281-5419

Goergen's Gun Shop, Inc., Rt. 2, Box 182BB, Austin, MN 55912/507-433-9280

GOEX, Inc., 1002 Springbrook Ave., Moosic, PA 18507/717-457-6724; FAX: 717-457-1130

Golden Age Arms Co., 115 E. High St., Ashley, OH 43003/614-747-2488

Gonic Arms, Inc., 134 Flagg Rd., Gonic, NH 03839/603-332-8456, 603-332-8457

Gonzalez Guns, Ramon B., P.O. Box 370, Monticello, NY 12701/914-794-4515

Goodling's Gunsmithing, R.D. 1, Box 1097, Spring Grove, PA 17362/717-225-3350

Goodwin, Fred, Silver Ridge Gun Shop, Sherman Mills, ME 04776/207-365-4451

Gordie's Gun Shop, 1401 Fulton St., Streator, IL 61364/815-672-7202

Gotz Bullets, 7313 Rogers St., Rockford, IL 61111

Goudy Classic Stocks, Gary, 263 Hedge Rd., Menlo Park, CA 94025-1711/415-322-1338

Gould & Goodrich, P.O. Box 1479, Lillington, NC 27546/919-893-2071; FAX: 919-893-4742

Gournet, Geoffroy, 820 Paxinosa Ave., Easton, PA 18042/215-559-0710

Gozon Corp., P.O. Box 6278, 152 Bittercreek Dr., Folsom, CA 95630/916-983-1807; FAX: 916-983-9500

Grace, Charles E., 6943 85.5 Rd., Trinchera, CO 81081/719-846-9435

Grace Metal Products, Inc., P.O. Box 67, Elk Rapids, MI 49629/616-264-8133

Grace Tool Co., 3661 E. 44th St., Tucson, AZ 85713/602-747-0213

"Gramps" Antique Cartridges, Box 341, Washago, Ont. L0K 2B0 CANADA/705-689-5348

Grand Falls Bullets, Inc., 1120 Forest Dr., Blue Springs, MO 64015/816-229-0112

Granger, Georges, 66 cours Fauriel, 42100 Saint Etienne, FRANCE/(77)25 14 73

Granite Custom Bullets, Box 190, Philipsburg, MT 59858/406-859-3245

Grant, Howard V., Hiawatha 15, Woodruff, WI 54568/715-356-7146

Graphics Direct, 18336 Gault St., Reseda, CA 91335/818-344-9002

Graves Co., 1800 Andrews Av., Pompano Beach, FL 33069/800-327-9103; FAX: 305-960-0301

Graybill's Gun Shop, 1035 Ironville Pike, Columbia, PA 17512/717-684-2739

Great 870 Co., The, P.O. Box 6309, El Monte, CA 91734
Great Lakes Airguns, 6175 S. Park Ave., Hamburg, NY 14075/716-648-6666;
  FAX: 716-648-5279
Green, Arthur S., 485 S. Robertson Blvd., Beverly Hills, CA 90211/310-274-1283
Green, Roger M., P.O. Box 984, 435 E. Birch, Glenrock, WY 82637/307-436-9804
Green Bay Bullets, 1638 Hazelwood Dr., Sobieski, WI 54171/414-826-7760
Green Genie, Box 114, Cusseta, GA 31805
Green Head Game Call Co., RR 1, Box 33, Lacon, IL 61540/309-246-2155
Green Mountain Rifle Barrel Co., Inc., RFD 2, Box 8 Center, Conway, NH
  03813/603-356-2047; FAX: 603-356-2048
Greene, M.L., 17200 W. 57th Ave., Golden, CO 80403/303-279-2383
Greenwald, Leon E. "Bud", 2553 S. Quitman St., Denver, CO
  80219/303-935-3850
Greenwood Precision, P.O. Box 468, Nixa, MO 65714-0468/417-725-2330
Greg Gunsmithing Repair, 3732 26th Ave. North, Robbinsdale, MN
  55422/612-529-8103
Greg's Superior Products, P.O. Box 46219, Seattle, WA 98146
Greider Precision, 431 Santa Marina Ct., Escondido, CA 92029/619-480-8892
Gremmel Enterprises, 271 Sterling Dr., Eugene, OR 97404/503-688-3319
Grendel, Inc., P.O. Box 560909, Rockledge, FL 32956-0909/800-274-7427,
  407-636-1211; FAX: 407-633-6710
Griffin & Howe, Inc., 33 Claremont Rd., Bernardsville, NJ
  07924/908-766-2287; FAX: 908-766-1068
Griffin & Howe, Inc., 36 W. 44th St., Suite 1011, New York, NY
  10036/212-921-0980
Grifon, Inc., 58 Guinam St., Waltham, MS 02154
Grip-Master, P.O. Box 32, Westbury, NY 11490/800-752-0164; FAX:
  516-997-5142
Grizzly Bullets, 2137 Hwy. 200, Trout Creek, MT 59874/406-847-2627
Group Tight Bullets, 482 Comerwood Court, San Francisco, CA
  94080/415-583-1550
GRS Corp., Glendo, P.O. Box 1153, 900 Overlander St., Emporia, KS
  66801/316-343-1084
Grulla Armes, Apartado 453, Avda Otaloa, 12, Eiber, SPAIN
  (U.S. importer—American Arms, Inc.)
GSI, Inc., 108 Morrow Ave., P.O. Box 129, Trussville, AL
  35173/205-655-8299; FAX: 205-655-7078
G.U., Inc., 4325 S. 120th St., Omaha, NE 68137/402-330-4492
Guardsman Products, 411 N. Darling, Fremont, MI 49412/616-924-3950
Gun City, 212 W. Main Ave., Bismarck, ND 58501/701-223-2304
Gun Doctor, The, 435 East Maple, Roselle, IL 60172/708-894-0668
Gun Doctor, The, P.O. Box 39242, Downey, CA 90242/310-862-3158
Gun Hunter Books, Div. of Gun Hunter Trading Co., 5075 Heisig St.,
  Beaumont, TX 77705/409-835-3006
Gun Leather Limited, 116 Lipscomb, Ft. Worth, TX 76104/817-334-0225;
  800-247-0609
Gun List (See Krause Publications)
Gun Locker, Div. of Airmold, W.R. Grace & Co.-Conn., Becker Farms Ind.
  Park,, P.O. Box 610/Roanoke Rapids, NC 27870/800-344-5716; FAX:
  919-536-2201
Gun Parts Corp., The, 226 Williams Lane, West Hurley, NY
  12491/914-679-2417; FAX: 914-679-5849
Gun Room Press, The, 127 Raritan Ave., Highland Park, NJ
  08904/908-545-4344; FAX: 908-545-6686
Gun Room, The, 1121 Burlington, Muncie, IN 47302/317-282-9073; FAX:
  317-282-9073
Gun Shop, The, 5550 S. 900 East, Salt Lake City, UT 84117/801-263-3633
Gun Shop, The, 62778 Spring Creek Rd., Montrose, CO 81401
Gun South, Inc. (See GSI, Inc.)
Gun Works, The, 236 Main St., Springfield, OR 97477/503-741-4118
Gun-Alert, Master Products, Inc., 1010 N. Maclay Ave., San Fernando, CA
  91340/818-365-0864; FAX: 818-365-1308
Guncraft Books (See Guncraft Sports, Inc.)
Guncraft Sports, Inc., 10737 Dutchtown Rd., Knoxville, TN
  37932/615-966-4545; FAX: 615-966-4500
Gunfitters, The, P.O. 426, Cambridge, WI 53523-0426/608-764-8128
Gun-Ho Sports Cases, 110 E. 10th St., St. Paul, MN 55101/612-224-9491
Gunline Tools, P.O. Box 478, Placentia, CA 92670/714-528-5252; FAX:
  714-572-4128
Gunnerman Books, P.O. Box 214292, Auburn Hills, MI 48321/810-879-2779
Guns, 81 E. Streetsboro St., Hudson, OH 44236/216-650-4563
Guns, Div. of D.C. Engineering, Inc., 8633 Southfield Fwy., Detroit, MI
  48228/313-271-7111, 800-886-7623 (orders only); FAX: 313-271-7112
Guns, Gear & Gadgets, L.L.C., P.O. Box 35722, Tucson, AZ
  85240-5222/602-747-9578; FAX: 602-747-9715
GUNS Magazine, 591 Camino de la Reina, Suite 200, San Diego, CA
  92108/619-297-5350; FAX: 619-297-5353
Guns Unlimited, Inc. (See G.U., Inc.)
Gunsight, The, 1712 North Placentia Ave., Fullerton, CA 92631
Gunsite Gunsmithy, P.O. Box 451, Paulden, AZ 86334/602-636-4565; FAX:
  602-636-1236
Gunsite Training Center, P.O. Box 700, Paulden, AZ 86334/602-636-4565;
  FAX: 602-636-1236
Gunsmith in Elk River, The, 14021 Victoria Lane, Elk River, MN
  55330/612-441-7761
Gunsmithing Ltd., 57 Unquowa Rd., Fairfield, CT 06430/203-254-0436
Gun-Tec, P.O. Box 8125, W. Palm Beach, FL 33407
Gurney, F.R., Box 13, Sooke, BC V0S 1N0 CANADA/604-642-5282
Gusdorf Corp., 11440 Lackland Rd., St. Louis, MO 63146/314-567-5249
Gusty Winds Corp., 2950 Bear St., Suite 120, Costa Mesa, CA
  92626/714-536-3587
Gutmann Cutlery Co., Inc., 120 S. Columbus Ave., Mt. Vernon, NY
  10553/914-699-4044
Gwinnell, Bryson J., P.O. Box 248C, Maple Hill Rd., Rochester, VT
  05767/802-767-3664
GZ Paintball Sports Products, P.O. Box 430, Andover, NH
  03216/603-735-5300; FAX: 603-735-5154

H

H&B Forge Co., Rt. 2 Geisinger Rd., Shiloh, OH 44878/419-895-1856
H&L Gun Works, 817 N. Highway 90 1109, Sierra Vista, AZ
  85635/602-452-0702
H&P Publishing, 7174 Hoffman Rd., San Angelo, TX 76905/915-655-5953
H&R 1871, Inc., 60 Industrial Rowe, Gardner, MA 01440/508-632-9393; FAX:
  508-632-2300
H&S Liner Service, 515 E. 8th, Odessa, TX 79761/915-332-1021
Hafner Creations, Inc., Rt. 1, P.O. Box 248A, Lake City, FL
  32055/904-755-6481
Hagn Rifles & Actions, Martin, P.O. Box 444, Cranbrook, B.C. V1C 4H9,
  CANADA/604-489-4861
Hakko Co. Ltd., 5F Daini-Tsunemi Bldg., 1-13-12, Narimasu, Itabashiku
  Tokyo 175, JAPAN/(03)5997-7870-2
Hale, Peter, 800 E. Canyon Rd., Spanish Fork, UT 84660/801-798-8215
Half Moon Rifle Shop, 490 Halfmoon Rd., Columbia Falls, MT
  59912/406-892-4409
Hall Manufacturing, 1801 Yellow Leaf Rd., Clanton, AL 35045/205-755-4094
Hall Plastics, Inc., John, P.O. Box 1526, Alvin, TX 77512/713-489-8709
Hallberg Gunsmith, Fritz, 33 S. Main, Payette, ID 83661
Hallowell & Co., 340 W. Putnam Ave., Greenwich, CT 06830/203-869-2190;
  FAX: 203-869-0692
Hally Caller, 443 Wells Rd., Doylestown, PA 18901/215-345-6354
Halstead, Rick, RR4, Box 272, Miami, OK 74354/515-236-5904
Hamilton, Alex B. (See Ten-Ring Precision, Inc.)
Hamilton, Keith, P.O. Box 871, Gridley, CA 95948/916-846-2316
Hammans, Charles E., P.O. Box 788, 2022 McCracken, Stuttgart, AR
  72106/501-673-1388
Hämmerli Ltd., Seonerstrasse 37, CH-5600 Lenzburg,
  SWITZERLAND/064-50 11 44; FAX: 064-51 38 27
  (U.S. importers—Beeman Precision Ariguns, Inc.; Hammerli USA; Mandall
  Shooting Supplies, Inc.)
Hammerli USA, 19296 Oak Grove Circle, Groveland, CA
  95321/209-962-5311; FAX: 209-962-5931
Hammets VLD Bullets, P.O. Box 479, Rayville, LA 71269/318-728-2019
Hammond Custom Guns Ltd., Guy, 619 S. Pandora, Gilbert, AZ
  85234/602-892-3437
Hammonds Rifles, RD 4, Box 504, Red Lion, PA 17356/717-244-7879
Hand Engravers Supply Co., 601 Springfield Dr., Albany, GA
  31707/912-432-9683
Handgun Press, P.O. Box 406, Glenview, IL 60025/708-657-6500; FAX:
  708-724-8831
HandiCrafts Unltd. (See Clements' Custom Leathercraft, Chas)
Handloader's Journal, 60 Cottage St. 11, Hughesville, PA 17737
Hands, Barry Lee, 26184 E. Shore Route, Bigfork, MT 59911/406-837-0035
Hank's Gun Shop, Box 370, 50 West 100 South, Monroe, UT
  84754/801-527-4456
Hanned Line, The, P.O. Box 161565, Cupertino, CA 95016-1565/408-345-3414
Hanned Precision (See Hanned Line, The)
Hansen & Co. (See Hansen Cartridge Co.)
Hansen Cartridge Co., 244 Old Post Rd., Southport, CT 06490/203-259-5424
  ext. 260
Hanson's Gun Center, Dick, 233 Everett Dr., Colorado Springs, CO 80911
Hanusin, John, 3306 Commercial, Northbrook, IL 60062/708-564-2706
Hardin Specialty Dist., P.O. Box 338, Radcliff, KY 40159-0338/502-351-6649
Hardison, Charles, P.O. Box 356, 200 W. Baseline Rd., Lafayette, CO
  80026-0356/303-666-5171
Harold's Custom Gun Shop, Inc., Rt. 1, Box 447, Big Spring, TX
  79720/915-394-4430
Harper, William E. (See Great 870 Co., The)
Harper's Custom Stocks, 928 Lombrano St., San Antonio, TX
  78207/512-732-5780
Harrell's Precision, 5756 Hickory Dr., Salem, VA 24133/703-380-2683
Harrington & Richardson (See H&R 1871, Inc.)
Harrington Cutlery, Inc., Russell, Subs. of Hyde Mfg. Co., 44 River St.,
  Southbridge, MA 01550/617-765-0201
Harris Engineering, Inc., Rt. 1, Barlow, KY 42024/502-334-3633; FAX:
  502-334-3000
Harris Enterprises, P.O. Box 105, Bly, OR 97622/503-353-2625
Harris Hand Engraving, Paul A., 10630 Janet Lee, San Antonio, TX
  78230/512-391-5121
Harrison-Hurtz Enterprises, Inc., P.O. Box 268, RR1, Wymore, NE
  68466/402-645-3378; FAX: 402-645-3606
Hart & Son, Inc., Robert W., 401 Montgomery St., Nescopeck, PA
  18635/717-752-3655; FAX: 717-752-1088
Hart Rifle Barrels, Inc., RD 2, Apulia Rd., P.O. Box 182, Lafayette, NY
  13084/315-677-9841; FAX: 315-677-9610
Hartmann & Weiss GmbH, Rahlstedter Bahnhofstr. 47, 22143 Hamburg,
  GERMANY/(40) 677 55 85; FAX: (40) 677 55 92
Harwood, Jack O., 1191 S. Pendlebury Lane, Blackfoot, ID 83221/208-785-5368
Haselbauer Products, Jerry, P.O. Box 27629, Tucson, AZ 85726/602-792-1075
Hastings Barrels, 320 Court St., Clay Center, KS 67432/913-632-3169; FAX:
  913-632-6554
Hatfield Gun Co., Inc., 224 N. 4th St., St. Joseph, MO 64501/816-279-8688;
  FAX: 816-279-2716
Hawk Co., P.O. Box 1689, Glenrock, WY 82637/307-436-5561
Hawken Shop, The (See Dayton Traister)
Haydel's Game Calls, Inc., 5018 Hazel Jones Rd., Bossier City, LA
  71111/318-746-3586; FAX: 318-746-3711
Haydon Shooters' Supply, Russ, 15018 Goodrich Dr. NW, Gig Harbor, WA
  98329/206-857-7557
Heatbath Corp., P.O. Box 2978, Springfield, MA 01101/413-543-3381
Hebard Guns, Gil, 125-129 Public Square, Knoxville, IL 61448
HEBB Resources, P.O. Box 999, Mead, WA 99021-09996/509-466-1292
Hecht, Hubert J., Waffen-Hecht, P.O. Box 2635, Fair Oaks, CA
  95628/916-966-1020

Heckler & Koch, Inc., 21480 Pacific Blvd., Sterling, VA 20166/703-450-1900; FAX: 703-450-8160

Heckler & Koch GmbH, Postfach 1329, D-7238 Oberndorf, Neckar, GERMANY (U.S. importer—Heckler & Koch, Inc.)

Hege Jagd-u. Sporthandels, GmbH, P.O. Box 101461, W-7770 Ueberlingen a. Bodensee, GERMANY

Heidenstrom Bullets, Urds GT 1 Heroya, 3900 Porsgrunn, NORWAY

Heilmann, Stephen, P.O. Box 657, Grass Valley, CA 95945/916-272-8758

Heinie Specialty Products, 323 W. Franklin St., Havana, IL 62644/309-543-4535; FAX: 309-543-2521

Heintz, David, 800 N. Hwy. 17, Moffat, CO 81143/719-256-4194

Hellweg Ltd., 40356 Oak Park Way, Suite H, Oakhurst, CA 93644/209-683-3030; FAX: 209-683-3422

Helwan (See U.S. importer—Interarms)

Henckels Zwillingswerk, Inc., J.A., 9 Skyline Dr., Hawthorne, NY 10532/914-592-7370

Hendricks, Frank E., Master Engravers, Inc., HC03, Box 434, Dripping Springs, TX 78620/512-858-7828

Henigson & Associates, Steve, 2049 Kerwood Ave., Los Angeles, CA 90025/213-305-8288

Henriksen Tool Co., Inc., 8515 Wagner Creek Rd., Talent, OR 97540/503-535-2309

Hensler, Jerry, 6614 Country Field, San Antonio, TX 78240/210-690-7491

Hensley & Gibbs, Box 10, Murphy, OR 97533/503-862-2341

Hensley, Darwin, P.O. Box 329, Brightwood, OR 97011/503-622-5411

Heppler, Keith M., Keith's Custom Gunstocks, 540 Banyan Circle, Walnut Creek, CA 94598/510-934-3509; FAX: 510-934-3143

Heppler's Machining, 2240 Calle Del Mundo, Santa Clara, CA 95054/408-748-9166; FAX: 408-988-7711

Hercules, Inc., Hercules Plaza, 1313 N Market St., Wilmington, DE 19894/800-276-9337

Heritage Firearms, 4600 NW 135th St., Opa Locka, FL 33054/305-685-5966; FAX: 305-687-6721

Hermann Leather Co., H.J., Rt. 1, P.O. Box 525, Skiatook, OK 74070/918-396-1226

Herrett's Stocks, Inc., P.O. Box 741, Twin Falls, ID 83303/208-733-1498

Hertel & Reuss, Werk für Optik und Feinmechanik GmbH, Quellhofstrabe 67, 34 127 Kassel, GERMANY/0561-83006; FAX: 0561-893308

Herter's Manufacturing, Inc., 111 E. Burnett St., P.O. Box 518, Beaver Dam, WI 53916/414-887-1765; FAX: 414-887-8444

Hesco-Meprolight, 2821 Greenville Rd., LaGrange, GA 30240/706-884-7967; FAX: 706-882-4683

Heydenberk, Warren R., 1059 W. Sawmill Rd., Quakertown, PA 18951/215-538-2682

Heym GmbH & Co. KG, Friedrich Wilh, Coburger Str.8, D-97702 Muennerstadt, GERMANY (U.S. importers—JägerSport, Ltd.; Swarovski Optik North America Ltd.)

HH Engineering, Box 642, Dept. HD, Narberth, PA 19072-0642

Hickman, Jaclyn, Box 1900, Glenrock, WY 82637

Hidalgo, Tony, 12701 SW 9th Pl., Davie, FL 33325/305-476-7645

High Bridge Arms, Inc., 3185 Mission St., San Francisco, CA 94110/415-282-8358

High North Products, Inc., P.O. Box 2, Antigo, WI 54409

High Performance International, 5734 W. Florist Ave., Milwaukee, WI 53218/414-466-9040

Highline Machine Co., 654 Lela Place, Grand Junction, CO 81504/303-434-4971

Hi-Grade Imports, 8655 Monterey Rd., Gilroy, CA 95021/408-842-9301; FAX: 408-842-2374

Hill, Loring F., 304 Cedar Rd., Elkins Park, PA 19117

Hill Speed Leather, Ernie, 4507 N. 195th Ave., Litchfield Park, AZ 85340/602-853-9222; FAX: 602-853-9235

Hillmer Custom Gunstocks, Paul D., 7251 Hudson Heights, Hudson, IA 50643/319-988-3941

Hindman, Ace, 1880 ½ Upper Turtle Creek Rd., Kerrville, TX 78028/512-257-4290

Hinman Outfitters, Bob, 1217 W. Glen, Peoria, IL 61614/309-691-8132

Hi-Point Firearms, 174 South Mulberry, Manfield, OH 44902/419-522-8830

Hiptmayer, Heidemarie, RR 112 750, P.O. Box 136, Eastman, Quebec J0E 1PO, CANADA/514-297-2492

Hiptmayer, Klaus, RR 112 750, P.O. Box 136, Eastman, Quebec J0E 1P0, CANADA/514-297-2492

Hirtenberger Aktiengesellschaft, Leobersdorferstrasse 31, A-2552 Hirtenberg, AUSTRIA/43(0)2256 81184; FAX: 43(0)2256 81807

HiTek International, 490 El Camino Real, Redwood City, CA 94063/800-54-NIGHT; FAX: 415-363-1408

Hiti-Schuch, Atelier Wilma, A-8863 Predlitz, Pirming Y1 AUSTRIA/0353418278

HJS Arms, Inc., P.O. Box 3711, Brownsville, TX 78523-3711/800-453-2767, 210-542-2767

H.K.S. Products, 7841 Founion Dr., Florence, KY 41042/606-342-7841

Hoag, James W., 8523 Canoga Ave., Suite C, Canoga Park, CA 91304/818-998-1510

Hobaugh, Wm. H. (See Rifle Shop, The)

Hobbie Gunsmithing, Duane A., 2412 Pattie Ave., Wichita, KS 67216/316-264-8266

Hobson Precision Mfg. Co., Rt. 1, Box 220-C, Brent, AL 35034/205-926-4662

Hoch Custom Bullet Moulds (See Colorado Shooter's Supply)

Hodgdon Powder Co., Inc., P.O. Box 2932, Shawnee Mission, KS 66201/913-362-9455; FAX: 913-362-1307

Hodgman, Inc., 1750 Orchard Rd., Montgomery, IL 60538/708-897-7555; FAX: 708-897-7558

Hodgson, Richard, 9081 Tahoe Lane, Boulder, CO 80301

Hoehn Sales, Inc., 75 Greensburg Ct., St. Charles, MO 63304/314-441-4231

Hoelscher, Virgil, 11047 Pope Ave., Lynwood, CA 90262/310-631-8545

Hoenig & Rodman, 6521 Morton Dr., Boise, ID 83704/208-375-1116

Hofer Jagdwaffen, P., Buchsenmachermeister, Kirchgasse 24, A-9170 Ferlach, AUSTRIA/04227-3683

Hoffman New Ideas, 821 Northmoor Rd., Lake Forest, IL 60045/312-234-4075

Hogue Grips, P.O. Box 1138, Paso Robles, CA 93446/800-438-4747; FAX: 805-466-7329

Holden Co., J.B., P.O. Box 700320, 975 Arthur, Plymouth, MI 48170/313-455-4850; FAX: 313-455-4212

Holland, Dick, 422 NE 6th St., Newport, OR 97365/503-265-7556

Holland's, Box 69, Powers, OR 97466/503-439-5155; FAX: 503-439-5155

Hollis Gun Shop, 917 Rex St., Carlsbad, NM 88220/505-885-3782

Hollywood Engineering, 10642 Arminta St., Sun Valley, CA 91352/818-842-8376

Holster Outpost, 950 Harry St., El Cajon, CA 92020/619-588-1222

Holster Shop, The, 720 N. Flagler Dr., Ft. Lauderdale, FL 33304/305-463-7910; FAX: 305-761-1483

Holston Ent., Inc., P.O. Box 493, Piney Flats, TN 37686

Homak Mfg. Co., Inc., 3800 W. 45th, Chicago, IL 60632/312-523-3100

Home Shop Machinist, The, Village Press Publications, P.O. Box 1810, Traverse City, MI 49685/800-447-7367; FAX: 616-946-3289

Hondo Ind., 510 S. 52nd St.,I04, Tempe, AZ 85281

Hoppe's Div., Penguin Industries, Inc., Airport Industrial Mall, Coatesville, PA 19320/251-384-6000

Horizons Unlimited, P.O. Box 426, Warm Springs, GA 31830/706-655-3603; FAX: 706-655-3603

Hornady Mfg. Co., P.O. Box 1848, Grand Island, NE 68801/800-338-3220, 308-382-1390

Horseshoe Leather Products, Andy Arratoonian, The Cottage Sharow, Ripon HG4 5BP ENGLAND/0765-605858

Horst, Alan K., 3221 2nd Ave. N., Great Falls, MT 59401/406-454-1831

Horton Dist. Co., Inc., Lew, 15 Walkup Dr., Westboro, MA 01581/508-366-7400

House of Muskets, Inc., The, P.O. Box 4640, Pagosa Springs, CO 81157/303-731-2295

Houtz & Barwick, P.O. Box 435, W. Church St., Elizabeth City, NC 27909/800-775-0337, 919-335-4191; FAX: 919-335-1152

Howa Machinery, Ltd., Sukaguchi, Shinkawa-cho, Nishikasugai-gun, Aichi 452, JAPAN (U.S. importer—Interarms)

Howell Machine, 815 1/2 D St., Lewiston, ID 83501/208-743-7418

Hoyt Holster Co., Inc., P.O. Box 69, Coupeville, WA 98239-0069/206-678-6640; FAX: 206-678-6549

H-S Precision, Inc., 1301 Turbine Dr., Rapid City, SD 57701/605-341-3006; FAX: 605-342-8964

HT Bullets, 244 Belleville Rd., New Bedford, MA 02745/508-999-3338

Hubertus Schneidwarenfabrik, P.O. Box 180 106, D-42626 Solingen, GERMANY/0149-212-59-19-94: FAX: 01149-212-59-19-92

Huebner, Corey O., Box 6, Hall, MT 59837/406-721-1658

Huey Gun Cases, Marvin, P.O. Box 22456, Kansas City, MO 64113/816-444-1637

Hugger Hooks Co., 3900 Easley Way, Golden, CO 80403/303-279-0600

Hughes, Steven Dodd, P.O. Box 11455, Eugene, OR 97440/503-485-8869

Hume, Don, P.O. Box 351, Miami, OK 74355/918-542-6604

Hungry Horse Books, 4605 Hwy. 93 South, Whitefish, MT 59937/406-862-7997

Hunkeler, A. (See Buckskin Machine Works)

Hunter Co., Inc., 3300 W. 71st Ave., Westminster, CO 80030/303-427-4626

Hunter's Specialties, Inc., 6000 Huntington Ct. NE, Cedar Rapids, IA 52402-1268/319-395-0321

Hunterjohn, P.O. Box 477, St. Louis, MO 63166/314-531-7250

Hunting Classics Ltd., P.O. Box 2089, Gastonia, NC 28053/704-867-1307; FAX: 704-867-0491

Huntington Die Specialties, 601 Oro Dam Blvd., Oroville, CA 95965/916-534-1210; FAX: 916-534-1212

Hydrosorbent Products, P.O. Box 437, Ashley Falls, MA 01222/413-229-2967; FAX: 413-229-8743

Hyper-Single, Inc., 520 E. Beaver, Jenks, OK 74037/918-299-2391

Hy-Score Arms Co. Ltd., 40 Stonar Industrial Estate, Sandwich, Kent CT13 9LN, ENGLAND/0304-61.12.21

I

IAI, 6226 Santos Diaz St., Irwindale, CA 91702/818-334-1200

Ibberson (Sheffield) Ltd., George, 25-31 Allen St., Sheffield, S3 7AW ENGLAND/0742-766123; FAX: 0742-738465

ICI-America, P.O. Box 751, Wilmington, DE 19897/302-575-3000

Idaho Ammunition Service, 2816 Mayfair Dr., Lewiston, ID 83501/208-743-0270; FAX: 208-743-4930

Idaho Bullets, 4344 Cavendish Hwy., Lenore, ID 83541/208-476-5046

IGA (See U.S. importer—Stoeger Industries)

Illinois Lead Shop, 7742 W. 61st Place, Summit, IL 60501

IMI, P.O. Box 1044, Ramat Hasharon 47100, ISRAEL/972-3-5485222 (U.S. importer—Magnum Research, Inc.)

IMI Services USA, Inc., 2 Wisconsin Circle, Suite 420, Chevy Chase, MD 20815/301-215-4800; FAX: 301-657-1446

Impact Case Co., P.O. Box 9912, Spokane, WA 99209-0912/800-262-3322, 509-467-3303; FAX: 509-326-5436

Imperial Magnum Corp., 1417 Main St., Oroville, WA 98844/604-495-3131; FAX: 604-495-2816

Imperial Schrade Corp., 7 Schrade Ct., Box 7000, Ellenville, NY 12428/914-647-7600

IMR Powder Co., 1080 Military Turnpike, Suite 2, Plattsburgh, NY 12901/518-563-2253; FAX: 518-563-6916

I.N.C., Inc. (See Kick Eez)

Incor, Inc., P.O. Box 132, Addison, TX 75001/214-931-3500; FAX: 214-458-1626

Independent Machine & Gun Shop, 1416 N. Hayes, Pocatello, ID 83201

INDESAL, P.O. Box 233, Eibar, SPAIN 20600/43-751800; FAX: 43-751962 (U.S. importer—American Arms, Inc.)

Industria de la Escopeta S.A.L. (See INDESAL)

Info-Arm, P.O. Box 1262, Champlain, NY 12919

Ingle, Ralph W., 4 Missing Link, Rossville, GA 30741/404-866-5589

Innovative Weaponry, Inc., 337 Eubank NE, Albuquerque, NM 87123/800-334-3573, 505-296-4645; FAX: 505-271-2633
Innovision Enterprises, 728 Skinner Dr., Kalamazoo, MI 49001/616-382-1681; FAX: 616-382-1830
InSights Training Center, Inc., 240 NW Gilman Blvd., Issaquah, WA 98027/206-391-4834
INTEC International, Inc., P.O. Box 5828, Sparks, NV 89432-5828/602-483-1708
Interarms, 10 Prince St., Alexandria, VA 22314/703-548-1400
Intermountain Arms & Tackle, Inc., 105 E. Idaho St., Meridian, ID 83642/208-888-4911; FAX: 208-888-4381
International Shooters Service (See I.S.S.)
International Shootists, Inc., P.O. Box 5354, Mission Hills, CA 91345/818-891-1723
Intratec, 12405 SW 130th St., Miami, FL 33186/305-232-1821; FAX: 305-253-7207
Iosso Products, 1485 Lively Blvd., Elk Grove Villiage, IL 60007/708-437-8400
Iron Mountain Knife Co., P.O. Box 2146, Sparks, NV 89432-2146/702-356-3632; FAX: 702-359-2785
Ironside International Publishers, Inc., P.O. Box 55, 800 Slaters Lane, Alexandria, VA 22313/703-684-6111; FAX: 703-683-5486
Irwin, Campbell H., 140 Hartland Blvd., East Hartland, CT 06027/203-653-3901
Irwindale Arms, Inc. (See IAI)
Israel Military Industries Ltd. (See IMI)
I.S.S., P.O. Box 185234, Ft. Worth, TX 76181/817-595-2090
I.S.W., 106 E. Cairo Dr., Tempe, AZ 85282
Ithaca Aquisition Corp., Ithaca Gun Co., 891 Route 34B, King Ferry, NY 13081/315-364-7171; FAX: 315-364-5134
Ivanoff, Thomas G. (See Tom's Gun Repair)

J

J-4, Inc., 1700 Via Burton, Anaheim, CA 92806
J&D Components, 75 East 350 North, Orem, UT 84057-4719/801-225-7007
J&J Products, Inc., 9240 Whitmore, El Monte, CA 91731/818-571-5228; FAX: 818-571-8704
J&L Superior Bullets (See Huntington Die Specialties)
J&R Enterprises, 4550 Scotts Valley Rd., Lakeport, CA 95453
J&S Heat Treat, 803 S. 16th St., Blue Springs, MO 64015/816-229-2149; FAX: 816-228-1135
J.A. Blades, Inc. (See Christopher Firearms Co., Inc., E.)
Jackalope Gun Shop, 1048 S. 5th St., Douglas, WY 82633/307-358-3441
JACO Precision Co., 11803 Indian Head Dr., Austin, TX 78753/512-836-4418
Jaeger, Inc. Paul, /Dunn's, P.O. Box 449, 1 Madison Ave., Grand Junction, TN 38039/901-764-6909; FAX: 901-764-6503
JägerSport, Ltd., One Wholesale Way, Cranston, RI 02920/800-426-3089, 401-944-9682; FAX: 401-946-2587
Jamison's Forge Works, 4527 Rd. 6.5 NE, Moses Lake, WA 98837/509-762-2659
Jansma, Jack J., 4320 Kalamazoo Ave., Grand Rapids, MI 49508/616-455-7810; FAX 616-455-5212
Jantz Supply, P.O. Box 584, Davis, OK 73030/405-369-2316; FAX: 405-369-3082
Jarrett Rifles, Inc., 383 Brown Rd., Jackson, SC 29831/803-471-3616
Jarvis Gunsmithing, Inc., 1123 Cherry Orchard Lane, Hamilton, MT 59840/406-961-4392
JAS, Inc., P.O. Box 0, Rosemount, MN 55068/612-890-7631
Jason Empire, Inc., 9200 Cody, Overland Park, KS 66214-3259/913-888-0220; FAX: 913-888-0222
Javelina Products, P.O. Box 337, San Bernardino, CA 92402/714-882-5847; FAX: 714-434-6937
J/B Adventures & Safaris, Inc., P.O. Box 3397, Englewood, CO 80155/303-771-0977
J-B Bore Cleaner, 299 Poplar St., Hamburg, PA 19526/610-562-2103
JBM Software, P.O. Box 3648, University Park, NM 88003
Jeffredo Gunsight, P.O. Box 669, San Marcos, CA 92079/619-728-2695
Jenco Sales, Inc., P.O. Box 1000, Manchaca, TX 78652/512-282-2800; FAX: 512-282-7504
Jenkins Recoil Pads, Inc., RR 2, Box 471, Olney, IL 62450/618-395-3416
Jennings Firearms, Inc., 17692 Cowan, Irvine, CA 92714/714-252-7621; FAX: 714-252-7626
Jensen Bullets, 86 North, 400 West, Blackfoot, ID 83221/208-785-5590
Jensen's Custom Ammunition, 5146 E. Pima, Tucson, AZ 85712/602-325-3346; FAX: 602-322-5704
Jensen's Firearms Academy, 1280 W. Prince, Tucson, AZ 85705/602-293-8516
Jester Bullets, Rt. 1 Box 27, Orienta, OK 73737
Jett & Co., Inc., 104 W. Water St., Litchfield, IL 62056-2464/217-324-3779
Jewell, Arnold W., 1490 Whitewater Rd., New Braunfels, TX 78132/210-620-0971
J-Gar Co., 183 Turnpike Rd., Dept. 3, Petersham, MA 01366-9604
JGS Precision Tool Mfg., 1141 S. Summer Rd., Coos Bay, OR 97420/503-267-4331; FAX:503-267-5996
Jim's Gun Shop (See Spradlin's)
Jim's Precision, Jim Ketchum, 1725 Moclips Dr., Petaluma, CA 94952/707-762-3014
J.I.T., Ltd., P.O. Box 749, Glenview, IL 60025/708-998-0937
JLK Bullets, RR1, Box 310C, Dover, AR 72837/501-331-4194
J.O. Arms & Ammunition Co., 5709 Hartsdale, Houston, TX 77036/713-789-0745; FAX: 713-789-7513
Johanssons Vapentillbehor, Bert, S-430 20 Veddige, SWEDEN
John's Custom Leather, 523 S. Liberty St., Blairsville, PA 15717/412-459-6802
Johns, Bill, 1412 Lisa Rae, Round Rock, TX 78664/512-255-8246
Johnson Gunsmithing, Inc., Neal G., 111 Marvin Dr., Hampton, VA 23666/804-838-8091; FAX: 804-838-8157
Johnson Wood Products, RR 1, Strawberry Point, IA 52076/319-933-4930
Johnston, James (See North Fork Custom Gunsmithing)

Johnston Bros., 1889 Rt. 9, Unit 22, Toms River, NJ 08755/800-257-2595; FAX: 800-257-2534
Jonad Corp., 2091 Lakeland Ave., Lakewood, OH 44107/216-226-3161
Jonas Appraisals & Taxidermy, Jack, 1675 S. Birch, Suite 506, Denver, CO 80222/303-757-7347
Jones Co., Dale, 680 Hoffman Draw, Kila, MT 59920/406-755-4684
Jones Custom Products, Neil, RD 1, Box 483A, Saegertown, PA 16433/814-763-2769; FAX: 814-763-4228
Jones, J.D. (See SSK Industries)
Jones Moulds, Paul, 4901 Telegraph Rd., Los Angeles, CA 90022/213-262-1510
Joy Enterprises (See Fury Cutlery)
J.P. Enterprises, Inc., P.O. Box 26324, Shoreview, MN 55126/612-486-9064, 800-528-9886; FAX: 612-482-0970
JP Sales, Box 307, Anderson, TX 77830
JRW, 2425 Taffy Ct., Nampa, ID 83687
JSL (Hereford) Ltd., 35 Church St., Hereford HR1 2LR ENGLAND/0432-355416; FAX: 0432-355242 (U.S. importer—Specialty Shooters Supply, Inc.)
Juenke, Vern, 25 Bitterbush Rd., Reno, NV 89523/702-345-0225
Jumbo Sports Products (See Bucheimer, J.M.)
Jungkind, Reeves C., 5001 Buckskin Pass, Austin, TX 78745/512-442-1094
Jurras, L.E., P.O. Box 680, Washington, IN 47501/812-254-7698
Just Brass, Inc., 121 Henry St., P.O. Box 112, Freeport, NY 11520/516-378-8588

K

K&K Ammo Wrist Band, R.D. 1, P.O. Box 448-CA18, Lewistown, PA 17044/717-242-2329
K&M Industries, Inc., Box 66, 510 S. Main, Troy, ID 83871/208-835-2281; FAX: 208-835-5211
K&M Services, 5430 Salmon Run Rd., Dover, PA 17315
K&P Gun Co., 1024 Central Ave., New Rockford, ND 58356/701-947-2248
K&T Co., Div. of T&S Industries, Inc., 1027 Skyview Dr., W. Carrollton, OH 45449/513-859-8414
Ka Pu Kapili, P.O. Box 745, Honokaa, HI 96727/808-776-1644; FAX: 808-776-1731
KA-BAR Knives, 31100 Solon Rd., Solon, OH 44139/216-248-7000; 800-321-9316, ext. 329; FAX: 216-248-8651
Kahles U.S.A., P.O. Box 81071, Warwick, RI 02888/800-752-4537: FAX: 401-946-2587
Kahr Arms, P.O. Box 220, Blauvelt, NY 10913/914-353-5996; FAX: 914-353-7833
Kalispel Case Line, P.O. Box 267, Cusick, WA 99119/509-445-1121
Kamik Outdoor Footwear, 554 Montee de Liesse, Montreal, Quebec, H4T 1P1 CANADA/514-341-3950; FAX: 514-341-1861
Kamyk Engraving Co., Steve, 9 Grandview Dr., Westfield, MA 01085-1810/413-568-0457
Kane Products, Inc., 5572 Brecksville Rd., Cleveland, OH 44131/216-524-9962
Kapro Mfg. Co., Inc. (See R.E.I.)
Kasenit Co., Inc., 13 Park Ave., Highland Mills, NY 10930/914-928-9595; FAX: 914-928-7292
Kasmarsik Bullets, 152 Crstler Rd., Chehalis, WA 98532
Kassnar (See U.S. importer—K.B.I., Inc.)
Kaswer Custom, Inc., 13 Surrey Drive, Brookfield, CT 06804/203-775-0564; FAX: 203-775-6872
K.B.I., Inc., P.O. Box 5440, Harrisburg, PA 17110-0440/717-540-8518; FAX: 717-540-8567
K-D, Inc., Box 459, 585 N. Hwy. 155, Cleveland, UT 84518/801-653-2530
KDF, Inc., 2485 Hwy. 46 N., Seguin, TX 78155/210-379-8141; FAX: 210-379-5420
KeeCo Impressions, Inc., 346 Wood Ave., North Brunswick, NJ 08902/800-468-0546
Keeler, R.H., 817 "N" St., Port Angeles, WA 98362/206-457-4702
Kehr, Roger, 2131 Agate Ct. SE, Lacy, WA 98503/206-456-0831
Keith's Bullets, 942 Twisted Oak, Algonquin, IL 60102/708-658-3520
Keith's Custom Gunstocks (See Heppler, Keith M.)
Kelbly, Inc., 7222 Dalton Fox Lake Rd., North Lawrence, OH 44666/216-683-4674; FAX: 216-683-7349
Keller Co., The, 4215 McEwen Rd., Dallas, TX 75244/214-770-8585
Kelley's, P.O. Box 125, Woburn, MA 01801/617-935-3389
Kellogg's Professional Products, 325 Pearl St., Sandusky, OH 44870/419-625-6551; FAX: 419-625-6167
Kelly, Lance, 1723 Willow Oak Dr., Edgewater, FL 32132/904-423-4933
Ken's Finn Knives, Rt. 1, Box 338, Republic, MI 49879/906-376-2132
Ken's Gun Specialties, Rt. 1, Box 147, Lakeview, AR 72642/501-431-5606
Ken's Kustom Kartridges, 331 Jacobs Rd., Hubbard, OH 44425/216-534-4595
Ken's Rifle Blanks, Ken McCullough, Rt. 2, P.O. Box 85B, Weston, OR 97886/503-566-3879
Keng's Firearms Specialty, Inc., 875 Wharton Dr. SW, Atlanta, GA 30336/404-691-7611; FAX: 404-505-8445
Kennebec Journal, 274 Western Ave., Augusta, ME 04330/207-622-6288
Kennedy Firearms, 10 N. Market St., Muncy, PA 17756/717-546-6695
Kennerknecht, Rick "KK", Randall Firearms Historian, P.O. Box 1586, Lomita, CA 90717-5586/310-781-9199; FAX: 310-781-9266
KenPatable Ent., Inc., P.O. Box 19422, Louisville, KY 40259/502-239-5447
Kent Cartridge Mfg. Co. Ltd., Unit 16, Branbridges Industrial Estate, East, Peckham/Tonbridge, Kent, TN12 5HF ENGLAND/622-872255; FAX: 622-872645
Keowee Game Calls, 608 Hwy. 25 North, Travelers Rest, SC 29690/803-834-7204
Kershaw Knives, 25300 SW Parkway Ave., Wilsonville, OR 97070/503-682-1966; FAX: 503-682-7168
Kesselring Gun Shop, 400 Hwy. 99 North, Burlington, WA 98233/206-724-3113; FAX: 206-724-7003
Kick Eez, P.O. Box 12767, Wichita, KS 67277/316-721-9570; FAX: 316-721-5260
Kilham & Co., Main St., P.O. Box 37, Lyme, NH 03768/603-795-4112

Kimball, Gary, 1526 N. Circle Dr., Colorado Springs, CO 80909/719-634-1274
Kimber of America, Inc., 9039 SE Jannsen Rd., Clackamas, OR 97015/503-656-1704; FAX: 503-657-5695
Kimel Industries, 3800 Old Monroe Rd., P.O. Box 335, Matthews, NC 28105/800-438-9288; FAX: 704-821-6339
King & Co., Box 1242, Bloomington, IL 61701/309-473-3964
King's Gun Works, 1837 W. Glenoaks Blvd., Glendale, CA 91201/818-956-6010
Kingyon, Paul L., 607 N. 5th St., Burlington, IA 52601/319-752-4465
Kirk Game Calls, Inc., Dennis, RD1, Box 184, Laurens, NY 13796/607-433-2710; FAX: 607-433-2711
Kirkpatrick Leather Co., 1910 San Bernardo, Laredo, TX 78040/512-723-6631; FAX: 512-725-0672
KJM Fabritek, Inc., P.O. Box 162, Marietta, GA 30061
KK Air International (See Impact Case Co.)
K.K. Arms Co., Star Route Box 671, Kerrville, TX 78028/210-257-4718; FAX: 210-257-4891
Kleen-Bore, Inc., 20 Ladd Ave., Northampton, MA 01060/413-586-7240; FAX: 413-586-0236
Klein Custom Guns, Don, 433 Murray Park Dr., Ripon, WI 54971/414-748-2931
Kleinendorst, K.W., RR 1, Box 1500, Hop Bottom, PA 18824/717-289-4687; FAX: 717-289-4687
Klingler Woodcarving, P.O. Box 141, Thistle Hill, Cabot, VT 05647/802-426-3811
Kmount, P.O. Box 19422, Louisville, KY 40259/502-239-5447
Kneiper Custom Guns, Jim, 334 Summit Vista, Carbondale, CO 81623/303-963-9880
Knife Importers, Inc., P.O. Box 1000, Manchaca, TX 78652/512-282-6860
Knight & Hale Game Calls, Box 468 Industrial Park, Cadiz, KY 42211/502-522-3651; FAX: 502-522-0211
Knight's Mfg. Co., 7750 9th St. SW, Vero Beach, FL 32968/407-778-3700; FAX: 407-569-2955
Knippel, Richard, 5924 Carnwood, Riverbank, CA 95367/209-869-1469
Knock on Wood Antiques, 355 Post Rd., Darien, CT 06820/203-655-9031
Kodiak Custom Bullets, 8261 Henry Circle, Anchorage, AK 99507/907-349-2282
Kodiak Safe, 468 N. 1200 W., Lindon, UT 84042/801-785-9113
Koevenig's Engraving Service, Box 55 Rabbit Gulch, Hill City, SD 57745
KOGOT, 410 College, Trinidad, CO 81082/719-846-9406
Kokolus, Michael M., 7005 Herber Rd., New Tripoli, PA 18066/215-298-3013
Kolpin Mfg., Inc., P.O. Box 107, 205 Depot St., Fox Lake, WI 53933/414-928-3118; FAX: 414-928-3687
Kopec Enterprises, John (See Peacemaker Specialists)
Kopp, Terry K., 1301 Franklin, Lexington, MO 64067/816-259-2636
Koppco Industries, 1301 Franklin, Lexington, MO 64067/816-259-3239
Korth, Robert-Bosch-Str. 4, P.O. Box 1320, 23909 Ratzeburg, GERMANY/0451-4991497; FAX: 0451-4993230 (U.S. importer—Mandall Shooting Supplies, Inc.)
Korzinek Riflesmith, J., RD 2, Box 73, Canton, PA 17724/717-673-8512
Koval Knives, 460 D Schrock Rd., Columbus, OH 43229/614-888-6486; FAX: 614-888-8218
Kowa Optimed, Inc., 20001 S. Vermont Ave., Torrance, CA 90502/310-327-1913; FAX: 310-327-4177
Kramer Designs, 302 Lump Gulch, Clancy, MT 59634/406-933-8658; FAX: 406-933-8658
Kramer Handgun Leather, P.O. Box 112154, Tacoma, WA 98411/206-564-6652; FAX: 206-564-1214
Krause Publications, 700 E. State St., Iola, WI 54990/715-445-2214; FAX: 715-445-4087
Krico/Kriegeskorte GmbH, A., Kronacherstr. 63, 85 W. Fürth-Stadeln, D-8510 GERMANY/0911-796092; FAX: 0911-796074 (U.S. importer—Mandall Shooting Supplies, Inc.)
Krieger Barrels, Inc., N114 W18697 Clinton Dr., Germantown, WI 53022/414-255-9593; FAX: 414-255-9586
Kriegeskorte GmbH., A. (See Krico/Kriegeskorte GmbH., A.)
Krieghoff Gun Co., H., Bosch Str. 22, 7900 Ulm, GERMANY (U.S. importer—Krieghoff International, Inc.)
Krieghoff International, Inc., 7528 Easton Rd., Ottsville, PA 18942/215-847-5173; FAX: 215-847-8691
Kris Mounts, 108 Lehigh St., Johnstown, PA 15905/814-539-9751
K-Sports Imports, Inc., 2755 Thompson Creek Rd., Pomona, CA 91767/909-392-2345; FAX: 909-392-2354
Kudlas, John M., 622 14th St. SE, Rochester, MN 55904/507-288-5579
Kulis Freeze Dry Taxidermy, 725 Broadway Ave., Bedford, OH 44146/216-232-8352; FAX: 216-232-7305
KVH Industries, Inc., 110 Enterprise Center, Middletown, RI 02842/401-847-3327; FAX: 401-849-0045
Kwik Mount Corp., P.O. Box 19422, Louisville, KY 40259/502-239-5447
Kwik-Site Co., 5555 Treadwell, Wayne, MI 48184/313-326-1500; FAX: 313-326-4120

L

L&R Lock Co., 1137 Pocalla Rd., Sumter, SC 29150/803-775-6127
L&S Technologies, Inc. (See Aimtech Mount Systems)
LaBounty Precision Reboring, P.O. Box 186, 7968 Silver Lk. Rd., Maple Falls, WA 98266/206-599-2047
Lachaussee, S.A., 29 Rue Kerstenne, Ans, B-4430 BELGIUM/041-63 88 77
La Clinique du .45, 1432 Rougemont, Chambly, Quebec, J3L 2L8 CANADA/514-658-1144
LaCrosse Footwear, Inc., P.O. Box 1328, La Crosse, WI 54602/608-782-3020
LaFrance Specialties, P.O. Box 178211, San Diego, CA 92117/619-293-3373
Lage Uniwad, Inc., P.O. Box 446, Victor, IA 52327/319-647-3232
Lair, Sam, 520 E. Beaver, Jenks, OK 74037/918-299-2391
Lake Center, P.O. Box 38, St. Charles, MO 63302/314-946-7500
Lakefield Arms Ltd., 248 Water St., Lakefield, Ont. K0L 2H0, CANADA/705-652-6735, 705-652-8000; FAX: 705-652-8431

Lakewood Products, Inc., P.O. Box 1527, 1445 Eagle St., Rhinelander, WI 54501/715-369-3445
Lampert, Ron, Rt. 1, Box 177, Guthrie, MN 56461/218-854-7345
Lamson & Goodnow Mfg. Co., 45 Conway St., Shelburne Falls, MA 03170/413-625-6331
Lan Orchards, 3601 10th St. SE, Ewenatchee, WA 98801
Lanber Armes S.A., Calle Zubiaurre 5, Zaldibar, SPAIN/34-4-6827702; FAX: 34-4-6827999
Lane Bullets, Inc., 1011 S. 10th St., Kansas City, KS 66105/913-621-6113, 800-444-7468
Lane Publishing, P.O. Box 759, Hot Springs, AR 71902/501-525-7514; FAX: 501-525-7519
Langenberg Hat Co., P.O. Box 1860, Washington, MO 63090/800-428-1860; FAX: 314-239-3151
Lansky Sharpeners & Crock Stick, P.O. Box 800, Buffalo, NY 14231/716-877-7511; FAX: 716-877-6955
LAP Systems Groups, N.A., P.O. Box 162, Marietta, GA 30061
Lapua Ltd., P.O. Box 5, Lapua, FINLAND SF-62101/64-310111; FAX: 64-4388951
L.A.R. Manufacturing, Inc., 4133 W. Farm Rd., West Jordan, UT 84088/801-255-7106; FAX: 801-569-1972
LaRocca Gun Works, Inc., 51 Union Place, Worcester, MA 01608/508-754-2887; FAX: 508-754-2887
Laser Devices, Inc., 2 Harris Ct. A-4, Monterey, CA 93940/408-373-0701; FAX: 408-373-0903
Laseraim, Inc. (See Emerging Technologies, Inc.)
Laseraim Arms, Inc., Sub. of Emerging Technologies, Inc., P.O. Box 3548, Little Rock, AR 72203/501-375-2227; FAX: 501-372-1445
LaserMax, 3495 Winton Place, Bldg. B, Rochester, NY 14623/716-272-5420
Lassen Community College, Gunsmithing Dept., P.O. Box 3000, Hwy. 139, Susanville, CA 96130/916-257-6181 ext. 109; FAX: 916-257-8964
Lathrop's, Inc., 5146 E. Pima, Tucson, AZ 85712/602-881-0226, 800-875-4867
Laughridge, William R. (See Cylinder & Slide, Inc.)
Laurel Mountain Forge, P.O. Box 224, Romeo, MI 48065/313-749-5742
Laurona Armas S.A., P.O. Box 260, 20600 Eibar, SPAIN/34-43-700600; FAX: 34-43-700616 (U.S. importer—Galaxy Imports Ltd., Inc.)
Law Concealment Systems, Inc., P.O. Box 3952, Wilmington, NC 28406/919-791-6656, 800-373-0116 orders
Lawrence Brand Shot (See Precision Reloading, Inc.)
Lawrence Leather Co., P.O. Box 1479, Lillington, NC 27546/910-893-2071; FAX: 910-893-4742
Lawson, John G. (See Sight Shop, The)
Lawson Co., Harry, 3328 N. Richey Blvd., Tucson, AZ 85716/602-326-1117
LBT, HCR 62, Box 145, Moyie Springs, ID 83845/208-267-3588
Lea Mfg. Co., 237 E. Aurora St., Waterbury, CT 06720/203-753-5116
Lead Bullets Technology (See LBT)
Leather Arsenal, 27549 Middleton Rd., Middleton, ID 83644/208-585-6212
Leatherman Tool Group, Inc., P.O. Box 20595, Portland, OR 97220/503-253-7826; FAX: 503-253-7830
Leatherwood-Meopta, Inc., 751 W. Lamar Blvd. Suite 102, Arlington, TX 76012-2010/817-965-3253
Lebeau-Courally, Rue St. Gilles, 386, 4000 Liege, BELGIUM/041 52 48 43; FAX: 041 52 20 08 (U.S. importer—New England Arms Co.
Lectro Science, Inc., 6410 W. Ridge Rd., Erie, PA 16506/814-833-6487; FAX: 814-833-0447
Ledbetter Airguns, Riley, 1804 E. Sprague St., Winston Salem, NC 27107-3521/919-784-0676
Leding Loader, RR 1, Box 645, Ozark, AR 72949
Lee Co., T.K., One Independence Plaza, Suite 520, Birmingham, AL 35209/205-913-5222
Lee Precision, Inc., 4275 Hwy. U, Hartford, WI 53027/414-673-3075
Lee Supplies, Mark, 9901 France Ct., Lakeville, MN 55044/612-461-2114
Lee's Red Ramps, Box 291240, Phelan, CA 92329-1240/619-868-5731
LeFever Arms Co., Inc., 6234 Stokes, Lee Center Rd., Lee Center, NY 13363/315-337-6722; FAX: 315-337-1543
Leibowitz, Leonard, 1205 Murrayhill Ave., Pittsburgh, PA 15217/412-361-5455
Leica USA, Inc., 156 Ludlow Ave., Northvale, NJ 07647/201-767-7500; FAX: 201-767-8666
LEM Gun Specialties, Inc., P.O. Box 2855, Peachtree City, GA 30269-2024
Lem Sports, Inc., P.O. Box 2107, Aurora, IL 60506/708-897-7382, 800-688-8801 (orders only)
Lenahan Family Enterprise, P.O. Box 46, Manitou Springs, CO 80829
Lethal Force Institute (See Police Bookshelf)
Letschnig, Franz, RR 1, Martintown, Ont. K0C 1S0, CANADA/613-528-4843
Leupold, P.O. Box 688, Beaverton, OR 97075/503-526-1491; FAX: 503-526-1475
Lever Arms Service Ltd., 2131 Burrard St., Vancouver, B.C. V6J 3H7 CANADA/604-736-0004; FAX: 604-738-3503
Lewis, Ed, P.O. Box 875, Pico Rivera, CA 90660
Liberty Antique Gunworks, 19 Key St., P.O. Box 183, Eastport, ME 04631/207-853-4116
Liberty Metals, 2233 East 16th St., Los Angeles, CA 90021/213-581-9171; FAX: 213-581-9351
Liberty Safe, 316 W. 700 S., Provo, UT 84601/801-373-0727
Liberty Shooting Supplies, P.O. Box 357, Hillsboro, OR 97123/503-640-5518
Liberty Trouser Co., 3500 6 Ave S., Birmingham, AL 35222-2406/205-251-9143
Lightfield Ammunition Corp., The Slug Group, P.O. Box 376, Paris, PA 15554/814-839-4517; FAX: 814-839-2601
Lightforce U.S.A., P.O. Box 488, Vaughn, WA 98394/206-876-3225; FAX: 206-876-3249
Lilja Precision Rifle Barrels, P.O. Box 372, Plains, MT 59859/406-826-3084; FAX: 406-826-3083
Lincoln, Dean, Box 1886, Farmington, NM 87401
Lind Custom Guns, Al, 7821 76th Ave. SW, Tacoma, WA 98498/206-584-6361
Linder Solingen Knives, 4401 Sentry Dr., Tucker, GA 30084/404-939-6915
Lindner Custom Bullets, 325 Bennetts Pond La., Mattituck, NY 11952

Lindsay, Steve, RR 2 Cedar Hills, Kearney, NE 68847/308-236-7885
Lindsley Arms Ctg. Co., P.O. Box 757, 20 College Hill Rd., Henniker, NH 03242/603-428-3127
Linebaugh Custom Sixguns & Rifle Works, P.O. Box 1263, Cody, WY 82414/307-587-8010
Lite Tek International, 133-30 32nd Ave., Flushing, NY 11354/718-463-0650; FAX: 718-762-0890
Lithi Bee Bullet Lube, 1885 Dyson St., Muskegon, MI 49442/616-726-3400
"Little John's" Antique Arms, 1740 W. Laveta, Orange, CA 92668
Littler Sales Co., 20815 W. Chicago, Detroit, MI 48228/313-273-6888; FAX: 313-273-1099
Ljutic Industries, Inc., 732 N. 16th Ave., Yakima, WA 98902/509-248-0476; FAX: 509-457-5141
L.L. Bean, 386 Main St., Freeport, ME 04032/207-865-3111
Llama Gabilondo Y Cia, Apartado 290, E-01080, Victoria, SPAIN (U.S. importer—SGS Importers International, Inc.)
Load From A Disk, 9826 Sagedale, Houston, TX 77089/713-484-0935
Loadmaster, P.O. Box 1209, Warminster, Wilts. BA12 9XJ ENGLAND/(0985)218544; FAX: (0985)214111
Loch Leven Industries, P.O. Box 2751, Santa Rosa, CA 95405/707-573-8735; FAX: 707-573-6369
Lock's Philadelphia Gun Exchange, 6700 Rowland Ave., Philadelphia, PA 19149/215-332-6225; FAX: 215-332-4800
Lodewick, Walter H., 2816 NE Halsey St., Portland, OR 97232/503-284-2554
Lofland, James W., 2275 Larkin Rd., Boothwyn, PA 19061/610-485-0391
Log Cabin Sport Shop, 8010 Lafayette Rd., Lodi, OH 44254/216-948-1082
Logan, Harry M., Box 745, Honokaa, HI 96727/808-776-1644
Logan Security Products Co., 4926 Annhurst Rd., Columbus, OH 43228-1341
Lohman Mfg. Co., Inc., 4500 Doniphan Dr., P.O. Box 220, Neosho, MO 64850/417-451-4438; FAX: 417-451-2576
Lomont Precision Bullets, 4236 W. 700 South, Poneto, IN 46781/219-694-6792; FAX: 219-694-6797
London Guns Ltd., Box 3750, Santa Barbara, CA 93130/805-683-4141; FAX: 805-683-1712
Lone Star Gunleather, 1301 Brushy Bend Dr., Round Rock, TX 78681/512-255-1805
Long, George F., 1500 Rogue River Hwy., Ste. F, Grants Pass, OR 97527/503-476-7552
Lorcin Engineering Co., Inc., 10427 San Sevaine Way, Ste. A, Mira Loma, CA 91752/909-360-1406; FAX: 909-360-0623
Lortone, Inc., 2856 NW Market St., Seattle, WA 98107/206-789-3100
Loweth, Richard, 29 Hedgegrow Lane, Kirby Muxloe, Leics. LE9 9BN ENGLAND
L.P.A. Snc, Via V. Alfieri 26, Gardone V.T. BS, ITALY 25063/(30)8911481; FAX: (30)8910951
LPS Laboratories, Inc., 4647 Hugh Howell Rd., P.O. Box 3050, Tucker, GA 30084/404-934-7800
Lucas, Edward E., 32 Garfield Ave., East Brunswick, NJ 08816/201-251-5526
Lucas, Mike, 1631 Jessamine Rd., Lexington, SC 29073/803-356-0282
Lutz Engraving, Ron, E. 1998 Smokey Valley Rd., Scandinavia, WI 54977/715-467-2674
Lyman Instant Targets, Inc. (See Lyman Products Corp.)
Lyman Products Corporation, Rt. 147, Middlefield, CT 06455/800-22-LYMAN, 203-349-3421; FAX: 203-349-3586
Lynn's Custom Gunstocks, RR 1, Brandon, IA 52210/319-474-2453

M

M&D Munitions Ltd., 127 Verdi St., Farmingdale, NY 11735/516-752-1038; FAX: 516-752-1905
M&M Engineering (See Hollywood Engineering)
M&N Bullet Lube, P.O. Box 495, 151 NE Jefferson St., Madras, OR 97741/503-255-3750
MA Systems, P.O. Box 1143, Chouteau, OK 74337/918-479-6378
Mac-1 Distributors, 13974 Van Ness Ave., Gardena, CA 90249/310-327-3582
Mac's .45 Shop, P.O. Box 2028, Seal Beach, CA 90740/310-438-5046
Macbean, Stan, 754 North 1200 West, Orem, UT 84057/801-224-6446
Madis, David, 2453 West Five Mile Pkwy., Dallas, TX 75233/214-330-7168
Madis, George, P.O. Box 545, Brownsboro, TX 75756
MAG Instrument, Inc., 1635 S. Sacramento Ave., Ontario, CA 91761/714-947-1006; FAX: 714-947-3116
Magma Engineering Co., P.O. Box 161, Queen Creek, AZ 85242/602-987-9008; FAX: 602-987-0148
Mag-Na-Port International, Inc., 41302 Executive Dr., Harrison Twp., MI 48045-3448/810-469-6727; FAX: 810-469-0425
Magnolia Sports, Inc., 211 W. Main, Magnolia, AR 71753/800-530-7816; FAX: 501-234-8117
Magnum Grips, Box 801G, Payson, AZ 85547
Magnum Power Products, Inc., P.O. Box 17768, Fountain Hills, AZ 85268
Magnum Research, Inc., 7110 University Ave., Minneapolis, MN 55432/612-574-1868; FAX: 612-574-0109
Magnus Bullets, P.O.Box 239, Toney, AL 35773/205-828-5089; FAX: 205-828-7756
Mag-Pack Corp., P.O. Box 846, Chesterland, OH 44026
MagSafe Ammo Co., 2725 Friendly Grove Rd NE, Olympia, WA 98506/206-357-6383
MAGTECH Recreational Products, Inc., 5030 Paradise Rd., Suite C211, Las Vegas, NV 89119/702-795-7111, 800-466-7191; FAX: 702-795-2769
Mahony, Philip Bruce, 67 White Hollow Rd., Lime Rock, CT 06039-2418/203-435-9341
Maine Custom Bullets, RFD 1, Box 1755, Brooks, ME 04921
Mains Enterprises, Inc., 3111 S. Valley View Blvd., Suite B120, Las Vegas, NV 89102-7790/702-876-6278; FAX: 702-876-1269
Maionchi-L.M.I., Via Di Coselli-Zona Industriale Di Guamo, Lucca, ITALY 55060/011 39-583 94291
Maki School of Engraving, Robert E., P.O. Box 947, Northbrook, IL 60065/708-724-8238

Makinson, Nicholas, RR 3, Komoka, Ont. N0L 1R0 CANADA/519-471-5462
Malcolm Enterprises, 1023 E. Prien Lake Rd., Lake Charles, LA 70601
Mallardtone Game Calls, 2901 16th St., Moline, IL 61265/309-762-8089
M.A.M. Products, Inc., 153 B Cross Slope Court, Englishtown, NJ 07726/908-536-3604
Mandall Shooting Supplies, Inc., 3616 N. Scottsdale Rd., Scottsdale, AZ 85252/602-945-2553; FAX: 602-949-0734
Mandarino, Monte, 205 Fifth Ave. East, Kalispell, MT 59901/406-257-6208
Manley Shooting Supplies, Lowell, 3684 Pine St., Deckerville, MI 48427/313-376-3665
Manufacture D'Armes Des Pyrenees Francaises (See Unique/M.A.P.F.)
Mar Knives, Inc., Al, 5755 SW Jean Rd., Suite 101, Lake Oswego, OR 97035/503-635-9229
Marathon Rubber Prods. Co., Inc., 510 Sherman St., Wausau, WI 54401/715-845-6255
Marble Arms Corp., 420 Industrial Park, P.O. Box 111, Gladstone, MI 49837/906-428-3710; FAX: 906-428-3711
Marchmon Bullets, 8191 Woodland Shore Dr., Brighton, MI 48116
Marek, George, 55 Arnold St., Westfield, MA 01085/413-562-5673
Marent, Rudolf, 9711 Tiltree St., Houston, TX 77075/713-946-7028
Markell, Inc., 422 Larkfield Center 235, Santa Rosa, CA 95403/707-573-0792; FAX: 707-573-9867
Marksman Products, 5482 Argosy Dr., Huntington Beach, CA 92649/714-898-7535, 800-822-8005; FAX: 714-891-0782
Marlin Firearms Co., 100 Kenna Dr., New Haven, CT 06473/203-239-5621; FAX: 203-234-7991
Marocchi F.lli S.p.A., Via Galileo Galilei, I-25068 Zanano di Sarezzo, ITALY (U.S. importers—PSI, Inc.; Sile Distributors)
Marple & Associates, Dick, 21 Dartmouth St., Hooksett, NH 03106/603-627-1837; FAX: 603-641-4837
Marquart Precision Co., Inc., Rear 136 Grove Ave., Box 1740, Prescott, AZ 86302/602-445-5646
Marsh, Johnny, 1007 Drummond Dr., Nashville, TN 37211/615-833-3259
Marsh, Mike, Croft Cottage, Main St., Elton, Derbyshire DE4 2BY, ENGLAND/0629 650 669
Marshall Enterprises, 792 Canyon Rd., Redwood City, CA 94062
Martin Bookseller, J., P.O. Drawer AP, Beckley, WV 25802/304-255-4073; FAX: 304-255-4077
Martin's Gun Shop, 937 S. Sheridan Blvd., Lakewood, CO 80226/303-922-2184
Martz, John V., 8060 Lakeview Lane, Lincoln, CA 95648/916-645-2250
Marvel, Alan, 3922 Madonna Rd., Jarretsville, MD 21084/301-557-6545
Maryland Munitions, P.O. Box 1711, Ellicott City, MD 21041-1711/410-744-3533
Masen Co., John, P.O. Box 5050, Suite 165, Lewisville, TX 75057/817-430-8732
Masker, Seely, 54 Woodshire S., Getzville, NY 14068/716-689-8894
MAST Technology, P.O. Box 97274, Las Vegas, NV 89193/702-362-5043
Master Class Bullets, 4110 Alder St., Eugene, OR 97405/503-687-1263
Master Engravers, Inc. (See Hendricks, Frank E.)
Master Lock Co., 2600 N. 32nd St., Milwaukee, WI 53245/414-444-2800
Master Products, Inc. (See Gun-Alert/Master Products, Inc.)
Match Prep, P.O. Box 155, Tehachapi, CA 93581/805-822-5383
Matco, Inc., 1003-2nd St., N. Manchester, IN 46962/219-982-8282
Mathews & Son, Inc., George E., 10224 S. Paramount Blvd., Downey, CA 90241/310-862-6719; FAX: 310-862-6719
Matthews Cutlery, 4401 Sentry Dr., Tucker, GA 30084
Mauser-Werke Oberndorf GmbH, P.O. Box 1349 1360, 78722 Oberndorf/Neckar GERMANY
Maverick Arms, Inc., 7 Grasso Ave., P.O. Box 497, North Haven, CT 06473/203-230-5300; FAX: 203-230-5420
Maxi-Mount, P.O. Box 291, Willoughby Hills, OH 44094-0291/216-946-3105
Maximum Security Corp., 32841 Calle Perfecto, San Juan Capistrano, CA 92675/714-493-3684; FAX: 714-496-7733
Mayville Engineering Co. (See MEC, Inc.)
Mazur Restoration, Pete, 13083 Drummer Way, Grass Valley, CA 95949/916-268-2412
MCA Sports, P.O. Box 8868, Palm Springs, CA 92263/619-770-2005
McCament, Jay, 1730-134th St. Ct. S., Tacoma, WA 98444/206-531-8832
McCann's Muzzle-Gun Works, 14 Walton Dr., New Hope, PA 18938/215-862-9180
McCluskey Precision Rifles, 10502 14th Ave. NW, Seattle, WA 98177/206-781-2776
McCombs, Leo, 1862 White Cemetery Rd., Patriot, OH 45658/614-256-1714
McCormick Corp., Chip, 1825 Fortview Rd., Ste. 115, Austin, TX 78704/800-328-CHIP, 512-462-0004; FAX: 512-462-0009
McCormick's Custom Gun Bluing, 609 NE 104th Ave., Vancouver, WA 98664/206-896-4232
McCullough, Ken (See Ken's Rifle Blanks)
McDonald, Dennis, 8359 Brady St., Peosta, IA 52068/319-556-7940
McFarland, Stan, 2221 Idella Ct., Grand Junction, CO 81505/303-243-4704
McGowen Rifle Barrels, 5961 Spruce Lane, St. Anne, IL 60964/815-937-9816; FAX: 815-937-4024
McGuire, Bill, 1600 N. Eastmont Ave., East Wenatchee, WA 98802/509-884-6021
McKee Publications, 121 Eatons Neck Rd., Northport, NY 11768/516-575-8850
McKenzie, Lynton, 6940 N. Alvernon Way, Tucson, AZ 85718/602-299-5090
McKillen & Heyer, Inc., 35535 Euclid Ave. Suite 11, Willoughby, OH 44094/216-942-2044
McMillan Bros. Rifle Co., Inc., P.O. Box 66549, Phoenix, AZ 85080/602-780-2115; FAX: 602-581-3825
McMillan Fiberglass Stocks, Inc., 21421 N. 14th Ave., Phoenix, AZ 85027/602-582-9635; FAX: 602-582-3825
McMillan Gunworks, Inc., 302 W. Melinda Lane, Phoenix, AZ 85027/602-582-9627; FAX: 602-582-5178
McMillan Optical Gunsight Co., 28638 N. 42nd St., Cave Creek, AZ 85331/602-585-7868; FAX: 602-585-7872
McMillan Rifle Barrels, P.O. Box 3427, Bryan, TX 77805/409-690-3456; FAX: 409-690-0156
McMurdo, Lynn (See Specialty Gunsmithing)

MCRW Associates Shooting Supplies, R.R. 1 Box 1425, Sweet Valley, PA 18656/717-864-3967; FAX: 717-864-2669
MCS, Inc., 34 Delmar Dr., Brookfield, CT 06804/203-775-1013; FAX: 203-775-9462
McWelco Products, 6730 Santa Fe Ave., Hesperia, CA 92345/619-244-8876; FAX: 619-244-9398
MDS, P.O. Box 1441, Brandon, FL 33509-1441/813-894-3512; FAX: 813-684-5953
Meadow Industries, P.O. Box 754, Locust Grove, VA 22508/703-972-2175; FAx: 703-972-2175
Measurement Group, Inc., Box 27777, Raleigh, NC 27611
MEC, Inc., 715 South St., Mayville, WI 53050/414-387-4500
MEC-Gar S.R.L., Via Madonnina 64, Gardone V.T. (BS), ITALY 25063/39-30-8911719; FAX: 39-30-8910065 (U.S. importer—MEC-Gar U.S.A., Inc.)
MEC-Gar U.S.A., Inc., Box 112, 500B Monroe Turnpike, Monroe, CT 06468/203-635-8662; FAX: 203-635-8662
Meier Works, P.O. Box 423, Tijeras, NM 87059/505-281-3783
Mele, Frank, 201 S. Wellow Ave., Cookeville, TN 38501/615-526-4860
Melton Shirt Co., Inc., 56 Harvester Ave., Batavia, NY 14020/716-343-8750
Menck, Thomas W., 5703 S. 77th St., Ralston, NE 68127-4201
Mendez, John A., P.O. Box 620984, Orlando, FL 32862/407-282-2178
Men-Metallwerk Elisenhuette, GmbH, P.O. Box 1263, D-56372 Nassau/Lahn, GERMANY/2604-7819
Meprolight (See Hesco-Meprolight)
Mercer Custom Stocks, R.M., 216 S. Whitewater Ave., Jefferson, WI 53549/414-674-3839, 800-704-4447
Merit Corp., Box 9044, Schenectady, NY 12309/518-346-1420
Merkel Freres, Strasse 7 October, 10, Suhl, GERMANY (U.S. importer—GSI, Inc.)
Merkuria Ltd., Argentinska 38, 17005 Praha 7, CZECH REPUBLIC/422-875117; FAX: 422-809152
Metal Products Co. (See MPC/McMinnville, TN)
Metalife Industries, Box 53 Mong Ave., Reno, PA 16343/814-436-7747; FAX: 814-676-5662
Michael's Antiques, Box 591, Waldoboro, ME 04572
Michaels of Oregon Co., P.O. Box 13010, Portland, OR 97213/503-255-6890; FAX: 503-255-0746
Micro Sight Co., 242 Harbor Blvd., Belmont, CA 94002/415-591-0769; FAX: 415-591-7531
Micro-Lube, Rt. 2, P.O. Box 201, Deming, NM 88030/505-546-9116
Mid-America Recreation, Inc., 1328 5th Ave., Moline, IA 52807/309-764-5089; FAX: 309-764-2722
Middlebrooks Custom Shop, 7366 Colonial Trail East, Surry, VA 23883/804-357-0881; FAX: 804-365-0442
Midway Arms, Inc., P.O. Box 1483, Columbia, MO 65205/800-243-3220, 314-445-6363; FAX: 314-446-1018
Midwest Gun Sport, 1108 Herbert Dr., Zebulon, NC 27597/919-269-5570
Midwest Sport Distributors, Box 129, Fayette, MO 65248
Military Armament Corp., P.O. Box 120, Mt. Zion Rd., Lingleville, TX 76461/817-965-3253
Millenium Safety Products, P.O. Box 9802-916, Austin, TX 78766/512-346-3876
Miller Arms, Inc., P.O. Box 260 Purl St., St. Onge, SD 57779/605-642-5160; FAX: 605-642-5160
Miller Co., David, 3131 E. Greenlee Rd., Tucson, AZ 85716/602-326-3117
Miller Custom, 210 E. Julia, Clinton, IL 61727/217-935-9362
Miller Engineering, R&D Engineering & Manufacturing, P.O. Box 6342, Virginia Beach, VA 23456/804-468-1402
Miller Enterprises, Inc., R.P., 1557 E. Main St., P.O. Box 234, Brownsburg, IN 46112/317-852-8187
Miller Gun Woods, 1440 Peltier Dr., Point Roberts, WA 98281/206-945-7014
Miller Single Trigger Mfg. Co., R.D.1, P.O. Box 99, Millersburg, PA 17061/717-692-3704
Millett Sights, 16131 Gothard St., Huntington Beach, CA 92647/800-645-5388; FAX: 714-843-5707
Milliron Custom Machine Carving, Earl, 1249 NE 166th Ave., Portland, OR 97230/503-252-3725
Mills Jr., Hugh B., 3615 Canterbury Rd., New Bern, NC 28560/919-637-4631
Miniature Machine Co. (See MMC)
Minute Man High Tech Industries, 3005B 6th Ave., Tacoma, WA 98406/800-233-2734
Mirador Optical Corp., P.O. Box 11614, Marina Del Rey, CA 90295-7614/310-821-5587; FAX: 310-305-0386
Miroku, B.C./Daly, Charles (See U.S. importers—Bell's Legendary Country Wear; British Sporting Arms; U.S. distributor—Outdoor Sports Headquarters, Inc.)
Mitchell Arms, Inc., 3400 W. MacArthur Blvd., Ste. 1, Santa Ana, CA 92704/714-957-5711; FAX: 714-957-5732
Mitchell Bullets, R.F., 430 Walnut St., Westernport, MD 21562
Mitchell Leatherworks, 1220 Black Brook Rd., Dunbarton, NH 03045/603-774-6283
Mitchell's Accuracy Shop, 68 Greenridge Dr., Stafford, VA 22554/703-659-0165
Mi-Te Bullets, R.R. 1 Box 230, Ellsworth, KS 67439/913-472-4575
Mittermeier, Inc., Frank, P.O. Box 2G, 3577 E. Tremont Ave., Bronx, NY 10465/718-828-3843
Mixson Leathercraft, Inc., 7435 W. 19th Ct., Hialeah, FL 33014/305-821-5190; FAX: 305-558-9318
MJK Gunsmithing, Inc., 417 N. Huber Ct., E. Wenatchee, WA 98802/509-884-7683
MJM Mfg., 3283 Rocky Water Ln. Suite B, San Jose, CA 95148/408-270-4207
MKL Service Co., 610 S. Troy St., P.O. Box D, Royal Oak, MI 48068/810-548-5453
MKS Supply, Inc., 174 S. Mulberry St., Mansfield, OH 44902/419-522-8330
MMC, 606 Grace Ave., Ft. Worth, TX 76111/817-831-0837
MMP, Rt. 6, Box 384, Harrison, AR 72601/501-741-5019; FAX: 501-741-3104
Mo's Competitor Supplies (See MCS, Inc.)
M.O.A. Corp., 2451 Old Camden Pike, Eaton, OH 45320/513-456-3669
M.O.A. Maximum, P.O. Box 185, Dayton, OH 45404/513-456-3669

Modern Gun Repair School, 2538 N. 8th St., P.O. Box 5338, Dept. GNX95, Phoenix, AZ 85010/602-990-8346
Modern MuzzleLoading, Inc., 234 Airport Rd., P.O. Box 130, Centerville, IA 52544/515-856-2626; FAX: 515-856-2628
Moeller, Steve, 1213 4th St., Fulton, IL 61252/815-589-2300
Molin Industries, Tru-Nord Division, P.O. Box 365, 204 North 9th St., Brainerd, MN 56401/218-829-2870
MoLoc Bullets, P.O. Box 2810, Turlock, CA 95381-2810/209-632-1644
Monell Custom Guns, Red Mill Road, Pine Bush, NY 12566/914-744-3021
Moneymaker Guncraft Corp., 1420 Military Ave., Omaha, NE 68131/402-556-0226
Montana Armory, Inc., 100 Centennial Dr., Big Timber, MT 59011/406-932-4353
Montana Outfitters, Lewis E. Yearout, 308 Riverview Dr. E., Great Falls, MT 59404/406-761-0859
Montana Precision Swaging, P.O. Box 4746, Butte, MT 59702/406-782-7502
Montana Vintage Arms, 2354 Bear Canyon Rd., Bozeman, MT 59715
Monte Kristo Pistol Grip Co., P.O. Box 85, Whiskeytown, CA 96095/916-623-4019
Montgomery Community College, P.O. Box 787, Troy, NC 27371/919-572-3691
Moore & Co., Wm. Larkin, 31360 Via Colinas, Suite 109, Westlake Village, CA 91361/818-889-4160
Moran, Jerry, P.O. Box 357, Mt. Morris, MI 45458-0357
Moreton/Fordyce Enterprises, P.O. Box 940, Saylorsburg, PA 18353/717-992-5742; FAX: 717-992-8775
Morini (See U.S. importer—Mandall Shooting Shpplies, Inc.)
Morrison Custom Rifles, J.W., 4015 W. Sharon, Phoenix, AZ 85029/602-978-3754
Morrow, Bud, 11 Hillside Lane, Sheridan, WY 82801-9729/307-674-8360
Morton Booth Co., P.O. Box 123, Joplin, MO 64802/417-673-1962
Moschetti, Mitchell R., P.O. Box 27065, Denver, CO 80227/303-733-9593
Moss Double Tone, Inc., P.O. Box 1112, 2101 S. Kentucky, Sedalia, MO 65301/816-827-0827
Mossberg & Sons, Inc., O.F., 7 Grasso Ave., North Haven, CT 06473/203-288-6491; FAX: 203-288-2404
Mountain Bear Rifle Works, Inc., 100 B Ruritan Rd., Sterling, VA 20164/703-430-0420
Mountain Hollow Game Calls, Box 121, Cascade, MD 21719/301-241-3282
Mountain South, P.O. Box 381, Barnwell, SC 29812/FAX: 803-259-3227
Mountain State Muzzleloading Supplies, Box 154-1, Rt. 2, Williamstown, WV 26187/304-375-7842; FAX: 304-375-3737
Mountain States Engraving, Kenneth W. Warren, P.O. Box 2842, Wenatchee, WA 98802/509-663-6123
Mountain View Sports, Inc., Box 188, Troy, NH 03465/603-357-9690; FAX: 603-357-9691
Mowrey Gun Works, P.O. Box 246, Waldron, IN 46182/317-525-6181; FAX: 317-525-6181
Mowrey's Guns & Gunsmithing, RR1, Box 82, Canajoharie, NY 13317/518-673-3483
MPC, P.O. Box 450, McMinnville, TN 37110-0450
MPI Stocks, P.O. Box 83266, Portland, OR 97283-0266/503-226-1215; FAX: 503-216-2661
MSC Industrial Supply Co., 151 Sunnyside Blvd., Plainview, NY 11803-9915/516-349-0330
Mt. Alto Outdoor Products, Rt. 735, Howardsville, VA 24562
Mt. Baldy Bullet Co., HC 87, Box 10A, Keystone, SD 57751/605-666-4725
MTM Molded Products Co., Inc., 3370 Obco Ct., Dayton, OH 45414/513-890-7461; FAX: 513-890-1747
Mulhern, Rick, Rt. 5, Box 152, Rayville, LA 71269/318-728-2688
Mullins Ammo, Rt. 2, Box 304K, Clintwood, VA 24228/703-926-6772
Mullis Guncraft, 3523 Lawyers Road E., Monroe, NC 28110/704-283-6683
Multipax, 8086 S. Yale, Suite 286, Tulsa, OK 74136/918-496-1999; FAX: 918-492-7465
Multiplex International, 26 S. Main St., Concord, NH 03301/FAX: 603-796-2223
Multipropulseurs, La Bertrandiere, 42580 L'Etrat, FRANCE/77 74 01 30; FAX: 77 93 19 34
Multi-Scale Charge Ltd., 3269 Niagara Falls Blvd., N. Tonawanda, NY 14120/905-566-1255; FAX: 416-276-6295
Mundy, Thomas A., 69 Robbins Road, Somerville, NJ 08876/201-722-2199
Munsch Gunsmithing, Tommy, Rt. 2, P.O. Box 248, Little Falls, MN 56345/612-632-6695
Murmur Corp., 2823 N. Westmoreland Ave., Dallas, TX 75222/214-630-5400
Murphy Co., Inc., R., 13 Groton-Harvard Rd., P.O. Box 376, Ayer, MA 01432/617-772-3481
Murray State College, 100 Faculty Dr., Tishomingo, OK 73460/405-371-2371
Muscle Products Corp., 188 Freeport Rd., Butler, PA 16001/800-227-7049, 412-283-0567; FAX: 412-283-8310
Museum of Historical Arms, Inc., 1038 Alton Rd., Miami Beach, FL 33139/305-672-7480
Mushroom Express Bullet Co., 601 W. 6th St., Greenfield, IN 46140/317-462-6332
Mustra's Custom Guns, Inc., Carl, 1002 Pennsylvania Ave., Palm Harbor, FL 34683/813-785-1403
Muzzlelite Corp., P.O. Box 987, DeLeon Springs, FL 32130
Muzzleload Magnum Products (See MMP)
Muzzleloaders Etcetera, Inc., 9901 Lyndale Ave. S., Bloomington, MN 55420/612-884-1161
Muzzle-Nuzzle Co., 609 N. Virginia Ave., Roswell, NM 88201/505-624-1260

N

N&J Sales, Lime Kiln Rd., Northford, CT 06472/203-484-0247
Nagel's Bullets, 9 Wilburn, Baytown, TX 77520
Nastoff's 45 Shop, Inc., Steve, 12288 Mahoning Ave., P.O. Box 446, North Jackson, OH 44451/216-538-2977
National Bullet Co., 1585 E. 361 St., Eastlake, OH 44095/216-951-1854; FAX: 216-951-7761

National Security Safe Co., Inc., P.O. Box 39, 620 S. 380 E., American Fork, UT 84003/801-756-7706

National Survival Game, Inc., P.O. Box 1439, New London, NH 03257/603-735-6165; FAX: 603-735-5154

National Target Co., 4690 Wyaconda Rd., Rockville, MD 20852/800-827-7060, 301-770-7060; FAX: 301-770-7892

Nationwide Airgun Repairs (See Airgun Repair Centre)

Nationwide Sports Distributors, 70 James Way, Southampton, PA 18966/215-322-2050; FAX: 215-322-5972

Naval Ordnance Works, Rt. 2, Box 919, Sheperdstown, WV 25443/304-876-0998

Navy Arms Co., 689 Bergen Blvd., Ridgefield, NJ 07657/201-945-2500; FAX: 201-945-6859

N.C. Ordnance Co., P.O. Box 3254, Wilson, NC 27895/919-237-2440

NCP Products, Inc., 721 Maryland Ave. SW, Canton, OH 44710

Necessary Concepts, Inc., P.O. Box 571, Deer Park, NY 11729/516-667-8509; 800-671-8881

NECO, 1316-67th St., Emeryville, CA 94608/510-450-0420

Necromancer Industries, Inc., 14 Communications Way, West Newton, PA 15089/412-872-8722

NEI Handtools, Inc., 51583 Columbia River Hwy., Scappoose, OR 97056/503-543-6776; FAX: 503-543-6799

Nelson, Gary K., 975 Terrace Dr., Oakdale, CA 95361/209-847-4590

Nelson, Stephen, 7365 NW Spring Creek Dr., Corvallis, OR 97330/503-745-5232

Nelson Combat Leather, Bruce, P.O. Box 8691 CRB, Tucson, AZ 85738/602-825-9047

Nelson/Weather-Rite, 14760 Santa Fe Trail Dr., Lenexa, KS 66215/913-492-3200

Nesci Enterprises, Inc., P.O. Box 119, Summit St., East Hampton, CT 06424/203-267-2588

Nesika Bay Precision, 22239 Big Valley Rd., Poulsbo, WA 98370/206-697-3830

Nettestad Gun Works, RR 1, Box 160, Pelican Rapids, MN 56572/218-863-4301

Neumann GmbH, Am Galgenberg 6, 90575 Langenzenn, GERMANY/09101/8258; FAX: 09101/6356

Neutralizer Police Munitions, 5029 Middle Rd., Horseheads, NY 14845-9568/607-739-8362; FAX: 607-594-3900

Nevada Cartridge Co., 44 Montgomery St., Suite 500, San Francisco, CA 94104/415-925-9394; FAX: 415-925-9396

New Advantage Arms Corp., 2843 N. Alvernon Way, Tucson, AZ 85712/602-881-7444; FAX: 602-323-0949

New Democracy, Inc., 751 W. Lamar Blvd., Suite 102, Arlington, TX 76012-2010

New England Ammunition Co., 1771 Post Rd. East, Suite 223, Westport, CT 06880/203-254-8048

New England Arms Co., Box 278, Lawrence Lane, Kittery Point, ME 03905/207-439-0593; FAX: 207-439-6726

New England Custom Gun Service, Brook Rd., RR2, Box 122W, W. Lebanon, NH 03784/603-469-3450; FAX: 603-469-3471

New England Firearms, 60 Industrial Rowe, Gardner, MA 01440/508-632-9393; FAX: 508-632-2300

New Historians Productions, The, 131 Oak St., Royal Oak, MI 48067/313-544-7544

New Orleans Arms Co., 5001 Treasure St., New Orleans, LA 70186/504-944-3371

New Orleans Jewelers Supply Co., 206 Charters St., New Orleans, LA 70130/504-523-3839

New Win Publishing, Inc., Box 5159, Clinton, NJ 08809/201-735-9701; FAX: 201-735-9703

Newark Electronics, 4801 N. Ravenswood Ave., Chicago, IL 60640

Newell, Robert H., 55 Coyote, Los Alamos, NM 87544/505-662-7135

Newman Gunshop, 119 Miller Rd., Agency, IA 52530/515-937-5775

NgraveR Co., The, 67 Wawecus Hill Rd., Bozrah, CT 06334/203-823-1533

Nichols Sports Optics, P.O. Box 37669, Omaha, NE 68137/402-339-3530; FAX: 402-330-8029

Nicholson Custom, Rt. 1, Box 176-3, Sedalia, MO 65301/816-826-8746

Nickels, Paul R., 4789 Summerhill Rd., Las Vegas, NV 89121/702-435-5318

Nicklas, Ted, 5504 Hegel Rd., Goodrich, MI 48438/810-797-4493

Nielsen Custom Cases, P.O. Box 26297, Las Vegas, NV 89126/800-377-1341, 702-878-5611; FAX: 702-877-4433

Niemi Engineering, W.B., Box 126 Center Road, Greensboro, VT 05841/802-533-7180 days, 802-533-7141 evenings

Nikon, Inc., 1300 Walt Whitman Rd., Melville, NY 11747/516-547-4200

Nitex, Inc., P.O. Box 1706, Uvalde, TX 78801/512-278-8843

Noble Co., Jim, 1305 Columbia St., Vancouver, WA 98660/206-695-1309

Nolan, Dave, Fox Valley Range, P.O. Box 155, Dundee, IL 60118/708-426-5921

Noreen, Peter H., 5075 Buena Vista Dr., Belgrade, MT 59714/406-586-7383

Norica, Avnda Otaola, 16, Apartado 68, 20600 Eibar, SPAIN (U.S. importers—American Arms, Inc.)

Norinco, 7A, Yun Tan N Beijing, CHINA (U.S. importers—Century International Arms, Inc.; ChinaSports, Inc.; Interarms)

Norma (See U.S. importer—Paul Co., The)

Norman Custom Gunstocks, Jim, 14281 Cane Rd., Valley Center, CA 92082/619-749-6252

Normark Corp., 1710 E. 78th St., Minneapolis, MN 55423/612-869-3291

Norrell Arms, John, 2608 Grist Mill Rd., Little Rock, AR 72207/501-225-7864

North American Arms, 2150 South 950 East, Provo, UT 84606-6285/800-821-5783, 801-374-9990; FAX: 801-374-9998

North American Correspondence Schools, The Gun Pro School, Oak & Pawney St., Scranton, PA 18515/717-342-7701

North American Shooting Systems, P.O. Box 306, Osoyoos, B.C. V0H 1V0 CANADA/604-495-3131; FAX: 604-495-2816

North American Specialties, 25442 Trabuco Rd., 105-328, Lake Forest, CA 92630/714-837-4867

North Devon Firearms Services, 3 North St., Braunton, EX33 1AJ ENGLAND

North Fork Custom Gunsmithing, James Johnston, 428 Del Rio Rd., Roseburg, OR 97470/503-673-4467

North Mountain Pine Training Center (See Executive Protection Institute)

North Specialty Products, 2664-B Saturn St., Brea, CA 92621/714-524-1665

North Star West, P.O. Box 488, Glencoe, CA 95232/209-293-7010

North Wind Decoys Co., 1005 N. Tower Rd., Fergus Falls, MN 56537/218-736-4378; FAX: 218-736-4378

Northern Precision Custom Swaged Bullets, 329 S. James St., Carthage, NY 13619/315-493-1711

Northlake Outdoor Footwear, P.O. Box 10, Franklin, TN 37065-0010/615-794-1556; FAX: 615-790-8005

No-Sho Mfg. Co., 10727 Glenfield Ct., Houston, TX 77096/713-723-5332

Nosler, Inc., P.O. Box 671, Bend, OR 97709/800-285-3701, 503-382-3921; FAX: 503-388-4667

Novak's, Inc., 1206 1/2 30th St., P.O. Box 4045, Parkersburg, WV 26101/304-485-9295; FAX: 304-428-6722

Nowlin Custom Mfg., Rt. 1, Box 308, Claremore, OK 74017/918-342-0689; FAX: 918-342-0624

NRI Schools, 4401 Connecticut Ave. NW, Washington, D.C. 20008

Nu-Line Guns, Inc., 1053 Caulks Hill Rd., Harvester, MO 63304/314-441-4500; FAX: 314-447-5018

Null Holsters Ltd., K.L., 161 School St. NW, Hill City Station, Resaca, GA 30735/706-625-5643; FAX: 706-625-9392

Numrich Arms Corp., 203 Broadway, W. Hurley, NY 12491

Nu-Teck, 30 Industrial Park Rd., Box 37, Centerbrook, CT 06409/203-767-3573; FAX: 203-767-9137

NW Sinker and Tackle, 380 Valley Dr., Myrtle Creek, OR 97457-9717

Nygord Precision Products, P.O. Box 8394, La Crescenta, CA 91224/818-352-3027; FAX: 818-352-3378

O

Oakland Custom Arms, Inc., 4690 W. Walton Blvd., Waterford, MI 48329/810-674-8261

Oakman Turkey Calls, RD 1, Box 825, Harrisonville, PA 17228/717-485-4620

Oakshore Electronic Sights, Inc., P.O. Box 4470, Ocala, FL 32678-4470/904-629-7112; FAX: 904-629-1433

Obermeyer Rifled Barrels, 23122 60th St., Bristol, WI 53104/414-843-3537; FAX: 414-843-2129

O'Connor Rifle Products Co., Ltd., 2008 Maybank Hwy., Charleston, SC 29412/803-795-8894

October Country, P.O. Box 969, Dept. GD, Hayden Lake, ID 83835/208-772-2068

Oehler Research, Inc., P.O. Box 9135, Austin, TX 78766/208-772-2068, 800-531-5125

Oglesby & Oglesby Gunmakers, Inc., RR 5, Springfield, IL 62707/217-487-7100

Oil Rod and Gun Shop, 69 Oak St., East Douglas, MA 01516/508-476-3687

Ojala Holsters, Arvo, P.O. Box 98, N. Hollywood, CA 91603/503-669-1404

OK Weber, Inc., P.O. Box 7485, Eugene, OR 97401/503-747-0458; FAX: 503-747-5927

Oker's Engraving, 365 Bell Rd., P.O. Box 126, Shawnee, CO 80475/303-838-6042

Oklahoma Ammunition Co., 4310 W. Rogers Blvd., Skiatook, OK 74070/918-396-3187; FAX: 918-396-4270

Oklahoma Leather Products, Inc., 500 26th NW, Miami, OK 74354/918-542-6651

Old Dominion Engravers, 100 Progress Drive, Lynchburg, VA 24502/804-237-4450

Old Wagon Bullets, 32 Old Wagon Rd., Wilton, CT 06897

Old West Bullet Moulds, P.O. Box 519, Flora Vista, NM 87415/505-334-6970

Old West Reproductions, Inc., 446 Florence S. Loop, Florence, MT 59833/406-273-2615

Old Western Scrounger, Inc., 12924 Hwy. A-I2, Montague, CA 96064/916-459-5445; FAX: 916-459-3944

Old World Gunsmithing, 2901 SE 122nd St., Portland, OR 97236/503-760-7681

Old World Oil Products, 3827 Queen Ave. N., Minneapolis, MN 55412/612-522-5037

Olde Pennsylvania, P.O. Box 912, New Kensington, PA 15068/412-337-1552

Ole Frontier Gunsmith Shop, 2617 Hwy. 29 S., Cantonment, FL 32533/904-477-8074

Olsen Development Lab, 111 Lakeview Ave., Blackwood, NJ 08012

Olson, Myron, 989 W. Kemp, Watertown, SD 57201/605-886-9787

Olson, Vic, 5002 Countryside Dr., Imperial, MO 63052/314-296-8086

Olt Co., Philip S., P.O. Box 550, 12662 Fifth St., Pekin, IL 61554/309-348-3633; FAX: 309-348-3300

Olympic Arms, Inc., 624 Old Pacific Hwy. SE, Olympia, WA 98503/206-456-3471; FAX: 206-491-3447

Olympic Optical Co., P.O. Box 752377, Memphis, TN 38175-2377/901-794-3890, 800-238-7120; FAX: 901-794-0676

Omark Industries, Div. of Blount, Inc., 2299 Snake River Ave., P.O. Box 856, Lewiston, ID 83501/800-627-3640, 208-746-2351

Omnishock, 2219 Verde Oak Drive, Hollywood, CA 90068

OMR Feinmechanik, Jagd-und Sportwaffen, GmbH, Postfach 1231, Schutzenstr. 20, D-5400 Koblenz, GERMANY/0261-31865-15351

One Of A Kind, 15610 Purple Sage, San Antonio, TX 78255/512-695-3364

Op-Tec, P.O. Box L632, Langhorn, PA 19047/215-757-5037

Optolyth-USA, Inc., 18805 Melvista Lane, Hillsboro, OR 97123/503-628-0246; FAX: 503-628-0797

Orchard Park Enterprise, P.O. Box 563, Orchard Park, NY 14227/616-656-0356

Ordnance Works, The, 2969 Pidgeon Point Road, Eureka, CA 95501/707-443-3252

Oregon Arms, Inc., 790 Stevens St., Medford, OR 97504-6746/503-560-4040

Original Mink Oil, Inc., P.O. Box 20191, 11021 NE Beach St., Portland, OR 97220/503-255-2814, 800-547-5895; FAX: 503-255-2487

Orion Rifle Barrel Co., RR2, 137 Cobler Village, Kalispell, MT 59901/406-257-5649

Or-Ün, Tahtakale Menekse Han 18, Istanbul, TURKEY 34460/90212-522-5912; FAX: 90212-522-7973

Orvis Co., The, Rt. 7, Manchester, VT 05254/802-362-3622 ext. 283; FAX: 802-362-3525

Ottmar, Maurice, Box 657, 113 E. Fir, Coulee City, WA 99115/509-632-5717

Outa-Site Gun Carriers, 219 Market, Laredo, TX 78040/210-722-4678, 800-880-9715; FAX: 210-726-4858

Outdoor Connection, Inc., The, 201 Douglas, P.O. Box 7751, Waco, TX 76712/800-533-6076; 817-772-5575; FAX: 817-776-6076
Outdoor Edge Cutlery Corp., 2888 Bluff St., Suite 130, Boulder, CO 80301/303-530-3855; FAX: 303-530-3855
Outdoor Sports Headquarters, Inc., 967 Watertower Lane, Dayton, OH 45449/513-865-5855; FAX: 513-865-5962
Outdoorsman's Bookstore, The, Llangorse, Brecon, Powys LD3 7UE, U.K./44-87484-660; FAX: 44-87484-650
Outers Laboratories, Div. of Blount, Inc., Route 2, Onalaska, WI 54650/608-781-5800
Owen, Harry, Sport Specialties, 100 N. Citrus Ave. 412, W. Covina, CA 91791-1614/818-968-5806
Ox-Yoke Originals, Inc., 34 Main St., Milo, ME 04463/800-231-8313; FAX: 207-943-2416
Ozark Gun Works, 11830 Cemetery Rd., Rogers, AR 72756/501-631-6944; FAX: 501-631-6944

P

P&M Sales and Service, 5724 Gainsborough Pl., Oak Forest, IL 60452/708-687-7149
P&S Gun Service, 2138 Old Shepardsville Rd., Louisville, KY 40218/502-456-9346
Pace Marketing, Inc., 9474 NW 48th St., Sunrise, FL 33351-5137/305-741-4361; FAX: 305-741-2901
Pachmayr Ltd., 1875 S. Mountain Ave., Monrovia, CA 91016/818-357-7771, 800-423-9704; FAX: 818-358-7251
Pacific Pistolcraft, 1810 E. Columbia Ave., Tacoma, WA 98404/206-474-5465
Pacific Tool Co., P.O. Box 2048, Ordnance Plant Rd., Grand Island, NE 68801
Pac-Nor Barreling, 99299 Overlook Rd., P.O. Box 6188, Brookings, OR 97415/503-469-7330; FAX: 503-469-7331
Paco's (See Small Custom Mould & Bullet Co.)
P.A.C.T., Inc., P.O. Box 531525, Grand Prairie, TX 75053/214-641-0049
Page Custom Bullets, P.O. Box 25, Port Moresby Papua, NEW GUINEA
Pagel Gun Works, Inc., 1407 4th St. NW, Grand Rapids, MN 55744/218-326-3003
Palmer Manufacturing Co., Inc., C., P.O. Box 220, West Newton, PA 15089/412-872-8200; FAX: 412-872-8302
Palmer Metal Products, 2930 N. Campbell Ave., Chicago, IL 60618/800-788-7725; FAX: 312-267-8080
Palmer Security Products, 2930 N. Campbell Ave., Chicago, IL 60618/800-788-7725; FAX: 312-267-8080
Palmgren Steel Products, 8383 S. Chicago Ave., Chicago, IL 60617/312-721-9675; FAX: 312-721-9739
Palsa Outdoor Products, P.O. Box 81336, Lincoln, NE 68501/402-456-9281, 800-456-9281; FAX: 402-488-2321
PanaVise Products, Inc., 1485 Southern Way, Sparks, NV 89431/702-353-2900; FAX: 702-353-2929
Para-Ordnance, Inc., 1919 NE 45th St., Ft. Lauderdale, FL 33308
Para-Ordnance Mfg., Inc., 3411 McNicoll Ave., Unit 14, Scarborough, Ont. M1V 2V6, CANADA/416-297-7855; FAX: 416-297-1289 (U.S. importer—Para-Ordnance, Inc.)
Paragon Sales & Services, Inc., P.O. Box 2022, Joliet, IL 60434/815-725-9212; FAX: 815-725-8974
Pardini Armi Commerciale Srl, Via Italica 154, 55043 Lido Di Camaiore Lu, ITALY/584-90121; FAX: 584-90122 (U.S. importers—MCS, Inc.; Nygord Precision Products)
Paris, Frank J., 17417 Pershing St., Livonia, MI 48152-3822
Parke-Bernet (See Sotheby's)
Parker, Mark D., 1240 Florida Ave. 7, Longmont, CO 80501/303-772-0214
Parker Div. Reageant Chemical (See Parker Reproductions)
Parker Gun Finishes, 9337 Smokey Row Rd., Strawberry Plains, TN 37871/615-933-3286
Parker Reproductions, 124 River Rd., Middlesex, NJ 08846/908-469-0100; FAX: 908-469-9692
Parker-Hale (See U.S. distributor—Navy Arms Co.)
Parsons Optical Mfg. Co., P.O. Box 192, Ross, OH 45061/513-867-0820
Partridge Sales Ltd., John, Trent Meadows, Rugeley, Staffordshire, WS15 2HS ENGLAND/0889-584438
Parts & Surplus, P.O. Box 22074, Memphis, TN 38122/901-683-4007
Pasadena Gun Center, 206 E. Shaw, Pasadena, TX 77506/713-472-0417; FAX: 713-472-1322
PAST Sporting Goods, Inc., P.O. Box 1035, Columbia, MO 65205/314-445-9200
Paterson Gunsmithing, 438 Main St., Paterson, NJ 07502/201-345-4100
Pathfinder Sports Leather, 2920 E. Chambers St., Phoenix, AZ 85040/602-276-0016
Patrick Bullets, P.O. Box 172, Warwick QSLD 4370 AUSTRALIA
Patriot Manufacturing, P.O. Box 50065, Lighthouse Point, FL 33074/305-783-4849
Pattern Control, 114 N. Third St., Garland, TX 75040/214-494-3551
Paul Co., The, 27385 Pressonville Rd., Wellsville, KS 66092/913-883-4444; FAX: 913-883-2525
Paulsen Gunstocks, Rt. 71, Box 11, Chinook, MT 59523/406-357-3403
Payne Photography, Robert, P.O. Box 141471, Austin, TX 78714/512-272-4554
PC Co., 5942 Secor Rd., Toledo, OH 43623/419-472-6222
Peacemaker Specialists, John Kopec Enterprises, P.O. Box 157, Whitmore, CA 96096/916-472-3438
Pease Accuracy, Bob, P.O. Box 310787, New Braunfels, TX 78131/210-625-1342
Peasley, David, P.O. Box 604, 2067 S. Hiway 17, Alamosa, CO 81101
PECAR Herbert Schwarz, GmbH, Kreuzbergstrasse 6, 10965 Berlin, GERMANY/004930-785-7383; FAX: 004930-785-1934
Pecatonica River Longrifle, 5205 Noddingham Dr., Rockford, IL 61111/815-968-1995; FAX: 815-968-1996
Pedersen, C.R., 2717 S. Pere Marquette Hwy., Ludington, MI 49431/616-843-2061
Pedersen, Rex C., 2717 S. Pere Marquette Hwy., Ludington, MI

49431/616-843-2061
Pedersoli Davide & C., Via Artigiani 53, Gardone V.T. (BS) ITALY 25063/030-8912402; FAX: 030-8911019 (U.S. importers—Beauchamp & Son, Inc.; Cabela's; Dixie Gun Works; EMF Co., Inc.; Navy Arms Co.)
Peerless Alloy, Inc., 1445 Osage St., Denver, CO 80204/303-825-6394, 800-253-1278
Peet Shoe Dryer, Inc., 130 S. 5th St., St. Maries, ID 83861/800-222-PEET; FAX: 208-245-5441
Pejsa Ballistics, 2120 Kenwood Pkwy., Minneapolis, MN 55405/612-374-3337; FAX: 612-374-3337
Pell, John T., 410 College, Trinidad, CO 81082/719-846-9406
Peltor, Inc., 41 Commercial Way, E. Providence, RI 02914/401-438-4800; FAX: 800-EAR-FAX1
PEM's Mfg. Co., 5063 Waterloo Rd., Atwater, OH 44201/216-947-3721
Pence Precision Barrels, 7567 E. 900 S., S. Whitley, IN 46787/219-839-4745
Pend Oreille Sport Shop, 3100 Hwy. 200 East, Sandpoint, ID 83864/208-263-2412
Pendleton Royal, 4/7 Highgate St., Birmingham, ENGLAND B12 0X5/44 21 440 3060; FAX: 44 21 446 4165
Pendleton Woolen Mills, P.O. Box 3030, 220 N.W. Broadway, Portland, OR 97208/503-226-4801
Penguin Industries, Inc., Airport Industrial Mall, Coatesville, PA 19320/215-384-6000
Penn Bullets, P.O. Box 756, Indianola, PA 15051
Penn's Woods Products, Inc., 19 W. Pittsburgh St., Delmont, PA 15626/412-468-8311
Pennsylvania Gun Parts, 638 Whiskey Spring Rd., Boiling Springs, PA 17007/717-258-5683
Pennsylvania Gunsmith School, 812 Ohio River Blvd., Avalon, Pittsburgh, PA 15202/412-766-1812
Penrod Precision, 312 College Ave., P.O. Box 307, N. Manchester, IN 46962/219-982-8385
Pentax Corp., 35 Inverness Dr. E., Englewood, CO 80112/303-799-8000
Pentheny de Pentheny, 2352 Baggett Ct., Santa Rosa, CA 95401/707-573-1390; FAX: 707-573-1390
Perazzi m.a.p. S.P.A., Via Fontanelle 1/3, 1-25080 Botticino Mattina, ITALY (U.S. importer—Perazzi USA, Inc.)
Perazzi USA, Inc., 1207 S. Shamrock Ave., Monrovia, CA 91016/818-303-0068
Performance Specialists, 308 Eanes School Rd., Austin, TX 78746/512-327-0119
Peripheral Data Systems (See Arms)
Personal Protection Systems, RD 5, Box 5027-A, Moscow, PA 18444/717-842-1766
Perugini Visini & Co. s.r.l., Via Camprelle, 126, 25080 Nuvolera (Bs.), ITALY 97004/503-654-8532
Peters & Hosea Gunmakers, 18255 Red Fox Dr., Beaver Creek, OR 97004/503-654-8532
Peters Stahl GmbH, Stettiner Str. 42, D-4790 Paderborn, GERMANY/05251-750025-27; FAX: 05251-75611 (U.S. importers—McMillan Gunworks, Inc.; Olympic Arms)
Petersen Publishing Co., 6420 Wilshire Blvd., Los Angeles, CA 90048
Peterson Gun Shop, A.W., Inc., 4255 W. Old U.S. 441, Mt. Dora, FL 32757-3299/904-383-4258
Petro-Explo, Inc., 7650 U.S. Hwy. 287, Suite 100, Arlington, TX 76017/817-478-8888
Pettinger Books, Gerald, Rt. 2, Box 125, Russell, IA 50238/515-535-2239
Pflumm Mfg. Co., 6139 Melrose Ln., Shawnee, KS 66203/800-888-4867; FAX: 913-631-3343
PFRB Co., P.O. Box 1242, Bloomington, IL 61701/309-473-3964
Phelps Mfg. Co., Box 2266, Evansville, IN 47714/812-476-8791
Phil-Chem, Inc., 2950 NW 29th, Portland, OR 97210/800-553-3022
Phillippi Custom Bullets, Justin, P.O. Box 773, Ligonier, PA 15658/412-238-9671
Phoenix Arms, 1420 S. Archibald Ave., Ontario, CA 91761/909-947-4843; FAX: 909-947-6798
Phoenix Arms Co. Ltd. (See Hy-Score Arms Co. Ltd.)
Photronic Systems Engineering Company, 6731 Via De La Reina, Bonsall, CA 92003/619-758-8000
Phyl-Mac, 609 NE 104th Ave., Vancouver, WA 98664/206-256-0579
Piedmont Community College, P.O. Box 1197, Roxboro, NC 27573/910-599-1181
Pierce Pistols, 2326 E. Hwy. 34, Newnan, GA 30263/404-253-8192
Pilgrim Pewter, Inc. (See Bell Originals, Sid)
Pilkington, Scott, Little Trees Ramble, P.O. Box 97, Monteagle, TN 37356/615-924-3475; FAX: 615-924-3489
Pilkington Gun Co., P.O. Box 1296, Muskogee, OK 74402/918-683-9418
Pine Technical College, 1100 4th St., Pine City, MN 55063/800-521-7463; FAX: 612-629-6766
Pioneer Arms Co., 355 Lawrence Rd., Broomall, OA 19008/215-356-5203
Pioneer Guns, 5228 Montgomery Rd., Norwood, OH 45212/513-631-4871
Pioneer Research, Inc., 216 Haddon Ave., Westmont, NJ 08108/609-854-2424, 800-257-7742; FAX: 609-858-8695
Piotti (See U.S. importer—Moore & Co., Wm. Larkin)
Piquette, Paul R., 80 Bradford Dr., Feeding Hills, MA 01030/413-781-8300, Ext. 682
Plaxco, J. Michael, Rt. 1, P.O. Box 203, Roland, AR 72135/501-868-9787
Plaza Cutlery, Inc., 3333 Bristol, 161, South Coast Plaza, Costa Mesa, CA 92626/714-549-3932
Plum City Ballistic Range, N2162 80th St., Plum City, WI 54761-8622/715-647-2539
P.M. Enterprises, Inc., 146 Curtis Hill Rd., Chehalis, WA 98532/206-748-3743; FAX: 206-748-1802
PMC/Eldorado Cartridge Corp., P.O. Box 62508, 12801 U.S. Hwy. 95 S., Boulder City, NV 89006-2508/702-294-0025; FAX: 702-294-0121
Pointing Dog Journal, Village Press Publications, P.O. Box 968, Dept. PGD, Traverse City, MI 49685/800-272-3246; Fax: 616-946-3289
Police Bookshelf, P.O. Box 122, Concord, NH 03301/603-224-6814; FAX: 603-226-3554

Policlips North America, 59 Douglas Crescent, Toronto, Ont. CANADA M4W 2E6/800-229-5089, 416-924-0383; FAX: 416-924-4375
Poly Technologies, Inc. (See U.S. importer—Keng's Firearms Specialty, Inc.)
Polywad, Inc., P.O. Box 7916, Macon, GA 31209/912-477-0669
Pomeroy, Robert, RR1, Box 50, E. Corinth, ME 04427/207-285-7721
Ponsness/Warren, P.O. Box 8, Rathdrum, ID 83858/208-687-2231; FAX: 208-687-2233
Pony Express Reloaders, 608 E. Co. Rd. D, Suite 3, St. Paul, MN 55117/612-483-9406; FAX: 612-483-9884
Pony Express Sport Shop, Inc., 16606 Schoenborn St., North Hills, CA 91343/818-895-1231
Porta Blind, Inc., 2700 Speedway, Wichita Falls, TX 76308/800-842-5545
Portus, Robert, 130 Ferry Rd., Grants Pass, OR 97526/503-476-4919
Potts, Wayne E., 912 Poplar St., Denver, CO 80220/303-355-5462
Powder Horn, Inc., The, P.O. Box 114 Patty Drive, Cusseta, GA 31805/404-989-3257
Powder Horn Antiques, P.O. Box 4196, Ft. Lauderdale, FL 33338/305-565-6060
Powell & Son (Gunmakers) Ltd., William, 35-37 Carrs Lane, Birmingham B4 7SX ENGLAND/21-643-0689; FAX: 21-631-3504 (U.S. importer—Bell's Legendary Country Wear)
Power Custom, Inc., RR 2, P.O. Box 756AB, Gravois Mills, MO 65037/314-372-5684
PPC Corp., 627 E. 24th St., Paterson, NJ 07514/201-278-5428
Practical Tools, Inc., Div. Behlert Precision, 7067 Easton Rd., P.O. Box 133, Pipersville, PA 18947/215-766-7301; FAX: 215-766-8681
Pragotrade, 307 Humberline Dr., Rexdale, Ontario, CANADA M9W 5V1/416-675-1322
Pranger, Ed G., 1414 7th St., Anacortes, WA 98221/206-293-3488
Precise International, 15 Corporate Dr., Orangeburg, NY 10962/914-365-3500
Precise Metalsmithing Enterprises, 146 Curtis Hill Rd., Chehalis, WA 98532/206-748-3743; FAX: 206-748-8102
Precision, Jim, 1725 Moclip's Dr., Petaluma, CA 94952/707-762-3014
Precision Airgun Sales, Inc., 5139 Warrensville Center Rd., Maple Hts., OH 44137-1906/216-587-5005
Precision Ballistics Co., P.O. Box 4374, Hamden, CT 06514/203-373-2293
Precision Bullet Co., 5200 A. Florence Loop, Dunsmuir, CA 96025/916-235-0565
Precision Cartridge, 176 Eastside Rd., Deer Lodge, MT 59722/800-397-3901, 406-846-3900
Precision Cast Bullets, 101 Mud Creek Lane, Ronan, MT 59864/406-676-5135
Precision Castings & Equipment, Inc., P.O. Box 326, Jasper, IN 47547-0135/812-634-9167
Precision Components and Guns, Rt. 55, P.O. Box 337, Pawling, NY 12564/914-855-3040
Precision Components, 3177 Sunrise Lake, Milford, PA 18337/717-686-4414
Precision Delta Corp., P.O. Box 128, Ruleville, MS 38771/601-756-2810; FAX: 601-756-2590
Precision Metal Finishing, John Westrom, P.O. Box 3186, Des Moines, IA 50316/515-288-8680; FAX: 515-244-3925
Precision Munitions, Inc., P.O. Box 326, Jasper, IN 47547
Precision Ordnance, 1316 E. North St., Jackson, MI 49202
Precision Reloading, Inc., P.O. Box 122, Stafford Springs, CT 06076/203-684-7979; FAX: 203-684-6788
Precision Rifles, Inc., 9814 Harney Bkwy. N., Omaha, NE 68114/402-397-3009; FAX: 402-393-7705
Precision Rifles, Inc., 19303 Ossenfort Ct., St. Louis, MO 63038/314-273-5159; FAX: 314-273-5149
Precision Sales International, Inc., P.O. Box 1776, Westfield, MA 01086/413-562-5055; FAX: 413-562-5056
Precision Shooting, Inc., 5735 Sherwood Forest Dr., Akron, OH 44319/216-882-2515; FAX: 216-882-2614
Precision Small Parts, Inc., 155 Carlton Rd., Charlottesville, VA 22902/804-293-6124
Precision Specialties, 131 Hendom Dr., Feeding Hills, MA 01030/413-786-3365; FAX: 413-786-3365
Precision Sport Optics, 15571 Producer Lane, Unit G, Huntington Beach, CA 92649/714-891-1309; FAX: 714-892-6920
Premier Reticles, 920 Breckinridge Lane, Winchester, VA 22601-6707
Prescott Projectile Co., 1808 Meadowbrook Road, Prescott, AZ 86303
Preslik's Gunstocks, 4245 Keith Ln., Chico, CA 95926/916-891-8236
Pre-Winchester 92-90-62 Parts Co., P.O. Box 8125, W. Palm Beach, FL 33407
Price Bullets, Patrick W., 16520 Worthley Drive, San Lorenzo, CA 94580/510-278-1547
Prime Reloading, 30 Chiswick End, Meldreth, Royston SG8 6LZ UK
Primos Wild Game Calls, Inc., P.O. Box 12785, Jackson, MS 39236-2785/601-366-1288; FAX: 601-362-3274
Pro Load Ammunition, Inc., 5180 E. Seltice Way, Post Falls, ID 83854/208-773-9444; FAX: 208-773-9441
Pro-Mark, Div. of Wells Lamont, 6640 W. Touhy, Chicago, IL 60648/312-647-8200
Pro-Port Ltd., 41302 Executive Dr., Harrison Twp., MI 48045-3448/810-469-7323; FAX: 810-469-0425
Pro-Shot Products, Inc., P.O. Box 763, Taylorville, IL 62568/217-824-9133; FAX: 217-824-8861
Professional Firearms Record Book Co. (See PFRB Co.)
Professional Gunsmiths of America, Inc., 1301 Franklin, Lexington, MO 64067/816-259-2636
Professional Hunter Supplies (See Star Custom Bullets)
Prolix, P.O. Box 1348, Victorville, CA 92393/800-248-LUBE, 619-243-3129; FAX: 619-241-0148
Protecto Plastics, Div. of Penguin Ind., Airport Industrial Mall, Coatesville, PA 19320/215-384-6000
Protector Mfg. Co., Inc., The, 443 Ashwood Place, Boca Raton, FL 33431/407-394-6011
Protektor Model, 1-11 Bridge St., Galeton, PA 16922/814-435-2442
Prototech Industries, Inc., Rt. 1, Box 81, Delia, KS 66418/913-771-3571; FAX: 913-771-2531

ProWare, Inc., 15847 NE Hancock St., Portland, OR 97230/503-239-0159
P.S.M.G. Gun Co., 10 Park Ave., Arlington, MA 02174/617-646-8845; FAX: 617-646-2133
PWL Gunleather, P.O. Box 450432, Atlanta, GA 31145/404-822-1640; FAX: 404-822-1704
Pyramid, Inc., 3292 S. Highway 97, Redmond, OR 97786

Q

Quack Decoy & Sporting Clays, 4 Ann & Hope Way, P.O. Box 98, Cumberland, RI 02864/401-723-8202; FAX: 401-722-5910
Quaker Boy, Inc., 5455 Webster Rd., Orchard Parks, NY 14127/716-662-3979
Qualigraphics, Inc., 25 Ruta Ct., P.O. Box 2306, S. Hackensack, NJ 07606/201-440-9200
Quality Arms, Inc., Box 19477, Dept. GD, Houston, TX 77224/713-870-8377; FAX: 713-870-8524
Quality Firearms of Idaho, Inc., 114 13th Ave. S., Nampa, ID 83651/208-466-1631
Quality Parts Co./Bushmaster Firearms, 999 Roosevelt Trail, Bldg. 3, Windham, ME 04062/800-998-7928, 207-892-2005; FAX: 207-892-8068
Quartz-Lok, 13137 N. 21st Lane, Phoenix, AZ 85029
Queen Cutlery Co., 507 Chestnut St., Titusville, PA 16354/800-222-5233
Quigley's Personal Protection Strategies, Paxton, 9903 Santa Monica Blvd.,, 300/Beverly Hills, CA 90212/310-281-1762
Quinetics Corp., P.O. Box 13237, San Antonio, TX 78213/512-684-8561; FAX: 512-684-2912

R

R&C Knives & Such, P.O. Box 1047, Manteca, CA 95336/209-239-3722
R&J Gun Shop, 133 W. Main St., John Day, OR 97845/503-575-2130
R&S Industries Corp., 8255 Brentwood Industrial Dr., St. Louis, MO 63144/314-781-5400
Rabeno, Martin, 92 Spook Hole Rd., Ellenville, NY 12428/914-647-4567
Radiator Specialty Co., 1900 Wilkinson Blvd., P.O. Box 34689, Charlotte, NC 28234/800-438-6947; FAX: 800-421-9525
Radical Concepts, P.O. Box 10731, Canoga Park, CA 91309-1731
Rainier Ballistics Corp., 4500 15th St. East, Tacoma, WA 98424/800-638-8722, 206-922-7589; FAX: 206-922-7854
Ram-Line, Inc., 545 Thirty-One Rd., Grand Junction, CO 81504/303-434-4500; FAX: 303-434-4004
Ranch Products, P.O. Box 145, Malinta, OH 43535/313-277-3118; FAX: 313-565-8536
Randall Firearms Research, P.O. Box 1586, Lomita, CA 90717-5586/310-325-0102; FAX: 310-325-0298
Randall-Made Knives, P.O. Box 1988, Orlando, FL 32802/407-855-8075
Randco UK, 286 Gipsy Rd., Welling, Kent DA16 1JJ, ENGLAND/44 81 303 4118
Randolph Engineering, Inc., 26 Thomas Patten Dr., Randolph, MA 02368/800-541-1405; FAX: 617-986-0337
Ranger Mfg. Co., Inc., 1536 Crescent Dr., Augusta, GA 30919/404-738-3469
Ranger Shooting Glasses, 26 Thomas Patten Dr., Randolph, MA 02368/800-541-1405; FAX: 617-986-0337
Ranging, Inc., Routes 5 & 20, East Bloomfield, NY 14443/716-657-6161
Ransom International Corp., P.O. Box 3845, 1040-A Sandretto Dr., Prescott, AZ 86302/602-778-7899; FAX: 602-778-7993
Rapine Bullet Mould Mfg. Co., 9503 Landis Lane, East Greenville, PA 18041/215-679-5413; FAX: 215-679-9795
Rattlers Brand, P.O. Box 311, Thomaston, GA 30286/800-652-1341; FAX: 404-647-2742
Ravell Ltd., 289 Diputacion St., 08009, Barcelona SPAIN
Ray's Gunsmith Shop, 3199 Elm Ave., Grand Junction, CO 81504/303-434-6162
Raytech, Div. of Lyman Products Corp., Rt. 32 Stafford Ind. Park, Box 6, Stafford Springs, CT 06076/203-684-4273; FAX: 203-684-7938
RCBS, Div. of Blount, Inc., 605 Oro Dam Blvd., Oroville, CA 95965/800-533-5000, 916-533-5191
R.D.P. Tool Co., Inc., 49162 McCoy Ave., East Liverpool, OH 43920/216-385-5129
Reagent Chemical & Research, Inc. (See Calico Hardwoods, Inc.)
Reardon Products, P.O. Box 126, Morrison, IL 61270/815-772-3155
Red Ball, 100 Factory St., Nashua, NH 03060/603-881-4420
Red Diamond Dist. Co., 1304 Snowdon Dr., Knoxville, TN 37912
Red River Frontier Outfitters, P.O. Box 241, Dept. GD, Tujunga, CA 91043/818-821-3167
Red Star Target Co., 4519 Brisebois Dr. NW, Calgary AB T2L 2G3 CANADA/403-289-7939; FAX: 403-289-3275
Redding Reloading Equipment, 1089 Starr Rd., Cortland, NY 13045/607-753-3331; FAX: 607-756-8445
Redfield, Inc., 5800 E. Jewell Ave., Denver, CO 80224/303-757-6411; FAX: 303-756-2338
Redman's Rifling & Reboring, Rt. 3, Box 330A, Omak, WA 98841/509-826-5512
Redmist Rifles, 316 W. Olive, Fresno, CA 93728/209-266-6363; FAX: 209-266-4638
Redwood Bullet Works, 3559 Bay Rd., Redwood City, CA 94063/415-367-6741
Reed, Dave, Rt. 1, Box 374, Minnesota City, MN 55959/507-689-2944
Reedy & Assoc., C.L., 2485 Grassmere Dr., Melbourne, FL 32904
Refrigiwear, Inc., 71 Inip Dr., Inwood, Long Island, NY 11696
Regional Associates, 6932 Little River Turnpike, Annandale, VA 22003/703-914-9338
Re-Heater, Inc., 15828 S. Broadway, C, Gardena, CA 90248
R.E.I., P.O. Box 88, Tallevast, FL 34270/813-755-0085
Reiswig, Wallace E., Claro Walnut Gunstock Co., 1235 Stanley Ave., Chico, CA 95928/916-342-5188
Reloaders Equipment Co., 4680 High St., Ecorse, MI 48229
Reloading Specialties, Inc., Box 1130, Pine Island, MN 55963/507-356-8500; FAX: 507-356-8800
Remington Arms Co., Inc., 1007 Market St., Wilmington, DE 19898/302-773-5291

Rencher Bullets, 5161 NE 5th St., Redmond, OR 97756
Renegade, P.O. Box 31546, Phoenix, AZ 85046/602-482-6777; FAX:
602-482-1952
Renfrew Guns & Supplies, R.R. 4, Renfrew, Ontario K7V 3Z7
CANADA/613-432-7080
Renner Co., R.J./Radical Concepts, P.O. Box 10731, Canoga Park, CA
91309/818-700-8131
Reno, Wayne, 2808 Stagestop Rd., Jefferson, CO 80456/719-836-3452
R.E.T. Enterprises, 2608 S. Chestnut, Broken Arrow, OK
74012/918-251-GUNS; FAX: 918-251-0587
Retting, Inc., Martin B., 11029 Washington, Culver City, CA
90232/213-837-2412
Reynolds, Lois M., 321 Lindenwood Ln. S., Hewitt, TX 76643/817-669-9686
R.G.-G., Inc., P.O. Box 1261, Conifer, CO 80433-1261/303-697-4154; FAX:
303-697-4154
Rhodeside, Inc., 1704 Commerce Dr., Piqua, OH 45356/513-773-5781
Rice, Keith (See White Rock Tool & Die)
Richards Classic Oil Finish, John, Rt. 2, Box 325, Bedford, KY
40006/502-255-7222
Richards Micro-Fit Stocks, 8331 N. San Fernando Rd., P.O. Box 1066, Sun
Valley, CA 91352/818-767-6097
Rickard, Inc., Pete, RD 1, Box 292, Cobleskill, NY 12043/800-282-5663; FAX:
518-234-2454
Ridgetop Sporting Goods, P.O. Box 306, 42907 Hilligoss Ln. East, Eatonville,
WA 98328/206-832-6422
Riebe Co., W.J., 3434 Tucker Rd., Boise, ID 83703
Ries, Chuck, 415 Ridgecrest Dr., Grants Pass, OR 97527/503-476-5623
Rifle Shop, The, Wm. H. Hobaugh, P.O. Box M, Philipsburg, MT
59858/406-859-3515
Rifle Works & Armory, 707 N 12 St., Cody, WY 82414/307-587-4914
RIG Products, 87 Coney Island Dr., Sparks, NV 89431-6334/702-331-5666;
FAX: 702-331-5669
Rigby & Co., John, 66 Great Suffolk St., London SE1 OBU, ENGLAND (U.S.
importer—Griffin & Howe, Inc.)
Riggs, Jim, 206 Azalea, Boerne, TX 78006/210-249-8567
Riling Arms Books Co., Ray, 6844 Gorsten St., P.O. Box 18925, Philadelphia,
PA 19119/215-438-2456
Rim Pac Sports, Inc., 1034 N. Soldano Ave., Azusa, CA 9170222-2135
Rimrock Rifle Stocks, P.O. Box 589, Vashon Island, WA 98070/206-463-5531
Ringler Custom Leather Co., P.O. Box 206, Cody, WY 82414/307-645-3255
R.I.S. Co., Inc., 718 Timberlake Circle, Richardson, TX 75080/214-235-0933
River Road Sporting Clays, Bruce Barsotti, P.O. Box 3016, Gonzales, CA
93926/408-675-2473
Rizzini, F.LLI (See U.S. importers—Moore & Co., Wm. Larkin; New England
Arms Co.)
Rizzini Battista, Via 2 Giugno, 7/7Bis-25060 Marcheno (Brescia), ITALY
(U.S. importer—Alessandri & Son, Lou)
RLCM Enterprises, 110 Hill Crest Drive, Burleson, TX 76028
RMS Custom Gunsmithing, 4120 N. Bitterwell, Prescott Valley, AZ
86314/602-772-7626
Robar Co.'s, Inc., The, 21438 N. 7th Ave., Suite B, Phoenix, AZ
85027/602-581-2648; FAX: 602-582-0059
Robbins Scent, Inc., P.O. Box 779, Connellsville, PA 15425/412-628-2529;
FAX: 412-628-9598
Roberts, J.J., 7808 Lake Dr., Manassas, VA 22111/703-330-0448
Roberts Products, 25238 SE 32nd, Issaquah, WA 98027/206-392-8172
Robinson, Don, Pennsylvania Hse., 36 Fairfax Crescent, Southowram,
Halifax, W. Yorkshire HX3 9SQ, ENGLAND/0422-364458
Robinson Firearms Mfg. Ltd., RR2, Suite 51, Comp. 24, Winfield, B.C.
CANADA V0H 2C0/604-766-5353
Robinson H.V. Bullets, 3145 Church St., Zachary, LA 70791/504-654-4029
Rochester Lead Works, 76 Anderson Ave., Rochester, NY 14607/716-442-8500
Rockwood Corp., Speedwell Division, 136 Lincoln Blvd., Middlesex, NJ
08846/908-560-7171
Rocky Fork Enterprises, P.O. Box 427, 878 Battle Rd., Nolensville, TN
37135/615-941-1307
Rocky Mountain Arms, Inc., 600 S. Sunset, Unit C, Longmont, CO
80501/303-768-8522; FAX: 303-678-8766
Rocky Mountain High Sports Glasses, 8121 N. Central Park Ave., Skokie, IL
60076/708-679-1012; FAX: 708-679-0184
Rocky Mountain Rifle Works Ltd., 1707 14th St., Boulder, CO 80302/303-443-9189
Rocky Mountain Target Co., 3 Aloe Way, Leesburg, FL 34788/904-365-9598
Rocky Mountain Wildlife Products, P.O. Box 999, La Porte, CO
80535/303-484-2768; FAX: 303-223-9389
Rocky Shoes & Boots, 294 Harper St., Nelsonville, OH 45764/800-421-5151,
614-753-1951; FAX: 614-753-4042
Rod Guide Co., Box 1149, Forsyth, MO 65653/800-952-2774
Rogers Gunsmithing, Bob, P.O. Box 305, 344 S. Walnut St., Franklin Grove,
IL 61031/815-456-2685; FAX: 815-288-7142
Rohner, Hans, 1148 Twin Sisters Ranch Rd., Nederland, CO 80466-9600
Rohner, John, 710 Sunshine Canyon, Boulder, CO 80302/303-444-3841
Rolston Jr., Fred W., 210 E. Cummins St., Tecumseh, MI
49286/517-423-6002; FAX: 517-423-6002
Romain's Custom Guns, RD 1, Whetstone Rd., Brockport, PA
15823/814-265-1948
Rooster Laboratories, P.O. Box 412514, Kansas City, MO
64141/816-474-1622; FAX: 816-474-1307
Rorschach Precision Products, P.O. Box 151613, Irving, TX
75015/214-790-3487
Rosenberg & Sons, Jack A., 12229 Cox Lane, Dallas, TX 75234/214-241-6302
Rosenthal, Brad and Sallie, 19303 Ossenfort Ct., St. Louis, MO
63038/314-273-5159; FAX: 314-273-5149
Ross, Don, 12813 West 83 Terrace, Lenexa, KS 66215/913-492-6982
Rosser, Bob, 267 W. Valley Ave., Suite 158, Birmingham, AL
35209/205-870-4422
Rossi S.A., Amadeo, Rua: Amadeo Rossi, 143, Sao Leopoldo, RS, BRAZIL
93030-220/051-592-5566 (U.S. importer—Interarms)

Roto Carve, 2754 Garden Ave., Janesville, IA 50647
Round Edge, Inc., P.O. Box 723, Lansdale, PA 19446/215-361-0859
Rowe Engineering, Inc. (See R.E.I.)
Roy's Custom Grips, Rt. 3, Box 174-E, Lynchburg, VA 24504/804-993-3470
Royal Arms, 5126 3rd Ave. N., Great Falls, MT 59405/406-453-1149
RPM, 15481 N. Twin Lakes Dr., Tucson, AZ 85737/602-825-1233; FAX:
602-825-3333
Rubright Bullets, 1008 S. Quince Rd., Walnutport, PA 18088/215-767-1339
Rucker Ammunition Co., P.O. Box 479, Terrell, TX 75160
Rudnicky, Susan, 8714 Center St., Holland, NY 14080/716-941-3259
Ruger (See Sturm, Ruger & Co.)
Ruko Products, Inc., P.O. Box 1181, Buffalo, NY 14240-1181/905-874-2707;
FAX: 905-826-1353
Rundell's Gun Shop, 6198 Frances Rd., Clio, MI 48420/313-687-0559
Runge, Robert P., 94 Grove St., Ilion, NY 13357/315-894-3036
Rupert's Gun Shop, 2202 Dick Rd., Suite B, Fenwick, MI 48834/517-248-3252
Russell Knives, Inc., A.G., 1705 Hwy. 71B North, Springdale, AR
72764/501-751-7341
Rusteprufe Laboratories, 1319 Jefferson Ave., Sparta, WI
54656/608-269-4144
Rusty Duck Premium Gun Care Products, 7785 Founion Dr., Florence, KY
41042/606-342-5553
Rutgers Book Center, 127 Raritan Ave., Highland Park, NJ
08904/908-545-4344; FAX: 908-545-6686
Rutgers Gun & Boat Center, 127 Raritan Ave., Highland Park, NJ
08904/908-545-4344; FAX: 908-545-6686
Ruvel & Co., Inc., 4128-30 W. Belmont Ave., Chicago, IL 60641/312-286-9494
R.V.I., P.O. Box 8019-56, Blaine, WA 98230/206-595-2933
RWS (See U.S. importer—Dynamit Nobel-RWS, Inc.)
Ryan, Chad L., RR 3, Box 72, Cresco, IA 52136/319-547-4384
Rybka Custom Leather Equipment, Thad, 32 Havilah Hill, Odenville, AL 35120

S

S&B Industries, 11238 McKinley Rd., Montrose, MI 48457/313-639-5491
S&H Arms Mfg. Co., Rt. 3, Box 689, Berryville, AR 72616/501-545-3511
S&K Mfg. Co., P.O. Box 247, Pittsfield, PA 16340/814-563-7808; FAX:
814-563-7808
S&S Firearms, 74-11 Myrtle Ave., Glendale, NY 11385/718-497-1100; FAX:
718-497-1105
Sabertooth Industries, P.O. Box 772, Santa Clara, CA 95052
SAECO (See Redding Reloading Equipment)
Safari Arms/SGW (See Olympic Arms, Inc.)
Safari Outfitters Ltd., 71 Ethan Allan Hwy., Ridgefield, CT 06877/203-544-9505
Safari Plus, 218 Quinlan, Suite 322, Kerrville, TX 78028-5314/210-367-5209
Safari Press, Inc., 15621 Chemical Lane B, Huntington Beach, CA
92649/714-894-9080; FAX: 714-894-4949
Safariland Ltd., Inc., 3120 E. Mission Blvd., P.O. Box 51478, Ontario, CA
91761/909-923-7300; FAX: 909-923-7400
SAFE, P.O. Box 864, Post Falls, ID 83854/208-773-3624
Safesport Manufacturing Co., 1100 W. 45th Ave., Denver, CO
80211/303-433-6506; FAX: 303-433-4112
Safety Speed Holster, 910 S. Vail Ave., Montebello, CA
90640/213-723-4140; FAX: 213-726-6973
Sako Ltd., P.O. Box 149, SF-11101, Riihimaki, FINLAND
(U.S. importer—Stoeger Industries)
Salter Calls, Inc., Eddie, Hwy. 31 South-Brewton Industrial Park, Brewton, AL
36426/205-867-2584; FAX: 206-867-9005
Samco Global Arms, Inc., 6995 NW 43rd St., Miami, FL 33166/305-593-9782
Sampson, Roger, 430 N. Grove, Mora, MN 55051/612-679-4868
San Angelo Sports Products, Inc., 909 W. 14th St., San Angelo, TX
76903/915-655-7126; FAX: 915-653-6720
San Francisco Gun Exchange, 124 Second St., San Francisco, CA
94105/415-982-6097
San Marco (See U.S. importers—Cape Outfitters; EMF Co., Inc.)
Sanders Custom Gun Service, 2358 Tyler Ln., Louisville, KY
40205/502-454-3338
Sanders Gun and Machine Shop, 145 Delhi Road, Manchester, IA 52057
Sandia Die & Ctg. Co., 37 Atancacio Rd. NE, Albuquerque, NM
87123/505-298-5729
Sandy's Custom Gunshop, Rt. 1, P.O. Box 4, Rockport, IL
62370/217-437-4241
Sarco, Inc., 323 Union St., Stirling, NJ 07980/908-647-3800
Sauer (See U.S. importer—Paul Co., The)
Sauer Sporting Rifles, P.O. Box 37669, Omaha, NE 68137
Saunders Gun & Machine Shop, R.R. 2, Delhi Road, Manchester, IA 52057
Savage Arms, Inc., Springdale Rd., Westfield, MA 01085/413-568-7001;
FAX: 413-562-7764
Savana Sports, Inc., 5763 Ferrier St., Montreal, Quebec,
CANADA/514-739-1753; FAX: 514-739-1755
Saville Iron Co. (See Greenwood Precision)
Scanco Environmental Systems, 5000 Highlands Parkway, Suite 180,
Atlanta, GA 30082/404-431-0025; FAX: 404-431-0028
Scansport, Inc., P.O. Box 700, Enfield, NH 03748/603-632-7654
Scattergun Technologies, Inc., 518 3rd Ave. S., Nashville, TN
37210/615-254-1441
Sceery Co., E.J., 2308 Cedros Circle, Sante Fe, NM 87505/505-983-2125
Schaefer Shooting Sports, 2280 Grand Ave., Baldwin, NY
11510/516-379-4900; FAX: 516-379-6701
Scharch Mfg., Inc., 10325 Co. Rd. 120, Unit C, Salida, CO 81201/719-539-7242
Scherer, Box 250, Ewing, VA 24248/615-733-2615; FAX: 615-733-2073
Schiffman, Curt, 3017 Kevin Cr., Idaho Falls, ID 83402/208-524-4684
Schiffman, Mike, 8233 S. Crystal Springs, McCammon, ID
83250/208-254-9114
Schiffman, Norman, 3017 Kevin Cr., Idaho Falls, ID 83402/208-524-4684
Schmidpke, Karl, P.O. Box 51692, New Berlin, WI 53151
Schmidt & Bender, Inc., Brook Rd., P.O. Box 134, Meriden, NH

03770/603-469-3565, 800-468-3450; FAX: 603-469-3471
Schmidt, Herbert (See U.S. importer—Sportarms of Florida)
Schmidtman Custom Ammunition, 6 Gilbert Court, Cotati, CA 94931
Schneider Bullets, 3655 West 214th St., Fairview Park, OH 44126
Schneider Rifle Barrels, Inc., Gary, 12202 N. 62nd Pl., Scottsdale, AZ
    85254/602-948-2525
School of Gunsmithing, The, 6065 Roswell Rd., Atlanta, GA
    30328/800-223-4542
Schrimsher's Custom Knifemaker's Supply, Bob, P.O. Box 308, Emory, TX
    75440/903-473-3330; FAX: 903-473-2235
Schulz Industries, 16247 Minnesota Ave., Paramount, CA
    90723/213-439-5903
Schumakers Gun Shop, William, 512 Prouty Corner Lp. A, Colville, WA
    99114/509-684-4848
Schwartz Custom Guns, David W., 2505 Waller St., Eau Claire, WI
    54703/715-832-1735
Schwartz Custom Guns, Wayne E., 970 E. Britton Rd., Morrice, MI
    48857/517-625-4079
Scobey Duck & Goose Calls, Glynn, Rt. 3, Box 37, Newbern, TN
    38059/901-643-6241
Scope Control, Inc., 5775 Co. Rd. 23 SE, Alexandria, MN 56308/612-762-7295
ScopLevel, 977 E. Stanley Blvd. 365, Livermore, CA 94550/510-449-5052;
    FAX: 510-373-0861
Scot Powder Co., Rt. 1, Box 167, McEwen, TN 37101/615-729-4207; FAX:
    615-729-4217
Scotch Hunting Products Co., Inc., 6619 Oak Orchard Rd., Elba, NY
    14058/716-757-9958; FAX: 716-757-9066
Scott, Dwight, 23089 Englehardt St., Clair Shores, MI 48080/313-779-4735
Scott, McDougall & Associates, 7950 Redwood Dr., Cotati, CA
    94931/707-546-2264
Scott Fine Guns, Inc., Thad, P.O. Box 412, Indianola, MS 38751/601-887-5929
S.C.R.C., P.O. Box 660, Katy, TX 77492-0660/713-492-6332; FAX:
    713-578-3134
Scruggs' Game Calls, Stanley, Rt. 1, Hwy. 661, Cullen, VA
    23934/804-542-4241, 800-323-4828
Seattle Binocular & Scope Repair Co., P.O. Box 46094, Seattle, WA
    98146/206-932-3733
Second Chance Body Armor, P.O. Box 578, Central Lake, MI
    49622/616-544-5721; FAX: 616-544-9824
Security Awareness & Firearms Education (See S.A.F.E.)
Seebeck Assoc., R.E., P.O. Box 59752, Dallas, TX 75229
Seecamp Co., Inc., L.W., P.O. Box 255, New Haven, CT 06502/203-877-3429
Seligman Shooting Products, Box 133, Seligman, AZ 86337/602-422-3607
Selsi Co., Inc., 40 Veterans Blvd., Carlstadt, NJ 07072-0497/201-935-5851
Semmer, Charles, 7885 Cyd Dr., Denver, CO 80221/303-429-6947
Serva Arms Co., Inc., RD 1, Box 483A, Greene, NY 13778/607-656-4764
Service Armament, 689 Bergen Blvd., Ridgefield, NJ 07657
Servus Footwear Co., 1136 2nd St., Rock Island, IL
    61204-3610/309-786-7741; FAX: 309-786-9808
SGS Importers International, Inc., 1750 Brielle Ave., Unit B1, Wanamassa, NJ
    07712/908-493-0302; FAX: 908-493-0301
S.G.S. Sporting Guns Srl., Via Della Resistenza, 37, 20090 Buccinasco (MI)
    ITALY/2-45702446; FAX: 2-45702464
Shappy Bullets, 76 Milldale Ave., Plantsville, CT 06479/203-621-3704
Sharon Rifle Barrel Co., 14396 D. Tuolumne Rd., Sonora, CA
    95370/209-532-4139
Sharp Shooter, Inc., P.O. Box 21362, St. Paul, MN 55121/612-452-4687
Sharps Arms Co., Inc., C. (See Montana Armory, Inc.)
Shaw, Inc., E.R. (See Small Arms Mfg. Co.)
Shay's Gunsmithing, 931 Marvin Ave., Lebanon, PA 17042
Sheffield Knifemakers Supply, P.O. Box 141, Deland, FL
    32721/904-775-6453; FAX: 904-774-5754
Shell Shack, 113 E. Main, MT 59044/406-628-8986
Shepherd Scope Ltd., Box 189, Waterloo, NE 68069/402-779-2424; FAX:
    402-779-4010
Sheridan USA, Inc., Austin, P.O. Box 577, Durham, CT 06422
Sherk, Dan A., 1311-105 Ave., Dawson Creek, B.C. V1G 2L9,
    CANADA/604-782-3720
Sherwood, George, 46 N. River Dr., Roseburg, OR 97470/503-672-3159
Sherwood Intl. Export Corp., 18714 Parthenia St., Northridge, CA
    91324/818-349-7600
Shilen Rifles, Inc., P.O. Box 1300, 205 Metro Park Blvd., Ennis, TX
    75120/214-875-5318; FAX: 214-875-5402
Shiloh Creek, Box 357, Cottleville, MO 63338/314-447-2900; FAX:
    314-447-2900
Shiloh Rifle Mfg., P.O. Box 279, Big Timber, MT 59011/406-932-4454; FAX:
    406-932-5627
Shirley Co. Gun & Riflemakers Ltd., J.A., P.O. Box 368, High Wycombe,
    Bucks. HP13 6YN, ENGLAND/0494-446883; FAX: 0494-463685
Shockley, Harold H., 204 E. Farmington Rd., Hanna City, IL
    61536/309-565-4524
Shoemaker & Sons, Inc., Tex, 714 W. Cienega Ave., San Dimas, CA
    91750/714-592-2071; FAX: 714-592-2378
Shooter Shop, The, 221 N. Main, Butte, MT 59701/406-723-3842
Shooter's Choice, 16770 Hilltop Park Place, Chagrin Falls, OH
    44023/216-543-8808; FAX: 216-543-8811
Shooter's Edge, Inc., P.O.Box 769, Trinidad, CO 81082
Shooter's Supply, RR1, Box 333B, Rt. 55, Poughquag, NY
    12570/914-724-3088; FAX: 914-724-3454
Shooter's World, 3828 N. 28th Ave., Phoenix, AZ 85017/602-266-0170
Shooters Supply, 1120 Tieton Dr., Yakima, WA 98902/509-452-1181
Shootin' Accessories, Ltd., P.O. Box 6810, Auburn, CA 95604/916-889-2220
Shootin' Shack, Inc., 1065 Silver Beach Rd., Riviera Beach, FL
    33403/407-842-0990
Shooting Arts Ltd., Box 621399, Littleton, CO 80162/303-933-2539
Shooting Chrony, Inc., 3269 Niagara Falls Blvd., N. Tonawanda, NY
    14120/905-276-6292; FAX: 416-276-6295

Shooting Gallery, The, 8070 Southern Blvd., Boardman, OH 44512/216-726-7788
Shooting Specialties (See Titus, Daniel)
Shooting Star, 1825 Fortview Rd., Ste. 115, Austin, TX 78747/512-462-0009
Shoptask, P.O. Box 591, Montesano, WA 98563/800-343-5775
Shotgun Bullets Mfg., Rt. 3, Box 41, Robinson, IL 62454/618-546-5043
Shotgun Shop, The, 14145 Proctor Ave., Suite 3, Industry, CA
    91746/818-855-2737; FAX: 818-855-2735
Shotguns Unlimited, 2307 Fon Du Lac Rd., Richmond, VA 23229/804-752-7115
Shurkatch Corp., P.O. Box 850, Richfield Springs, NY 13439/315-858-1470;
    FAX: 315-858-2969
Siegrist Gun Shop, 8754 Turtle Road, Whittemore, MI 48770
Sierra Bullets, 1400 W. Henry St., Sedalia, MO 65301/816-827-6300; FAX:
    816-827-4999
Sierra Specialty Prod. Co., 1344 Oakhurst Ave., Los Altos, CA 94024
SIG, CH-8212 Neuhausen, SWITZERLAND (U.S. importer—Mandall
    Shooting Supplies, Inc.)
Sigarms, Inc., Industrial Drive, Exeter, NH 03833/603-772-2302; FAX:
    603-772-9082
Sight Shop, The, John G. Lawson, 1802 E. Columbia Ave., Tacoma, WA
    98404/206-474-5465
Sightron, Inc., 9000 W. Sheridan St., Pembroke Pines, FL
    33024/305-438-4227; FAX: 305-438-3465
Signet Metal Corp., 551 Stewart Ave., Brooklyn, NY 11222/718-384-5400;
    FAX: 718-388-7488
SIG-Sauer (See U.S. importer—Sigarms, Inc.)
Sile Distributors, Inc., 7 Centre Market Pl., New York, NY
    10013/212-925-4389; FAX: 212-925-3149
Silencio/Safety Direct, 56 Coney Island Dr., Sparks, NV 89431/800-648-1812,
    702-354-4451; FAX: 702-359-1074
Silent Hunter, 1100 Newton Ave., W. Collingswood, NJ 08107/609-854-3276
Silhouette Leathers, P.O. Box 1161, Gunnison, CO 81230/303-641-6639
Silver Eagle Machining, 18007 N. 69th Ave., Glendale, AZ 85308
Silver Ridge Gun Shop (See Goodwin, Fred)
Silver-Tip Corp., RR2, Box 184, Gloster, MS 39638-9520
Simmons, Jerry, 715 Middlebury St., Goshen, IN 46526/219-533-8546
Simmons Enterprises, Ernie, 709 East Elizabethtown Rd., Manheim, PA
    17545/717-664-4040
Simmons Outdoor Corp., 2120 Killearney Way, Tallahassee, FL
    32308-3402/904-878-5100; FAX: 904-878-0300
Sinclair, W.P., Box 1209, Warminster, Wiltshire BA12 9XJ,
    ENGLAND/01044-985-218544; FAX: 01044-985-214111
Sinclair International, Inc., 2330 Wayne Haven St., Fort Wayne, IN
    46803/219-493-1858; FAX: 219-493-2530
Single Shot, Inc. (See Montana Armory, Inc.)
Singletary, Kent, 7516 W. Sells, Phoenix, AZ 85033/602-849-5917
Sioux Bullets, P.O. Box 3696, Midland, TX 79702
Sipes Gun Shop, 7415 Asher Ave., Little Rock, AR 72204/501-565-8480
Siskiyou Gun Works (See Donnelly, C.P.)
Six Enterprises, 320-D Turtle Creek Ct., San Jose, CA 95125/408-999-0201;
    FAX: 408-999-0216
S.K. Guns, Inc., 3041A Main Ave., Fargo, ND 58103/701-293-4867; FAX:
    701-232-0001
Skaggs, R.E., 1217 S. Church St., Princeton, IL 61356/815-875-8207
SKB Arms Co., C.P.O. Box 1401, Tokyo, JAPAN (U.S. importer—G.U., Inc.)
Skeoch, Brian R., P.O. Box 279, Glenrock, WY 82637/307-436-9804; FAX:
    307-436-9804
Skip's Machine, 364 29 Road, Grand Junction, CO 81501/303-245-5417
Sklany, Steve, 566 Birch Grove Dr., Kalispell, MT 59901/406-755-4257
SKR Industries, POB 1382, San Angelo, TX 76902/915-658-3133
S.L.A.P. Industries, P.O. Box 1121, Parklands 2121, SOUTH
    AFRICA/27-11-788-0030; FAX: 27-11-788-0030
Slezak, Jerome F., 1290 Marlowe, Lakewood (Cleveland), OH
    44107/216-221-1668
Slings & Arrows, RR1, Box 95, Derby Line, VT 05830
Slings 'N Things, Inc., 8909 Bedford Circle, Suite 11, Omaha, NE
    68134/402-571-6954; FAX: 402-571-7082
Slipshot MTS Group, P.O. Box 5, Postal Station D, Etobicoke, Ont., CANADA
    M9A 4X1/FAX: 416-762-0962
Slug Site Co., Ozark Wilds, Rt. 2, Box 158, Versailles, MO
    65084/314-378-6430
Small Arms Mfg. Co., 611 Thoms Run Rd., Bridgeville, PA
    15017/412-221-4343; FAX: 412-221-8443
Small Custom Mould & Bullet Co., Box 17211, Tucson, AZ 85731
Small Group Bullets, P.O. Box 20, Mertzon, TX 76941/915-835-4751
Smires, C.L., 28269 Old Schoolhouse Rd., Columbus, NJ 08022/609-298-3158
Smith & Wesson, 2100 Roosevelt Ave., Springfield, MA 01102/413-781-8300
Smith, Art, P.O. Box 13, Hector, MN 55342/612-848-2760
Smith, Mark A., 200 N. 9th, Sinclair, WY 82334/307-324-7929
Smith, Michael, 620 Nye Circle, Chattanooga, TN 37405/615-267-8341
Smith, Ron, 5869 Straley, Ft. Worth, TX 76114/817-732-6768
Smith, Sharmon, 4545 Speas Rd., Fruitland, ID 83619/208-452-6329
Smith Saddlery, Jesse W., 3601 E. Boone Ave., Spokane, WA
    99202-4501/509-325-0622
Smith Whetstone Co., Inc., 1700 Sleepy Valley Rd., P.O. Box 5095, Hot
    Springs, AR 71902-5095/501-321-2244; FAX: 501-321-9232
Smokey Valley Rifles (See Lutz Engraving, Ron)
Snapp's Gunshop, 6911 E. Washington Rd., Clare, MI 48617/517-386-9226
Snider Stocks, Walter S., Rt. 2 P.O. Box 147, Denton, NC 27239
Sno-Seal (See Atsko/Sno-Seal)
Societa Armi Bresciane Srl., Via Artigiani 93, Gardone Val Trompia, ITALY
    25063/30-8911640, 30-8911648 (U.S. importer—Cape Outfitters)
Solothurn (See U.S. importer—Sile Distributors)
Sonderman, Robert, 735 Kenton Dr., Charleston, IL 61920/217-345-5429
Soque River Knives, P.O. Box 880, Clarkesville, GA 30523/706-754-8500;
    FAX: 706-754-7263
SOS Products Co. (See Buck Stix—SOS Products Co.)
Sotheby's, 1334 York Ave. at 72nd St., New York, NY 10021

Sound Technology, P.O. Box 1132, Kodiak, AK 99615/907-486-8448
South Bend Replicas, Inc., 61650 Oak Rd., South Bend, IN 46614/219-289-4500
Southeastern Community College, 1015 S. Gear Ave., West Burlington, IA 52655/319-752-2731
Southern Ammunition Co., Inc., Rt. 1, Box 6B, Latta, SC 29565/803-752-7751; FAX: 803-752-2022
Southern Armory, The, Rt. 2, Box 134, Woodlawn, VA 24381/703-236-7835; FAX: 703-236-3714
Southern Bloomer Mfg. Co., P.O. Box 1621, Bristol, TN 37620/615-878-6660; FAX: 615-878-8761
Southern Security, 1700 Oak Hills Dr., Kingston, TN 37763/615-376-6297; 800-251-9992
Southwest Institute of Firearms Training (See S.W.I.F.T.)
Southwind Sanctions, P.O. Box 445, Aledo, TX 76008/817-441-8917
Sparks, Milt, 605 E. 44th St. No. 2, Boise, ID 83714-4800
Spartan-Realtree Products, Inc., 1390 Box Circle, Columbus, GA 31907/706-569-9101; FAX: 706-569-0042
Specialty Gunsmithing, Lynn McMurdo, P.O. Box 404, Afton, WY 83110/307-886-5535
Specialty Shooters Supply, Inc., 3325 Griffin Rd., Suite 9mm, Fort Lauderdale, FL 33317
Speedfeed, Inc., P.O. Box 258, Lafayette, CA 94549/510-284-2929; FAX: 510-284-2879
Speer Products, Div. of Blount, Inc., P.O. Box 856, Lewiston, ID 83501/208-746-2351; FAX: 208-746-2915
Spegel, Craig, P.O. Box 108, Bay City, OR 97107/503-377-2697
Speiser, Fred D., 2229 Dearborn, Missoula, MT 59801/406-549-8133
Spence, George W., 115 Locust St., Steele, MO 63877/314-695-4926
Spencer Reblue Service, 1820 Tupelo Trail, Holt, MI 48842/517-694-7474
Spencer's Custom Guns, Rt. 1, Box 546, Scottsville, VA 24590/804-293-6836
SPG Lubricants, Box 761-H, Livingston, MT 59047
Sphinx Engineering SA, Ch. des Grandes-Vies 2, CH-2900 Porrentruy, SWITZERLAND/41 66 66 73 81; FAX: 41 66 66 30 90
Spokhandguns, Inc., 1206 Fig St., Benton City, WA 99320/509-588-5255
Sport Flite Manufacturing Co., P.O. Box 1082, Bloomfield Hills, MI 48303/818-647-3747
Sport Specialties (See Owen, Harry)
Sportarms of Florida, 5555 NW 36 Ave., Miami, FL 33142/305-635-2411; FAX: 305-634-4536
Sporting Arms Mfg., Inc., 801 Hall Ave., Littlefield, TX 79339/806-385-5665; FAX: 806-385-3394
Sports Innovations, Inc., P.O. Box 5181, 8505 Jacksboro Hwy., Wichita Falls, TX 76307/817-723-6015
Sports Support Systems, Inc., 28416 Pacheco, Mission Viejo, CA 92692/714-472-1105
Sportsman Safe Mfg. Co., 6309-6311 Paramount Blvd., Long Beach, CA 90805/800-266-7150, 310-984-5445
Sportsman Supply Co., 714 East Eastwood, P.O. Box 650, Marshall, MO 65340/816-886-9393
Sportsman's Communicators, 588 Radcliffe Ave., Pacific Palisades, CA 90272/800-538-3752
Sportsmatch Ltd., 16 Summer St., Leighton Buzzard, Bedfordshire, LU7 8HT ENGLAND/0525-381638; FAX: 0525-851236
Sportsmen's Exchange & Western Gun Traders, Inc., 560 S. "C" St., Oxnard, CA 93030/805-483-1917
Spradlin's, 113 Arthur St., Pueblo, CO 81004/719-543-9462
Springfield, Inc., 420 W. Main St., Geneseo, IL 61254/309-944-5631; FAX: 309-944-3676
Springfield Sporters, Inc., RD 1, Penn Run, PA 15765/412-254-2626; FAX: 412-254-9173
Spyderco, Inc., P.O. Box 800, Golden, CO 80402/800-525-7770
SSK Co., 220 N. Belvidere Ave., York, PA 17404/717-854-2897
SSK Industries, 721 Woodvue Lane, Wintersville, OH 43952/614-264-0176; FAX: 614-264-2257
St. Lawrence Sales, Inc., 12 W. Fint St., Lake Orion, MI 48035/313-693-7760; 313-693-7718
Stackpole Books, P.O. Box 1831, Harrisburg, PA 17105/717-234-5041; FAX: 717-234-1359
Stafford Bullets, 1920 Tustin Ave., Philadelphia, PA 19152
Stalker, Inc., P.O. Box 21, Fishermans Wharf Rd., Malakoff, TX 75148/903-489-1010
Stalwart Corporation, P.O. Box 357, Pocatello, ID 83204/208-232-7899; FAX: 208-232-0815
Stanley Bullets, 2085 Heatheridge Ln., Reno, NV 89509
Star Bonifacio Echeverria S.A., Torrekva 3, Eibar, SPAIN 20600/43-117340; FAX: 43-111524 (U.S. importer—Interarms)
Star Custom Bullets, P.O. Box 608, 468 Main St., Ferndale, CA 95536/707-786-9140; FAX: 707-786-9117
Star Machine Works, 418 10th Ave., San Diego, CA 92101/619-232-3216
Star Reloading Co., Inc., 5520 Rock Hampton Ct., Indianapolis, IN 46268/317-872-5840
Stark's Bullet Mfg., 2580 Monroe St., Eugene, OR 97405
Starlight Training Center, Inc., Rt. 1, P.O. Box 88, Bronaugh, MO 64728/417-843-3555
Starline, 1300 W. Henry St., Sedalia, MO 65301/816-827-6640; FAX: 816-827-6650
Starnes, Ken, 32900 SW Laurelview Rd., Hillsboro, OR 97123/503-628-0705
Starrett Co., L.S., 121 Crescent St., Athol, MA 01331/617-249-3551
Starshot Holduxa, Bolognise 125, Miraflores, Lima PERU
State Arms Gun Co., 815 S. Division St., Waunakee, WI 53597/608-849-5800
Steel Reloading Components, Inc., P.O. Box 812, Washington, IN 47501/812-254-3775; FAX: 812-254-7269
Steelman's Gun Shop, 10465 Beers Rd., Swartz Creek, MI 48473/313-735-4884
Steffens, Ron, 18396 Mariposa Creek Rd., Willits, CA 95490/707-485-0873
Stegall, James B., 26 Forest Rd., Wallkill, NY 12589
Steger, James R., 1131 Dorsey Pl., Plainfield, NJ 07062

Steves House of Guns, Rt. 1, Minnesota City, MN 55959/507-689-2573
Stewart Game Calls, Johnny, Inc., P.O. Box 7954, 5100 Fort Ave., Waco, TX 76714/817-772-3261
Stewart's Gunsmithing, P.O. Box 5854, Pietersburg North 0750, Transvaal, SOUTH AFRICA/01521-89401
Steyr Mannlicher AG, Mannlicherstrasse 1, P.O.B. 1000, A-4400 Steyr, AUSTRIA/0043-7252-896-0; FAX: 0043-7252-68621 (U.S. importer—GSI, Inc.)
Steyr-Daimler-Puch, Schonauerstrasse 5, A-4400 Steyr AUSTRIA (U.S. importer—GSI, Inc.)
Stiles Custom Guns, RD3, Box 1605, Homer City, PA 15748/412-479-9945, 412-479-8666
Stillwell, Robert, 421 Judith Ann Dr., Schertz, TX 78154
Stock Shop, The, 134 Zimmerman Rd., Kalispell, MT 59901/406-257-9003
Stoeger Industries, 55 Ruta Ct., S. Hackensack, NJ 07606/201-440-2700, 800-631-0722; FAX: 201-440-2707
Stoeger Publishing Co. (See Stoeger Industries)
Stone Enterprises Ltd., Rt. 609, P.O. Box 335, Wicomico Church, VA 22579/804-580-5114; FAX: 804-580-8421
Stoney Baroque Shooters Supply, John Richards, Rt. 2, Box 325, Bedford, KY 40006/502-255-7222
Stoney Point Products, Inc., 124 Stoney Point Rd., P.O. Box 5, Courtland, MN 56021-0005/507-354-3360; FAX: 507-354-7236
Storage Tech, 1254 Morris Ave., N. Huntingdon, PA 15642/800-437-9393
Storey, Dale A. (See DGS, Inc.)
Storm, Gary, P.O. Box 511, Richardson, TX 75083/214-385-0862
Stott's Creek Armory, Inc., RR1, Box 70, Morgantown, IN 46160/317-878-5489
Stott's Creek Printers (See Stott's Creek Armory, Inc.)
Stratco, Inc., 200 E. Center St., Kalispell, MT 59901/406-755-4034; FAX: 406-257-4753
Strawbridge, Victor W., 6 Pineview Dr., Dover, NH 03820/603-742-0013
Streamlight, Inc., 1030 W. Germantown Pike, Norristown, PA 19403/215-631-0600
Strong Holster Co., 105 Maplewood Ave., Gloucester, MA 01930/508-281-3300; FAX: 508-281-6321
Strutz Rifle Barrels, Inc., W.C., P.O. Box 611, Eagle River, WI 54521/715-479-4766
Stuart, V. Pat, 2351 River Road West, Maidens, VA 23102/804-556-3845
Stuart Products, Inc., P.O. Box 1587, Easley, SC 29641/803-859-9360
Sturm, Ruger & Co., Inc., Lacey Place, Southport, CT 06490/203-259-7843
Sullivan, David S. (See Westwind Rifles, Inc.)
Summit Specialties, Inc., P.O. Box 786, Decatur, AL 35602/205-353-0634
Sun Jammer Products, Inc., 9600 N. IH-35, Austin, TX 78753/512-837-8696
Sun Welding Safe Co., 290 Easy St. No.3, Simi Valley, CA 93065/805-584-6678
Sundance Industries, Inc., 25163 W. Avenue Stanford, Valencia, CA 91355/805-257-4807
"Su-Press-On," Inc., P.O. Box 09161, Detroit, MI 48209/313-842-4222 7:30-11p.m. Mon-Thurs.
Sure Shot of LA, Inc., 103 Coachman Dr., Houma, LA 70360/504-876-6709
Surecase Co., The, 233 Wilshire Blvd., Ste. 900, Santa Monica, CA 90401/800-92ARMLOC
Sure-Shot Game Calls, Inc., P.O. Box 816, 6835 Capitol, Groves, TX 77619/409-962-1636; FAX: 409-962-5465
Survival Arms, Inc., 4500 Pine Cone Place, Cocoa, FL 32922/407-633-4880; FAX: 407-633-4975
Survival Books/The Larder, 11106 Magnolia Blvd., North Hollywood, CA 91601/818-763-0804
Svon Corp., 280 Eliot St., Ashland, MA 01721/508-881-8852
Swampfire Shop, The (See Peterson Gun Shop, Inc., A.W.)
Swann, D.J., 5 Orsova Close, Eltham North, Vic. 3095, AUSTRALIA/03-431-0323
Swanndri New Zealand, 152 Elm Ave., Burlingame, CA 94010/415-347-6158
SwaroSports, Inc. (See JägerSports, Ltd.)
Swarovski Optik North America Ltd., One Wholesale Way, Cranston, RI 02920/401-946-2220, 800-426-3089; FAX: 401-946-2587
Sweet Home, Inc., P.O. Box 900, Orrville, OH 44667-0900
Swenson's 45 Shop, A.D., P.O. Box 606, Fallbrook, CA 92028
S.W.I.F.T., 4610 Blue Diamond Rd., Las Vegas, NV 89118/702-897-1100
Swift Bullet Co., P.O. Box 27, 201 Main St., Quinter, KS 67752/913-754-3959; FAX: 913-754-2359
Swift Instruments, Inc., 952 Dorchester Ave., Boston, MA 02125/617-436-2960; FAX: 617-436-3232
Swift River Gunworks, Inc., 450 State St., Belchertown, MA 01007/413-323-4052
Swiss Army Knives, Inc., 151 Long Hill Crossroads, 37 Canal St., Shelton, CT 06484/800-243-4032
Swivel Machine Works, Inc., 167 Cherry St., Suite 286, Milford, CT 06460/203-926-1840; FAX: 203-874-9212
Synchronized Shooting Systems, P.O. Box 52481, Knoxville, TN 37950-2481/800-952-8649
Szweda, Robert (See RMS Custom Gunsmithing)

T

Tabler Marketing, 2554 Lincoln Blvd. 555, Marina Del Rey, CA 90291-5082/818-366-7485; FAX: 818-831-3441
TacStar Industries, Inc., P.O. Box 70, Cottonwood, AZ 86326/800-762-7471
TacTell, Inc., P.O. Box 5654, Maryville, TN 37802/615-982-7855; FAX: 615-558-8294
Tactical Training Center, 574 Miami Bluff Ct., Loveland, OH 45140/513-677-8229
Talley, Dave, P.O. Box 821, Glenrock, WY 82637/307-436-8724
Talmage, William G., RR16, Box 102A, Brazil, IN 47834/812-442-0804
Talon Mfg. Co., Inc., 575 Bevans Industrial Ln., Paw Paw, WV 25434
Tamarack Products, Inc., P.O. Box 625, Wauconda, IL 60084/708-526-9333; FAX: 708-526-9353

Tanfoglio S.r.l., Fratelli, via Valtrompia 39, 41, 25068 Gardone V.T., Brescia, ITALY/30-8910361; FAX: 30-8910183 (U.S. importer—E.A.A. Corp.)

Tanglefree Industries, 16102 Duggans Rd., Grass Valley, CA 95949

Tank's Rifle Shop, 1324 Ohio St., P.O. Box 474, Fremont, NE 68025/402-727-1317; FAX: 402-721-2573

Tanner (See U.S. importer—Mandall Shooting Supplies, Inc.)

Tapco, Inc., P.O. Box 818, Smyrna, GA 30081/404-435-9782, 800-359-6195; FAX: 404-333-9798

Taracorp Industries, Inc., 16th & Cleveland Blvd., Granite City, IL 62040/618-451-4400

Targot Man, Inc., 49 Gerald Dr., Manchester, CT 06040/203-646-8335; FAX: 203-646-8335

Tar-Hunt Custom Rifles, Inc., RR3, Box 572, Bloomsburg, PA 17815/717-784-6368; FAX: 717-784-6368

Tasco Sales, Inc., 7600 NW 84th Ave., Miami, FL 33122/305-591-3670; FAX: 305-592-5895

Taurus Firearms, Inc., 16175 NW 49th Ave., Miami, FL 33014/305-624-1115; FAX: 305-623-7506

Taurus International Firearms (See U.S. importer—Taurus Firearms, Inc.)

Taurus S.A., Forjas, Avenida Do Forte 511, Porto Alegre, BRAZIL 91360/55-51-340-22-44; FAX: 55-51-340-49-81

Taylor & Robbins, P.O. Box 164, Rixford, PA 16745/814-966-3233

Taylor's & Co., Inc., 299 Broad Ave., Winchester, VA 22602/703-722-2017; FAX: 703-722-2018

TCCI, P.O. Box 302, Phoenix, AZ 85001/602-237-3823; FAX: 602-237-3858

TCSR, 3998 Hoffman Rd., White Bear Lake, MN 55110-4626/800-328-5323; FAX: 612-429-0526

TDP Industries, Inc., 603 Airport Blvd., Doylestown, PA 18901/215-345-8687

Techni-Mec, Via Gitti s.n., 25060 Marcheno, ITALY (U.S. importer—Mandall Shooting Supplies, Inc.)

Tecnolegno S.p.A., Via A. Locatelli, 6, 10, 24019 Zogno, ITALY/0345-91114; FAX: 0345-93254

Tejas Resource, 104 Tejas Dr., Terrell, TX 75160/214-563-1220

Teledyne Co., 290 E. Prairie St., Crystal Lake, IL 60014

Tele-Optics, 5514 W. Lawrence Ave., Chicago, IL 60630/312-283-7757; FAX: 312-283-7757

Tennessee Valley Mfg., P.O. Box 1175, Corinth, MS 38834/601-286-5014

Ten-Ring Precision, Inc., Alex B. Hamilton, 1449 Blue Crest Lane, San Antonio, TX 78232/512-494-3063; FAX: 512-494-3066

10-X Products Group, 2915 Lyndon B. Johnson Freeway, Suite 133, Dallas, TX 75234/214-243-4016

Tepeco, P.O. Box 342, Friendswood, TX 77546/713-482-2702

Testing Systems, Inc., 220 Pegasus Ave., Northvale, NJ 07647

Teton Arms, Inc., P.O. Box 411, Wilson, WY 83014/307-733-3395

Tetra Gun Lubricants, 1812 Margaret Ave., Annapolis, MD 21401/410-268-6451; FAX: 410-268-8377

Texas Arms, P.O. Box 154906, Waco, TX 76715/817-867-6972

Texas Longhorn Arms, Inc., 5959 W. Loop South, Suite 424, Bellaire, TX 77401/713-660-6323; FAX: 713-660-0493

Texas Platers Supply Co., 2453 W. Five Mile Parkway, Dallas, TX 75233/214-330-7168

T.F.C. S.p.A., Via G. Marconi 118, B, Villa Carcina, Brescia 25069, ITALY/030-881271; FAX: 030-881826

Theis, Terry, P.O. Box 535, Fredericksburg, TX 78624/210-997-6778

Theoben Engineering (See U.S. importer—Air Rifle Specialists)

Thiewes, George W., 1846 Allen Lane, St. Charles, IL 60174/708-584-1383

Things Unlimited, 235 N. Kimbau, Casper, WY 82601/307-234-5277

Thirion Hand Engraving, Denise, P.O. Box 408, Graton, CA 95444/707-829-1876

Thomas, Charles C., 2600 S. First St., Springfield, IL 62794/217-789-8980; FAX: 217-789-9130

Thompson, Norm, 18905 NW Thurman St., Portland, OR 97209

Thompson, Randall (See Highline Machine Co.)

Thompson Bullet Lube Co., P.O. Box 472343, Garland, TX 75047/214-271-8063; FAX: 214-840-6743

Thompson Precision, 110 Mary St., P.O. Box 251, Warren, IL 61087/815-745-3625

Thompson Target Technology, 618 Roslyn Ave., SW, Canton, OH 44710/216-453-7707; FAX: 216-478-4723

Thompson/Center Arms, P.O. Box 5002, Rochester, NH 03867/603-332-2394; FAX: 603-332-5133

3-D Ammunition & Bullets, 112 W. Plum St., P.O. Box J, Doniphan, NE 68832/402-845-2285; FAX: 402-845-6546

300 Gunsmith Service, Inc., 6850 S. Yosemite Ct., Englewood, CO 80112/303-773-0300

3-Ten Corp., P.O. Box 269, Feeding Hills, MA 01030/413-789-2086

T.H.U. Enterprises, Inc., P.O. Box 418, Lederach, PA 19450/215-256-1665; FAX: 215-256-9718

Thunder Mountain Arms, P.O. Box 593, Oak Harbor, WA 98277/206-679-4657; FAX: 206-675-1114

Thunderbird Cartridge Co. (See TCCI)

Thurston Sports, Inc., RD 3 Donovan Rd., Auburn, NY 13021/315-253-0966

Tiger-Hunt, Michael D. Barton, Box 379, Beaverdale, PA 15921/814-472-5161

Tikka (See U.S. importer—Stoeger Industries)

Tillinghast, James C., P.O. Box 405DG, Hancock, NH 03449/603-525-4049

Timber Heirloom Products, 618 Roslyn Ave. SW, Canton, OH 44710/216-453-7707; FAX: 216-478-4723

Time Precision, Inc., 640 Federal Rd., Brookfield, CT 06804/203-775-8343

Timney Mfg., Inc., 3065 W. Fairmont Ave., Phoenix, AZ 85017/602-274-2999; FAX: 602-241-0361

Tink's Safariland Hunting Corp., P.O. Box 244, Madison, GA 30650/404-342-4915

Tinks & Ben Lee Hunting Products (See Wellington Outdoors)

Tioga Engineering Co., Inc., P.O. Box 913, 13 Cone St., Wellsboro, PA 16901/717-724-3533, 717-662-3347

Tippman Pneumatics, Inc., 3518 Adams Center Rd., Fort Wayne, IN 46806/219-749-6022; FAX: 219-749-6619

Tirelli, Snc Di Tirelli Primo E.C., Via Matteotti No. 359, Gardone V.T., Brescia, ITALY 25063/030-8912819; FAX: 030-832240

Titus, Daniel, Shooting Specialties, 872 Penn St., Bryn Mawr, PA 19010/215-525-8829

TM Stockworks, 6355 Maplecrest Rd., Fort Wayne, IN 46835/219-485-5389

TMI Products, 930 S. Plumer Ave., Tucson, AZ 85719/602-792-1075; FAX: 602-792-0093

Tom's Gun Repair, Thomas G. Ivanoff, 76-6 Rt. Southfork Rd., Cody, WY 82414/307-587-6949

Tom's Gunshop, 3601 Central Ave., Hot Springs, AR 71913/501-624-3856

Tomboy, Inc., P.O. Box 846, Dallas, OR 97338/503-623-6955

Tonoloway Tack Drives, HCR 81, Box 100, Needmore, OA 17238

Tooley Custom Rifles, 516 Creek Meadow Dr., Gastonia, NC 28054/704-864-7525

Top-Line USA, Inc., 7920-28 Hamilton Ave., Cincinnati, OH 45231/513-522-2992, 800-346-6699; FAX: 513-522-0916

Torel, Inc., 1053 N. South St., P.O. Box 592, Yoakum, TX 77995/512-293-2341; FAX: 512-293-3413

Totally Dependable Products (See TDP Industries, Inc.)

Track of the Wolf, Inc., P.O. Box 6, Osseo, MN 55369-0006/612-424-2500; FAX: 612-424-9860

Tradewinds, Inc., P.O. Box 1191, 2339-41 Tacoma Ave. S., Tacoma, WA 98401/206-272-4887

Traditions, P.O. Box 235, Deep River, CT 06417/203-526-9555; FAX: 203-526-4564

Trafalgar Square, P.O. Box 257, N. Pomfret, VT 05053/802-457-1911

Traft Gunshop, P.O. Box 1078, Buena Vista, CO 81211

Trail Guns Armory, 1422 E. Main St., League City, TX 77573

Trail Visions, 5800 N. Ames Terrace, Glendale, WI 53209/414-228-1328

TrailTimer Co., 1992-A Suburban Ave., P.O. Box 19722, St. Paul, MN 55119/612-738-0925

Trammco, 839 Gold Run Rd., Boulder, CO 80302

Trappers Trading, P.O. Box 26946, Austin, TX 78755/800-788-9334

Trax America, Inc., P.O. Box 898, 1150 Eldridge, Forrest City, AR 72335/800-232-2327; FAX: 501-633-4788

Treadlok Gun Safe, Inc., 1764 Granby St. NE, Roanoke, VA 24012/800-729-8732, 703-982-6881; FAX: 703-982-1059

Treemaster, P.O. Box 247, Guntersville, AL 35976/205-878-3597

Treso, Inc., P.O. Box 4640, Pagosa Springs, CO 81157/303-731-2295

Trevallion Gunstocks, 9 Old Mountain Rd., Cape Neddick, ME 03902/207-361-1130

Trico Plastics, 590 S. Vincent Ave., Azusa, CA 91702

Trijicon, Inc., P.O. Box 6029, Wixom, MI 48393-6029/810-960-7700; FAX: 810-960-7725

Trinidad State Junior College, Gunsmithing Dept., 600 Prospect St., Trinidad, CO 81082/719-846-5631; FAX: 719-846-5667

Triple-K Mfg. Co., Inc., 2222 Commercial St., San Diego, CA 92113/619-232-2066; FAX: 619-232-7675

Trius Traps, P.O. Box 25, 221 S. Miami Ave., Cleves, OH 45002/513-941-5682; FAX: 513-941-7970

Trophy Bonded Bullets, Inc., 900 S. Loop W., Suite 190, Houston, TX 77054/713-645-4499; FAX: 713-741-6393

Trotman, Ken, 135 Ditton Walk, Unit 11, Cambridge CB5 8QD, ENGLAND/0223-211030; FAX: 0223-212317

Tru-Balance Knife Co., 2155 Tremont Blvd. NW, Grand Rapids, MI 49504/616-453-3679

Tru-Square Metal Prods., Inc., 640 First St. SW, P.O. Box 585, Auburn, WA 98001/206-833-2310

True Flight Bullet Co., 5581 Roosevelt St., Whitehall, PA 18052/800-875-3625; FAX: 215-262-7806

Trulock Tool, Broad St., Whigham, GA 31797/912-762-4678

T.S.W. Conversions, Inc., E. 115 Crain Rd., Paramus, NJ 07650-4017/201-265-1618

Tucker, James C., P.O. Box 15485, Sacramento, CA 95851/916-923-0571

Turkish Firearms Corp., 8487 Euclid Ave., Suite 1, Manassas Park, VA 22111/703-369-6848; FAX: 703-257-7709

Turnbull Restoration, Doug, 6426 County Rd. 30, Bloomfield, NY 14469/716-657-6338

Tuscano, Tony, P.O. Box 461, Wickliffe, OH 44092/216-943-1175

Twin Pine Armory, P.O. Box 58, Hwy. 6, Adna, WA 98522/206-748-4590; FAX: 206-748-7011

Tyler Mfg.-Dist., Melvin, 1326 W. Britton Rd., Oklahoma City, OK 73114/405-842-8044

Tyler Scott, Inc., 313 Rugby Ave., Terrace Park, OH 45174/513-831-7603; FAX: 513-831-7417

U

Uberti, Aldo, Casella Postale 43, I-25063 Gardone V.T., ITALY (U.S. importers—American Arms, Inc.; Christopher Firearms Co., Inc., E.; Cimarron Arms; Dixie Gun Works; EMF Co., Inc.; Mitchell Arms, Inc.; Navy Arms Co; Uberti USA, Inc.)

Uberti USA, Inc., 362 Limerock Rd., P.O. Box 469, Lakeville, CT 06039/203-435-8068; FAX: 203-435-8146

U.F.A., Inc., 7655 Evans Rd. Suite Z, Scottsdale, AZ 85260/602-998-3941; FAX: 602-998-3941

Ugartechea S.A., Ignacio, Chonta 26, Eibar, SPAIN 20600/43-121257; FAX: 43-121669 (U.S. importer—Mandall Shooting Supplies, Inc.)

Ulrich, Doc & Bud (See D.O.C. Specialists, Inc.)

Ultimate Accuracy, 121 John Shelton Rd., JAcksonville, AR 72076/501-985-2530

Ultra Light Arms, Inc., P.O. Box 1270, 214 Price St., Granville, WV 26534/304-599-5687

UltraSport Arms, Inc., 1955 Norwood Ct., Racine, WI 53403/414-554-3237; FAX: 414-554-9731

Uncle Mike's (See Michaels of Oregon Co.)

Unertl Optical Co., Inc., John, 308 Clay Ave., P.O. Box 818, Mars, PA 16046-0818/412-625-3810

Unick's Gunsmithing, 5005 Center Rd., Lowellville, OH 44436/216-536-8015

Unique/M.A.P.F., 10, Les Allees, 64700 Hendaye, FRANCE 64700/33-59 20 71 93 (U.S. importer—Nygord Precision Products)

UniTec, 1250 Bedford SW, Canton, OH 44710/216-452-4017

United Binocular Co., 9043 S. Western Ave., Chicago, IL 60620

United Cutlery Corp., 1425 United Blvd., Sevierville, TN 37862/615-428-2532

United States Ammunition Co. (See USAC)

United States Optics Technologies, Inc., 1501 E. Chapman Ave. 306, Fullerton, CA 92631/714-879-8922; FAX: 714-449-0941

United States Products Co., 518 Melwood Ave., Pittsburgh, PA 15213/412-621-2130

Universal Clay Pigeon Traps, Unit 5, Dalacre Industrial Estate, Wilbarston, ENGLAND LE16 8QL/011-44536771625; FAX: 011-44536771625

Upper Missouri Trading Co., 304 Harold St., Crofton, NE 68730/402-388-4844

U.S. General Technologies, Inc., 145 Mitchell Ave., South San Francisco, CA 94080/415-634-8440; FAX: 415-634-8452

U.S. Optics Technologies, Inc., Div. of Zeitz Optics, U.S.A., 1501 E. Chapman Ave. Suite 306/Fullerton, CA 92631/714-944-4901; FAX: 714-944-4904

U.S. Repeating Arms Co., Inc., 275 Winchester Ave., New Haven, CT 06511/203-789-5000; FAX: 203-789-5071

USA Magazines, P.O. Box 39115, Downey, CA 90241/800-872-2577

USA Sporting, 1330 N. Glassell, Suite M, Orange, CA 92667/714-538-3109, 800-538-3109; FAX: 714-538-1334

USAC, 4500-15th St. East, Tacoma, WA 98424/206-922-7589

Utica Cutlery Co., 820 Noyes St., Utica, NY 13503/315-733-4663

Uvalde Machine & Tool, P.O. Box 1604, Uvalde, TX 78802

V

Valade, Robert B., 931 3rd Ave., Seaside, OR 97138/503-738-7672

Valmet (See Tikka/U.S. importer—Stoeger Industries)

Valor Corp., 5555 NW 36th Ave., Miami, FL 33142/305-633-0127

Van Epps, Milton, Rt. 69-A, Parish, NY 13131/315-625-7251

Van Gorden & Son, Inc., C.S., 1815 Main St., Bloomer, WI 54724/715-568-2612

Van Horn, Gil, P.O. Box 207, Llano, CA 93544

Van Patten, J.W., P.O. Box 145, Foster Hill, Milford, PA 18337/717-296-7069

Vann Custom Bullets, 330 Grandview Ave., Novato, CA 94947

Varmintmasters, P.O. Box 839, Arthur, Ont. N0G 1A0 CANADA/519-848-3374

Varner's Shop, 102 Shaffer Rd., Antwerp, OH 45813/419-258-8631

Vega Tool Co., 1840 Commerce St. Unit H, Boulder, CO 80301/303-443-4750

Venco Industries, Inc. (See Shooter's Choice)

Venus Industries, P.O. Box 246, Sialkot-1, PAKISTAN/FAX: 92 432 85579

Verdemont Fieldsports, 3035 Jo An Dr., San Bernardino, CA 92407-2022/714-880-8255; FAX: 714-880-8255

Verney-Carron, B.P. 72, 54 Boulevard Thiers, 42002 St. Etienne Cedex 1, FRANCE/33-77791500; FAX: 33-77790702

Vest, John, P.O. Box 1552, Susanville, CA 96130/916-257-7228

VibraShine, Inc., Rt. 1, P.O. Box 64, Mt. Olive, MS 39119/601-733-5614; FAX: 601-733-2226

Vibra-Tek Co., 1844 Arroya Rd., Colorado Springs, CO 80906/719-634-8611; FAX: 719-634-6886

Vic's Gun Refinishing, 6 Pineview Dr., Dover, NH 03820-6422/603-742-0013

Victory USA, P.O. Box 1021, Pine Bush, NY 12566/914-744-2060; FAX: 914-744-5181

Vihtavuori Oy, FIN-41330 Vihtavuori, FINLAND/358-41-3779211; FAX: 358-41-3771643

Vihtavuori Oy/Kaltron-Pettibone, 1241 Ellis St., Bensenville, IL 60106/708-350-1116; FAX: 708-350-1606

Viking Leathercraft, Inc., 1579A Jayken Way, Chula Vista, CA 91911/800-262-6666; FAX: 619-429-8268

Viking Video Productions, P.O. Box 251, Roseburg, OR 97470

Vincent's Shop, 210 Antoinette, Fairbanks, AK 99701

Vintage Arms, Inc., 6003 Saddle Horse, Fairfax, VA 22030/703-968-0779; FAX: 703-968-0780

Vintage Industries, Inc., 781 Big Tree Dr., Longwood, FL 32750/407-831-8949; FAX: 407-831-5346

VIP Products, 488 East 17th St., Ste. A-101, Costa Mesa, CA 92627/714-722-5986

Viramontez, Ray, 601 Springfield Dr., Albany, GA 31707/912-432-9683

Visible Impact Targets, Rts. 5 & 20, E. Bloomfield, NY 14443/716-657-6161

Vitt/Boos, 2178 Nichols Ave., Stratford, CT 06497/203-375-6859

Voere-KGH m.b.H., P.O. Box 416, A-6333 Kufstein, Tirol, AUSTRIA/0043-5372-62547; FAX: 0043-5372-65752 (U.S. importers—JägerSport, Ltd.; Swarovski Optik North America Ltd.)

Volquartsen Custom Ltd., RR 1, Box 33A, P.O. Box 271, Carroll, IA 51401/712-792-4238; FAX: 712-792-2542

Vom Hofe (See Old Western Scrounger, Inc., The)

Von Minden Gunsmithing Services, 2403 SW 39 Terrace, Cape Coral, FL 33914/813-542-8946

Vorhes, David, 3042 Beecham St., Napa, CA 94558/707-226-9116

VSP Publishers, P.O. Box 887, McCall, ID 83638/208-634-4104

Vulpes Ventures, Inc., Fox Cartridge Division, P.O. Box 1363, Bolingbrook, IL 60440-7363/708-759-1229

W

Waffen-Weber Custom Gunsmithing, 4-1691 Powick Rd., Kelowna, B.C. CANADA V1X 4L1/604-762-7575; FAX: 604-861-3655

Wagoner, Vernon G., 2325 E. Encanto, Mesa, AZ 85213/602-835-1307

Wakina by Pic, 24813 Alderbrook Dr., Santa Clarita, CA 91321/805-295-8194

Waldron, Herman, Box 475, 80 N. 17th St., Pomeroy, WA 99347/509-843-1404

Walker Arms Co., Inc., 499 County Rd. 820, Selma, AL 36701/205-872-6231

Walker Mfg., Inc., 8296 S. Channel, Harsen's Island, MI 48028

Walker Shoe Co., P.O. Box 1167, Asheboro, NC 27203-1167/919-625-1380

Wallace, Terry, 385 San Marino, Vallejo, CA 94589/707-642-7041

Waller & Son, Inc., W., 142 New Canaan Ave., Norwalk, CT 06850/203-838-4083

Walls Industries, P.O. Box 98, Cleburne, TX 76031/817-645-4366

Walnut Factory, The, 235 West Rd. No. 1, Portsmouth, NH 03801/603-436-2225; FAX: 603-433-7003

Walt's Custom Leather, Walt Whinnery, 1947 Meadow Creek Dr., Louisville, KY 40218/502-458-4361

Walters, John, 500 N. Avery Dr., Moore, OK 73160/405-799-0376

Walters Industries, 6226 Park Lane, Dallas, TX 75225/214-691-6973

Walther GmbH, Carl, B.P. 4325, D-89033 Ulm, GERMANY (U.S. importer—Interarms)

WAMCO, Inc., Mingo Loop, P.O. Box 337, Oquossoc, ME 04964-0337/207-864-3344

WAMCO—New Mexico, P.O. Box 205, Peralta, NM 87042-0205/505-869-0826

Ward & Van Valkenburg, 114 32nd Ave. N., Fargo, ND 58102/701-232-2351

Ward Machine, 5620 Lexington Rd., Corpus Christi, TX 78412/512-992-1221

Wardell Precision Handguns Ltd., 48851 N. Fig Springs Rd., New River, AZ 85027-8513/602-465-7995

Warenski, Julie, 590 E. 500 N., Richfield, UT 84701/801-896-5319; FAX: 801-896-5319

Warne Manufacturing Co., 9039 SE Jannsen Rd., Clackamas, OR 97015/503-657-5590; FAX: 503-657-5695

Warren & Sweat Mfg. Co., P.O. Box 350440, Grand Island, FL 32735/904-669-3166; FAX: 904-669-7272

Warren, Kenneth W. (See Mountain States Engraving)

Warren Muzzleloading Co., Inc., Hwy. 21 North, P.O. Box 100, Ozone, AR 72854/501-292-3268

Washita Mountain Whetstone Co., P.O. Box 378, Lake Hamilton, AR 71951/501-525-3914

WASP Shooting Systems, Rt. 1, Box 147, Lakeview, AR 72642/501-431-5606

Waterfield Sports, Inc., 13611 Country Lane, Burnsville, MN 55337/612-435-8339

Watson Trophy Match Bullets, 2404 Wade Hampton Blvd., Greenville, SC 29615/803-244-7948

Watsontown Machine & Tool Co., 309 Dickson Ave., Watsontown, PA 17777/717-538-3533

Wayland Precision Wood Products, P.O. Box 1142, Mill Valley, CA 94942/415-381-3543

Wayne Firearms for Collectors and Investors, James, 2608 N. Laurent, Victoria, TX 77901/512-578-1258; FAX: 512-578-3559

Wayne Specialty Services, 260 Waterford Drive, Florissant, MO 63033/413-831-7083

W.C. Wolff Co., P.O. Box I, Newtown Square, PA 19073/610-359-9600, 800-545-0077

WD-40 Co., P.O. Box 80607, San Diego, CA 92138-0607/619-275-1400; FAX: 619-275-5823

Weather Shield Sports Equipment, Inc., Rt. 3, Petoskey Rd., Charlevoix, MI 49720

Weatherby, Inc., 2781 Firestone Blvd., South Gate, CA 90280/213-569-7186, 800-227-2023; FAX: 213-569-5025

Weaver Arms Corp., P.O. Box 8, Dexter, MO 63841/314-568-3101

Weaver Products, Div. of Blount, Inc., P.O. Box 39, Onalaska, WI 54650/800-635-7656; FAX: 608-781-0368

Weaver Scope Repair Service, 1121 Larry Mahan Dr., Suite B, El Paso, TX 79925/915-593-1005

Weaver's Gun Shop, P.O. Box 8, Dexter, MO 63841/314-568-3101

Webb, Bill, 6504 North Bellefontaine, Kansas City, MO 64119/816-453-7431

Weber Jr., Rudolf, P.O. Box 160106, D-5650 Solingen, GERMANY/0212-592136

Webley and Scott Ltd., Frankley Industrial Park, Tay Rd., Rubery Rednal, Birmingham B45 OPA, U.K./021-453-1864; FAX: 021-457-7846 (U.S. importer—Beeman Precision Airguns, Inc.)

Webster Scale Mfg. Co., P.O. Box 188, Sebring, FL 33870/813-385-6362

Weems, Cecil, P.O. Box 657, Mineral Wells, TX 76067/817-325-1462

Weigand Combat Handguns, Inc., P.O. Box 239, Crestwood Industrial Park, Mountain Top, PA 18707/717-474-9804; FAX: 717-474-9987

Weihrauch KG, Hermann, Industriestrasse 11, 8744 Mellrichstadt, GERMANY/09776-497-498 (U.S. importers—Beeman Precision Airguns; E.A.A. Corp.)

Weisz Antique Gun Parts, P.O. Box 311, Arlington, VA 22210/703-243-9161

Welch, Sam, CVSR 2110, Moab, UT 84532/801-259-8131

Wellington Outdoors, P.O. Box 244, Madison, GA 30650/404-342-4915; FAX: 404-342-4656

Wells, Fred F., Wells Sport Store, 110 N. Summit St., Prescott, AZ 86301/602-445-3655

Wells, Rachel, 110 N. Summit St., Prescott, AZ 86301/602-445-3655

Wells Creek Knife & Gun Works, 32956 State Hwy. 38, Scottsburg, OR 97473/503-587-4202

Wells Custom Gunsmith, R.A., 3452 1st Ave., Racine, WI 53402/414-639-5223

Welsh, Bud, 80 New Road, E. Amherst, NY 14051/716-688-6344

Wenig Custom Gunstocks, Inc., 103 N. Market St., Lincoln, MO 65338/816-547-3334; FAX: 816-547-2881

Wenoka/Seastyle, P.O. Box 10969, Riviera Beach, FL 33419/407-845-6155; FAX: 407-842-4247

Wentling Co., S.A., 546 W. Chocolate Ave., P.O. Box 355P, Hershey, PA 17033/717-533-2468; FAX: 717-534-1252

Werner, Carl, P.O. Box 492, Littleton, CO 80160

Werth, T.W., 1203 Woodlawn Rd., Lincoln, IL 62656/217-732-1300

Wescombe, P.O. Box 488, Glencoe, CA 95232/209-293-7010

Wessinger Custom Guns & Engraving, 268 Limestone Rd., Chapin, SC 29036/803-345-5677

Wesson Firearms Co., Inc., Maple Tree Industrial Center, Rt. 20, Wilbraham, Rd./Palmer, MA 01069/413-267-4081; FAX: 413-267-3601

West, Robert G., 3973 Pam St., Eugene, OR 97402/503-344-3700

Westchester Carbide, 148 Wheeler Ave., Pleasantville, NY 10570/914-769-1445

Western Cutlery (See Camillus)
Western Design, 1629 Via Monserate, Fallbrook, CA 92028/619-723-9279
Western Gunstock Mfg. Co., 550 Valencia School Rd., Aptos, CA 95003/408-688-5884
Western Missouri Shooters Alliance, P.O. Box 11144, Kansas City, MO 64119/816-597-3950; FAX: 816-229-7350
Westfield Engineering, 6823 Watcher St., Commerce, CA 90040/FAX: 213-928-8270
Westley Richards & Co., 40 Grange Rd., Birmingham, ENGLAND B29 6AR/010-214722953 (U.S. importer—Cape Outfitters)
Westrom, John (See Precise Metal Finishing)
Westwind Rifles, Inc., David S. Sullivan, P.O. Box 261, 640 Briggs St., Erie, CO 80516/303-828-3823
Weyer International, 2740 Nebraska Ave., Toledo, OH 43607/419-534-2020; FAX: 419-534-2697
Wheel Weights Corp., 2611 Hwy. 40 East, Inglis, FL 34449/904-447-3571
Whildin & Sons Ltd., E.H., RR2, Box 119, Tamaqua, PA 18252/717-668-6743; FAX: 717-668-6745
Whinnery, Walt (See Walt's Custom Leather)
White Flyer, Div. of Reagent Chemical & Research, Inc., 9139 W. Redfield Rd., Peoria, AZ 85381/800-647-2898
White Flyer Targets, 124 River Rd., Middlesex, NJ 08846/908-469-0100; FAX: 908-469-9692
White Laboratory, Inc., H.P., 3114 Scarboro Rd., Street, MD 21154/410-838-6550; FAX: 410-838-2802
White Owl Enterprises, 2583 Flag Rd., Abilene, KS 67410/913-263-2613; FAX: 913-263-2613
White Pine Photographic Services, Hwy. 60, General Delivery, Wilno, Ontario K0J 2N0 CANADA/613-756-3452
White Rock Tool & Die, 6400 N. Brighton Ave., Kansas City, MO 64119/816-454-0478
White Shooting Systems, Inc., P.O. Box 277, Roosevelt, UT 84066/801-722-3085; FAX: 801-722-3054
Whitehead, James D., 204 Cappucino Way, Sacramento, CA 95838
Whitestone Lumber Corp., 148-02 14th Ave., Whitestone, NY 11357/718-746-4400; FAX: 718-767-1748
Whitetail Design & Engineering Ltd., 9421 E. Mannsiding Rd., Clare, MI 48617/517-386-3932
Whits Shooting Stuff, Box 1340, Cody, WY 82414
Wichita Arms, Inc., 923 E. Gilbert, P.O. Box 11371, Wichita, KS 67211/316-265-0661; FAX: 316-265-0760
Wick, David E., 1504 Michigan Ave., Columbus, IN 47201/812-376-6960
Widener's Reloading & Shooting Supply, Inc., P.O. Box 3009 CRS, Johnson City, TN 37602/615-282-6786; FAX: 615-282-6651
Wideview Scope Mount Corp., 26110 Michigan Ave., Inkster, MI 48141/313-274-1238; FAX: 313-274-2814
Wiebe, Duane, 3715 S. Browns Lake Dr. 106, Burlington, WI 53105-7931
Wiest, M.C., 10737 Dutchtown Rd., Knoxville, TN 37932/615-966-4545
Wilcox All-Pro Tools & Supply, RR 1, Montezuma, IA 50171/515-623-3138
Wild Bill's Originals, P.O. Box 13037, Burton, WA 98013/206-463-5738
Wilderness Sound Products Ltd., 4015 Main St. A, Springfield, OR 97478/503-741-0263; FAX: 503-741-7648
Wildey, Inc., P.O. Box 475, Brookfield, CT 06804/203-355-9000; FAX: 203-354-7759
Wildlife Research Center, Inc., 4345 157th Ave. NW, Anoka, MN 55304/612-427-3350
Wilkinson Arms, 26884 Pearl Rd., Parma, ID 83660/208-722-6771; FAX: 208-722-5197
Will-Burt Co., 169 S. Main, Orrville, OH 44667
William's Gun Shop, Ben, 1151 S. Cedar Ridge, Duncanville, TX 75137/214-780-1807
Williams Bullet Co., J.R., 2008 Tucker Rd., Perry, GA 31069/912-987-0274
Williams Gun Sight Co., 7389 Lapeer Rd., Box 329, Davison, MI 48423/810-653-2131, 800-530-9028; FAX: 810-658-2140
Williams Mfg. of Oregon, P.O. Box 98, 561 Upper Smith River Rd., Drain, OR 97435/503-836-7461; FAX: 503-836-7245
Williams Shootin' Iron Service, The Lynx-Line, 8857 Bennett Hill Rd., Central Lake, MI 49622/616-544-6615
Williamson Precision Gunsmithing, 117 W. Pipeline, Hurst, TX 76053/817-285-0064; FAX: 817-285-0064
Willig Custom Engraving, Claus, D-97422 Schweinfurt, Siedlerweg 17, GERMANY/01149-9721-41446; FAX: 01149-9721-44413
Willow Bend, P.O. Box 203, Chelmsford, MA 01824/508-256-8508; FAX: 508-256-9765
Willson Safety Prods. Div., P.O. Box 622, Reading, PA 19603-0622/610-376-6161; FAX: 610-371-7725
Wilson, Inc., L.E., Box 324, 404 Pioneer Ave., Cashmere, WA 98815/509-782-1328
Wilson Arms Co., The, 63 Leetes Island Rd., Branford, CT 06405/203-488-7297; FAX: 203-488-0135
Wilson Case, Inc., P.O. Box 1106, Hastings, NE 68902-1106/800-322-5493; FAX: 402-463-5276
Wilson's Gun Shop, Box 578, Rt. 3, Berryville, AR 72616/501-545-3635; FAX: 501-545-3310
Winchester (See U.S. Repeating Arms Co., Inc.)
Winchester Div., Olin Corp., 427 N. Shamrock, E. Alton, IL 62024/618-258-3566; FAX: 618-258-3599
Winchester Press (See New Win Publishing, Inc.)

Winchester Sutler, Inc., The, 270 Shadow Brook Lane, Winchester, VA 22603/703-888-3595
Windish, Jim, 2510 Dawn Dr., Alexandria, VA 22306/703-765-1994
Windjammer Tournament Wads, Inc., 750 W. Hampden Ave. Suite 170, Englewood, CO 80110/303-781-6329
Wingshooting Adventures, 4320 Kalamazoo Ave. SE, Grand Rapids, MI 49508/616-455-7810; FAX: 616-455-5212
Winkle Bullets, R.R. 1 Box 316, Heyworth, IL 61745
Winter & Associates (See Olde Pennsylvania)
Winter, Robert M., P.O. Box 484, Menno, SD 57045/605-387-5322
Wise Guns, Dale, 333 W. Olmos Dr., San Antonio, TX 78212/210-828-3388
Wiseman and Co., Bill, P.O. Box 3427, Bryan, TX 77805/409-690-3456; FAX: 409-690-0156
Wisner's Gun Shop, Inc., 287 NW Chehalis Ave., Chehalis, WA 98532/206-748-8942; FAX: 206-748-7011
Wolf's Western Traders, 40 E. Works #3F, Sheridan, WY 82801/307-674-5352
Wolfe Publishing Co., 6471 Airpark Dr., Prescott, AZ 86301/602-445-7810, 800-899-7810; FAX: 602-778-5124
Wolverine Boots & Outdoor Footwear Div., Wolverine World Wide, 9341 Cour, land Dr./Rockford, MI 49351/616-866-5500
Wood, Frank (See Classic Guns)
Wood, Mel, P.O. Box 1255, Sierra Vista, AZ 85636/602-455-5541
Woodleigh (See Huntington Die Specialties)
Woods Wise Products, P.O. Box 681552, 2200 Bowman Rd., Franklin, TN 37068/800-735-8182; FAX: 615-790-3581
Woodstream, P.O. Box 327, Lititz, PA 17543/717-626-2125; FAX: 717-626-1912
Woodworker's Supply, 1108 North Glenn Rd., Casper, WY 82601/307-237-5354
Woolrich Woolen Mills, Mill St., Woolrich, PA 17779/717-769-6464
World of Targets (See Birchwood Laboratories, Inc.)
World Trek, Inc., P.O. Box 11670, Pueblo, CO 81001-0670/719-546-2121; FAX: 719-543-6886
Worthy Products, Inc., RR 1, P.O. Box 213, Martville, NY 13111/315-324-5298
Wosenitz VHP, Inc., Box 741, Dania, FL 33004/305-923-3748; FAX: 305-925-2217
Wostenholm (See Ibberson [Sheffield] Ltd., George)
Wright's Hardwood Sawmill, 8540 SE Kane Rd., Gresham, OR 97080/503-666-1705
Wyant Bullets, Gen. Del., Swan Lake, MT 59911
Wyant's Outdoor Products, Inc., P.O. Box B, Broadway, VA 22815
Wyoming Armory, Inc., Box 28, Farson, WY 82932/307-273-5556
Wyoming Bonded Bullets, Box 91, Sheridan, WY 82801/307-674-8091
Wyoming Custom Bullets, 1626 21st St., Cody, WY 82414
Wyoming Knife Corp., 101 Commerce Dr., Ft. Collins, CO 80524/303-224-3454

X, Y

X-Spand Target Systems, 26-10th St. SE, Medicine Hat, AB T1A 1P7 CANADA/403-526-7997; FAX: 403-526-7997
Yankee Gunsmith, 2901 Deer Flat Dr., Copperas Cove, TX 76522/817-547-8433
Yavapai College, 1100 E. Sheldon St., Prescott, AZ 86301/602-776-2359; FAX: 602-776-2193
Yavapai Firearms Academy Ltd., P.O. Box 27290, Prescott Valley, AZ 86312/602-772-8262
Yearout, Lewis E. (See Montana Outfitters)
Yee, Mike, 29927 56 Pl. S., Auburn, WA 98001/206-839-3991
Yellowstone Wilderness Supply, P.O. Box 129, W. Yellowstone, MT 59758/406-646-7613
Yesteryear Armory & Supply, P.O. Box 408, Carthage, TN 37030
York M-1 Conversions, 803 Mill Creek Run, Plantersville, TX 77363/800-527-2881, 713-477-8442
Young Country Arms, P.O. Box 3615, Simi Valley, CA 93093

Z

Zabala Hermanos S.A., P.O. Box 97, Eibar, SPAIN 20600/43-768085, 43-768076; FAX: 43-768201 (U.S. importer—American Arms, Inc.)
Zanoletti, Pietro, Via Monte Gugielpo, 4, I-25063 Gardone V.T., ITALY (U.S. importer—Mandall Shooting Supplies, Inc.)
Zanotti Armor, 123 W. Lone Tree Rd., Cedar Falls, IA 50613/319-232-9650
Z-Coat Industrial Coatings, Inc., 3375 U.S. Hwy. 98 S. No. A, Lakeland, FL 33803-8365/813-665-1734
Zeeryp, Russ, 1601 Foard Dr., Lynn Ross Manor, Morristown, TN 37814/615-586-2357
Zeiss Optical, Carl, 1015 Commerce St., Petersburg, VA 23803/804-861-0033; FAX: 804-733-4024
Zero Ammunition Co., Inc., 1601 22nd St. SE, P.O. Box 1188, Cullman, AL 35056-1188/800-545-9376; FAX: 205-739-4683
Ziegel Engineering, 2108 Lomina Ave., Long Beach, CA 90815/310-596-9481; FAX: 310-598-4734
Zim's Inc., 4370 S. 3rd West, Salt Lake City, UT 84107/801-268-2505
Zoli, Antonio, Via Zanardelli 39, Casier Postal 21, I-25063 Gardone V.T., ITALY
Zufall, Joseph F., P.O. Box 304, Golden, CO 80402-0304